Digital Marketing

Visit the *Digital Marketing, Strategy, Implementation and Practice*, Fifth Edition Companion Website at **www.pearsoned.co.uk/chaffey** to find valuable student learning material including:

- Multiple choice questions for every chapter
- Links to video material, on YouTube and FT.com, that demonstrates marketing practice
- Annotated weblinks which provide examples for further study
- A comprehensive online glossary and flashcards which help define key terms and phrases

Digital Marketing

Strategy, Implementation and Practice

Dave Chaffey
Fiona Ellis-Chadwick

Fifth Edition

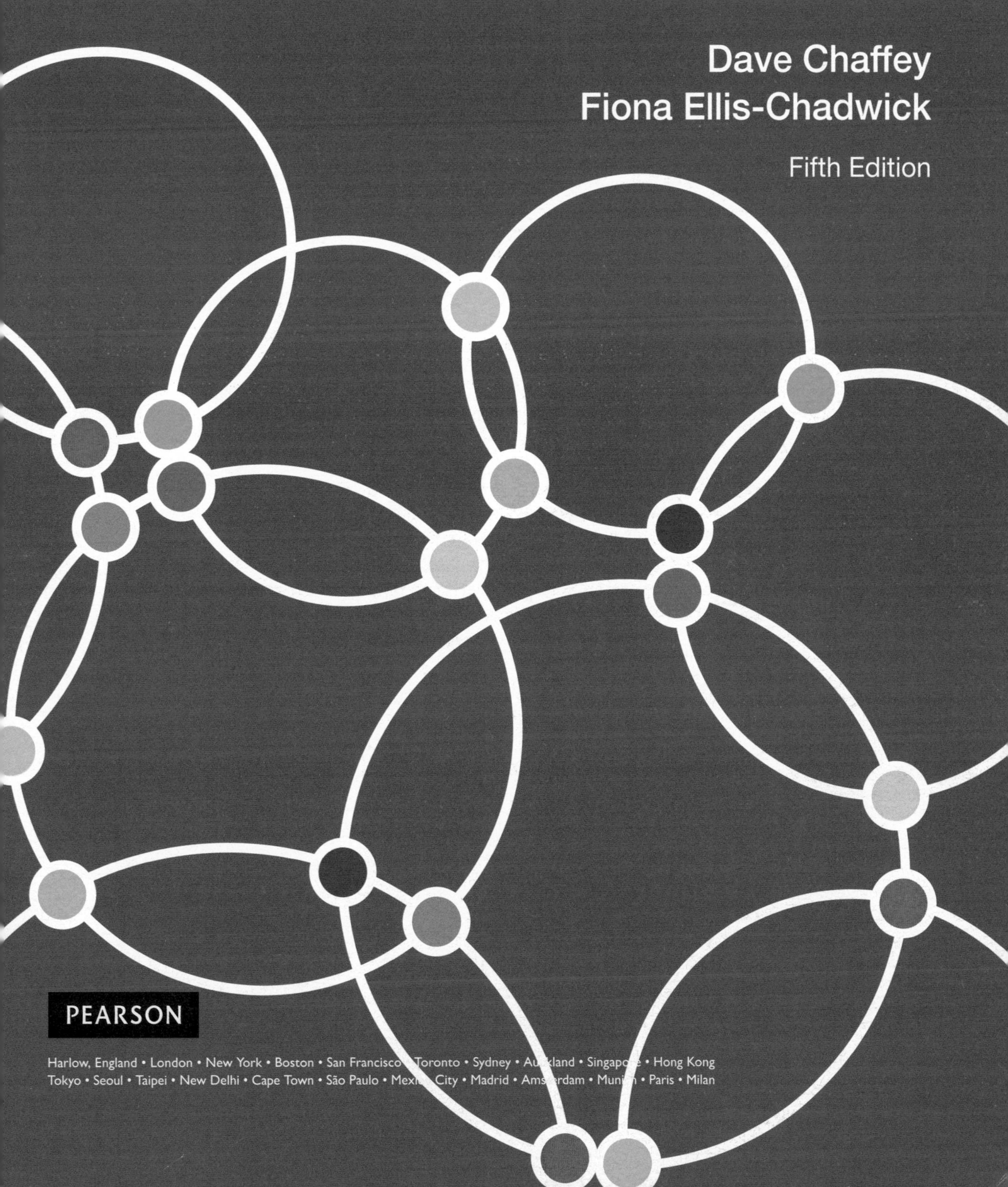

PEARSON

Harlow, England • London • New York • Boston • San Francisco • Toronto • Sydney • Auckland • Singapore • Hong Kong
Tokyo • Seoul • Taipei • New Delhi • Cape Town • São Paulo • Mexico City • Madrid • Amsterdam • Munich • Paris • Milan

Pearson Education Limited
Edinburgh Gate
Harlow
Essex CM20 2JE
England

and Associated Companies throughout the world

Visit us on the World Wide Web at:
www.pearsoned.com/uk

First published 2000
Second edition published 2003
Third edition published 2006
Fourth edition published 2009
Fifth edition published 2012

ISBN: 978-0-273-74610-2

British Library Cataloguing-in-Publication Data
A catalogue record for this book is available from the British Library

Library of Congress Cataloging-in-Publication Data
A catalog record for this book is available from the Library of Congress

10 9 8 7 6 5 4 3 2
16 15 14 13

Typeset in 10/12pt Minion by 30
Printed and bound by L.E.G.O. S.p.A., Italy

Brief contents

Contents

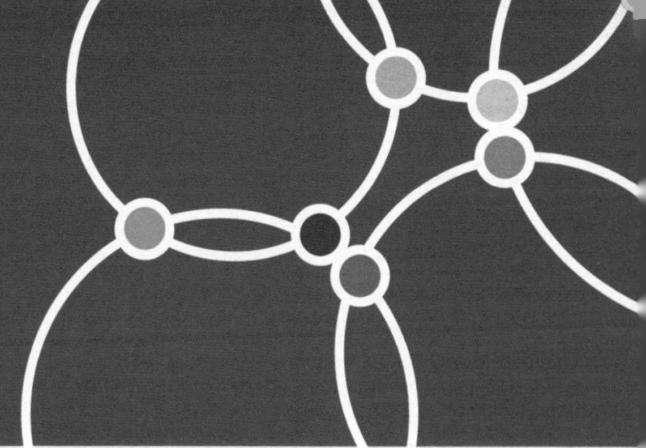

Part 3 Digital marketing: implementation and practice 365

7 Delivering the online customer experience 368

8 Campaign planning for digital media 426

Supporting resources

Visit **www.pearsoned.co.uk/chaffey** to find valuable online resources:

Companion Website for students
- Multiple choice questions for every chapter
- Links to video material, on YouTube and FT.com, that demonstrates marketing theory
- Annotated weblinks which provide examples for further study
- A comprehensive online glossary and flashcards which help define key terms and phrases

For instructors
- A complete, downloadable Instructor's Manual
- PowerPoint slides which are downloadable and available to use for teaching
- A Testbank of question material, which you can use to test your students

Also: The Companion Website also provides the following features:
- Search tool to help locate specific items of content
- E-mail results and profile tools to send results of quizzes to instructors
- Online help and support to assist with website usage and troubleshooting

For more information please contact your local Pearson Education sales representative or visit **www.pearsoned.co.uk/chaffey**

Preface

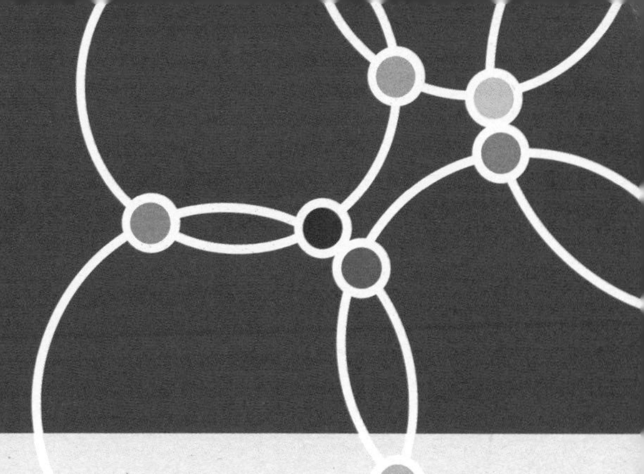

The Internet – opportunity and threat

The Internet and other digital media have transformed marketing. For customers, they give a much wider choice of products, services and prices from different suppliers and the means to select and purchase items more readily. There is also a choice of technology platforms from desktops and laptops to mobile and tablet devices for consumers to use. For organisations, digital media and new technology platforms give the opportunity to expand into new markets, offer new services, apply new online communications techniques and compete on a more equal footing with larger businesses. For those working within these organisations it gives the opportunity to develop new skills and to use the Internet to improve the competitiveness of the company.

At the same time, the Internet and related digital technology platforms gives rise to many threats to organisations. For example, online companies such as ASOS.com (clothing), Amazon.com (books and retail) and Expedia (travel) have captured a significant part of their market and struck fear into the existing players. Many consumers now regularly use social networks like Facebook, Google+, LinkedIn and Twitter as part of their daily lives. Engaging these consumers is an ongoing challenge, but as we will see, companies like ASOS have taken advantage of these opportunities to interact with customers and this has helped them develop as a worldwide brand.

Management of digital marketing

With the success stories of companies capturing market share following the rapidly increasing adoption of the Internet by consumers and business buyers has come a fast-growing realisation that all organisations must have an effective online presence to prosper, or possibly even survive! Michael Porter has said:

> The key question is not whether to deploy Internet technology – companies have no choice if they want to stay competitive – but how to deploy it.

What are these challenges of deploying Internet and digital technology? Figure P.1 gives an indication of the marketing activities that need to be managed effectively and which are covered in this book.

The figure shows the range of different marketing activities or operating processes needed to support acquiring new customers through communicating with them on third-party websites, attracting them to a company website, converting website visits into sales and then using online media to encourage further sales. You can see that applying social media is a part of each of acquisition, conversion and retention and as one of the key management challenges in digital marketing, we consider approaches to managing social media marketing throughout the book. Applying digital platforms as part of multichannel marketing to support customer journeys through different media is also a major theme throughout this text. Management processes related to digital marketing include planning how Internet marketing can be best resourced to contribute to the organisation and integrate with other marketing activities. The increased adoption of digital marketing also implies a significant programme of change that needs to be managed. New objectives need to be set, new communications strategies developed and staff developed through new responsibilities and skills.

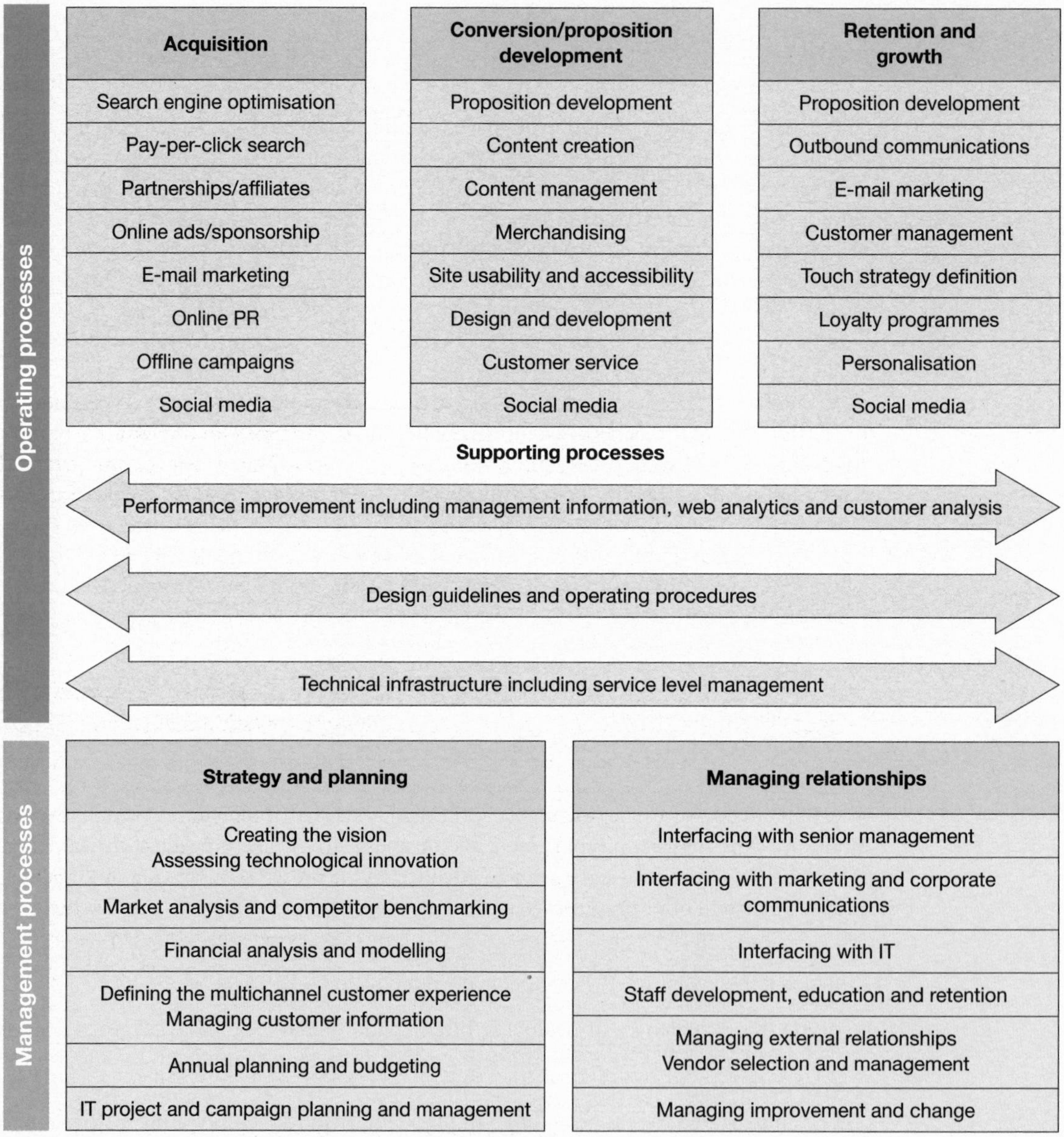

Operating processes
Acquisition
Search engine optimisation
Pay-per-click search
Partnerships/affiliates
Online ads/sponsorship
E-mail marketing
Online PR
Offline campaigns
Social media
Conversion/proposition development
Proposition development
Content creation
Content management
Merchandising
Site usability and accessibility
Design and development
Customer service
Social media
Retention and growth
Proposition development
Outbound communications
E-mail marketing
Customer management
Touch strategy definition
Loyalty programmes
Personalisation
Social media
Supporting processes
Performance improvement including management information, web analytics and customer analysis
Design guidelines and operating procedures
Technical infrastructure including service level management
Management processes
Strategy and planning
Creating the vision
Assessing technological innovation
Market analysis and competitor benchmarking
Financial analysis and modelling
Defining the multichannel customer experience
Managing customer information
Annual planning and budgeting
IT project and campaign planning and management
Managing relationships
Interfacing with senior management
Interfacing with marketing and corporate communications
Interfacing with IT
Staff development, education and retention
Managing external relationships
Vendor selection and management
Managing improvement and change

Figure P.1 Key marketing activities managed for digital marketing
Source: EConsultancy (2008), author Dave Chaffey

Digital marketing – new skills required?

The aim of this text is to provide you with a comprehensive guide to the concepts, techniques and best practice to support all the digital marketing processes shown in Figure P.1. This book is based on emerging academic models together with best practice from leading adopters of digital media. The practical knowledge developed through reviewing these concepts and best practice is intended to enable graduates entering employment and marketing professionals to exploit the opportunities of marketing using the Internet while minimising the risks.

Specifically, this book addresses the following needs:

- There is a need to know to what extent the Internet changes existing marketing models and whether new models and strategies can be applied to exploit the medium effectively.
- Marketing practitioners need practical Internet marketing skills to market their products effectively. Knowledge of the new jargon – terms such as 'portal', 'click-through', 'cookie', 'hits' and 'page impressions'– and of effective methods of site design and promotion such as search engine marketing will be necessary, either for direct 'hands-on' development of a site or to enable communication with other staff or agencies that are implementing and maintaining the site.
- Given the rapidly changing market characteristics and best practices of Internet marketing, web-based information sources are needed to update knowledge regularly. This text and the supporting companion website contain extensive links to websites to achieve this.

The content of this book assumes some existing knowledge of marketing in the reader, perhaps developed through experience or by students studying introductory modules in marketing fundamentals, marketing communications or buyer behaviour. However, the text outlines basic concepts of marketing, communications theory, buyer behaviour and the marketing mix.

Summary of changes for the fifth edition

The acclaimed structure of previous editions has been retained since this provides a clear sequence to the stages of strategy development and implementation that are required to plan successfully for Internet marketing in existing and start-up companies.

In the fifth edition we have changed the title from *Internet Marketing* to use the term *Digital Marketing*, in line with increased usage of this term and since it better suggests the application of a range of digital platforms used today to engage audiences.

In the UK, Europe, Asia and Oceania in particular, 'digital marketing' has become the preferred term in both professional and academic areas. For example, in the UK, the majority of professional masters qualifications are now know as 'Digital Marketing Diplomas'.

The main changes made for the fifth edition, based on feedback from reviews and prompted by continued innovation in the use of the web for marketing, are:

Chapter 1 – Introducing digital marketing

- New interview/case study covering mobile location review service Qype.
- New introduction to communications through paid, earned and owned digital media.
- Increased coverage of social media marketing and social commerce.
- More coverage on non-desktop digital marketing platforms including mobile, tablet and gaming platforms.
- Underpinning digital marketing communications techniques such as permission, content and engagement marketing are introduced.

Chapter 2 – Online marketplace analysis: micro-environment

- A new interview about the growth of Blackcircles.com, a UK start-up company.
- Updates to tools for marketplace analysis including search, benchmarking and buzz-monitoring tools.

Chapter 3 – The Internet macro-environment

- The structure of the chapter has been updated with the PESTLE factors re-ordered to give more emphasis to how technology creates opportunity for marketing.
- Mobile marketing and the use of smartphones for multichannel marketing through techniques such as contactless payment using NFC, location-based marketing and QR codes.
- Content on privacy law updated to address the latest legislation on cookies and social media marketing.

Chapter 4 – Digital marketing strategy

- Many of the models and strategy options in this chapter remain valid and have been retained.
- There is a new decision point 5 on customer engagement and social media strategy.

Chapter 5 – The Internet and the marketing mix

- New interview with Roberto Hortal who has managed digital marketing at UK and global enterprises including EDF Energy, RSA insurance group, MORE TH>N, easyJet and Nokia. He explains how the marketing mix concept is still applicable when taking real-world decisions in companies to shape their online proposition and increase their commercial value.
- Five new Digital marketing insight examples added.

Chapter 6 – Relationship marketing using digital platforms

- Restructured to explain e-CRM, social CRM and the permission marketing concept at the outset.
- New Mini Case Study about how Zappos.com built their business around customer service quality.
- Permission marketing coverage updated to show how it be supported through social media.
- Gamification.
- Discussion of how companies can use social networks like Facebook, Twitter, LinkedIn, Google+ and YouTube to build community.
- Dell case study updated to review how Dell use social media.

Chapter 7 – Delivering the online customer experience

- Overall learning objectives and content updated to reflect other forms of online presence such as social network company pages, mobile apps and sites.
- Three new Mini Case studies and three new activities illustrate how design can enhance marketing.
- Major new section on content strategy.

Chapter 8 – Campaign planning for digital media

- New interview on how digital creative supports brands.
- New section on types of campaign integration.
- Update to Facebook case study.

Chapter 9 – Marketing communications using digitial media channels

- New section on social media marketing.
- Updated Digital marketing insights.

Chapter 10 – Evaluation and improvement of digital channel performance

- More discussion of the challenges of using web analytics data to improve performance.
- Measurement of social media marketing effectiveness.
- New section on customer feedback tools in the section on marketing research.

Chapter 11 – Business-to-consumer digital marketing practice

- The chapter starts with a template checklist summarising key operational issues for managing digital marketing which acts as a 'healthcheck' for different types of companies – it applies both to Chapters 11 and 12.
- There is a major new case study on online fashion retailer ASOS reviewing how they have developed their marketing mix to sell in many markets globally.

Chapter 12 – Business-to-business digital marketing practice

- New discussion of the differences between B2C marketing and B2B marketing.
- Summary of B2B communications approaches for customer acquisition, conversion and retention.
- New examples from Cisco, Euroffice and Perfect Commerce.

New features included across all chapters:

- Smart Insights Interviews: new interviews where specialist practising digital marketers share their experiences of what makes for effective approaches in the areas covered in the chapter.
- Digital marketing insights: research highlighting customer behaviour or adoption of digital technologies.
- Use of QR codes to link to the latest resources for each chapter.

Table P.1 In-depth case studies in Digital Marketing, 5th edition

Chapter	Case study	Themes
1 Introduction	eBay thrives in the global marketplace	Business and revenue model, proposition, competition, objectives and strategies, risk management
2 Micro-environment	Boo hoo – learning from the largest European dot-com failure	Assessing a consumer market, business models, marketing communications
3 Macro-environment	Zopa launches a new lending model	Companion vision, branding, target market, communicating the proposition, challenges and reasons for failure
4 Internet marketing strategy	Tesco online development strategy supports global expansion	Business models, proposition and online product range, target market strategy
5 Internet marketing mix	The re-launched Napster changes the music marketing mix	Peer-to-peer services, revenue models, proposition design, strategy, competition, risk factors
6 Relationship marketing	Dell gets closer to its customers through its social media strategy	Influence of website design on conversion, retention marketing, personalisation, e-CRM, RFM analysis
7 Online customer experience	Refining the online customer experience at i-tot.com	Strategy, proposition, site design, on-site search capabilities
8 Campaign planning	A short history of Facebook	Ad revenue models, privacy
9 Digital media channels	Innovation at Google	Technology, ad revenue models, innnovation
10 Evaluation and improvement of digital channel performance	Learning from Amazon's culture of metrics	Strategy, measurement, online marketing communications, personalisation approach
11 Business-to-consumer marketing	ASOS reinvents fashion retail	Online consumer profiles, purchasing behaviour and expectations and e-retailing
12 Business-to-business marketing	Covisint – typical history of a B2B marketplace?; B2B adoption of the Internet: Inspirational Cosmetics	B2B trading environment, business markets, trading partnerships and digital marketing strategies

A new series of cases 'Digital Marketing in Practice – 'Smart Insights interview' are included at the start of each chapter. These are presented in question and answer format and focus on the practical challenges and opportunities facing practitioners working in digital media:

- *Chapter 1* Richard Dennys, Marketing Director of Qype UK
- *Chapter 2* Michael Welch of Blackcircles.com
- *Chapter 3* Fred Bassett of Blue Latitude
- *Chapter 4* Lisa Woods, Marketing Manager of HSBC International
- *Chapter 5* Robert Hortal of EDF Energy
- *Chapter 6* Guy Stephens of Foviance
- *Chapter 7* Ben Jesson and Karl Blands of Conversion Rate Experts
- *Chapter 8* Mike O'Brien of the Jam Partnership
- *Chapter 9* Katie Webb, online Marketing Manager at Vision Express
- *Chapter 10* Avinash Kaushik of Google.

All interviews are available online at: **www.smartinsights.com.**

The structure and content of this book

The book is divided into three parts, each covering a different aspect of how organisations use the Internet for marketing to help them achieve competitive advantage. Table P.2 shows how the book is related to established marketing topics.

Part 1 Digital marketing fundamentals (Chapters 1–3)

Part 1 relates the use of the Internet to traditional marketing theories and concepts, and questions the validity of existing models given the differences between the Internet and other media.

- Chapter 1 *Introducing digital marketing* introduces using the Internet as part of customer-centric, multichannel marketing; it also reviews the relationship between Internet marketing, digital marketing, e-commerce and e-business, and the benefits the Internet can bring to adopters, and outlines differences from other media and briefly introduces the technology.
- Chapter 2 *Online marketplace analysis: micro-environment* reviews how the Internet changes the immediate environment of an organisation, including marketplace and channel structure. It describes the type of situation analysis needed to support Internet strategy by examining how customers, competitors and intermediaries and the interplay between them can be evaluated.
- Chapter 3 *The Internet macro-environment* reviews the impact of social, technological, economic, political and legal environmental influences on Internet strategy and its implementation. The emphasis is on privacy and data protection regulations and managing technology innovation.

Part 2 Digital strategy development (Chapters 4–6)

Part 2 describes the emerging models for developing strategy and provides examples of the approaches companies have used to integrate the Internet into their marketing strategy.

- Chapter 4 *Digital marketing strategy* considers how the Internet strategy can be aligned with business and marketing strategies and describes a generic strategic approach with phases of situation review, goal setting, strategy formulation and resource allocation and monitoring.

- Chapter 5 *The Internet and the marketing mix* assesses how the different elements of the marketing mix can be varied in the online environment as part of strategy formulation.
- Chapter 6 *Relationship marketing using digital platforms* details the strategies and tactics for using the Internet to build and sustain 'one-to-one' relationships with customers.

Part 3 Digital marketing: implementation and practice (Chapters 7–11)

Part 3 of the book explains practical approaches to implementing an Internet marketing strategy. Techniques for communicating with customers, building relationships and facilitating electronic commerce are all reviewed in some detail. Knowledge of these practical techniques is essential for undergraduates on work placements involving a website, and for marketing managers who are dealing with suppliers such as design agencies.

- Chapter 7 *Delivering the online customer experience* explains how an online presence is developed to support branding and customer service quality objectives. The stages, including analysis of customer needs, design of the site structure and layout, and creating

Table P.2 Coverage of marketing topics in different chapters

	Chapter											
Topic	**1**	**2**	**3**	**4**	**5**	**6**	**7**	**8**	**9**	**10**	**11**	**12**
Advertising								✓		✓		
Branding				✓	✓	✓				✓	✓	
Consumer behaviour	✓	✓					✓	✓	✓	✓	✓	✓
Channel and market structure	✓	✓		✓						✓	✓	✓
Communications mix				✓				✓	✓			
Communications theory	✓							✓	✓			
Customer service quality						✓	✓	✓			✓	✓
Direct marketing						✓		✓	✓			
International marketing		✓	✓	✓			✓				✓	✓
Marketing mix		✓		✓	✓			✓				
Marketing research	✓	✓	✓							✓		
Evaluation and measurement	✓			✓			✓	✓	✓	✓		
Pricing strategy		✓		✓	✓							
Promotion	✓	✓		✓				✓	✓			
Public relations								✓	✓			
Relationship marketing						✓	✓					
Segmentation		✓		✓	✓	✓		✓		✓		
Services marketing					✓		✓					
Strategy and planning	✓	✓	✓	✓	✓	✓	✓	✓	✓	✓	✓	✓
Technology background including Web 2.0	✓		✓						✓	✓		

Note: A blue tick ✓ indicates fairly detailed coverage; a black tick ✓ indicates a brief direct reference or indirect coverage.

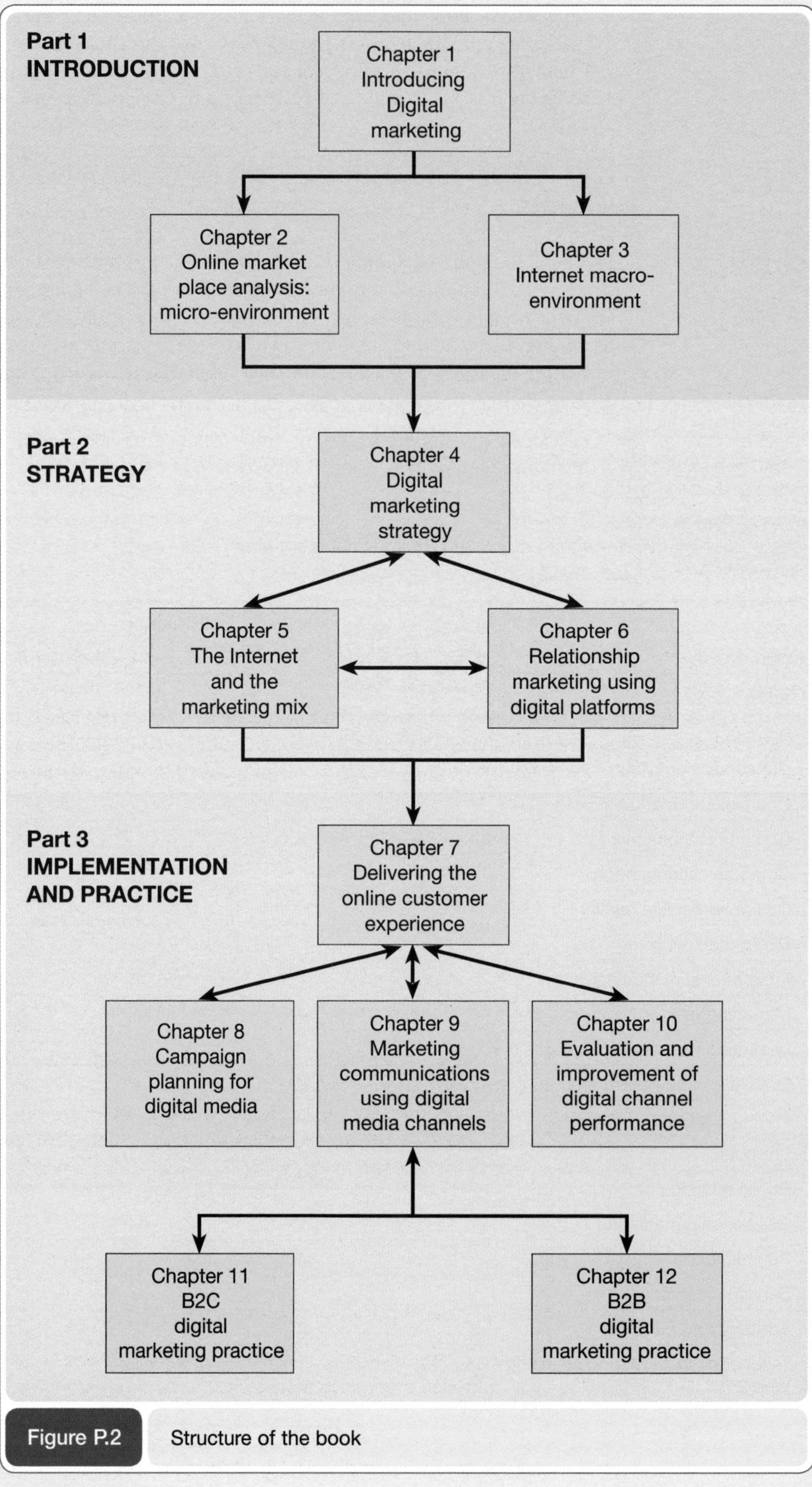

Figure P.2 Structure of the book

the site, are covered together with key techniques such as user-centred design, usability and accessibility design. It also covers different service quality models used to assess experience.
- Chapter 8 *Campaign planning for digital media* describes the novel characteristics of digital media, and then goes on to different aspects of marketing communications which then need to be considered for a successful online campaign.
- Chapter 9 *Marketing communications using digital media channels.* Among the techniques covered are banner advertising, affiliate networks, promotion in search engines, co-branding and sponsorship, e-mail, online PR, viral and word-of-mouth marketing with particular reference to social networks.
- Chapter 10 *Evaluation and improvement of digital channel performance* reviews methods for assessing and improving the effectiveness of a site and communications in delivering business and marketing benefits. The chapter briefly covers process and tools for updating sites.
- Chapter 11 *Business-to-consumer digital marketing practice* examines models of marketing to consumers and provides case studies of how retail businesses are tackling such marketing.
- Chapter 12 *Business-to-business digital marketing practice* examines the different area of marketing to other businesses and provides many examples of how companies are achieving this to support international marketing.

Who should use this book?

Students

This book has been created primarily as the main student text for undergraduate and postgraduate students taking specialist marketing courses or modules which cover e-marketing, Internet and digital marketing, electronic commerce and e-business. The book is relevant to students who are:

- *undergraduates on business programmes* which include modules on the use of the Internet and e-commerce. This includes specialist degrees such as Internet marketing, electronic commerce, marketing, tourism and accounting or general business degrees such as business studies, business administration and business management;
- *undergraduate project students* who select this topic for final-year projects or dissertations – this book is an excellent supporting text for these students;
- *undergraduates completing a work placement* in a company using the Internet to promote its products;
- *students at college aiming for vocational qualifications* such as the HNC or HND in Business Management or Computer Studies;
- *postgraduate students* taking specialist masters degrees in electronic commerce or Internet marketing, generic MBAs and courses leading to qualifications such as the Certificate in Management or Diploma in Digital Marketing or Management Studies which involve modules on electronic commerce and digital marketing.

Practitioners

Previous editions have been widely used by digital marketing practitioners including:

- *marketing managers or specialists such as e-commerce managers or e-marketing managers* responsible for defining digital marketing strategy and implementing and maintaining the company website;
- *senior managers and directors* wishing to understand the potential of digital marketing for a company and who need practical guidelines on how to exploit this potential;

- *technical project managers or webmasters* who may understand the technical details of building a site, but have a limited knowledge of marketing fundamentals and how to develop an Internet marketing strategy.

What does the book offer to lecturers teaching these courses?

The book is intended to be a comprehensive guide to all aspects of using the Internet and other digital media to support marketing. The book builds on existing marketing theories and concepts, and questions the validity of models in the light of the differences between the Internet and other media. The book references the emerging body of literature specific to Internet marketing. It can therefore be used across several modules. Lecturers will find the book has a good range of case studies, activities and exercises to support their teaching. Website links are given in the text and at the end of each chapter to provide important information sources for particular topics.

Student learning features

A range of features has been incorporated into this book to help the reader get the most out of it. Each feature has been designed to assist understanding, reinforce learning and help readers find information easily, particularly when completing assignments and preparing for exams. The features are described in the order in which you will find them in each chapter.

At the start of each chapter

The 'Chapter at a glance' page provides easy navigation for each chapter. It contains:

- *Main topics*: the main topics and their page numbers.
- *Case studies:* the main cases and their page numbers.
- *Learning objectives*: a list describing what readers can learn through reading the chapter and completing the exercises.
- *Questions for marketers*: explaining the relevance of the chapter for practitioners.
- *Links to other chapters*: a summary of related information in other chapters.

In each chapter

- *Definitions*: when significant terms are first introduced the main text contains succinct definitions in the margin for easy reference.
- *Web references*: where appropriate, web addresses are given to enable readers to obtain further information. They are provided in the main text where they are directly relevant as well as at the end of the chapter.
- *Case studies*: real-world examples of how companies are using the Internet for marketing. Questions at the end of the case study are intended to highlight the main learning points from the example.
- *Mini case studies*: short features which give a more detailed example, or explanation, than is practical in the main text. They do not contain supplementary questions.
- *Activities*: exercises in the main text which give readers the opportunity to practise and apply the techniques described in the text.
- *Chapter summaries*: intended as revision aids to summarise the main learning points from the chapter.

At the end of each chapter

- *Self-assessment exercises*: short questions which will test understanding of terms and concepts described in the chapter.
- *Essay questions*: conventional essay questions.
- *Discussion questions*: these require longer essay-style answers discussing themes from the chapter. They can be used either as topics for individual essays or as the basis for seminar discussion.
- *Examination questions*: typical short-answer questions of the type that are encountered in exams. These can also be used for revision.
- *References*: these are references to books, articles or papers referred to within the chapter.
- *Further reading*: supplementary texts or papers on the main themes of the chapter. Where appropriate, a brief commentary is provided on recommended supplementary reading on the main themes of the chapters.
- *Web links*: these are significant sites that provide further information on the concepts and topics of the chapter. This list does not repeat all the website references given within the chapter, for example company sites. For clarity, the website address prefix 'http://' is generally omitted.

At the end of the book

- *Glossary*: comprehensive definitions of all key terms and phrases used within the main text, cross-referenced for ease of use.
- *Index*: all key words and abbreviations referred to in the main text.

Support material

Free supplementary materials are available via the Pearson Education companion website at **www.pearsoned.co.uk/chaffey** and Dave Chaffey's website at **www.davechaffey.com** to support all users of the book. This regularly updated website contains advice, comment, support materials and hyperlinks to reference sites relevant to the text. There is a password-protected area for lecturers only to discuss issues arising from using the text; additional examination-type questions and answers; a multiple-choice question bank with answers; additional cases with suggestions for discussion; and a downloadable version of the Lecturer's Guide and OHP Masters.

References

EConsultancy (2005) Managing an e-commerce team. Integrating digital marketing into your organisation. 60-page report. Author: Dave Chaffey. Available from **www.econsultancy.com**.

EConsultancy (2008) Managing digital channels. Integrating digital marketing into your organisation (190-page report). Author: Dave Chaffey. Available from **www.econsultancy.com**.

Guided tour

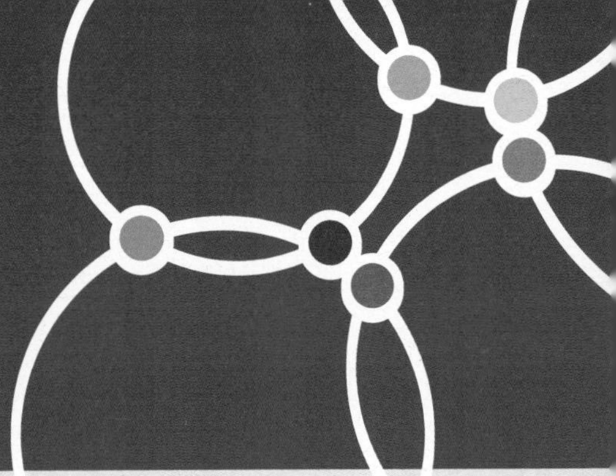

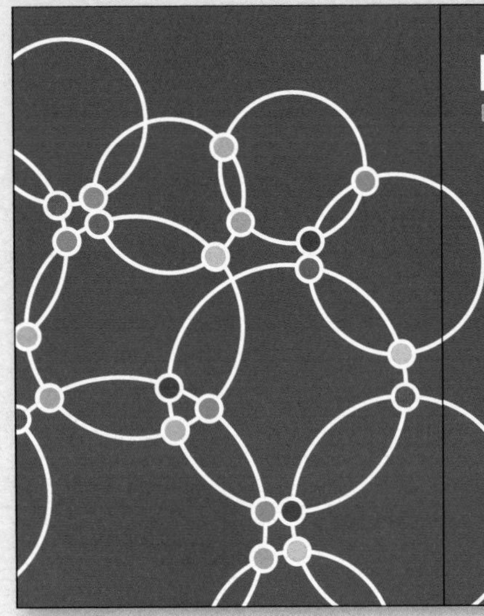

Part openers summarise the main themes with brief chapter contents.

Questions for marketers will stimulate further reading and thought.

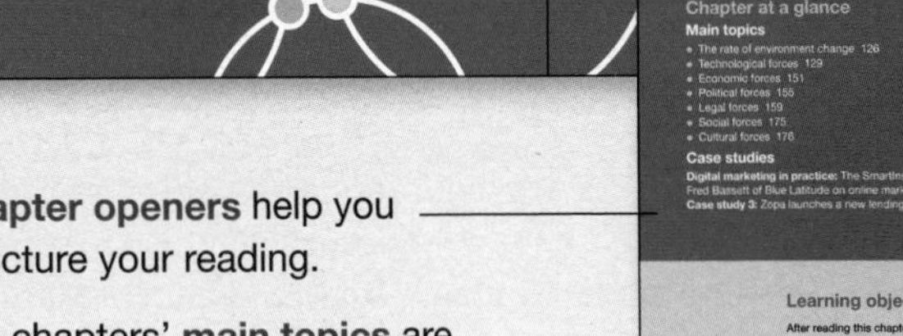

Chapter openers help you structure your reading.

The chapters' **main topics** are listed for quick and easy reference.

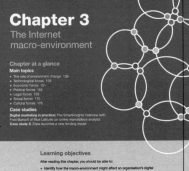

Learning objectives enable you to focus on what you can gain from reading the chapter.

Links to other chapters help you to integrate your reading.

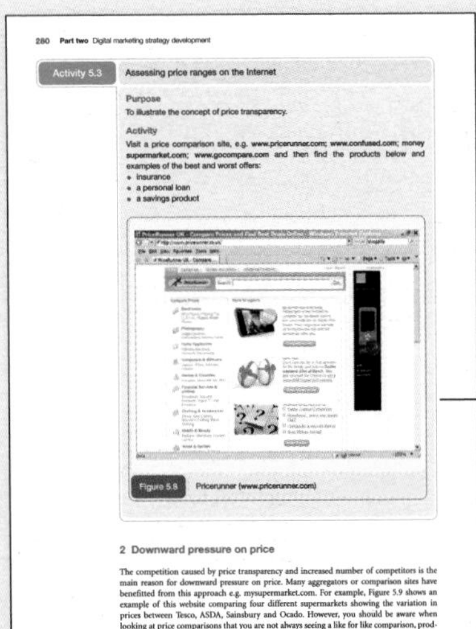

Activities give readers the opportunity to practise and apply the techniques described in the text.

Mini case studies encourage debate and classroom discussion.

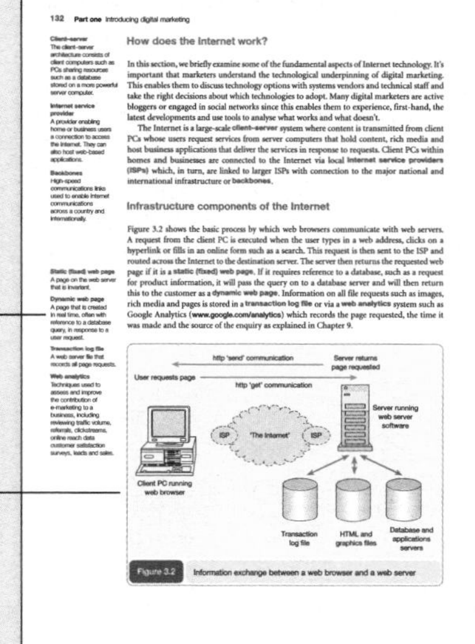

Margin definitions help emphasise the concepts covered in the body of the text.

Figures and **tables** illustrate key concepts and processes, visually reinforcing your learning.

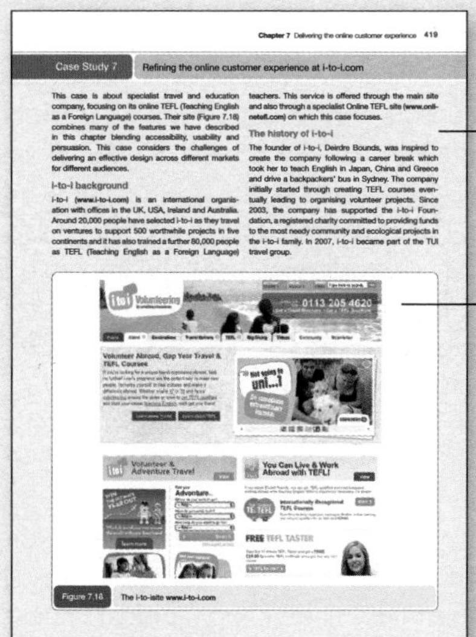

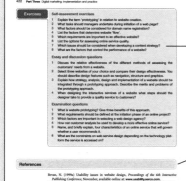

Case studies are positioned at the end of each section, showcasing relevant theories and themes.

Full-colour screenshots from genuine websites help to connect theory with real-life practical examples.

Summaries clinch the important concepts that have been presented in each section.

Each chapter ends with a number of **Exercises**, designed for use in class, as essay questions, and in exams.

At the end of each chapter you will also find a full list of **References**.

Suggested articles and texts for your **Further reading** are listed, as are a number of useful **Weblinks**.

About the authors

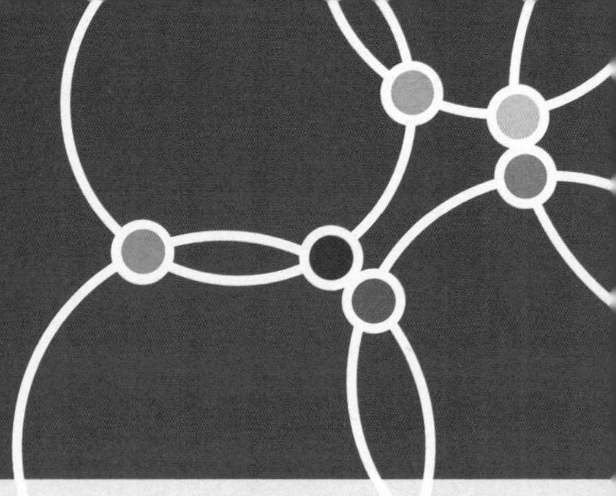

Dave Chaffey BSc, PhD, FCIM, MIDM

Dave is CEO of Smart Insights (**www.smartinsights.com**), an online publisher and analytics company providing advice and alerts on best practice and industry developments for digital marketers and Ecommerce managers. The advice is also created to help readers of Dave's books. The most relevant information is highlighted at **www.smartinsights.com/book-support.**

Dave also works as an independent Internet marketing trainer and consultant for Marketing Insights Limited. He has consulted on digital marketing and Ecommerce strategy for companies of a range of sizes from larger organisations like 3M, Barclaycard, HSBC, Mercedes-Benz, Nokia and The North Face to smaller organisations like Arco, **Confused.com**, Euroffice, Hornbill and i-to-i.

Dave's passion is educating students and marketers about latest and best practices in digital marketing, so empowering businesses to improve their online performance through getting the most value from their web analytics and market insight. In other words making the most of online opportunities and avoiding waste.

He is proud to have been recognized by the Department of Trade and Industry as one of the leading individuals who have provided input and influence on the development and growth of E-commerce and the Internet in the UK over the last 10 years. Dave has also been recognised by the Chartered Institute of Marketing as one of 50 marketing 'gurus' worldwide who have helped shape the future of marketing. He is also proud to be an Honorary Fellow of the IDM.

Dave is a visiting lecturer on E-commerce courses at different universities including Birmingham, Cranfield, Derby, Manchester Metropolitan and Warwick Universities. He is also a tutor on the IDM Diploma in *Digital marketing, for which he is senior examiner.*

In total, Dave is author of five best-selling business books including Ebusiness and Ecommerce Management, Digital Marketing: Strategy, Implementation and Practice, eMarketing eXcellence (with PR Smith) and Total E-mail Marketing. Many of these books have been published in new editions since 2000 and translations include Chinese, Dutch, German, Italian and Serbian.

When offline Dave enjoys fell-running, indie guitar music and travelling with his family.

Fiona Ellis PhD, BSc, PGCE

Fiona-Ellis Chadwick (**www.ellis-chadwick.com**) is a Senior lecturer at the Open University Business School, where she leads the Retail management and marketing programme. As part of this role she is also an academic consultant for the BBC and has worked on highly successful and award wining series: The Virtual Revolution, Foods that make billions, Evans Business Challenges and radio 4's the Bottom Line programme. Fiona has also made a series of educational films for the Open University and has interviewed business leaders about the role of technology in driving economic growth. She had a successful commercial career before becoming an academic and completing her PhD. Having made a significant contribution in the area of online retailing she continues to focus her research and academic publication in the areas of strategic adoption of the internet. Her work on these topics has been published in *Journal of Business Research, European Journal of Marketing, Internet research, International Journal of Retail Distribution and Management* plus additional textbooks, and practitioner journals. Fiona is passionate about how technology and education can help business development in the future.

Acknowledgements

I am fortunate to have shared my journey of understanding how to best use digital marketing with thousands of students and marketing professionals and I thank you for sharing your experiences with me. I'd particularly like to thank all the practitioners who have shared their experiences on applying digital marketing in the opening case study interviews in each chapter and on **SmartInsights.com.**

Likewise, I appreciate the effort made by the digital marketing specialists who have shared their knowledge as Expert commentators on Smart Insights including Mike Berry and Richard Sedley (Marketing Strategy), Dan Barker, Ben Jesson and Pritesh Patel (Analytics), Dan Bosomworth, Paul Fennemore, Katy Howell and Marie Page (Social media marketing), Rene Power (B2B marketing), Rob Thurner (Mobile Marketing), Chris Soames, James Gurd and John Newton (Search marketing), Mel Henson (copywriting), Paul Rouke (usability) and Mark Brownlow, Kath Pay and Tim Watson (Email Marketing). Also to the many occasional contributors who have shared their expertise and experiences.

The authors would like to thank the team at Pearson Education in Harlow for their help in the creation of this book, especially Rachel Gear, Amanda McPartlin (our acquisitions editors) and Elizabeth Wright who managed the book through the production process.

As always, special thanks go to my family for supporting me in the ongoing updates.

Dave Chaffey

Publisher's Acknowledgements

The publishers are grateful to the reviewers of this book for their valuable comments.

We are grateful to the following for permission to reproduce copyright material:

Figures

Figure 1.1 from www.google.com/about/corporate/company/history.html Google; Figure 1.12 fromhttp://novaspivack.typepad.com/nova_spivacks_weblog/2007/02/steps_towards_a.html., Nova Spivack; Figures 2.4 and 2.12 from *Googling the Present, Economic and Labour Review* (Chamberlin, G. 2010), Office for National Statistics, contains public sector information licensed under the Open Government Licence (OGL) v1.0.http://www.nationalarchives.gov.uk/doc/open-government-licence/open-government; Figure 2.8 from New GfK ROPO study with Vodafone. Published on Google Barometer Blog October 20th 2010.; Figure 2.20 from www.bowencraggs.com, Bowen Craggs & Co.; Figure 2.22 fromhttp://www.bowencraggs.com/downloads/ft/BC FTIndex 2011 booklet.pdf, www.bowencraggs.com; Figure 2.27 from SmartInsights.com; Figure 4.4 from *EMarketing Excellence: Planning and optimizing your digital marketing.* 3 ed, Butterworth Heinemann, Oxford (Chaffey, D. and Smith, P.R. 2008); Figure 5.2 from www.osselect.co.uk, Ordnance Survey, Reproduced from Ordnance Survey map data by permission of Ordnance Survey, © Crown copyright.; Figure 6.19 from Applying RFM Segmentation to the SilverMinds Catalogue, *Interactive Marketing (New name is Journal of Direct Data and Digital Marketing Practice)*, 5 (3) (Patron 2004), Palgrave Macmillan; Figure 6.20 from CIPD; Figure 7.1 from Succeeding with brands on the internet, *Journal of Brand Management*, 8(3), 186-95 (de Chernatony, L. 2001), Palgrave Macmillan; Figure 7.15 from Scene 7 (2008) Adobe, © 2012 Adobe Systems Incorporated. All rights reserved. Adobe and Scene 7 is/are either [a] registered trademark[s] of Adobe Systems Incorporated in the United States and/or other countries.; Figure 8.6 from Millward Brown Qualitative; Figure 8.12 from www.centreforintegratedmarketing.com, Centre for Integrated Marketing, CODAR is a registered trademark of Stepping Stones Consultancy Ltd.; Figures 9.1, 9.8 from Smart Insights.com; Figure 9.17 from The Hitwise UK Media Impact Report, September 2006; Figure 10.7 from Altimeter (2011) with permission (Creative commons).; Figure 10.9 from National Express, Test reports courtesy of Maxymiser Content Intelligence, www.maxymiser.com; Figure 10.10 from Maxymiser Ltd, Test reports courtesy of Maxymiser Content Intelligence, www.maxymiser.com

Screenshots

Screenshot 1.5 from http://www.northwestsupplies.co.uk, North West Supplies; Screenshot 1.12 from FT.com/View from the Top, FT.com; Screenshot 1.17 from www.travelrepublic.co.uk; Screenshot 2.14 from www.dulux.co.uk, Dulux is a trademark of ICI. © ICI; Screenshot 2.16 from Google 2011; Screenshot 2.21 from www.allthingsgreen.net, All things green; Screenshot 4.2 from Expat Zone (HSBC); Screenshot 4.18 adapted from the company website press releases and Revolution (2005a), Euroffice; Screenshot 5.5 from www.dorsetcereals.co.uk, Dorset Cereals; Screenshot 5.9 from www.mysupermarket.co.uk; Screenshot 5.13 from www.google.com/products; Screenshot 6.1 from Zappos.com Inc,© 2013 Zappos.com, Inc. or its affiliates; Screenshot 6.13 from www.ctshirts.co.uk, Charles Tyrwhitt LLP; Screenshot 7.5 fromwww.smartinsights.com; Screenshot 7.5 from Google; Screenshot 7.10 from Zen Garden; Screenshot 7.14 from Wine.com; Screenshot 7.18 from itoi; Screenshot 8.3 from www.threadless.com; Screenshot 8.21 from www.tourismirelandtaxichallenge.com, Tourism Ireland; Screenshot 9.3 from Google; Screenshot 9.11 from Blog post, www.amnavigator.com/blog/2011/09/12/back-to-affiliate-cookie-duration-return-days-question/, E Prussakov; Screenshot 9.13 from www.bannerblog.com.au, www.bannerblog.com.au; ; Screenshot 9.16 from SmartFOCUS DIGITAL, Reproduced by kind permission of smartFOCUS DIGITAL; Screenshot 10.8 from Hootsuite; Screenshot 12.5 from Lead forensics

Slides

Slide 4.9 from Arena flowers, ArenaFlowers.com

Tables

Table 1.2 from *E marketing Excellence, Planning and Optimising Your Digital Marketing*, 3ed, P.R. Smith and D. Chaffey © Elsevier (2008); Table 1.3 from *Managing an E-commerce team. Integrating digital marketing into your organisation.*, Econsultancy.com Ltd (Dave Chaffey 2005) Econsultancy; Table 2.1 from *Correlation between search volume in Google Trends and retail sales volume*, Office for National Statistics (2010) ONS, Contains public sector information licensed under the Open Government Licence (OGL) v1.0.http://www.nationalarchives.gov.uk/doc/open-government-licence/open-government; Table 2.4 from European Commission 2007, © European Union, 1995-2012 ; Table 2.5 from Multi-channel experience consistency: evidence from Lexus, *Interactive Marketing (Journal of Direct Data and Digital Marketing Practice)*, 64 (4), 317-25 (Menteth et al 2005), Palgrave Macmillan; Table 2.8 from CNET works study, YGS Group; Table 4.2 adapted from Managing Digital Channels Research Report. Econsultancy (2008); Table 5.2 reprinted from Journal of Interactive Marketing 20(2), Xing, X., Yang, S. and Tang, F., A comparison of time-varying online price and price dispersion between multichannel and dotcom DVD retailers, 3-20, © (2006), with permission from Elsevier.; Table 7.5 from Measuring online service quality, *Journal of Targeting, Analysis and Measurement for Marketing*, 8(40) (Chaffey, D. and Edgar, M. 2000), Palgrave Macmillan; Table 8.4 fromwww.cs.manchester.ac.uk/research/vicram/studies/eyetracking.php, Harper, S. (2006), School of Computer Science web research summary, University of Manchester;

Table 8.7 from www.iab.net/xmos, Interactive Advertising Bureau; Table 10.1 from www.abce.org.uk, ABCe (www.abce.org.uk); ; Table 11.4 from Allegra Strategies (2005); Table 11.5 adapted from *Journal of Retailing and Consumer Services* 15(3), Weltevreden, J. and Boschma, R. Internet strategies and performance of Dutch retailers 63-178, © 2008, with permission from Elsevier

Text

Interview on pages 8-10 from Richard Dennys Smartinsights Interview; Interview on pages 54-56 from Michael Welch SmartInsights; Case Study 2.1 after Case study developed by Agency.com; available through the IAB (www.iabuk.net) and presented at Engage 2007; Interview on pages 125-126 from Fred Bassett SmartInsights; Interview on pages 193-195 from Lisa Woods Smart Insights; Interview on pages 260-263 from Smart Insights; Interview on pages 315-319 from Guy Stephens Smart Insights; Case Study on page 332 after Smart Insights; Interview on pages 372-374 from Ben Jesson and Karl Blanks Smart Insights; Interview 8. from Mike O'Brien Smart Insights; Case Study 9. from www.buzzparadise.com/case-studies/pr-2-0-event-for-renault-le-web-2010/, Buzz Paradise; Interview 9. from Smart Insights.com; Case Study on pages 642-643 excerpt reprinted by permission of Harvard Business Review from *Transforming Strategy One Customer at a Time* by R. Harrington and A. Tjan, March 2008. Copyright © 2008 by The Harvard Business School Publishing Corporation; all rights reserved.

In some instances we have been unable to trace the owners of copyright material, and we would appreciate any information that would enable us to do so.

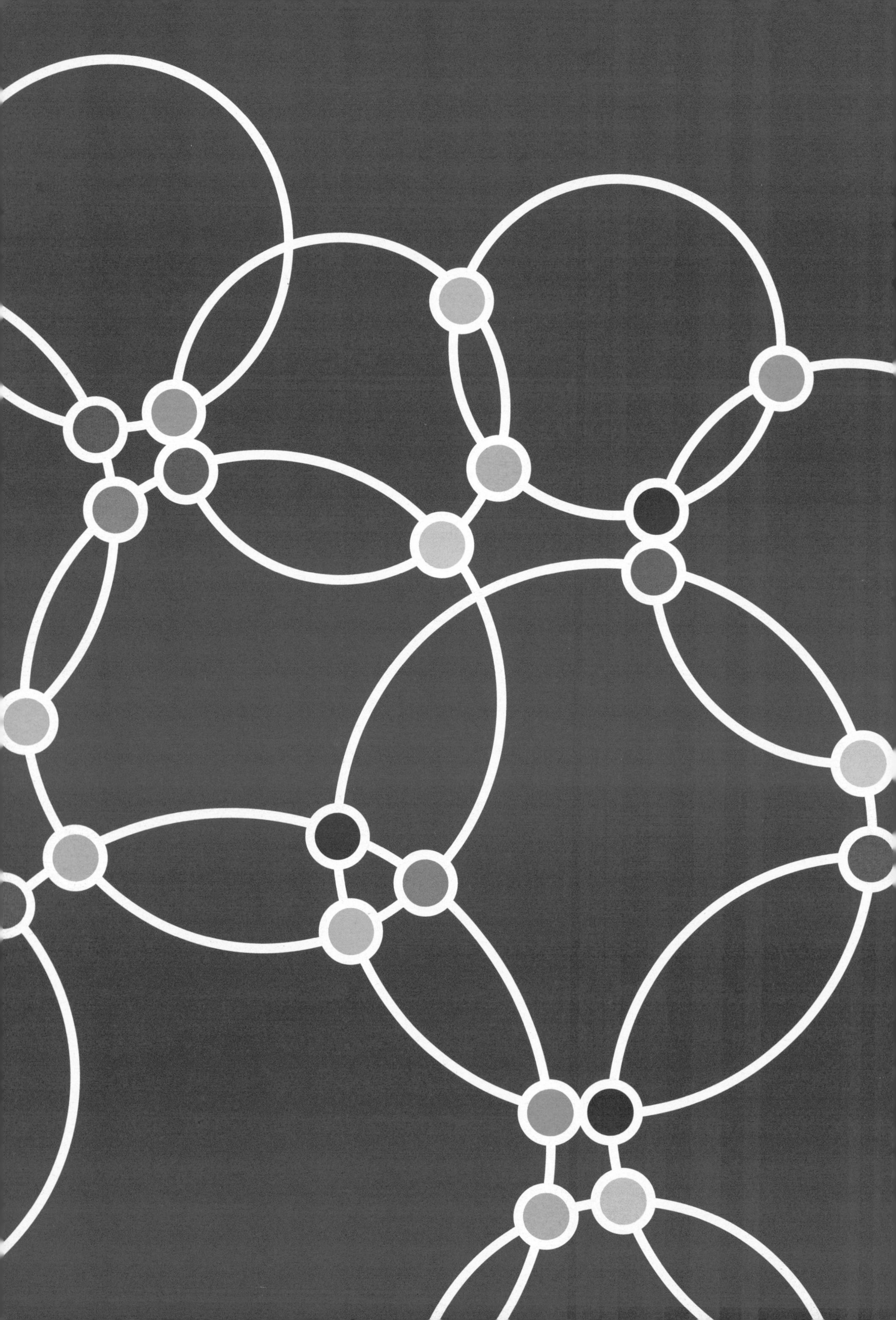

Part 1
Digital marketing fundamentals

Chapter 1 introduces the opportunities and challenges of digital marketing, as well as the different types of digital marketing platforms and media channels available to engage organisations online. It also introduces a planning framework that can be used to structure digital marketing strategies and student case studies. Chapters 2 and 3 provide a foundation for Internet marketing strategy development by reviewing how the online micro- and macro-environment of an organisation can be assessed as part of situation analysis.

Chapter 1
Introducing digital marketing

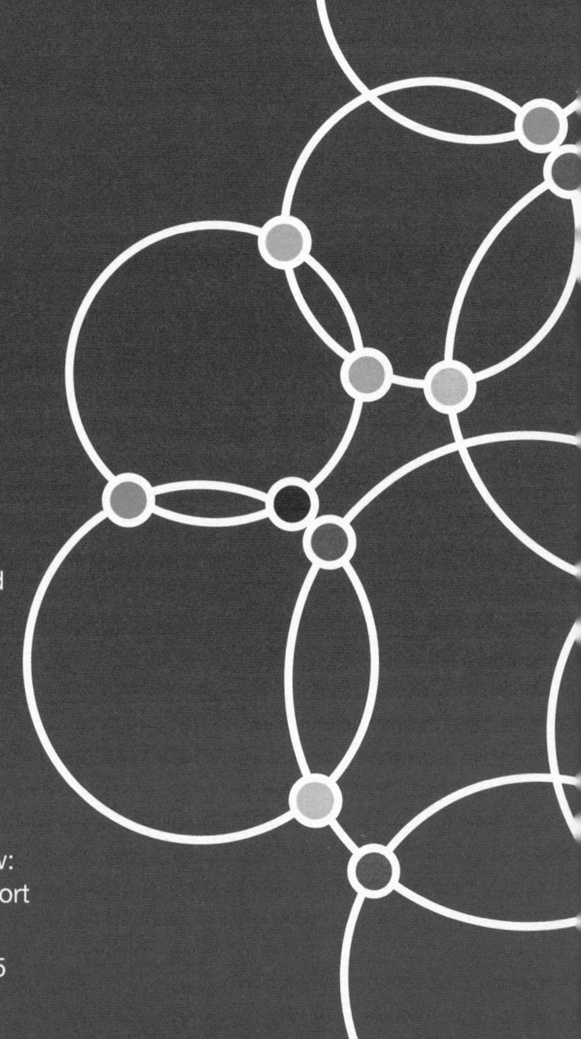

Chapter at a glance

Main topics

Case studies

Learning objectives

After reading this chapter, you should be able to:

- Evaluate the relevance of digital platforms and digital media to marketing
- Evaluate the advantages and challenges of digital media
- Identify the key differences between customer communications digital marketing and traditional marketing.

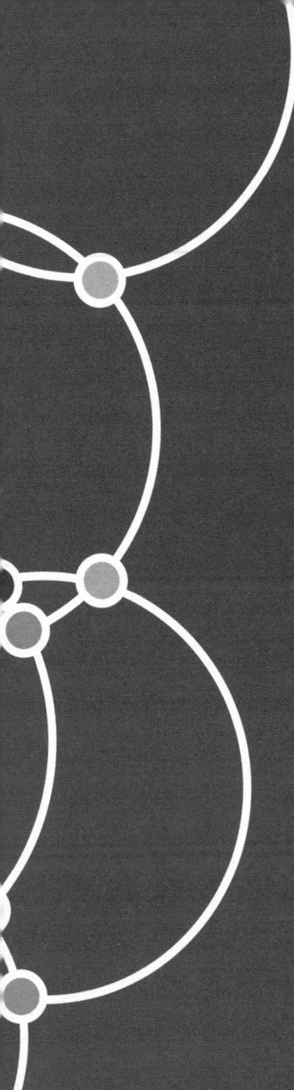

Questions for marketers

Key questions for marketing managers related to this chapter are:

- What are the options for digital marketing to grow our business?
- What are the key benefits of digital marketing?
- What differences do digital media introduce compared to existing marketing communications models?

Scan code to find the latest updates for topics in this chapter

Links to other chapters

This chapter provides an introduction to Internet marketing, and the concepts introduced are covered in more detail later in the book, as follows:

- Chapters 2 and 3 explain marketplace analysis for digital marketing planning
- Chapters 4, 5 and 6 in Part 2 describe how digital marketing strategy can be developed
- Chapters 7, 8, 10 and 11 in Part 3 describe strategy implementation
- Chapters 11 and 12 in Part 3 describe B2C and B2B applications.

Introduction – how have digital technologies transformed marketing?

The Internet and digital media have transformed marketing and business since the first website (**http://info.cern.ch**) went live in 1991. With over one billion people around the world regularly using the web to find products, entertainment and soulmates, consumer behaviour and the way companies market to both consumers and businesses have changed dramatically.

To succeed in the future, organisations will need marketers, strategists and agencies with up-to-date knowledge of how to apply digital media such as the web, e-mail, mobile and Internet TV. The aim of *Digital Marketing: Strategy, Implementation and Practice* is to support students and professionals in gaining and developing this knowledge. In the text, we will show how traditional marketing models and concepts can be applied to help develop digital marketing strategies and plans and where new models are appropriate. We will also give many practical examples and tips of best practice in applying online communications tools to effectively market an organisation's products and services using the Internet and other digital media.

For the authors of this book, digital marketing is an exciting area to be involved with, since it poses many new opportunities and challenges yearly, monthly and even daily. Innovation is a given with the continuous introduction of new technologies, new business models and new communications approaches. For example, Google innovates relentlessly. Its service has developed a long way since 1998 (Figure 1.1) with billions of pages now indexed and other services such as web mail, pay-per-click adverts, analytics and social networks all part of its offering. Complete Activity 1.1 or view Table 1.1 to see other examples of the rate at which new innovations occur.

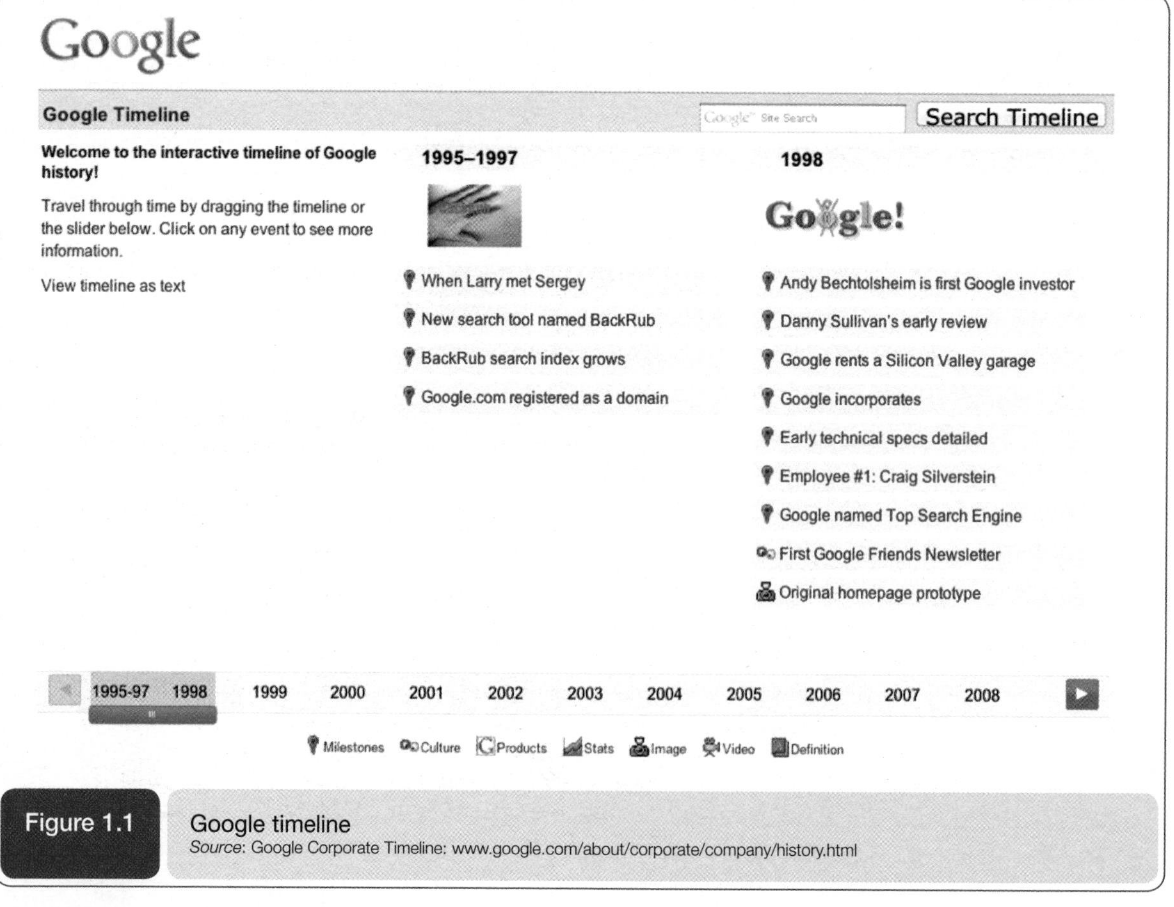

Figure 1.1 Google timeline
Source: Google Corporate Timeline: www.google.com/about/corporate/company/history.html

Activity 1.1 Innovation in digital marketing

Purpose

To illustrate innovation in online business models and communications approaches.

Questions

1 Think about the innovation that you have witnessed during the time you have used the Internet, World Wide Web and mobile platforms. What would you say are the main sites used in your country that have been created which have changed the way we spend our time or buy online? In Table 1.1 are the sites that we believe have had a biggest influence on online business models in the US and Europe, with more emphasis on the most recent ones.

2 What do these sites have in common that you think has made them successful?

Table 1.1 Timeline of online services indicating innovation in business model or marketing communications approach

Year founded	Company/service	Category of innovation
1994	Amazon	Retailer
1995 (March)	Yahoo! (**yahoo.com**)	Directory and portal
1995 (September)	eBay	Online auction
1995 (December)	Altavista (**altavista.com**)	Search engine
1996	Hotmail (**hotmail.com**)	Web-based e-mail Viral marketing (using e-mail signatures to promote service) Purchased by Microsoft in 1997
1998	GoTo.com (**goto.com**) Overture (2001)	First pay-per-click search marketing Purchased by Yahoo! in 2003
1998	Google (**google.com**)	Search engine
1999	Blogger (**blogger.com**)	Blog publishing platform Purchased by Google in 2003
1999	Alibaba (**alibaba.com**)	B2B marketplace with $1.7 billion IPO on Hong Kong stock exchange in 2007. See case in Chapter 2, p. 97
1999	MySpace (**myspace.com**) Formerly eUniverse	Social network Purchased by News Corp in 2005
2001	Wikipedia (**wikipedia.com**)	Open Encyclopedia
2002	Last.fm	A UK-based Internet radio and music community website, founded in 2002. On 30 May 2007, CBS Interactive acquired Last.fm for £140m (US$280m)
2003	Skype (**skype.com**)	Peer-to-peer Internet telephonyVOIP – Voice over Internet Protocol Purchased by eBay in 2005
2003	Second Life (**secondlife.com**)	Immersive virtual world
2004	Facebook (**facebook.com**)	Social network applications and groups
2005	YouTube (**youtube.com**)	Video sharing and rating
2007	Hulu (**hulu.com**)	Quality video broadcast service IPTV – Internet Protocol TV
2008	Groupon (**groupon.com**)	A group-buying service based on use of discounted gift certificates
2009	Foursquare (**foursquare.com**)	A location-based social media website designed for mobile access through 'check-ins'
?	The future	The last entry here is 2009 since it generally takes 1+ year for start-ups to gain prominence. See **www.thenextweb.com** for the current brightest start-ups.

The challenge for marketers is to assess which innovations are most relevant to their organisation and to seek to gain advantage through introducing them to a company such that the digital marketing techniques integrate effectively with traditional marketing communications.

This book will take you through the questions to ask and potential solutions step by step to enable you to develop appropriate strategies. In this introductory chapter, after an initial scoping of digital marketing, we review two main aspects of managing digital marketing. In the first part of this chapter, we review the main strategic challenges of digital marketing that must be managed by organisations. We then go on to introduce the oppor-tunities for promoting companies online through digital technology platforms such as desktop, mobile and digital media communications (for example, Search Engine Marketing (SEM), and social media and display advertising) using the unique characteristics of digital media. The following practitioner interview with Richard Dennys, marketing director of Qype, highlights some of the challenges and opportunities of marketing an online business.

Digital marketing in practice — The Smart Insights interview

Richard Dennys, Marketing Director of Qype UK on how marketing drives support development of this mobile service

Overview and main concepts covered

Founded in 2006 in Hamburg, Germany, Qype (Figure 1.2) is Europe's largest site for user-generated reviews and recommendations of places, events and experiences. Qype has 18 million unique users per month and over 2.2 million user-generated reviews covering business categories in more than 166,000 cities with locations worldwide. Qype allows users to search for and read reviews about a restaurant, shop, service or experience and, with the Qype App, users can read and add reviews on their phone and use the application as a personal sat-nav to find places nearby. Available in seven different languages, Qype is a pan-European local review site able to offer its international users a multi-lingual platform.

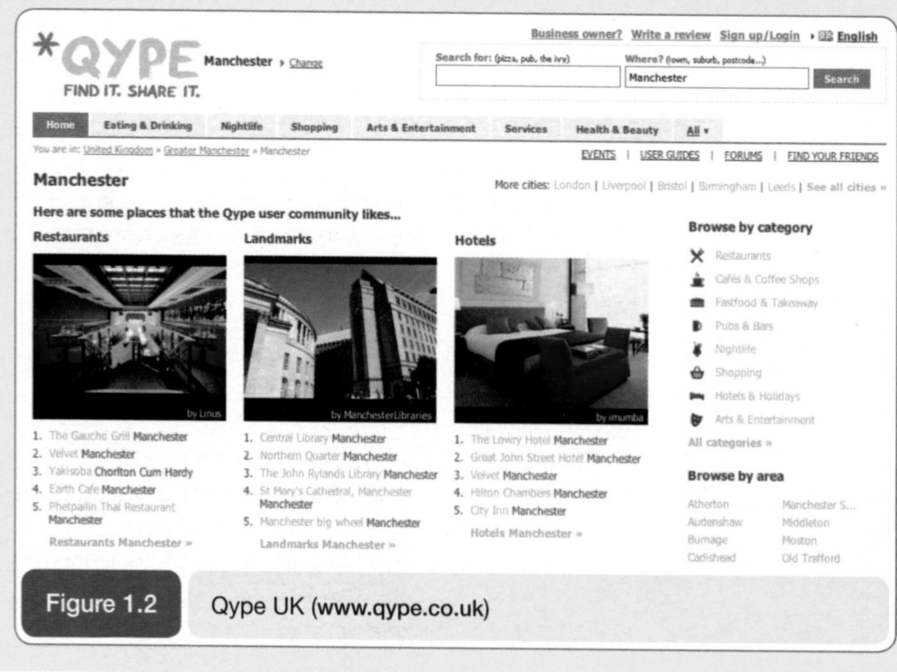

Figure 1.2 Qype UK (www.qype.co.uk)

The interview

Q. What do you see as the main success factors that have fuelled the growth of Qype that other types of businesses could learn from?

Richard Dennys: Qype is currently benefiting from a number of market factors. Principally, it's the rapid move to mobile as the number one medium for social exchange. Google noticed this a while back and then more recently plonked its 'Places' at the heart of its search results.

On top of this is a general growth in consumers to expect their voice to be heard. In the past, TV shows like *Watchdog* and consumer magazines like *Which?* acted as social champions representing groups of disaffected consumers who were dissatisfied with their lack of representation. Now sites like Qype offer a direct route to voice complaints.

Q. If you had to select three, which are the key commercial and marketing measures you look at to review the effectiveness of your marketing strategies?

Richard Dennys: We review and monitor absolutely everything. Each week I receive a multi-layer report with data on everything we can lay our hands on. As ever it's the insight and intelligence that's actually the hard part to put into context:

1 *Our engaged customers: how many people are doing stuff on Qype*. We see tens of millions of users arriving each month, but our challenge is to grow (and retain) the fully engaged central group of registered, contributing users at a faster rate than the overall rate of traffic growth.
2 *Numbers (and spread) of reviewed places*. Just having a list of businesses is easy; anyone can do that and sites like Yell.com do it so well. The whole point of Qype is to search, find and share experiences of places, venues and services so we keep a very close eye on this. Third party API mashups like MaptheQ.com, and also as recently launched on the Gatwick airport website, are also great to see.
3 *Money in! It's the reason we are here*. I have set up metrics to track how every new landing behaves on its conversion journey through to our bottom line.

Q. Could you share some practical tips on campaigns or offers which have been effective in engaging your audience?

Richard Dennys: On the consumer level, our positioning is that we are a fantastic media for forcing a positive change in customer service. We are in the age of the 'social majority' in most European cities now and our message is that Qype provides a brilliant vehicle for all of us to finally express our lack of tolerance of poor value as we move from place to place.

Awareness is the foil of deceit, and our vision for Qype is that cowboys, rip-off merchants and scam artists are quickly forced out of our lives for good. We need more reviews and we need everyone's help to join in and force the change.

On the business side, we are fortunate in that our audience profile is largely populated with urban high-earning, high-spending consumers. We have them looking to spend, while they are spending and just after their spending event; all the time talking about the experiences on the brand or service provider. That's a pretty tough offer to resist for any business owner.

Other than that, we are keeping aware of what's going on around us, staying relevant with an eye always just beyond the horizon, as seen by our recent acquisition of a couponing/voucher business.

→

Q. With Qype available through mobile apps, via the mobile and desktop web, what trends do you see in the relative popularity of these platforms?

Richard Dennys: We have mobile apps in all three major platforms, as well as a few others. We are fast approaching the point where place reviews added via our mobile app outnumber those added via the web. We are also surprised at the rapid growth of our income from mobile advertising. Add this to Geo-marketing, our new couponing offer to our 22 million visitors via their mobiles based on where they are without compromising personal data integrity, it is pretty exciting!

Q. What are the implications of the growth of Facebook location services for local mobile services brands like Qype?

Richard Dennys: We can co-exist. Personally speaking, I think Facebook is in danger of selling itself to death. My own feed on it now is pretty much all promotional messages from things I have liked! The value of me keeping in touch with people is still there, but the novelty has definitely faded.

Facebook also has a challenge on how to monetise its local offer to SMEs around the world. We shall see how it all pans out in the next phase of Web 2.0 or whichever scene we move to next!

Definitions – what are digital marketing and multichannel marketing?

Digital media
Communications are facilitated through content and interactive services delivered by different digital technology platforms including the Internet, web, mobile phone, interactive TV, IPTV and digital signage.

Digital marketing
The application of the Internet and related digital technologies in conjunction with traditional communications to achieve marketing objectives.

Online company presence
Different forms of online media controlled by a company including their website, blogs, e-mail list and social media presences. Also known as 'owned media'.

Electronic customer relationship management (E-CRM)
Using digital communications technologies to maximise sales to existing customers and encourage continued usage of online services through techniques including database, personalised web messages, customer services, e-mail and social media marketing.

The use of the Internet and other **digital media** to support marketing has given rise to a bewildering range of labels and jargon created by both academics and professionals. It has been called digital marketing, Internet marketing, e-marketing and web marketing. In the fifth edition we have changed the title of this text from *Internet Marketing* to *Digital Marketing* since it shows the use of a range of digital platforms to interact with audiences and for other reasons explained in the preface. Of course, what is important within a company is not the term, but the activities that comprise digital marketing, which must be prioritised according to their relevance. So in this chapter we focus on introducing these different digital marketing activities.

Digital marketing can be simply defined as:

Achieving marketing objectives through applying digital technologies.

This succinct definition helps remind us that it is the results delivered by technology that should determine investment in Internet marketing, not the adoption of the technology! These digital technologies include the desktop, mobile, tablet and other digital platforms introduced later in the chapter.

In practice, digital marketing includes managing different forms of **online company presence**, such as company websites and social media company pages in conjunction with online communications techniques introduced later in this chapter, including search engine marketing, social media marketing, online advertising, e-mail marketing and partnership arrangements with other websites. These techniques are used to support the objectives of acquiring new customers and providing services to existing customers that help develop the customer relationship through **E-CRM**. However, for digital marketing to be successful there is still a necessity for integration of these techniques with traditional media such as print, TV and direct mail as part of multichannel marketing communications.

The role of digital platforms in supporting **multichannel marketing** is another recurring theme in this book and in Chapter 2 we explore its role in supporting different **customer journeys** through alternative communications and distribution channels. Online channels can also be managed to support the whole buying process from pre-sale to sale to post-sale and further development of customer relationships.

Owned, earned and paid media

Multichannel marketing Customer communications and product distribution are supported by a combination of digital and traditional channels at different points in the buying cycle.

Customer journeys The sequence of online and offline touchpoints a customer takes during a buying process or broader customer experience. Online this may include a range of digital platforms, communications media, websites, pages and engagement devices.

Paid media Also known as bought media, a direct payment occurs to a site owner or an ad network when they serve an ad, a sponsorship or pay for a click, lead or sale generated.

Earned media The audience is reached through editorial, comments and sharing online.

Owned media Different forms of online media controlled by a company including their website, blogs, e-mail list and social media presence.

To develop a sound digital strategy today involves understanding a more complex, more competitive buying environment than ever before, with customer journeys involving many different forms of online presence. To help develop a strategy to reach and influence potential customers online it's commonplace to refer to three main types of media channels marketers need to consider today (Figure 1.3):

1 **Paid media.** These are bought media where there is investment to pay for visitors, reach or conversions through search, display ad networks or affiliate marketing. Offline, traditional media like print and TV advertising and direct mail remain important, accounting for the majority of paid media spend.
2 **Earned media.** Traditionally, earned media has been the name given to publicity generated through PR invested in targeting influencers to increase awareness about a brand. Now earned media also includes word-of-mouth that can be stimulated through viral and social media marketing, and conversations in social networks, blogs and other communities. It's useful to think of earned media as being developed through different types of partners such as publishers, bloggers and other influencers including customer advocates. Another way of thinking about earned media is as different forms of conversations between consumers and businesses occurring both online and offline.
3 **Owned media.** This is media owned by the brand. Online this includes a company's own websites, blogs, e-mail list, mobile apps or their social presence on Facebook, LinkedIn or Twitter. Offline owned media may include brochures or retail stores. It's useful to think of a company's own presence as media in the sense that they are an alternative investment to other media and they offer opportunities to promote products using similar ad or editorial formats to other media. It emphasises the need for all organisations to become multi-channel publishers.

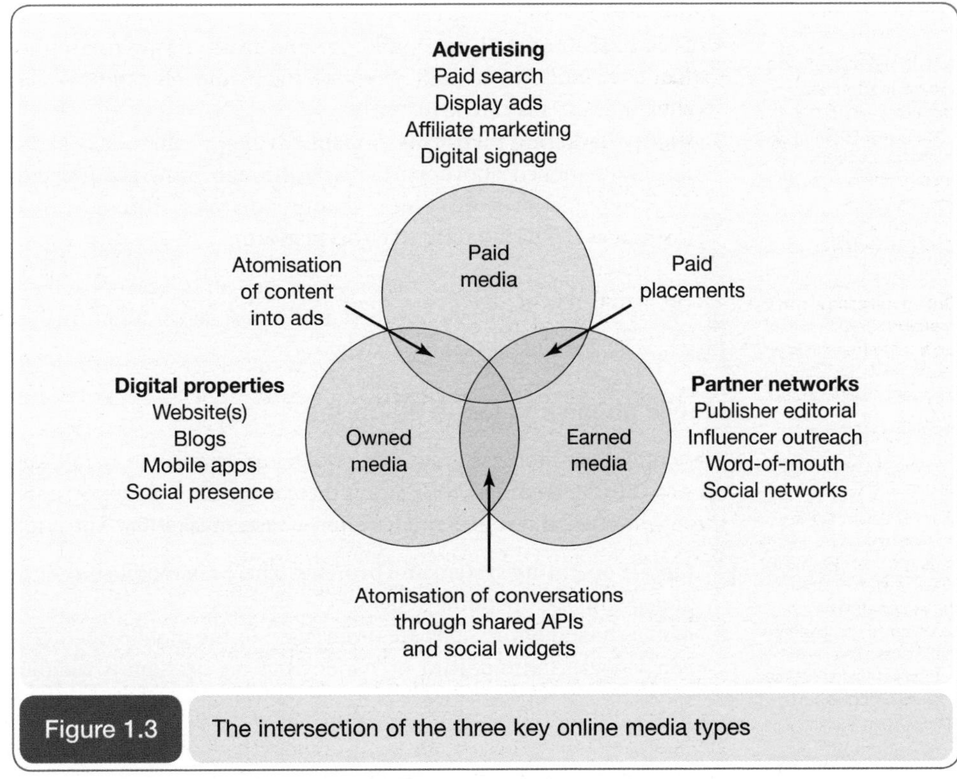

Figure 1.3 The intersection of the three key online media types

You can see on the diagram above that there is overlap between the three different types of media. It is important to note this since achieving this overlap requires integration of campaigns, resources and infrastructure. Content on a content hub or site can be broken down (atomised) and shared between other media types through widgets powered by program and data exchange APIs (**Application Programming Interfaces**) such as the Facebook API.

Application Programming Interfaces
Method of exchanging data between systems such as website services.

The growing range of digital marketing platforms

If you think of the options to reach and interact with audiences when they are online, we have traditionally used digital media channels like search, social media or display ads on media sites accessed via desktop or laptop-based hardware platforms.The desktop access platform has been dominant for years and remains so for now, but with mobile Internet access predicted to exceed desktop Internet access by 2014 or 2015, a range of mobile platforms will become available. Combining with these hardware platforms, there are also different software platforms which marketers can use to reach and interact with their audience through content marketing or advertising, so let's look at the range of options that are available:

Desktop, laptop and notebook platforms

1 **Desktop browser-based platform**. This is traditional web access through the consumer's browser of choice, whether Internet Explorer, Google Chrome or Safari.
2 **Desktop apps**. We don't hear this platform talked about much, but with the launch of Apple Lion many Apple users are accessing paid and free apps from their desktop too via the Apple App Store or the Microsoft equivalent, like Gadgets. This gives opportunities for brands to engage via these platforms.
3 **E-mail platforms**. While e-mail isn't traditionally considered a platform, it does offer an opportunity separate from browser and app-based options to communicate with prospects or clients, whether through editorial or advertising, and e-mail is still widely used for marketing.
4 **Feed-based and API data exchange platforms**. Many users still consume data through RSS feeds, and Twitter and Facebook status updates can be considered a form of feed or stream where ads can be inserted.
5 **Video-marketing platforms**. Streamed video is often delivered through the other platforms mentioned above, particularly through browsers and plug-ins, but it represents a separate platform. Television channels delivered through streaming over the Internet (known as IPTV) are related to this platform.

Mobile marketing
Marketing to encourage consumer engagement when using mobile phones (particularly smartphones) or tablet devices.

Location-based marketing
Location or proximity-based marketing is mobile marketing based on the GPS built into phones or based on interaction with other local digital devices.

Mobile-based apps
A software application that is designed for use on a mobile phone, typically downloaded from an app store. iPhone apps are best known, but all smartphones support the use of apps which can provide users with information, entertainment or location-based services such as mapping.

It could be argued that the major social networks Facebook, LinkedIn and Twitter also provide a form of platform, but these really exist across all of these technology platforms so they haven't been identified separately.

Mobile phone and tablet platforms

The options on mobile hardware platforms are similar in many ways to the desktop. Since they can be used in different locations there are many new opportunities to engage consumers through **mobile marketing** and **location-based marketing**. The main platforms are:

1 **Mobile operating system and browser**. There are mobile browsers which are closely integrated with the operating system.
2 **Mobile-based apps.** Apps are proprietary to the mobile operating system, whether Apple iOS, Google Android, RIM or Windows. A big decision is whether to deliver content and experience through a browser and/or a specific app which provides an improved experience.

Other hardware platforms

Apart from desktop and mobile access, there are a host of other and growing platforms to communicate with customers through. For example:

1 *Gaming platforms.* Whether it's a Playstation, Nintendo or Xbox, there are increasing options to reach gamers through ads or placements within games, for example in-game ads.
2 *Indoor and outdoorkiosk-type apps.* For example, interactive kiosks and augmented reality options to communicate with consumers.
3 *Interactive signage.* The modern version of signage is closely related to kiosk apps and may incorporate different methods such as touch-screen, Bluetooth or QR codes to encourage interactive. Mini Case Study 1.1.gives a futuristic example.

Mini Case Study 1.1 Tesco Homeplus opens subway virtual store in South Korea

In South Korea, Tesco Homeplus has signficantly fewer stores than the market leader E-mart. Based on research which showed that many Koreans tend to shop in stores near their homes for convenience, Tesco trialled a virtual store to reach these shoppers.

Virtual displays were implemented in a similar way to actual stores, from the display to merchandise, but with smartphone QR code readers used to shop and the goods delivered home after checkout (Figure 1.4).

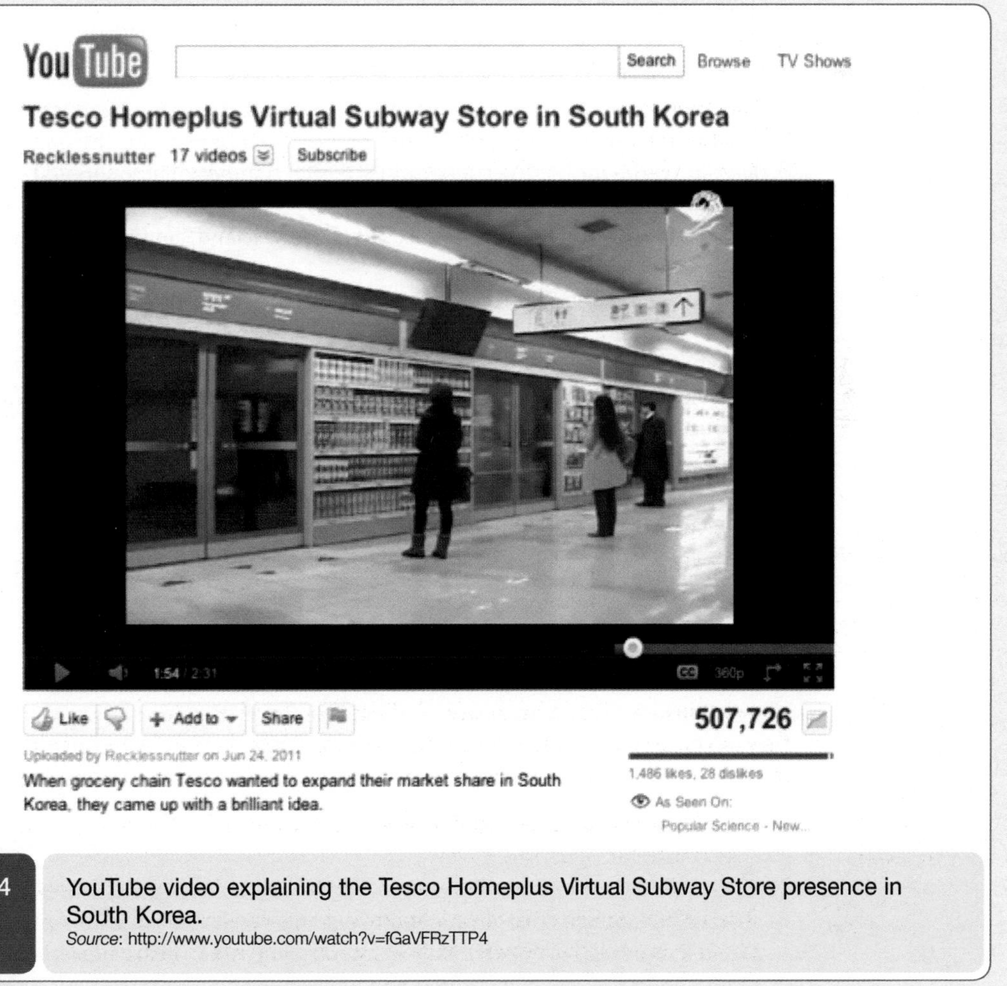

Figure 1.4 YouTube video explaining the Tesco Homeplus Virtual Subway Store presence in South Korea.
Source: http://www.youtube.com/watch?v=fGaVFRzTTP4

Introduction to digital marketing strategy

Positioning
Customers' perception of the product and brand offering relative to those of competitors.

Target marketing strategy
Evaluation and selection of appropriate customer segments and the development of appropriate offers.

Online value proposition (OVP)
A statement of the benefits of online services that reinforces the core proposition and differentiates from an organisation's offline offering and those of competitors.

Multichannel marketing
Defines how different marketing channels should integrate and support each other in terms of their proposition development and communications based on their relative merits for the customer and the company.

Value proposition
The benefits or value a brand offers to customers in its products and services.

The key strategic decisions for digital marketing are in common with traditional business and marketing strategy decisions. As we will see in Chapter 4, which defines a process for developing an Internet marketing strategy, customer segmentation, targeting and **positioning** are all key to effective digital marketing. These familiar **target marketing strategy** approaches involve selecting target customer groups and specifying how to deliver value to these groups as a proposition of services and products. As we will see in Chapter 7, as well as positioning of the core product or brand proposition, online development of a compelling *extended product* or **online value proposition (OVP)** is also important. This defines how the online experience of a brand is delivered through content, visual design, interactivity, sharing, rich media and how the online presence integrates with the offline presence. All of the companies referenced in Table 1.1 have a clear, compelling OVP. Strategic decisions about the future OVP a company offers is a key part of Internet marketing strategy.

Key features of digital marketing strategy

The interaction and integration between Internet channels and traditional channels is a key part of Internet marketing strategy development. Internet marketing strategy is essentially a channel marketing strategy and it needs to be integrated with other channels as part of **multichannel marketing**. It follows that an effective Internet marketing strategy should:

- Be aligned with business strategy (for example, many companies use a rolling three-year plan and vision), with more specific annual business priorities and initiatives.
- Use clear objectives for business and brand development and the online contribution of leads and sales for the Internet or other digital channels. These should be based on models of the number using the channels.
- Be consistent with the types of customers who use and can be effectively reached through the channel.
- Define a compelling, differential **value proposition** for the channel which must be effectively communicated to customers.
- Specify the mix of online and offline communication tools used to attract visitors to the company website or interact with the brand through other digital media such as e-mail or mobile.
- Support the customer journey through the buying process as they select and purchase products using the digital channel in combination with other channels.
- Manage the online customer lifecycle through the stages of attracting visitors to the website, converting them to customers and retention and growth.

Applications of digital marketing

For established multichannel organisations, digital media offer a range of opportunities for marketing products and services across the purchase cycle which companies need to review as part of their digital strategy. For example, companies such as easyJet and BP illustrate the applications of Internet marketing since they show how organisations can use online communications such as their website, third-party websites and e-mail marketing in the following ways:

- *Advertising medium.* For example, BP plc and its subsidiary companies, such as Castrol Limited, use large-format display or interactive ads on media sites to create awareness of brands and products such as fuels and lubricants.

- *Direct-response medium.* For example, easyJet uses sponsored links when a user is researching a flight using a search engine to prompt them to directly visit the easyJet site by clicking through to it. Similarly the easyJet e-mail newsletter sent to customers can encourage them to click through to a website to generate sales.
- *Platform for sales transactions.* For example, easyJet sells flights online to both consumers and business travellers.
- *Lead-generation method.* For example, BP offers content to business car managers about selecting the best fuel for company cars in order to identify interest from a car fleet manager.
- *Distribution channel.* For example, for distributing digital products. This is often specific to companies with digital products to sell such as online music resellers such as Napster (**www.napster.com**) and Apple iTunes (**www.itunes.com**) or publishers of written or video content.
- *Customer service mechanism.* For example, customers serve themselves on easyJet.com by reviewing frequently asked questions.
- *Relationship-building medium* where a company can interact with its customers to better understand their needs and publicise relevant products and offers. For example, easyJet uses its e-mail newsletter and tailored alerts about special deals to help keep its customers and engage them in a dialogue to understand their needs through completing surveys and polls.

Benefits of digital marketing

The benefits of digital marketing in supporting marketing is suggested by applying the definition of marketing by the Chartered Institute of Marketing (**www.cim.co.uk**):

> Marketing is the management process responsible for identifying, anticipating and satisfying customer requirements profitably.

This definition emphasises the focus of marketing on the customer, while at the same time implying a need to link to other business operations to achieve this profitability. Chaffey and Smith (2008) note that e-marketing can be used to support these aims as follows:

- *Identifying* – the Internet can be used for marketing research to find out customers' needs and wants (Chapters 7 and 10).
- *Anticipating* – the Internet provides an additional channel by which customers can access information and make purchases – evaluating this demand is key to governing resource allocation to e-marketing as explained in Chapters 2, 3 and 4.
- *Satisfying* – a key success factor in e-marketing is achieving customer satisfaction through the electronic channel, which raises issues such as: is the site easy to use, does it perform adequately, what is the standard of associated customer service and how are physical products dispatched? These issues of customer relationship management are discussed further in Chapters 6 and 7.

In Chapter 4, we show how to quantify different goals as part of developing digital marketing strategy. To introduce the typical types of goals for digital marketing, see Table 1.2 which gives a basic framework for reviewing the types of goals based on the 5 Ss of Chaffey and Smith (2008).

A powerful method of evaluating the strategic marketing opportunities of using the Internet is to apply the strategic marketing grid of Ansoff (1957) as discussed in the strategy formulation section of Chapter 4 (Figure 4.12). This shows how the Internet can potentially be used to achieve four strategic directions:

1. *Market penetration.* The Internet can be used to sell more existing products into existing markets.
2. *Market development.* Here the Internet is used to sell into new geographical markets, taking advantage of the low cost of advertising internationally without the necessity for a supporting sales infrastructure in the customers' countries.

Table 1.2 The 5 Ss of Internet marketing

Benefit of e-marketing	How benefit is delivered	Typical objectives
Sell – Grow sales	Includes direct online sales and sales from offline channels influenced online. Achieved through wider distribution to customers you cannot readily service offline or perhaps through a wider product range than in-store, or lower prices compared to other channels	• Achieve 10% of sales online in market • Increase online sales for product by 20% in year
Serve – Add value	Achieved through giving customers extra benefits online or inform product development through online dialogue and feedback	• Increase interaction with different content on site • Increase dwell-time duration on site by 10% (sometimes known as 'stickiness') • Increasing number of customers actively using online services (at least once per month) to 30%
Speak – Get closer to customers	Creating a two-way dialogue through web interactions like forums and surveys and conducting online market research through formal surveys and informally monitoring conversations to learn about them	• Grow e-mail coverage to 50% of current customer database • Survey 1000 customers online each month • Increase visitors to community site section by 5%
Save – Save costs	Achieved through online e-mail communications, sales and service transactions to reduce staff, print and postage costs. Savings also accrue through 'web self-service' where customers answers queries through online content	• Generate 10% more sales for same communications budget • Reduce cost of direct marketing by 15% through e-mail • Increase web self-service to 40% of all service enquiries and reduce overall cost-to-serve by 10%
Sizzle – Extend the brand online	Achieved through providing new propositions, new offers and new experiences online including building communities	• Improve branding metrics such as brand awareness, reach, brand favourability and purchase intent

Source: Chaffey and Smith, 2008

3 *Product development.* New products or services are developed which can be delivered by the Internet. These are typically digital products.
4 *Diversification.* In this sector, the Internet supports selling new products which are developed and sold into new markets.

Geyskens *et al.* (2002) suggested in an alternative perspective that there are three main forms of demand expansion for an existing company when they adopt direct Internet channels. These are: (1) *Market expansion* which occurs when new segments of customers are reached who did not previously buy in a category – they give the example of Estée Lauder who hopes that the Clinique.com site will attract customers who avoid buying at a cosmetics counter because they find the experience intimidating; (2) *Brand switching* which is by winning customers from competitors; and (3) *Relationship deepening* which is selling more to existing customers. For well-established brands with a loyal customer-base price reduction relative to other channels is not necessarily essential or some web-channel price reductions can be used, but they note that often competitive pressures may require lower online prices. These authors also note the potential benefits of reduction in transactional and distribution costs through introducing a direct Internet channel once initial startup costs are incurred.

As well as assisting large corporate organisations develop their markets, perhaps the most exciting potential of the Internet is to help existing small and medium enterprises (SMEs) expand. Read Mini Case Study 1.2 'North West Supplies extends its reach online', which also illustrates some of the challenges of managing an online business and highlights the need for continual review and investment in functionality.

Mini Case Study 1.2 North West Supplies extends its reach online

NWS commenced operations in March 1999 when Andrew Camwell, a member of the RAF Volunteer Reserve at the time, spotted a gap in the UK market for mail-order supplies of military garments to people active in the Volunteer Reserve and the Air Cadet Force. Andrew, his wife Carys and her sister Elaine Hughes started running a mail-order business out of shop premises in the village of Cemaes Bay.

The web store (**www.northwestsupplies.co.uk**, Figure 1.5) has been online since November 2002. As it can take several months for a website to be indexed by search engines, NWS used pay-per-click advertising (PPC – see Chapter 8) as a method of very quickly increasing the website's presence in the major search engines. This marketing method proved successful. The directors were pleasantly surprised as they had previously been somewhat dubious about the prospect of the Internet generating sales in their sector. Within six months of running the website, the company had increased turnover by £20,000, but further advances would incur a high advertising cost. Following an eCommerce Review by Opportunity Wales, the company decided to tackle the issues by implementing search engine optimisation (SEO – see Chapter 9) and a site re-design which included:

- *Improved graphic design* – this was to be changed to a more professional and up-to-date look.
- *Best, featured and latest products* – the introduction of a dynamic front page to entice customers to re-visit the site on a regular basis. The contents of this page would feature the best sellers, and latest or featured products.
- *Reviews and ratings* – to provide confidence to consumers and allow some kind of interaction with them, which would allow users to review products they have purchased and give them a star rating.
- *Cross-selling* – when customers view a product there may be other products or categories that may be of interest or be complementary, hence there was a proposal to allow staff to link products and categories so that these would be displayed.
- *Segmentation* – the site would be split into two sections emphasising the segmentation of product lines into military wear and outdoor wear, thus being less confusing and easier to use for the respective users.
- *Navigation by sub-categories* – as the product range had expanded, the additional pages created in each category made it harder for customers to find specific items or have to browse many pages before finding a suitable product. The introduction of sub-categories would provide a clear link to the areas of interest and contain fewer pages to browse thus helping the customer to make a choice more easily and more quickly.

Benefits

The owners describe the benefits of the improvements to their multichannel business as follows:

- *Increased direct sales*: '*The new launch increased sales and appealed to a broader audience – young and old*.' The annual turnover of the business has increased from £250,000 to £350,000 and this is mainly attributable to the new website. The high profile launch aimed at existing customers, the greater visibility in search engines, and the greater usability of the site have all contributed to this.
- *Improved promotion of the whole range of stock*: '*We started selling stuff that we hadn't sold before*.' The changes in navigation, particularly division into two market segments (military and outdoors) and greater use of sub-categories, meant that products were easier to find and hence easier to buy, leading to increased sales of products that had previously been slow sellers.
- *New customers*: '*We now send more items abroad*.' The better performance of the site in search engines has led to an increase in orders from new customers and from abroad. The company now has regular sales to Canada, Australia, New Zealand and various European states. Some 60 per cent of orders are from new customers – not bad for a business that initially set up on the premise of a niche market for UK-based cadet forces.

→

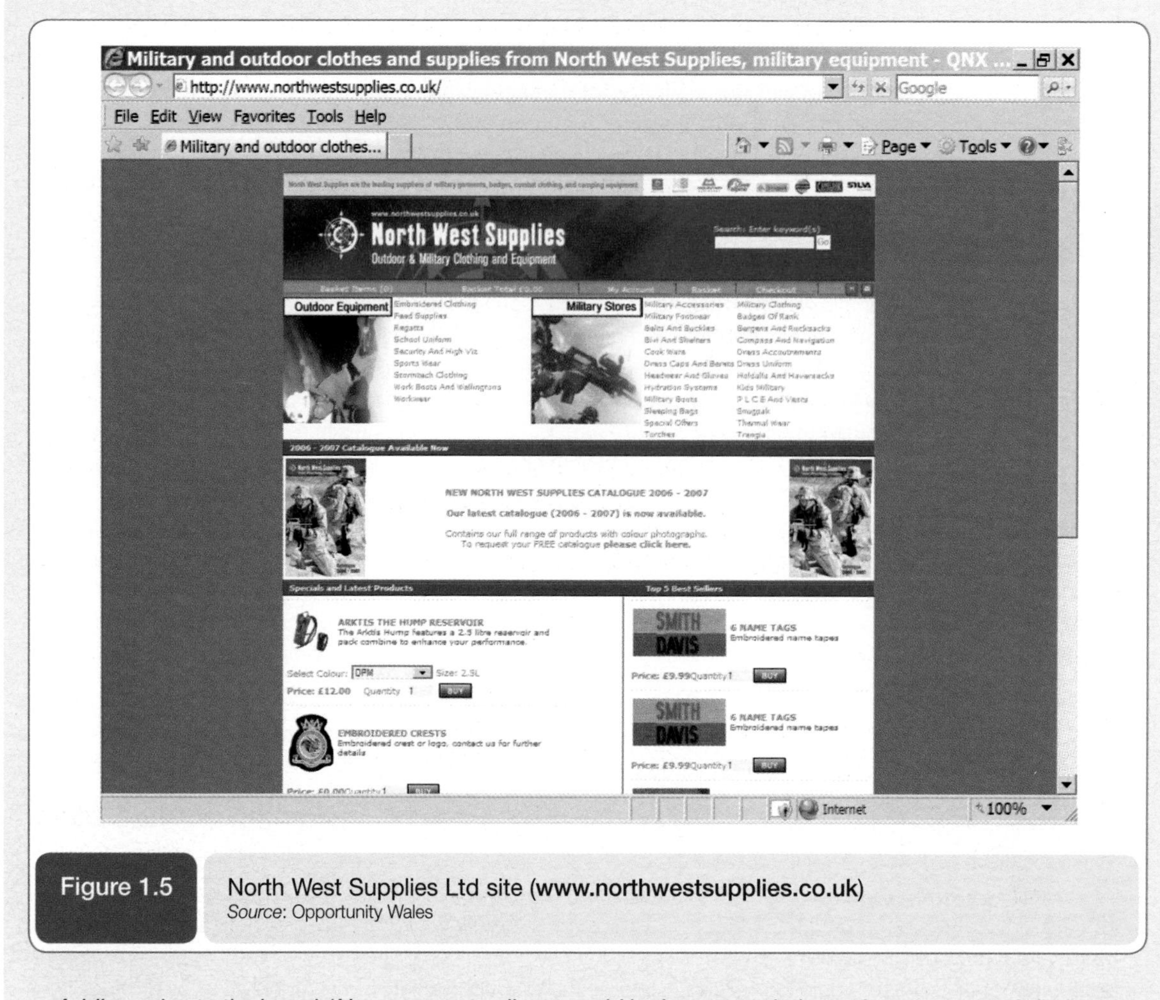

Figure 1.5 North West Supplies Ltd site (www.northwestsupplies.co.uk)
Source: Opportunity Wales

- *Adding value to the brand*: *'New corporate clients could look at our website and see we weren't fly-by-night and that we meant business.'* Improvements to the design have raised confidence levels in visitors and this has led to increased sales. But perhaps more significantly, the professional image of the site was a good boost to confidence for potential business partners in the emerging business-to-business division that started to trade as North Star Contracts.

Alternative digital business models

As part of strategy development, organisations require clarity on the type of business model they will develop.

Business-to-consumer (B2C)
Commercial transactions between an organisation and consumers.

Business-to-business (B2B)
Commercial transactions between an organisation and other organisations (inter-organisational marketing).

Business and consumer business models

A fundamental aspect of the business model is whether the proposition developed appeals to consumers or business. So Internet marketing opportunities are described in terms of the extent to which an organisation is transacting with consumers (**business-to-consumer – B2C**) or other businesses (**business-to-business – B2B**).

Reference to the well-known online companies in Table 1.1 initially suggests these companies are mainly focused on B2C markets. However, B2B communications are still important for many of these companies since business transactions may occur, as for example with eBay

Business (**http://business.ebay.com/**), or the B2C service may need to be sustained through advertising provided through B2B transactions, for example Google's revenue is largely based on its B2B AdWords (**http://adwords.google.com/**). Advertising service and advertising-based revenue is also important to sites such as YouTube, MySpace and Facebook.

Figure 1.6 gives examples of different companies operating in the business-to-consumer (B2C) and business-to-business (B2B) spheres. Often companies such as easyJet and BP will have products that appeal to both consumers and businesses, so will have different parts of their site to appeal to these audiences. Figure 1.6 also presents two additional types of transaction – those where consumers transact directly with other consumers (**Consumer-to consumer – C2C**) and where they initiate trading with companies (**Consumer-to-business – C2B**). Common C2C interactions include transactional exchange (e.g eBay, **www.ebay.com**), financial services (e.g. Zopa, **www.zopa.com**) and betting (e.g. Betfair, **www.betfair.com**). Hoffman and Novak (1996) suggested that C2C interactions are a key characteristic of the Internet that it is important for companies to consider, but their assertion has only been borne out more recently by the growth of the social networks), as is shown by Activity 1.2.

Consumer-to-consumer (C2C)
Informational or financial transactions between consumers, but usually mediated through a business site.

Consumer-to-business (C2B)
Consumers approach the business with an offer.

E-government
The use of Internet technologies to provide government services to citizens.

The diagram also includes government and public services organisations which deliver online or **e-government** services. As well as the models shown in Figure 1.6, it has also been suggested that employees should be considered as a separate type of consumer through the use of intranets, which is referred to as employee-to-employee or E2E.

To: Consumer of content/service \ From: Supplier of content/service	*Consumer or citizen*	*Business (organisation)*	*Government*
Consumer or citizen	**Consumer-to-Consumer (C2C)** • eBay • Peer-to-peer (Skype) • Blogs and communities • Product recommendations Social network (Bebo, Facebook Google+)	**Business-to-Consumer (B2C)** • Transactional: Amazon • Relationship-building: BP • Brand-building: Unilever • Media owner – News Corp • Comparison intermediary: Kelkoo, Pricerunner	**Government-to-Consumer (G2C)** • National government transactional: Tax – Inland Revenue • National government information • Local government information • Local government services
Business (organisation)	**Consumer-to-Business (C2B)** • Priceline • Consumer-feedback, communities or campaigns	**Business-to-Business (B2B)** • Transactional: Euroffice • Relationship-building: BP • Media owned: Emap business productions • B2B marketplaces: EC21 Social network (Linked-In, Plaxo)	**Government-to-Business (B2B)** • Government services and transactions: tax • Legal regulations
Government	**Consumer-to-Government (C2G)** • Feedback to government through pressure group or individual sites	**Business-to-Government (B2G)** • Feedback to government businesses and non-governmental organisations	**Government-to-government (G2G)** • Inter-government services • Exchange of information

Figure 1.6 Summary and examples of transaction alternatives between businesses, consumers and governmental organisations

Activity 1.2 Why are C2C interactions important?

Purpose

To highlight the relevance of C2C transactions to B2C companies.

Activity

Consult with fellow students and share experience of C2C interactions online. Think of C2C on both independent sites and organisational sites. How can C2C communications assist these organisations?

Electronic commerce
All financial and informational electronically mediated exchanges between an organisation and its external stakeholders.

Sell-side e-commerce
E-commerce transactions between a supplier organisation and its customers.

Buy-side e-commerce
E-commerce transactions between a purchasing organisation and its suppliers.

Social commerce
Social commerce is a subset of e-commerce which encourages participation and interaction of customers in rating, selecting and buying products through group-buying. This participation can occur on an e-commerce site or on third-party sites.

What is the difference between e-commerce and e-business?

Electronic commerce (e-commerce) refers to *both financial and informational* electronically mediated transactions between an organisation and any third party it deals with (Chaffey, 2011). So e-commerce involves management not only online of sales transactions, but also of non-financial transactions such as inbound customer service enquiries and outbound e-mail broadcasts, so you can argue that e-commerce is open to all online organisations.

E-commerce is often further subdivided into a **sell-side e-commerce** perspective which refers to transactions involved with selling products to an organisation's customers and a **buy-side e-commerce** perspective which refers to business-to-business transactions to procure resources needed by an organisation from its suppliers. This is shown in Figure 1.7.

Social commerce is an increasingly important part of e-commerce for site owners since incorporating reviews and ratings into a site and linking to social networking sites can help understand customers' needs and increase conversion to sale. It can also involve group buying using a coupon service like Groupon. There is much discussion on the extent to which social media interactions between consumers directly influence sales. Digital marketing insight 2.1 gives some researching hinting at the complexity of understanding this relationship. We introduce social media marketing later in this chapter.

Digital marketing insight 1.1 Social commerce – how much do social networks influence purchase?

Research published by the Harvard Business School quoting Iyengar *et al.* (2009) found that in Korea, where social networking and commerce is more established, that social networks do influence purchase, but the degree of influence depends on the usage level and connectedness of a user. In summary, the research shows:

- For light users of social networks with few connections (48 per cent of users), purchases are unaffected by social network activity.
- For moderate users of social networks with average connections (40 per cent), purchases are influenced by social network interaction, boosting vendor sales for this group by 5 per cent.
- For heavy users of social networks with a high number of connections (12 per cent), purchases are also influenced by social network interaction, but *negatively*; these users avoid buying what their friends have bought and are talking about, leading to a 14% drop in sales from this group for vendors.

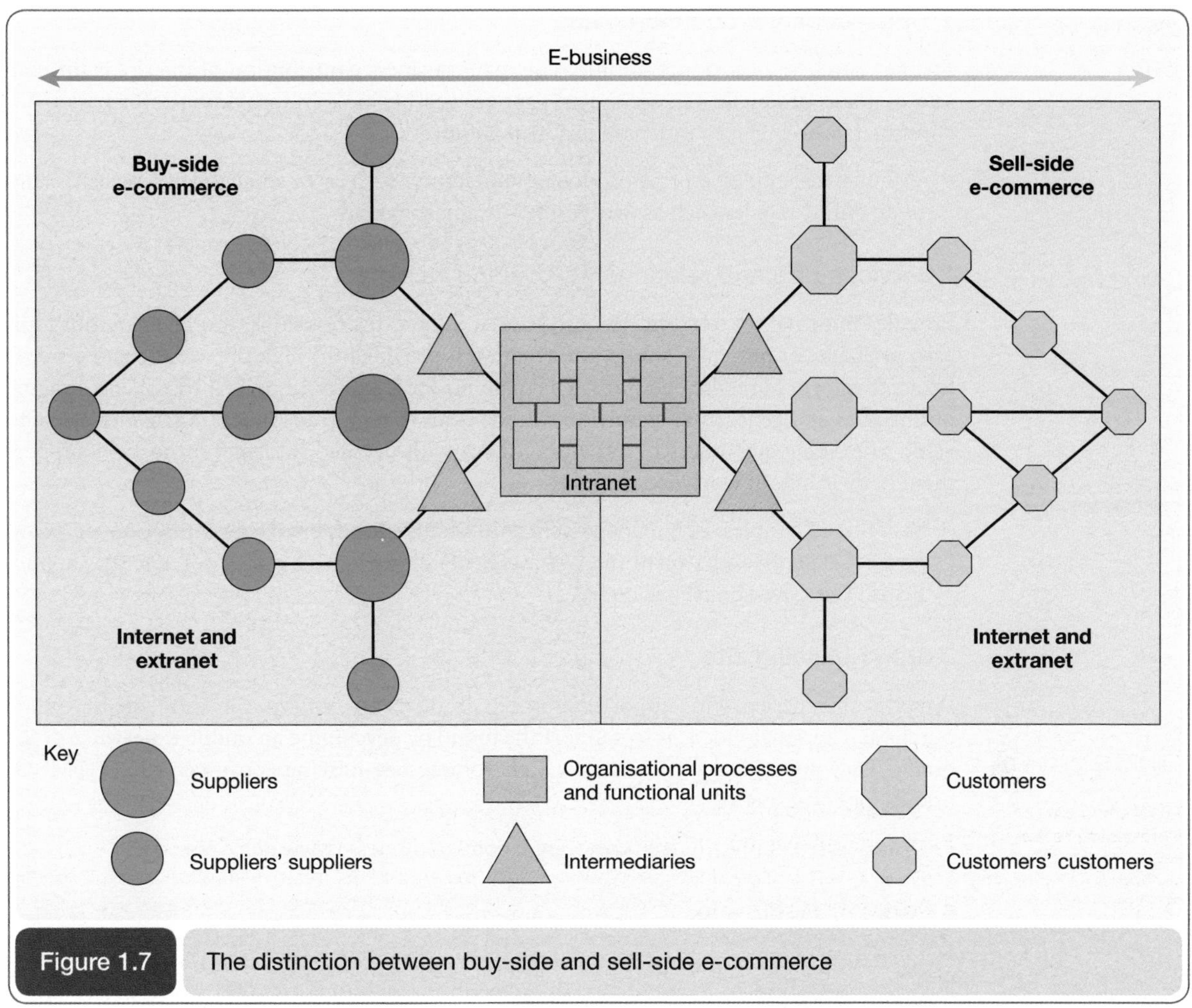

Figure 1.7 The distinction between buy-side and sell-side e-commerce

Electronic business (e-business)
Electronically mediated information exchanges, both within an organisation and with external stakeholders supporting the range of business processes.

E-business (e-business) is similar to e-commerce but broader in scope and refers to using digital technology to manage a range of business processes incorporating the sell-side and buy-side e-commerce shown in Figure 1.7, and also other key supporting business processes including research and development, marketing, manufacturing and inbound and outbound logistics.

Different forms of online presence

The form of digital strategy developed by a company will depend on the nature of a business. Chaffey (2011) identifies different types of online presence which each have different objectives and are appropriate for different markets. Note that these are not clear-cut categories of websites since any company may combine these types as part of their business model, but with a change in emphasis according to the market they serve. Increasingly companies are using their company pages on social networks such as Facebook, Google+ and LinkedIn to similar purposes. As you review websites and company social presences, note how organisations have different parts of the site focusing on these functions of sales transactions, services, relationship-building, brand-building and providing news and entertainment. The five main types of site are as follows.

1 Transactional e-commerce site

Enables purchase of products online. The main business contribution of the site is through sale of these products. The sites also support the business by providing information for consumers who prefer to purchase products offline.

- Visit these examples: an end-product manufacturer such as Vauxhall (**www.vauxhall.co.uk**) or an online retailer such as Amazon (**www.amazon.com**).

2 Services-oriented relationship-building website

Provides information to stimulate purchase and build relationships. Products are not typically available for purchase online. Information is provided through the website and e-newsletters to inform purchase decisions. The main business contribution is through encouraging offline sales and generating enquiries or leads from potential customers. Such sites also add value to existing customers by providing them with detailed information to help support them in their lives at work or at home.

- Visit these examples: B2B management consultants such as PricewaterhouseCooper (**www.pwcglobal.com**) and Accenture (**www.accenture.com**), B2C portal for energy supplier British Gas (**www.britishgas.co.uk**).

3 Brand-building site

Provides an experience to support the brand. Products are not typically available for online purchase. Their main focus is to support the brand by developing an online experience of the brand. They are typical for low-value, high-volume fast-moving consumer goods (FMCG) brands for consumers.

- Visit these examples: Tango (**www.tango.com**), Guinness (**www.guinness.com**).

4 Portal or media site

Provides information or news about a range of topics. 'Portal' refers to a gateway of information. This is information both on the site and through links to other sites. Portals have a diversity of options for generating revenue including advertising, commission-based sales, sale of customer data (lists).

- Visit these examples: Yahoo! (**www.yahoo.com**) (B2C) and Silicon (**www.silicon.com**) (B2B).

Each of these different types of sites tend to increase in sophistication as organisations develop their Internet marketing. In Chapters 2 and 4 we look at **stage models** of the development of Internet marketing services, from static **brochureware sites** to dynamic **transactional e-commerce sites** that support interactions with customers.

Stage models
Models for the development of different levels of Internet marketing services.

Brochureware site
A simple site with limited interaction with the user that replicates offline marketing literature.

Transactional e-commerce sites
Sites that support online sales.

5 Social network or community site

These sites or parts of sites focus on enabling community interactions between different consumers (C2C model). Typical interactions include posting comments and replies to comments, sending messages, rating content and tagging content in particular categories.

Well-known examples include Facebook, LinkedIn and Twitter. Other start-ups also have a social network element such as Delicious (social bookmarking or rating web pages), Digg (comment on blog postings), Flickr (image tagging), Technorati (blog postings) and YouTube (videos). B2B social networks to keep business professionals in contact include LinkedIn and Plaxo although some are turning to Facebook for this function. (Large social networks such as Facebook or MySpace are effectively media owners and this is their main revenue source and in previous editions of this book were included in that category.) In addition to distinct social network sites such as these, social networks can also be integrated into other site types. For example, travel and insurance company Saga Group, which provides products primarily to the over-50s market, has developed Saga Zone (**www2.saga.co.uk/sagazone**) where users can chat or post photos.

Challenges in developing and managing digital marketing strategy

Some of the challenges in managing Internet marketing strategy which are commonly seen in many organisations (and should be managed) include:

- *Unclear responsibilities* for the many different Internet marketing activities shown in Figure P.1 in the Preface.
- *No specific objectives* are set for Internet marketing.
- *Insufficient budget* is allocated for Internet marketing because customer demand for online services is underestimated and competitors potentially gain market share through superior online activities.
- *Budget is wasted* as different parts of an organisation experiment with using different tools or suppliers without achieving economies of scale.
- *New online value propositions for customers* are not developed since the Internet is treated as 'just another channel to market' without review of opportunities to offer improved, differentiated online services.
- *Results from digital marketing are not measured or reviewed* adequately, so actions cannot be taken to improve effectiveness.
- An experimental rather than planned approach is taken to using e-communications with poor integration between online and offline marketing communications.

Research by EConsultancy (2008) investigated the challenges of managing Internet marketing. The research found that many companies were experiencing problems of deploying the right resources for Internet marketing. Challenges were rated by respondents as follows:

- gaining senior management buy-in or resource (67% agreed)
- gaining buy-in or resource from traditional marketing functions or brands (66% agreed)
- gaining IT resource or technical support (61% agreed)
- finding suitable staff (75% agreed)
- finding suitable digital media agencies (54% agreed).

You can see that there are challenges both in managing different types of internal resources and finding suitable staff. The main challenges mentioned included gaining buy-in and budget along with conflicts of ownership and tensions between a digital marketing team and other teams such as traditional marketing, IT, finance and senior management. Coordination with different channels in conjunction with teams managing marketing programmes elsewhere in the business was also challenging.

Applying the 7 Ss

The 7 Ss are a useful framework for reviewing an organisation's existing and future capabilities to meet the challenges posed by the new digital channels and some of the aspects of this are shown in Table 1.3.

You may have encountered the 7 S framework, summarised by Waterman *et al.* (1980) and developed by McKinsey consultants in the 1980s. It is often referenced when referring to the management of a business. EConsultancy (2005) has summarised some of the strategic resource management issues that require consideration, as shown in Table 1.3.

Table 1.3 Summary of some of the organisational challenges of digital marketing that need to be managed in the context of the 7 S framework.

Element of 7 S model	Application to digital marketing strategy	Key issues from practice and literature
Strategy	The significance of digital marketing in influencing and supporting the organisation's strategy	Gaining appropriate budgets and demonstrating/ delivering value and ROI from budgets. Annual planning approach. Techniques for using digital marketing to impact organisation strategy. Techniques for aligning digital strategy with organisational and marketing strategy.
Structure	The modification of organisational structure to support digital marketing	Integration of team with other management, marketing (corporate communications, brand marketing, direct marketing) and IT staff. Use of cross-functional teams and steering groups. Insourcing vs outsourcing.
Systems	The development of specific processes, procedures or information systems to support digital marketing	Campaign planning approach–integration. Managing/sharing customer information. Managing content quality. Unified reporting of digital marketing effectiveness. In-house vs external best-of-breed vs external integrated technology solutions.
Staff	The breakdown of staff in terms of their background and characteristics such as IT vs marketing, use of contractors/ consultants, age and sex	Insourcing vs outsourcing. Achieving senior management buy-in/ involvement with digital marketing. Staff recruitment and retention. Virtual working. Staff development and training.
Style	Includes both the way in which key managers behave in achieving the organisation's goals and the cultural style of the organisation as a whole	Relates to role of digital marketing team in influencing strategy – is it dynamic and influential or conservative and looking for a voice.
Skills	Distinctive capabilities of key staff, but can be interpreted as specific skill sets of team members	Staff skills in specific areas: supplier selection, project management, content management, specific e-marketing approaches (SEO, PPC, affiliate marketing, e-mail marketing, online advertising).
Superordinate goals	The guiding concepts of the digital marketing organisation which are also part of shared values and culture. The internal and external perception of these goals may vary	Improving the perception of the importance and effectiveness of the digital marketing team among senior managers and staff it works with (marketing generalists and IT).

Source: EConsultancy (2005)

A strategic framework for developing a digital marketing strategy

To realise the benefits of Internet marketing and avoid the pitfalls that we have described, an organisation needs to develop a planned, structured approach. Consequently, this book defines a strategic approach to Internet marketing which is intended to manage these risks and deliver the opportunities available from online channels. In Figure 1.8 we suggest a process for developing and implementing an Internet marketing plan which is based on our experience of strategy definition in a wide range of companies. This diagram highlights the

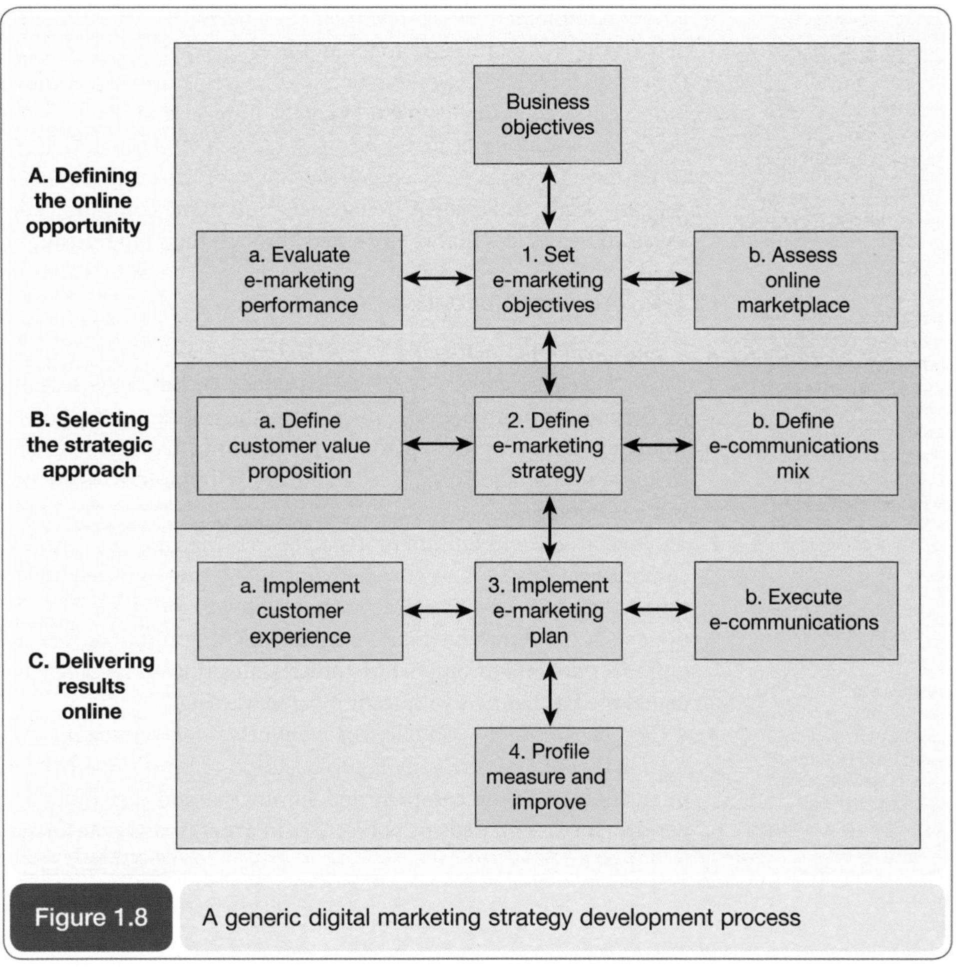

Figure 1.8 A generic digital marketing strategy development process

key activities and their dependencies which are involved for the creation of a typical Internet marketing strategy and relates them to coverage in different chapters in this book:

A: Defining the online opportunity

Setting objectives to define the potential is the core of this phase of strategy development. Key activities are:

- *1 Set e-marketing objectives (Chapters 4 and 8)*. Companies need to set specific numerical objectives for their online channels and then resource to deliver these objectives. These objectives should be informed by and influence the business objectives and also the following two activities.
- *1a Evaluate e-marketing performance (Chapters 4 and 10)*. Apply web analytics tools to measure the contribution of leads, sales and brand involvement currently delivered by online communications such as search engine marketing, online advertising and e-mail marketing in conjunction with the website.
- *1b Assess online marketplace (Chapters 2, 3 and 4)*. Situation analysis review of the micro-environment (customers, competitors, intermediaries, suppliers and internal capabilities and resources) and the broader macro-environment which influences strategy such as legal requirements and technology innovation.

B: Selecting the strategic approach

- *2 Define e-marketing strategy (Chapter 4)*. Select appropriate strategies to achieve the objectives set at stage A1.

- *2a Define customer value proposition (Chapters 4 to 7).* Define the value proposition available through the online channel and how it relates to the core proposition delivered by the company. Review segmentation and targeting options. Review the marketing mix and brand values to evaluate how they can be improved online.
- *2b Define e-communications mix (Chapters 4, 8 and 9).* Select the offline and online communications tools to encourage usage of an organisation's online services and to generate leads and sales. Develop new outbound communications and event-triggered touch strategies to support customers through their relationship with the company.

Digital media channels
Online communications techniques used to achieve goals of brand awareness, familiarity, favourability and to influence purchase intent by encouraging users of digital media to visit a website to engage with the brand or product, and ultimately to purchase online or offline through traditional media channels such as by phone or in-store.

Display ads
Use of graphical or *rich media ad units* within a web page to achieve goals of delivering brand awareness, familiarity, favourability and purchase intent. Many ads encourage interaction through prompting the viewer to *rollover* to play videos, complete an online form or to view more details before clicking through to a site.

C: Delivering results online

- *3 Implement e-marketing plan (Part 3).* This details the implementation of the strategy.
- *3a Implement customer experience (Chapter 7).* Build the website and create the e-mail marketing communications which form the online interactions customers make with a company. Create online customer relationship management capabilities to understand customers' characteristics, needs and behaviours and to deliver targeted, personalised value (Chapter 6).
- *3b Execute e-communications (Chapter 8).* Manage the continuous online marketing communications such as search engine marketing, partnerships social media marketing, sponsorships and affiliate arrangements, and campaign-based e-marketing communications such as online advertising, e-mail marketing and microsites to encourage usage of the online service and to support customer acquisition and retention campaigns. Integrate the digital media channels with traditional marketing.
- *4 Customer profiling (Chapter 6), monitoring and improving online activities and maintaining the online activities (Chapter 9).* Capture profile and behavioural data on customer interactions with the company and summarise and disseminate reports and alerts about performance compared with objectives in order to drive performance improvement.

You will see that in the process diagram, Figure 1.8, many double-headed arrows are used, since the activities are often not sequential but rather inform each other, so activity 1, set e-marketing objectives, is informed by the activities around it but may also influence them. Similarly, activity 4, profile, measure and improve, is informed by the execution of online activities but there should be a feedback loop to update the tactics and strategies used.

Introduction to digital marketing communications

Pay-per-click
PPC refers to when a company pays for text ads to be displayed on the search engine results pages as a sponsored link (typically above, to the right of or below the natural listings) when a specific keyphrase is entered by the search users. It is so called because the marketer pays each time the hypertext link in the ad is clicked on. If a link is clicked repeatedly, then this will be detected by the search engine as click fraud and the marketer will not be charged.

For many years, marketing campaigns were based on traditional media including TV, print and radio ads, and direct mail supported by public relations. But, in a few short years, since the web concept was first proposed in the late 1980s by Sir Tim Berners-Lee, there have been great changes in marketing communications. The digital equivalents of these traditional media, which are known as **digital media channels**, are vital components of most marketing campaigns. For example, in an online campaign, marketers can use ads and content on social media to engage audiences; **display ads**, the familiar banner and skyscraper ads seen on many online publisher sites; **pay-per-click (PPC)** ads such as the Sponsored Links in Google; **search engine optimisation (SEO)** to gain higher positions in the natural listings of Google; **affiliate marketing** where sites which generate a sale for a merchant gain commission and e-mail marketing, which is most effective when messages are sent to an existing customer base, i.e. customers who have given their permission to receive them. Many of these digital communications techniques are analogous to their traditional equivalents, for example, display ads are broadly equivalent to print or display ads and **e-mail marketing** is equivalent to direct mail.

But the approaches used to target the online audience are potentially very different with personalisation based on the customer profile and previous interactions with communications giving many options to deliver more timely, relevant messages. (Personalised communications are also effective on the website where **landing pages** are commonly used to make the page more relevant to what the customer is seeking.) Leading websites also provide great opportunities to engage the visitor through in-depth text content, **rich media** such as video and audio and participation in customer communities.

Search engine optimisation
A structured approach used to increase the position of a company or its products in search engine natural or organic results listings (the main body of the search results page) for selected keywords or phrases.

Affiliate marketing
A commission-based arrangement where referring sites (publishers) receive a commission on sales or leads by merchants (retailers). Commission is usually based on a percentage of product sale price or a fixed amount for each sale, but may also be based on a per-click basis, for example when an aggregator refers visits to merchants.

E-mail marketing
Typically applied to outbound communications from a company to prospects or customers to encourage purchase or branding goals. E-mail marketing is most commonly used for mailing to existing customers on a house-list, but can also be used for mailing prospects on a rented or co-branded list. E-mails may be sent as part of a one-off campaign or can be automated event-based triggered e-mails such as a welcome strategy which can be broadcast based on rules about intervals and customer characteristics.

Landing page
A destination page when a user clicks on an ad or other form of link from a *referring site*. It can be a home page but more typically and desirably, a landing page is a page with the messaging focused on the offer in the ad. This will maximise conversion rates and brand favourability.

Rich media
Advertisements or site content that are not static, but provide animation, sound or interactivity. An example of this would be a display advertisement for a loan in which a customer can type in the amount of loan required, and the cost of the loan is calculated immediately.

The relationship between digital and traditional communications

It is helpful to understand the relationship between the new digital communications techniques and traditional communications, in order that new opportunities are not missed and campaigns can be planned in an integrated fashion. As Jenkinson and Sain (2001) explain:

> A variety of concepts and terms are used across both academics and practitioners. For example, within our research into media neutral planning, some people referred to media, some to contact points or channels as methods of distributing communication. Similarly, some referred to tools and others to channels, disciplines or methods as the techniques by which the media could be used.

To illustrate the relationship between different levels of marketing communications consider Table 1.4 which is based on terminology introduced by Jenkinson and Sain (2001) and increasingly adopted by practioners and academics.

Table 1.4 Key marketing communications concepts

Marketing communications term	Definition	Examples from traditional and digital media
Medium (media)	*'Anything that conveys a message'* The carrier of the message or method of transmission. Can be conceived as the touchpoint with the customer	Broadcast (television, radio), press, direct mail, cinema, poster, digital (web, e-mail, mobile)
Discipline	'A body of craft technique biased *towards a facet of marketing communication'* These are traditionally known as 'promotion tools' or the different elements of the communications mix	Advertising, direct marketing, public relations, market research, personal selling, sales promotion, sponsorship, packaging, exhibitions and trade shows. All are also used online
Channel (tools)	The combination of a discipline with a medium	Direct mail, direct response TV, television brand advertising. Digital channels: different forms of search marketing, affiliate marketing, display advertising, e-mail marketing, social media, blogs and feeds
Vehicle	A specific channel used to reach a target audience	TV (ITV, Channel 4), newspaper (*The Sun*, *Metro*, *The Times*), magazine (*The Economist*, *Radio Times*), radio (Virgin Radio, BBC Radio 5) and their website equivalents. Different search engines such as Google fit, or aggregators of product from other suppliers such as Moneysupermarket, also fit here

Activity 1.3 Innovation in Digital marketing

Purpose

To illustrate similarities and differences between digital and traditional media.

Activity

Make two columns. On the left, write down different digital media channels and, on the right, the corresponding communications disciplines such as advertising, direct marketing or PR which are most appropriate.

Using digital media channels to support business objectives

Before we explain the different digital media channels, it's important to consider how they can support business goals. RACE (Figure 1.9) is a practical framework developed by Smart Insights (2010) to help marketers manage and improve the commercial value that their organisations gain from digital marketing. RACE is an evolution of the REAN (Reach Engage Activate Nurture) framework originally developed by Xavier Blanc and popularised by Steve

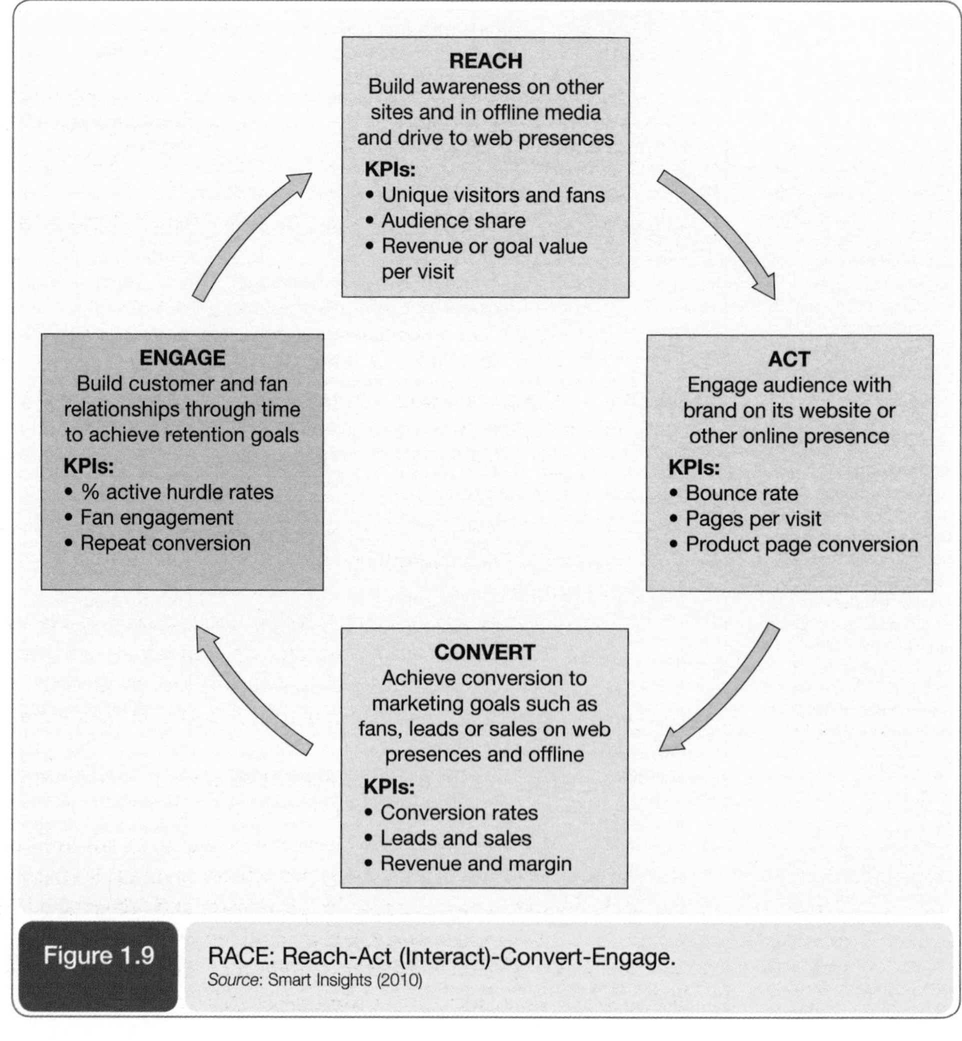

Figure 1.9 RACE: Reach-Act (Interact)-Convert-Engage.
Source: Smart Insights (2010)

Jackson in his book *Cult of Analytics* (Jackson, 2009). It is intended to help create a simplified approach to reviewing the performance of online marketing and taking actions to improve its effectiveness. The measures introduced in Figure 1.9 are covered in more depth in chapters 4 and 10 where we explore the power of using **web analytics** for improving marketing performance.

RACE consists of four steps designed to help engage prospects, customers and fans with brands throughout the customer lifecycle.

- *Step 1: Reach* – Build awareness of a brand, its products and services on other sites and in offline media and build traffic by driving visits to web presences.
- *Step 2: Interact* – Engage audience with brand on its website or other online presence to encourage them to act or interact with a company or other customers.
- *Step 3: Convert* – Achieve conversion to marketing goals such as new fans, leads or sales on web presences and offline.
- *Step 4: Engage* – Build customer relationships through time to achieve retention goals.

Digital channels always work best when they are integrated with other channels, so where appropriate digital channels should be combined with the traditional offline media and channels. The most important aspects of integration are first using traditional media to raise awareness of the value of the online presences at the Reach and Interact stages, and second at the 'Convert' and 'Engage' steps where customers may prefer to interact with customer representatives.

Web analytics
Techniques used to assess and improve the contribution of digital marketing to a business, including reviewing traffic volume, referrals, clickstreams, online reach data, customer satisfaction surveys, leads and sales.

Social networks
A site that facilitates peer-to-peer communication within a group or between individuals through providing facilities to develop user-generated content (UGC) and to exchange messages and comments between different users.

Blog
Personal online diary, journal or news source compiled by one person, an internal team or external guest authors. Postings are usually in different categories. Typically comments can be added to each blog posting to help create interactivity and feedback.

Podcast
Individuals and organisations post online media (audio and video) which can be viewed in the appropriate players (including the iPod which first sparked the growth in this technique). The latest podcast updates can be automatically delivered by RSS.

Feeds (or RSS feed)
Blog, news or other content is published by an XML standard and syndicated for other sites or read by users in RSS reader services such as Google Reader, personalised home pages or e-mail systems. RSS stands for Really Simple Syndication.

Viral marketing
A marketing message is communicated from one person to another, facilitated by different media, such as word of mouth, e-mail or websites, in particular social network or blog sites. Viral marketing implies rapid transmission of messages is intended.

The key types of digital media channels

There are many online communications tools which marketers must review as part of their communications strategy or as part of planning an online marketing campaign. To assist with planning, Chaffey and Smith (2008) recommend that these online marketing tools are divided into the six main groups shown in Figure 1.10.

In Chapters 8 and 9, we review these tools in detail, but this is the essence of each digital media channel:

1. *Search engine marketing.* Placing messages on a search engine to encourage click-through to a website when the user types a specific keyword phrase. Two key search marketing techniques are paid placements or sponsored links using pay-per-click, and placements in the natural or organic listings using search engine optimisation (SEO) where no charge is made for clicks from the search engine.
2. *Online PR.* Maximising favourable mentions of your company, brands, products or websites on third-party websites such as **social networks**, **blogs**, **podcasts** or **feeds** that are likely to be visited by your target audience. Also includes responding to negative mentions and conducting public relations via a site through a social media newscentre or blog, for example.
3. *Online partnerships.* Creating and managing long-term arrangements to promote your online services on third-party websites or through e-mail communications. Different forms of partnership include link building, affiliate marketing, aggregators such as price comparison sites like Moneysupermarket (**www.moneysupermarket.com**), online sponsorship and co-branding.
4. *Display advertising.* Use of online ads such as banners and rich media ads to achieve brand awareness and encourage click-through to a target site.
5. *Opt-in e-mail marketing.* Renting e-mail lists or placing ads in third-party e-newsletters or the use of an in-house list for customer activation and retention.
6. *Social media marketing.* Companies participate and advertise within social networks and communities to reach and engage their audience. **Viral marketing** or online word of mouth – messages is closely related to this. Here content is shared or messages are forwarded to help achieve awareness and, in some cases, drive response.

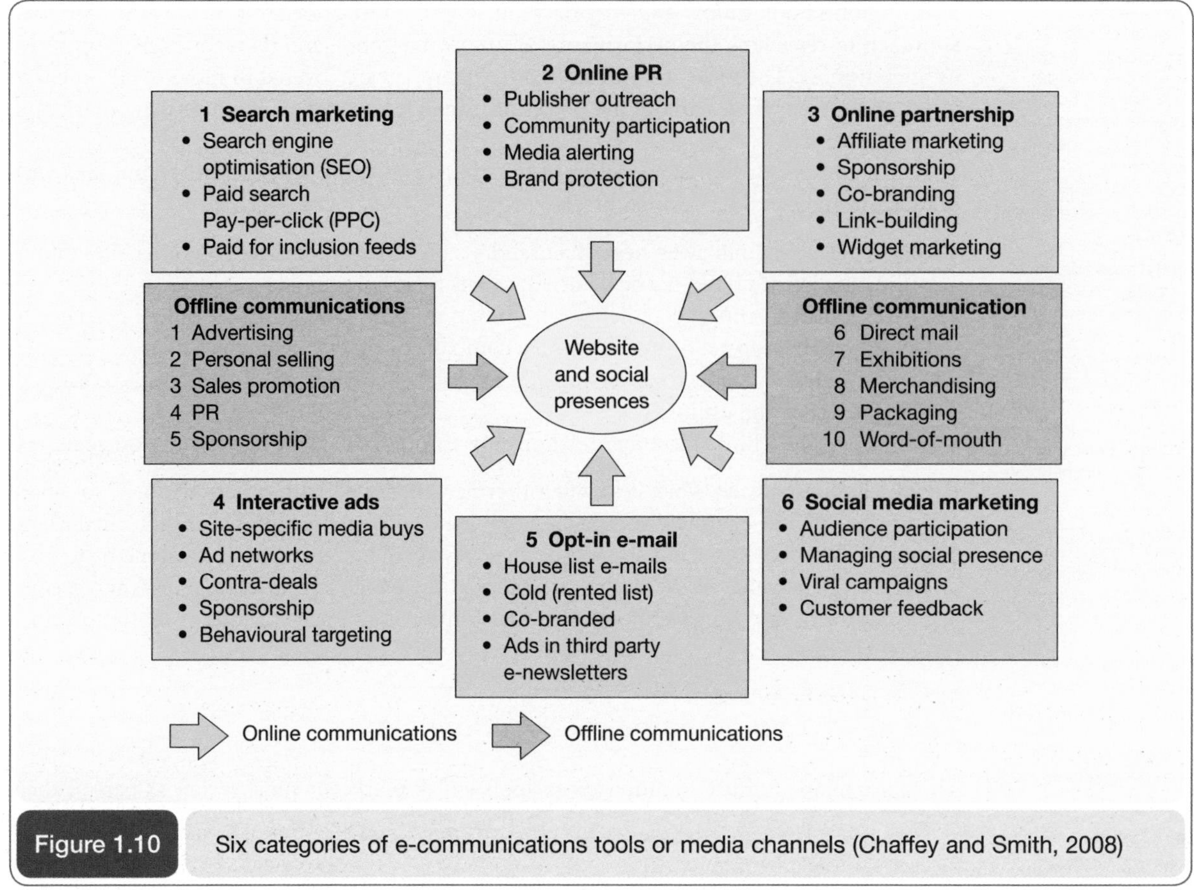

Figure 1.10 Six categories of e-communications tools or media channels (Chaffey and Smith, 2008)

Social media marketing Monitoring and facilitating customer-customer interaction and participation throughout the web to encourage positive engagement with a company and its brands. Interactions may occur on a company site, social networks and other third-party sites.

Social media marketing is an important category of digital marketing which involves encouraging customer communications on a company's own site, or social presences such as Facebook or Twitter or in specialist publisher sites, blogs and forums. It can be applied as a traditional broadcast medium, for example companies can use Facebook or Twitter to send messages to customers or partners who have opted in. However to take advantage of the benefits of social media it is important to start and participate in customer conversations. These can be related to products, promotions or customer service and are aimed at learning more about customers and providing support so improving the way a company is perceived.

The growth of social networks has been documented by Boyd and Ellison (2007) who describe social networking sites (SNS) as:

> Web-based services that allow individuals to (1) construct a public or semi-public profile within a bounded system, (2) articulate a list of other users with whom they share a connection, and (3) view and traverse their list of connections and those made by others within the system.

The interactive capabilities to post comments or other content and rate content are surprisingly missing from this definition.

Digital marketing insight 1.2 Social media matters – the Cluetrain Manifesto sparks the social media marketing revolution

Creating a social media or customer engagement strategy is challenging because it requires a change in mindset for the company wishing to exploit it. The challenge is that the company may have to give up some control of their messaging to enable them to communicate with customers effectively. The change in approach required is clear from a movement that originated in the USA in 1999, known as the Cluetrain manifesto (**www.cluetrain.com**). The authors, Levine *et al.* (2000), say

> *Conversations among human beings sound human. They are conducted in a human voice. Most corporations, on the other hand, only know how to talk in the soothing, humorless monotone of the mission statement, marketing brochure, and your-call-is-important-to-us busy signal. Same old tone, same old lies. No wonder networked markets have no respect for companies unable or unwilling to speak as they do. Corporate firewalls have kept smart employees in and smart markets out. It's going to cause real pain to tear those walls down. But the result will be a new kind of conversation. And it will be the most exciting conversation business has ever engaged in.*

Different types of social media marketing tools

There are many, many sites and tools which comprise what we call 'social media'. To gain an idea of just how many, complete Activity 1.4 which lists hundreds of tools in 25 categories.

A social media site is much more than simply a website. From a technology viewpoint, most of these sites can be considered as software applications or web services which give access to users at different levels of permission and then enable management and storage of different forms of user-generated content. Messaging is also an important feature of many of these sites, particularly the main social networks which will alert users when new content related to their content or connections is published. APIs for exchanging data with other web services interfaces are also a key feature of social networks which enable them to be more useful and allow them and their members to extend their reach and influence by incorporating social comments into other sites.

Activity 1.4 Assessing social media marketing platforms

Purpose

To explore the range of social media sites and tools, to categorise them and assess their business applications.

Activity

Visit the Conversation Prism (**www.conversationprism.com**) and compare this to Figure 1.11. Identify the types of social media sites you and your colleagues use. How do you think the popularity of tools would differ for different types of B2B and B2C sites? Discuss how businesses should decide on the most important to invest in to achieve their goals.

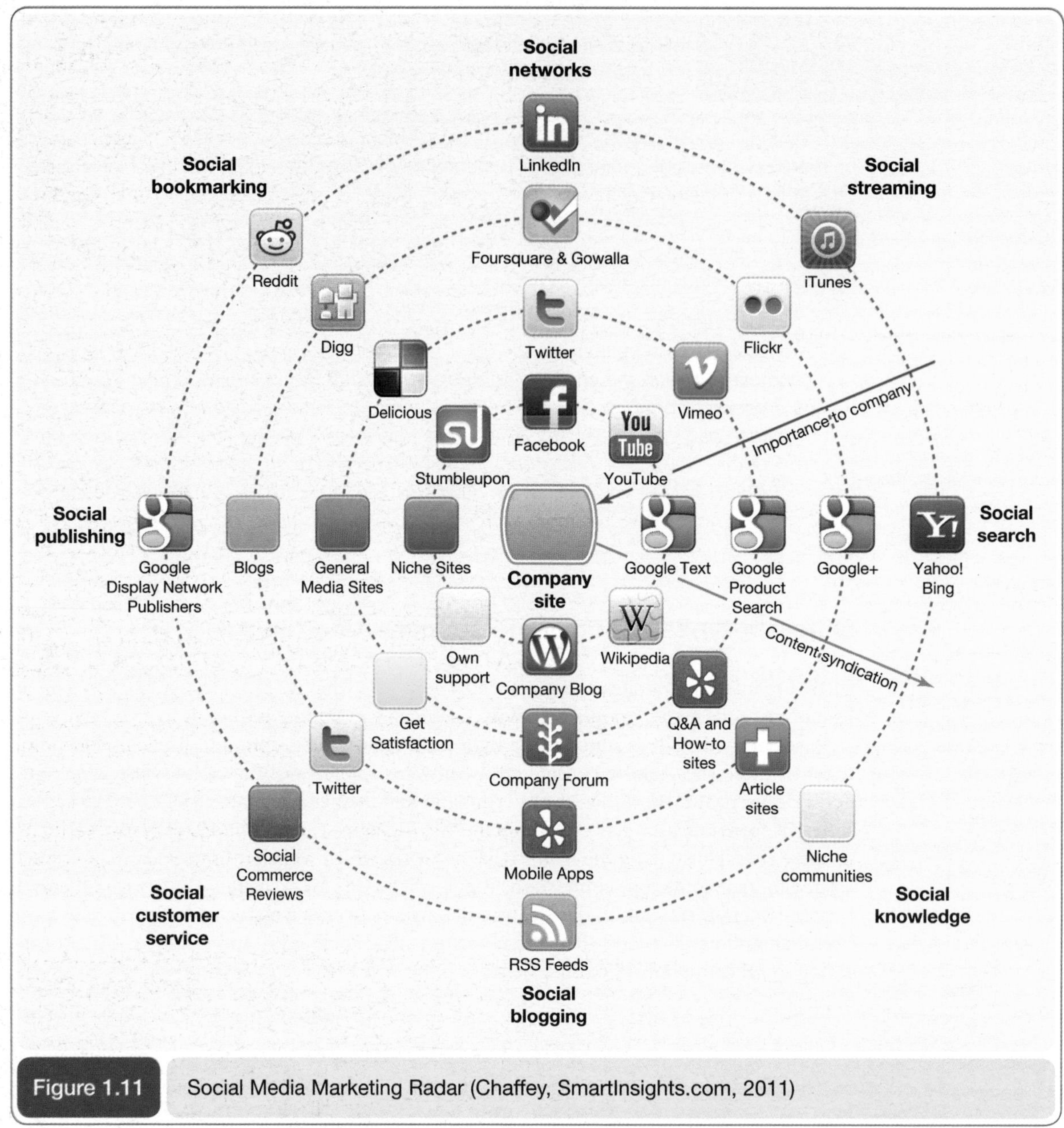

Figure 1.11 Social Media Marketing Radar (Chaffey, SmartInsights.com, 2011)

Since there are so many types of social presence, it's helpful to simplify the options to manage. For this we recommend reviewing these ten forms of online social presence shown in Figure 1.11 (first eight). Weinberg (2010) defines six similar categories. You can see there's more to social media then social networks...

1 *Social networks.* The core social platforms in most countries where people interact through social networks are Facebook for consumer audiences, LinkedIn for business audiences, Google+ and Twitter for both.
2 *Social publishing and news.* Nearly all newspapers and magazines, whether broad or niche, now have an online presence with the option to participate through comments on articles, blogs or communities.
3 *Social commenting in blogs.* A company blog can form the hub of your social media strategy and you can look at tapping into others blogs whether company or personal or through blog outreach.

4 *Social niche communities.* These are communities and forums independent of the main networks, although these do support sub-groups. You can create your own community this way.
5 *Social customer service.* Sites like GetSatisfaction as well as companies own customer support forums are increasingly important for responding to customer complaints.
6 *Social knowledge.* These are reference social networks like Yahoo! Answers, Quora and similar, plus Wikipedia. They show how any business can engage their audience by solving their problems and subtly showing how products have helped others.
7 *Social bookmarking.* The bookmarking sites like Delicious (**www.delicious.com**) which are relatively unimportant in the UK except if you are engaging technical audiences.
8 *Social streaming.* Rich and streaming media social sites – photos, video and podcasting.
9 *Social search.* Search engines are becoming more social with the ability to tag, comment on results and most recently, vote for them through Google+1.
10 *Social commerce.* We've left this one until last, because it's mainly relevant for the retail sector. It involves reviews and ratings on products and sharing of coupons about details.

Web 2.0

Web 2.0 concept
A collection of web services that facilitate interaction of web users with sites to create user-generated content and encourage behaviours such as community or social network participation, mashups, content rating, use of widgets and tagging.

Web 2.0 is a concept which is closely related to social media marketing. Since 2004, the **Web 2.0 concept** has been used to show the change in how experiences are created online through technology among website owners and developers. The main technologies and principles of Web 2.0 have been explained in an influential article by Tim O'Reilly (O'Reilly, 2005). Behind the label, Web 2.0, lies a bewildering range of interactive tools and social communications techniques like those we have just mentioned such as blogs, podcasts and social networks which have engaged many web users. These are aimed at increasing user participation and interaction on the web. With the widespread adoption of high-speed broadband in many countries, rich media experiences are increasingly used to engage customers with the hope they will have a *viral effect*, i.e. they will be discussed online or offline and more people will become aware of or interact with the brand campaign.

Web 2.0 also references methods of exchanging data between sites in standardised formats, such as the feeds merchants use to supply shopping comparison sites with data about products offered and their prices.

The main characteristics of Web 2.0 are that it typically involves:

- Web services or interactive applications hosted on the web such as Flickr (**www.flickr.com**), Google Maps™ (**http://maps.google.com**) or blogging services such as Blogger.com or Typepad (**www.typepad.com**).
- Supporting participation – many of the applications are based on altruistic principles of community participation.
- Encouraging creation of user-generated content – blogs are the best example of this. Another example is the collaborative encyclopedia Wikipedia (**www.wikipedia.com**).
- Enabling rating of content and online services – services such as delicious (**http://del.icio.us**) and traceback comments on blogs support this. These services are useful given the millions of blogs that are available – rating and tagging (categorising) content help indicate the relevance and quality of the content.
- Ad funding of neutral sites – web services such as Google Mail/GMail™ and many blogs are based on contextual advertising such as Google Adsense™ or Overture/Yahoo! Content Match.
- Data exchange between sites through XML-based data standards. RSS is based on XML, but has relatively little semantic markup to describe the content. An attempt by Google to facilitate this which illustrates the principle of structured information exchange and searching is Google Base™ (**http://base.google.com**). This allows users to upload data about particular services, such as training courses, in a standardised format based on XML. New classes of content can also be defined.

- Use of rich media or creation of rich internet applications (RIA) which provide for a more immersive, interactive experience. These may be integrated into web browsers or may be separate applications like that downloaded for Second Life (**www.secondlife.com**). **Video marketing** is an increasingly important tactic both through videos hosted by video sites like YouTube and VideoJug, and also embedded into a companies own sites.
- Rapid application development using interactive technology approaches known as 'Ajax' (Asynchronous JavaScript and XML). The best-known Ajax implementation is Google Maps which is responsive since it does not require refreshes to display maps.

Video marketing
The use of video to gain visibility in search marketing, video hosting sites and to engage site visitors.

Participation and interaction is at the heart of Web 2.0 with site users encouraged to create their own 'user generated content' whether this is a guest blog posting, a comment or a product rating. Web 2.0 techniques include blogs, communities, mashups, RSS feeds, podcasts, tagging, social networks, video streams, virtual worlds, widgets and Wikis.

Figure 1.12 summarises the evolution of digital and web-related technologies. Not all terms are explained at this point in the book, but the majority are included in the Glossary (see page 648). The terms related to technology are explained further in Chapter 3 and Web 2.0 in the online PR section of Chapter 9.

Web 3.0 concept
Next generation web incorporating high-speed connectivity, complex cross-community interactions and an intelligent or semantic web where automated applications can access data from different online services to assist searchers perform complex tasks of supplier selection.

Web 3.0

Since the Web 2.0 concept has been widely applied, it is natural that commentators would try to develop it to the **Web 3.0 concept**, although the term has not been widely applied to date. We can suggest that, as web functionality evolves, these approaches which could be deemed 'Web 3.0' will become more important:

- *Web applications.* Usage of web-based applications and services (like Google word processor and spreadsheets) using the web in this way is sometimes termed *cloud computing*

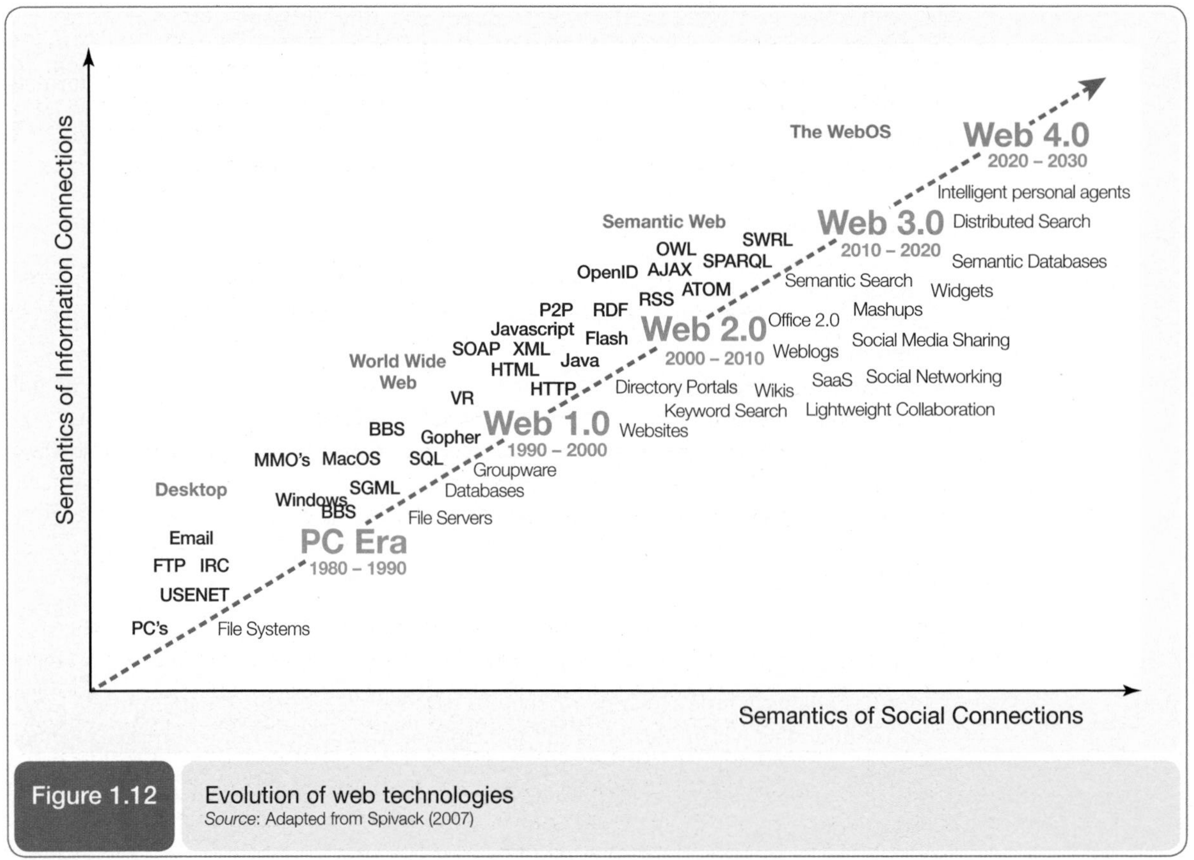

Figure 1.12 Evolution of web technologies
Source: Adapted from Spivack (2007)

where all that is really needed for many activities is a computer with a web browser with local software applications used less widely.

- *Syndication.* Increased incorporation of syndicated content and services from other sites or a network into a site (using tools such as Yahoo! Pipes and XML exchange between widgets). We refer to this concept as 'atomisation' in Chapter 9.
- *Streamed video or IPTV.* Increased use of streamed video from existing TV providers and user-generated content (as suggested by use of YouTube and IPTV services such as Joost).
- *Virtual worlds.* Increased use of immersive virtual environments such as Second Life.
- *Personal data integration.* Increased exchange of data between social networks fulfilling different needs (as indicated by the recent Google development of OpenSocial).
- *The semantic web.* Increased use of semantic mark-up leading to the semantic web envisioned by Tim Berners-Lee over ten years ago. It seems semantic mark-up will be needed to develop artificial intelligence applications which recommend content and services to web users without them actively having to seek them and apply their own judgement as to the best products and brands (i.e. an automated shopping comparison service) (as suggested by the use of standardised data feeds between shopping comparison sites and Google Base).

Benefits of digital media

In the section on digital marketing strategy, we described some of the applications of Internet marketing to support communications with customers across the purchase cycle from generating awareness, achieving direct response for lead generation or sale and supporting customer service and relationship marketing. In this section we explore key differences between digital media and traditional media which savvy marketers exploit.

Digital marketing communications differs significantly from conventional marketing communications because digital media enable new forms of interaction and new models for information exchange. A useful summary of the differences between new media and traditional media was developed by McDonald and Wilson (1999) – they describe the '6 Is of the e-marketing mix'. Note that these can be used as a strategic analysis tool, but they are not used in this context here. The 6 Is are useful since they highlight factors that apply to practical aspects of Internet marketing such as personalisation, direct response and marketing research, but also strategic issues of industry restructuring and integrated channel communications.

1 Interactivity

John Deighton was one of the first authors to summarise this key characteristic of the Internet. He identified the following characteristics inherent in a digital medium (Deighton, 1996) which are true for much online marketing activity:

- the customer initiates contact
- the customer is seeking information or an experience (*pull*)
- it is a high-intensity medium – the marketer will have 100 per cent of the individual's attention when he or she is viewing a website
- a company can gather and store the response of the individual
- individual needs of the customer can be addressed and taken into account in future *dialogues.*

Figure 1.13(a) shows how traditional media are predominantly *push media* where the marketing message is broadcast from company *to* customer and other stakeholders. During this process, there is limited interaction with the customer, although interaction is encouraged in some cases such as the direct-response advert or mail-order campaign. On the Internet it is often the customer who initiates contact and is *seeking* information through researching information on a website. In other words it is a '*pull*' mechanism where it is particularly important to have good visibility in search engines when customers are entering search terms relevant to a company's products or services. Amongst marketing professionals this powerful

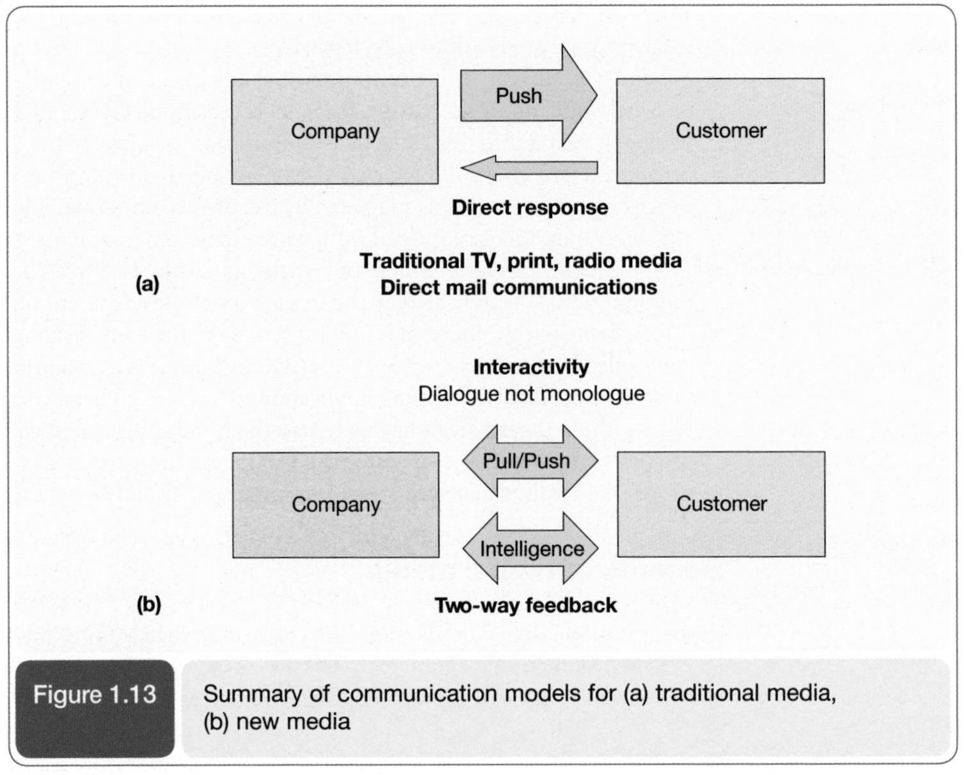

Figure 1.13 Summary of communication models for (a) traditional media, (b) new media

Inbound marketing
The consumer is proactive in actively seeking out information for their needs and interactions with brands are attracted through content, search and social media marketing.

new approach to marketing is now commonly known as Inbound marketing (Shah and Halligan, 2009). **Inbound marketing** is powerful since advertising wastage is reduced. Content and search marketing can be used to target prospects with a defined need – they are proactive and self-selecting. But this is a weakness since marketers may have less control than in traditional communications where the message is pushed out to a defined audience and can help generate awareness and demand. Advocates of inbound marketing such as Dharmesh Shah, and Brian Halligan argue that content, social media and search marketing do have a role to play in generating demand.

Note though that outbound e-mail marketing and online advertising can be considered as 'push' broadcast techniques. Figure 1.13(b) shows how the Internet should be used to encourage two-way communications, which may be extensions of the direct-response approach. For example, FMCG suppliers use their website or Facebook presence as a method of generating interaction by providing incentives such as competitions and sales promotions to encourage the customer to respond with their names, addresses and profile information such as age and sex.

Hoffman and Novak (1997) believe that digital media represent such a shift in the model of communication that it is a new model or paradigm for marketing communications. They suggest that the facilities of the Internet represent a computer-mediated environment in which the interactions are not between the sender and receiver of information, but with the medium itself. They say:

> Consumers can interact with the medium, firms can provide content to the medium and, in the most radical departure from traditional marketing environments, consumers can provide commercially-oriented content to the media.

It has taken ten years of the growth in use of individual recommendations, auction sites, community sites and more recently blogs and podcasts for the full extent of this shift to become apparent. In 2005, a *Business Week* cover feature article referred to the 'Power of us' to explain this change and showed that although relatively few consumers are creating blogs (low single-figure percentages), a large proportion of Internet users are accessing them.

2 Intelligence

The Internet can be used as a relatively low-cost method of collecting marketing research, particularly about customer perceptions of products and services. In the competitions referred to above, Nestlé are able to profile their customers' characteristics on the basis of questionnaire response.

A wealth of marketing research information is also available from the website itself. Marketers use the web analytics approaches described in Chapter 9 to build their knowledge of customer preferences and behaviour according to the types of sites and content which they consume when online. Every time a website visitor downloads content, this is recorded and analysed as 'site statistics' as described in Chapter 9 in order to build up a picture of how consumers interact with the site.

3 Individualisation

Personalisation
Delivering individualised content through web pages or e-mail.

Sense and respond communications
Customer behaviour is monitored at an individual level and the marketer responds with communications tailored to the individual's need.

Another important feature of the interactive marketing communications is that they can be tailored to the individual (Figure 1.14(b)) at relatively low costs, unlike in traditional media where the same message tends to be broadcast to everyone (Figure 1.14(a)). Importantly, this individualisation can be based on the intelligence collected about site visitors and then stored in a database and subsequently used to target and personalise communications to customers to achieve *relevance* in all media. The process of tailoring is also referred to as **personalisation** – Amazon is the most widely known example where the customer is greeted by name on the website and receives recommendations on site and in their e-mails based on previous purchases. This ability to deliver '**sense and respond communications**' is another key feature of digital marketing.

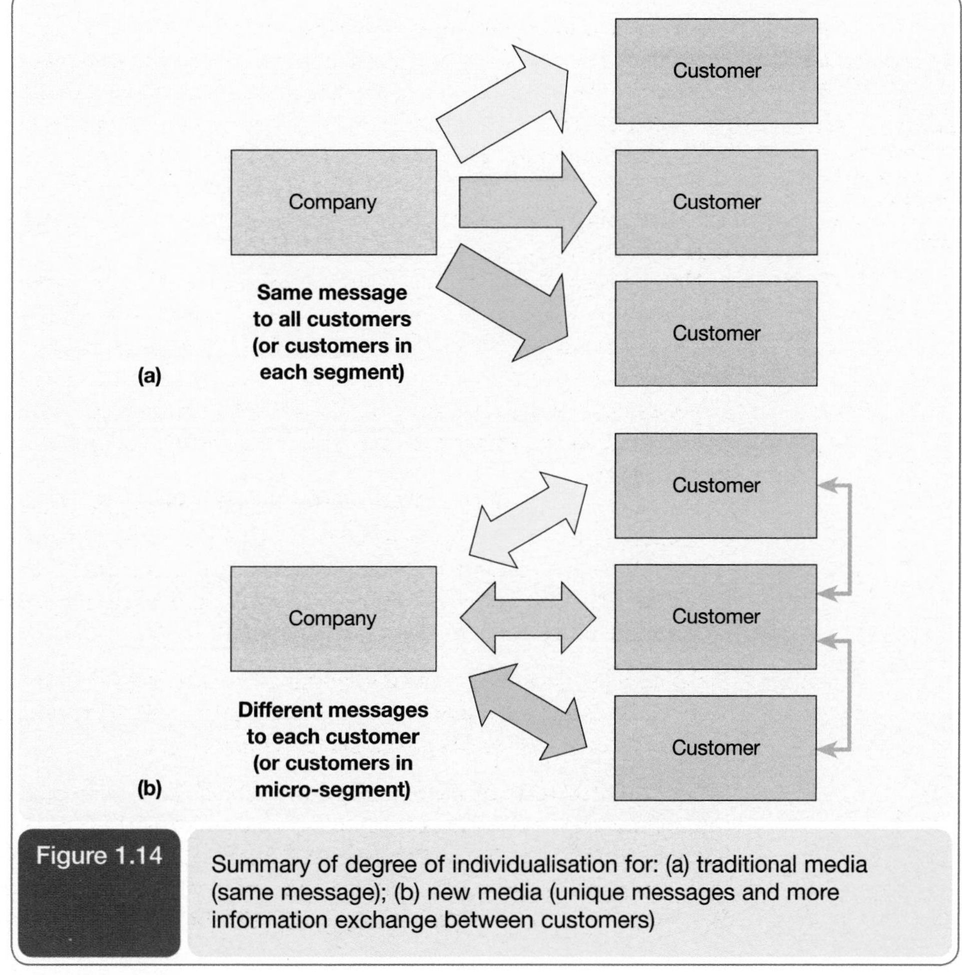

Figure 1.14 Summary of degree of individualisation for: (a) traditional media (same message); (b) new media (unique messages and more information exchange between customers)

Another example of personalisation is that achieved by business-to-business e-tailer RS Components (**www.rswww.com**). Every customer who accesses their system is profiled according to their area of product interest and information describing their role in the buying unit. When they next visit the site information will be displayed relevant to their product interest, for example office products and promotions if this is what was selected. This is an example of what is known as **mass customisation** where generic customer information is supplied for particular segments, i.e. the information is not unique to individuals, but is relevant to those with a common interest. Personalisation and mass customisation concepts are explored further in Chapter 6.

Mass customisation
Delivering customised content to groups of users through web pages or e-mail.

4 Integration

The Internet provides further scope for integrated marketing communications. Figure 1.15 shows the role of the Internet in multichannel marketing. When assessing the marketing effectiveness of a website, the role of the Internet in communicating with customers and other partners can best be considered from two perspectives. First, there is **outbound Internet-based communications** from *organisation to customer*. We need to ask how does the Internet complement other channels in communicating the proposition for the company's products and services to new and existing customers with a view to generating new leads and retaining existing customers? Second, **inbound Internet-based communications** from *customer to organisation*: how can the Internet complement other channels to deliver customer service to these customers? Many companies have now integrated e-mail response and website callback into their existing call centre or customer service operation.

Outbound Internet-based communications
The website and e-mail marketing are used to send personalised communications to customers.

Inbound Internet-based communications
Customers enquire through web-based forms and e-mail.

Some practical examples of how the Internet can be used as an integrated communications tool as part of supporting a multichannel customer journey (Figure 1.16) are the following:

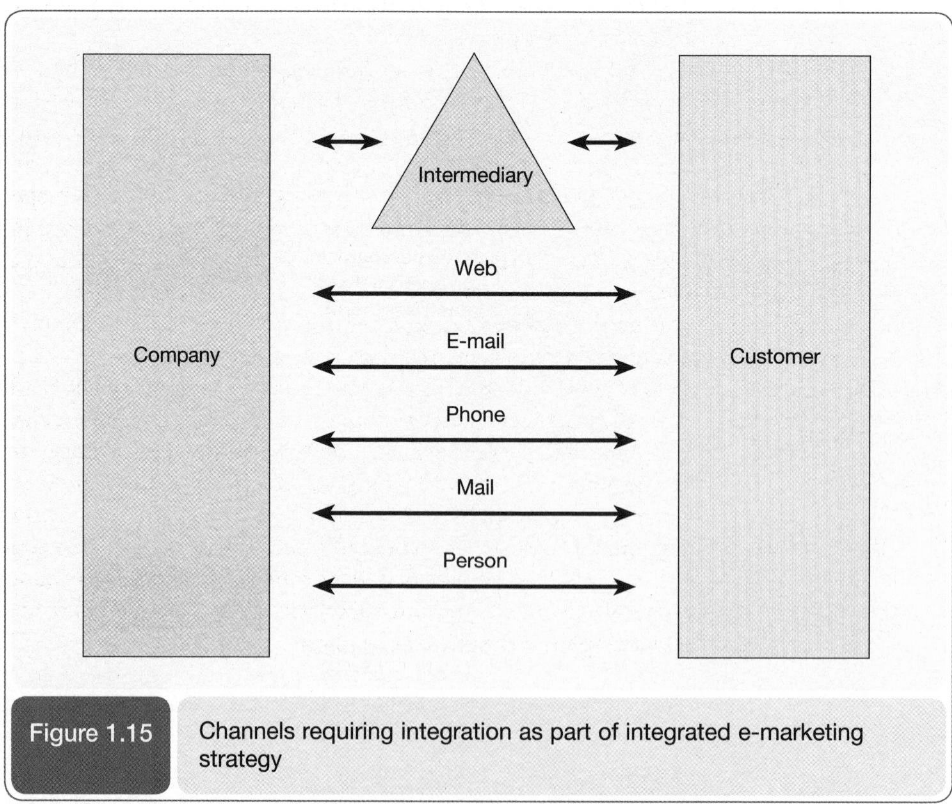

Figure 1.15 Channels requiring integration as part of integrated e-marketing strategy

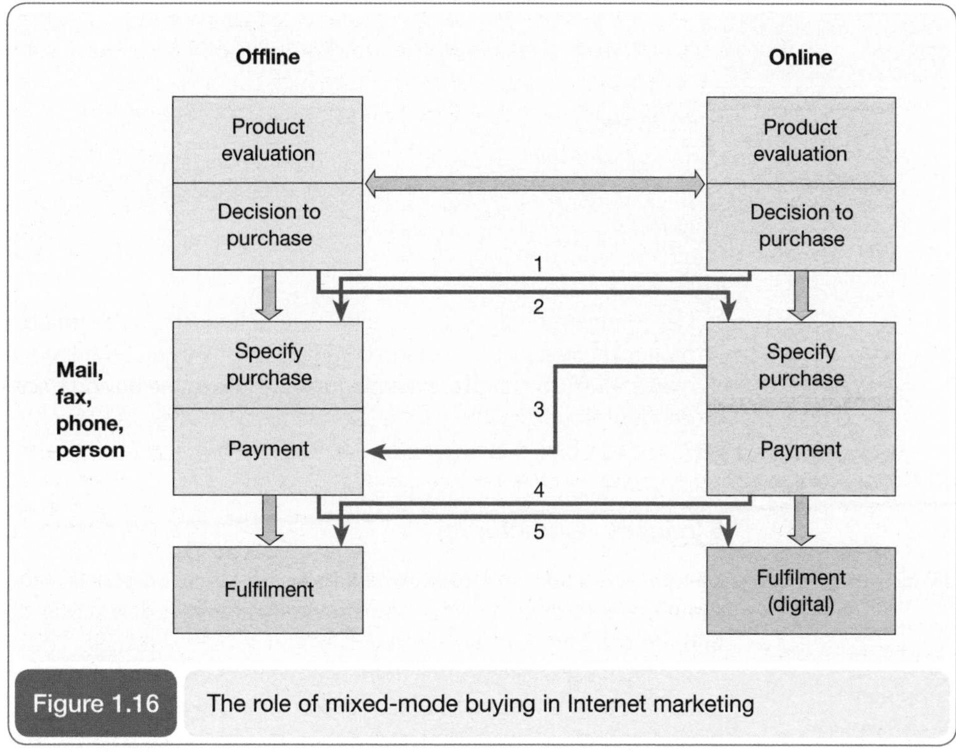

Figure 1.16 The role of mixed-mode buying in Internet marketing

- The Internet can be used as a direct-response tool, enabling customers to respond to offers and promotions publicised in other media.
- The website can have a direct response or callback facility built into it. The Automobile Association has a feature where a customer service representative will contact a customer by phone when the customer fills in their name, phone number and a suitable time to ring.
- The Internet can be used to support the buying decision even if the purchase does not occur via the website. For example, Dell has a prominent web-specific phone number on their website that encourages customers to ring a representative in the call centre to place their order. This has the benefits that Dell is less likely to lose the business of customers who are anxious about the security of online ordering and Dell can track sales that result partly from the website according to the number of callers on this line. Considering how a customer changes from one channel to another during the buying process, this is referred to as **mixed-mode buying**. It is a key aspect of devising online marketing communications since the customer should be supported in changing from one channel to another.

Mixed-mode buying
The process by which a customer changes between online and offline channels during the buying process.

- Customer information delivered on the website must be integrated with other databases of customer and order information, such as those accessed via staff in the call centre to provide what Seybold (1999) called a '360 degree view of the customer'.
- The Internet can be used to support customer service. For example easyJet (**www.easyjet.com**), which receives over half of its orders electronically, encourages users to check a list of frequently asked questions (FAQ) compiled from previous customer enquiries before contacting customer support by phone.

Activity 1.5 Integrating online and offline communications

Purpose

To highlight differences in marketing communications introduced through the use of the Internet as a channel and the need to integrate these communications with existing channels.

Activity

List communications between a PC vendor and a home customer over the lifetime of a product such as a PC. Include communications using both the Internet and traditional media. Refer to channel-swapping alternatives in the buying decision in Figure 1.16 to develop your answer.

5 Industry restructuring

Disintermediation
The removal of intermediaries such as distributors or brokers that formerly linked a company to its customers.

Reintermediation
The creation of new intermediaries between customers and suppliers providing services such as supplier search and product evaluation.

Disintermediation and **reintermediation** are key concepts of industry restructuring that should be considered by any company developing an e-marketing strategy and are explored in more detail in Chapters 2, 4 and 5.

For the marketer defining their company's communications strategy it becomes very important to consider the company's representation on these intermediary sites by answering questions such as 'Which intermediaries should we be represented on?' and 'How do our offerings compare to those of competitors in terms of features, benefits and price?'

6 Independence of location

Electronic media also introduce the possibility of increasing the reach of company communications to the global market. This gives opportunities to sell into international markets which may not have been previously possible. The Internet makes it possible to sell to a country without a local sales or customer service force (although this may still be necessary for some products). In such situations and with the restructuring in conjunction with disintermediation and reintermediation, strategists also need to carefully consider channel conflicts that may arise. If a customer is buying direct from a company in another country rather than via the agent, this will marginalise the business of the local agent who may want some recompense for sales efforts or may look for a partnership with competitors.

Kiani (1998) has presented a useful perspective to differences between the old and new media, which are shown as a summary to this section in Table 1.5.

Table 1.5 An interpretation of the differences between the old and digital media

Old media	Digital media	Comment
One-to-many communication model	One-to-one or many-to-many communication model	Hoffman and Novak (1996) state that theoretically the Internet is a many-to-many medium, but for company-to-customer organisation(s) communications it is best considered as one-to-one or one-to-many
Mass-marketing push model	Individualised marketing or mass customisation. Pull model for web marketing	Personalisation possible because of technology to monitor preferences and tailor content (Deighton, 1996). Pull occurs through targeted search engine marketing which tends to have lower wastage. Personalised e-mails used for push communications

Table 1.5 Continued

Old media	Digital media	Comment
Monologue	Dialogue	Indicates the interactive nature of the World Wide Web, with the facility for feedback and participation through social networks and forums.
Branding	Communication	Increased involvement of customer in defining brand characteristics. Opportunities for adding value to brand
Supply-side thinking	Demand-side thinking	Customer pull becomes more important
Customer as a target	Customer as a partner	Customer has more input into products and services required, particularly through surveys and product ratings
Segmentation	Communities	Aggregations of like-minded consumers rather than arbitrarily defined target segments

Source: After Kiani (1998)

Mini Case Study 1.3 Travel Republic achieves growth through taking advantage of benefits of digital marketing

Online travel agent Travel Republic topped *The Sunday Times* Virgin Fast Track 100 list just four years after the company was launched. The company was the UK's fastest growing privately owned company boasting 284.23 per cent annual sales growth. The Kingston-upon-Thames based business was set up in 2003 and is the brainchild of three university friends – Paul Furner, managing director, Chris Waite, IT director and Kane Pirie, finance and operations director.

The company employs more than 150 staff. TravelRepublic.co.uk appears in the IMRG-Hitwise Hot Shops List which ranks the UK's top 50 most popular internet retailers, across all sectors (ranked by number of web visitors). In the online travel agency sector TravelRepublic.co.uk is more popular than the likes of Opodo and ebookers.com. Only Expedia.co.uk and lastminute.com rank higher.

A major reason for the growth of Travel Republic is that it has taken advantage of the 'pull' effect of web communications. Through using sponsored links in search networks such as Google AdWords it has been able to target its offering precisely to an online audience looking for a competitive price on a holiday or a flight to a particular destination. Of course, this has to be backed up by a strong proposition, an easy to use, high performance website and trust in the brand indicated by user reviews and holiday guarantees (Figure 1.17).TravelRepublic.co.uk caters for a broad range of customers including families, couples and groups. The website offers charter, low-cost and scheduled airlines, powerful rate shopping technology for hotel rooms and apartments, plus hotel reviews and resort guides written by its customers.

Customers can save up to 50% on the price of a comparable package holiday purchased online or on the high street. TravelRepublic.co.uk works with over 100 different flight operators and offers flights to more than 200 destinations. The website also offers over 30,000 discounted hotels, apartments and villas plus a wide range of other services such as taxi transfers, airport parking and car hire. The website gives customers complete flexibility with flights, hotels and durations.

Paul Furner, managing director of TravelRepublic.co.uk explains:

> *Chris, Kane and I met at university but then followed very different careers – Chris in software development, Kane in corporate finance/private equity and me in software quality assurance. These differing backgrounds, all outside of the travel industry, have allowed us to take a fresh new look at the sector and become one of its leading innovators.*

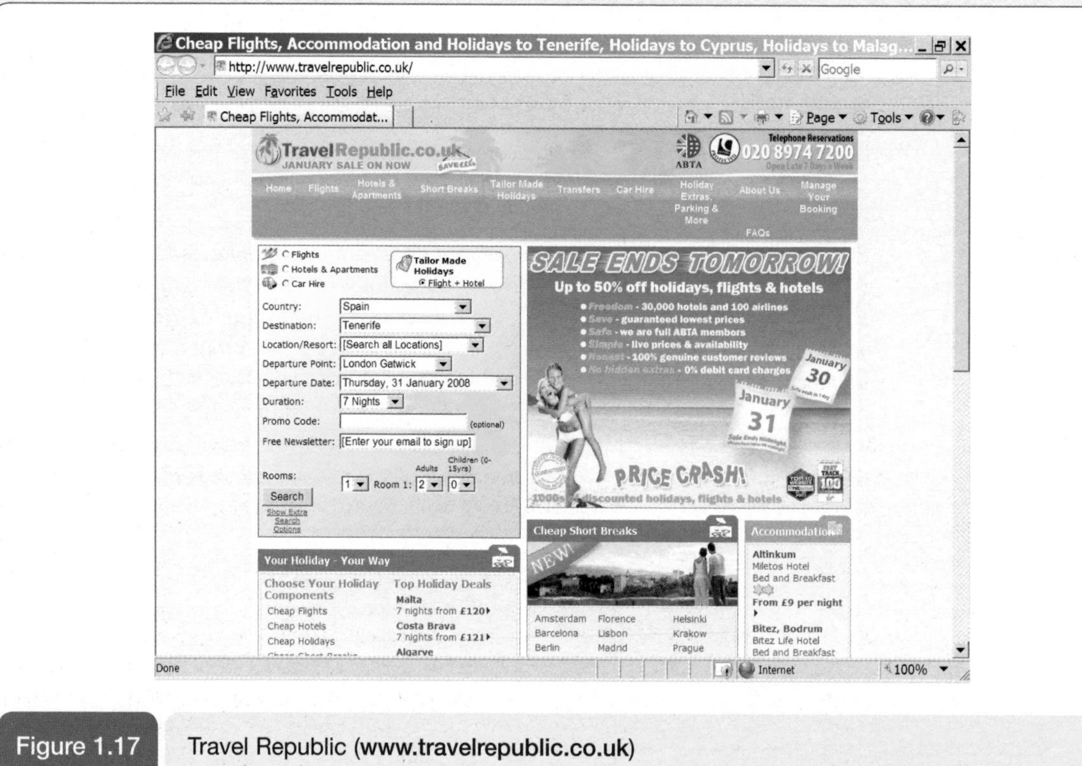

Figure 1.17 Travel Republic (**www.travelrepublic.co.uk**)

However, equally important has been our commitment, from the outset, to deliver gold standard customer service to our customers. At a time when it is often said that there is no loyalty on the web we would beg to differ. Our levels of repeat and recommended business suggest that we have a real affinity with our customers which we plan to build upon in the coming months.

Source: Travel Republic press release, 2 December 2007, Travel Republic is the UK's Fastest Growing Private Company, http://www.travelrepublic.co.uk/help/pressReplace_003.aspx

In terms of deploying campaigns, there are other key differences and benefits of digital media which we can illustrate through the Google AdWords (**http://adwords.google.com**) paid search advertising programme or similar programmes from Microsoft Bing Facebook and Twitterwhich we will reference in more detail in Chapter 9:

- *Accountability*. Digital media are potentially more accountable through the use of measurement systems known collectively as web analytics. Google provides a free tool known as Google Analytics (**www.google.com/analytics**) to enable its advertisers to test the value generated from its ads.
- *Testing*. Potentially, testing becomes more straightforward at a lower cost with the option to trial alternative creative executions, messaging or offers. Google offers another free tool – the Website Optimiser – to test alternative landing pages.
- *Flexibility*. Campaigns can be more flexible with the capability to change, copy or offers during a campaign. Alternative ads can be served within Google to evaluate which works best. Google AdWords also offers dayparting where ads can be displayed at different times of the day.
- *Micro-targeting*. Alternative messages can be delivered for different audiences according to what they are searching for. Potentially a company can show a different advert in Google AdWords for each term searched on.
- *Cost-control*. Costs can be controlled for each group of search terms entered by customers through the search engine, managed collectively, and bids made can be increased or decreased with the aid of software.

Key challenges of digital communications

It is sometimes suggested by some suppliers of digital media that they are 'quick, cheap and easy' to deploy. This is a great misconception since there are many challenges which need to be overcome when managing digital campaigns. Again referring to a Google AdWords campaign as an example, these include:

- *Complexity.* To enable the benefits we have mentioned above – such as personalisation, testing and dynamic variation in ads through time – time has to go into configuring the campaign although the search engines provide defaults to enable easy setup. This requires specialist expertise either in-house or at an agency to manage the campaign.
- *Responding to competitors.* Since competitors can also change their approach readily, more resource has to be used to monitor competitor activity. Automated tools known as bid management tools can assist with this – they will automatically check amounts competitors are paying and then adjust them according to pre-defined rules.
- *Responding to changes in technology.* Google and the other ad-serving companies innovate to offer better capabilities for their customers. This means that staff managing campaigns need training to keep up-to-date. Google offers 'Adwords Qualified Professionals' so that companies can be certain of a minimum skills level.
- *Cost.* Although costs can be readily controlled, in competitive categories, the costs can be high, exceeding €10 per click.
- *Attention.* While online paid search ads are highly targeted and there is arguably little wastage, not everyone will view paid adverts, indeed there is a phenomenon known as 'banner blindness' where web users ignore online ads (see Chapter 9 for more details). Engaging with the audience with advertising is also a problem in social networks and other publisher sites which can lead to a very low rate of people clicking on ads.

Key communications concepts for digital marketing

In this section, we introduce three key concepts which underpin digital communications across the digital media we have introduced in this chapter.

1 Customer engagement.
2 Permission marketing.
3 Content marketing.

1 Customer engagement

Customer engagement
Repeated interactions that strengthen the emotional, psychological or physical investment a customer has in a brand.

This difficulty in gaining attention online on all types of sites has led to the emergence of the concept of **customer engagement** as a key challenge with which digital marketers are increasingly concerned. cScape (2008) describe customer engagement as:

> repeated interactions that strengthen the emotional, psychological or physical investment a customer has in a brand.

while for Haven (2007) customer engagement is:

> the level of involvement, interaction, intimacy, and influence an individual has with a brand over time.

Arguably, the biggest difference in communications introduced by the growth of digital media and the web is the capability, or many would say necessity, to include customer's conversations as an integral part of communications. Today, proactively managing consumer participation which occurs through social networks such as Facebook, Google+ and LinkedIn video postings and comments on YouTube and myriad blogs and forums is essential since, when a positive sentiment is expressed by a real person independent from a company this confers credibility on the company.

Equally, there are negative sentiments or comments made by consumers on the web that need to be managed. For example, on one site (**www.haveyoursay.com**) a purchaser of a car was highly critical about a make of car and the comments appeared near the top of the Google search results page when someone searched for the brand, yet for several years the manufacturer did nothing to manage this.

2 Permission marketing

Permission marketing Customers agree (opt in) to be involved in an organisation's marketing activities, usually as a result of an incentive.

Interruption marketing Marketing communications that disrupt customers' activities.

Permission marketing is an established approach to online marketing which is still highly relevant today as a practical foundation for CRM and online customer engagement.'Permission marketing' was a term coined by Seth Godin. Godin (1999) noted that while research used to show we were bombarded by 500 marketing messages a day, with the advent of the web and digital TV this has now increased to over 3000 a day! From an organisation's viewpoint, this leads to a dilution in the effectiveness of the messages – how can the communications of any one company stand out? From the customer's viewpoint, time is seemingly in ever-shorter supply, customers are losing patience and expect reward for their attention, time and information. Godin refers to the traditional approach as **interruption marketing**. Permission marketing is about seeking the customer's permission before engaging them in a relationship and providing something in exchange. The classic exchange is based on information or entertainment – a B2B site can offer a free report in exchange for a customer sharing their e-mail address or 'Liking' a brand, while a B2C site can offer a newsletter or access to their wall with valuable content and offers. We cover the principles of permission marketing in more detail and with examples related to CRM in Chapter 6.

3 Content marketing

Content marketing The management of text, rich media, audio and video content aimed at engaging customers and prospects to meet business goals published through print and digital media including web and mobile platforms which is repurposed and syndicated to different forms of web presence such as publisher sites, blogs, social media and comparison sites.

Success in permission marketing requires exceptional, compelling content. To emphasise the importance of content marketing to gaining permission, encouraging sharing and ongoing engagement through websites and social media, the concepts of **content marketing** and content strategy have developed to describe best practice approaches. Today, by content we refer to the combination of static content forming web pages, but also dynamic rich media content which encourages interaction. Videos, podcasts, user-generated content and interactive product selectors should also be considered as content which should be refined to engage issues.

You can see the challenge content strategy presents since today there are so many different types of content delivered in different forms to different places on different access platforms, yet it is increasingly important to engage customers in social media.

The definition suggests these elements of content management that need to be planned and managed:

1 *Content engagement value.* Which types of content will engage the audience – is it simple product or services information, a guide to buying product, or a game to engage your audience?
2 *Content media.* Plain text, rich media such as Flash or Rich Internet applications or mobile apps (see Chapter 3), audio (podcasts) and hosted and streamed video. Even plain text offers different format options from HTML text to ebook formats and PDFs.
3 *Content syndication.* Content can be syndicated to different type of sites through feeds, APIs, microformats or direct submission by email. Content can be embedded in sites through widgets displaying information delivered by a feed.
4 *Content participation.* Effective content today is not simply delivered for static consumption, it should enable commenting, ratings and reviews. These also need to be monitored and managed both in the original location and where they are discussed elsewhere.
5 *Content access platform.* The different digital access platforms such as desktops and laptops of different screen resolution and mobile devices. Paper is also a content access platform for print media.

To conclude this chapter, read Case Study 1 for the background on the success factors which have helped build one of the biggest online brands.

Case Study 1 eBay thrives in the global marketplace

Context

It's hard to believe that one of the most well-known dot-coms has now been established 15 years. Pierre Omidyar, a 28-year-old French-born software engineer living in California, coded the site while working for another company, eventually launching the site for business on Monday, 4 September 1995 with the more direct name 'Auction Web'. Legend reports that the site attracted no visitors in its first 24 hours. The site became eBay in 1997. In 2009, eBay had 90 million active users globally, with the total worth of goods sold on eBay $60 billion which is equivalent to $2,000 every second. Total revenue was $8.7 billion.

Mission

eBay describes their purpose as to 'pioneer new communities around the world built on commerce, sustained by trust, and inspired by opportunity'.

At the time of writing eBay comprises two major businesses:

1 *The eBay Marketplaces (approximately 66 per cent of net revenues in 2009).* The mission for the core eBay business is to 'create the world's online marketplace'. The marketplace platforms include an average of 100 million products for sale each day! In 2007, eBay's SEC filing notes some of the success factors for this business for which eBay seeks to manage the functionality, safety, ease-of-use and reliability of the trading platform. By 2011 the strategic priorities had changed to trust, value, selection and convenience.
2 *PayPal (approximately 34 per cent of net revenues in 2009).* The mission is to 'create the new global standard for online payments'. This company was acquired in 2003.

Advertising and other net revenues represented 4 per cent of total net revenues during 2007.

This case focuses on the best known eBay business, the eBay Marketplace.

Revenue model

The vast majority of eBay's revenue is for the listing and commission on completed sales. For PayPal purchases an additional commission fee is charged. The margin on each transaction is phenomenal since once the infrastructure is built, incremental costs on each transaction are tiny – all eBay is doing is transmitting bits and bytes between buyers and sellers.

Advertising and other non-transaction net revenues represent a relatively small proportion of total net revenues and the strategy is that this should remain the case. Advertising and other net revenues totalled $94.3 million in 2004 (just 3 per cent of net revenue).

Proposition

The eBay marketplace is well known for its core service which enables sellers to list items for sale on an auction or fixed-price basis giving buyers the opportunity to bid for and purchase items of interest. At the end of 2007, there were over 532,000 online storefronts established by users in locations around the world.

Software tools are provided, particularly for frequent traders, including Turbo Lister, Seller's Assistant, Selling Manager and Selling Manager Pro, which help automate the selling process, the Shipping Calculator, Reporting tools, etc. Today over 60 per cent of listings are facilitated by software, showing the value of automating posting for frequent trading.

Fraud is a significant risk factor for eBay. BBC (2005) reported that around 1 in 10,000 transactions within the UK were fraudulent. 0.0001 per cent is a small percentage, but scaling this up across the number of transactions makes a significant volume.

eBay has developed 'Trust and Safety Programs' which are particularly important to reassure customers since online services are prone to fraud. For example, the eBay feedback forum can help establish credentials of sellers and buyers. Every registered user has a feedback profile that may contain compliments, criticisms and/or other comments by users who have conducted business with that user. The Feedback Forum requires feedback to be related to specific transactions and Top Seller status was introduced in 2010 to increase trust in the service. There is also a Safe Harbor data protection method and a standard purchase protection system.

eBay obtained increased use of mobile e-commerce in 2009 and into 2010. The eBay mobile app for iPhone was downloaded seven million times by January 2010. Consumers are shopping more and more via their mobile phones with more than $600 million worth of sales transacted through mobile applications in 2009.

According to the SEC filing, eBay summarises the core messages to define its proposition as follows:

➔

For buyers:

- trust
- value
- selection
- convenience

For sellers:

- access to broad markets
- cost effective marketing and distribution
- access to large buyer base
- good conversion rates.

In 2007, eBay introduced Neighbourhoods (**http://neighborhoods.ebay. com**) where groups can discuss brands and products they have a high involvement with.

In January 2008, eBay announced significant changes to its Marketplaces business in three major areas: fee structure, seller incentives and standards, and feedback. These changes have been controversial with some sellers, but are aimed at improving the quality of experience. Detailed Seller Ratings (DSRs) enable sellers to be reviewed in four areas: (1) item as described, (2) communication, (3) delivery time, and (4) postage and packaging charges. This is part of a move to help increase conversion rate by increasing positive shopping experiences, for example by including more accurate descriptions with better pictures and avoiding excessive shipping charges. Powersellers with positive DSRs will be featured more favourably in the search results pages and will gain additional discounts.

Competition

Although there are now few direct competitors of online auction services in many countries, there are many indirect competitors. SEC (2008) describes competing channels as including online and offline retailers, distributors, liquidators, import and export companies, auctioneers, catalogue and mail-order companies, classifieds, directories, search engines, products of search engines, virtually all online and offline commerce participants and online and offline shopping channels and networks.

BBC (2005) reports that eBay is not complacent about competition. It has already pulled out of Japan due to competition from Yahoo! and within Asia and China is also facing tough competition by Yahoo! which has a portal with a broader range of services more likely to attract subscribers.

Objectives and strategy

The overall eBay aims are to increase the gross merchandise volume and net revenues from the eBay Marketplace. More detailed objectives are defined to achieve these aims, with strategies focusing on:

1 *Acquisition* – increasing the number of newly registered users on the eBay Marketplace.
2 *Activation* – increasing the number of registered users that become active bidders, buyers or sellers on the eBay Marketplace.
3 *Activity* – increasing the volume and value of transactions that are conducted by each active user on the eBay Marketplace. eBay had approximately 83 million active users at the end of 2007, compared to approximately 82 million at the end of 2006. An active user is defined as any user who bid on, bought or listed an item during the most recent 12-month period.

The focus on each of these three areas will vary according to strategic priorities in particular local markets.

eBay Marketplace growth is also driven by defining approaches to improve performance in these areas. First, category growth is achieved by increasing the number and size of categories within the marketplace, for example: Antiques, Art, Books and Business & Industrial. Second, formats for interaction. The traditional format is auction listings, but it has been refined now to include the 'Buy-It-Now' fixed price format. This fix priced listing now accounts for 53 per cent of all transactions, suggesting adaptability into the eBay offering. Another format is the 'Dutch Auction' format, where a seller can sell multiple identical items to the highest bidders. eBay Stores was developed to enable sellers with a wider range of products to showcase their products in a more traditional retail format. eBay say they are constantly exploring new formats, often through acquisition of other companies, for example through the acquisition in 2004 of mobile. de in Germany and Marktplaats.nl in the Netherlands, as well as investment in craigslist, the US-based classified ad format. Another acquisition is Rent.com, which enables expansion into the online housing and apartment rental category. In 2007, eBay acquired StubHub, an online ticket marketplace, and it also owns comparison marketplace Shopping.com. Finally Marketplace growth is achieved through delivering specific sites localised for different geographies as follows. You can see there is still potential for greater localisation, for example in parts of Scandinavia, Eastern Europe and Asia.

Localised eBay marketplaces:

- Australia
- Austria
- Belgium
- Canada
- China
- France
- Germany
- Hong Kong
- India
- Ireland
- Italy
- Malaysia
- The Netherlands
- New Zealand
- The Philippines
- Singapore
- South Korea
- Spain
- Sweden
- Switzerland
- Taiwan
- United Kingdom
- United States

eBay's growth strategy

In its SEC filing, success factors eBay believes are important to enable it to compete in its market include:

- ability to attract buyers and sellers
- volume of transactions and price and selection of goods
- customer service
- brand recognition.

According to its 2010 SEC filing:

> *'Our growth strategy is focused on reinvesting in our customers by improving the buyer experience and seller economics by enhancing our products and services, improving trust and safety and customer support, extending our product offerings into new formats, categories and geographies, and implementing innovative pricing and buyer retention strategies.*
>
> *Over the course of 2009, we continued to make significant changes that were designed to improve the user experience on all of our sites, including changes to pricing and shipping policies. In 2009, we also made significant steps to create a faster and more streamlined search experience with a greater focus on relevance when sorting search results. Pricing changes reduced the upfront cost of listing fixed price items on eBay so that fees are now based more on the successful sale of items, for both smaller and larger sellers. We encourage sellers to offer free or inexpensive shipping to our buyers by promoting their listings through our "Best Match" search algorithm.'*

It also notes that in the context of its competitors, other factors it believes are important are:

- community cohesion, interaction and size
- system reliability
- reliability of delivery and payment
- website convenience and accessibility
- level of service fees
- quality of search tools.

This implies that eBay believes it has optimised these factors, but its competitors still have opportunities for improving performance in these areas which will make the market more competitive.

Risk management

The SEC filing lists the risks and challenges of conducting business internationally as follows:

- regulatory requirements, including regulation of auctioneering, professional selling, distance selling, banking and money transmitting
- legal uncertainty regarding liability for the listings and other content provided by users, including uncertainty as a result of less Internet-friendly legal systems, unique local laws and lack of clear precedent or applicable law
- difficulties in integrating with local payment providers, including banks, credit and debit card associations, and electronic fund transfer systems
- differing levels of retail distribution, shipping and communications infrastructures
- different employee/employer relationships and the existence of workers' councils and labour unions
- difficulties in staffing and managing foreign operations
- longer payment cycles, different accounting practices and greater problems in collecting accounts receivable
- potentially adverse tax consequences, including local taxation of fees or of transactions on websites
- higher telecommunications and Internet service provider costs
- strong local competitors
- different and more stringent consumer protection, data protection and other laws
- cultural ambivalence towards, or non-acceptance of, online trading
- seasonal reductions in business activity
- expenses associated with localising products, including offering customers the ability to transact business in the local currency
- laws and business practices that favour local competitors or prohibit foreign ownership of certain businesses
- profit repatriation restrictions, foreign currency exchange restrictions and exchange rate fluctuations
- volatility in a specific country's or region's political or economic conditions
- differing intellectual property laws and taxation laws.

Question

Assess how the characteristics of the digital media and the Internet, together with strategic decisions taken by its management team, have supported eBay's continued growth.

Summary

1. Digital marketing refers to the use of digital technology platforms, combined with traditional media, to achieve marketing objectives. Digital marketing involves using digital media channels and using other technologies, such as databases for customer relationship management (e-CRM). We reviewed ten key digital hardware platforms including desktop, mobile, tablet and other hardware platforms.
2. A customer-centric approach to digital marketing considers the needs of a range of customers using techniques such as persona and customer scenarios (Chapter 2) to understand customer needs in a multichannel buying process. Tailoring to individual customers may be practical using personalisation techniques.
3. Electronic commerce refers to both electronically mediated financial and informational transactions.
4. Electronic business is a broader term referring to how technology can benefit all internal business processes and interactions with third parties. This includes buy-side and sell-side e-commerce and the internal value chain.
5. E-commerce transactions include business-to-business (B2B), business-to-consumer (B2C), consumer-to-consumer (C2C) and consumer-to-business (C2B) transactions.
6. There are six key digital media channels: search marketing; online PR; partnership (affiliate) marketing; display advertising; e-mail; and social media marketing. These communications techniques can be deployed across paid, earned and owned digital media.
7. The Internet is used to develop existing markets through enabling an additional communications and/or sales channel with potential customers. It can be used to develop new international markets with a reduced need for new sales offices and agents. Companies can provide new services and possibly products using the Internet.
8. Digital marketing can support the full range of marketing functions and in doing so can help reduce costs, facilitate communication within and between organisations and improve customer service.
9. Interaction with customers, suppliers and distributors occurs across the Internet. The web and e-mail are particularly powerful if they can be used to create *relevant, personalised communications.*
10. The marketing benefits the Internet confers are advantageous both to the large corporation and to the small or medium-sized enterprise. These include:
    - a new medium for advertising and PR
    - a new channel for distributing products
    - opportunities for expansion into new markets
    - new ways of enhancing customer service
    - new ways of reducing costs by reducing the number of staff in order fulfilment.

Exercises

Self-assessment exercises

1. Explain the main types of digital marketing platform.
2. Identify different ways in which a website or social media presence is used for marketing in different markets.
3. Outline different applications of digital marketing which can help meet business goals.
4. Explain what is meant by electronic commerce, social commerce and electronic business. How do they relate to the marketing function?

5 Six digital media channels are introduced in this chapter. What are they and how do they work to reach, engage and convert an audience?
6 Summarise the main communications difference between digital and traditional media.
7 Distinguish between social media marketing inbound and content marketing.
8 How is the Internet used to develop new markets and penetrate existing markets? What types of new products can be delivered by the Internet?

Essay and discussion questions

1 Some would see digital media primarily as a means of advertising and selling products. What are the opportunities for other use of the Internet and digital media for marketing?
2 'The World Wide Web represents a *pull* medium for marketing rather than a *push* medium.' Discuss.
3 You are a newly installed marketing manager in a company selling products in the business-to-business sector. Currently, the company has only a limited website containing electronic versions of its brochures. You want to convince the directors of the benefits of investing in the website to provide more benefits to the company. How would you present your case?
4 Explain the main benefits that a company selling fast-moving consumer goods could derive by creating a website.

Examination questions

1 Explain electronic commerce and social commerce and how they relate.
2 Which techniques can be used to increase awareness of a brand and encourage interaction with the brand?
3 A digital marketing manager must seek to control and accommodate all the main methods by which consumers may visit a company website. Describe these methods.
4 Imagine you are explaining the difference between the digital marketing and Ecommerce to a marketing manager. How would you explain these two terms?
5 What is the relevance of 'conversion marketing' for digital marketing?
6 Explain how digital platforms can be used to increase market penetration in existing markets and develop new markets.

References

Ansoff, H. (1957) Strategies for diversification, *Harvard Business Review*, September–October, 113–24.

BBC (2005) eBay's 10-year rise to world fame. Robert Plummer story from BBC News, 2 September: **http://news.bbc.co.uk/go/pr/fr/-/1/hi/business/4207510.stm.** Published: 2 September 2005.

Boyd, D. and Ellison, N. (2007) Social network sites: definition, history and scholarship, *Journal of Computer-Mediated Communication*, 13(1), 210–30.

Business Week (2005) The Power of Us. Mass collaboration on the Internet is shaking up business. **http://www.businessweek.com/magazine/content/05_25/63938601.htm**, 20 June 2005.

Chaffey, D. (2006) *E-Business and E-Commerce Management*, 3rd edn. Financial Times/Prentice Hall, Harlow.

Chaffey, D. (2011) *E-business and E-commerce Management*, Financial Times/Prentice Hall, Harlow.

Chaffey, D. and Smith, P.R. (2008) *Emarketing Excellence, Planning and optimising your digital marketing*, 3rd edn. Butterworth-Heinemann, Oxford. Copyright Elsevier.

cScape (2008) Second Annual Online Customer Engagement Report 2008. Produced by EConsultancy in association with cScape. Published online at **www.econsultancy.com.**

Deighton, J. (1996) The future of interactive marketing, *Harvard Business Review*, November–December, 151–62.

EConsultancy (2005) Managing an e-commerce team: integrating digital marketing into your organisation. Author: Dave Chaffey. Available from **www.econsultancy.com.**

EConsultancy (2008) Managing Digital Channels Research Report. Author: Dave Chaffey. Available from **www.econsultancy.com.**

Geyskens, I., Gielens, K. and Dekimpe, M. (2002) The market valuation of internet channel additions, *Journal of Marketing*, 66 (April), 102–19.

Godin, S. (1999), *Permission Marketing*, Simon and Schuster, New York.

Haven, B. (2007) Marketing's new key metric: Engagement, 8 August, Forrester.

Hoffman, D.L. and Novak, T.P. (1996) Marketing in hypermedia computer-mediated environments: conceptual foundations, *Journal of Marketing*, 60 (July), 50–68.

Hoffman, D.L. and Novak, T.P. (1997) A new marketing paradigm for electronic commerce. *The Information Society*, Special issue on electronic commerce, 13 (January–March), 43–54.

Iyengar, R., Han, S. and Gupta, S. (2009) Do friends influence purchases in a social network? Harvard Business School working paper 09–123.

Jackson, S. (2009) *Cult of Analytics, Driving online marketing strategies using web analytics*, Elsevier, Oxford, UK.

Jenkinson, A. and Sain, B. (2001) *Getting words clear – marketing needs a clear and consistent terminology*. White paper available from Centre for Integrated Marketing, (**www.integrated marketing.org.uk**).

Kiani, G. (1998) Marketing opportunities in the digital world, *Internet Research: Electronic Networking Applications and Policy*, 8(2), 185–94.

Levine, R., Locke, C., Searls, D. and Weinberger, D. (2000) *The Cluetrain Manifesto*. Perseus Books, Cambridge, MA.

McDonald, M. and Wilson, H. (1999) *E-Marketing: Improving Marketing Effectiveness in a Digital World*. Financial Times/Prentice Hall, Harlow.

O'Reilly, T. (2005) What Is Web 2? Design Patterns and Business Models for the Next Generation of Software. Web article, 30 September. O'Reilly Publishing, Sebastopol, CA.

SEC (2008) United States Securities and Exchange Commission submission Form 10-K. eBay submission for the fiscal year ended December 31, 2007.

Shah, D. and Halligan, B. (2009) *Inbound Marketing: Get Found Using Google, Social Media, and Blogs*, Wiley, NJ.

Smart Insights (2010) Introducing RACE: a practical framework to improve your digital marketing. Blog post by Dave Chaffey, 15 July 2010. Available from: **www.smartinsights.com/digital-marketing-strategy.**

Smart Insights (2011) Digital marketing statistics. Blog post by Dave Chaffey, 6 March 2011. For latest updates, see **www.smartinsights.com/mobile-marketing.**

Seybold, P. (1999) *Customers.com*. Century Business Books, Random House, London.

Spivack (2007) How the WebOS Evolves? Nova Spivack blog posting, 9 February 2007, **http://novaspivack.typepad.com/nova_spivacks_weblog/2007/02/steps_towards_a.html.**

Waterman, R.H., Peters, T.J. and Phillips, J.R. (1980) Structure is not organisation. *McKinsey Quarterly in-house journal*. McKinsey & Co., New York.

Weinberg, T. (2010) *The New Community Rules: Marketing on The Social Web*, Wiley, Hoboken, NJ.

Weblinks

Leading portals and blogs covering digital marketing developments

- **ClickZ Experts** (www.clickz.com/experts). An excellent collection of articles on online marketing communications. US-focused.
- **Direct Marketing Association UK** (www.dma.org.uk). Source of up-to-date data protection advice and how-to guides about online direct marketing.
- **Econsultancy.com** (www.econsultancy.com). UK-focused portal with extensive supplier directory, best-practice white papers and forum.
- **eMarketer** (www.emarketer.com). Includes reports on media spend based on compilations of other analysts. Fee-based service.
- **iMediaConnection** (www.imediaconnection.com). Articles covering best practice in digital media channels.
- **Interactive Advertising Bureau** (www.iab.net). Best practice on interactive advertising. See also www.iabuk.net in the UK.
- **The Interactive Media in Retail** (www.imrg.org). Trade body for e-retailers reporting on growth and practice within UK and European e-commerce.
- **Journal of Computer Mediated Communications** (http://www.blackwell-synergy.com/loi/jcmc). A free online peer-reviewed journal describing developments in interactive communications.
- **Marketing Sherpa** (www.marketingsherpa.com). Case studies and news about online marketing.
- **Mashable** (www.mashable.com). The largest site covering developments in digitial media and technology.
- **Smart Insights** (www.smartinsights.com). Covers all developments in digital marketing to support this book. Edited by Dave Chaffey.

Print trade publications with online resources

- **New Media Age** (www.newmediazero.com/nma). A weekly magazine reporting on the UK new media interest. Full content available online.

Chapter 2
Online marketplace analysis: micro-environment

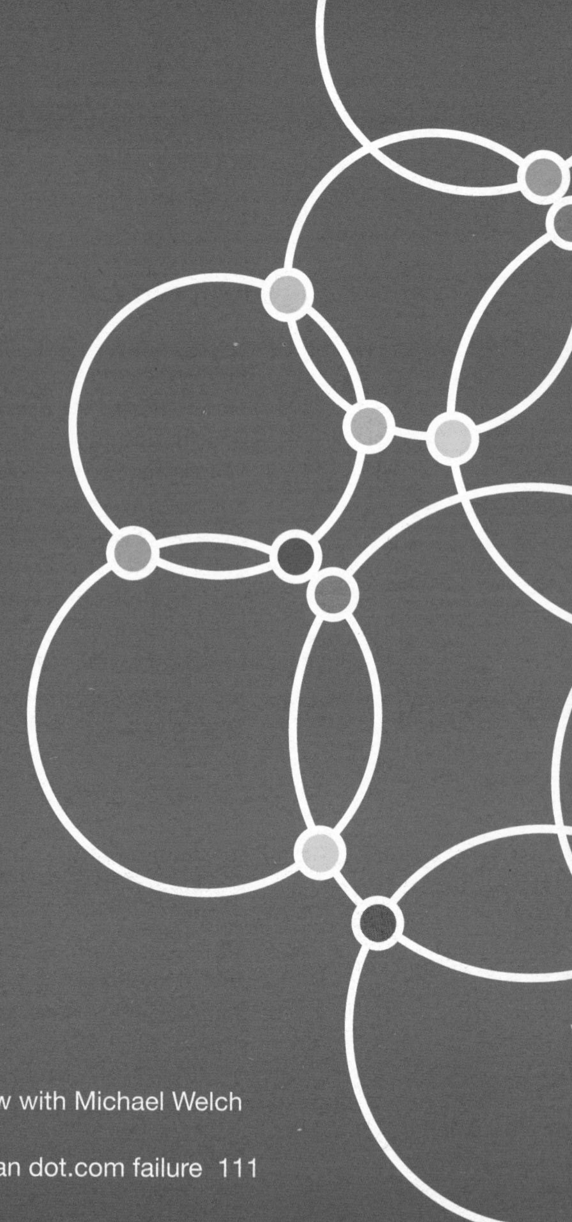

Chapter at a glance

Main topics

Case studies

Learning objectives

After reading this chapter, you should be able to:

- Identify the elements of an organisation's online marketplace that have implications for developing a digital marketing strategy
- Evaluate techniques for reviewing the importance of different actors in the microenvironment: customers, intermediaries, suppliers and competitors as part of the development of digital marketing strategy
- Review changes to business and revenue models enabled by digital markets.

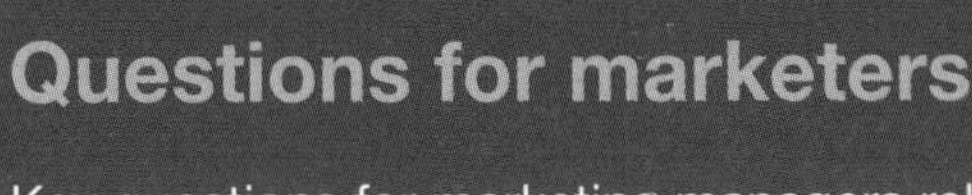

Questions for marketers

Key questions for marketing managers related to this chapter are:

- What are our capabilities for understanding our online marketplace?
- How relevant is the behaviour of the actors in the micro-environment to the future of our business?
- How do I complete a marketplace analysis and how does this inform our digital marketing planning?
- How are customers' needs changing as digital platforms develop and what are the implications of such changes?
- How do I compare our online marketing with that of our competitors?
- How do we find suitable intermediaries at the planning stage of a digital marketing strategy?

Scan code to find the latest updates for topics in this chapter

Links to other chapters

- Chapters 2 and 3 provide a foundation for later chapters on Internet marketing strategy and implementation.
- Chapter 3 builds on the concepts, frameworks and ideas introduced in this chapter.
- Chapter 4 explains how environment analysis is used as part of strategy development.
- Chapter 5 considers the principle functions of the mix in digital strategy development.

Introduction

Situation analysis
Collection and review of information about an organisation's external environment and internal resources and processes in order to refine its strategy.

All organisations operate within an environment that influences the performance of their business. Organisations that monitor, understand and respond appropriately to changes in the environment have the greatest opportunities to compete effectively in the online marketplace. Understanding an organisation's environment is a key part of **situation analysis**, and forms a solid foundation for all types of marketing planning but especially when devising a digital marketing strategy (process introduced in Figure 1.8 and covered in more detail in Chapter 4).

In the next two chapters we look at how organisations assess the digital environment and identify implications for digital marketing strategy and planning. To be successful in online trading environments it is important to respond effectively changes in the trading environment as the interview with Michael Welch of online startup Blackcircles.com shows.

Digital marketing in practice — The Smart Insights Interview

Michael Welch of Blackcircles.com on creating a new online business

Overview and concepts covered

Michael Welch created Blackcircles.com (Figure 2.1) as a new way for consumers to buy tyres at competitive prices either over the Internet or on the telephone. From the site, consumers can find the best deal from a network of over 1000 local dealerships.

Blackcircles.com now has a turnover of £18 million and is growing rapidly, so we thought it would be interesting to learn the approaches its founder, Michael Welch has used to grow and sustain the business.

The interview

Q. Which factors were important to the initial success of Blackcircles.com?

Michael Welch: At the very beginning it was mainly about hard work, determination and not 'taking no for an answer'. If I'm honest there was no real difference between me and the next guy walking down the street – I just wanted it more.

A key factor in the company getting to where it is today though was also having a strong USP (unique selling point). There were a couple of other companies around at the same time with a similar USP and there are now countless smaller operations that seem to have modelled their USP on ours.

Providing a culture of excellent customer service is an obvious way to go, back when you are a new company – at times – it is all you have. When brand awareness is zero to slim, you have to work as hard as possible to show the customers that first use you – and in reality are taking a gamble – that you give a damn and that their gamble has paid off. I worked hard to make sure customers came first.

Q. Which marketing activities are important to your continued growth?

Michael Welch: The base of our continued growth actually hasn't altered much from those early days. Customer satisfaction is still very much key, the desire to make the company a success is there and our USP is just as strong as it was back at the start of the last decade.

I suppose there has been a shift in that we were once the under dogs and now we are leading the pack. Implementing new ideas and technologies has played a major

Figure 2.1 Blackcircles.com

part in helping us to stay on top i.e. making sure we are up to date with the best SEO techniques, embracing the world of social media and continually trying to offer more attractive services to our customers – the launch of car servicing being one such evolution on the original 'tyre retailer' tag that Blackcircles.com started with.

Underneath all that though the company is supported by a foundation of 'getting the basics right'.

Q. How do you manage and improve service quality?

Michael Welch: It's a vital ongoing process. The most obvious way in which we check on the site's service quality is through customer feedback. This has been the backbone of many changes we've made over the years. Our customers are a great resource and I'm often surprised at the number of people I meet who don't listen to what their customers are saying to them – it's free advice, why wouldn't you take it?

We recently placed Trustpilot on our website which is the online retail industry's equivalent of Trip Advisor. This shows independent customer reviews and an overall rating. This is a further commitment from us and a great message to customers that we will be doing everything possible to give them a great service. We are passionate about great service.

On top of listening to what our customers are saying we also actively take part in user testing. We've been working with a company recently which records anonymous users (which you can define i.e. British person in mid-30s who doesn't often use the Internet to shop) on our site.

Not only are we able to see what they are doing, but they are also giving a narration of their thoughts. Its early days but we've already discovered areas of the site that can be improved due to this.

The newest form of testing we're just beginning to get involved with is a heat map style technology. Seeing where users are clicking and where they are not is great. It makes you ask why certain areas of a page are receiving attention whilst the rest is being ignored.

Q. How do you review the success of your site? Which approaches do you use?

Michael Welch: As far as I'm concerned if you don't include web analytics in your marketing plan, then quite simply, you don't have a marketing plan. Gone are the days when all website owners ever worried about was visitor numbers – good riddance too as it means we don't have to put up with those horrible 'visitor counters' that you used to see banded about everywhere.

Understanding not just how many visitors you have, but also how they are using your site is invaluable. We actively check out this information on a regular basis. A quick example would be: what percentage of our visitors search for tyres? From this, what percentage then adds a set of tyres to their basket and then how many actually end up on the payment confirmation page?

Looking at these stats we can see at what point in an order process people exit our site. Then we ask ourselves what content is on each page, are there enough call to actions? Is there enough information? Is it easy to navigate? Could we add in new content to encourage people to buy? If we come up with a potential change that we believe will help a page perform better we then track to see the difference. If conversions go up, great – but how can we improve it further? If they drop – back to the drawing board.

Not only do we see the importance on an 'order process' based analysis, but also using it for certain technical aspects. For instance, customers with one browser end up buying in greater percentages than those with a different browser. Ok, so is there a piece of code on a page that is affecting the customers' experience? Or is it even a demographic thing?

All this is just scratching the surface. Web analytics can answer so many questions you didn't even know you needed to ask. The trick is not getting overawed – it is too easy to get lost in an ocean of statistics.

Q. Which new approaches in the marketplace are you reviewing currently?

Michael Welch: The use of video is an interesting avenue that we are keenly pursuing at the moment. Audio and Visual are right up there in terms of brand development and with the sheer number of opportunities available on the web online videos have never been more exciting. We're still testing the water at the moment with a new 'Blackcircles.com TV' channel on YouTube, but I'm pleased with the results so far.

In a bit of a more traditions sense we are also enhancing our e-mail campaigns. However, I'm very wary of over-saturating our customers with information that they will just mark as spam. The key goal for us at the moment is engaging our customers with the brand. Social media is playing a large role in this as well, as you would expect.

The digital marketing environment

Micro-environment
The *actors* (stakeholders) and their interactions which influence how an organisation responds in its marketplace.

Research suggests the traditional marketing environment consists of two separate parts (Porter (1980) on corporate strategy or Kotler *et al.* (2001) on marketing strategy): 1) **micro-environment** and 2) **macro-environment** (Figure 2.2) The micro-environment, is known as '*the operating environment*', and focuses on the actors which shape the immediate trading environment. These actors include the customers whose needs and wants are to be satis-

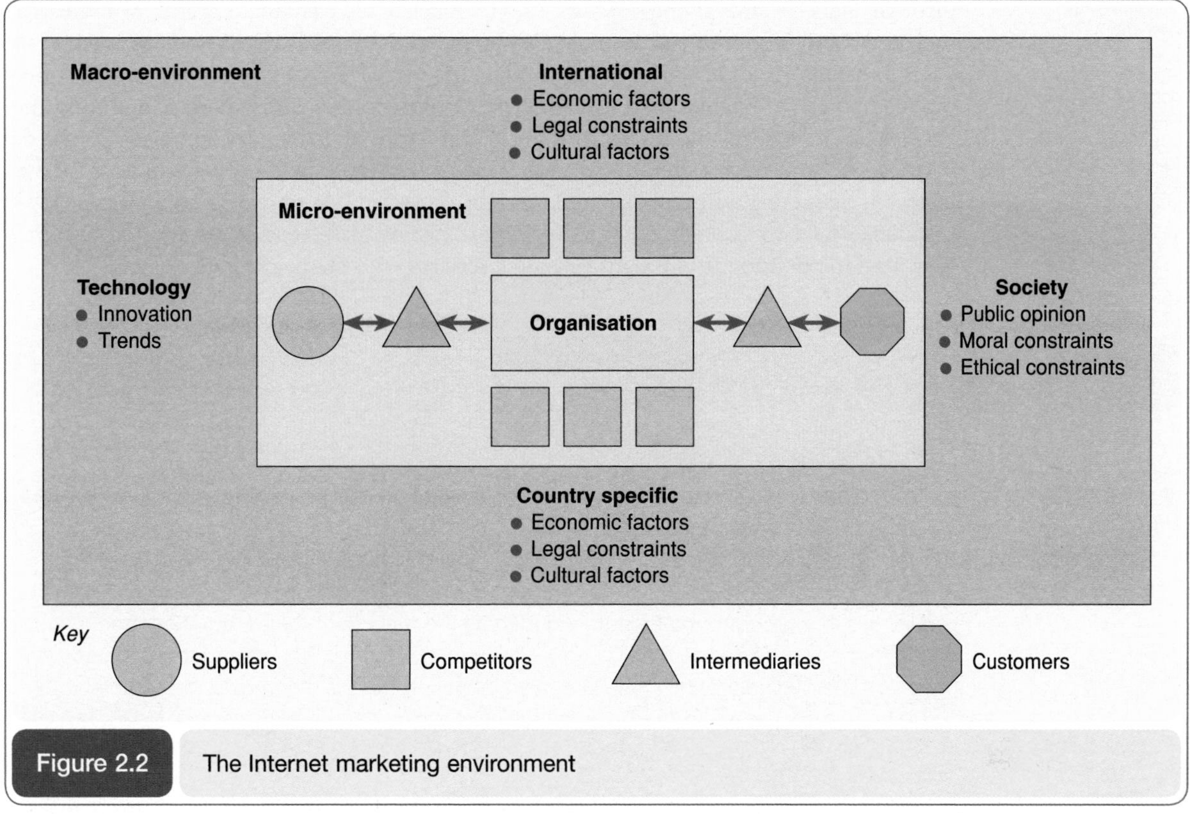

Figure 2.2 The Internet marketing environment

Macro-environment Broad forces affecting all organisations in the marketplace, including social, technological, economic, political, legal and ecological influences.

Environmental scanning The process of continuously monitoring and analysing events in an organisation environment(s), which have implications for planning.

fied, along with the competitors, intermediaries and suppliers. These groups of actors shape the online marketplace and a digital marketer needs to understand their behaviour and the implication of changes if an organisation is to develop an effective digital marketing strategy.

The macro-environment is sometimes known as '*the remote environment*' and consists of five key forces which can significantly affect organisational success. These forces originate from the marketplace which is largely beyond the immediate control of an organisation, e.g. economic conditions, changes to international trade legislation, technological developments and innovations, social change and political interventions. These are examples of possible areas of change which if ignored could have a significant impact on the future success of an organisation. We study the macro-environment and its significance in Chapter 3. In this chapter, we explore the actors in the micro-environment and the implications for marketing managers.

The trading environment can have a profound impact on performance; consequently an organisation should continually monitor the environment (micro and macro). This process is often referred to as **environmental scanning**.

Environmental scanning and online marketplace analysis

Click ecosystem Describes the customer behaviour or flow of online visitors between search engines, media sites, other intermediaries to an organisation and its competitors.

Analysis of the online marketplace or 'marketspace' is a key part of developing a long-term strategic digital marketing plan and/or creating a shorter-term marketing communications campaign. Marketplace analysis helps to define the nature of the competitive market or **click ecosystem** and provides a means of monitoring the online trading environment. In Chapter 1 we saw that there are a range of digital technology platforms within the mobile and desktop hardware platforms. Major online players such as Facebook, Google and Salesforce have developed their own infrastructure or **online market ecosystem** which connects websites

Online market ecosystem
Interactions between different online systems related to a specific hardware or software technology which may be independent or developed by a particular brand.

through data exchange giving opportunities to enhance the customer experience and extend their reach and influence. For example, Facebook has developed an API system known as the Facebook platform to enable exchange of data between websites and applications including mobile apps. This enables other site owners to incorporate information about consumer Facebook interactions into their own websites and apps and share social objects across the Facebook ecosystem to extend their reach. Google has developed its own ecosystem related to search marketing and mobile – the Android ecosystem. As part of marketplace analysis, companies have to evaluate the relative importance of these ecosystems and the resources they need to put into integrating their online services with them, to create a plan.

Activity 2.1 Online ecosystems

Purpose

To explore the increasing importance of facilitating communications through online platforms and service providers.

Activity

Discuss in a group, or make notes to identify the main companies (e.g. Facebook) and platforms (e.g. tablet devices) used by consumers that are important for companies to review their presence on. Once you have identified the main company or service types group them together so that their overall importance can be reviewed.

Analysing the impact of different ecosystems on online consumer behaviour or customer journeys is, today, as important as observing their physical behaviour in the real world. For example, potential online customers regularly turn to search engines to find products, services, information about brands and entertainment. Search engines can act as a conduit connecting together buyers and sellers through different 'search phrases'. So, organisations need to understand consumer use of key phrases entered from generic searches for products or services, more specific phrases and brand phrases incorporating their own key words and competitor names (see Chapter 9 for an explanation of tools to gain this information).

To help understand and summarise the linkages between online businesses and customer journeys it is worthwhile producing an online marketplace map as shown in Figure 2.3. This shows the linkages between different online intermediaries in the marketplace; the flow of clicks between different customer segments, a company's online presences and different competitors' sites.

The main elements of the online marketplace map presented in Figure 2.3 are:

1 *Customer segments.* The marketplace analysis helps identify and summarise different target segments for an online business in order to understand their online media consumption, behaviour and the type of content and experiences they want online. In a digital campaign or website design project, personas are used to understand the preferences, characteristics and online behaviours of different groups (as described in the section on online buyer behaviour later in this chapter).
2 *Search intermediaries.* These are the main search engines in each country. Typically Google, Yahoo!, Bing and Ask, but others are important in some markets such as China (Baidu), Russia (Yandex) and South Korea (Naver). There are companies which provide specialist audience data to enable a digital marketer to discover the relative importance of particular search engines (and other types of site) in different countries, e.g. ComScore (**www.comscore.com**), Experian Hitwise (**www.hitwise.com**), Google AdPlanner data (**www.google.com/adplanner**), Nielsen online (**www.nielsen.com**). Indeed, search engines have

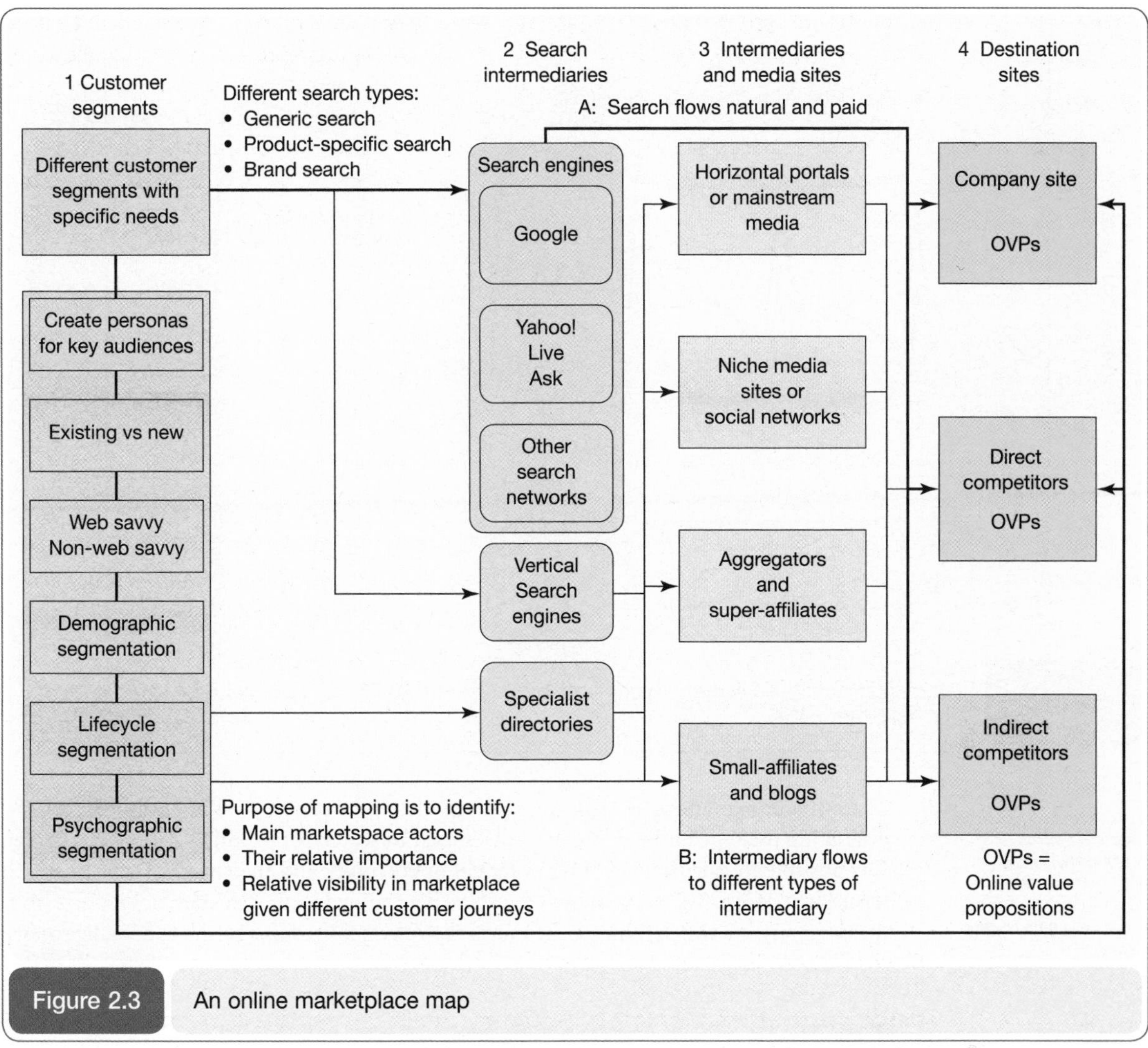

Figure 2.3 An online marketplace map

become so significant that search trends are used to predict sales future sales volume. Choi and Varian (2009) note that Google Trends data on search volumes through time is very useful for predicting levels of spending. They argue that:

> because Google Trends data are practically available in real time, any statistical relationship between actual sales and Google Trends can be exploited to produce more timely estimates of data. For example, official retail sales data are only available with a lag of several weeks, whereas a model based on Google Trends data could produce estimates much faster. This approach to producing more rapid estimates of present data is commonly referred to as *nowcasting*, as the idea is to predict the present rather than the future (forecasting).

Figure 2.4 shows Office for National Statistics sales data for textile clothing and footware mapped against apparel searches, e.g. top searches for dress, clothes, shoes and boots.

Companies need to know which sites are effective in harnessing search traffic and either partner with them or try to obtain a share of the search traffic using the search engine marketing and affiliate marketing techniques explained in Chapter 9. Well known, trusted brands which have developed customer loyalty are in a good position to succeed online since a common consumer behaviour is to go straight to the site through entering a URL

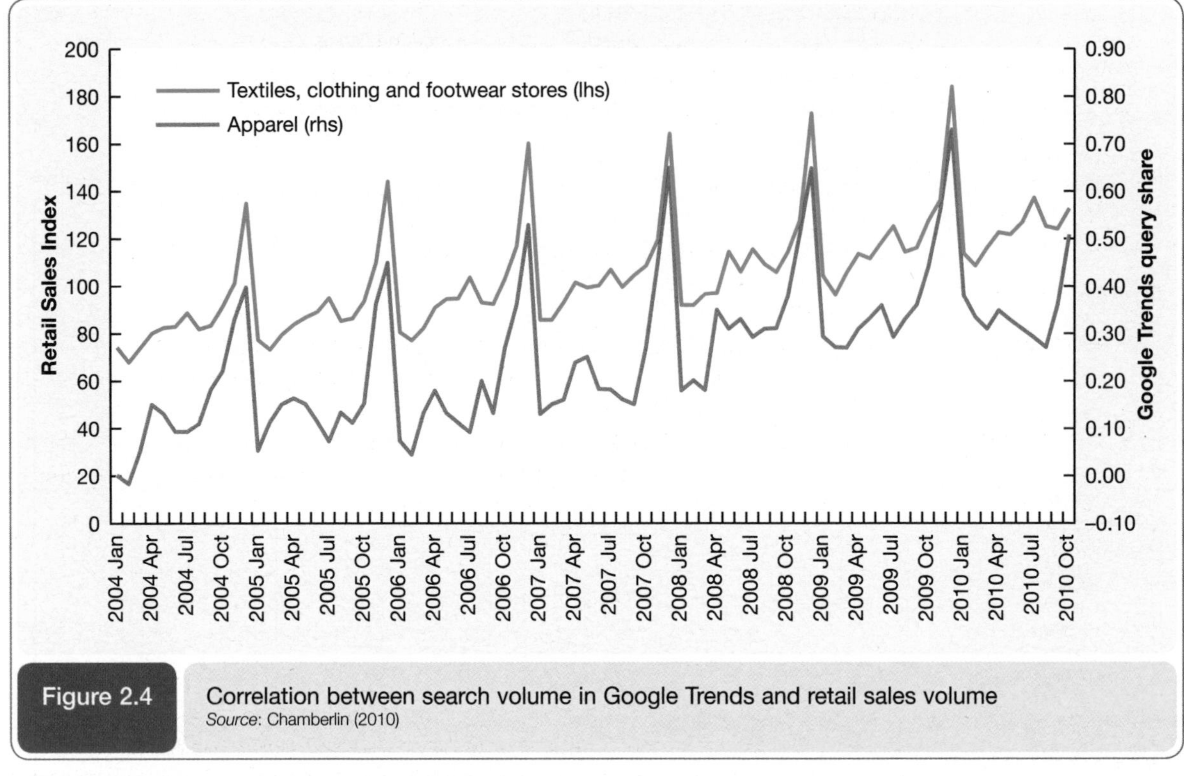

Figure 2.4 Correlation between search volume in Google Trends and retail sales volume
Source: Chamberlin (2010)

Share of search
The audience share of Internet searchers achieved by a particular audience in a particular market.

or from a bookmark or e-mail. Alternatively they may search for the brand or URL. By evaluating the type and volume of phrases used to search for products in a given market, it is possible to calculate the total potential opportunity and the current share of search terms for a company. **Share of search** can be determined from web analytics reports from the company site which indicate the precise key phrases used by visitors to actually reach a site from different search engines.

Table 2.1 Top 10 search terms for all retailing and for apparel

Search term	Food retailers	Volume of search relative to the top term	Textiles clothing and footware	Volume of search relative to the top term
1 top term	Tesco	100	Shoes	100
2	Asda	50	Boots	75
3	Tesco Direct	15	Dress	55
4	Morrisions	10	Clothes	45
5	Sainsbury's	10	Next	40
6	Aldi	5	Dresses	35
7	Clubcard	5	Nike	35
8	George Asda	5	River Island	35
9	Ocado	5	Watches	35
10	Sainsbury	5	New Look	30

Source: Chamberlin (2010)

Aggregators
An alternative term to price comparison sites. Aggregators include product, price and service information comparing competitors within a sector such as financial services, retail or travel. Their revenue models commonly include affiliate revenues (CPA), pay-per-click advertising (CPC) and display advertising (CPM).

Affiliates
Companies promoting a merchant typically through a commission-based arrangement either direct or through an affiliate network.

Key online influencers
Individuals or publishers who an online target audience listens to and interacts with. Online influencer outreach or 'blogger outreach' can help companies reach and engage a wider audience.

3 *Intermediaries and media or publisher sites.* Media sites and other intermediaries such as social networks, **aggregators** and **affiliates** are often successful in attracting visitors via customer search or direct to their web sites if they are mainstream brands. Companies need to assess potential online media and distribution partners in the categories shown in Figure 2.2 such as:

- *Mainstream news media sites or portals.* These include traditional (for example, FT.com, *The Times*, *Guardian*) or Pureplay (like Google News).
- *Niche/vertical media sites.* For example EConsultancy, ClickZ.com in B2B.
- *Social networks.* For example, Facebook, Google+, Twitter and LinkedIn. We saw through Digital marketing insight 1.1 that there is discussion on how influential interactions between consumers in social networks are in driving sales.
- *Price comparison sites (also known as aggregators).* For example, Moneysupermarket, Kelkoo, Shopping.com, confused.com, mysupermarket.com.
- *Super-affiliates.* Affiliates gain revenue from a merchant they refer traffic to by being paid commission based on a proportion of the sale or a fixed amount. They are important in e-retail markets, accounting for tens of % of sales.
- *Niche affiliates or bloggers.* These are often individuals but they may be very influential, for example, in the UK Martin Lewis of Moneysavingexpert.com receives millions of visits every month. Smaller affiliates and bloggers can be important collectively. With the growth in readership and social interactions on blogs, identifying **key online influencers** within a market is important to help reach and engage target audiences.

4 *Destination sites and platforms.* These are the sites that the marketer is trying to attract visitors to, including transactional sites by retail, financial service, travel, manufacturers and other companies or non-transactional sites like brand or relationship-building sites as introduced in Chapter 1. Destination sites also include presence on other social sites like Facebook and Twitter or mobile apps. Figure 2.3 refers to OVP or 'online value proposition' which is a summary of the unique features offered by brands in their online services and presences which are described in more detail in Chapter 4. The OVP is a key aspect to consider within planning – marketers should evaluate their OVPs against competitors and think about how they can refine them to develop a unique online experience.

Digital marketing insight 2.1 Resources for analysing the online marketplace

How to make sense of the volume of available data can be a big challenge for any online marketer. However, it makes sense when planning digital marketing campaigns to take up the opportunity to plan based on the actual marketplace characteristics rather than intuition. Nevertheless, in order to do this a digital marketer needs to know how and where they can tap into the wealth of research about current Internet use and future trends. Typically, businesses use different tools for analysis of the online marketplace and customer behaviour as they access different websites as part of their customer journey. There are both free and paid-for analytical services available to help. Table 2.2, shows a selection of free and paid-for services which can be used for online marketplace analysis, and these resources can be used to assess the number of people searching for information and the popularity of different types of sites measured by the number of **unique visitors**.

Unique visitors
Individual visitors to a site measured through cookies or IP addresses on an individual computer.

Table 2.2 Research tools for assessing digital markets

Search tool provider and sources of information	Focus and services
1 **Google tools** (www.google.com/ads/agency/toolkit.html	Google is one of the best sources of accurate tools for marketplace analysis including: • Google Adplanner (site popularity and demographics) • Google Insights for search – trends in search volume by country (similar to Google Trends) • Keyword Tool – for comparing keyphrase volume.
2 **Alexa** (www.alexa.com)	Free tool (see also **www.compete.com**). Also use the Google syntax related:domain.com to find related sites Owned by Amazon which provides traffic ranking of individual sites compared to all sites. Works best for sites in top 100,000. Sample dependent on users of the Alexa toolbar.
3 **Experian Hitwise** (www.hitwise.com)	Paid-for tool, but free research available at **http://weblogs.hitwise.com**, available in many countries to compare audience size and search/site use. Works through monitoring IP traffic to different sites through ISPs.
4 **Nielsen**	Paid-for tool but free data on search engines and intermediaries available from press release section focus in on what consumers buy. Panel service based on at-home and at-work users who have agreed to have their web use tracked by software. Top rankings on site gives examples of most popular sites in several countries.
5 **Comscore** (www.comscore.com)	Paid-for tool but free data on search engines and intermediaries available from press release section. Source of global digital marketing intelligence. Services provide insight into behaviour and lifestyle of consumers, e.g. demographics, attitudes, offline behaviour.
6 **Google Analytics**	Free and paid-for services, which provide insights into website traffic.
7 **Internet or Interactive Advertising Bureau (IAB)** US: **www.iab.net** UK: **www.iabuk.net** Europe: **www.europe.uk.net** (see also **www.eiaa.net**)	Research focusing on investment in different digital media channels, in particular display ads and search marketing. Paid-for services.
8 **Internet Media in Retail Group (IMRG)** (www.imrg.org)	The IMRG provides statistics on UK e-retail sales. Their e-retail sales index, offers a range of measurements, e.g. total sales, number of shoppers online, conversion rates. The services are free to members.

By scanning the detailed results from searching information providers a digital marketing planner can build an informed picture of what is happening at any given time and also make forecasts for strategic planning.

In the remainder of this chapter we examine the actors who shape the micro-environment We also consider ideas and methods of analysis and highlight implications for digital marketing planning. Table 2.3 provides an overview of the issues.

Table 2.3 The micro-environment: issues for digital marketers

Micro-environment	Issues
Customers	• Access to digital platforms • Level of use of digital platforms and services • Behaviour, characteristics and profiles • Service expectations
Suppliers and intermediaries	• Level of technology adoption • Integration and connectedness • Service provision • Trading relationships
Competitors	• Strategic intentions and planning • Resources and capabilities • Levels of service provision • Supplier and intermediary relationships • Performance

Customer analysis

Consumer behaviour analysis
In digital markets, this type of analysis involves research into the motivations, media consumption preferences and selection processes used by consumers as they use digital channels together with traditional channels to purchase online products and use other online services.

Customer insight
Knowledge about customers' needs, profile, preferences and digital experiences from analysis of qualitative and quantitative data. Specific insights can be used to inform marketing tactics directed at groups of customers with shared characteristics.

Customer segments
Groups of customers sharing similar characteristics, preferences and behaviours that are meaningful in terms of various market propositions, and which are defined as part of *target marketing strategy and planning*.

In marketing, understanding the trading situation is very important for setting realistic business and marketing objectives. Customers' attitudes towards the Internet have changed significantly during the last two decades. In consumer markets, shoppers are becoming more attuned to buying online and digital technologies enable them to be well-informed when making purchasing decisions. Moreover, this is one of the reasons, it is suggested that 'there will be a significant struggle for power between the retailer and the consumer' (Doherty and Ellis-Chadwick, 2011) in the future as the consumer becomes more and more informed and more demanding. In business markets, some of the same principles apply but the balance of power is less likely to be determined by the Internet *per se*, as the technology plays a more facilitative role in the purchasing and communication; this is because personal relationships currently tend to be of greater importance when negotiating sales than remotely transacted arrangements. However, social networks play an increasingly important role in linking together both consumers and potential business partners. Complete Activity 2.2 to get a feel for how business networks are changing the way we make connections.

Customers are important actors in a company's immediate trading environment, and analysis of their behaviour is central to understanding of the trading situation and ultimately digital planning. **Customer behaviour analysis** can be considered from two perspectives:

1 *Demand analysis*. This involves understanding the potential and actual volume of visitors to an online presence and the extent to which prospects convert to tactical and strategic outcomes, e.g. lead generation and sales.
2 *Digital consumer behaviour*. Here a marketer wants to understand the needs, characteristics and digital experiences or behaviours of target consumers. These variables are often collectively referred to as **customer insight**. Based on this analysis, **customer segments** can be created which will be used to develop targeting approaches as part of strategy and planning (described in Chapter 4 onwards).

Activity 2.2 LinkedIn: making processional connections

Purpose

To consider the business potential of online networks.

Activity

Businesses rely on their connections to other business and key individuals to develop their business. In 2002, Reid Hoffman had an idea, which he turned into the largest professional network in the world, LinkedIn. In March 2011, there were over 100 million professional individuals signed up to the network.

Visit **http://press.linkedin.com/success-stories** and read 'Success stories of LinkedIn members' who have used this network to grow their business.

Now answer these questions:

1 How have the successful LinkedIn members used the network to their advantage?
2 Suggest to how being a member of the LinkedIn network might help a company to develop better customer knowledge.

Demand analysis and implications for marketing planning

Demand analysis
Quantitative determination of the potential use and business value from online customers of an organisation. Qualitative analysis of perceptions of online channels is also assessed.

Digital marketing managers should understand current trends and levels of use of the Internet and different online services and how they relate to services and products the organisation wishes to deliver online. Additionally, marketers need to be aware of factors that affect how customers actively use the digital services on offer. This evaluation process is called **demand analysis**. The benefits of this form of analysis are that companies can identify opportunities for influencing and delivering sales online based on actual use of digital media by individuals in the company's target market. Demand analysis can reduce guesswork, and improve the effectiveness of digital marketing communications campaigns.

Demand analysis research has identified some important generic factors that influence adoption and use of the Internet:

- cost of access
- value proposition
- perception of ease of use
- perceptions of security.

Assessing demand for digital services by looking at these generic factors should enable marketers to set realistic strategic objectives for each target segment, but in order to do this the digital marketer also needs to assess the volume and share of customers who:

- have access to the digital channel
- use specific online services which may affect the purchase decision like price comparison sites, social networks and specialist blogs
- are influenced by using the digital channel but purchase using another channel as part of the multichannel buyer behaviour
- purchase or use other services using the digital channel.

Using information sources and tools, like those suggested in Table 2.2, plus any primary research a company decides to carry out, a digital marketer should be able to develop a sound understanding of the characteristics, needs and wants of the individuals (and/or companies) in the target market and their propensity to engage with digital channels. Once this foundation level of understanding is developed it is possible to consider how to achieve marketing goals and objectives through the use of digital communications.

Implications for marketing planning: conversion models

Conversion marketing
Using marketing communications to maximise conversion of potential customers to actual customers.

As part of situation analysis and objective setting, experienced digital marketers build conversion or waterfall models of the efficiency of their web marketing. Using this approach, the total potential online demand for a service in a particular market can be estimated and then the success of the company in achieving a share of this market determined. **Conversion marketing** tactics can then be used to convert as many *potential* site visitors into *actual* visitors and then convert these into leads, customers and repeat customers.

Berthon *et al.* (1998) suggested the online purchasing decision process could be looked at using the hierarchy of effects model (originally developed for assessing the efficiency of offline marketing communications). The model assumes that different types of communications can be used based on where the customer is in the purchasing decision process, e.g. at the beginning of the purchasing process advertising can be used to raise awareness, further through the process sales promotion techniques can be used to elicit action.

Figure 2.5 shows an adapted version of Berthon *et al.* (1998) model from Chaffey (2001) and it highlights the conversion metrics, which act as drivers of performance. The key ratios to consider are:

- *awareness efficiency*: target web users/all web users
- *attractability efficiency*: number of individual visits/number of seekers
- *engagement efficiency*: number of active visitors/number of visits
- *conversion efficiency*: number of purchases/number of active visits

This model is instructive for improving digital marketing within an organisation since these different types of conversion efficiencies are key to understanding how effective online and offline marketing communications are in achieving marketing outcomes. An additional and important ratio is *retention efficiency*, which involves calculating the relationship between the *number of re-purchases/number of purchases.*

The model is useful to the digital marketer as it highlights the significance of how conversion effectiveness differs between first-time users and repeat users. It also shows the stages a

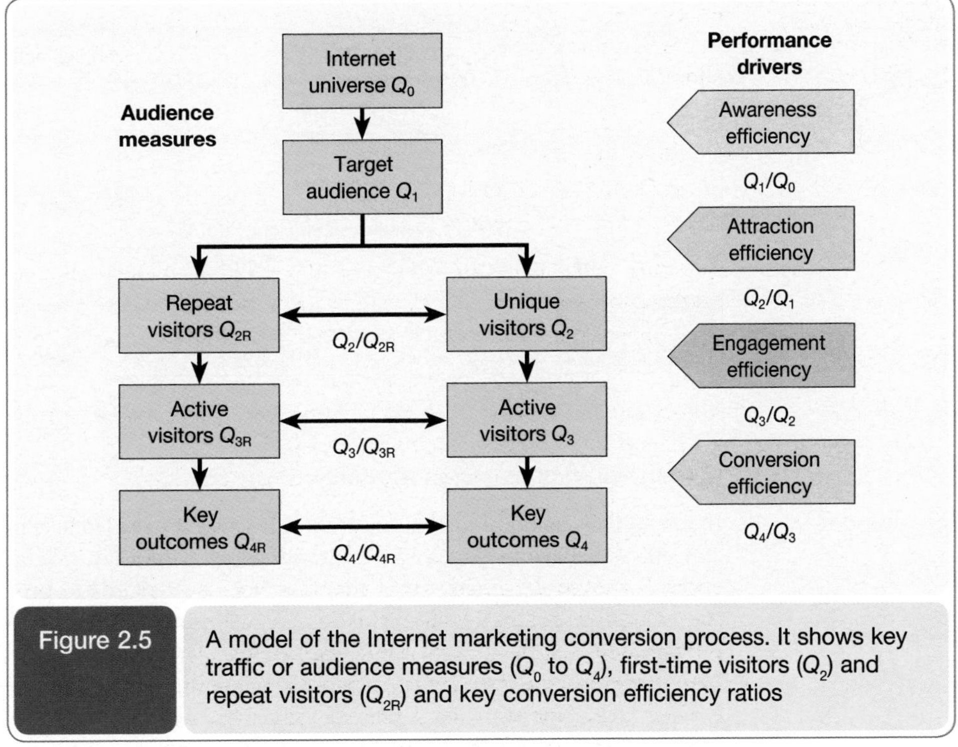

Figure 2.5 A model of the Internet marketing conversion process. It shows key traffic or audience measures (Q_0 to Q_4), first-time visitors (Q_2) and repeat visitors (Q_{2R}) and key conversion efficiency ratios

Clickstream
The sequence of clicks made by a visitor to the site to make a purchase.

customer may take in a virtual purchasing journey. An additional important aspect of online buyer behaviour not shown in the figure is the site path or **clickstream** for different audience types or segments. Analysing the clickstream reveals which pages a website visitor looks at before leaving the site.

Figure 2.6 shows an example of how measuring conversion rates can be used to improve web marketing. Numbers are across a fixed time period of one month. If for a particular market there is a potential audience (market) of 200,000 (Q_1), then if online and offline promotion techniques achieve 100,000 visitors to the site (Q_2), marketers have achieved an impressive conversion rate of 50 per cent. The online marketers are then looking to convert these visitors to action. Before this is achieved, the visitors must be engaged. Data from log files show that many visitors leave when they first visit the home page of a site if they do not find the site acceptable or they are not happy with the experience. The number of visitors engaged (Q_3) is 50,000, which is half of all visitors. For the visitors that are engaged, the next step is to convert them to action. This is achieved for 500 visitors (Q_4), giving a conversion rate (Q_4/Q_3) of 1 per cent. If what is calculated (as is most common) is (Q_4/Q_2), this gives a conversion rate of 0.5 per cent.

An organisation in the position depicted in Figure 2.6 is attracting visitors to the site, but not converting them into active customers. Many companies fall into the trap of building websites which are aesthetically pleasing but fail to deliver improvements against marketing objectives. By looking more closely at the conversion ratios an organisation could considerably improve the performance on their digital offer. It is important to ensure that marketing objectives are being achieved through digital marketing action. We discuss different approaches in relation to communications goals in Chapter 8.

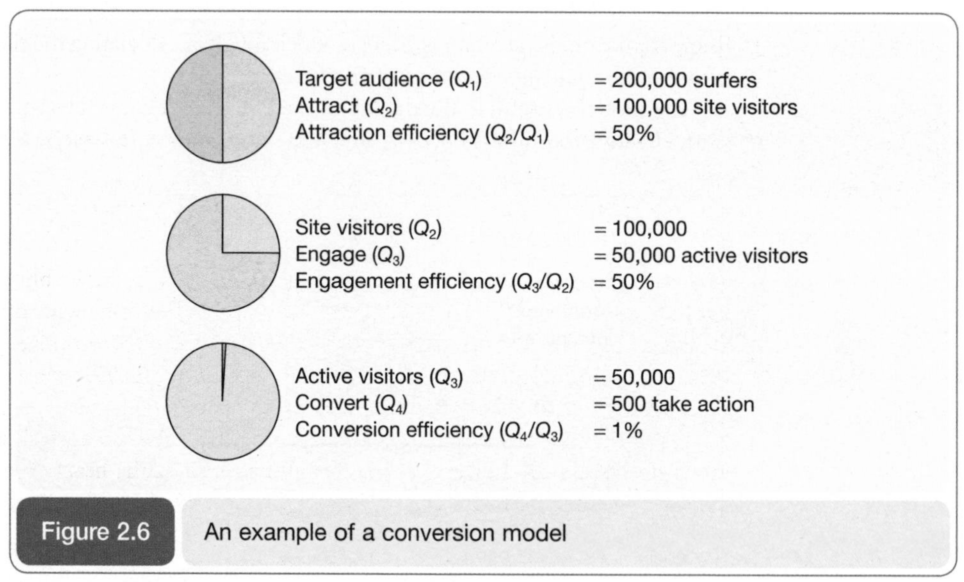

Figure 2.6 An example of a conversion model

Multichannel conversion models

In reality, conversion modelling is complex because it needs to take into account both online and offline behaviour. Figure 2.5 is simplified as it does not take account of offline influences. For example, an advertiser may use Google AdWords to promote their product but some shoppers will buy online while others will prefer to use other channels to make their purchase, e.g. use the phone or buy instore. Some online retailers in the UK have been very keen to monitor the effects of conversion rates and multichannel shopping behaviour as there is evidence to suggest there are potential gains, Brand Republic (2011):

> 'brands with multichannel offerings saw the largest growth of 19% in March, compared to 6% for online-only brands. Jonathan Brown, head of online selling, John Lewis, said: 'While overall traffic saw slightly slower growth than we have been used to, customers who were on our website were converting at a higher rate, spending more each time they shopped with us.'

Therefore, it is useful to put in place the means of monitoring cross-channel conversions at different stages in the buying process as it can help a business to understand how it might improve performance in both online and offline channels by making the marketing spend more effective.

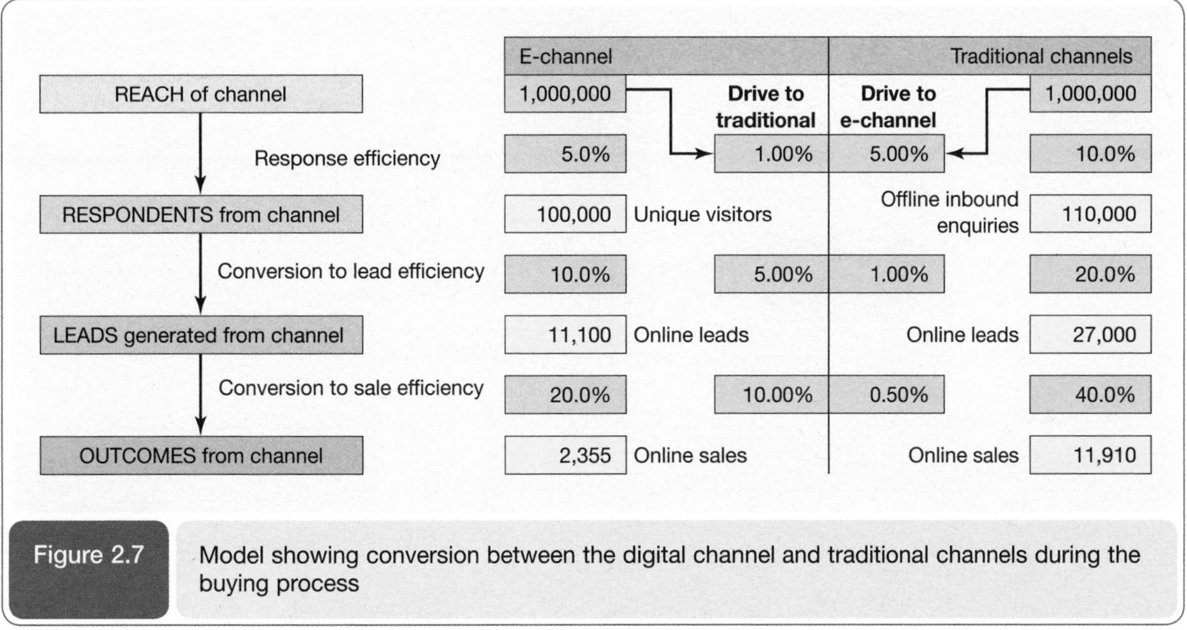

Figure 2.7 Model showing conversion between the digital channel and traditional channels during the buying process

Figure 2.7 shows a model of how this might work. For example, phone numbers which are unique to the website can be used as an indication of the volume of callers to a contact centre influenced by the website. This insight can then be built into budget models of sales levels such as that shown in Figure 2.6. This shows that of the 100,000 unique visitors in a period we can determine that 5000 (5%) may actually become offline leads.

In this section we have been discussing complex models for analysing customer conversion strategies. There are however three core dimensions at the heart of such models which are important to be aware of: 'Access : Choose : Transact' (ACT). We will now review each dimension, firstly from the perspective of B2C marketplace and then B2B.

Digital marketing insight 2.2 — ROPO models highlight consumer behaviour in the consumer phone market

ROPO is a term coined to describe research published by Google (2010) meaning 'Research Online Purchase Offline'. This study reviewed the role of the Internet in the decision process for mobile and broadband contracts involving the Vodafone website and stores in Germany based on a panel of 16,000 web users and questionnaires about their intent and purchase. For both of these services, the contract was signed online by around a third of the audience. However, a significant proportion signed the contract offline. The matrix presented in Figure 2.8 is a good framework for evaluating and summarising multichannel behaviour since it also shows the situation where research is offline and purchase occurs online. This behaviour is particularly common where products such as in this case, handsets, consumers want to evaluate their purchase online.

Mobile buyer		Research... Online	Research... Offline
Purchase...	Online	22%	9%
Purchase...	Offline	37%	32%

Figure 2.8 Research Online Purchase Online example
Source: Google, 2010

Evaluating demand levels

Access to digital platforms

E-commerce provides a global marketplace, and digital marketers should review user access in terms of frequency of access, location and channel.

Location of access

The networks which provide user access to digital services are continuing to grow and in doing so provide better, faster and more flexible links to digital service providers and other Internet users. Telegeography has been mapping the networks, Internet backbone, undersea cables, IP VPN and Ethernet services, broadband and 4G wireless which enable access since 1989. In 2000, the key areas for international data traffic were between the eastern seaboard of USA and Europe; there was limited traffic between Africa and other parts of the world. Whilst the USA continues to account for a major proportion of global data traffic, links between Asia, Africa and Australasia have been significantly improved and this is reflected in the increase in data traffic flows. Take a look at Activity 2.3 to find out more about Internet access around the world.

Type of access: broadband

The type of access is becoming increasingly important as more wireless technological innovations emerge. A variety of access devices are being developed which enable users to use the Internet from a greater range of locations for an ever-increasing range of applications. However, it is important to note that the type of access varies based on global location; some parts of the world do not have significant levels of high-speed, always-on, broadband Internet

Activity 2.3 Internet access around the world

Purpose

To consider the distribution and spread of global online communities.

Activity

Internetworldstats provide useful tables of Internet usage statistics from around the world, showing percentage of populations online, growth in user populations and much more information. Visit **http://www.internetworldstats.com** and find answers to the following questions:

1. Which part of the world has the highest number of Internet users?
2. What percentage of users are in Europe compared to the rest of the world?
3. Which region of the world has the least number of Internet users?

access and the bandwidth of the Internet backbone can vary significantly depending on where you are in the world. Figure 2.9 shows the trends over the last decade in broadband penetration in Denmark, Germany, France, Italy and the total for 27 EU countries.

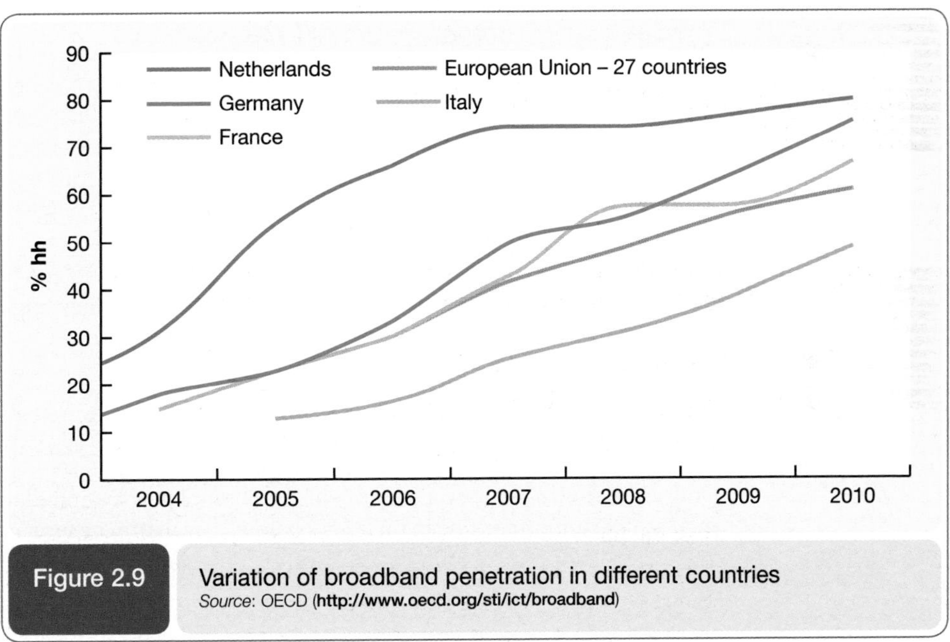

Figure 2.9 Variation of broadband penetration in different countries
Source: OECD (**http://www.oecd.org/sti/ict/broadband**)

Broadband access permits more sophisticated sites and streaming media such as music and video. Use of the Internet also tends to increase with broadband because of the 'always-on' connection. Therefore, it is important for a digital marketer to understand the opportunities and limitations afforded by various locations.

Types of access: mobile

Technological innovation has meant that mobile Internet access has become a feasible option for many Internet users. Consumers have been quick to respond and many retail sectors are seeing high rates of access to services through mobile platforms. Doherty & Ellis-Chadwick, (2010) suggest demand for access to the Internet whilst on the move is growing and businesses 'will face growing pressure from consumers to allow their services to be accessed flexibly from a growing array of mobile devices, as they want to be able to shop on the move.' Predictions by Morgan Stanley (2010) suggested that the number of people with mobile access (including smartphone and tablet devices) to the Internet would exceed those with fixed desktop access by 2014.

As an example of this on one business sector, ComScore, Inc. (2011) released figures showing that 20 million mobile users across the five leading European markets (UK, France, Spain, Germany and Italy), which represents 8.5 per cent of mobile subscribers in these markets, accessed their bank account via a mobile phone in March 2011. Smartphone owners have been driving this rapid rate of adoption and accounted for 70 per cent of the mobile banking market in the same period. *Among smartphone owners the number of banking users has risen by 40 per cent since August 2010.*

> 'Consumers want to be able to access information on the go at any time, and with mobile banking becoming more user-friendly through apps and mobile optimised pages, people are gradually becoming accustomed to it', said Jeremy Copp, vice president mobile for ComScore Europe. 'It will be important for service providers, such as banks and credit card providers, to watch this development as it can certainly be seen as an indicator of increased trust in mobile services.' (M: Metrics, 2011)

This example demonstrates the importance of understanding how different segments behave when accessing digital web-based services. Not only are online banking services benefiting from consumers having mobile Internet access, leading grocery retailers Tesco.com has been quick to respond to increasing use of mobile Internet access and has developed a mobile app which allow consumers to swipe the bar codes of products, which are then automatically added to their online shopping cart.

Once the opportunities and limitations of access are understood, the next dimension to examine is how customers select and choose which services they might use.

Consumer choice and digital influence

Consumer choice is a crucial step in the purchasing process and digital media now plays an increasingly important role in buying decisions. For many consumers the Internet is the first place to look for information that will inform what they buy, so the Internet:

- *is a vital part of the research process, as Internet users now spend longer researching product online*
- *is used at every stage of the research process from the initial scan to the more detailed comparison and final checking of specifications before purchase.*

The result of this change in behaviour means that consumers are more informed and they are referring to a multiplicity of sources to find information which will inform their final purchasing decision. See Figure 9.2, which summarises research which shows that the most important sources of information shaping purchase decisions are personal recommendations and information posted online by other consumers. So companies have to think carefully how they can maximise favourable mentions through product and service quality and brand preference.

Understanding the potential reach of a website and its role in influencing purchasing is clearly important in setting digital marketing budgets. Moreover, as consumers become more familiar with using the Internet the more likely they are to spend more time online and to make wider use of the Internet. Figure 2.10 shows the range of activities Internet users were engaging in 2010, when 31 million UK adults ordered goods and services online and over half spent their money on clothing and sports goods.

Figure 2.11 shows that when consumers first use the web they tend to limit use of the web to searching for product information, but as they become more confident they are not only likely to involve the Internet at a greater number of points in the purchasing process but are also likely to increase the value of the products they buy and the frequency with which they make purchases.

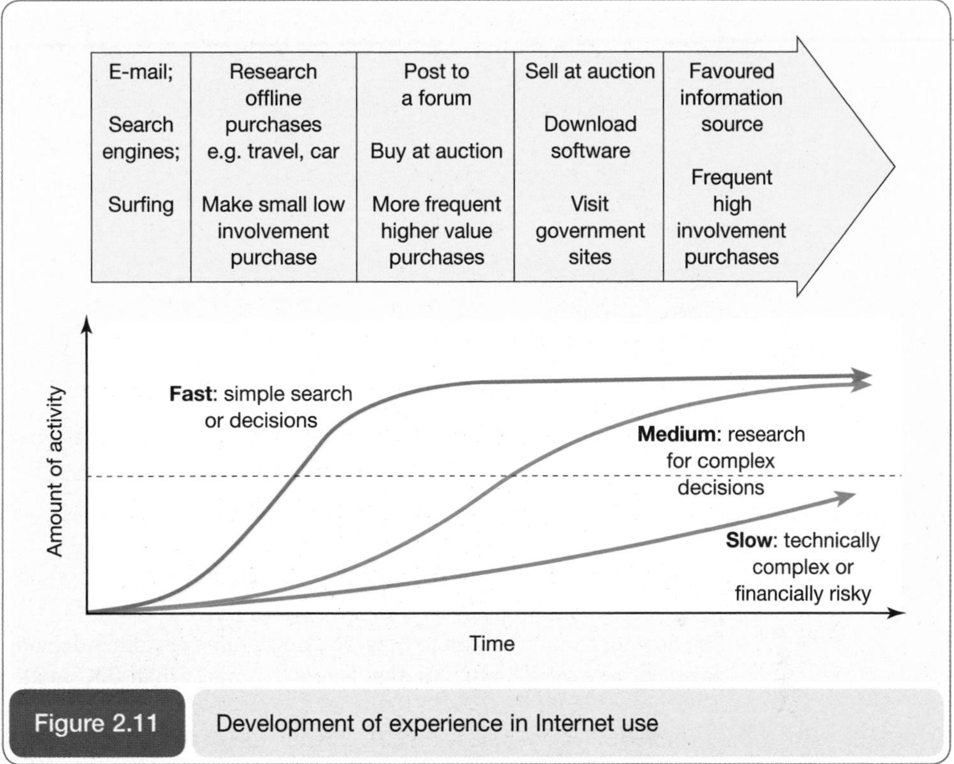

Figure 2.11 Development of experience in Internet use

Developing an understanding of the processes involved in customer choice should enable marketers to identify how to tailor services to meet the needs of the customers so that they move to the transaction dimension.

Consumer transactions

The proportion of Internet users who will purchase different types of products online varies considerably based on the characteristics and demographic profile of the consumers, the product category and the past experiences of the shopper. There have also been many predictions about the development of online retailing and how it might fuel demand for online transactions. Convenience remains the biggest driver for online shoppers, whilst preferring to shop instore and not seeing the need to shop online are the largest barriers to adoption. Figure 2.12 shows the types of purchases consumers have made in the UK in 2010 and the reasons which have encouraged them either to buy online or not.

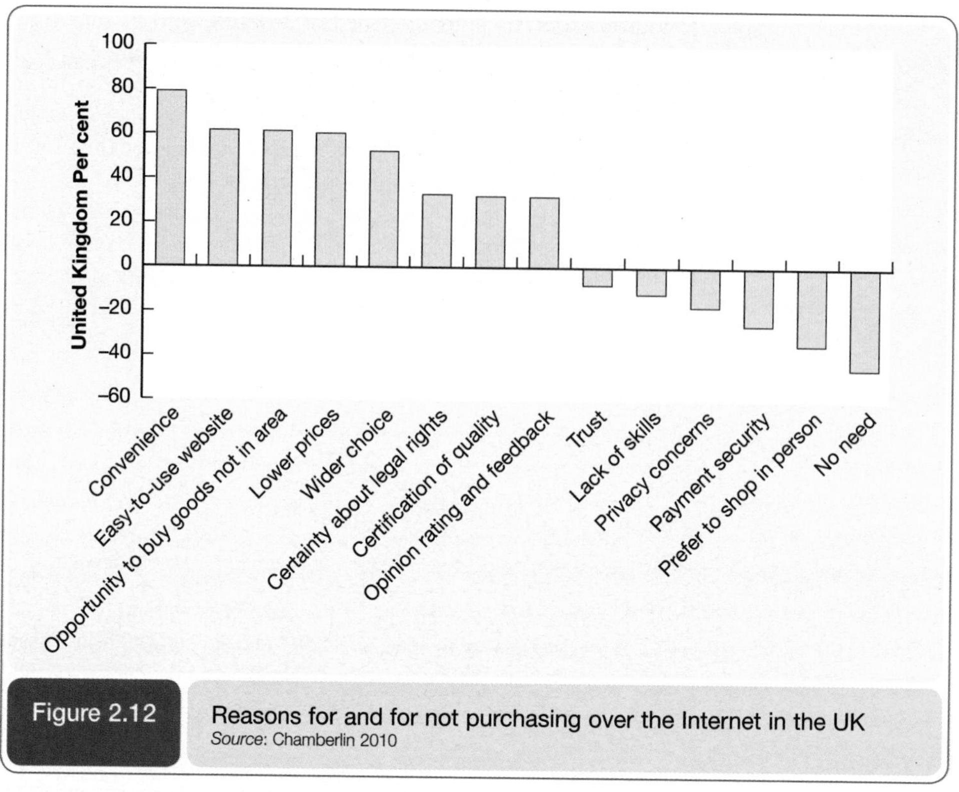

Figure 2.12 Reasons for and for not purchasing over the Internet in the UK
Source: Chamberlin 2010

By understanding the dimensions which affect how consumers interact with online trading environments, digital markets can identify key points where they can seek to manage conversion.

Business access and digital influence

We now turn our attention to how we assess online customer demand and characteristics for business services. The B2B market is more complex than B2C markets in so far as variation in online demand or research in the buying process will occur according to different types of organisation and people within the buying unit in the organisation. We need to profile business demand according to:

Variation in organisation characteristics:

- *size of company – employees or turnover*
- *industry sector and products*
- *organisation type – private, public, government, not-for-profit*
- *application of service – which business activities do purchased products and services support?*
- *country and region.*

Individual role:

- *role and responsibility – job title, function or number of staff managed*
- *role in buying decision – purchasing influence*
- *department*
- *product interest*
- *demographics – age, sex and possibly social group.*

For generating demand estimates, we can also profile business users of the Internet in a similar way to consumers by assessing the following three dimensions.

1 The percentage of companies with access

In the business-to-business market, Internet access levels are higher than for business-to-consumer. European Commission Information Society has a Digital Agenda strategy which aims to develop the growing digital economy and as part of the initiative research is monitoring use of the Internet by business. Whilst the headline figure for Internet access of businesses in the majority of countries is found to be around 95 per cent (see Figure 2.13), it should be noted that there is significant variation depending on the size of the company, the sector it trades in and the type of organisation.

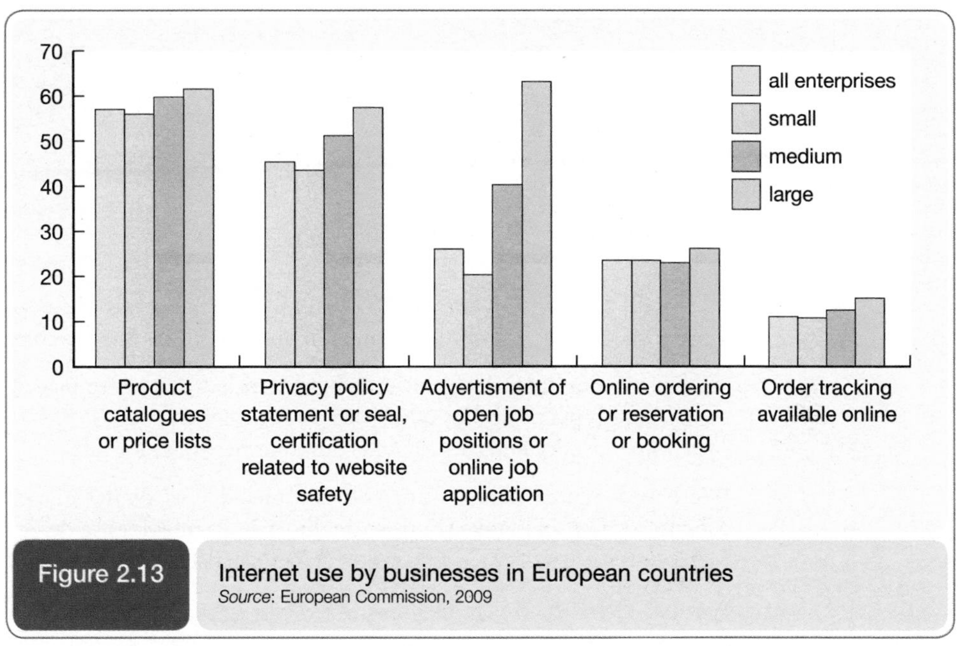

Figure 2.13 Internet use by businesses in European countries
Source: European Commission, 2009

Understanding access for different members of the organisational buying unit among their customers is also important for marketers. Although the Internet seems to be used by many companies we also need to ask whether it reaches the right people in the buying unit. The answer is 'not necessarily' – access is not available to all employees. This can be an issue if marketing to particular types of staff who have shared PC access, e.g. healthcare professionals.

2 Business choice and influence

In B2B marketing, the high level of access is consistent with a high level of use. Most business now have a website as this helps identify suppliers, and there is a trend towards using the Internet for communications in the first instance.

Research into the reasons limiting adoption are shown in Table 2.4. The perceived cost of implementing the technology is the most important factor across companies of different sizes, with security and legal issues also being significant.

3 Business transactions

Research by the European Commission (2011) reveals a large variation between how businesses in different countries order online, with the figure substantially higher in some countries such as Sweden and Germany in comparison to Italy and France. This shows the importance of understanding differences in the environment for e-commerce in different countries since this will dramatically affect the volume of leads and orders.

Table 2.4 Reasons for limited adoption of e-business services in Europe

Barrier to e-business adoption (size of company)	Total	1–9	10–49	50–249	250+
Company too small	68	75	54	36	19
E-business technologies too expensive	40	46	30	37	40
Technology too complicated	35	37	31	33	13
Compatibility problems with partners	26	31	19	34	20
Security issues	33	36	25	31	35
Legal challenges	21	25	17	23	24
Reliability of IT suppliers	22	22	24	30	19

Source: European Commission, 2007

Across all 27 countries surveyed in 2010, the average levels of Internet transactions give an idea of the potential for future growth in business-to-business e-commerce:

- 13.9 per cent total electronic sales by enterprises as a percentage of their total turnover
- 26.8 per cent enterprises purchased on the Internet
- 13.4 per cent of enterprises used computer networks for sales.

We have explored demand analysis, considered how digital marketers might use conversion modelling and looked at the core dimensions of assessing demand from a B2C and B2B perspective. The next section considers online consumer behaviour.

Online consumer behaviour and implications for marketing

So far we have considered the different stages at which an individual or a business might engage with digital environments by using the dimensions of access choice and transaction. In order to build a more complete picture it is important for digital marketers to gain an appreciation of the online behaviour of their specific target audiences and to understand how their customers' characteristics affect the way they might interact with different digital marketing channels. There can be significant difference in the ways an individual uses digital platforms.

Personas
A thumbnail summary of the characteristics, needs, motivations and environment of typical website users.

We recommend creating **personas** as an essential tool to help understand online customer characteristics and behaviour. Creating personas is a powerful technique for developing customer-centred online strategies, company presences and campaigns. It is a key part of marketplace analysis.

Personas are essentially a 'thumbnail' description of a type of person. They have been used for a long time in research for segmentation and advertising, but in recent years have also proved effective for improving website design by companies that have applied the technique.

Customer scenarios (online customer journeys)
Alternative tasks or outcomes required by a customer. Typically accomplished in a series of stages or different tasks involving different information needs across different sites and platforms.

Additionally **customer scenarios (online customer journeys)** can be developed for different personas which describe their overall online customer journeys. Patricia Seybold, in her book with Ronni Marshak, *The Customer Revolution* (2001), explains them as follows:

> A customer scenario is a set of tasks that a particular customer wants or needs to do in order to accomplish his or her desired outcome.

You will see that scenarios can be developed for each persona. For an online bank, scenarios might include:

- new customer opening an online account
- existing customer transferring an account online
- existing customer finding an additional product.

Each scenario is split up into a series of steps or tasks before the scenario is completed. These steps can be best thought of as a series of questions a visitor asks. By identifying questions, website designers identify the different information needs of different customer types at different stages in the buying process.

The use of scenarios is a simple, but very powerful, web design technique that is still relatively rare in website design. They can also be used when benchmarking competitor sites as part of situation analysis.

Here are two simple examples of a commercial bank offering business services which show an experienced user (persona 1) and less experienced user (persona 2).

Online banking persona 1 – Switcher

Chris Barber owns a top-quality restaurant, and in the long term would like to build up a small chain of country hotels and restaurants. As the owner–manager, Chris currently uses a competitor (Barclays) for his business banking. He is thinking of moving to business Internet banking since he has used Barclays Internet banking for his personal banking. He will use the Internet to select the best offering for his needs. His main interest is to minimise bank charges by switching. Chris has been using the Internet for five years.

Online banking persona 2 – Start-up

John Smith has just registered Gifts-R-Us as a new business. The company will be a wholesale gift supplier selling a range of imported gift products, such as candles and decorations to small shops and stores. He has worked as a marketing director in a similar business previously, but is now seeking to start up his own business with the operations manager of the other company as his partner. John is selecting a business bank, but is not sure whether to use Internet banking or not. He wants to assess the benefits. He has no preferences for a business bank – he wants to review all the options and find the easiest to use. He also wants one with favourable banking rates. He is not an experienced Internet user since previously his secretary accessed the Internet for him.

The customer persona/scenario approach has the following benefits:

- fosters customer-centricity
- identifies detailed information needs and steps required by customers
- can be used to test existing website designs or prototypes and to devise new designs
- can be used to compare and test the strength and clarity of communication of proposition on different websites
- can be linked to specific marketing outcomes required by site owners.

Here are some guidelines and ideas on what can be included when developing a persona. The start or end point is to give each persona a name.

1. Build personal attributes into personas:
   - demographic – age, sex, education, occupation and, for B2B, company size, position in buying unit
   - psychographic – goals, tasks, motivation
   - webographics – web experience (months), usage location (home or work), usage platform (dial-up, broadband), usage frequency, favourite sites.

2 Remember that personas are only models of characteristics and environment:
   - design targets
   - stereotypes
   - three or four usually suffice to improve general usability, but more may be needed for specific behaviours;
   - choose one **primary persona** whom, if satisfied, means others are likely to be satisfied.

Primary persona
A representation of the typical site user.

3 Different scenarios can be developed for each persona as explained further below. Write three or four, for example:
   - information-seeking scenario (leads to site registration)
   - purchase scenario – new customer (leads to sale)
   - purchase scenario – existing customer (leads to sale).

Once different personas have been developed that are representative of key site-visitor types or customer types, a primary persona is sometimes identified. Wodtke (2002) says:

> Your primary persona needs to be a common user type who is both important to the business success of the product and needy from a design point of view – in other words, a beginner user or a technologically challenged one.

She also says that secondary personas can also be developed, such as super-users or complete novices. Complementary personas are those that don't fit into the main categories and which display unusual behaviour. Such complementary personas help 'out-of-box thinking' and offer choices or content that may appeal to all users.

For another example of the application of personas, see Mini Case Study 2.1 about paint manufacturer, Dulux, which uses personas to design its site and to integrate with offline media campaigns.

Mini Case Study 2.1 Dulux paint a picture of consumers with personas

Campaign aims

The aims behind this brand initiative were to reposition Dulux from a paint brand to a colour help brand by meeting customer needs, in a way competitors don't, to help differentiate the Dulux brand. The aim was to position Dulux.co.uk (Figure 2.14) as 'the online destination for colour scheming and visualisation to help you achieve your individual style from the comfort of your home'. Specific outcomes on the site are to browse colours, add colours to a personal scrapbook, use the paint calculator and find a stockist. Further aims were to 'win the war before the store', i.e. to provide colour help tools that can develop a preference for Dulux before consumers are instore and to prompt other ideas to sell more than one colour at a time.

Specific SMART objectives were to increase the number of unique visitors from 1 million p.a. in 2003 to 3.5 million p.a. in 2006 and to drive 12 per cent of visitors to a desired outcome (e.g. ordering swatches).

Target audience

Based on research, it was found that the main audience for the site was female with these typical demographics and psychographics:

- would-be adventurous 25–44 women, online
- lack of confidence with previous site:
  - gap between inspiration (TV, magazines, advertising) and lived experience (DIY sheds, nervous discomfort)
  - no guidance or reassurance previously available currently on their journey
- colours and colour combining is key
- online is a well-used channel for help and guidance on other topics
- twelve-month decorating cycle
- propensity to socialise
- quality, technical innovation and scientific proficiency of Dulux is a given.

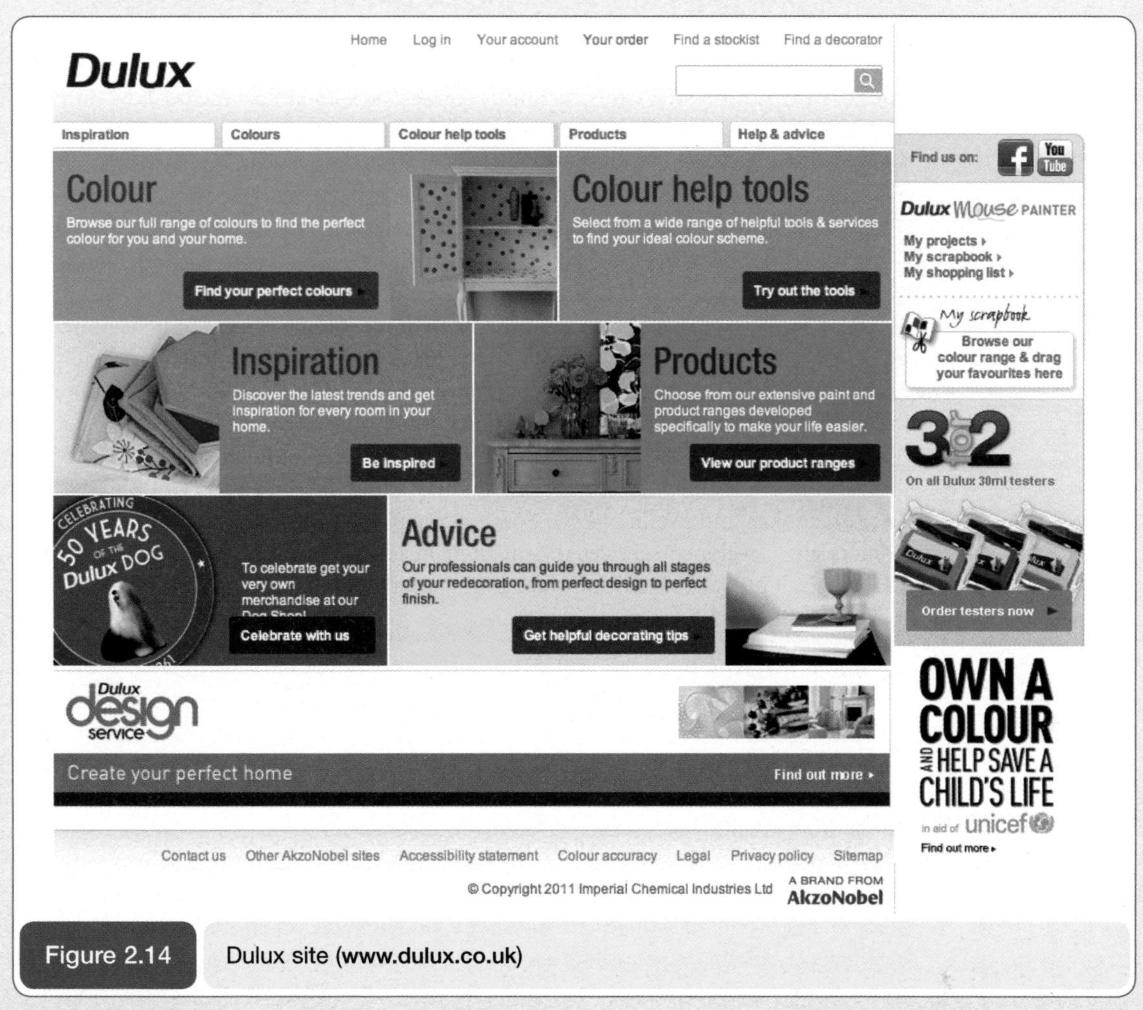

Figure 2.14 Dulux site (**www.dulux.co.uk**)

Specific personas were developed as follows:

- *First time buyer*. Penny Edwards, age 27; partner, Ben; location – north London; occupation – sales assistant.
- *Part-time mum*. Jane Lawrence, age: 37; husband, Joe; location – Manchester; occupation – part-time PR consultant.
- *Single mum*. Rachel Wilson, age 40; location – Reading; occupation – business analyst.

Each has a different approach to interacting with the brand, for Penny it is summarised by the statement:

> *I've got loads of ideas and enthusiasm, I just don't know where to start.*

Each persona was also characterised by their media consumption and preferences such as types of websites, TV, magazines and radio channels and their favourite hobbies and socialising activities.

Brand campaign

To support the relaunch of the site, digital channels such as online banner advertising and interactive TV were used, with traditional channels such as press, instore and PR. The main theme of the ads was 'colour chemistry' which was developed through featuring personas in the ads such as Candy Love, Forest Lake and Treacle Tart. The ads had a clear call-to-action to visit the website to find the right match for the consumer's personality and style.

Source: Case study developed by Agency.com; available through the IAB (**www.iabuk.net**) and presented at Engage 2007.

Other approaches for reviewing customer characteristics

Understanding the individual nature of customers is fundamental to marketing practice and planning. In Chapter 4 you can read about segmentation approaches and how they can be used successfully as part of an integrated marketing strategy. In this section we explore the actual consumer behaviour variables which help build segmentation profiles for the later stages in the planning process.

Research has identified that there are many factors which influence online behaviour (Keen *et al.*, 2004) and over time the market segments that use the Internet and digital services has changed significantly, so it is important for digital markets to a) be aware of important behaviour variables, and b) to understand how to model online consumer behaviour.

According to Doherty and Ellis-Chadwick (2010) it is possible to look back and see that the types of individuals using the web have changed significantly since 1995. In those early days, online shoppers tended to be young males, who were generally better educated and wealthier than their contemporaries. They also had both the confidence and desire to experiment with the Internet, which at the time was an exciting new channel (Donthu and Garcia, 1999; Korgaonkar and Wolin, 1999). Some companies specifically targeted these types of customers and developed services to suit their needs. Research suggests there are two key areas which can prove very fruitful when aiming to identify consumer variables:

1 *Demographic variables.* Doherty and Ellis-Chadwick (2010) suggest that any personal attributes that tend to remain static throughout an individual's life time, or evolve slowly over time – such as age, gender, race etc. – can be defined as *demographic variables.* Key elements of a consumers' demographic profile that have been found to influence online behaviour include variables such as: income, education, race, age (Hoffman *et al.*, 2000); gender (Slyke, 2002); and life-style (Brengman *et al.*, 2005), cultural and social make-up that influnces online behaviour (e.g. Shiu and Dawson, 2004).
2 *Psychographic and behavioural variables.* Any aspect of a consumer's perceptions, beliefs and attitudes that might influence online behaviour, and in particular a consumer's intention to shop, can be defined as a *psychographic/behavioural variables.* Indeed, there has now been a significant amount of recent work to explore how the consumer's character or personality might influence their online behaviour (George, 2004). Cheung *et al.* (2005) suggest that the impact of a wide range of behavioural characteristics, such as knowledge, attitude, innovativeness, risk aversion, can have a significant effect on a consumer's intention to shop. For example, it has been found that consumers who are primarily motivated by convenience were more likely to make purchases online, whilst those who value social interactions were found to be less interested (Swaminathan *et al.*, 1999).

In addition to *studying* demographic, psychographic and behavioural variables, the consumer's actual experience of the online environment also helps to identify further variables which can prove fruitful when targeting certain segments. These variables include:

- ease of use
- usefulness
- perceived control
- interactivity
- shopping enjoyment.

Each of these variables has been found to have an affect on an individual's intention to continue to use digital services and to shopping on-line (Wolfinbarger and Gilly, 2003). For example the impact of consumers' personal experiences of say convenience, site design and security might affect their overall satisfaction with a particular website. Another important point is that by studying variables associated with a consumer's experiences, digital marketers begin to understand how to increase loyalty and trust through websites and online services.

Having considered some of the variables that might help digital marketers identify online target segments, the remainder of this section reviews different models of online buyer behaviour which suggest ways to apply this knowledge. The models we are going to consider are:

1 information/experience-seeking behaviour models
2 hierarchy of response buying process models
3 multichannel buying models
4 trust-based models
5 social interaction communication models.

1 Information/experience-seeking behaviour models focus on type of behaviour

Standard models of consumer buyer behaviour have been developed by Bettman (1979) and Booms and Bitner (1981). In these models, consumers process and interpret marketing stimuli such as the 4 Ps (page 258) and environmental stimuli according to their personal characteristics, such as their culture, social group and personal and psychological make-up. Together these characteristics will affect the consumers' response to marketing messages.

Lewis and Lewis (1997) found that it is possible to group Internet users by studying their online behaviour. They identified five different types of web users or rather modes of use of the Internet which remain valid today:

1 *Directed information-seekers.* These users will be looking for product, market or leisure information such as details of their football club's fixtures. They are not typically planning to buy online.
2 *Undirected information-seekers.* These are the users, usually referred to as 'surfers', who like to browse and change sites by following hyperlinks. Members of this group tend to be novice users (but not exclusively so) and they may be more likely to click on banner advertisements.
3 *Directed buyers.* These buyers are online to purchase specific products online. For such users, brokers or cybermediaries that compare product features and prices will be important locations to visit.
4 *Bargain hunters.* These users (sometimes known as 'compers') want to find the offers available from sales promotions such as free samples or competitions. For example, the MyOffers site (**www.myoffers.co.uk**) is used by many brands to generate awareness and interest from consumers.
5 *Entertainment seekers.* These are users looking to interact with the web for enjoyment through entering contests such as quizzes, puzzles or interactive multi-player games.

Lewis and Lewis (1997) are not the only researchers to suggest online consumers can be grouped by behaviour. Styler (2001) describes four consumer-buying behaviours: 1) brand-focused; 2) price-sensitive; 3) feature-savvy; 4) advice-led. But their work focuses on the characteristics of the shopper, based on the products they are seeking. Moe and Fader (2004) believe that through analysing clickstream behaviour and patterns of repeated visits, it may be possible to identify directed buying, browsing or searching behaviour and make prompts accordingly online in a similar manner to watching shopper behaviour in a physical store.

Another useful model is the revised Web Motivation Inventory (WMI) identified by Rodgers *et al.* (2007) this framework examines different motivations for using the web which will differ for different parts of a web session. The four motives which cut across cultures are research (information acquisition), communicate (socialisation), surf (entertainment) and shop and these are broken down further below.

1 Community
   - get to know other people
   - participate in an online chat
   - join a group.

2 Entertainment
- amuse myself
- entertain myself
- find information to entertain myself.

3 Product trial
- try on the latest fashions
- experience a product
- try out a product.

4 Information
- do research
- get information I need
- search for information I need.

5 Transaction
- make a purchase
- buy things
- purchase a product I've heard about.

6 Game
- play online games
- entertain myself with internet games
- play online games with individuals from other countries.

7 Survey
- take a survey on a topic I care about
- fill out an online survey
- give my opinion on a survey.

8 Downloads
- download music
- listen to music
- watch online videos.

9 Interaction
- connect with my friends
- communicate with others
- instant message others I know.

10 Search
- get answers to specific questions
- find information I can trust.

11 Exploration
- find interesting web pages
- explore new sites
- surf for fun.

12 News
- read about current events and news
- read entertainment news.

Web advertisers and site owners can use this framework to review the suitability of facilities to meet these needs. In a report on benchmarking the user experience of UK retail sites, EConsultancy (2004) identified a useful classification of online shopping behaviour to test how well website design matches different consumer behaviours. In a similar way to previous studies, three types of potential behaviour were identified which are trackers, hunters and explorers. Note that these do not equate to different people, since according to the type of product or occasion, the behaviour of an individual may differ:

Tracker

Knows exactly which product they wish to buy and uses an online shopping site to track it down and check its price, availability, delivery time, delivery charges or after-sales support. The tracker is looking for specific information about a particular product.

The report says:

> If they get the answers they are seeking they need little further persuasion or purchase-justification before completing the purchase.

While this may not be true, since they may compare on other sites, this type of shopper will be relatively easy to convert.

Hunter

Doesn't have a specific product in mind but knows what type of product they are looking for (e.g. digital camera, cooker) and probably has one or more product features they are looking for. The hunter uses an online shopping site to find a range of suitable products, compare them and decide which one to buy. The hunter needs more help, support and guidance to reach a purchasing decision.

The report says:

> Once a potential purchase is found, they then need to justify that purchase in their own minds, and possibly to justify their purchase to others. Only then will confirmation of the purchase become a possibility.

Explorer

Doesn't even have a particular type of product in mind. They may have a well-defined shopping objective (buying a present for someone or treating themselves), a less-resolved shopping objective (buying something to 'brighten up' the lounge) or no shopping objective at all (they like the high street store and thought they would have a look at the online site).

The report suggests that the explorer has a range of possible needs and many uncertainties to be resolved before committing to purchase, but the following may be helpful in persuading these shoppers to convert:

> Certain types of information, however, are particularly relevant. Suggested gift ideas, guides to product categories, lists of top selling products and information-rich promotions (What's New? What's Hot?) – these could all propel them towards a purchasing decision.

From this brief review of online buyer behaviours, we can suggest that online marketers need to take into account the range of behaviours when developing digital marketing strategy and when executing it through site design.

2 Hierarchy of response buying process models – focus on stage in the buying process

An alternative view of consumer behaviour in using the Internet during different stages of the buying process relates to the well-documented 'hierarchy of response model', summarised for example by Kotler *et al.* (2001), as made up of the following stages:

- awareness
- interest
- evaluation
- trial
- adoption.

Breitenbach and van Doren (1998) also suggest that audience members of an individual website tend to pass through these stages, while Chaffey and Smith (2008) describe them as:

1. problem recognition
2. information search
3. evaluation

4 decision
5 action (sale or use of online service)
6 post purchase.

Figure 2.15 gives a summary of how the Internet can be used to support the different stages in the buying process. The boxes on the left show the typical stages that a new prospect passes through, according to, for example, Robinson *et al.* (1967). A similar analysis was performed by Berthon *et al.* (1998), who speculated that the relative communications effectiveness of using a website in this process gradually increased from 1 to 6.

It is worthwhile reviewing each of the stages in the buying process referred to in Figure 2.15 in order to highlight how effective the Internet can be when used at different stages to support the marketing communications objectives. Of course, the exact stage of the buying decision varies for different products and different types of customers, so an alternative approach is to develop channel chains (Figure 2.25) which reflect these differences. In general, digital media support the consumer buying process as follows.

1 Consumer: unaware. Company: generates awareness (of need, product or service)

Generating awareness of need is conventionally achieved principally through the mass media used in offline advertising. The Internet is relatively ineffective at this since it tends to have a more limited impact and reach than television, radio or print media. However, display

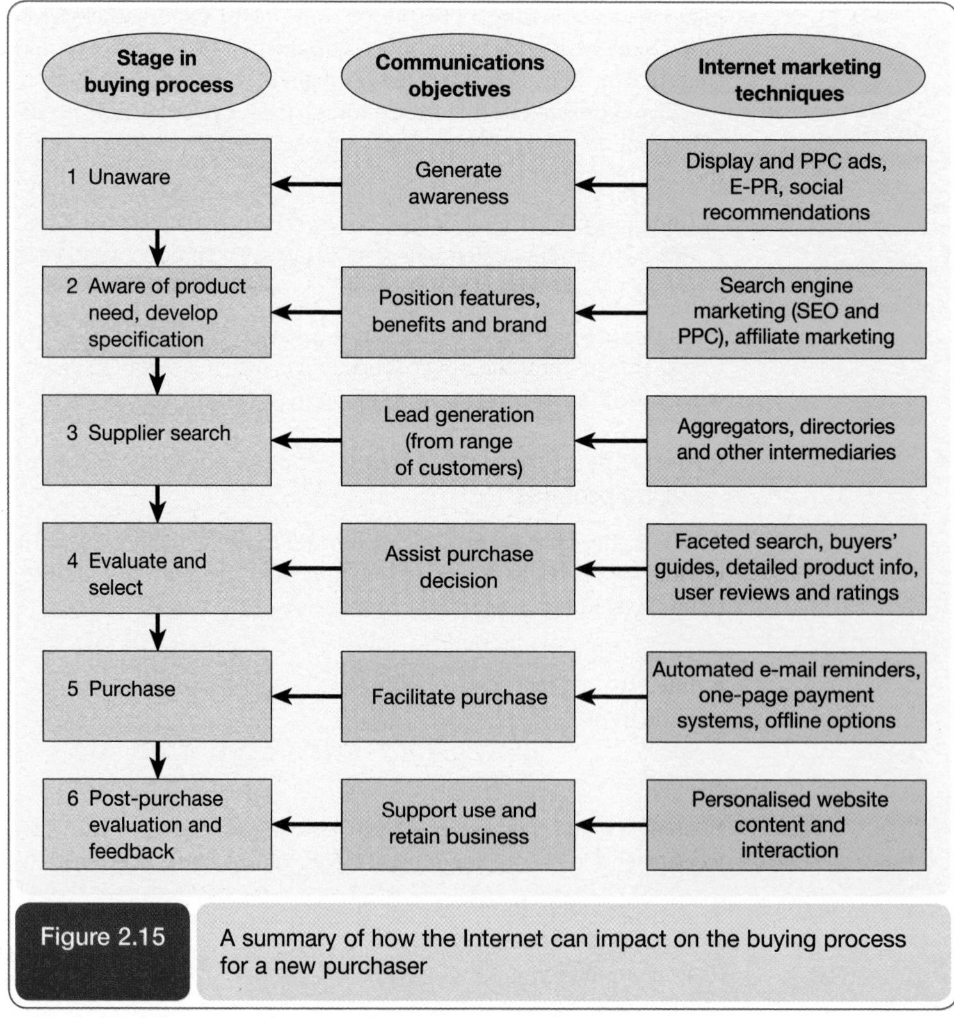

Figure 2.15 A summary of how the Internet can impact on the buying process for a new purchaser

advertising or paid search marketing can be used to supplement offline awareness-building as explained in Chapter 8. Online equivalents of word-of-mouth or recommendations from friends or colleagues, perhaps influenced by a viral marketing campaign, can also create awareness of need. Some companies have effectively developed brand awareness by means of PR and media mentions concerning their success on the Internet, with the result that even if a customer does not have a current need for a product, that customer may be aware of the source when the need develops.

2 Consumer: aware of need, develops specification. Company: position features, benefits and brand

Once a consumer is aware of a need and is considering what features and benefits he or she requires from a product or online service, then they may turn straight to the web to start identifying the range of features available from a particular type of product through using a generic search using search engines such as Google,and Yahoo! So influencing consumers through search engine marketing and affiliate marketing is important at this stage. Specification development effectively happens at the same time as supplier search and more suppliers can be evaluated in greater depth than traditionally. For example, Figure 2.16 shows e-retailers available in paid search for an initial product search on fridges. Retailers such as Currys are displayed in the natural listings (see Chapter 8) while others such as John Lewis, Appliances online, AEG are displayed in the sponsored links.

Intermediaries well known within a sector, such as Kelkoo (**www.kelkoo.com**), are quite important in supplier search and can also help in evaluation. For example, aggregators or comparison sites appear in Figure 2.16. It can be difficult for these aggregators or manufacturers such as Whirlpool to afford to feature high in the paid listings. On the web, if companies have the right permission marketing incentives described in Chapter 6, such as an

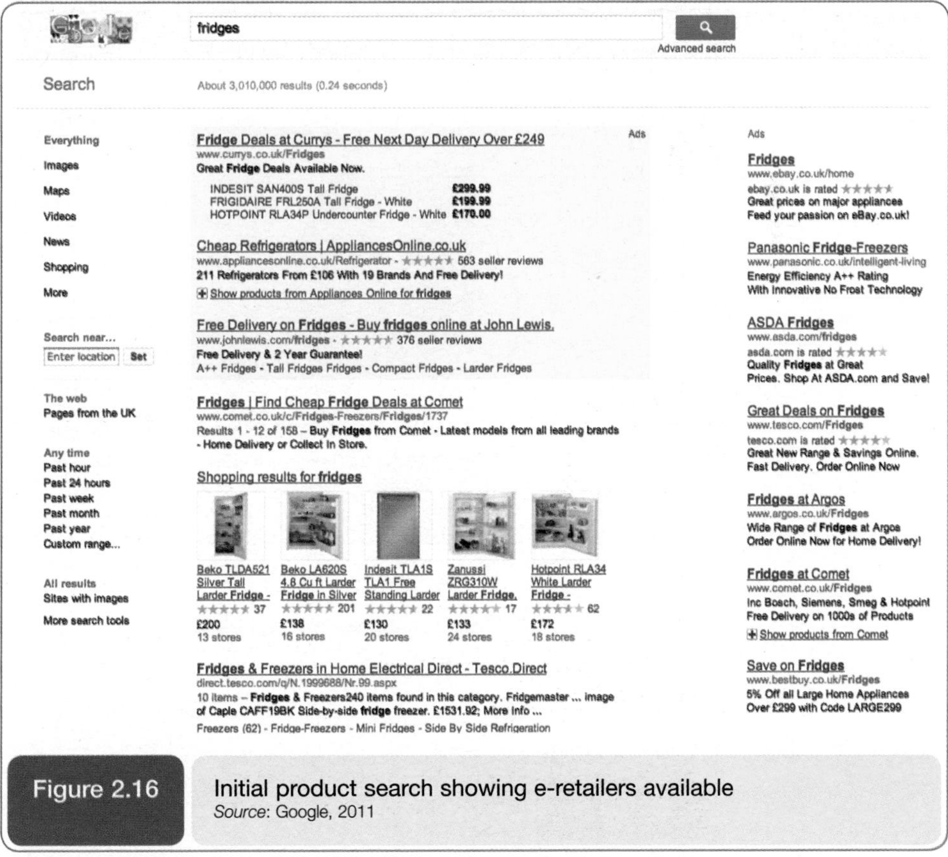

Figure 2.16 Initial product search showing e-retailers available
Source: Google, 2011

opt-in e-newsletter or coupon discount, then they may effectively gain interest earlier in the lifecycle in comparison with traditional channels.

3 Consumer: supplier search. Company: generate leads (engage and capture interest)

Once customers are actively searching for products (the directed information-seeker of Lewis and Lewis, 1997), the web provides an excellent medium to help them do this. It also provides a good opportunity for companies to describe the benefits of their websites and obtain qualified leads. The Internet marketer must consider the methods that a customer will choose for searching and then ensure that the company or its product is featured prominently on these sites whether they are search engines, aggregators or affiliate intermediaries.

4 Consumer: evaluate and select. Supplier: assist purchase decision

One of the most powerful features of websites is their facility to carry a large amount of content at relatively low cost. This can be turned to advantage when customers are looking to identify the best product. By providing relevant information in a form that is easy to find and digest, a company can use its website to help in persuading the customer. For example, the Currys site (Figure 2.17) enables customers to readily compare product features side-by-side, so they can decide on the best products for them. Thanks to the web, this stage can now overlap with earlier stages. Brand issues are important here, as proved by research in

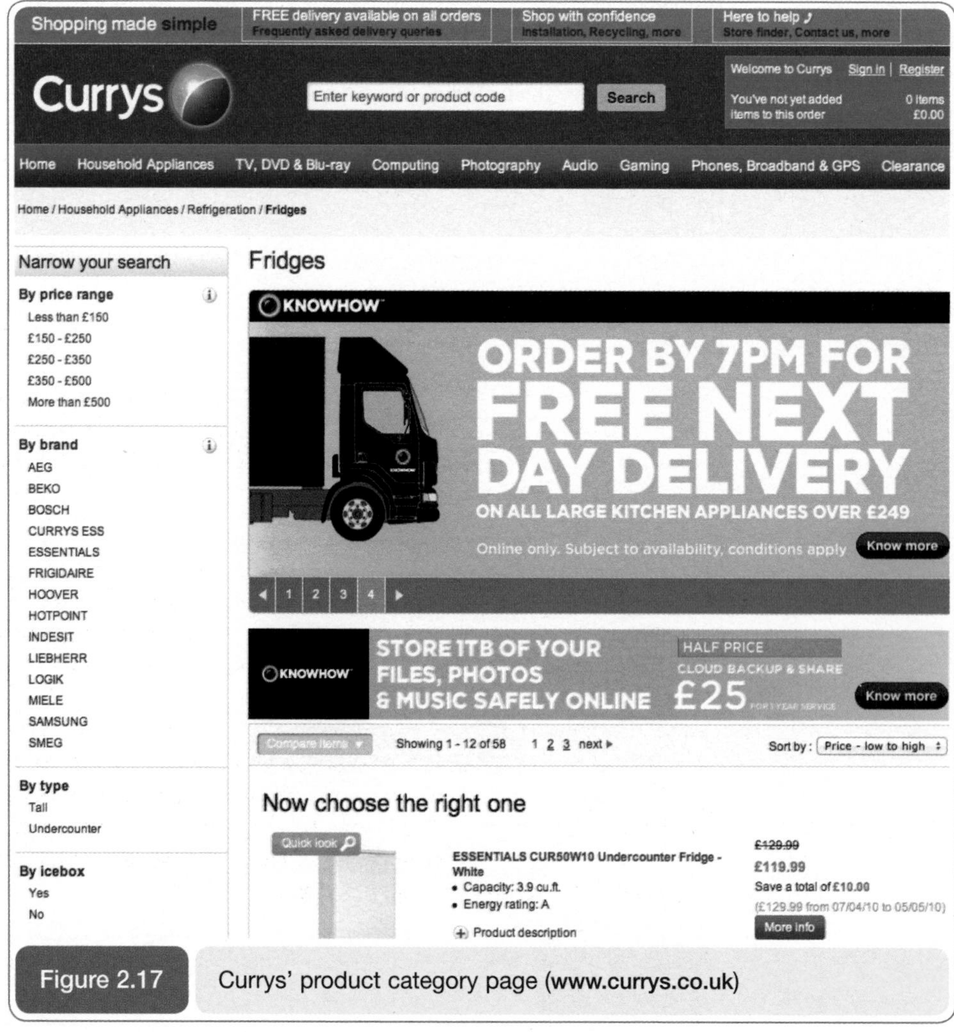

Figure 2.17 Currys' product category page (www.currys.co.uk)

the branding section of Chapter 5, since a new buyer naturally prefers to buy from a familiar supplier with a good reputation – it will be difficult for a company to portray itself in this way if it is unknown and has a slow, poorly designed or shoddy website.

5 Consumer: purchase. Company: facilitate purchase

Once a customer has decided to purchase, then the company will not want to lose the custom at this stage! The website should enable standard credit-card payment mechanisms with the option to place the order by phone or mail. Online retailers pay great attention to identifying factors that encourage customers to convert once they have added a product to their 'shopping basket'. Security guarantees, delivery choices and free delivery offers, for example, can help increase conversion rates.

6 Consumer: post-purchase evaluation and feedback. Company: support product use and retain business

The Internet also provides great potential for retaining customers, as explained in Chapter 6 since:

- value-added services such as free customer support can be provided by the website and these encourage repeat visits and provide value-added features
- feedback on products can be provided to customers; the provision of such information will indicate to customers that the company is looking to improve its service
- e-mail can be used to give regular updates on products and promotions and encourage customers to revisit the site
- repeat visits to sites provide opportunities for cross-selling and repeat selling through personalised sales promotions messages based on previous purchase behaviour.

In this section we have reviewed simple models of the online buying process that can help Internet marketers convert more site visitors to lead and sale; however, in many cases the situation is not as simple as the models.

Activity 2.4 Changes in consumer buyer behaviour caused by digital channels

Although the model shown in Figure 2.15 provides a useful starting point for assessing buyer behaviour, it is right to remember that the Internet has changed behaviour and in some ways the model is not an accurate reflection of reality. What do you think are its main weaknesses? We would suggest:

- The process is not necessarily sequential.
- The process is compressed – for low-involvement products, the decision can be made straightaway. The process will often start with a search and is mediated through search engines throughout, with the searches refined iteratively from generic to specific plus brand, for example 'fridge', 'upright fridge', 'comets fridge', 'whirlpool fridge', 'whirlpool 20TB L4'.
- The participation on the web and the creation of user-generated content (UGC), such as reviews and ratings on the retail site and comparison intermediaries such as Revoo (**www.revoo.com**), are important in the decision process.
- Viral marketing and online PR can be important for generating awareness. In a virtual environment, trust becomes important, as we will see below, so the strength and familiarity of brands will be important.

3 Multichannel buying models

It's important to recognise that a user journey through a website is only part of a wider customer experience which involves multiple channels (Brashear *et al.*, 2009). The importance of multichannel strategies should also be built into assessing customer behaviour and their perception of the online customer experience. The importance of digital channels in influencing the overall customer experience is indicated in Digital marketing insight 2.5.

Digital marketing insight 2.5 Lexus assesses multichannel experience consistency

The luxury car brand Lexus has worked with the Multichannel Marketing Best Practice Club at the Cranfield School of Management, UK to assess the relative importance of consistency between channels. The pertinent results of this study are presented in Table 2.5. It can be seen that, as might be expected, the showroom experience is very important to the overall attitude towards the brand and purchase intent. The importance of the website experience quality is also notable and especially its role in the propensity to recommend – the Lexus customer can readily recommend the website to a friend or a colleague. So, it is the interactive channels that deliver the best experience, as would be expected.

Table 2.5 The impact of channel experience on customer relationship

Lexus communication channel	Attitude towards the brand	Future purchase intention	Propensity to recommend
TV experience quality	0.362**	0.360**	0.185
Print experience quality	0.203	0.133	0.023
Direct mail experience quality	0.343*	0.204	0.072
Showroom experience quality	0.447**	0.292*	0.217
Contact centre experience quality	0.431*	0.566	0.147
Website experience quality	0.452**	0.315*	0.309*

* Correlation is significant at the 0.05 level
** Correlation is significant at the 0.01 level

Source: Menteth *et al.*, 2005. Reprinted by permission of Macmillan Publishers Ltd: *Interactive Marketing*, 6(4) 317–25, copyright 2005, published by Palgrave Macmillan. (The new name of this journal is *Journal of Direct Data and Digital Marketing Practice*).

Since online interactions on a website often happen with limited consumer experience of a site, site owners and designers need to understand how they can develop trusting relationships with target audiences through the use of multiple channel strategies.

4 Trust-based models focus on trust and commitment

Online, purchasers lack the physical reassurance they have when purchasing from a store or talking to someone over a phone. This is compounded because of stories of fraud and security problems. It follows that consumers are looking for cues of trust when they are on a site and marketers need to understand the nature of these. These cues can include brand familiarity, site design, type of content, accreditation and recommendations by other customers. Bart

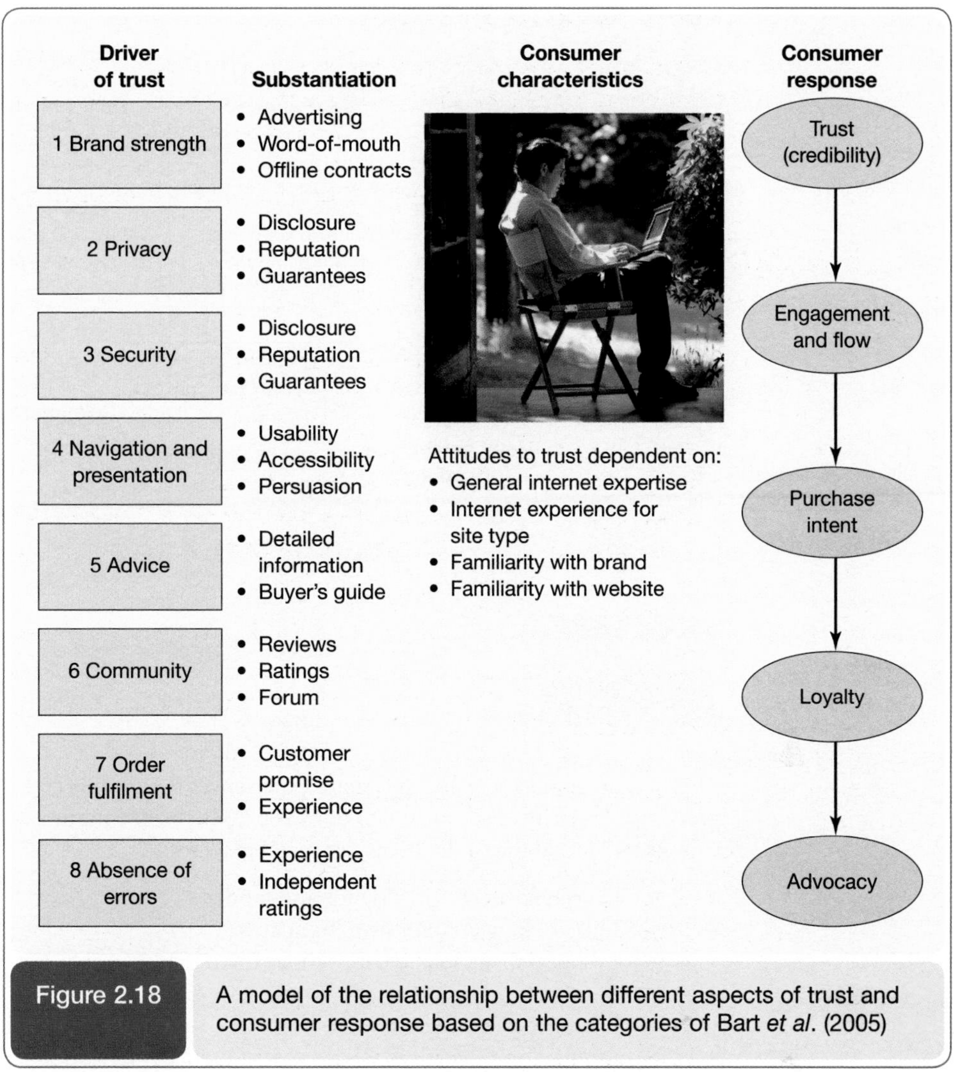

Figure 2.18 A model of the relationship between different aspects of trust and consumer response based on the categories of Bart *et al.* (2005)

et al. (2005) developed a conceptual model that links website and consumer characteristics, online trust and behaviour and found that external sources indicated are very important in building trusting, e.g. search engines listing, personal recommendations, brand identity. Figure 2.18 summarises the key drivers of trust identified by Bart *et al.* (2005) and the model has been adapted to show how elements of trust can be substantiated online.

When reviewing products on a destination site, web users will differ in their decision-making style which will vary according to their knowledge of the web and their attitude to risk and trust. To evaluate these issues, a useful framework has been developed by Forrester for the financial services market to segment customers. This is summarised in Figure 2.19. It shows how customers will generally fall into four groups, first based on those who gather detailed information and those who rely on less information and then based on those who value advice from advisers.

5 Social interaction communication models update

Throughout this section we have seen evidence of the increased the role of digital media in our daily lives (both socially and in the workplace). The use of social media, such as Facebook and Twitter, has risen substantially in the last four years. Social media have become important as means of communicating and interacting online and also as a source of peer recommendations. Generally, as humans we are keen to join together and participate in sharing information.

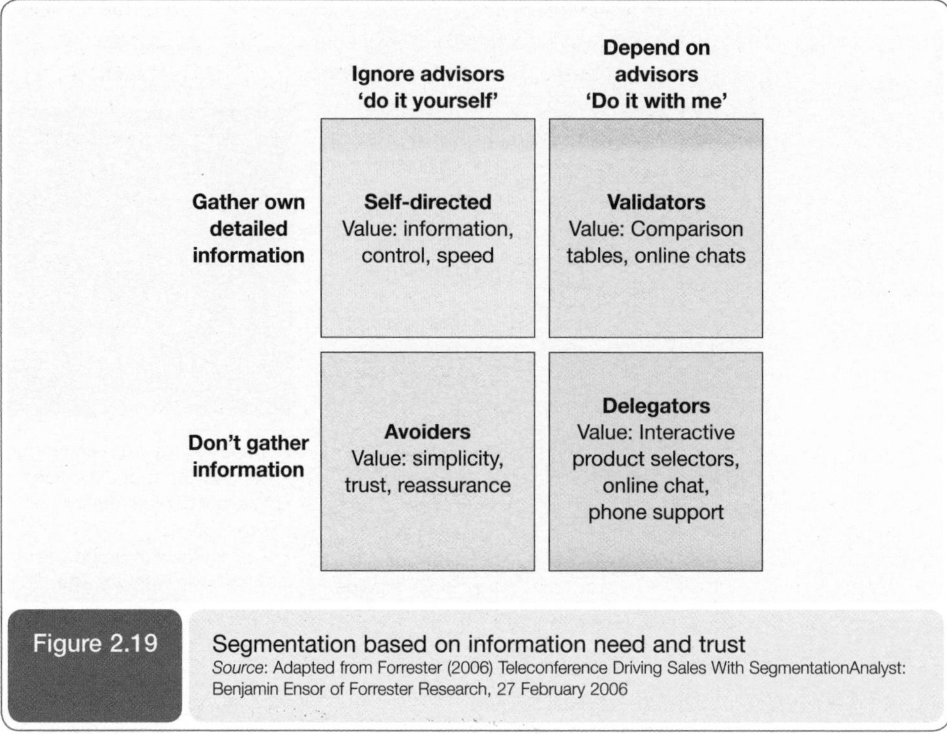

Figure 2.19 Segmentation based on information need and trust
Source: Adapted from Forrester (2006) Teleconference Driving Sales With SegmentationAnalyst: Benjamin Ensor of Forrester Research, 27 February 2006

This human wish to socialise and share experiences is an important underlying driver of the growing popularity of social networks. In 2007, Microsoft conducted a study looking at motivations and found that individuals use social networks:

- 59% – to keep in touch with friends and family
- 57% – I like looking at other people's spaces
- 47% – I want to meet people with similar interests
- 46% – to express my opinions and views on topics
- 20% – it is a good way to date
- 17% – using it for a specific reason, e.g. wedding, job networking.

Members of a community or social network will differ in the extent to which they are connected with others. The most influential network members will be highly connected and will discuss issues of interests with a wider range of contacts than those who are less connected (Table 2.6).

Table 2.6 Variations in number of connections in a sample

Mean number of people communicated with monthly by each method	Less connected 10 or fewer connections	Moderately connected 11 to 99 connections	Highly connected 100+ or fewer connections
E-mail	5	21	84
See in person	4	20	88
Talk on the phone	4	14	46
Instant message	1	5	16
Text message	1	4	15

Source: Understanding Influence, and Making It Work For You: A CNET Networks Study, Published 2007

It is generally believed by PR professionals seeking to influence marketplace perceptions that it is important to target the highly connected individuals since they are typically trusted individuals who other members of the community may turn to for advice. However, Watts and Dodds (2007) suggest that consideration should also be given to the *herding* instinct as 'most social change is driven not by influentials, but by easily influenced individuals influencing other easily influenced individuals'.

Although there is a clear wish to socialise online, site owners need to remember that it is not straightforward to engage an online audience as they move between different sites.

This section has considered customers and their behaviour, as well as how to analyse demand for digital services and the models a digital market might apply to gain better understanding of customers in the micro-environment. The next section explores another set of actors, who shape the micro-environment: competitors.

Competitors

For any marketer, a key consideration is developing an understanding of how to satisfy customers better than the competition. In Chapter 4 we explore developing competitive advantage and the value chain in some detail. In this section, the focus is on the structure of competitive markets and way the competitors behave.

The shape and nature of online competitive markets

According to Jobber (2010), 'an industry is a group of firms that market products that are close substitutes for each other'. However, some industries are more profitable than others, some are reasonably stable, while others are highly volatile. The variance between industrial sectors and specific markets is not all down to the abilities of the companies within the market to product customer satisfaction. There are various forces that *shape the rules of competition*. Porter's five forces model has been widely used to help analyse the shape and competition and it is the nature of the forces and how they combine, he suggests, that ultimately determines how companies compete. In 2001, Porter updated his model to encompass the influence of the Internet. The rest of this sub-section explores his ideas following the five forces which make up the model. Table 2.7 summarises the impact of the Internet on the five forces.

Bargaining power of buyers

The increase in customer power and knowledge is perhaps the single biggest threat posed by electronic trading. This force is important in both B2C and B2B trading situations. From a B2C perspective, the bargaining power of retail shopper is greatly increased when they are using the Internet as they are able to evaluate products and compare prices. This is particularly true for standardised products where offers from different suppliers can be readily compared through online intermediaries such as search engines and price comparison sites, e.g. Kelkoo (**www.kelkoo.com**) or Pricerunner (**www.pricerunner.com**), compare the market (**www.comparethemarket.com**), confused (**www.confused.com**). From a B2B perspective online auctions and business-to-business exchanges can also have a similar effect of driving down price of commodities. The Internet has not only opened up opportunities for more customers (in both sectors B2C and B2B) to take advantage of comparing prices but has also extended the scope to commodities products. Purchase of some products that have not traditionally been thought of as commodities, may become more price-sensitive. This process is known as **commoditisation**. Examples of goods that are becoming commoditised include electrical goods and cars.

Commoditisation
The process whereby product selection becomes more dependent on price than on differentiating features, benefits and value-added services.

In the business-to-business arena, a further issue is that the ease of use of the Internet channel makes it potentially easier for customers to swap between suppliers – switching costs

Table 2.7 Impact of the Internet on the five competitive forces

Bargaining power of buyers	Bargaining power of suppliers	Threat of substitute products and services	Barriers to entry	Rivalry between existing competitors
• The power of online buyers is increased since they have a wider choice and prices are likely to be forced down through increased customer knowledge and price transparency (see Chapter 5)	• When an organisation purchases, the bargaining power of its suppliers is reduced since there is a wider choice and increased commoditisation due to e-procurement and e-marketplaces	• Substitution is a significant threat since new digital products or extended products can be readily introduced	• Barriers to entry are reduced, enabling new competitors, particularly for retailers or service organisations that have traditionally required a high-street presence or a mobile sales force	• The Internet encourages commoditisation which makes it less easy to differentiate products
• For a B2B organisation, forming electronic links with customers may deepen a relationship and it may increase switching costs, leading to 'soft lock-in'	• The reverse arguments regarding bargaining power of buyers	• The introduction of new substitute products and services should be carefully monitored to avoid erosion of market share • Internet technology enables faster introduction of products and services • This threat is related to new business models which are covered in a later section in this chapter	• New entrants must be carefully monitored to avoid erosion of market share • Internet services are easier to imitate than traditional services, making it easy for 'fast followers'	• Rivalry becomes more intense as product lifecycles decrease and lead times for new product development decrease • The Internet facilitates the move to the global market, increasing the number of competitors

Soft lock-in
Electronic linkages between supplier and customer that increase switching costs.

are lower. With the Internet, which offers a more standard method for purchase through web browsers, the barriers to swapping to another supplier will be lower. With a specific EDI (electronic data interchange) link that has to be set up between one company and another, there may be reluctance to change this arrangement (**soft lock-in** due to switching costs). Commentators often glibly say 'online, your competitor is only a mouse click away', but it should be remembered that soft lock-in still exists on the web – there are still barriers and costs to switching between suppliers since, once a customer has invested time in understanding how to use a website to select and purchase a particular type of products, they may not want to learn another service.

A significant downstream channel threat is the potential loss of partners or distributors if there is a channel conflict resulting from disintermediation (see the sections on new channel structures, pages 100 and 291). For example, a car distributor could switch to an alternative manufacturer if its profitability were threatened by direct sales from the manufacturer.

Bargaining power of suppliers

Internet EDI
Use of electronic data interchange standards delivered across non-proprietary Internet protocol networks.

Business-to-business exchanges or marketplaces
Virtual intermediaries with facilities to enable trading between buyers and sellers.

This can be considered as an opportunity rather than a threat. Companies can insist, for reasons of reducing cost and increasing supply chain efficiency, that their suppliers use electronic links such as EDI or **Internet EDI** to process orders. Additionally, the Internet tends to reduce the power of suppliers since barriers to migrating to a different supplier are reduced, particularly with the advent of **business-to-business exchanges**. However, if suppliers insist on proprietary technology to link companies, then this creates soft lock-in due to the cost or complexity of changing suppppliers.

Threat of substitute products and services

This threat can occur from established or new companies. The Internet is particularly good as a means of providing information-based services at a lower cost. The greatest threats are likely to occur where digital product and/or service fulfilment can occur over the Internet. These substitutes can involve new online channel essentially replicating an existing service as is the case with online banking or e-books. But, often, online can involve adding to the proposition. For example, compared to traditional music retailers, online legal subscription music services such as iTunes (www.iTunes.com) offers a much wider choice of products with different delivery modes (real-time streaming to a PC or the capability to burn onto a CD or download to a portable music device such as an MP3 player). In banking, new facilities have been developed to help customers manage their finances online by aggregating services from different providers into one central account. Such added-value digital services can help lock customers into a particular supplier.

Barriers to entry

For traditional companies, new online entrants have been a significant threat for retailers selling products such as books and financial services. For example, for the banking sector in Europe, traditional banks were threatened by the entry of completely new start-up competitors, such as First-e (www.first-e.com) which later became financially unviable, or of traditional companies from one country that use the Internet to facilitate their entry into another country. US company Citibank (www.citibank.com) and ING Direct (www.ingdirect.co.uk) from the Netherlands used the latter approach. New companies were also created by traditional competitors – for example, Prudential created Egg (www.egg.com), Abbey National created Cahoot (www.cahoot.com), and the Co-operative bank created Smile (www.smile.co.uk). ING Direct has acquired millions of customers in new markets such as Canada, Australia and the UK through a combination of offline advertising, online advertising and an online or phone application process and account servicing.

In the past it has been argued that it is particularly easy and low cost for new entrants to challenge the market. The logic behind the argument its that these new entrants have been able to enter the market rapidly since they do not have the cost of developing and maintaining a distribution network to sell their products and these products do not require a manufacturing base.

However, to succeed, new entrants need to be market leaders in executing marketing and customer service. These are sometimes described as *barriers to success* or *hygiene factors* rather than *barriers to entry*. The costs of achieving these will be high, for example First-e has not survived as an independent business. This competitive threat is less common in vertical business-to-business markets involving manufacture and process industries such as the chemical or oil industries since the investment barriers to entry are much higher.

Intensity of rivalry

The Internet has encouraged the commitisation of more products making it harder to differentiate between product offers. However, as Internet markets have evolved so has the number of companies providing services via the Internet. As a result, in some market sectors there is an increasing number of companies (existing and new entrants) competing for their share of the available business. The nature of the rivalry between the companies trading online is largely determined by the number of players in a market and their relative sizes, the structure of costs and pricing, the switching costs customers will encounter if they change, strategic objectives and exit barriers. For example, in the online book market, Amazon is a major player accounting for a large proportion of the spend on books. Many book retailers find it hard to compete as their operating costs are higher than Amazon, which restricts the opportunity to cut costs and sell at lower prices for sustained periods, Amazon has also differentiated from its competitors as it is able to offer the largest selection of books on the planet and speedy delivery services. Shoppers are also encouraged to stay with Amazon as the online interface makes, it very easy for the shopper to buy and pay for books. Moreover, Amazon has developed the Kindle, an electronic book reader, which is now accounting for more sales of e-books than paper printed ones. In the UK, where Amazon launched its Kindle Store only in 2010, the company has sold 242 e-books for every 100 hardbacks since 1 April 2011, even though there has been a growth in hardback sales (Edgecliffe-Johnson, 2011). The Internet has also increased the opportunity for global players to expand into new local markets.

By using the five forces model for analysing the structure and nature of the competition, digital marketers can gain an understanding of the marketplace. However, it is important to be aware that actions have consequences, for example a price reduction may stimulate a response from a competitor (the same applies to promotional activities and advertising) – *wars* can be very costly. Therefore, the next step for the digital marketer is to develop understanding of their competitors and how they might respond. The next sub-section explores how to analyse competitors and assess their potential.

Competitor analysis and benchmarking

Competitor analysis
Involves identifying the companies which are competing for our business and then reviewing what they are good at, what are their strengths, where are their weaknesses; what are they planning, where do they want to take the company and how do they behave when other companies try to take their market share.

Competitor benchmarking
A structured analysis of the online services, capabilities and performance of an organisation within the areas of customer acquisition, conversion, retention and growth.

Competitor analysis and benchmarking of competitor use of Internet marketing for acquisition and retention of customers is especially important because of the dynamic nature of the Internet medium. As Porter (2001) has pointed out, this dynamism enables new services to be launched and elements of the marketing mix, such as price and promotion, to be changed much more frequently than was traditionally the case. Copying of concepts and approaches within sectors is rife, but can sometimes be controlled through patenting. For example, Amazon.com has patented the 'One Click' approach to purchase, so this term and approach is not seen on other sites. The implications of this dynamism are that competitor benchmarking is not a one-off activity while developing a strategy, but needs to be continuous.

Competitor benchmarking is the term used for structured comparison of digital marketing approaches of an organisation's services within a market. Its purpose is to identify threats posed by changes to competitor offerings, but also to identify opportunities for enhancing a company's own web services through looking at innovative approaches in non-competing companies. Competitor benchmarking is closely related to developing the customer proposition and brand experience and is informed by understanding the requirements of different customer personas, as introduced earlier in this chapter.

Benchmarking of services has different perspectives which serve different purposes:

1 *Internal capabilities* such as resourcing, structure and processes vs *external customer facing* features of the sites.
2 *Different aspects of the customer lifecycle*: customer acquisition, conversion to retention. Capabilities are benchmarked in all the activities of each shown in Figure P.1 in the Preface. For example, what are the capabilities of a competitor within search marketing through reviewing their presence in the paid and natural listings of the search engines.
3 *Qualitative to quantitative*: from qualitative assessments by customers through surveys and focus groups through to quantitative analysis by independent auditors of data across customer acquisition (e.g. number of site visitors or reach within market, cost of acquisition,

number of customers, sales volumes and revenues and market share); conversion (average conversion rates) and retention such as repeat conversion and number of active customers.

4 *In-sector and out-of-sector*: benchmarking against similar sites within sector and reviewing out-of-sector to sectors which tend to be more advanced, e.g. online publishers, social networks and brand sites. Benchmarking services are available for this type of comparison from analysts such as Bowen Craggs Index (**www.bowencraggs.com**). An example of one of their benchmark reports is shown in Figure 2.20. You can see that this is based on the expert evaluation of the suitability of the site for different audiences as well as measures under the overall construction (which includes usability and accessibility), message (which covers key brand messages and suitability for international audiences) and contact (which shows integration between different audiences). Although some research into site types is based on the presence or absence of a feature, but Figure 2.20 is based on an expert review taking ten hours. The methodology states: 'it is not "tick box": every metric is judged by its existence, its quality and its utility to the client, rather than "Is it there or is it not?"'

5 *Financial to non-financial measures*. Through reviewing competitive intelligence sources such as company reports or tax submissions additional information may be available on turnover and profit generated by digital channels. But other forward-looking aspects of the company's capability which are incorporated on the balanced score measurement framework (see Chapter 4) should also be considered, including resourcing, innovation and learning.

6 *From user experience to expert evaluation*. Benchmarking research should take two alternative perspectives, from actual customer reviews of content and usability to expert evaluations.

In the physical world, a company's competitors tend to be visibly active in any given market and therefore are well known. However, in digital environments there may be new entrants that have the potential to achieve significant market share, which are less visible until they grow to a significant size. This is particularly the case with retail sales. For example, successful new companies have developed on the Internet that sell books, music, CDs and electronic components. As a consequence, companies need to review the Internet-based performance of both existing and new players. Companies should review:

- well-known local competitors (for example, UK or European competitors for British companies)
- well-known international competitors
- new Internet companies – local and worldwide (within sector and out of sector).

As well as assessing competitors on performance criteria, it is also worthwhile categorising them in terms of their capability to respond. Deise *et al.* (2000) suggest an equation that can be used in combination to assess the capability of competitors to respond:

Pos	Company	Construction	Message	Contact	Serving society	Serving investors	Serving the media	Serving job seekers	Serving customers	Total	URL	Country
	maximum score	60	48	12	32	32	32	32	32	280		
1	Siemens	47	40	10	27	21	28	24	24	221	www.siemens.com	Germany
2	Royal Dutch Shell	46	41	7	26	22	21	24	22	209	www.shell.com	Netherlands
3	BP	41	39	10	28	27	18	19	25	207	www.bp.com	UK
4	Nokia	44	36	8	26	24	24	16	25	203	www.nokia.com	Finland
5	AstraZeneca	48	33	9	20	20	27	16	27	200	www.astrazeneca.com	France
	Total	44	39	11	25	27	12	22	21	200	www.total.com	UK/Sweden
7	IBM	41	36	11	23	26	26	12	24	199	www.ibm.com	US
8	ING	43	40	8	22	25	21	16	22	197	www.ing.com	Netherlands
9	UBS	37	36	6	20	27	22	26	20	194	www.ubs.com	Switzerland
10	General Electric	42	37	10	25	17	19	17	24	191	www.ge.com	US

Figure 2.20 Benchmark comparison of corporate websites
Source: Bowen Craggs & Co (**www.bowencraggs.com**)

$$\text{Competitive capability} = \frac{\text{agility} \times \text{reach}}{\text{time-to-market}}$$

'Agility' refers to the speed at which a company is able to change strategic direction and respond to new customer demands. 'Reach' is the ability to connect to or to promote products and generate new business in new markets. 'Time-to-market' is the product lifecycle from concept through to revenue generation or more generally, it can be considered how long it takes to implement new digital marketing services, e.g. social network integration. Companies with a high competitive capability within their market and competitive markets are arguably the most important ones to watch.

In summary, it is important for digital markets to be able to identify and understand their competitors and in doing so be able to infer what their strategies and future activities might be. We revisit competitor benchmarking in more detail in Chapters 4, 7 and 10.

Suppliers

Suppliers deliver the goods and services a business needs to carry out its business activities further down the supply chain. In the digital marketplace, the supply chain can take many different forms depending on whether physical or digital products are involved. The most significant aspect of monitoring suppliers in the context of digital marketing is with respect to the effect suppliers have on the value of quality of product or service delivered to the end customer. Key issues include the effect of suppliers on product price, availability and features. This topic is not discussed further since it is less significant than other factors in an Internet marketing context. However, the Internet has had a significant impact in some business activity sectors insofar as it has resulted in new channel structures for supply chains and new types of suppliers, which offer specialist service to the digital industry as a whole. The new suppliers act as intermediaries and offer a wide range of specialist services: website development, technology management and integration.

Online marketing intermediaries

Marketing intermediaries
Firms that can help a company to promote, sell and distribute its products or services, for example media sites, comparison sites, search engines, social networks and blogs.

Destination sites
Sites typically owned by merchants, product manufacturers or retailers providing product information.

Online intermediary sites
Websites that facilitate exchanges between consumer and business suppliers.

Online social network
A service facilitating the connection, collaboration and exchange of information between individuals.

Marketing intermediaries are firms that can help a company to promote, sell and distribute its products or services. They should not be confused with Internet service providers, who develop websites and provide hosting services. In the Internet context, online marketing intermediaries can be contrasted with destination sites which are typically merchant sites owned by manufacturers or retailers which offer information and products (in reality any type of site can be a **destination site**, but the term is generally used to refer to merchant and brand sites).

Online intermediary sites provide information about destination sites and are a means of connecting Internet users with product information. The best known online intermediaries are the most popular sites such as Google, MSN and Yahoo! These are known as 'portals' and are described further below. Other consumer intermediaries such as Kelkoo (**www.kelkoo.com**) and Bizrate (**www.bizrate.com**) provide price comparison for products, as described earlier in this chapter. Most newspapers, e.g., *The Times*, *Guardian*, *The Telegraph* and magazine publishers, and Emap (**www.greatmagazines.co.uk**), now provide online versions of their publications. These are as important in the online world in promoting products as newspapers and magazines are in the offline world.

Online intermediaries are businesses which support business and consumer audiences, so they can serve both B2B and B2C information exchanges. Auction sites are another type of online intermediary that support the B2B and the C2C exchanges introduced in Chapter 1. Online intermediaries sometimes support **online social networks** which are a form of online community described in more detail in the section on virtual communities at the end of Chapter 6. The Google Orkut service (**www.orkut.com**) is an example of a personal social network, while LinkedIn (**www.linkedin.com**) and Ecademy (**www.ecademy.com**) are examples of business networks.

Mini Case Study 2.2 Alibaba provides a global markets for all

Alibaba.com is one of the leaders of e-commerce transactions in China. It provides a marketplace connecting small and medium-sized buyers and suppliers from China and around the world. Its web presence includes an international marketplace (**www.alibaba.com**) which focuses on global importers and exporters and a China marketplace (**www.alibaba.com.cn**) which focuses on suppliers and buyers trading domestically in China.

From a launch in 1999 the marketplaces have a community of more than 24 million registered users and over 255,000 paying members. In November 2007, Alibaba launched on the Hong Kong stock exchange and raised HK$13.1 billion (US$1.7 billion) in gross proceeds before offering expenses making it the largest Internet IPO in Asia and the second largest globally.

Jack Ma, the founder of Alibaba, first saw the Internet in 1995 when he went to Seattle as an interpreter for a trade delegation and a friend showed him the Internet. They searched for the word 'beer' on Yahoo! and discovered that there was no data about China. He decided to launch a website and registered the name China Pages.

He borrowed $2000 to set up his first company and at the time knew nothing about personal computers or e-mails and had never touched a keyboard before. He described the experience as a 'blind man riding on the back of a blind tiger'.

Figure 2.21 Taobao (www.allthingsgreen.net)

Initially, the business did not fare well, since it was a part of China Telecom and Jack Ma reflects that: 'everything we suggested, they turned us down; it was like an elephant and an ant'.

He resigned, but in 1999 he gathered 18 people in his apartment and spoke to them for two hours about his vision. Everyone put their money on the table, and he got $60,000 to start Alibaba. He chose Alibaba as the name since it was easy to spell and associated with 'Open Sesame', the command that AliBaba used to open doors to hidden treasures in *One Thousand and One Nights*.

During the dot-com bubble there were layoffs, such that by 2002 there was only enough cash to survive for 18 months. We had a lot of free members using our site, and we didn't know how we'd make money. But they then developed a product for China exporters to meet US buyers online which Ma said saved the company. By the end of 2002, Alibaba made $1 in profits! Each year since it has improved in profitability to the position where it was launched on the stock market.

Jack Ma's driving vision was to build an e-commerce ecosystem that allows consumers and businesses to do all aspects of business online. By 2006 he had done so well its caused one of it major competitors eBay to close its operation in China. The Alibaba Group's flagship company is a world-leading B2B e-commerce company and Taobao (part of the group – see Figure 2.21) is China's largest online retail website, which provides a portal for shopping, socialising and sharing information. Alibaba also now provides cloud computing, and a range of other computing services and has become one of China's leading Internet portals.

Source: You can view the video of CEO Jack Ma talking about the business on FT.com (search on Jack Ma), **http://www.ft.com/cms/8a38c684-2a26-11dc-9208-000b5df1062.html**

Ali Baba Press releases, Alibaba.com Limited Trading Debut, 7 November 2007, **http://resources.alibaba.com/article/225276/ Alibaba_com_Limited_Trading_Debut_.htm**

Riding the Blind Tiger: The Unlikely Rise of Alibaba CEO, Jack Ma, 8 January 2008, **http://resources.alibaba.com/article/246718/ Riding_the_Blind_Tiger_The_Unlikely_Rise_of_Alibaba_CEO_Jack_MA.htm**

Sarkar *et al.* (1996) identified many different types of potential online intermediaries (mainly from a B2C perspective) which used to be referred to as 'cybermediaries'. Whilst this term is no longer widely used the types of intermediaries remain relevant and include:

Directories
Structured listings of registered sites in different categories.

- **directories** (such as Yahoo! directory, Open Directory, Business.com)
- search engines (Google, Yahoo! Search Bing)
- virtual resellers (own inventory and sells direct, e.g. Amazon, CDWOW)
- financial intermediaries (offering digital cash and payment services such as PayPal)
- forums, fan clubs and user groups (referred to collectively as 'virtual communities') or social networks such as HabboHotel for youth audiences (**www.habbo.com**)
- evaluators (sites which act as reviewers or comparison of services) such as **www.tripadvisor.com**.

Since Sarkar *et al.* (1996) identified the different types of intermediaries there has been much diversification and new intermediaries provide services to other intermediaries.

Activity 2.5 Tripadvisor.com

VisitBritain, the UK's national tourist board, is promoting travel review site TripAdvisor. The idea is that travellers who use the VisitBritain website can now click on a link to a 'dedicated UK tourism destination page in TripAdvisor (**http://www.tripadvisor.co.uk/Tourism-g186216-United_Kingdom-Vacations.html**). Each attraction, hotel and tourist destination is given a rating based on customers reviews. A great idea or an own goal? Some hoteliers are very dissatisfied. Traditionally, in Britain, hotels are rated from one star to five stars, and these stars are given out by tourist board hotel inspectors who (unannounced) stay over night to do an assessment of a hotel and then award (if applicable) the appropriate star rating. Hotels pay to be included in the scheme and generally feel that there is a guarantee of standards across the industry. Hoteliers feel the TripAdvisor system is open to corruption, does not offer consistent standards, and they have no form of recourse if a customer gives a bad review.

Purpose

To examine the marketing opportunities provided by an Evaluator intermediary site

Activity

1 Visit the TripAdvisor for your country and search for a hotel in your home town. See how TripAdvisor reviews rate the hotel.
2 Now imagine you are responsible for the online communications for the hotel. Make a list of the positive and negative points raised in the reviews
3 Suggest how you might use these comments positively to generate visitor traffic to the hotel website.

Portals

Portal
An online publisher that acts as a gateway to information and services available on the Internet by providing search engines, directories and other services such as personalised news or free e-mail.

An Internet **portal** is a type of publisher that acts as a gateway to information and services available on the Internet. Essentially, it is an alternative term for online intermediary, but the main emphasis is on providing access to information on the portal site and other sites.

Portals are important to Internet marketers since portals are where users spend a good deal of time online when they are not on merchant or brand sites. Situation analysis involves assessing which portals target customers with different demographics and psychographics use. It also relates to competitor benchmarking, since the sponsorship deals and co-branding arrangements set up by competitors should also be reviewed.

For marketers to extend the visibility or reach of their company online, they need to be well represented on a range of portals through using sponsorships, online adverts and search marketing, as explained in Chapter 8. Portals also enable targeted communications. Specialist portals enable markets to target a particular audience through advertising, sponsorship and PR, while general portals often have sections or 'channels' which indicate a particular product interest. For example, moneysavingexpert.com. Main portals such as newspapers and trade magazines also have registration, so can provide options for delivering messages and news updates.

Types of portals

Portals vary in scope and in the services they offer, so naturally terms have evolved to describe the different types of portals. It is useful, in particular, for marketers to understand these terms since they act as a checklist that companies are represented on the different types of portals. Table 2.8 shows different types of portals. It is apparent that there is overlap between the different types of portal. Yahoo! for instance is a horizontal portal since it offers a range of services, but it has also been developed as a geographical portal for different countries and, in the USA, even for different cities. There are also vertical and marketplace portals such as VertMarkets (**www.vertmarkets.com**).

In this sub-section, we have considered some of the marketing intermediaries and the implications for digital marketing. However, it is also important to understand how marketing channels are structured. The final section of the chapter investigates channel structures.

Table 2.8 Portal characteristics

Type of portal	Characteristics	Example
Access portal	Associated with ISP or telco	Orange (**www.orange.co.uk**) AOL (**www.aol.com**)
Horizontal or functional portal	Range of services: search engines, directories, news recruitment, personal information management, shopping, etc.	Yahoo! (**www.yahoo.com**) MSN (**www.msn.com**) Lycos (**www.lycos.com**)
Vertical	A vertical portal covers a particular market, such as construction, with news and other services	Construction Plus (**www.constructionplus.co.uk**) Chem Industry (**www.chemindustry.com**)
Media portal	Main focus is on consumer or business news or entertainment	BBC (**www.bbc.co.uk**) Guardian (**www.guardian.co.uk**) Sky News (**http://news.sky.com/skynews/**)
Social network portal	Providing a community	Facebook, LinkedIn, Google+
Geographical (region, country, local) Marketplace	May be: • horizontal • vertical May be: • horizontal • vertical • geographical	 Yahoo! country and city versions Countyweb (**www.countyweb.com**) Alibaba (**www.alibaba.com**) EC21 (**www.ec21.com**) eBay (**www.eBay.com**)
Educational portal	Vertical and horizontal	The Open University (**www.open.ac.uk**)
Search portal	Main focus is on search Ask Jeeves (www.ask.com)	Google (**www.google.com**)
Media type	May be: • voice • video Delivered by streaming media or downloads of files	YouTube (**www.youtube.com**) Rocketboom (**www.rocketboom.com**)

New channel structures

Channel structure
The configuration of partners in a distribution channel.

Disintermediation
The removal of intermediaries such as distributors or brokers that formerly linked a company to its customers.

Channel structures describe the way a manufacturer or selling organisation delivers products and services to its customers. The distribution channel will consist of one or more intermediaries, such as wholesalers and retailers. For example, a music company is unlikely to distribute its CDs directly to retailers, but will use wholesalers that have a large warehouse of titles that are then distributed to individual branches according to demand. A company selling business products may have a longer distribution channel involving more intermediaries.

The relationship between a company and its channel partners can be dramatically altered by the opportunities afforded by the Internet. This occurs because the Internet offers a means of bypassing some of the channel partners. This process is known as **disintermediation** or, in plainer language, 'cutting out the middleman'.

Figure 2.22 illustrates disintermediation in a graphical form for a simplified retail channel. Further intermediaries, such as additional distributors, may occur in a business-to-business market. Figure 2.22 shows the former position where a company marketed and sold its products by 'pushing' them through a sales channel. Figure 2.22 shows two different types of disintermediation in which the wholesaler (b) or the wholesaler and retailer (c) are bypassed, allowing the producer to sell and promote direct to the consumer. The benefits of disintermediation to the producer are clear – it is able to remove the sales and infrastructure cost of selling through the channel. and some of these cost savings can be passed on to the customer in the form of cost reductions.

The Internet's potential to change channel structures has been debated and in disintermediation, the rise of a new breed of virtual merchants and the cannibalising of customers were all quoted as potential threats to the highstreet. More specifically, according to Doherty and Ellis-Chadwick (2010) "Disintermediation" was the word on many commentators' lips, in the early days of Internet retailing, when it was envisaged that manufacturers could simply target their consumers directly, and in so doing, cut the retailer, as "middle man", out of the equation [Malone *et al.*, 1997].' By interacting directly with customers, via the Internet, manufacturers would have the opportunity to dramatically change the structure and dynamic of retail channels [Ettorre, 1996], and in so doing, allow both producers and customers to benefit from a

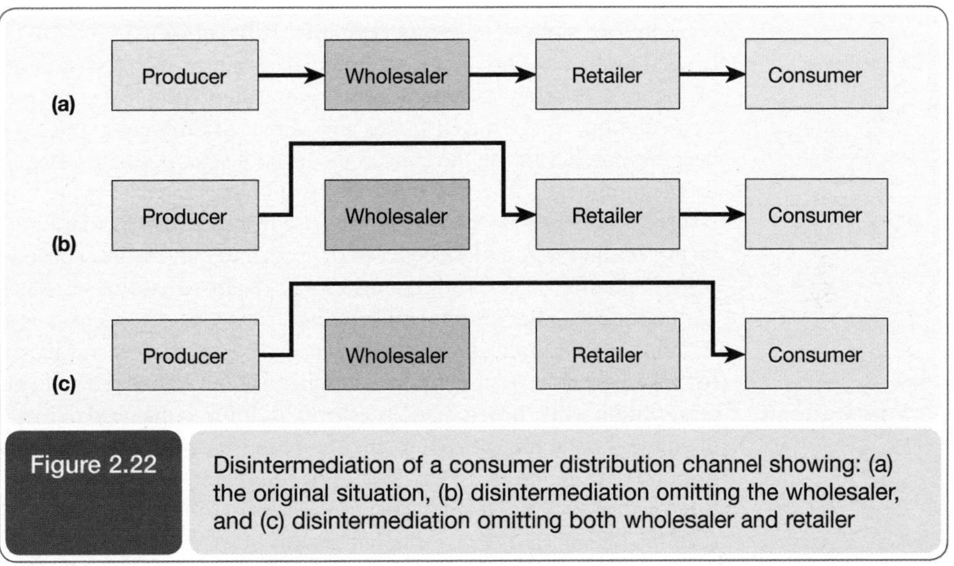

Figure 2.22 Disintermediation of a consumer distribution channel showing: (a) the original situation, (b) disintermediation omitting the wholesaler, and (c) disintermediation omitting both wholesaler and retailer

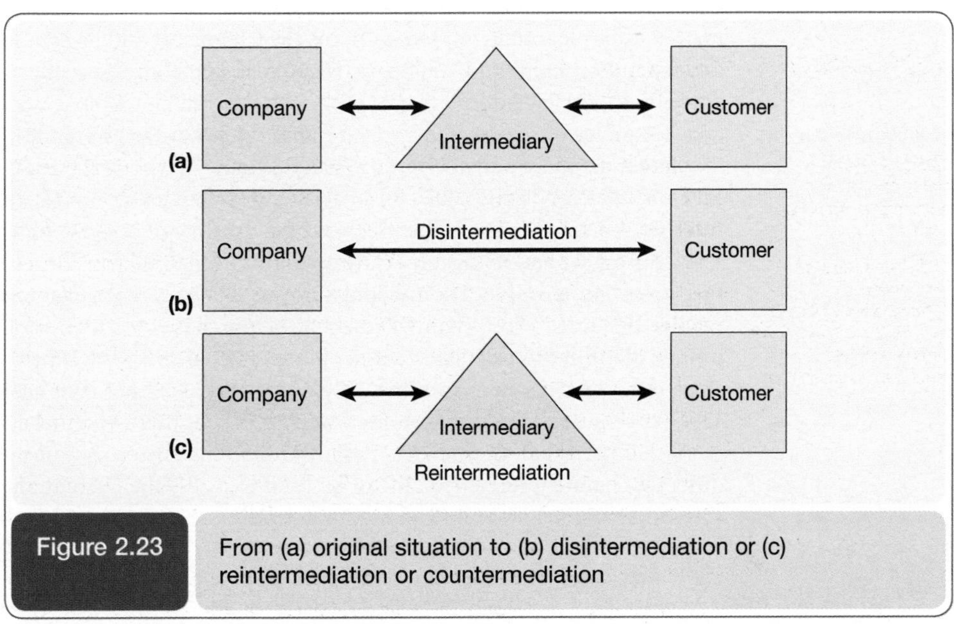

Figure 2.23 From (a) original situation to (b) disintermediation or (c) reintermediation or countermediation

more direct form of contact [Benjamin & Wigand, 1995]. It was envisaged that this form of 'pirating the value chain' [Ghosh, 1998] could ultimately change the balance of power within electronic retail channels. Indeed, Alba *et al.* [1997] suggested that 'disintermediation' might be the 'the most important structural change brought about by interactive home selling'.

The reality is that the early concerns that the Internet would replace the high street and that established retailers would be under threat from the disintermediation of the supply-chain, are generally felt to have been rather overblown [Rosenbloom, 2002; Hurt, 2007]. By and large, the high street has weathered the storm, and the global economy has been left with the reality that the impact of retail disintermediation has been fairly modest [Wrigley & Currah, 2006]. Although in overall terms, disintermediation may not have had a marked impact on the high street, there are particular segments, such as music, entertainment, printing/publishing and traditional travel agents, in which its impact has already been highly significant [Constantinides *et al.*, 2008]. In particular, when it comes to the purchase of computer equipment, very large numbers of consumers are now heading straight for web-sites such as: Apple.com, HP.com or Dell.com, to satisfy their requirements. (Doherty and Ellis-Chadwick, 2010)

Moreover, since purchasers of products still require assistance in the selection of products, this led to the creation of new intermediaries, a process referred to as **reintermediation.**

Reintermediation
The creation of new intermediaries between customers and suppliers providing services such as supplier search and product evaluation.

Figure 2.23 shows the operation of reintermediation in a graphical form. Following disintermediation, where the customer goes direct to different suppliers to select a product, this becomes inefficient for the consumer. Take, the example of someone buying insurance – to decide on the best price and offer, they would have to visit say five different insurers and then return to the one they decide to purchase from. Reintermediation removes this inefficiency by placing an intermediary between the purchaser and seller. This intermediary performs the price evaluation stage of fulfilment since its database has links updated from prices contained within the databases of different suppliers.

What are the implications of reintermediation for the Internet marketer? First, it is necessary to make sure that a company, as a supplier, is represented with the new intermediaries operating within your chosen market sector. This implies the need to integrate, using the Internet, databases containing price information with that of different intermediaries. Secondly, it is important to monitor the prices of other suppliers within this sector (possibly by using the intermediary website for this purpose). Thirdly, long-term partnering arrangements such as sponsorships need to be considered. Finally, it may be appropriate to create your own intermediary to compete with existing intermediaries or to pre-empt similar intermediaries. For example, the Thomson Travel Group set up Latedeals.com (**http://www.thomson.co.uk/late-deals/late-deals.html**) in direct competition with Lastminute.com (**www.lastminute.com**). A further example is that, in the UK, Boots the Chemist set up its own intermediaries Handbag (**www.handbag.com**) and Wellbeing (**www.wellbeing.com**). This effectively created barriers to entry for other new intermediaries wishing to operate in this space. Such tactics to counter or take advantage of reintermediation are sometimes known as **countermediation.**

Countermediation
Creation of a new intermediary by an established company.

Market mapping and developing channel chains is a powerful technique recommended by McDonald and Wilson (2002) for analysing the changes in a marketplace introduced by the Internet. A market map can be used to show the flow of revenue between a manufacturer or service provider and its customers through traditional intermediaries and new types of intermediaries. For example, Thomas and Sullivan (2005) give the example of a US multichannel retailer that used cross-channel tracking of purchases through assigning each customer a unique identifier to calculate channel preferences as follows: 63 per cent bricks-and-mortar store only, 12.4 per cent Internet-only customers, 11.9 per cent catalogue-only customers, 11.9 per cent dual-channel customers and 1 per cent three-channel customers.

A channel chain is similar – it shows different customer journeys for customers with different channel preferences. It can be used to assess the current and future importance of these different customer journeys. An example of a channel chain is shown in Figure 2.24.

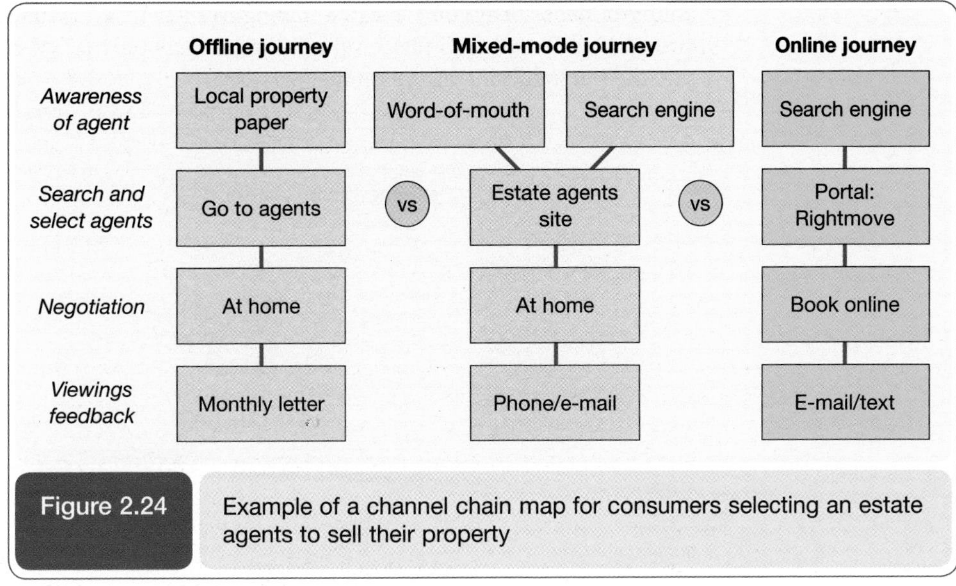

Figure 2.24 Example of a channel chain map for consumers selecting an estate agents to sell their property

Location of trading

Electronic marketspace
A virtual marketplace such as the Internet in which no direct contact occurs between buyers and sellers.

Representation
The locations on the Internet where an organisation is located for promoting or selling its services.

While traditional marketplaces have a physical location, Internet-based markets have no physical presence – it is a virtual marketplace. Rayport and Sviokla (1996) used this distinction to coin the new term **electronic marketspace**. This has implications for the way in which the relationships between the different actors in the marketplace occur.

The new electronic marketspace has many alternative virtual locations where an organisation needs to position itself to communicate and sell to its customers. Thus, one tactical marketing question is 'What representation do we have on the Internet?' A particular aspect of **representation** that needs to be reviewed is the different types of marketplace location. Berryman *et al.* (1998) have identified a simple framework for this. They identify three key online locations for promotion of services and for performing e-commerce transactions with customers (Figure 2.25). The three options are:

a *Supplier-controlled sites (sell-side at supplier site, one supplier to many customers).* This is the main website of the company and is where the majority of transactions take place. Most e-tailers such as Amazon (**www.amazon.com**) or Dell (**www.dell.com**) fall into this category.

b *Buyer-controlled sites (buy-side at buyer site, many suppliers to one customer).* These are intermediaries that have been set up so that it is the buyer that initiates the market-making. This can occur through procurement posting where a purchaser specifies what they wish to purchase, it is sent by e-mail to suppliers registered on the system and then offers are awaited. Aggregators involve a group of purchasers combining to purchase a multiple order, thus reducing the purchase cost. General Electric Trading Post Network was the first to set up this type of arrangement (**http://tpn.geis.com**, although this site is no longer available) but it remains uncommon in comparison to the other two alternatives.

c *Neutral sites or intermediaries (neutral location – many suppliers to many customers).* For consumers, evaluator intermediaries that enable price and product comparison have become commonplace as we have seen. B2B intermediaries are known as *trading exchanges, marketplaces* or *hubs.* Examples of independent B2B exchanges mentioned in the previous edition are Vertical Net (**www.vertical.net**), Commerce One Marketsite (**www.commerceone.com**) and Covisint (**www.covisint.net**), none of which now exist in their original form. While some B2B intermediaries remain for some commodities or simple services (for example, EC21 (**www.ec21.com**), Elance (**www.elance.com**), eBay Business (**http://business.ebay.com**)) the new trading arrangements have not developed as predicted by many analysts due to the complexity of business purchase decisions and negotiations and their destabilising nature on markets.

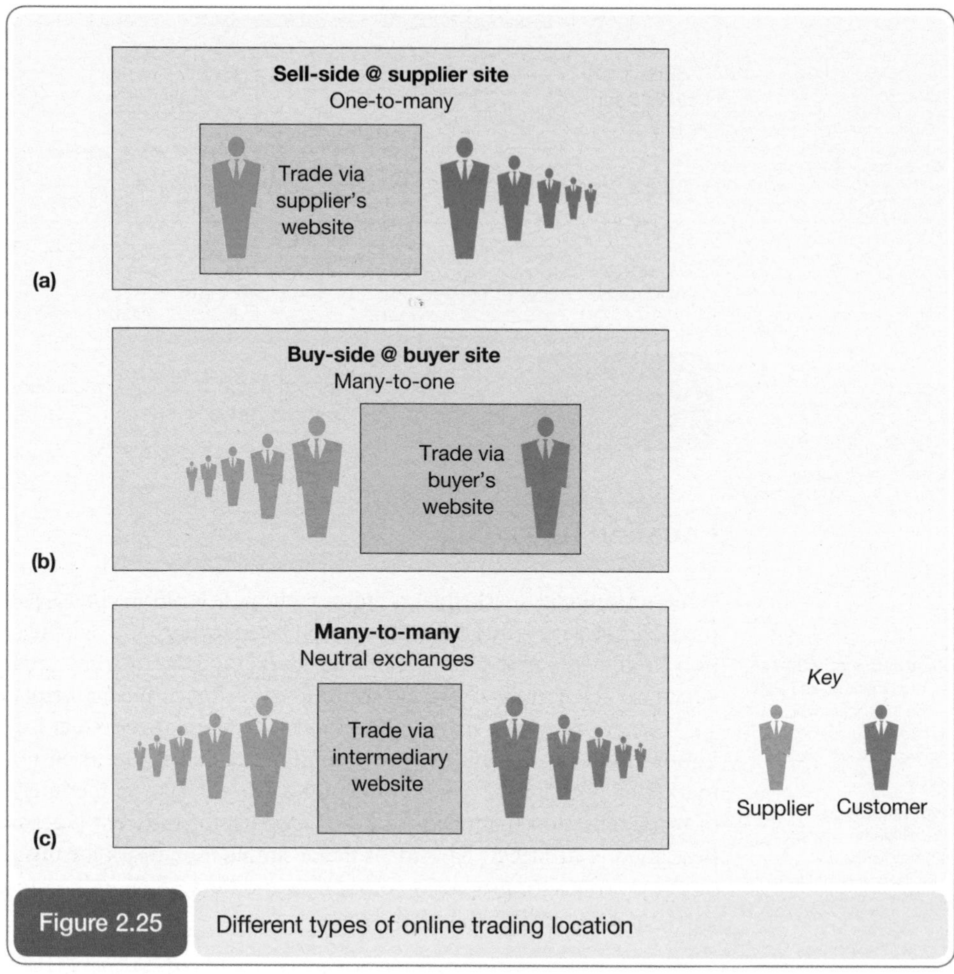

Figure 2.25 Different types of online trading location

Commercial arrangement for transactions

Markets can also be considered from another perspective – that of the type of commercial arrangement that is used to agree a sale and price between the buyer and supplier. The main alternative commercial arrangements are shown in Table 2.9.

It can be seen from Table 2.9 that each of these commercial arrangements is similar to a traditional arrangement. Although the mechanism cannot be considered to have changed, the relative importance of these different options has changed with the Internet. Owing to the ability to rapidly publish new offers and prices, auction has become an important means of selling on the Internet. A turnover of billions of dollars has been achieved by eBay from consumers offering items ranging from cars to antiques. Many airlines have successfully trialled auctions to sell seats remaining on an aircraft just before a flight.

Research suggests that participants in auctions do not necessarily behave rationally. In a study of the consumer approach to auctions which assessed the type of value assessments and decision dynamics made at each stage of the auction, Ariely and Simonson (2003) suggested that participants in auctions do not always get the bargain they may be looking for – their study of purchases of DVDs and electronic equipment found that:

Table 2.9 Commercial mechanisms and online transactions

Commercial (trading) mechanism	Online transaction mechanism of Nunes *et al.* (2000)
1 **Negotiated deal** Example: can use similar mechanism to auction as on Commerce One (**www.ec21.com**)	• Negotiation – bargaining between single seller and buyer • Continuous replenishment – ongoing fulfilment of orders under preset terms
2 **Brokered deal** Example: intermediaries such as Screentrade (**www.screentrade.co.uk**)	• Achieved through online intermediaries offering auction and pure markets online
3 **Auction** C2C: eBay (**www.ebay.com**) B2B: eBay business (**http://business.ebay.com**)	• Seller auction – buyers' bids determine final price of sellers' offerings • Buyer auction – buyers request prices from multiple sellers • Reverse – buyer posts desired price for seller acceptance
4 **Fixed price sale** Example: all e-tailers	• Static call – online catalogue with fixed prices • Dynamic call – online catalogue with continuously updated prices and features
5 **Pure markets** Example: electronic share dealing	• Spot – buyers' and sellers' bids clear instantly
6 **Barter** Example: **www.intagio.com**	• Barter – buyer and seller exchange goods

(a) due to a focus on the narrow auction context, consumers under-search and, consequently, overpay for widely available commodities (CDs, DVDs) and (b) higher auction starting prices tend to lead to higher winning bids, particularly when comparable items are not available in the immediate context.

Business models for e-commerce

Online business model
A summary of how a company will generate a profit identifying its core product or service value proposition, target customers in different markets, position in the competitive online marketplace or value chain and its projections for revenue and costs.

A review of the different **online business models** made available through e-commerce is of relevance to existing companies, but in particular, start-up companies and online intermediaries. Venkatram (2000) pointed out that existing businesses needed to use the Internet to build on current business models, while at the same time experimenting with new business models. New business models may be important to gain a competitive advantage over existing competitors, while at the same time heading off similar business models created by new entrants. More commonly, they may simply offer a different revenue stream through advertising or charging for services in a new way. For Internet start-ups the viability of a business model and in particular their sources of revenue will be crucial to funding from venture capitalists. But what is a business model? Timmers (1999) defines a 'business model' as:

> An architecture for product, service and information flows, including a description of the various business actors and their roles; and a description of the potential benefits for the various business actors; and a description of the sources of revenue.

Investors will require eight key elements of the business model to be defined which will summarise the organisation's e-business strategy:

1 *Value proposition.* Which products and or services will the company offer? This is supplemented by the added value defined using the online value proposition described in Chapter 5.
2 *Market or audience.* Which audience will the company serve and target with its communications? For example, business-to-business, business-to-consumer or not-for-profit? Within these categories are there particular audience segments that will be targeted. The scope of geographical markets such as countries, regions or towns need to be defined. A communications plan as described in Chapters 8 and 9 will detail how the audience will be reached and influenced using online communications and offline communications such as advertising and public relations.
3 *Revenue models and cost base.* What are the specific revenue models that will generate different income streams? What are the main costs of the business forming its budget? How are these forecast to change through time?
4 *Competitive environment.* Who are the direct and indirect competitors for the service and which range of business models do they possess?
5 *Value chain and marketplace positioning.* How is the company and its services positioned in the value chain between customers and suppliers and in comparison with direct and indirect competitors?
6 *Representation in the physical and virtual world.* What is its relative representation in the physical and virtual world, e.g. high-street presence, online only, intermediary, mixture? How will the company influence its audience through a multichannel buying process
7 *Organisational structure.* How will the organisation be internally structured to create, deliver and promote its service (See Chapter 10)? How will it partner with other companies to provide services, for example through outsourcing?
8 *Management.* What experience in similar markets and companies do the managers have? Will they attract publicity?

Timmers (1999) identifies no less than eleven different types of business model that can be facilitated by the web. These are described mainly in terms of their revenue models and value chain or marketplace positioning. You will notice that many of these are in common with the intermediary types identified by Sarkar which we reviewed earlier in the chapter:

1 *e-shop* – marketing of a company or shop via the web
2 *e-procurement* – electronic tendering and procurement of goods and services
3 *e-malls* – a collection of e-shops such as Indigo Square (**www.indigosquare.com**)
4 *e-auctions* – eBay (**www.ebay.com**) is the best-known example and offers both B2B and B2C offerings
5 *virtual communities* – these can be B2C communities such as the major social networks or B2B communities such as those built around trade publishers; these are important for their potential in e-marketing and are described in the section on virtual communities in Chapter 9
6 *collaboration platforms* – these enable collaboration between businesses or individuals, e.g. e-groups, now part of Yahoo! (**www.yahoo.com**) services
7 *third-party marketplaces* – marketplaces are described in Chapter 7
8 *value-chain integrators* – offer a range of services across the value chain
9 *value-chain service providers* – specialise in providing functions for a specific part of the value chain, such as the logistics company UPS (**www.ups.com**)
10 *information brokerage* – provide information for consumers and businesses, often to assist in making the buying decision or for business operations or leisure
11 *trust and other services* – examples of trust services include Internet Shopping is Safe (ISIS) (**www.imrg.org/isis**) or TRUSTe (**www.truste.org**) which authenticate the quality of service provided by companies trading on the web.

Publishers are a major type of business model that is not clearly represented in the Timmers categories. We examine the revenue models for these below. Riggins and Mitra (2007) have a more recent evaluation of alternative online marketplace players which we review in Chapter 7. Regardless of the descriptors used, the important point is that as part of strategy development, organisations should identify relevant partners and develop tactics for working with them appropriately.

Figure 2.26 suggests a different perspective for reviewing alternative business models. There are three different perspectives from which a business model can be viewed. Any individual organisation can operate in different categories, as the examples below show, but most will focus on a single category for each perspective. Such a categorisation of business models can be used as a tool for *formulating e-business strategy*. The three perspectives, with examples, are:

1 *Marketplace position perspective.* The book publisher here is the manufacturer, Amazon is a retailer and Yahoo! is both a retailer and a marketplace intermediary.
2 *Revenue model perspective.* The book publisher can use the web to sell direct whileYahoo! and Amazon can take commission-based sales. Yahoo! also has advertising as a revenue model.
3 *Commercial arrangement perspective.* All three companies offer fixed-price sales, but, in its place as a marketplace intermediary, Yahoo! also offers alternatives.

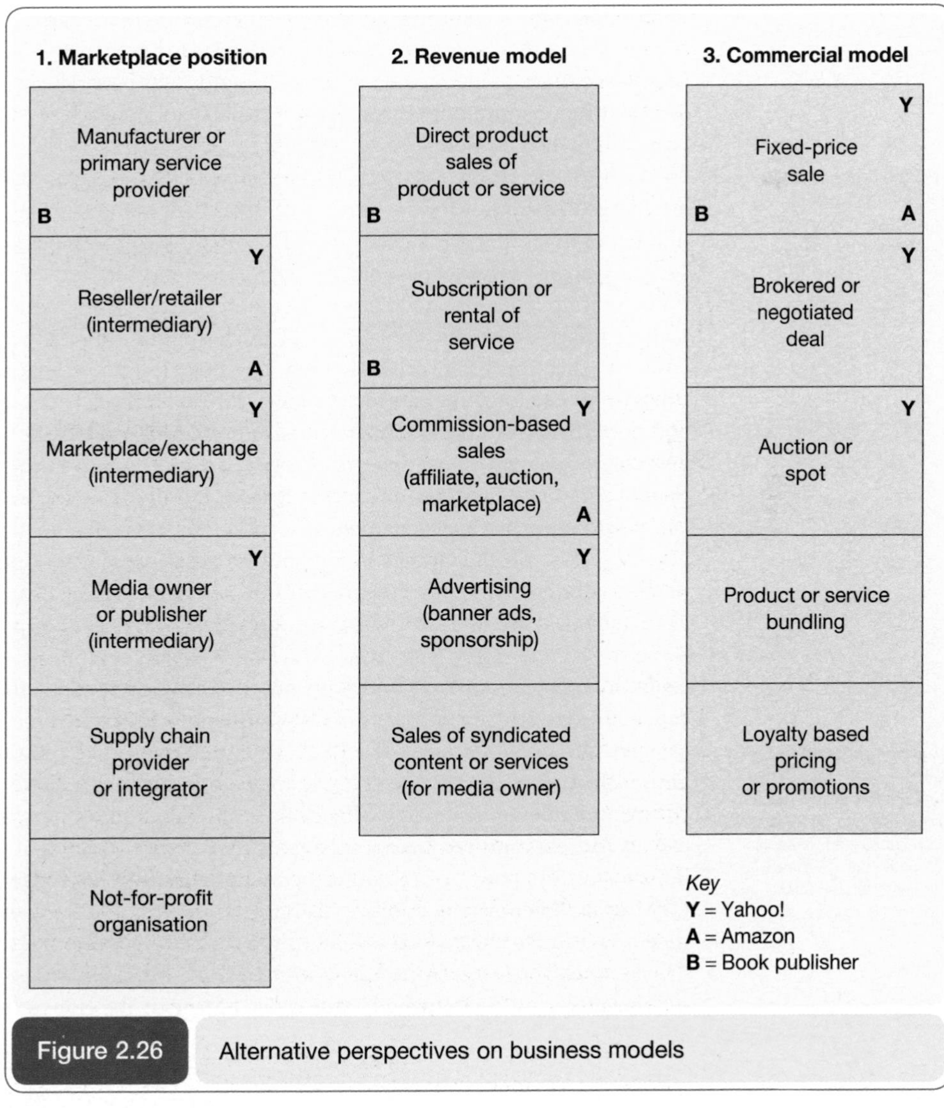

Figure 2.26 Alternative perspectives on business models

Revenue models

Revenue models
Describe methods of generating income for an organisation.

Revenue models specifically describe different techniques for generation of income. For existing companies, revenue models have mainly been based upon the income from sales of products or services. This may be either for selling direct from the manufacturer or supplier of the service or through an intermediary that will take a cut of the selling price. Both of these revenue models are, of course, still crucial in online trading. There may, however, be options for other methods of generating revenue; a manufacturer may be able to sell advertising space or sell digital services that were not previously possible.

Online publisher and intermediary revenue models

For a publisher, there are many options for generating revenue online based around advertising and fees for usage of the online service. These options, particularly the first four in the list below, can also be reviewed by other types of business such as price comparison sites, aggregators, social networks and destination sites which can also carry advertising to supplement revenue. The main types of online revenue model are:

CPM (cost per thousand)
The cost to the advertiser (or the revenue received by the publisher) when an ad is served 1000 times.

CPC (cost per click)
The cost to the advertiser (or the revenue received by the publisher) of each click of a link to a third-party site.

Cost per acquisition (CPA)
The cost to the advertiser (or the revenue received by the publisher) for each outcome such as a lead or sale generated after a click to a third-party site.

1 *CPM display advertising on site.* **CPM** stands for 'cost per thousand' where M denotes 'mille'. This is the traditional method by which site owners charge a fee for advertising. The site owner charges advertisers a rate card price (for example £50 CPM) according to the number of times ad are served to site visitors. Ads may be served by the site owner's own ad server or more commonly through a third-party ad network service such as DoubleClick (which is owned by Google).
2 *CPC advertising on site (pay-per-click text ads).* **CPC** stands for 'cost per click'. Advertisers are charged not simply for the number of times their ads are displayed, but according to the number of times they are clicked upon. These are typically text ads served by a search engine such as Google (**www.google.com**) on what is known as its content network. Google has its AdSense (**http://adsense.google.com**) program for publishers which enables them to offer text- or image-based ads typically on a CPC basis, but optionally on a CPM basis. Typical costs per click can be surprisingly high, i.e. they are in the range £0.10 to £4, but sometimes up to £20 for some categories such as 'life insurance'. The revenue for search engines and publishers from these sources can also be significant: Google's annual reports (**http://investor.google.com**) show that this is between a quarter and a third of Google's revenue.
3 *Sponsorship of site sections or content types (typically fixed fee for a period).* A company can pay to advertise a site channel or section. For example, the bank HSBC sponsors the Money section on the Orange broadband provider portal (**www.orange.co.uk**). This type of deal is often struck for a fixed amount per year. It may also be part of a reciprocal arrangement, sometimes known as a 'contra-deal' where neither party pays.
4 *Affiliate revenue (CPA, but could be CPC).* Affiliate revenue is commission-based, for example, I display Amazon books on my site **DaveChaffey.com** and receive around 5 per cent of the cover price as a fee from Amazon. Such an arrangement is sometimes known as **cost per acquisition (CPA)**. Increasingly, this approach is replacing CPM or CPC approaches where the advertiser has more negotiating power. For example, manufacturing company Unilever negotiates CPA deals with online publishers where it paid for every e-mail address captured by a campaign rather than a traditional CPM deal. However, it depends on the power of the publisher, who will often receive more revenue overall for CPM deals. After all, the publisher cannot influence the quality of the ad creative or the incentivisation to click which will affect the clickthrough rate and so earnings from the ad.
5 *Transaction fee revenue.* A company receives a fee for facilitating a transaction. Examples include eBay and PayPal who charge a percentage of the transaction cost between buyer and seller.
6 *Subscription access to content or services.* A range of documents can be accessed from a publisher for a fixed period. These are often referred to as premium services on websites.

7 *Pay-per-view access to documents.* Here payment occurs for single access to a document, video or music clip which can be downloaded. It may or may not be protected with a password or **digital rights management (DRM)**. I pay to access detailed best-practice guides on Internet marketing from Marketing Sherpa (**www.marketingsherpa.com**).

Digital rights management (DRM)
The use of different technologies to protect the distribution of digital services or content such as software, music, movies or other digital data.

8 *Subscriber data access for e-mail marketing.* The data a site owner has about its customers are also potentially valuable since it can send different forms of e-mail to its customers if they have given their permission that they are happy to receive e-mail from either the publisher or third parties. The site owner can charge for adverts placed in its newsletter or can deliver a separate message on behalf of the advertiser (sometimes known as 'list rental'). A related approach is to conduct market research with the site customers.

Calculating revenue for an online business

Site owners can develop models of potential revenue depending on the mix of revenue-generating techniques from the four main revenue options they use on the site given in the options above.

Consider the capacity of a site owner to maximise revenue or 'monetise' their site – which factors will be important? The model will be based on assumptions about the level of traffic and number of pages viewed plus the interaction with different types of ad unit. Their ability to maximise revenue will be based on these factors which can be modelled in the spreadsheet shown in Figure 2.27:

- *Number and size of ad units.* This is a delicate balance between the number of ad units in each site section or page – too many obtrusive ad units may present a bad experience for site users, too few will reduce revenue. Figure 2.27 has a parameter for the number of ad units or containers in each ad revenue category. There is a tension with advertisers who know that the awareness and response they generate from their ads is maximised when they are as large as practical and in prominent placements. A more accurate revenue model would develop revenue for different page types such as the home page and different page categories, e.g. the money or travel sections.
- *Capacity to sell advertising.* Figure 2.27 also has a parameter for the percentage of ad inventory sold in each category – for example, for the CPM ad display revenue only 40 per cent of inventory may be sold. This is why you may see publisher sites with their own 'house ads' – it is a sign they have been unable to sell all their ad space. A benefit of using the Google AdSense publisher program is that inventory is commonly all used.
- *Fee levels negotiated for different advertising models.* These will depend on the market competition or demand for advertising space. For 'pay-per-performance' advertising options such as the CPC and CPA models, it also depends on the response. In the first case, the site owner only receives revenue when the ad is clicked upon and in the second case, the site owner only receives revenue when the ad is clicked upon and a product is purchased on the destination merchant site.
- *Traffic volumes.* More visitors equate to more opportunities to generate revenue through serving more pages (which helps with CPM based advertising) or more clicks to third-party sites (which helps generate revenue from CPC and CPA deals).
- *Visitor engagement.* The longer visitors stay on a site (its 'stickiness'), the more page views that will accumulate, which again gives more opportunities for ad revenue. For a destination site a typical number of page views per visit would be in the range 5 to 10, but for a social network, media site or community the figure could be greater than 30.

Considering all of these approaches to revenue generation together, the site owner will seek to use the best combination of these techniques to maximise the revenue. An illustration of this approach is shown in Figure 2.27.

To assess how effective different pages or sites in their portfolio are at generating revenue using these techniques, site owners will use two approaches. The first is eCPM, or effective cost per thousand. This looks at the total the advertiser can charge (or cost to advertisers) for each page or site. Through increasing the number of ad units on each page this value will increase. The other alternative to assess page or site revenue-generating effectiveness is

Ad revenue option	Measure	Site
	Pages served	**100,000**
Display advertising (CPM)	CPM (Cost Per Thousand)	£2
	% Inventory served	40%
	Avg. Clickthrough (CTR %)	0.10%
	Ad units served per page	2
	Clicks – CPM ads	80
	Revenue – display ads	**£160**
	Earnings per 100 clicks (EPC)	**£200.0**
	eCPM – display ads	**£1.60**
Fixed run-of-site sponsorship	% Inventory served	100%
	Avg. Clickthrough (CTR %)	0.30%
	Ad units served 1	1
	Clicks – fixed	300
	Revenue – fixed sponsorship	**£3,000**
	Earnings per 100 clicks (EPC)	**£1,000.0**
	eCPM – fixed	**£30.00**
Text ad advertising (CPC)	% Inventory served	100%
	Avg. Clickthrough (CTR %)	1.00%
	Avg. Cost Per Click	£0.30
	Ad units served per page	1
	Clicks – CPC ads	1,000
	Revenue – CPC ads	**£300**
	Earnings per 100 clicks (EPC)	**£30.0**
	eCPM – CPC ads	**£3**
Affiliate commission	% Inventory served	100%
	Avg. Clickthrough (CTR %)	0.50%
	Ad units served per page	1
	Clicks – Affiliates	500
	Desination conversion rate (%)	3%
	Average order value	£100
	Commission %	10%
	Revenue – affiliates	**£150**
	Earnings per 100 clicks (EPC)	**£30.0**
	eCPM – affiliates	**£1.50**
Overall metrics for site	**Clicks – total**	**1,880**
	Revenue – total	**£3,610**
	Earnings per 100 clicks (EPC) – total	**£192.02**
	eCPM – total	**£36.10**

Blue cells = input variables – vary these for 'what-if' analysis

Orange cells = Output variables (calculated – **do not overtype**)

Figure 2.27 Revenue model spreadsheet
Source: SmartInsights.com

revenue per click (RPC), also known as 'earnings per click' (EPC). Alternatively, revenue can be calculated as ad revenue per 1000 site visitors. This is particularly important for affiliate marketers who make money through commission when their visitors click through to third-party retail sites, and then purchase there.

Activity 2.6 explores some of the revenue models that are possible.

Activity 2.6 Revenue models at marketing membership sites

Purpose

To illustrate the range of revenue-generating opportunities for an online publisher. This site looks at three alternative approaches for publishing, referencing three different types of portal.

Visit The International Telecoms Union, free statistics section (**http://www.itu.int**) and find answers to these questions:

1. Which regions of the world have the highest and lowest number of Internet users as a proportion of the total population?
2. Which regions of the world have the highest and lowest number of mobile users as a proportion of the total population?
3. What are the implications for a digital strategist in a large organisation?

To conclude this chapter, read the following Case Study 2 about dot-com failure Boo.com. We can learn from studying the mistakes of others, and have chosen this example since it shows what can happen when a company does not understand the marketplace and does not have clear goals.

Case Study 2 Boo hoo – learning from the largest European dot-com failure

Context

'Unless we raise $20 million by midnight, boo.com is dead.' So said boo.com CEO Ernst Malmsten on 18 May 2000. Half the investment was raised, but this was too little, too late, and at midnight, less than a year after its launch, Boo.com closed. The headlines in the *Financial Times* the next day read: 'Boo.com collapses as investors refuse funds. Online sports retailer becomes Europe's first big Internet casualty.'

The Boo.com case remains a valuable case study for all types of businesses, since it doesn't only illustrate the challenges of managing e-commerce for a clothes retailer, but rather highlights failings in e-commerce strategy and management that can be made in any type of organisation.

Company background

Boo.com was founded in 1998 by three Swedish entrepreneurs, Ernst Malmsten, Kajsa Leander and Patrik Hedelin. Malmsten and Leander had previous business experience in publishing where they created a specialist publisher and had also created an online bookstore, bokus.com, which in 1997 became the world's third largest book e-retailer behind Amazon and Barnes & Noble. They became millionaires when they sold the company in 1998. At Boo.com, they were joined by Patrik Hedelin who was also the financial director at bokus, and at the time they were perceived as experienced European Internet entrepreneurs by the investors who backed them in their new venture.

Company vision

The vision for Boo.com was for it to become the world's first online global sports retail site. It would be a European brand, but with a global appeal. Think of it as a sports and fashion retail version of Amazon. At launch it would open its virtual doors in both Europe and America with a view to 'amazoning the sector'. Note, though, that Amazon did not launch simultaneously in all markets. Rather it became established in the US before providing local European distribution.

→

The Boo.com brand name

According to Malmsten *et al.* (2001), the boo brand name originated from film star Bo Derek, best known for her role in the movie *10*. The domain name 'bo.com' was unavailable, but adding an 'o', they managed to procure the domain 'boo.com' for $2,500 from a domain name dealer. According to Rob Talbot, director of marketing for Boo.com, Boo were '*looking for a name that was easy to spell across all the different countries and easy to remember ... something that didn't have a particular meaning*'.

Target market

The audience targeted by Boo.com can be characterised as 'young, well-off and fashion-conscious' 18-to-24-year-olds. The concept was that globally the target market would be interested in sports and fashion brands stocked by Boo.com.

The market for clothing in this area was viewed as very large, so the thought was that capture of only a small part of this market was required for Boo.com to be successful. The view at this time on the scale of this market and the basis for success is indicated by *New Media Age* (1999):

> *The $60b USD industry is dominated by Gen Xers who are online and according to market research in need of knowing what is in, what is not and a way to receive such goods quickly. If boo.com becomes known as the place to keep up with fashion and can supply the latest trends then there is no doubt that there is a market, a highly profitable one at that, for profits to grow from.*

The growth in market was also supported by retail analysts, with Verdict predicting online shopping in the United Kingdom to grow from £600 million in 1999 to £12.5 billion in 2005.

However, *New Media Age* (2005) does note some reservations about this market, saying:

> *Clothes and trainers have a high rate of return in the mail order/home shopping world. Twenty-year-olds may be online and may have disposable income but they are not the main market associated with mail order. To date there is no one else doing anything similar to boo.com.*

The Boo.com proposition

In their proposal to investors, the company stated that 'their business idea is to become the world-leading Internet-based retailer of prestigious brand leisure and sportswear names'. They listed brands such as Polo, Ralph Lauren, Tommy Hilfiger, Nike, Fila, Lacoste and Adidas. The proposition involved sports and fashion goods alongside each other. The thinking was that sports clothing has more standardized sizes with less need for a precise fit than designer clothing.

The owners of Boo.com wanted to develop an easy-to-use experience which re-created the offline shopping experience as far as possible. As part of the branding strategy, an idea was developed of a virtual salesperson, initially named Jenny and later Miss Boo. She would guide users through the site and give helpful tips. When selecting products, users could drag them on to models, zoom in and rotate them in 3D to visualise them from different angles. The technology to achieve this was built from scratch along with the stock control and distribution software. A large investment was required in technology with several suppliers being replaced before launch which was six months later than promised to investors, largely due to problems with implementing the technology.

Clothing the mannequin and populating the catalogue was also an expensive challenge. For 2000, about $6 million was spent on content about spring/summer fashion wear. It cost $200 to photograph each product, representing a monthly cost of more than $500,000.

Although the user experience of Boo.com is often criticised for its speed, it does seem to have had that wow factor that influenced investors. Analyst Nik Margolis, writing in *New Media Age* (1999), illustrates this by saying:

> *What I saw at Boo.com is simply the most clever web experience I have seen in quite a while. The presentation of products and content are both imaginative and offer an experience. Sure everything loads up fast in an office but I was assured by those at Boo.com that they will keep to a limit of eight seconds for a page to download. Eight seconds is not great but the question is will it be worth waiting for?*

Of course, today, the majority of European users have broadband, but in the late 1990s the majority were on dial-up and had to download the software to view products.

Communicating the Boo.com proposition

Early plans referred to extensive 'high-impact' marketing campaigns on TV and newspapers. Public relations were important in leveraging the novelty of the concept and human side of the business – Leander was previously a professional model and had formerly been Malmsten's partner. This PR was initially focused within the fashion and sportswear trade and then rolled out to publications likely to be read by the target audience. The success of this PR initiative can be judged by the 350,000 e-mail pre-registrations who wanted to be notified of launch.

For the launch Malmsten *et al*. (2001) explains that '*with a marketing and PR spend of only $22.4 million we had managed to create a worldwide brand*'.

To help create the values of the Boo.com brand, Boom, a lavish online fashion magazine, was created, which required substantial staff for different language versions. The magazine wasn't a catalogue which directly supported sales, rather it was a publishing venture competing with established fashion titles. For existing customers the Look Book, a 44-page print catalogue was produced which showcased different products each month.

The challenges of building a global brand in months

The challenges of creating a global brand in months are illustrated well by Malmsten *et al*. (2001). After an initial round of funding, including investment from JP Morgan, LMVH Investment and the Benetton family, which generated around $9 million, the founders planned towards launch by identifying thousands of individual tasks, many of which needed to be completed by staff yet to be recruited. These tasks were divided into twenty-seven areas of responsibility familiar to many organisations including office infrastructure, logistics, product information, pricing, front-end applications, call centres, packaging, suppliers, designing logos, advertising/PR, legal issues, and recruitment. At its zenith, Boo.com had 350 staff, with over one hundred in London and new offices in, Munich, New York, Paris and Stockholm. Initially boo.com was available in UK English, US English, German, Swedish, Danish and Finnish with localized versions for France, Spain and Italy added after launch. The website was tailored for individual countries using the local language and currency and also local prices. Orders were fulfilled and shipped out of one of two warehouses: one in Louisville, Kentucky and the other in Cologne, Germany. This side of the business was relatively successful with on-time delivery rates approaching 100 per cent achieved.

Boo possessed classic channel conflicts. Initially, it was difficult getting fashion and sports brands to offer their products through Boo.com. Manufacturers already had a well-established distribution network through large high-street sports and fashion retailers and many smaller retailers. If clothing brands permitted Boo.com to sell their clothes online at discounted prices, then this would conflict with retailers' interests and would also portray the brands in a negative light if their goods were in an online 'bargain bucket'. A further pricing issue is where local or *zone pricing* in different markets exists, for example lower prices often exist in the US than Europe and there are variations in different European countries.

Making the business case to investors

Today it seems incredible that investors were confident enough to invest $130 million in the company and, at the high point, the company was valued at $390 million. Yet much of this investment was based on the vision of the founders to be a global brand and achieve 'first-mover advantage'. Although there were naturally revenue projections, these were not always based on an accurate detailed analysis of market potential. Immediately before launch, Malmsten *et al*. (2001) explains a meeting with would-be investor Pequot Capital, represented by Larry Lenihan who had made successful investments in AOL and Yahoo! The Boo.com management team were able to provide revenue forecasts, but unable to answer fundamental questions for modelling the potential of the business, such as '*How many visitors are you aiming for? What kind of conversion rate are you aiming for? How much does each customer have to spend? What's your customer acquisition cost? And what's your payback time on customer acquisition cost?*' When these figures were obtained, the analyst found them to be 'far-fetched' and reputedly ended the meeting with the words. '*I'm not interested. Sorry for my bluntness, but I think you're going to be out of business by Christmas*.'

When the site launched on 3 November 1999, around 50,000 unique visitors were achieved on the first day, but only 4 in 1000 placed orders (a 0.25 per cent conversion rate). This shows the importance of modelling conversion rates accurately. This low conversion rate was also symptomatic of problems with technology. It also gave rise to negative PR. One reviewer explained how he waited: '*Eighty-one minutes to pay too much money for a pair of shoes that I still have to wait a week to get?*' These rates did improve as problems were ironed out – by the end of the week 228,848 visits had resulted in 609 orders with a value of $64,000. In the six weeks from launch, sales of $353,000 were made and conversion rates had more than doubled to 0.98 per cent before Christmas. However, a relaunch was required within six months to cut download times and to introduce a 'low-bandwidth version' for users using dial-up connections. This led to conversion rates of nearly 3 per cent on sales promotion. Sales results were disappointing in some regions, with US sales accounting for 20 per cent compared to the planned 40 per cent.

The management team felt that further substantial investment was required to grow the business from a presence in 18 countries and 22 brands in November to 31 countries and 40 brands the following spring. Turnover was forecast to rise from $100 million in 2000/01 to $1,350 million by 2003/04 which would be driven by $102.3 million in marketing in 2003/04. Profit was forecast to be $51.9 million by 2003/4.

→

The end of Boo.com

The end of Boo.com came on 18 May 2000, when investor funds could not be raised to meet the spiralling marketing, technology and wage bills.

Source: Prepared by Dave Chaffey from original sources including Malmsten *et al*. (2001) and *New Media Age* (1999).

Questions

1 Which strategic marketing assumptions and decisions arguably made Boo.com's failure inevitable? Contrast these with other dot-com era survivors that are still in business, for example lastminute.com, Egg.com and Fire box.com

2 Using the framework of the marketing mix to appraise the marketing tactics of Boo.com in the areas of Product, Pricing, Place, Promotion, Process, People and Physical evidence.

3 In many ways, the vision of Boo's founders were 'ideas before their time'. Give examples of e-retail techniques used to create an engaging online customer experience which Boo adopted that are now becoming commonplace.

Summary

1 The constantly changing Internet environment should be monitored by all organisations in order to be able to respond to changes in the micro-environment or the immediate marketplace. The micro-enviroment is largely within the reach of an organisation and therefore digital marketers should be aware of the management implications that arise from this arena. To be successful it is important to understand consumer and competitor behaviour and which suppliers and intermediaries offer services which will enable a company to achieve its digital marketing goals.

2 In this chapter, we have explored each of the groups of actors in the micro-environment. From a consumer perspective we have identified variables that are likely to be the most effective foundation for developing targeting strategies. We have also considered how to analyse consumer demand and the importance of developing conversion strategies.

3 Competitors are an importance group of actors in the micro environment and the Internet has created major changes to the competitive environment. This chapter has considered how organisations should deploy tools such as Porter's five forces to assess the nature and structure of competition in online markets.

4 We have examined techniques for competitive benchmarking and how to analyse competitor behaviour, which has highlighted how it is important to understand the potential strengths and weakness of the companies a company might compete with online.

5 Suppliers and intermediaries also have an important role to play in digital marketing. We have explored the services provided by these actors and considered the opportunities provided.

6 Finally, we considered the impact of the Internet on marketing channels. The Internet can encourage the formation of new channel structures. These include *disintermediation* within the marketplace as organisations' channel partners such as wholesalers or retailers are bypassed. Alternatively, the Internet can cause *reintermediation* as new intermediaries with a different purpose are formed to help bring buyers and sellers together in a *virtual marketplace* or *marketspace.*

Trading in the marketplace can be sell-side (seller-controlled), buy-side (buyer-controlled) or at a neutral marketplace.

7 This chapter has provided a foundation for analysing the immediate trading environment and provides a foundation for Chapter 3, which focuses on the macro environment.
8 A business model is a summary of how a company will generate revenue, identifying its product offering, value-added services, revenue sources and target customers. Exploiting the range of business models made available through the Internet is important to both existing companies and start-ups.
9 The Internet may also offer opportunities for new revenue models such as commission on affiliate referrals to other sites or banner advertising.
10 The opportunity for new commercial arrangements for transactions includes negotiated deals, brokered deals, auctions, fixed-price sales, and pure spot markets; and barters should also be considered.
11 Customer analysis is an important part of situation analysis. It involves assessing demand for online services, characteristics of existing online customers and the multichannel behaviour of customers as they select and purchase products.
12 Regular competitive benchmarking should be conducted to compare services.
13 The role of intermediaries like publishers, media sites, comparison sites and bloggers should also be carefully reviewed as part of strategic analysis.

Exercises

Self-assessment exercises

1 Explain the components of the digital market environment.
2 Why is environmental scanning necessary?
3 Summarise how each of the micro-environment factors may directly drive the content and services provided by a website.
4 How would you analyse demand for digital marketing services?
5 Why is it important to understand conversion marketing models?
6 What is the difference between demographic variables and behavioural variables?
7 What are the main aspects of customer adoption of the Internet that managers should be aware of?
8 What are the main changes to channel structures that are facilitated through the Internet?
9 How should a marketing manager benchmark the online performance of competitors?
10 How can the Internet be used to support the different stages of the buying process?

Essay and discussion questions

1 Competition is intensified when trading online. Discuss the extent to which you feel this assertion is true.
2 Internet access varies from country to country; explain the key factors which might influence different levels of access.
3 Discuss how an Internet entrepreneur might identify market opportunities online.

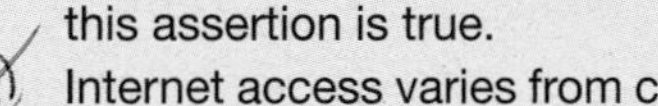

4 Perform a demand analysis for e-commerce services for a product sector and geographical market of your choice.
5 Perform competitor benchmarking for online services for an organisation of your choice.

Examination questions

1 The relationship between intermediaries, suppliers and resellers are crucial to every business. Discuss how the Internet potentially changes supply-chain relationships?
2 Trading online increasingly involves developing multichannel strategies. Give three examples of potential channel conflicts that might arise from using the Internet. Illustrate your answer with examples.

3 Discuss the extent to which it is possible to operate as a *virtual* organisation.
4 Using examples, suggest different ways that a company might use the Internet to build market share.
5 There are numerous variables, which can be used to identify potential target segments that can be used for marketing strategy and planning. Suggest which variables have the most potential for identifying online consumers and justify your answer with examples.
7 Discuss the extent to which Porter's five forces model is applicable for analysing competition in digital markets.
8 Compare the physical and digital trading environments by identifying the similarities and differences.
9 Imagine you are about to set up a business online. Explain how you would go about investigating the micro environment as part of your situation analysis.
10 Suggest how you would advise a business that has a website which is not delivering a benefit to the company.

References

Alba, J., Lynch, J., Weitz, B., Janiszewski, C., Lutz, R., Sawyer, A. and Wood, S. (1997) Interactive home shopping: consumer, retailer and manufacturer incentives to participate in electronic market places, *Journal of Marketing*, 61, 38–53.

Ariely, D. and Simonson, I. (2003) Buying, bidding, playing or competing, *Journal of Consumer Psychology*, 13(1&2), 113–23.

Bart, Y., Shankar, V., Sultan, F. and Urban, G. (2005) Are the drivers and the role of online trust the same for all websites and consumers? A large-scale exploratory empirical study, *Journal of Marketing*, October, 133–52.

Benjamin, R. and Wigand, R. (1995) Electronic markets and virtual value-chains on the information superhighway, *Sloan Management Review*, Winter, 62–72.

Berryman, K., Harrington, L., Layton-Rodin, D. and Rerolle, V. (1998) Electronic commerce: three emerging strategies, *McKinsey Quarterly*, No. 1, 152–9.

Berthon, P., Lane, N., Pitt, L. and Watson, R. (1998) The World Wide Web as an industrial marketing communications tool: models for the identification and assessment of opportunities, *Journal of Marketing Management*, 14, 691–704.

Bettman, J. (1979) *An Information Processing Theory of Consumer Choice*. Addison-Wesley, Reading, MA.

Booms, B. and Bitner, M. (1981) Marketing strategies and organisation structure for service firms. In J. Donelly and W. George (eds) *Marketing of Services*. American Marketing Association, New York.

Bowen Craggs & Co, **www.bowencraggs.com**.

Brand Republic (2011), **http://www.brandrepublic.com/news/1065727/Online-sales-top-5bn-March/?DCMP=ILC-SEARCH_** accessed 31 may 2011.

Brashear, T. G., Kashyap, V., Musante, M. D. and Donthu, N. (2009) A profile of the internet shopper: evidence from six countries, *Journal of Marketing Theory and Practice*, 17(3), 267–81.

BRC (2011) BRC – Google Online Retail Monitor Q1 2011, British Retail Consortium: **http://www.brc.org.uk/bis/downloads/orm/2011Q1_ORM_jd48n.pdf**, accessed July 2011.

Breitenbach, C. and van Doren, D. (1998) Value-added marketing in the digital domain: enhancing the utility of the Internet, *Journal of Consumer Marketing*, 15(6), 559–75.

Brengman, M., Geuensb, M., Weijtersc, C., Smith, S. and Swinyardd, W. (2005) Segmenting Internet shoppers based on their web-usage-related lifestyle: a cross-cultural validation, *Journal of Business Research*, 58(1), 79–88.

Chaffey, D. (2001) Optimising e-marketing performance – a review of approaches and tools. In *Proceedings of IBM Workshop on Business Intelligence and E-marketing*. Warwick, 6 December.

Chaffey, D. and Smith, P.R. (2008) *Emarketing Excellence. Planning and optimising your digital marketing*, 3rd edn, Butterworth-Heinemann, Oxford.

Chamberlin, G. (2010) Googling the Present, *Economic & Labour Review*, December 2010, Office for National Statistics.

Cheung, C.M.K., Chan G.W.W. and Limayem, M. (2005) A Critical Review of Online Consumer Behaviour: Empirical Research, *Journal of Electronic Commerce in Organizations*; 3(4), 1–19.

Choi, H. and Varian, H. (2009) Predicting the present with Google Trends, Google Inc, available at: **http://static.googleusercontent.com/external_content/untrusted_dlcp/www.google.com/en//googleblogs/pdfs/google_predicting_the_present.pdf.**

ComScore (2011) Press release: Europe sees 40 per cent growth in mobile banking through smartphones, 27 May.

Constantinides, E., Romero, C. and Boria, M. (2008) Social media: a new frontier for retailers? *European Retail Research*, 22, 1–28.

Dennis, C., Merrilees, B. Jayawardhena, C. and Wright, L.T. (2009) E-consumer behaviour, *European Journal of Marketing*, 43(9/10), 1121–39.

Doherty N.F and Ellis-Chadwick F.E (2010) Internet retailing: the past the present and the future, *International Journal of Retail & Distribution Management*, 38(11/12) 943–65.

Donthu, N. and Garcioa, A. (1999) The Internet Shopper, *Journal of Advertising Research*, 39(3), 316–33.

EConsultancy (2004) Online Retail 2004, benchmarking the user experience of UK retail sites. Report, July, London. Available online from **www.e-consultancy.com.**

Edgecliffe-Johnson, A. (2011) Kindle e-book sales soar for Amazon, **http://www.ft.com/cms/s/0/efb8670a-8240-11e0-961e-00144feabdc0.html**, 19 May.

Ettorre, B. (1996), 2002: what's the world coming to (how technological developments affect industries)? *Management Review*, 85(9), 33.

European Commission (2007) i2010 Annual Information Society Report 2007, published at: **http://ec.europa.eu/information_society/eeurope/i2010/index_en.htm.**

European Commission (2011) Digital Agenda Scoreboard, available at: **http://ec.europa.eu/information_society/digital-agenda/scoreboard/graphs/index_en.htm.**

George, J. (2004) The theory of planned behaviour and Internet purchasing, *Internet Research* 14(3), 198–211.

Ghosh, S. (1998) Making business sense of the Internet, *Harvard Business Review*, March–April, 126–35.

Google (2010) New GfK ROPO study with Vodafone. Published on Google Barometer Blog, 20 October: **http://googlebarometer.blogspot.com/2010/10/new-gfk-ropo-study-with-vodafone.html.**

Hoffman, D., Novak, T. and Schlosser, A. (2000) 'The evolution of the digital divide: how gaps in Internet access may impact electronic commerce, *Journal of computer-mediated Communications* 5(3), 000.

Hurt, C. (2007), Initial public offerings and the failed promise of disintermediation, *Entrepreneurial Business Law Journal* 2(2), 703–42.

Jobber, D. (2010) *Principles and Practices of Marketing*, McGraw-Hill, Maidenhead.

Keen, C., Wetzels, M., de Ruyter, K. and Feinberg, R. (2004) E-tailers versus retailers: which factors determine consumer preferences, *Journal of Business Research*, 57(7), 635–95.

Korgaonkar, P.K. and Wolin, L.D. (1999) A multivariate analysis of web usage, *Journal of Advertising Research*, 39(2), 53–68.

Kotler, P., Armstrong, G., Saunders, J. and Wong, V. (2001) *Principles of Marketing*, 3rd European edn., Financial Times/Prentice Hall, Harlow.

Lewis, H. and Lewis, R. (1997) Give your customers what they want, selling on the Net, *Executive Book Summaries*, 19(3), March.

Malmsten, E., Portanger, E. and Drazin, C. (2001) *Boo Hoo. A Dot.com Story from Concept to Catastrophe.* Random House, London.

Malone, T.W., Yates, J. and Benjamin, R.I. (1997) Electronic markets and electronic hierarchies, *Communications of the ACM*, 30(6), 484–97.

McDonald, M. and Wilson, H. (2002) *New Marketing: Transforming the Corporate Future.* Butterworth-Heinemann, Oxford.

Menteth, H., Arbuthnot, S. and Wilson, H. (2005) Multi-channel experience consistency: evidence from Lexus, *Interactive Marketing*, 6(4), 317–25.

M: Metrics (2011), **http://www.mmetrics.com/layout/set/popup/Press_Events/Press_Releases/2011/5/Europe_Sees_40_Percent_Growth_in_Mobile_Banking_Through_Smartphones**, accessed May 2011.

Moe, W. and Fader, P. (2004) Dynamic conversion behaviour at e-commerce sites, *Management Science*, 50(3), 326–35.

Morgan Stanley (2010) Mary Meeker: mobile Internet will soon overtake fixed Internet, Report published 12 April: **http://gigaom.com/2010/04/12/mary-meeker-mobile-internet-will-soon-overtake-fixed-internet/**.

New Media Age (1999) Will boo.com scare off the competition? by Budd Margolis, 22 July.

New Media Age (2005) Personal lender, by Dominic Dudley, 18 August.

Nunes, P., Kambil, A. and Wilson, D. (2000) The all in one market, *Harvard Business Review*, May–June, 2–3.

Porter, M. (1980) *Competitive Strategy.* Free Press, New York.

Porter, M. (2001) Strategy and the Internet, *Harvard Business Review*, March, 62–78.

Rayport, J. and Sviokla, J. (1996) Exploiting the virtual value-chain, *McKinsey Quarterly*, No. 1, 20–32.

The Retailer (2011) Market trends: Verdict Research's e-retail report, July/August, 28.

Riggins, F. and Mitra S. (2007) An evaluation framework for developing net-enabled business metrics through functionality interaction, *Journal of Organizational Computing and Electronic Commerce*, 17(2), 175–203.

Robinson, P., Faris, C. and Wind, Y. (1967) *Industrial Buying and Creative Marketing.* Allyn and Bacon, Boston.

Rodgers, S., Chen, Q., Wang, Y. Rettie, R. and Alpert, F. (2007) The Web Motivation Inventory, *International Journal of Advertising*, 26(4), 447–76.

Rosenbloom, B. (2002) The ten deadly myths of e-commerce, *Business Horizon*, 45, 1–6.

Sarkar, M., Butler, B. and Steinfield, C. (1996) Intermediaries and cybermediaries. A continuing role for mediating players in the electronic marketplace, *Journal of Computer Mediated Communication*, issue 1.

Seybold, P. and Marshak, R. (2011) *The Customer Revolution*, Crown Business, New York.

Shui, E. and Dawson, J. (2004) Comparing the Impacts of Technology and National Culture on Online Usage and Purchase from a four country Perspective, *Journal of Retailing and Consumer Services*, 11(6), 385–94.

Slyke, C.V. (2002) Gender differences in perceptions of web-based shopping, *Communications of the ACM*, 47, 82–6.

Styler, A. (2001) Understanding buyer behaviour in the 21st century, *Admap*, 23–6 September.

Swaminathan, V., Lepkowska-White, E. and Rao, B.P. (1999) Browsers or buyers in cyberspace? An investigation of factors influencing electronic exchange *Journal of Computer-Mediated Communication*, 5(2), 1–19.

Thomas, J. and Sullivan, U. (2005) Managing marketing communications with multichannel customers, *Journal of Marketing*, 69(October), 239–51.

Timmers, P. (1999) *Electronic Commerce Strategies and Models for Business-to-Business Trading*, Wiley, Chichester.

Venkatraman, N. (2000) Five steps to a dot-com strategy: how to find your footing on the web, *Sloan Management Review*, Spring, 15–28.

Watts, D. and Dodds, S. (2007) Influentials, networks, and public opinion formation, *Journal of Consumer Research*, 34(4), 441–58.

Wodtke, C. (2002) *Information Architecture: Blueprints of the Web*, New Riders, IN.

Wolfinbarger, M. and Gilly, M (2003) etailQ: dimensionalizing, measuring and predicting etail Quality, *Journal of Retailing*, 79(3), 183–98.

Wrigley, N. and Currah, A. (2006) Globalizing retail and the 'new e-conomy': the organizational challenge of e-commerce for the retail TNCs, *Geoforum*, 37, 340–51.

Further reading

Jobber, D. (2010) *Principles and Practice of Marketing*, 6th eds, McGraw Hill. *See* Chapter 18, Digital Marketing.

Porter, M. (2001) Strategy and the Internet, *Harvard Business Review*, March, 62–78. A retrospective assessment of how the Internet has changed Porter's model, first proposed in the 1980s.

Doherty, N.F., and Ellis-Chadwick, F. (2010), Internet retailing: the past, the present and the future, *International Journal of Retail & Distribution Management*, 38(11/12), 943–65.

Weblinks

A directory of Internet marketing links, including sources for statistics from the Internet environment, is maintained by Dave Chaffey at http://www.smartinsights.com.

Sources for Internet adoption statistics

Online research aggregators and publishers

- **ClickZ Internet research** (www.clickz.com/stats).
- **EConsultancy** (www.econsultancy.com). See their Internet statistics compendium. Fee-based service with some free data available.
- **eMarketer** (www.emarketer.com). Includes reports on media spend based on compilations of other analysts. Fee-based service with some free data available.
- **Internet World Stats** (www.internetworldstats.com). Compiles global statistics by region country from other sources on this list.
- **Marketing Charts** (www.marketingcharts.com). Has an online media section with visual summaries of reports mainly from the audience media panels.

Government sources on Internet use and adoption

- **European government** (http://europa.eu.int/comm/eurostat).
- **OECD** (www.oecd.org). OECD broadband research (http://www.oecd.org/sti/ict/broadband).
- **UK government** (wwww.statistics.gov.uk).
- **Ofcom** (www.ofcom.org.uk). Ofcom is the independent regulator and competition authority for the UK communications industries, with responsibilities across television, radio, telecommunications and wireless communications services and has in-depth reports on communications markets.
- **US government** (www.usa.gov) government business and general national statistics.

Online audience panel media consumption and use data

These are fee-based data, but contain useful free data within press release sections.

- **Comscore** (www.comscore.com).
- **ExperianHitwise** (www.hitwise.com). Hitwise blog (http://weblogs.hitwise.com). Sample reports from Hitwise on consumer search behaviour and importance of different online intermediaries. Netratings (www.netratings.com).

Other major online research providers

- **The European Interactive Advertising Association** (www.eiaa.net). The EIAA and IAB have merged to form a powerful pan-European trade organisation with surveys of media consumption.
- **The Pew Internet & American Life Project** (www.pewinternet.org), produces reports that explore the impact of the Internet on families, communities, work and home, daily life, education, healthcare, and civic and political life.

Chapter 3
The Internet macro-environment

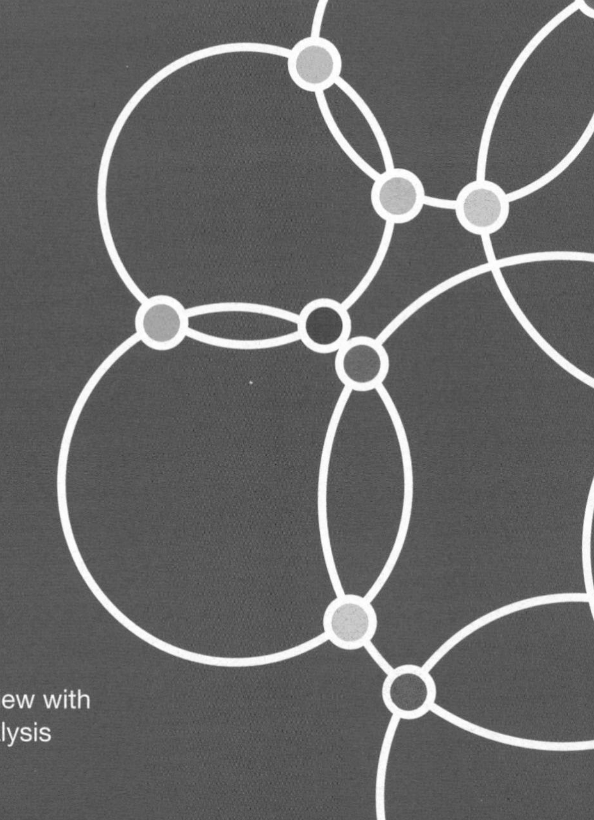

Chapter at a glance

Main topics

Case studies

Learning objectives

After reading this chapter, you should be able to:

- Identify how the macro-environment might affect an organisation's digital marketing strategy, planning, implementation and performance
- Consider legal, moral and ethical constraints of digital marketing
- Evaluate the wider significance of macro-environmental forces
- Identify aspects of each of the macro-environmental forces that are particularly relevant to digital marketing.

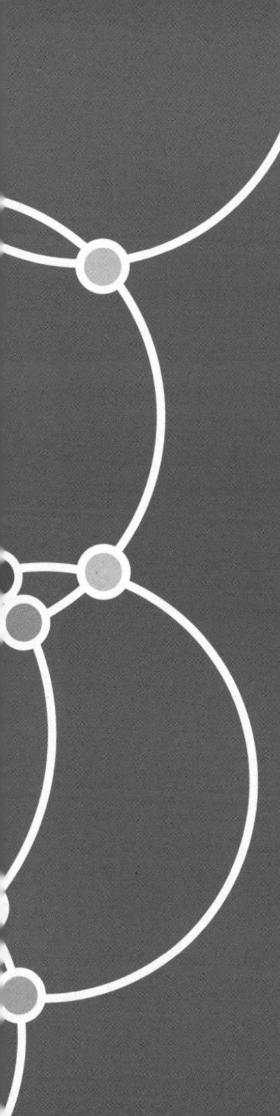

Questions for marketers

Key questions for marketing managers related to this chapter are:

- How important are macro-environmental changes to my digital marketing strategy?
- How can I ensure my online marketing activities are consistent with evolving culture and ethical standards of online communities?
- How important is it for me to understand technological innovations?
- Which laws am I subject to when marketing online?
- How is social media marketing likely to impact on my business and what changes do I need to make in order to react to social changes in the online market place?
- What are the political influences which could influence my digital marketing planning?
- How do I keep up in a constantly changing marketing environement?

Scan code to find the latest updates for topics in this chapter

Links to other chapters

This chapter provides a foundation for later chapters on digital marketing strategy and implementation:

- Chapter 4 looks at the development of a digital marketing strategy
- Chapter 5 considers the Internet and the marketing mix
- Chapter 6 explores relationship marketing using the Internet
- Chapter 7 looks at how to deliver the online customer experience
- Chapter 8 describes campaign planning for digital media

Introduction

In the previous chapter, we reviewed the influence of actors who shape the immediate trading environment. In this chapter, we review how macro-economic forces can influence digital marketing. These are forces which affect the trading environment but companies operating have limited direct influence over.

We explore the macro-environment forces focusing on the potential relevance of each to digital marketing strategy. In the marketing literature, there are widely used mnemonics, which aim to act as an *aide-memoire* for the macro-environmental forces, e.g. PEST, SLEPT, PESTLE, where each letter represents a slightly different arrangement of the following macro forces:

- Political forces
- Economic forces
- Social forces
- Technological forces
- Legal forces
- Environmental forces

Each variant of the mnemonic puts the macro-environmental forces in a slightly different order. For the digital marketer, the most important to task is to carry out a thorough assessment of the forces that are shaping the online marketing environment and identify which forces have implications for their own marketing planning and strategic initiatives. The chapter proceeds by exploring each of the macro-enviromnetal forces in the following order:

- *Technological forces* changes in technology which influence marketing opportunities; create new product development opportunities; introduce new ways to access target markets through channel integration; create new forms of access platforms and applications.
- *Economic forces* cause variation in economic conditions; affect trading opportunites; influence consumer spending and business performance; have significant implications for digital marketing planning.
- *Political forces* national governments and transnational organisations have an important role in determining the future adoption and control of the Internet and the rules by which it is governed.
- *Legal forces* determine the methods by which products can be promoted and sold online. Laws and ethical guidelines that seek to safeguard individuals' rights to privacy and business to free trade.
- *Social forces* cultural diversity among digital communities, which influences use of the Internet and the services businesses provided online.

The main reason for keeping track of changes in the macro-environment is to be aware of how changes in social behaviour, new laws and technological innovation can create opportunities or threats. Organisations that monitor and respond effectively to their macro-environment can create differentiation and competitive advantages which enable the business to survive and prosper. Given the significance of technology, we begin with this force as it is arguably a top priority for digital marketing planning.

Digital marketing in practice | The Smart Insights interview

Fred Bassett of Blue Latitude on online marketplace analysis

Overview and main concepts

This interview with Fred Bassett of digital strategy consulting strategy firm Blue Latitude outlines a structured approach to online marketplace analysis in order to inform digital marketing strategy.

The interview

Q. Fred, you say there is an increasing demand for e-marketplace analysis today. Why do you think this is, surely most companies already understand their marketplace?

Fred Bassett: The main driver is simply competitive pressure. Many companies have now optimised essential processes such as search marketing, e-mail marketing and site conversion. This has led to many online markets becoming highly competitive environments in which improving performance is increasingly challenging.

Marketplace analysis helps identify opportunities for growth from discovering gaps in the market that competitors aren't exploiting. In strategic terms, situation analysis helps identify gaps where customer segments aren't well served by existing propositions.

At a more tactical level we also identify quick wins in terms of online media allocation, PR and partnership opportunities – where media investments such as paid search or display ads could be better spent.

Q. What process do you follow in your environment analysis and mapping?

Fred Bassett: We have developed a five-stage situation analysis process. This starts with Business Insight analysis which aims to identify the current goals and the challenges of the business as highlighted by an Internet SWOT analysis. Next is User Insight, since our approach is centred on the customer, we spend a lot of time understanding different customer clusters. We use existing research and data, or perform new qualitative and quantitative research to define segments and personas for different customer groups.

Then we turn to Competitive Insight where we analyse purchase behaviour in the context of the journeys web users take as they as they select products or seek information online and offline. For example, what sequence of search terms do they use as they visit different sites, which types of sites do they visit and how does the whole customer journey map out. The competitive insight analysis also involves benchmarking of the propositions of different competitors and sites.

We use a proprietary predictive modelling tool to assess which are the most influential types of site which make an impact on purchase. This could involve analysis of tens of thousands of user journeys.

For each persona, we then create a probability model which indicates the influencing effect of each type of site. This is validated against data available from web analytics.

The final output is an environment mapping for each persona which summarises the influence of different sites such as portals, blogs, social media sites, search engines, etc. against their current and future potential value for the business in terms of opportunities for partnering, PR or media spend.

Q. Wow, that must require integration of many data sources. Which data sources typically inform the predictive model?

Fred Bassett: Well, it will vary a fair bit between sectors, but there are certainly many sources we leverage – over 20 in some cases.

Typical external data includes audience data from the likes of Hitwise and ComScore and keyword usage tools. This is blended with internal data such as historical search data, web analytics and purchase data. For customer insights within a sector we will also use analyst sources such as Forrester or Gartner.

One of the benefits of using data in this way is that we can work in and compare a brands' online activities in different territories. We have performed situation analyses in over 22 territories across Europe, Asia, North and South America.

Q. How is the output from the model used by businesses?

Fred Bassett: We find the environment map gives marketing directors the confidence to present a clear digital strategy based on evidence based insights. We use the environment map to help formulate a strategy with the client and then we map this strategy against different business objectives in areas of customer acquisition, conversion and retention.

Within each of these areas, tactics are developed which may cover a number of areas from targeting new audiences, refining customer propositions and content or developing long-term partnership arrangements.

The visual mapping we use makes it easier for others in the business to understand and buy-in to the approaches used.

Q. Which types of sectors have you applied this model?

Fred Bassett: The model scales well across different markets. We have used this approach on markets as varied as retail, pharmaceutical, not-for-profit and financial services.

The rate of environment change

Digital marketing insights 3.1 highlights the importance of understanding the trading environment and how it can affect the potential success of digital ventures. The lesson from this case for digital marketers is that understanding the macro-environment can help them to spotlight opportunities. Furthermore, to be effective businesses and individuals need to constantly scan the environment and assess which changes might have an effect on their trading environment.

Digital marketing insight 3.1 Monetise PLC

Mobile phones are changing the way we shop and access online services and *mobile money* could be a new method for making online payments.

According to the Office of National Statistics Survey (2011) 14 per cent more people accessed the Internet via their mobile phone than in 2010, bringing the total to around 45 per cent. Younger people (16–24 year olds) are mainly driving this growth as older Internet users are either happy with their computer-based connections or are not interested in getting online at all. In the UK, 23 per cent of households do not have an

Internet connection (ONS, 2011). But are they in danger of being left behind as banks, retailers and many consumers increasingly turn to mobile devices in almost every aspect of their daily lives?

According to Alistair Lukies, CEO and founder of Monitise PLC, a start-up company which now provides global mobile banking and payments, currently, there are three forms of mobilemoney:

1 *Mobile banking*. Allows you to access your bank account via your mobile phone, check statements, move money around between your accounts. Alistair says, 'mobile only accounts for a small proportion of digital banking at the moment, i.e. 3–5 per cent, but this percentage is growing all the time'.
2 *Mobile payments*. Paying your bills via your mobile, whether it is your credit card, gas or telephone bill. Interestingly, this service is growing slowly in developed countries where there are well-established banking infrastructures. However, these services are really taking off in emerging markets where there are less well developed banking infrastructures, e.g. in India and Brazil. Alistair says, 'Monitise PLC offers mobile money services that are fully interoperable and open source technology which means everyone can get access. He emphasises that this is really exciting for the less well-developed part of the world. In India, there are 220 million people with a bank account and 500 million that have a mobile phone but no bank account. The key reason for not having an account is the lack of a banking infrastructure so being able to transfer and make payments via a mobile phone and a local agent who provides a key code to facilitate the transaction across even the remotest parts of India has the potential to revolutionise millions of people's lives.
3 *Mobile commerce*. Shopping online in the UK has become very popular and increasingly our favourite retailers are sending us offers via mobile phones, which aim to encourage our spending. In the UK, M-commerce is growing quickly especially in the retail sector

Near Field Communications (NFC)
Enables data exchange through wireless connections between two devices in close proximity to each other. Use of NFC enabled smartphones can facilitate contactless payments.

A fourth category is contactless payments enabled through **Near Field Communications (NFC)**.

Some of the largest online businesses are looking to take advantage of this interest in mobile money. For example, Google launched its Google Wallet (Figure 3.1) in 2011 which uses a relatively new technology known as Near Field Communications (NFC). This offers the capability for sales promotions in combination with Google Offers that enables merchants to offer coupons redeemable via the Google Wallet. According to Smart Insights (2011b), contactless payments are predicted to reach $50 billion by 2014 although Barlclaycard announced in 2010 that only around 2 million contactless payments were transacted in 2010.

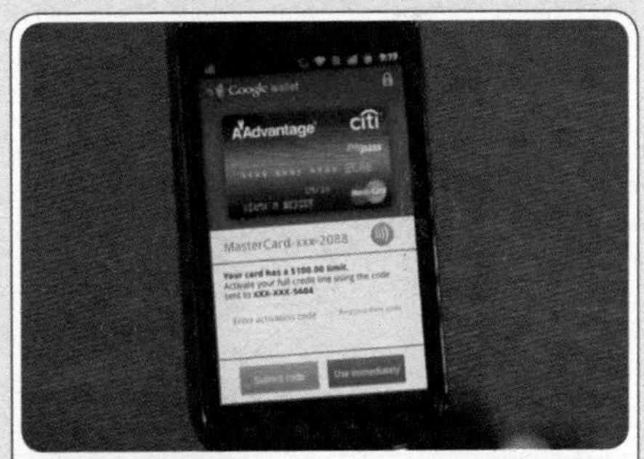

Figure 3.1 Google Wallet

Digital payment systems and currencies are nothing new – InternetCash.com developed prepaid cards (physical or electronic which the user could top-up with cash and which could be spent at participating retailers). InternetCash opted to build its own payment network and make money to sustain and grow the business from transaction fees and advertising revenue. The founders were optimistic that this was a robust alternative to credit payments online. Unfortunately the company ran out of money and by 2001 closed down. Beenz.com offered an alternative solution and e-currency which worked by shoppers earning *beenz* by visiting websites and shopping online. The beenz e-currency could then be spent with participating digital merchants. Beenz.com encountered many barriers, not least the legalities involved in launching a new currency (illegal in many countries). The company managed to operate in 12 countries, including the USA, Sweden, Italy and Singapore, but despite management changes and a buyout the company failed. Many other digital cash and e-currency solutions, e.g. flooz.com (a type of loyalty programme), bitcoin (peer-to-peer digital currency that enables low cost payments), have emerged since shopping and trading via the Internet has become popular. Most have either failed due to technological constraints, legal issues or the public's lack of confidence in the services offered. So does this mean Monitise Plc is likely to suffer the same fate or are we all going to use our mobile phones to manage our loose change?

What makes this *mobile money* system different from InternetCash and other e-currencies is arguably the trading environment. One billion mobile phone users around the globe have a mobile phone but not a bank account, which create a huge market for these new services. Moreover these users are familiar with the access technology (mobile phone) and can benefit significantly from having access to financial services. Mobile technology provides tremendous flexibility for both the users and the service providers. Encryption and security is more robust, so Monitise's *mobile money* can become more reliable. *Mobile money* uses existing global currencies to facilitate transactions thereby avoiding having to deal with legal issues. Early indications are that the trading environment, particularly the technology forces, are favourable for this form of digital payment to succeed. Monitise has identified an opportunity to become the world leader for mobile money, but they are not the only company to have spotted the opportunities for providing financial services to the underdeveloped world. Currently there are around 65 mobile money systems (GMSA, 2010) trying to get a share of the market.

Find out more about Monitise, and hear what Alistair Lukies, founder and CEO, has to say about how *mobile money* is changing the way we spend at: **http://www.monitisegroup.com/about_us.**

Sources: BBC News, Mobile Internet use nearing 50%: **http://www.bbc.co.uk/news/technology-14731757**; Mobile banking closes the poverty gap: **http://www.bbc.co.uk/news/10156667**.

In the digital world, changes in social culture and particularly pop culture (what's 'hot' and what's not) tend to be very rapid. Introduction of new technologies and changes in their popularity tend to occur frequently. Government and legal changes tend to happen over longer time scales. Therefore, digital marketers need to be alert to the forces that are important in the context of their own trading environment so they can aim to ensure the competitiveness of the business. They should also develop the capacity to respond to environmental changes and the emerging opportunities and threats by developing **strategic agility**, a concept strongly associated with knowledge management theory and based on developing a sound process for reviewing marketplace opportunities and threats and then selecting the appropriate strategy options.

Strategic agility
The capability to innovate and so gain competitive advantage within a marketplace by monitoring changes within an organisation's marketplace, and then efficiently evaluating alternative strategies, selecting, reviewing and implementing appropriate candidate strategies.

Strategic agility is important for digital marketers to understand and they should consider how to ensure:

1. collection, dissemination and evaluation of different information sources from the micro- and macro-environment
2. processes for generating and reviewing the relevance of new strategies based on creating new value for customers
3. research into potential customer value against the business value generated

4 implementation of prototypes of new functionality to deliver customer value
5 measurement and review of results from prototypes to revise further to improve proposition or to end a trial.

Technological forces

Marketers need to understand digital and Internet technology and terminology, as making mistakes can have significant consequences. In this section, we explore digital technology, the Internet and web technology; we will also consider digital security; technology convergence and emerging technology. These are key factors, which currently have significant implications for digital marketing planning. As an example of the impact of the opportunities afforded by technology, Activity 3.1 explores the options for delivering mobile services to customers, which is a current concern for marketers.

Activity 3.1 Environmental forces: Impact of the mobile web

Context

Many years have been heralded as 'The year of mobile' where adoption of the mobile web access and mobile commerce would grow rapidly. As long ago as 1999/2000 this was the case, yet if companies had invested in mobile facilities then, it's unlikely they would have seen a return from their investment. Today, use of mobile devices and smartphones is commonplace, so it's important for companies to consider how they can use these technologies within their marketing. This activity explores some of the possibilities based on your experience.

Activity

Identify a company with which you are familiar, either as a customer or an employee, or one that interests you. Make a list of how this company is currently using web technology, e.g. does the company have a mobile-optimised website? What type of services does it offer online?

Identify which of these services might be offered via a mobile phone, e.g. booking an appointment.

Finally, assess which of these technology options are most appropriate for this company by considering the costs in comparison with the benefits. What would be considered in the business case for the mobile technology?

Internet
The physical network that links computers across the globe. It consists of the infrastructure of network servers and communication links between them that are used to hold and transport the vast amount of information.

World Wide Web
The World Wide Web is a medium for publishing information and providing services on the Internet. It is accessed through *web browsers*, which display site *content* on different *web pages*. The content making up *websites* is stored on web servers.

Web server
Used to store the web pages accessed by web browsers. They may also contain databases of customer or product information, which can be queried and retrieved using a browser.

Web browser
Browsers such as Google Chrome, Mozilla Firefox, Apple Safari and Microsoft Internet Explorer provide an easy method of accessing and viewing information stored as HTML web documents on different web servers.

A short introduction to Internet technology

The **Internet** has existed since the late 1960s when a limited number of computers were connected for military and research purposes in the United States to form the ARPAnet.

The recent dramatic growth in the use of the Internet has occurred because of the development of the **World Wide Web.** This became a commercial proposition in 1993 after development of the original concept by Tim Berners-Lee, a British scientist working at CERN in Switzerland in 1989. Today, the main principles of web technology hold true. Web content is stored on **web server** computers and then accessed by users who run **web browser** software such as Microsoft Internet Explorer, Apple Safari or Mozilla Firefox which display the information and allow users to interact and select links to access other websites. Rich media, such

Streaming media server
A specialist server used to broadcast audio (e.g. podcasts) or video (e.g. IPTV or webcast presentations). Served streams can be unicast (a separate copy of stream is served for each recipient), multicast (recipients share streams) or peer-to-peer where the media is shared between different recipient's computers using a Bitorrent or Kontiki approach favoured by distributors of TV programmes such as the BBCs iPlayer.

Uniform (universal) resource locator (URL)
A web address used to locate a web page on a web server.

as Flash applications, audio or video content, can also be stored on a web server, or a specialist **streaming media server.**

Promoting website addresses is important to marketing communications. The technical name for web addresses is **uniform (universal) resource locator (URL)**. URLs can be thought of as a standard method of addressing, similar to postal codes, that make it straightforward to find the name of a site.

Web addresses are structured in a standard way as follows:

http://www.domain-name.extension/filename.html

The 'domain-name' refers to the name of the web server and is usually selected to be the same as the name of the company, and the extension will indicate its type. The 'extension' is also commonly known as the generic top-level domain (gTLD).

Common gTLDs are:

- **.com** represents an international or American company (e.g. www.travelocity.com)
- **.org** are not-for-profit organisations (e.g. www.greenpeace.org)
- **.mobi** was introduced in 2006 for sites configured for mobile phones
- **.net** is a network provider (e.g. www.amakai.net)

There are also country code top-level domains (ccTLDs) maintained by ICANN e.g.:

- **.co.uk** represents a company based in the UK (e.g. www.thomascook.co.uk)
- **.au, .ca, .de, .es,.fi, .fr, .it,.nl,** etc. represent other countries (the **co.uk** syntax is an anomaly!)
- **.ac.uk** is a UK-based university or other higher education institution (e.g. www.cranfield.ac.uk)
- **.org.uk** is for an organisation focusing on a single country (e.g. www.mencap.org.uk)

In 2011, Internet Corporation for Assigned Names and Numbers (ICANN), the not-for-profit organisation dedicated to registering, maintaining and coordinating the Internet addressing system began a programme of expansion for gTLD names. According to Beckstrom (2011), their aim is to give Internet users more choice and create business opportunities. Between 1998 and 2010, 22 gTLDs have come into general use but ICANN's expansion programme for new gTLDs will allow the introduction of many more domains. Corporate marketers, investors, local municipalities and non-governmental organisations are on the list of potential applicants expected to apply to register and manage their own top level domains. This move by ICANN is intended to change the Internet landscape and open up competition for domain registrations by creating hundreds of new gTLDs, but the use of country level domains names (ccTLDs) such as .au, .ca, .cn, co.uk, co.nz, .de, .fr and the universal .com for US and pureplay companies is likely to remain dominant since marketers perceive that consumers like the familiarity and trust of companies using these domains.

Domain names are part of a company's brand property and digital brand managers should protect brand abuse of domains by other companies who might register variants of competitors' brand domain names. In the early days of online commerce, high-profile cases spotlighted the importanceof protecting domain names and registering variant, e.g. Microsoft Corporation and .win95.com; harrods .co .uk. In both these case, the brands eventually regained control of their domains and created legal precedents for registering domain names. However, domain names do not only represent threats to business and organisations (see Digital marketing insights 3.2).

URL strategy

The 'filename.html' part of the web address refers to an individual web page, for example 'products.html' for a web page summarising a company's products. When a web address is typed in without a filename, for example www.bt.com, the browser automatically assumes the user is looking for the home page, which by convention is referred to as index.html. When

Digital marketing insight 3.2 — tv: economic boost from a ccTLD

Tuvalu is a group of tiny islands in the South Pacific where the 11,000 islanders rely on collecting rain for essential water supplies as there are no lakes and rivers to provide fresh water and few opportunities to generate income. Until recently, the Tuvulans' relied on foreign aid and eking out a living from selling dried coconut kernels, and issuing tuna fishing licenses. However, the islands were allocated the ccTLD of .tv and this has provided a windfall. In 2000, Tuvalu made an exclusive agreement with a Californian company dotTV allowing them to register tv domain names. In October 2000, .tv set a record of being the fastest growing top level domain by registering over 100,000 names in less than six months. This was a shrewd move by the islanders as the domain registrations generate income for the islands. Many of the .tv domains belong to television broadcasters. Royalties from the domain registrations generated more than 2 million dollars in 2006 and currently Tuvalu has over 109,478 making it 77th in the world in country Internet host rankings (CIA, 2011).

Source: Tuvalu country profile: **http://news.bbc.co.uk/1/hi/world/asia-pacific/country_profiles/1249549.stm**; Domain news: **http://www.domainlot.com/about/news.php**; World Factbook: **https://www.cia.gov/library/publications/the-world-factbook/geos/tv.html**.

URL strategy
A defined approach to forming URLs including the use of capitalisation, hyphenation and subdomains for different brands and different locations. This has implications for promoting a website offline through promotional or vanity URLs, search engine optimisation and findability.

A clean URL which fits many of these aims is **http://www.domain.com/folder-name/document-name**. Care must be taken with capitalisation since Linux servers parse capitals differently from lower-case letters.

creating sites, it is therefore vital to name the home page index.html (or an equivalent such as index.asp or index.php). The file index.html can also be placed in sub-directories to ease access to information. For example, to access a support page a customer would type **www.bt.com/support** rather than **www.bt.com/support/index.htm.** In offline communications sub-directories are publicised as part of a company's **URL strategy** (see Digital marketing insight 3.3).

Digital marketing insight 3.3 — What's in a URL?

A great example of different URL components is provided by Google engineer Matt Cutts (Cutts, 2007). He gives this example:

http://video.google.co.uk:80/videoplay?docid=-7246927612831078230&hl=en#00h02m30s

Here are some of the components of the url:

- The *protocol* is http. Other protocols include https, ftp, etc.
- The *host* or *hostname* is video.google.co.uk.
- The *subdomain* is video.
- The *domain name* is google.co.uk.
- The *top-level domain or TLD* is uk (also known as gTLD). The uk domain is also referred to as a country-code top-level domain or ccTLD. For google.com, the TLD would be com.
- The *second-level domain* (SLD) is co.uk.
- The *port* is 80, which is the default port for web servers (not usually used in URLs, when it is the default although all web servers broadcast on ports).
- The *path* is /videoplay. Path typically refers to a file or location on the web server, e.g. /directory/file.html.
- The URL parameter is docid and the value of that parameter is -7246927612831078230. These are often called the name, value pair. URLs often have lots of parameters. Parameters start with a question mark (?) and are separated with an ampersand (&).
- The *anchor* or fragment is '#00h02m30s'.

Client–server
The client–server architecture consists of client computers such as PCs sharing resources such as a database stored on a more powerful server computer.

Internet service provider
A provider enabling home or business users a connection to access the Internet. They can also host web-based applications.

Backbones
High-speed communications links used to enable Internet communications across a country and internationally.

How does the Internet work?

In this section, we briefly examine some of the fundamental aspects of Internet technology. It's important that marketers understand the technological underpinning of digital marketing. This enables them to discuss technology options with systems vendors and technical staff and take the right decisions about which technologies to adopt. Many digital marketers are active bloggers or engaged in social networks since this enables them to experience, first-hand, the latest developments and use tools to analyse what works and what doesn't.

The Internet is a large-scale **client–server** system where content is transmitted from client PCs whose users request services from server computers that hold content, rich media and host business applications that deliver the services in response to requests. Client PCs within homes and businesses are connected to the Internet via local **Internet service providers (ISPs)** which, in turn, are linked to larger ISPs with connection to the major national and international infrastructure or **backbones**.

Infrastructure components of the Internet

Static (fixed) web page
A page on the web server that is invariant.

Dynamic web page
A page that is created in real time, often with reference to a database query, in response to a user request.

Transaction log file
A web server file that records all page requests.

Web analytics
Techniques used to assess and improve the contribution of e-marketing to a business, including reviewing traffic volume, referrals, clickstreams, online reach data customer satisfaction surveys, leads and sales.

Figure 3.2 shows the basic process by which web browsers communicate with web servers. A request from the client PC is executed when the user types in a web address, clicks on a hyperlink or fills in an online form such as a search. This request is then sent to the ISP and routed across the Internet to the destination server. The server then returns the requested web page if it is a **static (fixed) web page**. If it requires reference to a database, such as a request for product information, it will pass the query on to a database server and will then return this to the customer as a **dynamic web page**. Information on all file requests such as images, rich media and pages is stored in a **transaction log file** or via a **web analytics** system such as Google Analytics (**www.google.com/analytics**) which records the page requested, the time it was made and the source of the enquiry as explained in Chapter 9.

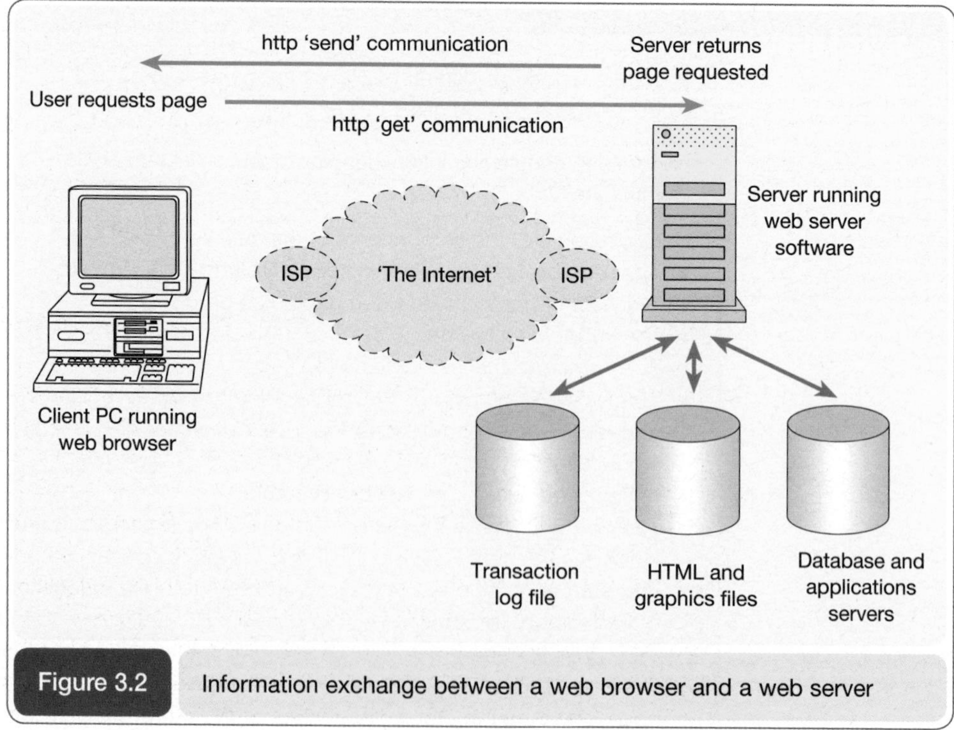

Figure 3.2 Information exchange between a web browser and a web server

Web page standards

The information, graphics and interactive elements that make up the web pages of a site are collectively referred to as **content**. Different standards exist for text, graphics and multimedia.

Digital marketing insight 3.4 W3C

The World Wide Web Consortium (W3C) community is enabling the web to expand and develop by building an Open Web Platform to support and foster innovations and future sustainability for the web. Founded by Tim Berners-Lee, the inventor of HTTP protocol, which underpins web technology, W3C is an organisation which works to maintain international standards for the web. W3C provides a forum for discussion on the development and growth of the web, facilitates software development and acts as an educational platform. W3C aims to ensure that protocols and standards are maintained between its members and organisations across the globe.

Source: **http://www.w3.org/2011/01/w3c2011.html**; and **http://en.wikipedia.org/wiki/World_Wide_Web_Consortium**.

Content
Content is the design, text and graphical information that forms a web page. Good content is the key to attracting customers to a website and retaining their interest or achieving repeat visits.

HTML (Hypertext Markup Language)
A standard format used to define the text and layout of web pages. HTML files usually have the extension .HTML or .HTM.

Cascading style sheets (CSS)
Enable web designers to define standard styles (e.g. fonts, spacing and colours) to hypertext mark-up language documents. By separating the presentation style of documents from the content of documents, CSS simplifies web authoring and site maintenance since style can be defined across a whole site (or sections of sites).

Text information – HTML (Hypertext Markup Language)

Web page content is formatted and rendered by the browser software using **HTML** (or XHTML) **Hypertext Markup Language.** HTML is an international standard established by the World Wide Web Consortium (published at **www.w3.org**) intended to ensure that any web page written according to the definitions in the standard will appear the same in any web browser.

A description of HTML markup is outside the scope of this book, see www.w3schools.com for tutorials. In brief, HTML code is used to construct pages using codes or instruction tags, such as <title>, to indicate to the web browser what is displayed. The <title> tag indicates what appears at the top of the web browser window. Each starting tag has a corresponding end tag, usually marked by a '/', for example <strong>bold text</strong> is used to embolden 'bold text'.

Cascading Style Sheets (CSS) are now used by most web sites to enable standard styling and interaction features across a site. Figure 7.10 show hows CSS effectively decouples style from content.

Text information and data – XML (eXtensible Markup Language)

When the early version of HTML was designed by Tim Berners-Lee at CERN, he based it on the existing standard for representation of documents. This standard was SGML, the Standard Generalised Markup Language, which was ratified by the ISO in 1986. SGML uses tags to identify the different elements of a document such as title and chapters. While HTML proved powerful in providing a standard method of displaying information that was easy to learn, it was purely presentational. It lacked the ability to describe the data on web pages. A **metadata** language providing data about data contained within pages is much more powerful and is provided by **XML** or **eXtensible Markup Language**, produced in February 1998. This is also based on SGML. The key word describing XML is 'extensible'. This means that new markup tags can be created that facilitate the searching and exchange of information. For example, product information on a web page could use the XML tags <NAME>, <DESCRIPTION>, <COLOUR> and <PRICE>. The tags can effectively act as a standard set of database field descriptions so that data can be exchanged through price comparison sites.

Metadata
Literally, data about data – a format describing the structure and content of data.

XML or eXtensible Markup Language
A standard for transferring structured data, unlike HTML which is purely presentational.

The importance of XML for data integration is indicated by its incorporation by Microsoft into its BizTalk server for B2B integration and the creation of the ebXML (electronic business XML) standard by their rival Sun Microsystems. We will see in Chapter 9 that the basic metadata that each page of a website can use is important for search engine optimisation (SEO). SEO is increasingly used by digital markets to ensue their websites get noticed by target audiences.

Graphical images (GIF, JPEG and PNG files)

GIF (Graphics Interchange Format)
A graphics format and compression algorithm best used for simple graphics.

JPEG (Joint Photographic Experts Group)
A graphics format and compression algorithm best used for photographs.

Graphics produced by graphic designers or captured using digital cameras can be readily incorporated into web pages as images. **GIF (Graphics Interchange Format)** and **JPEG (Joint Photographic Experts Group)** refer to two standard file formats most commonly used to present images on web pages. GIF files are limited to 256 colours and are best used for small, simple graphics, such as banner adverts, while JPEG is best used for larger images where image quality is important, such as photographs. Both formats use image compression technology to minimise the size of downloaded files. Portable Network Graphics (.PNG) is growing in popularity since it is a patent and licence-free standard file format approved by the World Wide Web Consortium to replace the GIF file format.

Animated graphical information (Flash and plug-ins)

Plug-in
An add-on program to a web browser providing extra functionality such as animation.

Plug-ins are additional programs, sometimes referred to as 'helper applications', and work in association with the web browser to provide features not present in the basic web browser. The best-known plug-ins are probably that for Adobe Acrobat which is used to display documents in .pdf format (**www.adobe.com**) and the Macromedia Flash and Shockwave products for producing interactive graphics (**www.macromedia.com**).

Audio and video standards

Traditionally, sound and video or 'rich media' have been stored as the Microsoft standards .WMA and .AVI. Alternative standards are RM3, MP3 MPEG. Film content and images are increasingly used as a means of creating engaging digital communications as explored in Activity 3.2.

Activity 3.2 Using video for digital marketing

Purpose

To consider the scope for using film for digital marketing initiatives.

Activity

Nitromedia is an innovative company, which aims to bring together film, sound and the web. Visit: **www.nitromedia.co.uk** (see Figure 3.3) and watch the film clip by Nitromedia a specialist film production company. Then answer the following questions.

1. How does Nigel Douglas suggest digital marketers might use film to enhance the performance of a website?
2. What are the wider implications of using film rather than text-based content in company website?

Figure 3.3 Nitromedia (www.nitromedia.co.uk)

Intranet
A network within a single company that enables access to company information using the familiar tools of the Internet such as e-mail and web browsers. Only staff within the company can access the intranet, which will be password-protected.

Extranet
Formed by extending the intranet beyond a company to customers, suppliers, collaborators or even competitors. This is again password-protected to prevent access by general Internet users.

From the Internet to intranets and extranets and beyond

Intranet and **extranet** are two terms that arose in the 1990s to describe applications of Internet technology with specific audiences, rather than anyone with access to the Internet. They are commonly used for marketing. Access to an intranet is limited by username and password to company staff, while an extranet can only be accessed by authorised third parties such as registered customers, suppliers and distributors. This relationship between the Internet, intranets and extranets is indicated by Figure 3.4. You can see that an intranet is effectively a private company internet with access available to staff only. An extranet permits access to trusted third parties, and the Internet provides global access.

Extranets such as Dell's Premier Pages provide exciting opportunities to communicate with major customers since tailored information such as special promotions, electronic catalogues and order histories can be provided on a web page personalised for each customer. Vlosky *et al.* (2000) examine in more detail how extranets impact business practices and relationships.

Web application frameworks
A standard programming framework based on reusable library functions for creating dynamic websites through a programming language.

Web application frameworks and application servers

Web application frameworks provide a foundation for building dynamic interactive websites and web services. They use standard programming conventions or Application Programming Interface (APIs) in combination with data storage to achieve different tasks such as simply adding a user to a system or rendering the different page elements of a

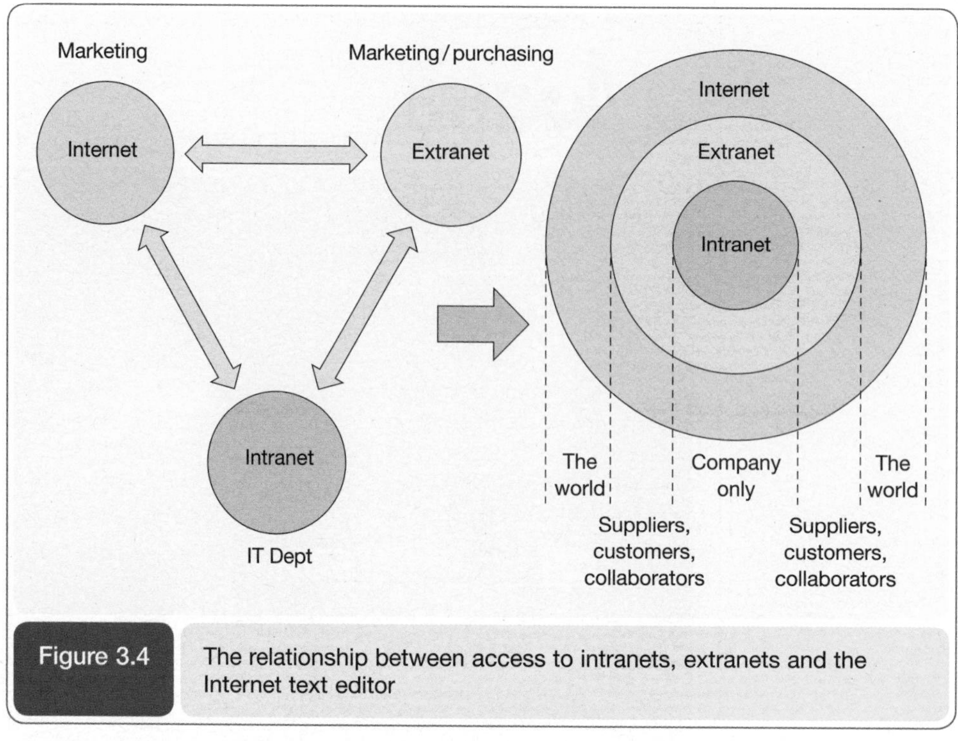

Figure 3.4 The relationship between access to intranets, extranets and the Internet text editor

site. They provide standard functions in libraries to make it quicker to develop functionality than starting from lower-level coding. Functions in the web application framework are executed by **web application servers** which are software processes running on the server which accept and action requests via the principal web server software (e.g. Apache or Microsoft Information Server). The Common Gateway Interface (CGI) was a forerunner of this concept since it enabled standard functions to be accessed on a server, for example to perform form validation.

Web application server Software processes which is accessed by a standard programming interface (API) of a web application framework to serve dynamic website functionality in response to requests received from browsers.

Examples:

- *Adobe ColdFusion* (**www.adobe.com/products/coldfusion/**) – an established commercial framework.
- *Microsoft ASP.Net* (**www.asp.net**) – an evolution of the former Micosoft ASP script-based approach to an entirely different approach based on running compiled code on a server.
- *PHP* (**www.php.net**) – an open-source script-based alternative for development of web applications which can be used to create web applications. Open-source CMS such as Drupal (**www.drupal.org**) are based on this.
- *JavaBeans Enterprise and Java Server Pages* – widely used enterprise open-source system promoted by Sun Microsystems which are implemented using the Java language (**www.java.com**). The ERP system SAP makes extensive use of this framework within its web application versions.
- *Zope* (**www.zope.org**) – an object-based open-source application server using the Python language on which the widely used Plone (**www.plone.org**) CMS is based.
- Ruby on Rails (**www.rubyonrails.org**) – another relatively new open-source application framework feted for its rapid production of systems and re-usability of modules as part of agile development.

Digital security

Security is a key technology factor to consider as it is a major concern for Internet users everywhere. Digital marketers needs to understand security issues and the risks they might encounter in order to manage their online operations effectively. Strictly speaking, security *per se* is a factor over which a company has control but it is the risks of trading and communicating online which are much less controllable and can present high levels of risk to a digital marketing initiative. This is part of the reason why we are discussing security in this chapter. From a consumer or merchant point of view, these are the main security risks involved in an e-commerce transaction:

- Confidential details or passwords accessed on user's computer, for example through keylogging software or malware.
- Transaction or credit card details stolen in transit, for example through 'packet sniffing' software.
- Customer's credit card details stolen from merchant's server, for example through hacking.
- Customer's details accessed by company staff (or through a hacker who is in the building and has used 'social engineering' techniques to find information).
- Merchants or customers are not who they claim to be and the innocent party can be drawn into a fraudulent trading situation.

As Internet derived commerce and communications play an increasingly important role in economic growth, the burden of ensuring secure and safe passage through the internet is increasing. According to Rueda-Sabater and Derosby (2011) there are five features of the Internet's evolution to consider which add to risks of what they call the *Axes of uncertainty*:

1 Growth in the global economy and in the markets around the Internet will occur primarily in countries that we now categorise as 'emerging'.
2 Governance of the Internet with its loose structure will be open to occasional Internet disruptions, including malicious ones.
3 Digital natives – people who have been raised on the Internet since late 1990 – will relate to the Internet in markedly different ways than do most of today's adults. Members of these web-savvy 'Net generations' will tend to view the Internet as an extender of their own cognitive capabilities and as a portal to a virtual experience.
4 Today's QWERTY keyboard and the language and interface hurdles it represents will no longer be the primary means of relating to the Internet. A combination of voice recognition, bio-sensing, gestural interfaces, touch-screen versatility and other technologies will allow us to input data and commands without keys. One major consequence of this change will be an explosion in the number of people who can use the Internet, as well as in the types of things they can do.
5 Consumers will pay for the Internet connectivity in a much wider range of ways, both direct and indirect, compared to today's predominant flat-price subscriptions. As high band-width applications explode, the need to allocate available network capacity efficiently across time and users will be a major issue. The spread of wireless connectivity will also open up many new pricing models for network access, such as easily bundling connectivity and services.

The potential increase in security risks reinforces the need for everyone, not just digital marketers to understand and be able to assess security risks. In this section we assess the measures that can be taken to reduce the risk of these breaches of e-commerce security. We start by reviewing some of the theory of online security and then review the techniques used.

For a summary of the main security risks for a website owner that must be managed within the design, see the summary in Digital marketing insight 3.4.

Digital marketing insight 3.5 The main website security risks

This summary is provided by specialist website security consultants Watson Hall (**www.watsonhall.com**). They consider the top ten Internet security risks to be:

1 Validation of input and output data

All data used by the website (from users, other servers, other websites and internal systems) must be validated for type (e.g. numeric, date, string), length (e.g. 200 characters maximum, or a positive integer), syntax (e.g. product codes begin with two letters and are followed by five digits) and business rules (e.g. televisions can only cost between £100 and £2000, an order can contain at most 20 items, daily credit limit must not be exceeded). All data written as output (displayed) needs to be safe to view in a browser, e-mail client or other software and the integrity of any data that is returned must be checked. Utilising Asynchronous JavaScript and XML (AJAX) or Adobe Flex increases complexity and the possible attack vectors.

2 Direct data access (and theft)

If data exists, they can potentially be viewed or extracted. Avoid storing data that you do not need on the website and its database(s), for example some data relating to payment cards should never be stored. Poorly developed systems may allow access to data through SQL injection compromises, insufficient input and output data validation (see point 1 above) or poor system security.

3 Data poisoning

If users can amend or delete data inappropriately and this is then used to update your internal systems, business information is being lost. This can be hard to detect and it is important that the business rules are examined and enforced to validate data changes to ensure that poisoning is not occurring. If poisoning is not detected until well after it has occurred, it may be impossible to recover the original data.

4 Malicious file execution

Uploaded files or other data feeds may not be what they seem. Never allow user-supplied input to be used in any file name or path (e.g. URLs or file system references). Uploaded files may also contain a malicious payload so should not be stored in web accessible locations.

5 Authentication and session management

Websites rely on identifying users to provide access permissions to data and functions. If authentication (verification of identity, registration and logging in), authorisation (granting access rights) and session management (keeping track of the identity of a logged in user while browsing a website) can be circumvented or altered, then a user could access resources that are prohibited. Beware especially of how password reminders, remember-me, change password, log out and updating account details are handled, how session tokens are used and always have login forms on dedicated and encrypted (SSL) pages.

6 System architecture and configuration

The information system architecture model should address the sensitivity of data identified during the requirements and specification phase of a website project. This may entail having separate web, application and database servers or involve clustering, load balancing or virtualisation. Additional security issues can be created through the way

Phishing
(Pronounced 'fishing') is a specialised form of online identity theft. The most common form of 'phishing' is where a spam e-mail is sent out purporting to be from an organisation such as a bank or payment service.

Denial of service attack
Also known as a distributed denial of service (DDOS) attack, these involve a hacker group taking control of many 'zombie' computers attached to the Internet whose security has been compromised. This '**botnet**' is then used to make many requests to a target server, so overloading it and preventing access to other visitors.

Botnet
Independent computers, connected to the Internet, are used together, typically for malicious purposes through controlling software. For example, they may be used to send out spam or for a denial of service attack where they repeatedly access a server to degrade its software. Computers are often initially infected through a virus when effective anti-virus measures are not in place.

the live environment is configured. Sufficient and safe logging, monitoring and alerting facilities need to be built in to allow audit.

7 Phishing

Phishing, where users are misled into believing some other entity is or belongs to an own organisation (e-mail messages and websites are the most common combination), is best tackled through user education, but the way the website is designed, its architecture and how it communicates with users can reduce the risk.

8 Denial of service

While malicious users might try to swamp the web server with a vast number of requests or actions that degrade its performance (filling up logs, uploading large files, undertaking tasks that require a lot of memory repeatedly), **denial of service attacks** include locking out valid user accounts or those caused by coding problems (e.g. memory leaks, resources not being released).

9 System information leakage

Web servers, errors, staff, partner organisations, search engines and rubbish can all be the source of important information about your website – its technologies, business logic and security methods. An attacker can use such information to their advantage so it is important to avoid system information leakage as far as possible.

10 Error handling

Exceptions such as user data validation messages, missing pages and server errors should be handled by the code so that a custom page is displayed that does not provide any system information to the user (see item 9 above). Logging and alerting of unusual conditions should be enabled and these should allow subsequent audit.

Activity 3.3 Security breaches

Purpose

To reflect on the significance of security risks to the digital trading environment.

Activity

Choose two of the top ten security risks listed above and find an example reported in the news, e.g. leading high street banks have been exposed to phishing attacks when spoof e-mails are sent inviting recipients to provide the banking details and security passwords, which will then allow the cyber-criminals to gain access to bank accounts.

Make a list of the threats the security risk posed to the business in your examples, e.g. loss of trade, disruption to services, business closure.

Finally, assess the severity and long-term impact of these incidents.

Approaches to developing secure systems

Faced with the growing likelihood of security risks there are various actions which might help reduce the risks.

Digital certificates

Digital certificates (keys)
Consist of keys made up of large numbers that are used to uniquely identify individuals.

Symmetric encryption
Both parties to a transaction use the same key to encode and decode messages.

Asymmetric encryption
Both parties use a related but different key to encode and decode messages.

There are two main methods of encryption using **digital certificates** or 'keys':

1 Secret-key or **symmetric encryption** involves both parties having an identical (shared) key known only to them. Only this key can be used to encrypt and decrypt messages. The secret key has to be passed from one party to the other before use, in much the same way that a copy of a secure attaché case key would have to be sent to a receiver of information. This approach has traditionally been used to achieve security between two separate parties, such as major companies conducting EDI. Here the private key is sent out electronically or by courier to ensure it is not copied.

   This method is not practical for general e-commerce since it would not be safe for a purchaser to give a secret key to a merchant because control of it would be lost and it could not then be used for other purposes. A merchant would also have to manage many customer keys.

2 Public-key or **asymmetric encryption**. Asymmetric encryption is so called since the keys used by the sender and receiver of information are different. The two keys are related by a numerical code, so only the *pair* of keys can be used in combination to encrypt and decrypt information. Figure 3.5 shows how public-key encryption works in an e-commerce context. A customer can place an order with a merchant by automatically looking up the public key of the merchant and then using this key to encrypt the message containing their order. The scrambled message is then sent across the Internet and on receipt is read using the merchant's private key. In this way only the merchant who has the only copy of the private key can read the order. In the reverse case the merchant could confirm the customer's identity by reading identity information such as a digital signature encrypted with the private key of the customer using their public key.

Digital signatures

Digital signature
A method of identifying individuals or companies using public-key encryption.

Digital signatures can be used to create commercial systems by using public-key encryption to achieve authentication: the merchant and purchaser can prove they are genuine. The purchaser's digital signature is encrypted before sending a message using their private key, and on receipt the public key of the purchaser is used to decrypt the digital signature. This proves the customer is genuine. Digital signatures are not widely used currently due to the difficulty of setting up transactions, but will become more widespread as the public-key infrastructure (PKI) stabilises and the use of certificate authorities increases.

The public-key infrastructure (PKI) and certificate authorities

For digital signatures and public-key encryption to be effective it is necessary to ensure the public key intended for decryption of a document actually belongs to the genuine person who you believe is sending you the document. A system of Trusted Third Party (TTP) certificates are used as a means of containing owner identification information and a copy of the public

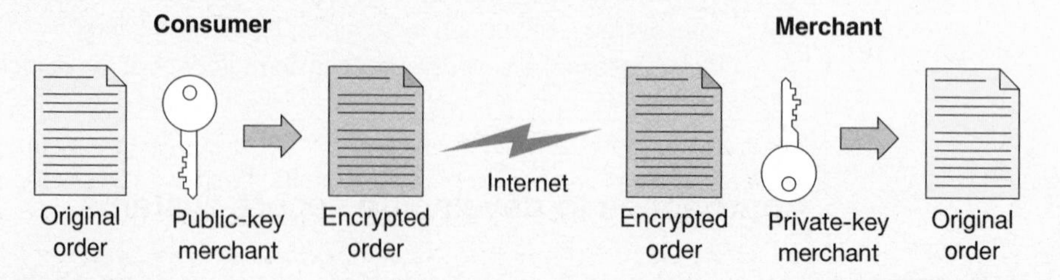

Consumer
Merchant
Original order
Public-key merchant
Encrypted order
Internet
Encrypted order
Private-key merchant
Original order

Figure 3.5 Public-key or asymmetric encryption

Certificate and certificate authorities
A certificate is a valid copy of a public key of an individual or organisation together with identification information. It is issued by a trusted third party (TTP) or certificate authority (CA). CAs make public keys available and also issue private keys.

key used to unlock the information. The TTPs are usually referred to as **certificate authorities (CAs)** – an example is VeriSign (**www.verisign.com**). The message is called a *certificate* and typically includes user and issuing authority identification data, users public key, date and class of certificate.

In addition to validating identification technology software solutions are also available to ensure the security of e-commerce transactions.

Secure Sockets Layer protocol (SSL)

SSL is the most common security mechanism used on transactional websites in association with CAs like VeriSign who issue an SSL certificate that verifies the identity of the certificate owner. The SSL approach enables encryption of sensitive information during online transactions using PKI and digital certificates to ensure privacy and authentication. SSL is more widely used than the rival S-HTTP method. Here, when encryption is occurring they will see that the web address prefix in the browser changes from 'http://' to 'https://' and a padlock appears at the bottom of the browser window.

Secure Electronic Transaction
A standard for public-key encryption intended to enable secure e-commerce transactions, lead-developed by Mastercard and Visa.

Secure Electronic Transaction (SET)

Secure Electronic Transaction (SET) is a security protocol based on digital certificates, originally developed by a consortium led by Mastercard and Visa, which allows parties to a transaction to confirm each other's identity. Due to complexity of implementation, SET is not widely used and SSL has become the *de facto* standard.

Digital marketing insight 3.6 Alternative payment systems: PayPal

Payment system
Method of transferring funds from a customer to a merchant.

Micropayment
Digital cash systems that allow very small sums of money to be transferred, but with lower security such small sums do not warrant credit card payment because processing is too costly.

One **payment system** that has succeeded is PayPal (**www.paypal.com**). PayPal enables individuals and business to transfer funds via the Internet. In 2002, PayPal became a wholly owned subsidiary of eBay and provides a major revenue stream since it is used for payment by many eBay users. Part of PayPal's success was that it offered an easy payment solution for individuals who did not have access to a credit card. Currently, PayPal operates more than 232 million accounts and enables financial transactions and **micropayments** between 24 different currencies worldwide and has revenue streams from transaction fees and merchant services.

PayPal protects its customers by using VeriSign identity protection and security keys and has recently enabled the use of mobile transactions numbers (MITAN) which allows financial transaction to be made using a mobile phone. PayPal is keen to ensure ongoing security of its services. Recently, Michael Barrett, the Chief Technical Officer has collaborated with Andy Steingruebl and Bill Smith on a White Paper on CyberCrime, which they all feel is on the increase. The paper explores the principles, policies and programmes for combating cyber crime. Read the full paper at: **https://www.paypal-media.com/assets/pdf/fact_sheet/PayPal_CombatingCybercrime_WP_0411_v4.pdf.**

Source: Paypal **http://en.wikipedia.org/wiki/PayPal#cite_note-paypal-media.com-29.**

Ultimately, digital marketers should ensure safe passage for its users. Once the security measures are in place, content on the merchant's site can be used to reassure the customer, for example Amazon (**www.amazon.com**) takes customer fears about security seriously judging by the prominence and amount of content it devotes to this issue. Some of the approaches used indicate good practice in allaying customers' fears. These include:

- use of customer guarantee to safeguard purchase
- clear explanation of SSL security measures used

- highlighting the rarity of fraud ('ten million customers have shopped safely without credit card fraud')
- the use of alternative ordering mechanisms such as phone or fax
- the prominence of information to allay fears – the guarantee is one of the main menu options.

Firewall
A specialised software application mounted on a server at the point where the company is connected to the Internet. Its purpose is to prevent unauthorised access into the company from outsiders.

Companies can also use independent third parties that set guidelines for online privacy and security. The best-known international bodies for privacy are TRUSTe (**www.truste.org**) and VeriSign for payment authentication (**www.verisign.com**). Macafee (**www.macafee.com**) and Avast (**www.avast.com**) are examples of commercial organisations which provide encryption, antivirus software, **firewalls** and a range of protection services. Avast provide maps showing infected domains around the globe at: **http://www.avast.com/en-gb/maps**.

Technology convergence

Technology convergence
A trend in which different hardware devices such as TVs, computers and phones merge and have similar functions.

Technology convergence is an important consideration for the digital marketer as consumers are increasingly using multiple platforms to access digital services. Mobile phone and tablet computer technology is rapidly developing and facilitating access to thousands of different online services, which go beyond texting and making phone calls. New services include accessing and reading daily newspapers, music playing system, e-mail reading platform, camera, personal organiser, live satellite navigation, Internet access and global positioning system (GPS). Individuals, are keen to make use of these new services and Apple has introduced the Appstore where tens of thousands of different apps are available. Due to rapid advances and development in technology, digital marketers should be able to assess emerging technologies and applications, especially those which have implications for how users interact with the Internet. The implications of users having access to digital marketing offers via mobile and wireless devices is a key point to consider.

Activity 3.4 Flexible internet access

Purpose

To consider how and why you access the Internet and reflect on how free are you when it comes to accessing the Internet?

Activity

Answer the following questions:

1. How many hours a week do you spend accessing the Internet?
2. Where do you access the Internet most frequently, e.g. from a fixed computer, wireless access or via a mobile device?
3. What are your main reasons for accessing the Internet, e.g. socialising, shopping, work related, booking travel, finding locations?

SMS messaging

Short Message Service (SMS)
The formal name for text messaging.

In addition to offering voice calls and data transfer, mobile phones have increasingly been used for e-mail and the **Short Message Service (SMS)**, commonly known as 'texting'. SMS is, of course, a simple form of e-mail that enables messages to be transferred between mobile phones.

Texting is increasingly popular as a means of communicating with customers. High street banks notify customers of current account balances, when they approach an overdraft limit, retailers send delivery notifications and airlines send boarding and flight details using SMS. Text is also used by consumer brands to market their products and texting can also be used in supply chain management applications for notifying managers of problems or deliveries.

Digital marketing insight 3.7 SMS Text and picture messaging

Text.it (**www.text.it**) is the Mobile Phones Association's website and provides news, information and data on mobile phone use. The number of texts sent on a daily basis is increasing annually, as is the growth in picture messaging. In the UK, over 11 million text messages are sent in an hour. Currently seasonal events appear to drive picture messaging.

Christmas Day 2009	Increase on 2008	New Year's Eve/ Day 2009/2010	Increase on 2008
441,805,870	31 %	874,033,799	21 %

Source: **http://www.text.it/mediacentre/press_release_list.cfm?thePublicationID=749C769E-15C5-F4C0-99E6A252A5A98607**.

However, the generation of touch screen handsets, social media and innovative phone tariff packages that reduce the cost of sending images are driving the use of texting and making it more accessible to many more users. This is creating opportunities for marketers to interact directly with their target audiences. Fast food chains regularly use text messaging to entice their target customers to enjoy the chains latest offers. McDonald's uses text and iPhone applications to promote their latest breakfast menu offers, and Starbucks run time-limited offers using Quick response codes to tempt their customers. For the digital marketer the opportunities are seemingly limitless when it comes to finding innovative ways to engage the end consumer.

SMS applications

For the creative marketer who respects opt-in and privacy legislation, SMS has proved a great way to get closer to customers, particularly those in the youth market who are difficult to reach with other media. These are some of the applications showcased on Text.it (**www.text.it**):

1 *Database building/direct response to ads/direct mail or on-pack.* This is one of the most significant applications.
2 *Location-based services.* Text for the nearest pub, club, shop or taxi. In London you can now text for the nearest available taxi, and pay the congestion charge through texting, once accounts are set up via the web!
3 *Sampling/trial.* Use for encouraging consumers to trial new products through promotions.
4 *Sales promotions.* Timed e-coupons can be sent out to encourage footfall in real and virtual stores.
5 *Rewarding with offers for brand engagement.* Valuable content on mobiles can be offered via SMS, for example free ringtones, wallpaper, Java games or credits can be offered to consumers via text.

Short code
Five-digit number combined with text that can be used by advertisers or broadcasters to encourage consumers to register their interest. They are typically followed-up by an automated text message from the advertiser with the option to opt-in to further information by e-mail or to link through to a WAP site.

Mobile apps
A software application that is designed for use on a mobile phone, typically downloaded from an App store. iPhone apps are best known, but all smartphones support the use of apps which can provide users with information, entertainment or location-based services such as mapping.

6 *Short codes.* **Short codes** are easy-to-remember five-digit numbers combined with text that can be used by advertisers or broadcasters to encourage consumers to register their interest.
7 *Offering paid-for WAP services and content.* Any service such as a ringtone delivered by WAP can be invoked from a text message.

Mobile apps

Mobile apps are a highly significant development in mobile communications, indeed all digital communications, since they highlight a change in the method of delivering interactive services and content via mobile phones. Until the advent of apps, popularised by Apple iPhone, the web browser had been seen as the main model by most for delivering content via mobile phones.

For this author, the growth in popularity of apps for the iPhone has been incredible, with Apple announcing in January 2010 that 3 billion apps had been downloaded in the 18 months following the launch of the AppStore. iPhoneDev (2010) compiled a summary of the growth based on official figures from the Apple App Store and showed these characteristics of Apps from the App Store in June 2010:

- number of apps downloaded per month = 500M
- number of iOS users = 100 Million
- average number of apps downloaded by an iOS user = 5 per month
- of which paid apps are 25 per cent, i.e. 1.25 apps
- average spend by an iOS user = 1.25*$1.25 = $1.5 per month
- total paid apps sales amount = $1.5*100 million = $150 million

These figures show the potential benefits of apps to marketers in reaching audiences and in selling apps, although the latter will be generally limited to publishers or specialist software developers. It's also worth remembering that other handsets use other operating systems which in total are nearly as popular as the iPhone in terms of apps downloaded. The most significant of these include Android OS from Google, Symbian OS from Nokia and Blackberry. So app producers also have to decide whether to support these. For example, Tesco launched a Nokia Grocery App (**http://www.tesco.com/apps/**) in advance of its iPhone app to reach the substantial audience of non iPhone App users.

Through reviewing the types of apps which have proved popular, businesses can assess the potential for them to develop applications for their audiences.

The key questions to ask are:

1 *Are apps a strategic priority for us?* The goal of apps for most organisations will be to increase awareness and sales, or for publishers revenue from advertising or subscriptions. For many companies, this won't be a priority because they will have to put budget into higher priority areas such as improving the experience on site or in their social network presence. Owing to volume of users reached through these other platforms incremental improvements here are likely to give better returns. But the figures presented above show the potential benefits of apps to marketers in reaching audiences and potentially in selling apps, although the latter will be generally limited to publishers or specialist software developers. For these types of organisations, apps are likely to be a priority.
2 *Do we build our own app and/or leverage existing apps?* Creating an app is only one of the marketing options – advertising and sponsorship options may be a more cost-effective method to build reach and awareness of a brand. A good example of sponsorship fit is the Canon Sponsorship of the excellent Guardian Eyewitness photography app. There are also options of new iAds from Apple and Google AdSense mobile display networks.
3 *Free or paid apps?* Retailers will generally offer free apps offering choice and convenience in return for loyalty. Brands offering entertainment will likely also go the free route to increase

customer engagement. But for publishers or software houses, a freemium approach of free app showcasing the service and paid app for improved features or content is the standard approach.

4 *Which category of application to target?* As you would expect, accessing social networks and music via apps is popular, but for most organisations, you can see from the chart below that Games and Entertainment are the main options.

5 *How to best promote mobile apps?* The options for marketing apps were also research by Nielsen who found that the most popular methods of app discovery are:

- searching the app store
- recommendations from friends and family
- mention on device or network carrier page
- e-mail promotion
- offline mention in TV and print.

6 *How to refine apps in line with feedback.* The success of apps is very dependent on feedback in the App stores and the need to fix bugs and add enhancements to compete shows the need for an ongoing development cycle with frequent updates. A whole new area of app analytics and new solutions will no doubt develop but a challenge with apps similar to that of Flash apps before them is that measurement functionality needs to be specified in advance. Careful review of hurdle rates for % user base who are using the app or its different function is going to be a KPI here.

Social location-based marketing
Where social media tools give users the option of sharing their location, and hence give businesses the opportunity to use proximity or location-based marketing to deliver targeted offers and messages to consumers and collect data about their preferences and behaviour. Businesses can offer consumers benefits to check-in, for example, to gain points, be the most regular visitor to that location, to gain rewards and prizes from advertisers, to share their location with friends, and, in the case of events, to meet like-minded people. Of course the privacy implications of this relatively new technology must be carefully reviewed.

Social location-based marketing through mobile

In **social location-based marketing** there is a fusion of social and mobile marketing. Foursquare, Gowalla, Facebook Places and Twitter Locations are all options available to consumers. There's also Google Latitude which has an API which can be used to ask users for access to update their Latitude location or view their current location if they have enabled their location history in Google.

Mini Case Study 3.1 Location-based marketing

If you're thinking that location-based marketing is just for corporates with large budgets, the likes of Starbucks and McDonalds, then think again. ClickZ (2010) has reported how AJ Bombers, a speciality burger bar in Milwaukee attributed a sale increase of 110 Percent to Foursquare. It has 1400 people on its Foursquare page who have checked in 6000 times. The mayor gets a free burger, and currently that's 'Amy' – who has had to check-in 40 times in the last 60 days at the one-location establishment in order to achieve the distinction.

Engagement is also increased through people who add a tip to the restaurant's Foursquare page getting rewarded with a free cookie when they show it to a waiter or cashier.

The sales increase figure is based on a single campaign which saw 161 check-ins on Feb. 28 – a 110 percent sales increase when compared to a normal Sunday. Joe Sorge, owner of the restaurant, promoted an AJ Bombers-branded 'Swarm Badge' event to his Foursquare-using regulars. Such a custom badge is awarded to users who check in at a location where at least 50 other users are simultaneously checked in.

The restaurant owner advised that success involves implementing Foursquare as a regular part of operations:

Our staff encourages the use and engagement of Foursquare by virtue of our Foursquare specials being very prominent throughout our business. It encourages our customers to ask questions of our staff. Education of that staff is the key.

QR Codes

Quick Response code
A-two-dimensional matrix bar code. QR codes were invented in Japan where they are a popular type of two-dimensional code used for direct response.

Quick Response (QR) codes are barcodes published in newspapers or billboards which can be scanned by a mobile phone camera and then linked directly through to a website. Figure 3.6 shows an example. They give exciting opportunities for integrating customer journeys. QR codes can be used in promotional initiatives to allow target consumers to have quick access to a variety of information e.g., instant access to email addresses; phone number or business card.

Figure 3.6 QR Codes

Wi-Fi (wireless fidelity)
A high-speed wireless local-area network enabling wireless access to the Internet for mobile, office and home users.

Wi-Fi

Wi-Fi (wireless fidelity) is the shorthand often used to describe a high-speed wireless local area network. Wi-Fi can be deployed in an office or home environment where it removes the need for cabling and adds flexibility. However, it has attracted most attention for its potential for offering wireless access in airports, shopping centres, cities and towns without the need for a fixed connection.

Bluetooth technology
A wireless standard for transmission of data between devices over short ranges (less than 10m).

Proximity marketing
Marketing messages are delivered in real-time according to customers' presence based on the technology they are carrying, wearing or have embedded. Bluecasting is the best known example.

Bluetooth wireless applications

Bluetooth technology has potential for different forms of local marketing campaigns known as **proximity marketing**: (1) viral communication; (2) community activities (dating or gaming events); (3) location-based services – electronic coupons as you pass a store.

Activity 3.5 Assessing new technology options

Purpose

To illustrate the process for reviewing the relevance of new technology options.

Activity

You work for an FMCG (fast-moving consumer goods) brand and are attending an industry trade show where you see a presentation about the next-generation (3G) mobile phones which are due to launch in your country in one year's time. You need to decide whether your organisation adopts the new phone and if so when. Complete the following:

1 How would you assess the significance of this new technology?
2 Summarise the proposition of the new access devices for both consumers and your organisation.
3 What recommendations would you make about when to adopt and which services to offer?

Emerging technologies

In addition to mobile and wi-fi access, Internet access technologies to television and radio is available digitally. Internet TV, or IPTV, is increasingly popular and as bandwidth, download speeds and access devices improve, the number and range of users is increasing. This technology creates challenges for the digital marketer as they need to access which technology their target audience is using to access which type of content, information and or digital services.

Nielsen (2010) found that on average each home in the USA owns more than two televisions; 66 per cent of the population has access to the internet through broadband and or cable and there are over 228 million mobile phone users over the age of 13. Additionally, usage of mobile phones has been changing and while voice calls usage remains static SMS messaging is increasing significantly.

Activity 3.6 Using the *right* technology

Purpose

To consider how audience vary for different technologies.

Activity

Imagine you are planning a series of digital marketing campaigns. Using the information provided from Nielsen (2010) for the following products and audiences suggest which media you would recommend:

1 Discount vouchers for a pizza from an international fast-food retailer to a target audience of 14–18-year-olds?
2 Latest version of a tablet computer to target audience of men over the age of 30?
3 Health foods supplements for a target audience of women and men between 60 and 75?

Assessing the marketing value of technology innovation

One of the challenges for digital marketers is how to successfully assess which new technological innovations can be applied to give competitive advantage. For example, personalisation technology (Chapter 6) is intended to enhance the customer's online experience and increase their loyalty. However, personalisation may require a large investment in proprietary software and hardware technology for effective implementation. How does the manager decide whether to proceed and which technological solutions to adopt? There is more to digital marketing than establishing and managing a website, and in Chapter 4, strategy decisions are examined while in Chapter 8 how to make decisions to achieve the best media mix is considered.

A manager may have read articles in the trade and general press or spoken to colleagues which have highlighted the potential of a new technology-enabled marketing technique. They then face a difficult decision as to whether to:

- ignore the use of the technique completely, perhaps because it is felt to be too expensive or untried, or because they simply don't believe the benefits will outweigh the costs
- ignore the technique for now, but keep an eye on the results of other companies that are starting to use it

- evaluate the technique in a structured manner and then make a decision whether to adopt it according to the evaluation
- enthusiastically adopt the technique without a detailed evaluation since the hype alone convinces the manager that the technique should be adopted.

Depending on the attitude of the manager, this behaviour can be summarised as:

1 Cautious, a 'wait and see' approach.
2 Intermediate, sometimes referred to as 'fast-follower' approach. Let others take the majority of the risk, but if they are proving successful then rapidly adopt the technique, i.e. copy them.
3 Risk-taking, an early-adopter approach.

Early adopters
Companies or departments that invest in new technologies and techniques.

Different behaviours by different adopters will result in different numbers of adopters through time. This diffusion–adoption process (represented by the bell curve in Figure 3.7) was identified by Rogers (1983) who classified those trialling new products as being innovators, **early adopters**, early majority, late majority, through to the laggards.

The diffusion–adoption curve can be used in two main ways as an analytical tool to help managers:

1 to understand the stage at which customers are in adoption of a technology, or any product. For example, the Internet is now a well-established tool and in many developed countries we are into the late majority phase of adoption with large numbers of users of services. This suggests it is essential to use this medium for marketing purposes. But if we look at WAP technology (see below) it can be seen that we are in the innovator phase, so investment now may be wasted since it is not clear how many will adopt the product.
2 to look at adoption of a new technique by other businesses – from an organisational perspective. For example, an online supermarket could look at how many other e-tailers have adopted personalisation to evaluate whether it is worthwhile adopting the technique.

Hype cycle
A graphic representation of the maturity, adoption and business application of specific technologies.

A commercial application of the diffusion of innovation curve was developed by technology analyst Gartner (2011) and has been applied to different technologies since 1995. They describe a **hype cycle** as a graphic representation of the maturity, adoption and business application of specific technologies.

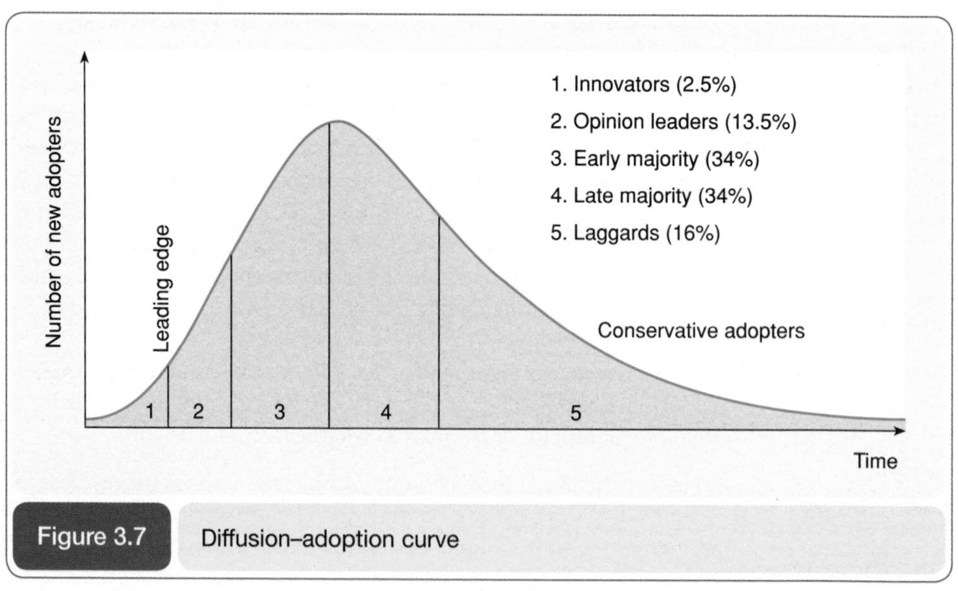

Figure 3.7 Diffusion–adoption curve

Gartner (2011) recognises the following stages within the hype cycle (Figure 3.8):

1 *Technology trigger.* The first phase of a hype cycle is the 'technology trigger' or breakthrough, product launch or other event that generates significant press and interest.
2 *Peak of inflated expectations.* In the next phase, a frenzy of publicity typically generates over-enthusiasm and unrealistic expectations. There may be some successful applications of a technology, but there are typically more failures.
3 *Trough of disillusionment.* Technologies enter the 'trough of disillusionment' because they fail to meet expectations and quickly become unfashionable. Consequently, the press usually abandons the topic and the technology.
4 *Slope of enlightenment.* Although the press may have stopped covering the technology, some businesses continue through the 'slope of enlightenment' and experiment to understand the benefits and practical application of the technology.
5 *Plateau of productivity.* A technology reaches the 'plateau of productivity' as the benefits of it become widely demonstrated and accepted. The technology becomes increasingly stable and evolves in second and third generations. The final height of the plateau varies according to whether the technology is broadly applicable or benefits only a niche market.

The problem with being an early adopter (as an organisation) is that being at the leading edge of using new technologies is often also referred to as the 'bleeding edge' due to the risk

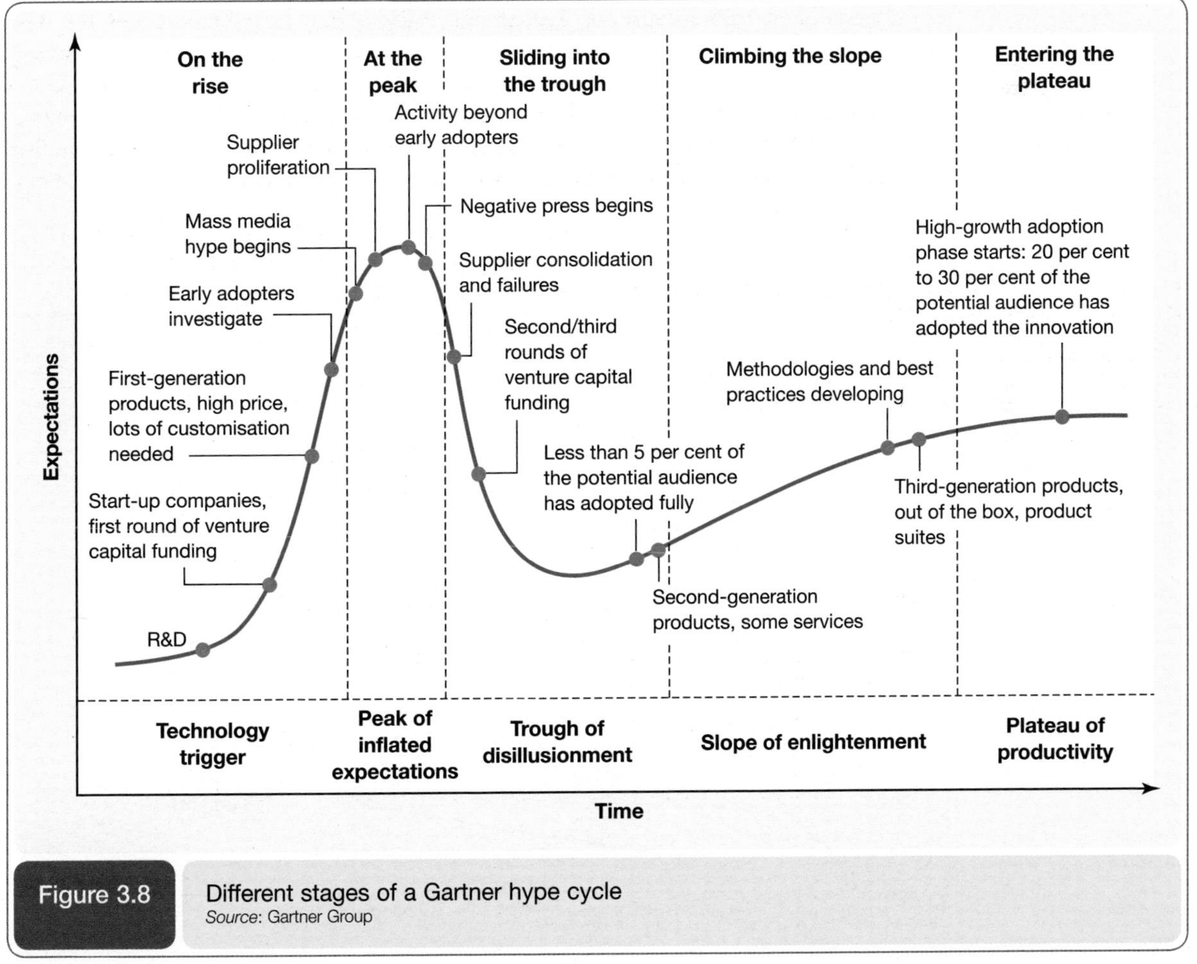

Figure 3.8 Different stages of a Gartner hype cycle
Source: Gartner Group

of failure. New technologies will have bugs, may integrate poorly with the existing systems or the marketing benefits may simply not live up to their promise. Of course, the reason for risk taking is that the rewards are high – if you are using a technique that your competitors are not, then you will gain an edge on your rivals. For example, RS Components (**www.rswww.com**) was one of the first UK suppliers of industrial components to adopt personalisation as part of their e-commerce system. They have learned the strengths and weaknesses of the product and now know how to position it to appeal to customers. It offers facilities such as customised pages, access to previous order history and the facility to place repeat orders or modified re-buys. This has enabled them to build up a base of customers who are familiar with using the RS Components online services and are then less likely to swap to rival services in the future.

It may also be useful to identify how rapidly a new concept is being adopted. When a product or service is adopted rapidly this is known as *rapid diffusion*. The access to the Internet is an example of this. In developed countries the use of the Internet has become widespread more rapidly than the use of TV, for example. It seems that interactive digital TV and Internet-enabled mobile phones are relatively slow-diffusion products! Activity 3.1 (page 126) considers this issue further.

So, what action should e-commerce managers take when confronted by new techniques and technologies? There is no straightforward rule of thumb, other than that a balanced approach must be taken. It would be easy to dismiss many new techniques as fads, or classify them as 'not relevant to my market'. However, competitors are likely to be reviewing new techniques and incorporating some, so a careful review of new techniques is required. This indicates that benchmarking of 'best of breed' sites within a sector and in different sectors is essential as part of environmental scanning. However, by waiting for others to innovate and review the results on their website, a company has probably already lost 6 to 12 months. Figure 3.9 summarises the choices. The stepped curve I shows the variations in technology through time. Some changes may be small incremental ones such as a new operating system; others, such as the introduction of personalisation technology, are more significant in delivering value to customers and so improving business performance. Line A is a company that is using innovative business techniques, adopts technology early, or is even in advance of what the technology can currently deliver. Line C shows the conservative adopter whose use of technology lags behind the available potential. Line B, the middle ground, is probably the ideal situation where a company monitors new ideas as early adopters, trials them and then adopts those that will positively impact the business.

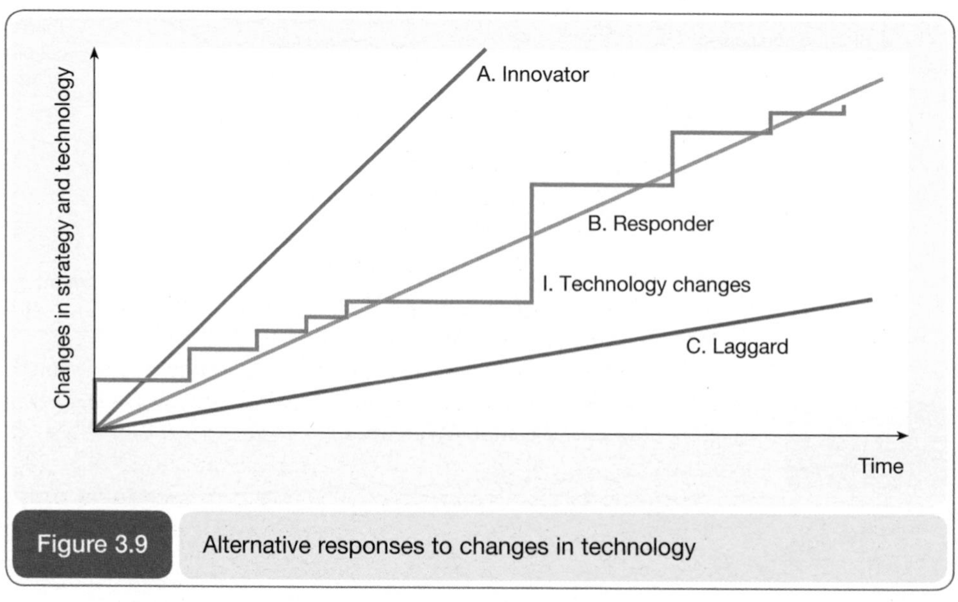

Figure 3.9 Alternative responses to changes in technology

Technological forces are significant and can influence digital marketing success significantly. In this section we have considered major factors which make up the forces likely to affect the digital marketer. In the next section, we examine economic forces.

Economic forces

Globally economic influences affect the level of success of business. Economic forces affect supply and demand and consequently it is important for digital markets to identify which economic influences they need to monitor. Classic economic factors e.g., growth and unemployment, interest and exchange rates can affect every aspect of business activity and are equally pertinent to off and online businesses. International market growth and emerging economies, for example central and eastern European markets and the BRIC economies, also have the potential to influence digital marketing activities. In this section we explore the implications of the classic economic factors, market growth and emerging markets for digital marketers.

Market growth and employment

According to Varley (2001), 'Modern societies are organised around consumption and so the trends in patterns of consumption that emerge over time are very important for marketers to observe and understand.'

The impact of changes in demand can have far-reaching implications for digital marketing initiatives as this will affect the strength of market growth so it is important to anticipate demand. Sophisticated technology enables companies to analyse purchasing patterns and forecast future demand. But this is only part of the picture of consumption that drives modern global economies. It is also important to monitor changes to trends (which affect market growth) in order to be able to make realistic predictions about how consumers and companies are going to behave in the future.

The changing nature of a population's age profile, changes to working life and changing lifestyles are beyond the control of the digital marketer but such changes are relatively slow-moving so as long as these trends are identified they can be accommodated in long-term strategic plans.

Demographics is the study of populations, which uses measurable variables to monitor and analyse population trends. Demographic variables include:

- age profiles
- birth rates
- education levels
- gender
- household structures
- lifestage (e.g. single, married, divorced)
- total income and expenditure
- working patterns and occupations.

In developed economies, populations are living longer and the age profile of a consumer market can be very important for the digital marketer's business.

Nevertheless, Tim Berners-Lee (inventor of the web) had a vision that everyone everywhere should be able to access the web; the reality is that there is significant variation in the ability of the users based on their age profile. W3C (2008) suggests that web developers and marketers should not stereotype older adults as technophobes, In fact Fox (2004) goes as far as stating: 'Wired seniors are often as enthusiastic as younger users in the major activities which define online life such as email and the use of search engines to answer specific questions.' However, whilst enthusiasm for using the web may be similar across age groups, what the users are doing online and how they do it varies. According to Fox (2004), older users are more likely to use the web for product research, to make travel reservations and visit government websites than their younger counterparts. Furthermore, there are age-related functional limitations, e.g. visual decline, hearing loss, motor skills diminishment and cognitive effects which have implications for web design (W3C, 2008). This means developers and marketers should pay careful attention to the level of interaction, the information architecture and organisation and visual design (Chapter 7).

Employment and working patterns

An emerging economic trend relating to employment is that there are more women working across Europe. According to the Office of National statistics (ONS, 2010), in the UK:

> Over the past four decades, the proportion of women in employment has grown markedly. At the start of 1971, the employment rate for women was 56 per cent compared with 70 per cent in the three months to December 2008. This increase compares with a similar-sized decrease in the employment rate for men over the same period, with the male employment rate falling from 92 per cent to 78 per cent.

Furthermore, the types of work individuals are engaged in is changing from traditional manufacturing to the service sector industries. Work in the service sector can involve part-time, flexible working hours and be lighter than that of traditional manufacturing industries. The trend towards more women working in both part-time and full-time occupations has implications for digital marketing planning.

Activity 3.7 Employment patterns and e-mail marketing campaigns

Purpose

To reflect on the potential impact of working patterns for the timing of e-mail marketing campaigns.

Activity

According to research (Ellis-Chadwick and Doherty, 2011), frequency and timing of sending e-mail marketing messages is critically important when seeking to grab the attention of the receiver of the email message.

For the following target groups discuss the best time (in terms of specific hours and days) to send e-mail marketing messages:

1. Shift-worker working in the health industry whose shift patterns alternate on a weekly basis from 10 pm to 8 am (week 1) and 8 am to 4 pm (week 2).
2. Administrative assistant who starts work at 8.30 am and finishes at 5 pm Monday to Thursday.
3. Senior Manager for a motor dealership who works flexible hours Monday to Friday, all day Saturday and occasionally on a Sunday.

Other economic factors from the macro-environment that influence consumer spending are changes in the rate of taxation, e.g. income tax and VAT and or interest rates.

Income and expenditure

The majority of consumers in developed societies in Europe and the USA have seen an increase in the level of personal *disposable* income during the last 50 years. This means spending *proportionally* less on the essentials of life such as housing and food, and being in a position to spend more on discretionary purchases such as fashion goods, household appliances, eating out, holidays and entertainment. Companies selling consumer goods have benefited by encouraging consumers to trade-up in their essential purchases (remember how Tesco has benefited from selling its premium priced ranges during the 2008–2009 recession) and by making discretionary purchases appear to be essential (e.g. flat-screen colour televisions).

International market growth and emerging economies

Globalisation
The increase of international trading and shared social and cultural values.

Globalisation refers to the move towards international trading in a single global marketplace and the blurring of social and cultural differences between countries. In Chapter 2 we saw that there is wide variation in the level of use of the Internet in different continents and countries, particularly from the consumer perspective. Furthermore, according to Doherty *et al.* (2003), a major driver of Internet adoption by commercial organisations is the opportunity for market expansion in domestic and international markets. However, digital marketers need to be aware of the implications of trading in global markets and consider whether to develop bespoke, branding and marketing campaigns or whether to apply a standardised approach. These issues are considered in more detail in Chapter 5.

Economic disruption

Throughout history there have been periods of strong economic growth followed by economic downturn and recession. The dot-com period of boom and bust at the beginning of the 21st century highlighted the fragility of high-tech markets and many of the emerging Internet companies, which had high value stock market valuations, crashed and no longer exist. However, from such disruption has emerged an online economy which is fuelling growth. According to Gorell (2011) there are lessons leading innovators can learn, which can help them to steer their businesses through economic turbulence and take advantage of emerging markets. Gorell's observations are that in order to be able to manage in periods of economic change business leaders should focus on developing the ability to:

1 anticipate and act on market uncertainty and unmet customer needs by applying a focused business model
2 focus on innovations and how they can deliver value to the company's business model
3 expect opportunities to emerge from uncertainty and develop strategies which can maximise any emerging market advantage (Gorell, 2011).

The world's best performing companies are adept at spotting opportunities in times of economic disruption but according to Gorell (2011): 'By adoption of their best practices, almost any company can learn to out-compete their rivals by creating new products, finding white-space markets and imagining new business models even in the toughest of times.' However, in order to achieve success companies should:

- focus on improving opportunities and innovations, which already exist within the business
- be selective about which innovations are likely to bring early gains and carefully manage company resources – innovations which require limited resources can be very useful in challenging economic times
- get everyone in the company involved in working towards a common goal.

These ideas pose challenges for digital marketers; on the one hand the advice suggests economic restraint and engaging in low cost initiative but on the other hand it suggests developing high growth innovations. According to Inder Sidh (vice president of worldwide strategy and planning, Cisco Systems Inc) it is possible to do both and this approach is followed throughout the organisation by looking at 'every opportunity not as a choice between apparent conflicting goals but rather a way of obtaining a multiplier effect by seeking and meeting two apparently conflicting goals' (Davidson, 2011). Now complete Activity 3.8.

Activity 3.8 Time-value economics: competing for customer attention

Purpose

To explore the importance of time to online consumers.

Activity

Read the following section discussing time-value economics and then answer the following questions.

According to Ott (2011) consumers spend on average 28 minutes each day researching and buying goods and services (in all contexts real world and online), and what makes this figure even more interesting is that the amount of time has remained fairly constant since the 1960s. However, the number of products, marketing messages and platforms over which consumers receive marketing messages has increased significantly during the last 50 years. The result is that it is increasingly difficult to attract a shopper's attention with marketing messages online or offline. Ott (2011) suggests that 'rather than fighting against the barriers of time and attention, why not use them to build advantage?' He advocates that companies should move away from targeting consumers using demographic and psychographic variables and instead 'view customers through a time-value economics perspective'. The benefit of this approach is gaining better insight into how consumers think and act. There are two concepts which are central to Ott's theory: 1) the time-value trade-off which helps us to understand how consumers act and think; 2) the Time-ographics framework, which marketers can use to design their offering.

1 *The time-value trade off* – the basic premise is that as we shop we are constantly evaluating what we buy and how many different items we buy based on the time it takes to make the purchase weighted against the value of each item and its price. This appears to be an elegant solution that can help marketers to design more effective communication campaigns. But there is an additional layer of complexity. We all value time differently depending on what we are doing, e.g. *hours spent playing with the kids are considered 'well spent', but time used standing in line at the post office is 'wasted'*. Furthermore, our attention varies as well and it has been discovered that nearly half our time each day is spent on *repetitive and unthinking activities*. This is where Ott's time-ographics framework comes into play.
2 *The Time-ographics framework*. The time-ographics matrix consists of four quadrants and encompasses a customer's propensity to spend time engaged in purchasing and their willingness to be attentive towards the product (or service in question).

The time–magnet quadrant indicates that consumers are willing to devote time and attention to making the purchase. According to Ott (2011): 'Google is reportedly teaming up with Zynga for the imminent launch of Google Games, which aims to capture some of the online social and fun time that people spend on sites like Facebook. Google is betting that customers will spend more of their time and attention on these activities and try to provide the company with opportunities to monetize the relationship.'

Time-on-autopilot quadrant – here the consumers carry out routine behaviour and are almost immune to marketing messages that are the focus. Supermarkets rely on routine and habitual purchasing behaviour for the sale of many of their products. The challenge for other marketers is to tap into this quadrant by identifying and then reinforcing product relevant habitual behaviour, e.g. how often do you check your e-mail via your smartphone?

The time-saver quadrant – these consumers are careful with their attention as their primary focus is likely to be saving time. To engage with these customers, marketers are looking for time saving propositions which are attractive to this target group, e.g.

Garde Robe (**http://www.garderobeonline.com/garderobepage/sortingpage.php**) is a luxury wardrobe storage and valeting service, which can have your garments delivered to your door ready to wear in less than 2 hours.

The time-minimised quadrant – products and services in this quadrant tend to have standardised features or require limited information processing.

The proposition is that *time* and *attention* are at a premium and as a result the time consumers spend considering product and service offers are severely restricted so digital marketers should reflect on how to develop new ways to maximise the opportunities in the time-value economy.

Questions

1 To get a feel for the distractions which interrupt our attention try to make a list of the technology driven distractions you might encounter on a typical shopping trip to a local department store e.g., mobile phone advertisements.
2 Then visit the web site of either your chosen store or one selling similar product ranges. Make a note of the number and type of distractions you encounter when visiting the store online.
3 Compare your experiences and the number of distractions you have identified and then reflect upon into which quadrants the shopping experience fits.

In Chapter 4 strategic implications and planning issues are explored further.

This section has identified key economic factors and considered their potential impact for digital marketers and the online trading environment. There are close links between economic factors such as interest rates and inflation on political influences. Some of the issues raised will be returned to later in this chapter. In the next section we explore social forces and how online communities are changing.

Political forces

The political environment is shaped by the interplay of government agencies, public opinion and consumer pressure groups (e.g. Mediawatch-UK) and industry-backed organisations such as TRUSTe (**www.truste.org**). Interaction between these organisations helps to create a trading environment with established regulations. The political environment has many factors which influence the trading environment, such as taxation, investment and management of business and public affairs. Political forces are closely intertwined with economic forces, e.g. the government sets financial goals for the Bank of England, which in turn sets interest rates to control inflation. The government's influence over the economy has an impact on overall economic performance and also business investment (see Digital marketing insight 3.8).

Digital marketing insight 3.8 Investment in high-speed broadband

According to eGov monitor (2011) the Government has unveiled a £530 million investment plan, which aims to improve high-speed broadband access in rural areas throughout the UK. They state that 'Wales, Northern Ireland and some other parts were already allocated around £150 million and the DMCS announced £362 million would be invested in 40 areas in England as well as some parts in Scotland.'

The target for the investment is British households, which do not have internet access and also to improve the minimum speed of access so that '90 per sent of homes have access speeds over 24Mbps' (eGov monitor, 2011).

Chief Secretary to the Treasury Danny Alexander, speaking at the Liberal Democrat conference in September 2011, said that the government feels business development and economic recovery (from the 2008–10 economic recession) is being held back by poor-quality infrastructure. Indeed he is quoted as saying: 'Too many business are being held back by congested roads, slow railways and inadequate broadband' (*Telegraph*, 2011). As a result, the government is focusing attention on scaling up its plans for high-speed broadband provision across the UK and the overarching aim is for Britain to have the best broadband infrastructure in Europe.

It is important for digital marketers to beware that political action enacted through government agencies to control the adoption of the Internet includes:

- promoting the benefits of adopting the Internet for consumers and business to improve a country's economic prosperity
- sponsoring research leading to dissemination of best practice among companies, for example the DTI international benchmarking survey
- enacting legislation to regulate the environment, for example to protect privacy or control taxation
- involvement in setting up international bodies to coordinate the Internet such as ICANN (the Internet Corporation for Assigned Names and Numbers, **www.icann.com**) which has introduced new domains such as .biz and .info.

e-government
The use of Internet technologies to provide government services to citizens.

The type of initiative launched by government is highlighted by the launch in the UK in September 1999 of a new 'UK online' campaign, a raft of initiatives and investment aimed at moving people, business and government itself online (**e-government**). E-envoy posts and an e-minister have also been appointed. The prime minister said in 1999:

> There is a revolution going on in our economy. A fundamental change, not a dot.com fad, but a real transformation towards a knowledge economy. So, today, I am announcing a new campaign. Its goal is to get the UK online. To meet the three stretching targets we have set: for Britain to be the best place in the world for e-commerce, with universal access to the Internet and all government services on the net. In short, the UK online campaign aims to get business, people and government online.

The government continued to invest in developing their online proposition and by 2005 billions of pounds had been invested in getting public services online. The 2000 strategy was designed to build a smarter and more efficient public service infrastructure. However, the government faces challenging issues: how to identify citizens online; sharing of information between departments; how to establish 'online' as the main channel of communication for all UK citizens.

A central plank of the e-government regulatory strategy is the Digital Economy Act. However, the Act has been at the centre of a controversy, led by telecoms companies BT and Talk Talk who were appealing to the high court that the Act contravened European law on commerce and privacy (BBC, 2011). The heart of the problem is illegal downloading of copyrighted material, e.g. music and film, and prior to the introduction of the Act content producers argued for legislation to control this type of Internet piracy. The Act requires Internet service providers to make provision for policing this type of action. However, opponents of the Act are unhappy that it can sanction individual computer users and favour the demands of large corporations. One group that is very happy about the recent ruling that the Act is in line with European law is the British Pornographic Institute, and Geoff Taylor, Chief

Executive, feels this is a positive move that 'gives the green light for action to tackle illegal downloading in the UK' (BBC, 2011).

Political control and democracy

Government action that can have a significant impact on the online marketplace is control of intermediaries. This depends on the amount of regulation in a given country and in individual markets. Taking the UK as example, regulation of different marketplaces occurs through these groups:

- *Financial Services Authority* – controls providers of banking products such as current accounts, savings and loans.
- *Ofgem* – controls provision of energy such as electricity and gas.
- *Ofcom* – controls providers of mobile phone and broadband services.

In the financial services market, it is not necessary for a price comparison intermediary to show all providers, so, for example, one major insurance provider, Direct Line, has decided not to be included. However, in the energy industry it is required that all providers are to be included due to the industry regulators, although links between the intermediary and the suppliers do not.

However, government intervention can extend beyond such control and raise questions about democracy and freedom. Visit and watch the following two films:

1 The enemy of the state – what China fears, at: **http://www.bbc.co.uk/virtualrevolution/3dexplorer_start.shtml.**
2 Ross Anderson discussing how governments such as in China are going about controlling the web: **http://www.bbc.co.uk/blogs/digitalrevolution/2009/11/rushes-sequences-ross-anderson.shtml.**

These films raise many questions about the role of government and democracy online. Now try Activity 3.9.

Activity 3.9 Is Digital democracy a fallacy?

Purpose

To consider the contribution of the web and the extent to which it is a force for democratisation.

Activity

Watch *The Great Levelling*?, a documentary produced by the BBC and Open University to explore how the Internet and the web impacts on the world, democracy and global populations.

Now reflect on the extent to which Internet megabrands are exercising their power, and the extent to which these brands are giving the world's population equal access to information.

Internet governance

Internet governance
Control of the operation and use of the Internet.

Internet governance describes the control put in place to manage the growth of the Internet and its usage. Governance is traditionally undertaken by government, but the global nature of the Internet makes it less practical for a government to control online.

Taxation

How to change tax laws to reflect the globalisation through the Internet is a problem that many governments are grappling with. The fear is that the Internet may cause significant reductions in tax revenues to national or local governments if existing laws do not cover changes in purchasing patterns. In Europe, the use of online betting in lower-tax areas such as Gibraltar has resulted in lower revenues to governments in the countries where consumers would have formerly paid gaming tax to the government via a betting shop. Large UK bookmakers such as William Hill and Victor Chandler are offering Internet-based betting from 'offshore' locations such as Gibraltar. The lower duties in these countries offer the companies the opportunity to make betting significantly cheaper than if they were operating under a higher-tax regime. This trend has been dubbed LOCI or Location Optimised Commerce on the Internet by Mougayer (1998). Meanwhile, the government of the country from which a person places the bet will face a drop in its tax revenues. In the UK the government has sought to reduce the revenue shortfall by reducing the differential between UK and overseas costs.

According to Omar *et al.* (2009):

> The tax-free status of most items purchased online has resulted in significant loss of tax revenues to state and local government. Our research indicated that the loss of taxes amounting to $13.3 billion in 2001 will rise to $62.1 billion by 2011, unless taxation policies are changed. Changing the tax laws governing online trading is problematic. One significant aspect concerns the one who collects the revenues: should the taxes on items purchased online be collected by the state and local government, as is now done in traditional brick-and-mortar trades, or should this be done by a concerted, standardised federal effort?

Since the Internet supports the global marketplace it could be argued that it makes little sense to introduce tariffs on goods and services delivered over the Internet. Such instruments would, in any case, be impossible to apply to products delivered electronically. This position is currently that of the USA. In the document 'A Framework for Global Electronic Commerce', former President Clinton stated that:

> The United States will advocate in the World Trade Organisation (WTO) and other appropriate international fora that the Internet be declared a tariff-free zone.

Tax jurisdiction

Tax jurisdiction determines which country gets the tax income from a transaction. Under the current system of international tax treaties, the right to tax is divided between the country where the enterprise that receives the income is resident ('residence' country) and that from which the enterprise derives that income ('source' country). Laws on taxation are rapidly evolving and vary dramatically between countries. A proposed EU directive intends to deal with these issues by defining the place of establishment of a merchant as where they pursue an economic activity from a fixed physical location. At the time of writing, the general principle that is being applied is that tax rules are similar to those for a conventional mail-order sale; for the UK, the tax principles are as follows:

- **a** if the supplier (residence) and the customer (source) are both in the UK, VAT will be chargeable
- **b** exports to private customers in the EU will attract either UK VAT or local VAT
- **c** exports outside the EU will be zero-rated (but tax may be levied on import)
- **d** imports into the UK from the EU or beyond will attract local VAT, or UK import tax when received through customs
- **e** services attract VAT according to where the supplier is located. This is different from products and causes anomalies if online services are created. For example, a betting service located in Gibraltar enables UK customers to gamble at a lower tax rate than with the same company in the UK.

This section has explored some factors that contribute to the economic forces which can affect digital marketing initiatives. The next section considers legal forces.

Legal forces

Laws develop in order to provide a framework of control and regulations that aim to enable individuals and businesses to go about their business in a legal and ethical manner. However, laws are open to interpretation and there are many legal and ethical considerations in the online trading environments. Many laws aim to prevent unethical marketing practice, so marketers have to understand and work within this regulatory framework. This section considers six of the most important legal issues for digital marketers (see Table 3.1).

Table 3.1 Significant laws which control digital marketing

Legal issue	Digital marketing activities affected
1 Data protection and privacy law	• Collection, storage, usage and deletion of personal information directly through data capture on forms and indirectly through tracking behaviour through web analytics • E-mail marketing and SMS mobile marketing • Use of viral marketing to encourage transmission of marketing messages between consumers • Use of cookies and other techniques for personalising content and tracking on site • Use of cookies for tracking between sites, for example for advertising networks • Use of digital assets installed on a user's PC for marketing purposes, e.g. toolbars or other downloadable utilties sometimes referred to as 'malware'
2 Disability and discrimination law	• Accessibility of content such as images for the visually impaired within different digital environments: – website – e-mail marketing – mobile marketing – IPTV • Accessibility affecting other forms of disability including hearing difficulties and motor impairment
3 Brand and trademark protection	• Use of trademarks and brand names within: – domain names – content on site (for search engine optimisation) – paid search advertising campaigns (e.g. Google AdWords) • Representation of a brand on third-party sites including partners, publishers and social networks • Defamation of employees
4 Intellectual property rights	• Protection of digital assets such as text content, images, audio and sounds through digital rights management (DRM)
5 Contract law	• Validity of electronic contracts relevant to: – cancellations – returns – errors in pricing • Distance selling law • International taxation issues where the e-commerce service provider is under a different tax regime to the purchaser
6 Online advertising law	• Similar issues to traditional media: – representation of offer – causing offence (e.g. viral marketing)

Legal activities can be considered unethical

Ethical standards
Practices and behaviours which are morally acceptable to society.

Digital marketers should be compliant with the law and adhere to **ethical standards** but since the rate of technological innovation is rapid and consequently the law is often unclear. In this case, marketers need to tread carefully since unethical action can result in serious damage to the reputation of a company and negative sentiment can result in a reduction in online audience or sales.

1 Data protection and privacy law

Privacy
A moral right of individuals to avoid intrusion into their personal affairs.

Identity theft
The misappropriation of the identity of another person, without their knowledge or consent.

Privacy refers to a moral right of individuals to avoid intrusion into their personal affairs by third parties. Privacy of personal data, such as our identities, likes and dislikes, is a major concern to consumers, particularly with the dramatic increase in **identity theft**.

Digital marketers can better understand their customers' needs by using this type of very valuable information. Through collecting personal information it becomes possible to develop highly targeted communications and develop products that are more consistent with users' needs. Therefore how should marketers respond to this dilemma? An obvious step is to ensure that marketing activities are consistent with the latest data protection and privacy laws. Although compliance with the laws may sound straightforward, in practice different interpretations of the law are possible and since these are new laws they have not been tested in court. As a result, companies have to make their own business decisions based on the business benefits of applying particular marketing practices against the financial and reputational risks of less strict compliance (see Activity 3.10).

Activity 3.9 Security, censorship on the web

Purpose

To consider the right to privacy and freedom of information argument.

Activity

Visit: The Virtual Revolution and hear what John Perry has to say about the freedom of information: **www.bbc.co.uk/blogs/digitalrevolution/2009/10/rushes-sequences-john-perry-ba.shtml.**

Now reflect on whether you agree with John's views on the freedom of information and then suggest what implications his views have for digital marketing.

Effective e-commerce requires establishing a balance between the benefits the individual customer will gain to their online experience through providing personal information and the amount and type of information that they are prepared for companies to hold about them.

The main information types used by the digital marketer which are governed by ethics and legislation, are:

1 *Contact information.* This is the name, postal address, e-mail address and, for B2B companies, website address.
2 *Profile information.* This is information about a customer's characteristics that can be used for segmentation. They include age, sex and social group for consumers, and company characteristics and individual role for business customers (see Chapter 6).
3 *Platform usage information.*Through web analytics systems it is possible to collect information on type of computer, browser and screen resolution used by site users (see Chapter 7).

4 *Behavioural information (on a single site).* This is purchase history and the whole of buying process. Web analytics (Chapter 10) can be used to assess the web and e-mail content accessed by individuals.
5 *Behavioural information (across multiple sites).* This can potentially show how a user accesses multiple sites and responds to adverts across sites. Typically this data is collected and used through an anonymous profile based on cookie or IP addresses which is not related to an individual.

Table 3.2 summarises how these different types of customer information are collected and used through technology. The main issue to be considered by the marketer is *disclosure* of the types of information collection and tracking data used. The first two types of information in the table are usually readily explained through a privacy statement at the point of data collection and, as we will see, this is usually a legal requirement. However, with the other types of information, users would only know they were being tracked if they have cookie monitoring software installed or if they seek out the privacy statement of a publisher which offers advertising.

Table 3.2 Types of information collected online and the related technologies

Type of information	Approach and technology used to capture and use information
1 Contact information	• Online forms – online forms linked to a customer database • Cookies – are used to remember a specific person on subsequent visits
2 Profile information including personal information	• Online forms • Cookies can be used to assign a person to a particular segment by linking the cookie to a customer database record and then offering content consistent with their segment
3 Access platform usage	• Web analytics system – identification of computer type, operating system and screen characteristics based on http attributes of visitors
4 Behavioural information on a single site	• Purchase histories are stored in the sales order database • Web analytics store details of IP addresses against clickstreams of the sequence of web pages visited • Web beacons in e-mail marketing – a single pixel GIF is used to assess whether a reader opened an e-mail • First-party cookies are also used for monitoring visitor behaviour during a site visit and on subsequent visits • **Malware** can collect additional information such as passwords
5 Behavioural information across multiple sites	• Third-party cookies used for assessing visits from different sources such as online advertising networks or affiliate networks (Chapter 9) • Search engines such as Google use cookies to track advertising through its AdWords pay-per-click programme • Services such as Hitwise (**www.hitwise.com**) monitor IP traffic to assess site usage of customer groups within a product category

Malware
Malicious software or toolbars, typically downloaded via the Internet, which act as a 'Trojan horse' by executing unwanted activites such as keylogging of user passwords or viruses which may collect e-mail addresses.

All of these issues arise in the next section which reviews actions that marketers should take to achieve privacy and trust.

Data protection law

Personal data
Any information about an individual stored by companies concerning their customers or employees.

Data protection legislation is enacted to protect the individual, to protect their privacy and to prevent misuse of their personal data. Indeed, the first article of the European Union Directive 95/46/EC (see **http://ec.europa.eu/justice_home/fsi/privacy/**) on which legislation in individual European countries is based, specifically refers to **personal data.** It says:

> Member states shall protect the fundamental rights and freedoms of natural persons [i.e. a named individual at home or at work], and in particular their right to privacy with respect to the processing of personal data.

In the UK, the enactment of the European legislation is the Data Protection Act 1984, 1998 (DPA), which is managed by the legal requirements of the 1998 UK Data Protection Act and the Information Commissioner's office is the UK's independent authority which 'upholds information rights in the public interest, promoting openness by public bodies and data privacy for individuals', (ICO 2011). The ICO provides detailed information at: **www.ico.gov.uk**. This law is typical of laws that have evolved in many countries to help protect personal information. Any company that holds personal data on computers or on file about customers or employees must be registered with a data protection registrar (although there are some exceptions which may exclude small businesses). This process is known as **notification.**

Notification
The process whereby companies register with the data protection registrar to inform about their data holdings.

The guidelines on the eight data protection principles which marketers need to consider are produced by Information Commissioner (1998) on which this overview is based. These principles state that personal data should be:

1 Fairly and lawfully processed

In full:

> Personal data shall be processed fairly and lawfully and, in particular, shall not be processed unless at least one of the conditions in Schedule 2 is met; and in the case of sensitive personal data, at least one of the conditions in Schedule 3 is also met.

The Information Commissioner has produced a 'fair processing code' which suggests how an organisation needs to achieve 'fair and lawful processing' under the details of Schedules 2 and 3 of the Act. This requires:

Data controller
Each company must have a defined person responsible for data protection.

Data subject
The legal term to refer to the individual whose data are held.

- Appointment of a **data controller** who is the person with defined responsibility for data protection within a company.
- Clear details in communications such as on a website or direct mail of how a **data subject** can contact the data controller or a representative.
- Before data processing 'the data subject has given his consent' or the processing must be *necessary* either for a 'contract to which the data subject is a party' (for example, as part of a sale of a product) or because it is required by other laws. Consent is defined in the published guidelines as 'any freely given specific and informed indication of his wishes by which the data subject signifies his agreement to personal data relating to him being processed'.
- Sensitive personal data requires particular care, this includes:
  - the racial or ethnic origin of the data subject
  - political opinions
  - religious beliefs or other beliefs of a similar nature
  - membership of a trade union
  - physical or mental health or condition
  - sexual life
  - the commission or alleged commission or proceedings of any offence.
- No other laws must be broken in processing the data.

2 Processed for limited purposes

In full:

> Personal data shall be obtained only for one or more specified and lawful purposes, and shall not be further processed in any manner incompatible with that purpose or those purposes.

This implies that the organisation must make it clear why and how the data will be processed at the point of collection. For example, an organisation has to explain how your data will be used if you provide your details on a website when entering a prize draw. You would also have to agree (give consent) for further communications from the company.

Figure 3.10 suggests some of the issues that should be considered when a data subject is informed of how the data will be used. Important issues are:

- whether future communications will be sent to the individual (explicit consent is required for this in online channels; this is clarified by the related Privacy and Electronic Communications Regulation Act which is referred to below)
- whether the data will be passed on to third parties (again explicit consent is required)
- how long the data will be kept.

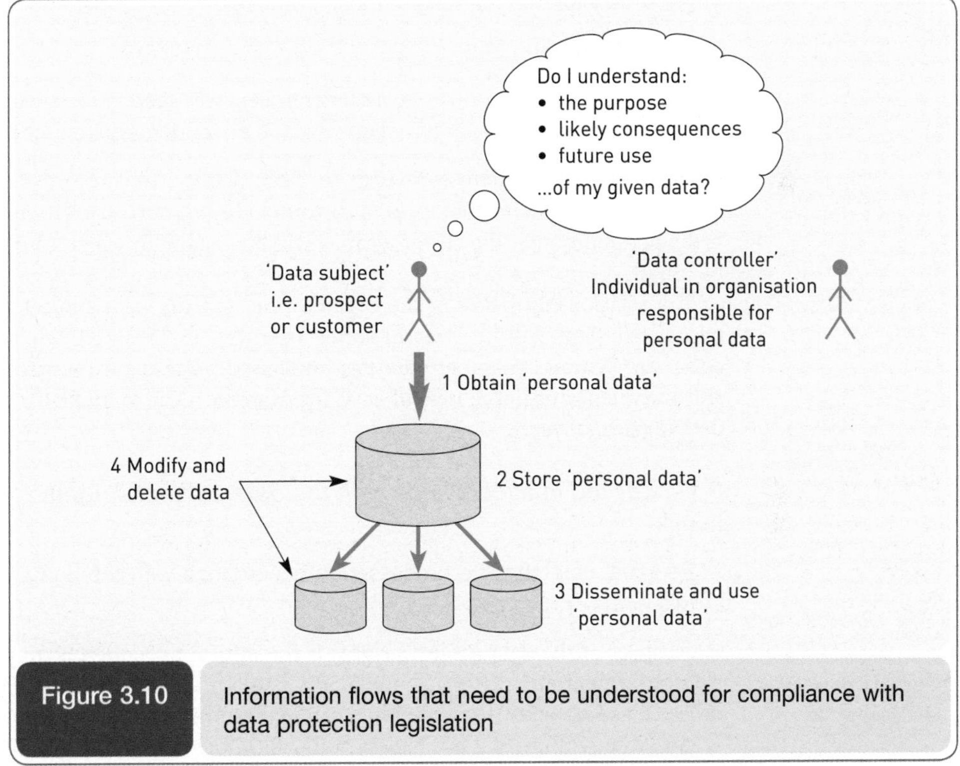

Figure 3.10 Information flows that need to be understood for compliance with data protection legislation

3 Adequate, relevant and not excessive

In full:

> Personal data shall be adequate, relevant and not excessive in relation to the purpose or purposes for which they are processed.

This specifies that the minimum necessary amount of data is requested for processing. There is difficulty in reconciling this provision between the needs of the individual and the needs of the company. The more details that an organisation has about a customer, then the better they can understand that customer and so develop products and marketing communications specific to that customer which they are more likely to respond to.

4 Accurate

In full:

> Personal data shall be accurate and, where necessary, kept up to date.

It is clearly also in the interest of an organisation in an ongoing relationship with a partner that the data be kept accurate and up-to-date. The guidelines on the Act suggest that additional steps should be taken to check data are accurate, in case they are in error, for example due to mis-keying by the data subject or the organisation or for some other reason. Inaccurate data are defined in the guidelines as 'incorrect or misleading as to any matter of fact'.

The guidelines go on to discuss the importance of keeping information up-to-date. This is only necessary where there is an ongoing relationship and the rights of the individual may be affected if they are not up-to-date. This implies, for example, that a credit-checking agency should keep credit scores up-to-date.

5 Not kept longer than necessary

In full:

> Personal data processed for any purpose or purposes shall not be kept for longer than is necessary for that purpose or those purposes.

The guidelines state:

> To comply with this Principle, data controllers will need to review their personal data regularly and to delete the information which is no longer required for their purposes.

It might be in a company's interests to 'clean data' so that records that are not relevant are archived or deleted, for example if a customer has not purchased for ten years. However, there is the possibility that the customer may still buy again, in which case the information would be useful.

If a relationship between the organisation and the data subject ends, then data should be deleted. This will be clear in some instances, for example when an employee leaves a company. With a consumer who has purchased products from a company this is less clear since frequency of purchase will vary, for example a car manufacturer could justifiably hold data for several years.

6 Processed in accordance with the data subject's rights

In full:

> Personal data shall be processed in accordance with the rights of data subjects under this Act.

Subject access request
A request by a data subject to view personal data from an organisation.

One aspect of the data subject's rights is the option to request a copy of their personal data from an organisation; this is known as a **subject access request**. For payment of a small fee, such as £10 or £30, an individual can request information which must be supplied by the organisation within 40 days. This includes all information on paper files and on computer. If you requested this information from your bank there might be several boxes of transactions!

Other aspects of a data subject's rights which the law upholds are designed to prevent or control processing which:

- causes damage or distress (for example, repeatedly sending mailshots to someone who has died)
- is used for direct marketing (for example, in the UK consumers can subscribe to the mail, e-mail or telephone preference services to avoid unsolicited mailings, e-mails or phone calls); this invaluable service is provided by the Direct Marketing Association (**www.dmaconsumers.org**) – if you subscribe to these services, organisations must check against these 'exclusion lists' before contacting you; if they don't, and some don't, they are breaking the law
- is used for automatic decision making – automated credit checks, for example, may result in unjust decisions on taking a loan. These can be investigated if you feel the decision is unfair.

7 Secure

In full:

> Appropriate technical and organisational measures shall be taken against unauthorised or unlawful processing of personal data and against accidental loss or destruction of, or damage to, personal data.

The Data Protection Law guidelines place a legal imperative on organisations to prevent unauthorised internal or external access to information and also its modification or destruction. Of course, most organisations would want to do this anyway since the information has value to the organisation and the reputational damage of losing customer information or being subject to a hack attack can be severe. For example in late 2006, online clothing retail group TJX Inc. (owner of TK Maxx) was hacked resulting in loss of credit card details of over 45 million customer in the US and Europe. TJX later said in its security filing that its potential liability (loss) from the computer intrusion(s) was $118 million.

8 Not transferred to countries without adequate protection

In full:

> Personal data shall not be transferred to a country or territory outside the European Economic Area, unless that country or territory ensures an adequate level of protection of the rights and freedoms of data subjects in relation to the processing of personal data.

Transfer of data beyond Europe is likely for multinational companies. This principle prevents export of data to countries that do not have sound data processing laws. If the transfer is required in concluding a sale or contract, or if the data subject agrees to it, then transfer is legal. Data transfer with the US is possible through companies registered through the Safe Harbor Scheme (**http://export.gov/safeharbour/index.asp**).

Anti-spam legislation

Spam
Unsolicited e-mail (usually bulk-mailed and untargeted).

Opt-in
A customer proactively agrees to receive further information.

Opt-out
A customer declines the offer to receive further information.

Cold list
Data about individuals that are rented or sold by a third party.

House list
Data about existing customers used to market products to encourage future purchase.

Laws have been enacted in different countries to protect individual privacy and with the intention of reducing spam or unsolicited commercial e-mail (UCE). Originally, the best-known **spam** was tinned meat (a contraction of 'spiced ham'), but a modern version of this acronym is 'sending persistent annoying e-mail'. Spammers rely on sending out millions of e-mails in the hope that even if there is only a 0.01 per cent response they may make some money, if not get rich.

Anti-spam laws do not mean that e-mail cannot be used as a marketing tool but the recipient has to agree to receive the mailing. This approach is called Permissive Marketing. Permissive e-mail marketing is based on consent or **opt-in** by customers, and the option to unsubscribe or **opt-out** is the key to successful e-mail marketing. E-mail lists can also be rented where customers have opted in to receive e-mail. This is known as a **cold list**, so called because the company that purchases the data from a third party does not know you. Your name will also potentially be stored on an opt-in **house list** within companies you have purchased from where you have given your consent to be contacted by the company or given additional consent to be contacted by its partners.

European regulations on privacy and electronic communications

While the Data Protection Directive 95/46 and Data Protection Act afford a reasonable level of protection for consumers, they were quickly superseded by advances in technology and the rapid growth in spam. As a result, in 2002 the European Union passed the '2002/58/EC Directive on Privacy and Electronic Communications' to complement previous data protection law. This Act is significant for marketers since it applies specifically to electronic communications such as e-mail and the monitoring of websites.

Clauses 22 to 24 are the main clauses relevant to e-mail communications.

Activity 3.10 Privacy and social media

Purpose

To consider the implications of personal privacy in social media countries.

Activity

Watch Martha Lane Fox, founder of LastMinute.com at: **http://goo.gl/urkvB/**

Question

What are the implications for digital marketers of what Martha says about how different age groups are using the web?

Digital marketing insight 3.9 UK and European e-mail marketing law

As an example of European privacy law which covers use of e-mail, SMS and cookies for marketing, we review the implications for managers of the UK enactment of 2002/58/EC Directive on Privacy and Electronic Communications. We will contrast this with the law in other European countries. This came into force in the UK on 11 December 2003 as the Privacy and Electronic Communications Regulations (PECR) Act. The law is published at: **www.legislation.gov.uk/uksi/2003/2426/contents/made**. Consumer marketers in the UK also need to heed the Code of Advertising Practice from the Advertising Standards Agency (**www.asa.org.uk/advertising-codes.aspx**). This has broadly similar aims and places similar restrictions on marketers to the PECR law. We will summarise the main implications of the law by picking out key phrases. The new PECR law:

1 Applies to consumer marketing using e-mail or SMS text messages

22(1) applies to *individual subscribers*. 'Individual subscribers' means consumers, although the Information Commissioner has stated that this may be reviewed in future to include business subscribers, as is the case in some other countries such as Italy and Germany.

Although this sounds like great news for business-to-business (B2B) marketers – and some take the view 'great, the new law doesn't apply to us' – this could be dangerous. There has been adjudication by the Advertising Standards Agency which found against a B2B organisation that had unwittingly e-mailed consumers from what they believed was an in-house list of B2B customers.

2 Is an 'opt-in' regime

The law applies to '*unsolicited communications*' (22(1)). It was introduced with a view to reducing spam, although we all know its impact will be limited on spammers beyond Europe. The relevant phrase is part of 22(2) where the recipient must have 'previously notified the sender that he consents' or has proactively agreed to receiving commercial e-mail. This is **opt-in**. Opt-in can be achieved online or offline through asking people whether they want to receive e-mail. Online this is often done through a tick box.

The approach required by the law has, in common with many aspects of data protection and privacy law, been used by many organisations for some time. In other words, sending unsolicited e-mails was thought to be unethical and also not in the best

Permission marketing
Customers agree (opt-in) to be involved in an organisation's marketing activities, usually as a result of an incentive

Viral marketing
A marketing message is communicated from one person to another, facilitated by different media, such as word of mouth, e-mail or websites. It implies rapid transmission of messages is intended.

interests of the company because of the risk of annoying customers. In fact, the law conforms to an established approach known as **permission marketing**, a term coined by US commentator Seth Godin (1999, Chapter 6 – first four chapters available free from **www.permission.com**).

Viral marketing

One widespread business practice that is not covered explicitly in the PECR law is **viral marketing** (Chapter 9). In the guidelines for marketers for the law, the commissioner states that it 'takes a dim view' of viral marketing, especially when it is incentivised and the marketer needs to be careful that consent of the friend is agreed.

3 Requires an opt-out option in all communications

An **opt-out** or method of 'unsubscribing' is required so that the recipient does not receive future communications. In a database this means that a 'do not e-mail' field must be created to avoid e-mailing these customers. The law states that a 'simple means of refusing' future communications is required both when the details were first collected and in each subsequent communication.

4 Does not apply to existing customers when marketing similar products

This common-sense clause (22(3)(a)) states that previous opt-in is not required if the contact details were obtained during the course of the sale or negotiations for the sale of a product or service. This is sometimes known as the 'soft or implied opt-in exception'. This key soft opt-in caveat is interpreted differently in different European countries, with seven countries, Italy, Denmark, Germany, Austria, Greece, Finland and Spain not including it. The differences mean that marketers managing campaigns across Europe need to take the differences in different countries into account.

Clause 22(3)(b) adds that when marketing to existing customers, the marketer may market 'similar products and services only'. Case law will help in clarifying this. For example, for a bank, it is not clear whether a customer with an insurance policy could be targeted for a loan.

5 Requires contact details must be provided

It is not sufficient to send an e-mail with a simple sign-off from 'the marketing team' or 'the web team' with no further contact details. The law requires a name, address or phone number to whom a recipient can complain.

6 Requires the 'from' identification of the sender to be clear

Spammers aim to disguise the e-mail originator. The law says that the identity of the person who sends the communication must not be 'disguised or concealed' and that a valid address to 'send a request that such communications cease' should be provided.

7 Applies to direct marketing communications

The communications that the legislation refers to are for 'direct marketing'. This suggests that other communications involved with customer service, such as an e-mail about a monthly phone statement, are not covered, so the opt-out choice may not be required here.

Cookies
Cookies are small text files stored on an end-user's computer to enable websites to identify the user.

8 Restricts the use of cookies

Some privacy campaigners consider that the user's privacy is invaded by planting **cookies** or electronic tags on the end-user's computer. The concept of the cookie and its associated law is not straightforward, so it warrants separate discussion.

Persistent cookies Cookies that remain on the computer after a visitor session has ended. Used to recognise returning visitors.

Session cookies A cookie used to manage a single visitor session.

First-party cookies Served by the site currently in use – typically for e-commerce sites.

Third-party cookies Served by another site to the one being viewed – typically for portals where an ad network will track remotely or where the web analytics software places a cookie.

Digital marketing insight 3.10 Understanding cookies

A cookie is a data file placed on your computer that identifies that individual computer. 'Cookie' derives from the Unix operating system term 'magic cookie' which meant something passed between routines or programs that enables the receiver to perform some operation.

Types of cookies

The main cookie types are:

- **Persistent cookies** – these stay on a user's computer between multiple sessions and are most valuable for marketers to identify repeat visits to sites.
- Temporary or **session cookies** (single session) – useful for tracking within pages of a session such as on an e-commerce site.
- **First-party cookies** – served by the site currently in use, typically for e-commerce sites. These can be persistent or session cookies.
- **Third-party cookies** – served by another site to the one being viewed, typically for portals where an ad network will track remotely or where the web analytics software places a cookie. These are typically persistent cookies.

Cookies are stored as individual text files in a directory on a personal computer. There is usually one file per website. For example: **dave_chaffey@british-airways.txt**. This file contains encoded information as follows:

FLT_VIS |K:bapzRnGdxBYUUID:Jul-25-1999| british-airways.com/ 0 425259904 29357426 1170747936 29284034 *

The information in the cookie file is essentially just an identification number and the date of the last visit, although other information can be stored.

Cookies are specific to a particular browser and computer, so if a user connects from a different computer, such as at work or starts using a different browser, the website will not identify him or her as a similar user.

What are cookies used for?

Common marketing applications of cookies include:

- *Personalising a site for an individual*. Cookies are used to identify individual users and retrieve their preferences from a database according to an identifier stored in the cookie. For example, I subscribe to the EConsultancy service (**www.e-consultancy.com**) for the latest information about e-business; each time I return I do not have the annoyance of having to log in because it remembers my previous visit. Many sites feature a 'Remember Me' option which implies using a cookie to recognise a returning visitor. Retailers such as Amazon can use cookies to recognise returning visitors and can recommend related books purchased by other readers. This approach generally has good benefits for both the individual (it is a hassle to sign in again and relevant content can be delivered) and the company (tailored marketing messages can be delivered).
- *Online ordering systems*. This enables a site such as Tesco.com to track what is in your basket as you order different products.
- *Tracking within a site*. Web analytics software such as Webtrends (**www.webtrends.com**) or analyses statistics on visitors to websites and relies on persistent cookies to find the proportion of repeat visitors to a website. Webtrends and other tools increasingly use first-party cookies since they are more accurate and less likely to be blocked. Marketers should check whether use of first-party cookies is possible on their site.

- *Tracking across sites*. Advertising networks use cookies to track the number of times a particular computer user has been shown a particular banner advertisement; they can also track adverts served on sites across an ad network. There was an individual rights outcry in the late 1990s since Doubleclick was using this to profile customers. Doubleclick no longer operates an ad network, partly due to this.

Affiliate networks and pay-per-click ad networks such as Google AdWords and Yahoo! Search services may also use cookies to track through from a click on a third-party site to a sale or lead being generated on a destination or merchant site. These approaches tend to use third-party cookies. For example, if conversion tracking is enabled in Google Adwords, Google sets a cookie when a user clicks through on an ad. If this user buys the product, then the purchase confirmation page will include script code supplied by Google to make a check for a cookie placed by Google. If there is a match, the sale is attributed to AdWords. An alternative approach using third-party tracking is that different online campaigns have different tracking parameters or codes within the links through to the destination site, and when the user arrives on a site from a particular source (such as Google AdWords) this is identified and a cookie set. When purchase confirmation occurs, this can then be attributed back to the original source, e.g. Google AdWords, and the particular referrer.

Owing to the large investments made now in pay-per-click marketing and affiliate marketing by many companies, this is the area of most concern for marketers since the tracking can become inaccurate. However, a sale should still occur even if the cookies are blocked or deleted, so the main consequence is that the ROI (return on investment) of online advertising or pay-per-click marketing may look lower than expected. In affiliate marketing, this phenomenon may benefit the marketer in that payment may not need to be made to the third party if a cookie has been deleted (or blocked) between the time of original click-through and sale.

Privacy issues with cookie use

The problem for digital marketers is that, despite these important applications, blocking by browsers, such as Internet Explorer, or security software and deletion by users has increased dramatically. In 2005 Jupiter Research claimed that 39 per cent of online users may be deleting cookies from their primary computer monthly, although this is debated.

Many distrust cookies since they indicate a 'big brother' is monitoring their actions. Others fear that their personal details or credit card details may be accessed by other websites. This is very unlikely since all the cookies contain is a short identifier or number that is used to link you to your record in a database. Anyone who found the cookie wouldn't be able to log on to the database without your password. Cookies do not contain passwords, credit card information or any personal details as many people seem to think. These are held on the site servers, protected by firewalls and usernames and passwords. In most cases, the worst that someone can do who gets access to your cookies is to find out which sites you have been visiting.

It is possible to block cookies if the user finds out how to block them, but this is not straightforward and many customers either do not know how or do not mind that their privacy may be infringed.

Legal constraints on cookies

The UK implementation of the PECR law from European law introduced in 2003 was one of the first to limit the use of cookies. It states:

> *a person shall not use an electronic communications network to store information, or to gain access to information stored, in the terminal equipment of a subscriber or user unless the following requirements are met.*

The requirements are: (a) the user is provided with clear and comprehensive information about the purposes of the storage of, or access to, that information; and b is given the opportunity to refuse the storage of or access to that information. (a) suggests that it is important that there is a clear **privacy statement** and (b) suggests that opt-in to cookies is required. In other words, on the first visit to the site, a box would have to be ticked to agree to the use of cookies. This was thought by many commentators to be a curious provision since this facility is already available in the web browser. A further provision clarifies this. The law states: 'where such storage or access is strictly necessary for the provision of an information society service requested by the subscriber or user'. This indicates that for an e-commerce service session cookies are legitimate without the need for opt-in. It is arguable whether the identification of return visitors is 'strictly necessary' and this is why some sites have a 'remember me' tick box next to the log-in. Through doing this they are compliant with the law. Using cookies for tracking return visits alone would seem to be outlawed, but we will have to see how case law develops over the coming years before this is resolved.

With continuing use of cookies with limited information about their usage, another attempt was made in 2011 by European legislators to control their usage for marketing. Smart Insights (2011a) describes the guidance on this law to be enforced from 25 May 2012. This new law could have significant implications for marketers who currently make use display advertising, behavioural targeting and web analytics. The new law followed press articles about cookie-based targeting and the 'Do Not Track Us' (**http://donottrack.us/**) campaign in the US supported by the Electronic Frontier Federation which aims to introduce a universal web tracking opt-out.

Privacy statement
Information on a website explaining how and why individuals' data are collected, processed and stored.

Worldwide regulations on privacy and electronic communications

In the US in January 2004, a new federal law known as the CAN-SPAM Act was introduced to assist in the control of unsolicited e-mail. CAN-SPAM stands for 'Controlling the Assault of Non-Solicited Pornography and Marketing' (an ironic juxtaposition between pornography and marketing). This harmonised separate laws in different US states, but was less strict than in some states such as California. The Act requires unsolicited commercial e-mail messages to be labelled (though not by a standard method) and to include opt-out instructions and the sender's physical address. It prohibits the use of deceptive subject lines and false headers in such messages. Current details of CAN-SPAM act compliance guidelines can be found at: **http://business.ftc.gov/documents/bus61-can-spam-act-compliance-guide-business.** Anti-spam legislation in other countries can be accessed at:

- **www.privacy.gov.au** (Australia enacted a SPAM act in 2003)
- **www.privcom.gc.ca** (Canada has a privacy act)
- **www.privacy.org.nz** (New Zealand Privacy Commissioner)
- **www.spamlaws.com** (summary for all countries).

We conclude this section on privacy legislation with a checklist summary of the practical steps that are required to audit a company's compliance with data protection and privacy legislation. Companies should:

1. Follow privacy and consumer protection guidelines and laws in all local markets. Use local privacy and security certification where available.
2. Notify or inform the site visitor before asking for information on:
   - who the company is
   - what personal data are collected, processed and stored
   - the purpose of collection

- how the site visitor can opt-out (be unsubscribed from e-mail lists or cookies)
- how the site visitor can obtain information held about them.

3 Ask for consent for collecting sensitive personal data, and it is good practice to ask before collecting any type of data.
4 Reassure customers by providing clear and effective privacy statements and explaining the purpose of data collection.
5 Let individuals know when 'cookies' or other covert software are used to collect information about them.
6 Never collect or retain personal data unless it is strictly necessary for the organisation's purposes. For example, a person's name and full address should not be required to provide an online quotation. If extra information is required for marketing purposes this should be made clear and the provision of such information should be optional.
7 Amend incorrect data when informed and tell others. Enable correction on site.
8 Only use data for marketing (by the company or third parties) when a user has been informed this is the case and has agreed to this. (This is opt-in.)
9 Provide the option for customers to stop receiving information. (This is opt-out.)
10 Use appropriate security technology to protect the customer information on your site.

2 Disability and discrimination law

Accessibility legislation
Legislation intended to protect users of websites with disabilities including visual disability.

Laws relating to discriminating against disabled users who may find it more difficult to use websites because of audio, visual or motor impairment are known as **accessibility legislation**. This is often contained within disability and discrimination acts. In the UK, the relevant act is the Disability Discrimination Act 2010.

Web accessibility refers to enabling all users of a website to interact with it regardless of disabilities they may have or the web browser or platform they are using to access the site. The visually impaired or blind are the main audience that designing an accessible website can help. Coverage of the requirements that accessibility places on web design are covered in Chapter 7.

3 Brand and trademark protection

Online brand and trademark protection covers several areas, including use of a brand name within domain names and use of trademarks within other websites and in online adverts.

Domain name registration

Domain name registration
The process of reserving a unique web address that can be used to refer to the company website.

Most companies are likely to own several domains, perhaps for different product lines or countries or for specific marketing campaigns. Domain name disputes can arise when an individual or company has registered a domain name which another company claims they have the right to. This is sometimes referred to as 'cybersquatting'.

One of the best-known cases was brought in 1998 by Marks and Spencer and other high street retailers, since another company, 'One In a Million Limited', had registered names such as marks&spencer.com, britishtelecom.net and sainsbury.com. It then tried to sell these names for a profit. The companies already had sites with more familiar addresses, such as marksandspencers.co.uk, but had not taken the precaution of registering all related domains with different forms of spelling and different top-level domains, such as .net. Unsurprisingly, an injunction was issued against One in a Million which was no longer able to use these names.

The problem of companies' names being misappropriated was common during the 1990s, but companies still need to be sure to register all related domain names for each brand since new top-level domain names are created through time, such as .biz and .eu.

If you are responsible for websites, you need to check that domain names are automatically renewed by your hosting company (as most are today). For example, the .co.uk domain must be renewed every two years. Companies that don't manage this process potentially risk losing their domain name since another company could potentially register it if the domain name lapsed. A further option with domain registration is to purchase generic domain names of established sites which may perform well in the search engines.

Digital marketing insight 3.11 How much is a domain worth?

One of the highest values attached to a domain in Europe was paid in 2008 when the website cruise.co.uk paid the German travel company Nees Reisen £560,000 for the rival name cruises.co.uk. *Guardian* (2008) reported the new owner of cruises.co.uk as saying that he hopes to use the new domain differently – by turning the site into an online intermediary or community for cruising enthusiasts while its existing cruise.co.uk will concentrate on offering the best deals for voyages. Explaining the valuation, cruise.co.uk's managing director, Seamus Conlon stated:

> *'Cruises' is consistently ranked first on Google, with 'cruise' just behind. We wanted the top positions so that when Internet users are searching for cruise deals, reviews or news we are the first port of call. The cruise market is one of the fastest and most consistently growing sectors in the travel industry.*

Since the commercialisation of the web, domain names have changed hands for high prices, for example:

- business.com for $7.5 million, December 1999
- AsSeenOnTv.com for $5.1 million, January 2000
- Credcards.com for $2.7 million, July 2004
- sex.com for $12 million, October 2010
- casino.tt for $2.0 million, May 2011

Using competitor names and trademarks in meta-tags (for search engine optimisation)

Meta-tags, which are part of the HTML code of a site, are used to market websites by enabling them to appear more prominently in search engines as part of search engine optimisation (SEO) (see Chapter 8). Some companies have tried putting the name of a competitor company within the meta-tags. This is not legal since case law has found against companies that have used this approach. A further issue of marketing-related law is privacy law for e-mail marketing which was considered in the previous section.

Using competitor names and trademarks in pay-per-click advertising

Pay-per-click search marketing
Refers to when a company pays for text ads to be displayed on the search engine results pages when a specific keyphrase is entered by the search users. It is so called since the marketer pays for each time the hypertext link in the ad is clicked on.

A similar approach can potentially be used in **pay-per-click marketing** (explained in Chapter 9) to advertise on competitors' names and trademarks. For example, if a search user types 'Dell laptop' can an advertiser bid to place an ad offering an 'HP laptop'? There is less case law in this area and differing findings have occurred in the US and France (such advertising is not permitted in France).

Reputational damage in advertising

Companies fear reputational damage through advertising on sites with which they wouldn't want their brand associated because of ad buys on social networks or ad networks (Chapter 9) where it was not clear what content their ads would be associated with. For example, Vodafone removed all its advertising from the social network Facebook after its ads appeared on the group profile for the British National Party. Many other advertisers withdrew their advertising as a result.

Monitoring brand conversations in social networks and blogs

Online brand reputation management and alerting software tools offer real-time alerts when comments or mentions about a brand are posted online in different locations, including blogs and social networks. Some basic tools are available including:

- Googlealert (**www.googlealert.com**) and Google Alerts (**www.google.com/alerts**) which will alert companies when any new pages appear that contain a search phrase such as your company or brand names.
- Nielsen BuzzMetrics' BlogPulse (**www.blogpulse.com**) gives trends and listings of any phrase and individual postings can be viewed.

There are also more sophisticated online reputation-management services which offer more in-depth analysis on whether the sentiment is positive or negative and cover other issues such as unauthorised use of logos and use of trademarks. Examples include Mark Monitor, Reputation Intelligence, Brand Intelligence, Big Mouth Media and Market Sentinel.

The challenges of policing online trademark infringement, given the range of opportunities for this and the lag between what the law stipulates and what is possible through the technology, is evident from Mini Case Study 3.5.

4 Intellectual property rights

Intellectual property rights
Protect the intangible property created by corporations or individuals that is protected under copyright, trade secret and patent laws.

Intellectual property rights (IPRs) protect designs, ideas and inventions and include content and services developed for e-commerce sites. Closely related is copyright law which is designed to protect authors, producers, broadcasters and performers by ensuring they see some returns from their works every time they are experienced. The European Directive of Copyright (2001/29/EC) came into force in many countries in 2003. This is a significant update to the law which covers new technologies and approaches such as streaming a broadcast via the Internet.

IP can be misappropriated in two senses online. First, an organisation's IP may be misappropriated and you need to protect against this. For example, it is relatively easy to copy web content and re-publish on another site, and this practice is not unknown among smaller businesses. Reputation management services can be used to assess how an organisation's content, logos and **trademarks** are being used on other websites.

Trademark
A trademark is a unique word or phrase that distinguishes your company. The mark can be registered as plain or designed text, artwork or a combination. In theory, colours, smells and sounds can also be trademarks.

Secondly, an organisation may misappropriate content inadvertently. Some employees may infringe copyright if they are not aware of the law. Additionally, some methods of designing transactional websites have been patented. For example, Amazon has patented its 'One-click' purchasing option which is why you do not see this labelling and process on other sites.

5 Contract law

We will look at two aspects of forming an electronic contract – the country of origin principle and distance selling laws.

Country of origin principle

The contract formed between a buyer and a seller on a website will be subject to the laws of a particular country. In Europe, many such laws are specified at the regional (European Union) level, but are interpreted differently in different countries. This raises the issue of the jurisdiction in which law applies – is it that for the buyer, for example located in Germany, or the seller (merchant) whose site is based in France? Although this has been unclear, in 2002 attempts were made by the EU to adopt the 'country of origin principle'. This means that the law for the contract will be that where the merchant is located. The Out-Law site produced by lawyers Pinsent Mason gives more information on jurisdiction (**http://www.out-law.com/page-479**).

Distance-selling law

Sparrow (2000) advises different forms of disclaimers to protect the retailer. For example, if a retailer made an error with the price or the product details, then the retailer is not bound to honour a contract, since it was only displaying the products as 'an invitation to treat', not a fixed offer.

A well-known case was when an e-retailer offered televisions for £2.99 due to an error in pricing a £299 product. Numerous purchases were made, but the e-retailer claimed that a contract had not been established simply by accepting the online order, although the customers did not see it that way! Unfortunately, no legal precedent was established in this case since the case did not come to trial.

Disclaimers can also be used to limit liability if the website service causes a problem for the user, such as a financial loss resulting from an action based on erroneous content. Furthermore, Sparrow suggests that terms and conditions should be developed to refer to issues such as timing of delivery and damage or loss of goods.

The distance-selling directive also has a bearing on e-commerce contracts in the European Union. It was originally developed to protect people using mail order (by post or phone). The main requirements, which are consistent with what most reputable e-retailers would do anyway, are that e-commerce sites must contain easily accessible content which clearly states:

- the company's identity including address
- the main features of the goods or services
- price information, including tax and, if appropriate, delivery costs
- the period for which the offer or price remains valid
- payment, delivery and fulfilment performance arrangements
- right of the consumer to withdraw, i.e. cancellation terms
- the minimum duration of the contract and whether the contract for the supply of products or services is to be permanent or recurrent, if appropriate
- whether an equivalent product or service might be substituted, and confirmation as to whether the seller pays the return costs in this event.

After the contract has been entered into, the supplier is required to provide written confirmation of the information provided. An e-mail confirmation is now legally binding provided both parties have agreed that e-mail is an acceptable form for the contract. It is always advisable to obtain an electronic signature to confirm that both parties have agreed the contract, and this is especially valuable in the event of a dispute. The default position for services is that there is no cancellation right once services begin.

The Out-Law site produced by lawyers Pinsent Mason gives more information on distance-selling (**http://www.out-law.com/page-430**).

6 Online advertising law

Advertising standards that are enforced by independent agencies such as the UK's Advertising Standards Authority Code also apply in the Internet environment (although they are traditionally less strongly policed, leading to more 'edgy' creative executions online which are intended to have a viral effect).

The Out-Law site produced by lawyers Pinsent Mason gives more information on online advertising law (**www.out-law.com/page-5604**).

In this section we have considered ethical standards and have explored in more detail the legislation that is likely to affect digital marketers.

Social forces

Social forces are closely linked with culture and have significant implications for digital marketing. Broadly speaking the key factors which make up these forces are: social communities based on demographic profile; social exclusion; and cultural factors.

In the previous chapter, we looked at demographics and consumer adoption of the web and found great variation in terms of levels of Internet access, amount of usage, and engagement in online purchases. In this chapter, our interest is in the wider impact of demographic influences: changes in populations. Why this is important is that the size and growth rates of populations have implications for digital marketing strategy and planning. One highly important shift in demographic trends is that for the first time in the history of the world over 50 per cent of the population lives in an urban setting.

The world population is estimated at just under 7 billion, with 26.3 per cent being 14 and under, 65.9 per cent between the ages of 15–64 and 7.9 per cent over the age of 65. Population growth is estimated to be 1.09. The expanding population means there is increasing demand on finite resources. Changes in population are important to marketers as they create new market opportunities. Currently, emerging marketing in Russia, India, Brazil and China represent market growth but there are other demographic factors before making a major investment in developing and access emerging markets, e.g. two thirds of the world's illiterate adults live in just eight countries: Bangladesh, China, Egypt, Ethiopia, India, Indonesia, Nigeria and Pakistan (CIA, 2011).

Analysis of demographic trends can reveal important issues, e.g. there is a significant group in each national population of at least a quarter of the adult population that does not envisage ever using the Internet. Clearly, the lack of demand for Internet services from this group needs to be taken into account when forecasting future demand. Furthermore, this raises the questions of social isolation, or what the Oxford Internet Institute have called in their research into Internet usage 'Internet disengagement'. Others consider this to be an aspect of 'social exclusion'.

Social exclusion

Social exclusion
Part of society is excluded from the facilities available to the remainder.

The social impact of the Internet has also concerned many commentators because the Internet has the potential effect of accentuating differences in quality of life, both within a society in a single country and between different nations, essentially creating 'information haves' and 'information have-nots'. This may accentuate **social exclusion** where one part of society is excluded from the facilities available to the remainder and so becomes isolated. The United Nations noted, as early in the growth of the Internet as 1999, that parallel worlds are developing where:

> those with income, education and – literally – connections have cheap and instantaneous access to information. The rest are left with uncertain, slow and costly access . . . the advantage of being connected will overpower the marginal and impoverished, cutting off their voices and concerns from the global conversation.

Developed countries with the economies to support it are promoting the use of IT and the Internet through social programmes, such as the UK government's UK Online initiative, which operated between 2000 and 2004 to promote the use of the Internet by business and consumers. The European Commission (2007) believe that 'e-Inclusion policies and actions have made significant progress in implementing the goal of an inclusive knowledge-based society (Europa (2007))'. They recommend that governments should focus on three aspects of e-Inclusion:

1 The access divide (or 'early digital divide') which considers the gap between those with and those without access. Governments will encourage competition to reduce costs and give a wider choice of access through different platforms (e.g. mobile phone or interactive TV access in addition to fixed PC access).
2 The usage divide ('primary digital divide') concentrating on those who have access but are non-users. Governments promote learning of basic Internet skills through ICT courses to those with the highest risks of disengagement.
3 The divide stemming from quality of use ('secondary digital divide') focusing on differentials in participation rates of those people who have access and are users. Training can also be used to reduce this divide.

To assist with social exclusion due to lack of technology, The One Laptop Per Child initiative (OLPC, **www.laptop.org**) was founded as a non-profit organisation in 2005. The original concept was to offer a $100 laptop in developed and developing countries. The first, low-power XO which has WiFi, a Linux operating system and an Advanced Micro Devices chip, is closer to $200 in US.

Like other innovations, such as mechanised transport, electricity or the phone, the Internet has been used to support social progress. Those with special needs and interests can now communicate on a global basis and empowering information sources are readily available to all. For example, visually impaired people are no longer restricted to Braille books but can use screen readers to hear information available to sighted people on the web. The use of social networks and virtual worlds may also appeal to those who are disabled, although some of the social networks have been criticised for not being easy to access for the visually impaired. As we will see, this has implications for disability discrimination laws which impact accessibility. However, these same technologies, including the Internet, can have negative social impacts such as changing traditional social ideals and being used as a conduit for crime. The Internet has facilitated the publication of and access to information, which has led to many benefits, but it has also led to publication of and access to information which most in society would deem inappropriate. Well-known problems include the use of the Internet to incite racial hatred and terrorism, support child pornography and for identity theft. Such social problems can have implications for marketers who need to respond to laws or the morals established by society and respond to the fears generated. For example, portals such as MSN (**www.msn.com**) and Yahoo! (**www.yahoo.com**) discontinued their use of unmoderated chatrooms in 2003 since paedophiles were using them to 'groom' children for later real-world meetings. These issues are explored in more detail in Case Study 3.

Cultural forces

The local language and culture of a country or region can dramatically affect the requirements of users of a web service. We discuss this issue further in Chapter 7 on website design. The types of sites used (media consumption) and search engines used can also vary dramatically by country as discussed in Chapter 9. So it is important for situation analysis to review country differences.

Environmental and green issues related to Internet usage

The future state of our planet is a widely held social concern that is closely related to economic issues. Although technology is generally seen as detrimental to the environment – think long- and short-haul flights, TVs and electronic gadgets burning fuel when left on standby – there are some arguments that e-commerce and digital communications can have environment benefits. These benefits are also often beneficial to companies in that they can make cost-savings while positioning themselves as environmentally concerned – see Digital marketing insight 3.12.

Digital marketing insight 3.12 HSBC customers plant Virtual Forest

HSBC has committed to improving the environment since it became a climate-neutral company globally. Through the use of green technologies and emission-offset trading, HSBC counteracts all CO_2 emissions generated by its building operations and corporate travel. In 2006, 35 per cent of operations in North America were offset by investments in Renewable Energy Certificates from wind power alone.

Another aspect of its green policy is its online banking service, where it encourages paperless billing. For example, in the UK in 2007 over 400,000 customers switched from paper statements to online delivery, creating a virtual tree each time, and for every 20 virtual trees HSBC promised to plant a real one.

Potentially, online shopping through transactional e-commerce can also have environment benefits. Imagine a situation where we no longer travelled to the shops, and 100 per cent of items were efficiently delivered to us at home or at work. This would reduce traffic considerably! Although this situation is inconceivable since most of us enjoy shopping in the real world too much, online shopping is growing considerably and it may be having an impact. Research by the Internet Media in Retail Group (**www.imrg.org**) shows the growing importance of e-commerce in the UK where over 10 per cent of retail sales are now online. In 2007 it launched a Go Green, Go Online campaign where it identified six reasons why it believes e-commerce is green. They are:

1 *Fewer vehicle miles*. Shopping is the most frequent reason for car travel in Great Britain, accounting for 20 per cent of all trips, and for 12 per cent of mileage. A study by the Swiss Online Grocer LeShop.ch calculated that each time a customer decides to buy online rather than go shopping by car, 3.5 kg of CO_2 emissions are saved.
2 *Lower inventory requirements*. The trend towards pre-selling online – i.e. taking orders for products before they are built, as implemented by Dell – avoids the production of obsolete goods that have to be disposed of if they don't sell, with associated wastage in energy and natural resources.
3 *Fewer printed materials*. Online e-newsletters and brochures replace their physical equivalent so saving paper and distribution costs. Data from the Direct Mail Information Service (**www.dmis.co.uk**) shows that direct mail volumes have fallen slightly in the last two years reversing an upward trend in the previous ten years. This must be partly due to marketing e-mails, which the DMA e-mail benchmarks (**www.dma.org.uk**) show number in their billions in the UK alone.
4 *Less packaging*. Although theoretically there is less need for fancy packaging if an item is sold online this argument is less convincing, since most items like software or electronic items still come in packaging to help convince us we have bought the right thing – to reduce post-purchase dissonance. At least those billions of music tracks downloaded from iTunes and Napster don't require any packaging or plastic.
5 *Less waste*. Across the whole supply chain of procurement, manufacturing and distribution, the Internet can help reduce product and distribution cycles. Some even claim that auction services like eBay and Amazon Marketplace which enable redistribution of second-hand items can promote recycling.
6 *Dematerialisation*. Better known as digitisation, this is the availability of products like software, music and video in digital form.

If companies trading online can explain these benefits to their customers effectively, as HSBC have done, then this can benefit these online channels.

But what does the research show about how much e-shopping reduces greenhouse gas emissions? A study by Finnish researchers Siikavirta *et al.* (2003), limited to e-grocery shopping, has suggested that, depending on the home delivery model used, it is theoretically possible to reduce the greenhouse gas emissions generated by grocery shopping by 18 per cent to 87 per cent compared with the situation in which household members go to the store. Some of the constraints that were used in the simulation model include: maximum of 60 orders per route, maximum of 3000 L per route, working time maximum 11 hours per van, working time maximum 5 hours per route, loading time 20 minutes per route, drop-off time 2 minutes per customer. The researchers estimated that this would lead to a reduction of all Finland's greenhouse gas emissions by as much as 1 per cent, but in reality the figure is much lower since only 10 per cent of grocery shopping trips are online. Cairns (2005) has completed a study for the UK which shows the importance of grocery shopping – she estimates that car travel for food and other household items represents about 40 per cent of all UK shopping trips by car, and about 5 per cent of all car use. She considers that a direct substitution of car trips by van trips could reduce vehicle-km by 70 per cent or more. A broader study by Ahmed and Sharma (2006) has used value-chain analysis to assess the role of the Internet in changing the amount of energy and materials consumed by businesses for each part of the supply chain. However, no estimates of savings are made.

As a conclusion to this chapter, consider Case Study 3, which highlights the marketplace issues faced by a new e-business launched in 2005.

Case Study 3 Zopa launches a new lending model

This case shows how it is still possible to develop radical new online business models. It shows how an online business can be launched without large-scale expenditure on advertising and how it needs to be well targeted at its intended audience.

Context

It might be thought that innovation in business models was left behind in the dot-com era, but still fledgling businesses are launching new online services. Zopa is an interesting example of a pureplay social or peer-to-peer lending service launched in March 2005 with US and Italian sites launching in 2007 and a Japanese site launched in 2008.

Zopa is an online service which enables borrowers and lenders to bypass high street banks. There are over 150,000 UK members and 200,000 worldwide. Zopa is an example of a consumer-to-consumer (peer-to-peer) exchange intermediary.

Zopa stands for 'zone of possible agreement', which is a term from business theory. It refers to the overlap between one person's bottom line (the lowest they're prepared to receive for something they are offering) and another person's top line (the most they're prepared to pay for something). This approach underpins negotiations about the majority of types of products and services.

The business model

The exchange provides a matching facility between people who want to borrow with people who want to lend. Each lender's money is parcelled out between at least 50 borrowers. Zopa revenue is based on charging borrowers 1 per cent of their loan as a fee, and from commission on any repayment protection insurance that the borrower selects. At the time of launch, Zopa estimated it needed to gain just a 0.2 per cent share of the UK loan market to break even, which it could achieve within 18 months of launch.

In 2007, listings were launched (**http://uk.zopa.com/ZopaWeb/Listings/**) where loans can be requested by individuals in a similar way to eBay listings.

Borrowers can borrow relatively cheaply over shorter periods for small amounts. This is the reverse of banks, where if you borrow more and for longer it gets cheaper. The service will also appeal to borrowers who have difficulty gaining credit ratings from traditional financial services providers.

For lenders, returns are in the range of 20 to 30 per cent higher than putting money in a deposit account, but there is the risk of bad debt. Lenders choose the minimum interest rate that they are prepared to accept after bad debt has been taken into account for different markets within Zopa. Borrowers are placed in different risk categories with different interest rates according to their credit histories (using the same Equifax-based credit ratings as used by the banks) and lenders can decide which balance of risk against return they require.

Borrowers who fail to pay are pursued through the same mechanism as banks use and also get a black mark against their credit histories. But, for the lender, their investment is not protected by any compensation scheme, unless they have been defrauded.

The *Financial Times* reported that banks don't currently see Zopa as a threat to their high-street business. One financial analyst said Zopa was 'one of these things that could catch on but probably won't'.

Zopa does not have a contact centre. According to its website, enquiries are restricted to e-mail in order to keep its costs down. However, there is a service promise of answering e-mails within three hours during working hours.

Although the service was launched initially in the UK in 2005, *Financial Times* (2005) reported that people in 20 countries want to set up franchises, including China, New Zealand, India and some South American countries.

The peer-to-peer lending marketplace now has several providers. The social lending site Kiva allows lenders to give to a specific entrepreneur in a poor or developing world country. In the US, Prosper (**www.prosper.com**) has over 600,000 members and uses a loan listing model.

About the founders

The three founders of Zopa are chief executive Richard Duvall, chief financial officer James Alexander and David Nicholson, inventor of the concept and business architect. All were involved with Egg, with Richard Duvall creating the online bank for Prudential in 1998. Mr Alexander had been strategy director at Egg after joining in 2000, and previously had written the business plan for Smile, another online bank owned by the Co-operative Bank. The founders were also joined by Sarah Matthews, who was Egg's brand development director.

Target market

The idea for the business was developed from market research that showed there was a potential market of 'freeformers' to be tapped.

Freeformers are typically not in standard employment, rather they are self-employed or complete project-based or freelance work. Examples include consultants and entrepreneurs. Consequently, their incomes and lifestyles may be irregular, although they may still be assessed as creditworthy. According to James Alexander, 'they're people who are not understood by banks, which value stability in people's lives and income over everything else'. Institute of Directors (IOD) (2005) reported that the research showed that freeformers had 'much less of a spending model of money and much more of an asset model'.

Surprisingly, the research indicated a large number of freeformers. *New Media Age* reported Duvall as estimating that in the UK there may be around 6 million freeformers (of a population of around 60 million). Duvall is quoted as saying: 'It's a group that's growing really quickly. I think in 10 or 15 years time most people will work this way. It's happening right across the developed world. We've been doing some research in the US and we think there are some 30 or 40 million people there with these attitudes and behaviours.'

Some of the directors see themselves as freeformers: they have multiple interests and do not only work for Zopa; James Alexander works for one day a week in a charity and Sarah Matthews works just three days a week for Zopa. You can see example personas of typical borrowers and lenders on the web site: **www.zopa.com/ZopaWeb/public/how/zopamembers.shtml**.

From reviewing the customer base, lenders and borrowers are often united by a desire to distance themselves from conventional institutions. James Alexander says: 'I spend a lot of time talking to members and have found enormous goodwill towards the idea, which is really like lending to family members or within a community.' But he also says that some of the lenders are simply entrepreneurs who have the funds, understand portfolio diversification and risk and are lending on Zopa alongside other investments.

Business status

The *Financial Times* (2005) reported that Zopa had just 300 members at launch, but within four months it had 26,000 members. According to James Alexander, around 35 per cent are lenders, who between them have £3 million of capital waiting to be distributed. The company has not, to date, revealed how much has been lent, but average loans have been between £2,000 and £5,000. **Moneyfacts.co.uk** isn't showing any current accounts with more than 5 per cent interest, but Zopa is a riskier product, so you'd expect better rates. Unlike a deposit account, it's not covered by any compensation schemes.

Marketing communications

The launch of Zopa was quite different from Egg and other dot-coms at the turn of the millennium. Many companies at that time invested large amounts in offline media such as TV and print to rapidly grow awareness and to explain their proposition to customers.

Instead, Zopa relied on word of mouth and PR with some online marketing activities where the cost of customer acquisition can be controlled. The launch of such a model and the history of its founders made it relatively easy to have major pieces about the item in relevant newspapers and magazines such as the *Guardian*, *Financial Times*, *The Economist* and the Institute of Directors house magazine, which its target audience may read. Around launch, IOD (2005) reported that Duvall's PR agency, Sputnik, achieved 200 million opportunities for the new company to be read about. Of course, not all coverage is favourable: many of the articles explored the risk of lending and the viability of the start-up. However, others pointed out that the rates for the best-rated 'A category' borrowers are better than any commercial loan offered by a bank and for lenders, rates are better than any savings account. The main online marketing activities that Zopa uses are search engine marketing and affiliate marketing. In 2007 Zopa created its own Facebook application 'People Like You', which lets Facebookers compare their personality with other people's. Zopa communicates with its audience in an informal way through its blogs (**http://blog.zopa.com**).

Funding

Zopa initially received funding from two private equity groups, Munich-based Wellington Partners and Benchmark Capital of the US. Although the model was unique within financial services, its appeal was increased by the well-publicised success of other peer-to-peer Internet services such as Betfair, the gambling website, and eBay, the auction site.

Sources: *Financial Times* (2005), *New Media Age* (2005), Institute of Directors (2005), Zopa website (**www.zopa.com**) and blog (**http://blog.zopa.com**).

Question

Imagine you are a member of the team at the investors reviewing the future viability of the Zopa business. On which criteria would you assess the future potential of the business and the returns in your investment based on Zopa's position in the marketplace and its internal capabilities?

Summary

1 Environmental scanning and analysis of the macro-environment are necessary in order that a company can respond to environmental changes and act on the forces which shape the trading environment.

2 Technological forces are arguably the most likely and most important for digital marketers to watch and assess. Rapid variation in technology requires constant monitoring of adoption of the technology by customers and competitors and appropriate responses.

3 Economic forces considered in this chapter include classic economic factors, i.e. employment, interest rates and market growth and emerging markets for digital marketers. Different economic conditions in different markets are considered in developing e-commerce budgets.

4 Political forces involve the role of governments in promoting e-commerce, but also in trying to restrict it, which raises the question of democracy and the Internet.

5 Legal forces to be considered by e-commerce managers include privacy and data protection, distance-selling rules, taxation, brand reputation protection including domain name registration and copyright.

6 Social forces include variation in usage of the Internet while ethical issues include the need to safeguard consumer privacy and security of details. Privacy issues include collection and dissemination of customer information, cookies and the use of direct e-mail. Marketers must act within current law, reassure customers about their privacy and explain the benefits of collection of personal information.

Exercises

Self-assessment exercises

1 Summarise the key elements of the macro-environment that should be scanned by an e-commerce manager.
2 Give an example of how each of the macro-environment forces may directly drive the content and services provided by a website.
3 What actions should e-commerce managers take to safeguard consumer privacy and security?
4 Give three examples of techniques websites can use to protect the user's privacy.
5 How do governments attempt to control the adoption of the Internet and to what extent does this impact on the democracy of information?
6 Suggest approaches to managing the rapid change of technological innovation.

Essay and discussion questions

1 You recently started a job as e-commerce manager for a bank. Produce a checklist of all the different legal issues that you need to check for compliance on the existing website of the bank.
2 How should the e-commerce manager monitor and respond to technological innovation?
3 Benchmark different approaches to achieving and reassuring customers about their privacy and security using three or four examples for a retail sector such as travel, books, toys or clothing.
4 Select a new Internet-access technology (such as phone, kiosks or TV) that has been introduced in the last two years and assess whether it will become a significant method of access.

Examination questions

1 Summarise the macro-environment variables a company needs to monitor when operating an e-commerce site.
2 Discuss the potential significance of economic influences on the development of digital marketing initiatives.
3 Explain the purpose of environmental scanning in an e-commerce context.
4 Give three examples of how websites can use techniques to protect the user's privacy.
5 Explain the significance of the diffusion–adoption concept to the adoption of new technologies to:
   a consumers purchasing using technological innovations
   b businesses deploying technological innovations.
6 What action should an e-commerce manager take to ensure compliance with ethical and legal standards of their site?

References

Ahmed, N.U. and Sharma, S.K. (2006) Porter's value chain model for assessing the impact of the internet for environmental gains, *Int. J. Management and Enterprise Development*, 3(3), 278–95.

BBC (2011) Digital Economy Act court challenge fails, **http://www.bbc.co.uk/news/technology-13141986**, 20 April 2011.

Beckstrom (2011) gTLD Applicant Guide Book, http://www.icann.org/en/topics/new-gtlds/rfp-new-gtld-global-awareness-campaign-05jul11-en.pdf.

Cairns, S. (2005) Delivering supermarket shopping: more or less traffic? *Transport Reviews*, 25(1), 51–84, January .

CIA (2011) The World Factbook, https://www.cia.gov/library/publications/the-world-factbook/geos/xx.html, accessed, September 2011.

ClickZ (2010) Foursquare Marketing Hits and Misses: 5 Case Studies, Christopher Heine, 28 September 28: http://www.clickz.com/clickz/news/1735591/foursquare-marketing-hits-misses-case-studies.

Cutts, M. (2007) Talk like a Googler: parts of a url, Blog posting, 14 August 2007, http://www.mattcutts.com/blog/seo-glossary-url-definitions/.

Davidson, A. (2011) Interviewing Innovation by 'doing both': Cisco manages contradiction that drive growth and profit, http://www.emeraldinsight.com.libezproxy.open.ac.uk/journals.htm?issn=1087-8572&volume=39&issue=1&articleid=1896872&show=html.

Doherty, N.F., Ellis-Chadwick, F. and Hart, C.A. (2003) An analysis of the factors affecting the adoption of the Internet in the UK retail sector, *Journal of Business Research*, 56(11), 887–97.

eGov monitor (2011) Government unveils £530 million investment to boost high-speed broadband in rural areas across the UK, http://www.egovmonitor.com/node/43298, accessed September 2011.

Ellis-Chadwick, F. and Doherty, N. (2011) Web advertising: the role of email marketing, *Journal of Business.*

European Commission (2007) i2010 Annual Information Society Report 2007, published at: http://ec.europa.eu/information_society/eeurope/i2010/index_en.htm.

Fox, S. (2004) Older Americans and the Internet, Pew Internet Project: 24 March 2004, presented at presentation at 'Older Adults and the Web' event for usability.gov, July 19–20, 2004

Financial Times (2005) Lending exchange bypasses high street banks, Paul J. Davies, 22 August.

Gartner (2011) Hype Cycle Special Report for 2011. Report published 2 August 2011,
http://www.gartner.com/DisplayDocument?id=1758314&ref=g_noreg.

Godin, S. (1999) *Permission Marketing*. Simon and Schuster, New York.

Gorell, C. (2011) Quick Takes, *Strategy & Leadership*, 39(1).

GMSA (2010) Mobile banking closes the poverty gap: http://www.bbc.co.uk/news/10156667.

Guardian (2008) Porn? Sex? Britons value cruises much more, *Guardian*, Richard Wray, 6 February 2008.

ICO (2011) Promoting openness by public bodies and data privacy for individuals
An information rights strategy for the Information Commissioner's Office. May 2011 v1.0

Information Commissioner (1998) *Legal guidelines on the 1998 UK Data Protection Act*, available from: www.informationcommissioner.gov.uk.

Institute of Directors (2005) Profile – Richard Duvall, IOD house magazine, *Director*, pp. 51–5.

iPhoneDev (2010) App Store average earning per month per paid app is $700, http://iphone-dev.tumblr.com/post/754296222/appstore-average-earning Blog post, 30 June 2010

Mougayer, W. (1998) *Opening Digital Markets – Battle Plans and Strategies for Internet Commerce*, 2nd edn, CommerceNet Press, McGraw-Hill, New York.

New Media Age (2005) Personal lender, Dominic Dudley, 18 August.

Nielsen (2010) Homes add even more TV sets in 2010, blog post, 28 April: http://blog-nielsen/nom/nielsenwire.

Omar, A., Khurrum, M., Bhutta, S. and Sanchez, T. (2009) The impact of e-taxation policy on state and local government revenue, *Electronic Government, an International Journal 2009*, 6(4), 378–90.

ONS – Office for National Statistics (2010) Women in the Labour Market: http://www.statistics.gov.uk/cci/nugget.asp?id=2145, accessed 15 March 2011.

ONS – Office for National Statistics (2011) Households and individuals: http://www.ons.gov.uk/ons/rel/rdit2/internet-access---households-and-individuals/2011/stb-internet-access-2011.html, accessed 31 August 2011.

Ott, A. (2011) Time-value economics: competing for customer time and attention, *Strategy & Leadership*, 39(1), 24–31.

Rogers, E. (1983) *Diffusion of Innovations*, 3rd edn. Free Press, New York.

Rueda-Sabater, E. and Derosby, D. (2011) The evolving Internet in 2025: four scenarios, *Strategy & Leadership*, 39(1), 32–38.

Siikavirta, H., Punakivi, M., Karkkainen, M. and Linnanen, L. (2003) Effects of e-commerce on greenhouse gas emissions: a case study of grocery home delivery in Finland, *Journal of Industrial Ecology*, 6(2), 83–97.

Sparrow, A. (2000) E-Commerce and the Law. The legal implications of doing business online. *Financial Times* Executive Briefings.

Smart Insights (2011a), New privacy law on cookies – do we need to take action?, blog post by Dave Chaffey, 1 March 2011: http://www.smartinsights.com/marketplace-analysis/digital-marketing-laws/cookie-privacy-law.

Smart Insights (2011b) Contactless payment using Near Field Communications, blog post by Dave Chaffey, 26 September 2011: http://www.smartinsights.com/mobile-marketing/proximity-marketing/contactless-payments-near-field-communications-nfc/.

Telegraph (2011) Liberal Democrat Party Conference 2011: Danny Alexander's speech in full, http://www.telegraph.co.uk/news/politics/liberaldemocrats/8771863/Liberal-Democrat-Party-Conference-2011-Danny-Alexanders-speech-in-full.html.

Varley, R. (2001) *Retail Product Management*, Routledge, London.

Vlosky, R., Fontenot, R. and Blalock, L. (2000) Extranets: impacts on business practices and relationships, *Journal of Business & Industrial Marketing*, 15(6), 438–57.

W3C (2008) Web accessibility for older users: a literature review, http://www.w3.org/TR/wai-age-literature/#arfl, accessed 10 August 2011.

Weblinks

- **M:Metrics** (www.mmetrics.com). Provider of research about mobile phone usage.
- **New Media Age** (www.newmediazero.com/nma). A weekly magazine reporting on the UK new media developments specialising in mobile media and IPTV.
- **Oxford Internet Survey (OxIS)** (www.oii.ox.ac.uk/microsites/oxis). Research and statistics from the Oxford Internet Institute is designed to offer detailed insights into the influence of the Internet on society in Britain including 'Internet disengagement'.
- **Pew Internet and American Life Project** (www.pewinternet.org). Funds and publishes original, academic-quality research that explores the impact of the Internet on society. Also highlights adoption trends such as social networks, online video and chat.
- **Brand Republic** (http://www.brandrepublic.com/). A weekly magazine available for the UK, covering a range of new media platforms.
- **Text.It** (www.text.it). Portal from Mobile Data Association with examples of how SMS is used in the UK for consumer and business campaigns. Text.It (www.text.it). Portal from Mobile Data Association with examples of how SMS is used in the UK for consumer and business campaigns.

New digital law developments

- **iCompli** (www.icompli.co.uk). Portal and e-newsletter concentrating on e-commerce law.
- **Marketing Law** (www.marketinglaw.co.uk). Up-to-date source on all forms of law related to marketing activities.
- **OUT-LAW** (www.out-law.com). This site has 8000 pages of free legal news and guidance, mostly on IT and e-commerce issues produced by UK Law firm Pinsent Masons.
- **Privacy International** (www.privacyinternational.org). Group campaigning for privacy which contains information on legal developments in different countries.

Country-specific privacy laws

- Australia also enacted a SPAM act in 2003 (www.privacy.gov.au).
- Canada also has a privacy act (www.privcom.gc.ca).
- European Commission Data Protection and privacy legal resources (http://ec.europa.eu/justice_home/fsj/privacy).
- New Zealand Privacy Commissioner (www.privacy.org.nz).
- United States (CAN-SPAM Act, www.ftc.gov/spam).
- United Kingdom (Information Commissioner, www.ico.gov.uk).
- Summary of all countries (www.spamlaws.com).

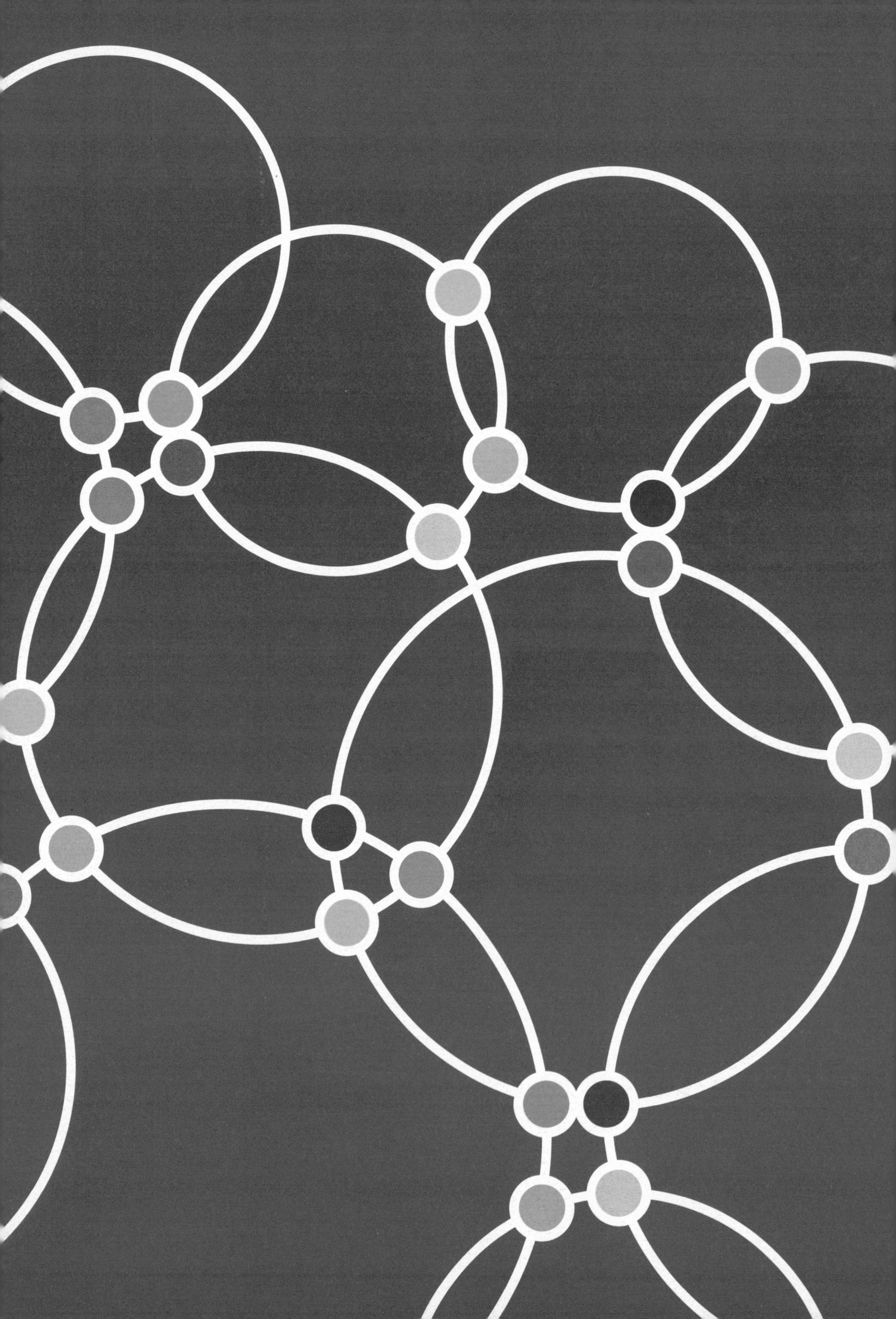

Part 2

Digital marketing strategy development

In Part 2, approaches for developing a digital marketing strategy are explored. These combine traditional approaches to strategic marketing planning with specific Internet-related issues that need to be considered by digital marketers. In Chapter 4 a framework for developing digital marketing is described, Chapter 5 discusses the opportunities for varying the marketing mix online and Chapter 6 reviews strategies for online customer relationship management.

Chapter 4
Digital marketing strategy

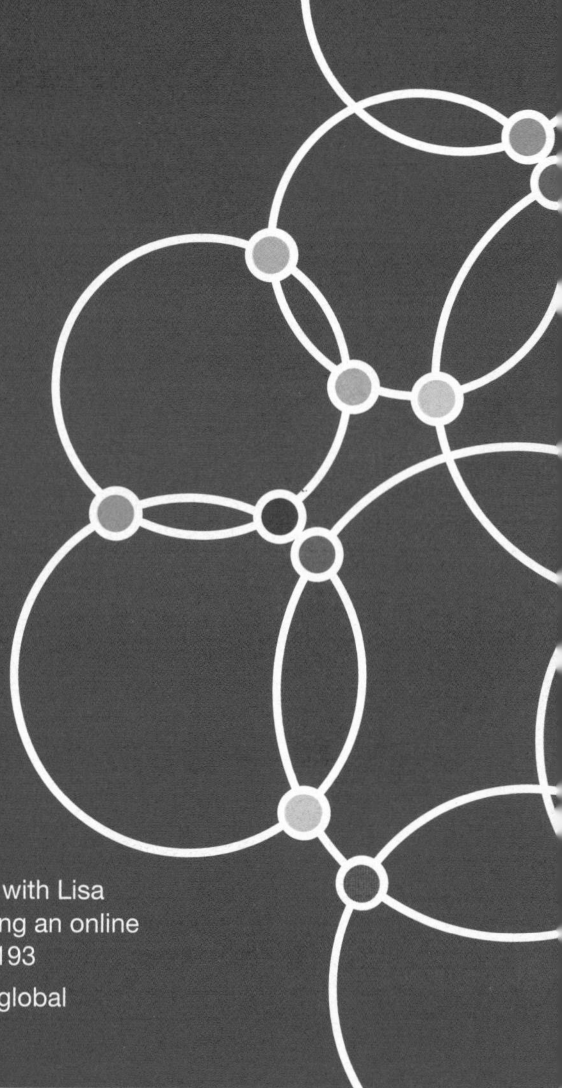

Chapter at a glance

Main topics

Case studies

Learning objectives

After reading this chapter, the reader should be able to:

- Relate digital marketing strategy to marketing and business strategy
- Identify opportunities and threats arising from digital technology platforms
- Evaluate alternative strategic approaches for using digital platforms

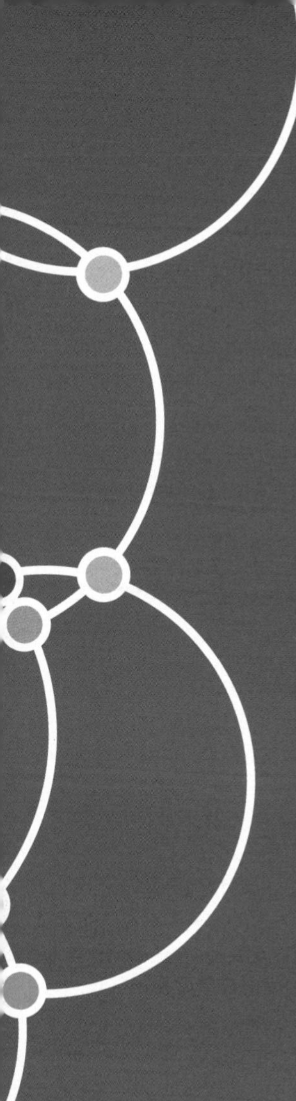

Questions for marketers

Key questions for marketing managers related to this chapter are:

- What approaches can be used to create digital marketing strategies?
- How does digital marketing strategy relate to other strategy development?
- What are the key strategic options for digital marketing?

Scan code to find the latest updates for topics in this chapter

Links to other chapters

This chapter is related to other chapters as follows:

- It builds on the evaluation of the Internet environment from Chapters 2 and 3
- Chapter 5 describes the potential for varying different elements of the marketing mix as part of digital marketing strategy
- Chapter 6 describes customer relationship management strategies
- Options for segmenting online customers by activity levels are covered in Chapter 6. Options for segmenting site visitors through web analytics systems are covered in Chapter 10
- Chapter 8 gives examples of goal setting for digital campaigns and strategies for developing the right communications mix

Introduction

The importance of the Internet to modern business strategy was underlined by Michael Porter (2001), who famously said:

> The key question is not whether to deploy Internet technology – companies have no choice if they want to stay competitive – but how to deploy it.

Digital marketing strategy
Definition of the approach by which applying digital technology platforms will support marketing and business objectives.

A **digital marketing strategy** is needed to provide consistent direction for an organisation's online marketing activities so that they integrate with its other marketing activities and support its overall business objectives. The digital marketing strategy has many similarities to the typical aims of traditional marketing strategies, in that it will:

- provide a future direction to digital marketing activities
- involve analysis of the organisation's external environment, internal resources and capabilities to inform strategy
- define digital marketing objectives that support marketing objectives
- involve selection of strategic options to achieve digital marketing objectives and create sustainable differential competitive advantage
- include strategy formulation to address typical marketing strategy options such as target markets, positioning and specification of the marketing mix
- help identify which strategies NOT to pursue and which marketing tactics are not suitable to implement
- specify how resources will be deployed and how the organisation will be structured to achieve the strategy.

This chapter examines each of these elements of strategy and begins by considering, an appropriate process for developing a digital marketing strategy, and then considers the following aspects of strategy development:

1 situation review (drawing on our coverage in Chapters 2 and 3)
2 goal setting
3 strategy formulation.

Figure 4.1 indicates the context for digital marketing strategy development. The internal influences include corporate objectives and strategy, and these in turn influence marketing strategy that should directly influence the digital marketing strategy. Key external influences include the market structure and demand, competitor strategies and the current and evolving opportunities and threats, in particular those enabled by new digital technologies (e.g. mobile marketing and IPTV) and marketing approaches (e.g. search engine marketing and use of social media). Methods for monitoring the external environment to anticipate external opportunities and threats and competitors' actions have been introduced in Chapters 2 and 3, as were methods of assessing the demand of the market for Internet-delivered services.

Channel marketing strategy
Defines how a company should set specific objectives for a channel such as the Internet and vary its proposition and communications for this channel.

Digital marketing strategy as a channel marketing strategy

Customer touchpoints
Communications channels with which companies interact directly with prospects and customers. Traditional touchpoints include face-to-face (instore or with sales representatives), phone and mail. Digital touchpoints include web services, e-mail and, potentially, mobile phone.

Digital marketing strategy is primarily a **channel marketing strategy** which defines how a company should set *channel-specific objectives* and develop a *differential channel-proposition* and *channel-specific communications* consistent with the characteristics of the channel and end user requirements. The strategy determines the strategic significance of the Internet relative to other communications channels that are used to communicate directly with customers at different **customer touchpoints**. Some organisations, such as low-cost airlines, use virtual channels, e.g. websites and e-mail marketing, for delivering services and communicating with customers, whereas others may follow a strategy which uses a mix of digital and offline channels, e.g. supermarkets which use face-to-face, telephone, mobile, direct mail communications and the web.

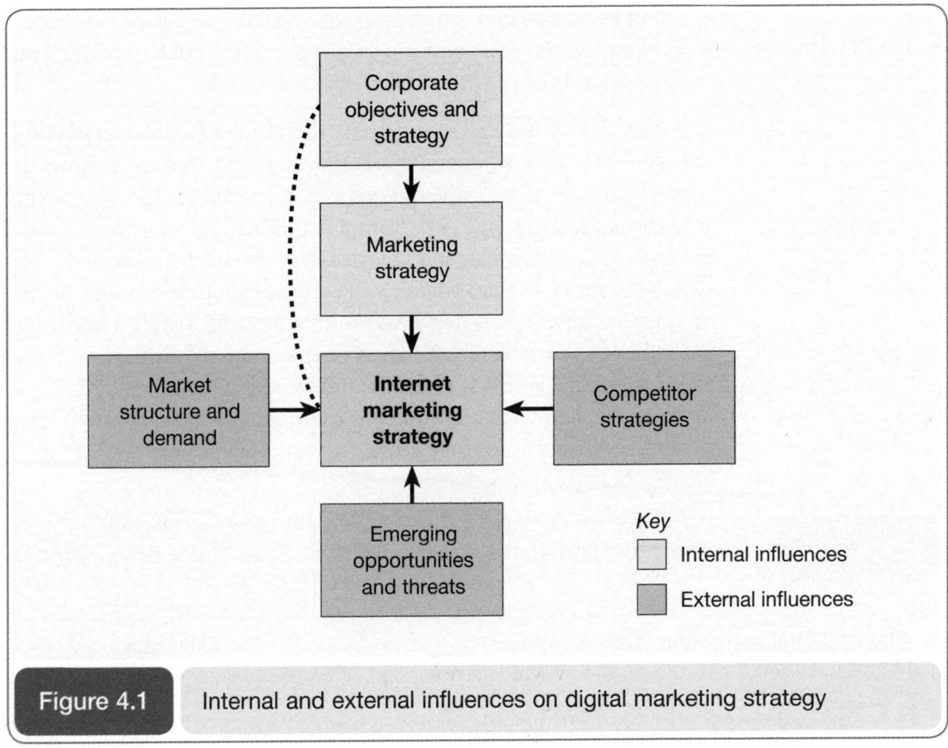

Figure 4.1 Internal and external influences on digital marketing strategy

So the focus of digital marketing strategy is decisions about how to use the channel to support existing marketing strategies, how to exploit its strengths and manage its weaknesses, and to use it in conjunction with other channels as part of a **multichannel marketing strategy**. This multichannel marketing strategy defines how different marketing channels should integrate and support each other in terms of their proposition development and communications based on their relative merits for the customer and the company.

Multichannel marketing strategy
Defines how different marketing channels should integrate and support each other in terms of their proposition development and communications based on their relative merits for the customer and the company.

The scope of digital marketing strategy

When reviewing options for online strategy, it is useful consider that this involves more than the narrow focus of a strategy to develop website functionality. Although, developing a website can be a central part of the strategy, digital marketers should also examine broader issues of how to:

- maximise the benefits of partnering with online intermediaries such as portals and social networks or influencers such as bloggers
- harness social media marketing both through use on its own site through user-generated content and within the main social networks like Facebook, Google+, LinkedIn and Twitter
- use e-mail, mobile, apps and databases strategically as communications and relationship-building tools which must integrate with other marketing communications.

Developing a digital marketing strategy may also involve redesigning business processes to integrate with partners such as suppliers and distributors in new ways. This point is made by Sultan and Rohm (2004) who, based on a study of three organisations, identify different forms of aligning online strategies with business goals, their framework identifying these strategic objectives:

- *Cost reduction and value chain efficiencies.* B2B supplier AB Dick used the Internet to sell printer supplies via the Internet to reduce service calls.
- *Revenue generation.* Reebok uses the Internet for direct licensed sales of products such as treadmills which do not have strong distribution deals.

- *Channel partnership.* Partnering with distributors using extranets.
- *Communications and branding.* Car company Saturn developed the MySaturn site to foster close relationships with customers.

Figure P.1 in the Preface suggests the range of digital marketing activities that must be managed as part of an digital marketing strategy. The figure shows that the operational activities which need to be implemented and managed as part of strategy can be usefully divided into those focusing on (1) customer acquisition, (2) customer conversion, proposition and experience development, and (3) customer retention and growth. Improving the capability to execute many of these activities will be decided upon through the review process of creating an digital marketing strategy. An output from the digital strategy will be a series of strategic e-commerce initiatives in the areas of customer acquisition, conversion or retention such as those shown in Table 4.1. These e-commerce initiatives will typically be prioritised and placed as part of a long-term e-commerce 'roadmap' defining required developments over a longer period, say one year to three years.

Table 4.1 Summary of typical focus for main types of e-commerce-related strategic initiatives

Type of digital marketing strategy initiative	Commentary	Examples
New customer proposition (product and pricing)	New site features or other online communications which are directly related to offering new products or services that will generate revenue	• Bank – introducing new product requiring different quotations • Portal – introducing a price comparison service • Magazine or music service offering new pricing options
Customer acquisition strategic initiatives	Strategic projects designed to enhance a site's capability and deliver different online marketing techniques aimed to attract new customers	• SEO • PPC • Affiliate marketing • Aggregators
Customer conversion and customer experience strategic initiatives	Investments in new customer features designed to engage the audience and increase conversion rates and average order values New functionality, e.g. new online store; special functionality, e.g. real time stock checking Strategic initiatives aimed at improving the customers' brand experience	• Implement online shop/secure payment • Introduce customer reviews and ratings • Merchandising capability for offer tailored promotions • Interactive tools to help product selection • Buyers' guides
Customer development and growth strategic initiatives	Investments to improve the experience and delivery of offers to existing customers	• Personalised recommendations and services for existing customers • Email contact strategy focused on the customer journey and level of brand awareness • Communities, social media, blogs or RSS feeds to encourage return visitors
Enhance marketing capabilities through site infrastructure improvements	These typically involve 'back-end or back-office features' which won't be evident to users of the site, but will help in the management or administration of the site	• CRM or personalisation • Content management system • Performance improvement – improve management information, web analytics systems including systems for multivariate and AB testing • Improve customer feedback facilities

In terms of scope, it is important to consider the extent to which digital marketing strategies blend together many elements of marketing and information technology strategies. In common with marketing strategy, digital marketing strategy must determine the best value propositions to offer to online customers and how to integrate with other channels to achieve strategic goals. But in common with IT strategy, many of the decisions of digital marketing strategy involve selection of the most appropriate investments in software or functionality and hardware technology and resources to provide an improved customer experience and to provide an infrastructure to gain better results from digital channels. Furthermore, media selection becomes a more strategic decision when planning a digital marketing strategy. In traditional marketing, media is selected based on its potential to deliver the objectives of a specific promotional initiative. However, digital marketing strategies often require a longer term view when making media investments, as techniques used to attract visitors to a website are often *continuous* or 'always-on' activities. See Chapter 8 for further discussion of these techniques.

Digital marketing in practice — The Smart Insights interview

Lisa Woods, Marketing Manager, HSBC International on creating an online engagement programme to raise awareness of its services

Overview and main concepts

Lisa Woods, marketing manager at HSBC International, describes a strategic approach for increasing awareness and engaging a key audience of Expats through the HSBC Expat Explorer (Figure 4.2). Expats are 'expatriates' of a country who live and work abroad.

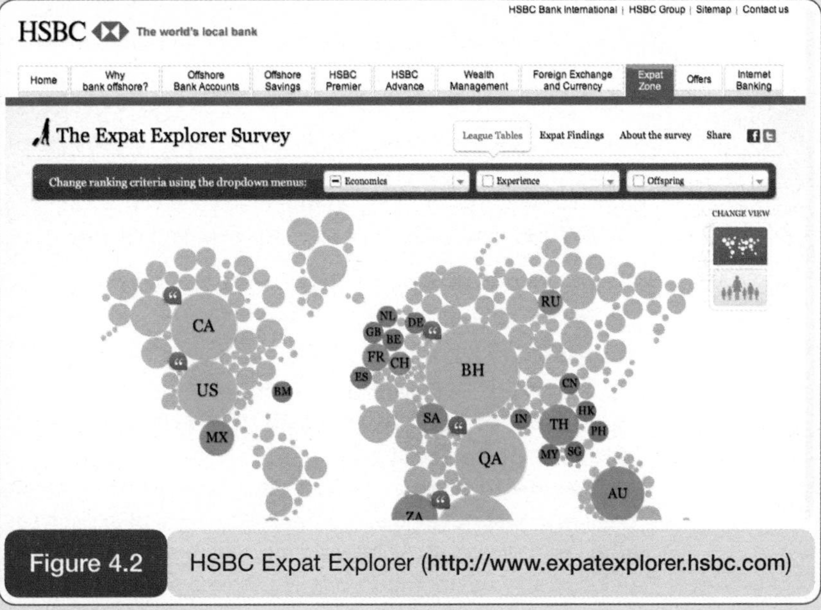

Figure 4.2 HSBC Expat Explorer (http://www.expatexplorer.hsbc.com)

The interview

Q. I know that the HSBC Expat Explorer is an established approach for HSBC International to engage its audience. What was the original thinking behind it?

Lisa Woods: 2011 is the fourth year of Expat Explorer since its conception in 2008. Since the launch, we've watched it grow into the world's largest survey of expats with

over 4000 respondents in 2010. The survey was devised because as a business we wanted to better understand the expat community and the issues and challenges they face whilst living or relocating overseas. Expat Explorer has provided us with some fascinating insights and because it covers all aspects of expat life has allowed us to better tailor the services we offer to our existing and potential customer base.

Q. How do you justify the return-on-investment for a branding activity such as this which doesn't directly link to online leads and sales?

Lisa Woods: Our main objective is to demonstrate that HSBC really does understand expat life. Establishing this credibility is important to us. It means we can build trust with both our existing and potential customer base increasing loyalty to our brand and giving our customers the confidence that we know the types of financial products and services they need.

We also hope to gain online leads and sales indirectly in a number of ways. We are investing in compelling content designed to pull people into the website, as opposed to spending money to 'push' people to us.

By creating something that is genuinely useful we hope that expats will want to share it with their peers in expat forums and communities, and thus generate additional traffic to the website at no extra cost. Likewise, we've had a large amount of press coverage for Expat Explorer which leads to more traffic being driven to the site. Encouraging media and social media sites to link to us also helps with our natural rankings in search engines for expat-related keywords.

Q. You run the survey across many countries, how do you approach tailoring communications before, during and after the survey so they resonate with local markets?

Lisa Woods: The survey is truly global and in 2010 we had respondents from over 100 countries complete the questionnaire. Tailoring communications is an extremely important part of the process and we use our local offices to translate all our press and survey launch materials to make them relevant to regional markets. Our social media channels also allow us to reach a global audience and we've built a community of followers from all over the world meaning we can keep them informed of the survey and its key findings as and when these are released.

Q. In recent years, you have used social media to support the survey and disseminating the results – how do you use social media?

Lisa Woods: We've been using social media since early 2009. It was a big step for us as a bank but it's delivered some fantastic results for us. We have three main channels which consist of an Expat Explorer blog, Twitter feed and YouTube platform and these are used in a variety of ways.

We look to position the blog as a central hub of expat related content. It's got a range of posts looking at the whole spectrum of expat issues and often helps us share the insights we've gained from our recent surveys. Quite often we'll also invite guest bloggers to contribute to our site. These contributions come from a wide variety of people, from expats who have moved abroad and have an interesting story to share to Expat life coaches, authors and business leaders. They're a great way of providing unique expat relevant content to our readers and the feedback we've had has been extremely positive.

The Twitter feed allows us to engage directly with the expat community helping us build the relationships with them more effectively. Our tweets range from flagging interesting articles, to responding to our follower's queries or issues, promoting our recent blog posts or simply saying a cheery hello. From a brand perspective it's allowed us to develop a much more personable face and we've seen our community grow to over 2300 followers which is testament to how positively we've been received.

The YouTube platform, a more recent addition to our social media channels, is where as you'd expect we host all of our video content. We generally develop one piece of film around each of the survey reports detailing the key findings and the insights we've developed on the back of this. We've also just launched an animated, infographic video bringing together the key highlights from the survey, which is also on YouTube. The videos are a lot of fun to work on and allow us to put a human face to the business. We then utilise the blog and Twitter feed to drive engagement and traffic.

We're about to launch an interactive version of Expat Explorer, which serves as a focal point on our own website for our social media activity and has Share functionality to enable users to share interesting findings from the survey on social media sites.

Q. Your activity this year uses some innovative approaches. What's new and which approaches have you found are successful that other companies could apply?

Lisa Woods: This year we really wanted to build upon the success of our previous Expat Explorer surveys. We wanted to bring the wealth of information we had from the survey to life online, in a visually rich and engaging way.

We took inspiration from other sites, particularly media sites, which use data visualisation to help readers make sense of large amounts of data. Working with our digital agency HeathWallace, we've developed an interactive tool based on the data from the survey.

The tool lets users explore the differences between their home country and other countries. They can compare countries based on 55 criteria ranging from quality of life to disposable income and the cost of educating their children abroad. Each output generates its own specific URL which can be shared through a number of social media sites. Users can also read key themes from the survey in a series of articles, illustrated with infographics.

We tested the tool with focus groups of expats and the responses were very positive. In particular, expats commented that they would trust the tool more than other country comparison tools as it reflects the views of real expats, people like them in similar circumstances.

As I mentioned, we have also created a non-commercial, animated video which highlights some of the interesting findings from the survey. By avoiding using commercial marketing messages and overt branding we hope that expats will be more inclined to watch and share the video and to come to our website to find out more.

We've also allowed a select group of bloggers and journalists, who write about expat issues, to have an exclusive preview of the new Expat Explorer before launch. The response has been great – we even enlisted some expat bloggers to help with content creation, providing us with case studies about their experiences of life abroad.

Brands such as HSBC have huge amounts of data, which can be used to create interesting and compelling content. We wanted to find ways to make that data accessible and useful for customers, which is what we have aimed to achieve with Expat Explorer. We have been able to mobilise HSBC's development and marketing resources in order to create something that we believe brings value for our customers and expats in general.

An integrated digital marketing strategy

The scope of digital marketing is widening and becoming increasingly pervasive, but the integration of an digital marketing strategy into business and marketing strategies often represents a significant challenge for many organisations. A possible explanation for this is because typically organisations have considered the Internet in isolation and sometimes try to bolt on digital marketing initiatives to existing promotional campaigns. The Econsultancy (2008) research highlighted the challenges of digital marketing strategy. The research involved e-commerce managers at companies in markets where their products could be sold online, e.g. mobile phones (Orange, Carphone Warehouse), travel (Tui and MyTravel), financial services (Lloyds TSB and Bradford & Bingley) and direct marketers such as BCA. Respondents were asked what their main challenges were and these highlighted the issues of gaining sufficient resource for Internet marketing. Challenges mentioned included:

- *gaining buy-in and budget* consistent with audience media consumption and value generated
- *conflicts of ownership and tensions* between a digital marketing team and other teams such as traditional marketing, IT, finance and senior management
- *coordination with different channels* in conjunction with teams managing marketing programmes elsewhere in the business
- *managing and integrating customer information* about characteristics and behaviours collected online
- *achieving consistent reporting*, review, analysis and follow-up actions of digital marketing results throughout the business
- *structuring the specialist digital team* and integrating into the organisation by changing responsibilities elsewhere in the organisation
- '*time to market*' for implementing new functionality on a site
- insourcing vs outsourcing online marketing tactics, i.e. search, affiliate, e-mail marketing, PR
- staff recruitment and retention.

Ultimately, it is important for organisations to integrate all of their strategic plans and it is important to clearly understand how and where the digital marketing strategy fits into the organisations overall corporate objectives. Figure 4.3. shows a planning hierarchy for an organisation, from a corporate or business plan which informs a marketing plan which in turn informs a communications plan and campaign briefs for different markets or brands. Figure 4.3 suggests that an e-marketing plan may be useful to manage the 'e-campaign components', which refers to online communications tools such as online advertising or e-mail marketing or continuous e-marketing activities which may be conducted throughout the year to achieve awareness or engagement on a website or social media presence, e.g. affiliate, search engine or social media marketing.

You may be thinking that the marketer already has enough plans to deal with. Surely the practical approach for companies that are embracing digital marketing initiatives is to integrate e-marketing activities within their existing planning frameworks? But we believe that in many organisations, a distinct digital marketing plan is initially essential if the organisation is to effectively harness digital marketing. Since online channels are new, it is even more imperative to have clarity within the organisation. An e-marketing specialist can create an e-marketing plan to help inform and influence not only senior managers or directors and other non-marketing functions, but also to achieve buy-in from fellow marketers.

The impact of digital in the marketing function has increased significantly in recent years and the Internet is no longer considered as 'just another channel to market'. Furthermore, it is important for organisations to plan how to manage the strategic contribution of digital channels to business objectives. Failure to plan how to manage digital channels can lead to a number of problems:

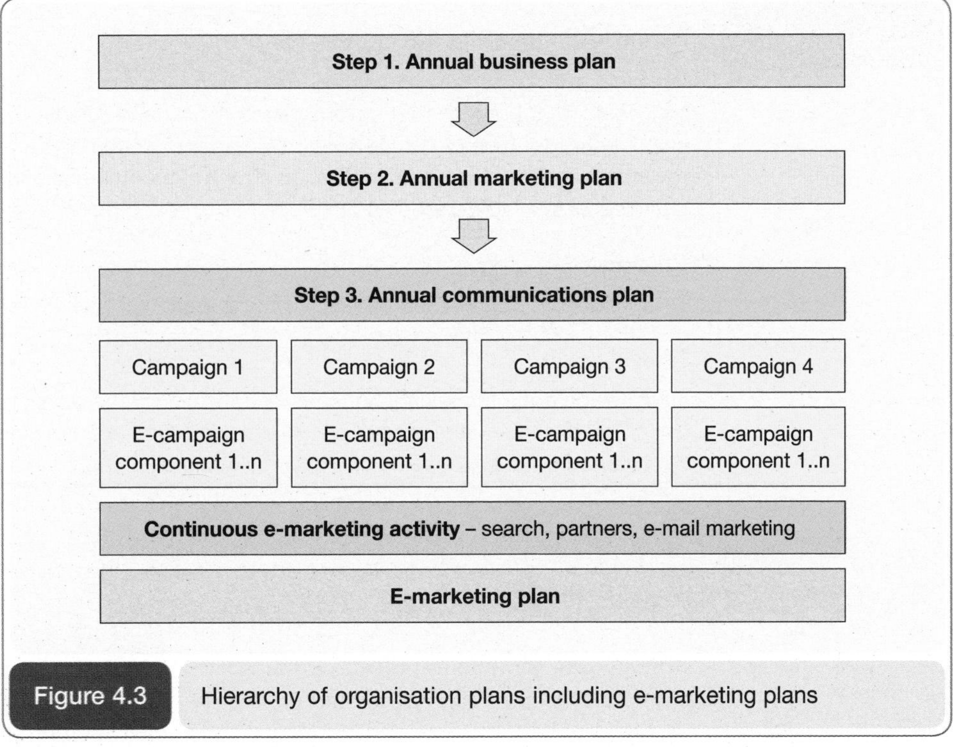

Figure 4.3 Hierarchy of organisation plans including e-marketing plans

1. Customer demand for online services will be underestimated if this has not been researched and it is under-resourced, and no or unrealistic objectives are set to achieve online marketing share.
2. Existing and start-up competitors will gain market share if insufficient resources are devoted to e-marketing and no clear strategies are defined.
3. Duplication of resources can occur, e.g. different parts of the marketing organisation purchasing different tools or different agencies for performing similar online marketing tasks.
4. Insufficient resource will be devoted to planning and executing e-marketing and there is likely to be a lack of specific specialist e-marketing skills, making it difficult to respond to competitive threats effectively.
5. Insufficient customer data are collected online as part of relationship building and these data are not integrated well with existing systems.
6. Efficiencies available through online marketing will be missed, e.g. lower communications costs and enhanced conversion rates in customer acquisition and retention campaigns.
7. Opportunities for applying online marketing tools, such as search marketing or e-mail marketing, will be missed or the execution may be inefficient if the wrong resources are used or marketers don't have the right tools.
8. Changes required to internal IT systems by different groups will not be prioritised accordingly.
9. The results of online marketing are not tracked adequately on a detailed or high-level basis.
10. Senior management support of e-marketing is inadequate to drive what often needs to be a major strategic initiative.

Activity 4.1 Benefits of digital-marketing planning

McDonald (2003) suggested several reasons why a marketing plan is useful, e.g. to help identify sources of competitive advantage, to encourage an organised approach towards marketing functions, to develop strong customer relationships. However, many organisations fail to develop and implement marketing plans (at all levels) effectively.

Purpose

To consider the barriers and benefits to the adoption of digital marketing planning.

Task

Imagine you are a marketing manager responsible for the development of your organisation's digital market strategy. Using an organisation you are familiar with, outline the barriers and potential benefits of digital maketing planning.

A generic strategic approach

Strategy process model A framework for approaching strategy development.

Marketing planning A logical sequence and a series of activities leading to the setting of marketing objectives and the formulation of plans for achieving them.

A **strategy process model** provides a framework that gives a logical sequence to follow to ensure inclusion of all key activities of strategy development and implementation. In a marketing context, these strategy development and implementation activities are coordinated through a marketing plan, and the process of creating this is known as **marketing planning**. McDonald (2003) defines marketing planning simply as:

> the planned application of marketing resources to achieve marketing objectives ... Marketing planning is simply a logical sequence and a series of activities leading to the setting of marketing objectives and the formulation of plans for achieving them.

McDonald (2003) distinguishes between strategic marketing plans which cover a period beyond the next financial year (typically three to five years) and tactical marketing plans which cover detailed actions over a shorter time period of one year or less and this is equally applicable to digital marketing planning. Furthermore, we suggest that a strategic digital marketing plan should place emphasis on three key areas:

1. Identification of changes to competitive forces in the micro-environment and macro-environment which will influence customer demand for online experiences and products.
2. Developing value propositions for customers using online services as part of their buying process.
3. Definition of the technology infrastructure and information architecture to deliver these value propositions as a customer experience.

Such an approach requires a long-term plan that can provide a *roadmap* to guide digital marketing activities for the eighteen months to three years. Whilst many organisations produce longer-term plans of say three to five years, it is important to consider that digital environments are highly dynamic and operational plans should aim to promote strategic agility (see Chapter 3).

Figure 4.4 shows an overall strategy process model for strategic Internet marketing by Chaffey and Smith (2008). An alternative perspective was presented in Figure 1.8 in order to introduce the role of strategy development into the first three chapters. SOSTAC® stands for Situation, Objectives and Strategy, Tactics, Action and Control. Chaffey and Smith (2008) note that each stage is not discrete, rather there is some overlap during each stage of planning – previous stages may be revisited and refined, as indicated by the reverse arrows in Figure 4.4. The elements of SOSTAC® planning in the context of how they are described in this text with respect to digital marketing strategy are:

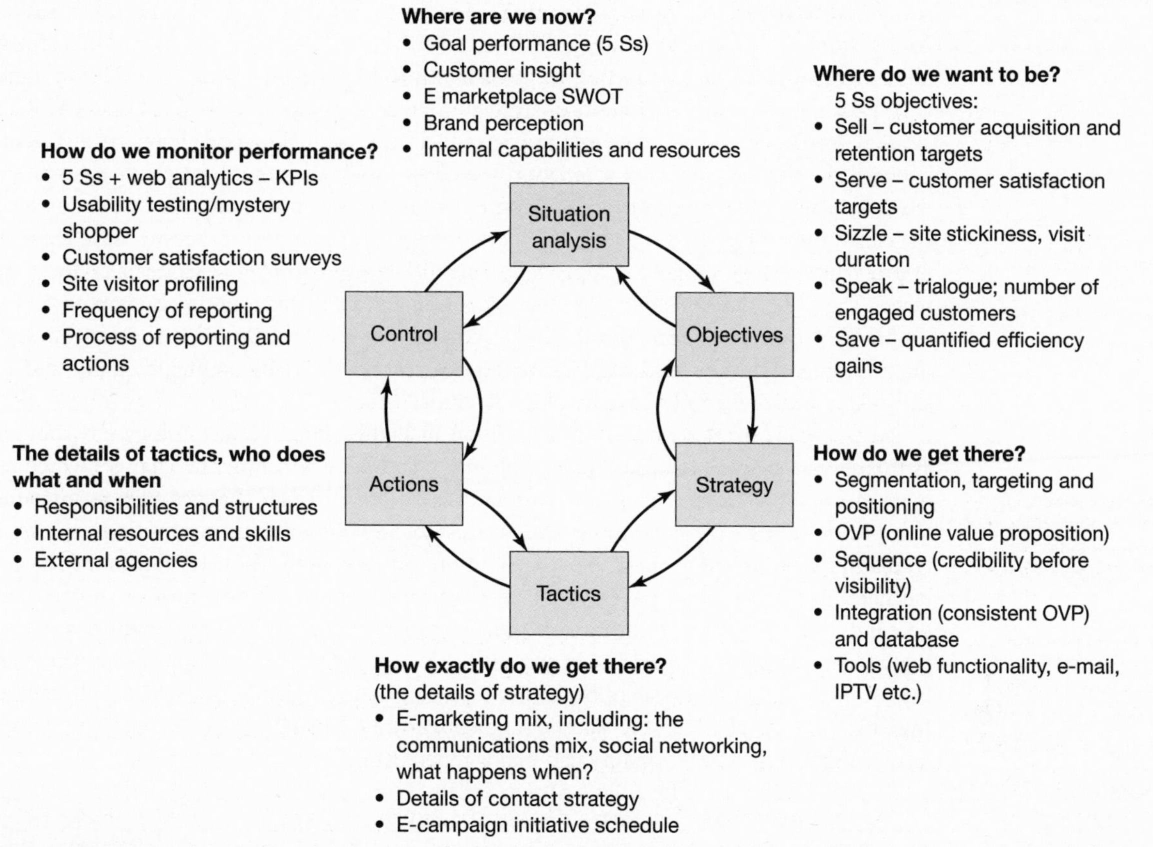

Figure 4.4 The SOSTAC® planning framework applied to digital Digital marketing strategy development
Source: Chaffey and Smith (2008)

1 *Situation analysis means 'where are we now?'* Planning activities involved at this stage include performing an Internet-specific SWOT analysis, and reviewing the different aspects of the micro-environment (Chapter 2) including customers, competitors and intermediaries. Situation analysis also involves review of the macro-environment (Chapter 3).
2 *Objectives means 'where do we want to be?'* This can include a vision for digital channels, and also specific numerical objectives for the digital channels such as projections of sales volumes and cost savings (see Chapter 9).
3 *Strategy means 'how do we get there?'* Strategy summarises how to achieve the objectives for the different decision points explained in this chapter including segmentation, targeting, proposition development (including the elements of the marketing mix described in more detail in Chapter 5 and e-CRM described in Chapter 6).
4 *Tactics defines the usage of tactical digital communications tools.* This includes specific details of the marketing mix (Chapter 5), e-CRM (Chapter 6), experience (Chapter 7) and digital communications (Chapters 8 and 9).
5 *Actions refers to action plans, change management and project management skills.* We refer to some of the issues of modifications to organisational roles and structures later in this chapter.
6 *Control looks at the use of management information including web analytics to assess whether strategic and tactical objectives are achieved and how improvements can be made to enhance results further.* This is closely related to goal setting as described in this chapter and in Chapter 8, and also the coverage of web analytics and tracking in Chapter 9.

Prescriptive strategy The three core areas of strategic analysis, strategic development and strategy implementation are linked together sequentially.

Emergent strategy Strategic analysis, strategic development and strategy implementation are interrelated and are developed together.

Arguably, due to the speed of development of digital technologies, there is a need for a more responsive approach to strategy planning. Mintzberg and Quinn (1991) and other authors commenting on corporate strategy, such as Lynch (2000), distinguish between prescriptive and emergent strategy approaches. In the **prescriptive strategy** approach, similar to Figure 4.4, Lynch identifies three elements of strategy – strategic analysis, strategic development and strategy implementation, and these are linked together sequentially. Where the distinction between the three elements of strategy is less clear, this is the **emergent strategy** approach where strategic analysis, strategic development and strategy implementation are interrelated. In reality, most organisational strategy development and planning processes have elements of prescriptive and emergent strategy reflecting different planning and strategic review timescales. The prescriptive elements are the structured annual or six-monthly budgeting process or a longer-term three-year rolling marketing planning process. But on a shorter timescale, organisations naturally also need an emergent process to enable strategic agility and the ability to rapidly respond to marketplace dynamics.

Strategic windows Opportunities arising through a significant change in environment.

An emergent strategy approach is essential in highly dynamic technology environment as this should enable organisations to respond to sudden environmental changes which can open **strategic windows**. Strategic windows may occur through changes such as introduction of new technology, e.g. mobile and wireless technology or cloud computing, changes in regulation of an industry, changes to distribution channels in the industry (again the Internet has had this impact), emerging target groups of customers who have a new set of needs and demands. The danger in creating a responsive capability for technology-enabled change is that mistakes may be made either in evaluating the significance of new approaches (in which case strategic investments may be wasted) or in the implementation, which will degrade the customer experience (the Facebook case study in Chapter 8 shows how the privacy implications of new functionality had major repercussions for customer trust).

Based on preliminary findings by Brian Smith, Daniel *et al.* (2001) suggested that planning styles adopted by organisations for e-commerce will be governed by a combination of market complexity, turbulence and the personal styles of company leaders. Smith identifies three main modes of strategy development:

- *Logical rational planning.* Uses analytical tools and frameworks to formulate and implement strategy.
- *Pragmatic incremental.* Strategy develops in response to minor adjustments to the external environment.
- *Subjective visionary.* Strategy is the result of a leader, typically dominant or charismatic.

Daniel *et al.* (2001) suggest that in low-complexity, high-turbulence markets vision and incrementalism will be dominant, that in high-complexity, low-turbulence markets rational planning approaches are dominant, and that in highly complex, turbulent markets all three styles may be required.

Econsultancy (2008) has researched approaches used to encourage emergent strategies or strategic agility (see Chapter 3) based on interviews with e-commerce practitioners. Some of the approaches used by companies to support emergent strategy development are summarised in Table 4.2.

Competitive intelligence (CI) A process that transforms disaggregated information into relevant, accurate and usable strategic knowledge about competitors, position, performance, capabilities and intentions.

Kalakota and Robinson (2000) have also recommended a dynamic, emergent strategy process specific to e-business. The elements of this strategy approach are shown in Figure 4.5. The emphasis is on responsiveness with continuous review and prioritisation of investment in new Internet applications. Clearly, the quality of environment scanning and information collection, dissemination and analysis and the speed of response will be key for organisations following such a responsive, emergent approach. One example of an approach to collecting this market event data is **competitive intelligence** or **CI**.

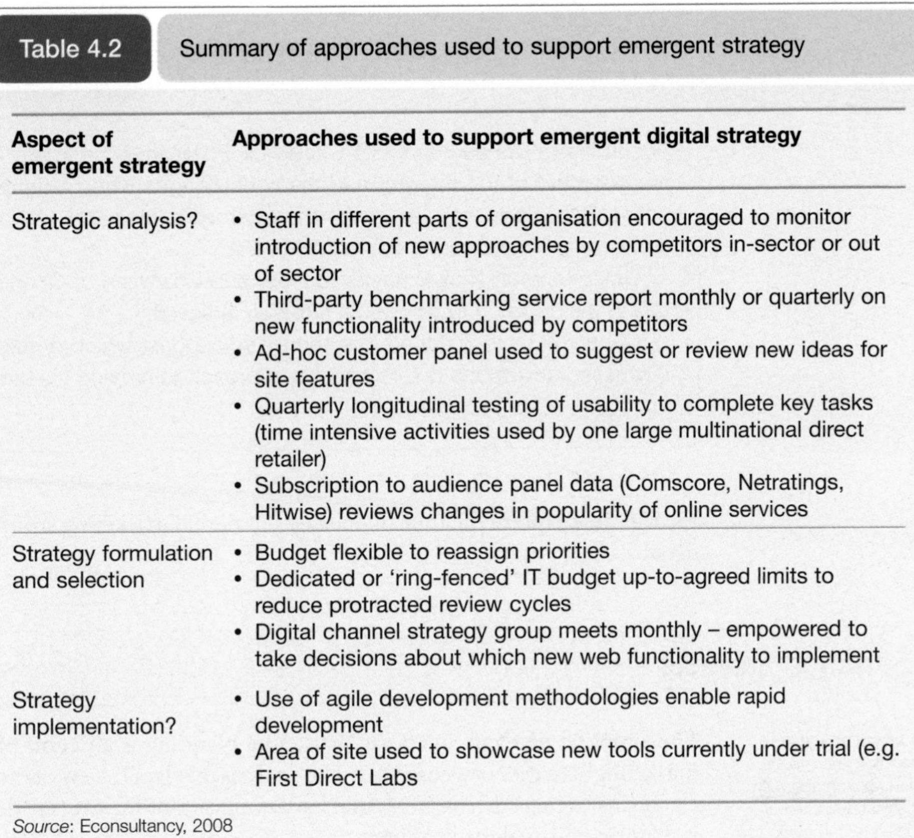

Table 4.2 Summary of approaches used to support emergent strategy

Aspect of emergent strategy	Approaches used to support emergent digital strategy
Strategic analysis?	• Staff in different parts of organisation encouraged to monitor introduction of new approaches by competitors in-sector or out of sector • Third-party benchmarking service report monthly or quarterly on new functionality introduced by competitors • Ad-hoc customer panel used to suggest or review new ideas for site features • Quarterly longitudinal testing of usability to complete key tasks (time intensive activities used by one large multinational direct retailer) • Subscription to audience panel data (Comscore, Netratings, Hitwise) reviews changes in popularity of online services
Strategy formulation and selection	• Budget flexible to reassign priorities • Dedicated or 'ring-fenced' IT budget up-to-agreed limits to reduce protracted review cycles • Digital channel strategy group meets monthly – empowered to take decisions about which new web functionality to implement
Strategy implementation?	• Use of agile development methodologies enable rapid development • Area of site used to showcase new tools currently under trial (e.g. First Direct Labs

Source: Econsultancy, 2008

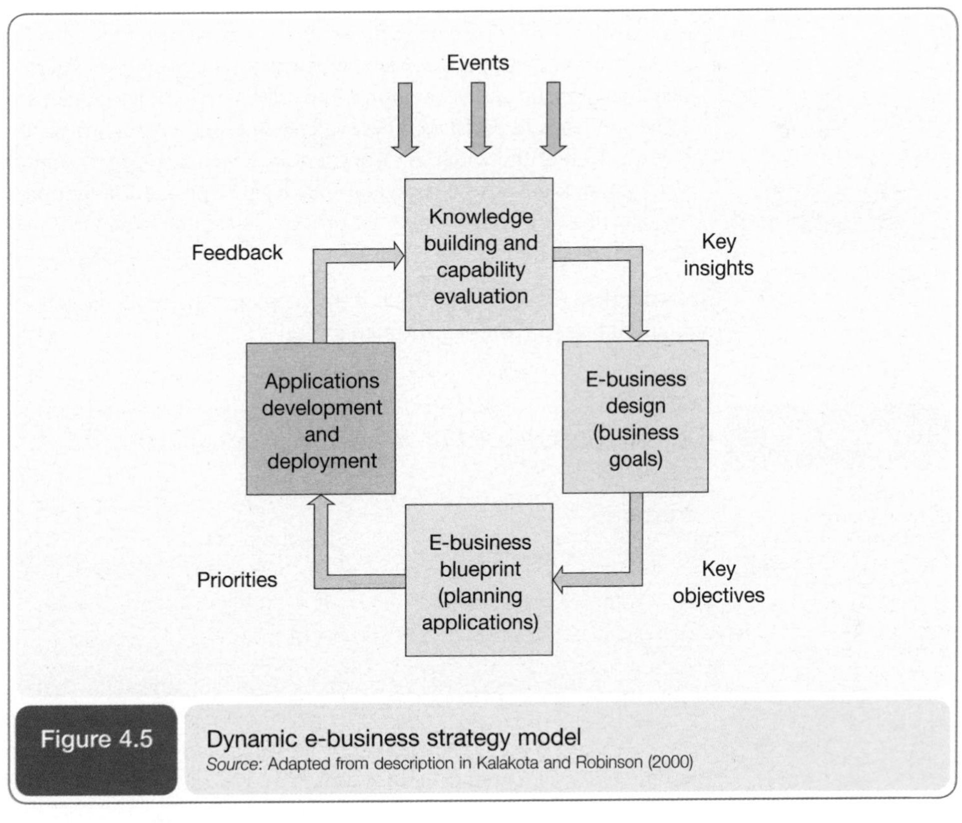

Figure 4.5 Dynamic e-business strategy model
Source: Adapted from description in Kalakota and Robinson (2000)

Activity 4.2 Taking the strategic decision to integrate use of the Internet into business operations

According to Doherty and Ellis-Chadwick (2010) there are many drivers and barriers to the adoption of the Internet and many challenges when attempting to be successful online. Therefore, how to adopt the Internet is probably the biggest decision most companies have taken in the last 15 years.

Listen to what Nick Wheeler founder and Chairman of Charles Tyrwhitt says about taking the decision to go online: **http:goo.gl/9cvL6**.

Once you have watched this short film, suggest which of the strategic approaches discussed above best explain Nick's approach to moving his business online.

We will now explore the four main stages of digital marketing strategy development in more detail.

Situation analysis

Situation analysis
Collection and review of information about an organisation's internal processes and resources and external marketplace factors in order to inform strategy definition.

The **situation analysis** in classic marketing planning is an audit of current effectiveness of marketing activities of a company. The analysis involves review of internal and external factor, i.e. the marketing environment, that have implications for strategy development. More specifically situation analysis involves:

- Assessment of internal capabilities, resources and processes of the company and a review of its activity in the marketplace – the 7 S framework introduced in Chapter 1 (Table 1.3) is a useful way of considering these internal capabilities to deliver strategy.
- Consideration of the immediate competitive environment (micro-environment) including customer demand and behaviour, competitor activity, marketplace structure and relationships with suppliers and partners. These micro-environment factors were reviewed in Chapter 2.
- Investigation of the wider environment in which a company operates, including economic development, government regulations, legal issues and taxation, social and ethical issues, e.g. data protection and consumer privacy. These macro-environment factors were reviewed in detail in Chapter 3.

Now complete Activity 4.3, which illustrates the type of analysis that needs to be performed for an digital marketing situation analysis.

Activity 4.3 Situation analysis for an e-commerce operation

Purpose

To introduce the different types of Internet marketing analysis required as part of the situation review.

Activity

You are a new e-commerce manager in an organisation that has operated a B2B e-commerce presence for two years in all the major European countries. The organisation sells office equipment and has been an established mail-order catalogue operation for 25 years. The UK, Germany, France and Italy each have their own localised content.

List the e-commerce-related questions you would ask of your new colleagues and the research you would commission under these headings:

- internal analysis
- external analysis (micro-economic factors)
- external analysis (macro-economic factors).

Internal audit for digital marketing

The internal audit involves reviewing the existing contribution that the digital channels are currently delivering.

Assessing the current contribution of the digital marketing to the organisation

To assess the contribution and the effectiveness of digital marketing involves the organisation in reviewing how well its online presence is meeting its goals. So this activity overlaps with that on strategic goal-setting discussed in the next section. Assessing effectiveness also requires a performance measurement or web analytics system to collect and report on marketing effectiveness. These different levels of measures can be usefully used to assess effectiveness:

1 Business effectiveness

This will include the contribution of the site directly or indirectly to sales and profit and how well it is supporting business objectives. The relative costs of producing, updating and promoting the site will also be reviewed as part of a cost–benefit analysis.

2 Marketing effectiveness

These measures may include:

- leads (qualified enquiries)
- sales
- customer retention and loyalty, including lifetime value
- online market (or audience share)
- brand enhancement
- customer service.

For large organisations, these measures can be assessed for each of the different markets a company operates in or for product lines produced on the website.

3 Digital marketing effectiveness

These are specific measures that are used to assess the way in which the website is used, and the characteristics of the audience. They are described in more detail in Chapter 9. According to Chaffey and Smith (2008) key performance indicators (KPIs) for an online presence include:

- *unique visitors* – the number of separate, individual visitors to the site
- total numbers of *sessions* or *visits* to the website
- *repeat visits* – average number of visits per individual
- *duration* – average length of time visitors spend on the site
- *subscription rates* such as the number of visitors subscribing for services such as an opt-in e-mail and newsletters and the response rates for these e-newsletters
- *conversion rates* – the percentage of visitors converting to subscribers (or becoming customers)
- *attrition rates* through the online buying process
- *churn rates* – percentage of subscribers withdrawing or unsubscribing
- *click-through rates (CTR)* from third-party sites to your own.

Customer research

Persona
A thumbnail summary of the characteristics, needs, motivations and environment of a typical website user.

Customer scenarios
Alternative tasks or outcomes required by a visitor to a website. Typically accomplished in a series of stages of different tasks involving different information needs or experiences.

Research into customers should not be restricted to quantitative demand analysis. Varianini and Vaturi (2000) point out that qualitative research about existing customers provides insights that can be used to inform strategy. Research suggests using user profiling, to capture the core characteristics of target customers involves more than using demographics. It also includes using customer needs, attitudes experiences and abilities of using digital technologies and the Internet (Doherty and Ellis-Chadwick, 2010). In Chapter 2 we reviewed how customer **personas** and **customer scenarios** are developed to help inform understanding of online buyer behaviour.

More recently, Sam Decker, formerly e-commerce manager at Dell, who helped develop the customer-centric strategy for Dell's US consumer business, has stressed the importance of this activity by referencing this approach as 'customer oxygen'. In Econsultancy (2008) he says:

> Your company needs to breathe 'customer oxygen'. The word 'oxygen' is important, because it reflects the idea that the customer's perspective should infuse just about every business decision you make each day. This oxygen should flow from the CEO and beyond, as a customer-centric culture affects every division, department and function.

He believes this is an ongoing activity rather than the sporadic customer insights collected by many organisations:

> Occasional research insights are important to guide the corporate ship like a compass, but not enough to sustain its course.

Instead he advises:

> For a corporate system to digest the perspective of the customer, a programme needs to integrate into processes, reporting, performance plans and other methods of day-to-day work and accountability. It becomes a programme that people in the company can continuously improve, which is something employees are good at doing. Your managers, colleagues and employees can feed on daily customer-focused tactics and metrics that can be part of their job and performance; weaving it into the overall fabric of your company.

Resource analysis

Resource analysis
Review of the technological, financial and human resources of an organisation and how they are utilised in business processes.

Resource analysis involves assessing the capabilities of the organisation to deliver its digital services. The 7 S framework introduced in Chapter 1 in (Table 1.3) is a useful way of considering the suitability of internal capabilities to achieve strategic aims. Other aspects of resource analysis that can be reviewed include:

- *Financial resources* – the cost components of running an online presence, including site development, promotion and maintenance. Mismatch between current spend and required spend to achieve visibility within the online marketplace should be reviewed using tools such as Hitwise and Netratings which can be used to assess online market share.
- *Technology infrastructure resources* – availability and performance (speed) of website and service-level agreements with the ISP. The need for different applications to enhance the customer experience or increase conversion rates can be assessed (e.g. on-site search, customer review or customisation facilities). The infrastructure to manage sites such as content management, customer relationship management and web analytics should also be considered.
- *Human resources* – availability for an e-retailer includes service and fulfilment resources for answering customer queries and dispatching goods. For all companies there is a challenge of possibly recruiting new staff or re-skilling marketing staff to manage online marketing activities such as merchandising, search engine marketing, affiliate marketing and e-mail marketing. We return to this topic later in this chapter.
- *Structure* – what are the responsibilities and control mechanisms used to co-ordinate Internet marketing across different departments and business units? We again return to this topic later in the chapter.

- *Strengths and weaknesses* – SWOT analysis is referred to in the next section where generic strengths and weaknesses are summarised in Figure 4.7 and an example is given in Figure 4.8. Companies will also assess their distinctive competencies.

Stage models of the digital marketing capability

Stage models of capability delivered through the online presence can help assess digital marketing capabilities. Companies tend to follow a natural progression in developing their website to support their marketing activities. The following levels of digital marketing can be identified:

- **Level 0.** No website or social presence. Some small businesses may still not have any online presence, although the number in this category are decreasing.
- **Level 1.** Company places an entry in a directory website that lists company names such as Yellow Pages (**www.yell.co.uk**) to make people searching the web aware of the existence of the company or its products.
- **Level 2.** Simple static website created containing basic company contact and product information (sometimes referred to as **brochureware**).
- **Level 3.** Simple interactive site where users are able to search the site and make queries to retrieve information such as product availability and pricing. Enquiries submitted by a form and transmitted by e-mail may also be supported.
- **Level 4.** Interactive site supporting transactions with users. The functions offered will vary according to the company. If products can be sold direct then an electronic commerce or online store option for online sales will be available. Other functions might include user-generated content, social sharing of blog or product pages or an interactive customer-service helpdesk.
- **Level 5.** Fully interactive site providing relationship marketing with individual customers and facilitating the full range of marketing functions relevant for the sector.

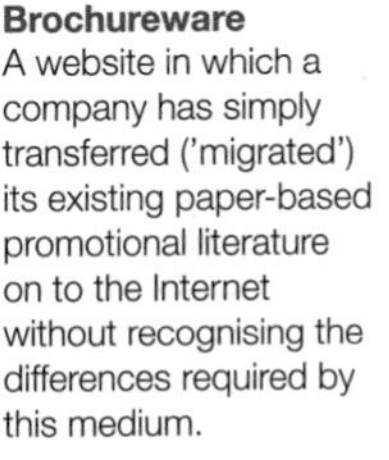

Brochureware
A website in which a company has simply transferred ('migrated') its existing paper-based promotional literature on to the Internet without recognising the differences required by this medium.

A variety of online stage models have been produced since the classic stage model created by Quelch and Klein (1996) – they noted the sequence in which websites develop for different types of company. They distinguish between existing major companies (see Figure 4.6(a)) and start-up companies (see Figure 4.6(b)) that start as Internet companies. The main differ-

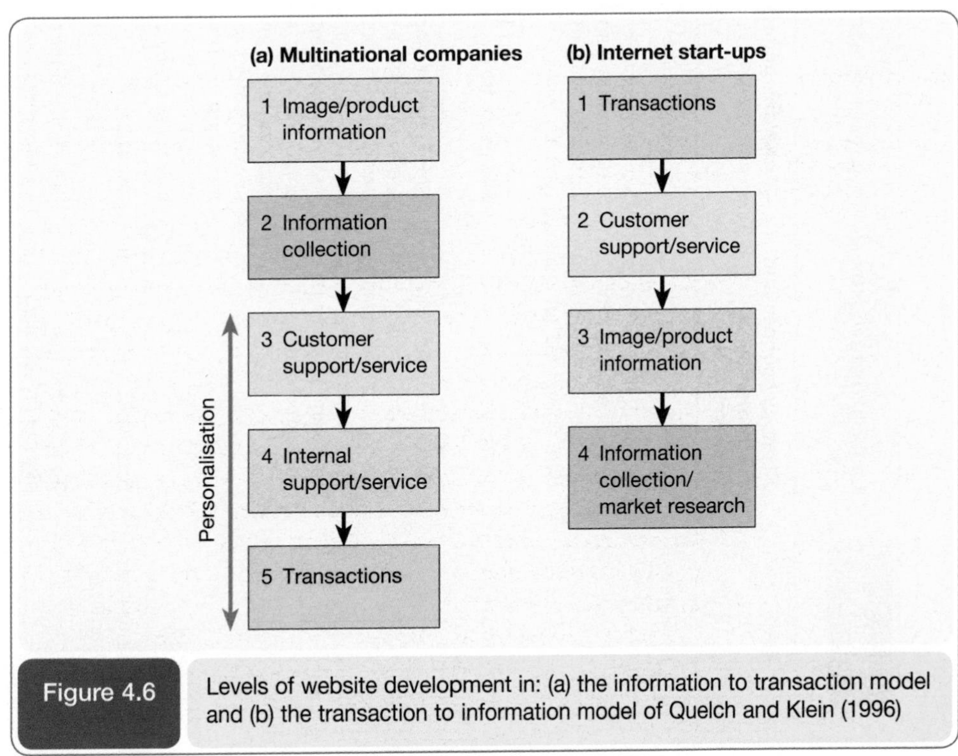

Figure 4.6 Levels of website development in: (a) the information to transaction model and (b) the transaction to information model of Quelch and Klein (1996)

Table 4.3 Capability maturity model of e-commerce adoption based on Econsultancy (2008) research

Level	Strategy process and performance improvement	Structure: location of e-commerce	Senior management buy-in	Marketing integration	Online marketing focus
1 Unplanned	*Limited*	*Experimentation*	*Limited*	*Poor integration*	*Content focus*
	Online channels not part of business planning process. Web analytics data collected, but unlikely to be reviewed or actioned	No clear centralised e-commerce resources in business. Main responsibility typically within IT	No direct involvement in planning and little necessity seen for involvement	Some interested marketers may experiment with e-communications tools	Creation of online brochures and catalogues. Adoption of first style guidelines
2 Diffuse management	*Low-level*	*Diffuse*	*Aware*	*Separate*	*Traffic focus*
	Online referenced in planning, but with limited channel-specific objectives. Some campaign analysis by interested staff	Small central e-commerce group or single manager, possibly with steering group controlled by marketing. Many separate websites, separate online initiatives, e.g. tools adopted and agencies for search marketing, e-mail marketing. E-communications funding from brands/businesses may be limited	Management becomes aware of expenditure and potential of online channels	Increased adoption of e-communications tools and growth of separate sites and microsites continues. Media spend still dominantly offline	Increased emphasis on driving visitors to site through pay-per-click search marketing and affiliate marketing
3 Centralised management	*Specific*	*Centralised*	*Involved*	*Arm's-length*	*Conversion and customer experience focus*
	Specific channel objectives set. Web analytics capability not integrated to give unified reporting of campaign effectiveness	Common platform for content management, web analytics Preferred-supplier list of digital agencies. Centralised, independent e-commerce function, but with some digital-specific responsibilities by country/product/brand	Directly involved in annual review and ensures review structure involving senior managers from marketing, IT, operations and finance	Marketing and e-commerce mainly work together during planning process. Limited review within campaigns. Senior e-commerce team-members responsible for encouraging adoption of digital marketing throughout organisation	Initiatives for usability, accessibility and revision of content management system (including search engine optimisation) are common at this stage

4 Decentralised operations	*Refined*	*Decentralised*	*Driving performance*	*Partnership*	*Retention focus*
	Close cooperation between e-commerce and marketing. Targets and performance reviewed monthly. Towards unified reporting. Project debriefs	Digital marketing skills more developed in business with integration of e-commerce into planning and execution at business or country level. E-retailers commonly adopt direct-channel organisation of which e-commerce is one channel. Online channel profit and loss accountability sometimes controlled by businesses/brands, but with central budget for continuous e-communications spend (search, affiliates, e-communications)	Involved in review at least monthly	Marketing and e-commerce work closely together through year. Digital media spend starts to reflect importance of online channels to business and consumers	Initiatives on analysis of customer purchase and response behaviour and Implementation of well-defined touch strategies with emphasis on e-mail marketing. Loyalty drivers well known and managed
5 Integrated and optimised	*Multichannel process*	*Integrated*	*Integral*	*Complete*	*Optimisation focus*
	The interactions and financial contribution of different channels are well understood and resourced and improved accordingly	Majority of digital skills within business and e-commerce team commonly positioned within marketing or direct marketing teams	Less frequent in-depth involvement required. Annual planning and six-monthly quarterly review and improvement	Marketing has full complement of digital marketing skills, but calls on specialist expertise from agencies or central team	Initiatives to improve acquisition, conversion and retention according to developments in access platform and customer experience

ence is that Internet start-ups are likely to introduce transaction facilities earlier than existing companies. However, they may take longer to develop suitable customer service facilities.

Dave Chaffey writing for Econsultancy (2008) developed a modern stage-model framework for assessing internal digital marketing capabilities in large organisations (Table 4.3 above). This was inspired by the capability maturity models devised by the Carnegie Mellon Software Engineering Institute (**www.sei.cmu.edu/cmm/cmm.html**) to help organisations improve their software development practices.

Table 4.3 is intended to help:

1 review current approaches to digital marketing to identify areas for improvement
2 benchmark with competitors who are in the same market sector or industry and in different sectors
3 identify best practice from more advanced adopters
4 set targets and develop strategies for improving capabilities.

Of the companies assessed within the research, the majority were at Level 3 or 4 overall, although companies may occupy different levels according to different criteria. We return to assessing capabilities using the 7 Ss to implement digital marketing strategy at the end of the chapter.

Competitor analysis

In Chapter 2 we showed that competitor analysis or the monitoring of competitor use of e-commerce to acquire and retain customers is especially important in the online marketplace due to the dynamic nature of the Internet medium. This enables new services to be launched and prices and promotions changed much more rapidly than through print communications.

Intermediary analysis

Chapter 2 highlighted the importance of web-based intermediaries such as publisher sites and blogs in increasing awareness and driving traffic to an organisation's website. Situation analysis will also involve identifying relevant intermediaries for a particular marketplace and look at how the organisation and its competitors are using the intermediaries to build traffic and provide services. For example, an e-tailer needs to assess where its target customers might encounter their competitors (at comparison services such as Kelkoo, (**www.kelkoo.com**) or know whether competitors have any special sponsorship arrangements or microsites created with intermediaries. The other aspect of situation analysis for intermediaries is to consider the way in which the marketplace is operating. To what extent are competitors using disintermediation or reintermediation? How are existing channel arrangements being changed?

Assessing opportunities and threats

Performing a structured SWOT analysis to summarise the external opportunities and threats that are presented by digital platforms is a core activity for situation analysis. Companies should also consider their own strengths and weaknesses in the Internet marketing environment. Summarising the results through digital channel-specific SWOT analysis (internal Strengths and Weaknesses and external Opportunities and Threats) will clearly highlight the opportunities and threats. Appropriate planning to counter the threats and take advantage of the opportunities can then be built into the Internet marketing plan. An example of a typical SWOT analysis of digital marketing-related strengths and weaknesses is shown in Figure 4.7. As is often the case with SWOT analysis, the opportunities available to a company are the opposites of the threats presented by other companies. The strengths and weaknesses will vary according to the company involved, but many of the strengths and weaknesses are dependent

The organisation	Stengths – S 1. Existing brand 2. Existing customer base 3. Existing distribution	Weaknesses – W 1. Brand perception 2. Intermediary use 3. Technology/skills 4. Cross-channel support
Opportunities – O 1. Cross-selling 2. New markets 3. New services 4. Alliances/co-branding	**SO strategies** Leverage strengths to maximise opportunities **= Attacking strategy**	**WO strategies** Counter weaknesses through exploiting opportunities **= Build strengths for attacking strategy**
Threats – T 1. Customer choice 2. New entrants 3. New competitive products 4. Channel conflicts	**ST strategies** Leverage strengths to minimise threats **= Defensive strategy**	**WT strategies** Counter weaknesses and threats **= Build strengths for defensive strategy**

Figure 4.7 A generic digital channel-specific SWOT analysis showing typical opportunities and threats presented by digital media

on the capacity of senior management to acknowledge and act on change. The SWOT can be reviewed in the main areas of online marketing activity, namely areas of customer acquisition, conversion, retention and growth.

This form of presentation of the Internet-specific SWOT shown in Figure 4.7 is a powerful technique since it not only indicates the SWOT, but can be used to generate appropriate strategies. Often, the most rewarding strategies combine Strengths and Opportunities or counter Threats through Strengths. Figure 4.8 on the next page gives an example of a typical digital SWOT analytics for an established multichannel brand.

Strategic goal setting

Any marketing strategy should be based on clearly defined corporate objectives, but there has been a tendency for Internet marketing to be conducted separately from other business and marketing objectives. Porter (2001) has criticised the lack of goal setting when many organisations have developed Internet strategies. He notes that many companies, responding to distorted market signals, have used 'rampant experimentation' that is not economically sustainable. This resulted in the failure of many 'dot-com' companies and also poor investments by many established companies. He suggests that economic value or sustained profitability for a company is the final arbiter of business success.

It is best, of course, if the digital marketing strategy is consistent with and aligns with business and marketing objectives, e.g. business objectives such as increasing market share in an overseas market or introducing a new product to market can and should be supported by the Internet communications channel. See Mini Case Study 4.1.

As a starting point for setting specific objectives, it is useful to think through the benefits of the Internet channel so that these benefits can be converted into objectives. It is useful to identify both *tangible benefits*, for which monetary savings or revenues can be identified, and *intangible benefits*, for which it is more difficult to calculate financial benefits and costs, but are still important, e.g. customer service quality. Table 4.4 presents a summary of typical benefits of digital marketing.

The organisation	**Strengths – S** 1 Existing brand 2 Existing customer base 3 Existing distribution	**Weaknesses – W** 1 Brand perception 2 Intermediary use 3 Technology/skills (poor web experience) 4 Cross-channel support 5 Churn rate
Opportunities – O 1 Cross-selling 2 New markets 3 New services 4 Alliances/co-branding	**SO strategies** Leverage strengths to maximise opportunities = attacking strategy **Examples:** 1 Migrate customers to web strategy 2 Refine customer contact strategy across customer lifecycle or commitment segmentation (e-mail, web) 3 Partnership strategy (co-branding, linking) 4 Launch new web-based products or value-adding experiences, e.g. video streaming	**WO strategies** Counter weaknesses through exploiting opportunities = build strengths for attacking strategy **Examples:** 1 Countermediation strategy (create or acquire) 2 Search marketing acquisition strategy 3 Affiliate-based acquisition strategy 4 Refine customer contact strategy (e-mail, web)
Threats – T 1 Customer choice (price) 2 New entrants 3 New competitive products 4 Channel conflicts 5 Social network	**ST strategies** Leverage strengths to minimise threat = defensive strategy **Examples:** 1 Introduce new Internet-only products 2 Add value to web services – refine OVP 3 Partner with complementary brand 4 Create own social network/customer reviews	**WT strategies** Counter weaknesses and threats: = build strengths for defensive strategy **Examples:** 1 Differential online pricing strategy 2 Acquire/create pure-play company with lower cost-base 3 Customer engagement strategy to increase conversion, average order value and lifetime value 4 Online reputation management strategy/E-PR

Figure 4.8 An example of an digital channel specific SWOT for an established multichannel brand showing how the elements of SWOT can be related to strategy formulation

An alternative way of thinking through the goals of digital marketing, is to review the 5 Ss of Chaffey and Smith (2008) who suggest there are five broad benefits of e-marketing:

- *Sell* – grow sales through wider distribution to customers you can't service offline, or perhaps through a wider product range than instore, or better prices.
- *Serve* – add value by giving customers extra benefits online, or inform them of product development through online dialogue and feedback.
- *Speak* – get closer to customers by tracking them, asking them questions, conducting online interviews, creating a dialogue, monitoring chat rooms, learning about them.
- *Save* – save costs of service, sales transactions and administration, print and post. Can you reduce transaction costs and therefore either make online sales more profitable or use cost savings to enable you to cut prices, which in turn could enable you to generate greater market share?

Table 4.4 Tangible and intangible benefits from Internet marketing

Tangible benefits	Intangible benefits
Increased sales from new sales leads giving: • New customers, new markets • Existing customers (repeat-selling) • Existing customers (cross-selling) Cost reductions from: • reduced time in customer service • (customer self-service online) • online sales • reduced printing and distribution costs of marketing communications	Corporate image communication rise due to increased revenue from: • Enhanced brand • More rapid, more responsive marketing communications including PR • Improved customer service • Learning for the future • Meeting customer expectations to have a website • Identifying new partners, supporting existing partners better • Better management of marketing information and customer information • Feedback from customers on products

- *Sizzle* – extend the brand online. Reinforce brand values in a totally new medium. The web scores very highly as a medium for creating brand awareness, recognition and involvement, as explained further in Chapter 5.

Mini Case Study 4.1 Arena Flowers expands Overseas

Arena Flowers (Figure 4.9) is an online florist based in London. The business was incorporated in July 2006 and went live with a transactional website in September 2006. In 2008, the company began moving into European markets, e.g. the Netherlands, Germany, Belgium, France. Overseas sales now represent about a fifth of the company's annual sales (Graham, 2011). The essence of the Arena Flowers' business proposition is to cut out all middlemen and buy direct from growers, so they can get great prices and because the flowers are exceedingly fresh.

Figure 4.9 Will Wynne, Arena Flowers (www.arenaflowers.com)

> *There are no 'relay' fees with us and, because of our high stock turnover, we get fresh flowers in daily and they go straight to the customer, rather than sitting in a hot shop window. Arena Flowers offer free delivery on all of our products and we were the first online florist in the UK to offer FFP-accredited, ethically sourced flowers.*

That has been a good 'unique selling point' and enables Arena to offer something different from other suppliers such as supermarkets.

Strategic development

The company delivered £2 million net sales in its first year and broke even within the first 12 months of trading. Arena forecast sales of £4 million in year 2, which would bring a healthy profit. The head of design and development, Sam Barton, explained how he sees opportunities to keep growing both sales and profitability at a similar rate going forward through various initiatives. The company developed a Facebook application that provided 15 per cent of the site traffic – an opportunity that has been missed by many of its more established rivals.

A can do approach to developing their business online has enabled arena Flowers to enter European and other international markets even though the competition is very tough. Will Wynne, Arena's co-founder and current managing director, feels strongly about the importance of getting the language right in order to be success online in European markets:

> *I think the language is a no-brainer. You're not going to have any success if you don't adapt to the local language.*
>
> *It's almost a matter of respect. If you think there's 60 million people in France and 80 million in Germany, and the idea that they would use our website if we didn't translate is probably a bit ambitious,*

See more about the team at Arena Flowers at by watching Nick discussing the development of the business and what it stands for at: **http://www.youtube.com/watch?v=4SsnC5dRklg&NR=1**.

Sources: Econsultancy (2008); Arena Flowers' Sam Barton on web design and development, E-newsletter interview, 12 March 2008; Graham, F. (2011), Firms Ignore the foreign language Internet at their peril, BBC News, **http://www.bbc.co.uk/news/business-13878064** (accessed September 2011).

The online revenue contribution

Online revenue contribution
An assessment of the direct contribution of the Internet or other digital media to sales, usually expressed as a percentage of overall sales revenue.

A key objective for digital marketing is the **online revenue contribution** since this gives a simple measure of the proportion of online sales achieved in different product categories. This is a measure of the extent to which a company's online presence directly impacts the sales revenue (or better profit) of the organisation. By understanding the contribution of online revenue business planners should be able to determine future resource needs to online channels. Online revenue contribution objectives can be specified for different types of products, customer segments and geographic markets. For example, in 1997, low-cost airline easyJet set an online contribution objective of 50 per cent by the year 2000. This established a clear vision and resources could be put in place to achieve this. EasyJet now has an online revenue contribution of 95 per cent:

- Services 15% (32%)
- Manufacturers 15% (32%)
- Financial services 15% (28%)
- Retail 14% (21%)
- Total 15% (29%).

Allowable cost per acquisition
A target maximum cost for generating leads or new customers profitably.

It is important that companies set sales and revenue goals for online channels for which costs are controlled through an **allowable cost per acquisition**. This takes into account the cost of attracting visitors through techniques such as affiliate marketing, paid search advertising or display advertising as explained in budget models presented in Chapter 8.

For some companies, such as an FMCG manufacturer, a beverage company or a B2B manufacturer, it is unrealistic to expect a direct online revenue contribution. In this case, an indirect online contribution can be stated. This considers the Internet as part of the promotional mix and its role in reaching and influencing a proportion of customers to purchase the product, generating trials, or in the case of a B2B company, leads. In this case a company could set an **online promotion contribution** or indirect online revenue contribution of 5 per cent of its target market visiting the website or social media presence and interacting with the brand. Bazett *et al.* (2005) give the example of a high-street chain that for every £1 of revenue it takes on the web, £3 is spent in the store after browsing online – so it has objectives for this and works equally hard to help these customers through such facilities as store locators and information on the nearest store with a particular product in stock. Complete Activity 4.4 to explore the factors that impact online revenue contribution in different markets.

Online promotion contribution
This is an assessment of the proportion of customers (new or retained) who are influenced and reached by online communications.

The contribution should also reference the contribution to customer service transaction as this reflects reduction in costs. Speaking to the Econsultancy Marketing Masterclass in November 2007, Paul Say, formerly head of e-marketing at First Direct, explained how his vision for the bank had included clear targets for online acquisition, transactions and recommendations. These translated into the following results by November 2007:

- 40% of total sales now being through electronic channels
- 71% of its customer base actively using electronic channels (measured as 90-day active)
- 72% of all customer transactions (e.g. bill payments) made electronically
- 75% would recommend friends to use the service (compared to 30% UK banking average).

Activity 4.4 Assessing the significance of digital channels

Purpose

To illustrate the issues involved with assessing the suitability of the Internet for e-commerce.

Activity

For each of the products and services in Table 4.5, assess the suitability of the Internet for delivery of the product or service and position it on the grid in Figure 4.10 overleaf with justification. Make estimates in Table 4.5 for the direct and indirect online revenue contribution in 5 and 10 years' time for different products in your country. Choose specific products within each category shown.

Table 4.5 Vision of online revenue contribution for different types of company

Products/services	Now	2 years' time	5 years' time	10 years' time
Example: Cars, US				
Direct online sales	5%	10%	25%	50%
Indirect online sales	50%	70%	90%	95%
Financial services				
Direct online sales				
Indirect online sales				
Clothing				
Direct online sales				
Indirect online sales				
Business office supplies				
Direct online sales				
Indirect online sales				

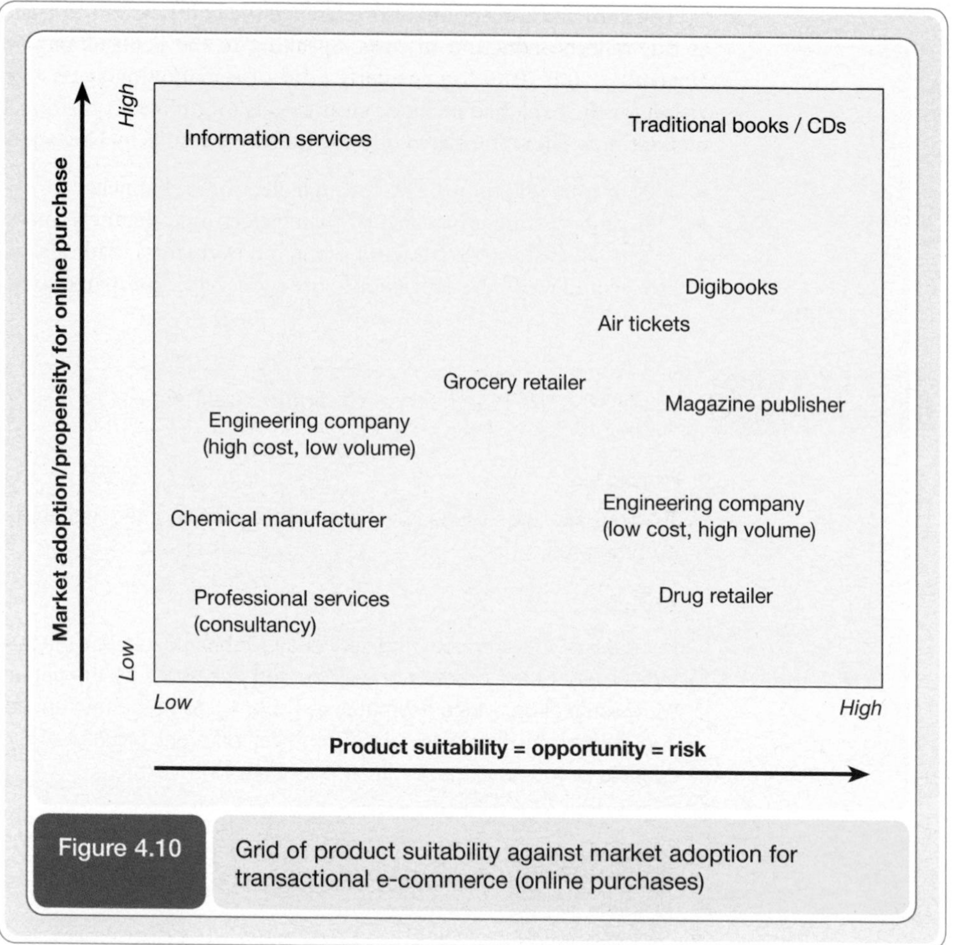

Figure 4.10 Grid of product suitability against market adoption for transactional e-commerce (online purchases)

Setting SMART objectives

You have probably heard before that effective objectives and measures to set objectives and assess performance against these goals are SMART. SMART is used to assess the suitability of objectives set to drive different strategies or the improvement of the full range of business processes.

- *Specific.* Is the objective sufficiently detailed to measure real-world problems and opportunities?
- *Measurable.* Can a quantitative or qualitative attribute be applied to create a metric?
- *Actionable.* Can the information be used to improve performance? If the objective doesn't change behaviour in staff to help them improve performance, there is little point in it!
- *Relevant.* Can the information be applied to the specific problem faced by the manager?
- *Time-related.* Can the information be constrained through time?

With SMART objectives, everyone is sure exactly what the target is and progresses towards it and, if necessary, action can be taken to put the company back on target. Here are some typical examples of SMART objectives, including those to support goal-setting in customer acquisition, conversion and retention categories for digital marketing strategy:

- *Digital channel contribution objective.* Achieve 10% online revenue (or profit) contribution within two years.
- *Acquisition objective.* Acquire 50,000 new online customers this financial year at an average cost per acquisition (CPA) of £30 with an average profitability of £5.

- *Acquisition or conversion objective.* Migrate 40% of existing customers to using online 'paperless' bill payment services within 3 years (e.g., for a bank or utilities company).
- *Acquisition objective.* Increase by 20% within one year the number of sales arising from a certain target market, e.g. 18–25-year-olds.
- *Conversion objective.* Increase the average order value of online sales to £42 per customer.
- Conversion objective. Increase site conversion rate to 3.2% (would be based on model of new and existing customers in different categories).
- *Conversion objective.* Increase percentage of online service enquiries fulfilled online by 'web self-service' from 85% to 90%.
- *Retention objective.* Increase annual repeat new customer conversion rate by 20%.
- *Retention objective.* Increase percentage of active users of service transacting (purchasing or using other electronic services) within a 180-day period from 20% to 25%.
- *Retention objective.* Increase customer satisfaction rating for channel from 70% to 80%.
- *Growth objective.* Increase new prospects recommended by friends (viral marketing or 'member get member') by 10,000 per annum.
- *Growth objective.* Increase propensity to recommend online service from 60% to 70%.
- *Penetration objective.* Achieve first or second position in category penetration in the countries within which the company operates (this is effectively online audience or market share and can be measured through visitor rankings such as Hitwise or Netratings (Chapter 2) or, better, by online revenue share).
- *Cost objective.* Achieve a cost reduction of 10% in marketing communications within two years.
- Improve customer service by providing a response to a query within 2 hours, 24 hours per day, 7 days a week.

Specific digital communications objectives are also described in Chapter 8.

Frameworks for objective setting

A significant challenge of objective setting for Internet marketing is that there will potentially be many different measures such as those listed above and these will have be to grouped to be meaningful. Categorisation of objectives into groups is also useful since it can be used to identify suitable objectives. In this chapter, we have already seen two methods of categorising objectives. First, objectives can be set at the level of business effectiveness, marketing effectiveness and Internet marketing effectiveness as explained in the section on internal auditing as part of the situation analysis. Second, the 5 S framework of Sell, Speak, Serve, Save and Sizzle provides a simple framework for objective setting. A further five-part framework for goal setting and analysis is presented in Chapter 9.

Some larger companies will identify objectives for digital marketing initiatives which are consistent with existing business measurement frameworks, e.g. the **balanced scorecard**, but research has identified widespread variation in the use and level of uptake of performance measures (Gunawan *et al.*, 2008). Nevertheless, the balanced business scorecard is a well-known and widely used framework and it can be helpful as a guide.

Balanced scorecard
A framework for setting and monitoring business performance. Metrics are structured according to customer issues, internal efficiency measures, financial measures and innovation.

Efficiency
Minimising resources or time needed to complete a process. 'Doing the thing right.'

Effectiveness
Meeting process objectives, delivering the required outputs and outcomes. 'Doing the right thing.'

The balanced scorecard was popularised in a *Harvard Business Review* article by Kaplan and Norton (1993), can be used to translate vision and strategy into objectives and then, through measurement, assessing whether the strategy and its implementation are successful. In addition to financial data, the balanced scorecard uses operational measures such as customer satisfaction, efficiency of internal processes and also the organisation's innovation and improvement activities including staff development. This framework has since been applied to IT (Der Zee and De Jong, 1999), e-commerce (Hasan and Tibbits, 2000) and multichannel marketing (Bazett *et al.*, 2005).

Table 4.6 illustrates specific Internet marketing measures within the four main areas of organisational performance managed through the balanced scorecard. In our presentation we have placed objectives within the areas of **efficiency** ('doing the thing right') and **effectiveness**

Table 4.6 Example allocation of Internet marketing objectives within the balanced scorecard framework for a transactional e-commerce site

Balanced scorecard sector	Efficiency	Effectiveness
Financial results (Business value)	• Channel costs • Channel profitability	• Online contribution (direct) • Online contribution (indirect) • Profit contributed
Customer value	• Online reach (unique visitors as % of potential visitors) • Cost of acquisition or cost per sale (CPA/CPS) • Customer propensity	• Sales and sales per customer • New customers • Online market share • Customer satisfaction ratings • Customer loyalty index
Operational processes	• Conversion rates • Average order value • List size and quality • E-mail active %	• Fulfilment times • Support response times
Operational processes	• Conversion rates • Average order value • List size and quality • E-mail active %	• Fulfilment times • Support response times

('doing the right thing'), e.g. efficiency involves increasing conversion rates and reducing costs of acquisition. Effectiveness involves supporting broader marketing objectives and often indicates the contribution of the online channel.

Performance drivers

Performance metrics
Measures that are used to evaluate and improve the efficiency and effectiveness of business processes.

Key performance indicators (KPIs)
Metrics used to assess the performance of a process and/or whether set goals are achieved.

Specific **performance metrics** are used to evaluate and improve the efficiency and effectiveness of a process. **Key performance indicators (KPIs)** are a special type of performance metric which indicate the overall performance of a process or its sub-processes. An example of KPIs for an online electrical goods retailer is shown in Figure 4.11. Improving the results from the e-commerce site involves using the techniques on the left of the diagram to improve the performance drivers, and so the KPI. The KPI is the total online sales figure. For a traditional retailer, this could be compared as a percentage to other retail channels such as mail order or retail stores. It can be seen that this KPI is dependent on performance drivers such as number of site visits or average order value which combine to govern this KPI.

Leading and lagging performance indicators

When developing goals and measurement systems used to review and improve performance of digital channels, it is also helpful to consider which are leading and lagging indicators of performance. Trends should be identified within these, e.g. are they increasing or decreasing year-on-year (often used as a good like-for-like comparison), or compared to the previous week, month or average for a recent period.

Leading performance indicator
A measure which is suggestive of future performance and so can be used to take proactive action to shape future performance.

A **leading performance indicator** is a metric that is suggestive of future performance – think of the amber preceding the green light on traffic lights on a short timescale. The benefit of leading indicators is that they enable managers to be proactive in shaping future performance. There tend to be fewer leading performance indicators, but these can be applied to e-commerce:

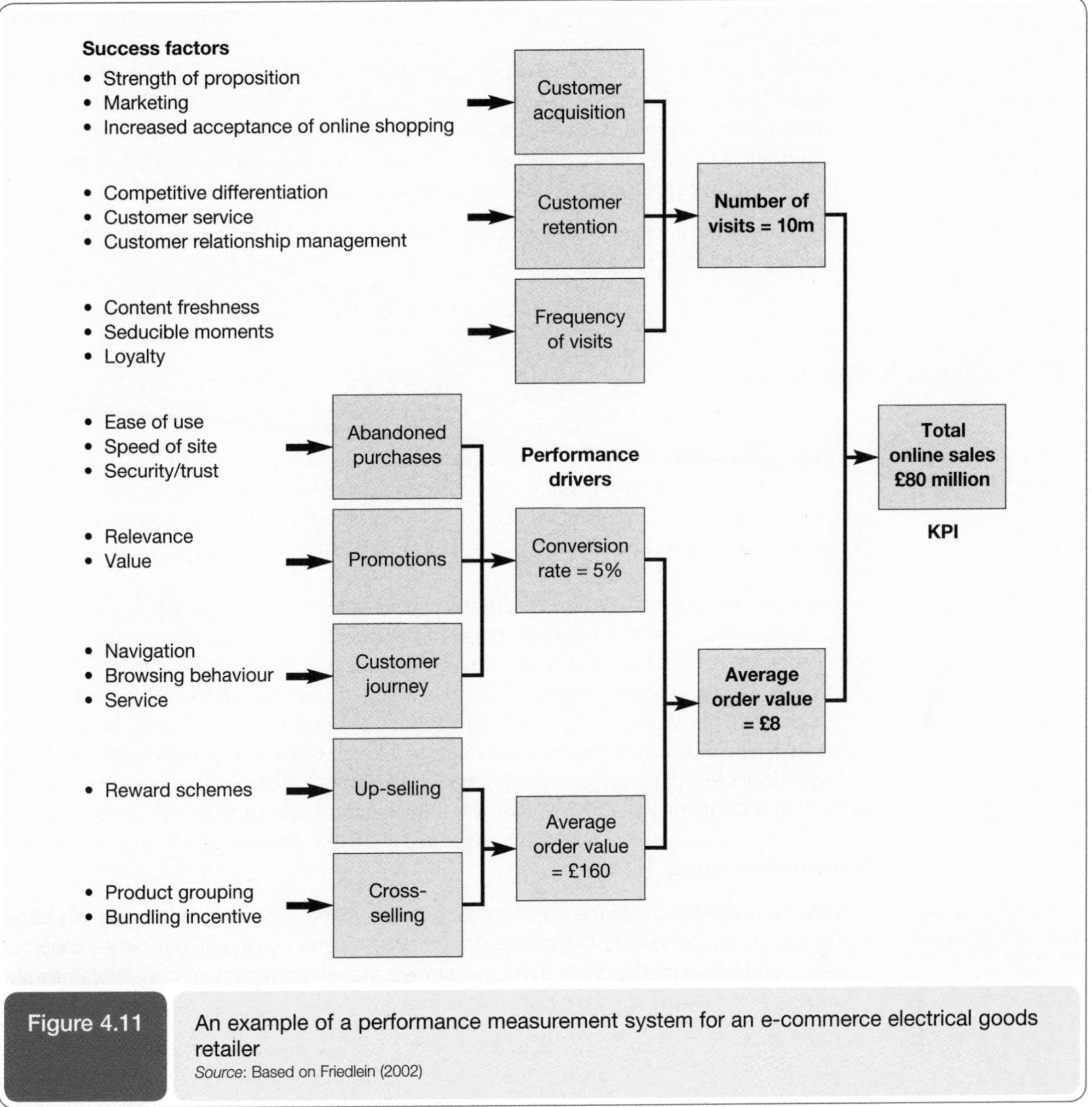

Figure 4.11 An example of a performance measurement system for an e-commerce electrical goods retailer
Source: Based on Friedlein (2002)

- *Repeat sales metrics.* If repeat conversion rates are falling or the average time between sales (sales latency) is falling, then these are warning signs of future declining sales volume for which proactive action can be taken, e.g. through a customer e-mail marketing programme.
- *Customer satisfaction or advocacy ratings such as the Net Promoter Score.* If these are trending downwards or return rates are increasing, this may be a sign of a future decline in repeat sales since more customers are dissatisfied.
- *Sales trends compared to market audience trends.* If, for example, online sales are increasing at a lower rate than overall online audiences for a product category are indicated, e.g. through panel data, Hitwise or searches in particular categories, then this is a warning sign that needs to be acted upon.

Lagging performance indicator
A measure which indicates past performance. Corrective action can then be applied to improve performance.

A **lagging performance indicator** is one where the measure indicates past performance. Lagging indicators enable corrective action to be taken. Some also identify a coincident performance indicator which is more suggestive of current performance. Lagging performance indicators for a transactional retail site include:

- *Sales volume, revenue and profitability.* These are typically compared against target or previous periods.
- *Cost per acquisition (CPA).* The cost of gaining each new customer will also be compared against target. Variations in trends in CPA for different referrers (traffic sources) and between different product categories can potentially be used as leading indicators.
- *Conversion efficiency metrics.* For an e-commerce site these include process efficiency metrics such as conversion rate, average order and landing page bounce rates.

These lagging indicators are used operationally on a daily or weekly basis so that performance can be diagnosed and reviewed.

Strategy formulation

Strategy formulation
Gerneration, review and selection of strategies to achieve strategic objectives.

Strategy formulation involves the identification of alternative strategies, a review of the merits of each of these options and then selecting the strategy that has the best fit with a company's trading environment, its internal resources and capabilities. Companies should be realistic about what their strategies can achieve and must base digital strategies on sound logic and thorough analysis.

Strategies are agreed to be most effective when they support specific business objectives, e.g. increasing the online contribution to revenue, or increasing the number of online sales enquiries. A useful technique to help align strategies and objectives is to present them together in a table, together with the insight developed from situation analysis which may have informed the strategy. Table 4.7 shows how objectives, strategies and performance indicates can be matched to produce this logical and connected flow of activity.

Digital marketing strategy formulation typically involves making *adjustments* to marketing strategy to take advantage of the benefits of online channels rather than wholescale changes. Porter (2001) attacks those who have suggested that the Internet invalidates well-known approaches to strategy. He says:

> Many have assumed that the Internet changes everything, rendering all the old rules about companies and competition obsolete. That may be a natural reaction, but it is a dangerous one . . . [resulting in] decisions that have eroded the attractiveness of their industries and undermined their own competitive advantages.

The key strategic decisions for digital marketing are the same as strategic decisions for traditional marketing. They involve selecting target customer groups and specifying how to deliver value to these groups. Segmentation, targeting, differentiation and positioning are all key to effective digital marketing.

For us, the main thrust of digital marketing strategy development is taking the right decisions on the selective targeting of customer groups and different forms of value delivery for online channels. But rather than selective development of online propositions, a common strategic option is to replicate existing offline segmentation, targeting, differentiation and positioning in the online channels. While this is a relatively easy strategic approach to implement, the company is likely to lose market share relative to more nimble competitors that modify their approach for online channels. An example of where companies have followed a 'do-nothing strategy' is grocery shopping where some have not rolled out home shopping to all parts of the country or do not offer the service at all. These supermarkets will lose customers to the most enthusiastic adopters of online channels such as Tesco.com and Sainsbury which will be difficult to win back in the future.

As mentioned at the start of the chapter, we should remember that digital marketing strategy is a channel marketing strategy and it needs to operate in the context of multichannel marketing. It follows that it is important that the digital marketing strategy should:

Table 4.7 An example of the relationship between objectives, strategies and performance indicators

Objectives	**Substantiation (informed by situation analysis or insight, example)**	**Strategies to achieve goals**	**Key performance indicators (critical success factors)**
1 *Acquisition objective*. Acquire 50,000 new online based on current sales of customers this financial year at an average cost per acquisition (CPA) of £30 with an average profitability of 5%	Based on growth forecast 40,000 sales per year, but with incremental sales arising from new affiliate programme and SEO development	Start affiliate marketing programme and improve SEO. Existing media mix based on pay-per-click and display advertising supported by offline media. Use social media engagement to generate leads.	Overall CPA for online sales Incremental number and % of sales from affiliate marketing programme Number of strategic keywords ranked for in top positions in natural search results page
2 *Acquisition (or conversion) objective*. Migrate 40% of existing customers to using online 'paperless' bill payment services services and e-mail communications within three years	Extrapolation of current natural migration coupled with increased adoption from offline direct marketing campaign	Direct marketing campaign using direct mail, phone prompts and online persuasion to encourage adoption. Use of incentive to encourage change	Number and percentage of existing customers registering to use online service Number and percentage of customers actively using online services at different points after initially registering
3 *Conversion objective*. Increase the average order value of online sales to £42 per customer	Growth estimate based on current AOV of £35 plus model suggesting 20% increase in AOV	Use of new merchandising system to show users related 'next best product' for different product categories	% of site visitors responding to merchandising/cross-selling messages
4 *Conversion objective*. Increase site conversion rate to 3.2%	Model showing separate increase in conversion for new and existing customers based on strategies shown right	Combination of strategies: • Incentivised e-mail follow-up on checkout abandonments for new customers • Introduction of more competitive pricing strategy on best sellers • AB and multivariate messaging improvement of landing pages • Refinement to quality of traffic purchased through pay-per-click programme	Variations in conversion rates for new and existing customers in different product categories
5 *Retention objective*. Increase annual repeat new customer conversion rate by 20%	Business case based on limited personalisation of offers to encourage repeat purchases via e-mail	• Delivery of personalised product offers by e-mail • 5% second purchase discount voucher	• Increased conversion rate of retention e-mail contact programme • Conversion to sale for second purchase discount campaigns
6 *Growth objective*. Increase new prospects recommended by friends (viral marketing or 'member get member') by 10,000 per annum	Model based on encouraging 2% of customers to recommend friends annually (based on trial scheme)	Supported by direct mail and e-mail recommendation programme	Response rate to direct mail campaign

Online tactical marketing segmentation
Tactical segmentation enables targeting based on customer journey behaviour such as search behaviour, content accessed and contribution to social media.

- be based on objectives for online contribution of leads and sales for this channel
- be consistent with the types of customers that use and can be effectively reached through the channel
- support the customer journey as they select and purchase products using this channel in combination with other channels
- define a unique, differential proposition for the channel
- specify how we communicate this proposition to persuade customers to use online services in conjunction with other channels
- manage the online customer lifecycle through the stages of attracting visitors to the website, converting them to customers and retention and growth.

Furthermore, digital marketing strategy development involves reappraising a company's approach to strategy based on familiar elements of marketing strategy. We believe these are eight important decisions to consider:

- *Decision 1*: Market and product development strategies
- *Decision 2*: Business and revenue models strategies
- *Decision 3*: Target marketing strategy
- *Decision 4*: Positioning and differentiation strategy (including the marketing mix)
- *Decision 5*: Customer engagement and social media strategy
- *Decision 6*: Multichannel distribution strategy
- *Decision 7*: Multichannel communications strategy
- *Decision 8*: Online communications mix and budget
- *Decision 9*: Organisational capabilities and governance (7 S framework).

The first four decisions are concerned with fundamental questions of how an organisation delivers value to customers online and which products are offered to which markets online. The next four decisions are more concerned with the mix of marketing communications used to communicate with customers across multiple channels.

Decision 1: Market and product development strategies

In Chapter 1, we introduced the Ansoff matrix as a useful analytic tool for assessing online strategies for manufacturers and retailers. This tool is also fundamental to marketing planning and it should be the first decision point because it can help companies think about how online channels can support their marketing objectives, and also suggest innovative use of these channels to deliver new products and more markets (the boxes help stimulate 'out-of-box' thinking which is often missing with digital marketing strategy). Fundamentally, the market and product development matrix (Figure 4.12) can help identify strategies to grow sales volume through varying what is sold (the product dimension on the horizontal axis of Figure 4.12) and who it is sold to (the market dimension on the vertical axis). Specific objectives need to be set for sales generated via these strategies, so this decision relates closely to that of objective setting. Let us now review these strategies in more detail.

1 Market penetration

This strategy involves using digital channels to sell more existing products into existing markets. The Internet has great potential for achieving sales growth or maintaining sales by the market penetration strategy. As a starting point, many companies will use the Internet to help sell existing products into existing markets, although they may miss opportunities indicated by the strategies in other parts of the matrix. Figure 4.12 indicates some of the main ways in which the Internet can be used for market penetration:

- *Market share growth* – companies can compete more effectively online if they have websites that are efficient at converting visitors to sale as explained in Chapter 7, and mastery of the online marketing communications techniques reviewed in Chapter 8, such as search engine marketing, affiliate marketing and online advertising.

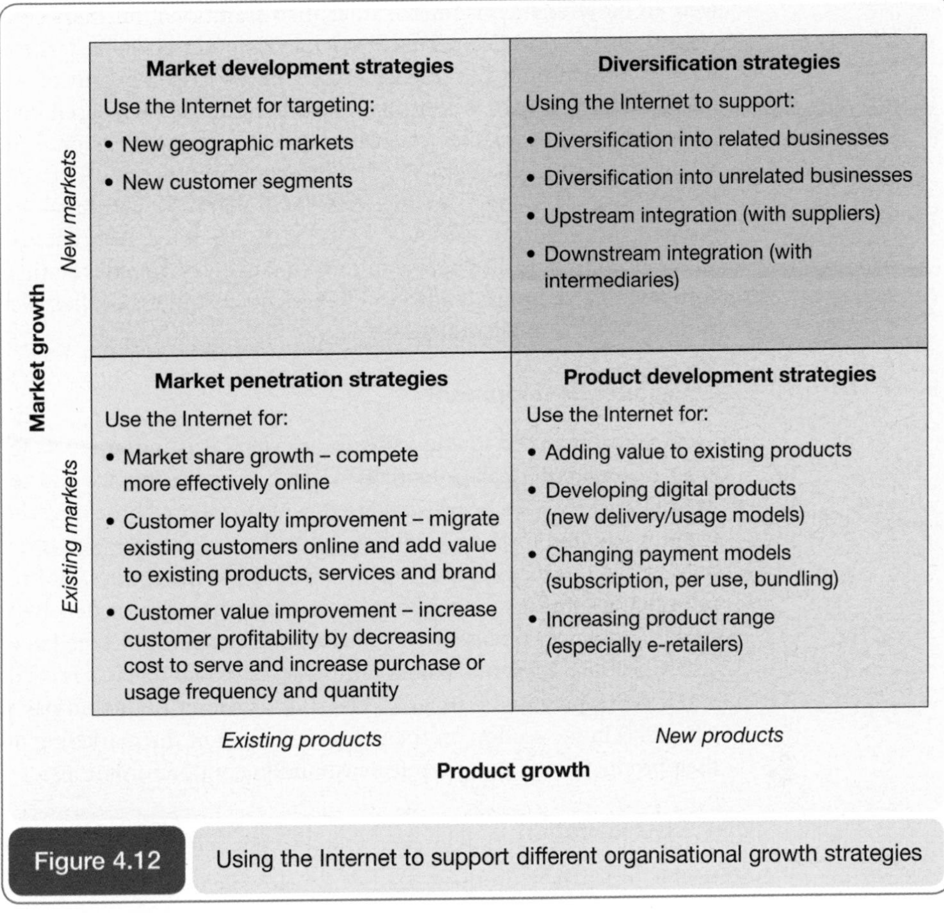

Market development strategies
Use the Internet for targeting:
• New geographic markets
• New customer segments
Diversification strategies
Using the Internet to support:
• Diversification into related businesses
• Diversification into unrelated businesses
• Upstream integration (with suppliers)
• Downstream integration (with intermediaries)
Market penetration strategies
Use the Internet for:
• Market share growth – compete more effectively online
• Customer loyalty improvement – migrate existing customers online and add value to existing products, services and brand
• Customer value improvement – increase customer profitability by decreasing cost to serve and increase purchase or usage frequency and quantity
Product development strategies
Use the Internet for:
• Adding value to existing products
• Developing digital products (new delivery/usage models)
• Changing payment models (subscription, per use, bundling)
• Increasing product range (especially e-retailers)
Market growth
New markets
Existing markets
Existing products
New products
Product growth

Figure 4.12 Using the Internet to support different organisational growth strategies

- *Customer loyalty improvement* – companies can increase their value to customers and so increase loyalty by migrating existing customers online by adding value to existing products, services and brand by developing their online value proposition (see Decision 4).
- *Customer value improvement* – the value delivered by customers to the company can be increased by increasing customer profitability by decreasing cost to serve (and so price to customers) and at the same time increasing purchase or usage frequency and quantity. These combined effects should drive up sales. Many companies will offer competitive online prices or discounts to help increase their market share. Approaches to specifying online pricing are covered in Chapter 5.

2 Market development

Online channels are used to sell into new markets, taking advantage of the low cost of advertising internationally without the necessity for a supporting sales infrastructure in the customer's country. The Internet has helped low-cost airlines such as easyJet and Ryanair to enter new markets served by their routes cost-effectively. This is a relatively conservative use of the Internet but is a great opportunity for SMEs to increase exports at a low cost, though it does require overcoming the barriers to exporting.

Existing products can also be sold to new market segments or different types of customers. Virtual inventory enables new offerings to be made available to smaller segment sizes, an approach known as micro-targeting. This may happen simply as a by-product of having a website, e.g. RS Components (**www.rswww.com**), a supplier of a range of MRO (maintenance, repair and operations) items, found that 10 per cent of the web-based sales were to individual consumers rather than traditional business customers. It also uses the website to offer additional facilities for customers placing large orders online. The UK retailer Argos found the opposite was true with 10 per cent of website sales being from businesses when their traditional market was consumer-based. EasyJet also has a section of its website to serve business customers. The Internet may offer further opportunities for selling to market sub-segments that have not been previously targeted, e.g. a product sold to large businesses may also appeal to SMEs that they have previously been unable to serve because of the cost of sales via a specialist sales force. Alternatively a product targeted at young people could also appeal to some members of an older audience and vice versa. Many companies have found that the audience and customers of their website are quite different from their traditional audience.

3 Product development

The web can be used to add value to or extend existing products for many companies, e.g. a car manufacturer can potentially provide car performance and service information via a website. Facilities can be provided to download tailored brochures, book a test drive or tailor features required from a car model. But truly new products or services that can be delivered only by the Internet apply for some types of products. These are typically digital media or information products, e.g. online trade magazine *Construction Weekly* diversified to a B2B portal Construction Plus (**www.constructionplus.com**) which had new revenue streams. Similarly, music and book publishing companies have found new ways to deliver products through a new development and usage model such as subscription and pay-per-use, as explained in Chapter 5 in the section on the product element of the marketing mix. Retailers can extend their product range and provide new bundling options online also.

4 Diversification

In this sector, new products are developed which are sold into new markets. The Internet alone cannot facilitate these high-risk business strategies, but it can facilitate them at lower costs than have previously been possible. The options include:

- *Diversification into related businesses.* A low-cost airline can use the website and customer e-mails to promote travel-related services such as hotel booking, car rental or travel insurance at relatively low costs either through its own brand or through partner companies, e.g. Ryanair offers it customers discounts if they book car hire with Hertz car rentals.
- *Diversification into unrelated businesses.* Again the website can be used to promote less-related products to customers, which is the approach used by the Virgin brand, although it is relatively rare.
- *Upstream integration with suppliers.* This is achieved through data exchange between a manufacturer or retailer and its suppliers to enable a company to take more control of the supply chain.
- *Downstream integration with intermediaries.* Again, this is achieved through data exchange with distributors such as online intermediaries.

The benefits and risks of market and product development are highlighted by the creation of **smile** (Figure 4.13), an Internet-specific bank set up by The Co-operative Bank in the UK. **smile** opened for business in October 1999 and in its first year added 200,000 customers at a rate of 20,000 per month. Significantly, 80 per cent of these customers were market development in the context of the parent, since they were not existing Co-operative Bank customers and typically belonged to a higher-income segment.

The risks of the new approach to banking were highlighted by the cost of innovation; with it being estimated that in its first year, the creation and promotion of **smile** increased overall costs at the Co-operative Bank by 5 per cent. However, within five years **smile** was on target, profitable and growing strongly.

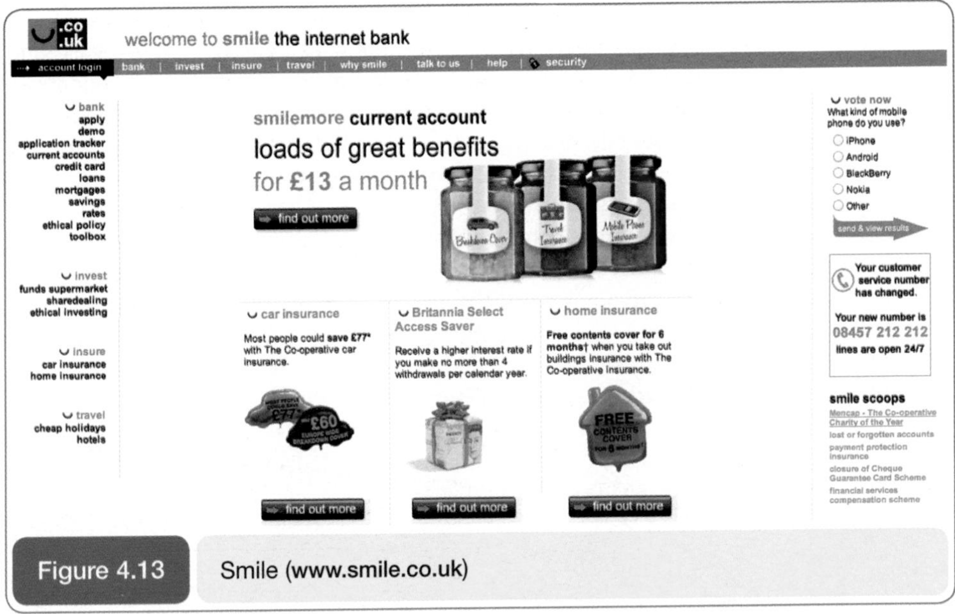

Figure 4.13 Smile (www.smile.co.uk)

Decision 2: Business and revenue models strategies

Business model
A summary of how a company will generate revenue, identifying its product offering, value-added services, revenue sources and target customers.

Strategy formulation often requires companies to evaluate new models since to survive in the digital age means companies need to constantly innovate in order to defend market share for competitors and new entrants. Andy Grove of Intel famously said: 'Only the paranoid will survive', alluding to the need to review new revenue opportunities and competitor innovations. A willingness to test and experiment with new **business models** using calculations like those covered in Chapter 2 is also required. Dell is another example of a technology company that regularly reviews and modifies its business model as shown in Mini Case Study 4.2. Companies at the bleeding edge of technology such as Facebook and Google constantly innovate through acquiring other companies and internal research and development (witness Google Labs (**http://labs.google.com**) which was used to showcase and test new propositions, but is now no longer publicly available). Case Study 4 on Tesco.com at the end of this chapter also highlights innovation in the Tesco business model facilitated through online channels.

To sound a note of caution, flexibility in the business model should not be to the company's detriment through losing focus on the core business. A survey of CEOs of leading UK Internet companies (Durlacher, 2000) showed that, even at the time of the dot-com boom, although flexibility is useful this may not apply to business models. The report states:

> A widely held belief in the new economy in the past has been that change and flexibility is good, but these interviews suggest that it is actually those companies who have stuck to a single business model that have been to date more successful . . . CEOs were not moving far from their starting vision, but that it was in the marketing, scope and partnerships where new economy companies had to be flexible.

Early (first) mover advantage
An early entrant into the marketplace.

Mini Case Study 4.2 Innovation in the Dell business model

One example of how companies can review and revise their business model is provided by Dell Computers. Dell gained **early-mover advantage** in the mid-1990s when it became one of the first companies to offer PCs for sale online. Its sales of PCs and peripherals rapidly grew from the mid-1990s with online sales of $1 million per day to sales of $50 million per day in 2000. Based on this success it has looked at new business models it can use in combination with its powerful brand to provide new services to its existing customer base and also to generate revenue through new customers. In September 2000, Dell announced plans to become a supplier of IT consulting services through linking with enterprise resource planning specialists such as software suppliers, systems integrators and business consulting firms. This venture will enable the facility of Dell's PremierPages to be integrated into the procurement component of ERP systems such as SAP and Baan, thus avoiding the need for rekeying and reducing costs.

In a separate initiative, Dell launched a B2B marketplace (formerly **www.dellmarketplace.com**) aimed at discounted office goods and services procurements including PCs, peripherals, software, stationery and travel. This strategic option did not prove sustainable.

Dell launched Ideastorm (**www.ideastorm.com**, see Figure 4.14), as a site encouraging user participation where anyone can suggest new products and features which can be voted on. Importantly, Dell 'closes the loop' through a separate *Ideas in Action* section where they update consumers on actions taken by the company. For example, as well as improvements to customer service, they explain how they have introduced new systems such as a non-Windows Linux operating system in response to suggestions on Ideastorm. They also explain ideas they haven't implemented and why.

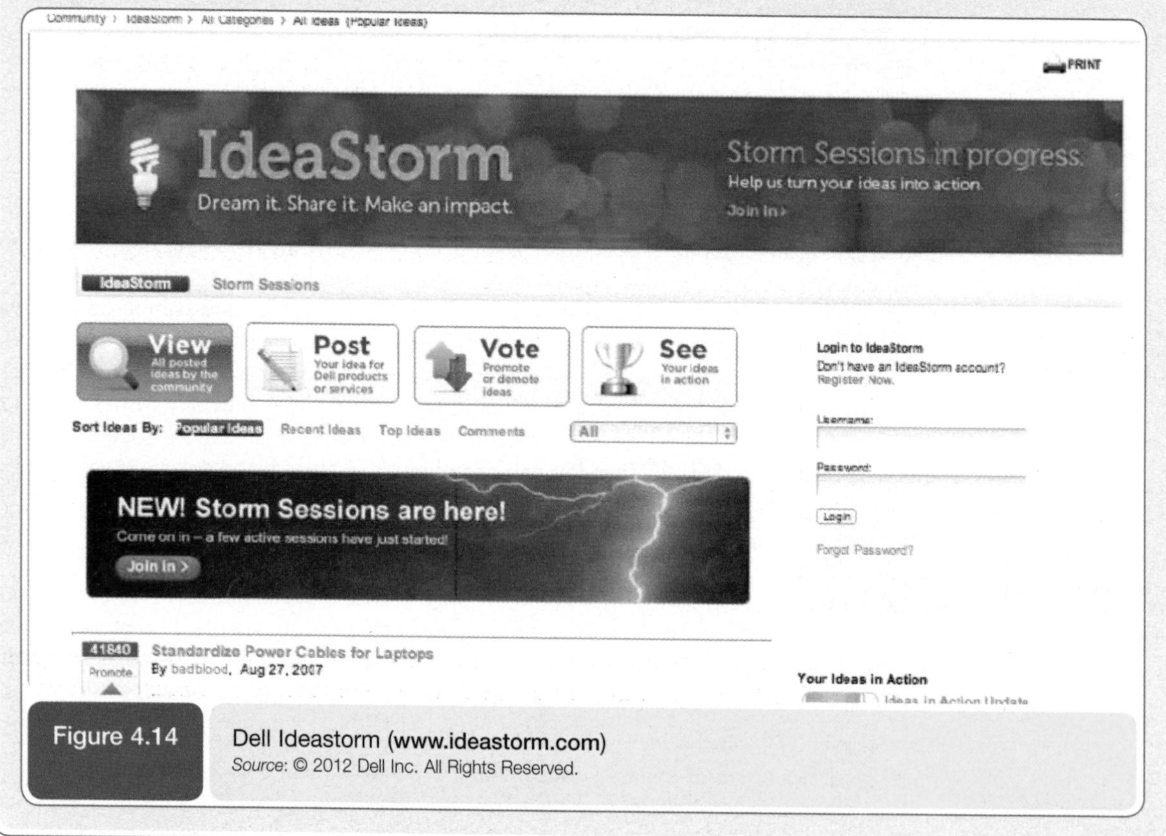

Figure 4.14 Dell Ideastorm (www.ideastorm.com)
Source: © 2012 Dell Inc. All Rights Reserved.

Furthermore, where companies including transactional sites such as Amazon.com or Lastminute.com, have introduced advertising as part of their revenue model, the amount of revenue generated tends to be low compared to overall revenue (although it may be used as leverage for other co-branding work) or insight generated about customer response.

So with all strategy options, managers should also consider the 'do-nothing option'. Here, a company will not risk a new business model, but adopt a 'wait-and-see' or 'fast-follower' approach to see how competitors perform, and then respond rapidly if the new business model proves sustainable.

Revenue model
Describes methods of generating income for an organisation.

Finally, we can note that companies can make less radical changes to their **revenue models** through the Internet which are less far-reaching, but may nevertheless be worthwhile. For example:

- Transactional e-commerce sites (e.g. Tesco.com and Lastminute.com) can sell advertising space or run co-branded promotions on site or through their e-mail newsletters or lists to sell access to their audience to third parties.
- Retailers or media owners can sell-on white-labelled services through their online presence such as ISP, e-mail services or photo-sharing services.
- Companies can gain commission through selling products which are complementary (but not competitive to their own), e.g. a publisher can sell its books through an affiliate arrangement through an e-retailer.

Activity 4.5 Advertising as a revenue model

Google, Amazon and many other successful online corporations have successfully used advertising for their revenue model.

Listen to what Chris Anderson, editor of *Wired* magazine, has to say about the additional *trade-offs* which consumers are making when they visit websites and look at the products and adverts on offer: **http://www.bbc.co.uk/blogs/digitalrevolution/2009/11/rushes-sequences-chris-anderson.shtml.**

Activity

Discuss what extent do you think it is reasonable that advertisers use data collected from website visitors to provide increasingly targeted advertising.

Decision 3: Target marketing strategy

Target marketing strategy
Evaluation and selection of appropriate segments and the development of appropriate offers.

Strategic market segmentation
Selection of key audiences to target with value propositions developed for these audiences

Deciding on which markets to target is a key strategic consideration when planning a digital marketing strategy in the same way it is key to marketing strategy. We will see that a company's web presence and e-mail marketing enables them to target more focused audiences than may be possible with other channels. **Target marketing strategy** involves the four stages shown in Figure 4.15, but the most important decisions are:

- *Segmentation/targeting strategy* – a company's online customers will often have different demographic characteristics, needs and behaviours from its offline customers. It follows that online different approaches to **strategic market segmentation** may be an opportunity and specific segments may need to be selectively targeted through online media channels, the company website or e-mail communications. As we will see, personal development and lifecycle targeting are common approaches for online targeting.
- *Positioning/differentiation strategy* – competitors' product and service offerings will often differ in the online environment. Developing an appropriate online value proposition as described below is an important aspect of this strategy. However, there should also be clarity on the core brand proposition.

The first stage in Figure 4.15 is *segmentation.* Segmentation is a management technique which allows businesses to focus their efforts on the customers they can serve best. When creating digital marketing plans it is useful to distinguish between strategic market segmentation and online tactical segmentation which is used for online targeting.

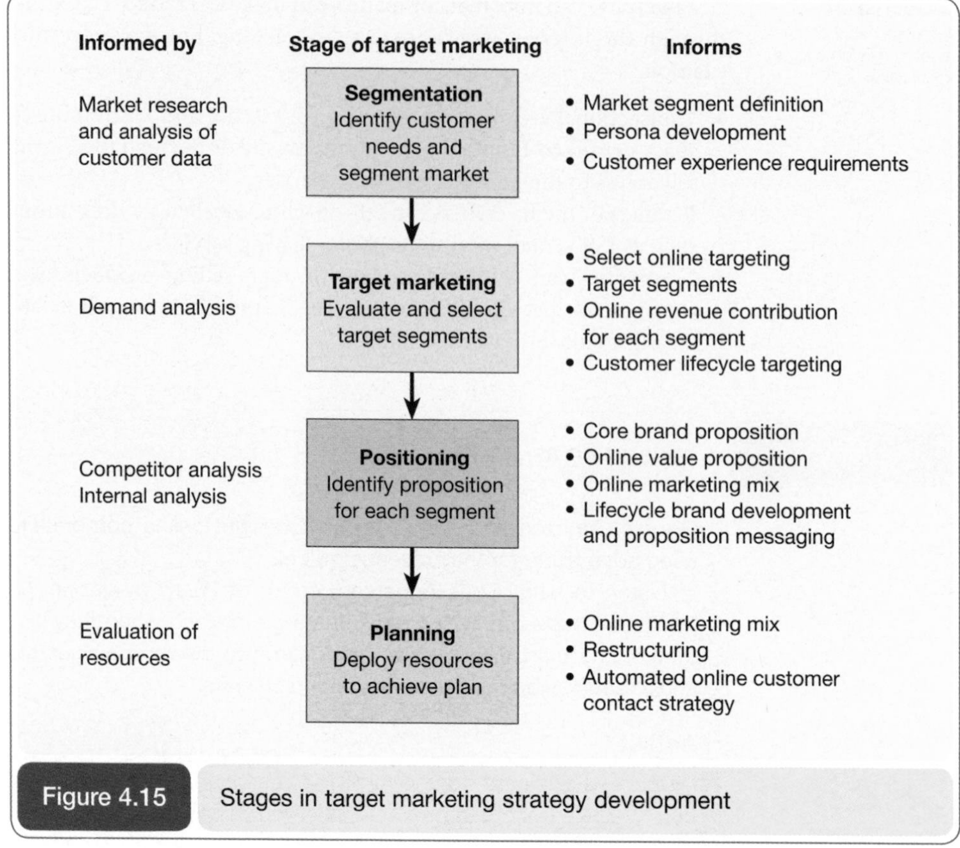

Figure 4.15 Stages in target marketing strategy development

Strategic market segmentation can be defined as (Jobber, 2010):

> the identification of individuals or organisations with similar characteristics that have significant implications for determining marketing strategy.

In an Internet marketing planning context, market segments should be reviewed to assess:

- the current market size or value, future projections of size
- the organisation's current and future market share within the segment
- needs of each segment, in particular, unmet needs
- competitor market shares within the segment
- organisation and competitor offers and propositions
- likelihood of a segment engaging with the organisations offer across all aspects of the buying process;
- usage of the site and conversion to action through web analytics.

online tactical marketing segmentation
Please supply

Options for segmenting online customers by activity levels, which is an **online tactical marketing segmentation** approach, are covered in more detail in Chapter 6 and segmenting site visitors through web analytics systems are covered in Chapter 10.

Stage 2 in Figure 4.15 is target marketing. Here we can select segments for targeting online that are most attractive in terms of growth and profitability. These may be similar or different compared with groups targeted offline. Some examples of customer segments that are targeted online include:

- *The most profitable customers* – using the Internet to provide tailored offers to the top 20 per cent of customers by profit may result in more repeat business and cross-sales.
- *Larger companies (B2B)* – an extranet could be produced to service these customers and increase their loyalty.

- *Smaller companies (B2B)* – large companies are traditionally serviced through sales representatives and account managers, but smaller companies may not warrant the expense of account managers. However, the Internet can be used to reach smaller companies more cost effectively. The number of smaller companies that can be reached in this way may be significant, so although the individual revenue of each one is relatively small, the collective revenue achieved through Internet servicing can be large.
- *Particular members of the buying unit (B2B)* – the site should provide detailed information for different interests which supports the buying decision, e.g. technical documentation for users of products, information on savings from e-procurement for IS or purchasing managers, and information to establish the credibility of the company for decision makers.
- *Customers that are difficult to reach using other media* – an insurance company looking to target younger drivers could use the web as a vehicle for this.
- *Customers that are brand-loyal* – services to appeal to brand loyalists can be provided to support them in their role as advocates of a brand, as suggested by Aaker and Joachimsthaler (2000).
- *Customers that are not brand-loyal* – conversely, incentives, promotion and a good level of service quality could be provided by the website to try and retain such customers.

Some segments can be targeted online by using navigation options to different content groupings such that visitors *self-identify*. This is the approach used as the main basis for navigation on the Dell site (Figure 4.16) and has potential for subsidiary navigation on other sites. Dell targets by geography and then tailors the types of consumers or businesses according to country, the US Dell site having the most options. Other alternatives are to set up separate sites for different audiences, e.g. Dell Premier is targeted at purchasing and IT staff in larger organisations. Once customers are registered on a site, profiling information in a database can be used to send tailored e-mail messages to different segments, as we explain in the Euroffice example in Mini Case Study 4.2.

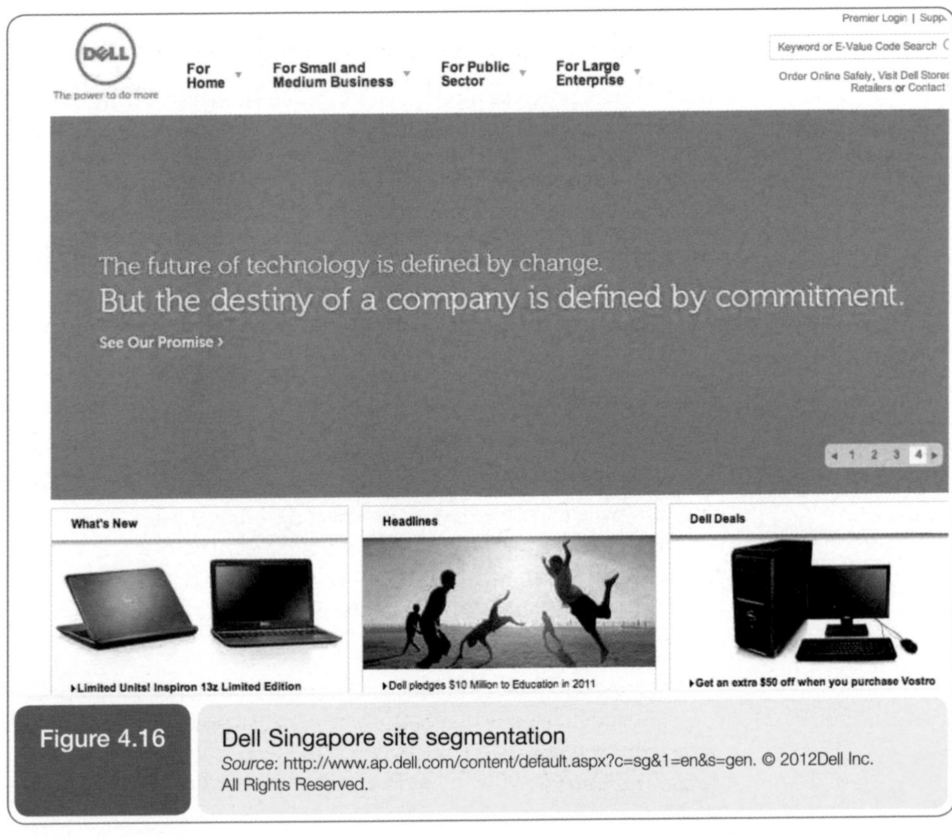

Figure 4.16 Dell Singapore site segmentation

Source: http://www.ap.dell.com/content/default.aspx?c=sg&1=en&s=gen. © 2012Dell Inc. All Rights Reserved.

The most sophisticated online tactical segmentation and targeting schemes are often used by e-retailers, which have detailed customer profiling information and purchase history data and seek to increase customer lifetime value through encouraging increased use of online services through time. However, the general principles of this approach can also be used by other types of companies online. The segmentation and targeting approach used by e-retailers is based on five main elements which in effect are layered on top of each other. The number of options used or segment layers, and so the sophistication of the approach will depend on resources available, technology capabilities and opportunities afforded by the following.

1 Identify customer profile-based demographic characteristics

This is a traditional segmentation based on the type of customer. For B2C companies this will include age, sex and geography. For B2B companies, it will include size of company and the industry sector or application they operate in.

2 Identify customer lifecycle groups

Figure 4.17 illustrates this approach. As visitors use online services they can potentially pass through seven or more stages. Once companies have defined these groups and set up the customer relationship management infrastructure to categorise customers in this way, they can then deliver targeted messages, either by personalised on-site messaging or through e-mails that are triggered automatically by different rules. First-time visitors can be identified by whether they have a cookie placed on their PC. Once visitors have registered, they can be tracked through the remaining stages. Two particularly important groups are customers that have purchased one or more times. For many e-retailers, encouraging customers to move from the first purchase to the second purchase and then on to the third purchase is a key challenge. Specific promotions can be used to encourage further purchases. Similarly, once customers become inactive (i.e. they have not purchased for a defined period such as three months) further follow-ups are required.

3 Identify behaviour in response and purchase value

As customers progress through the lifecycle shown in Figure 4.17, database analysis can be used by the marketer to build up a detailed response and purchase history which considers

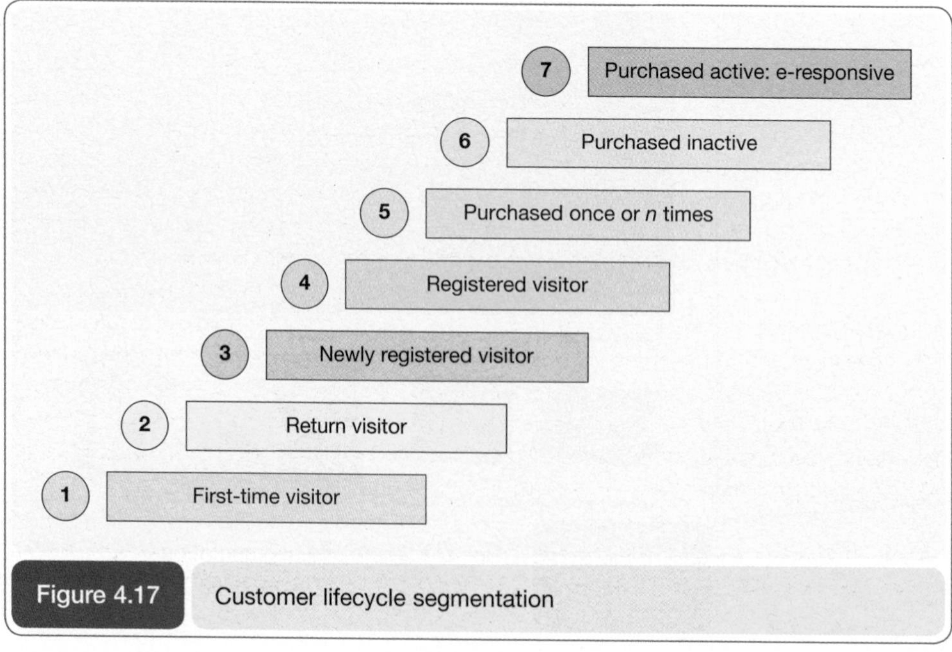

Figure 4.17 Customer lifecycle segmentation

the details of recency, frequency, monetary value and category of products purchased. As explained in Chapter 6, grouping customers by their current and future value and techniques such as FRAC and RFM analysis can be used to develop strategies to retain valuable customers and migrate lower value customers to higher value in future.

4 Identify multichannel behaviour (channel preference)

Regardless of the enthusiasm of the company for online channels, some customers will prefer using online channels and others will prefer traditional channels. Drawing a channel chain (Figure 2.24) for different customers is useful to help understand this. It is also useful to have a flag within the database which indicates the customer's channel preference and, by implication, the best channel to target them through. Customers who prefer online channels can be targeted mainly by online communications such as e-mail, while those who prefer traditional channels can be targeted by traditional communications such as direct mail or phone.

5 Tone and style preference

In a similar manner to channel preference, customers will respond differently to different types of message. Some may like a more rational appeal, in which case a detailed e-mail explaining the benefits of the offer may work best. Others will prefer an emotional appeal based on images and with warmer, less formal copy. Sophisticated companies will test for this in customers or infer it using profile characteristics and response behaviour and then develop different creative treatments accordingly. Companies that use polls can potentially use this to infer style preferences. To summarise this section, read Mini Case Study 4.3 which illustrates the combination of these different forms of communication.

Mini Case Study 4.3 Euroffice segment office supplies purchasers using a 'touch marketing funnel' approach

Euroffice (**www.euroffice.co.uk**) targets small and medium-sized companies. According to George Karibian, CEO, 'getting the message across effectively required segmentation' to engage different people in different ways. The office sector is fiercely competitive with relatively little loyalty since company purchasers will often simply buy on price. However, targeted incentives can be used to reward or encourage buyers' loyalty. Rather than manually developing campaigns for each segment, which is time-consuming, Euroffice mainly uses an automated event-based targeting approach based on the system identifying the stage at which a consumer is in the lifecycle, i.e. how many products they have purchased and the types of product within their purchase history. Karibian calls this a '*touch marketing funnel*' approach, i.e. the touch strategy is determined by customer segmentation and response. Three main groups of customers are identified in the lifecycle and these are broken down further according to purchase category. Also layered on this segmentation is breakdown into buyer type – are they a small home-user, an operations manager at a mid-size company or a purchasing manager at a large company? Each will respond to different promotions.

The first group, at the top of the funnel and the largest, are '*Group 1: Trial customers*' who have made one or two purchases. For the first group, Euroffice believes that creating impulse buying through price promotions is most important. These will be based on categories purchased in the past. The second group, '*Group 2: The nursery*', have made three to eight purchases. A particular issue, as with many e-retailers, is encouraging customers from the third to fourth purchase – there is a more significant drop-out at this point which the company uses marketing to control. Karibian says: 'When they get to Group 2: it's about creating frequency of purchase to ensure they don't forget you'. Euroffice sends a printed catalogue to Group 2 separately from their merchandise as a reminder about the company. The final group, '*Group 3: Key accounts*', have made nine or more orders. They also tend to have a higher basket value. These people are 'the Crown Jewels' and will spend an average of £135 per order compared to an average of £55 for trial customers. They have a 90%

probability of re-ordering within a six-month period. For this group, tools have been developed on the site to make it easier for them to shop. The intention is that these customers find these tools help them in making their orders and they become reliant on them, so achieving 'soft lock-in'.

Subject: Storming Savings at Euroffice

To ensure you don't miss future email updates, please add **offers@euroffice.co.uk** to your email address book or safe list.

euroffice
We love office stuff

Search Go

Home | Office Products | Toners & Cartridges | Electronics | Furniture | Business Cards | Flowers | Rewards | Clearance

Dear Dave

Like the rest of the country, a storm is brewing up at Euroffice this week.

We have slashed prices on some of your favourite products like A4 copier paper at our **lowest price** ever of £1.75 a pack.

There's also the added bonus of double reward points on all orders, so grab these competition beating offers while you can as they will end on Friday.

reward points x2 claim now

Storming Savings
Many more on site. click here

5 Packs Copier Paper
ONLY £8.75
only £1.75 per pack
Our Lowest Price EVER!
more info

DL Envelopes + Avery Labels
ONLY £19.99
45% cheaper than Viking
more info

5 Binders + Dividers
ONLY £9.98

A4 Notebook + 12 Pens
ONLY £7.98

Figure 4.18 Euroffice e-mail (www.euroffice.co.uk)
Source: Adapted from the company website press releases and *Revolution* (2005a)

Decision 4: Positioning and differentiation strategy (including the marketing mix)

Positioning
Customers' perception of the product offer relative to those of competitors.

Stage 3 in Figure 4.15 is **positioning.** Deise *et al.* (2000) suggest that in an online context, companies can position their products relative to competitor offerings according to four main variables: product quality, service quality, price and fulfilment time. They suggest it is useful to review these through an equation of how they combine to influence customer perceptions of value or brand:

$$\text{customer value (brand perception)} = \frac{\text{product quality} \times \text{service quality}}{\text{price} \times \text{fulfilment time}}$$

Strategies should review the extent to which increases in product and service quality can be balanced against variations in price and fulfilment time. Chaston (2000) argues that there are four options for strategic focus to position a company in the online marketplace. It is evident that these are related to the different elements of Deise *et al.* (2000). He says that online these should build on existing strengths, and can use the online facilities to enhance the positioning as follows:

- *Product performance excellence.* Enhance by providing online product customisation.
- *Price performance excellence.* Use the facilities of the Internet to offer favourable pricing to loyal customers or to reduce prices where demand is low (e.g. British Midland Airlines uses auctions to sell under-used capacity on flights).
- *Transactional excellence.* A site such as that of software and hardware e-tailer dabs.com offers transactional excellence through combining pricing information with dynamic availability information on products, listing number in stock, number on order and when they are expected.
- *Relationship excellence.* Personalisation features to enable customers to review sales order history and place repeat orders. An example is RS Components (**www.rswww.com**).

These positioning options have much in common with Porter's generic competitive strategies of cost leadership or differentiation in a broad market and a market segmentation approach focusing on a more limited target market (Porter, 1980). Porter has been criticised because many commentators believe that to remain competitive it is necessary to combine excellence in all of these areas. It can be suggested that the same is true for sell-side e-commerce. These are not mutually exclusive strategic options, rather they are prerequisites for success. Customers will be unlikely to judge on a single criterion, but on the balance of multiple criteria. This is the view of Kim *et al.* (2004) who concluded that for online businesses 'integrated strategies that combine elements of cost leadership and differentiation will outperform cost leadership or differentiation strategies'. It can be seen that Porter's original criteria are similar to the strategic positioning options of Chaston (2000) and Deise *et al.* (2000). Figure 4.19 summarises the positioning options described in this section, showing the emphasis on the three main variables for online differentiation – price, product and relationship-building services. The diagram can be used to show the mix of the three elements of positionings. EasyJet has an emphasis on price performance, but with a component of product innovation. Amazon is not positioned on price performance, but rather on relationship building and product innovation. We will see in Chapter 5, in the section on price, that although it would be expected that pricing is a key aspect determining online retail sales, there are other factors about a retail brand, such as familiarity, trust and service, which are also important.

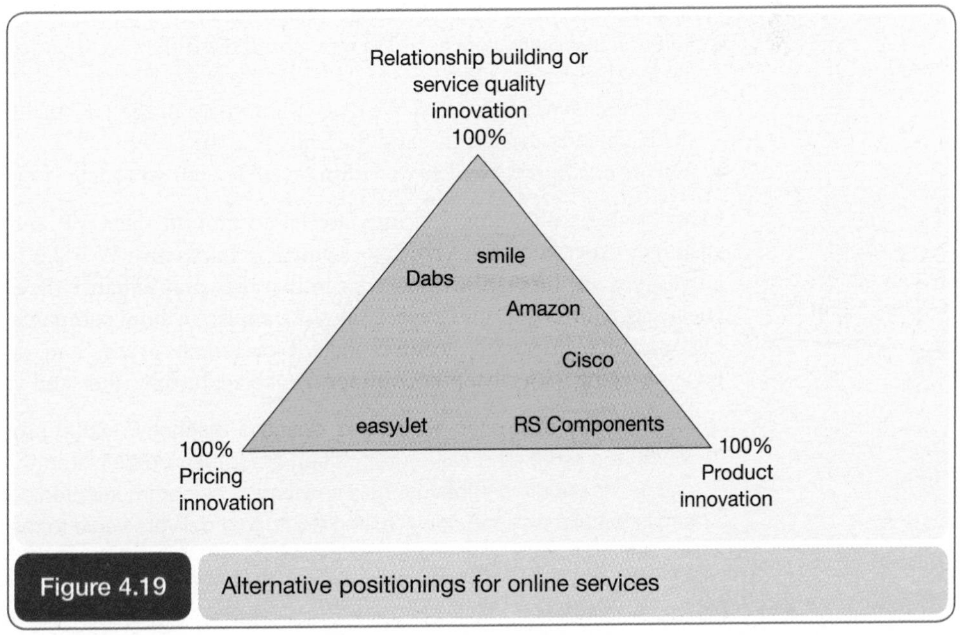

Figure 4.19 Alternative positionings for online services

Differential advantage

Differential advantage
A desirable attribute of a product offering that is not currently matched by competitor offerings.

The aim of positioning is to develop a **differential advantage** over competitors. Jobber (2010) suggests that market segmentation is at the heart of developing a differential marketing strategy. Marking strategists use elements from the marketing mix to establish the difference between their company and their rivals. Many business' have differentiated their own line offer by using price, for example:

- *Retailers* offering lower prices online. Examples: Tesco.com (price promotions on selected products), Comet (discounts relative to instore pricing on some products).
- *Airlines* offering lower-cost flights for online bookings. Examples: easyJet, Ryanair, BA.
- *Financial services companies* offering higher interest rates on savings products and lower interest rates on credit products such as credit cards and loans. Examples: Nationwide, Alliance and Leicester.
- *Mobile phone network* providers or utilities offering lower-cost tariffs or discounts for customers accounts who are managed online without paper billing. Examples: O2, British Gas.

It is important to note that price is not the only way to stand out online, quality of brand experience and quality of service is equally important for creating differential advantage.

In a digital marketing context differential advantage and positioning can be clarified and communicated by developing an **online value proposition (OVP)**. Developing an OVP, involves:

Online value proposition (OVP)
A statement of the benefits of online services reinforces the core proposition and differentiates from an organisation's offline offering and those of competitors.

- Developing online content and service and explaining them through messages which:
  - reinforce core brand proposition and credibility
  - communicate what a visitor can get from an online brand that they can't get from the brand offline and they can't get from competitors or intermediaries.
- Communicating these messages to all appropriate online and offline customers with touch points in different levels of detail from straplines to more detailed content on the website or in print.

Communicating the OVP on the site can help create a customer-centric website. Look at how Webuyanycar.com does this for different types of visitors and services in Figure 4.20. Virgin Wines used an OVP to communicate its service promise as follows:

- And what if . . . *You are out during the day*? We promise that our drivers will find a safe place to leave your wine; but if it does get stolen, we just replace it.
- *You find it cheaper elsewhere*? We will refund the difference if you are lucky enough to find a wine cheaper elsewhere.
- *You live somewhere obscure*? We deliver anywhere in the UK, including Northern Ireland, the Highlands and Islands, and the Scilly Isles for £5.99.
- *You are in a hurry*? We deliver within seven days, or your delivery is free.

Many strategic planning decisions are based around the OVP and the quality of online customer experience delivered by a company. Interactive Web 2.0 features can be particularly important for transactional sites in that they may enhance the user's experience and so encourage conversion and repeat sales. Examples of how companies have developed their OVP through interactive features include customer reviews and ratings; podcast product reviews; a blog with customer comments enabled; buyers guide and video reviews.

> First identify customer needs and define a distinctive value proposition that will meet them, at a profit. The value proposition must then be delivered through the right product and service and the right channels and it must be communicated consistently. The ultimate aim is to build a strong, long-lasting brand that delivers value to the company marketing it.

Figure 4.20 WeBuyAnyCar (www.webuyanycar.co.uk) clearly communicates its proposition

Having a clear online value proposition has several benefits:

- It helps distinguish an e-commerce site from its competitors (this should be a website design objective).
- It helps provide a focus to marketing efforts so that company staff are clear about the purpose of the site.
- If the proposition is clear it can be used for PR, and word-of-mouth recommendations may be made about the company, e.g. the clear proposition of Amazon on its site is that prices are reduced by up to 40 per cent and that a wide range of three million titles are available.
- It can be linked to the normal product propositions of a company or its product.

We look further into options for varying the proposition and marketing mix in Chapter 5.

Activity 4.6 Online value proposition

Visit the websites of the following companies and, in one or two sentences each, summarise their Internet value proposition. You should also explain how they use the content of the website to indicate their value proposition to customers.

- Tektronix (www.tektronix.com)
- Handbag.com (www.handbag.com)
- Harrods (www.harrods.com)
- Guinness (www.guinness.com)

Multichannel prioritisation
Assesses the strategic significance of the Internet relative to other communications channels and then deploys resources to integrate with marketing channels.

Customer communications channels
The range of media used to communicate directly with a customer.

Decisions 5 and 6 relate to **multichannel prioritisation** which assesses the strategic significance of the Internet relative to other communications channels. In making this prioritisation it is helpful to distinguish between **customer communications channels** and distribution channels.

Decision 5: Customer engagement and social media strategy

Customer engagement strategy
A strategy to encourage interaction and participation of consumers with a brand through developing content and experiences with the aim of meeting commercial objectives. It is closely related to the development of content marketing and social media strategy.

Social media strategy
A definition of the marketing communications used to achieve interaction with social network users to meet business goals. The scope of social media optimisation also includes incorporation of social features such as status updates and sharing widgets into company websites.

Each day there are millions of social network status updates, new blog posts, videos and news articles published. As consumers spend more time online reading and interacting with this content, the challenge of engaging them increases. Given this, we believe that every company must develop a **customer engagement strategy** as a key part of their digital marketing strategy. This customer engagement strategy reviews approaches to create compelling content and experiences that form the online value proposition.

Increasingly, it's most straightforward to achieve online engagement not on a company website, but a social presence in one of the main social networks like Facebook, Google+, LinkedIn, Twitter or specialist networks. Given the popularity of these social networks, many companies will seek to develop an overall **social media strategy.**

When developing an approach for using each social network to build engagement and community, there are some common decisions across the networks that focus on the types of content and how it is published. The answers for each social network will vary, but there are some common themes that should be part of an overall engagement and content marketing strategy. We recommend that companies review these 12 questions to help define their social media marketing strategy:

- *Question 1. Who are our target audience?* For a single company, the typical audience of each social network will differ in terms of demographics. If you review a sample of profiles for your own followers or competitors, you will get a feel for the typical audience and can develop typical customer personas you are targeting.
- *Question 2. What are the content preferences of our audiences?* The type of content that audiences like to see on each network is shown by the content they share or rate highly. For example on Facebook it may be that videos work well, on Twitter infographics and on LinkedIn posting a provocative statement. Benchmarking to establish the popularity of different types of messages is worthwhile.
- *Question 3. Strategic business goals for social network presences?* Ask which of the 5 Ss is the emphasis on: Sell, Speak, Serve, Save or Sizzle? On some platforms such as Twitter, a separate presence can be created for sales and service. But the majority of communications are to engage through speaking, so it's important to establish which types of content will help create sharing and dialogue.
- *Question 4. Which content types should have priority?* Based on your analysis of customer needs and competitor benchmarking, you can set out the topics that will work best when covered in your content stream. For example, for the American Express Open Forum (**www.openforum.com**, a community that is independent of social networks) their content focuses on innovation, marketing and finance though it can cover health and lifestyle too.
- *Question 5. How to differentiate the social channel from other communications channels?* We have seen that the audience for each network will differ and will have different preferences for types of content that fit the channel. If you can define a powerful offer for the social channel it will encourage people to subscribe to that channel even if they are already using other channels. It's important to communicate clearly what the channel offers to encourage sign-up. For example, retailer Asda (**www.facebook.com/GeorgeatAsdaOfficial**) offers 'Previews, competitions and exclusive offers' if someone 'Likes' its page. It also has more tactical campaigns to encourage sign-up which require e-mail addresses to be collected which can be assigned as a Facebook user. Communicating the value offered can happen both on the page and in other channels such as e-mail, direct mail or print advertising.
- *Question 6. How to integrate social channels?* This is a complex question since customers use social media sites in combination with other channels like the website, e-mail, apps and traditional communications like advertising. Since the user-generated content of social media is engaging, companies will often want to incorporate social content within their website or e-mails. This is facilitated by APIs created by the social networks to enable

sharing such as the Facebook platform. Incorporating social sign-on (Chapter 6) is increasingly important to enable integration.

- *Question 7. Content frequency and editorial calendar?* To engage an audience requires regular content, but what does regular mean? Will there be several status updates a day or only several updates a week? How do these link to other content like that on a blog? There will be many different types of content, some will be quick to create, others will take much longer and need planning or resourcing; this is where an editorial calendar is essential.
- *Question 8. Sourcing content?* Creating content takes time, even if it is only a 140 character tweet or status update. Often the content will need to link to more indepth content on the company website or blog. This will take yet more time to create and will have to be of sufficient quality to engage the audience to encourage sharing and will reflect well on the brand. Some of this can be originated in-house, but it may need an agency to create it.
- *Question 9. How to manage publication and interaction?* Each social platform needs someone to update the content, but also to respond and interact on other social networks. A decision has to be taken as to whether this happens in-house or whether some of it can be outsourced to a third-party.
- *Question 10. Software for managing the publishing process?* Software can't create content for you, but it can streamline the process. Tools like Hootsuite or Tweetburner enable status updates to be shared across different networks. For example status updates can be shared across Facebook, LinkedIn or Twitter. However, a personalised approach is recommended also.
- *Question 11. Tracking the business impact of social network activity?* Tools are available from each of the platforms to help marketers review their effectiveness. For example Facebook Insights is a service available to page owner on Facebook. There are also analytics features within tools like Hootsuite showing which messages were popular based on sharing and clickthrough rate. To review how these translate to business value, tagging of messages to show the source of visitors in analytics systems are also needed.
- *Question 12. How to optimise the social presence?* Tracking isn't worthwhile unless it is reviewed and acted upon. The insights available will enable you to test, learn and refine marketing activities. This is known as **social media optimisation (SMO)**. To get the most from social media marketing requires time to be ring-fenced to make changes and then review them.

Social media optimisation (SMO)
A process to review and improve the effectiveness of social media marketing through reviewing approaches to enhance content and communications quality to generate more business value.

Distribution channels
The mechanism by which products are directed to customers either through intermediaries or directly.

Decision 6: Multichannel distribution strategy

Distribution channels refer to flow of products from a manufacturer or service provider to the end customer. At the centre of any distribution channel are the movement of goods and the flow of information between different organisations involved in moving goods from the point of manufacture and the point of consumption. Depending on the *players* who make up the supply chain its structure can vary and this structure will determine whether goods get to the right place at the right time. Players in a supply chain can include: retailers, suppliers, intermediaries, third-party logistic solution providers and transportation companies who provide transportation, warehousing and distribution management facilities for their retailer clients. In retailing, the principle function of a distribution channel is the *breaking of bulk*. Fernie *et al.* (2010) tell us that:

> the aim for retailers (and their supply partners) is to manage this chain to create value for the customer at an acceptable cost. The managing of this so-called 'pipeline' has been a key challenge for logistics professionals, especially with the realisation that the reduction of time not only reduces costs, but also gives competitive advantage.

Mini Case Study 4.4 discusses how Tesco plc leveraged competitive advantages from making effective decision for their multi channel strategy.

Mini Case Study 4.4 Distribution and the online grocery retailer

Fernie *et al*. (2010) have identified many challenges, which grocery retailers face when setting up and managing online sales operations. Grocery retailers wanting to sell online must typically decide how to select goods that will fulfil customer orders. On average a typical customer order will about 60–80 items. But, the complexity of managing the products is more than just selecting items: selling groceries means selling products which are from three different temperature zones (ambient, chilled and frozen) from a total range of 10–25,000 products within 12–24 hours for delivery to customers within one- to two-hour time-slots. For example, Tesco is currently picking and delivering an average of 250,000 such orders every week. New logistical techniques have had to be devised to support e-grocery retailing on this scale. Tesco has a logistical network, which links into satellite technology and enables the organisation to know precisely where all of its goods are all of the time in order to ensure availability of good to fulfil individual orders, which are selected in-store. Adopting this strategy has enabled Tesco to rapidly expand its online operation in the UK and Europe.

According to Ellis-Chadwick *et al*. (2007), Tesco's channel strategy decisions were critical to its future success. The company maximised the benefits of having a national network of retail stores and trained its staff well to establish store based product selection for all its online shopping orders. This strategy facilitated rapid expansion of its online shopping operation across Britain. Other retailers, such as Sainsbury's, initially adopted a centralised distribution network to support its online shopping operation and this strategy decision limited growth and expansion. Tesco have been able to leverage advantage from being a first mover and by establishing highly efficient systems to support their online operations. This strategic approach to distribution channels has enabled Tesco to become the no 1 grocery retailer in the world.

Clicks and mortar
A business combining an online and offline presence.

Clicks-only (Internet pureplay)
An organisation with principally an online presence. It does not operate a mail-order operation or promote inbound phone orders.

The general options for the mix of 'bricks and clicks' are shown in Figure 4.21. The online revenue contribution estimate is informed by the customer demand analysis of propensity to purchase a particular type of product. If the objective is to achieve a high online revenue contribution of greater than 70 per cent then this will require fundamental change for the company to transform to a **clicks and mortar** or **clicks-only (Internet pureplay)** company.

Kumar (1999) suggests that a company should decide whether the Internet will primarily *complement* the company's other channels or primarily *replace* other channels. Clearly, if it is believed that the Internet will primarily replace other channels, then it is important to invest in the promotion and infrastructure to achieve this. This is a key decision as the company is essentially deciding whether the Internet is 'just another communications and/or sales channel' or whether it will fundamentally change the way it communicates and sells to its customers.

Figure 4.22 summarises the main decisions on which a company should base its commitment to the Internet. Kumar (1999) suggests that replacement is most likely to happen when:

- customer access to the Internet is high
- the Internet can offer a better value proposition than other media
- the product can be delivered over the Internet (it can be argued that this condition is not essential for replacement, so it is not shown in the figure)
- the product can be standardised (the user does not usually need to view to purchase).

Only if all four conditions are met will there primarily be a replacement effect. The fewer conditions met, the more likely it is that there will be a complementary effect.

From an analysis such as that in Figure 4.22 it should be possible to state whether the company strategy should be directed as a complementary or as a replacement scenario. As mentioned in relation to the question of the contribution of the Internet to its business, the company should repeat the analysis for different product segments and different markets. It will then be possible to state the company's overall commitment to the Internet. If the future strategic importance of the Internet is high, with replacement likely, then a significant

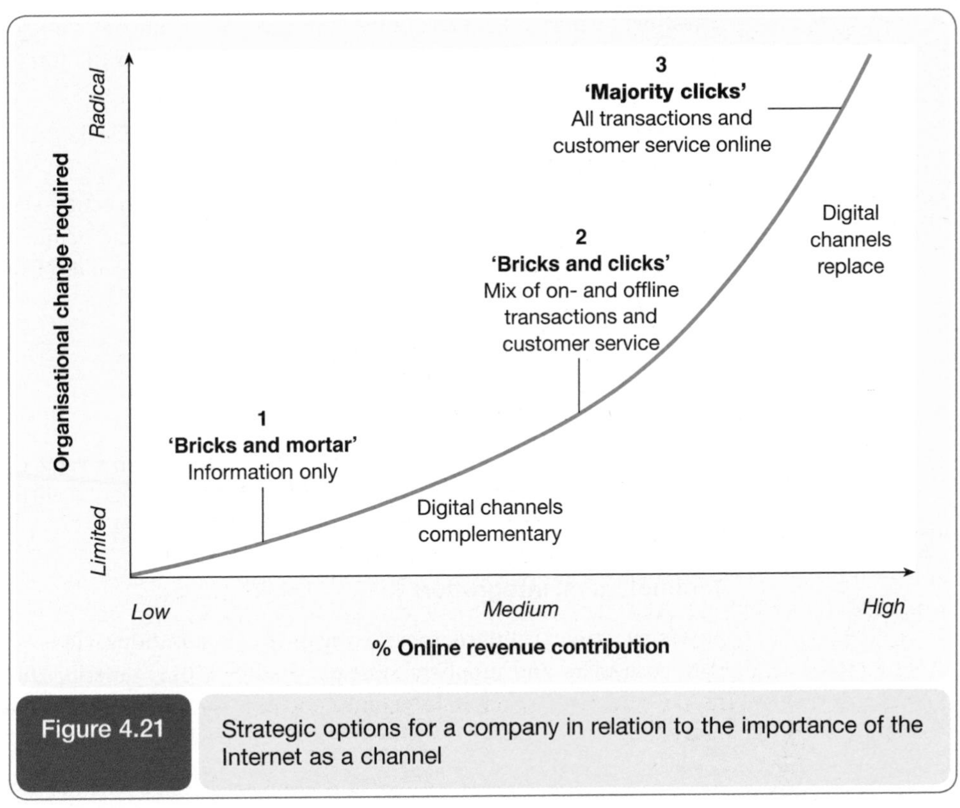

Figure 4.21 Strategic options for a company in relation to the importance of the Internet as a channel

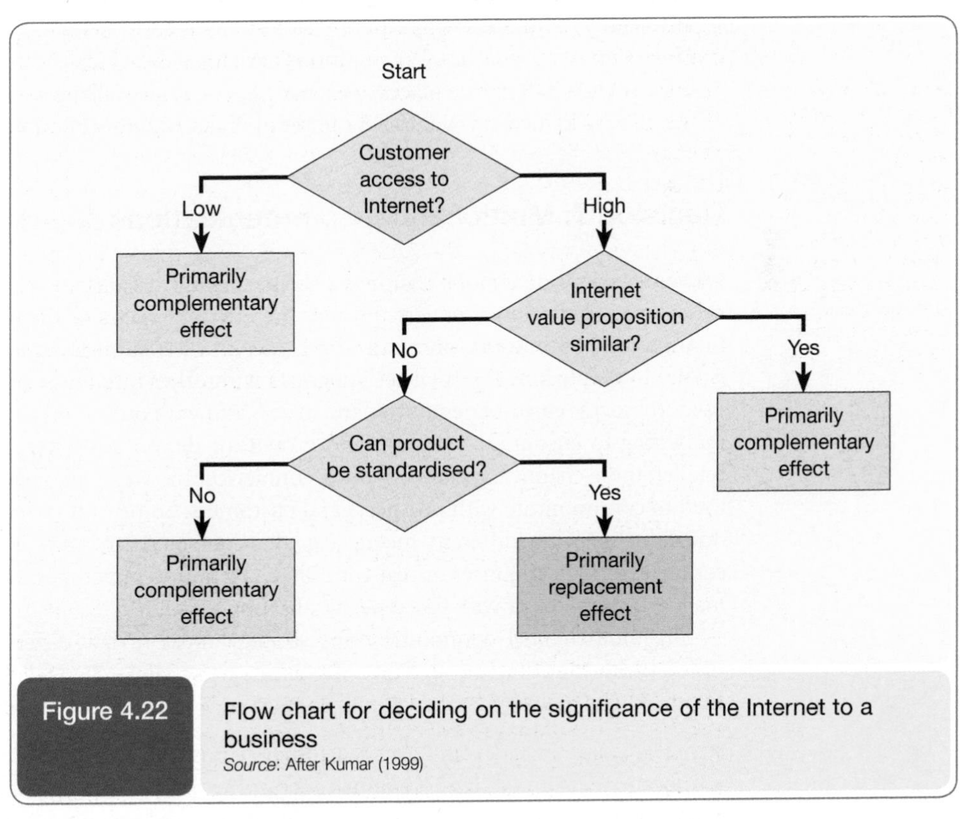

Figure 4.22 Flow chart for deciding on the significance of the Internet to a business

Source: After Kumar (1999)

investment needs to be made in the Internet, and a company's mission needs to be directed towards replacement. If the future strategic importance of the Internet is low then this still needs to be recognised and appropriate investment made.

Changes to marketplace structure

Strategies to take advantage of changes in marketplace structure should also be developed. These options are created through disintermediation and reintermediation (Chapter 2) within a marketplace. The strategic options have already been discussed in Chapter 2, e.g.:

- disintermediation (sell direct)
- create new online intermediary (countermediation)
- partner with new online or existing intermediaries
- do nothing!

Prioritising strategic partnerships as part of the move from a value chain to a value network should also occur as part of this decision. For all options, tactics will be needed to manage the channel conflicts that may occur as a result of restructuring.

Technological integration

To achieve strategic Internet marketing goals, organisations will have to plan for integration with customers' and suppliers' systems. Chaffey (2011) describes how a supplier (in a B2B market) may have to support technical integration with a range of customer e-procurement needs, e.g.:

- *Links with single customers.* Organisations will decide whether a single customer is large enough to enforce such linkage, e.g. supermarkets often insist that their suppliers trade with them electronically. However, the supplier may be faced with the cost of setting up different types of links with different supermarket customers.
- *Links with intermediaries.* Organisations have to assess which are the dominant intermediaries, such as B2B marketplaces or exchanges, and then evaluate whether the trade resulting from the intermediary is sufficient to set up links with this intermediary.

Decision 7: Multichannel communications strategy

Customer communications channels refer to how an organisation influences its customers to select products and suppliers through the different stages of the buying process through inbound and outbound communications. As part of creating a digital marketing strategy, it is vital to define how the Internet integrates with other inbound communications channels used to process customer enquiries and orders and with outbound channels which use direct marketing to encourage retention and growth or deliver customer service messages. For a retailer, these channels include in-store, contact-centre, web and outbound direct messaging used to communicate with prospects and customers. Some of these channels may be broken down further into different media, e.g. the contact-centre may involve inbound phone enquiries, e-mail enquiries or real-time chat. Outbound direct messaging may involve direct mail, e-mail media or web-based personalisation.

The multichannel communications strategy must review different types of customer contact with the company and then determine how online channels will best support these channels. The main types of customer contact and corresponding strategies will typically be:

- inbound sales-related enquiries (customer acquisition or conversion strategy)
- inbound customer-support enquiries (customer service strategy)
- outbound contact strategy (customer retention and development strategy).

For each of these strategies, the most efficient mix and sequence of media to support the business objectives must be determined. Typically the short-term objective will be conversion to outcome such as sale or satisfactorily resolved service enquiry in the shortest possible time with the minimum cost. However, longer-term objectives of customer loyalty and growth also need to be considered. If the initial experience is efficient, but unsatisfactory to the customer, then they may not remain a customer!

The multichannel communications strategy must assess the balance between:

- *Customer channel preferences* – some customers will prefer online channels for product selection or making enquiries while others will prefer traditional channels.
- *Organisation channel preferences* – traditional channels tend to be more expensive to service than digital channels for the company; however, it is important to assess effectiveness and the ability of channels to convert the customer to sale (e.g. a customer who responds to a TV ad to buy car insurance may be more likely to purchase if they enquire by phone in comparison to web enquiry) or in developing customer loyalty (the personal touch available through face-to-face or phone contact may result in a better experience for some customers which engenders loyalty).

Channels and media have become increasing sophisticated and diverse in recent years and these developments have led to increasingly complex patterns of consumer behaviour. For an organisation to begin to understand customer behaviour online they need to identify target market segments, develop customer profiles, and select channels and media which might be suitable for communicating with the chosen segment. As 'consumer segmentation is a critical aspect of effective multichannel strategy design' (Neslin *et al.*, 2006) organisations are faced with making difficult and challenging decisions.

Figure 4.23 is based on the work of Dholakia *et al.* (2010) who suggest there are eight dimensions to consider when making channel choice. This figure shows these dimensions and suggests the factors that affect consumer decision making. The channel dimensions have

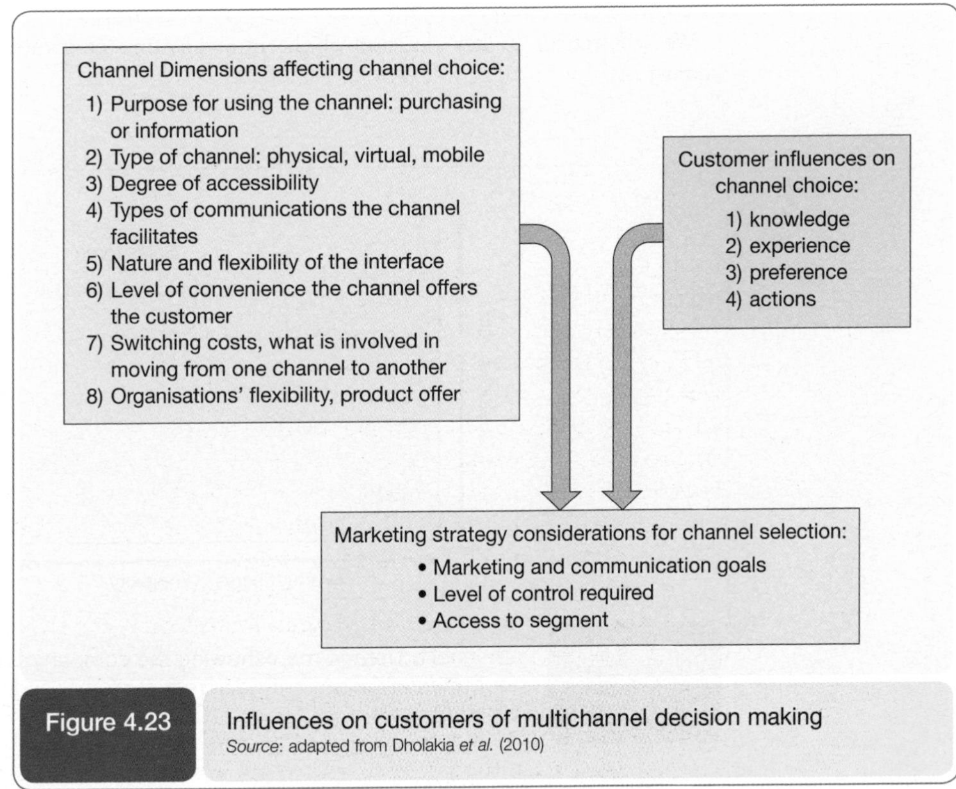

Figure 4.23 Influences on customers of multichannel decision making
Source: adapted from Dholakia *et al.* (2010)

implications for planning and point to key decision areas for an organisation that is developing its channel and communication strategies. For example, dimension 3 – accessibility – is becoming increasingly important with the widespread adoption of wireless technology and mobile phones; dimension 5 – flexibility of the interface – some channels offer limited flexibility whereas others can be instantaneously tailored, e.g. advertising which through emotional recognition software can potentially provide personal message as a customer passes by an outdoor billboard. Customer influences affect their channel choice based on their personal characteristics which affect how they interact with technology. Both the channel dimensions and customer will shape the strategy decisions a marketer makes but there are also marketing strategy considerations which will influence final channels selection, e.g. goals and objectives.

Multichannel communications strategy needs to specify the extent of communications choices made available to customers and the degree to which a company uses different channels to communicate with particular customer segments. Deciding on the best combination of channels is a complex challenge for organisations. Consider your mobile phone company – when purchasing you may make your decision about handset and network supplier in-store, on the web or through phoning the contact centre. Any of these contact points may either be direct with the network provider or through a retail intermediary. After purchase, if you have support questions about billing, handset upgrades or new tariffs you may again use any of these touchpoints to resolve your questions. Managing this multichannel challenge is vital for the phone company for two reasons, both concerned with customer retention. First, the experience delivered through these channels is vital to the decision whether to remain with the network supplier when their contract expires – price is not the only consideration. Second, outbound communications delivered via website, e-mail, direct mail and phone are critical to getting the customer to stay with the company by recommending the most appropriate tariff and handset with appropriate promotions, but which is the most appropriate mix of channels for the company (each channel has a different level of cost-effectiveness for customers which contributes different levels of value to the customer) and the customer (each customer will have a preference for the combinations of channels they will use for different decisions)?

We will return to key decision about implementing customer contact strategies in Chapter 6.

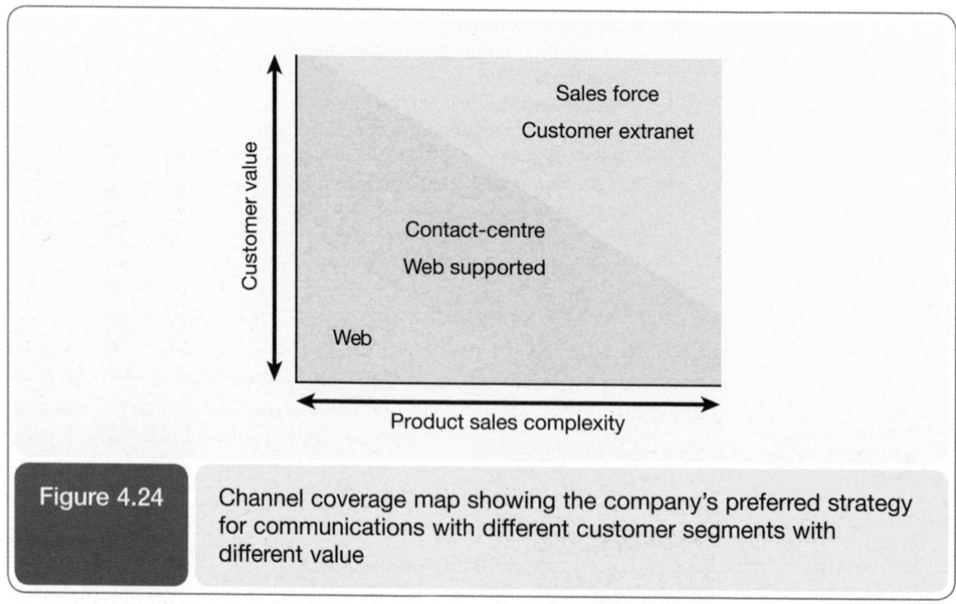

Figure 4.24 Channel coverage map showing the company's preferred strategy for communications with different customer segments with different value

Decision 8: Online communications mix and budget

The decision on the amount of spending on online communications and the mix between the different communications techniques such as search engine marketing, affiliate marketing, e-mail marketing and online advertising closely relates to Decision 6. In Chapter 2 we discussed the changes in levels of adoption of different channels and media and these changes have a cascade effect in terms of implications for planning the communication mix.

Making these decisions requires digital marketers to decide the focus of their communications and whether the primary purpose, is customer acquisition, retention or relationship building.

In the case of e-commerce operations Agrawal *et al.* (2001) suggests success can be modelled and controlled based on the customer lifecycle of customer relationship management. They suggest using a scorecard, which is based on **performance drivers** or critical success factors, e.g. costs for acquisition and retention, conversion rates of visitors to buyers to repeat buyers, together with churn rates. There are three main parts to their scorecard:

Performance drivers
Critical success factors that determine whether business and marketing objectives are met.

1 *Attraction.* Size of visitor base, visitor acquisition cost and visitor advertising revenue (e.g. media sites).
2 *Conversion.* Customer base, customer acquisition costs, customer conversion rate, number of transactions per customer, revenue per transaction, revenue per customer, customer gross income, customer maintenance cost, customer operating income, customer churn rate, customer operating income before marketing spending.
3 *Retention.* This uses similar measures to those for conversion customers.

Agrawal *et al.* (2001) also used a net present value model to show the relative importance of these drivers:

1 Attraction
   - Visitor acquisition cost: 0.74% change in NPV.
   - Visitor growth: 3.09% change in NPV.
2 Conversion
   - Customer conversion rate: 0.84% change in NPV.
   - Revenue per customer: 2.32% change in NPV.
3 Retention
   - Cost of repeat customer: 0.69% change in NPV.
   - Revenue per repeat customer: 5.78% change in NPV.
   - Repeat customer churn rate: 6.65% change in NPV.
   - Repeat customer conversion rate: 9.49% change in NPV.

This research remains important as it highlights on-site marketing communications and the quality of service delivery in converting browsers to buyers and buyers into repeat buyers. It is apparent that marketing spend is large relative to turnover initially, to achieve customer growth, but is then carefully controlled to achieve profitability.

We will return to this topic in Chapter 8, where we will review the balance between **campaign-based e-communications** which are often tied into a particular event such as the launch or re-launch of a website or a product, e.g. an interactive (banner) advert campaign may last for a period of two months following a site re-launch or for a five-month period around a new product launch.

Campaign-based e-communications
Digital communications that are executed to support a specific marketing campaign such as a product launch, price promotion or a website launch.

In addition to campaign-based e-communications, we also need **continuous e-communications.** Organisations need to ensure that there is sufficient investment in continuous online marketing activities such as search marketing, affiliate marketing and sponsorship.

Continuous e-communications
Long-term use of e-marketing communications for customer acquisition (such as, search engine and affiliate marketing) and retention (e.g. e-newsletter marketing).

Companies wishing to advertise using digital channels are also making changes they are having to invest in new staff with the required skills to understand the new media and many established brand images need to be changed to be succeed online.

Decision 9: Organisational capabilities (7 S framework) and governance

A useful framework for reviewing an organisation's capabilities to implement digital marketing strategy is shown in Table 1.3 (page 24) applied to digital marketing. Which are the main challenges in implementing strategy? Econsultancy (2008) surveyed UK e-commerce managers to assess their views on the main challenges of managing e-commerce within an organisation. In the context of the 7 Ss, we can summarise the main challenges as follows:

- *Strategy* – limited capabilities to integrate into Internet strategy within core marketing and business strategy as discussed earlier in this chapter is indicated by frustration on gaining appropriate budgets.
- *Structure* – structural and process issues are indicated by the challenges of gaining resource and buy-in from traditional marketing and IT functions.
- *Skills and staff* – these issues were indicated by difficulties in finding specialist staff or agencies.

To help manage the internal capabilities for improving the results from digital channels, Econsultancy (2008) has developed a useful checklist for auditing current internal capabilities, resources and processes and then putting in place a programme to improve results. Econsultancy (2008) recommends these steps in a digital channel performance audit and improvement plan:

- *Step 1 – Senior management commitment.* Assess and encourage senior management commitment. What is the level of understanding of digital channels and physical commitment and sponsorship among the senior management team? Develop a plan to educate and influence the senior management team.
- *Step 2 – Digital channel contribution.* What are the digital channels delivering across different markets and product categories now to support business goals in terms of sales, cost of acquisition, profitability and customer loyalty?
- *Step 3 – Brand alignment.* Reviewing how digital channels and website functionality can support traditional brand values but also enhance the brand through development of online value propositions (OVP).
- *Step 4 – Marketplace analysis.* Customer insight is key, i.e. qualitative and quantitative research of customer characteristics, behaviours and opinions. Also includes benchmarking of competitors' proposition, marketing communications and capabilities. Develop detailed understanding of online intermediaries, e.g. key portals, search engines and social networks which influence audience.
- *Step 5 – Technology infrastructure.* Review capability of technology infrastructure to support online marketing innovation. Is an acceptable 'time to market' for new functionality available dependent on legacy system integration, business case authorisation and prioritisation, dedicated development resource and agile technical development processes?
- *Step 6 – Vision and goals.* Develop a long-term vision for how digital channels will contribute to the development business. Set short-term goals for digital channels in areas of customer acquisition, conversion and customer experience, retention and growth.
- *Step 7 – Strategy and planning.* Ensure digital marketing is integrated into different planning cycles (i.e. long-term three to five-year plans, annual plans and quarterly/monthly operational planning reviews). Establish method and budget sources for identifying, reviewing business case and prioritisation for new site and campaign functionality.
- *Step 8 – Review capability of marketing resources to deliver efficient, integrated cross-channel communications.* Including organisation structure, staff roles and responsibilities, skills levels of staff, agency capability, marketing campaign management and review process.
- *Step 9 – Refine management information and reporting.* Ensure web analytics and other business reporting tools maximise understanding of the influence of different digital media channels on delivering leads or sales. Implement a culture and process for integrating review and action based on defined key performance indicators and structured tests.

- *Step 10 – Identify and implement 'quick wins'*. Based on strategic analysis performed, identify short-term projects to deliver business results across areas of customer acquisition (e.g. improvements to digital media channels such as search engine marketing, aggregators or affiliate marketing); conversion (improvements to landing page messaging and usability through small findability improvements to navigation or search labelling possibly based on AB or multivariate testing or customer journey improvements on home page, category, product or other landing pages and basket, registration or checkout process) or retention and growth (encouraging repeat site visits or purchases through e-mail marketing or on site merchandising).

Change management
Controls to minimise the risks of project-based and organisational change.

Organisational structure decisions form two main questions. The first is 'How should internal structures be changed to deliver e-marketing?'; and the second 'How should the structure of links with partner organisations be changed to achieve e-marketing objectives?' Once structural decisions have been made attention should be focused on effective **change management**. Many e-commerce initiatives fail, not in their conceptualisation, but in their implementation. Chaffey (2008) describes approaches to change management and risk management in Chapter 10.

Internal structures

There are several alternative options for restructuring within a business such as the creation of an in-house digital marketing or e-commerce group. This issue has been considered by Parsons *et al.* (1996) from a sell-side e-commerce perspective. They recognise four stages in the growth of what they refer to as 'the digital marketing organisation' which are still useful for benchmarking digital marketing capabilities. A more sophisticated e-commerce capability assessment was presented earlier in this chapter in the section on situation review (Table 4.3). The stages are:

1. *Ad-hoc activity.* At this stage there is no formal organisation related to e-commerce and the skills are dispersed around the organisation. It is likely that there is poor integration between online and offline marketing communications. The website may not reflect the offline brand, and the website services may not be featured in the offline marketing communications. A further problem with ad-hoc activity is that the maintenance of the website will be informal and errors may occur as information becomes out-of-date.
2. *Focusing the effort.* At this stage, efforts are made to introduce a controlling mechanism for Internet marketing. Parsons *et al.* (1996) suggest that this is often achieved through a senior executive setting up a steering group which may include interested parties from marketing and IT and legal experts. At this stage the efforts to control the site will be experimental, with different approaches being tried to build, promote and manage the site.
3. *Formalisation.* At this stage the authors suggest that Internet marketing will have reached a critical mass and there will be a defined group or separate business unit within the company that will manage all digital marketing.
4. *Institutionalising capability.* This stage also involves a formal grouping within the organisation, but is distinguished from the previous stage in that there are formal links created between digital marketing and the company's core activities.

Although this is presented as a stage model with evolution implying that all companies will move from one stage to the next, many companies will find that true formalisation with the creation of a separate e-commerce or e-business department is unnecessary. For small and medium companies with a marketing department numbering a few people and an IT department perhaps consisting of two people, it will not be practical to have a separate group. Even large companies may find it is sufficient to have a single person or small team responsible for e-commerce with their role being to co-ordinate the different activities within the company using a matrix management approach.

Activity 4.5 reviews different types of organisational structures for e-commerce. Table 4.8 reviews some of the advantages and disadvantages of each.

Table 4.8 Advantages and disadvantages of the organisational structures shown in Figure 4.25

Organisational structure	Circumstances	Advantages	Disadvantages
(a) No formal structure for e-commerce	Initial response to e-commerce or poor leadership with no identification of need for change	Can achieve rapid response to e-commerce	Poor-quality site in terms of content quality and customer service responses (e-mail, phone). Priorities not decided logically. Insufficient resources
(b) A separate committee or department manages and co-ordinates e-commerce	Identification of problem and response in (a)	Co-ordination and budgeting and resource allocation possible	May be difficult to get different departments to deliver their input because of other commitments
(c) A separate business unit with independent budgets	Internet contribution (Chapter 6) is sizeable (>20%)	As for (b), but can set own targets and not be constrained by resources. Lower-risk option than (d)	Has to respond to corporate strategy. Conflict of interests between department and traditional business
(d) A separate operating company	Major revenue potential or flotation. Need to differentiate from parent	As for (c), but can set strategy independently. Can maximise market potential	High risk if market potential is overestimated due to start-up costs

Where the main e-commerce function is internal, the Econsultancy (2008) research suggested that it was typically located in one of four areas (see Figure 4.25) in approximate decreasing order of frequency:

a Main e-commerce function in separate team.
b Main e-commerce function part of operations or direct channel.
c Main e-commerce function part of marketing, corporate communications or other central marketing function.
d Main e-commerce function part of information technology.

There is also often one or several secondary areas of e-commerce competence and resource, e.g. IT may have a role in applications development and site build and each business, brand or country may have one or more e-commerce specialists responsible for managing e-commerce in their unit. Which was appropriate depended strongly on the market(s) the company operated in and their existing channel structures.

For the specialist skills needed to plan and manage digital marketing, it may be more efficient to outsource some skills. These are some of the main options for external suppliers for these Internet marketing skills:

1 Full-service digital agency.
2 Specialist digital agency.
3 Traditional agency.
4 In-house resource.

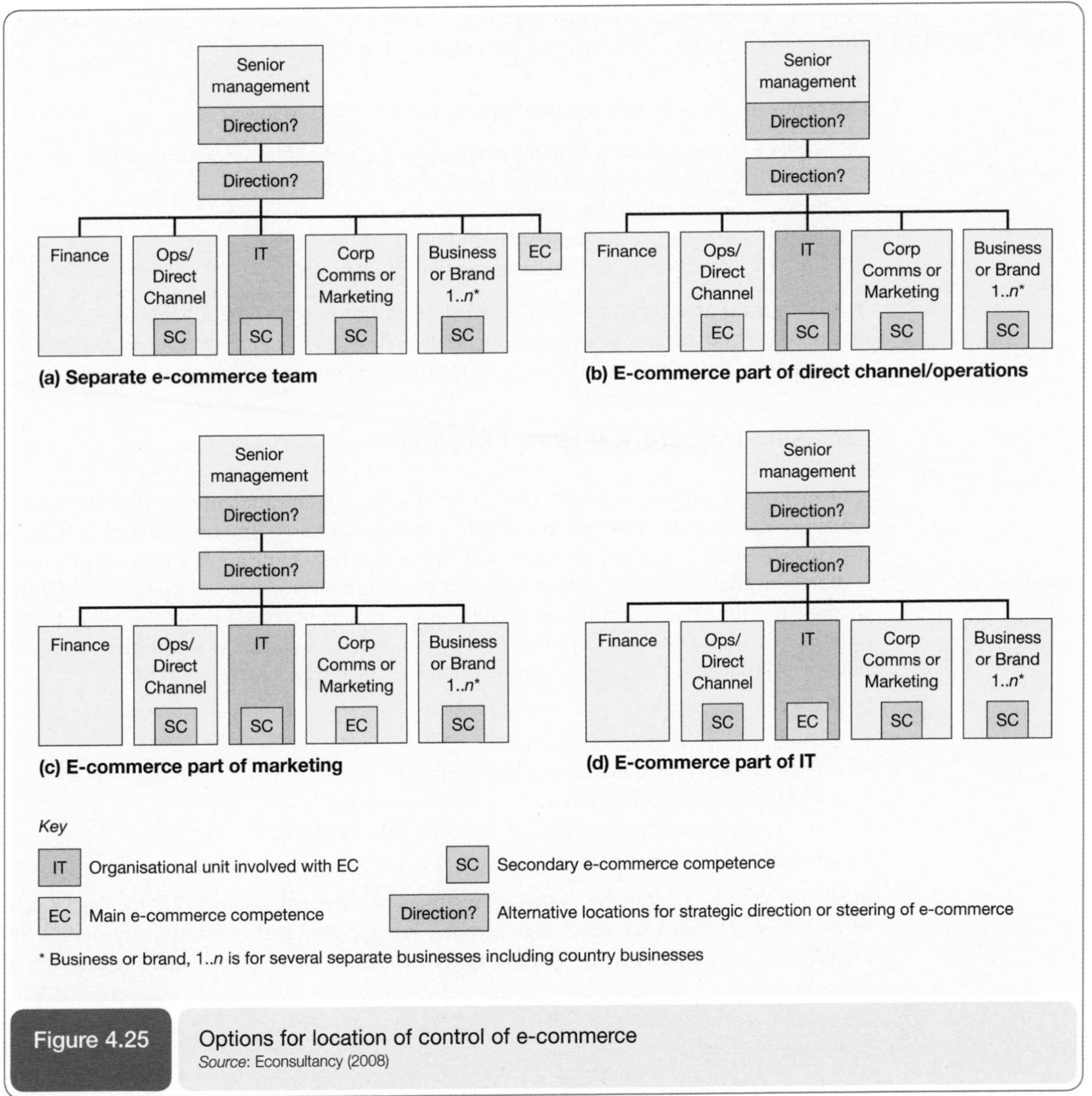

Figure 4.25 Options for location of control of e-commerce
Source: Econsultancy (2008)

When deciding on supplier or resource, suppliers need to consider the level and type of marketing activities they will be covering. The level typically ranges through:

1 Strategy.
2 Analysis and creative concepts.
3 Creative or content development.
4 Executing campaign, including reporting analysis and adjustment.
5 Infrastructure (e.g. web hosting, ad-serving, e-mail broadcasting, evaluation).

Options for outsourcing different e-marketing activities are reviewed in Activity 7.1 (page 374).

Strategy implementation

This forms the topic for subsequent chapters in this book as follows:

- Chapter 5 – options for varying the marketing mix in the Internet environment.
- Chapter 6 – implementing customer relationship management.
- Chapter 7 – delivering online services via a website.
- Chapter 8 – interactive marketing communications.
- Chapter 9 – monitoring and maintaining the online presence.

In each of these areas, such as CRM or development of website functionality, it is common that different initiatives will compete for budget. The next section reviews techniques for prioritising these projects and deciding on the best portfolio of e-commerce applications.

Assessing different Internet projects

A further organisational capability issue is the decision about different information systems marketing applications. Typically, there will be a range of different Internet marketing alternatives to be evaluated. Limited resources will dictate that only some applications are practical.

Portfolio analysis
Identification, evaluation and selection of desirable marketing applications.

Portfolio analysis can be used to select the most suitable projects, e.g. Daniel *et al.* (2001) suggest that potential e-commerce opportunities should be assessed for the value of the opportunity to the company against its ability to deliver. Typical opportunities for digital marketing strategy for an organisation which has a brochureware site might be:

- online catalogue facility
- e-CRM system – lead generation system
- e-CRM system – customer service management
- e-CRM system – personalisation of content for users
- partner relationship management extranet for distributors or agents
- transactional e-commerce facility.

Such alternatives can then be evaluated in terms of their risk against reward. Figure 4.26 shows a possible evaluation of strategic options. It is apparent that with limited resources, the e-CRM lead generation, partner extranet and customer services options offer the best mix of risk and reward.

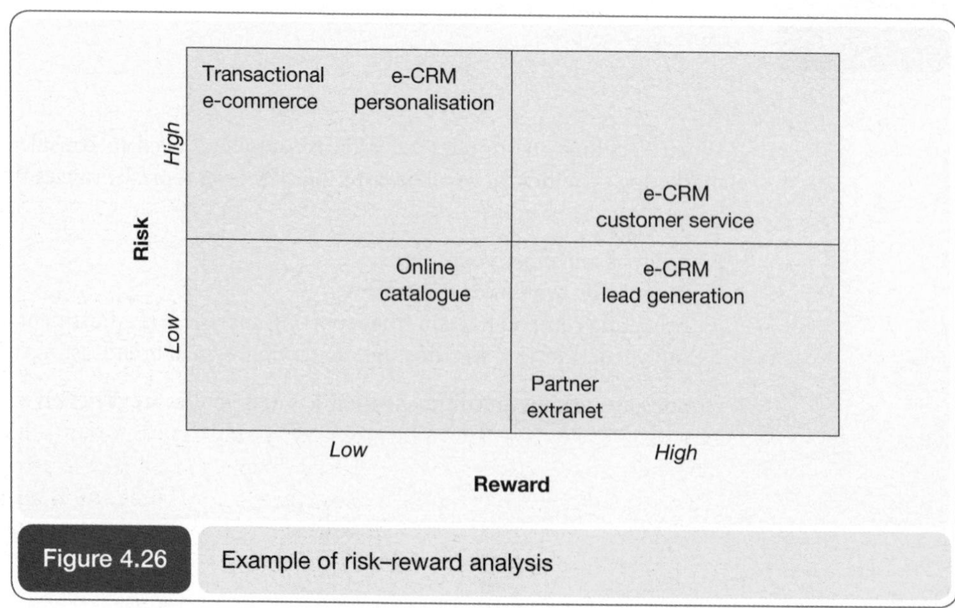

Figure 4.26 Example of risk–reward analysis

For information systems investments, the model of McFarlan (1984) has been used extensively to assess the future strategic importance applications in a portfolio. This model has been applied to the e-commerce applications by Daniel *et al.* (2008) and Chaffey (2011). Potential e-commerce applications can be assessed as:

- *Key operational* – essential to remain competitive. Example: partner relationship management extranet for distributors or agents.
- *Support* – deliver improved performance, but not critical to strategy. Example: e-CRM system – personalisation of content for users.
- *High-potential* – may be important for achieving future success. Example: e-CRM system – customer service management.
- *Strategic* – critical to future business strategy. Example: e-CRM system – lead generation system is vital to developing new business.

Portfolio analysis
Evaluation of value of current e-commerce services or applications.

A further **portfolio analysis** suggested by McDonald and Wilson (2002) is a matrix of attractiveness to customer against attractiveness to company, which will give a similar result to the risk–reward matrix. Finally, Tjan (2001) has suggested a matrix approach of viability (return on investment) against fit (with the organisation's capabilities) for Internet applications. He presents five metrics for assessing viability and fit. Viability is ideally based on a quantitative business case assessment of the value of a new application that will be generated through increasing conversion and retention rates. Fit is a more subjective measure based on the ease of implementation given the fit of an application with an organisation's existing processes, capabilities and culture. Additional criteria are developed for viability and fit. For 'viability', the criteria used to assess the potential value of an investment are rated between 100 (positive) and 0 (unfavourable) in each of these areas:

- market value potential
- time to positive cash flow
- personnel requirement
- funding requirement.

For 'fit', the criteria are rated as low to medium to high to assess the value of a potential investment:

- alignment with core capabilities
- alignment with other company initiatives
- fit with organisational structure
- fit with company's culture and value
- ease of technical implementation.

The online lifecycle management grid

Earlier in the chapter, in the section on objective setting, we reviewed different frameworks for identifying objectives and metrics to assess whether they are achieved. We consider the online lifecycle management grid at this point since Table 4.9 acts as a good summary that integrates objectives, strategies and tactics.

The columns isolate the key performance areas of site visitor acquisition, conversion to opportunity, conversion to sale and retention. The rows isolate more detailed metrics such as the tracking metrics and performance drivers from higher-level metrics such as the customer-centric key performance indicators (KPIs) and business-value KPIs. In the bottom two rows we have also added in typical strategies and tactics used to achieve objectives which show the relationship between objectives and strategy. Note, though, that this framework mainly creates a focus on efficiency of conversion, although there are some effectiveness measures also.

These are some of the generic Internet marketing main strategies to achieve the objectives in the grid which apply to a range of organisations:

Table 4.9 Online performance management grid for an e-retailer

Metric and growth	Visitor acquisition	Conversion to opportunity	Conversion to sale	Customer retention
Tracking metrics	• Unique visitors • New visitors • Conversation volume	• Opportunity volume	• Sales volume	• E-mail list quality • E-mail response quality transactions
Performance drivers (diagnostics)	• Bounce rate • Conversion rate: new visit to start quote • Brand/direct visits	• Macro-conversion rate to opportunity and micro-conversion efficiency	• Conversion rate to sale • E-mail conversion rate	• Active customers % (site and e-mail active) • Repeat conversion rate for different purchases
Customer-centric KPIs	• Cost per click and per sale • Brand awareness • Conversation polarity	• Cost per opportunity • Customer satisfaction	• Cost per sale • Customer satisfaction • Average order value (AOV)	• Lifetime value • Customer loyalty index and advocacy • Products per customer
Business value KPIs	• Audience share • Share of voice	• Online product requests (n, £, % of total)	• Online originated sales (n, £, % of total)	• Retained sales growth and volume
Strategy	• Online targeted reach strategy • Offline targeted reach strategy	• Lead generation strategy)	• Online sales generation • Offline sales impact strategy	• Retention and customer growth strategy
Tactics	• Continuous communications mix • Campaign communications mix • Online value Proposition	• Usability • Personalisation • Inbound contact strategy (customer service)	• Usability • Personalisation • Inbound contact strategy (customer service) • Merchandising • Triggered e-mails	• Database/list quality • Targeting • Outbound contact strategy (e-mail) • Personalisation

Source: Adapted from Neil Mason's Applied Insights (www.applied-insights.co.uk) Acquisition, Conversion, Retention approach

- *Online value proposition strategy* – defining the value proposition for acquisition and retention to engage with customers online. Includes informational and promotional incentives used to encourage trial. Also defines programme of value creation through time, e.g. business white papers published on partner sites.
- *Online targeted reach strategy* – the aim is to communicate with relevant audiences online to achieve communications objectives. The communications commonly include campaign communications such as online advertising, PR, e-mail, viral campaigns and continuous communications such as search engine marketing or sponsorship or partnership arrangements. The strategy may involve (1) driving new, potential customers to the company site, (2) migrating existing customers to online channels or (3) achieving reach to enhance brand awareness, favourability and purchase intent through ads and sponsorships on third-party sites. Building brand awareness, favourability and purchase intent on third-party sites may be a more effective strategy for low-involvement FMCG brands where it will be difficult to encourage visitors to the site.
- *Offline targeted reach strategy* – the objective is to encourage potential customers to use online channels, i.e. visit website and transact where relevant. The strategy is to communicate with selected customer segments offline through direct mail, media buys, PR and sponsorship.

- *Online sales efficiency strategy* – the objective is to convert site visitors to engage and become leads (e.g. through registering for an e-newsletter or placing the first item in the shopping basket) to convert them to buy products and maximise the purchase transaction value.
- *Offline sales impact strategy* – the aim is to achieve sales offline from new or existing customers. Strategy defines how online communications through the website and e-mail can influence sales offline, i.e. by phone, mail-order or in-store.

Case Study 4 Tesco online development strategy supports global expansion

Context

Tesco is a leading global online retail operation and is Britain's leading food retail group. Tesco has a substantial European and international network of retailer operations and has recently begun selling non-food goods, e.g. clothing in over 20 countries. In 2010, Tesco's online operations enjoyed significant growth in online sales; its non-food operation Tesco Direct saw sales rise by 30 per cent. International sales are a fundamental part of Tesco's growth strategy and in Korea, for example, sales grew by 15 per cent. Going forward Tesco states its vision for online retailing in 2011 and beyond takes account of customer needs (Tesco, 2011):

> *Customers expect to be able to shop where and when they want – as shopping habits have changed over the years we've changed too. As we've grown from a UK supermarket chain towards becoming an international multi-channel retailer we've continued to innovate every step of the way.*
>
> *We were viewed as pioneers when we first launched an online grocery business 11 years ago. It's now the largest, most profitable business of its kind in the world.*
>
> *Using their smartphones, our customers can now scan the barcode of grocery items, order online and have their shopping delivered to their home.*

Currently, Tesco Plc is one of the world's top three retailer's competing with WalMart and Carrefour for the leading position. Tesco operates in over 14 countries globally in Europe, Asia and has recently begun to establish a presence in North America. Founded in 1919 by Jack Cohen, the company grew rapidly and has a history of delivering innovations to the UK retail sector so it is no surprise that once it became feasible to offer online shopping that Tesco was quick to determine how it might trade online. By the early 1990s, Tesco was one of the few UK retailers that had invested in a specialist e-commerce department to spearhead its online developments. In 1994 Tesco started offering online shopping to its customers but strategically the organisation had big plans for online shopping.

Tesco's chief executive, Terry Leahy, was quoted in The *Sunday Times* as saying: 'We will be the world's biggest online grocery retailer and we intend to become the UK's No.1 e-commerce business'. A goal quickly achieved, by December 2000, Tesco offered a wide range of products to 90 per cent of the UK population. The online shopping service, Tesco.com was established soon afterwards and operated as an independent subsidiary to Tesco. Tesco then started to diversify its online product range, offering many non-food products ranges and the result was a significant increase in sales. To support logistical operations, Tesco developed a sophisticated semi-automated in-store picking service, supported by local refrigerated delivery vans using existing facilities rather than building high-tech dedicated warehouses and, according to Ellis-Chadwick *et al.* (2007), this created a strategic advantage that enabled faster geographical expansion of the online shopping services and a distinct advantage of extended national coverage of Tesco's online shopping service provision. By 2003, 96 per cent of the UK population could shop online with Tesco.com, giving the company 65 per cent of the UK online grocery shopping market and further diversification of product ranges, e.g. financial services and telecoms. It started to expand and offered its online services internationally, for example, in South Korea through Homeplus.co.kr.

Tesco constantly focuses on technology innovation in order to streamline services, provide new features and extend the range of points at which customers can access (Ellis-Chadwick *et al.*, 2007). Diversification and expansion of the online product portfolio and customer services continues with the addition of a series of innovations such as: DVDs to your door (a rental service), energy utilities (thousands of customers save money on their gas and electricity bills), getting healthy online by using the e-diets service (which, helps customers tailor their eating plans to what's right for them, taking into account lifestyles, food preferences and health recommendations), and Internet telephony.

Tesco's new chief executive, Philip Clarke, has a vision to lead the world's largest retailer, saying that Tesco must be a highly successful multichannel retailer if it is to remain successful globally. In his vision of the future, he sees the Internet be even more of a mainstream retail cahnnel and envisages that more use will be made of mobile and wireless channels. He goes further to say that retail sales are migrating to the Internet and that Tesco and other companies in the retail sector must embrace this change and devise multichannel strategies if they wish to remain in business (Wood, 2011).

The online grocery market and competitors

Tesco currently leads the UK's other leading grocery retailers in terms of off and online market share, but according to Wood (2011), Clarke (CEO of Tesco):

> *has promised to nurture its domestic business, which despite ringing up almost one pound in every seven spent on the UK high street has lagged behind rivals such as Sainsbury's and Morrisons in sales growth. Despite its recent underperformance, Tesco remains the dominant force in UK retail, with a market share of more than 30 per cent. It is estimated that 13 per cent of all the MasterCard and Visa credit card transactions in the UK are made on a Tesco credit card.*

The implications are that as more retailers migrate online, the competition is likely to intensify. According to IGD (2011), around 25 per cent of grocery manufacturers are considering creating their own online stores and these manufacturers are anticipating about 10 per cent of turnover to come from direct consumer sales. Despite the growing competition the online grocery market is relatively small as it is only predicted to account for 5.4 per cent of online sales by 2015 even though this represents £9.9 billion.

Tesco has been at the the forefront of the development of online shopping and while it has been making a significant contribution to the growth in online retail, it has also enabled more retailers and consumers to feel that they can shop and trade online. Tesco is likely to face challenges from different sources of competition as the online shopping market grows and matures.

Staying ahead: How does Tesco promote its online offer?

As with other online retailers, Tesco.online operations rely to a certain extent on instore advertising and marketing to the supermarket's Clubcard loyalty scheme's customer base. The linkages between Clubcard mailings (off and online) act as a trigger for shoppers to engage with both channels. E-mail marketing is an important part of Tesco's promotions and according to Doherty and Ellis-Chadwick (2010) using e-mail marketing is a complex activity, which is largely focused on 'grabbing customer attention' but it can be used to achieve a number of communication and sales objectives. Humby and Hunt (2003), describe how Tesco.com uses 'commitment-based segmentation' or 'loyalty ladder' based on recency of purchase, frequency of purchase and value to drive Tesco's communication campaigns. They identified six lifecycle categories which are then further divided to target communications:

- 'Logged-on'
- 'Cautionary'
- 'Developing'
- 'Established'
- 'Dedicated'
- 'Logged-off' (the aim here is to win back).

Tesco then uses automated event-triggered messaging which can be created to encourage continued purchase, e.g. Tesco.com has a touch strategy which includes a sequence of follow-up communications triggered after different events in the customer lifecycle. In the example given below, communications after event 1 are intended to achieve the objective of converting a website visitor to action; communications after event 2 are intended to move the customer from a first-time purchaser to a regular purchaser, and for event 3 to reactivate lapsed purchasers.

Trigger event 1: Customer first registers on site (but does not buy)

Auto-response (AR) 1: Two days after registration e-mail sent offering assistance and discounts to encourage the first purchase..

Trigger event 2: Customer first purchases online

AR1: Immediate order confirmation.

AR2: Five days after purchase e-mail sent with link to online customer satisfaction survey asking about quality of service from driver and picker (e.g. item quality and substitutions).

AR3: Two weeks after first purchase – direct mail offering tips on how to use service and £5 discount on next purchases, intended to encourage re-use of online services.

AR4: Generic monthly e-newsletter with online exclusive offers encouraging cross-selling.

AR5: Bi-weekly alert with personalised offers for customer.

AR6: After two months – financial discount to encourage the next shop.

AR7: Quarterly mailing of coupons encouraging repeat sales and cross-sales.

Trigger event 3: Customer does not purchase for an extended period

AR1: Dormancy detected – reactivation e-mail with survey of how the customer is finding the service (to identify any problems) and a £5 incentive.

AR2: A further discount incentive is used in order to encourage continued usage to shop after the first shop after a break.

By using this stages approach to keeping track of its customers online Tesco has established a robust strategy for attracting attention and retaining customers using e-mail marketing. According to Doherty and Ellis-Chadwick (2010) this form of digital communication is increasingly important as a mechanism for developing and maintaining mutually beneficial relationships with customers. Furthermore, advertising research discovered a large proportion of the message recipient's attention is determined by the structural, executional elements of a message rather than its content, e.g. length, size, layout (Rossiter and Bellman, 2005) which has implications for developing effective email marketing messages.

Summary and conclusions

Tesco has played a major role in building the online shopping market for groceries in the UK. The company made a very important strategy decision to select the goods needed to fulfil the customer instore. This strategy enabled Tesco to expand rapidly and it soon had an online operation which stretched the length and breadth of the UK and beyond. However, Tesco is likely to face increasing competition not only from retailers but also from food manufacturers in lucrative online markets. Tesco's CEO suggests that the way forward is to strengthen links between online and offline operations, something which has been increasingly done – from a promotional perspective – through the online communications, especially e-mail marketing. Given that Tesco is a highly innovative company we are likely to see many new features, and techniques that will aim to ensure that Tesco remains ahead of the game.

Question

Based on the case study and your own research, discuss where you think Tesco should focus to ensure it can continue to achieve success online and protect market share.

Summary

1. The development of the online presence follows stage models from basic static 'brochure-ware' sites through simple interactive sites with query facilities to dynamic sites offering personalisation of services for customers.
2. The digital marketing strategy should follow a similar form to a traditional strategic marketing planning process and should include:
   - goal setting
   - situation review
   - strategy formulation
   - resource allocation and monitoring.

   A feedback loop should be established to ensure the site is monitored and modifications are fed back into the strategy development.
3. Strategic goal setting should involve:
   - setting business objectives that the Internet can help achieve
   - assessing and stating the contribution that the Internet will make to the business in the future, both as a proportion of revenue and in terms of whether the Internet will complement or replace other media
   - stating the full range of business benefits that are sought, such as improved corporate image, cost reduction, more leads and sales, and improved customer service.
4. The situation review will include assessing internal resources and assets, including the services available through the existing website.
5. Strategy formulation involves defining a company's commitment to the Internet; setting an appropriate value proposition for customers of the website; and identifying the role of the Internet in exploiting new markets, marketplaces and distribution channels and in delivering new products and services. In summary:
   - Decision 1: Market and product development strategies
   - Decision 2: Business and revenue models strategies

- Decision 3: Target market strategy
- Decision 4: Positioning and differentiation strategy (including the marketing mix)
- Decision 5: Customer engagement and social media strategy
- Decision 6: Multichannel distribution strategy
- Decision 7: Multichannel communications strategy
- Decision 8: Online communications mix and budget
- Decision 9: Organisational capabilities (7 S framework)

Exercises

Self-assessment exercises

1. What is meant by the 'Internet contribution', and what is its relevance to strategy?
2. What is the role of monitoring in the strategic planning process?
3. Summarise the main tangible and intangible business benefits of the Internet to a company.
4. What is the purpose of a digital marketing audit? What should it involve?
5. What does a company need in order to be able to state clearly in the mission statement its strategic position relative to the Internet?
6. What are the market and product positioning opportunities offered by the Internet?
7. What are the distribution channel options for a manufacturing company?

Essay and discussion questions

1. Discuss the frequency with which an digital marketing strategy should be updated for a company to remain competitive.
2. 'Setting long-term strategic objectives for a website is unrealistic since the rate of change in the marketplace is so rapid.' Discuss.
3. Explain the essential elements of an digital marketing strategy.
4. Summarise the role of strategy tools and models in formulating a company's strategic approach to the Internet.

Examination questions

1. How might a retail business use the Internet to develop an effective digital marketing strategy?
2. Discuss the extent to which Porter's five forces model can help to identify sources of competition online.
3. Which factors will affect whether the Internet has primarily a complementary effect or a replacement effect on a company?
4. Describe different stages in the sophistication of development of a website, giving examples of the services provided at each stage.
5. Briefly explain the purpose and activities involved in an external audit conducted as part of the development of an digital marketing strategy.
6. Which factors would a financial services sector company consider when assessing the suitability of its product for Internet sales?
7. Explain what is meant by the online value proposition, and give two examples of the value proposition for websites with which you are familiar.

References

Aaker, D. and Joachimsthaler, E. (2000) *Brand Leadership*. Free Press, New York.

Agrawal, V., Arjona, V. and Lemmens, R. (2001) E-performance: the path to rational exuberance, *McKinsey Quarterly*, No. 1, 31–43.

Bazett, M., Bowden, I., Love, J., Street, R. and Wilson, H. (2005) Measuring multichannel effectiveness using the balanced scorecard. *Interactive Marketing*, 6(3) (January–March), 224–31.

Chaffey, D. (2011) *E-Business and E-Commerce Management*, 5th edn. Financial Times/Prentice Hall, Harlow.

Chaffey, D. and Smith, P.R. (2008) *EMarketing Excellence: Planning and Optimizing Your Digital Marketing*, 3rd edn. Butterworth-Heinemann, Oxford.

Chaston, I. (2000) *E-Marketing Strategy*. McGraw-Hill, Maidenhead.

Daniel, E., Wilson, H., McDonald, M. and Ward, J. (2001) *Marketing Strategy in the Digital Age*. Financial Times/Prentice Hall, Harlow.

Daniel, E., Wilson, H., Ward, J. and McDonald, M. (2008) Innovation @nd integration: developing an integrated e-enabled business strategy. Preliminary findings from an industry-sponsored research project for the Information Systems Research Centre and the Centre for E-marketing. Cranfield University School of Management, January.

Deise, M., Nowikow, C., King, P. and Wright, A. (2000) *Executive's Guide to E-Business. From Tactics to Strategy*. Wiley, New York.

Der Zee, J. and De Jong, B. (1999) Alignment is not enough: integrating business and information technology management with the balanced business scorecard, *Journal of Management Information Systems*, 16(2), 137–57.

Dholakia, U., Kahn, B., Reeves, R., Rindfleisch, A., Stewart, D. and Taylor, E. (2010) Consumer behaviour in a multichannel, multimedia retailing environment, *Journal of Interactive Marketing* 24, 86–95.

Doherty, N.F. and Ellis-Chadwick, F. (2010) Internet retailing: the past, the present and the future, *International Journal of Retail & Distribution Management*, 38(11/12), 943–65.

Durlacher (2000) Trends in the UK new economy, *Durlacher Quarterly Internet Report*, November, 1–12.

Econsultancy (2008) Managing Digital Channels Research Report. Author: Dave Chaffey. Available from **www.e-consultancy.com**.

Ellis-Chadwick, F., Doherty, N. F. and Anastasakis, L. (2007) E-strategy in the UK retail grocery sector: a resource-based analysis, *Managing Service Quality*, 17(6), 702–27.

Fernie, J., Sparks, L. and Mckinnon, A.C. (2010) Retail logistics in the UK: past, present and future, *International Journal of Retail and Distribution Management*, 38(11/12), 894–914.

Gunawan, G., Ellis-Chadwick, F. and King, M. (2008) An empirical study of the uptake of performance measurement by Internet retailers, *Internet Research*, 18(4), 361–81.

Hasan, H. and Tibbits, H. (2000) Strategic management of electronic commerce: an adaptation of the balanced scorecard, *Internet Research*, 10(5), 439–50.

Humby, C. and Hunt, T. (2003) *Scoring points. How Tesco Is Winning Customer Loyalty*. Kogan Page, London.

Jobber, D. (2010) *Principles and Practice of Marketing*, 6th edn. McGraw-Hill.

Kalakota, R. and Robinson, M. (2000) *E-Business: Roadmap for Success*. Addison-Wesley, Reading, MA.

Kaplan, R.S. and Norton, D.P. (1993) Putting the balanced scorecard to work, *Harvard Business Review*, September–October, 134–42.

Kim, E., Nam, D. and Stimpert, D. (2004) The applicability of Porter's generic strategies in the digital age: assumptions, conjectures and suggestions, *Journal of Management*, 30(5).

Kumar, N. (1999) Internet distribution strategies: dilemmas for the incumbent, *Financial Times*, Special Issue on mastering information management, no 7. Electronic Commerce, (**www.ftmastering.com**).

Lynch, R. (2000) *Corporate Strategy*. Financial Times/Prentice Hall, Harlow.

McDonald, M. (2003) *Marketing Plans: How To Prepare Them, How To Use Them*, 5th edn. Butterworth-Heinemann, Oxford.

McDonald, M. and Wilson, H. (2002) *New Marketing: Transforming the Corporate Future*. Butterworth-Heinemann, Oxford.

McFarlan, F.W. (1984) Information technology changes the way you compete, *Harvard Business Review*, May–June, 54–61.

Mintzberg, H. and Quinn, J.B. (1991) *The Strategy Process*, 2nd edn. Prentice Hall, Upper Saddle River, NJ.

Neslin, S., Grewal, D., Leghorn, R., Venkatesh, S., Teerling, L. and Thomas, J. (2006) Challenges and opportunities in multichannel customer management *Journal of Science Research* 9(2), 95–112.

Parsons, A., Zeisser, M. and Waitman, R. (1996) Organizing for digital marketing, *McKinsey Quarterly*, No. 4, 183–92.

Porter, M. (1980) *Competitive Strategy*. Free Press, New York.

Porter, M. (2001) Strategy and the Internet, *Harvard Business Review*, March, 62–78.

Quelch, J. and Klein, L. (1996) The Internet and international marketing, *Sloan Management Review*, Spring, 61–75.

Revolution (2005a) E-mail marketing report, by Justin Pugsley. *Revolution*, September, 58–60.

Rossiter, J.R. and Bellman, S. (2005) *Marketing Communications: Theory and Practice*, Pearson Prentice-Hall, Sydney.

Sultan, F. and Rohm, A. (2004) The evolving role of the Internet in marketing strategy. *Journal of Interactive marketing*, 19(2), Spring.

Tesco (2011) published online at: **http://www.tescoplc.com/media/417/tesco_annual_report_2011_final.pdf**, accessed October 2011.

The Telegraph (2011) Online grocery sales will double within five years, **http://www.telegraph.co.uk/finance/newsbysector/retailandconsumer/8374998/Online-grocery-sales-will-double-within-five-years.html**, assessed 16 October.

Tjan, A. (2001) Finally, a way to put your Internet portfolio in order, *Harvard Business Review*, February, 78–85.

Varianini, V. and Vaturi, D. (2000) Marketing lessons from e-failures, *McKinsey Quarterly*, No. 4, 86–97.

Wood, Z. (2011) Tesco Boss: Internet sales and stores can work together, *Guardian*, 8 June, **http://www.guardian.co.uk/business/2011/jun/08/new-tesco-boss-says-internet-sales-and-stores-must-support-each-other.**

Weblinks

See Chapter 2 Web links which covers developments in business models, and Chapter 3 Web links for developments in technology.

- **SmartInsights.com** (**www.smartinsights.com**). Updates about all aspects of digital marketing including strategy edited by Dave Chaffey.
- **E-commerce Times** (**www.ecommercetimes.com**). An online newspaper specific to e-commerce developments.
- **Econsultancy.com** (**www.Econsultancy.com**). A good compilation of reports and white papers many of which are strategy-related.
- **Forrester Marketing Blog** (**http://blogs.forrester.com/marketing**). Forrester analysts write about developments in technology.
- **Knowledge@Wharton Wharton** (**http://knowledge.wharton.upenn.edu/www**). Knowledge@Wharton is an online resource that offers the latest business insights, information, and research from a variety of sources.
- ***Financial Times* Digital Business** (**http://news.ft.com/reports/digitalbusiness**). Monthly articles based on case studies.
- ***McKinsey Quarterly*** (**www.mckinseyquarter.com**). Articles regularly cover digital marketing strategy.

Chapter 5

The Internet and the marketing mix

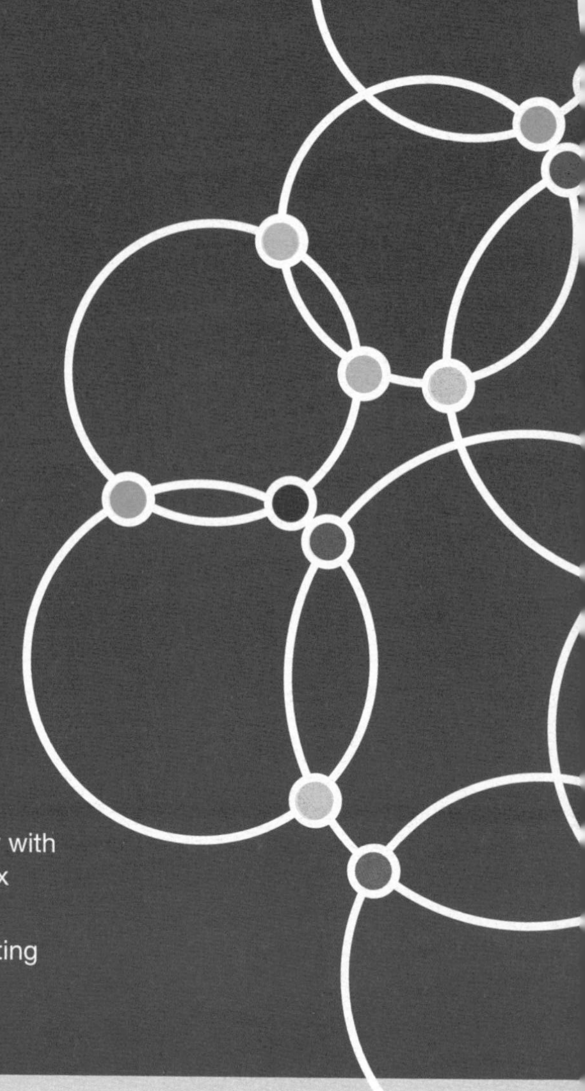

Chapter at a glance

Main topics

Case studies

Learning objectives

After reading this chapter, the reader should be able to:

- Apply the elements of the marketing mix in an online context
- Evaluate the opportunities that the Internet makes available for varying the marketing mix
- Assess the opportunities for online brand-building

Questions for marketers

Key questions for marketing managers related to this chapter are:

- How are the elements of the marketing mix varied online?
- What are the implications of the Internet for brand development?
- Can the product component of the mix be varied online?
- How are companies developing online pricing strategies?
- Does 'place' have relevance online?

Scan code to find the latest updates for topics in this chapter

Links to other chapters

This chapter is related to other chapters as follows:

- Chapter 2 introduces the impact of the Internet on market structure and distribution channels
- Chapter 4 describes how digital marketing strategies can be developed
- Chapters 6 and 7 explain the service elements of the mix in more detail
- Chapter 7 explains site design can be used to support and enhance brand values
- Chapters 8 and 9 explain the promotion elements of the mix in more detail

Introduction

Marketing mix
The series of seven key variables – Product, Price, Place, Promotion, People, Process and Physical evidence – that are varied by marketers as part of the customer offering.

Online branding
How online channels are used to support brands that, in essence, are the sum of the characteristics of a product or service as perceived by a user.

This chapter shows how the well-established strategic framework of the **marketing mix** can be applied by marketers to inform their digital marketing strategy. It explores this key issue of digital marketing strategy in more detail than was possible in Chapter 4. As well as the marketing mix, **online branding** is another major topic covered in Chapter 5. As part of our discussion of product we will review how the Internet can be used to support and impact the way brands are developed.

The marketing mix – widely referred to as the 4 Ps of Product, Price, Place and Promotion – was originally proposed by Jerome McCarthy (1960) and is still used as an essential part of formulating and implementing marketing strategy by many practitioners. The 4 Ps have since been extended to the 7 Ps, which include three further elements that better reflect service delivery: People, Process and Physical evidence (Booms and Bitner, 1981), although others argue that these are subsumed within the 4 Ps. Figure 5.1 summarises the different sub-elements of the 7 Ps.

The marketing mix is applied frequently in discussion of marketing strategy since it provides a simple strategic framework for varying different elements of an organisation's product offering to influence the demand for products within target markets. For example, if the aim is to increase sales of a product, options include decreasing the price and changing the amount or type of promotion, or some combination of these elements.

Digital media provides many new opportunities for the marketer to vary the marketing mix, as suggested by Figure 5.1 and Activity 5.1. Digital media also have far-reaching implications for the relative importance of different elements of the mix for many markets, regardless of whether an organisation is involved directly in transactional e-commerce. Consequently, the marketing mix is a useful framework to inform strategy development. First, it gives a framework for comparing an organisation's existing services with competitors' in and out of sector as part of the benchmarking process described in Chapter 1. As well as a tool for benchmarking, it can also be used as a mechanism for generating alternative strategic approaches.

Given the potential implications of the Internet on the marketing mix, a whole chapter is devoted to examining its impact and strategies that companies can develop to best manage this situation.

Using the Internet to vary the marketing mix

Product	Promotion	Price	Place	People	Process	Physical evidence
• Quality • Image • Branding • Features • Variants • Mix • Support • Customer service • Use occasion • Availability • Warranties	• Marketing communications • Personal promotion • Sales promotion • PR • Branding • Direct marketing	• Positioning • List • Discounts • Credit • Payment methods • Free or value-added elements	• Trade channels • Sales support • Channel number • Segmented channels	• Individuals on marketing activities • Individuals on customer contact • Recruitment • Culture/image • Training and skills • Remuneration	• Customer focus • Business-led • IT-supported • Design features • Research and development	• Sales/staff contact experience of brand • Product packaging • Online experience

Figure 5.1 The elements of the marketing mix

Activity 5.1 How can the Internet be used to vary the marketing mix?

Purpose

An introductory activity which highlights the vast number of areas which the Internet impacts.

Activity

Review Figure 5.1 and select the *two* most important ways in which the Internet gives new potential for varying the marketing mix for *each* of product, price, promotion, place, people and processes. State:

- new opportunities for varying the mix
- examples of companies that have achieved this
- possible negative implications (threats) for each opportunity.

Digital marketing affects all aspects of the traditional and service marketing mix. The elements in this chapter are:

- *Product* – looking at opportunities for modifying the core or extended product for digital environments.
- *Price* – focusing on the implications for setting prices in digital markets; new pricing models and strategies.
- *Place* – considering the implications for distribution for digital marketing.
- *Promotion* – exploring promotional techniques in advance of more detailed coverage of new techniques in Chapters 8 and 9.
- *People, process and physical evidence* – reviewing the principle ideas in advance of more detailed discussion in Chapters 6, 7 and 10, where the focus is on how these elements of the mix relate to customer-relationship management and managing an organisation's digital presence.

The marketing mix concept is widely used in marketing management. The 4 Ps (Product, Price, Place and Promotion) present a robust and easy to apply framework, which can aid marketing strategy development, but before reviewing the relevance of the Internet for each of the 7 Ps, it is worth briefly considering some criticisms of applying the marketing mix as a single tool for marketing strategy. First and perhaps most importantly, the marketing mix, because of its origins in the 1960s, is symptomatic of a push approach to marketing and does not explicitly acknowledge the needs of customers. As a consequence, the marketing mix tends to lead to a product orientation rather than focusing on the needs of the customer. To mitigate this effect, Lautenborn (1990) suggested the 4 Cs framework which considers the 4 Ps from a customer perspective. In brief, the 4 Cs are:

- Customer needs and wants (from the product)
- Cost to the customer (price)
- Convenience (relative to place)
- Communication (promotion).

Focusing on the customer is equally important both on and offline, although it is important to remember that the customer base and the individual needs of the customer can vary significantly from the physical to the virtual environment. It follows that the selection of the marketing mix should be based on detailed knowledge of buyer behaviour collected through market research. Furthermore, it should be remembered that the mix is often adjusted according to different target markets or segments to better meet the needs of these customer groupings.

As you read this chapter, you should consider which are the key elements of the mix that vary online for the different types of online presence introduced in Chapter 1, i.e. transactional e-commerce, relationship-building, brand-building, media owner portals and social networks. Allen and Fjermestad (2001) and Harridge-March (2004) have reviewed how the Internet has impacted the main elements of the marketing mix, particularly for digital products. There is no denying that all of the elements are still important, but Chaffey and Smith (2008) have said that, online, partnerships is the eighth P because this is so important in achieving reach and affiliation. In this text, though, partnerships will be considered as part of Place and Promotion. We begin our discussion of the mix by looking at the product element of the mix.

Digital marketing in practice — The Smart Insights interview

Roberto Hortal explains why the marketing mix remains relevant today

Overview and main concepts

Roberto Hortal has worked as an e-business director with many years of experience in different types of businesses operating in different countries. Examples of the UK and global enterprises he has worked for including EDF Energy, RSA insurance group, MORE TH>N, easyJet and Nokia. Here he shares his experience of how the marketing mix concept is still applicable when taking real-world decisions in companies to shape their online proposition and increase their commercial value.

The interview

Q. We often hear that the concept of the marketing mix isn't that useful any longer in this era of customer-first. What's your view on its relevance today? Are there any particular aspects of the mix which lend themselves to refining online?

Roberto Hortal: The marketing mix is a conceptual framework, and as such it is useful since it enables a common language to be used in the planning, execution and measurement of a number of coordinated activities that deliver the desired marketing outcomes. Customer-centricity demands that organisations becomes a lot better at collecting and reacting to customer insight and adapt their offering to best suit an ever growing number of narrowing customer segments – ever approaching the ideal of the completely personalised product. As complexity increases exponentially, it is crucial to be able to rely on tried and tested concepts like the marketing mix.

I use the basic components of the marketing mix (such as the 4 Ps) at work daily, and as such for me the marketing mix remains a practical tool. In a digital environment routinely identifying and profiling individual consumers over time and adapting to their needs and wants, the 4 Ps become elastic. Is my website a Place, or is it an integral part of the Product? When more efficient digital channels directly influence my ability to Price, do Place and Price become synonymous? This elasticity needs to be managed effectively to avoid the pitfalls of too rigidly applying the model. One must always challenge the validity of every tool in the Digital Marketing armoury; adding, changing and discarding as business and customers evolve. Proposed evolutions of the marketing mix concept (such as the 4 Cs) may ensure it remains relevant today. My personal view is we're still some distance from seeing the end of its useful life.

Q. Could you give some examples of where you applied new ways of applying the mix online.

Roberto Hortal: In my view, the key insight is that digital media can contribute to every element of the mix. Therefore we must avoid a narrow categorisation of digital as contributing solely (or even primarily) to a single component of the mix.

While I haven't come across an organisation that fundamentally disagrees with that view, some organisations find it easier than others to put it into practice. I have worked in organisations where the mix is embedded in the corporate structure with separate Pricing, Product, Distribution (Place) and Marketing (Promotion) departments. Embedding a digital mindset across those silos can be a daunting task.

I've experimented with channel pricing, as pricing is a critical driver of conversion and business value in a services organisation. Straight online discounts have proven difficult to justify. Online discounts aren't valued by customers (in the age of price comparison, they focus on the total price, rather than its components) and often do not reflect a real lower cost to the business (lower costs to sell and serve are offset by lower transaction value and lower retention rates). Using channel data as a pricing factor has proven a lot more successful: as historical data is accumulated, it is possible to really offer competitive prices to those customers identified as high value at the point of application. An accurate value/propensity model can use the wealth of information available from digital visitors (geography, visit trigger/campaign, past visits, customer history, etc.) to drive truly personalised pricing. In this example, price follows place and both price and promotion reflect the individual customer.

I've successfully extended the data-driven approach to other elements of the mix: dynamic packaging (the creation of a personalised offering from the basis of a modular product) has proven successful many times: at easyJet we built a product that included car hire recommendations based on a predictive model that took destination, seasonality and party size as inputs – increasing car hire uptake very significantly. More recently I've applied the same insight-driven dynamic packaging approach to RSA's Central and Eastern European businesses, increasing sales of optional covers and add-ons very significantly.

Further opportunities exist around selecting which default base products to present: are you more likely to want a cheap energy tariff that tracks price rises or a fixed price deal that ensures protection against future rises? What we know about you from your digital 'shadow' may provide the clues we need.

Q. Online channels bring great opportunities to test propositions online. Can you advise on approaches to testing propositions?

Roberto Hortal: I have used online channels to test propositions in a couple of ways. I assign propositions randomly to visitors on first arrival to test interest/sales. I would typically run this against a large control group (being offered the current main proposition) to both protect commercial results and detect the effect of any external influences that maybe otherwise wrongly influence the experiment. This approach can be extended beyond the site, via randomised allocation of marketing messages on Display, Search etc. to measure a proposition's attractiveness. It's important to test all aspects of the proposition: a proposition successful at attracting interest may convert badly if it can't be priced at a level that matches customer expectations. I also provide a modular proposition platform and allow customers to combine proposition elements.

We can easily analyse popular combinations as well as secondary correlations such as the propensity to add a certain ancillary product to a particular proposition configuration, and understand the compound impact on profitability, retention and advocacy from what we know about each of the modular components in isolation.

I've found that proposition testing rarely fits neatly an A/B scenario, with tests quickly developing into complex multivariate experiments with a significant number of variables. It is important to ensure the tests are solidly planned, rigorously executed and statistically significant. Free tools like Google Website Optimiser provide information to test and get the best out of website contact. However, such tools will not prevent badly designed experiments from yielding wrong data. In my experience, the only way to ensure valid tests and improved business results is to bring in the best analytical brain you can find. Analytics is the first role I fill when I build a digital team from scratch, it's that important.

Q. Many organisations are now developing social media strategies. How do you see the intersection between social media and the marketing mix since it clearly impacts on product decision making and service?

Roberto Hortal: If I only had the answer ... I take a radically different view of social media than many of my peers. While most people see social media as a branding and customer service channel, I see social media's largest potential in the areas of awareness, consideration and acquisition. This is not to say the best way to use social media sites is to advertise in them. Far from it. The social nature of the Internet demands that brands engage in conversation, and identify and incentivise brand ambassadors to help amplify our messages. There is general acceptance of this, but also a general shyness about steering conversations and seeking to extract immediate commercial value in the form of direct sales. Risk-aversion takes over and anecdotes used to prove the point that there is a risk that poor execution may lead to a social backlash.

The risk is clearly real but there is also an opportunity to execute well and generate significant amounts of business and positive buzz. I recently ran a campaign with Poland's largest social network (Nasza Klassa). A fairly simple personality quiz mechanism was executed beautifully by my Polish team, resulting in what our partners characterised as the country's most successful campaign in terms of reach and engagement, one that generated levels of sales comparable to those contributed by mainstream E-marketing channels.

Social media spaces require nurture and respect, but we must not forget that so do physical locations. In the same way that people like to go to the village's Post Office for a chat but also do their banking, branded social media environments have the potential to merge conversation and commerce in a seamless, altogether better proposition for both consumers and brands.

Q. Many organisations now are looking at providing new mobile propositions. A key decision is whether to implement them as mobile app or mobile site. How do you approach this platform decision?

Roberto: Hortal: I start from the point of view of the user: Why would they use this proposition? Where would they use the proposition? How would they find it first time, and subsequently? Would they accept/appreciate the added engagement possibilities of an app (alerts, updates, a permanent place on the home screen)?

Some scenarios where I have used this approach in the past include:

- **Insurance/energy sales**. Website – neither mobile app nor mobile site. In this particular case I think the best option is to provide a solidly usable, accessible web sales capability that works well across devices. Rather than building separate sites/capabilities for separate devices I prefer to ensure the basis of the experience is optimised – this principle ensures that device-specificity doesn't catch me off-guard: sales websites I have managed worked well on iPhone the day it came out as they were built of solid principles and standards that apply across devices. I do use extensively the principles of progressive enhancement to provide a great experience to segments of people on particular channels/devices such as modern PC browsers and mobile browsers. However, the underlying principle of a solid, accessible, easy-to-use site has never let me down.
- **Regular/emergency transaction**. Apps – I look at regular events such as submitting an electricity meter reading or unpredictable ones such as registering a motor insurance claim as ideal candidates for a mobile app. Regularity breeds familiarity, and regular events can benefit from app characteristics such as local storage, transparent login, notifications and a permanent place on the user's screen. These same characteristics, together with the reassurance of being completely contained on the device and not requiring uninterrupted Internet access support the use of apps for functionality perceived as critical. HTML5 may make these distinctions technically irrelevant, but I expect customer behaviour will lag significantly so they will effectively apply for a long while yet.
- **Seamless access vs perceived value**. An app's installation is quite a disruptive process: you need to open the shop interface, confirm credentials, find the app, start a possibly long download (which may impact on your monthly limits), find the app on the phone screens, start it, watch it initialise (including possibly entering username and password for initial configuration) and finally access it – and from now on it will take space permanently on your device, competing with your music and movies. Quite an expensive process, from a usability point of view. Therefore an app must have quite a high perceived value in order to get installed. On the other hand, if casual use (particularly in conjunction with web searching/browsing) is what is sought, then a mobile site is the best solution.
- **Fragmentation is finally the last of my current worries**. We used to have to contend with the iPhone and the iPad – two screen sizes in a universal app is manageable. Suddenly we have myriad versions of iOS, Android, Windows Phone on a continuum of screen sizes and very variable device capabilities (processor speed, camera/s, GPS, NFC, etc.). This is turning into a big argument for HTML5 and mobile sites. Major platform/device combos will continue to be relevant for apps, but I also expect the relative size of this group of devices to shrink in relation to the universe of mobile devices – serving most of which will only be practical through mobile web.

Product

Product variable
The element of the marketing mix that involves researching customers' needs and developing appropriate products.

Core product
The fundamental features of the product that meet the user's needs.

Extended product
Additional features and benefits beyond the core product.

The **Product variable** of the marketing mix refers to characteristics of a product, service or brand. Product decisions should be informed by market research where customers' needs are assessed and the feedback is used to modify existing products or develop new products. There are many alternatives for varying the product in the online context when a company is developing its online strategy. Internet-related product decisions can be usefully divided into decisions affecting the **core product** and the **extended product**. The core product refers to the main product purchased by the consumer to fulfil their needs, while the extended or augmented product refers to additional services and benefits that are built around the core of the product.

The main implications of the Internet for the product element of the mix are:

1 options for varying the core product
2 options for offering digital products
3 options for changing the extended product
4 conducting research online
5 speed of new product development
6 speed of new product diffusion.

1 Options for varying the core product

For some companies, there may be options for new digital products which will typically be information products that can be delivered over the web. Ghosh (1998) talks about developing new products or adding 'digital value' to customers. The questions he posed still prove useful today:

- *Can I offer additional information or transaction services to my existing customer base?* For example, a bookseller can provide customer book reviews, new title previews or sell books online. A travel company can provide video tours of resorts and accommodation.
- *Can I address the needs of new customer segments by repackaging my current information assets or by creating new business propositions using the Internet?* For an online bookseller, creating an electronic book service, or a DVD rental service.
- *Can I use my ability to attract customers to generate new sources of revenue such as advertising or sales of complementary products?* Lastminute.com, which sells travel-related services, has a significant advertising revenue; it can also sell non-travel services.
- *Will my current business be significantly harmed by other companies providing some of the value I currently offer?* Considers the consequences if other companies use some of the product strategies described above.

Of course, the markets transformed most by the Internet are those where products themselves can be transformed into digital services. Such products include music (download or streaming of digital tracks – see the iTunes case study at the end of the chapter), books (electronic books), newspaper and magazine publishing (online access to articles) and software (digital downloads and online subscription services).

Mass customisation
Using economies of scale enabled by technology to offer tailored versions of products to individual customers or groups of customers.

Prosumer
'Producer + consumer'. The customer is closely involved in specifying their requirements in a product.

The Internet also introduces options for **mass customisation** of products, particularly digital products or products that can be specified online. The Internet has provided a channel through which manufacturers can not only sell the personalised product but also use the Internet as a source of information for developing the latest catwalk designs (see Activity 5.1).

Mass customisation or personalisation of products in which a customer takes a more active role in product design is part of the move to the **prosumer**. An example of a customised digital product is shown in Figure 5.2. Further details on the prosumer concept are given in Digital marketing insight 5.1.

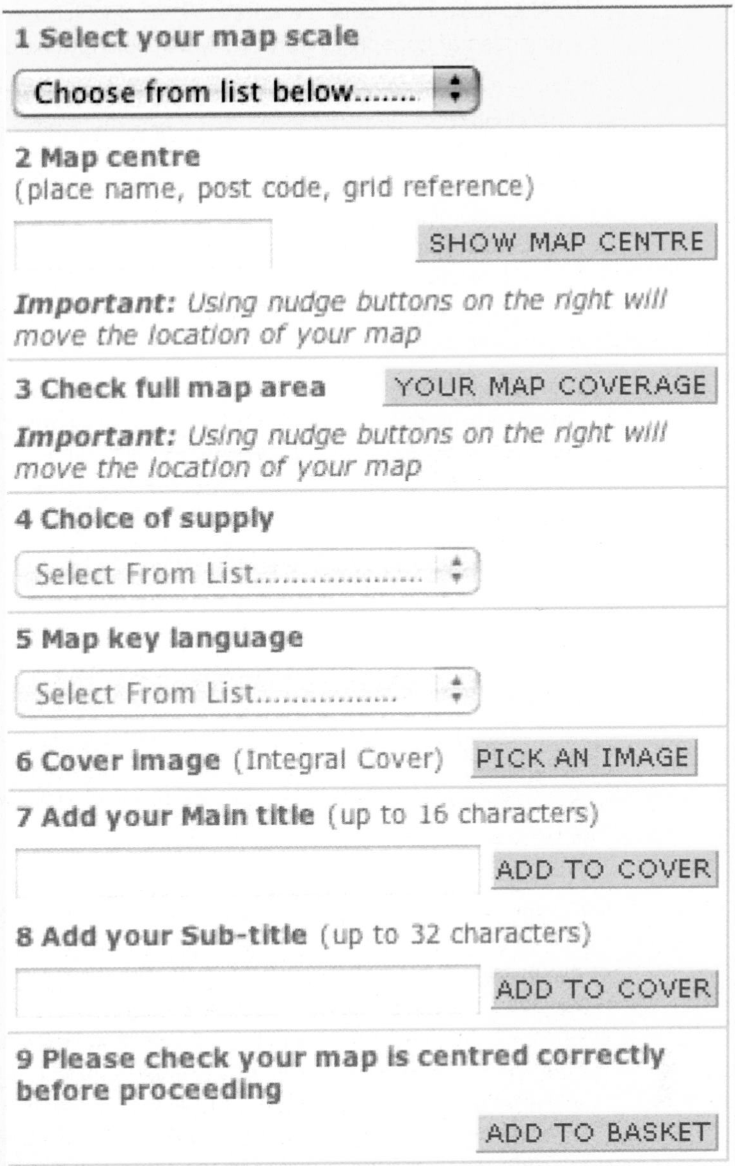

1 Select your map scale

Choose from list below.......

2 Map centre
(place name, post code, grid reference)

SHOW MAP CENTRE

Important: *Using nudge buttons on the right will move the location of your map*

3 Check full map area YOUR MAP COVERAGE

Important: *Using nudge buttons on the right will move the location of your map*

4 Choice of supply

Select From List...................

5 Map key language

Select From List................

6 Cover image (Integral Cover) PICK AN IMAGE

7 Add your Main title (up to 16 characters)

ADD TO COVER

8 Add your Sub-title (up to 32 characters)

ADD TO COVER

9 Please check your map is centred correctly before proceeding

ADD TO BASKET

Figure 5.2 Customising maps according to customers' preferences
Source: Ordnance Survey OS Select (**www.osselect.co.uk**)

Digital marketing insight 5.1 The prosumer

The prosumer concept was introduced in 1980 by futurist Alvin Toffler in his book *The Third Wave*. According to Toffler, the future would once again combine production with consumption. In *The Third Wave*, Toffler saw a world where interconnected users would collaboratively 'create' products. Note that he foresaw this over ten years before the web was invented!

Alternative notions of the prosumer, all of which are applicable to e-marketing, are catalogued at Logophilia WordSpy (**www.wordspy.com**):

1 A consumer who is an amateur in a particular field, but who is knowledgeable enough to require equipment that has some professional features: ('professional' + 'consumer').
2 A person who helps to design or customise the products they purchase: ('producer' + 'consumer').
3 A person who creates goods for their own use and also possibly to sell: ('producing' + 'consumer').
4 A person who takes steps to correct difficulties with consumer companies or markets and to anticipate future problems: ('proactive' + 'consumer').

An example of the application of the prosumer is provided by BMW who used an interactive website prior to launch of their Z3 roadster where users could design their own preferred features. The information collected was linked to a database and as BMW had previously collected data on its most loyal customers, the database could give a very accurate indication of which combinations of features were the most sought after and should therefore be put into production.

Dominos Pizza provide a further example of supporting the prosumer. They have introduced an online promotion called BFD, or *Big Fantastic Deal*, which lets pizza lovers ornament a pizza any way they like through a Flash-based microsite.

Users can specify crust type, amount of sauce and cheese, and any number of a series of toppings. Users can also name and register their pizzas for other users to try. Dominos report that over 12,000 pizzas have been registered, some with names like 'Happy Birthday Aaron' and 'Rhonda Half Doug Half,' according to Springwise. The most popular custom pizza is 'Ciao Bella,' which has been ordered 83,000 times.

Bundling
Offering complementary services.

Companies can also consider how the Internet can be used to change the range or combination of products offered. Some companies such as online fashion retailers may only offer a subset of products online. Alternatively, a company may have a fuller catalogue available online than is available through offline brochures. **Bundling** is a further alternative. For example, low-cost airlines, e.g. easyJet, Ryanair, offer complementary travel-related services including flights, hotel packages, car hire insurance and a range of other product offers.

Finally, the Internet is a platform for providing information about the core features of the product. However, the availability of information can impact on price as the price has become more transparent. Comparison sites like Comparethemarket.com, enable online shoppers to assess the price of car insurance from many suppliers in one location.

2 Options for offering digital products

Companies such as publishers, TV companies and other media owners who can offer digital products such as published content, music or videos now have great flexibility to offer a range of product purchase options at different price points including:

- *Subscription.* This is a traditional publisher revenue model, but subscription can potentially be offered for different periods at different price points, e.g. three months, twelve months or two years.
- *Pay-per-view.* A fee for a single download or viewing session at a higher relative price than the subscription service, e.g. music products from iTunes, customers can enjoy instant download in a similar way to a mobile company 'pay-as-you-go' model. Travel publisher Lonely Planet enables visitors to a destination to download an introduction for a fraction of the price of a full printed guide.

- *Bundling*. Different channels or content can be offered as individual products or grouped at a reduced price compared to pay-per-view.
- *Ad supported content*. There is no direct price set here, instead, the publisher's main revenue source is through adverts on the site (either CPM display advertising on-site using banner ads and skyscrapers) a fixed sponsorship arrangement or CPC, which stands for 'cost-per-click' more typical when using search ad network publishing such as Google Adsense (**www.google.com/adsense.com**) which accounts for around a third of Google's revenue. Other options include affiliate revenue from sales on third party sites or offering access to subscriber lists. Three of the UK's most popular quality newspapers are now successfully using subscriptions as described in Digital marketing insight 5.2 including the *Guardian* (**www.guardian.co.uk**) *The Telegraph*, and *The Times*.

Digital marketing insight 5.2 | **Does the Internet herald the end for newspapers?**

On the one hand, predictions are being made that the Internet signals the end for newspapers. According to Keen (2009), the Internet is throwing many challenges at traditional journalism and cites Shirky's book *Everything Changes* stating that:

> The Internet undermines traditional news bundling, forever unstitching the necessity of combining disparate content in a single product. Internet technology does away with the oligarchy of newspaper publishers, enabling anyone to publish anything they like in real-time at minimal cost on an always-on global network.

However, on the other hand Rupert Murdoch, chairman of News Corporation, has introduced a charging policy for downloading newspapers to iPads and other digital devices. The potential coverage afforded by the Internet is immense and extends around the globe. So although the Internet may be changing how people access newspapers, there are benefits in terms of reach and also production and distribution efficiency gains to be made. In its first month the Guardian app (which offers the *Guardian* newspaper in a digitised format) was downloaded 68,976 times, a figure which delighted Emily Bell, the paper's Director of Digital Content. The *Guardian* is now available for download via the iphone and Android and during 2011 the App has been activated over 150 million times.

3 Options for changing the extended product

When a customer buys a new computer, it consists not only of the tangible computer, monitor and cables, but also the information provided by the computer salesperson, the instruction manual, the packaging, the warranty and the follow-up technical service. These are elements of the extended product. Chaffey and Smith (2008) suggest these examples of how the Internet can be used to vary the extended product:

- endorsements
- awards
- testimonies
- customer lists
- customer comments
- warranties
- guarantees
- money-back offers
- customer service (see people, process and physical evidence)
- incorporating tools to help users during their selection and use of the product.

Peppard and Rylander (2005) have researched how people assimilate information online when selecting products and point out it is important that the site replicates information about product selection that would normally be provided by interaction in other channels by a member of sales staff by phone or face-to-face. These facilities can be replicated online. For example, the bank First Direct uses an interactive dialogue to recommend the best options on their portfolio of financial products, e.g. savings, investments, mortgage insurance.

Organisations should aim to identify sources of value to engage customers before they have to pay for the products and services on offer. Ghosh (1998) suggested this was an important trigger to encourage site visitors to engage with a brand on a first visit to a site and or to encourage return visits. He refers to this process as 'building a customer *magnet*' and the concepts he identified remain central to 'portal' or 'community' websites. Once customers are attracted to a site and have begun to learn about the brand offer, the next step is to provide extensions to the freely available offer. Ideally, customers will be encouraged to enter into a paid-for relationship with the organisation. In other cases a premium may be charged for new services. Amazon (**www.amazon.com**) for instance is active in identifying new revenue sources through product innovation – for example it has always charged a premium for its wrapping service, but more recently has introduced related products including a credit card and offers Amazon Prime for customers who use the service frequently. For business audiences it offers advertising on its site or hosting and application support through Amazon Web Services.

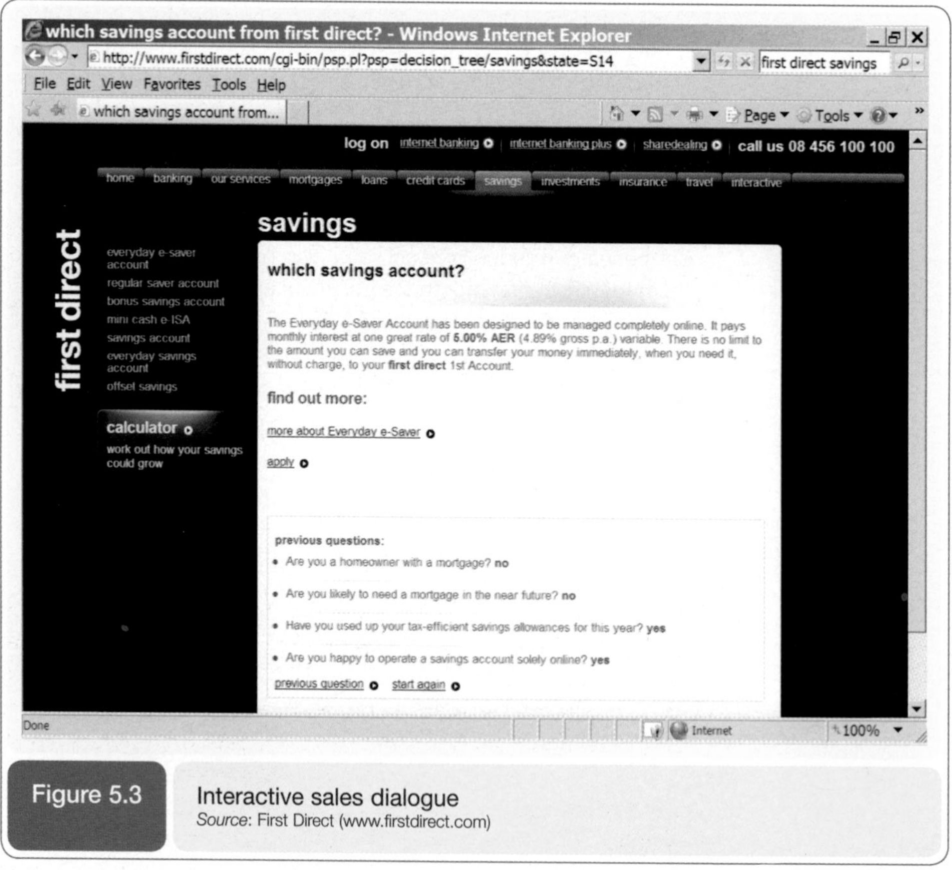

Figure 5.3 Interactive sales dialogue
Source: First Direct (www.firstdirect.com)

4 Conducting research online

The Internet provides many options for learning about product preferences and it can be used as a relatively low-cost method of collecting marketing research, particularly when trying to discover customer perceptions of products and services. Sawhney *et al.* (2005) have reviewed the options for using digital media for new product innovation where they contrast the traditional new product research process with a digitally augmented co-creation process. They suggest that online research tools should be evaluated according to how they can be used (1) front-end developments of ideation and concept against back-end developments involving product design and testing, and (2) the nature of collaboration – broad/high reach against deep/high richness.

Options for performing new product development research online include:

- *Online focus group.* A moderated focus group can be conducted to compare customers' experience of product use. Many companies now have permanent customer panels they can use to ask about new ideas.
- *Online questionnaire survey.* These typically focus on the site visitors' experience, but can also include questions relating to products.
- *Customer feedback or support forums.* Comments posted to the site or independent sites such as social networks may give suggestions about future product innovation. Dell launched IdeaStorm with the idea of talking directly to customers in 2007. The aim was to give customers a voice and provide a conduit to connect ideas about new products from the customer to the manufacturer (Dell).
- *Web analytics.* A wealth of marketing research information is also available from response data from e-mail and search campaigns and the website itself, since every time a user clicks on a link offering a particular product, this indicates a preference for products and related offers. Such information can be used indirectly to assess customers' product preferences.

Approaches for undertaking these types of research are briefly reviewed in Chapter 10.

5 Velocity of new product development

The Internet provides a platform which enables new products to be developed more rapidly as it is possible to test new ideas and concepts and explore different product options through online market research. Companies can use their own panels of consumers to test opinion more rapidly and often at lower costs than for traditional market research. Google is a highly innovative company and it has had many successes and failures e.g., GoogleAdwords (success) and Google Buzz and Wave (failure). Another aspect of the velocity of new product development is that the network effect of the Internet enables companies to form partnerships more readily to launch new products.

6 Velocity of new product diffusion

Quelch and Klein (1996) also noted that the implication of the Internet and globalisation is that to remain competitive, organisations will have to roll out new products more rapidly to international markets. More recently, Malcolm Gladwell in his book *The Tipping Point* (2000) has shown how word-of-mouth communication has a tremendous impact on the rate of adoption of new products and we can suggest this effect is often enhanced or facilitated through the Internet. In Chapter 9, we will see how marketers seek to influence this effect through what is known as 'viral marketing'. Marsden (2004) provides a good summary of the implications of the **tipping point** for marketers. He says that 'using the science of social epidemics, *The Tipping Point* explains the three simple principles that underpin the rapid spread of ideas, products and behaviours through a population'. He advises how marketers should help create a 'tipping point' for a new product or service, the moment when a domino effect is triggered and an epidemic of demand sweeps through a population like a highly contagious virus.

Tipping point
Using the science of social epidemics explains principles that underpin the rapid spread of ideas, products and behaviours through a population.

There are three main laws that are relevant from *The Tipping Point*:

1 The law of the few

This suggests that the spread of any new product or service is dependent on the initial adoption by 'connectors' who are socially connected and who encourage adoption through word-of-mouth and copycat behaviour. In an online context, these connectors may use personal blogs, e-mail newsletters and podcasts to propagate their opinions.

2 The stickiness factor

Typically, this refers to how 'glued' we are to a medium such as a TV channel or a website, but in this context it refers to attachment to the characteristics and attributes of a product or a brand. Gladwell stresses the importance of testing and market research to make the product effective. Marsden suggests that there are key cross-category attributes which are key drivers for product success and he commends the work of Morris and Martin (2000) which summarises these attributes as:

- *Excellence*: perceived as best of breed
- *Uniqueness*: clear one-of-a-kind differentiation
- *Aesthetics*: perceived aesthetic appeal
- *Association*: generates positive associations
- *Engagement*: fosters emotional involvement
- *Expressive value*: visible sign of user values
- *Functional value*: addresses functional needs
- *Nostalgic value*: evokes sentimental linkages
- *Personification*: has character, personality
- *Cost*: perceived value for money.

You can see that this list is also a useful prompt about the ideal characteristics of a website or online service.

3 The power of context

Gladwell (2000) suggests that like infectious diseases, products and behaviours spread far and wide only when they fit the physical, social and mental context into which they are launched. He gives the example of a wave of crime in the New York subway that came to an abrupt halt by simply removing the graffiti from trains and clamping down on fare-dodging. It can be suggested that products should be devised and tested to fit their context, situation or occasion of use.

Activity 5.2 Assessing options online to vary product using the Internet

Purpose

To illustrate the options for varying the product element of the marketing mix online.

Activity

Select one of the sectors below. Use a search engine to find three competitors with similar product offerings. List ways in which each has used the Internet to vary its core and extended product. Which of the companies do you think makes best use of the Internet?

- computer manufacturers
- management consultants
- cosmetics and women's and men's fragrances
- higher education providers

The long tail concept

Long tail concept
A frequency distribution suggesting the relative variation in popularity of items selected by consumers.

The **long tail concept** is useful for considering the role of Product, Place, Price and Promotion online. The phenomenon, now referred to as the 'long tail', following an article by Anderson (2004), was arguably first applied to human behaviour by George Kingsley Zipf, professor of linguistics at Harvard who observed the phenomenon in word usage (see **http://en.wikipedia.org/wiki/Zipf%27s_law**). He found that if the variation in popularity of different words in a language is considered, there is a systematic pattern in the frequency of usage or popularity. Zipf's 'law' suggests that if a collection of items is ordered or ranked by popularity, the second item will have around half the popularity of the first one and the third item will have about a third of the popularity of the first one and so on. In general:

> The kth item is 1/k the popularity of the first.

Look at Figure 5.4 which shows how the 'relative popularity' of items is predicted to decline according to Zipf's law from a maximum count of 1000 for the most popular item to 20 for the 50th item.

In an online context, application of this 'law' is now known as 'the long tail' thanks to Anderson (2004). It can be applied to the relative popularity of a group of websites or web pages or products on an individual site, since they tend to show a similar pattern of popularity. There are a small number of sites (or pages within sites) which are very popular (the head which may account for 80 per cent of the volume) and a much larger number of sites or pages that are less popular individually, but still collectively important. Returning to the product context, Anderson (2004) argued that for a company such as Amazon, the long tail or Zipf's law can be applied to describe the variation in preferences for selecting or purchasing from a choice for products as varied as books, CDs, electronic items, travel or financial services. This pattern has also been identified by Brynjolfsson *et al.* (2003) who present a framework that quantifies the economic impact of increased product variety made available through electronic markets. They say:

> One reason for increased product variety on the Internet is the ability of online retailers to catalog, recommend, and provide a large number of products for sale. For example, the number of book titles available at Amazon.com is more than 23 times larger than the number of books on the shelves of a typical Barnes & Noble superstore, and 57 times greater than the number of books stocked in a typical large independent bookstore.

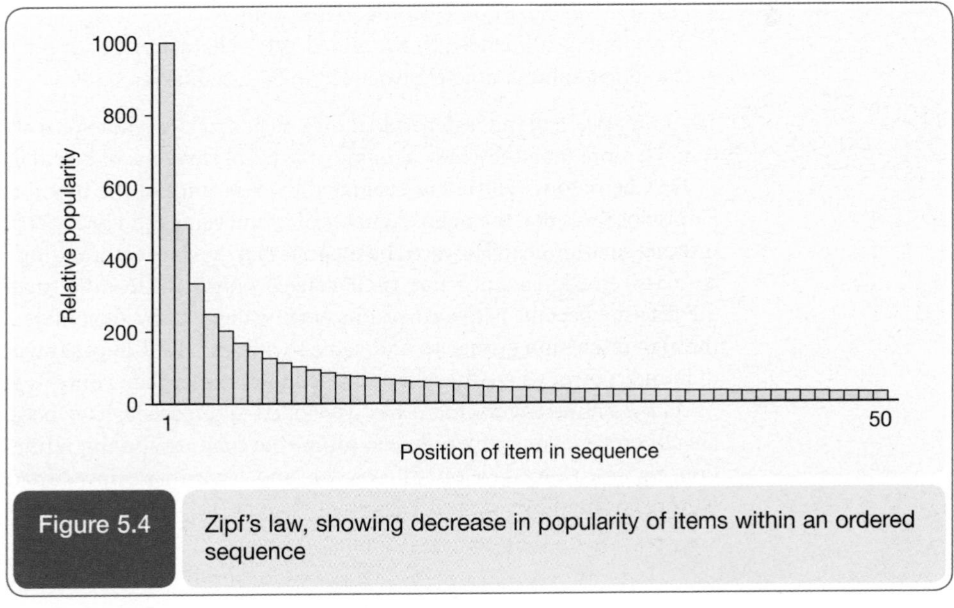

Figure 5.4 Zipf's law, showing decrease in popularity of items within an ordered sequence

Looking at the issue from another perspective, they estimate that 40 per cent of sales are from relatively obscure books with a sales rank of more than 100,000 (if you visit Amazon, you will see that every book has a sales rank from 1 for the most popular to over 1 million for the least popular). This indicates the importance of the long tail for online retailers like Amazon, since 40 per cent of sales are from these less popular books which cannot be stocked in a conventional bookstore (a large real-world book store would typically hold about 100,000 books). In a Pricing context, another benefit for online retailers is that less popular products cannot be readily obtained in the real world, so Amazon can justify higher prices for these books. Brynjolfsson *et al.* (2003) estimated that average Amazon prices for an item in the top 100,000 is $29.26 and in less popular titles $41.60.

In this section, we have seen that there are many opportunities to vary the Product element of the mix. Complete Activity 5.2 to apply these to different types of markets.

Branding in a digital environment

Branding
The process of creating and evolving successful brands.

Branding is important on and offline as it helps customers differentiate between products and services. Furthermore, branding is how companies set themselves apart from their competitors. Perhaps most importantly, 'branding affects perceptions since it is well-known that in blind product testing consumers fail to distinguish between brands' (Jobber, 2010). Consequently, how a brand is developed and presented online is particularly important because a website visitor has limited physical cues to help form an opinion about a company and its services, such as talking to a sales representative or the ambiance of the physical store. Branding can add value across the supply chain, act as a barrier to competition, increase consumer trust and generate high levels of profitability.

Brand
The sum of the characteristics of a product or service perceived by a user.

When building an online brand it is also important to remember that branding involves much more than the name or logo associated with a company or products. A **brand** is described by Leslie de Chernatony and Malcolm McDonald in their classic 1992 book *Creating Powerful Brands* as:

> an identifiable product or service augmented in such a way that the buyer or user perceives relevant unique added values which match their needs most closely. Furthermore, its success results from being able to sustain these added values in the face of competition.

This definition highlights three essential characteristics of a successful brand which we need to relate to the online environment:

- brand is dependent on customer perception
- perception is influenced by the added-value characteristics of the product
- the added-value characteristics need to be sustainable.

To summarise, a brand is dependent on a customer's psychological affinity for a product, and is much more than the physical name or symbol elements of brand identity.

De Chernatony (2001) has evaluated the relevance of the brand concept on the Internet. He also believes that the main elements of brand values and brand strategy are the same in the Internet environment. However, he suggests that the classical branding model where consumers are passive recipients of value is challenged online. Instead he suggests that consumers on the Internet become active co-producers of value where consumers can contribute feedback through discussion groups to add value to a brand. De Chernatony argues for a looser form of brand control where the company facilitates rather than controls customer discussion.

As the online environment has developed and markets have become more stable brands are not only moving from online to offline but they are also migrating in the alternative direction, e.g. Tesco have developed Tesco.com and Amazon are now developing High Street stores. Now read Mini Case Study 5.1.

Mini Case Study 5.1 Expansion of an online brand offline

According to Bravo *et al*. (2011), 'in recent years the offline and online spheres of strategic brand management are becoming more and more interconnected'. Part of the reason for this is that when offline companies decide to sell their product online they also need to establish the logistical and technical networks to support the operation. However, as companies seek to commercialise their products by using digital channels, the crossover from offline to online can lead to the creation of new online products. Apple is an example with its iPhone and the iTunes shop (Bravo *et al*., (2011). By operating offline, brands can build value in both environments. For an offline brand the core reasons for expanding online are accessing new markets, adding customer value and increasing flexibility through the use of multichannels. According to Burt (2010), established brands are 'getting more, rather than less important'. However, for a brand moving from online to offline the focus and opportunities are slightly different. Online brands can create awareness for their product and service offers and it may be possible to enhance consumer trust in the online brand (Delgado and Hernandez, 2008). Google has recently set up a physical store selling on London's Tottenham Court Road. The store sells Google chromebooks from a 'zone' within the Curry's PC World shop. Chromebooks are *cloud-centric* devices that provide computing power and almost constant internet access. Head of consumer marketing at Google UK, said they have 'found anecdotally that when people tried the Chromebook and played with it, that it made a huge difference to their understanding of what the Chromebook is all about' (Meyer, 2011).

Brand experience
The frequency and depth of interactions with a brand can be enhanced through the Internet.

Brand equity
The assets (or liabilities) linked to a brand's name and symbol that add to (or subtract from) a service.

Summarising the elements of online branding, de Chernatony (2001) suggests that successful online branding requires delivering three aspects of a brand: rational values, emotional values and promised **brand experience** (based on rational and emotional values). We return to the notion of brand promise at the start of Chapter 7 since this is closely related to delivering customer experience.

Another consideration is **brand equity,** which is a measure of the strength of a brand in the market place (Jobber, 2010) and Aaker and Joachimsthaler (2000) define it as:

> a set of brand assets and liabilities linked to a brand, its name and symbol, that add to or subtract from the value provided by a product or service to a firm and/or to that firm's customers.

Therefore, brand equity indicates the value provided to a company, or its customers, through a brand. Assessing brand equity on the web needs to address the unique characteristics of computer-mediated environments as Christodoulides and de Chernatony (2004) have pointed out. Based on expert interviews they have identified the additional measures of brand equity which are important online, as summarised in Table 5.1. As we would expect, this includes attributes of the digital medium such as interactivity and customisation which combine to form relevance and a great online brand experience. Content is not stressed separately, which is surprising, although they do mention its importance under site design and it is also a key aspect of other attributes such as customisation, relevance and the overall experience. A more recent analysis of online brand equity which can be used to survey customers on the quality of brand experience for retail and service sites by Christodoulides *et al.* (2006) is presented in the introduction to Chapter 7.

Table 5.1 Traditional measures of brand equity and online measures of brand equity

Traditional measures of brand equity (Aaker and Joachimsthaler, 2000)	Online measures of brand equity (Christodoulides and de Chernatony, 2004)
Price premium	Online brand experience
Satisfaction/loyalty	Interactivity
Perceived quality	Customisation
Leadership popularity	Relevance
Perceived value	Site design
Brand personality	Customer service
Organisational associations	Order fulfilment
Brand awareness	Quality of brand relationships
Market share	Communities
Market price and distribution coverage	Engagement measured through web analytics (see Chapter 9)

Success factors for brand sites

In Chapter 1, we identified a 'brand website' as one of five classes of website or parts of sites which support different organisational goals. Although other types of sites we mentioned in Chapter 1 including transactional sites, relationship building sites, portals and social networks will all seek to provide a favourable brand experience. In the case of pure 'brand sites', the manager of the site needs to carefully think the best way the brand can engage with consumers given lack of content naturally associated with low-involvement products.

Brand advocate
A customer who has favourable perceptions of a brand who will talk favourably about a brand to their acquaintances to help generate awareness of the brand or influence purchase intent.

For the site itself, it is not the quantity of visitors that is important, rather it is about the quality of visitors, since brand sites are most likely to attract **brand advocates** who can be important in influencing others to make them aware of the brand or trial the brand. As Ries and Ries (2000) have said, it is important that brand sites provide a home for the brand loyalists and advocates. It follows that brand owners should determine the type of content on a brand site which will encourage brand loyalists (and also the brand-neutral consumer) to visit and then return to the brand site. Flores (2004) has said that encouraging visitors to return is key and he suggests different aspects of a quality site experience to achieve this. Some of the methods he suggests to encourage visitors to return include:

- *Create a compelling, interactive experience including rich media which reflects the brand.* The research by Flores showed that a site which delivers an unsatisfactory experience will negatively affect brand perception. He notes that some brand sites which often contain rich media or video, although visually engaging may have poor usability or download speeds.
- *Consider how the site will influence the sales cycle by encouraging trial.* Trial will often be fulfilled offline so approaches such as samples, coupons or prize draws can be used. These response activators should be integrated throughout the site. For example, car brands will all have prominent options for taking a test drive, receiving a brochure or the option to win a car or a visit to a race circuit.
- *Developing an exchange (permission marketing) programme on your website to begin a 'conversation' with the most valuable customer segments.* Permission-based e-mail or text messages can be used to update consumers about new products or promotions.

Additionally we would stress the importance of achieving customer engagement with brand sites to encourage participation or co-creation of content. For example, brands can encourage users to share and submit their comments, stories, photos or videos. Once engaged in this way, visitors are more likely to return to a site to see other's comments.

Dorset Cereals (Figure 5.5, **www.dorsetcereals.co.uk**) gives a good example of how the opportunities for a consumer brand to engage its audiences have been well thought through. Some of the approaches used are indicated by the menu bar and other content and the associated goals can be inferred:

- *Buy things.* Goals – increase product usage. Provide content for brand advocates.
- *We make.* Goals – increase sales for new adoptions since product distribution is not as widespread as some brands.

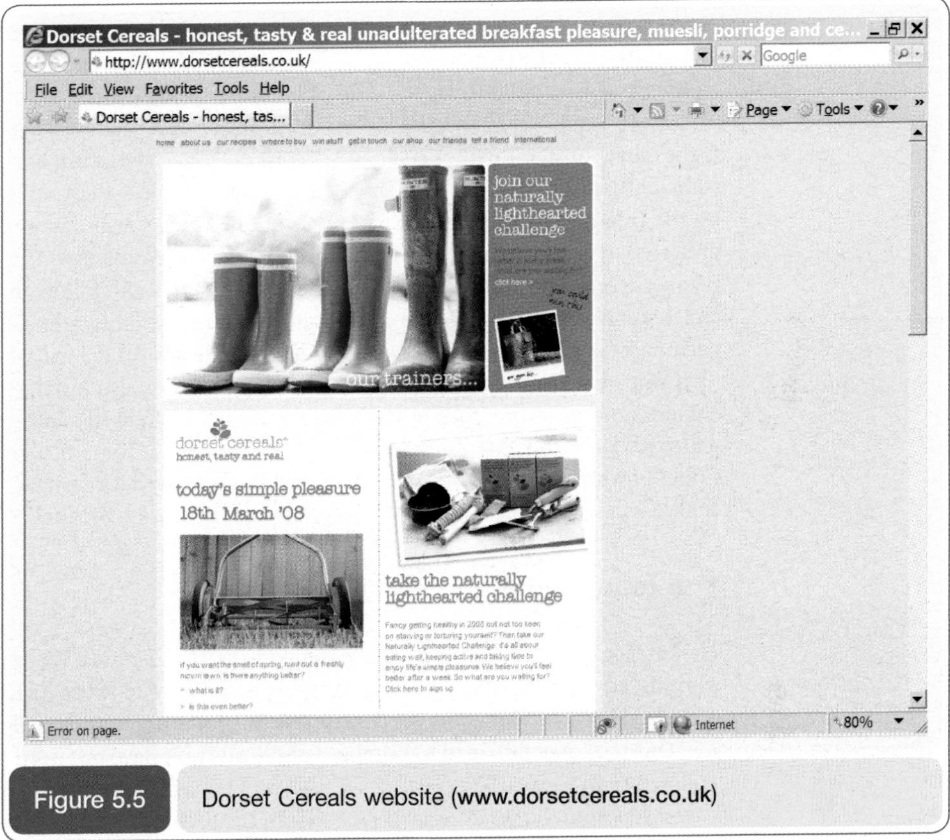

Figure 5.5 Dorset Cereals website (www.dorsetcereals.co.uk)

- *Win stuff.* Goals: encourage trial and reward loyalists. The company has not used sampling to-date, but instead has run prize draws related to the rural nature of its brand, e.g. win a Land Rover, win trips to flower shows, photo competitions. The current featured promotion is the 'Naturally lighthearted challenge' which is a seven-day permission e-mail supported programme to eat more healthily.
- *Blog.* Goal: engage site visitors and encourage involved customers to keep brand 'front-of-mind' through comments and posts
- *Get in touch.* Goals: encourage feedback and dialogue.
- *Online shop.* Goals: Direct sales of cereal and branded merchandise such as cereal bowls.
- *Our friends.* Goals: Partner with related brands and sites which explain brand values.
- *Sell our cereals.* Goal: Find additional distributors.
- *International.* Goal: Show international availability.

The success factors a brand uses should closely interlink with the brand's identity.

Brand identity

Brand identity
The totality of brand associations including name and symbols that must be communicated.

Aaker and Joachimsthaler (2000) also emphasise the importance of developing a plan to communicate the key features of the **brand identity** and increase brand awareness. Brand identity is again more than the name. These authors refer to it as a set of brand associations that imply a promise to customers from an organisation.

Brand names for online brands

Companies creating a new online brand or portal need to consider the characteristics of a successful brand name suggested by de Chernatony and McDonald (1992) for offline brands. Ideally, the name should be simple, distinctive, meaningful and compatible with the product. These principles can be readily applied to web-based brands. Examples of brands that fulfil most of these characteristics are CD WOW!, eBags and Travelocity. Others suggest that distinctiveness is most important: ASOS, Amazon, Yahoo!, Expedia,, E*Trade, and Fireand-Water (HarperCollins) books.

Ries and Ries (2000) suggest two rules for naming online brands. (1) The Law of the Common Name – they say 'the kiss of death for an Internet brand is a common name'. This argues that common names such as Art.com or Advertising.com are poor since they are not sufficiently distinctive. (2) The Law of the Proper Name – they say 'your name stands alone on the Internet, so you'd better have a good one'. This suggests that proper names are to be preferred to generic names, e.g. Handbag.com against Woman.com, or Moreover.com against Business.com. The authors suggest that the best names will follow most of these eight principles: short, simple, suggestive of the category, unique, alliterative, speakable, shocking and personalised. Although these are cast as 'immutable laws' there will of course be exceptions!

If you are registering a domain for a new company it is also worth remembering that search engines tend to favour sites in their listings which include the name of the service which is searched for within the domain name. For example, a domain name such as MyVoucher-Codes (**www.myvouchercodes.com**) will tend to rank well for 'voucher codes' since the search engine will see sites linking to it which contains the words 'voucher codes'.

The importance of brand online

The Internet presents a 'double-edged sword' to existing brands. We have seen that a consumer who already has knowledge of a brand is more likely to trust it. However, loyalty can be decreased because it encourages consumers to trial other brands. This is suggested by Figure 5.7. This trial may well lead to purchase of brands that have not been previously considered.

The BrandNewWorld (2004) survey showed that in some categories, a large proportion of buyers have purchased different brands from those they initially considered for example:

- large home appliances, 47%
- financial products and services, 39%
- holidays and travel, 31%
- mobile phones, 28%
- cars, 26%.

But, for other types of products, existing brand preferences appear to be more important:

- clothing/accessories, 22%
- computer hardware, 21%
- garden/DIY products, 17%
- home furnishings, 6%.

The survey also suggested that experienced Internet users were more likely to switch brands (52 per cent agreed they were more likely to switch after researching online) compared to less-experienced users (33 per cent).

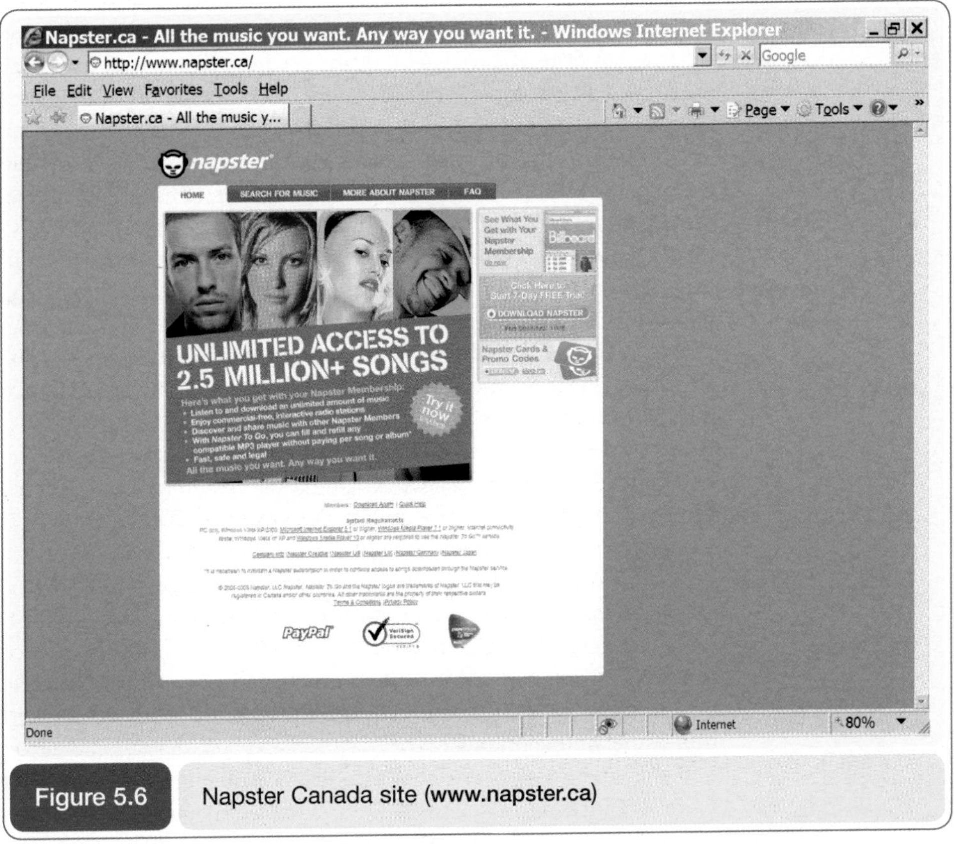

Figure 5.6 Napster Canada site (www.napster.ca)

Of course, the likelihood of a consumer purchasing will depend upon their knowledge of the retailer brand or the product brand. Figure 5.7 shows that many customers will still buy an unknown manufacturer brand if they are familiar with the retailer brand. This is less true if they don't know the retailer. Significantly, if they don't know the retailer or the brand, it is fairly unlikely they will buy.

When buying online, I will buy a product if...

I am familiar with the *retailer*	Yes	Yes	No	No
I am familiar with the *product brand*	Yes	No	Yes	No
	90%	82%	54%	13%

Figure 5.7 The influence of brand knowledge on purchase. Matrix for question 'I will buy a product if …'
Source: BrandNewWorld (2004)

Price

Price variable
The element of the marketing mix that involves defining product prices and pricing models.

Pricing models
Describe the form of payment such as outright purchase, auction, rental, volume purchases and credit terms.

The **Price variable** of the marketing mix refers to an organisation's pricing policies which are used to define **pricing models** and, of course, to set prices for products and services. The Internet has dramatic implications for pricing in many sectors and there is a lot of literature in this area. Baker *et al.* (2000) and more recently Xing *et al.* (2006) noted two approaches that have been commonly adopted for pricing on the Internet: start-up companies have tended to use low prices to gain a customer base, while many existing companies have transferred their existing prices to the web. Other existing companies have used differential pricing with lower prices for some of their products online. This has been the approach followed by online electrical retailers such as Comet (**www.comet.co.uk**). The Pricing element mix will often relate to the Product element since online pricing depends on the range of products offered and the point at which a product is in its lifecycle. Extending the product range may allow these products to be discounted online. Some organisations have launched new products online which have a lower Price element, for example banks have launched 'eSavings' products where higher interest rates are offered to online customers. Alternatively, they may offer insurance products with a 10 per cent online discount in order to encourage customers to use the digital channel. Often these agreements are dependent on the customer servicing their account online, which helps reduce the cost-base of the bank. This then relates to the service elements of the mix since service has to be delivered online.

However, as organisations are increasingly developing multichannel strategies in order to give their customers more opportunities to interact with brands it becomes more difficult to justify on and offline pricing policies, especially in consumer markets. Low-cost airlines sell the majority of their products online and penalise consumers with higher prices if they do not buy online. However for companies selling tangible goods, it is becoming harder to legitimise differential online pricing.

Remember that lower prices may imply reducing the level of customer service to reduce costs and this can in turn lead to a poor repeat purchase rate. Amazon, one of the most successful online brands, established its market dominance by being known for its range of products and quality of service rather than having the lowest prices; although pricing continues to be very competitive.

The main implications of the Internet for the price aspect of the mix, which we will review in this section, are:

1 increased price transparency and its implications on differential pricing
2 downward pressure on price (including commoditisation)
3 new pricing approaches (including dynamic pricing, price testing and auctions)
4 alternative pricing structure or policies.

1 Increased price transparency

Price transparency
Customer knowledge about pricing increases due to increased availability of pricing information.

Differential pricing
Identical products are priced differently for different types of customers, markets or buying situations.

Quelch and Klein (1996) describe two contradictory effects of the Internet on price that are related to **price transparency**. First, a supplier can use the technology for **differential pricing**, for example, for customers in different countries. However, if precautions are not taken about price, the customers may be able to quickly find out about the price discrimination and they will object to it.

Price elasticity of demand
Measure of consumer behaviour that indicates the change in demand for a product or service in response to changes in price. Price elasticity of demand is used to assess the extent to which a change in price will influence demand for a product.

Pricing online has to take into account the concept of **price elasticity of demand.** This is a measure of consumer behaviour based on economic theory that indicates the change in demand for a product or service in response to changes in price. Price elasticity of demand is determined by the price of the product, availability of alternative goods from alternative suppliers (which tends to increase online) and consumer income. A product is said to be 'elastic' (or responsive to price changes) if a small change in price increases or reduces the demand substantially. A product is 'inelastic' if a large change in price is accompanied by a small amount of change in demand.

Satisficing behaviour
Consumers do not behave entirely rationally in product or supplier selection. They will compare alternatives, but then may make their choice given imperfect information.

Although, intuitively, we would think that price transparency enabled through the Internet price comparison services such as Shopping.com (owned by eBay), which leads to searching by product rather than by store level, would lead to common comparisons of price and the selection of the cheapest product – but the reality seems different. Pricing online is relatively inelastic. There are two main reasons for this. First, pricing is only one variable – consumers also decide on suppliers according to other aspects about the brand such as familiarity, trust and perceived service levels. Second, consumers often display **satisficing behaviour.** The term 'satisfice' was coined by Herbert Simon in 1957 when he said that people are only 'rational enough' and that they suspend or relax their rationality if they feel it is no longer required. This is called 'bounded rationality' by cognitive psychologists. In other words, although consumers may seek to minimise some variable (such as price) when making a product or supplier selection, most may not try too hard. Online, this is supported by research by Johnson *et al.* (2004) who showed that by analysing panel data from over 10,000 Internet households and three commodity-like products (books, compact discs and air travel services), the amount of online search is actually quite limited. On average, households visit only 1.2 book sites, 1.3 CD sites and 1.8 travel sites during a typical active month in each category. Of course, these averages will reflect a range of behaviour. This is consistent with previous research quoted by Marn (2000) which suggested that only around 8% of active online consumers are 'aggressive price shoppers'. Furthermore, he notes that Internet price bands have remained broad. Online booksellers' prices varied by an average of 33 per cent and those of CD sellers by 25 per cent.

Aggregators
An alternative term to *price comparison sites or comparison search engines (CSE)*. Aggregators include product, price and service information comparing competitors within a sector such as financial services, retail or travel. Their revenue models commonly include affiliate revenues (CPA), pay-per-click advertising (CPC) and display advertising (CPM).

Retailers or other transactional e-commerce companies operating in markets where their products are readily reviewed online need to review their strategy towards the impact of **aggregators** which facilitate price comparison. One strategy for companies in the face of increased price transparency is to highlight the other features of the brand – such as the quality of the retail experience, fulfilment choice or customer service – to reduce the emphasis on cost as a differentiator. Another strategy is to educate the market about the limitations in aggregators such as incomplete coverage or limited information about delivery or service levels. This approach is highlighted by Mini Case Study 5.2 which shows the tensions between aggregators and the service provider brands they promote.

To the authors, this conflict shows the importance of companies that are featured within aggregators possessing a strong brand which can offer additional value in terms of customer service or trust. It also shows the continuing importance of offline advertising in shaping consumer perceptions of brands and to drive visitors directly to a destination site.

Commoditisation
The process whereby product selection becomes more dependent on price than on differentiating features, benefits and value-added services.

For business commodities, auctions on business-to-business exchanges can also have a similar effect of driving down price. Purchase of some products that have not traditionally been thought of as commodities may become more price sensitive. This process is known as **commoditisation**. Examples of goods that are becoming commoditised include electrical goods and cars.

Activity 5.3 Assessing price ranges on the Internet

Purpose

To illustrate the concept of price transparency.

Activity

Visit a price comparison site, e.g. **www.pricerunner.com; www.confused.com; moneysupermarket.com; www.gocompare.com** and then find the products below and examples of the best and worst offers:

- insurance
- a personal loan
- a savings product

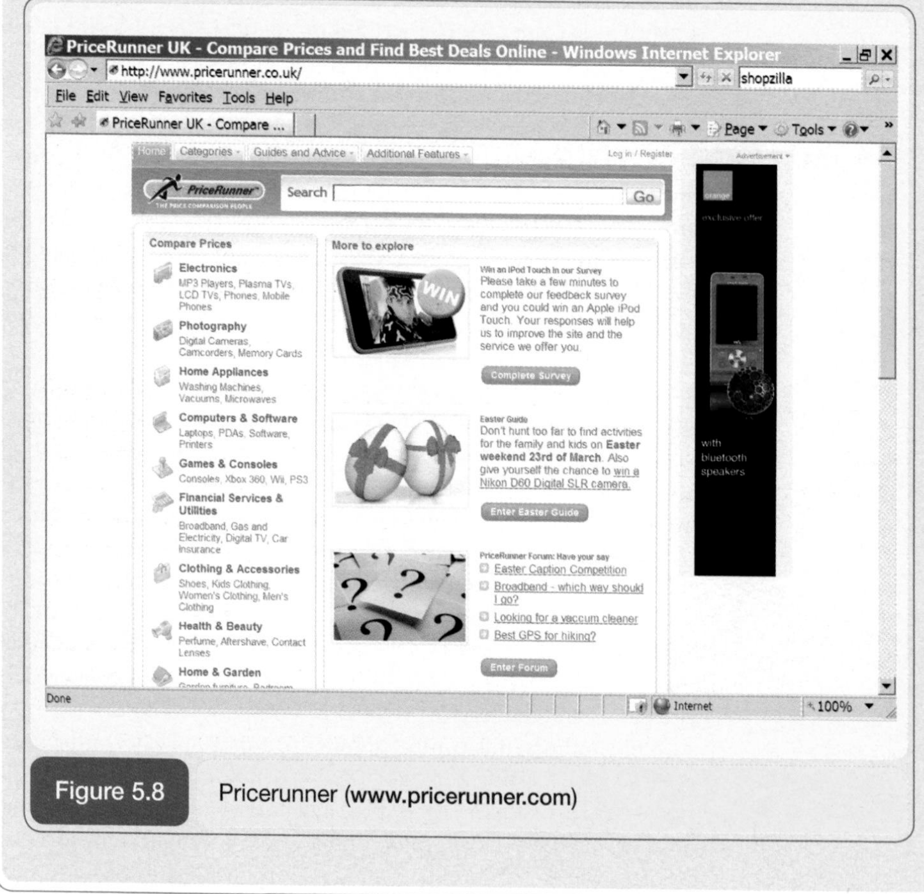

Figure 5.8 Pricerunner (www.pricerunner.com)

2 Downward pressure on price

The competition caused by price transparency and increased number of competitors is the main reason for downward pressure on price. Many aggregators or comparison sites have benefitted from this approach e.g. mysupermarket.com. For example, Figure 5.9 shows an example of this website comparing four different supermarkets showing the variation in prices between Tesco, ASDA, Sainsbury and Ocado. However, you should be aware when looking at price comparisons that you are not always seeing a like for like comparison, products, can vary especially when supermarket own brands are in the shopping basket.

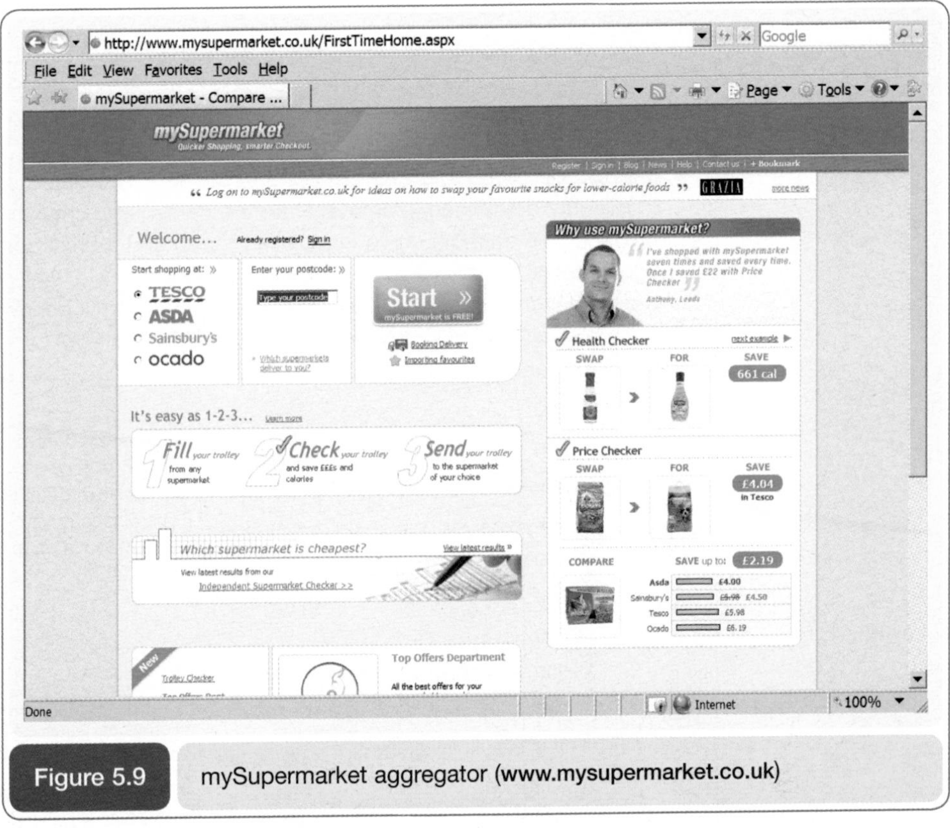

Figure 5.9 mySupermarket aggregator (www.mysupermarket.co.uk)

The Internet also tends to drive down prices since Internet-only retailers that do not have a physical presence do not have the overheads of operating stores and a retailer distribution network. This means that, in theory, online companies can operate at lower **pricing levels** than offline rivals. This phenomenon is prevalent in the banking sector where many banks have set up online companies or online only accounts offering better rates of interest on savings products. Online purchase discounts are a common approach in many markets.

Pricing level
The price set for a specific product or range of products.

Price elasticity of demand (see Digital marketing insight 5.3) assesses the extent to which a change in price will influence the demand for a product. It is calculated as the change in quantity demanded (expressed as a percentage) divided by the change in price as a percentage. Different products will naturally have different coefficients of price elasticity of demand depending on where they lie on the continuum of consumer tastes from relatively undifferentiated commodities to luxury, highly differentiated products where the brand perception is important.

Digital marketing insight 5.3 Price elasticity of demand

The formula for the price elasticity of demand is:

$$\text{Price elasticity of demand coefficient} = \frac{(\%\ \text{change in quantity demanded})}{(\%\ \text{change in price})}$$

Price elasticity for products is generally described as:

- *Elastic (coefficient of price elasticity > 1).* Here, the percentage change in quantity demanded is greater than the percentage change in price. In elastic demand, the demand curve is relatively shallow and a small percentage increase in price leads to a reduction in revenue. On balance overall, when the price is raised, the total revenue of producers or retailers falls since the rise in revenue does not compensate for the

fall in demand; and when the price is decreased, total revenue rises because the income from additional customers compensates in the decrease in revenue from reduced prices. Figure 5.10 shows the demand curve for a relatively elastic product (price elasticity = 1.67).

- *Inelastic demand (coefficient of price elasticity < 1).* Here, the percentage change in quantity demanded is smaller than the percentage change in price. In inelastic demand, the demand curve is relatively steep and a small percentage increase in price causes a small decrease in demand. On balance overall revenue increases as the price increases and falls as the price falls. Figure 5.11 shows the demand curve for a relatively inelastic product (price elasticity = 0.3125).

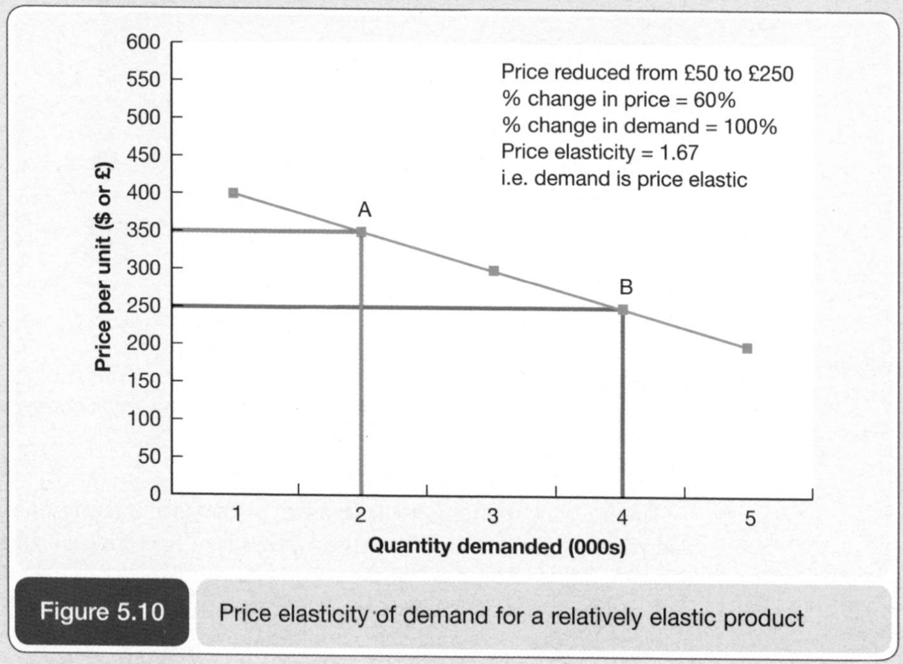

Figure 5.10 Price elasticity of demand for a relatively elastic product

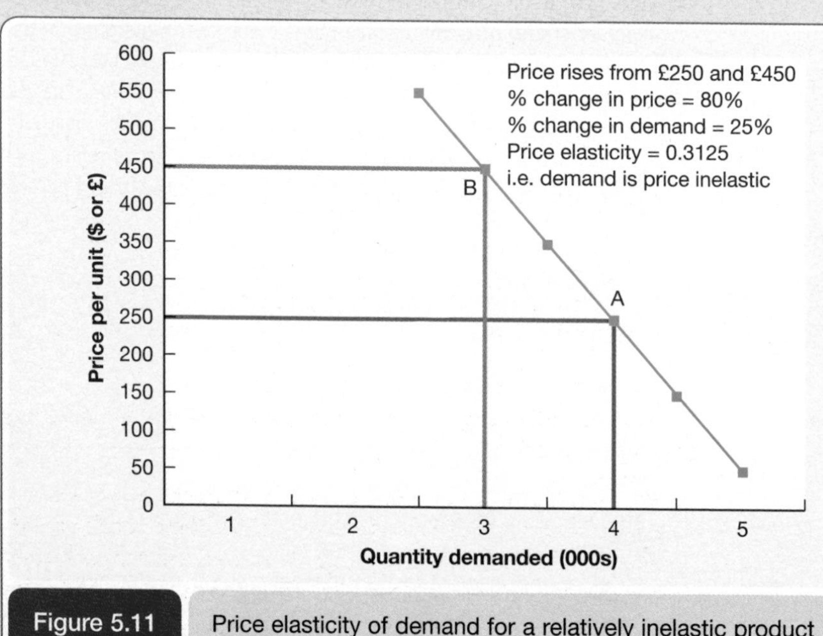

Figure 5.11 Price elasticity of demand for a relatively inelastic product

When the price elasticity coefficient is close to 1, this is described as unit elastic or unitary elastic. At the limits of elasticity, products will vary from:

- *Perfectly elastic (coefficient is not infinite)*, effectively shown as a horizontal line on demand curve graphs such as Figure 5.10 where any increase in the price will cause demand (and revenue for the goods) to drop to zero.
- *Perfectly inelastic (coefficient of price elasticity is zero)*, effectively shown as a vertical line on demand curve graphs such as Figure 5.11 where changes in the price do not affect the quantity demanded for the good.

When the price elasticity value is 1 of the demand for a good it is known as *unit elastic (or unitary elastic)*.

Discounting of the most popular products is another pricing approach used by both online and traditional retailers to acquire customers or drive sales. For example, online booksellers may decide to offer a discount of 50 per cent on the top 25 best-selling books in each category, for which no profit is made, but offer a smaller discount on less popular books to give a profit margin.

Xing *et al.* (2006) reported in their study of pricing levels for DVD merchants, summarised in Table 5.2, that traditional multichannel marketing companies tend to charge higher prices than pureplays or dot-com only companies, although pureplays will adjust their prices upwards more rapidly. However, they noted that this is market specific and when sales tax and shipping are taken into account, pureplays often charge more than multichannel merchants, as they found in a previous study of the consumer electronic market. They also found that **price dispersion** tended to be less for pureplays.

Price dispersion
The distribution or range of prices charged for an item across different retailers.

Table 5.2 A summary of the differences in pricing among DVD retailers from the research of Xing *et al.* (2006)

	All titles		Popular titles		Random titles	
Retailer type	**Average**	**Standard deviation**	**Average**	**Standard deviation**	**Average**	**Standard deviation**
Pureplay example – Amazon	21.51	3.90	21.05	3.72	21.99	4.02
Multichannel example – Borders	22.95	4.44	22.57	4.01	23.34	4.81
Pureplay average	20.54	3.75	20.42	3.60	20.6	63.90
Multichannel retailer average	22.28	4.27	22.02	4.19	22.55	4.33

Baker *et al.* (2000) suggest that companies should use the following three factors to assist in pricing.

1 *Precision.* Each product has a price-indifference band, where varying price has little or no impact on sales. The authors report that these bands can be as wide as 17 per cent for branded consumer beauty products, 10 per cent for engineered industrial components, but less than 10 per cent for some financial products. The authors suggest that while the cost of undertaking a survey to calculate price indifference is very expensive in the real world, it is more effective online.

2 *Adaptability.* This refers simply to the fact that it is possible to respond more quickly to the demands of the marketplace with online pricing. For some product areas, such as ticketing, it may be possible to dynamically alter prices in line with demand. Tickets.com adjusts concert ticket prices according to demand and has been able to achieve 45 per cent more revenue per event as a result. Arguably, in this case, and for other sought-after items such as computer games or luxury cars, the Internet can actually increase the price since there it is possible to reach more people.
3 *Segmentation.* This refers to pricing differently for different groups of customers. This has not traditionally been practical for B2C markets since at the point of sale, information is not known about the customer, although it is widely practised for B2B markets. One example of pricing by segments would be for a car manufacturer to vary promotional pricing, so that rather than offering every purchaser discount purchasing or cash-back, it is only offered to those for whom it is thought necessary to make the sale. A further example is where a company can identify regular customers and fill-in customers who only buy from the supplier when their needs can't be met elsewhere. In the latter case, up to 20 per cent higher prices are levied.

What then are the options available to marketers given this downward pressure on pricing? We will start by looking at traditional methods for pricing and how they are affected by the Internet. Bickerton *et al.* (2000) identify a range of options that are available for setting pricing.

1 *Cost-plus pricing.* This involves adding on a profit margin based on production costs. As we have seen above, a reduction in this margin may be required in the Internet era.
2 *Target-profit pricing.* This is a more sophisticated pricing method that involves looking at the fixed and variable costs in relation to income for different sales volumes and unit prices. Using this method the breakeven amount for different combinations can be calculated. For e-commerce sales the variable selling cost, i.e the cost for each transaction, is small. This means that once breakeven is achieved each sale has a large margin. With this model differential pricing is often used in a B2B context according to the volume of goods sold. Care needs to be taken that differential prices are not evident to different customers. One company, through an error on their website, made prices for different customers available for all to see, with disastrous results.
3 *Competition-based pricing.* This approach is common online. The advent of price-comparison engines such as Kelkoo (**www.kelkoo.com**) for B2C consumables has increased price competition and companies need to develop online pricing strategies that are flexible enough to compete in the marketplace, but are still sufficient to achieve profitability in the channel. This approach may be used for the most popular products, e.g. the top 25 CDs, but other methods, such as target-profit pricing; will be used for other products.
4 *Market-oriented pricing.* Here the response to price changes by customers making up the market are considered. This is known as 'the elasticity of demand'. There are two approaches. *Premium pricing* (or *skimming the market*) involves setting a higher price than the competition to reflect the positioning of the product as a high-quality item. Penetration pricing is when a price is set below the competitors' prices to either stimulate demand or increase penetration. This approach was commonly used by dot-com companies to acquire customers. The difficulty with this approach is that if customers are price-sensitive then the low price has to be sustained – otherwise customers may change to a rival supplier. This has happened with online banks – some customers regularly move to reduce costs of overdrafts for example. Alternatively if a customer is concerned by other aspects such as service quality it may be necessary to create a large price differential in order to encourage the customer to change supplier.

Whilst there is much research evidence that suggests the Internet has had a downwards impact on pricing, this may not be so prevalent in the future. As the Internet has become a more mainstream shopping channel, consumers are tending to focus more on the quality of the services provided rather than the price.

3 New pricing approaches (including auctions)

Forward auctions
Item purchased by highest bid made in bidding period.

Reverse auctions
Item purchased from lowest-bidding supplier in bidding period.

Offer
A commitment by a trader to sell under certain conditions.

Bid
A commitment by a trader to purchase under certain conditions.

The Internet has proved to have the technological capacity to create new pricing options. Figure 5.12 summarises different pricing mechanisms, which have been used effectively online. While many of these were available before the advent of the Internet and are not new, the Internet has made some models easier to apply. In particular, the volume of users makes traditional or **forward auctions** (B2C) and **reverse auctions** (B2B) more tenable – these have become more widely used than previously. Digital marketing insight 5.4 gives one example.

An **offer** is a commitment for a trader to sell under certain conditions, such as a minimum price. A **bid** is made by a trader to buy under the conditions of the bid, such as a commitment to purchase at a particular price. In a sealed-bid arrangement, suppliers submit their bids in response to an RFP posted to a website at a set time. In an open-bid arrangement, suppliers bid sequentially through a series of product lots or subgroups and can view their competitors' bids and respond in real time. A moving end-time (a 'soft close') is used for each lot, which means that any bid within the last minute of the closing time automatically extends the end time for a few minutes to allow other bidders to respond.

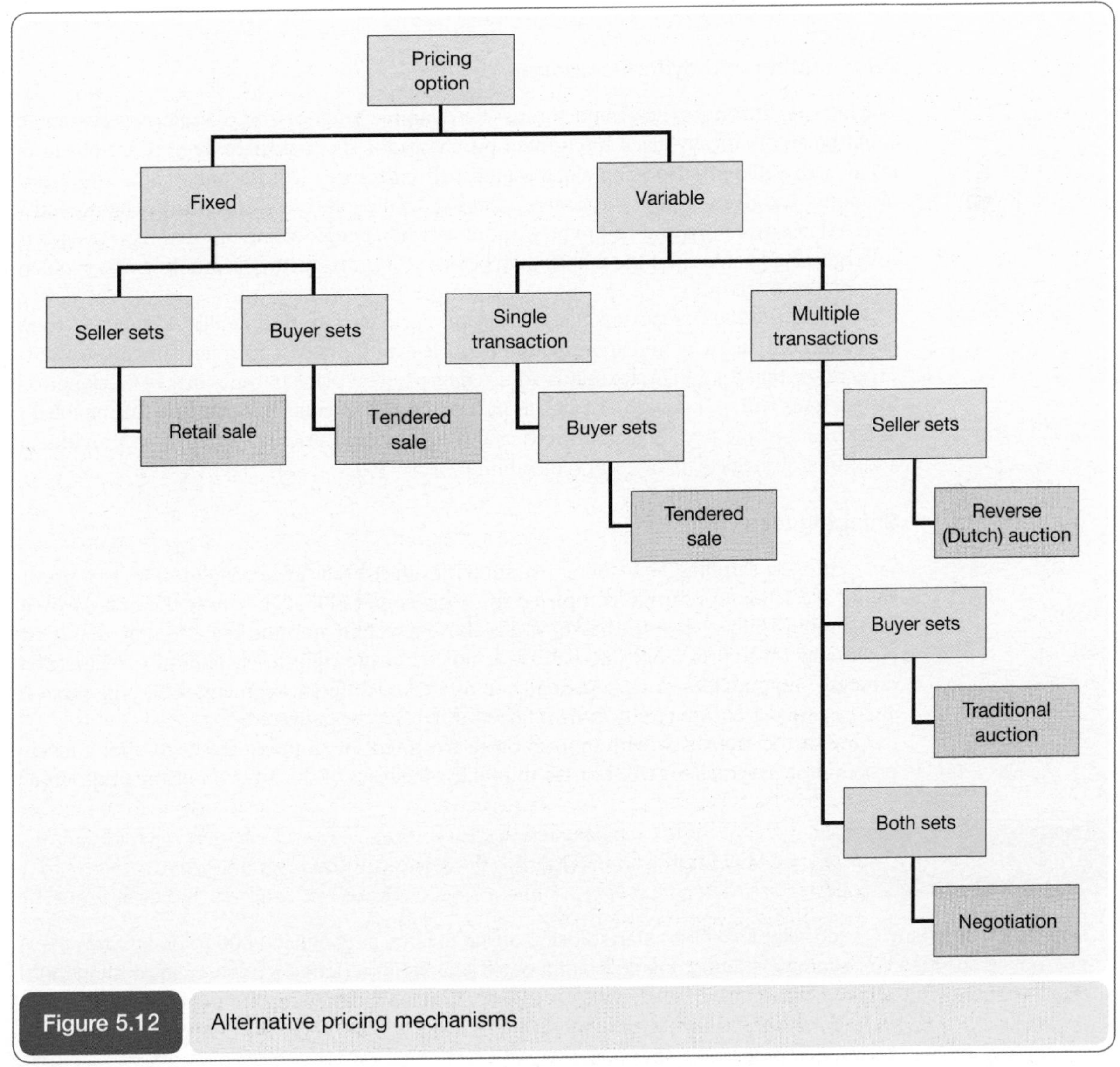

Figure 5.12 Alternative pricing mechanisms

Digital marketing insight 5.4 Dubli.com launches reverse auctions for consumer markets.

The Internet is creating opportunities for widescale application of different pricing models. The Dubli network is an example of a company which is applying the reverse auction concept to create consumer networks. Dubli is a marketing company, which originated in Germany, which aims to create retail shopping communities through the use of reverse auctions. The principle is that person-to-person referrals (word-of-mouth) is a very compelling way to spread commercial marketing messages. Consumers are invited to join reverse options and if they post the lowest bid they are able to but items are at significantly reduced prices. The aim for the marketing consultants is not selling products but gathering data.

Watch the Dubli promotional film to get an idea of how the company gets consumers to get involved at: **http://www.youtube.com/watch?v=7N4MTPYMC_g**.

Listen to what Michael Hanse has to say about Dubli and its future impact on shopping communities at: **http://www.globalonlineshoppingnetwork.net/dubli-shopping-2/michael-hansen-the-dubli-vision**.

Aggregated buying
A form of customer union where buyers collectively purchase a number of items at the same price and receive a volume discount.

Price testing and dynamic pricing

Dynamic pricing
Prices can be updated in real time according to the type of customer or current market conditions.

The Internet introduces new opportunities for **dynamic pricing** – for example, new customers could be automatically given discounted purchases for the first three items. Care has to be taken with differential pricing since established customers will be unhappy if significant discounts are given to new customers. Amazon trialled such a discounting scheme and it received negative press and had to be withdrawn when people found out that their friends or colleagues had paid less. If the scheme had been a clear introductory promotion this problem may not have arisen.

Baye *et al.* (2007) reported that European electronics online retailer Pixmania (**www.pixmania.com**) used price experimentation to learn about its customers' price sensitivity. They noted that for a PDA, Pixmania adjusted its product price 11 times in a 14-week period, from a low of £268 to a high of £283, as part of a series of small experiments that enabled it to learn about the price sensitivities of its customers. This pricing strategy also provides an additional strategic benefit – unpredictability.

Shipping fees

The setting of shipping fees can have a dramatic effect both on conversion rates and profitability according to research completed by Lewis *et al.* (2006). They note the popularity of free shipping offers when the basket size is above a certain amount, but also note that it can potentially cause profitability to fall if it is not set at the right level. They also suggest that different shipping fees could potentially be offered to different segments. Shipping fees can also be varied according to the time it takes for items to be delivered.

One further approach with innovation in treatment of shipping fees is to offer a loyalty programme in return for free express shipping – the basis of the Amazon Prime programme.

Mini Case Study 5.2 GlaxoSmithKline reduces prices through reverse auctions

Healthcare company GlaxoSmithKline (GSK) started using online reverse auctions in 2000 to drive down the price of its supplies. For example, it bought supplies of a basic solvent for a price 15 per cent lower than the day's spot price in the commodity market, and Queree (2000) reported that on other purchases of highly specified solvents and chemicals, SmithKline Beecham (prior to formation of GSK) regularly beat its own historic pricing by between 7 and 25 per cent. She says:

FreeMarkets, the company that manages the SmithKline Beecham auctions, quotes examples of savings achieved by other clients in these virtual marketplaces: 42% on orders for printed circuit boards, 41% on labels, 24% on commercial machinings and so on.

The reverse auction process starts with a particularly detailed Request for Proposals (RFP) from which suppliers ask to take part, and then selected suppliers are invited to take part in the auction. Once the bidding starts, the participants see every bid, but not the names of the bidders. In the final stages of the auction, each last bid extends the bidding time by one more minute. One auction scheduled for two hours ran for four hours and 20 minutes and attracted more than 700 bids!

4 Alternative pricing structure or policies

Different types of pricing may be possible on the Internet, particularly for digital, downloadable products. Software and music have traditionally been sold for a continuous right to use. As explained in more detail in the section on Product, the Internet offers new options such as payment per use, rental at a fixed cost per month, a lease arrangement and bundling with other products. The use of applications service providers (ASPs) to deliver service such as website traffic monitoring also gives new methods of volume pricing. Web analytics companies such as Adobe Ommiture (**www.ommiture.com**) and Webtrends (**www.webtrendslive.com**) charge in price bands based on the number of visitors to the purchaser's site.

Further pricing options which could be varied online include:

- basic price
- discounts
- add-ons and extra products and services
- guarantees and warranties
- refund policies
- order cancellation terms.

As a summary to the section on pricing, we summarise the research by Baye *et al.* (2007) which has many interesting examples of innovative online pricing approaches. They recommend that online retailers should ask the following questions when reviewing pricing online:

- *How many competitors are there at a point in time?* They suggest a product's markup should be increased when number of rivals falls and decreased when the number of rivals increases. They also recommend that since the identity of competitors online will differ from traditional offline rivals it is important to include key online competitors.
- *What is the position in the product lifecycle?* A product's markup should be decreased over its lifecycle or when new versions are introduced.
- *What is the price sensitivity or elasticity of a product?* They suggest continuously experimenting to learn from changes in the price sensitivity of a product.
- *What level is pricing set?* The optimal markup factor should be applied at the product rather than category or firm level based on price testing at the product level. They also note the variation of conversion rates and click-through fees from paid search engines and aggregators at the category or product level which makes it important to have micro-management of pricing.
- *Are rivals monitoring my price?* Be unpredictable if rivals are watching; exploit 'blind spots' if rivals are not watching.
- *Are we stuck in the middle?* A middle pricing point is sub-optimal particularly if prices can be set to target the lowest point in the market.

Place

Place variable
The element of the marketing mix that involves distributing products to customers in line with demand and minimising cost of inventory, transport and storage.

The **Place variable** of the marketing mix refers to how the product is distributed to customers. Typically, for offline channels, the aim of Place is to maximise the reach of distribution to achieve widespread availability of products while minimising the costs of inventory, transport and storage. In an online context, thanks to ease of navigating from one site to another, the scope of Place is less clear since Place also relates to Promotion and Partnerships. Take the example of a retailer of mobile phones. For this retailer to reach its potential audience to sell and distribute its product, it has to think beyond its own website to third-party websites where it can promote its services. Successful retailers are those that maximise their representation or visibility on third-party sites which are used by their target audiences. These third-party sites will include search engines, online portals reviewing mobile phones and product comparison sites. When thinking about representation on third-party sites, it is useful to think of the long-tail concept (Anderson, 2004) referenced in Figure 5.4. Across all Internet sites, there are a small number of sites including portals such as Google, MSN and Yahoo! which are very popular (the head which may theoretically account for 80 per cent of the volume of visitors) and a much larger number of sites that are less popular individually, but still collectively important. Similarly within a category of sites, such as automotive, there will be a few very popular sites, and then many niche sites which are collectively important in volume and may be more effective at reaching a niche target audience. When considering Place and Promotion, it is important to target both the head and the tail to maximise reach and to attract quality visitors to the destination site.

The main implications of the Internet for the Place aspect of the mix, which we will review in this section, are:

1. place of purchase
2. new channel structures
3. channel conflicts
4. virtual organisations.

1 Place of purchase

Suggesting the concept of place in relation to the Internet may seem peculiar; as it is a global virtual environment that crosses geographical boundaries, the issues associated with distribution, logistics and the point at which sales and other transactions take place are important for digital marketers. For example when selling physical goods there are cost and time issues associated with fulfilment (local, regional and international) together with issues of trust, culture and local support networks. However, in the case of sellers of digital products where there is no physical limitation on fulfilment – so, for example, Apple iTunes has proved successful in offering this service worldwide. Read Mini Case Study 5.3.

Mini Case Study 5.3 Internet retailing: the past, present and future

Retailers make a good case for exploring the impact of the Internet on the place element of the marketing. Since the beginning of the online shopping era there have been many predictions made about the likely impact of the Internet however, according to Doherty and Ellis-Chadwick (2010), not all of these have come to fruition. They state, 'Retailers are not cannibalising their own custom, virtual merchants do not dominate the market place and the high street has not been put out of business', but they are seeing a rise in the role of one to one marketing, increasing competition and a shift in power from the retailer to the consumer (Doherty and Ellis-Chadwick, 2010).

Currently, many academic studies are 'beginning to play down the chances of the Internet having a significant destabilising effect on the viability of the high street' (Doherty and Ellis-Chadwick, 2010). However, certain product activity sectors such as music, entertainment, printing publishing and travel agents have significantly reduced their high street presence due to the impact of the Internet. Furthermore, although in the majority of retail sectors the Internet is having less impact on the physicality of retailing it is widely agreed that consumer behaviour is changing in so far as shoppers are going online to find information about the products and services they wish to buy.

Whilst it may not be possible to determine the degree to which the Internet is going to impact on the physical high street it is clear that the influence of online shopping is set to rise.

Now listen to where UK retailers think they are going to be in the next five years: **http://itunes.apple.com/itunes-u/retail-management-marketing/id443383557.**

Source: Based on Doherty and Ellis-Chadwick (2010)

Evans and Wurster (1999) have argued that there are three aspects of 'navigational advantage' that are key to achieving competitive advantage online. These three, which all relate to the Place elements of the mix, are:

- *Reach.* Evans and Wurster say: 'It [reach] means, simply, how many customers a business can connect with and how many products it can offer to those customers'. Reach can be increased by moving from a single site to representation with a large number of different intermediaries. Allen and Fjermestad (2001) suggest that niche suppliers can readily reach a much wider market due to search-engine marketing (Chapter 8). Evans and Wurster also suggest that reach refers to the range of products and services that can be offered since this will increase the number of people the company can appeal to.
- *Richness.* This is the depth or detail of information which is both collected about the customer and provided to the customer. The latter is related to the richness of product information and how well it can be personalised to be relevant to the individual needs.
- *Affiliation.* This refers to whose interest the selling organisation represents – consumers' or suppliers' – and stresses the importance of forming the right partnerships. This particularly applies to retailers. The authors suggest that successful online retailers will reward customers who provide them with the richest information on comparing competitive products. They suggest this tilts the balance in favour of the customer.

Table 5.3 Different places for virtual marketplace representation

Place of purchase	Examples of sites
A Seller-controlled	• Vendor sites, i.e. home site of organisation selling products, e.g. **www.dell.com**
B Seller-oriented	• Intermediaries controlled by third parties to the seller such as distributors and agents, e.g. Opodo (**www.opodo.com**) represents the main air carriers. Amazon marketplace where third-parties can sell products
C Neutral	• Intermediaries not controlled by buyer's industry • Product-specific search engines, e.g. CNET (**www.computer.com**) • Comparison sites, e.g. uSwitch (**www.uswitch.com**), Auction space, e.g. eBay (**www.eBay.com**)
D Buyer-oriented	• My Supermarket (**www.mysupermarket.com**) • Intermediaries controlled by buyers, e.g. the remaining parts of the Covisint network of motor manufacturers • Discount sites for consumers such as voucher code sites, e.g. **www.myvouchercodes.com** and Cashback sites, e.g. GreasyPalm (**www.greasypalm.com**).
E Buyer-controlled	• Website procurement posting or reverse auctions on company's own site

Syndication

Syndication
Content or product information is distributed to third parties. Online this is commonly achieved through standard XML formats such as RSS.

Traditionally, **syndication** referred to articles or extracts from books being included in other publications such as newspapers and magazines. In an online context, this practice related to Place and partnerships needs to be reviewed for online content owners since there may be opportunities to generate additional revenue by re-publishing content on third-party sites through feeds, widgets or data exchange, or it may be possible to increase exposure on partner sites and so generate awareness or visits to the company site. For example, through its Connect service, Amazon.com enables authors to publish a blog on their site based on an RSS feed (see Chapter 1) from their own blog, so increasing awareness of the blog.

But syndication also has implications for other companies, and in particular retailers, since syndication of information from their product catalogues to third-party aggregators is important to extend their reach. This is also possible through feeds which have a particular format, for example the Google Base format (**http://base.google.com**) is used to provide results from Google Product Search (**www.google.com/products**) whose results are integrated into the Google search results pages. Figure 5.13 shows how some companies have used standard data feeds to promote their products within Google Product Search.

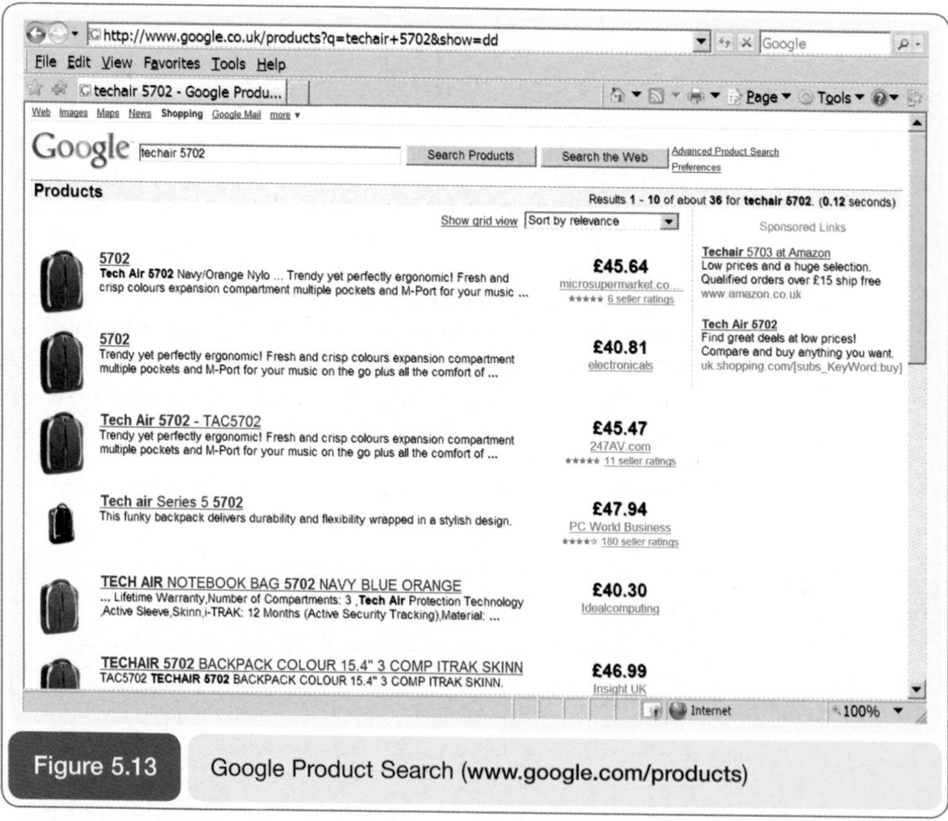

Figure 5.13 Google Product Search (**www.google.com/products**)

Since integrating product data with a range of aggregators which will require formats can be time consuming, some companies such as Channel Advisor (**www.channeladvisor.com**), now offer a service to upload data and track results across a range of aggregators.

Payment mechanisms – purchase place

Traditionally, online purchase will occur at the retailer through a partnership with an online secure payment provider such as Protx (**www.proxtx.com**) or Worldpay (**www.worldpay.com**). Effectively, the purchase transaction occurs on a different domain, but it is important that customers are reassured that the payment process is secure and to make it seamless. Retailers often offer payment mechanisms where the purchaser has already set up payment with another payment provider, e.g., of which PayPal (**www.paypal.com**) and Google Checkout (**www.google.com/checkout**) are dominant. This approach can assist with reassurance about privacy and security and increase purchase convenience and choice for the user, so these options also have to be reviewed.

Localisation

Localisation
Tailoring of website information for individual countries or regions. Localisation can include simple translation, but also cultural adaptation.

Providing a local site, with or without a language-specific version and additional cultural adaptations, is referred to as **localisation**. A site may need to support customers from a range of countries with:

- different product needs
- language differences
- cultural adaptation.

Some approaches used for cultural adaptation and localisation are described further in Chapter 7 in the section on localisation.

Activity 5.4 Place of purchase on the Internet

Purpose

To explore connections between physical and virtual locations.

Activity

Imagine you are going to purchase a new second hand car. Set out the stages in the process you might go through from thinking about the car you might buy to finding a place to purchase your car and then identifying the final car you might buy.

While you are going through this process try to identify when you will be using the Internet (virtual environment) and when you will be in the physical environment (e.g. visiting car dealers).

2 New channel structures

New channel structures enabled by the Internet have been described in detail in Chapters 2 and 4. The main types of phenomena that companies need to develop strategies for are:

- *Distintermediation.* Digital marketers should ask themselves the question; Is there an option for selling direct? But they should also remember that selling direct can lead to the channel conflicts (mentioned in the next section).
- *Reintermediation.* The new intermediaries created through reintermediation described by Sarkar *et al.* (1996) should be evaluated for suitability for partnering in affiliate arrangements, e.g. Kelkoo, who receive a commission on each click or sale resulting from a referral from their site.
- *Countermediation.* Countermediation refers to the strategic options to make better use of online intermediaries, for example through partnering with independent intermediaries, purchasing or creating its own independent intermediary. For example, a group of European airlines have joined forces to form Opodo (**www.opodo.com**) which is intended to counter independent companies such as Lastminute.com (**www.lastminute.com**) and eBookers (**www.ebookers.com**) in offering discount fares.

When considering channel structures it is important to remember that there may be implications for the physical distribution channel, e.g. grocery retailers have had to identify the best strategy for picking customers' goods prior to home delivery. Options include in-store picking (selection of items on customer orders) and regional picking centres. The former is proving more cost effective.

3 Channel conflicts

A significant threat arising from the introduction of an Internet channel is that while disintermediation gives a company the opportunity to sell direct and increase profitability on products, it can also threaten distribution arrangements with existing partners. Such channel conflicts are described by Frazier (1999), and need to be carefully managed. Frazier identifies some situations when the Internet should only be used as a communications channel. This is particularly the case where manufacturers offer an exclusive, or highly selective, distribution approach. To take an example, a company manufacturing expensive watches costing thousands of pounds will not in the past have sold direct, but will have used a wholesaler to distribute watches via retailers. If this wholesaler is a major player in watch distribution, then it is powerful and will react against the watch manufacturer selling direct. The wholesaler may even refuse to act as distributor and may threaten to distribute only a competitor's watches, which are not available over the Internet. Furthermore, direct sales may damage the product's brand or change its price positioning.

Further channel conflicts involve other stakeholders including sales representatives and customers. Sales representatives may see the Internet as a direct threat to their livelihood. In some cases, such as Avon cosmetics and Encyclopaedia Britannica, this has proved to be the case, with this sales model being partly or completely replaced by the Internet. For many B2B purchases, sales representatives remain an essential method of reaching the customer to support them in the purchase decision. Here, following training of sales staff, the Internet can be used as a sales support and customer education tool. Customers who do not use the online channels may also respond negatively if lower prices are available to their online counterparts. This is less serious than other types of channel conflict.

To assess channel conflicts it is necessary to consider the different forms of channel the Internet can take. These are:

- a communication channel only
- a distribution channel to intermediaries
- a direct sales channel to customers
- any combination of the above.

To avoid channel conflicts, the appropriate combination of channels must be arrived at. For example, Frazier (1999) notes that using the Internet as a direct sales channel may not be wise when a product's price varies considerably across global markets. In the watch manufacturer example, it may be best to use the Internet as a communication channel only.

Digital channel strategy will, of course, depend on the existing arrangements for the market. If a geographical market is new and there are no existing agents or distributors, there is unlikely to be channel conflict in that there is a choice of distribution through the Internet only or appointments of new agents to support Internet sales, or a combination of the two. Often SMEs will attempt to use the Internet to sell products without appointing agents, but this strategy will only be possible for retail products that need limited pre-sales and after-sales support. For higher-value products such as engineering equipment, which will require skilled sales staff to support the sale and after-sales servicing, agents will have to be appointed.

For existing geographical markets in which a company already has a mechanism for distribution in the form of agents and distributors, the situation is more complex, and there is the threat of channel conflict. The strategic options available when an existing reseller arrangement is in place have been described by Kumar (1999):

- *No Internet sales.* Neither the company nor any of its resellers makes sales over the Internet. This will be the option to follow when a company, or its resellers, feel that the number of buyers has not reached the critical mass thought to warrant the investment in an online sales capability.
- *Internet sales by reseller only.* A reseller who is selling products from many companies may have sufficient aggregated demand (through selling products for other companies) to justify the expenditure of setting up online sales. The manufacturer may also not have the infrastructure to fulfil orders direct to customers without further investment, whereas the reseller will be set up for this already. In this case it is unlikely that a manufacturer would want to block sales via the Internet channel.
- *Internet sales by manufacturer only.* It would be unusual if a manufacturer chose this option if it already had existing resellers in place. Were the manufacturer to do so, it would probably lead to lost sales as the reseller would perhaps stop selling through traditional channels.
- *Internet sales by all.* This option is arguably the logical future for Internet sales. It is also likely to be the result if the manufacturer does not take a proactive approach to controlling Internet sales.

Strategy will need to be reviewed annually and the sales channels changed as thought appropriate. Given the fast rate of change of e-commerce, it will probably not be possible to create a five-year plan! Kumar (1999) notes that history suggests that most companies have a tendency to use existing distribution networks for too long. The reason for this is that resellers may be powerful within a channel and the company does not want to alienate them, for fear of losing sales.

4 Virtual organisations

Benjamin and Wigand (1995) state that 'it is becoming increasingly difficult to delineate accurately the borders of today's organisations' and a further implication of the introduction of electronic networks such as the Internet is that it becomes easier to outsource aspects of the production and distribution of goods to third parties. This can lead to the boundaries within an organisation becoming blurred. Employees may work in any time zone, and customers are able to purchase tailored products from any location. The absence of any rigid boundary or hierarchy within the organisation should lead to a company becoming more responsive and flexible, and having a greater market orientation. Davidow and Malone (1992) describe the virtual corporation as follows:

> To the outside observer, it will appear almost edgeless, with permeable and continuously changing interfaces between company, supplier and customer. From inside the firm, the view will be no less amorphous, with traditional offices, departments, and operating divisions constantly reforming according to need. Job responsibilities will regularly shift.

Virtual organisation and virtualisation
A virtual organisation uses information and communications technology to allow it to operate without clearly defined physical boundaries between different functions. It provides customised services by outsourcing production and other functions to third parties.

Kraut *et al.* (1998) suggest the following features of a **virtual organisation**:

- Processes transcend the boundaries of a single form and are not controlled by a single organisational hierarchy.
- Production processes are flexible, with different parties involved at different times.
- Parties involved in the production of a single product are often geographically dispersed.
- Given this dispersion, co-ordination is heavily dependent on telecommunications and data networks.

Introna (2001) notes that a key aspect of the virtual organisation is strategic alliances or partnering. The ease of forming such alliances in the value network as described in Chapter 2 is one of the factors that has given rise to the virtual organisation.

Virtualisation
The process whereby a company develops more of the characteristics of a virtual organisation.

All companies tend to have some elements of the virtual organisation. The process whereby these characteristics increase is known as **virtualisation**. Malone *et al.* (1987) argued that the presence of electronic networks tends to lead to virtualisation since they enable the governance and co-ordination of business transactions to be conducted effectively at lower cost.

What are the implications for a marketing strategist of this trend towards virtualisation? Initially it may appear that outsourcing does not have direct relevance to market orientation. However, an example shows the relevance. Michael Dell relates (in Magretta, 1998) that Dell does not see outsourcing as getting rid of a process that does not add value, rather it sees it as a way of 'co-ordinating their activity to create the most value for customers'. Dell has improved customer service by changing the way it works with both its suppliers and its distributors to build a computer to the customer's specific order within just six days. This *vertical integration* has been achieved by creating a contractual vertical marketing system in which members of a channel retain their independence, but work together by sharing contracts.

So, one aspect of virtualisation is that companies should identify opportunities for providing new services and products to customers looking to outsource their external processes. The corollary of this is that it may offer companies opportunities to outsource some marketing activities that were previously conducted in-house. For example, marketing research to assess the impact of a website can now be conducted in a virtual environment by an outside company rather than by having employees conduct a focus group.

Referring to small and medium businesses, Azumah *et al.* (2005) indicate three levels of development towards what they term an e-organisation:

- 1/2-fusion organisations – minimum use of the Internet and network technologies.
- Fusion organisation – committed and intensive use of the Internet and network technologies.
- E-organisation – uses technologies as the core of the business for managing the entire business processes, from the point of receiving a customer order to processing the order and parts, and supplying and delivery.

Marshall *et al.* (2001) provide useful examples of different structures for the virtual organisation. These are:

- *Co-alliance model* – effort and risk are shared equally by partners.
- *Star alliance model* – here the effort and risk are centred on one organisation that subcontracts other virtual partners as required.
- *Value alliance model* – this is a partnership where elements are contributed across a supply chain for a particular industry. This is effectively the value network of Chapter 2.
- *Market alliance model* – this is similar to the value alliance, but is more likely to serve several different marketplaces.

Using the Internet to facilitate such alliances can provide competitive advantage to organisations operating in business-to-business markets since their core competences can be complemented by partnerships with third parties. This can potentially help organisations broaden their range of services or compete for work that on their own they may be unable to deliver. Such approaches can also be used to support business-to-consumer markets. For example, Dell can compete on price and quality in its consumer markets through its use of a star alliance model where other organisations are responsible for peripherals such as monitors or printers or distribution.

At a more practical level, electronic partnerships can be used to deliver the entire marketing mix referenced in this chapter through standardised data exchange interfaces which include:

- advertising through Paid Search networks (e.g. Google AdWords)
- promoting services through feeds on price comparison search engines (e.g. Kelkoo or Google Product Search)
- promoting services through affiliate networks (e.g. Commission Junction) or advertising networks (e.g. Google AdSense publishers programme)
- procuring expertise for short-term digital marketing work through an online web skills marketplace such as Elance (www.elance.com), Guru.com (www.guru.com), Scriptlance (www.scriptlance.com) or oDesk (www.oDesk.com)
- use of secure payment system services such as Paypal or Google Checkout
- analysis of web performance through online web analytics services (e.g Google analytics).

You can see that Google has been active in providing services to support businesses across many of these different aspects of the selling process.

Promotion

Promotion variable
The element of the marketing mix that involves communication with customers and other stakeholders to inform them about the product and the organisation.

The **Promotion variable** of the marketing mix refers to how marketing communications are used to inform customers and other stakeholders about an organisation and its products. The Internet and digital marketing techniques are important and have significant implications for marketing communication plan and for this reason digital promotions are covered in depth in Chapters 8 and 9. In this chapter the aim is to briefly outline the core components of Promotions.

Promotion is the element of the marketing mix that is concerned with communicating the existence of products or services to a target market. Burnett (1993) defines it as:

> the marketing function concerned with persuasively communicating to target audiences the components of the marketing program in order to facilitate exchange.

A broader view of promotion is given by Wilmshurst (1993):

> Promotion unfortunately has a range of meanings. It can be used to describe the marketing communications aspect of the marketing mix or, more narrowly, as in sales promotion. In its very broad sense it includes the personal methods of communications, such as face to face or telephone selling, as well as the impersonal ones such as advertising. When we use a range of different types of promotion – direct mail, exhibitions, publicity etc. we describe it as the promotional mix.

The main elements of the promotional or communications mix and their online equivalents summarised by Chaffey and Smith (2008) are shown in Table 5.4.

Table 5.4 The main elements of the promotional mix

Communications tool	Online implementation
Advertising	Interactive display ads, pay-per-click search advertising
Selling	Virtual sales staff, site merchandising, chat and affiliate marketing
Sales promotion	Incentives such as coupons, rewards, online loyalty schemes
Public relations	Online editorial, blogs, feeds, e-newsletters, newsletters, social networks, links and viral campaigns
Sponsorship	Sponsoring an online event, site or service
Direct mail	Opt-in e-mail using e-newsletters and e-blasts (solus e-mails)
Exhibitions	Virtual exhibitions and whitepaper distribution
Merchandising	Promotional ad-serving on retail sites, personalised recommendations and e-alerts
Packaging	Virtual tours, real packaging is displayed online
Word-of-mouth	Viral, affiliate marketing, e-mail a friend, links

Specification of the Promotion element of the mix is usually part of a communications strategy. This will include selection of target markets, positioning and integration of different communications tools. The Internet offers a new, additional marketing communications channel to inform customers of the benefits of a product and assist in the buying decision.

These are different approaches for looking at how the Internet can be used to vary the Promotion element of the mix:

1 reviewing new ways of applying each of the elements of the communications mix – such as advertising, sales promotions, PR and direct marketing
2 assessing how the Internet can be used at different stages of the buying process
3 using promotional tools to assist in different stages of customer relationship management from customer acquisition to retention. In a web context this includes gaining initial visitors to the site and gaining repeat visits through these types of communications techniques
   - reminders in traditional media campaigns why a site is worth visiting – such as online services and unique online offers and competitions
   - direct e-mail reminders of site proposition – new offers
   - frequently updated content – including promotional offers or information that helps your customer do their job or reminds them to visit.

The Promotion element of a marketing plan also requires three important decisions about investment for the online promotion or the online communications mix:

- *Investment in site promotion compared to site creation and maintenance.* Since there is often a fixed budget for site creation, maintenance and promotion, the e-marketing plan should specify the budget for each to ensure there is a sensible balance and the promotion of the site is not underfunded.
- *Investment in online promotion techniques in comparison to offline promotion.* A balance must be struck between these techniques. Typically, offline promotion investment often exceeds that for online promotion investment. For existing companies, traditional media such as print are used to advertise the sites, while print and TV will also be widely used by dot-com companies to drive traffic to their sites.
- *Investment in different online promotion techniques.* For example, how much should be paid for banner advertising as against online PR about online presence, and how much for search engine registration?

Digital marketing insight 5.5 Using data to shape advertising

Arguably, the promotional element of the mix has been affected significantly by the advent of the internet. Marketing communications in digital environments are a dialogue rather than a monologue and there can also be a high level of interaction. The implications of these changes are that marketers can create more focused, targeted and individual communication messages and campaigns. A key driver of such communications is data and the information it can reveal.

Listen to what Matt Brittin, head of Google operations has to say about the importance of data and how it can be used to shape advertising at: **http://www.open.ac.uk/openlearn/money-management/management/business-research-methods/matt-brittin-on-the-value-data.**

People, process and physical evidence

The people, process and physical evidence elements of the mix are closely related and often grouped as 'the service elements'. They are significant since the level of perceived service will impact a customer's loyalty and the probability of their recommending the service. Since this issue is closely related to the online customer experience, we also look at issues of website performance and response to customer e-mails in Chapter 7, including review of frameworks such as WEBQUAL and E-SERVQUAL for assessing service effectiveness.

Some of the key issues in improving the delivery of service online have been summarised by Rayport *et al.* (2005). They identify these questions that senior executives and managers should ask to assess the combination of technology and human assistance that is used to deliver service. We have added some typical examples of applications for each type:

1. *Substitution.* Deploying technology instead of people (or the opposite situation), for example:
   - frequently asked questions section on a website
   - in-site search engine
   - interactive sales dialogue recommending relevant products (Figure 5.3) based on human response
   - avatar offering answers to questions as in the Ikea Ask Anna feature
   - automated e-mail response or a series of 'Welcome' e-mails educating customers about how to use a service
   - using video to demonstrate products online.
2. *Complementarity.* Deploying technology in combination with people, for example:
   - call-back facility where the website is used to setup a subsequent call from contact centre
   - online chat facility – the user chats through text on the website
   - an employee using a WiFi-enabled hand-held device to facilitate easy rental car returns.
3. *Displacement.* Outsourcing or 'off-shoring' technology or labour, for example:
   - a fast-food chain centralising drive-through order taking in a remote call centre
   - the online chat or call-back systems referred to above can be deployed at a lower cost through outsourcing.

Note that this perspective doesn't stress another important aspect of the service elements of the online marketing mix, namely the participation by other customers in shaping a service through their feedback and the collaboration that occurs as customers will answer other customers questions in a forum.

We will now review the different elements of the service elements of the mix in more detail.

People

People variable
The element of the marketing mix that involves the delivery of service to customers during interactions with customers.

The **People variable** of the marketing mix relates to how an organisation's staff interact with customers and other stakeholders during sales and pre- and post-sales communications with them.

Chaffey and Smith (2008) make a similar point to Rayport *et al.* (2006) when they suggest that, online, the main consideration for the People element of the mix is the review of how staff involvement in the buying is changed, either through new roles such as replying to e-mails or online chat enquiries or through them being replaced through automated online services.

While the options for this form of customer service outlined above are straightforward, what is challenging is to implement the applications effectively. For example, if an FAQ doesn't have sufficient relevant answers or a call-back does not occur at the right time, then the result will be a dissatisfied customer who is unlikely to use a service again or will tell others about their experience either through ratings in shopping comparison engines (e.g. Figure 5.8) or sites created for this purpose such as Blagger (**www.blagger.com**).

To manage service, quality, organisations must devise plans to accommodate the five stages shown in Figure 5.14.

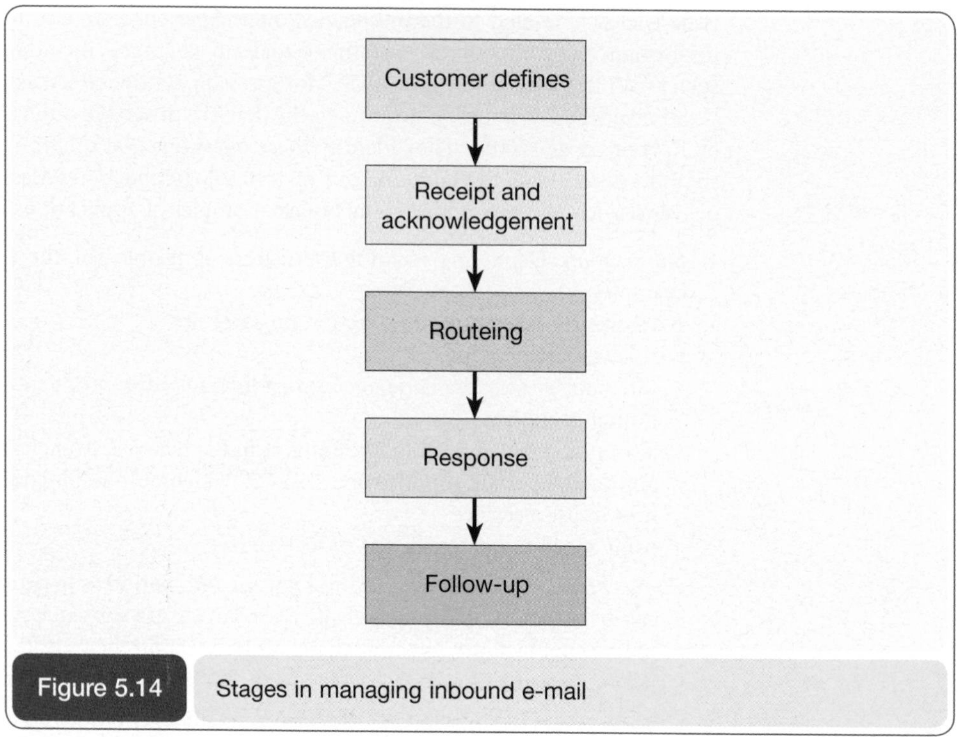

Figure 5.14 Stages in managing inbound e-mail

Stage 1: Customer defines support query

Companies should consider how easily the customer can find contact points and compose a support request on site. Best practice is clearly to find e-mail support options. Often, finding contact and support information on a website is surprisingly difficult. Standardised terminology on site is 'Contact Us', 'Support' or 'Ask a Question' (see Mini Case Study 5.4). Options should be available for the customer to specify the type of query on a web form or provide alternative e-mail addresses such as products@company.comor returns@company.comon site, or in offline communications such as a catalogue. Providing FAQs or automated diagnostic tools should be considered at this stage to reduce the number of inbound enquiries. Epson (**www.epson.co.uk**) provides an online tool to diagnose problems with printers and to suggest solutions.

Finally, the website should determine expectations about the level of service quality. For example, inform the customer that 'your enquiry will be responded to within 24 hours'.

Avatar
A term used in computer-mediated environments to mean a 'virtual person'. Derived from the word's original meaning: '*n.* the descendant of a Hindu deity in a visible form; incarnation; supreme glorification of any principle'.

Avatars are increasingly being used to reduce the need for enquiries such as 'Ask Anna' on the Ikea site. Research by Holzwarth *et al.* (2006) found that use of an avatar-based sales agent can lead to more satisfaction with the retailer, a more positive attitude towards the product and a greater purchase intent. They investigated the usage of 'attractive' versus 'expert' advisers dependent on the complexity of the purchase decision.

Stage 2: Receipt of e-mail and acknowledgement

Autoresponder or 'mailbots'
Software tool or 'agent' running on web servers that automatically sends a standard reply to the sender of an e-mail message.

Best practice is that automatic message acknowledgement occurs. This is usually provided by **autoresponder** software. While many autoresponders only provide a simple acknowledgement, more sophisticated responses can reassure the customer about when the response will occur and highlight other sources of information.

Stage 3: Routeing of e-mail

Best practice involves automated routeing or workflow. Routeing the e-mail to the right person is made easier if the type of query has been identified through the techniques described for Stage 1. It is also possible to use pattern recognition to identify the type of enquiry. For example, Nationwide (**www.nationwide.co.uk**) use Brightware's 'skill-based message routeing' so that messages are sent to a specialist adviser where specific enquiries are made. Such software can also be used at Stage 1 to give an autoresponse appropriate for the enquiry.

Mini Case Study 5.4 Online customer service at Barclays

In 2005, Barclays deployed web self-service to answer customers' questions online and reduce the 100,000 monthly calls to its helpdesk. Accessible on every page, via 'Ask a question', the Barclays solution allows customers to ask questions and receive meaningful, accurate answers on any subject from credit card offers to information about how the company scores credit.

In the first 12 months, 'Ask a question' was used by 350,000 customers and answered more than half-a-million questions. Only 8 per cent of customers escalated through to the call centre, pointing to high levels of customer satisfaction and resulting in improvements to call centre efficiency and quality of service. In 2007, more than two million customers used 'Ask a question' to find answers to their enquiries.

'Ask a question' is providing invaluable insight in the critical decision-making process about what concerns customers have and what products are of interest. For example, it identified a higher demand from personal banking customers for making foreign currency payments than was previously known to Barclays. This information is being used to inform the bank about customer trends and requirements, and for creating customer-driven website content.

It was apparent that website visitors who ask questions through web self-service were more than casual browsers but customers with genuine buying requirements. There was potential to increase sales conversion by putting the right information and product offer in front of these customers based on what they were asking about.'Ask a question' was enhanced to incorporate ad-serving, which serves up targeted advertising and sales promotions in response to questions asked by customers via the bank's website. The adverts change automatically depending on their relevance to customer questions, or to products and services Barclays wants to promote. For example, when customers ask questions about foreign currency accounts, 'Ask a question' will provide a specific answer and display adverts for travel insurance, the use of debit cards abroad and foreign mortgages. As well as promoting products directly relevant to the customer's search, ad-serving is used to cross-promote related products and services. These ads provide customers with an appealing call to action that speeds sales completion and increases response rates.

Advertising products alongside search results is producing high conversion rates with 12 per cent of customers responding to a product advertisement. 'Ask a question' is also improving usability, allowing customers to access all of the content relevant to them from a single click or question. By integrating ad-serving with 'Ask a question', Barclays have been able to achieve high levels of behavioural targeting that have previously only been available through expensive and complicated website analytics tools. Because advertisements and promotions are served in response to customer enquiries, there is no need for the system to log or track vast amounts of historical customer data to analyse and predict customer behaviour in order to deliver targeted information. This cuts the complexity of delivering targeted information and increases sales.

Source: Transversal (2008) *UK companies fail the multichannel customer service test*. Research report, March 2008, available online at www.transversal.com

Stage 4: Compose response

Best practice is to use a library of pre-prepared templates for different types of query. These can then be tailored and personalised by the contact centre employee as appropriate. The right type of template can again be selected automatically using the software referred to in

Stage 2. Through using such auto-suggestion, Nationwide has seen e-mail handling times reduced by 25 per cent for messages requiring adviser intervention. Sony Europe identifies all new support issues and adds them with the appropriate response to a central knowledge base.

Stage 5: Follow-up

Best practice is that if the employee does not successfully answer the first response, then the e-mail should suggest callback from an employee or a live chat. Indeed, to avoid the problem of 'e-mail ping-pong' where several e-mails may be exchanged, the company may want to proactively ring the customer to increase the speed of problem resolution, and so solve the problem. Finally, the e-mail follow-up may provide the opportunity for outbound contact and marketing, perhaps advising about complementary products or offers.

Process

Process variable
The element of the marketing mix that involves the methods and procedures companies use to achieve all marketing functions.

The **Process variable** of the marketing mix refers to the methods and procedures companies use to achieve all marketing functions – such as new product development, promotion, sales and customer service (as described in the previous section). The restructuring of the organisation and channel structures to accommodate online marketing which were described in the previous chapter are part of Process.

Customer contact strategies are a compromise between delivering quality customer service with the emphasis on customer choice and minimising the cost of customer contacts. Typical operational objectives that should drive the strategies and measure effectiveness are:

- to minimise average response time per e-mail and the range of response time from slowest to fastest. This should form the basis of an advertised service quality level.
- to minimise clear-up (resolution) time, for example number of contacts and elapsed time to resolution.
- to maximise customer satisfaction ratings with response.
- to minimise average staff time and cost per e-mail response.

Customer contact strategies for integrating web and e-mail support into existing contact centre operations usually incorporate elements of both of the following options:

- *Customer-preferred channel.* Here the company uses a customer-led approach where customers use their preferred channel for enquiry, whether it be phone call-back, e-mail or live chat. There is little attempt made to influence the customer as to which is the preferable channel. Note that while this approach may give good customer satisfaction ratings, it is not usually the most cost-effective approach, since the cost of phone support will be higher than customer self-service on the web, or an e-mail enquiry.
- *Company-preferred channel.* Here the company will seek to influence the customer on the medium used for contact. For example, easyJet encourages customers to use online channels rather than voice contact to the call centre for both ordering and customer service. Customer choice is still available, but the company uses the website to influence the choice of channel.

Physical evidence

Physical evidence variable
The element of the marketing mix that involves the tangible expression it is purchased and used.

The **Physical evidence variable** of the marketing mix refers to the tangible expression of a product and how it is purchased and used. In an online context, 'physical evidence' refers to the customer's experience of the company through the website. It includes issues such as site ease of use or navigation, availability and performance, which are discussed further in Chapter 7.

Case Study 5 The new Napster changes the music marketing mix

This case about the online music subscription service Napster illustrates how different elements of the mix can be varied online. It also highlights success factors for developing an online marketing strategy since Napster's proposition, objectives, competitors and risk factors are all reviewed.

The Napster brand has had a varied history. Its initial incarnation was as the first widely used service for 'free' peer-to-peer (P2P) music sharing. The record companies mounted a legal challenge to Napster due to lost revenues on music sales which eventually forced it to close. But the Napster brand was purchased and its second incarnation (*Figure 5.6*) offers a legal music download service in direct competition with Apple's iTunes. They also offer a music subscription service.

The original Napster

Napster was created between 1998 and 1999 by a 19-year-old called Shawn Fanning while he attended Boston's Northeastern University. He wrote the program initially as a way of solving a problem for a friend who wanted to find music downloads more easily online. The name 'Napster' came from Fanning's nickname.

The system was known as 'peer-to-peer' since it enabled music tracks stored on other Internet users' hard disks in MP3 format to be searched and shared with other Internet users. Strictly speaking, the service was not a pure P2P since central services indexed the tracks available and their locations in a similar way to which instant messaging (IM) works.

The capability to try a range of tracks proved irresistible and Napster use peaked with 26.4 million users worldwide in February 2001.

It was not long before several major recording companies backed by the RIAA (Recording Industry Association of America) launched a lawsuit. Of course, such an action also gave Napster tremendous PR and more users trialled the service. Some individual bands also responded with lawsuits. Rock band Metallica found that a demo of their song 'I disappear' began circulating on the Napster network and was eventually played on the radio. Other well-known artists who vented their ire on Napster included Madonna and Eminem by posting false 'Cuckoo Egg' files instead of music; Madonna asked the downloader: 'What the fuck do you think you're doing?'! However, not all artists felt the service was negative for them. UK band Radiohead pre-released some tracks of their album Kid A on to Napster and subsequently became Number 1 in the US despite failing to achieve this previously.

Eventually, as a result of legal action an injunction was issued on 5 March 2001 ordering Napster to cease trading in copyrighted material. Napster complied with this injunction, but tried to do a deal with the record companies to pay past copyright fees and to turn the service into a legal subscription service.

In the following year, a deal was agreed with German media company Bertelsmann AG to purchase Napster's assets for $8 million as part of an agreement when Napster filed for Chapter 11 bankruptcy in the United States. This sale was blocked and the web site closed. Eventually, the Napster brand was purchased by Roxio, Inc. which used the brand to rebrand their PressPlay service.

Since this time, other P2P services such as Gnutella, Grokster and Kazaa prospered, which have been more difficult for the copyright owners to pursue in court; however, many individuals have now been sued in the US and Europe and the association of these services with spyware and adware has damaged them, which has reduced the popularity of these services.

New Napster in 2010

In September 2008, Napster was purchased by US electronics retailer Best Buy for $US121 million. It has continued to innovate and develop distribution deals, for example:

- January 2010: Named primary music partner for My Coke Rewards
- January 2010: Release of an application programming interface (API), Consumer electronics and web developers of any size can easily integrate Napster content and services into their own products and web pages. Napster also used its own API to create a consistent look and feel to its services across all three screens – PC, mobile and TV.
- 2 October 2009: Dell consumer laptops and desktops in the US, UK and Germany to come with a Year of Napster
- 1 September 2009: Napster available on web-enabled phones via m.napster.com

However, competitors such as Spotify, Last.fm and of course iTunes tend to gain the largest number of mentions in the media and the Napster brand seems often to be still associated with the free download service.

The online music download environment has also changed with legal music downloading propelled through increasing adoption of broadband, the success of Apple iTunes and its portable music player, the iPod.

Napster gains its main revenues from online subscriptions and permanent music downloads. The Napster service offers subscribers on-demand access to over 6 million tracks that can be streamed or downloaded as well as the ability to purchase individual tracks or albums. Subscription fees are paid by end-user customers in advance. Napster also periodically licenses merchandising rights and resells hardware that its end-users use to store and replay their music.

BBC (2005) reports Brad Duea, president of Napster, as saying:

> *The number one brand attribute at the time Napster was shut down was innovation. The second highest characteristic was actually 'free'. The difference now is that the number one attribute is still innovation. Free is now way down on the list. People are able to search for more music than was ever possible at retail, even in the largest megastore.*

According to Security Exchange Commission 2008 10-K filing for Napstar, Napster had fiscal 2008 revenue of $127.5 million, an increase of 15 percent over the prior fiscal year; a loss of $16.5 million, an improvement compared with a loss of $36.8 million the prior fiscal year; and positive cash flow for the fiscal year ended 31 March 2008.

The Napster proposition

Napster subscribers can listen to as many tracks as they wish which are contained within the catalogue of over 6 million tracks. Napster users can listen to tracks on any compatible device that includes Windows Digital Rights Management (DRM) software, which includes MP3 players, computers, PDAs and mobile phones. Napster also has a store of 6 million MP3 tracks through its Napster Lite service.

Duea describes Napster as an 'experience' rather than a retailer. He says this because of features available such as:

- Napster recommendations
- Napster Radio based around songs by particular artists
- Napster Radio playlists based on the songs you have downloaded
- Swapping playlists and recommendations with other users.

iTunes and Napster are probably the two highest-profile services, but they have a quite different model of operating. There are no subscribers to iTunes, where users purchase songs either on a per-track basis or in the form of albums. By mid-2005, over half a billion tracks had been purchased on Napster. Some feel that iTunes locks people into purchasing Apple hardware; as one would expect, Duea of Napster says that Steve Jobs of Apple 'has tricked people into buying a hardware trap'.

But Napster's subscription model has also been criticised since it is a service where subscribers do not 'own' the music unless they purchase it at additional cost, for example to burn it to CD. The music is theirs to play either on a PC or on a portable player, but for only as long as they continue to subscribe to Napster. So it could be argued that Napster achieves lock-in in another form and requires a different approach to music ownership than some of its competitors.

Napster strategy

Napster (2005) describe their strategy as follows. The overall objective is to become the 'leading global provider of consumer digital music services'. They see these strategic initiatives as being important to achieving this:

- *Continue to Build the Napster Consumer Brand* – as well as increasing awareness of the Napster brand identity, this also includes promoting the subscription service which encourages discovery of new music. Napster (2005) say 'We market our Napster service directly to consumers through an integrated offline and online marketing program consistent with the existing strong awareness and perception of the Napster brand. The marketing message is focused on our subscription service, which differentiates our offering from those of many of our competitors. Offline marketing channels include television (including direct-response TV), radio and print advertising.'
- *Continue to Innovate by Investing in New Services and Technologies* – this initiative encourages support of a wide range of platforms from portable MP3 players, PCs, cars, mobile phones, etc. The large technical team in Napster shows the importance of this strategy. In the longer term, access to other forms of content such as video may be offered. Napster seem to view their ability to compete as depending substantially upon their intellectual property. They have a number of patents issued, but are also in dispute with other organizations over their patents.
- *Continue to Pursue and Execute Strategic Partnerships* – Napster has already entered strategic partnerships with technology companies (Microsoft and Intel), hardware companies (iRiver, Dell, Creative, Toshiba and IBM), retailers (Best Buy, Blockbuster, Radio Shack, Dixons Group, The Link, PC World, Currys, Target), and others (Molson, Miller, Energizer, Nestlé).
- *Continue to Pursue Strategic Acquisitions and Complementary Technologies* – this is another route to innovation and developing new services. Distribution partnerships with mobile providers are a key aspect of its strategy. In 2008, Napster launched Mobile music service with Telecom Italia which

serves more than 35 million subscribers; Entel PCS, the leading Chilean mobile operator with more than 5.5 million subscribers; and in Japan Napster Mobile for NTT DoCoMo.

Customers

The Register (2005) reported that in the UK, by mid-2005, Napster UK's 750,000 users had downloaded or streamed 55m tracks since the service launched in May 2004. The company said 80 per cent of its subscribers are over the age of 25, and half of them have kids. Some three-quarters of them are male. Its subscribers buy more music online than folk who buy one-off downloads do and research shows that one in five of them no longer buy CDs, apparently.

Describing its marketing strategy Napster says in its SEC filing:

> *We primarily focus our marketing efforts on online advertising, where we can most cost effectively reach our target audience of 25–40 year-olds, as well as strategic partnerships where we can market our service with complementary products. In the United Kingdom and Germany, we also market our paid Napster service directly to consumers through a predominately online marketing program, consistent with the existing strong awareness and perception of the Napster brand. The marketing message is focused on our subscription service, which differentiates our offering from many of our competitors. Our online marketing program includes advertising placements on a number of web sites (including affiliate partners) and search engines.*

Distribution

Napster's online music services are sold directly to end-users through the web site (**www.napster.com**). Affiliate networks and universities have procured site licences (in the US, a significant proportion of subscribers are university users). Prepaid cards are also available through retail partners such as Dixons in the UK, who also promote the service.

Napster also bundle its service with hardware manufacturers such as iRiver, Dell, Creative Labs, Gateway and Samsung.

Competition

Napster see their competitors for online music services in the US as Apple Computer's iTunes, Amazon, RealNetworks, Inc.'s Rhapsody, Yahoo! Unlimited, Sony Connect, AOL Music, MusicNet and MusicNow.

Napster (2005) believe that the main competitive factors affecting their market include programming and features, price and performance, quality of customer support, compatibility with popular hardware devices and brand.

Risk factors

In their annual report submission to the United States Securities and Exchange Commission, Napster is required to give its risk factors, which also give an indication of success factors for the business. Napster (2005) summarises the main risk factors as follows:

1. The success of our Napster service depends upon our ability to add new subscribers and reduce churn.
2. Our online music distribution business has lower margins than our former consumer software products business. Costs of our online music distribution business as a percentage of the revenue generated by that business are higher than those of our former consumer software products business. The cost of third-party content, in particular, is a substantial portion of revenues we receive from subscribers and end-users and is unlikely to decrease significantly over time as a percentage of revenue.
3. We rely on the value of the Napster brand, and our revenues could suffer if we are not able to maintain its high level of recognition in the digital music sector.
4. We face significant competition from traditional retail music distributors, from emerging paid online music services delivered electronically such as ours, and from 'free' peer-to-peer services.
5. Online music distribution services in general are new and rapidly evolving and may not prove to be a profitable or even viable business model.
6. We rely on content provided by third parties, which may not be available to us on commercially reasonable terms or at all.
7. We must provide digital rights management solutions that are acceptable to both content providers and consumers.
8. Our business could be harmed by a lack of availability of popular content.
9. Our success depends on our music service's interoperability with our customer's music playback hardware.
10. We may not successfully develop new products and services.
11. We must maintain and add to our strategic marketing relationships in order to be successful.
12. The growth of our business depends on the increased use of the Internet for communications, electronic commerce and advertising.
13. If broadband technologies do not become widely available or widely adopted, our online music distribution services may not achieve broad market acceptance, and our business may be harmed.

➜

14 Our network is subject to security and stability risks that could harm our business and reputation and expose us to litigation or liability.

15 If we fail to manage expansion effectively, we may not be able to successfully manage our business, which could cause us to fail to meet our customer demand or to attract new customers, which would adversely affect our revenue.

16 We may be subject to intellectual property infringement claims, such as those claimed by SightSound Technologies, which are costly to defend and could limit our ability to use certain technologies in the future.

Sources: BBC (2005), Napster (2005), Wikipedia (2005), *The Register* (2005) and *Wired* (2005). Reprinted by kind permission of Napster, LLC. Napster disclaims any obligation to update or correct any information provided here.

Question

Assess how Napster competes with traditional and online music providers by reviewing the approaches it uses for different elements of the marketing mix.

Summary

1 Evaluating the opportunities provided by the Internet for varying the marketing mix is a useful framework for assessing current and future digital marketing strategy.

2 *Product.* Opportunities for varying the core product through new information-based services and also the extended product should be reviewed.

3 *Price.* The Internet leads to price transparency and commoditisation and hence lower prices. Dynamic pricing gives the ability to test prices or to offer differential pricing for different segments or in response to variations in demand. New pricing models such as auctions are available.

4 *Place.* This refers to place of purchase and channel structure on the Internet. There are three main locations for e-commerce transactions: seller site, buyer site and intermediary. New channel structures are available through direct sales and linking to new intermediaries. Steps must be taken to minimise channel conflict.

5 *Promotion.* This aspect of the mix is discussed in more detail in Chapter 8.

6 *People, process and physical evidence.* These aspects of the mix are discussed in more detail in Chapters 6 and 7 where customer relationship management and service delivery are discussed.

Exercises

Self-assessment exercises

1 Select the two most important changes introduced by the Internet for each of the 7 Ps.

2 What types of product are most amenable to changes to the core and extended product?

3 Explain the implications of the Internet for Price.

4 What are the implications of the Internet for Place?

Essay and discussion questions

1 'The marketing mix developed as part of annual planning is no longer a valid concept in the Internet era.' Discuss.

2 Critically evaluate the impact of the Internet on the marketing mix for an industry sector of your choice.

3 Explain how the Internet has affected pricing policies.

4 Does 'Place' have any meaning for marketers in the global marketplace enabled by the Internet?

Examination questions

1 Describe three alternative locations for transactions for a B2B company on the Internet.
2 Explain two applications of dynamic pricing on the Internet.
3 How does the Internet impact an organisation's options for core and extended (augmented) product?
4 Briefly summarise the implications of the Internet on each of these elements of the marketing mix:
   a Product
   b Price
   c Place
   d Promotion.
5 Explain the reasons why the Internet could be expected to decrease prices online.
6 How can an organisation vary its promotional mix using the Internet?

References

Aaker, D. and Joachimsthaler, E. (2000) *Brand Leadership*. Free Press, New York.

Allen, E. and Fjermestad, J. (2001) E-commerce marketing strategies: a framework and case analysis, *Logistics Information Management*, 14(1/2), 14–23.

Anderson, C. (2004) The Long Tail. *Wired*. 12, October, **www.wired.com/wired/archive/ 12.10/tail.html.**

Azumah, G., Loh, S. and McGuire, S. (2005) E-organisation and its future implication for SMEs, *Production Planning & Control*, 6(6), September, 555–62

Baker, W., Marn, M. and Zawada, C. (2000) Price smarter on the Net, *Harvard Business Review*, February, 2–7.

Baye, M., Gatti, J., Kattuman, P. and Morgan, J. (2007) Dashboard for online pricing, *The California Management Review*, Fall, 50(1), 202–16.

BBC (2005) Napster boss on life after piracy, by Derren Waters, 22 August, **http://news.bbc.co.uk/1/hi/entertainment/music/4165868.stm.**

Benjamin, R. and Wigand, R. (1995) Electronic markets and virtual value-chains on the information superhighway, *Sloan Management Review*, Winter, 62–72.

Bickerton, P., Bickerton, M. and Pardesi, U. (2000) *CyberMarketing*, 2nd edn, Butterworth-Heinemann, Oxford.

Booms, B. and Bitner, M. (1981) Marketing strategies and organisation structures for service firms, in J. Donnelly and W. George (eds), *Marketing of Services*. American Marketing Association, New York.

BrandNewWorld (2004) AOL research published at: **www.brandnewworld.co.uk.**

Brynjolfsson, E., Smith, D. and Hu, Y. (2003) Consumer surplus in the digital economy: estimating the value of increased product variety at online booksellers, *Management Science*, 49(11), 1580–96, **http://ebusiness.mit.edu/research/papers/176_ErikB_Online-Booksellers2.pdf.**

Burnett, J. (1993), *Promotional Management*. Houghton Mifflin, Boston.

Burt, S. (2010) Retailing in Europe: 20 years on, *International Review of Retail, Distribution and Consumer Research*, 20(1), 9–27.

Chaffey, D. and Smith, P.R. (2008) *E-marketing Excellence: Planning and Optimising Your Digital Marketing*, 3rd edn, Butterworth-Heinemann, Oxford.

Christodoulides, G. and de Chernatony, L. (2004) Dimensionalising on- and offline brands' composite equity, *Journal of Product and Brand Management*, 13(3), 168–79.

Christodoulides, G, de Chernatony, L., Furrer, O., Shiu, E. and Temi, A. (2006) Conceptualising and measuring the equity of online brands, *Journal of Marketing Management*, September, 22,(7/8), 799–825.

Davidow, W.H. and Malone, M.S. (1992) *The Virtual Corporation. Structuring and Revitalizing the Corporation for the 21st Century*, HarperCollins, New York.

de Chernatony, L. (2001) Succeeding with brands on the Internet, *Journal of Brand Management*, 8(3), 186–95.

de Chernatony, L. and McDonald, M. (1992) *Creating Powerful Brands*. Butterworth-Heinemann, Oxford.

Delgado, E. and Hernandez, M. (2008) Building online brands through brand alliances in Internet, *European Journal of Marketing*, 42(9/10), 954–76.

Doherty, N.F. and Ellis-Chadwick, F. (2010) Internet retailing: the past, the present and the future, *International Journal of Retail & Distribution Management*, 38(11/12), 943–65.

Evans, P. and Wurster, T.S. (1999) Getting real about virtual commerce, *Harvard Business Review*, November, 84–94.

Flores, L. (2004) 10 Facts about the value of brand websites, AdMap, February, 26–8, **http://www.imediaconnection.com/content/wp/admap.pdf.**

Frazier, G. (1999) Organising and managing channels of distribution, *Journal of the Academy of Marketing Science*, 27(2), 222–40.

Ghosh, S. (1998) Making business sense of the Internet, *Harvard Business Review*, March–April, 127–35.

Gladwell, M. (2000) *The Tipping Point: How Little Things can Make a Big Difference*. Little, Brown, New York.

Harridge-March, S. (2004) Electronic marketing, the new kid on the block, *Marketing Intelligence and Planning*, 22(3), 297–309.

Holzwarth, M., Janiszewski, C. and Neumann, M. (2006) The influence of avatars on online consumer shopping behavior, *Journal of Marketing*, 70(October), 19–36.

Introna, L. (2001) Defining the virtual organisation, in S. Barnes and B. Hunt (eds), *E-Commerce and V-Business: Business Models for Global Success*, Butterworth-Heinemann, Oxford.

Jobber, D. (2010) *Principles and Practice of Marketing*, 6th edn. McGraw-Hill.

Johnson, E., Moe, W., Fader, P., Bellman, S. and Lohse, G. (2004) On the depth and dynamics of online search behavior, *Management Science*, 50(3), 299–308.

Keen, A. (2009) The Internet will devour newspapers, *The Telegraph*, Technology Section, 8 October, **http://www.telegraph.co.uk/technology/6271317/The-internet-will-devour-newspapers. html**, accessed October 2011.

Kraut, R., Chan, A., Butler, B. and Hong, A. (1998) Coordination and virtualisation: the role of electronic networks and personal relationships, *Journal of Computer Mediated Communications*, 3(4).

Kumar, N. (1999) Internet distribution strategies: dilemmas for the incumbent, *Financial Times*, Special issue on mastering information management, no. 7. Electronic Commerce (**www.ftmastering.com**).

Lautenborn, R. (1990) New marketing litany: 4Ps passes; C-words take over, *Advertising Age*, 1 October, 26.

Lewis, M., Singh, V. and Fay, S. (2006) An empirical study of the impact of nonlinear shipping and handling fees on purchase incidence and expenditure decisions, *Marketing Science*, 25(1), January–February, 51–64.

Magretta, J. (1998) The power of virtual integration. An interview with Michael Dell, *Harvard Business Review*, March–April, 72–84.

Malone, T., Yates, J. and Benjamin, R. (1987) Electronic markets and electronic hierarchies: effects of information technology on market structure and corporate strategies, *Communications of the ACM*, 30(6), 484–97.

Marn, M. (2000) Virtual pricing, *McKinsey Quarterly*, No. 4.

Marsden, P. (2004) Tipping point marketing: a primer, *Brand strategy*, April, available at: www.viralculture.com/pubs/tippingpoint2.htm.

Marshall, P., McKay, J. and Burn J. (2001) Structure, strategy and success factors in the virtual organisation, in S. Barnes and B. Hunt (eds) *E-Commerce and V-Business. Business Models for Global Success*, Butterworth-Heinemann, Oxford.

McCarthy, J. (1960) *Basic marketing: a managerial approach*, Richard D. Irwin, Homewood, Illinois.

Meyer, D. (2011) Google opens a 'Chrome Zone' shop in London, http://www.zdnet.co.uk/blogs/communication-breakdown-10000030/google-opens-a-chrome-zone-shop-in-london-10024474/, accessed October 2011.

Morris, R.J. and Martin, C.L. (2000) Beanie Babies: a case study in the engineering of a high involvement/relationship-prone brand, *Journal of Product and Brand Management*, 9(2), 78–98.

Napster (2005) Annual Report, published at Investor relations site (http://investor. napster.com).

Peppard, J. and Rylander, A. (2005) Products and services in cyberspace, *International Journal of Information Management*, 25(4).

Pitt, L., Berthorn, P., Watson, R. and Ewing, M. (2001) Pricing strategy and the net, *Business Horizons*, March–April, 45–54.

Quelch, J. and Klein, L. (1996) The Internet and international marketing, *Sloan Management Review*, Spring, 61–75.

Queree, A. (2000) *Financial Times*, Technology Supplement, 1 March.

Rayport, J., Jaworski, B. and Kyung, E. (2005) Best face forward: improving companies' service interfaces with customers, *Journal of Interactive Marketing*, 19(4), 67–80.

Ries, A. and Ries, L. (2000) *The 11 Immutable Laws of Internet Branding*. HarperCollins Business, London.

Sarkar, M., Butler, B. and Steinfield, C. (1996) Intermediaries and cybermediaries: a continuing role for mediating players in the electronic marketplace, *Journal of Computer Mediated Communication*, 1(3).

Sawhney, M., Verona, G. and Prandelli, E. (2005) Collaborating to create: the Internet as a platform for customer engagement in product innovation. *Journal of Interactive Marketing*, 19(4), Autumn, 4–17.

The Register (2005) Napster UK touts subscriber numbers. *The Register*, Tony Smith, 5 September. www.theregister.co.uk/2005/09/05/napster_numbers.

The Telegraph (2011) http://www.telegraph.co.uk/telegraphtv/6271276/VIDEO-EMBED-Whats-next-for-news-A-conversation-about-journalism.html, accessed October 2011.

Wilmshurst, J. (1993), *Below the Line Promotion*, Butterworth-Heinemann, Oxford.

Xing, X., Yang, S. and Tang, F. (2006) A comparison of time-varying online price and price dispersion between multichannel and dotcom DVD retailers, *Journal of Interactive Marketing*, 20(2), 3–20.

Further reading

Allen, E. and Fjermestad, J. (2001) E-commerce marketing strategies: a framework and case analysis, *Logistics Information Management*, 14(1/2), 14–23. Includes an analysis of how the 4 Ps are impacted by the Internet.

Baker, W., Marn, M. and Zawada, C. (2000) Price smarter on the Net, *Harvard Business Review*, February, 2–7. This gives a clear summary of the challenges and opportunities of Internet pricing.

Ghosh, S. (1998) Making business sense of the Internet, *Harvard Business Review*, March–April, 127–35. This paper gives many examples of how US companies have adapted their products to the Internet and asks key questions that should govern the strategy adopted.

Harridge-March, S. (2004) Electronic marketing, the new kid on the block. *Marketing Intelligence and Planning*, 22(3), 297–309. Like the Allen and Fjermestad (2001) paper, this gives a review of the impact of the Internet on different aspects of the marketing mix.

Kumar, N. (1999), Internet distribution strategies: dilemmas for the incumbent, *Financial Times*, Special issue on mastering information management, no. 7. Electronic Commerce (www.ftmastering.com). This article assesses the impact of the Internet on manufacturers and their distribution channels. The other articles in this special issue are also interesting.

Smith, P.R. and Chaffey, D. (2005) *E-Marketing Excellence: at the Heart of EBusiness*, 2nd edn. Butterworth-Heinemann, Oxford. Chapter 2 is devoted to applying the marketing mix to Digital marketing.

Weblinks

- **Chris Anderson** has a blog site (www.thelongtail.com), the Long Tail, to support his book on the topic published in 2006 by Hyperion, New York.
- **CIM 10-minute guide to achieving an effective marketing mix.** (http://www.cim.co.uk/filestore/resources/10minguides/marketingmix.pdf). A fairly detailed introduction to the marketing mix with further links.
- **ClickZ** (www.clickz.com). An excellent collection of articles on online marketing communications, US-focused. Relevant section for this chapter: brand marketing.
- **The culturally customized website** (www.theculturallycustomizedwebsite.com). Resources supporting the authors' book of this title.
- **Gladwell.com** (www.gladwell.com). Author's site with extracts from *The Tipping Point* and other books.
- **Paul Marsden's** Viral Culture site (www.viralculture.com). Articles related to *The Tipping Point* and connected marketing.

Chapter 6

Relationship marketing using digital platforms

Chapter at a glance

Main topics

Case studies

Learning objectives

After reading this chapter, the reader should be able to:

- Assess the relevance and alternative approaches for using digital platforms for customer relationship management
- Evaluate the potential of the Internet to support one-to-one marketing, and the range of techniques and systems available to support dialogue with the customer through digital media
- Assess how to integrate social and mobile interactions to develop social CRM capabilities

Questions for marketers

Key questions for marketing managers related to this chapter are:

- How can the digital platforms be used to increase the value of customers through the customer lifecycle?
- How do I implement permission marketing with mobile, social and messaging applications?
- How can I apply personalisation and mass customisation cost effectively in my marketing?

Scan code to find the latest updates for topics in this chapter

Links to other chapters

This chapter is related to other chapters as follows:

- Chapter 4 introduces customer lifecycle-based segmentation models
- Chapter 7 has guidelines on how to develop the right customer experience to assist in forming and maintaining relationships
- Chapter 8 describes methods of acquiring customers for one-to-one marketing
- Chapters 10 and 11 give examples of relationship marketing in the business-to-consumer and business-to-business markets

Introduction

Building long-term relationships with customers is essential for any sustainable business, and this applies equally to online elements of a business. Failure to build relationships to gain repeat visitors and sales largely caused the failure of many dot-coms following huge expenditure on customer acquisition. Research summarised by Reichheld and Schefter (2000) showed that acquiring online customers is so expensive (he suggested 20–30 per cent higher than for traditional businesses) that start-up companies may remain unprofitable for at least two to three years. The research also shows that by retaining just 5 per cent more customers, online companies can boost their profits by 25 per cent to 95 per cent.

Customer relationship management (CRM)
A marketing-led approach to building and sustaining long-term business with customers.

One-to-one marketing
A unique dialogue occurs between a company and individual customers (or groups of customers with similar needs).

Over the last two decades or more, relationship marketing, direct marketing and database marketing have combined to create a powerful new marketing paradigm. This paradigm is often referred to as **customer relationship management (CRM)**. A related approach is known as **one-to-one marketing** where, in theory, relationships are managed on an individual basis. But, owing to the costs of managing relationships on an individual level, many companies will apply CRM by using approaches which automate the tailoring of services to develop relationships with particular customer segments or groups, rather than individuals. These tailored messages can then be delivered by e-mail marketing or recommendations and promotions on the website. Delivering the relevant messages involves a company in developing a long-term relationship with each customer in order to better understand that customer's needs and then deliver services that meet these individual needs. How to achieve the levels of customer satisfaction necessary to encourage loyalty is a major focus within this chapter. Mini Case Study 6.1 shows an inspiring example of how relentless focus on the customer has built a company.

Mini Case Study 6.1 Zappos deliver customer happiness

Zappos are a US online clothing retailer often referred to as a pioneer in online marketing. Tony Hsieh, CEO of Zappos, puts their success down to a customer-centric approach. He says simply 'We pay more attention to our customers'. He explains,'People may not remember exactly what you did or what you said, but they will always remember how you made them feel'. Tony's summary of the evolution of the Zappos brand has seen it go from simply having a strong customer focus to their being really passionate about how they make their customers feel (Figure 6.1):

1999 Selection
2003 Customer Service
2005 Culture and Core Values as our platform
2007 Personal Emotional Connection
2009 Delivering Happiness

Overall, the approach seems to be successful. In 2009, Amazon purchased Zappos for $1.2 billion. Here is our summary of the five success factors we can take from Zappos' success which can be applied to other businesses:

1 **Customers come back, order more and more often.**
   - On any given day, about 75 per cent of purchases from Zappos are from returning customers.
   - Repeat customers order >2.5 × more from in the following 12 months.
   - Repeat customers spend more.

2 **Make it easy for customers to build your brand.**
   - Superior experience drives word of mouth, so do the unexpected.
   - Remove the risk of purchase and make it easy to return product for free.
   - Fast, accurate fulfilment is worth talking about.

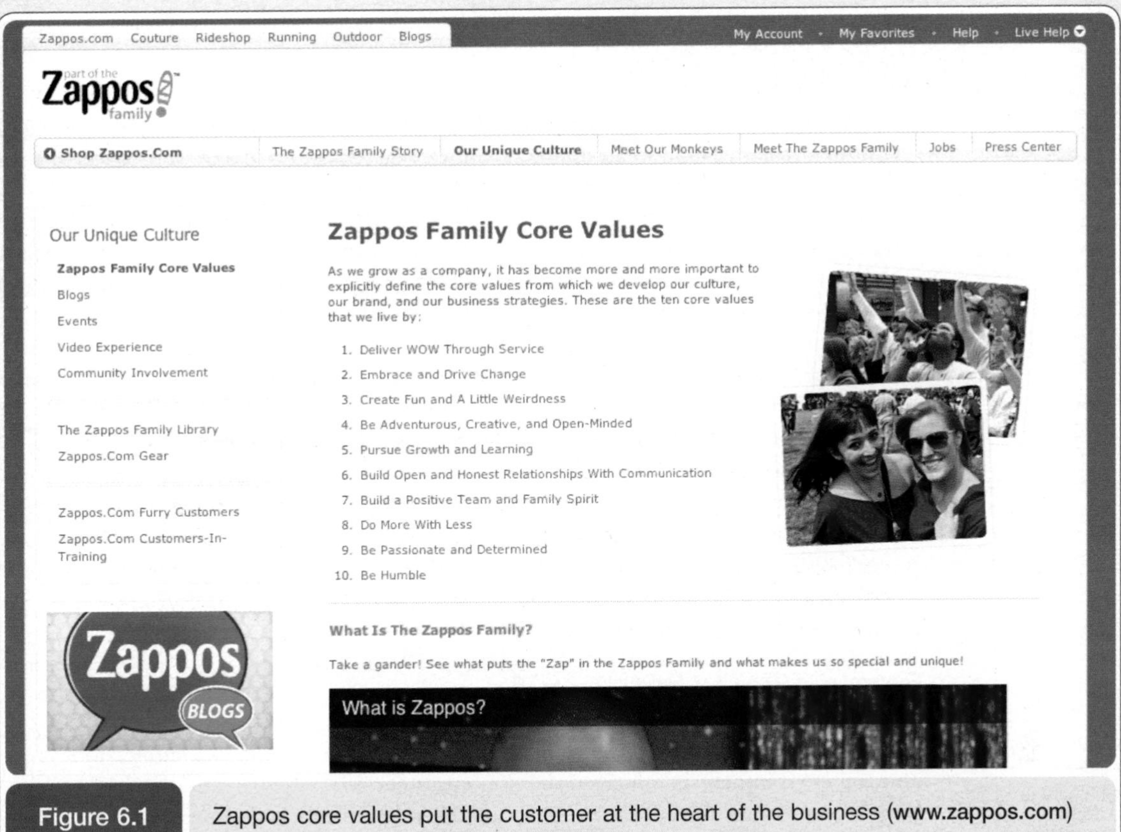

Figure 6.1 Zappos core values put the customer at the heart of the business (www.zappos.com)

- Deliver an 'above and beyond' customer service.
- Drive people to the phone, be contactable and be open.

3 **Talk to people!**
- 'The telephone is one of the best branding devices available.'
- Take time to talk to people properly.
- At Zappos there are no call times and no sales-based performance goals for sales reps.
- Zappos will also pay you $2000 to quit, so only the best people who enjoy the job stay.
- The Culture Book makes it clear how Zappos do business and even underpins performance management.

4 **Build a culture that envelops customers and internal staff**:
- Zappos have 'committable core values' that are clear, exciting and simple.
- It doesn't matter what your core values are as long as you commit to them and get internal alignment.
- Commit to a culture of transparency: 'An Ask Anything Culture'.
- Zappos insights.com focuses on lifting the lid for customers and future employees.

5 **Have a vision...**
- 'Whatever you're thinking, think bigger', comments Tony.
- Does your company vision have real meaning? Without is there little chance of achieving any of the above.
- 'What would you be passionate about doing for ten years even if you never made a dime?'

Source: Hsieh (2010), Delivering customer happiness: a presentation by Zappos CEO Tony Hsieh with Tony Robbins, http://www.slideshare.net/zappos/zappos-tony-robbins-business-mastery-011610, accessed October 2011.

Electronic customer relationship management (E-CRM) Using digital communications technologies to maximise sales to existing customers and encourage continued usage of online services through techniques including database, personalised web messages, customer services, email and social media marketing.

Electronic customer relationship management (E-CRM) involves creating strategies and plans for how digital technology and digital data can support CRM.

Digital marketing activities which are within the scope of E-CRM which we will cover in this chapter include:

- Using the *website and online social presences for customer development* from generating leads through to conversion to an online or offline sale using e-mail and web-based content to encourage purchase.
- *Managing customer profile information and e-mail list quality* (coverage of e-mail addresses and integration of customer profile information from other databases to enable targeting).
- Managing customer contact options through mobile, *e-mail and social networks* to support up-sell and cross-sell.
- *Data mining* to improve targeting.
- Providing online personalisation or *mass customisation* facilities to automatically recommend the 'next-best product'.
- Providing *online customer service facilities* (such as frequently asked questions, call-back and chat support).
- Managing *online service quality* to ensure that first-time buyers have a great customer experience that encourages them to buy again.
- Managing the *multichannel customer experience* as they use different media as part of the buying process and customer lifecycle.

From E-CRM to Social CRM

Electronic customer relationship management (E-CRM) Using digital communications technologies to maximise sales to existing customers and encourage continued usage of online services.

Social CRM The process of managing customer-to-customer conversations to engage existing customers, prospects and other stakeholders with a brand and so enhance customer-relationship management.

The interactive nature of the web combined with e-mail and mobile communications provides an ideal environment in which to develop customer relationships, and databases provide a foundation for storing information about the relationship and providing information to strengthen it by improved, personalised services. This online approach to CRM is often known as **electronic customer relationship management (E-CRM)**. E-CRM, can be characterised as sense and respond communications. The classic example of this is the personalisation facilities provided by Amazon where personal recommendations are provided through e-mail marketing and personalised messages to site visitors.

In previous chapters, we have seen the growing popularity of social media with consumers and as a marketing technique. It's natural that a new marketing approach, **social CRM** has developed to determine how social media can be applied to develop customer relationships and customer value. The scope of E-CRM and social CRM crosses many business processes as suggested by Figure 6.2.

The scope of each area shown in Figure 6.2 is:

1. *Marketing.* Monitoring, analysis and response of customer conversations through social listening tools.
2. *Sales.* Understanding where prospects are discussing selection of products and services offered by you and competitors and determining the best way to get involved in the conversation to influence sales and generate leads. Within B2B, Linked-In is an obvious location that should be monitored.
3. *Service and support.* Customer self-help through forums provided by you and neutral sites.
4. *Innovation.* Using conversations to foster new product development or enhance online offerings is one of the most exciting forms of social CRM.
5. *Collaboration.* This is e-business collaboration within an organisation through an intranet and other software tools to encourage all forms of collaboration which support business process.
6. *Customer experience.* This references the use of social CRM to enhance the customer experience and add value to a brand which is implied by many of the other aspects above. It gives the examples of using VIP programmes offering collaboration between customers with shared characteristics to add value and create advocacy.

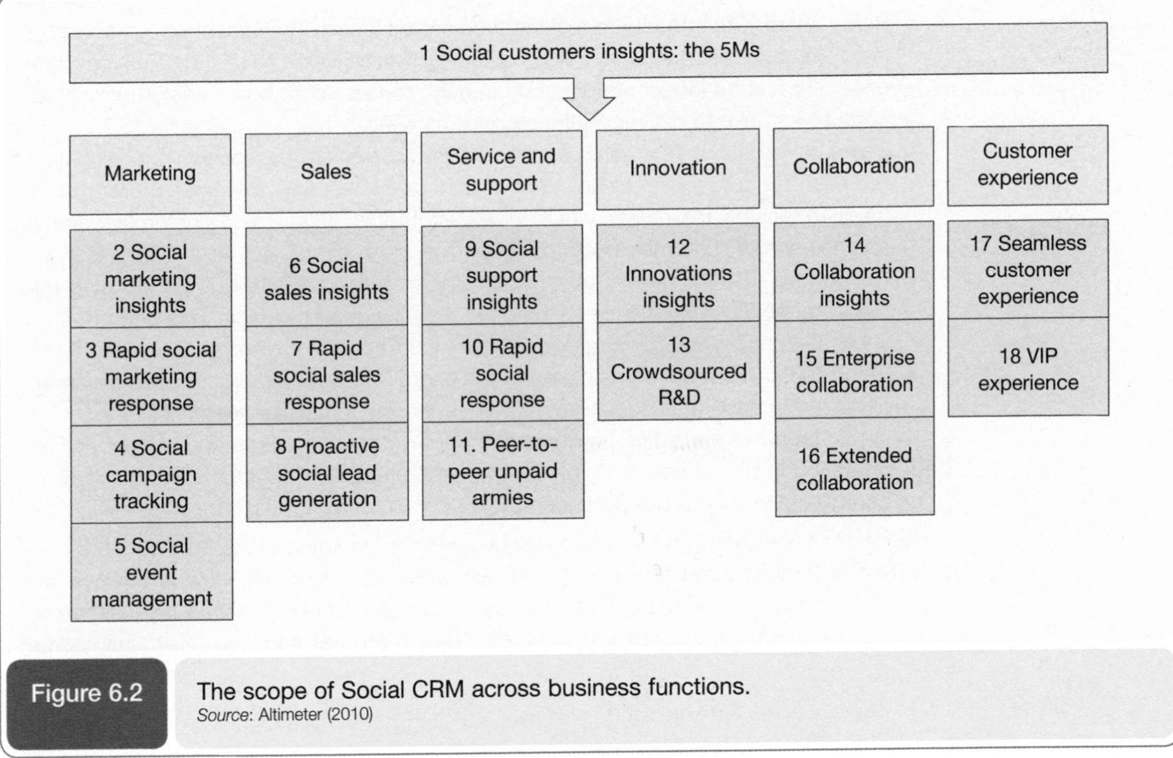

Figure 6.2 The scope of Social CRM across business functions.
Source: Altimeter (2010)

Structure of this chapter

We started the chapter by reviewing the challenges of customer engagement and introducing how E-CRM can be used to help encourage engagement. We then considered how e-CRM, permission marketing and social CRM can support customer marketing activities through the customer lifecycle. In the final part of the chapter, we show how advanced techniques are used to assess and increase customer value.

Digital marketing in practice — The Smart Insights interview

Guy Stephens of Foviance on using social media platforms to enhance customer service

Overview and main concepts

Guy Stephens championed customer service when he was at Carphone Warehouse where he was customer knowledge manager and also at Mars Drink UK when he was online marketing manager. Today, Guy is a senior consultant at Foviance and is active in sharing his expertise through various channels:

The interview

Q: Some customers are now using services like Twitter or Get Satisfaction to 'self-serve' their queries. But how important is it?

Guy Stephens: I think it's less a question of importance, as that implies it's the company deciding whether it is important or not, and ignores not only customer behaviour but also the fundamental shifts that are taking place within customer service through the impact of social media. These changes in behaviour require companies to think through:

- Being heard: Customers are making themselves heard. They have always shouted, but companies are no longer able to get away with as much selective hearing as they once did. It is no longer simply good enough to talk about being customer-centric, companies have to deliver on the promise as well
- Being there: The shift towards a customer-driven service proposition is highlighting the need for companies to go, to be and to deliver a customer service proposition that can feasibly take place wherever a customer is, whenever a customer wants it and however a customer so chooses
- Being now: The increasing ubiquity of smartphones and apps is condensing the customer service experience to the point at which it takes place. This brings with it implications on resourcing, agent skill levels, collaborative working amongst others
- Being seen: Customer service has always had a PR capability, but this has traditionally been overlooked. Social media forces the customer service interaction into a public arena where a fine line between opportunity and risk is an inherent part of operating in this space. The real-time characteristic of this adds a further layer of complexity that needs to be understood.

Social media is changing the way not only customer service is being provided, but how business is conducted between companies and customers. My view is that we will continue to see the mainstreaming of social media, and with it, the gradual questioning and subsequent erosion of the lines between customer service, sales, marketing, compliance, business operations.

Q: Which are the most common online service options companies should consider?

Guy Stephens: From what I have seen over the last two years, if a company is looking to deliver customer service through the use of social media, then the platforms they have got to include are: Twitter, blogs, YouTube and now Facebook.

For some reason, Facebook has come back into the frame and companies are interestingly treating it as a help destination point in its own right. In the UK, Thomas Cook has a help and support page within its Facebook offering. We are seeing a shift in thinking towards a deeper understanding and appreciation of the need to provide 'service at source' for customers. Traditionally, companies would have looked to bring the interaction back to their website or into the contact centre as soon as possible.

Take the case of BestBuy's Twelpforce. The next iteration of Twelpforce according to John Bernier of Best Buy is: '…for us to enable customers to answer questions that come from anywhere so that the customer doesn't have to find us, we find them. We don't want someone to have to leave Facebook to ask a question, we want them to ask it there.'

What I would say to companies looking to move into this space, is that whilst there exist what could loosely be termed a core set of tools, you've got to see what your customers are doing and where they are doing it. You set up a Twitter account or offer help and support on Facebook because your customers are there and in doing so you are meeting their needs, not yours.

Q: Many examples of customer service provided through social channels often involve retail. How important is customer service in other sectors?

Guy Stephens: There are some sectors which have a natural affinity with it because of the nature of their product or service. But in my mind it is simply understanding what you want to achieve, observing how your customers behave and then matching that to the available toolset.

Furthermore, I think there needs to be less thinking about sector and more about what it is that you are trying to do. Every sector requires the passing of information at some point between customer and company. Whether that is keeping people updated if their train is delayed, through to informing customers about changes to a returns policy, through to apologising for poor service.

On this point, and as a quick aside, I think companies also shouldn't overlook or underestimate the power of being 'signposts to the mundane' in a sense. What I mean by this is that many of the calls or e-mails that come into the contact centre every day are simple requests for information about delivery times, new products, product specifications etc. Information that can be responded to easily and quickly, without the need to really come into the call centre. Social channels like Twitter, Facebook and YouTube are fantastic assets for this and the upside in terms of immediate PR value often outweighs the actual issue itself.

Take the financial services or legal sectors. Traditionally we would have looked at these sectors and concluded that social media wouldn't work. We have a very open system in social media on the one hand, and come up against two heavily regulated sectors on the other. And yet, think about when you want to get a mortgage, renew your car insurance or understand some legal requirement relating to your work. Up until the point at which you actually have to pass sensitive data through to someone, I would have thought there's probably quite a lot of space in which social media could have a role to play in simply explaining a process or pointing someone in the right direction.

Think about someone buying a mortgage for the first time or a student opening up their first bank account. A lot of research is undertaken, particularly in the case of choosing a mortgage. A lot of hand-holding and explaining of terminology is needed. A lot of this hand-holding could be handled on the platforms that these potential customers use. So for a student opening their first bank account are they more likely to go to your website or Facebook?

Q: What about the smaller to mid-size business? Can Social CRM help here?

Guy Stephens: Absolutely, social media isn't an exclusive 'one size fits all' solution. There are many different platforms to choose from, and they can all be used individually or in combination in any number of different ways.

What's key is that in taking part you are offering something relevant and meaningful to your customers, whether that's a Wiggly Wrigglers recording a podcast, @OverheardAtMoo responding to customers' queries, or The Carphone Warehouse employees publishing helpful tips and hints about mobile phones via their Eyeopeners channel on YouTube.

I think these types of adopters share an openness to explore, an awareness of what their customers want, backed up by a willingness to actually respond. From a customer service point of view, there are obvious benefits in handling queries' and complaints via social channels. Not only are you handling and often resolving the issues or complaints at source, but you are also wrapping into the way you engage with your customers an automatic PR layer. For a small- to medium-sized company, this type of automatic PR, almost like a continual reputation feed, brings with it clear cost-saving implications as well.

At this point, many companies may well raise the spectre of negative comments as a reason for either not going down this route or at the very least being cautious of it. My response to them is this. People, your customers, will complain – that is their right, and that is what we all do. But the reason we complain is that a company has got it wrong somewhere along the way. Customers are simply letting you know where. This gives all companies the opportunity not only to respond in a positive and empathetic way, but also to actually rectify the problem as well. I think we need to re-evaluate not only the way we look at complaints, but also how we define them as well, regardless of the size of your company.

Customer-centric marketing
The approach to digital marketing based on deep understanding of customer behaviour and needs within the target audience and then seeking to deliver more relevant communications and services to meet the needs of customers.

Q: How should companies develop strategies to change the way they deliver customer service enquiries?

Guy Stephens: Fundamentally, for me, this is all about a change in mindset. Companies have long talked about being **customer-centric**, without having to really prove that they are or deliver on it. Customers are now holding mirrors up and exposing all parts of a company to scrutiny.

For me, once again it's about creating an open, enquiring and responsive environment to your customers' needs. This doesn't equate to chaos, or not being in control of what you are doing, or not understanding what success looks like. I like to think of this approach as 'freedom within a framework'.

It's not about looking at it in terms of what the company wants to achieve, but approaching it from the perspective of what your customers are trying to achieve, and then working that backwards. Once again, how well do you understand your customers? Do you understand what social platforms they are using? Do you understand what they are using them for? Do you understand what traditional platforms they are using and what they are using those for? Are they achieving what they set out to achieve? If not, why not? What are the barriers? Then flip it round and ask yourself: what are we trying to achieve?

Only then can you start to understand the gaps and begin to make changes. It's important that you understand what your baseline is before trying to plug in a new channel and avoid unintentionally creating subsequent issues around channel or process integration. If I think back to my time at The Carphone Warehouse, the reason we could try things out was simply because of our approach. Part of this is having people who 'get social'. And this touches on an important issue. From a resourcing perspective, it's apparent from talking to those who are going down this route that their approach is very much around hiring people who understand social media, and then training them in terms of the customer service skills they will need.

If we move onto the practical issues surrounding the use of social media for customer service the key issues for me are communication and integration.

- *Communicating expectations*: keeping customers informed so that you can manage their expectations. This is where empathy comes in to the picture as well. We are certainly seeing customers expecting companies to imbue a greater sense of empathy into customer service interactions than ever before. For a company, how do you 'productise' empathy in a way?
- *Integration*: ensuring the holistic customer experience helps them achieve what they set out to achieve without bluntly 'pissing them off' along the way. How do all the different channels – Twitter, phone, store visit, web, chat – that a customer might use in any one interaction work together? What takes precedence over another channel? How do you, or even, do you, build a response mechanism to Stephen Fry tweeting about your products, against any other customer tweeting in about the same product? What channels will you offer? What are your opening hours?

  For me, it comes back to looking to, working with and trusting your customers to help you find the answers to these questions. Companies no longer hold the dominant position they once did, and we are in a period where companies are being forced to re-evaluate, and in some instances re-engineer, the way in which they engage with their customers.

Q: What is the future potential of web self-service?

Guy Stephens: Companies must try to understand how people seek help. Traditionally if something went wrong we would go into a store, call or e-mail that company about it, or else ask our friends. Now, if something goes wrong we often turn to Google as our first port of call. From there we go to Twitter, forums, YouTube, blogs etc. Calling a company isn't necessarily your first step anymore. The idea of self-sufficiency is a very real threat and in some instances the role of the company is being marginalised; customer service in a sense is decentralising. But this decentralisation also brings with it opportunities.

I think what we will see are a few trends emerge which will require us to recognise and define new ways of working, and which will influence how support is provided by both customers to each other and companies to customers, and even to wider networks at large:

- Customer service will continue its move into the frontline and becoming a truly strategic part of the business. This is likely to be characterised by an element of friction at the point at which the customers' call for a greater degree of 'socialised' engagement rubs against the traditional drive for cost savings and lean efficiencies.
- There will be a continued move towards collaborative 'help/support' spaces built around the exchange of information and knowledge between people. This will continue the gradual erosion of the way we currently work. A by-product of this will be a blurring between the traditional divisions that separate not only a company from its customers, but also in the actual provision of the services themselves.
- The rise of 'ubiquitous connectivity' to not only one's own network, but networks in general will continue. The idea that I can literally plug in anytime anywhere. With this comes the idea of 'empowered me' – I am my own work force. Not only am I self sufficient, but I am also able to offer help as and when the inclination takes me.
- Social media will become increasingly embedded in the processes that underpin the products and services company's provide. The current novelty and associated awkwardness in the way we talk about and define customer service as being made up of traditional and social channels will gradually ebb as we simply see the customer service proposition as a natural combining of the two.

Read the full interview with Guy Stephens at: **http://goo.g/WS2W2.**

The challenge of customer engagement

Customer engagement
Repeated interactions that strengthen the emotional, psychological or physical investment a customer has in a brand.

Media fragmentation
Describes a trend to increasing choice and consumption of a range of media in terms of different channels such as web and mobile and also within channels, for example more TV channels, radio stations, magazines, more websites. Media fragmentation implies increased difficulty in reaching target audiences.

Forrester (2007) heralded **customer engagement** as 'marketing's new key metric', given the rapidly increasing online **media fragmentation** and the challenges of keeping customers engaged with brands given the proliferation of choice. Customer engagement is sometimes used to refer to engaging customers on a single touchpoint such as whether someone dwells on the site for a significant time or whether they convert to sale or other outcome. Instead engagement really refers to the long-term ability of a brand to gain a customer's attention on an ongoing basis whether the engagement could occur on site, in third-party social networks or in e-mail or traditional direct communications. Richard Sedley, commercial director of customer experience consultancy Foviance (**www.foviance.com**) has developed the definition of customer engagement as, 'Repeated interactions that strengthen the emotional, psychological or physical investment a customer has in a brand.'

The commercial aim of engagement is to maximise customer value through using customer interactions to lead to more profitable relationships.

Forrester (2007) has developed a framework to measure online engagement through the customer lifecycle and also away from a brand's own site, such as on publisher sites or social networks.

According to Forrester, engagement has four parts which can be measured both online and offline:

- *Involvement.* Forrester says that online this includes website visits, time spent, pages viewed.
- *Interaction.* This is contributed comments to blogs, quantity/frequency of written reviews, and online comments as well as comments expressed in customer service. [We could add the recency, frequency and category of product purchases, and also ongoing engagement in e-mail marketing programmes as discussed later in this chapter, are all important here.]
- *Intimacy.* This is sentiment tracking on third-party sites including blogs and reviews, as well as opinions expressed in customer service calls.
- *Influence.* This is advocacy indicated by measures such as likelihood to recommend, brand affinity, content forwarded to friends, etc.

It should be measured by data collected both online and offline. Forrester analyst Brian Haven says (Forrester, 2007)

> Using engagement, you get a more holistic appreciation of your customers' actions, recognising that value comes not just from transactions but also from actions people take to influence others. Once engagement takes hold of marketing, marketing messages will become conversations, and dollars will shift from media buying to customer understanding.

Benefits of using E-CRM to support customer engagement

Using digital platforms for relationship marketing involves integrating the customer database with websites and messaging to make the relationship targeted and personalised. Through doing this marketing can be improved through:

Inbound marketing
The customer is proactive in actively seeking out a solution and interactions with brands are attracted through content, search and social media marketing.

- *Targeting more cost-effectively.* Traditional targeting, for direct mail for instance, is often based on mailing lists compiled according to criteria that mean that not everyone contacted is in the target market. For example, a company wishing to acquire new affluent consumers may use postcodes to target areas with appropriate demographics, but within the postal district the population may be heterogeneous. The result of poor targeting will be low response rates, perhaps less than 1 per cent. *Permission marketing* or **Inbound marketing** has the benefit that the list of contacts is *self-selecting* or pre-qualified. A company will only aim to build relationships with those who have visited a website and expressed an interest in its products by registering their name and address.
- *Mass customisation of the marketing messages* (and possibly the product). This tailoring process is described in a subsequent section. Technology makes it possible to send tailored e-mails at much lower cost than is possible with direct mail and also to provide tailored web pages to smaller groups of customers (microsegments).
- *Increased depth and breadth of information and improve the nature of relationship.* Digital media enables more information to be supplied to customers as required through content marketing. For example, special pages such as Dell's Premier can be set up to provide customer groups with specific information. The nature of the relationship can be changed in that contact with a customer can be made more frequently. The frequency of contact with the customer can be determined by customers – whenever they have the need to visit their personalised pages – or they can be contacted by e-mail by the company.

Sense and respond communications
Delivering timely, relevant communications to customers as part of a contact strategy based on assessment of their position in the customer lifecycle and monitoring specific interactions with a company's website, e-mails and staff.

- *Deeper customer understanding and more relevant communications can be delivered through a sense and respond approach.* Examples of **sense and respond communications** include tools summarise products purchased on-site and the searching behaviour that occurred before these products were bought; online feedback forms about the site or products are completed when a customer requests free information; questions asked through forms or e-mails to the online customer service facilities; online questionnaires asking about product category interests and opinions on competitors; new product development evaluation – commenting on prototypes of new products.
- *Lower cost.* Contacting customers by e-mail or through their viewing web pages costs less than using physical mail, but perhaps more importantly, information needs to be sent only to those customers who have expressed a preference for it, resulting in fewer mail-outs.

Once personalisation technology has been purchased, much of the targeting and communications can be implemented automatically.

- *Delivering loyalty programmes.* Loyalty schemes are often used to encourage customer extension and retention. You will be familiar with schemes run by retailers such as the Tesco Clubcard or Nectar schemes or those of airlines and hotel chains. Such schemes are often used for E-CRM purposes as follows:
  a initial bonus points for sign-up to online services or initial registration
  b points for customer development or extension – more points awarded to encourage second or third online purchase
  c additional points to encourage reactivation of online services.
- Popular products are offered for a relatively low number of points to encourage repeat purchases.
- *Opportunities for gamification.* **Gamification** involves applying game-based thinking to a brand, business or organisation to engage and develop loyalty. Research shows that game play itself stimulates the human brain (releasing dopamine) and the now proven mechanics from gaming can be brought into marketing and especially mobile marketing. Some key features of gamification applied to digital marketing are:
  – creative and concept to engage
  – game mechanics to encourage play (badges, points, leader-boards, levels, interactions)
  – game dynamics can be altered to reward and even penalise
  – game currencies to provide the motivation – this can be financial, status, need for doing good, pleasure and influence.

Gamification
The process of applying game thinking and mechanics to engage an audience by rewarding them for achievements and sharing.

Mini Case Study 6.2 Chiquita uses gamification with film tie-in

The aim of this campaign according to Scott Faucheux, North America consumer marketing manager at Chiquita Brands was to 'create an engaging online playground for our Chiquita Banana consumer where the whole family could share in the fun of Chiquita-branded products, the film Rio, and win great prizes including tasty Chiquita Bananas and other nutritious products. The movie's colourful and exciting story continues online for Chiquita Banana consumers'.

Consumers that signed in to the site received a virtual passport and earned virtual badges for exploring pages including video clips from the movie, recipes, colouring pages, product information, games and a sweepstakes. The game mechanics includes five concepts from game designers to motivate player behaviour:

1. *Badges* are used as a way to reward players for accomplishing missions. They use the badges to fill their passports and complete levels of game play.
2. Players *work as a team*, collaborating to complete missions. Each time one player earns a badge, the total number of earned badges increases. As that total number of badges goes up, more prizes are unlocked with the prize packages becoming progressively better.
3. The *news feed* shows all player activity, a way of surfacing and cross promoting all of the content being consumed. It shows life and activity in the game and that there are other people playing. Players can see what others are doing and get clues to what they should do next.
4. *The leader board* shows the high scorers to help ramp up competition among players and sustain interest.
5. *Notification* – players get real-time feedback via an icon that pops up in the bottom of the window. This is an immediate reinforcement of the behaviour and the reward with a recommendation for the next action.

Source: http://www.empowermm.com/blog/2011/05/18/chiquita-rio-empower-gamification/

Figure 6.3 Chiquita Rio film campaign applies gamification
Source: http://www.bunchball.com/chiquita

Marketing applications of e-CRM

E-CRM systems supports the following marketing applications:

1 *Sales force automation (SFA)*. Sales representatives are supported in their account management through tools to arrange and record customer visits.
2 *Customer service management*. Representatives in contact centres respond to customer requests for information by using an intranet to access databases containing information on the customer, products and previous queries. It is more efficient and may increase customer convenience if customers are given the option of **web self-service**, i.e. accessing support data through a web interface.
3 *Managing the sales process*. This can be achieved through e-commerce sites, or in a B2B context by supporting sales representatives by recording the sales process (SFA).
4 *Customer communications management*. Managing communications integrated across different channels like direct mail, e-mail, mobile messaging, personalised web messages and social networks.

Web self-service
Customers perform information requests and transactions through a web interface rather than by contact with customer support staff.

5 *Analysis.* Through technologies such as data warehouses and approaches such as data mining, which are explained further later in the chapter, customers' characteristics, their purchase behaviour and campaigns can be analysed in order to optimise the marketing mix.

CRM technologies and data

Database technology is at the heart of delivering these CRM applications. Often the database is accessible through an intranet website accessed by employees or an extranet accessed by customers or partners providing an interface onto the entire customer relationship management system. E-mail is used to manage many of the inbound, outbound and internal communications managed by the CRM system. A workflow system is often used for automating CRM processes. For example, a workflow system can remind sales representatives about customer contacts or can be used to manage service delivery, such as the many stages of arranging a mortgage. The three main types of customer data held as tables in customer databases for CRM are typically:

1 *Personal and profile data.* These include contact details and characteristics for profiling customers, such as age and sex (B2C), and business size, industry sector and the individual's role in the buying decision (B2B).
2 *Transaction data.* A record of each purchase transaction including specific product purchased, quantities, category, location, date and time and channel where purchased.
3 *Communications data.* A record of which customers have been targeted by campaigns and their response to them (outbound communications). Also includes a record of inbound enquiries and sales representative visits and reports (B2B).

The behavioural data available through 2 and 3 are very important for targeting customers to more closely meet their needs.

Customer lifecycle management

Customer lifecycle
The stages each customer will pass through in a long-term relationship through acquisition, retention and extension.

Customer selection
Identifying key customer segments and targeting them for relationship building.

Customer acquisition
Strategies and techniques used to gain new customers.

Customer retention
Techniques to maintain relationships with existing customers.

Customer extension
Techniques to encourage customers to increase their involvement with an organisation.

In this section we will review methods of assessing the position of customers in the lifecycle and the use of 'sense and respond' communications to build customer loyalty at each stage of the customer lifecycle.

A high-level view of the classic **customer lifecycle** of select, acquire, retain, extend is shown in Figure 6.4.

1 **Customer selection** means defining the types of customers that a company will market to. It means identifying different groups of customers for which to develop offerings and to target during acquisition, retention and extension. Different ways of segmenting customers by value and by their detailed lifecycle with the company are reviewed.
2 **Customer acquisition** refers to marketing activities to form relationships with new customers while minimising acquisition costs and targeting high value customers. Service quality and selecting the right channels for different customers are important at this stage and throughout the lifecycle.
3 **Customer retention** refers to the marketing activities taken by an organisation to keep its existing customers. Identifying relevant offerings based on their individual needs and detailed position in the customer lifecycle (e.g. number and value of purchases) is key.
4 **Customer extension** refers to increasing the depth or range of products that a customer purchases from a company. This is often referred to as 'customer development'.

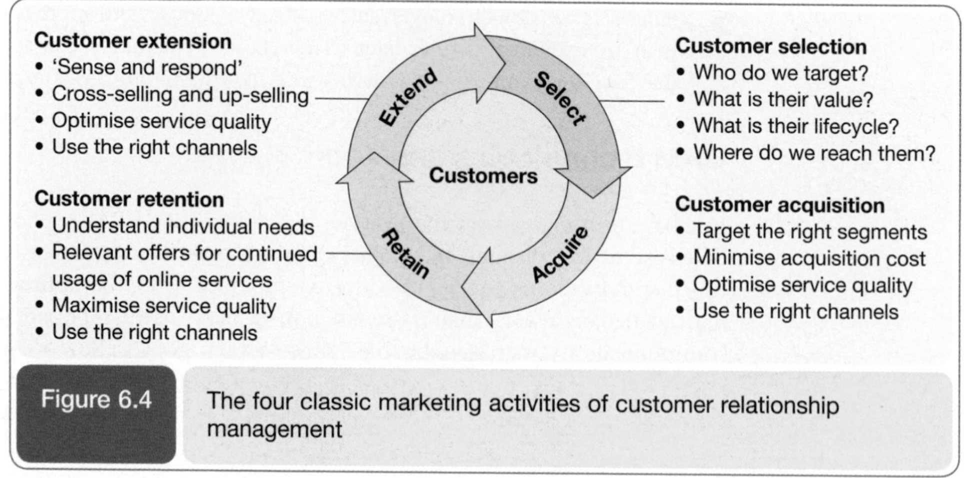

Figure 6.4 The four classic marketing activities of customer relationship management

There is a range of customer extension techniques that are particularly important to online retailers:

- *Re-sell.* Selling similar products to existing customers – particularly important in some B2B contexts as rebuys or modified rebuys.
- *Cross-sell.* Selling additional products which may be closely related to the original purchase, but not necessarily so.
- *Up-sell.* A subset of cross-selling, but in this case selling more expensive products.
- *Reactivation.* Customers who have not purchased for some time, or have lapsed can be encouraged to purchase again.
- *Referrals.* Generating sales from recommendations from existing customers – for example, member-get-member deals.

You can see that this framework distinguishes between customer retention and customer extension. Retention involves keeping the most valuable customers by selecting relevant customers for retention, understanding their loyalty factors that keep them buying and then developing strategies that encourage loyalty and cement the relationship. Customer extension is about developing customers to try a broader range of products to convert the most growable customers into the most valuable customers. You will also see that there are common features to each area – balancing cost and quality of service through the channels used according to the anticipated value of customers.

Peppers and Rogers (1997) recommend the following stages to achieve these goals, which they popularised as the 5 Is:

- *Identification.* It is necessary to learn the characteristics of customers in as much detail as possible to be able to conduct the dialogue. In a business-to-business context, this means understanding those involved in the buying decision.
- *Individualisation.* Individualising means tailoring the company's approach to each customer, offering a benefit to the customer based on the identification of customer needs. The effort expended on each customer should be consistent with the value of that customer to the organisation.
- *Interaction.* Continued dialogue is necessary to understand both the customer's needs and the customer's strategic value. The interactions need to be recorded to facilitate the learning relationship.
- *Integration.* Integration of the relationship and knowledge of the customer must extend throughout all parts of the company.
- *Integrity.* Since all relationships are built on trust it is essential not to lose the trust of the customer. Efforts to learn from the customer should not be seen as intrusive, and privacy should be maintained. (See Chapter 3 for coverage of privacy issues related to e-CRM.)

Permission marketing

Permission marketing
Customers agree (opt-in) to be involved in an organisation's marketing activities, usually as a result of an incentive.

Permission marketing is a significant concept that underpins online CRM in management of the customer lifecycle. 'Permission marketing' is a term coined by Seth Godin (1999). It is best characterised with just three (or four) words:

> Permission marketing is …
>
> anticipated, relevant and personal [and timely].

Godin (1999) notes that while research used to show we were bombarded by 500 marketing messages a day, with the advent of the web and digital TV this has now increased to over 3000 a day! From the marketing organisation's viewpoint, this leads to a dilution in the effectiveness of the messages – how can the communications of any one company stand out? Godin refers to the traditional approach as **interruption marketing.** Permission marketing is about seeking the customer's permission before engaging them in a relationship and providing something in exchange. The classic exchange is based on information or entertainment – a B2B site can offer a free report in exchange for a customer sharing their e-mail address which will be used to maintain a dialogue; a B2C site can offer a screensaver in exchange.

Interruption marketing
Marketing communications that disrupt customers' activities.

Opt-in
A customer proactively agrees to receive further information.

Opt-out
A customer declines the offer to receive further information.

From a practical e-commerce perspective, we can think of a customer agreeing to engage in a relationship when they check a box on a web form to indicate that they agree to receive further communications from a company. This approach is referred to as **opt-in.** This is preferable to **opt-out,** the situation where a customer has to consciously agree not to receive further information.

The importance of incentivisation in permission marketing has also been emphasised by Seth Godin who likens the process of acquisition and retention to dating someone. Likening customer relationship building to social behaviour is not new, as O'Malley and Tynan (2001) note; the analogy of marriage has been used since the 1980s at least. They also report on consumer research that indicates that while marriage may be analogous to business relationships, it is less appropriate for B2C relationships.

Godin (1999) suggests that dating the customer involves:

1. offering the prospect an *incentive* to volunteer
2. using the attention offered by the prospect, offering a curriculum over time, teaching the consumer about your product or service
3. reinforcing the *incentive* to guarantee that the prospect maintains the permission
4. offering additional *incentives* to get even more permission from the consumer
5. over time, using the permission to change consumer behaviour towards profits.

Figure 6.5 gives a summary of a common, effective process for permission-based online relationship building to support engagement through the different stages of the customer lifecycle.

The stages are:

- *Stage 1. Attract new and existing customers to online presence.* The online and offline communications channels described in Chapter 9, such as search, social media marketing and direct mail, are used to drive visitors to a website, Facebook or other form of presence such as an app that enables opt-in.
- *Stage 2a. Incentivise visitors to action.* Two key types of incentives to consider are: **lead generation offers** and **sales generation offers.** On Facebook, companies used gated pages where the visitor must 'Like' the brand before they can gain the incentive.

Lead generation offer
Offered in return for customers providing their contact details and characteristics. Commonly used in B2B marketing where free information such as a report or a seminar will be offered.

Sales generation offer
Encourage product trial. A coupon redeemed against a purchase is a classic example.

Types of offers marketers can devise include information value, entertainment value, monetary value and privileged access to information (such as that only available on an extranet). The beauty of digital marketing is that different offers can be tested for different audiences using AB or multivariate testing (Chapter 10) and the offers refined to increase response.

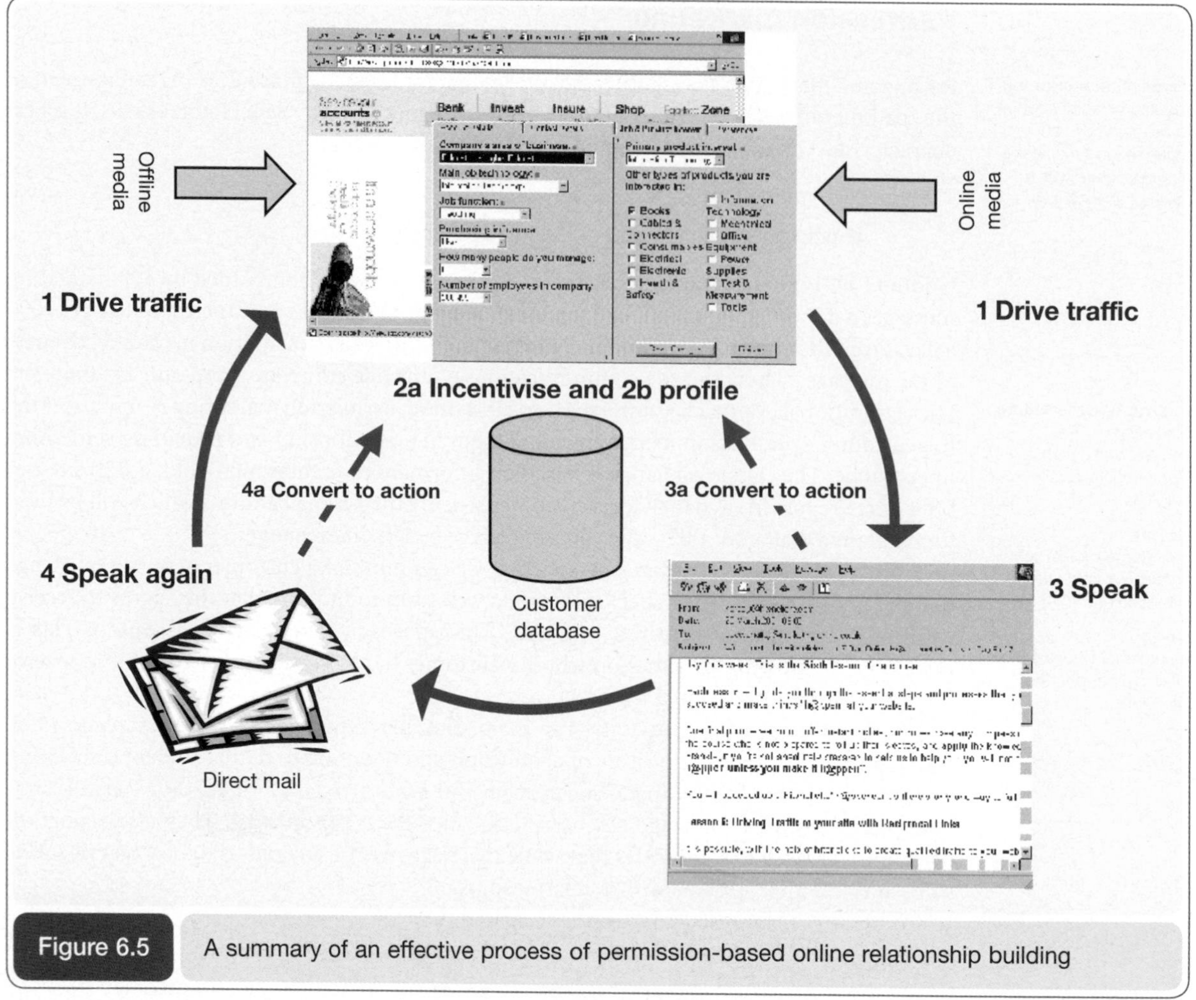

Figure 6.5 A summary of an effective process of permission-based online relationship building

- *Stage 2b: Capture customer information to maintain relationship.* Capturing profile information is commonly achieved through an online form such as shown in Figure 6.6 which the customer must complete to receive the offer. It is important to design these forms to maximise their completion. Factors which are important are:
  - *branding* to reassure the customer
  - *key profile fields* to capture the most important information to segment the customer for future communications, in this case postcode, airport and preferred activities (not too many questions should be asked)
  - *mandatory fields* – mark fields which must be completed or, as in this case, only include mandatory figures
  - *privacy* – 'we will not share' is the magic phrase to counter the customer's main fear of their details being passed on; a full privacy statement should be available for those who need it
  - *KISS* – 'Keep it simple, stupid' is a well-known American phrase
  - *WIFM* – 'What's in it for me?' Explain why the customer's data is being captured; what benefits it will give them?
  - *validation* – of e-mail, postcode etc., checking data as far as possible to make it accurate.

As well as online data capture, it is important to use all customer touchpoints to capture information and keep it up-to-date since this affects the ability to target customers accurately. Figure 6.7 provides a good way for a company to review all the possible methods of capturing e-mail addresses and other profile information.

Register for newsletter updates by email

Register your details with us to receive the latest travel deals and ideas direct to your inbox.

You...

Title: Mr | First Name: | Surname:

First line of address: | Post Code:

Email address: | Mobile Number*:

*In future, we may investigate innovative ways of communication with you by SMS, which could include exclusive access to competitions and offers. If you are interested in being part of this, please provide your mobile.

Your preferences...

How often would you prefer to receive updates? Please select

Please select
Weekly
Fortnightly
Monthly
Bi-Monthly

What airport do you prefer to fly from?

Do you have a particular interest ... ?

Summer Sun	Winter Sun	Ski
City Breaks	Lakes & Mountains	Villas
World Wide	Accommodation Only	Auctions
Flights	Cruises	Mobile Homes

Data Protection Notice

1. All details provided by you will be held by us and used in accordance with our Privacy Policy.
2. We may from time to time contact you **by post** with further information on the latest offers, brochures, products or services which we believe may be of interest to you, from Thomson (a division of TUI UK Limited), other hoiday divisions within and group companies of TUI UK limited.

Figure 6.6 Opt-in customer profiling form

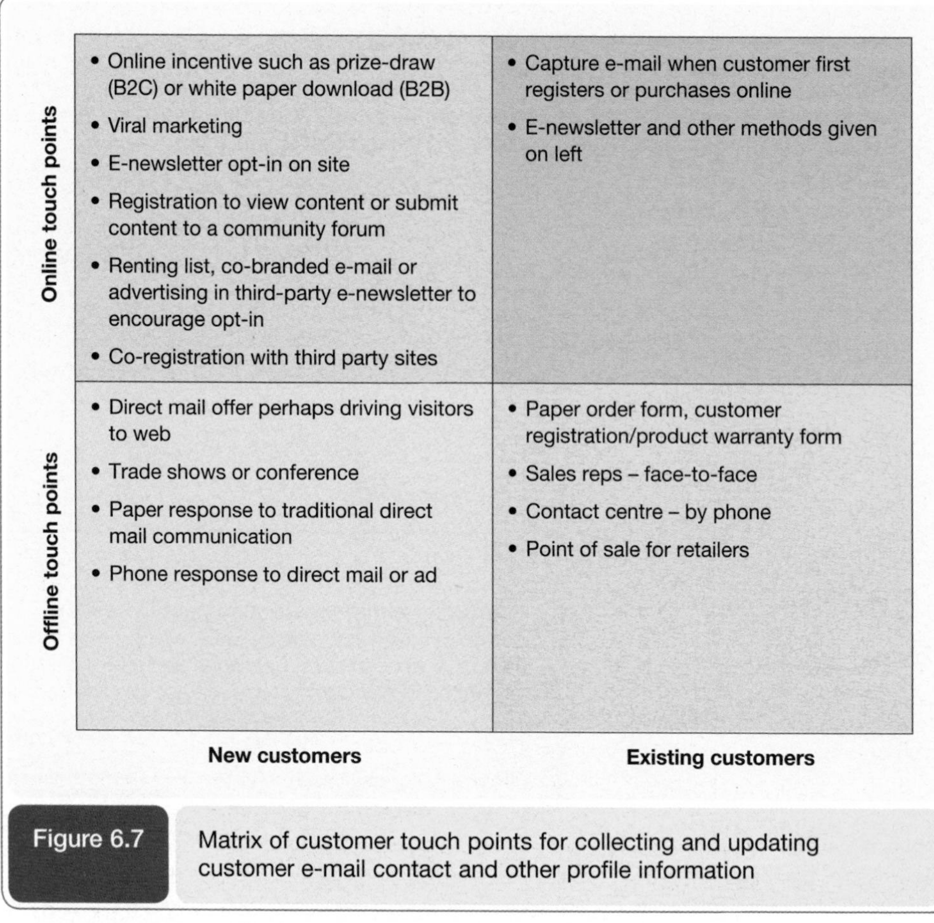

Online touch points
Offline touch points
New customers
Existing customers
• Online incentive such as prize-draw (B2C) or white paper download (B2B)
• Viral marketing
• E-newsletter opt-in on site
• Registration to view content or submit content to a community forum
• Renting list, co-branded e-mail or advertising in third-party e-newsletter to encourage opt-in
• Co-registration with third party sites
• Capture e-mail when customer first registers or purchases online
• E-newsletter and other methods given on left
• Direct mail offer perhaps driving visitors to web
• Trade shows or conference
• Paper response to traditional direct mail communication
• Phone response to direct mail or ad
• Paper order form, customer registration/product warranty form
• Sales reps – face-to-face
• Contact centre – by phone
• Point of sale for retailers

Figure 6.7 Matrix of customer touch points for collecting and updating customer e-mail contact and other profile information

Customer profiling
Using the website to find out a customer's specific interests and characteristics.

Apart from the contact information, the other important information to collect is a method of **customer profiling** so that relevant content and offers can be delivered to them. For example, B2B company RS Components asks for:

- industry sector
- purchasing influence
- specific areas of product interest
- how many people you manage
- total number of employees in company.

Single customer view
Customer profile information is kept consistent across systems to maintain customer data quality.

Once data has been initially collected, it should be added to gain a better understanding of customer needs and behaviours. The risk here is that if data is entered into different systems, data quality issues may arise with inaccurate data. Management measures should be put in place to create an accurate **single customer view**. This is a significant risk with ECRM systems since data can be collected offline and in different online systems such as on the website, transactional E-commerce or within social media and a separate email system.

- *Stage 3: Maintain dialogue using online communication.* To build the relationship between company and customer there are many digital methods of communication. These are:
  1. Send an e-mail to the customer which can be tailored based on the customers' disclosed profile information or information inferred from the type of content they have accessed on the site.
  2. Display specific information on the website when the customer logs in. This is referred to as 'personalisation'.

3 Use syndication technology such as RSS feeds or sharing via social networks to deliver content to the customer. Social networks have the limitation currently of not having a level of permission where profile information can be accessed and messages can't be personalised. Integration of e-mail and social network profiles is possible using a technique known as **social sign on** (Smart Insights, 2011) where a user logs-in to a site using their social network profile and this can be linked with profile information captured through traditional web forms. Smart Insights (2011) give the example of Sears Social (**http://social.sears.com**) where users reviews and ratings about products are included as part of their profile. This is an example of social commerce.

Social sign-on
A user logs-in to a site using a social network service user name and password. This can enable connection between social memberships and company profile information.

- *Stage 4. Maintain dialogue using offline communication.* Direct mail or phone contact may still be cost-effective forms of communication since these can also be tailored and may have more 'cut-through' compared to an e-mail. With direct mail campaigns the aim may be to drive traffic to the website in a web response campaign using techniques such as:
  - online competition
  - online web seminar (webinar)
  - sales promotion.

A further objective in stage 3 and stage 4 is to improve customer information quality. In particular, e-mails may bounce – in which case offline touch points as indicated in Figure 6.7 need to be planned to determine the latest addresses.

With the advent of social media marketing, the permission marketing concept has been applied to social networks where opt-in involves 'liking' a brand on Facebook or following a company on Twitter, LinkedIn or Google+. Within Facebook, 'Liking' or exchange of e-mail address can be encouraged through company pages as the campaign shown in Mini Case Study 6.3 about Princess Cruises. Of course, e-mail offers a key benefit over social media channels since it can be tailored to the individual.

Mini Case Study 6.3 Princess Cruises integrate Facebook and e-mail marketing activities

In this campaign, Princess Cruises used a classic 'blog to win' or 'share to win' campaign asking readers about their favourite travel destination and based around the hub of the company Facebook page (Figure 6.8).

The different waves of this integrated campaign were:

Step 1. Promote to existing customers through email
Subject line: *Just one week left to enter to win a dream holiday!*
The aim is to encourage subscribers to like the company on Facebook and then encourage entries – both which will have a viral effect.

Step 2. Facebook contest tab encourages like
The campaign is based around a 'Travel Bucket' wish list in which customers are encouraged to share through videos and write-ups.

Step 3. Engage through contest tabs to create, share and win
Company Facebook pages have different tabs like a company microsite within Facebook which encourage customers to interact and return to the site.

Step 4. Inspire through blog
Within the company site, the blog also generates ongoing interest through articles written about cruise destination positioned as written by staff rather than journalists to add a personal touch. For full creative examples for this campaign see: **http://goo.PLIkJ**

→

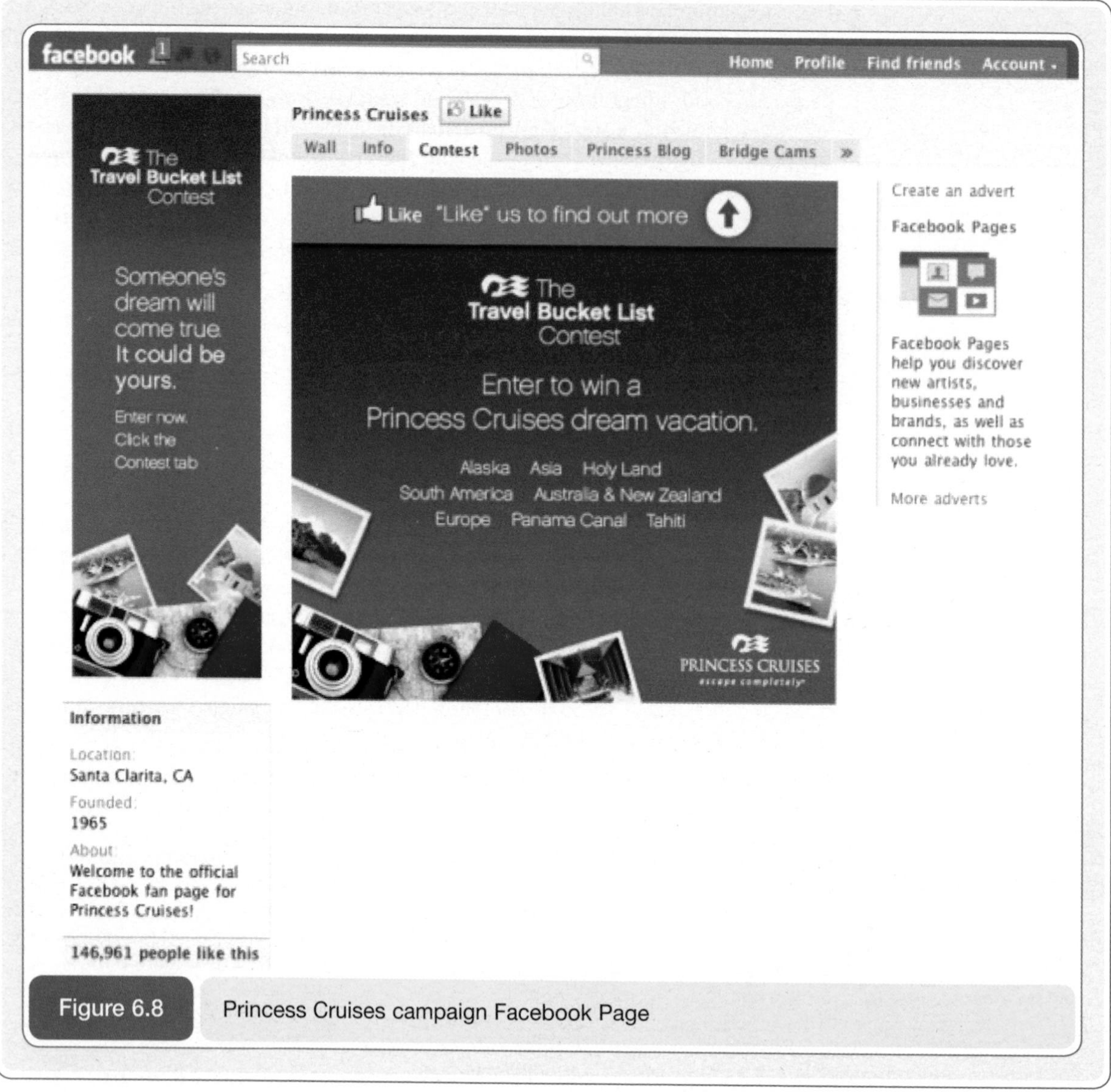

Figure 6.8 Princess Cruises campaign Facebook Page

Writing for the *What's New in Marketing* e-newsletter, Chaffey (2004) extended Godin's principles to E-CRM with his 'e-permission marketing principles' which remain relevant for reviewing use of e-mail marketing and social CRM communications strategy:

- **Principle 1** – *Consider selective opt-in to communications.* In other words, offer choice in *communications preferences* to the customer to ensure more relevant communications. Some customers may not want a weekly e-newsletter, rather they may only want to hear about new product releases. Remember opt-in is a legal requirement in many countries. Four key communications preferences options, selected by tick box are:
  - *Content* – news, products, offers, events
  - *Frequency* – weekly, monthly, quarterly, or alerts
  - *Channel* – e-mail, social network, direct mail, phone or SMS
  - *Format* – text vs HTML.
- **Principle 2** – *Create a 'common customer profile'.* A structured approach to customer data capture is needed otherwise some data will be missed, as is the case with the utility company that collected 80,000 e-mail addresses, but forgot to ask for the postcode for

geo-targeting! This can be achieved through a common customer profile – a definition of all the database fields that are relevant to the marketer in order to understand and target the customer with a relevant offering. The customer profile can have different levels to set targets for data quality (Level 1 is contact details and key profile fields only, Level 2 includes preferences and Level 3 includes full purchase and response behaviour).

- **Principle 3** – *Offer a range of opt-in incentives.* Many websites now have 'free–win–save' incentives to encourage opt-in, but often it is one incentive fits all visitors. Different incentives for different audiences will generate a higher volume of permission, particularly for business-to-business websites. We can also gauge the characteristics of the respondent by the type of incentives or communications they have requested, without the need to ask them.
- **Principle 4** – *Don't make opt-out too easy.* Often marketers make it too easy to unsubscribe. Although offering some form of opt-out is now a legal requirement in many countries due to privacy laws, a single click to unsubscribe is making it too easy. Instead, wise e-permission marketers such as Amazon use the concept of 'My Profile' or a 'selective opt-out'. Instead of unsubscribe, they offer a link to a 'communications preferences' or 'customer centre' web form to update a profile that includes the options to reduce communications, which may be the option taken rather than unsubscribing completely.
- **Principle 5** – *Watch, don't ask (or 'Sense and Respond').* The need to ask interruptive questions can be reduced through the use of monitoring clicks to better understand customer needs and to trigger follow-up communications. Some examples:
  - monitoring click-through to different types of content or offer
  - monitoring the engagement of individual customers with e-mail communications
  - follow-up reminder to those who don't open the e-mail first time.

Contact strategy
Definition of the sequence and type of outbound communications required at different points in the customer lifecycle.

- **Principle 6** – *Create an outbound contact strategy.* Online permission marketers need a plan for the number, frequency and type of online and offline communications and offers. This is a **contact** or **touch strategy** which is particularly important for large organisations with several marketers responsible for e-mail communications. We describe contact strategies in more depth in the next section.

An example of permission marketing in practice, and how to set goals for permission, is provided in Chapter 9 in Mini Case Study 9.2, 'Beep-beep-beep-beep, that'll be the bank then'. In this campaign to promote a new interactive banking service, the campaign objectives and results (in brackets) were to:

- capture 5000 mobile phone numbers from customers (200 per cent of plan)
- acquire 3000 e-mail addresses (176 per cent of plan)
- raise awareness about the new service (31,000 customers view demonstration)
- create 1000 new registrations (576 per cent of plan)

'Right touching' through developing online contact strategies

Given the difficulty in achieving customer engagement, with the increase in media fragmentation and the development of high attention media such as social networks, the need for developing a structured approach to communicating with customers across the lifecycle has become more urgent. Dave Chaffey has emphasised the importance for companies to build and refine an integrated multichannel touch or contact strategy which delivers customised communications to consumers by search ads, e-mail and web recommendations and promotions.

Every customer interaction or response to a communication should be followed-up by a series of relevant communications delivered by the right combinations of channel (web, e-mail, phone, direct mail) to elicit a response or further dialogue. This is contextual marketing, where the aim is to deliver relevant messages which fit the current context of what the customer is interested in according to the searches they have performed, the type of content they have viewed or the products they have recently purchased.

Digital marketing insight 6.1 Right touching can be summarised as:

A **Multichannel Communications Strategy**
Customised for Individual Prospects and Customers forming segments
Across a **defined customer lifecycle**
Which...
Delivers the **Right Message**
Featuring the **Right Value Proposition** (product, service or experience)
With the **Right Tone**
At the **Right Time** or context
With the Right **Frequency and Interval**
Using the Right **Media/Communications channels**
To achieve...
Right **balance of value between both parties**

A contact policy should be developed to manage and control communications so that they are at an acceptable level. The contact strategy should indicate the following:

- *Frequency* – e.g. minimum once per quarter and maximum once per month.
- *Interval* – e.g. there must be a gap of at least one week or one month between communications.
- *Content and offers* – we may want to limit or achieve a certain number of prize draws or information-led offers.
- *Links* – between online communications and offline communications.
- *A control strategy* – a mechanism to make sure these guidelines are adhered to, for example using a single 'focal point' for checking all communications before creation dispatch.

Examples of contact strategies for Euroffice and Tesco.com were discussed in Chapter 4. A simpler example of a contact strategy is shown in the following Mini Case Study 6.4.

Mini Case Study 6.4 WHSmith use behavioural e-mail to encourage engagement

Behavioural e-mail marketing or remarketing is a classic 'sense and respond' e-CRM approach. In this case, a classic abandoned shopping cart follow-up email, but with three alternative communications which were tested with these results:

1 *Generic branded follow-up e-mail*: + 10 per cent conversion rate.
2 *Personalised remarketing e-mail with a promotional code for a 5 per cent discount time limited to 72 hours*: + 100 per cent conversion rate.
3 *Personalised remarketing email with a promotional code for a 5% discount time limited to 48 hours*: + 200 per cent conversion rate.

A survey was conducted (VE interactive) of those customers who had clicked through from the remarketing e-mails and had made a purchase, but who hadn't actually used the promotional codes! Interestingly, it was found:

- These customers had still reacted to the remarketing email as a prompt to return to the WHSmith website.
- It was the expiry date of the call to action that had prompted them to return, even though they then did not take advantage of the 5 per cent discount promo code.

Source: VE Interactive Case Study published on SmartInsights: http://www.smartinsights.com/email-marketing-ecrm-alerts/email-remarketing-an-example-of-how-to-test/, accessed October 2011.

Table 6.1 shows a recommended approach for developing a contact strategy or e-mail communications sequence involving different behavioural trigger events which prompt broadcast of a personalised e-mail

Table 6.1 Example welcome contact strategy

	Message type	Interval/trigger condition	Outcomes required	Medium for message/ sequence
1	Welcome message	Guest site membership signup Immediate	• Encourage trial of site services • Increase awareness of range of commercial and informational offerings	E-mail, post transaction page
2	Engagement message	1 month inactive (i.e. < 3 visits)	• Encourage use of forum (good enabler of membership) • Highlight top content	E-mail, home page, side panels deep in site
3	Initial cross-sell message	1 month active	• Encourage membership • Ask for feedback	E-mail
4	Conversion	2 days after browsing content	• Use for range of services for guest members or full	Phone or e-mail

The 'emotionally unsubscribed' e-mail list members

The inactive members of an e-mail list are sometimes called the 'emotionally unsubscribed'. They represent a significant issue in the management of customer e-mail marketing programmes. Although unsubscribe rates are usually low (for example, less than 0.1 per cent per campaign) there can be upwards of 50 per cent of a list who are 'emotionally unsubscribed', i.e. they are not actually unsubscribed but rarely open or click, suggesting that e-mail is not an effective communications channel. To avoid this and to maintain the dialogue, it is important to ensure that the contact strategy has been planned and implemented to deliver relevant messages. Some other steps that can be taken to manage this issue include:

- Measure the level of activity in e-mail response at a more granular level, e.g. review open, click, purchase rates or other actions at different points in time compared to when the subscribers first signed up. Response rates from different segment types who have taken different actions can also be reviewed to see how engaging they find the e-newsletter.
- Test different frequencies. It may be appropriate to reduce frequency if customers become 'emotionally unsubscribed' and then e-mails received will have a large impact. List members can also be surveyed for their preferences, possibly as part of a reactivation campaign.
- Develop automated customer lifecycle e-mails which are part of the contact strategy which are relevant and tailored according to the interests of the subscriber. Lifecycle e-mails will include welcome e-mail contact strategies, reactivation e-mail strategies and other service messages such as customer feedback surveys.
- Ensure the fields that are used to customise messages are those that are most likely to be relevant. Often these won't be the obvious fields such as gender, but contextual information related to content or products which have been recently consumed, as shown by Figure 6.9
- Use offline communications such as direct mail and phone where list members express a preference for these (and see Stage 4 below).

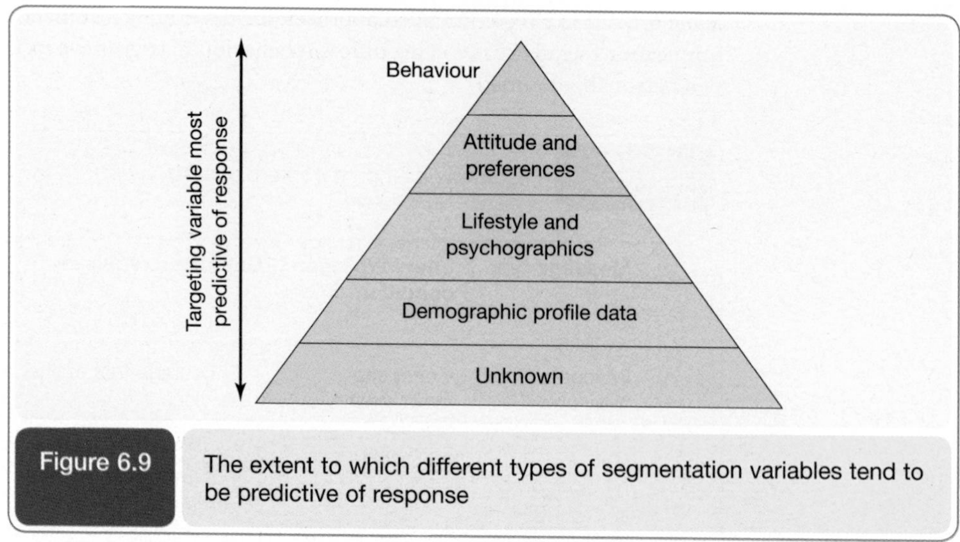

Figure 6.9 The extent to which different types of segmentation variables tend to be predictive of response

Personalisation and mass customisation

Personalisation
Web-based personalisation involves delivering customised content for the individual, through web pages, e-mail or push technology.

The potential power of **personalisation** is suggested by these quotes from Evans *et al.* (2000) that show the negative effects of lack of targeting of traditional direct mail:

> Don't like unsolicited mail ... haven't asked for it and I'm not interested.
> Female, 25–34

> Most isn't wanted, it's not relevant and just clutters up the table ... you have to sort through it to get to the 'real mail'.
> Male, 45–54

> It's annoying to be sent things that you are not interested in. Even more annoying when they phone you up ... If you wanted something you would go and find out about it.
> Female, 45–54

Mass customisation
The creation of tailored marketing messages or products for individual customers or groups of customers typically using technology to retain the economies of scale and the capacity of mass marketing or production.

Personalisation and **mass customisation** can be used to tailor information content on a website, or within an opt-in e-mail. 'Personalisation' and 'mass customisation' are terms that are often used interchangeably. In the strict sense, personalisation refers to customisation of information requested by a site customer at an *individual* level. Mass customisation involves providing tailored content to a *group* or *individuals* with similar interests. It uses technology to achieve this on an economical basis. An example of mass customisation is when Amazon recommends similar products according to what others in a segment have offered, or if it sent a similar e-mail to customers who had an interest in a particular topic such as e-commerce.

Collaborative filtering
Profiling of customer interest coupled with delivery of specific information and offers, often based on the interests of similar customers.

Other methods of profiling customers include collaborative filtering and monitoring the content they view. With **collaborative filtering**, customers are openly asked what their interests are, by checking boxes corresponding to their interests. A database then compares the customer's preferences with those of other customers in its database, and then makes recommendations or delivers information accordingly. The more information a database contains about an individual customer, the more useful its recommendations can be. The best-known example of this technology in action can be found on the Amazon website (**www.amazon.com**), where the database reveals that customers who bought book X also bought books Y and Z.

Figure 6.10 summarises the options available to organisations wishing to use the Internet for mass customisation or personalisation. If there is little information available about the customer and it is not integrated with the website then no mass customisation is possible (A). To achieve mass customisation or personalisation, the organisation must have sufficient information about the customer. For limited tailoring to groups of customers (B), it is necessary to have basic profiling information such as age, sex, social group, product category interest or, for B2B, role in the buying unit. This information must be contained in a database system that is directly linked to the system used to display website content. For personalisation on a one-to-one level (C) more detailed information about specific interests, perhaps available from a purchase history, should be available.

An organisation can use Figure 6.10 to plan their relationship marketing strategy. The symbols X_1 to X_3 show a typical path for an organisation. At X_1 information collected about customers is limited. At X_2 detailed information is available about customers, but it is in discrete databases that are not integrated with the website. At X_3 the strategy is to provide mass customisation of information and offers to major segments, since it is felt that the expense of full personalisation is not warranted.

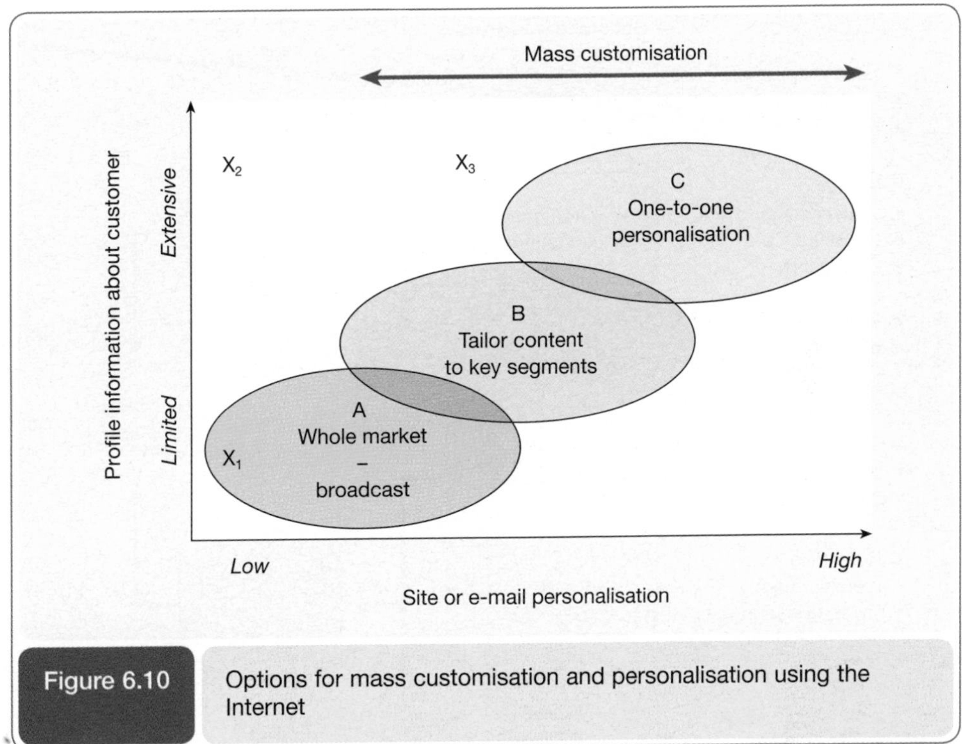

Figure 6.10 Options for mass customisation and personalisation using the Internet

Using digital media to increase customer loyalty and value

Customer loyalty
The desire on the part of the customer to continue to do business with a given supplier over time (Sargeant and West, 2001).

The ultimate commercial aim of relationship marketing approaches such as e-CRM and social CRM is to increase engagement with customers leading to increase **customer loyalty** and so direct sales from these customers and indirect sales through advocacy. Understanding the different levers that contribute to increased engagement and loyalty amongst different customer groups should be the starting point in developing a customer retention and growth strategy.

Determining what customers value

Emotional loyalty
Loyalty to a brand is demonstrated by favourable perceptions, opinions and recommendations.

Consider the different forms of online interaction a consumer can have with a brand that can determine their perceptions of satisfaction and influence loyalty. Figure 6.11 shows how, when using digital media for online retention marketing, our ultimate goal on the right of the diagram is customer loyalty. The factors on the left help to deliver two main drivers of loyalty. First, **emotional loyalty** where loyalty to a brand is demonstrated by favourable perceptions, opinions and recommendations including social sharing. The success factors at the top of the diagram that are all related to the customer experience of online services as we will explore further at the start of Chapter 7. These tend to influence emotional loyalty the most and these are important in determining customer satisfaction. Of course, a favourable customer experience is, very important to achieving repeat purchases – how many online sites have you continued to use after a poor level of service was delivered?

Behavioural loyalty
Loyalty to a brand is demonstrated by repeat sales and response to marketing campaigns.

The second type of loyalty is **behavioural loyalty** where loyalty relates to repeat sales, repeated site visits, social interactions and response to marketing campaigns. To achieve these repeat sales, companies work hard to deliver relevant marketing communications either through e-mail and social media communications, web-based personalisation or through traditional media.

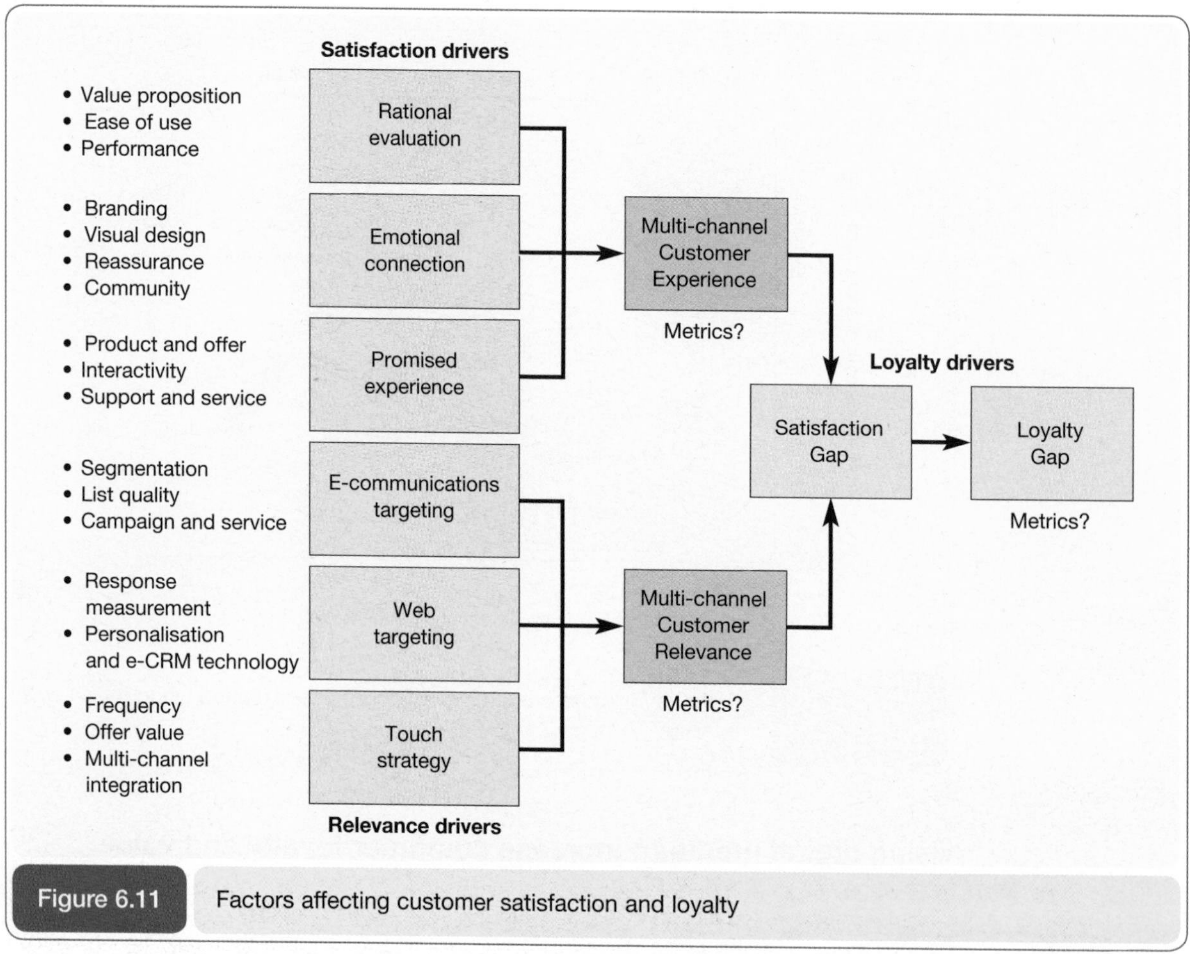

Figure 6.11 Factors affecting customer satisfaction and loyalty

Figure 6.11 shows typical loyalty drivers to review, but customer research is essential to understand how specific factors affect loyalty and how satisfaction influences loyalty.

The relationship between satisfaction and loyalty

Customer satisfaction
The extent to which a customer's expectations of product quality, service quality and price are met.

Although the terms 'satisfaction' and 'loyalty' are sometimes used interchangeably, we have seen that they do not necessarily correspond. **Customer satisfaction** refers to the degree a customer is happy about the quality of products and services. As a customer's satisfaction with products and/or services increases, so should their behavioural and emotional loyalty together with advocacy.

As we have seen, though, there may be customers with a high degree of satisfaction who don't exhibit behavioural loyalty and, conversely, customers who are loyal according to their behaviour that may be at risk of defection since they are not satisfied. The implications are that it is important not only to measure satisfaction with online services, but loyalty also. In this way we are able to identify customers at risk of defection who are likely to choose an alternative and those in the zone of indifference. This is an important category of customer who, although they may have a high degree of satisfaction, is not necessarily loyal.

To measure satisfaction ratings meaningfully, satisfaction must be benchmarked against other companies in and out-of-sector using standard questions. In the US, the American Satisfaction Index uses a standard methodology for different types of e-businesses shown in Figure 6.12 This diagram shows how behavioural measures which show how customers interact with brands online are often recorded through web analytics systems as described in Chapter 10, but they are lagging indicators that don't predict future success. Satisfaction measures tend to be more predictive of future success and purchase intent.

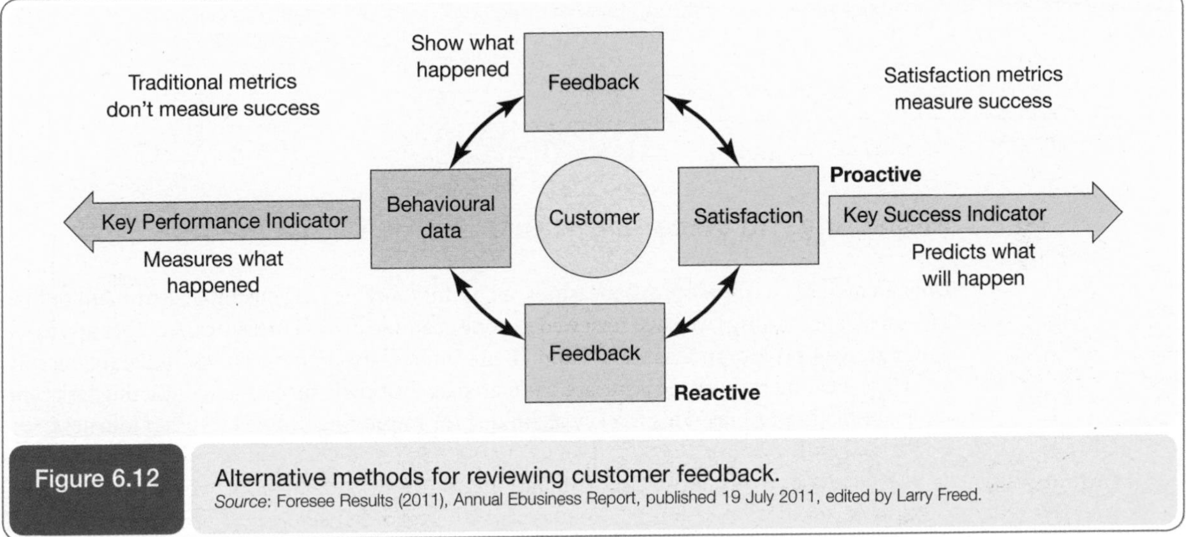

Figure 6.12 Alternative methods for reviewing customer feedback.
Source: Foresee Results (2011), Annual Ebusiness Report, published 19 July 2011, edited by Larry Freed.

Mini Case Study 6.5 How car manufacturers use loyalty-based segmentation

An approach to reconciling customer satisfaction, loyalty, value and potential is to use a value-based segmentation. This modelling approach is often used by car manufacturers and other companies who are assessing strategies to enhance the future value of their customer segments. This approach involves creating a segmentation model combining real data for each customer about their current value and satisfaction, and modelled values for future loyalty and value. Each customer is scored according to these four variables:

- current satisfaction
- repurchase loyalty
- current value
- future potential

Table 6.2 Loyalty-based segmentation for car manufacturer

SLVP score	Nature of customer	Segment strategy
Moderate satisfaction and loyalty. Moderate current and future potential value	An owner of average loyalty who replaces their car every three to four years and has a tendency to repurchase from brand	Not a key segment to influence. But should encourage to subscribe to e-newsletter club and deliver targeted messages around time of renewal
High satisfaction, moderate loyalty. Low future and potential value	A satisfied owner but tends to buy second-hand and keeps cars until they have a high mileage	Engage in dialogue via e-mail newsletter and use this to encourage advocacy and make aware of benefits of buying new
Low satisfaction and loyalty. High current and future potential value	A dissatisfied owner of luxury cars who is at risk of switching	A key target segment who needs to be contacted to understand issues and reassure about quality and performance

Measuring the voice of the customer in digital media

Online voice of customer (VoC)
Qualitative assessments of the effectiveness of digital presence based on direct customer feedback. They answer 'who and why' questions about how customers interact with brands online.

Net Promoter Score (NPS)
A measure of the number of advocates a company (or website) has who would recommend it compared to the number of detractors.

Online voice of customer (VoC) measures are useful for reviewing customer sentiment online. The satisfaction ratings we have reviewed are one example of VoC measures. Another approach which we will explore in Chapters 7 and 10 are intent-satisfaction surveys where the reasons for why a customer is visiting a site are compared against their success in completing tasks and their satisfaction ratings. This is a key technique for improving online customer journeys.

Net Promoter Score (NPS) is a key VoC measure of advocacy originally popularised by Reichheld (2006) in his book: 'the Ultimate Question' is essentially 'would you recommend us?' The aim is to work out techniques to maximise this NPS. Reichheld explains the main process for NPS as follows:

1 Systematically categorise customers into promoters, passives or detractors. If you prefer, you can call them loyal advocates, fair-weather friends and adversaries.

2 Creating closed-loop processes so that the right employees will directly investigate the root causes that drive customers into these categories.

3 Making the creation of more promoters and fewer detractors a top priority so employees up and down the organisation take actions based on their findings from these root-cause investigations.

In practice, consumers are asked 'Would you recommend [Brand/Company X] to a friend or colleague?', answered on a scale between 0 (not at all likely) and 10 (extremely likely). The actual score is calculated by subtracting the percentage of detractors (those giving 0–6 answers) from promoters (9–10s). The middle section, between 7 and 8, are the so-called passives.

The concept of NPS is based on economic analysis of the customer base of a company. For Dell, Reichheld estimates that the average consumer is worth $210 (five year, Net Present Value), whereas a detractor costs the company $57 and a promoter generates $328. Online, Dell uses software from Opinion Labs (**www.opinionlabs.com**) to both gather feedback and follow-up on negative experiences and so reduce the number of detractors with major negative sentiment.

So, the idea is that after surveying as many customers as possible (to make it representative) and show you are listening, to then work backwards to determine which aspects of the experience of interacting with a brand creates 'promoters' or 'detractors'. Some specific approaches that can be used to help manage NPS in the online environment are:

1. Facilitating online advocacy:
   - Page template contains 'Forward/recommend to a friend' options.
   - E-mail templates contain 'Forward to a friend option'.
   - Facilitate customer feedback through a structured programme of e-mailing customers for their opinions and NPS evaluations and by making it easy for site owners to comment.
   - Showcase positive experiences – for example, e-retail sites often contain options for rating and commenting on products.
   - Involve customers more in shaping your web services and core product offerings, such as the approach used by Dell in their IdeaStorm site (**www.ideastorm.com**).
2. Managing online detractors:
   - Use online reputation management tools (**www.davechaffey.com/online-reputation-management-tools**) for notification of negative (and positive) comments.
   - Develop a process and identify resources for rapidly responding to negative comments using a natural and open approach.
   - Assess and manage the influence of negative comments within the natural listings of search engines.
   - Practise fundamental marketing principles of listening to customer comments about products and services and aim to rectify them to win back the situation!

An example of a company that seeks feedback from customers and then makes this feedback available to all customers is shirt retailer Charles Tyrwhitt (Figure 6.13).

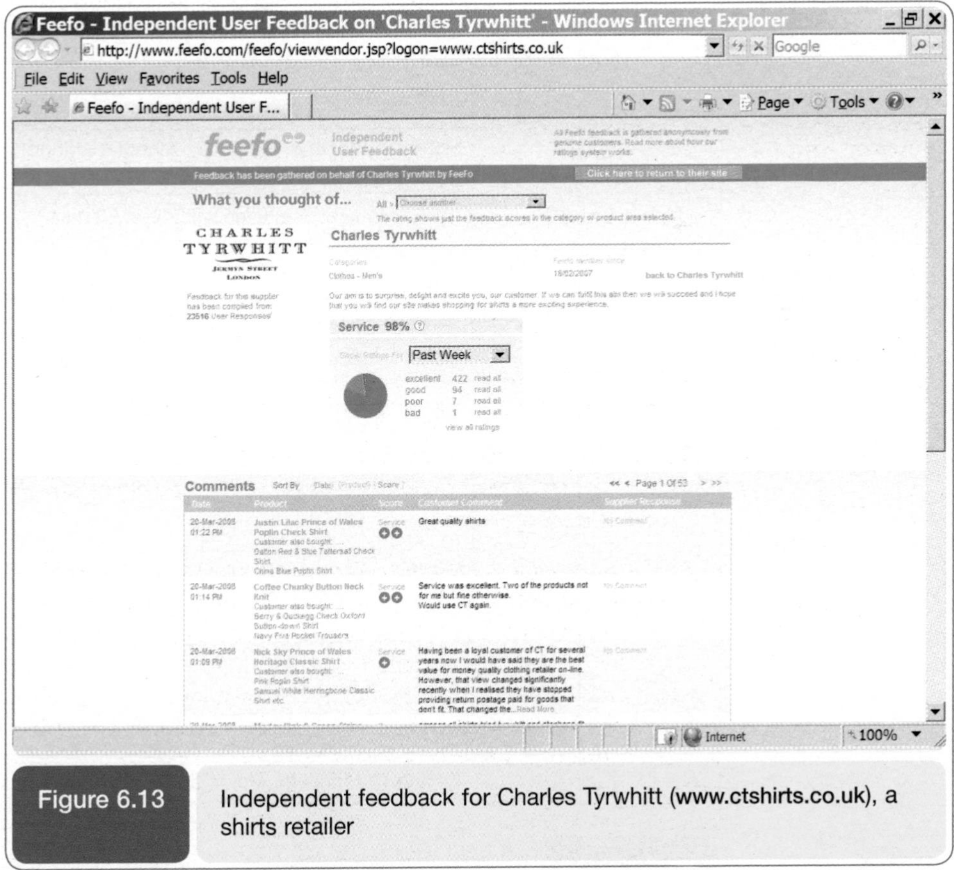

Figure 6.13 Independent feedback for Charles Tyrwhitt (www.ctshirts.co.uk), a shirts retailer

Kirby and Samson (2007) have critiqued the use of the NPS in practice. For example, they ask:

> is an NPS of 40, consisting of 70% promoters and 30% detractors, the same as the same NPS consisting of 40% promoters and 0% detractors?

They also quote research by Kumar *et al.* (2007) which shows that while about three-quarters of US telecoms and financial service customers may intend to recommend when asked, only about one-third actually follow through and only about 13 per cent of those referrals actually generate new customers. Keiningham *et al.* (2007) have assessed the value of recommendation metrics as determinants of customer lifetime value and also believe that the use of NPS could be misleading. They say the consequences of a simple focus on NPS are:

> the potential misallocation of customer satisfaction and loyalty resources due to flawed strategies that are guided by a myopic focus on customers' recommend intentions.

Differentiating customers by value and engagement

A core approach to relationship marketing is to focus our limited resources and marketing activities on the most valuable customers. Within the online customer base of an organisation, there will be customers who have different levels of activity or engagement with online services and purchasing. A good example is a bank – some customers may use the online account once a week, others much less frequently and some not at all. Figure 6.14 illustrates the different levels of activity in this case.

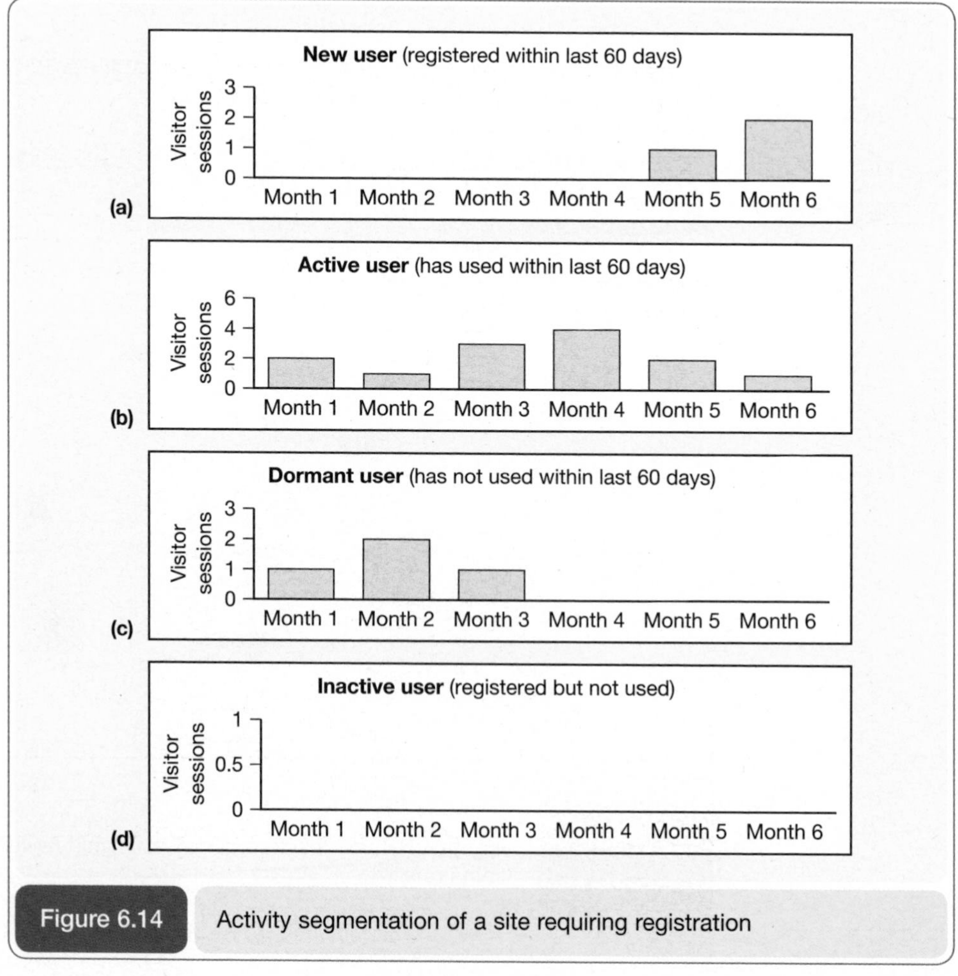

Figure 6.14 Activity segmentation of a site requiring registration

A key part of e-CRM strategy is to define measures that indicate activity levels and then develop tactics to increase activity levels through more frequent use. An online magazine could segment its customers in this way, also based on returning visitors. Even for companies without transactional service a similar concept can apply if they use e-mail marketing – some customers will regularly read and interact with the e-mail and others will not.

Objectives and corresponding tactics can be set for:

- Increasing the number of new users per month and annually (separate objectives will be set for existing bank customers and new bank customers) through promoting online services to drive visitors to the website.
- Increasing the percentage of active users (an appropriate threshold can be used – for different organisations it could be set at 7, 30 or 90 days). Using direct communications, such as e-mail, personalised website messages, direct mail and phone communications to new, dormant and inactive users, increases the percentage of active users.
- Decreasing the percentage of dormant users (once new or active – could be sub-categories) who have not used the service or responded to communications within a defined time period, such as three months.
- Decreasing the percentage of inactive users (or non-activated) users. These are those who signed up for a service such as online banking and had a username issued, but have not used the service.

You can see that corresponding strategies can be developed for each of these objectives.

Another key metric, in fact the *key* retention metric for e-commerce sites, refers to repeat business. The importance of retention rate metrics was highlighted by Agrawal *et al.* (2001). The main retention metrics they mention which influence profitability are:

- *repeat-customer base* – the proportion of the customer base that has made repeat purchases
- *number of transactions per repeat customer* – this indicates the stage of development of the customer in the relationship (another similar measure is number of product categories purchased)
- *revenue per transaction of repeat customer* – this is a proxy for lifetime value since it gives average order value.

Figure 6.15 gives a visual indication of this approach using the terminology suggested by Peppers and Rogers (2002). They identify three groups of customers with corresponding communications strategies:

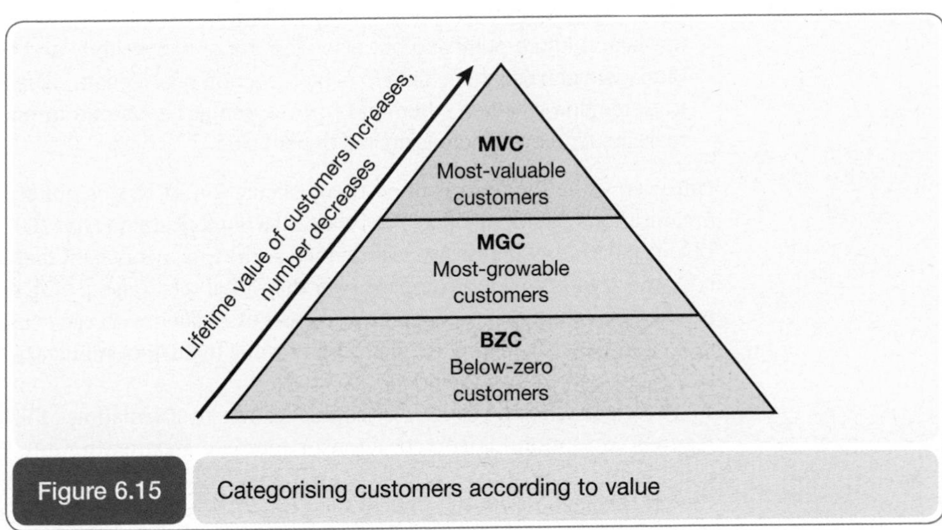

Figure 6.15 Categorising customers according to value

1 Most-valuable customers (MVCs)

These are the customers who contribute the most profit and are typically a small proportion of the total customer base as suggested by their position in the pyramid. These customers will likely have purchased more or higher-value products. The strategy for these customers focuses on retention rather than extension. In the case of a bank, personal relationship managers would be appointed for customers in this category to provide them with guidance and advice and to make sure they remain loyal. Often this strategy will work best using direct personal contact as the primary communication channel, but using online marketing for support where the customer has a propensity to use online channels.

2 Most-growable customers (MGCs)

These are customers who show potential to become more valuable customers. They are profitable when assessed in terms of lifetime value, but the number of product holdings or lifetime value is relatively low compared with the MVCs.

Strategies for these customers centre on extension, through making recommendations about relevant products based on previous purchases. Encouraging similar re-purchases could also be part of this. Online marketing offers great opportunities to make personalised recommendations through the website and e-mail.

3 Below-zero customers (BZCs)

BZCs are simply unprofitable customers. The strategy for these customers may vary – they can be encouraged to develop towards MGCs, but more typically expenditure will be minimised if it is felt that it will be difficult to change their loyalty behaviour or the source of their being unprofitable. Again, digital media can be used as a lower-cost form of marketing expenditure to encourage these customers to make repeat purchases or to allow them to self-serve online.

Lifetime value modelling

Lifetime value (LTV)
Lifetime value is the total net benefit that a customer or group of customers will provide a company over their total relationship with a company.

An appreciation of **lifetime value (LTV)** is key to the theory and practice of customer relationship management.

Digital technology has enabled marketers to become more sophisticated in how they can identify and target valuable customers. Kumar *et al.* (2007) explain it this way:

> By applying statistical models, they can predict not only when each customer is likely to make a future purchase but also what he or she will buy and through which channel. Managers can use these data to estimate a potential lifetime value for every customer and to determine whether, when and how to contact each one to maximise the chances of realising (and even increasing) his or her value.

However, while the term is often used, calculation of LTV is not straightforward, so many organisations do not calculate it. You are referred to Kumar *et al.* (2007) for an explanation of LTV calculations. Lifetime value is defined as the total net benefit that a customer, or group of customers, will provide a company over their total relationship with the company. Modelling is based on estimating the income and costs associated with each customer over a period of time, and then calculating the net present value in current monetary terms using a discount rate value applied over the period.

There are different degrees of sophistication in calculating LTV. These are indicated in Figure 6.16. Option 1 is a practical way or approximate proxy for future LTV, but the true LTV is the future value of the customer at an individual level.

Lifetime value modelling at segment level (4) is vital within marketing since it answers the question:

> How much can I afford to invest in acquiring a new customer?

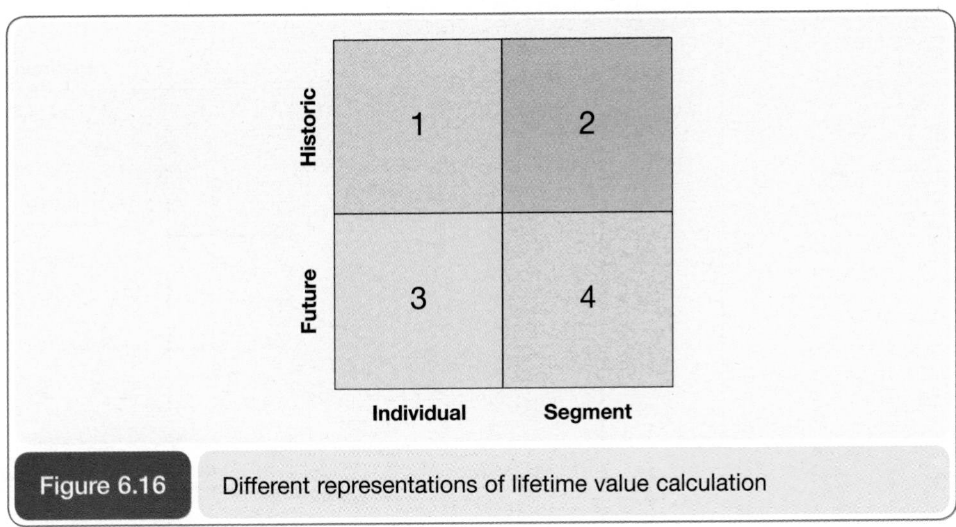

Figure 6.16 Different representations of lifetime value calculation

If online marketers try to answer this from a short-term perspective, as is often the case – i.e. by judging it based on the profit from a single sale on an e-commerce site – there are two problems:

- They become very focused on short-term return on investment (ROI) and so may not invest sufficiently to grow the business.
- They assume that each new customer is worth precisely the same and ignore differentials in loyalty and profitability between differing types of customer.

Lifetime value analysis enables marketers to:

- plan and measure investment in customer acquisition programmes
- identify and compare critical target segments
- measure the effectiveness of alternative customer retention strategies
- establish the true value of a company's customer base
- make decisions about products and offers
- make decisions about the value of introducing new E-CRM technologies.

Figure 6.17 gives an example of how LTV can be used to develop a CRM strategy for different customer groups. Four main types of customers are indicated by their current and future value as bronze, silver, gold and platinum. Distinct customer groupings (circles) are identified according to their current value (as indicated by current value) and future value as indicated by lifetime value calculations. Each of these groups will have a customer profile signature based on their demographics, so this can be used for customer selection. Different strategies are developed for different customer groups within the four main value groupings. Some bronze customers, such as groups A and B, realistically do not have development potential and are typically unprofitable, so the aim is to reduce costs in communications and if they do not remain as customers this is acceptable. Some bronze customers, such as group C, may have potential for growth so for these the strategy is to extend their purchases. Silver customers are targeted with customer extension offers and gold customers are extended where possible, although they have relatively little growth potential. Platinum customers are the best customers, so it is important to understand the communication preferences of these customers and to not over-communicate unless there is evidence that they may defect.

To illustrate another application of LTV and how it is calculated, take a look at the last example in Activity 6.1.

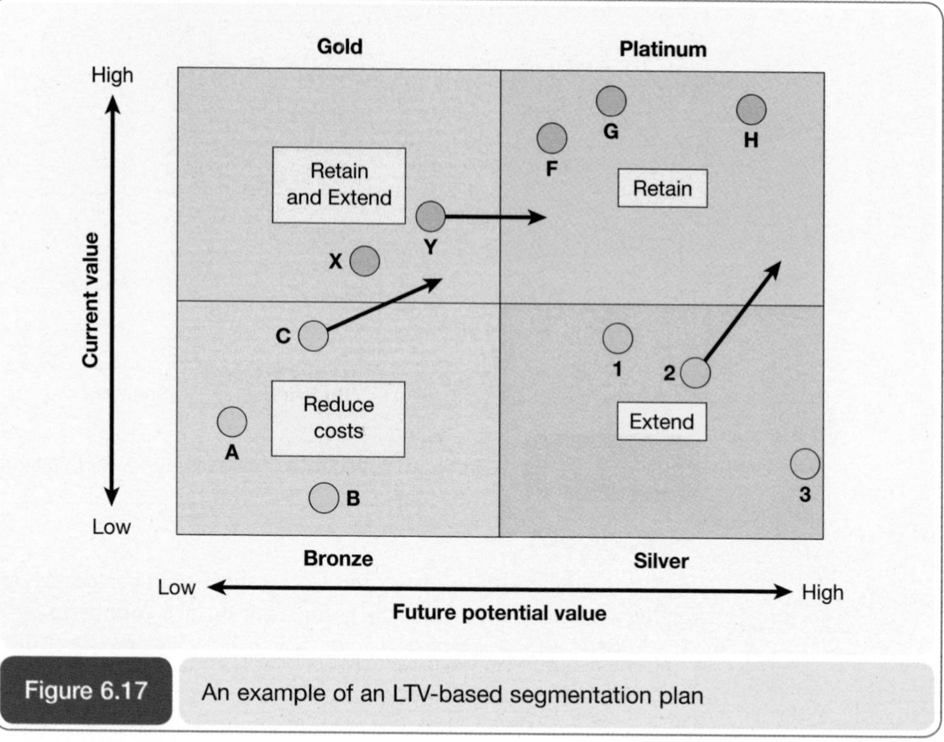

Figure 6.17 An example of an LTV-based segmentation plan

Activity 6.1 Charity uses lifetime value modelling to assess returns from new E-CRM system

A charity is considering implementing a new e-mail marketing system to increase donations from its donors. The charity's main role is as a relief agency which aims to reduce poverty through providing aid, particularly to the regions that need it most. Currently, its only e-mail activity is a monthly e-newsletter received by its 200,000 subscribers which features its current campaigns and appeals. It hopes to increase donations by using a more targeted approach based on previous customer behaviour. The e-mail system will integrate with the donor database which contains information on customer profiles and previous donations.

The company is considering three solutions which will cost between £50,000 and £100,000 in the first year. In the charity, all such investments are assessed using lifetime value modelling.

Table 6.3 is a lifetime value model showing customer value derived from using the current system and marketing activities.

A *Donors* – this is the number of initial donors. It declines each year dependent on the retention rate (row B).

B *Retention rate* – in lifetime value modelling this is usually found to increase year-on-year, since customers who stay loyal are more likely to remain loyal.

C *Donations per annum* – likewise, the charity finds that the average contributions per year increase through time within this group of customers.

D *Total donations* – calculated through multiplying rows A and C.

E *Net profit (at 20% margin)* – LTV modelling is based on profit contributed by this group of customers, row D is multiplied by 0.2.

Table 6.3 Lifetime value model for customer base for current system

	Year 1	Year 2	Year 3	Year 4	Year 5
A Donors	100,000	50,000	27,500	16,500	10,725
B Retention	50%	55%	60%	65%	70%
C Donations per annum	£100	£120	£140	£160	£180
D Total donations	£10,000,000	£6,000,000	£3,850,000	£2,640,000	£1,930,500
E Net profit (at 20% margin)	£2,000,000.0	£1,200,000.0	£770,000.0	£528,000.0	£386,100.0
F Discount rate	1	0.86	0.7396	0.636	0.547
G NPV contribution	£2,000,000.0	£1,032,000.0	£569,492.0	£335,808.0	£211,196.7
H Cumulative NPV contribution	£2,000,000.0	£3,032,000.0	£3,601,492.0	£3,937,300.0	£4,148,496.7
I Lifetime value at net present value	£20.0	£30.3	£36.0	£39.4	£41.5

F *Discount rate* – since the value of money held at a point in time will decrease due to inflation, a discount rate factor is applied to calculate the value of future returns in terms of current day value.

G *NPV contribution* – this is the profitability after taking the discount factor into account to give the net present value in future years. This is calculated by multiplying row E by row F.

H *Cumulative NPV contribution* – this adds the previous year's NPV for each year.

I *Lifetime value at net present value* – this is a value per customer calculated by dividing row H by the initial number of donors in Year 1.

Based on preliminary tests with improved targeting, it is estimated that with the new system, retention rates will increase from 50% to 51% in the first year, increasing by 5% per year as currently. It is estimated that in Year 1 donations per annum will increase from £100 per annum to £120 per annum, increasing by £20 per year as currently.

Question

Using the example of the lifetime value for the current donor base with the current system, calculate the LTV with the new system.

Kumar *et al.* (2007) note that the capability of a customer to generate value is divided into lifetime value of purchases (CLV) and what they term CRV, customer referral value. This concept is closely related to that of the 'net promoter score' identified earlier in the chapter.

These authors stress that there is not a clear correlation between CLV and CRV. For example, in their study they found that customers with the highest CLV did not have the highest CRV. So they suggest that customers should be segmented according to both attributes and then tactics developed. For one company they studied, they identified four groupings of customers presented in a customer value matrix plotting average CRV at one year on the *x* axis and average CLV after one year on the *y* axis to give these segments:

- *Champions (top-right) – 21% of customers*, CLV=$370, CRV=$590
- *Misers (bottom-left) – 21% of customers*, CLV=$130, CRV=$64
- *Affluents (top-left) – 29% of customers*, CLV=$1219, CRV=$49
- *Advocates (bottom-right) – 29% of customers*, CLV=$180, CRV=$670

You can see that it would be worthwhile using different tactics for each segment to encourage recommendation or purchase – for example to migrate misers to affluents or advocates, and advocates and affluents to champions.

Indepth analysis of customer data has traditionally been completed by catalogue retailers such as Argos, Littlewoods Index or retailers such as Boots (see Mini Case Study 6.6) using a technique known as 'RFM analysis'. This technique tends to be little known outside retail circles, but e-CRM gives great potential to apply it in a range of techniques since we can use it not only to analyse purchase history, but also visit or log-in frequency to a site or online service and response rates to e-mail communications.

Mini Case Study 6.6 Boots mine diamonds in their customer data

The high street retailer Boots launched its Advantage loyalty card in 1997. Today, there are over 15 million card holders of whom 10 million are active. Boots describes the benefits for its card holders as follows.

There are 23 analysts in the Customer Insight team, run by Helen James, who mine the data available about card users and their transactional behaviour. They use tools including MicroStrategy's DSS Agent and Andyne's GQL which are used for the majority of queries. IBM's Intelligent Miner for Data is used for more advanced data mining, such as segmentation and predictive modelling. Helen James describes the benefits of data mining as follows:

> *From our traditional electronic point-of-sale data we knew what was being sold, but now [through data mining] we can determine what different groups of customers are buying and monitor their behaviour over time.*

This case study gives these examples of the applications of data mining:

> *What interests the analysts most is the behaviour of groups of customers. They are interested, for example, in the effect of Boots' marketing activity on customers – such as the impact of promotional offers on buying patterns over time. They can make a valuable input to decisions about layout, ranging and promotions by using market basket analysis to provide insight into the product purchasing repertoires of different groups of customers.*

Like others, Boots has made a feature of multi-buy promotional schemes in recent years with numerous 'three for the price of two' and even 'two for the price of one' offers. Using the card data the Insight team has now been able to identify four groups of promotion buyers:

- the deal seekers who only ever buy promotional lines
- the stockpilers who buy in bulk when goods are on offer and then don't visit the store for weeks
- the loyalists – existing buyers who will buy a little more of a line when it is on offer but soon revert to their usual buying patterns
- the new market – customers who start buying items when on promotion and then continue to purchase the same product once it reverts to normal price.

'This sort of analysis helps marketeers to understand what they are achieving via their promotions, rather than just identifying the uplift. They can see whether they are attracting new long-term business or just generating short-term uplift and also the extent to which they are cannibalising existing lines,' says Helen. Analysing market basket trends by shopper over time is also providing Boots with a new view of its traditional product categories. Customers buying skin-care products, for example, often buy hair-care products as well so this is a good link to use in promotions, direct mail and in-store activity.

Other linkings which emerge from the data – as Helen says, quite obvious when one thinks about them – include films and suntan lotion; sensitive skin products – be they washing-up gloves, cosmetics or skincare; and films and photograph frames with new baby products. 'Like many large retailers we are still organised along product category lines,' she says, 'so it would never really occur to the baby products buyers to create a special offer linked to picture frames – yet these are the very thing which new parents are likely to want.'

'We're also able to see how much shoppers participate in a particular range,' says Helen. 'They may buy toothbrushes, but do they also buy toothpaste and dental floss?' It may well be more profitable to encourage existing customers to buy deeper in the range than to attract new ones.

Monitoring purchases over time is also helping to identify buying patterns which fuel further marketing effort. Disposable nappy purchases, for example, are generally limited by the number of packs a customer can carry. A shopper visiting Boots once a fortnight and buying nappies is probably buying from a number of supply sources, whereas one calling at the store twice a week probably gets most of her baby's nappy needs from Boots. Encouraging the first shopper to visit more often would probably also increase nappy sales. Boots combines its basic customer demographic data (data such as age, gender, number of children and postcode) with externally available data. However, according to Helen, 'the real power comes from being able to combine this with detailed purchase behaviour data – and this is now being used to fuel business decisions outside of the marketing arena.'

This helps Boots to understand the main drivers of customer value and identify which customers they should value and retain and which could be more valuable if they focused on them more.

Lifestage analysis provides insight into how a customer's value changes over their lifetime. Using it, Boots can identify which are the potentially valuable customers of the future. They can also see the point at which a customer might become less valuable and try to prevent this. It is also clear that some messages become very important at certain times (for example, vitamins to people over 35 who have realised they may not be immortal) and irrelevant at others (what mother is concerned about cosmetics within a couple of weeks of the birth of her child?). This informs the mix of messages the customer receives, for instance via direct mail.

Attitudinal insight from market research surveys and questionnaires gives Boots an understanding of the attitudes driving the behaviour they see on their database. It is pointless directing a lot of marketing effort at people whose attitudes mean that they are unlikely to become more valuable to Boots.

This diversity of data is being used to build up a multi-dimensional picture of customers that gets to the heart of what drives customer value both today and into the future. Analysis of attitudes and customer repertoires offers Boots pointers to influencing customer value in a positive way. This understanding of customers has many applications within Boots, from the way the Boots brand is communicated to specific cross-selling activities for store staff. One of the first applications of this segmentation was as a driver of the Boots relationship marketing programme enabled by the Advantage card.

The segmentation provides a framework for relationship marketing. Specific campaigns help Boots to deliver that framework. These could encourage customers to shop along different themes – summer holidays, Christmas shopping – and incentivise them to make a visit. They may simply raise awareness of a particular new product or service – Boots Health & Travel Cover launched in April is a good example of this. They could be an invitation to an exclusive shopping event where the customer can shop in peace and perhaps earn extra points as well.

To make all this happen Boots needed a campaign management system that could involve customers in the relationship marketing programme most relevant to them. The 'campaign management' component has been fully integrated within CDAS (Cross-domain Authentication Service) through a bespoke development by IBM. This means that direct marketing analysts are able to develop their target customer profiles without having to first create a separate extract of the data, and are also able to base these profiles on the full richness of information held within the database. Having defined these criteria, the system will automatically come up with a mailing list of matching card holders with no further intervention. The system not only automates the measurement of basic campaign response analysis, but also makes the list of customers actually mailed available within the analysis environment so that more sophisticated response analysis can be performed. 'The close integration of the campaign management system within the analytic environment of CDAS is one of its main strengths' – 'not only are we able to drive high response rates by tightly targeting relevant customer groups, but we are able to close the loop from initial customer analysis, through customer selection and campaign execution back to campaign response measurement and further campaign analysis.'

Computer Weekly (2001), Interactive Being. *Computer Weekly*, 2 May 2001, article by Lindsay Nicolle

Recency frequency monetary value (RFM) analysis

RFM is sometimes known as FRAC, which stands for: Frequency, Recency, Amount (obviously equivalent to monetary value), Category (types of product purchased – not included within RFM). We will now give an overview of how RFM approaches can be applied, with special reference to online marketing. We will also look at the related concepts of latency and hurdle rates.

Recency

This is the recency of customer action, e.g. purchase, site visit, account access, e-mail response. Novo (2003) stresses the importance of recency when he says:

> Recency, or the number of days that have gone by since a customer completed an action (purchase, log-in, download, etc., is the most powerful predictor of the customer repeating an action ... Recency is why you receive another catalogue from the company shortly after you make your first purchase from them.

Online applications of analysis of recency include monitoring through time to identify vulnerable customers, and scoring customers to preferentially target more responsive customers for cost savings.

Frequency

Frequency is the number of times an action is completed in a period of a customer action, e.g. purchase, visit, e-mail response – for example five purchases per year, five visits per month, five log-ins per week, five e-mail opens per month, five e-mail clicks per year. Online applications of this analysis include combining with recency for 'RF targeting'.

Monetary value

The monetary value of purchase(s) can be measured in different ways – for example average order value of £50, total annual purchase value of £5000. Generally, customers with higher monetary values tend to have a higher loyalty and potential future value since they have purchased more items historically. One example application would be to exclude these customers from special promotions if their RF scores suggested they were actively purchasing. Frequency is often a proxy for monetary value per year since the more products purchased, the higher the overall monetary value. It is possible, then, to simplify analysis by just using recency and frequency. Monetary value can also skew the analysis with high-value initial purchases.

Latency
The average length of time that different customers types takes between different activities, e.g. log-ins, paying bills, first and second purchase.

Latency

Latency is a powerful concept, closely related to frequency – it is the average time between customer events in the customer lifecycle. Examples include the average time between website visits, second and third purchase and e-mail click-throughs. Online applications of latency include putting in place triggers that alert companies to customer behaviour outside the norm, for example increased interest or disinterest, and then to manage this behaviour using e-communications or traditional communications. For example, if a B2B or B2C organisation with a long interval between purchases found that latency decreased for a particular customer, then they may be investigating an additional purchase via e-mail or website (their recency and frequency would likely increase also). E-mails, phone calls or direct mail could then be used to target this person with relevant offers according to what they were searching for.

Hurdle rate

Hurdle rate
The proportion of customers that fall within a particular level of activity. For example, the percentage of members of an e-mail list that click on the e-mail within a 90-day period, or the number of customers that have made a second purchase.

According to Novo (2003), **hurdle rate** refers to the percentage of customers in a group (such as in a segment or on a list) who have completed an action. It is a useful concept since it can be used to compare the engagement of different groups or to set targets to increase engagement with online channels as the examples below show:

- 20 per cent of customers have visited in the past six months
- 5 per cent of customers have made three or more purchases this year
- 60 per cent of registrants have logged on to system this year
- 30 per cent have clicked through on e-mail this year.

Grouping customers into different RFM categories

In the examples above, each division for recency, frequency and monetary value is placed in an arbitrary position to place a roughly equal number of customers in each group. This approach is also useful since the marketer can set thresholds of value relevant to their understanding of their customers.

RFM analysis involves two techniques for grouping customers:

1 Statistical RFM analysis

This involves placing an equal number of customers in each RFM category using quintiles of 20% (10 deciles can also be used for larger databases) as shown in Figure 6.18. The figure also shows one application of RFM with a view to using communications channels more effectively. Lower-cost e-communications can be used to correspond with customers who use only services more frequently since they prefer these channels, while more expensive offline communications can be used for customers who seem to prefer traditional channels.

2 Arbitrary divisions of customer database

This approach is also useful since the marketer can set thresholds of value relevant to their understanding of their customers.

For example, RFM analysis can be applied for targeting using e-mail according to how a customer interacts with an e-commerce site. Values could be assigned to each customer as follows:

Recency:
1 – Over 12 months
2 – Within last 12 months
3 – Within last 6 months
4 – Within last 3 months
5 – Within last 1 month

Frequency:
1 – More than once every 6 months
2 – Every 6 months
3 – Every 3 months
4 – Every 2 months
5 – Monthly

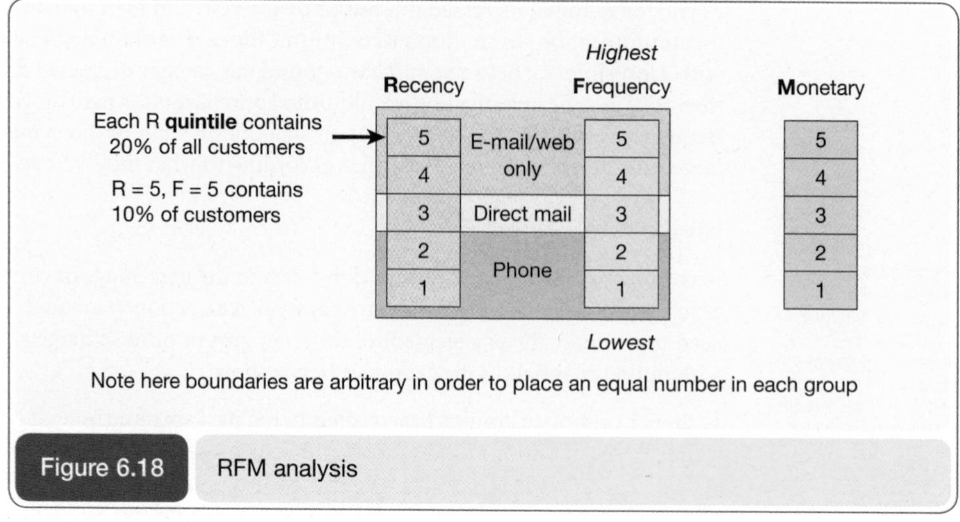

Figure 6.18 RFM analysis

Monetary value:
1 – Less than £10
2 – £10–£50
3 – £50–£100
4 – £100–£200
5 – More than £200

Simplified versions of this analysis can be created to make it more manageable – for example a theatre group uses these nine categories for its direct marketing:

Oncers (attended theatre once):

- Recent oncer — attended <12 months
- Rusty oncer — attended >12 but <36 months
- Very rusty oncer — attended in 36+ months

Twicers:

- Recent twicer — attended <12 months
- Rusty twicer — attended >12 but <36 months
- Very rusty twicer — attended in 36+ months

2+ subscribers:

- Current subscribers — booked 2+ events in current season
- Recent — booked 2+ last season
- Very rusty — booked 2+ more than a season ago

Another example, with real-world data, is shown in Figure 6.19. You can see that plotting customer numbers against recency and frequency in this way for an online company gives a great visual indication of the health of the business and groups that can be targeted to encourage more repeat purchases.

Product recommendations and propensity modelling

Propensity modelling The approach of evaluating customer characteristics and behaviour and then making recommendations for future products.

Propensity modelling is one name given to the approach of evaluating customer characteristics and behaviour, in particular previous products or services purchased, and then making recommendations for the next suitable product. However, it is best known as recommending the 'Next best product' to existing customers.

A related acquisition approach is to target potential customers with similar characteristics through renting direct mail or e-mail lists or advertising online in similar locations.

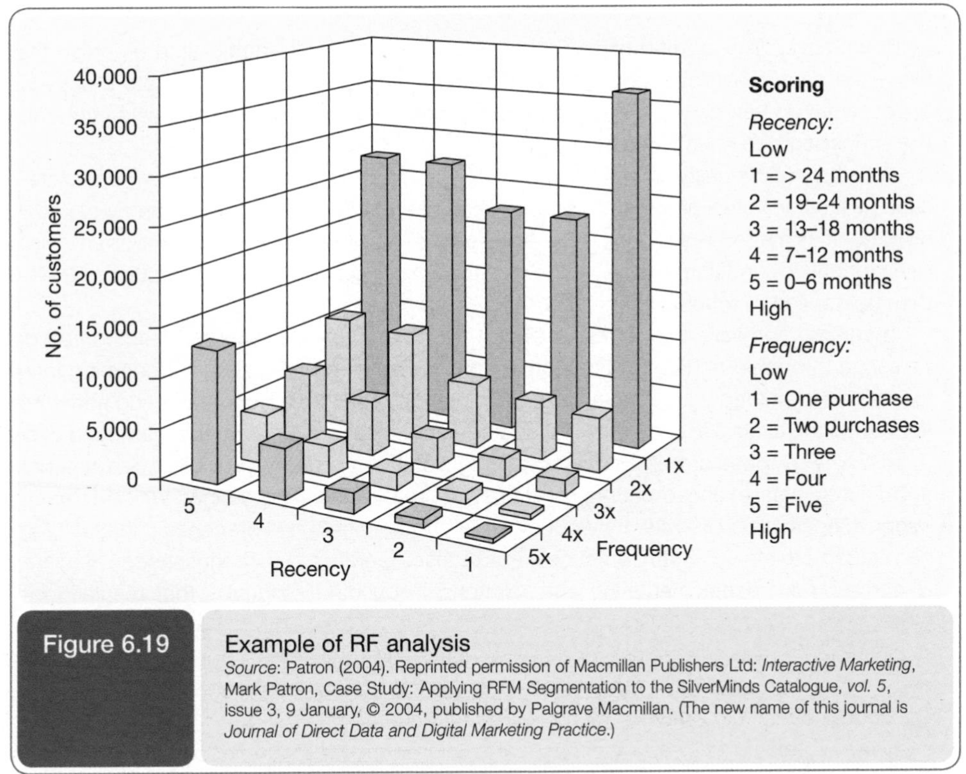

Figure 6.19 Example of RF analysis

Source: Patron (2004). Reprinted permission of Macmillan Publishers Ltd: *Interactive Marketing*, Mark Patron, Case Study: Applying RFM Segmentation to the SilverMinds Catalogue, *vol. 5*, issue 3, 9 January, © 2004, published by Palgrave Macmillan. (The new name of this journal is *Journal of Direct Data and Digital Marketing Practice*.)

The following recommendations are based on those in van Duyne *et al.* (2003):

1 *Create automatic product relationships* [i.e. Next best product]. A low-tech approach to this is, for each product, to group together products previously purchased together. Then for each product, rank product by number of times purchased together to find relationships.
2 *Cordon off and minimise the 'real estate' devoted to related products.* An area of screen should be reserved for 'Next best product prompts' for up-selling and cross-selling. However, if these can be made part of the current product they may be more effective.
3 *Use familiar 'trigger words'.* That is, familiar from using other sites such as Amazon. Such phrases include: 'Related products', 'Your recommendations', 'Similar', 'Customers who bought . . .', 'Top 3 related products'.
4 *Editorialise about related products.* That is, within copy about a product.
5 *Allow quick purchase of related products.*
6 *Sell related product during checkout.* And also on post-transaction pages, i.e. after one item has been added to the basket or purchased.

Note that techniques do not necessarily require an expensive recommendations engine except for very large sites.

Mini Case Study 6.7 Charity PDSA refines its understanding of its members

The context for this case is provided by Robin Prouse who is the training manager of Apteco Ltd, (**www.apteco.com**) a company that specialises in analytical marketing software. He is in a unique position to understand the difficulties and challenges facing many organisations in making sense of their customer data and has worked with PDSA.

Robin says, 'The starting place for most organisations is to gather and organise their data in one place. Once the data is available and in a suitable software tool such as FastStats Discoverer, the question then arises, what do you do with it? Understanding and being able to visualise who your current customers are is the springboard to effective marketing.

Software functionality allows for RFM information to be found and in turn calculate valuable knowledge, such as lifetime value, and identify segments at risk of attrition or churn. When you know your customers, the opportunities for cross-sell or up-sell become more apparent. Once these important customer segments have been identified, profiling tools give you the ability to find the key characteristics of their members, which can then be applied to other existing customers or prospects.

Integrated software now makes it easier for the marketer to take their segmented data and present their message through a number of different channels. E-mail broadcasting is becoming increasingly popular and being able to upload your contact list and content directly from your marketing software adds another link to the marketing cycle. By capturing and adding responses to your data, the marketing cycle is made complete.'

PDSA (**www.pdsa.org**) is the UK's leading veterinary charity providing free veterinary care for the sick and injured pets of those unable to afford veterinary fees. The charity, which is entirely funded by public support, operates a UK-wide network of 47 PetAid hospitals and branches and also works through some 348 contracted private veterinary practices. PDSA also operates 180 charity shops UK-wide, but its main income is derived from direct marketing and relationship-building programs that result in gifts in wills, voluntary donations and trading activities.

The charity uses Discoverer for detailed marketing analytics, supporter profiling, database segmentation and predictive modelling. The direct marketing and legacy teams also make extensive use of Discoverer's Cascade module for campaign planning and management.

PDSA holds a huge database of past transactional and promotional histories on nearly six million supporters. This data set is used to report lifetime value, patterns and trends in support, and for the identification of cross-sell and up-sell opportunities. In conjunction with third-party geo-demographic data, Discoverer has been used to build sophisticated legacy propensity models, donor profiles and channel attrition analysis.

As PDSA improves its online presence via its website (**www.pdsa.org.uk**) and dedicated e-mail marketing campaigns, Discoverer has increasingly been used to monitor and classify donor e-mail addresses. This allows marketers to combine online knowledge with that contained in transactional and operational systems – linking offline lifetime value, demographics and product propensity models with online marketing permissions and click-through analysis.

Applying virtual communities and social networks for CRM

We have discussed some of the psychological reasons for the popularity of social networks in Chapter 2 in the section on consumer buyer behaviour and in Chapter 9 we review some of the related Web 2.0 marketing techniques that can be used for customer acquisition. But in this section, we consider why social networks have developed and how they can be used to develop customer understanding and for relationship building.

Virtual community
An Internet-based forum for special-interest groups to communicate.

The reasons for the popularity of **virtual communities** today such as the social networks Facebook, Google+ and LinkedIn can be traced back to the nineteenth century. The German sociologist Ferdinand Tonnies (1855–1936) made the distinction between public society and private community (Loomis, 1957). Tonnies employed the terms *Gemeinschaft* meaning 'community' (informal, organic or instinctive ties typified by the family or neighbourhood) and *Gesellschaft* meaning 'society' (formal, impersonal, instrumental, goal-orientated relations typified by big cities, the state and large organisations). Membership of *Gemeinschaft* is self-fulfilling (intrinsic motivation) whereas being a member of a *Gesellschaft* is a means to further individual goals (extrinsic motivation).

Marshall McLuhan (1964) posited that 'cool' (meaning on-going and shared) and inclusive 'electric media' (meaning telephone and television, rather than books) would 'retribalise' human society into clusters of affiliation. Nicholas Negroponte (1995) predicted that in the near future 'we will socialise in digital neighbourhoods'. Manuel Castells (1996) has developed the concept of 'networked individualism', in which individuals build their networks on and off-line on the basis of values, interests and projects, and believes that 'our societies are increasingly structured around the bipolar opposition of the Net and the Self'.

Virtual communities are the emerging construct of the traditional social marketplaces where groups of people who share common interests and needs come together online. Most are drawn together by the opportunity to share a sense of community with like-minded individuals, regardless of where they live.

Virtual communities also provide opportunities for some companies to develop relationships with their customers. Since the publication of the article by Armstrong and Hagel in 1996 entitled 'The real value of online communities' and John Hagel's subsequent book (Hagel, 1997) there has been much discussion about using digital media to create virtual communities.

The power of the virtual communities, according to Hagel (1997), is that they exhibit a number of positive feedback loops (or 'virtuous circles'). Focused content attracts new members, who in turn contribute to the quantity and quality of the community's pooled knowledge. Member loyalty grows as the community grows and evolves. The purchasing power of the community grows and thus the community attracts more advertisers to fund it. The growing revenue potential attracts yet more vendors, providing more choice and attracting more members. As the size and sophistication of the community grow (while it still remains tightly focused) its data-gathering and profiling capabilities increase – thus enabling better-targeted marketing and attracting more vendors . . . and so on. In such positive feedback loops there is an initial start-up period of slow and uneven growth until critical mass in members, content, vendors and transactions is reached. The potential for growth is then exponential – until the limits of the focus of the community as it defines itself are reached.

All of these predictions are now a reality, particularly within the social networks which support rich interactions. When deciding on a strategic approach to online communities, companies essentially have two main options if they decide to use them as part of their efforts in relationship building. They can either create community through other sites (earned media, Chapter 1) or provide community facilities on their own site (owned media). We will look at the options for each separately, but it's worth noting that the overlap between the two is increasing due to capability for social sign-on that we introduced earlier in the chapter with the Sears Social example (SmartInsights, 2011).

1 Creating community through social networks

The main social media platforms which can offer a presence for companies are Facebook, Twitter, LinkedIn, Google+ and YouTube. Other social media platforms do exist, but they tend to have a smaller audience reach as they have a niche focus. The most commonly used options are:

1. *Facebook company page.* These are popular with many types of companies. See **http://statistics.allfacebook.com** for a compilation. Facebook pages are designed to help businesses engage an audience and so promote their products and services. The members of the page are referred to as 'fans' who 'Like' the page. These fans can then receive status update information from the business page within their news feeds. Paid Facebook ads can be used to recruit new fans, but fans will also be attracted as other fans like the page or share information.
2. *Twitter page.* Twitter enables companies to setup their own page with communication made through messages that can contain up to 140 characters. Currently the pages for companies are the same as those for indviduals with a short bio featuring the company. Crucially for communication, as with Facebook status updates, these messages can contain links through to the company website which contain relevant content or offers to engage the audience. Twitter is also commonly used for customer service. Some companies like retailers Dell and ASOS have separate channels for customer offers and support.

3 *LinkedIn Company pages and groups.* LinkedIn is the most popular network to track and maintain professional contacts within the business world. Therefore, it is often utilised by academics, corporate executives and professionals. It allows users to promote their experience and expertise through resumes and professional recommendations. Companies can set up a company page which similar to other networks has status updates to communicate new products and services and users can comment on these. Many companies also setup their own group on LinkedIn which can cover a topic but is branded by the company. For example, jobs company OnlyMarketingJobs.com set up a group called Digital/Online Marketing Professionals (DOMP) which raises awareness of the brand although discussions are about digital marketing practice more widely.
4 *Google+.* Google+ is more recently established and at the time of writing only has a limited number of company pages from companies like Ford. These follow a similar model to Facebook company pages.
5 *YouTube channels.* These enable companies to post and host videos which users can comment on. The level of usage of these channels tends to be lower than that for other social networks so consequently they are not so widely used.

Before investing a lot of time in trying to build a community within a social network, it's important for business to establish strategic priorities and processes that will give the best results. We covered some of these decisions in Chapter 4 (see key strategic decision 5 – engagement strategy).

2 Creating your own presence

If a company sets up a community facility on its own site or sets up a separately branded community like the American Express Open Forum (**www.openforum.com**), it is more closely aligned to the goals and brand values of the website. Since registered members of the community will be on the company database, the community will provide opportunities for email marketing and research about the company and its products as part of the learning relationship. However, the brand may be damaged if customers criticise products, so some moderation is required. Honda UK (**www.honda.co.uk/car**) gives a good example of a community created by their brand on their site. Rather than having a separate community section, the community is integrated within the context of each car as a 'second opinions' review menu option in the context of each car. Interestingly, some negative comments are permitted to make the discussion more meaningful.

A potential problem with a company-hosted forum is that it may be unable to get sufficient people to contribute to give the community 'critical mass'. An example where initial recruitment of contributors and moderation has been used to grow the forum successfully is shown in Figure 6.20. Communities are best suited to high-involvement brands, such as a professional body like CIPD, or those related to sports and hobbies and business-to-business.

Based on a study of some the first online communities, Durlacher (1999) suggested, that depending on market sector, an organisation has a choice of developing different types of community: communities of purpose, position and interest for B2C, and of profession for B2B.

- *Purpose* – people who are going through the same process or trying to achieve a particular objective. Examples include those researching cars, e.g. at Autotrader (**www.autotrader.co.uk**), or stocks online, e.g. at the Motley Fool (**www.motleyfool.co.uk**). Price or product comparison services such as Bizrate (**www.bizrate.com**) are also in this category.
- *Position* – people who are in a certain circumstance, such as a health disorder, or in a certain stage of life, such as communities set up specifically for young people or old people. Examples are teenage chat site Habbo Hotel (**www.habbohotel.com**), 50 Connect (**www.50connect.co.uk**) and MumsNet (**www.mumsnet.com**).
- *Interest* – this community is for people who share an interest or passion such as sport (**www.thefootballforum.net**), music (**www.pepsi.com**) or leisure (**www.ukclimbing.com**).
- *Profession* – these are important for companies promoting B2B services.

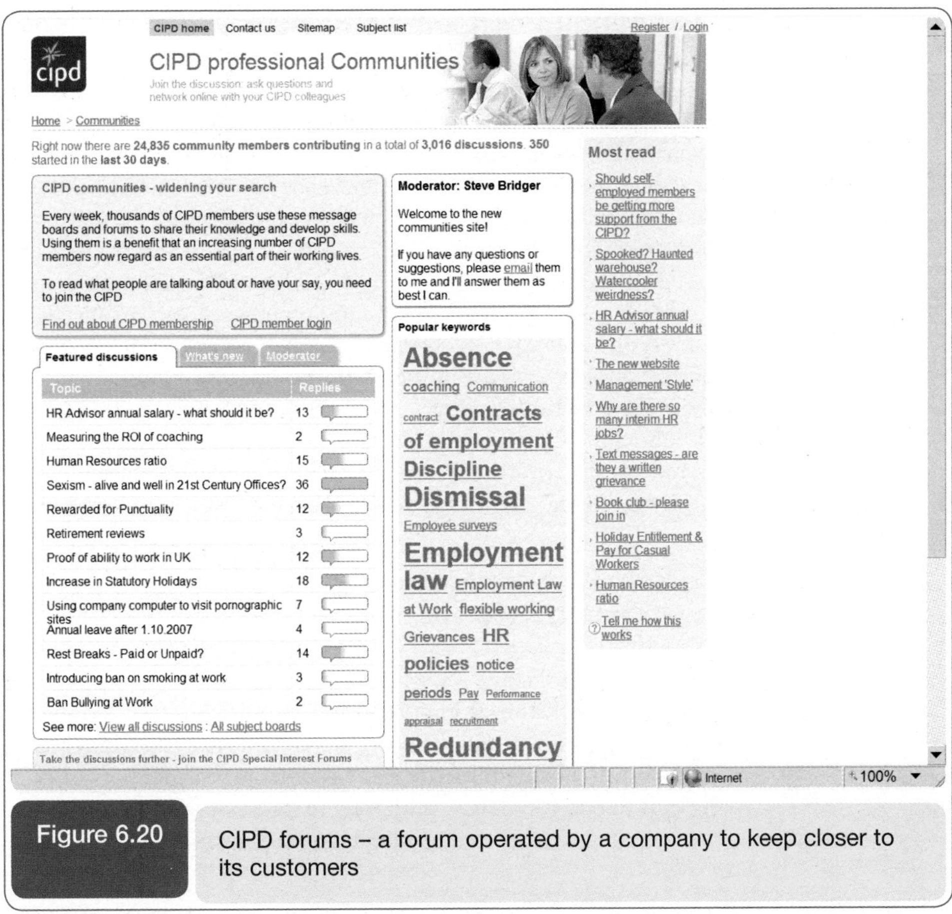

Figure 6.20 CIPD forums – a forum operated by a company to keep closer to its customers

A further classification of communities is that of Armstrong and Hagel (1996) which is arguably less useful and identifies communities of transaction, communities of interest, communities of fantasy and communities of relationship.

What tactics can organisations use to foster community? Despite the hype and potential, many communities fail to generate activity, and a silent community isn't a community. Parker (2000) suggests eight questions organisations should ask when considering how to create a customer community and encourage advocacy:

1 What interests, needs or passions do many of your customers have in common?
2 What topics or concerns might your customers like to share with each other?
3 What information is likely to appeal to your customers' friends or colleagues?
4 What other types of business in your area appeal to buyers of your products and services?
5 How can you create packages or offers based on combining offers from two or more affinity partners?
6 What price, delivery, financing or incentives can you afford to offer to friends (or colleagues) that your current customers recommend?
7 What types of incentives or rewards can you afford to provide for customers who recommend friends (or colleagues) who make a purchase?
8 How can you best track purchases resulting from word-of-mouth recommendations from friends?

These types of questions remain valid both for a company's own community and conversations hosted on social networks like Facebook and Twitter.

Marketing to consumers using independent social networks

One potential benefit of marketing to virtual communities is that they are naturally formed around problems shared, benefits sought, interests etc. and so are naturally self-segmented. Segmentation occurs at a microscopic level – for example, the biggest community on eBay Neighbourhoods is currently (**http://neighbourhoods.ebay.com/espresso-machines**) which has developed for aficionados of quality coffee to debate the merits of various strains of coffee beans, of methods of preparation, of coffee machines and of brands such as Starbucks. Each species of bean, each processing mode, each machine and each brand will have its enthusiasts.

The owners of many specialist communities will be seeking advertising revenue (see Case Study 8 on Facebook), so they may accept links to merchants and display advertising if the match of product/service and community interests is close enough and the advertising doesn't divert from the community.

Although social networks such as Facebook and MySpace use advertising as a revenue source, for the advertisers responses tend to be low because the focus of users is on interacting, not on the ads.

Customer experience – the missing element required for customer loyalty

We have in this chapter shown how delivering relevant timely communications as part of permission marketing is important to developing loyalty. However, even the most relevant communications will fail if another key factor is not taken into account – this is the *customer experience*. If a first-time or repeat customer experience is poor due to a slow-to-download difficult-to-use site, then it is unlikely that loyalty from the online customer will develop. In the next chapter we review techniques used to help develop this experience.

Case Study 6 Dell gets closer to its customers through its social media strategy

Dell is well known as a technology company, offering a broad range of product categories, including desktop computer systems, storage, servers and networking products, mobility products, software and peripherals, and services to manage IT infrastructure for large organisations.

Dell business strategy

Dell's vision is to 'strive to provide the best possible customer experience by offering: superior value; high-quality, relevant technology; customised systems; superior service and support; and differentiated products and services that are easy to buy and use'.

The core elements of the strategy which are evident in Dell's marketing communications are:

- *We simplify information technology for customers.* Making quality personal computers, servers, storage and services affordable is Dell's legacy. We are focused on making information technology affordable for millions of customers around the world. As a result of our direct relationships with customers, or 'customer intimacy', we are best positioned to simplify how customers implement and maintain information technology and deliver hardware, services and software solutions tailored for their businesses and homes.
- *We offer customers choice.* Customers can purchase systems and services from Dell via telephone, kiosks and our website, **www.dell.com**, where they may review, configure and price systems within our entire product line; order systems online, and track orders from manufacturing through shipping. We have recently launched a retail initiative and plan to expand that initiative by adding new distribution channels to reach additional consumers and small businesses through retail partners and value-added resellers globally.
- *Customers can purchase custom-built products and custom-tailored services.* Historically our flexible, build-to-order manufacturing process enabled us to turn over inventory every five days on average, thereby reducing inventory levels and rapidly bring the latest technology to our customers. The market and our competition has evolved and we are now exploring the utilisation of original design manufacturers and new distribution strategies to better meet

customer needs and reduce product cycle times. Our goal is to introduce the latest relevant technology more quickly and to rapidly pass on component cost savings to a broader set of our customers worldwide.

- *We are committed to being environmentally responsible in all areas of our business*. We have built environmental consideration into every stage of the Dell product lifecycle – from developing and designing energy-efficient products, to reducing the footprint of our manufacturing and operations, to customer use and product recovery.

Dell's sales and marketing

Dell sell products and services directly to customers through dedicated sales representatives, telephone-based sales and online at **www.dell.com**. Customer segments include large corporate, government, healthcare and education accounts, as well as small-to-medium businesses and individual consumers.

Dell stresses the importance of its direct business model in providing direct and continuous feedback from customers, thereby allowing them to develop and refine our products and marketing programmes for specific customer groups.

In its SEC filing, Dell emphasises how it listens to customers to develop relevant innovative technology and services they trust and value. Evidence for using the participative nature of Web 2.0 is that customers can offer suggestions for current and future Dell products, services and operations on an interactive portion of the Dell website called Dell IdeaStorm. It says: 'This constant flow of communication, which is unique to our direct business model, also allows us to rapidly gauge customer satisfaction and target new or existing products.'

For large business and institutional customers, Dell maintain a field sales force throughout the world. Dedicated account teams, which include field-based system engineers and consultants, form long-term relationships to provide our largest customers with a single source of assistance and develop specific tailored solutions for these customers. Dell also maintain specific sales and marketing programmes targeted at federal, state and local governmental agencies as well as specific healthcare and educational markets.

Dell Premier

For its large organisational customers, Dell offers Premier (**http://premier.dell.com**), which is a secure, customisable procurement and support site or extranet designed to save organisations time and money through all phases of I/T product ownership. The main benefits of Dell Premier are described as:

- *Easy ordering* – a custom online store ensures access to your products at your price.
- *Easy tracking* – view real-time order status, online invoices and purchase history details.
- *Easy control* – custom access groups define what users can see and do within Premier.

Marketing communications

Dell markets its products and services to small-to-medium businesses and consumers primarily by advertising on television and the Internet, advertising in a variety of print media and by mailing a broad range of direct marketing publications, such as promotional pieces, catalogues and customer newsletters. In certain locations Dell also operate stores or kiosks, typically located within shopping centres, that allow customers to view our products in person and purchase online with the assistance of a Dell expert.

Dell online communications

The management of the consumer site was presented to EConsultancy (2008). Dell has a three-stage order funnel:

- marketing communications execution measured by site visits
- site merchandising measured by *consideration* % (site visits to e-store visits)
- store merchandising measured by *conversion* % (e-store visits to e-receipts).

The presenter explained how Dell aims to understand and act on customer behaviour based on identification of a series of consideration drivers – for example, the quality of online advertising; path quality through site; merchandising/offers – and conversion drivers – for example, configurator 'ease of use'; accessibility of decision support tools and consistency of message through the entire path.

Dell will invest in strategic improvements to the site to improve these levers – examples mentioned included new merchandising approaches such as customer ratings and reviews, videos, major 'path' or customer journey changes created through decision support tools to 'Help me choose'. There are also more tactical initiatives to help deliver the right message to each customer including customisation/personalisation, real estate optimisation and message balancing.

More tactical persuasion of site visitors is based on price moves/optimised price position to market and the mix of product features. A wide range of different offers need to be managed. Tactical promotions which are driven by promotional 'end dates' which are weekly or bi-weekly include varying:

- free shipping
- money-off discounts
- free upgrades (e.g. memory)
- free accessories
- finance offers
- service upgrades.

The presenter also noted how, across Europe, the promotional mix has to vary to reflect the differences in buying psychology. He summarised the main differences between customers as follows:

- UK – all about price
- CH – add value over price
- DE – all about high-end products in mix
- IT – design is important (!)
- DK – cheap is good
- NO – added value is key
- FR – tailored for France.

Dell's use of digital media channels

The main digital media channels used by Dell.com in Europe are:

- Paid search through programmes such as Google AdWords, which are used to promote value through time-limited offers related to the phrase searched upon. For example, a Google search for 'cheapest Dell' displays an ad: 'Discount Dell Laptops **www.dell.co.uk/laptop** – Save up to £300 on selected Dell Laptops from £329. Buy online now!'
- Display advertising, for example advertising on technology websites, is particularly important for the corporate market.
- Affiliate marketing – used to protect the Dell brand by enabling affiliates to bid on terms such as 'Dell laptops' and to target niche audiences such as owners of gaming machines.
- E-mail marketing – an e-newsletter is used to keep in touch with existing customers and deliver targeted offers when their hardware may be renewed.

How Dell use social media marketing

Cory Edwards, director of social media and reputation team (SMART) at Dell has explained Dell's approach to social media marketing. He stresses the importance of commitment from senior managers which is exemplified for Dell by CEO Michael Dell who frequently emphasises the importance of social media marketing to Dell. Edwards (2011) contains this quote from Michael Dell:

> *Engaging in honest, direct conversations with customers and stakeholders is a part of who we are, who we've always been. The social web amplifies our opportunity to listen and learn and invest ourselves in a two-way dialogue, enabling us to become a better company with more to offer the people who depend on us.*

Edwards simply says, 'If content is king, then listening is queen'.

As an indication of the importance of social media listening to Dell, Dell has created a Social Media Listening Command Center which has six wall monitors tracking what Dell's most influential customers are saying, trending topics relating to Dell, market performance including share of voice and ratings of sentiment expressed about Dell. Around 25,000 posts in 11 languages are monitored daily by Dell's 'Ground Control Team'.

Dell have a social media governance workflow which reviews the potential importance of these customer comments and identifies those it is worth following up with. The Ground Control Team is tightly integrated with the @DellCares Twitter team who engage around 1000 customers per week. Their role is reach out to people complaining Dell on Twitter. Edwards notes that the team has a 30 per cent conversion rate of converting ranters to ravers.

As well as responding to negative mentions as part of customer service, Dell has created an Online Influencer Relations Program. This is managed by identifying influencers across business unit, region or topic area. Key influencers are identified using a Conversation tracker which is part of Dell's social media listening tool Radian 6. Influencers are provided with content and products which they may review or share. Dell has gone beyond virtual relationships introducing Dell Customer Advisory Panel (CAP) which Edwards describes as 'a ranters and ravers event'. Invitees are prioritised based on size of social media reach and their affinity with Dell.

Relationship owners are designated and involved with ongoing efforts to build advocates. Within CAP days, Dell not only listens, but gives feedback on how problems are addressed. For example, Dell heard that there were too many dropped calls and unnecessary transfers, so they explained how ePhone CRM software is being launched across sites, which will improve reporting capability to track telecom issues and queue mergers to eliminate certain types of transfers.

The reputation management we have described is only part of the social media marketing activities. If we review these activities according to the RACE framework (Chapter 1), we can see that Dell are involved in social media marketing activities across the customer lifecycle:

- *Reach*: Research, Network and advertise to reach and interact with customers and prospects on the social outposts, communities and blogs relevant to your audience.
- *(Inter) Act*: This involves determining your goals and then working out the engagement tools that will encourage your customers to interact and will inspire them. Dell have clear goals around a number

of financial and non-financial measures. They look at measures including operational savings through paid search and support savings and boosting customer loyalty measured through the Net Promoter Score.

When customers Interact, with Dell, their experiences are shared via their social graph of followers or fans, so there is this viral affect which helps customer acquisition.

- *Convert*: Here Dell are trying to leverage initial interaction to go through into real value of leads or sales. At a practical level, Dell have a clearance channel, Dell Outlet, that they use to sell through Twitter. They may also offer promotional coupons through social media like Groupon or deals sites to encourage sales.
- *Engage*: This is the big challenge with social media: how to keep customers engaged. For Dell engagement occurs on several platforms, but in particular within community forums which are users-to-user support postings where topics range from support to pre-purchase or enthusiast discussions. There are millions of members with tens of thousands of discussions and accepted solutions each week. The Direct2Dell Network is also used for B2B customers with separate blogs for Enterprise IT, Small Business, Education, Investers, etc. They encourage guest influencers to join the discussion. Finally another big part of engagement for Dell is IdeaStorm – one of the best examples of crowdsourcing through social media which encourages ideas, feedback, innovation and dialogue. Over tens of thousands of ideas have been generated with around 100,000 comments added, and a viral effect occurring through a Facebook app. Only several hundred ideas have been implemented, but the secret is that Dell close the loop by feeding back to customers what has worked and what hasn't.

Source: 2011 SEC Filing Econsultancy (2008); Dell case study; Online Marketing Masterclass, presented at the Royal Institute of British Architects, November 2008. Edwards (2011); Tackling corporate reputation with social media, presentation by Cory Edwards, director of social media and reputation team (SMART) February 2011, available to view online at **http://www.slideshare.net/KerryatDell/dell-social-media-nma-event-london-v2-feb-2011** See also: **http://www.slideshare.net/KerryatDell/dells-social-media-journey-econsultancy-masterclasses-november-2009** **http://content.dell.com/us/en/corp/our-story-company-timeline.aspx**

Question

Describe approaches used by Dell within their site design and promotion to deliver relevant offers for different types of online customers.

Summary

1. E-CRM enables 'sense and respond' communications where personalised e-mails or web-based messages can be delivered based on disclosed or inferred customers preferences stored as customer profiles.
2. E-CRM also involves management of online services to deliver customer service which is aimed at improving brand loyalty.
3. The classic model for permission marketing to support E-CRM is:
   - Step 1 – Attract customers to website, partner microsite or social presence such as Facebook.
   - Step 2a – Incentivise in order to gain contact and profile information.
   - Step 2b – Capture customer information to maintain the relationship and profile the customer.
   - Step 3 – Maintain dialogue through using online communications to achieve repeat site visits.
   - Step 4 – Maintain dialogue consistent with customer's profile using email, social media messaging or where cost-effective, direct mail or outbound phone contact.
4. Personalisation technologies enable customised e-mails (or direct mails) to be sent to each individual (or related groups) and customised web content to be displayed or distributed using push technology.
5. E-CRM also involves review of customer advocacy through techniques such as Net Promoter Score (NPS) and development of programmes to encourage customer advocacy.

6 The development of online communities through social networks, particularly Facebook company pages and LinkedIn groups or independent communities linked to the company site, is a key part of social CRM.
7 Development of an independent customer community may give additional benefits since the community will be more aligned with company goals and customer brand experience.
8 Management of customer value through customer lifetime value and Recency-Frequency-Monetary (RFM value analysis) is a core technique for targeting marketing programmes at customers who will generate the most future value for an organisation.

Exercises

Self-assessment exercises

1. Why are digital platforms so suitable for relationship marketing?
2. Explain 'personalisation' in an digital marketing context.
3. What is meant by 'customer profiling'?
4. Explain the concept and benefits of the 'sense and respond' approach to customer communications.
5. How can customer concerns about privacy be responded to when conducting one-to-one marketing using the Internet?
6. What are the key decisions when creating or improving an online community?
7. Explain the concept and applications of RFM analysis to different types of web presence.
8. Explain the concept and applications of lifetime analysis.

Essay and discussion questions

1. Explain the factors that influence the development of multichannel customer contact strategies.
2. Explain how customer lifetime value analysis can be applied to improve all aspects of the customer lifecycle.
3. Write a report summarising for a manager the necessary stages for transforming a static brochureware site to E-CRM and the benefits that can be expected.
4. Explore the legal and ethical constraints on implementing relationship marketing using the digital media.

Examination questions

1. Define and explain the scope and applications of E-CRM.
2. What characteristics of the Internet make it so conducive to the direct marketing approach?
3. Suggest how an organisation could review its E-CRM capabilities.
4. Explain the benefits to businesses of creating virtual communities and how such communities can be used as part of relationship marketing.
5. Suggest three measures a company can take to ensure that a customer's privacy is not infringed when conducting one-to-one marketing.
6. Explain how digital media can support customer advocacy. Suggest how advocacy can be proactively managed.
7. What is 'web self-service'? What are typical challenges in managing this?
8. Explore opportunities and methods for personalising the interactive web session and adding value for that individual customer.

References

Agrawal, V., Arjona, V. and Lemmens, R. (2001) E-performance: the path to rational exuberance, *McKinsey Quarterly*, No. 1, 31–43.

Altimeter (2010) Social CRM: The New Rules of Relationship Management, Whitepaper published April 2010, Editor Charlene Li.

Armstrong, A. and Hagel, J. (1996) The real value of online communities, *Harvard Business Review*, May–June, 134–41.

Castells, M. (1996) *The Rise of the Network Society*, Blackwell, Oxford.

Chaffey, D. (2004) E-permission marketing, Chartered Institute of Marketing, *What's New in Marketing*, e-newsletter, Issue 25, (**www.wnim.com**).

Duffy, D. (1998) Customer loyalty strategies, *Journal of Consumer Marketing*, 15(5), 435–48.

Durlacher (1999) UK online community, *Durlacher Quarterly Internet Report*, Q3, 7–11, London.

Evans, M., Patterson, M. and O'Malley, L. (2000) Bridging the direct marketing–direct consumer gap: some solutions from qualitative research, *Proceedings of the Academy of Marketing Annual Conference*, Derby, UK.

Forrester (2007) Marketing's new key metric: engagement, marketers must measure involvement, interaction, intimacy, and influence. *Forrester Analyst report*. Brian Haven, 8 August.

Godin, S. (1999) *Permission Marketing*, Simon and Schuster, New York.

Hagel, J. (1997) *Net Gain: Expanding Markets through Virtual Communities*, Harvard Business School Press, Boston.

Keiningham, T., Cooil, B., Aksoy, L., Andreassen, T. and Weiner, J. (2007) The value of different customer satisfaction and loyalty metrics in predicting customer retention, recommendation and share-of-wallet, *Managing Service Quality*, 17(4).

Kirby, K. and Samson, A. (2007) Customer advocacy metrics: the NPS theory in practice, *AdMap*, February 2007, 17–19.

Kumar, V., Petersen, J. and Leone, R. (2007) How valuable is word of mouth? *Harvard Business Review*, October, 85(10), 139–46.

Loomis, C.P. (1957) *Community and Society: Gemeinschaft und Gesellschaft*, Michigan State University Press.

McLuhan, M. (1964) *Understanding Media*, Routledge, London.

Negroponte, N. (1995) *Being Digital*, Hodder and Stoughton, London.

Novo, J. (2003) *Drilling Down: Turning customer data into profits with a spreadsheet*, available from: **www.jimnovo.com**.

O'Malley, L. and Tynan, C. (2001) Reframing relationship marketing for consumer markets, *Interactive Marketing*, 2(3), 240–6.

Parker, R. (2000), *Relationship Marketing on the Web*, Adams Streetwise, Cincinnati, OH.

Peppers, D. and Rogers, M. (1997) *Enterprise One-to-One: Tools for Building Unbreakable Customer Relationships in the Interactive Age*, Piatkus, London.

Peppers, D. and Rogers, M. (2002) *One to One B2B: Customer Relationship Management Strategies for the Real Economy*, Capstone, Oxford.

Reichheld, F. (2006) *The Ultimate Question: Driving Good Profits and True Growth*, Harvard Business School Publishing.

Reichheld, F. and Schefter, P. (2000) E-loyalty, your secret weapon, *Harvard Business Review*, July–August, 105–13.

Smart Insights (2011), Why social sign-on matters, blog post by Dave Chaffey, 26 September at: **http://www.smartinsights.com/social-media-marketing-alerts/why-social-sign-on-matters.**

van Duyne, D., Landay, J. and Hong, J. (2003), *The Design of Sites. Patterns, Principles, and Processes for Crafting a Customer-centered Web Experience*, Addison-Wesley, Reading, MA.

Further reading

Chaffey, D. (2003), *Total E-mail Marketing*, Butterworth-Heinemann, Elsevier, Oxford. A detailed, practical guide to permission-based e-mail marketing.

Peppers, D., Rogers, M. and Dorf, B. (1999), Is your company ready for one-to-one marketing? *Harvard Business Review*, January–February, 3–12. A fairly detailed summary of the IDIC approach.

Reichheld, F. and Schefter, P. (2000), E-loyalty, your secret weapon, *Harvard Business Review*, July–August, 105–13. An excellent review of the importance of achieving online loyalty and approaches to achieving it.

Tapp, A. (2005), *Principles of Direct and Database Marketing*, 3rd edn. Financial Times/Prentice Hall, Harlow. A well-structured guide to best practice in direct and interactive marketing.

Weblinks

- **ClickZ** (www.clickz.com). An excellent collection of articles on online marketing communications. US-focused. Relevant section for this chapter: CRM strategies.
- **CRM Today** (www.crm2day.com). A portal with articles about the practical aspects of deploying CRM technology.
- **Database Marketing Institute** (www.dbmarketing.com). Useful collection of articles on best practice.
- **Jim Novo** (www.jimnovo.com). A site by a US consultant that has a lot of detail on techniques to profile and target customers online.
- **MyCustomer** (www.mycustomer.com). Articles about the principles and technology of customer relationship management.
- **Net Promoter Score blog** (http://netpromoter.typepad.com/fred_reichheld). Multi-author blog and forum discussing the practicalities of implementing NPS.
- **Peppers and Rogers One-to-One marketing website** (www.1to1.com). A site containing a lot of information on the techniques and tools of relationship marketing.

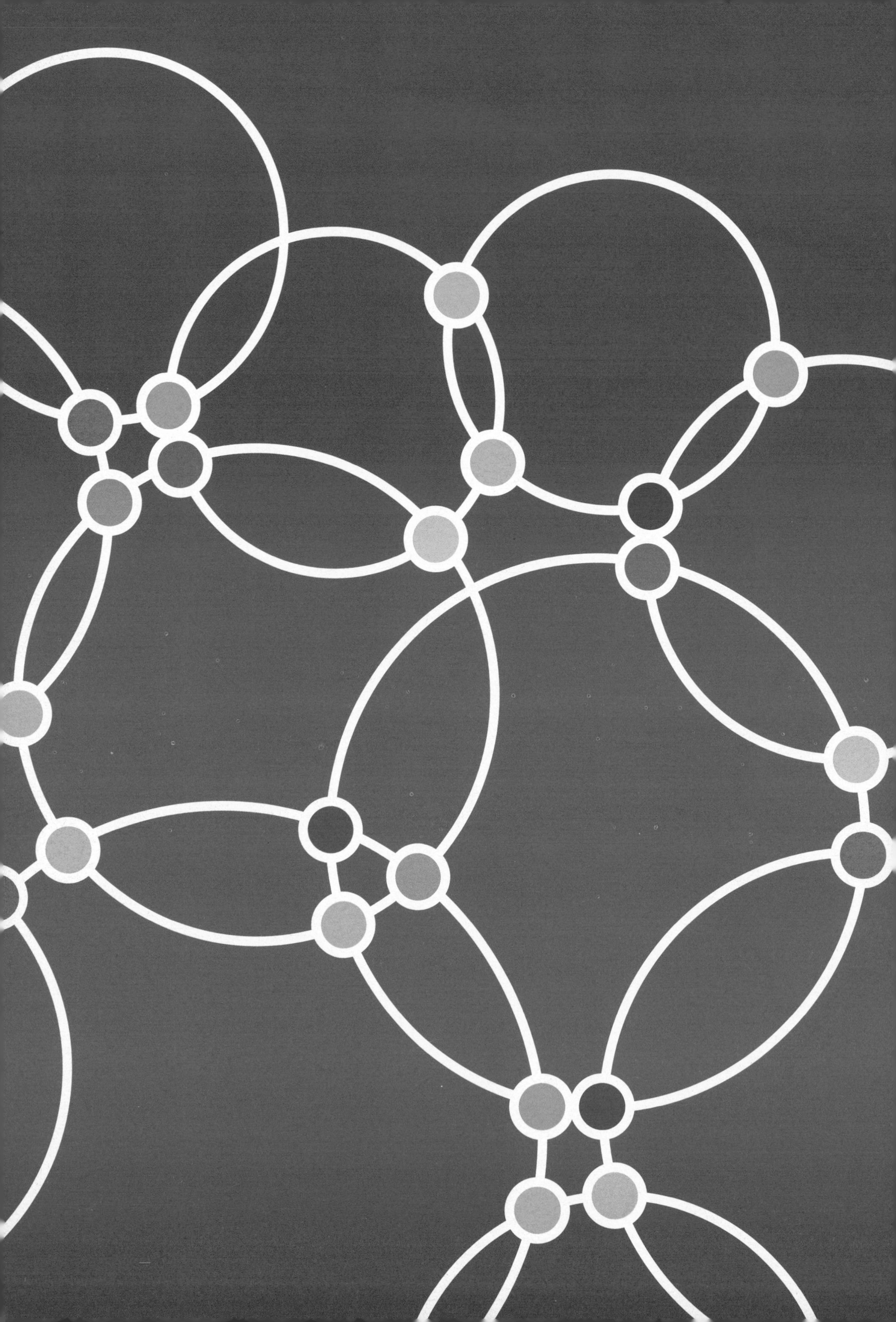

Part 3

Digital marketing: implementation and practice

In Part 3 particular issues regarding the execution of digital marketing strategy are described, including development of a website and ensuring a quality customer experience (Chapter 7), marketing communications to promote a site (Chapters 8 and 9) and the maintenance and evaluation as online presence (Chapter 10). In Chapters 11 and 12, specific examples are given of how business-to-consumer and business-to-business companies are using the Internet.

→

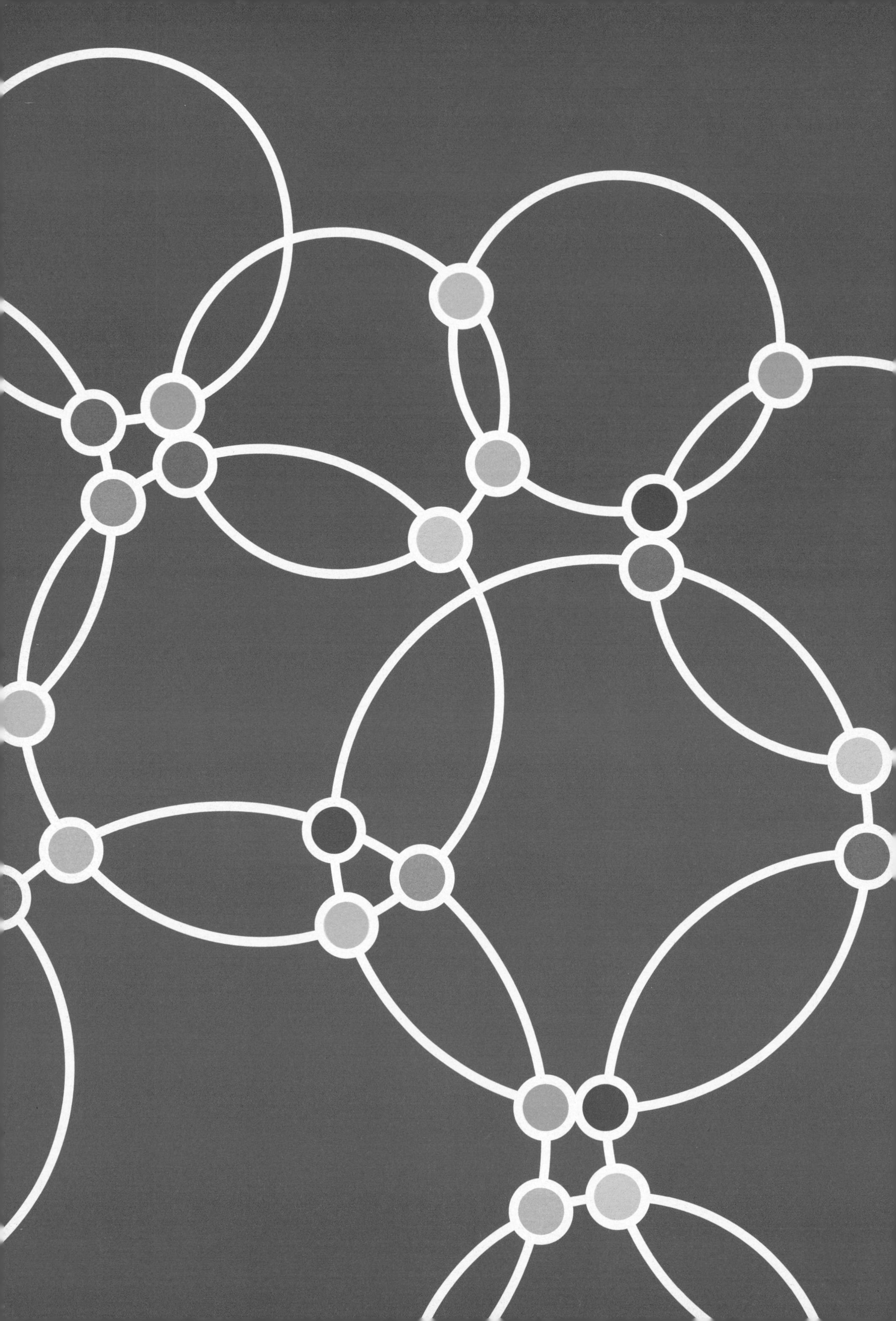

Chapter 7
Delivering the online customer experience

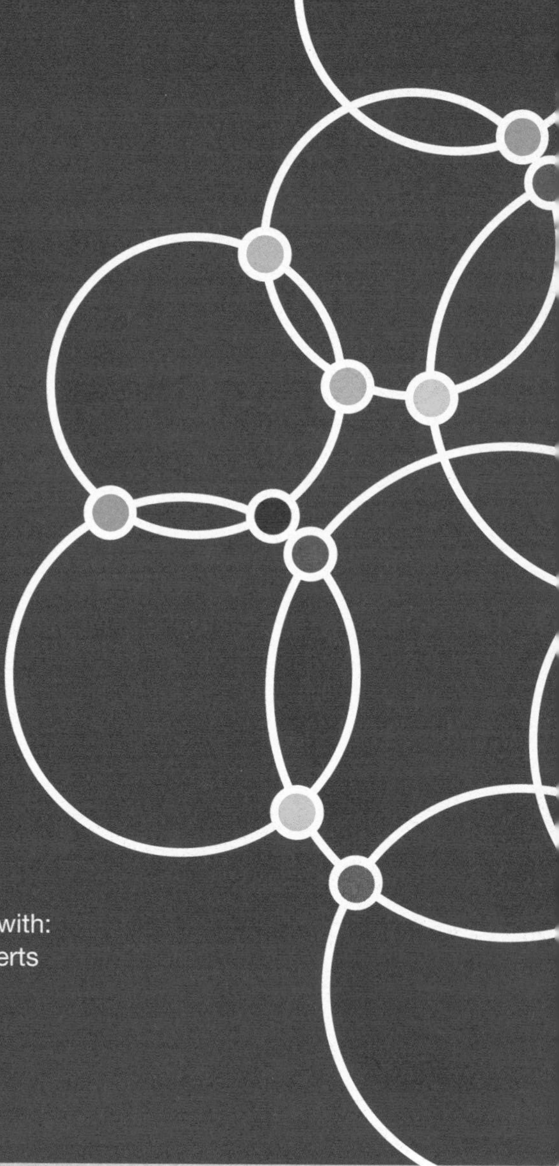

Chapter at a glance

Main topics

Case studies

Learning objectives

After reading this chapter, the reader should be able to:

- Describe the different stages needed to create an effective website, mobile site or social media presence
- Define the requirements that contribute to an effective site or presence
- Identify the similarities and differences in creating a website and other forms of online presence

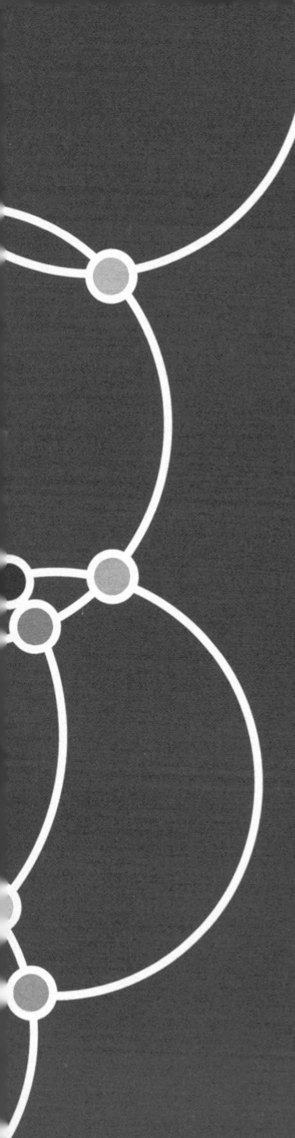

Questions for marketers

Key questions for marketing managers related to this chapter are:

- Which activities are involved in building a new site or updating an existing site?
- What are the key factors of online service quality and site design that will help my goals of customer acquisition and retention?
- Which techniques can I use to determine visitors' requirements and whether they are met?
- How should I integrate the different forms of online presence

Scan code to find the latest updates for topics in this chapter

Links to other chapters

Related chapters are:

- Chapters 4 and 5, which describe the development of the strategy and tactics that inform the design of the website
- Chapters 8 and 9, which describes approaches to promoting websites
- Chapter 10, which describes the analysis of a site and the maintenance of a site once it is created

Introduction

Developing the capability to create and maintain effective online brand presences is a key part of digital marketing. As digital media have evolved, there are an increasing number of online brand presences from company websites accessed over desktop computers to mobile sites and apps accessed via tablets and mobile phone to social presences on the major social networks like Facebook, Google+, LinkedIn and Twitter.

Online customer experience
The combination of rational and emotional factors of using a company's online services that influences customers' perceptions of a brand online.

Conversion rate optimisation (CRO)
Improving the commercial returns from a transactional site through increasing conversion to key goals such as sales, quotes or bookings or leads. CRO combines customer and competitor research with evaluation of customer behaviour using web analytics and AB and multivariate testing (see Chapter 10 for details).

'Effective' means that the presence must deliver relevance and a satisfactory **online customer experience** for its audience. At the same time, 'effective' means the presence must support and add value to the brand to deliver results for the company. **Conversion rate optimisation (CRO)** is increasingly being used by companies to improve the commercial contribution of online presence to a business as the Smart Insights interview introducing this chapter shows.

In this chapter, we will explore different practical actions that companies can take to create and maintain satisfactory online experiences. An indication of the need to produce a customer-centric online presence is given by Alison Lancaster, at the time the head of marketing and catalogues at John Lewis Direct and then marketing director at Charles Tyrrwhit (**www.ctshirts.co.uk**) who says:

> A good site should always begin with the user. Understand who the customer is, how they use the channel to shop, and understand how the marketplace works in that category. This includes understanding who your competitors are and how they operate online. You need continuous research, feedback and usability testing to continue to monitor and evolve the customer experience online. Customers want convenience and ease of ordering. They want a site that is quick to download, well-structured and easy to navigate.

You can see that creating effective online experiences is a challenge since there are many practical issues to consider, which we present in Figure 7.1. This is based on a diagram by de Chernatony (2001) who suggested that delivering the online experience promised by a brand requires delivering rational values, emotional values and promised experience (based on rational and emotional values). The factors that influence the online customer experience can be presented in a pyramid form of success factors as is shown in Figure 7.1 (the different success factors reflect current best-practice and differ from those of de Chernatony). The diagram also highlights the importance of delivering service quality online, as has been indicated by Trocchia and Janda (2003). More recently, Christodoulides *et al.* (2006) have tested the importance of a range of indicators of online brand equity for online retail and service companies. This analysis was performed across these five dimensions of brand equity assessed by asking the questions below – they provide an excellent framework which can be applied to assess and benchmark the quality of brand experience for different types of website:

1 **Emotional connection**
Q1: I feel related to the type of people who are [X]'s customers.
Q2: I feel as though [X] actually cares about me.
Q3: I feel as though [X] really understands me.

2 **Online experience**
Q4: [X]'s website provides easy-to-follow search paths.
Q5: I never feel lost when navigating through [X]'s website.
Q6: I was able to obtain the information I wanted without any delay.

3 **Responsive service nature**
Q7: [X] is willing and ready to respond to customer needs.
Q8: [X]'s website gives visitors the opportunity to 'talk back' to [X].

4 **Trust**
Q9: I trust [X] to keep my personal information safe.
Q10: I feel safe in my transactions with [X].

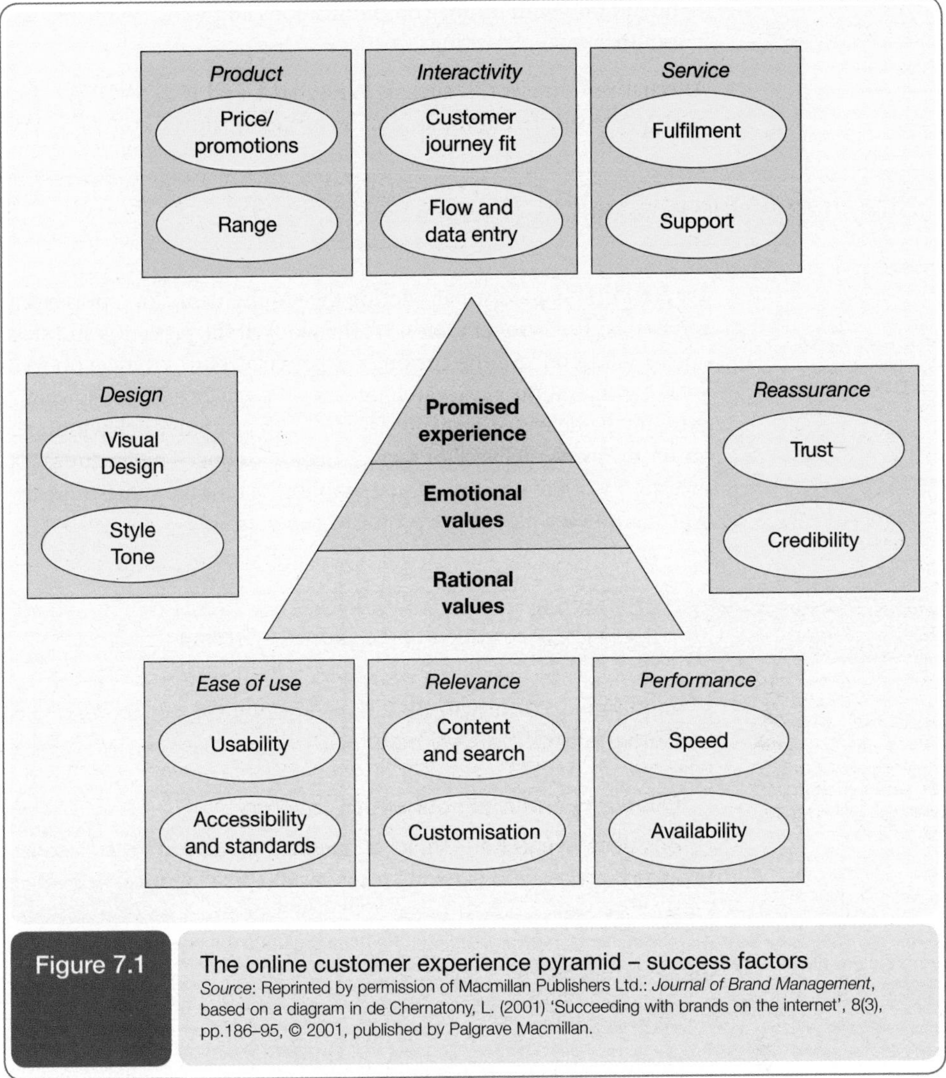

Figure 7.1 The online customer experience pyramid – success factors

Source: Reprinted by permission of Macmillan Publishers Ltd.: *Journal of Brand Management*, based on a diagram in de Chernatony, L. (2001) 'Succeeding with brands on the internet', 8(3), pp.186–95, © 2001, published by Palgrave Macmillan.

Web merchandising
The aims of web merchandising are to maximise the sales potential of an online store for each visitor. This means connecting the right products with the right offer to the right visitor, and remembering that the online store is part of a broader experience including online and offline advertising, instore visits, customer service and delivery.

Customer journey
The sequence of interactions across different media and online presences which a consumer takes as they use, seek information, products or entertainment online.

5 Fulfilment

Q11: I got what I ordered from [X]'s website.

Q12: The product was delivered by the time promised by [X].

Figure 7.1 incorporates many of the factors that are relevant for a transactional e-retail site such as price and promotions which together form **web merchandising** (see the end of the chapter), but you can see that many of the rational and emotional values are important to any website. Some of the terms such as 'usability' and 'accessibility' (which are delivered through an effective website design) you may not be familiar with, but these will all be explained later in this chapter.

In Figure 7.1 these factors are all associated with using the website, but the online customer experience extends beyond this, so effective designs are based on integrating with the entire **customer journey** for different audiences and different scenarios to achieve the best result. So design of online presence also needs to look at the bigger picture:

- ease of locating the site through search engines (Chapter 8)
- services provided by partners online on other websites
- quality of outbound communications such as e-newsletters
- quality of processing inbound e-mail communications from customers

- integration with offline communications and touchpoints like store and phone as part of multichannel marketing.

Alternative frameworks, such as WEBQUAL and E-SERVQUAL, for assessing website effectiveness are covered in the section on service quality.

Structure of the chapter

We start the chapter by considering the requirements for a presence that delivers appropriate rational and emotional values. We then look at the processes and stages involved in managing a project to improve the customer experience. Our coverage on website design is integrated with consideration of researching online buyer behaviour since an appropriate experience can only be delivered if it is consistent with customer behaviour, needs and wants. We then go on to review delivery of service quality online. This includes aspects such as speed and availability of the site itself which support the rational values, and also fulfilment and support which are a core part of the promised experience.

Digital marketing in practice — The Smart Insights Interview

Ben Jesson and Karl Blanks of agency Conversion Rate Experts on Conversion Rate Optimisation

Overview and main concepts covered

Ben Jesson and Karl Blanks of agency Conversion Rate Experts discuss how to optimise business and generate revenue with their ideas on Conversion Rate Optimisation.

The interview

Q: We're seeing a lot more companies working now on CRO. What is it and why is its use increasing?

Ben Jesson: Yes, it should be. Landing page optimisation focuses on one page. We coined the term Conversion Rate Optimisation ('CRO') in 2007 to describe the process of optimising the business itself. It's really commercial optimisation. A proper job of CRO includes the review of the entire process from the initial lead-generation ad, all the way through to the post-sale follow-up. The real goal is to identify which parts of the sales funnel will yield the greatest wins with the least work.

That means it's necessary to bring a lot of disciplines to the party, including understanding traffic sources, visitor psychology, and the company's position in the marketplace, including its core strengths and weaknesses. On top of that there's usability testing, copywriting, and web design factors to look at.

All these elements go into creating hypotheses for testing. We're maniacal about testing, because we've seen too many businesses merely throw a series of 'best practices' against the wall to see if anything sticks. Best practices should not be the answer to optimising a website, but merely one starting point for formulating a test strategy.

Once we determine what truly works for a particular website, then we examine how our findings might be used in other media channels. For instance a better series of benefit statements might be transferable to direct mail or email autoresponder campaigns – subject to testing in those media, of course.

Q. How do you help companies build a business case for returns from CRO?

Karl Blanks: It's easy. We explain that CRO allows companies to generate more revenue without spending more on advertising. It's about getting a higher return from the existing ad spend. Unlike certain industries like public relations, the entire foundation of CRO is based on data, measurement and testing. You don't need to present arguments when the data can do the talking for you. Once you measure the value of visitors, conversions, and sales, then it's simple arithmetic to show how, say, a 10 per cent boost in conversions would help the bottom line.

Here's another powerful side-benefit: when you optimise your funnel and bring in more revenues, you then have earned a luxury. You get to decide whether to pocket those profits or plough them back into even more advertising, thus distancing yourself even further from your competitors. It's a nice problem to have.

Q. Which approaches do you use to decide which part of a site needs most urgent attention?

Ben Jesson: *FORTUNE* magazine called what we do 'a combination of multivariate statistical analysis and good old-fashioned detective work' and that pretty well describes our approach.

It's often very useful to map out your entire sales/conversion funnel and make sure it's being comprehensively measured in whatever web analytics package you prefer.

Then you should look for the biggest drop-offs from one step to the next. We like to say that we look for the 'blocked arteries' (that is, pages – or page elements – that get loads of visitors but are underperforming). How do you know if something is underperforming? Clues come from a range of feedback mechanisms: the analytics data, usability tests, surveys, customer support feedback … and, of course, gut feel. Of course, we have the advantage of having been engaged by companies on several continents and in many industries, so we have a good knowledgebase of what's good and what's bad.

Q. What can limit conversion? Give some examples of the most common 'conversion rate killers' you see.

Karl Blanks: These are some of the most common mistakes we see:

- Killer #1: not split testing. Many people think they're done if they take action to make changes to their site. In reality they're only 'done' when tests show that the changes in fact improved conversions. Installing a 'best practice' magic button that another site swears by might actually lower conversions. Despite the popularity of video, Google once discovered through tests that video reduced conversions on one of its pages. You simply must test to find out.

  Not long ago, multivariate testing software cost more than £5000 per month. Now you can use Google Website Optimiser and other software packages for free, so there's really no excuse. We created a tool, called Which Multivariate, which helps you to select the best software for multivariate testing.
- Killer #2 is 'meek tweaking' – in other words, making changes that are never likely to have a significant effect.
- Killer #3 is asking for the sale on the first visit. It's often a good idea to test the creation of a multi-step conversion funnel, in which you provide great value before you ask for the order. Comparison charts, forums, special reports, and email marketing are examples of elements that allow you to provide good information, ask for names, cultivate a relationship and thereby improve the chances of a sale.

→

Q. Could you share some tools that readers could use on their sites?

Karl Blanks: Excellent design is a prerequisite for conversion, but the biggest breakthroughs tend to be the new tools and techniques for gathering insights into the visitor's mindset. For determining how visitors interact with a site we often useboth Clicktale and CrazyEgg for this.

KISSInsights and Ethnio are both good for asking your visitors to give you immediate feedback on your site. GazeHawk enables you to conduct an eye-tracking study on your site for a tiny fraction of the traditional cost.

Many of your readers will already know about how wireframing is important in order to get agreement on functional aspects before you take the time to make a site look good. We like Balsamiq for that purpose.

Planning website design and build

In the past, it has been a common mistake among those creating a new website for the first time, to 'dive in' and start creative design and content creation without sufficient forward planning. The design process (Figure 7.2) involves analysing the needs of owners and users of a site and then deciding on the best way to build the site to fulfil these needs. Without a structured plan and careful design costly reworking is inevitable, as the first version of a site will not achieve the needs of the end-users or the business. Follow Activity 7.1 to think through the problems you have experienced when using a site which does not meet your needs.

The process of website development summarised in Figure 7.2 is idealised because, for efficiency, many of these activities have to occur in parallel. Figure 7.3 gives an indication of the relationship between these tasks, and how long they may take, for a typical website project. We will explain some of the specialist design terminology later in this chapter. The main development tasks which need to be scheduled as part of the planning process are as follows:

1 *Pre-development tasks.* For a new site, these include domain name registration and deciding on the company to host the website. They also include preparing a brief setting out the aims and objectives of the site, and then – if it is intended to outsource the site – presenting the brief to rival agencies to bid for and pitch their offering.

Activity 7.1 What can go wrong without a planned approach to website design?

Purpose

To indicate potential problems to customers, partners and staff if the design of an online presence is not carefully planned.

Activity

Make a list of the potential problems related to a poorly planned design which may be faced by customers of an online retailer. Base your answer on problems you have experienced on a website that can be related to planning and implementation of site design.

The answers you identify all define the requirements for a new website design including: relevant content, acceptable performance, renders correctly in browser, findable within search engines (search engine optimisation (SEO)).

2 *Analysis and design.* This is the detailed analysis and design of the site, and includes clarification of business objectives, market research to identify the audience and typical customer personas and user journeys and their needs, defining the information architecture of different content types and prototyping different functional and visual designs to support the brand.
3 *Content development and testing.* Developing the site to create prototypes including integration of content management systems, database integration, usability and performance testing.
4 *Publishing or launching the site.* This is a relatively short stage. Often a **soft-launch** is used where the site is updated, but the version is not widely communicated until the owners are sure the site is stable. Some site owners such as Google test features with a limited number of users to assess their impact before the features are rolled out more widely.

Soft launch
Migration occurs from the development site to the live site, but it isn't widely communicated until live testing proves the site is stable.

5 *Pre-launch promotion or communications.* Search engine registration and optimisation is most important for new sites. Although search engines can readily index a new site, some place a penalty on new sites (sometimes known as 'the Google sandbox effect'), where the site is effectively on trial until it is established. Briefing the PR company to publicise the launch is another example of pre-launch promotion.
6 *Ongoing promotion.* The schedule should also allow for promotion after site launch. This might involve structured discount promotions on the site, or competitions which are planned in advance. Many now consider search engine optimisation and pay-per-click marketing (Chapter 9) as a continuous process, and will often employ a third party to help achieve this.

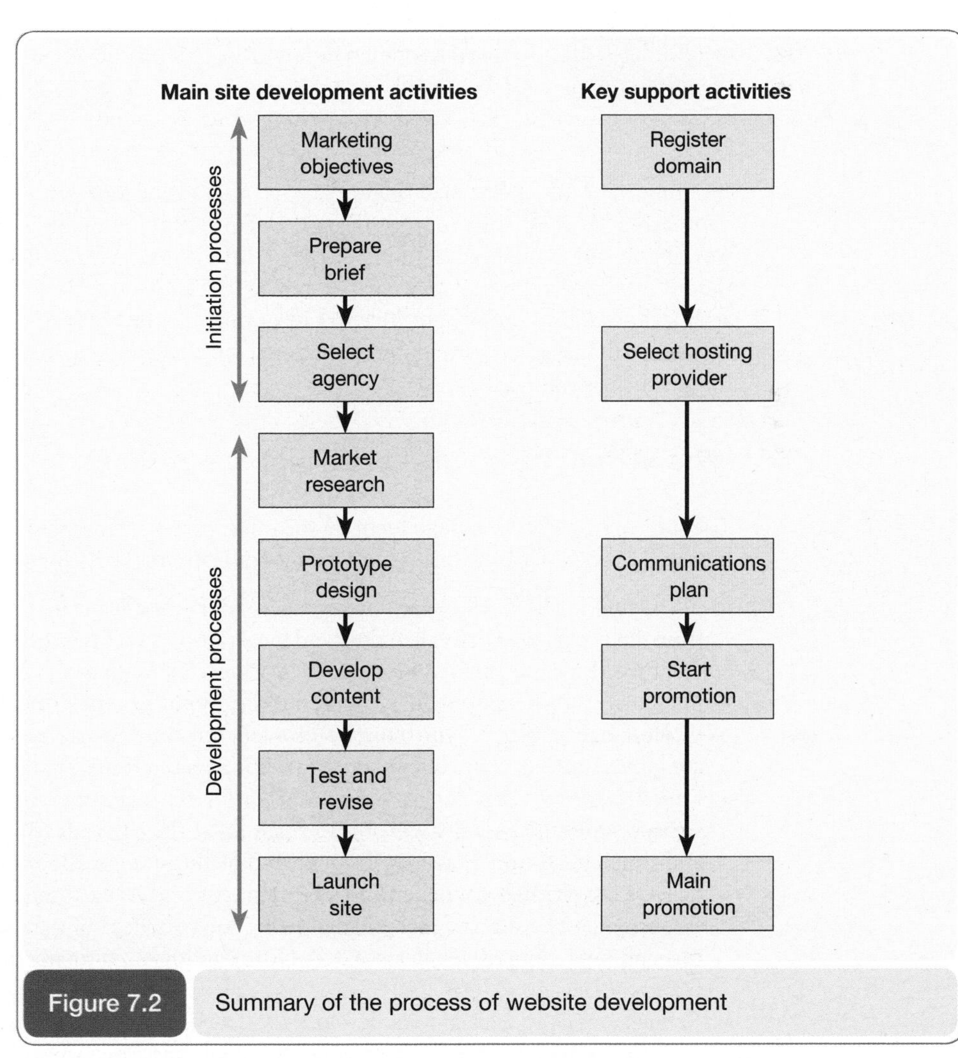

Figure 7.2 Summary of the process of website development

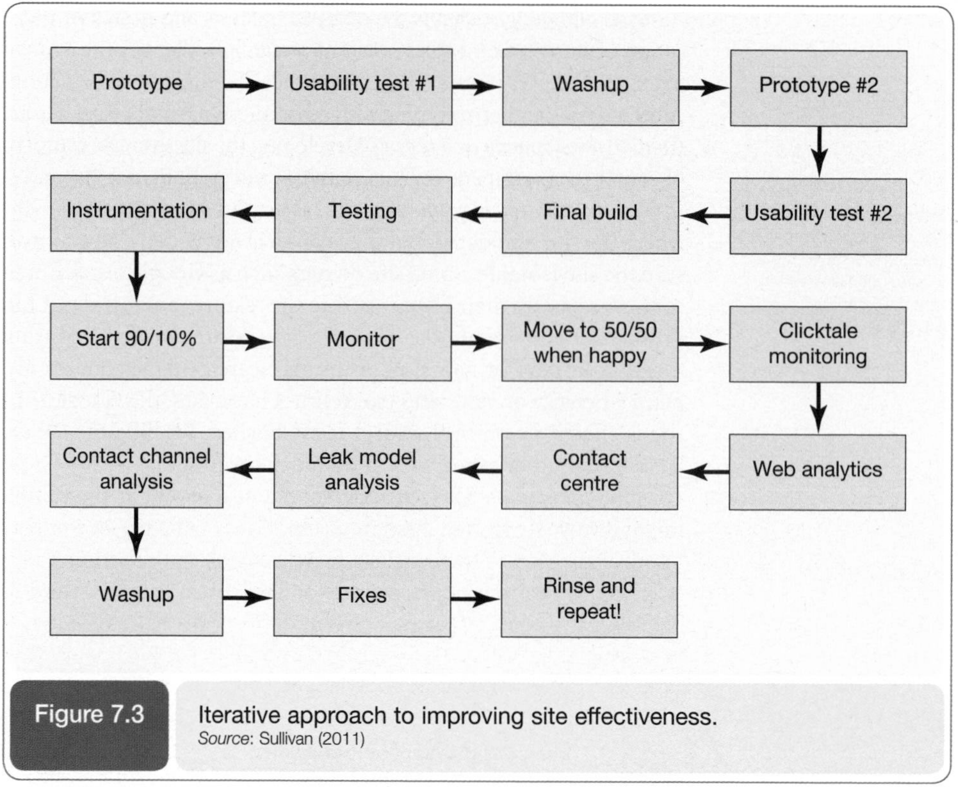

Figure 7.3 Iterative approach to improving site effectiveness.
Source: Sullivan (2011)

It's important to realise that Figure 7.2 is a simplification of real-world optimisation approaches. In reality, iteration of designs in a prototyping phase is required. Then once a working version is finalised it should be tested through user-testing and then live testing using the AB/multivariate testing approach described in Chapter 10. Figure 7.3 defines an iterative approach to improving site effectiveness recommended by Sullivan (2011). Craig Sullivan is e-business manager at Belron, an international windscreen repair service with local country brands such as Autoglass.

Who should be involved in a website project?

The success of a website is dependent on the range of people involved in its development, and how well they work as a team. Typical profiles of team members follow:

- *Site sponsors.* These will be senior managers who will effectively be paying for the system from their budgets. They will understand the strategic benefits of the system and will be keen that the site is implemented successfully to achieve the business objectives they have set.
- *Site owner.* 'Ownership' will typically be the responsibility of a marketing manager or e-commerce manager, who may be devoted full-time to overseeing the site in a large company; it may be part of a marketing manager's remit in a smaller company.
- *Project manager.* This person is responsible for the planning and co-ordination of the website project. He or she will aim to ensure that the site is developed within the budget and time constraints that have been agreed at the start of the project, and that the site delivers the planned-for benefits for the company and its customers.
- *Site designer.* The site designer will define the 'look and feel' of the site, including its styling through Cascading Style Sheets (CSS), layout and how company brand values are transferred to the web.
- *Content developer.* The content developer will write the copy for the website and convert it to a form suitable for the site. In medium or large companies this role may be split between

marketing staff or staff from elsewhere in the organisation who write the copy and a technical member of staff who converts it to the graphics and HTML documents forming the web page and does the programming for interactive content.
- *Webmaster.* This is a technical role. The webmaster is responsible for ensuring the quality of the site. This means achieving suitable availability, speed, working links between pages and connections to company databases. In small companies the webmaster may take on graphic design and content developer roles also.
- *Stakeholders.* The impact of the website on other members of the organisation should not be underestimated. Internal staff may need to refer to some of the information on the website or use its services.

While the site sponsor and site owner will work within the company, many organisations outsource the other resources since full-time staff cannot be justified in these roles. There are a range of different choices for outsourcing which are summarised in Activity 7.2.

We are seeing a gradual blurring between these different types of supplier as they recruit expertise so as to deliver a 'one-stop shop' or 'full-service agency', but they still tend to be strongest in particular areas. Companies need to decide whether to partner with the best of breed in each, or to perhaps compromise and choose the one-stop shop that gives the best balance and is most likely to achieve integration across different marketing activities – this would arguably be the new media agency, or perhaps a traditional marketing agency that has an established new media division. Which approach do you think is best?

Observation of the practice of outsourcing suggests that two conflicting patterns are evident:

- *Outside-in.* A company often starts using new digital marketing technologies by outsourcing some activities where there is insufficient in-house expertise. The company then builds up skills internally to manage these areas as digital marketing becomes an important contributor to the business. An outside-in approach will probably be driven by the need to reduce the costs of outsourcing, poor delivery of services by the supplier or simply a need to concentrate resource for a strategic core competence in-house.
- *Inside-out.* A company starts to implement digital marketing using existing resources within the IT department and marketing department in conjunction with recruitment of digital media specialists. They may then find that there are problems in developing a site that meets customers' needs or in building traffic to the site. At this point they may turn to outsourcing to solve the problems.

These approaches are not mutually exclusive and an outside-in approach may be used for some activities, such as SEO or content development, while an inside-out approach is used for other functions such as site promotion.

Activity 7.2 Options for outsourcing different digital marketing activities

Purpose

To highlight the outsourcing available for digital marketing and to gain an appreciation of how to choose suppliers.

Activity

A B2C company is trying to decide which of its e-business activities it should outsource. Select a single supplier that you think can best deliver each of these services indicated in Table 7.1. Justify your decision.

Table 7.1 Options for outsourcing different digital marketing activities

E-marketing function	Traditional marketing agency	Digital marketing agency	Traditional IT supplier	Management consultants
1 Strategy				
2 Design				
3 Content and service development				
4 Online promotion				
5 Offline promotion				
6 Infrastructure				

Prototyping and agile software development

Prototype
A preliminary version of part, or a framework of all, of a website, which can be reviewed by its target audience or the marketing team. Prototyping is an iterative process in which website users suggest modifications before further prototypes and the final version of the site are developed.

Prototypes are trial versions of a website that are gradually refined through an iterative process to become closer to the final version. Initial prototypes or 'mockups' may simply be paper prototypes or storyboards, perhaps of a 'wireframe' or screen layout. These may then be extended to include some visuals of key static pages using a tool such as Adobe Photoshop. Finally, working prototypes will be produced as HTML code is developed. The idea is that the design agency or development team and the marketing staff who commissioned the work can review and comment on prototypes, and changes can then be made to the site to incorporate these comments. Prototyping should result in a more effective final site which can be developed more rapidly than a more traditional approach with a long period of requirements determination.

Each iteration of the prototype typically passes through the stages shown in Figure 7.4, which are:

1 *Analysis.* Understanding the requirements of the audience of the site and the requirements of the business, defined by business and marketing strategy (and comments input from previous prototypes).
2 *Design.* Specifying different features of the site that will fulfil the requirements of the users and the business as identified during analysis.
3 *Develop.* The creation of the web pages and the dynamic content of the website.
4 *Test and review.* Structured checks are conducted to ensure that different aspects of the site meet the original requirements and work correctly.

Agile development
An iterative approach to developing software and website functionality with the emphasis on face-to-face communications to elicit, define and test requirements. Each iteration is effectively a mini-software project including stages of planning, requirements analysis, design, coding, testing and documentation.

Agile software development

Today, the concept of prototyping has been extended across the whole lifecycle for developing website functionality or software applications where it is known as **agile software development**. The goal of agile development is to be able to create stable releases more frequently than traditional development methodologies, i.e. new functionality will be introduced through several releases each month rather than a more significant release every few weeks, months or even years. The approach is sometimes known as 'permanent beta'. Another difference with

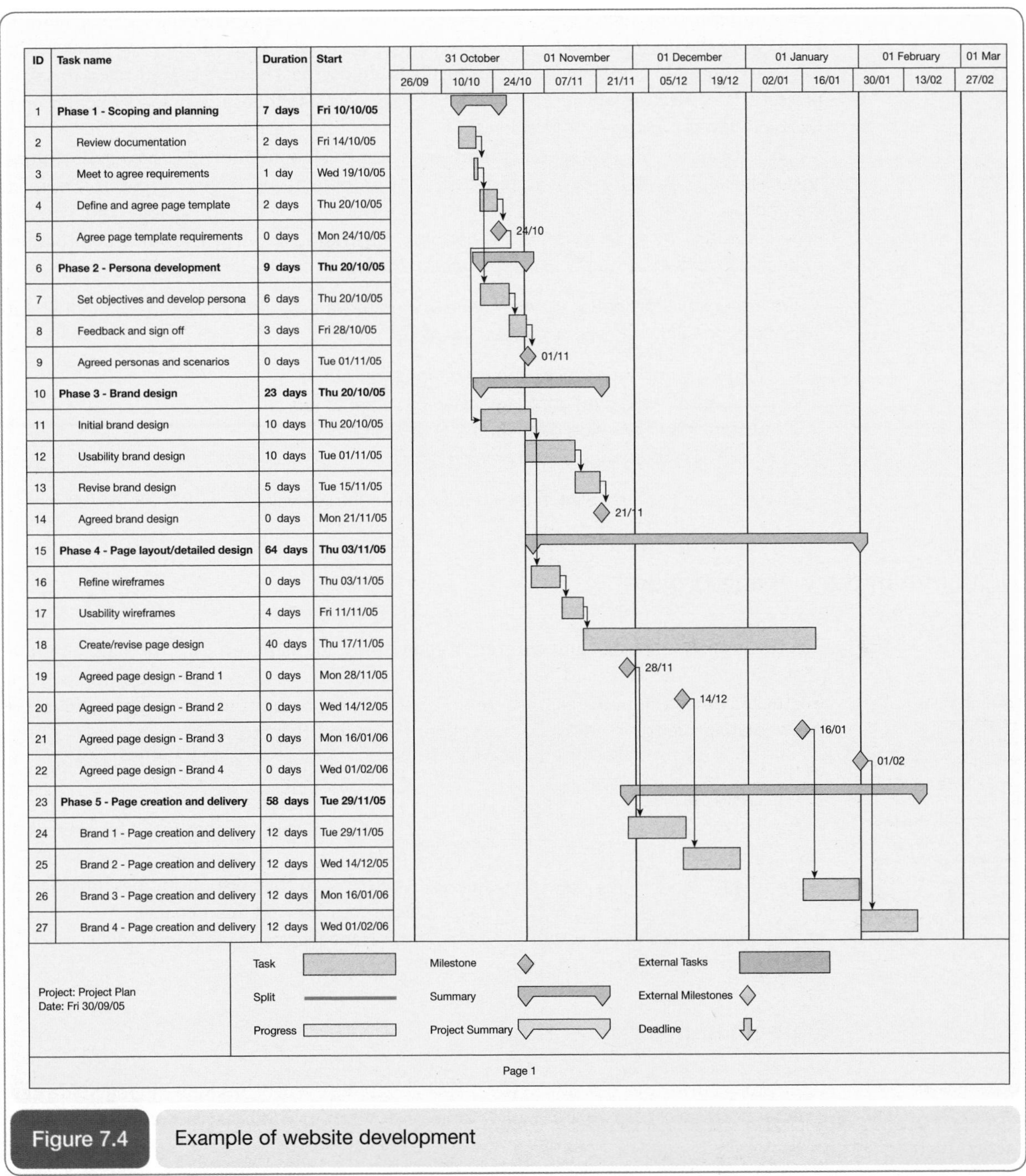

ID	Task name	Duration	Start
1	**Phase 1 - Scoping and planning**	**7 days**	**Fri 10/10/05**
2	Review documentation	2 days	Fri 14/10/05
3	Meet to agree requirements	1 day	Wed 19/10/05
4	Define and agree page template	2 days	Thu 20/10/05
5	Agree page template requirements	0 days	Mon 24/10/05
6	**Phase 2 - Persona development**	**9 days**	**Thu 20/10/05**
7	Set objectives and develop persona	6 days	Thu 20/10/05
8	Feedback and sign off	3 days	Fri 28/10/05
9	Agreed personas and scenarios	0 days	Tue 01/11/05
10	**Phase 3 - Brand design**	**23 days**	**Thu 20/10/05**
11	Initial brand design	10 days	Thu 20/10/05
12	Usability brand design	10 days	Tue 01/11/05
13	Revise brand design	5 days	Tue 15/11/05
14	Agreed brand design	0 days	Mon 21/11/05
15	**Phase 4 - Page layout/detailed design**	**64 days**	**Thu 03/11/05**
16	Refine wireframes	0 days	Thu 03/11/05
17	Usability wireframes	4 days	Fri 11/11/05
18	Create/revise page design	40 days	Thu 17/11/05
19	Agreed page design - Brand 1	0 days	Mon 28/11/05
20	Agreed page design - Brand 2	0 days	Wed 14/12/05
21	Agreed page design - Brand 3	0 days	Mon 16/01/06
22	Agreed page design - Brand 4	0 days	Wed 01/02/06
23	**Phase 5 - Page creation and delivery**	**58 days**	**Tue 29/11/05**
24	Brand 1 - Page creation and delivery	12 days	Tue 29/11/05
25	Brand 2 - Page creation and delivery	12 days	Wed 14/12/05
26	Brand 3 - Page creation and delivery	12 days	Mon 16/01/06
27	Brand 4 - Page creation and delivery	12 days	Wed 01/02/06

Figure 7.4 Example of website development

agile development is the emphasis on face-to-face communication to define requirements rather than detailed requirements specifications.

Scrum
Scrum is a methodology that supports agile software development based on 15–30 day sprints to implement features from a product backlog. 'Scrum' refers to a daily project status meeting during the sprint.

Scrum is a methodology that supports agile software development. Scrum involves stakeholders including the *scrum master* who is effectively a project manager, the *product owner* who represents the stakeholders such as the business owners and customers and the *scrum team* which includes the developers.

Scrum is based on focused sprints of a 15–30 day period where the team creates an increment of potentially releasable software. Potential functionality for each sprint are agreed at a *sprint planning meeting* from the *product backlog*, a prioritised set of high-level requirements.

The sprint planning meeting is itself iterative with the product owner stating their requirements from the product backlog and the technical team then determining how much of this they can commit to complete during the forthcoming sprint. The term 'scrum' refers to a daily project status meeting during the sprint. See **http://www.softhouse.se/hploads/ scrum_eng_webb.pdf** for an overview of the process.

The principles of agile development are encapsulated in the *Agile Manifesto* (**http://agilemanifesto.org/**) which was agreed in 2001 by proponents of previous rapid development methodologies including the Dynamic Systems Development Methodology and Extreme Programming. The Agile Manifesto is useful in illustrating the principles of agile programming it contrasts with traditional approaches. The text of the manifesto is:

> We are uncovering better ways of developing software by doing it and helping others do it. Through this work we have come to value:
>
> - individuals and interactions over processes and tools
> - working software over comprehensive documentation
> - customer collaboration over contract negotiation
> - responding to change over following a plan
>
> That is, while there is value in the items on the right, we value the items on the left more.

Initiation of the website project

Initiation of the website project
This phase of the project should involve a structured review of the costs and benefits of developing a website (or making a major revision to an existing website). A successful outcome to initiation will be a decision to proceed with the site development phase, with an agreed budget and target completion date.

Before the analysis, design and creation of the website, all major projects will have an initial phase in which the aims and objectives of the website are reviewed, to assess whether it is worthwhile investing in the website and to decide on the amount to invest. The **initiation of the website project** provides a framework for the project that ensures:

- there is management and staff commitment to the project
- objectives are clearly defined
- the costs and benefits are reviewed in order that the appropriate amount of investment in the site occurs
- the project will follow a structured path, with clearly identified responsibilities for different aspects such as project management, analysis, promotion and maintenance
- the implementation phase will ensure that important aspects of the project, such as testing and promotion, are not skimped.

Domain name registration

Domain name registration
The process of reserving a unique web address that can be used to refer to the company website, in the form of www.<company name>.com or www.<company name>.co.uk.

If the project involves a new site rather than an upgrade, it will be necessary to **register a new domain name**, more usually referred to as a 'web address' or 'uniform (or universal) resource locator' (URL).

Domain names are registered using hosting company or domain broker who use a domain name service, such as:

- *InterNIC* (**www.internic.net**). Registration for the .com, .org and .net domains.
- *Nominet* (**www.nominet.org.uk**). Registration for the .co.uk domain. All country-specific domains, such as .fr (France) or .de (Germany), have their own domain registration authority.

The following guidelines should be borne in mind when registering domain names:

1 *Campaign microsites may hinder findability and give maintenance problems.* If a new site is created specifically for a campaign this can cause problems since although Google's robots will crawl it rapidly, it will likely not rank highly without backlinks from other sites, so it will have poor visibility (as described in Chapter 8 in the section on SEO). For this reason

it is often better to redirect visitors typing in the domain name to a campaign subfolder on an existing site.

2 *Organisations should register multiple ccTLDs to protect their reputation.* As described in Chapter 3, 'domaineers' may seek to purchase domains extensions or ccTLDs which would rightly belong to the brand such as .org.uk or their equivalents in other countries.
3 *New startup companies should consider whether the company and domain name can assist in SEO.* While existing brands will use their main company or brand name for a site, new companies may benefit if the domain name contains a keyphrase that searchers will seek. As we saw in Chapter 3, about the legal constraints on domain purchase, companies may pay a lot to register a domain such as cruises.com for this reason.

Selecting a hosting provider

Selecting the right partner to host a website is an important decision since the quality of service provided will directly impact on the quality of service delivered to a company's customers. The partner that hosts the content will usually be a specialist hosting provider such as rackspace (**www.rackspace.com**) for the majority of small and medium companies, but for larger companies the web server used to host the content may be inside the company and managed by the company's IT department.

The quality of service of hosted content is essentially dependent on two factors: the performance of the website and its availability.

Website performance optimisation

Bandwidth
Indicates the speed at which data are transferred using a particular network medium. It is measured in bits per second (bps).

Content distribution (or delivery) networks (CDNs)
A systems of servers distributed globally with copies of data stored locally to enable more rapid download of content. Their use has increased with increased use of streaming video and more complex web applications.

It's important for site owners to recognise that page download performance is essential to the success of a site even when many users have broadband connections and sites are hosted to Internet with high **bandwidth**. Research by Strangeloop (2011) showed that the average user perception of acceptable download time is three seconds, while for the average Fortune 500 site it is seven seconds. But for more complex retail sites of the top US retailers, the average was 11.21 seconds with only a small number delivering acceptable sub-three second performance. The research also reveals that these larger sites often have poor performance despite use of **content distribution networks (CDNs)** like Akamai and Cloudflare indicating underlying technical issues in delivering content from the server.

Google clearly take this area of website management seriously; they want users to access relevant content quickly as part of their service and have stated that if a site is particularly slow it's ranking will be affected. To help site owners, Google has made available tools such as that shown in Figure 7.5 to show the relevant performance, so marketers should ask their agency to assess their performance.

The length of time is dependent on a number of factors, some of which cannot be controlled, but primarily depends on the bandwidth of the hosting company's connection to the Internet and the performance of the web server hardware and content management platform. It also depends on the 'page weight' of the site's pages measured in kilobytes (which is dependent on the number and complexity of images and animations).

Another factor for a company to consider when choosing a hosting provider is whether the server is *dedicated* to one company or whether content from several companies is located on the same server. A dedicated server is best, but it will attract a premium price.

The availability of the website

The availability of a website is an indication of how easy it is for a user to connect to it. In theory this figure should be 100 per cent but sometimes, for technical reasons such as failures in the server hardware or upgrades to software, the figure can drop substantially below this.

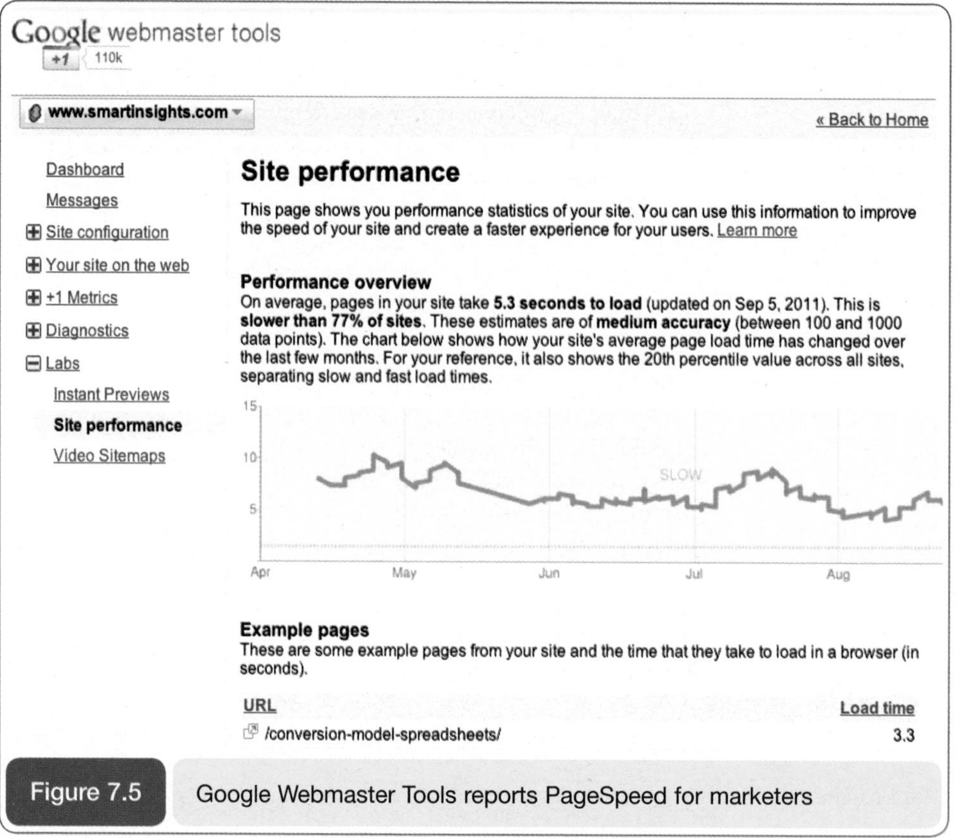

Figure 7.5 Google Webmaster Tools reports PageSpeed for marketers

SciVisum, a web-testing specialist, found that three-quarters of Internet marketing campaigns are impacted by website failures, with 14 per cent of failures so severe that they prevented the campaign meeting its objectives. The company surveyed marketing professionals from 100 UK-based organisations across the retail, financial, travel and online gaming sectors. More than a third of failures were rated as 'serious to severe', with many customers complaining or being unable to complete web transactions. These are often seen by marketers as technology issues which are owned by others in the business, but marketers need to ask the right questions. The SciVisum (2005) research showed that nearly two-thirds of marketing professionals did not know how many users who were making transactions their websites could support, despite an average transaction value of £50 to £100, so they were not able to factor this into campaign plans. Thirty-seven per cent could not put a monetary value on losses caused by customers abandoning web transactions. A quarter of organisations experienced website overloads and crashes as a direct result of a lack of communication between the two departments.

SciVisum recommends that companies do the following:

- Define the peak visitor throughput requirements for each customer journey on the site. For example, the site should be able to support at the same time: approximately ten checkout journeys per second, 30 add-to-basket journeys per second, five registration journeys per second, two check-my-order-status journeys per second.
- Service-level agreement – more detailed technical requirements need to be agreed for each of the transaction stages. Home-page delivery time and server uptime are insufficiently detailed.
- Set up a monitoring programme that measures and reports on the agreed journeys 24/7.

Defining site or app requirements

Analysis phase
The identification of the requirements of a website. Techniques to achieve this may include focus groups, questionnaires sent to existing customers or interviews with key accounts.

The **Analysis** phase involves using different marketing research techniques to find out the needs of the business and audience whether it's a website, mobile site, app or company social page. These needs can then be used to drive the design and content of the website.

Analysis is not a 'one-off' exercise, but is likely to be repeated for each iteration of the prototype. Although analysis and design are separate activities, there tends to be considerable overlap between the two phases. In analysis we are seeking to answer the following types of 'who, what, why, how, when, where' questions:

- Who are the key audiences for the site?
- Why should they use the site (what will appeal to them)?
- What should the content of site be? Which services will be provided?
- How will the content of the site be structured (information architecture)?
- How will navigation around the site occur?
- What are the main marketing outcomes we want the site to deliver (registrations, leads, sales)?
- When and where is the online presence accessed: at home, at work or while mobile?

User-centred design
A design approach which is based on research of user characteristics and needs.

To help answer these questions, web designers commonly use a research-based approach known as **user-centred design** which uses a range of techniques to ensure the site meets user needs. This often involves ethnographic research used to build the website design or customer personas we described in Chapter 2. See this section for more depth on the benefits of building personas which summarise different customer journeys.

A structured approach to user-centred design is defined in the standard: *ISO 13407: Human-centred design processes for interactive systems.* This was published in 1999 and also covers software and hardware systems.

We will now explore the key requirements for an online presence: business requirements and user requirements which comprise usability, accessibility and information needs.

Business requirements

Marketing-led site design
Site design elements are developed to achieve customer acquisition, retention and communication of marketing messages.

With a focus on user-centred design, there is a risk that business requirements to achieve marketing outcomes may be margninalised. A **marketing-led site design** is informed by marketing objectives and tactics. A common approach is to base the design on achieving the performance drivers of successful digital marketing referred to in Chapter 4 and the loyalty drivers referred to at the start of this chapter. Design will be led by these performance drivers as follows:

- *Customer acquisition* – the online value proposition must be clear. Appropriate incentives for customer acquisition and permission marketing such as those described in Chapter 6 must be devised.
- *Customer conversion* – the site must engage first-time visitors. Call to action for customer acquisition and retention offers must be prominent with benefits clearly explained. The fulfilment of the offer or purchase must be as simple as possible to avoid attrition during this process.
- *Customer retention* – appropriate incentives, content and customer service information to encourage repeat visits and business must be available (see Chapter 6).
- *Service quality* – this has been covered in this chapter. Service quality is affected by site navigation, performance, availability and responsiveness to enquiries.
- *Branding* – the brand offer must be clearly explained and interaction with the brand must be possible.

Persuasion marketing Using design elements such as layout, copy and typography together with promotional messages to encourage site users to follow particular paths and specific actions rather than giving them complete choice in their navigation.

Marketing-led site design is also known as **persuasion marketing.** Consultant Bryan Eisenberg of Future Now (**www.bryaneisenberg.com**) is an advocate of persuasion marketing alongside other design principles such as usability and accessibility. He says:

> during the wireframe and storyboard phase we ask three critical questions of every page a visitor will see:
>
> **1** What action needs to be taken?
> **2** Who needs to take that action?
> **3** How do we persuade that person to take the action we desire?

Fogg (2009) has developed a model to inform persuasive design. The FBM asserts that for a person to perform a target behaviour, he or she must (1) be sufficiently motivated, (2) have the ability to perform the behaviour, and (3) be triggered to perform the behaviour. These three factors must occur at the same moment, else the behaviour will not happen.

Before we review user-centred design processes, consider Mini Case Study 7.1 which shows how one company has developed a site that blends marketing-led and user-centric design.

Mini Case Study 7.1 Ultralase

Ultralase is one of the UK's largest laser eye treatments companies. The first Ultralase clinic was opened in January 1991 and there are now 31 locations in the UK. Its growth has been supported through its website and digital media since the content available online is a key part of the consumer decision making process and for the company lead generation.

Figure 7.6 Shows how Ultralase combines persuasion, usability and accessibility within it's home page to help meet business needs.

These are some of the design elements used by Ultralase to help it achieve it's goals:

1. *Carousel area (centre top of page).* Use to deliver key brand messages and position the brand through imagery.
2. *Customer journey highlighted (buttons below carousel).* The 'call-to-action' buttons for 'book a consultation', 'request a brochure' and 'find your local clinic' help highlight what the customer can do on the site and its goals.
3. *Intro text.* This helps show relevance for users, communicates key brand messages and is used for search engine optimisation to target the keyphrases laser eye surgery and treatment.
4. *Incentivised response-form (left side-bar).* Multiple incentives and prominent position consistent with eyetracking studies.
5. *Clear calls-to-action.* Again, prominent on the left-hand side, these are likely set up as conversion goals in Google Analytics. Containers blend image and text to avoid banner blindness. These containers all highlight the site online value proposition.
6. *Common questions answered (centre panel).* These 'points of resolution' are often hidden in an FAQ, but it is interesting that Ultralase highlights them on the home page. Key concerns are also highlighted in the main navigation.
7. *Prominent phone response (top right).* Vital for high-value, complex products since conversion tends to be higher via the phone channel. A unique web number can be used for tracking online influence.
8. *Social proof (right sidebar).* The right sidebar is used for the map to show the scale of the company through number of clinics and engaging containers for customer testimonials.
9. *MyUltralase (top right and right sidebar).* This site registration facility again shows the online value proposition. This is intended to encourage a deeper relationship and return visits.

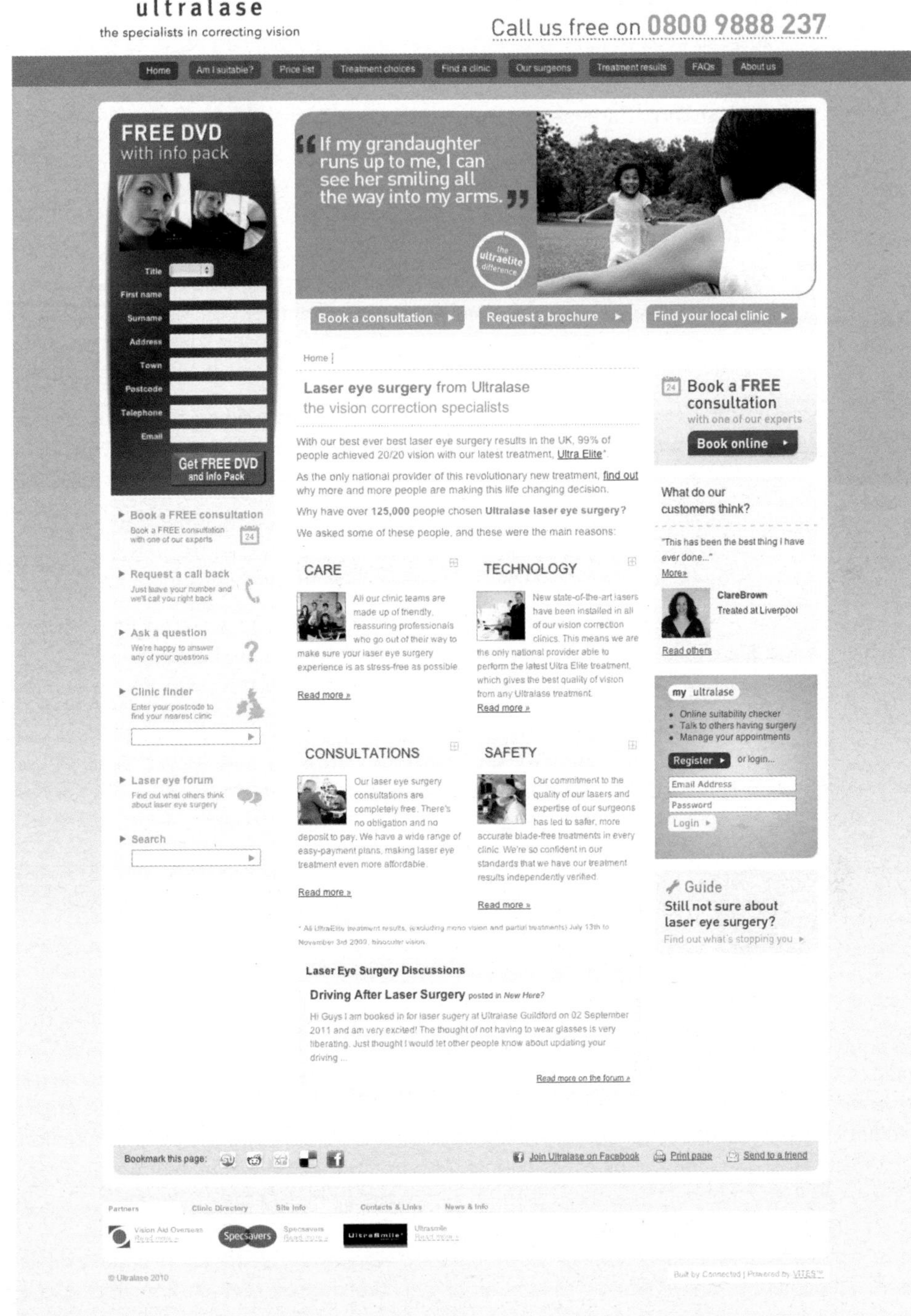

Figure 7.6 Ultralase website (www.ultralase.com)

Usability requirements

Usability
An approach to website design intended to enable the completion of user tasks.

Usability is a concept that can be applied to the analysis and design for a range of products which defines how easy they are to use. The British Standard/ISO Standard (1999): *Human Centred design processes for interactive systems* defines usability as:

> the extent to which a product can be used by specified users to achieve specified goals with effectiveness, efficiency and satisfaction in a specified context of use.

You can see how the concept can be readily applied to website design – web visitors often have defined *goals* such as finding particular information or completing an action such as booking a flight or viewing an account balance.

In Jakob Nielsen's classic book Designing Web Usability (Nielsen, 2000), he describes usability as follows:

> An engineering approach to website design to ensure the user interface of the site is learnable, memorable, error free, efficient and gives user satisfaction. It incorporates testing and evaluation to ensure the best use of navigation and links to access information in the shortest possible time. A companion process to information architecture.

Expert review
An analysis of an existing site or prototype by an experienced usability expert who will identify deficiencies and improvements to a site based on their knowledge of web design principles and best practice.

Usability/user testing
Representative users are observed performing representative tasks using a system.

In practice, usability involves two key project activities. **Expert reviews** are often performed at the beginning of a redesign project as a way of identifying problems with a previous design. **Usability testing** involves:

1. identifying representative users of the site (see, for example, Table 7.2) and identifying typical tasks
2. asking them to perform specific tasks such as finding a product or completing an order
3. observing what they do and how they succeed.

For a site to be successful, the user tasks or actions need to be completed:

- *Effectively* – web usability specialists measure task completion; for example, only three out of ten visitors to a website may be able to find a telephone number or other piece of information.
- *Efficiently* – web usability specialists also measure how long it takes to complete a task on-site, or the number of clicks it takes.

Mini Case Study 7.2 Thomas Cook Netherlands use 4Q to review and improve their customers' experience

To find out the customer satisfaction ratings for visitors to their site compared to their intent, Thomas Cook Netherlands used Voice of Customer Tool 4Q (Figure 7.7).

A sample of visitors were asked four questions after they had used the site to determine the gap between what they were looking for and whether they were successful. Thomas Cook noticed that website visitors were not able to find certain seasonal travel content such as destinations and specific accommodations from the homepage. Visitors also validated other research into web performance by suggesting that page load times could be improved. Using not only their own research, but also the voice of their customers, they were able to build a much stronger case to focus optimisation improvements in these areas.

'Because our work is very seasonal, we are constantly monitoring feedback in order to meet our visitors' content expectations,' said Matthew Niederberger, conversion specialist at Thomas Cook Netherlands. 'Thanks to our visitors' insights, we have been able to improve much of the content on the homepage to better meet their needs. We have also increased priority to several web performance improvement projects as we could clearly see that this was a major concern among our visitor base.'

Source: iPerceptions (2011), iPerceptions' 4Q Suite helps improve Thomas Cook Netherlands website performance and content, case study published at: http://www.iperceptions.com/news/iperceptions%E2%80%99-4q-suite-helps-improves-thomas-cook-netherlands-website-performance-and-content/.

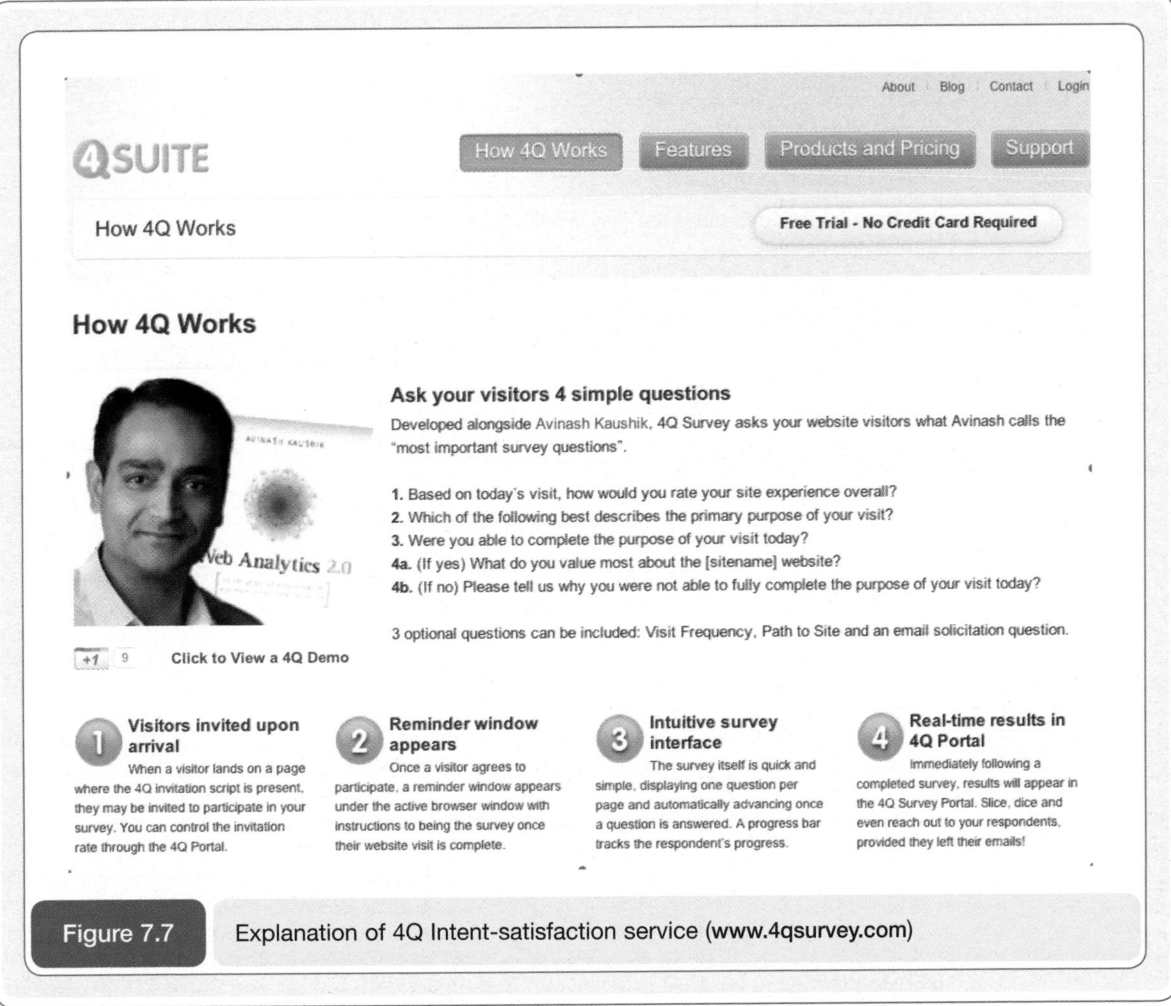

About | Blog | Contact | Login
4SUITE
How 4Q Works
Features
Products and Pricing
Support
How 4Q Works
Free Trial - No Credit Card Required
How 4Q Works
Ask your visitors 4 simple questions
Developed alongside Avinash Kaushik, 4Q Survey asks your website visitors what Avinash calls the "most important survey questions".
1. Based on today's visit, how would you rate your site experience overall?
2. Which of the following best describes the primary purpose of your visit?
3. Were you able to complete the purpose of your visit today?
4a. (If yes) What do you value most about the [sitename] website?
4b. (If no) Please tell us why you were not able to fully complete the purpose of your visit today?
3 optional questions can be included: Visit Frequency, Path to Site and an email solicitation question.
Web Analytics 2.0
+1 9
Click to View a 4Q Demo
1 Visitors invited upon arrival
When a visitor lands on a page where the 4Q invitation script is present, they may be invited to participate in your survey. You can control the invitation rate through the 4Q Portal.
2 Reminder window appears
Once a visitor agrees to participate, a reminder window appears under the active browser window with instructions to being the survey once their website visit is complete.
3 Intuitive survey interface
The survey itself is quick and simple, displaying one question per page and automatically advancing once a question is answered. A progress bar tracks the respondent's progress.
4 Real-time results in 4Q Portal
Immediately following a completed survey, results will appear in the 4Q Survey Portal. Slice, dice and even reach out to your respondents, provided they left their emails!

Figure 7.7 Explanation of 4Q Intent-satisfaction service (**www.4qsurvey.com**)

Jakob Nielsen explains the imperative for usability well in his 'Usability 101' (**www.useit.com/alertbox/20030825.html**). He said:

> On the web, usability is a necessary condition for survival. If a website is difficult to use, people leave. If the homepage fails to clearly state what a company offers and what users can do on the site, people leave. If users get lost on a website, they leave. If a website's information is hard to read or doesn't answer users' key questions, they leave. Note a pattern here?

For these reasons, Nielsen suggests that around 10 per cent of a design project budget should be spent on usability, but often actual spend is significantly less.

Some would also extend usability to including testing of the visual or brand design of a site in focus groups, to assess how well consumers perceive it reflects the brand. Often, alternative visual designs are developed to identify those which are most appropriate.

Additional website design research activities include the use of *personas* and *scenario-based design* as introduced in Chapter 2.

Web accessibility
An approach to site design intended to accommodate site usage using different browsers and settings – particularly required by the visually impaired and visitors with other disabilities including motor control, learning difficulties and deaf users. Users whose first language is not English can also be assisted.

Web accessibility requirements

Web accessibility is another core requirement for websites. It is about allowing all users of a website to interact with it regardless of disabilities they may have, or the web browser or

Table 7.2 Different potential audiences for a website

Customers vary by	Staff	Third parties
New or existing prospects	New or existing	New or existing
Size of prospect companies (e.g. small, medium or large)	Different departments Sales staff for different markets	Suppliers Distributors
Market type (e.g. different vertical markets)	Location (by country)	Investors Media
Members of buying process (decision makers, influencers, buyers)	Students	
Familiarity (with using the web, the company, its products and services or its website)		

platform they are using to access the site. The visually impaired are the main audience that designing an accessible website can help. However, increased usage of mobile devices also make consideration of accessibility important.

The following quote shows the importance of accessibility to a visually impaired user who uses a screen-reader which reads out the navigation options and content on a website.

> For me being online is everything. It's my hi-fi, it's my source of income, it's my supermarket, it's my telephone. It's my way in.
>
> (Lynn Holdsworth, screen-reader user, web developer and programmer)
>
> Source: RNIB

Accessibility legislation Legislation intended to protect users of websites with disabilities including visual disability.

Remember, as we explained in Chapter 3, that many countries now have specific **accessibility legislation** to which website owners are subject. This is often contained within disability and discrimination acts. In the UK, the relevant act is the Disability and Discrimination Act (DDA) 1995. Recent amendments to the DDA make it unlawful to discriminate against disabled people in the way in which a company recruits and employs people, provides services or provides education. Providing services is the part of the law that applies to website design. Providing accessible websites is a requirement of Part II of the Disability and Discrimination Act published in 1999 and required by law from 2002. In the 2002 code of practice there is a legal requirement for websites to be accessible. This is most important for sites which provide a service; for example, the code of practice gives this example:

> An airline company provides a flight reservation and booking service to the public on its website. This is a provision of a service and is subject to the Act.

Although there is a moral imperative for accessibility, there is also a business imperative to encourage companies to make their websites accessible. The main arguments in favour of accessibility are:

- *Number of visually impaired people.* In many countries there are millions of visually impaired people varying from 'colour blind' to partially sighted to blind. The number of web users with other disabilities is also significant.
- *Number of users of less popular browsers or variation in screen display resolution.* Microsoft Internet Explorer is now the dominant browser, but there are less well-known browsers which have a loyal following among the visually impaired (for example, screen-readers and Lynx, a text-only browser) and early-adopters (for example, Mozilla Firefox, Safari

and Opera). If a website does not display well in these browsers, then you may lose these audiences.

- *More visitors from natural listings of search engines.* Many of the techniques used to make sites more usable also assist in search engine optimisation. For example, clearer navigation, text alternatives for images and site maps can all help improve a site's position in the search engine rankings.
- *Legal requirements.* In many countries it is a legal requirement to make websites accessible. For example, the UK has a Disability Discrimination Act that requires this.

Guidelines for creating accessible websites are produced by the governments of different countries and non-government organisations such as charities. Internet standards organisations, such as the World Wide Web Consortium, have been active in promoting guidelines for web accessibility through the Website Accessibility Initiative (see **www.w3.org/WAI**). This describes common accessibility problems such as:

> images without alternative text; lack of alternative text for imagemap hot-spots; misleading use of structural elements on pages; uncaptioned audio or undescribed video; lack of alternative information for users who cannot access frames or scripts; tables that are difficult to decipher when linearised; or sites with poor colour contrast.

A fuller checklist for acessibility compliance for website design and coding using HTML is available from the World Wide Web Consortium (**http://www.w3.org/WAI/**).

Localisation

Localisation
Tailoring of website information for individual countries.

A further aspect of customer-centricity for website design is the decision whether to include specific content for particular countries. This is referred to as **localisation**. A site may need to support customers from a range of countries with:

- different product needs
- language differences
- cultural differences – this approach is also referred to as 'cultural adaptation'.

Localisation will address all these issues. It may be that products will be similar in different countries and localisation will simply involve converting the website to suit another country. However, in order to be effective this often needs more than translation, since different promotion concepts may be needed for different countries. Note that each company prioritises different countries according to the size of the market, and this priority then governs the amount of work it puts into localisation.

Singh and Pereira (2005) provide an evaluation framework for the level of localisation:

- *Standardised websites (not localised).* A single site serves all customer segments (domestic and international).
- *Semi-localised websites.* A single site serves all customers; however, contact information about foreign subsidiaries is available for international customers. Many sites fall into this category.
- *Localised websites.* Country-specific websites with language translation for international customers, wherever relevant. 3M (**www.3m.com**) has adapted the websites for many countries to local language versions. It initially focused on the major websites.
- *Highly-localised websites.* Country-specific websites with language translation; they also include other localisation efforts in terms of time, date, zip code, currency formats, etc. Dell (**www.dell.com**) provides highly-localised websites.
- *Culturally customised websites.* Websites reflecting complete 'immersion' in the culture of target customer segments; as such, targeting a particular country may mean providing multiple websites for that country depending on the dominant cultures present. Durex (**www.durex.com**) is a good example of a culturally customised website.

Deciding on the degree of localisation is a difficult challenge for managers since while it has been established that local preferences are significant, it is often difficult to balance localisation costs against the likely increase or conversion rate through localisation. In a survey published in *Multilingual* (2008), localisation was seen as important with 88 per cent of managers at multinational companies stating that localisation is a key issue and with 76 per cent of them saying that it is important specifically for international customer satisfaction. Yet over half of these respondents also admitted that they allocate only between 1 per cent and 5 per cent of their overall budget for localisation.

An indication of the importance of localisation in different cultures has been completed by Nitish *et al.* (2006) for the German, Indian and Chinese cultures assessing localised websites in terms not only of content, but cultural values such as collectivism, individualism, uncertainty avoidance and masculinity. The survey suggests that without cultural adaptation, confidence or flow decreased so resulting in lower purchase intent.

A further aspect of localisation to be considered is search engine optimisation (SEO, see Chapter 9) since sites which have local language versions will be listed more prominently within the search engine results pages for local versions of the search engines. Many specialist companies have been created to help manage these content localisation issues for companies – for example, agency Web Certain maintains a forum advising on localisation (**www.multilingual-seo.com**).

Reviewing competitors' websites

Benchmarking of competitors' websites is vital in positioning a website to compete effectively with competitors that already have websites. Given the importance of this activity, criteria for performing benchmarking have been described in Chapters 2 and 4.

Benchmarking should not only be based on the obvious tangible features of a website such as its ease of use and the impact of its design. Benchmarking criteria should include those that define the companies' marketing performance in the industry and those that are specific to web marketing as follows:

- *Financial performance* (available from About Us, investor relations and electronic copies of company reports) – this information is also available from intermediary sites such as finance information or share dealing sites such as Interactive Trader International (**www.iii.com.uk**) or Bloomberg (**www.bloomberg.com**) for major quoted companies.
- *Conversion efficiency* – sites can be compared to published results of average conversion rates (see, for example, SmartInsights.com).
- *Marketplace performance* – market share and sales trends and, significantly, the proportion of sales achieved through the Internet. This may not be available directly on the website, but may need the use of other online sources. For example, new entrant to European aviation easyJet (**www.easyjet.com**) achieved over two-thirds of its sales via the website and competitors needed to respond to this.
- *Business and revenue models* (see Chapter 5) – do these differ from other marketplace players?
- *Marketplace positioning* – the elements of the marketing mix covered in Chapter 5 including Product, Pricing and Place.
- *Marketing communications techniques* – is the customer value proposition of the site clear? Does the site support all stages of the buying decision from customers who are unfamiliar with the company through to existing customers? Are special promotions used on a monthly or periodic basis? Beyond the competitor's site, how do they promote their site? How do they make thorough use of intermediary sites to promote and deliver their services?
- *Services offered* – what is offered beyond brochureware? Is online purchase possible? What is the level of online customer support and how much technical information is available?
- *Implementation of services* – these are the practical features of site design that are described in this chapter, such as aesthetics, ease of use, personalisation, navigation, availability and speed.

A review of corporate websites suggests that, for most companies, the type of information that can be included on a website will be fairly similar. Many commentators make the point that some sites miss out the basic information that someone who is unfamiliar with a company may want to know, such as:

- *Who are you?* 'About Us' is now a standard menu option.
- *What do you do?* What products or services are available?
- *Where do you do it?* Are the products and services available internationally?
- *What makes you different?* Why should I use your site/services compared to your competitors? This includes communicating the online value proposition (OVP) we introduced in Chapter 4.

Designing the information architecture

Information architecture
The combination of organisation, labelling and navigation schemes constituting an information system.

Rosenfeld and Morville (2002) emphasised the importance of **information architecture** to an effective website design. They said:

> It is important to recognise that every information system, be it a book or an intranet, has an information architecture. 'Well developed' is the key here, as most sites don't have a planned information architecture at all. They are analogous to buildings that weren't architected in advance. Design decisions reflect the personal biases of designers, the space doesn't scale over time, technologies drive the design and not the other way around.

In their book, which is still the basis for good practice in web design, Rosenfeld and Morville give these alternative definitions of an information architecture:

1. The combination of organisation, labelling, and navigation schemes within an information system.
2. The structural design of an information space to facilitate task completion and intuitive access to content.
3. The art and science of structuring and classifying websites and intranets to help people find and manage information.
4. An emerging discipline and community of practice focused on bringing principles of design and architecture to the digital landscape.

Site map
A graphical or text depiction of the relationship between different groups of content on a website.

Findability
Supporting users to locate the content or offers they are looking for through search engines or when browsing or searching on a site.

In practice, creation of an information architecture involves creating a plan to group information logically – it involves creating a site structure which is often represented as a **site map**. A well-developed information architecture is very important to usability since it determines navigation options and **findability** (Morville, 2005). Mini Case Study 7.3 shows how research to improve findability and in-particular through optimising on-site search engines can yield major benefits to site owners.

Mini Case Study 7.3 Travel company Thomson improves findability through analytics and user feedback

This case study of TUI travel company Thomson highlights the importance of site search. It is based on a presentation by Sandra Leonhard given at the 2004 Econsultancy Online Marketing Masterclasses.

When Thomson calculate improvements derived from usability, two of the main measures they use is:

'Look to Book %' = Number of bookings/Unique users

'Search to Book %' = Number of bookings/Number of unique searches

Below is usability testing and customer feedback obtained as part of the project to optimise search. Customers tend to be frank – these are some of examples of the direct feedback you can get from tests like these which can be used to refine messaging and usability on a site to improve results:

- 'Your search and book could allow a range of dates and selection of details from all brochures. A dropdown for regional airports would help.'
- 'Search would be better if you could input destinations relevant to your departure airport.'
- 'It won't let me select any destination in search.'
- 'This is my third try. It will not show me anything!!! Useless site.'
- 'Search facility restricted to brochure. I wanted to search for any holidays within a date period but I had to state a destination – why when I wanted a good deal to any destination.'
- 'I find the website appalling to search for a holiday due to the fact that it appears to search in a very specific manner. I always get the message "sorry we aren't able…" I booked through Lunn Poly instead'.

Basic analytics showed the scope for improvement and the optimisation project delivered this. Although these problems have now been resolved we have included this example since many sites have not been optimised in this way.

A planned information architecture is essential to large-scale websites such as transactional e-commerce sites, media owner sites and relationship-building sites that include a large volume of product or support documentation. Information architectures are less important to small-scale websites and brand sites, but even here the principles can be readily applied and can help make the site more visible to search engines and more usable. It is also important for search engine optimisation (Chapter 8), since it determines how different types of content that users may search for are labelled and grouped.

The benefits of creating an information architecture include:

- A defined structure and categorisation of information will support user and organisation goals, i.e. it is a vital aspect of usability.
- It helps increase 'flow' on the site – a user's mental model of where to find content should mirror that of the content on the website.
- Search engine optimisation – a higher listing in the search rankings can often be used through structuring and labelling information in a structured way.
- Applicable for integrating offline communications – offline communications such as ads or direct mail can link to a product or campaign landing page to help achieve direct response, sometimes known as 'web response'. A sound URL strategy, as explained in Chapter 8, can help this.
- Related content can be grouped to measure the effectiveness of a website as part of design for analysis, which is also explained below.

Card sorting

Using card sorting is a way in which users can become actively involved in the development process of information architecture.

Card sorting is a useful approach since websites are frequently designed from the perspective of the designer rather than the information user, leading to labels, subject grouping and categories that are not intuitive to the user. **Card sorting** or **web classification** should categorise web objects (e.g. documents) in order to facilitate information task completion or information goals the user has set.

Card sorting or web classification
The process of arranging a way of organising objects on the website in a consistent manner.

Robertson (2003) explains an approach to card sorting which identifies the following questions when using the technique to aid the process of modelling web classification systems:

- Do the users want to see the information grouped by subject, task, business or customer groupings, or type of information?
- What are the most important items to put on the main menu?
- How many menu items should there be, and how deep should it go?
- How similar or different are the needs of the users throughout the organisation?

Selected groups of users or representatives will be given index cards with the following written on them, depending on the aim of the card sorting process:

- types of documents
- organisational key words and concepts
- document titles
- descriptions of documents
- navigation labels.

The user groups may then be asked to:

- Group together cards that they feel relate to each other.
- Select cards that accurately reflect a given topic or area.
- Organise cards in terms of hierarchy – high-level terms (broad) to low-level terms.

At the end of the session the analyst must take the cards away and map the results into a spreadsheet to find out the most popular terms, descriptions and relationships. If two or more different groups are used, the results should be compared and reasons for differences should be analysed.

Blueprints

Blueprint
Shows the relationships between pages and other content components, and can be used to portray organisation, navigation and labelling systems.

According to Rosenfeld and Morville (2002), **blueprints**:

> show the relationships between pages and other content components, and can be used to portray organisation, navigation and labelling systems.

They are often thought of, and referred to, as 'site maps' or 'site structure diagrams' and have much in common with these, except that they are used as a design device clearly showing grouping of information and linkages between pages, rather than a page on the website to assist navigation.

Refer to Figure 7.8 for an example of a site structure diagram for a toy manufacturer website which shows the groupings of content and an indication of the process of task completion also.

Wireframes

Wireframe
Also known as 'schematics', a way of illustrating the layout of an individual web page.

A related technique to blueprints is the **wireframes** which are used by web designers to indicate the eventual layout of a web page. Figure 7.9 shows that the wireframe is so called because it just consists of an outline of the page with the 'wires' of content separating different areas of content or navigation shown by white space.

Wodtke (2002) describes a wireframe (sometimes known as a 'schematic') as:

> a basic outline of an individual page, drawn to indicate the elements of a page, their relationships and their relative importance.

A wireframe will be created for all types of similar page groups, identified at the blueprint (site map) stage of creating the information architecture.

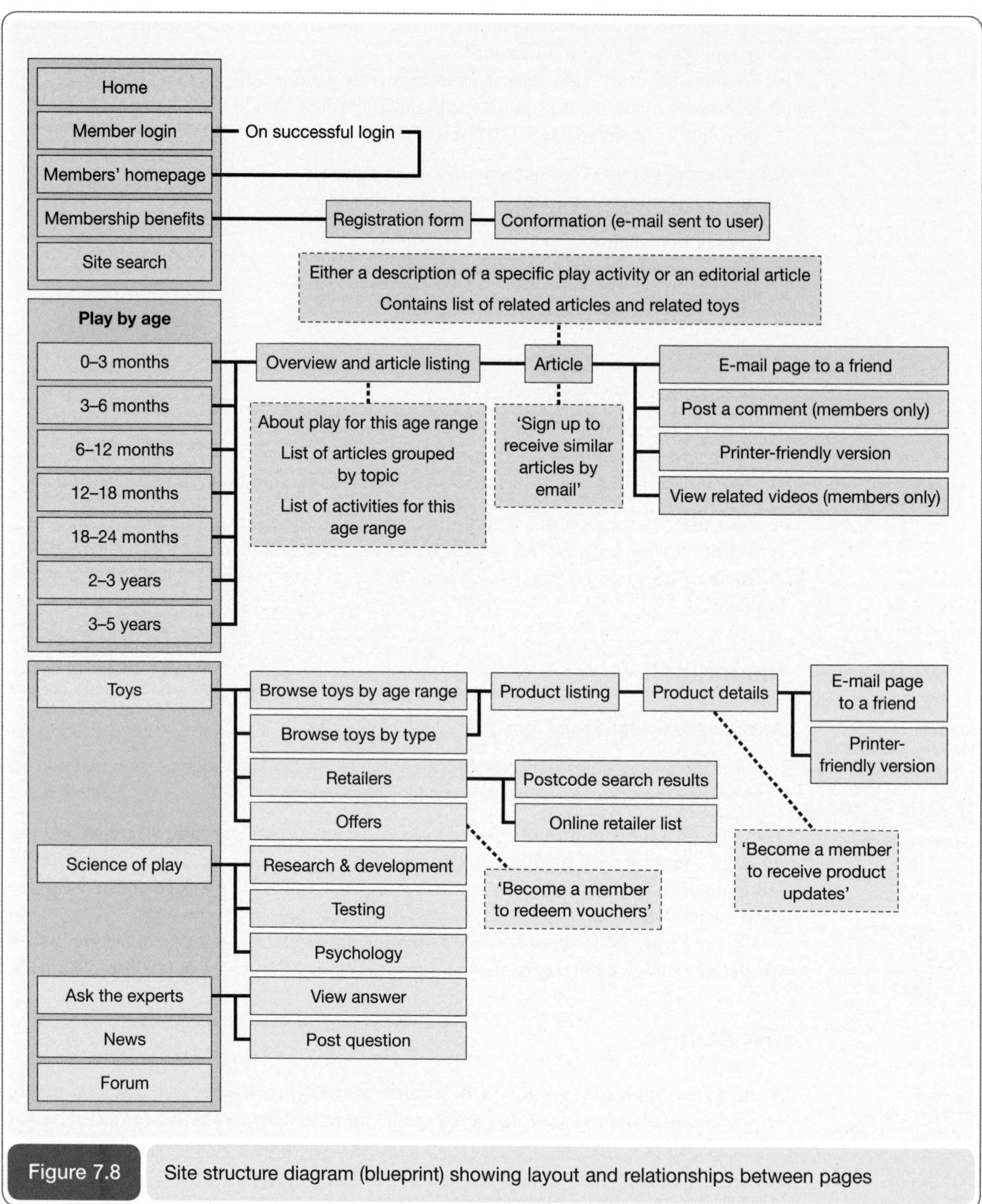

Figure 7.8 Site structure diagram (blueprint) showing layout and relationships between pages

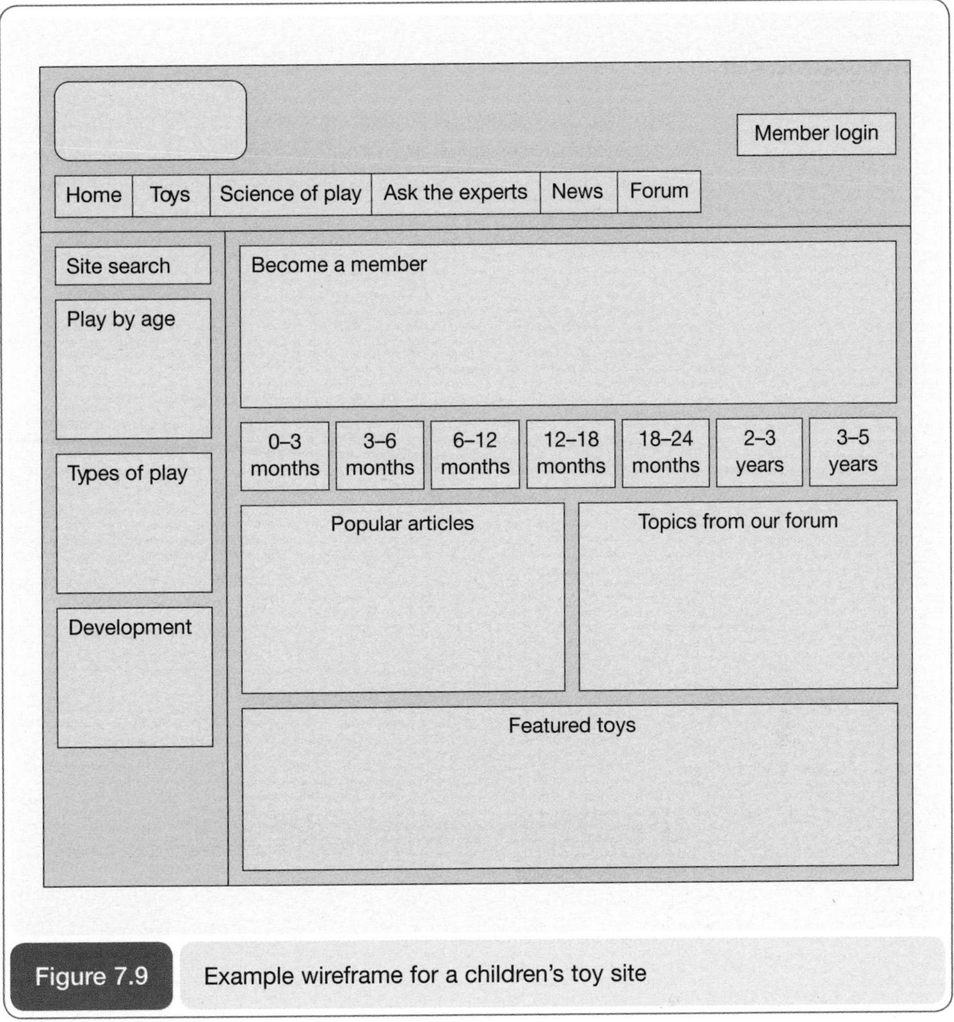

Figure 7.9 Example wireframe for a children's toy site

Site design page template (CSS)
A standard page layout format which is applied to each page of a website. Typically defined for different page categories (e.g. category page, product page, search page).

Cascading style sheets
A simple mechanism for adding style (e.g. fonts, colours, spacing) to web documents. CSS enables different style elements to be controlled across an entire site or section of site. Style elements that are commonly controlled include typography, background colour and images, and borders and margins.

Wireframes are then transformed into physical **site design page templates** which are now traditionally created using standardised **cascading style sheets (CSS)** which enable a standard look and feel to be enforced across different sections of the site. Complete Activity 7.3 to see the power of using CSS.

The standards body W3C (**www.w3.org**) defines cascading style sheets as:

> a simple mechanism for adding style (e.g. fonts, colors, spacing) to Web documents.

CSS enable different style elements to be controlled across an entire site or section of site. Style elements that are commonly controlled include:

- typography
- background colour and images
- borders and margins.

Activity 7.3 Using CSS to separate site style from design

Visit CSS ZenGarden (**www.csszengarden.com**) which shows how CSS can be used to separate presentation from content (Figure 7.10). Select the different designs from the right sidebar on the site to see how the design changes radically while the content remains the same.

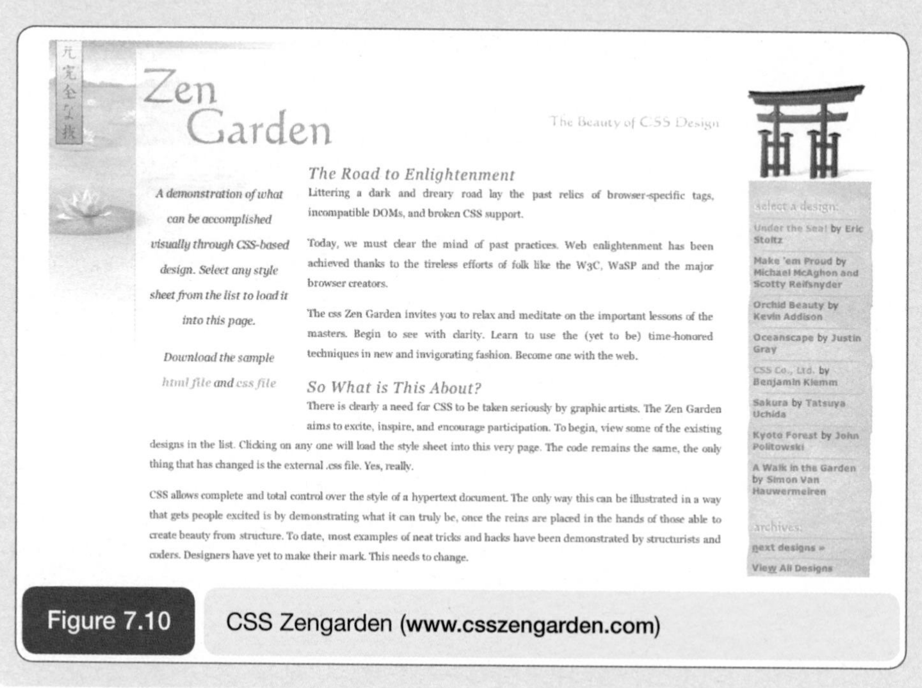

Figure 7.10 CSS Zengarden (**www.csszengarden.com**)

For example, CSS will use this syntax to enforce the standard appearance of body copy on a site:

```
body {
    margin:0;
    padding:0;
    color:#666666;
    background-color:#f3f3f3;
    font-family: Arial, 'Trebuchet MS', Verdana;
    font-size: 70%;
    background-repeat:repeat-x;
    background-position:top;
}
```

The benefits of CSS are:

- *Bandwidth* – pages download faster after initial page load since style definitions only need to be downloaded once as a separate file, not for each page.
- *More efficient development* – through agreeing site style and implementing in CSS as part of page templates, it is more efficient to design a site.
- *Reduces updating and maintenance time* – presentational markup is stored in one place separate from the content making it quicker to update the site globally with less scope for errors.
- *Increased interoperability* – by adhering to W3C recommendations; helps with support of multiple browsers.
- *Increases accessibility* – users can more readily configure the way a site looks or sounds using browsers and other accessibility support tools. The site is more likely to render on a range of access platforms like PDAs and smartphones.

Landing pages

Landing page
An entrance page to the site when a user clicks on an ad or other form of link from a referring site. It can be a home page but more typically, and desirably, a landing page is a page with the messaging focused on the offer in the ad. This will maximise conversion rates and brand favourability.

Deciding on the page template design for different forms of **landing pages** is particularly important for site owners seeking to maximise conversion rate since many first time visitors don't arrive on the home page, they arrive deeper in the site from search engines or links from other sites. Chaffey and Smith (2008) suggest these are typical aims and corresponding questions to consider for increasing landing page conversion rate:

- *Aim 1 – Generate response (online lead or sale & offline callback).* Does the page have a prominent call-to-action, such as a prominent button above the fold and repeated in text and image form?
- *Aim 2 – Engage different audience types (reduce bounce rate, increase value events, increase return rate).* Does the page have a prominent headline and subheads showing the visitor is in the right place? Does the page have scent-trail trigger messages, offers or images to appeal to different audiences? For example, Dell has links on its site to appeal to consumers and different types of businesses. A landing page containing form fields to fill in is often more effective than an additional click since it starts committed visitors on their journey.
- *Aim 3 – Communicate key brand messages (increase brand familiarity and favourability).* Does the page clearly explain who you are, what you do, where you operate and what makes you different? Is your online value proposition compelling? Do you use customer testimonials or ratings to show independent credibility? To help with this, use run-of-site messages (on all pages) across the top of the screen or in the left or right sidebars.
- *Aim 4 – Answer the visitor's questions (reduce bounce rates, increase conversion rates).* Different audiences will want to know different things. Have you identified personas (Chapter 4) and do you seek to answer their questions? Do you use FAQ or messages which say 'New to company'?
- *Aim 5 – Showcase range of offers (cross-sell).* Do you have recommendations on related or best selling products and do you show the full-range of your offering through navigation?
- *Aim 6 – Attract visitors through search engine optimisation (SEO).* How well do you rank for relevant search terms compared to competitors? Do your navigation, copy and page templates indicate relevance to search engines through on-page optimisation?

Blueprints illustrate how the content of a website is related and navigated while a wireframe focuses on individual pages; with a wireframe the navigation focus becomes where it will be placed on the page. Wireframes are useful for agencies and clients to discuss the way a website will be laid out without getting distracted by colour, style or messaging issues which should be covered separately as a creative planning activity.

Storyboarding
The use of static drawings or screenshots of the different parts of a website to review the design concept with user groups. It can be used to develop the structure – an overall 'map' with individual pages shown separately.

The process of reviewing wireframes is sometimes referred to as **storyboarding**, although the term is often applied to reviewing creative ideas rather than formal design alternatives. Early designs are drawn on large pieces of paper, or mock-ups are produced using a drawing or paint program.

At the wireframe stage, emphasis is not placed on use of colour or graphics, which will be developed in conjunction with branding or marketing teams and graphic designers and integrated into the site after the wireframe process.

According to Chaffey and Wood (2010), the aim of a wireframe will be to:

- integrate consistently available components on the web page (e.g. navigation, search boxes)
- order and group key types of components together
- develop a design that will focus the user on to core messages and content
- make correct use of white space to structure the page
- develop a page structure that can be easily reused by other web designers.

Common wireframe or template features you may come across are:

- navigation in columns on left or right and at top or bottom
- header areas and footer areas

- containers, 'slots' or 'portlets' – these are areas of content such as an article or list of articles placed in boxes on the screen. Often slots will be dynamically populated from a content management system
- containers on the homepage may be used to:
  - summarise the online value proposition
  - show promotions
  - recommend related products
  - feature news, etc.
  - contain ads.

Designing the user experience

Design phase
The design phase defines how the site will work in the key areas of website structure, navigation and security.

Once analysis has determined the business and user needs for a site, the site can be designed. The **design phase** is critical to a successful website since it will determine the quality of experience users of a site have; if they have a good experience they will return, if not they will not! A 'good experience' is determined by a number of factors such as those that affect how easy it is to find information: for example, the structure of the site, menu choices and searching facilities. It is also affected by less tangible factors such as the graphical design and layout of the site.

As mentioned at the start of the chapter, design is not solely a paper-based exercise, but needs to be integrated into the prototyping process. The design should be tested by review with the client and customer to ensure it is appropriate. Since the main reason given for returning to a website is high-quality content and content effects conversion too, it is important to determine, through analysis, that the content is correct. However, the quality of content is determined by more than the text copy. It is important to achieve high-quality content through design. To help in this it is useful to consider the factors that affect quality content. These are shown in Figure 7.11. All are determined by the quality of the information.
Nigel Bevan (1999a) says:

> Unless a website meets the needs of the intended users it will not meet the needs of the organisation providing the website. Website development should be user-centred, evaluating the evolving design against user requirements.

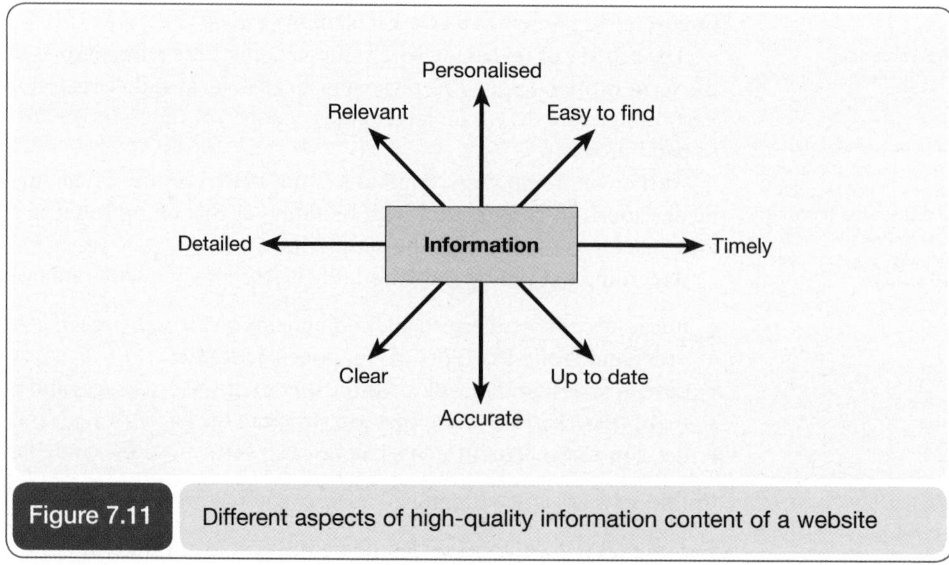

Figure 7.11 Different aspects of high-quality information content of a website

User-centred design
Design based on optimising the user experience according to all factors, including the user interface, which affect this.

How can this customer-oriented or user-centred content be achieved? **User-centred design** starts with understanding the nature and variation within the user groups. According to Bevan (1999a), issues to consider include:

- Who are the important users?
- What is their purpose for accessing the site?
- How frequently will they visit the site?
- What experience and expertise do they have?
- What nationality are they? Can they read your language?
- What type of information are they looking for?
- How will they want to use the information: read it on the screen, print it or download it?
- What type of browsers will they use? How fast will their communication links be?
- How large a screen or window will they use, with how many colours?

Rosenfeld and Morville (2002) suggest four stages of site design that also have a user-centred basis:

1. Identify different audiences.
2. Rank importance of each to business.
3. List the three most important information needs of audience.
4. Ask representatives of each audience type to develop their own wish lists.

We noted in Chapter 2 that customer persona and scenario analysis is a powerful technique of understanding different audiences which can be used to inform and test website design. Even without indepth analysis, every site owner should consider the key questions that a visitor will need answering when they are considering a service.

Evaluating designs

A test of effective design for usability is dependent on three areas according to Bevan (1999b):

- *Effectiveness* – can users complete their tasks correctly and completely?
- *Productivity (efficiency)* – are tasks completed in an acceptable length of time?
- *Satisfaction* – are users satisfied with the interaction?

Elements of site design

Once the requirements of the user and marketer are established we turn our attention to the design of the human–computer interface. Nielsen (2000) structures his book on web usability according to three main areas, which can be interpreted as follows:

1. *site design and structure* – the overall structure of the site
2. *page design* – the layout of individual pages
3. *content design* – how the text and graphic content on each page is designed.

There is also the additional area of branding and messaging which is a key part of persuasion as explained earlier in this chapter.

Site design and structure

The structures created by designers for websites will vary greatly according to their audience and the site's purpose, but we can make some general observations about common approaches to site design and structure and their influence on consumers. These are often known as best practice principles of website design and in this section we will summarise some of the main factors. Of course, there are exceptions to such rules of thumb or 'heuristics', but often a design approach that works on one type of site will work on another, particularly if it is a common feature across the majority of sites.

Rosen and Purinton (2004) assessed the design factors which influence a consumer (based on questionnaires of a group of students). They believe there are some basic factors that determine the effectiveness of an e-commerce site. They group these factors as follows:

- *Coherence* – simplicity of design, easy to read, use of categories (for browsing products or topics), absence of information overload, adequate font size, uncrowded presentation.
- *Complexity* – different categories of text.
- *Legibility* – use of 'mini home page' on every subsequent page, same menu on every page, site map.

You can see that these authors suggest that simplicity in design is important. Another example of research into website design factors supports the importance of design. Fogg *et al.* (2003) asked students to review sites to assess the credibility of different suppliers based on the website design. They considered these factors most important:

Design look	*46.1%*
Information design/structure	*28.5%*
Information focus	*25.1%*
Company motive	*15.5%*
Usefulness of information	*14.8%*
Accuracy of information	*14.3%*
Name recognition and reputation	*14.1%*
Advertising	*13.8%*
Bias of information	*11.6%*
Tone of the writing	*9.0%*
Identity of site sponsor	*8.8%*
Functionality of site	*8.6%*
Customer service	*6.4%*
Past experience with site	*4.6%*
Information clarity	*3.7%*
Performance on a test	*3.6%*
Readability	*3.6%*
Affiliations	*3.4%*

However, it should be borne in mind that such generalisations can be misleading based on the methodology used. Reported behaviour (e.g. through questionnaires or focus groups) may be quite different from actual observed behaviour. Leading e-retail sites (for example Amazon.com and eBay.com) and many media sites typically have a large amount of information and navigation choices available on-screen since the site designers know from testing alternative designs that consumers are quite capable of finding content relevant to them, and that a wider choice of links means that the user can find the information they need without clicking through a hierarchy. When performing a real-life product search, in-depth information on the products and reviews of the product are important in making the product decision and are one of the benefits that online channels can give. Although design look is top of the list of factors presented by Fogg *et al.* (2003), you can see that many of the other factors are based on the quality of information.

In the following coverage, we will review the general factors which designers consider in designing the style, organisation and navigation schemes for the site.

Site style

An effective website design will have a style that is communicated through use of colour, images, typography and layout. This should support the way a product is positioned or its brand.

Site personality

The style elements can be combined to develop a personality for a site. We could describe a site's personality in the same way we can describe people, such as 'formal' or 'fun'. This personality has to be consistent with the needs of the target audience . A business audience often requires detailed information and prefers an information-intensive style such as that of the Cisco site (Example: **www.cisco.com**). A consumer site is usually more graphically intensive. Before the designers pass on their creative designs to developers, they also need to consider the constraints on the user experience, such as screen resolution and colour depth, browser used and download speed.

Visual design

Despite modern browsers and broadband access, graphic design of websites still represents a challenge since designers of websites are severely constrained by a number of factors:

- *The speed of downloading graphics* – designers still need to allow for page download speed as we explained earlier in the chapter.
- *The screen resolutions of the computer* – designing for different screen resolutions is necessary, since some users with laptops may be operating at a low resolution such as 1024 × 768 pixels, while the majority will have a higher resolution.
- *The number of colours on screen* – the colour palettes available on web browsers.
- *The type of web browser used* – different browsers, such as Google Chrome, Microsoft Internet Explorer IE and Apple Safari, and different versions of browsers, such as IE8.0 or 9.0, may display graphics or text slightly differently or may support different plug-ins.
- *Different access devices* – with the increase in popularity of mobile and tablet browsers it has become very important to support users of these sites using techniques such as **adaptive web design**.

Adaptive web design
Also known as progressive enhancement, this design technique delivers different layouts and features according to what is supported by browser and screen resolution of the device.

As a result of these constraints, the design of websites is a constant compromise between what looks visually appealing and modern on the most advanced hardware platforms and highest speed network connections and what works for other systems. This is referred to as the 'lowest common denominator problem' since this is what the designer has traditionally had to do – design for the old browsers, using slow links and low screen resolutions. Adaptive website design is now a common method for avoiding the 'lowest common denominator problem' and is particularly pertinent to the design of mobile experiences as Digital Marketing Insights 7.1 shows.

Digital marketing insight 7.1 Taking the mobile site vs app decision

Despite advances in web development, frameworks such as CSS, the challenge of developing for different platforms has increased with the advent of new platforms such as smartphones and tablets. Consequently, key technology options include:

- mobile version of website (full site)
- mobile version of site (most popular pages linking through to traditional pages)
- separate mobile app
- which device formats and so screen sizes do we support?
- which mobile operating systems and mobile browser versions do we support? For example, Android, iOS, Symbian, etc?

It will only be cost-effective for the very largest organisations to design for all of these target platforms and devices, so companies need to balance the costs against the benefits and select carefully. The decision is complicated by the improving quality of screen resolution through smartphones and tablets. Many of these now have a size that enables viewing of sites designed for desktops, although zooming and panning can be frustrating.

The challenge has been nicely summarised by former eBay designer Luke Wroblewski (2011), now lead designer at start-up BagCheck (Figure 7.12) who says:

> *As use of mobile devices continues to skyrocket across the globe, we're seeing more ways to tackle the challenge of creating great web experiences across multiple devices. But which approach is right for any given project?*
>
> *For us site performance and speed of development were crucial. So many of the decisions we made were designed to make both of these as fast as possible. As part of our focus on performance, we also had a philosophy of 'just what's necessary'. This meant sending things to devices (and people) that didn't actually need them made us squeamish. We liked to optimize. With a dual template system we felt we had more optimization of: source order, media, URL structure, and application design*

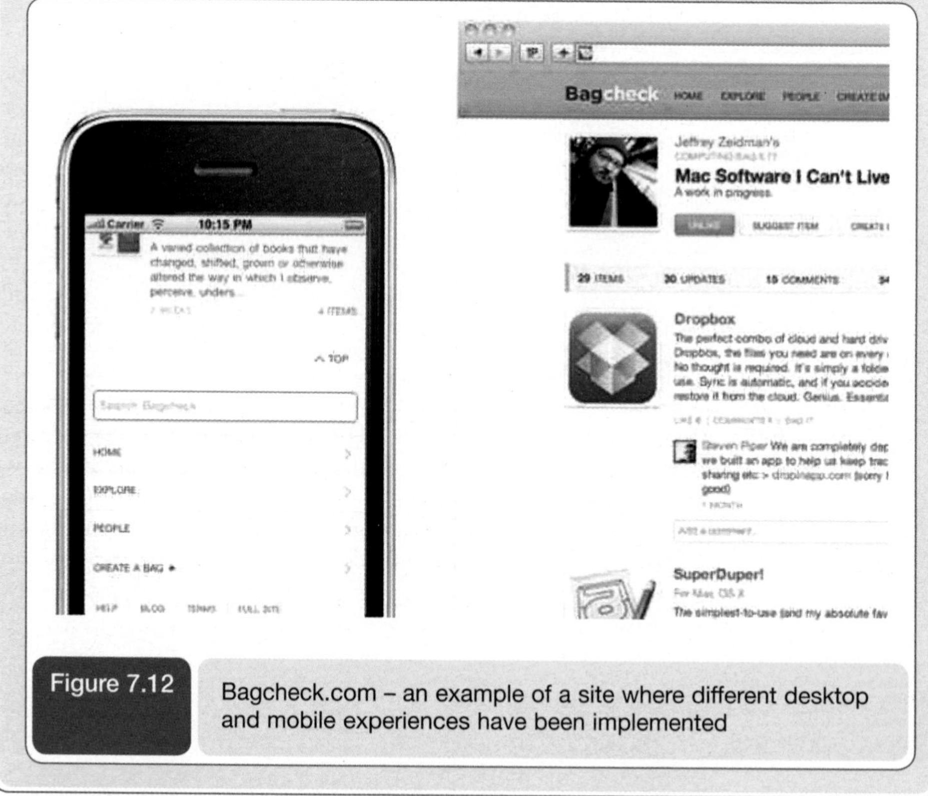

Figure 7.12 Bagcheck.com – an example of a site where different desktop and mobile experiences have been implemented

Site organisation

Information organisation scheme
A structure chosen to group and categorise information.

In their book *Information Architecture for the World Wide Web*, Rosenfeld and Morville (2002) identify several different **information organisation schemes**. These can be applied for different aspects of e-commerce sites, from the whole site through to different parts of the site.

Rosenfeld and Morville (2002) identify the following information organisation schemes:

- *Exact.* Here information can be naturally indexed. If we take the example of books, these can be alphabetical – by author or title; chronological – by date; or for travel books, for example, geographical – by place. Information on an e-commerce site may be presented alphabetically, but it is not suitable for browsing.
- *Ambiguous.* Here the information requires classification – again taking the examples of books, the Dewey Decimal System is an ambiguous classification scheme since librarians classify books into arbitrary categories. Such an approach is common on an e-commerce site since products and services can be classified in different ways. Other ambiguous information organisation schemes that are commonly used on websites are where content is broken down by topic, by task or by audience. The use of metaphors is also common, a metaphor being where the website corresponds to a familiar real-world situation. Microsoft Windows Explorer, where information is grouped according to Folders, Files and Trash is an example of a real-world metaphor. The use of the shopping basket metaphor is widespread within e-commerce sites. It should be noted though that Nielsen (2000) believes that metaphors can be confusing if the metaphor isn't understood immediately or is misinterpreted.
- *Hybrid.* Here there will be a mixture of organisation schemes, both exact and ambiguous. Rosenfeld and Morville (2002) point out that using different approaches is common on websites, but this can lead to confusion because the user is not clear what mental model is being followed. We can say that it is probably best to minimise the number of information organisation schemes.

Site navigation schemes

Site navigation scheme
Tools provided to the user to move between different information on a website.

Flow
Describes how easy it is for users of a site to move between the different pages of content of the site.

Devising a site that is easy to use is critically dependent on the design of the **site navigation scheme**. Hoffman and Novak (1997) and many subsequent studies (e.g. Rettie, 2001; Smith and Sivakumar, 2004) have stressed the importance of the concept of **flow** in governing site usability. The concept of 'flow' was first brought to prominence by Mihaly Csikszentmihalyi, a psychology professor at the University of Chicago. In his book, *Flow: The Psychology of Optimal Experience*, he explains his theory that people are most happy when they are in a state of flow – a Zen-like state of total oneness with the activity at hand. In an online marketing context, 'flow' essentially describes how easy it is for users to find the information or experiences they need as they move from one page of the site to the next, but it also includes other interactions such as filling in on-screen forms. Rettie (2001) has suggested that the quality of navigation is one of the prerequisites for flow, although other factors are also important. They include quick download time, alternative versions, auto-completion of forms, opportunities for interaction, navigation that creates choices, predictable navigation for control and segmenting content by Internet experience.

It can be suggested that there are three important aspects to a site that is easy to navigate. These are:

- *Consistency.* A site will be easier to navigate if the user is presented with a consistent user interface when viewing the different parts of the site. For example, if the menu options in the support section of the site are on the left side of the screen, then they should also be on the left when the user moves to the 'news section' of the site.
- *Simplicity.* Sites are easier to navigate if there are limited numbers of options. It is usually suggested that two or possibly three levels of menu are the most that are desirable. For example, there may be main menu options at the left of the screen that take the user to the different parts of the site, and at the bottom of the screen there will be specific menu options that refer to that part of the site. (Menus in this form are often referred to as 'nested'.)
- *Context.* Context is the use of 'signposts' to indicate to users where they are located within the site – in other words, to reassure users that they are not 'lost'. To help with this, the website designer should use particular text or colour to indicate to users which part of the

site they are currently using. Context can be provided by the use of JavaScript 'rollovers', where the colour of the menu option changes when the user positions the mouse over the menu option and then changes again when the menu option is selected. Many sites also have a site-map option that shows the layout and content of the whole site so the user can understand its structure. When using a well-designed site it should not be necessary to refer to such a map regularly.

Navigation
Describes how easy it is to find and move between different information on a website. It is governed by menu arrangements, site structure and the layout of individual pages.

Narrow and deep navigation
Fewer choices, more clicks to reach required content.

Broad and shallow navigation
More choices, fewer clicks to reach required content.

Deep linking
Jakob Nielsen's term for a user arriving at a site deep within its structure.

Most **navigation** systems are based upon a hierarchical site structure. When creating the structure, designers have to compromise between the two approaches shown in Figure 7.12. **Narrow and deep navigation** has the benefit of fewer choices on each page, making it easier for the user to make their selection, but more clicks are required to reach a particular piece of information. **Broad and shallow navigation** requires fewer clicks to reach the same piece of information, but the design of the screen potentially becomes cluttered. Figure 7.13(a) depict the narrow and deep approach and Figure 7.13(b) the broad and shallow approach. Note that in these cases the approaches are appropriate for both non-technical and technical audiences. A rule of thumb is that site designers should ensure it only takes three clicks to reach any piece of information on a site. This implies the use of a broad and shallow approach on most large sites. Lynch and Horton (1999) recommend a broad and shallow approach and note that designers should not conceive of a single home page where customers arrive on the site, but of different home pages according to different audience types. Each of the pages in the second row of Figure 7.13(b) could be thought of as an example of a home page which the visitors can bookmark if the page appeals to them. Nielsen (2000) points out that many users will not arrive on the home page, but may be referred from another site or according to a print or TV advert to a particular page such as www.b2b.com/jancomp. He calls this process **deep linking** and site designers should ensure that navigation and context are appropriate for users arriving on these pages.

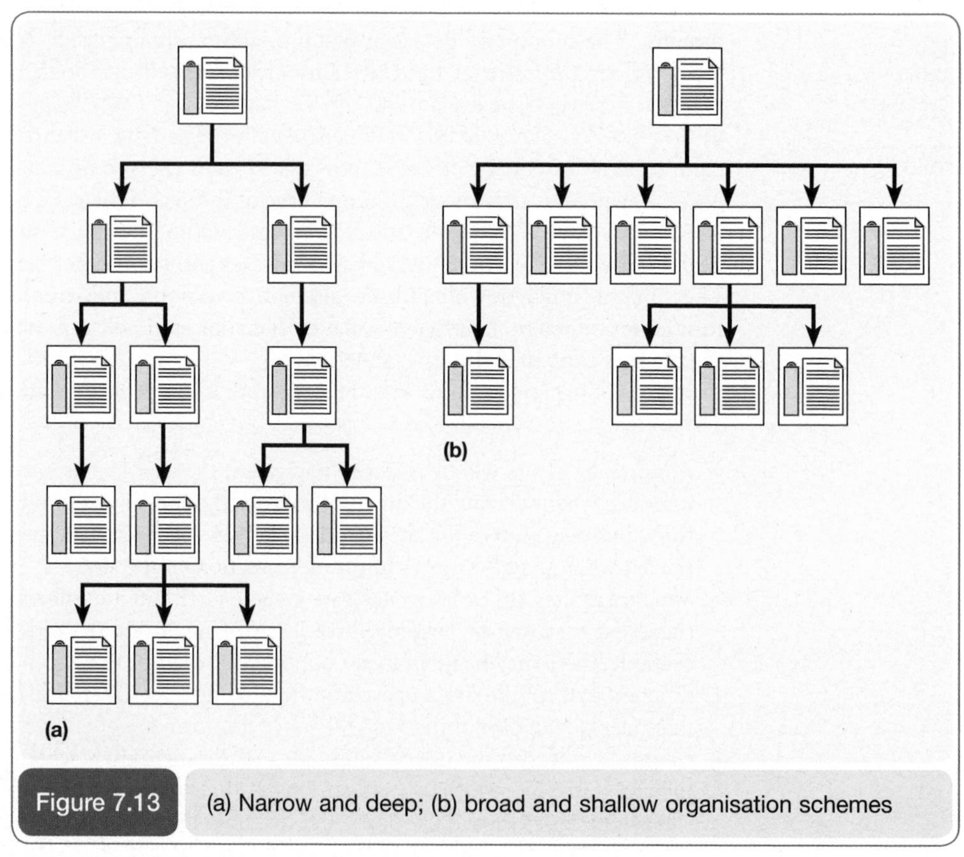

Figure 7.13 (a) Narrow and deep; (b) broad and shallow organisation schemes

As well as compromises on depth of links within a site, it is also necessary to compromise on the amount of space devoted to menus. Nielsen (1999) points out that some sites devote so much space to navigation bars that the space available for content is limited. Nielsen suggests that the designer of navigation systems should consider the following information that a site user wants to know:

- *Where am I?* The user needs to know where they are on the site and this can be indicated by highlighting the current location and clear titling of pages. This can be considered as *context. Consistency* of menu locations on different pages is also required to aid cognition. Users also need to know where they are on the web. This can be indicated by a logo, which by convention is at the top or top-left of a site.
- *Where have I been?* This is difficult to indicate on a site, but for task-oriented activities such as purchasing a product it can show the user that they are at the *n*th stage of an operation, such as making a purchase.
- *Where do I want to go?* This is the main navigation system which gives options for future operations.

To answer these questions, clear succinct labelling is required. Widely used standards such as Home, Main page, Search, Find, Browse, FAQ, Help and About Us are preferable. But for other particular labels it is useful to have what Rosenfeld and Morville (2002) call 'scope notes' – an additional explanation. These authors also argue against the use of iconic labels or pictures without corresponding text since they are open to misinterpretation and take longer to process.

Since using the navigation system may not enable the user to find the information they want rapidly, alternatives have to be provided by the site designers. These alternatives include search, advanced search, browse and site map facilities. Whatis.com (**www.whatis.com**) illustrates these features well.

Menu options

Designing and creating the menus to support navigation present several options. A combination of text-based menus graphical buttons or images is usually preferred in modern sites to meet the requirements of accessibility, persuasion, SEO and usability. Yet some sites are still-based solely on Flash or image-based menus which will reduce the business effectiveness of the site. Most large retail sites now use 'mega-menus' where there are a wide range of products and promotions to communicate.

Page design

The page design involves creating an appropriate layout of page elements to meet the goals of findability and usability as illustrated in the example in Activity 7.4. The main elements of a particular page layout are the title, navigation and content. Standard content, such as copyright information, may be added to every page as a footer. Common page templates will be created for pages which share similar characteristics such as home page, category/sub-category page, product page, search results page and checkout pages for a retail site. Through use of common templates improvements can be implemented more efficiently.

Issues in page design include:

- *Page elements.* We have to consider the proportion of a page devoted to content compared to all other material such as headers, footers and navigation elements. The location of these elements also needs to be considered. It is conventional for the main menu to be at the top or on the left. The use of a menu system at the top of the browser window allows more space for content below.
- *Resizing.* A good page layout design should allow for the user to change the size of text or work with different monitor resolutions.
- *Consistency.* Page layout should be similar for all areas of the site unless more space is required – for example for a discussion forum or product demonstration. Standards of colour and typography can be enforced through cascading style sheets.
- *Printing.* Layout should allow for printing or provide an alternative printing format.

Content design

Content strategy
The management of text, rich media, audio and video content aimed at engaging customers and prospects to meet business goals published through print and digital media including web and mobile platforms which is repurposed and syndicated to different forms of web presence such as publisher sites, blogs, social media and comparison sites.

It's evident that a compelling customer experience demands exceptional, compelling content and a well-planned **content strategy**. Today, by content we refer to the combination of static content forming web pages, but also dynamic rich media content which encourages interaction. Videos, podcasts, user-generated content and interactive product selectors should also be considered as content which should be refined to engage issues.

To create such resources requires a content strategy since there is a challenge of delivering so many different types of content delivered in different forms to different places on different access platforms.

The definition suggests these elements of content management that need to be planned and managed:

1 *Content engagement value.* Which types of content will engage the audience – is it simple product or services information, a guide to buying product, or a game to engage your audience.
2 *Content media.* Plain text, rich media such as Flash or Rich Internet applications or mobile apps, audio (podcasts) and hosted and streamed video. Even plain text offers different format options from HTML text to ebook formats and PDFs.
3 *Content syndication.* Content can be syndicated to different type of sites through feeds, APIs, microformats or direct submission by e-mail. Content can be embedded in sites through widgets displaying information delivered by a feed.
4 *Content participation.* Effective content today is not simply delivered for static consumption, it should enable commenting, ratings and reviews. These also need to be monitored and managed both in the original location and where they are discussed elsewhere.
5 *Content access platform.* The different digital access platforms such as desktops and laptops of different screen resolution and mobile devices. Paper is also a content access platform for print media.

Halvorson (2010) describes the importance of these activities. It can be seen that managing the creation of quality content is part of a broader customer engagement strategy which looks at delivering effective content across the whole customer lifecycle. As such it is an integral part of the CRM strategy development which we covered in Chapter 6. It is also an important marketing activity affecting both conversion optimisation, social media engagement and SEO, so increasing attention is directed at content strategy today.

To help implement a content strategy requires a change of mindset for many companies (Pulizzi, 2010). They need to think more like a publisher and so invest in quality content that's superior to that of their competitors. This requires:

- Quality, compelling content – content is still king!
- Quality writers to create quality content who may be internal staff or external freelance writers.
- An editorial calendar and appropriate process to schedule and deliver the content.
- Investment in software tools to facilitate the process.
- Investment in customer research to determine the content their different audiences will engage with.
- Careful tracking of which content engages and is effective for SEO and which doesn't.

Pulizzi and Barrett (2010) recommend creating a content marketing roadmap which is underpinned by the BEST principles. BEST stands for:

- *Behavioural.* Does everything you communicate with customers have a purpose? What do you want them to do as a result of interacting with content?
- *Essential.* Deliver information that your best prospects need if they are to succeed at work or in life.
- *Strategic.* Your content marketing efforts must be an integral part of your overall business strategy.
- *Targeted.* You must target your content precisely so that it's truly relevant to your buyers. Different forms of content will need to be delivered through different social platforms.

Copywriting for the web is an evolving art form, but many of the rules for good copywriting are as for any media. Common errors we see on websites are:

- too much knowledge assumed of the visitor about the company, its products and services
- using internal jargon about products, services or departments – using undecipherable acronyms.

Web copywriters also need to take account of the user reading the content on-screen. Approaches to dealing with the limitations imposed by the customer using a monitor include:

- writing more concisely than in brochures
- chunking, or breaking text into units of five to six lines at most, which allows users to scan rather than read information on web pages
- use of lists with headline text in larger font
- never including too much on a single page, except when presenting lengthy information such as a report which may be easier to read on a single page
- using hyperlinks to decrease page sizes or help achieve flow within copy, either by linking to sections further down a page or linking to another page.

Chaffey and Smith (2008) summarise the essentials of good copywriting for the web under the mnemonic 'CRABS', which stands for chunking, relevance, accuracy, brevity and scannability.

Hofacker (2000) describes five stages of human information processing when a website is being used. These can be applied to both page design and content design to improve usability and help companies get their message across to consumers. Each of the five stages summarised in Table 7.3 acts as a hurdle, since if the site design or content is too difficult to process then the customer cannot progress to the next stage. It is useful to consider the stages in order to minimise these difficulties.

Table 7.3 A summary of the characteristics of the five stages of information processing described by Hofacker (2000)

Stage	Description	Applications
1 Exposure	Content must be present for long enough to be processed	Content on banner ads may not be on screen long enough for processing and cognition
2 Attention	User's eyes will be drawn towards headings and content, not graphics and moving items on a web page (Nielsen, 2000)	Emphasis and accurate labelling of headings is vital to gain a user's attention. Evidence suggests that users do not notice banner adverts, suffering from 'banner blindness'
3 Comprehension and perception	The user's interpretation of content	Designs that use common standards and metaphors and are kept simple will be more readily comprehended
4 Yielding and acceptance	Is information (copy) presented accepted by customers?	Copy should refer to credible sources and present counter arguments as necessary
5 Retention	As for traditional advertising, this describes the extent to which the information is remembered	An unusual style or high degree of interaction leading to flow and user satisfaction is more likely to be recalled

Development and testing of content

Content management system (CMS)
A software tool for creating, editing and updating documents accessed by intranet, extranet or Internet.

It is not practical to provide details of the methods of developing content since marketers do not need an indepth understanding of development technologies since they will use specialists for this. What marketers do have to know is the aspects of customer experience that can be affected by the tools and development methodologies used. Then, when selecting suppliers, they can ask questions so that the type of constraints on the customer experience described in Activity 7.1 are accounted for. They can also test to make sure the systems have been built successfully. Selecting the right **content management system (CMS)** is important to provide a good user experience and is also important to an efficient method of publishing content since the facility can be made available to people throughout the company. Today there are two main forms of CMS, both of which are delivered as web services which can be accessed through a web browser. Enterprise CMSs can be used for large, complex sites (and other corporate documents) and as well as the standard page creation and editing facilities offer version control and review of documents through workflow systems which notify reviewers when new documents are ready for editing. CMS for smaller companies traditionally lack workflow or multi-author facilities, but offer many of the other features to create content. But blogging platforms such as WordPress and Moveable Type are increasingly used by smaller businesses for managing their entire site since they have enterprise features.

Criteria for selecting a content management system

A professional content management systems should provide these facilities:

- *Easy authoring system.* Editing of new and existing documents should be possible through a WYSIWYG (what you see is what you get) facility similar to a word processor which makes it easy to embed images and supports a range of markup necessary for SEO.
- *Search engine robot crawling.* The content must be stored and linked such that it can be indexed by search engine crawlers to add it to their index. Sometimes URL rewriting to a search-engine-friendly format without many parameters is required. The Google Webmaster pages describe the requirements: **www.google.com/webmasters.**
- *Search-engine-optimisation-friendly markup.* Some bespoke content management systems created by design agencies do not enable easy editing of the key fields, such as <title>, <h1> and <meta name= 'description' content='page description'>.
- *Different page templates.* The design and maintenance of content structure (sub-components, templates, etc.), web page structure and website structure. It should be possible to create different layouts and designs for different site sections or categories of pages.
- *Link management.* The maintenance of internal and external links through content change and the elimination of dead links.
- *Input and syndication.* The loading (spidering) of externally originating content and the aggregation and dissemination of content from a variety of sources.
- *Versioning.* The crucial task of controlling which edition of a page, page element or the whole site is published. Typically this will be the most recent, but previous editions should be archived and it should be possible to roll back to a previous version.
- *Security and access control.* Different permissions can be assigned to different roles of users and some content may only be available through log-in details. In these cases, the CMS maintains a list of users.
- *Use of plug-ins and widgets.* Mashups are possible through embedding widgets such as links to social networks or third-party applications. But a content management system may not readily support embedding within the main content or sidebars.
- *Publication workflow.* Content destined for a website needs to pass through a publication process to move it from the management environment to the live delivery

environment. The process may involve tasks such as format conversion (e.g. to PDF, or to WAP), rendering to HTML, editorial authorisation and the construction of composite documents in real time (personalisation and selective dissemination).

- *Tracking and monitoring.* Providing logs and statistical analysis of use to provide performance measures, tune the content according to demand and protect against misuse. It should also be possible to rapidly add tags to the page templates for web analytics tools such as Google Analytics.
- *Navigation and visualisation.* Providing an intuitive, clear and attractive representation of the nature and location of content using colour, texture, 3D rendering or even virtual reality. It should be possible to make changes to the navigation and containers holding content within the page template.
- *Flexibility to test new approaches.* It should be possible to test alternative designs and messaging using techniques such as AB and multivariate testing as described in Chapter 11.

Testing the experience

Development
The creation of a website by programmers. It involves writing the HTML content, creating graphics and writing any necessary software code such as JavaScript or ActiveX (programming).

Testing
Involves different aspects of the content such as spelling, validity of links, formatting on different web browsers and dynamic features such as form filling or database queries.

Marketing managers responsible for websites need to have a basic awareness of website **development** and **testing**. We have already discussed the importance of usability testing with typical users of the system. In brief, other necessary testing steps include:

- test that the content displays correctly on different types and versions of web browsers
- test plug-ins
- test all interactive facilities and integration with company databases
- test spelling and grammar
- test adherence to corporate image standards
- test to ensure all internal and links to external sites are valid.

Testing often occurs on a separate test web server (or directory) or *test environment*, with access to the test or prototype version being restricted to the development team. When complete, the website is released or published to the main web server or *live environment*.

Post-launch ongoing improvements to site effectiveness can be made through review of the web analytics and testing different page layouts, messaging and offers using the AB and multivariate testing tools as described in Chapter 10.

Online retail merchandising

Findability
An assessment of how easy it is for a web user to locate a single content object or to use browse the navigation and search system to find content. Like usability it is assessed through efficiency – how long it takes to find the content and effectiveness – how satisfied the user is with the experience and relevance of the content they find.

Faceted navigation
Enables users to rapidly filter results from a product search based on different ways of classifying the product by their attributes or features. For example by brand, by sub-product category, by price bands.

For online retail site owners, merchandising is a crucial activity, in the same way it is for physical retail store owners. In both cases, the aims are similar – to maximise sales potential for each store visitor. Online, this means presenting relevant products and promotions to site visitors which should help boost key measures of site performance such as conversion rate and average order value. You will see that many of these approaches are related to the concept of **findability**. Some of the most common approaches used are:

- *Expanding navigation through synonyms.* Through using a range of terms which may apply to the same product, the product may become easier to find if a site visitor is searching using a particular expression.
- *Applying faceted navigation or search approaches.* Search results pages are important in online merchandising since conversion rates will be higher if relevant products and offers are at the top of the list. **Faceted navigation** enables website users to 'drill-down' to easily select a relevant product by selecting different product attributes (Figure 7.14).
- *Featuring the bestselling products prominently.* Featuring strongest product lines prominently is a common approach, with retailers showing 'Top 10' or 'Top 20' products.

Figure 7.14 Faceted navigation at Wine.com

- *Use of bundling.* The classic retail approaches of buy-one-get-one-free (BOGOFF) is commonly applied online through showcasing complementary products. For example, Amazon discounts two related books it offers. Related products are also shown on the product page or in checkout, although care has to be taken here since this can reduce conversion rates.
- *Use of customer ratings and reviews.* Reviews can be important in influencing sales. Research from online ratings service Bazaar Voice showed that for one of its clients, CompUSA, the use of reviews achieved:
  - 60% higher conversion
  - 50% higher order value
  - 82% more page views per visitor.
- Mini Case Study 7.4 'Figleaves.com uncovers customer feedback to increase conversion' shows another example.
- *Use of product visualisation systems.* These systems enable web users to zoom in and rotate on products. Research by Scene7 (2008) summarised in Figure 7.15 shows the popularity and effectiveness ratings for these techniques.

Rich Internet applications (RIA)
Interactive applications which provide options such as product selectors or games. They may incorporate video or sound also. Typically built using technologies such as Adobe Flash, Ajax, Flex, Java or Silverlight.

Some of these techniques use Web 2.0 approaches with interactive **rich Internet applications (RIA)**. The research reports on an assessment of the measures that are used to assess the deployment of these applications which give a useful indication of how online merchandising approaches are evaluated. The full breakdown of effectiveness measures is:

- increased engagement (clicks/usage) = 63.3%
- increased conversion rate = 60.2% (reduced abandonment, 35.5%)
- increase revenues = 47.2%
- qualitative feedback = 41%

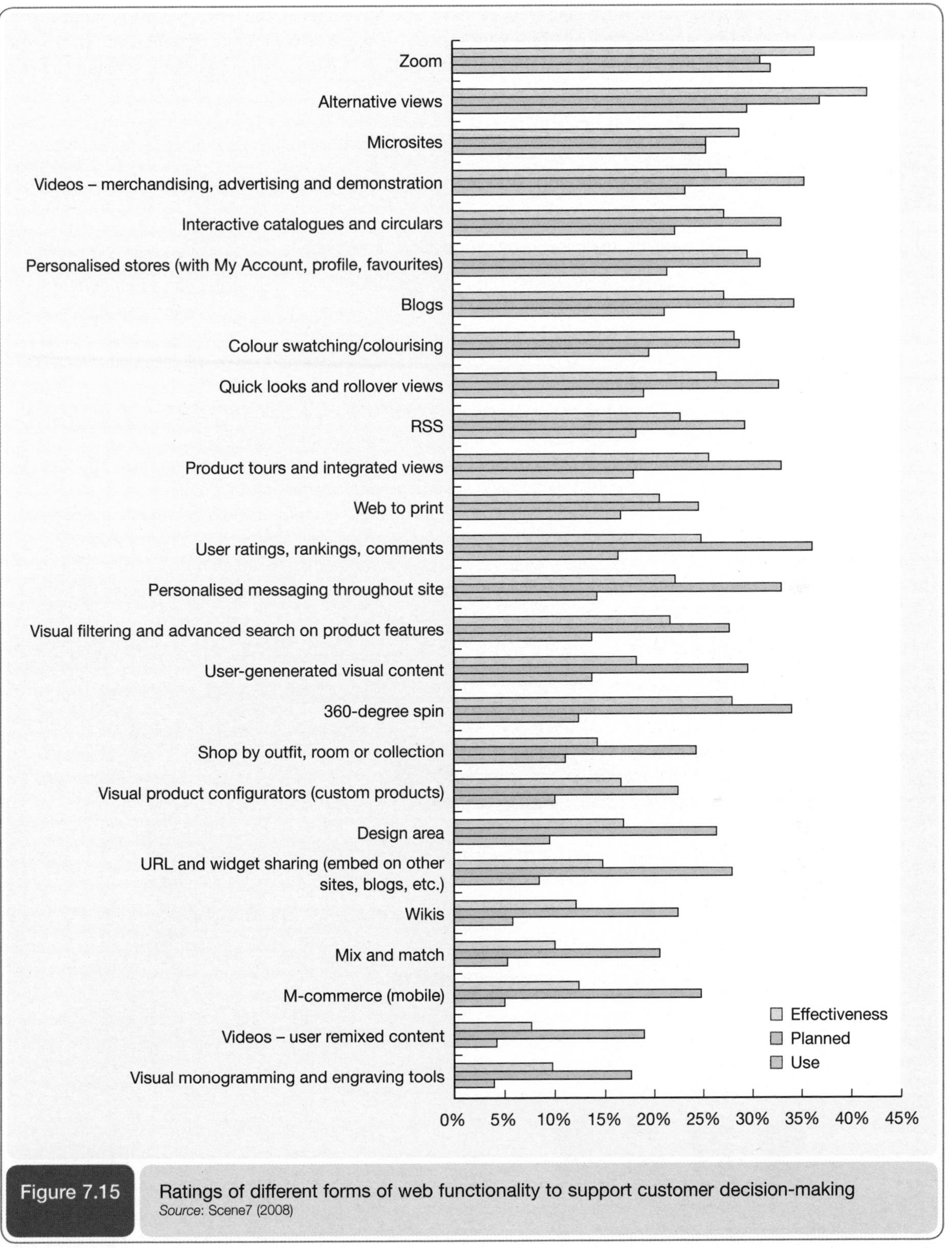

Figure 7.15 Ratings of different forms of web functionality to support customer decision-making
Source: Scene7 (2008)

- increase repeat purchase = 29.6%
- increase average order size = 28.4%
- reduce returns = 18.

Weathers and Makienko (2006) have also investigated the effect of merchandising on online store success rate based on a study of users of review site Bizrate.com. They found that features to enable searching for products were particularly important, as was a choice of ordering options.

Mini Case Study 7.4 figleaves.com uncovers customer feedback to increase conversion

figleaves.com (Figure 7.16) explains its online value proposition as follows:

- *figleaves.com is the world's largest online seller of branded intimate apparel. The retailer offers branded underwear, swimwear, exercisewear, nightwear and hosiery for men and women. [Core proposition and audience]*
- *While the choice is huge, it couldn't be easier to find what you are looking for. You can shop by brand, size, price, colour, style or occasion; or, if you know exactly what you are looking for, we will take you directly to it in one click. [Ease of use/findability]*
- *You can easily return goods if they don't fit or if they don't meet your expectation. It's our famous 'no hassle' returns policy. If you're in the UK we even pay the returns postage. [Returns policy]*
- *What's more, you can check out your purchases at home – no queuing for or embarrassing moments in luridly lit changing rooms. [Unique channel-specific advantage of online service]*
- *Underwear makes a great gift for both men and women. If you are buying for a loved one then we can send your present in a beautiful gift box along with a personalised message. Alternatively, you can send a gift certificate so that the recipient can choose exactly what they want themselves. [Gifting]*
- *We know how much you appreciate speedy delivery – in-stock items are usually dispatched within 24 hours. [Delivery]*

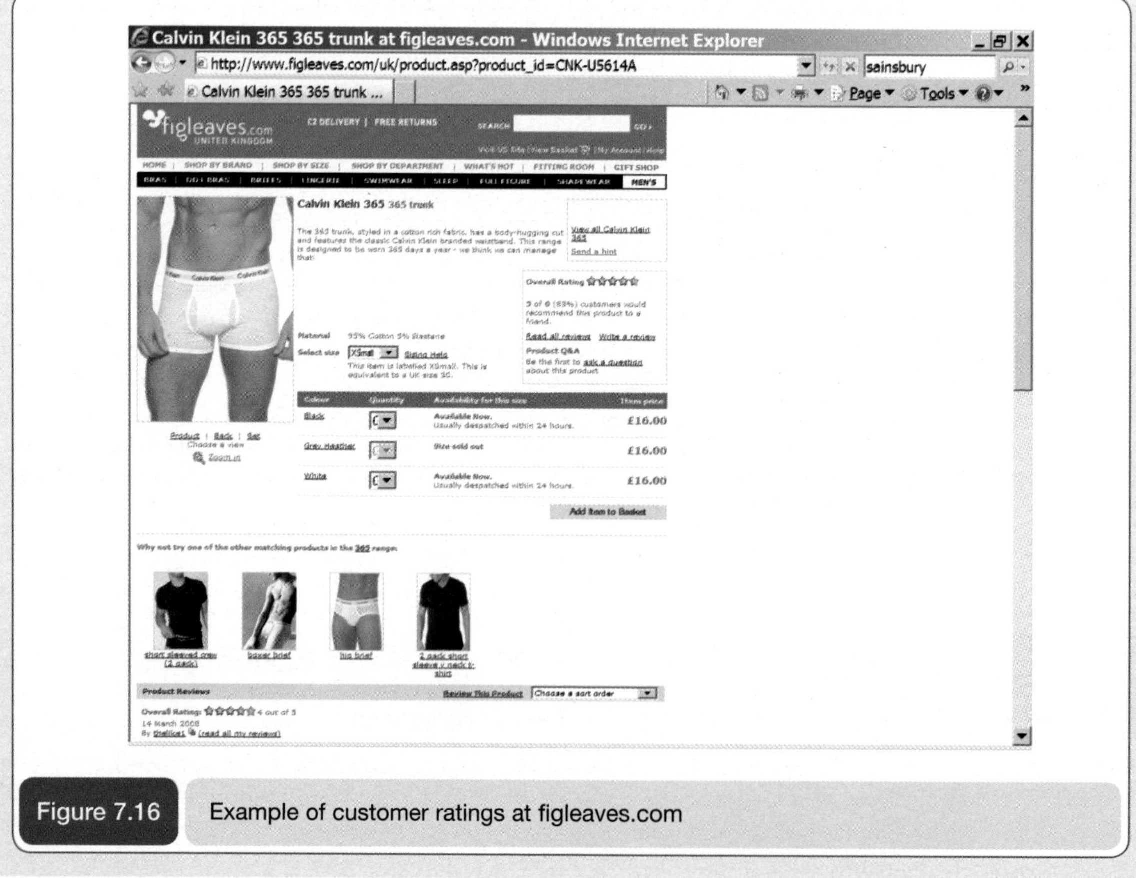

Figure 7.16 Example of customer ratings at figleaves.com

This research by Bazaarvoice shows the value of using customer reviews:

- Overall, products with reviews have a 12.5 per cent higher conversion rate than those without.
- Products with 20+ reviews have an 83.85 per cent higher conversion than those products without reviews. Note that products prompting the most reviews tend to be the best sellers and thus are generally higher converting.
- Analysing the session conversion for the same products before and after going live, the same products with reviews have a 35.27 per cent higher overall session conversion rate.
- Conversion was not negatively affected for products without reviews.
- The look-to-book ratio is four times lower (better) for products with reviews compared to those without.
- Overall look-to-book is 32.6 per cent higher (worse) for products without reviews.
- Since going live, products with reviews have seen a significant decrease (better) in the look-to-book ratio.
- Products without reviews saw no significant decrease.

Source: Bazaar Voice case study: **http://bazaarvoice.com/cs_rr_conversion_figleaves.html**

Promote site

Promotion of a site is a significant topic that will be part of the strategy of developing a website. It will follow the initial development of a site and is described in detail in Chapters 8 and 9. Particularly important issues that must be considered during the course of site design are search engine optimisation and the experience delivered on landing pages where the visitor arrives not on the home page, but deeper within the site.

Service quality

Delivering service quality in e-commerce can be assessed through reviewing existing marketing frameworks for determining levels of service quality. Those most frequently used are based on the concept of a 'service-quality gap' that exists between the customer's expected level of service (from previous experience and word-of-mouth communication) and their perception of the actual level of service delivery. We can apply the elements of service quality on which Parasuraman *et al.* (1985) suggest that consumers judge companies. Note that there has been heated dispute about the validity of this SERVQUAL instrument framework in determining service quality – see, for example, Cronin and Taylor (1992). Despite this it is still instructive to apply these dimensions of service quality to customer service on the web (see, for example, Chaffey and Edgar (2000), Kolesar and Galbraith (2000), Zeithaml *et al.* (2002) and Trocchia and Janda (2003)):

- *tangibles* – the physical appearance of facilities and communications
- *reliability* – the ability to perform the service dependably and accurately
- *responsiveness* – a willingness to help customers and provide prompt service
- *assurance* – the knowledge and courtesy of employees and their ability to convey trust and confidence;
- *empathy* – providing caring, individualised attention.

As well as applying these academic frameworks, organisations can use benchmarking services such as Foresee (**www.foreseeresults.com**) based on the American Customer Satisfaction Index methodology which assess satisfaction scores based on the gap between expectations and actual service (see Chapter 6, Figure 6.12).

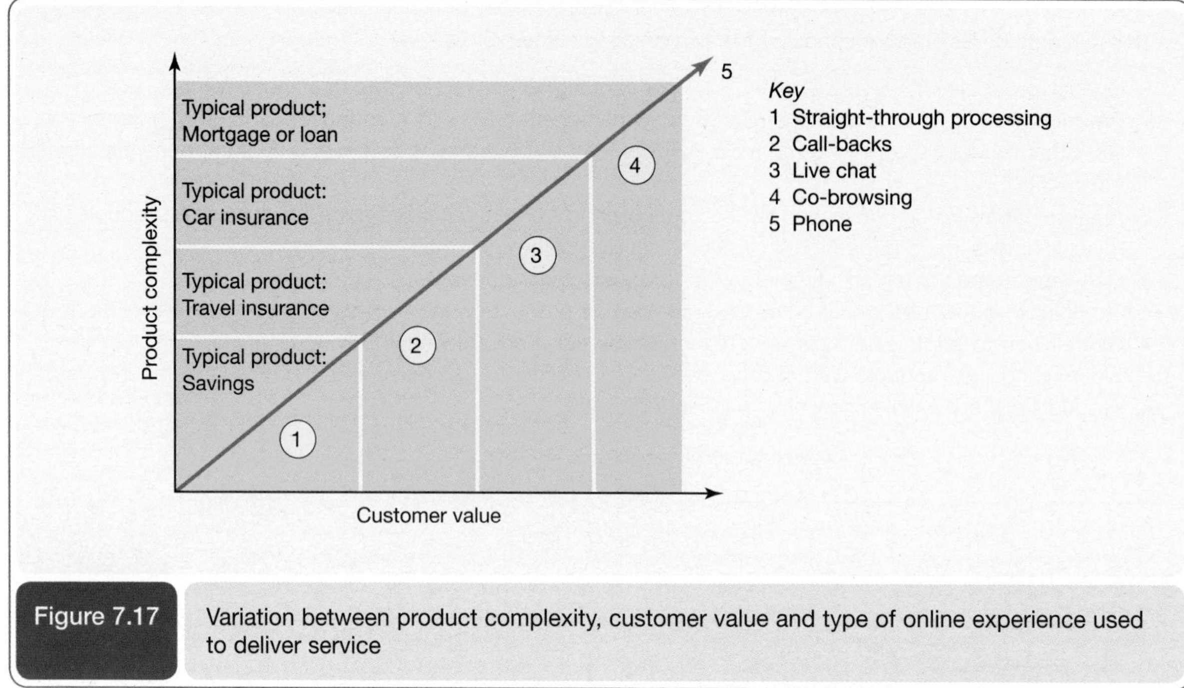

Figure 7.17 Variation between product complexity, customer value and type of online experience used to deliver service

It should also be remembered that the level of service selected by an online transactional service is based on the relationship between the costs to serve, the value of the product and the likelihood of the channel to increase conversion. Figure 7.17 shows the typical situation for a bank. Typically costs to serve increase to the top-right of the diagram, as does the capability to convert through a more extended dialogue and the value generated from sale. The figure shows a general pattern, but the options are often not mutually exclusive – for example, phone contact may be available for all levels, but emphasised for the most complex products. We introduced some of these methods of delivering service in Chapter 5:

1 *Straight-through processing.* Transaction typically occurs without intervention from staff for a relatively simple product such as a savings account.
2 *Call-backs.* The customer has the option to specify the bank call if there is anything they are unclear on.
3 *Live chat.* Online discussion between service representative and the client. This may be invoked proactively if analysis suggests the customer is having difficulty in deciding.
4 *Co-browsing.* Sharing of screen to walk through application process.
5 *Phone.* Typically this has the highest cost, but often the highest conversion rate.

Two of the most significant frameworks for assessing online service quality are:

- WEBQUAL (Loiacono *et al.*, 2000) which considers 14 dimensions. It has been criticised for relating too much to functional design issues rather than service issues. The dimensions are:
  1 *Information quality* – the concern that information provided is accurate, updated, and appropriate.
  2 *Functional fit to task* – the extent to which users believe that the website meets their needs.
  3 *Tailored communications* – communications can be tailored to meet the user's needs.
  4 *Trust* – secure communication and observance of information privacy.
  5 *Response time* – time to get a response after a request or an interaction with a website.
  6 *Ease of understanding* – easy to read and understand.
  7 *Intuitive operations* – easy to operate and navigate.

8 *Visual appeal* – the aesthetics of the site.
9 *Innovativeness* – the creativity and uniqueness of the website.
10 *Emotional appeal* – the emotional affect of using the website and intensity of involvement.
11 *Consistent image* – the website does not create dissonance for the user by an image incompatible with that projected by the firm through other media.
12 *Online completeness* – allowing all or most necessary transactions to be completed on-line (for example, purchasing over the website).
13 *Relative advantage* – equivalent to or better than other means of interacting with the company.
14 *Customer service* – the response to customer inquiries, comments and feedback when such response requires more than one interaction.

- E-SERVQUAL (Zeithaml *et al.*, 2002) which contains seven dimensions. The first four are classified as the core service scale, and the latter three dimensions are regarded as a recovery scale, since they are only relevant when online customers have questions or problems:
  1. *Efficiency* refers to the ability of the customers to get to the website, search for information or transact as requires.
  2. *Fulfilment* involves the accuracy of service promises, including products in-stock availability and delivering the products in the promised time.
  3. *Reliability* is associated with the technical functioning of the site, including availability and performance.
  4. *Privacy* is related to assurance that shopping behaviour data are not shared and that credit card information is secure.
  5. *Responsiveness* refers to the ability of e-tailers to provide appropriate support information to customers when requested.
  6. *Compensation* involves returns facilities for refunds and return shipping and handling costs.
  7. *Contact* is the ability of customers to talk to a live service agent online.

Both are useful frameworks which can still be applied to evaluate online service quality today, although arguably they omit the importance of accessibility, findability techniques, multichannel integration and customer reviews and ratings (as discussed in the later section on merchandising as a determinant of satisfactory experience).

Online marketers should assess what customers' expectations are in each of these areas, and identify where there is an **online service–quality gap** between the customer expectations and what is currently delivered.

Online service–quality gap
The mismatch between what is expected and delivered by an online presence.

We will now examine how the five determinants of online service quality apply online.

Tangibles

It can be suggested that the tangibles dimension is influenced by ease of use and visual appeal based on the structural and graphic design of the site. Design factors that influence this variable are described later in this chapter.

Reliability

The reliability dimension is dependent on the availability of a website – in other words, how easy it is to connect to the website as a user. Many companies fail to achieve 100 per cent availability and potential customers may be lost for ever if they attempt to use the site when it is unavailable.

Reliability of e-mail response is also a key issue. Transversal (2008), found the following reliability of response in a survey of UK businesses:

- Websites could only provide answers to 50 per cent of questions asked (when testing against FAQ and service content).
- The average response to an e-mail was 46 hours.
- Meanwhile 60 per cent of calls to contact centres were answered within three minutes.

Amongst business-to-business communications, InsideSales (2011) review response and found a similarly poor picture of response. Of the US companies surveyed, 55.3 per cent of the 159 companies never responded, but 40.1 per cent responded within 24 hours suggesting that these companies do have an acceptable response policy in place.

Responsiveness is closely related to the reliability of response to e-mail as described above. Responsiveness is also indicated by the performance of the website – the time it takes for a page request to be delivered to the user's browser as a page impression. Data from monitoring services such as Keynote (**www.keynote.com**) indicate that there is a wide variability in the delivery of information and hence service quality from web servers hosted at ISPs, and companies should be careful to monitor this and specify levels of quality with suppliers in service-level agreements (SLAs).

Assurance

In an e-mail context, assurance can best be considered as the quality of response. In a survey reported by Chaffey and Edgar (2000), of 180 responses received, 91 per cent delivered a personalised human response, with 9 per cent delivering an automated response which did not address the individual enquiry; 40 per cent of responses answered or referred to all three questions, with 10 per cent answering two questions and 22 per cent one. Overall, 38 per cent did not answer any of the specific questions posed!

Multichannel communications preferences

Upton (2008) reports on research where 1000 UK consumers aged 18+ were surveyed to identify the role and importance of customer services and communications for online businesses. Despite the growing popularity of e-mail as a communication tool, 53 per cent of those interviewed still prefer to communicate with businesses over the telephone, particularly for service enquiries, compared with 48 per cent for e-mail and 16 per cent for traditional mail. However, when asked about their experiences, three out of ten UK consumers stated they found it difficult to locate contact details on websites.

Surprisingly, 53 per cent of consumers consider three minutes waiting time a satisfactory period to speak with an agent over the telephone. Consumers particularly disliked ringing a contact centre only to be met with a computerised answering service. As Upton notes, replacing a skilled operator with an automated service might save money in the short term – however, in the long term companies risk losing brand advocacy and sales. Additionally, customers believe 24 hours is a respectable amount of time to wait for a response when contacting a business via e-mail.

He concludes:

> Overall the research shows that in this era of multi-communication, consumers are no longer allied to any particular mode of communication. They will select the most convenient or appropriate channel even if the retailer trades solely online.
>
> As a result, brands need to provide their contact centre agents with the tools to seamlessly combine different communication channels such as telephone, e-mail, v-mail, web chat and SMS to communicate with the consumer and meet their expectations of service.
>
> Agents also need to have real-time access to all past interactions with a customer. This should include text transcriptions of conversations and e-mails, scanned copies of letters received and despatched, as well as call recordings, comments and outcomes ensuring

that the agent is fully briefed on the existing relationship that the customer has with the brand. Importantly, this information can be further used to tailor all future contact with the customer, delivering greater levels of customer satisfaction. By employing the customer's preferred channel of communication, which has been identified using the data from real conversations with individuals, it is possible to meet customer expectations, and as a result maximise retention and brand advocacy.

A further assurance concern of e-commerce websites is the privacy and security of customer information (see Chapter 3). A company that adheres to the UK Internet Shopping Is Safe (ISIS) (**www.imrg.org/isis**) or TRUSTe principles (**www.truste.org**) will provide better assurance than one that does not. For security, 'hacker safe' accreditation is available from Scan Alert (**www.scanalert.com**) who are owned by McAfee security products. This involves automated daily scans to test site security.

Chaffey and Smith (2008) suggest that the following actions can be used to achieve assurance in an e-commerce site:

- provide clear and effective privacy statements
- follow privacy and consumer protection guidelines in all local markets
- make security of customer data a priority
- use independent certification bodies
- emphasise the excellence of service quality in all communications.

Empathy

Although it might be considered that empathy requires personal human contact, it can still be achieved, to an extent, through e-mail and web communications.

Provision of personalisation facilities is also an indication of the empathy provided by the website, but more research is needed as to customers' perception of the value of web pages that are dynamically created to meet a customer's information needs.

It can be suggested that for managers wishing to apply a framework such as SERVQUAL in an e-commerce context there are three stages appropriate to managing the process:

1 *Understanding expectations.* Customer expectations for the e-commerce environment in a particular market sector must be understood. The SERVQUAL framework can be used with market research and benchmarking of other sites to understand requirements such as responsiveness and empathy. Scenarios can also be used to identify customer expectations of using services on a site.
2 *Setting and communicating the service promise.* Once expectations are understood, marketing communications can be used to inform the customers of the level of service. This can be achieved through customer service guarantees or promises. It is better to under-promise than over-promise. A book retailer who delivers a book in two days when three days were promised will earn the customer's loyalty better than the retailer who promises one day but delivers in two! The enlightened company may also explain what it will do if it doesn't meet its promises – will the customer be recompensed? The service promise must also be communicated internally and combined with training to ensure that the service is delivered.
3 *Delivering the service promise.* Finally, commitments must be delivered through on-site service, support from employees and physical fulfilment. Otherwise, online credibility is destroyed and a customer may never return.

Tables 7.4 and 7.5 summarise the main concerns of online consumers for each of the elements of service quality. Table 7.4 summarises the main factors in the context of SERVQUAL and Table 7.5 presents the requirements from an e-commerce site that must be met for excellent customer service.

Table 7.4 Online elements of service quality

Tangibles	Reliability	Responsiveness	Assurance and empathy
Ease of use	Availability	Download speed	Contacts with call centre
Content quality	Reliability	E-mail response	Personalisation
Price	E-mail replies	Call-back	Privacy
		Fulfilment	Security

Table 7.5 Summary of requirements for online service quality

E-mail response requirements	Website requirements
• Defined response times and named individual responsible for replies	• Support for customer-preferred channel of communication in response to enquiries (e-mail, phone, postal mail or in person)
• Use of autoresponders to confirm query is being processed	• Clearly indicated contact points for enquiries via e-mail mailto: and forms
• Personalised e-mail where appropriate	• Company internal targets for site availability and performance
• Accurate response to inbound e-mail by *customer-preferred channel: outbound e-mail* or phone call-back	• Testing of site usability and efficiency of links, HTML, plug-ins and browsers to maximise availability
• Opt-in and opt-out options must be provided for promotional e-mail with a suitable offer in exchange for a customer's provision of information	• Appropriate graphic and structural site design to achieve ease of use and relevant content with visual appeal
• Clear layout, named individual and privacy statements in e-mail	• Personalisation option for customers • Specific tools to help a user to answer specific queries such as interactive support databases and frequently asked questions (FAQ)

Source: Chaffey and Edgar (2000)

The relationship between service quality, customer satisfaction and loyalty

As we discussed in Chapter 6 (see Figure 6.11), it is key for organisations to understand not only the levers that determines service quality and customer satisfaction, but also loyalty or repeat purchases.

Rigby *et al.* (2000) assessed repeat-purchase drivers in grocery, clothing and consumer electronics e-tail. It was found that the key loyalty drivers were similar to those of Dell, including correct delivery of order, but other factors such as price, ease of use and customer support were more important.

Case Study 7 Refining the online customer experience at i-to-i.com

This case is about specialist travel and education company, focusing on its online TEFL (Teaching English as a Foreign Language) courses. Their site (Figure 7.18) combines many of the features we have described in this chapter blending accessibility, usability and persuasion. This case considers the challenges of delivering an effective design across different markets for different audiences.

i-to-i background

i-to-i (**www.i-to-i.com**) is an international organisation with offices in the UK, USA, Ireland and Australia. Around 20,000 people have selected i-to-i as they travel on ventures to support 500 worthwhile projects in five continents and it has also trained a further 80,000 people as TEFL (Teaching English as a Foreign Language) teachers. This service is offered through the main site and also through a specialist Online TEFL site (**www.onlinetefl.com**) on which this case focuses.

The history of i-to-i

The founder of i-to-i, Deirdre Bounds, was inspired to create the company following a career break which took her to teach English in Japan, China and Greece and drive a backpackers' bus in Sydney. The company initially started through creating TEFL courses eventually leading to organising volunteer projects. Since 2003, the company has supported the i-to-i Foundation, a registered charity committed to providing funds to the most needy community and ecological projects in the i-to-i family. In 2007, i-to-i became part of the TUI travel group.

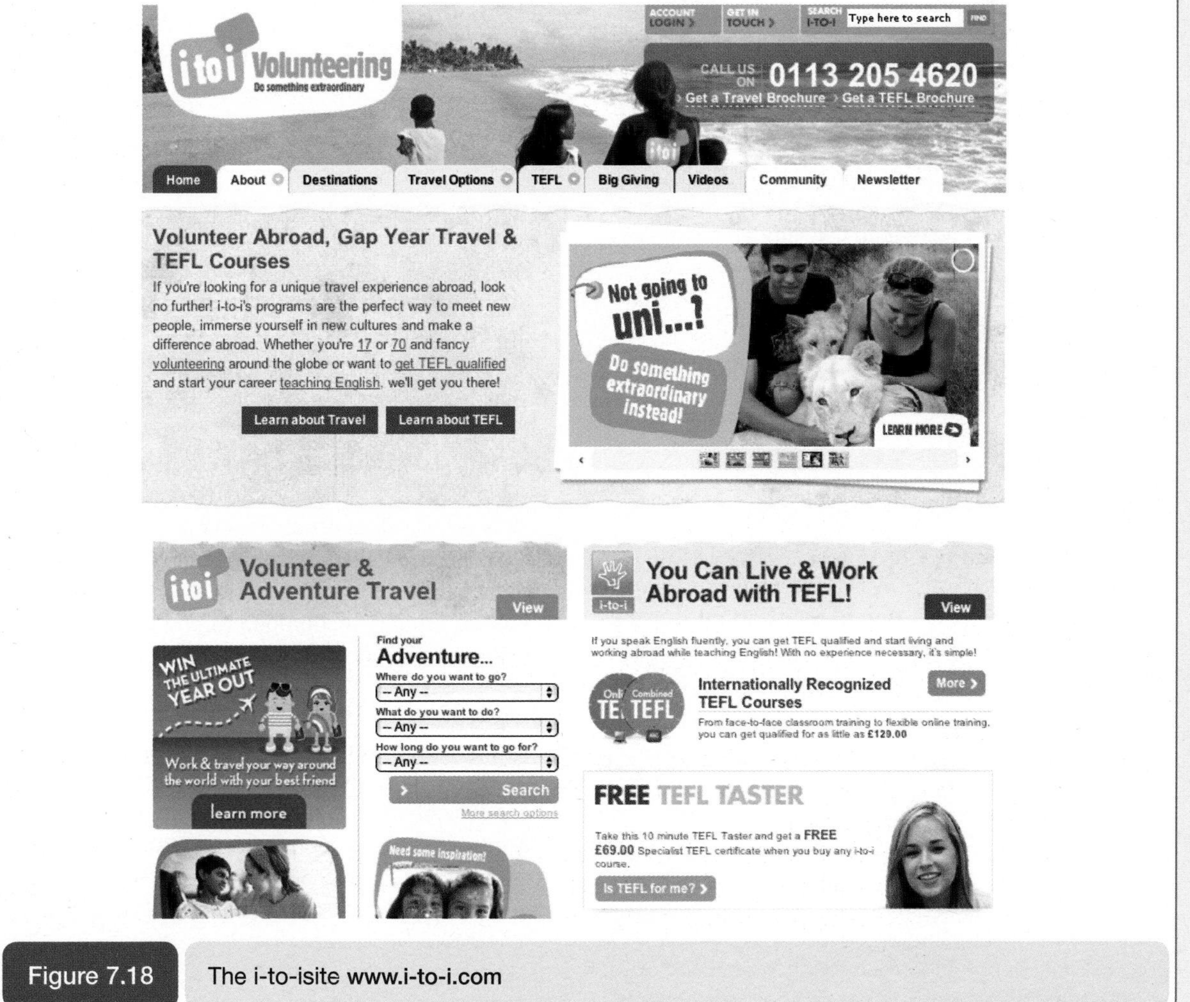

Figure 7.18 The i-to-isite www.i-to-i.com

Proposition

The main features of the i-to-i TEFL proposition communicated through its site are:

- *International accreditation*: i-to-i is externally accredited by the ODLQC in order to ensure that its courses are rigorously monitored and always meet the highest industry standards.
- *World-class reputation*: i-to-i has four offices worldwide and it has over 12 years experience teaching TEFL.
- *Partnership*: i-to-i is preferred TEFL course provider for STA Travel, Opodo and Lonely Planet.
- *Complete student support*: students receive advice on how to get work abroad, how best to prepare for their time away and up to the minute advice on current job opportunities.
- *Highly experienced tutors*: all i-to-i tutors have at least three years overseas teaching experience.

This proposition is backed up by 'the i-to-i TEFL Promise' which is communicated on the site.

- We will beat any equivalent and cheaper course by 150%.
- If you're not entirely satisfied after the first seven days, we'll give you a full refund.
- Our experience, our high academic standards and the quality of our courses means that i-to-i TEFL certificates are recognised by thousands of language schools worldwide.
- Additionally i-to-i can offer to help students find TEFL jobs abroad.

Audience segmentation

The main segmentation used by i-to-i is geographic:

- UK
- North America
- Europe
- Australia and New Zealand
- Rest-of-world (same as UK).

Different brochures are also available for each geographical area. Information is also collected on an optional basis about prospects' age and status, although these are not used for targeting emails. Status categories are:

- student
- employed
- self-employed
- career break
- unemployed
- retired.

Since optional information is restricted to certain lead tools it is not used to target e-mails. For weekend TEFL – post code/city is used to target courses to prospects.

Competitors

Some of the main competitors for online TEFL courses based in the UK and Australia include:

- **www.cactustefl.com**
- **www.teflonline.com**
- **www.eslbase.com**

In the US, competitors who also operate in the UK and other countries include:

- **www.teflcorp.com/**
- ITTP (International Tefl-Tesol-Online) **www.tefl-tesol-online.com**

Media mix

i-to-i use a combination of these digital media channels to drive visits, leads and sales:

- pay per click (PPC) (mainly Google AdWords)
- social media marketing using Facebook, Twitter and i-to-i's own traveller community
- natural search
- affiliate marketing
- display advertising
- e-mail marketing.

Customer experience and conversion process

Detailed content to help visitors decide on purchasing a course is available on the site. This includes module outlines, and videos. Specific landing pages are used to convert visitors from paid search or affiliates for example.

A number of engagement devices are blended into the design used to generate leads including brochures, 'TEFL tasters', an e-mail guide and campaign promotions such as winning a course. Customers have the choice of requesting a brochure (post or download), requesting a callback or a live chat.

Such leads are followed up through a series of welcome e-mails. Results are monitored, but e-mails are not proactively followed up on. There is no phone follow-up of leads due to the relative low value of the products, but site visitors are encouraged to ring or setup a call-back which often leads to higher conversion rates.

Marketplace challenges

The main marketplace challenges faced by i-to-i are:

- Increasing their presence and conversion effectiveness in a competitive market in different geographies:
- i-to-i have good exposure in the UK, its primary market, but operate in a cluttered marketplace with price being the main differentiator (products are similar and some competitors are just as established etc.).
- Research suggests that there is good opportunity within the US, but exposure is more limited because

of the cost of pay per click advertising and because presence in natural search favours the US.

- Rest-of-world sales (outside of UK, USA, Canada, Ireland/Europe, Australia, New Zealand) are increasing and is believed to be a growing market. i-to-i seek to penetrate these markets, but in a cost-effective way, that will not distract attention from main markets.
- Increasing demand through reaching and educating those considering travel, that are not aware of TEFL courses, and the opportunities they unlock. For example, many will look for casual work in other countries, e.g. in bars or in agriculture, but will be unaware of TEFL.

Questions

1 Select one country that i-to-I operates in closest to the area that you live. Define a persona based on their age and product needs and then identify the main customer journeys that form the customer for this persona. Which routes through the site would this user follow?

2 Review the range of engagement devices on the i-to-i to engage the audience to generate leads.

3 Identify key areas for improvement for i-to-i based on your use of the site.

Summary

1 An effective online customer experience is dependent on many factors, including the visual elements of the site design and how it has been designed for persuasion, usability, accessibility and performance.

2 Careful planning and execution of website implementation is important, in order to avoid the need for extensive reworking at a later stage if the design proves to be ineffective.

3 Analysis, design and implementation should form an iterative, prototyping approach based on usability testing that meets business and user requirements.

4 A feasibility study should take place before the initiation of a major website project. A feasibility study will assess:
   - the costs and benefits of the project
   - the difficulty of achieving management and staff commitment to the project
   - the availability of domain names to support the project
   - the responsibilities and stages necessary for a successful project.

5 The choice of host for a website should be considered carefully since this will govern the quality of service of the website.

6 Options for analysis of users' requirements for a website include:
   - interviews with marketing staff
   - questionnaire sent to companies
   - usability and accessibility testing
   - informal interviews with key accounts
   - focus groups
   - reviewing competitors' websites.

7 The design phase of developing a website includes specification of:
   - the information architecture, or structure, of the website using techniques such as site maps, blueprints and wireframes
   - the flow, controlled by the navigation and menu options
   - the graphic design and brand identity
   - content strategy
   - country-specific localisation
   - the service quality of online forms and e-mail messages.

Exercises

Self-assessment exercises

1. Explain the term 'prototyping' in relation to website creation.
2. What tasks should managers undertake during initiation of a web page?
3. What factors should be considered for domain name registration?
4. List the factors that determine website 'flow'.
5. Which requirements are important to an effective website?
6. List the options for assessing online service quality.
7. Which issues should be considered when developing a content strategy?
8. What are the factors that control the performance of a website?

Essay and discussion questions

1. Discuss the relative effectiveness of the different methods of assessing the customers' needs from a website.
2. Select three websites of your choice and compare their design effectiveness. You should describe design features such as navigation, structure and graphics.
3. Explain how strategy, analysis, design and implementation of a website should be integrated through a prototyping approach. Describe the merits and problems of the prototyping approach.
4. When designing the interactive services of a website what steps should the designer take to provide a quality service to customers?

Examination questions

1. What is website prototyping? Give three benefits of this approach.
2. What requirements should be defined at the initiation phase of an online project?
3. Which factors are important in selecting a web design agency?
4. How can customer analysis be used to develop a more effective online service?
5. Name, and briefly explain, four characteristics of an online service that will govern whether a user recommends it.
6. What are the constraints on web service design depending on the technology platform the service is accessed on?

References

Bevan, N. (1999a) Usability issues in website design, *Proceedings of the 6th Interactive Publishing Conference*, November, available online at: **www.usability.serco.com**.

Bevan, N. (1999b) Common industry format usability tests, *Proceedings of UPA'98*, Usability Professionals Association, Scottsdale, Arizona, 29 June–2 July 1999, available online at: **www.usability.serco.com**.

BSI (1999) BS 13407 Human-centred design processes for interactive systems, British Standards Institute.

Chaffey, D. and Edgar, M. (2000) Measuring online service quality, *Journal of Targeting, Analysis and Measurement for Marketing*, 8(4) (May), 363–78.

Chaffey, D. and Smith, P.R. (2008) *E-marketing Excellence. Planning and Optimizing your Digital Marketing – at the Heart of E-Business*, 3rd edn. Butterworth-Heinemann, Oxford.

Chaffey, D. and Wood, S. (2010) *Business Information Management*, 2nd ed. Financial Times/ Prentice Hall, Harlow.

Christodoulides, G., de Chernatony, L., Furrer, O., Shiu, E. and Temi, A. (2006) Conceptualising and measuring the equity of online brands, *Journal of Marketing Management*, September, 22(7/8), 799–825.

Cronin, J. and Taylor, S. (1992) Measuring service quality: a re-examination and extension, *Journal of Marketing*, 56, 55–63.

de Chernatony, L. (2001) Succeeding with brands on the Internet, *Journal of Brand Management*, 8(3), 186–95.

Fogg, B. (2009) In Proceedings of the 4th International Conference on Persuasive Technology, pp. 1–7, available from: **www.behaviormodel.org.**

Fogg, B., Soohoo, C., Danielson, D., Marable, L., Stanford, J. and Tauber, E. (2003) How do people evaluate a website's credibility? A Consumer WebWatch research report, prepared by Stanford Persuasive Technology Lab.

Halvorson, K. (2010) *Content Strategy for the Web*, New Riders, 1249 Eight Street, Berkeley, CA.

Hofacker, C. (2000) *Internet Marketing*, Wiley, New York.

Hoffman, D.L. and Novak, T.P. (1997) A new marketing paradigm for electronic commerce, *The Information Society*, Special issue on electronic commerce, 13, 43–54.

InsideSales (2011) Audit of response to sales leads, available from: **http://www.insidesales.com/resources.**

Kolesar, M. and Galbraith, R. (2000) A services-marketing perspective on e-retailing, *Internet Research: Electronic Networking Applications and Policy*, 10(5), 424–38.

Loiacono, E., Watson, R. and Goodhue, D. (2000) 'WEBQUAL: a measure of website quality', *Marketing Theory and Applications*, Vol. 13, K. Evans and L. Scheer (eds), American Marketing Association, Chicago, 2002, 432–439.

Lynch, P. and Horton, S. (1999) *Web Style Guide: Basic Design Principles for Creating Websites*, Yale University Press, New Haven, CT.

Morville, P. (2005) *Ambient Findability, What We Find Changes Who We Become*, O'Reilly Media, Sebastopol, CA.

Multilingual (2008) Localizing a localizer's website: the challenge, Jan/Feb, 30–33.

Nielsen, J. (1999) Details in study methodology can give misleading results, Jakob Nielsen's Alertbox, 21 February, **www.useit.com/alertbox/990221.html.**

Nielsen, J. (2000) *Designing Web Usability*. New Riders Publishing, USA.

Nitish, S., Fassott, G., Zhao, H. and Boughton, P. (2006) A cross-cultural analysis of German, Chinese and Indian consumers' perception of website adaptation, *Journal of Consumer Behaviour*, 5, 56–68.

Parasuraman, A., Zeithaml, V. and Berry, L. (1985) A conceptual model of service quality and its implications for future research, *Journal of Marketing*, 49, Fall, 48.

Pulizzi, J. and Barrett, T. (2010), *Get Content. Get Customers*, McGraw-Hill, Columbus, OH.

Rettie, R. (2001) An exploration of flow during Internet use, *Internet Research*, 11(2), 103–13.

Rigby, D., Bavega, S., Rastoi, S., Zook, C. and Hancock, S. (2000) The value of customer loyalty and how you can capture it, Bain and Company/Mainspring whitepaper, 17 March published at: **www.mainspring.com.**

Robertson, J. (2003) Information design using card sorting, Step Two, available online at: **www.steptwo.com.au/papers/cardsorting/index.html.**

Rosen, D. and Purinton, E. (2004) Website design: viewing the Web as a cognitive landscape, *Journal of Business Research*, 57(7), 787–94.

Rosenfeld, L. and Morville, P. (2002) *Information Architecture for the World Wide Web*, 2nd edn, O'Reilly, Sebastopol, CA.

Scene7 on demand survey: Web 2.0 experience 2008 and beyond, January 2008, **http://www.scene7.com/survey/Scene7_2008_Survey_Report.pdf.**

SciVisum (2005) Internet campaign effectiveness study, press release, July, **www.scivisum.co.uk.**

Singh, N. and Pereira, A. (2005) *The Culturally Customized Website, Customizing Websites for the Global Marketplace*, Butterworth-Heinemann, Oxford, UK.

Smith, D. and Sivakumar, K. (2004) Flow and Internet shopping behavior: a conceptual model and research propositions, *Journal of Business Research*, 57(10), 1199–208.

Strangeloop (2011) Report State of the Union: Study of the top 2000 retail websites reveals that the top sites are getting slower not faster, **http://www.strangeloopnetworks.com/resources/research/report-state-of-the-union-for-page-speed-and-website-performance/key-findings/.**

Sullivan (2011) Web design process infographic, SmartInsights blog post, 6 September: **www.smartinsights.com.**

Transversal (2008) Email black hole causing customer service crisis, **http://www.transversal.com/html/news/viewpress.php?article=81.**

Trocchia, P. and Janda, S. (2003) How do consumers evaluate Internet retail service quality? *Journal of Services Marketing*, 17(3).

Upton, N. (2008) Online customer service, *What's New in Marketing*, E-newsletter, Issue 66, February 2008, available online at: **www.wnim.com.**

Weathers, D. and Makienko, I. (2006) Assessing the relationships between e-tail success and product and website factors, *Journal of Interactive Marketing*, 2, 41–54.

Wodtke, C. (2002) *Information Architecture: Blueprints for the Web*, New Riders, IN.

Wroblewski, L. (2011) Why separate mobile and desktop web design, blog post, 1 September: **http://www.lukew.com/ff/entry.asp?1390.**

Zeithaml, V., Parasuraman, A. and Malhotra, A. (2002) Service quality delivery through websites: a critical review of extant knowledge, *Academy of Marketing Science*, 30(4), 368.

Further reading

Bevan, N. (1999) Usability issues in website design, *Proceedings of the 6th Interactive Publishing Conference*, November. Available online at **www.usability.serco.com.** Accessible lists of web-design pointers.

Noyes, J. and Baber, C. (1999) *User-centred Design of Systems*, Springer-Verlag, Berlin. Details the user-centred design approach.

Preece, J., Rogers, Y. and Sharp, H. (2002) *Interaction Design*, Wiley, New York. Clearly describes a structured approach to interaction design, including web interaction.

Weblinks

Accessibility

- **Royal National Institute for the Blind** (**www.rnib/org.uk/accessibility**) Web accessibility guidelines.
- **W3C** (**www.w3.org/WAI**) Guidelines and resources from the World Wide Web Consortium (W3C).

Information architecture

- **Boxes and Arrows** (**www.boxesandarrows.com**) A great collection of best practice articles and discussions about IA topics such as controlled vocabularies.
- **Peter Morville** (**www.semanticstudios.com/publications**) Blog of the author of the classic information architecture book. In-depth best practice articles.
- **Louis Rosenfeld site** (**www.louisrosenfeld.com**) Rosenfeld is also author of the classic Information Architecture book.
- **Jesse James Garrett** (**http://jjg.net/ia**) Design expert JJG's Articles on IA.
- **Step Two** (**www.steptwo.com.au**) This design company has introductory outlines and more detailed articles on information architecture and other aspects of usability.

Usability

- **UsabilityNet** (www.usabilitynet.org) A portal about usability with good links to other sites and an introduction to usability terms and concepts.
- **Usability.Gov** (www.usability.gov) A comprehensive US portal site covering every aspect of usability, from planning and analysing to designing, followed by testing and refining.
- **UseIt** (www.useit.com/alertbox) Ten years on, it is still worth subscribing for Jakob Nielsen's often trenchant views on web design, which are typically based on his user research.
- **UIE** (www.uie.com/articles) Jared Spool's user interface engineering articles provide good best practice summary articles.

Web development

- **Web Developers Handbook** (www.alvit.de/handbook) One of the best resources summarising all web development, how-to resources and blogs.
- **Sitepoint** (www.sitepoint.com) Online publisher with a range of blog articles in all web design categories.
- **Cre8asiteforums** (www.cre8asiteforums.com/forums) Popular forum covering many aspects of website design.
- **Webby Awards** (www.webbyawards.com) Best practice. The Oscars for the web – international.

Web standards

- **A List Apart** (www.alistapart.com) Explores the design, development and meaning of web content, with a special focus on web standards and best practices.
- **Web Standards Project (WASP)** (www.webstandards.org) A consortium that promotes web standards.
- **The World Wide Web Consortium** (www.w3.org) The global standards body prominent in defining web standards.
- **Zeldman.com** (www.zeldman.com) The blog of web standards advocate, Jeffrey Zeldman.

Chapter 8

Campaign planning for digital media

Chapter at a glance

Main topics

Case studies

Learning objectives

After reading this chapter, the reader should be able to:

- Assess the difference in communications characteristics between digital and traditional media
- Identify the main success factors in managing a digital campaign
- Understand the importance of integrating online and offline communications
- Relate promotion techniques to methods of measuring site effectiveness

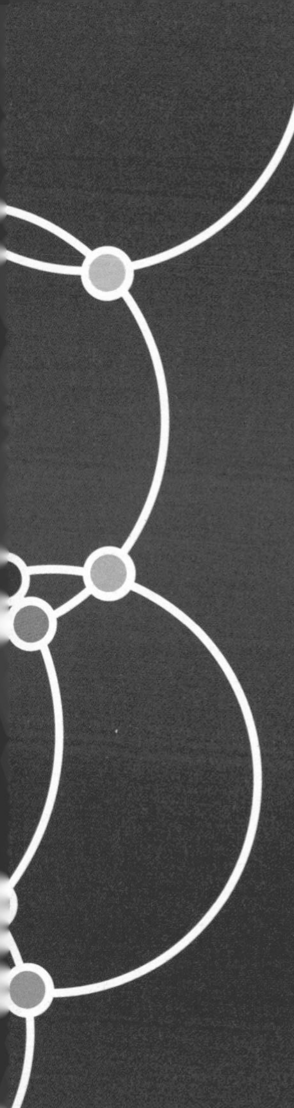

Questions for marketers

Key questions for marketing managers related to this chapter are:

- How do the characteristics of digital media differ from those of traditional media?
- How should I plan an online marketing campaign?
- How do I choose the best mix of online and offline communications techniques?

Scan code to find the latest updates for topics in this chapter

Links to other chapters

Related chapters are:

- Chapter 1 describes the 6 Is, a framework that introduces the characteristics of Internet marketing communications
- Chapter 2 introduces portals and search engines – one of the methods of online traffic building discussed in this chapter
- Chapter 3 introduces some of the legal and ethical constraints on online marketing communications
- Chapter 4 provides the strategic basis for Internet marketing communications
- Chapter 7 describes on-site communications
- Chapter 9 reviews the different digital media channels in detail
- Chapter 10 considers the measurement of communications effectiveness

Introduction

A company that has developed an effective online customer experience as discussed in Chapter 7 is only part-way to success in digital marketing. In the days of the dot-com boom a common expression was: 'If you build it, they will come.' This famous line proved true of a baseball stadium built in the film *Field of Dreams*, but unfortunately, it doesn't apply to websites or other forms of online presence like mobile apps or social media sites. Berthon *et al.* (1998) make the analogy between online communications and a trade fair. Effective promotion and achieving visibility of the stand is necessary to attract some of the many show visitors to that stand and encourage them to interact. Similarly, if you want to maximise quality visitors within a target audience to your online presences to acquire new customers online, Internet marketers have to select the appropriate online and offline marketing communications.

Continuous e-communications activities
Long-term use of e-marketing communications intended to generate site visitors for customer acquisition (such as search engine, affiliate marketing and online sponsorship) and retention (for example, e-newsletter marketing).

Planning for how digital media are used includes both short-term campaigns to support a particular goal such as launching a new product, promoting a sale or encouraging prospects to attend an event, and longer-term 'always-on' or **continuous e-communications activities** which review the best mix of communications to use to drive visitors to a site and achieve the main outcomes for the site such as product sales (for a retailer), lead generation (for a business-to-business company), engagement with a brand or subscriptions or ad revenue (for an online publisher or consumer brand).

Chaffey and Smith (2008) refer to the relevance of timing for traffic building. They say:

> Some e-marketers may consider traffic building to be a continuous process, but others may view it as a specific campaign, perhaps to launch a site or a major enhancement. Some methods tend to work best continuously; others are short term. Short-term campaigns will be for a site launch or an event such as an online trade show.

A similar sentiment is expressed in Mini Case Study 8.1 on the Alliance & Leicester which refers to use of 'drip' as against 'burst' communications.

Mini Case Study 8.1 Full rather than a burst online presence for Alliance & Leicester

Speaking to *New Media Age* (2006), Graham Findlay, Customer Acquisition Manager at bank Alliance & Leicester, highlighted the importance of continuous e-communications when he said:

> *A big part of my team's job is to continually monitor traffic to and from our sites. We work to maintain the bank's profile. Some of our competitors don't always have a full online presence, settling instead for bursts of activity. That's certainly not our strategy.*

This sentiment is backed up through investment in search and affiliate marketing. The article reported that Alliance & Leicester have increased their search engine marketing budget from 2001: £10,000 to £3 million in 2006 as part of a £13 million budget. About search he says:

> *I believe there's volume to be made from search and it's only right that a direct bank like us features in the top listings through search.*

The structure of this chapter

We begin Chapter 8 by reviewing the unique characteristics of digital media which must be applied for success in online campaigns. We then look at the different practical aspects of communications which must be reviewed as part of planning and managing a digital campaign and integrating it with traditional media. These are the sections of this chapter and the main questions we will be answering.

1 *Goal setting and tracking* – which specific goals should be set for online campaigns and how do we measure success? What response mechanisms will be most effective?
2 *Campaign insight* – which data about customer and competitor behaviour is available to inform our decision?
3 *Segmentation and targeting* – how can we target and reach our different audiences?
4 *Offer and message development* – how do we specify our offer and key messages?
5 *Budgeting and selecting the digital media mix* – how should we set the budget and invest in different forms of digital media?
6 *Integration into overall media schedule or plan* – how should we plan the media schedule which incorporates different waves of online and offline communications?

Digital media channel
Online communications technique used to achieve goals of brand awareness, familiarity, favourability, and to influence purchase intent by encouraging users of digital media to visit a website, where they will engage with the brand or product and ultimately purchase online or offline through traditional media channels such as by phone or instore.

Referrer or referring site
The source of a visitor to a site delivered via a digital media channel. Typically a specific site, e.g. Google AdWords, or a media site or an individual ad placement on the site.

In Chapter 9, we will review the success factors for the main **digital media channels** such as affiliate, search and social media marketing shown in Figure 1.9 which make up the tactics of digital marketing campaigns. When a visitor is directed to a site from another third-party site via a digital media channel, the origin is known as a **referrer or referring site**.

Digital marketing in practice The Smart Insights Interview

Mike O'Brien of the Jam Partnership on the ingredients for creating engaging digital campaigns

Overview and main concepts covered

Quality campaign creative engages. But, creating quality creative is far from simple. Mike O'Brien has been involved in creating many campaigns and this interview shows the power of digital media in creating engaging campaigns. As Mike says:

> I think we have reached the point where creative platforms are no longer hindering the free-flow of ideas. They are opening up to the point where even the most obscure brand, regardless of budget can create, execute and evaluate the most incredible interpersonal ideas and campaigns and create real time engagements with customers.

The interview

Q1: What are the ingredients for successful digital creative of a campaign?

Mike O'Brien: We should be on the lookout for campaigns that put the customer, not the brand, product or service, at the heart of everything. The future belongs to campaigns that transcend one-sided linear communication and push the boundaries of client/customer relationships into the realm of interpersonal communication. In linear communication, brands put themselves in a superior position to customers. They believe their job is to anticipate and satisfy customer needs, wants and desires, while the customers' subordinate role is simply to learn, spend and be grateful. Interpersonal communication, on the other hand, is a two-way process in which the brand and the customer learn to anticipate and satisfy each other's needs, wants and desires together in a process that rewards both parties for facilitation and engagement.

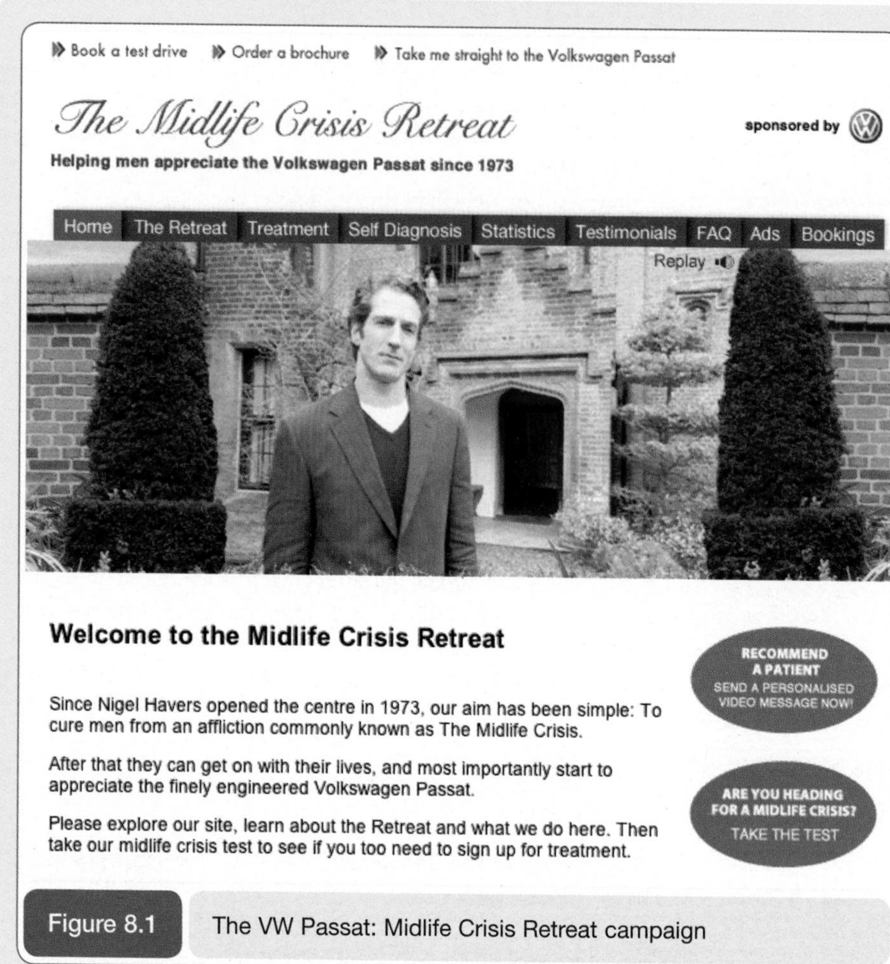

Figure 8.1 The VW Passat: Midlife Crisis Retreat campaign

Figure 8.1 shows a good example of this approach centred on a video-rich campaign hosted on a microsite (**www.midlife-crisis-retreat.co.uk**) and supported by a rich media ad campaign and email, with additional quiz and video content that can be personalised and sent to friends.

Q. Which campaign creative mistakes do you see most often?

Mike O'Brien: The total lack of relevance to the customer is all too apparent in most campaigns, especially in online display which seems, despite the billions being poured into it at the moment, to have virtually no demonstrable impact on the clients' business. I am also convinced that we tend to have too much interest in the platform and technology and not enough in the customer's journey. Whole page take-overs and interstitials that add nothing to the customers' context of engagement really make me blow a fuse. Our job is not to interrupt the customer but to work with them to achieve their key tasks. A great example of this supporting role is the Mini Banner campaign that drops a Cherished Mini search tab into the site's (Autotrader, MSN etc.) search tab structure. For the same reason, I like simple but effective dynamic, data feed and capture, contextual and RSS feed ads that augment and give direction to the customer's on-screen experience in the way that the Dominos app does on my iPhone when I am hungry. Don't expect me to look at car ads when my stomach is grumbling.

I suppose the other gripe I have is creative that shows little or no understanding of state of play between the brand and the customer. Are we in the awareness, conversion or engaged phase? How do I change my mode of engagement accordingly? Am I in a position to make the communication more relevant and individuated as the engagement deepens?

Q. What process do you recommend for getting the right creative for your audience?

Mike O'Brien: We need to help everyone involved in creating campaigns to see the world from the customer's perspective. We have a tribe of young digital creative specialists trying to communicate with an increasingly ageing population and the apparent disconnect is as misguided as Saga sending me a 'Welcome to the Club' mailing on my 50th birthday that all but suggested the onset of incontinence pants was imminent.

The root of this kind of creative incongruence is a lack of empathy and life experience and, to make matters worse, an industry-wide inability to bridge the gap through informative and inspirational briefing. I see far too many briefs written with little or no enthusiasm for the task, an optimistically heroic focus on the brand, product or service, a patronising and meagre view of the customer and an abundance of cut and paste edits from earlier scribbles and brain dumps.

So, let's look for briefs that are 80 per cent customer and 20 per cent us. Let's make sure that campaigns can be segmented into groups that allow us to create very specific responses to very specific audiences. Out there in the world of the customer are rich sources of unique campaign ideas that are Relevant, Original and Impactful waiting to be discovered.

Q. With the walled garden of Facebook a component of many campaigns do you think this hinders campaign creative?

Mike O'Brien: No. Facebook can be a great source of inspiration to the creative thinker. What better chance to engage with the language, visual culture and interests of the customer? As a young creative 30 years ago, I would have needed to virtually invent the world of the customer or, frankly, be indifferent to any reality that existed outside of my elitist agency experience. I'm not sure a lot has changed. Perhaps social marketing will help to bridge the gap. One campaign that works the social channel brilliantly is the IKEA Malmö store campaign (Figure 8.2).

When IKEA launched a brand new store in Malmö, Sweden, their agency chose to use an existing and very popular platform (Facebook) and technology (photo tagging) in an innovative way. They created a Facebook account for Gordon Gustavsson, the General Manager of the new store. Over the course of two weeks, they added a dozen photos of instore showrooms filled with IKEA products. Once the first photo was posted, they announced that people were free to tag the items in the photos, and the first person to tag an item would win said item. By tagging the photos, they would appear on the taggers' profile pages, links and news feeds, therefore exposing the 'campaign' to all of their Facebook friends. Soon everybody was anticipating the next photo in the series, spreading the word about the IKEA promotion. This is a stunning example of facilitated leverage campaigns built around ideas that see customers as an integral part of the creative process. If you make an idea sufficiently engaging the customers will do the heavy lifting for you.

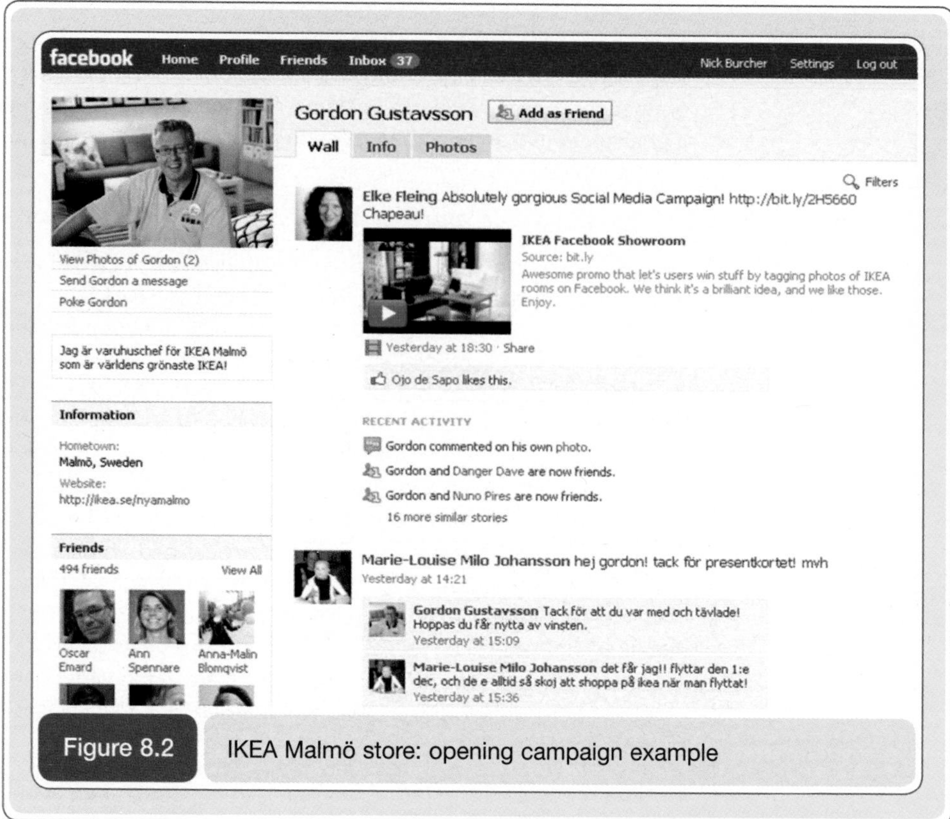

Figure 8.2 IKEA Malmö store: opening campaign example

The characteristics of digital media

Through understanding the key interactive communications characteristics enabled through digital media we can exploit these media while guarding against their weaknesses. In this section, we will describe eight key changes in the media characteristics between traditional and digital media. Note that the 6 Is in Chapter 1 (page 35) provide an alternative framework that is useful for evaluating the differences between traditional media and new media.

1 From push to pull

Push media
Communications are broadcast from an advertiser to consumers of the message, who are passive recipients.

Pull media and inbound marketing
The consumer is proactive in actively seeking out a solution and interactions with brands and are attracted through content, search and social media marketing.

Traditional media such as print, TV and radio are **push media** – one-way streets where information is mainly unidirectional, from company to customer unless direct response elements are built in. In contrast, many digital marketing activities like content, search and social media marketing are **pull media and inbound marketing**. Amongst marketing professionals this powerful new approach to marketing is now commonly known as inbound marketing (Shah and Halligan, 2009). Inbound marketing is powerful since advertising wastage is reduced. Content and search marketing can be used to target prospects with a defined need – they are proactive and self-selecting. But this is a weakness since marketers may have less control than in traditional communications where the message is pushed out to a defined audience and can help generate awareness and demand. Advocates of inbound marketing argue that content, social media and search marketing do have a role to play in generating demand. The implications are that stimuli to encourage online interactions are still important through online or traditional ads, direct mail, physical reminders or encouraging word-of-mouth. 'Push' from e-mail marketing remains important and is part of the inbound marketing approach:, it should be a priority objective of website design to capture customers' e-mail addresses in order that opt-in e-mail can be used to push relevant and timely messages to customers.

2 From monologue to dialogue to trialogue

Interactivity
The medium enables a dialogue between company and customer.

Creating a dialogue through **interactivity** is the next important feature of the web and digital media such as mobile and interactive TV which provide the opportunity for two-way interaction with the customer. This is a key distinguishing feature of the medium according to Peters (1998), and Deighton (1996) proclaimed the interactive benefits of the Internet as a means of developing long-term relationships with customers through what would later be defined as permission marketing by Godin (1999).

Trialogue
The interaction between company, customer and other customers facilitated through online community, social networks, reviews and comments.

Walmsley (2007) believes that the main impact of digital media has not been to find new ways to connect brands to consumers as originally anticipated, but in connecting those consumers to each other. In the age of **trialogue**; brands need to reinterpret themselves as facilitators. Walmsley believes this trialogue will influence every aspect of marketing, from product design through to product recommendation. An example where product design is influenced is Threadless.com, the online T-shirt store, which only carries designs its users have uploaded, and manufactures only those that get a critical mass of votes (see Figure 8.3).

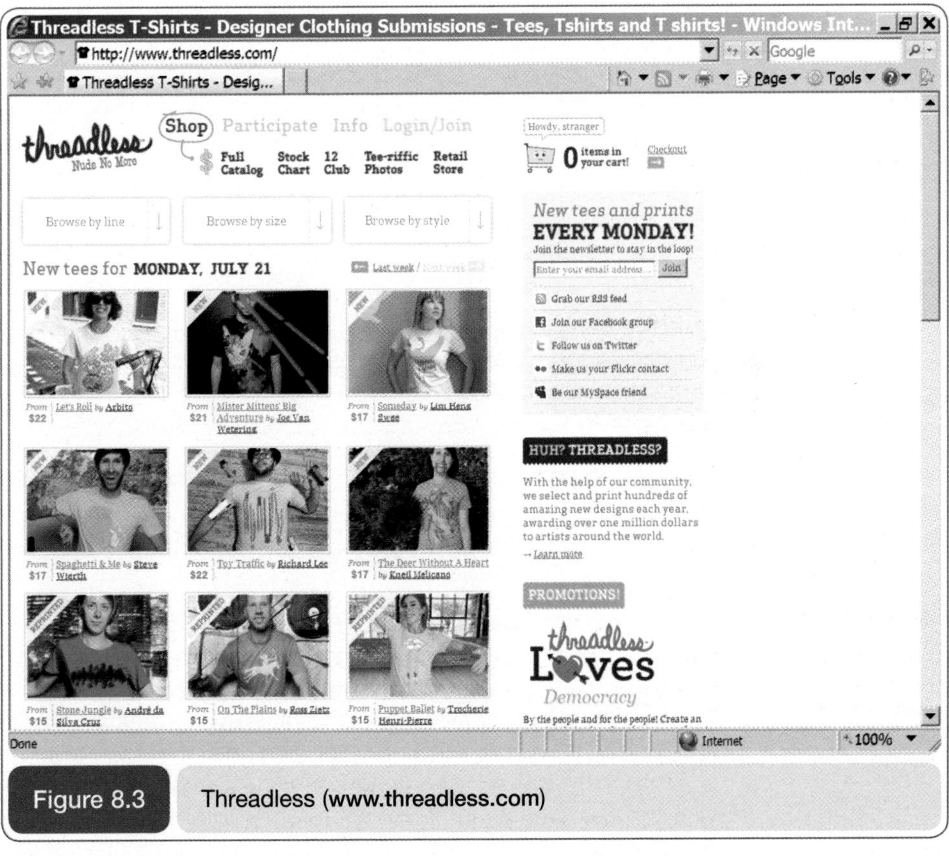

Figure 8.3 Threadless (www.threadless.com)

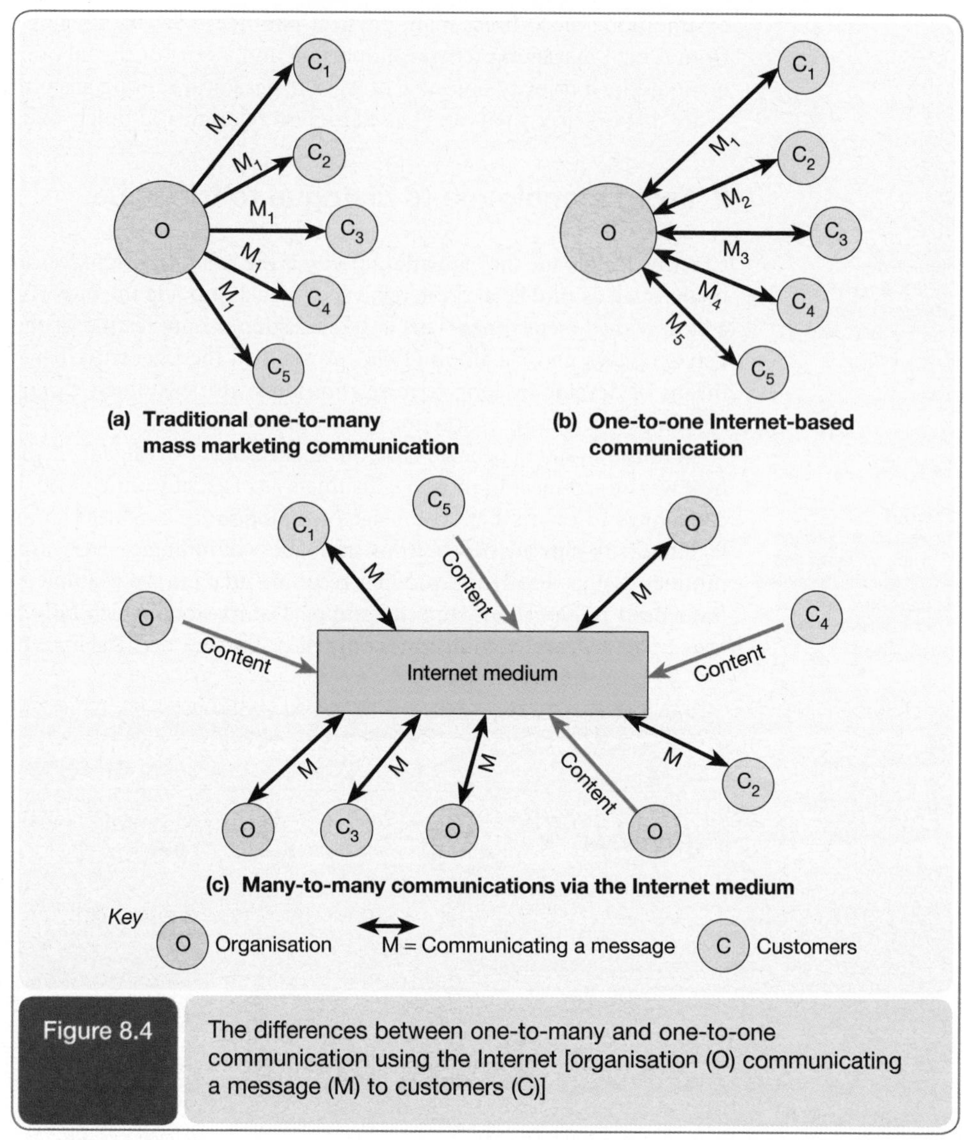

Figure 8.4 The differences between one-to-many and one-to-one communication using the Internet [organisation (O) communicating a message (M) to customers (C)]

3 From one-to-many to one-to-some and one-to-one

Mass customisation The creation of tailored marketing messages or products for individual customers or groups of customers typically using technology to retain the economies of scale and the capacity of mass marketing or production.

Personalisation Web-based personalisation involves delivering customised content for the individual through web pages, e-mail or push technology.

Traditional push communications are one-to-many, from one company to many customers, often the same message to different segments and often poorly targeted. With digital media 'one-to-some' – reaching a niche or micro-segment becomes more practical – e-marketers can afford to tailor and target their message to different segments through providing different site content or e-mail for different audiences through **mass customisation** and **personalisation** (Chapter 6).

Figure 8.4 illustrates the opportunities for mass customisation as interaction occurs between an organisation (O) communicating a message (M) to customers (C) for a single-step flow of communication. It is apparent that for traditional mass marketing in (a) a single message (M_1) is communicated to all customers (C_1 to C_5).

Hoffman and Novak (1997) believed that this change was significant enough to represent a new model for marketing, or a new 'marketing paradigm' (Figure 8.4 (c)). They suggest that the facilities of the Internet, including the web, represent a computer-mediated environment in which the interactions are not between the sender and receiver of information, but with the medium itself. Their vision of the future is now apparent in the popularity of social networks, blogs and specialist communities.

> consumers can interact with the medium, firms can provide content to the medium, and in the most radical departure from traditional marketing environments, consumers can provide commercially-oriented content to the media.

4 From one-to-many to many-to-many communications

Digital media also enable many-to-many communications. Hoffman and Novak (1996) noted that new media are many-to-many media. Here customers can interact with other customers via a website, in independent communities or on their personal websites and blogs. We will see in the section on online PR that the implications of many-to-many communications are a loss of control of communications requiring monitoring of information sources, but it opens more opportunities to reach out to influencers to expand reach.

5 From 'lean-back' to 'lean-forward'

Digital media are also intense media – they are interactive, lean-forward media where the customer wants to be in control and wants to experience flow and responsiveness to their needs. First impressions and devices to encourage the visitor to interact are important. If the visitor to your site does not find what they are looking for immediately, whether through poor design or slow speed, they will move on, probably never to return.

6 The medium changes the nature of standard marketing communications tools such as advertising

In addition to offering the opportunity for one-to-one marketing, the Internet can be, and widely still is, used for one-to-many advertising. The website or social media site can be considered as similar in function to an advertisement (since it can inform, persuade and remind customers about the offering, although it is not paid for in the same way as a traditional advertisement). Berthon *et al.* (1996) consider a website as a mix between advertising and direct selling since it can also be used to engage the visitor in a dialogue. Constraints on advertising in traditional mass media, such as paying for time or space, become less important. The wastage in traditional advertising where ads are either ignored or are not relevant for an audience is reduced in online marketing and search marketing in particular. In pay-per-click (PPC) advertising, display of ads can be controlled according to user need based on what searchers are looking for and cost is only incurred where interest is indicated by a click. Affiliate marketing is also a **pay-per-performance communications** technique where cost is only incurred where there is a response.

Pay-for-performance communications
The wastage from traditional media buys can be reduced online through advertising models where the advertisers only pay for a response (cost-per-click) as in pay-per-click search marketing or for a lead or sale as in affiliate marketing.

Peters (1998) suggests that communication via the new medium is differentiated from communication using traditional media in four different ways. First, *communication style* is changed with *immediate*, or synchronous, transfer of information through online customer service being possible. Asynchronous communication, where there is a time delay between sending and receiving information as through e-mail, also occurs. Second, *social presence* or the feeling that a communications exchange is sociable, warm, personal and active may be lower if a standard web page is delivered, but can be enhanced, perhaps by personalisation. Third, the consumer has more *control of contact*; and fourth the user has control of *content*, for example through personalisation facilities or posting their own user-generated content.

Although Hoffman and Novak (1996) point out that with the Internet the main relationships are not *directly* between sender and receiver of information, but with the web-based environment, the classic communications model of Schramm (1955) can still be used to help

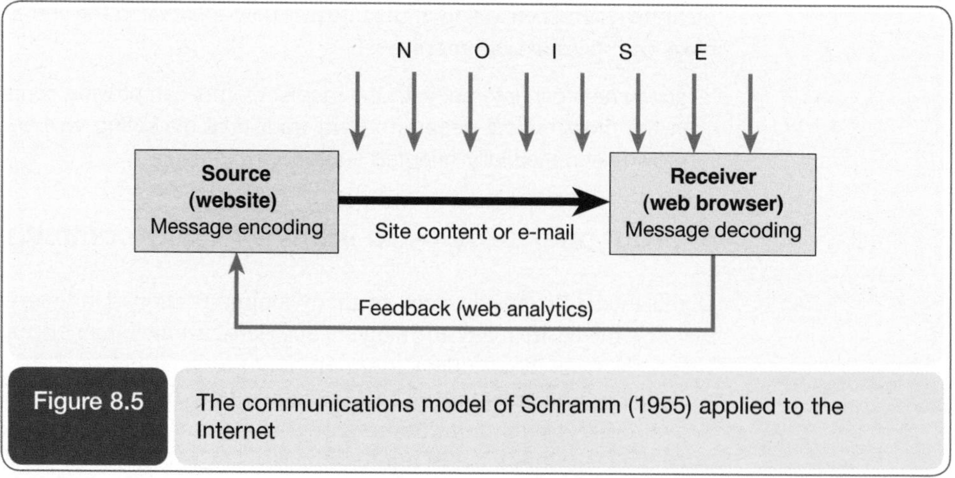

Figure 8.5 The communications model of Schramm (1955) applied to the Internet

understand the effectiveness of marketing communication using the Internet. Figure 8.5 shows the model applied to the Internet. Four of the elements of the model that can constrain the effectiveness of Internet marketing are:

- *Encoding* – this is the design and development of the site content or e-mail that aims to convey the message of the company, and is dependent on understanding of the target audience.
- *Noise* – this is the external influence that affects the quality of the message; in an Internet context this can be slow download times, the use of plug-ins that the user cannot use or confusion caused by too much information on-screen.
- *Decoding* – this is the process of interpreting the message, and is dependent on the cognitive ability of the receiver, which is partly influenced by the length of time they have used the Internet.
- *Feedback* – this occurs through online forms and through monitoring of on-site behaviour through web analytics (Chapter 10).

7 Increase in communications intermediaries

If we contrast traditional advertising and PR with digital media, there is an increase in options to reach audiences online through a large number of options for media and influencers. Traditional radio channels, newspapers and print titles have migrated online, but in addition there are a vast number of online-only publishers, bloggers and individual sharing through social networks. The concept of the long tail (Chapter 5) also applies to websites in any sector. There are a handful of key sites, but many others can also be used to reach customers. The online marketer needs to select the most appropriate of this plethora of sites which customers visit to drive traffic to their website.

8 Integration

Although digital media have distinct characteristics compared to traditional media, it does not follow that we should concentrate our communications solely on digital media. Rather we should combine and integrate traditional and digital media according to their strengths as explained in Step 6 in this chapter.

We conclude this section with our summary of some of the main differences between traditional and digital media (Table 8.1) and a review of how consumers perceive the Internet in comparison to traditional media (Digital marketing insights 8.1).

Table 8.1 Summary of differences in characteristics of traditional media and digital media (note that rows 10–12 are similarities between the two media types

Traditional media	Digital media
1 Push emphasis (e.g. TV and print ads and direct mail)	Pull emphasis. Relevance to context (search engine marketing (SEM))
2 One-way communications	Dialogue and interactivity and trialogue through user-generated content (UGC)
3 Targeting cost constrained by media placements	Micro-targeting and personalisation through SEM and media placements on niche sites
4 Limited customer-to-customer interactions	Participation: communities and social networks
5 Static campaigns – once campaigns have been booked with a media agency it is difficult to adjust them	Dynamic campaigns where it is possible to test alternative creative and targeting and then revise during campaign according to performance
6 Burst campaigns maximise ad impact over a short-term period	Continuous campaigns where a permanent presence is required in online media (e.g. in SEM and aggregators)
7 Limited media-buying opportunities with high degree of wastage	Limitless media-buying opportunities with pay-per-performance options
8 Detailed response measurement often limited to qualitative research	Potentially measurable at micro-level through web analytics and ad tracking systems
9 Pre-testing	Can also test and refine during campaign
10 Most communications to reach audience via media owners	Media owners are still important but communications also possible via website and non-media owned blogs and social networks
11 Integrated communications vital	Integrated communications vital
12 Not cheap, quick or easy	Not cheap, quick or easy

Digital marketing insight 8.1 Consumer perceptions of the Internet and different media

This study was completed when the web was a relatively new medium, but it's still worth referencing since it contrasts the differences between different media channels well. Review whether you think these differences remain valid in this era when social media marketing is dominant. Branthwaite *et al*. (2000) conducted a global qualitative project covering a sample of 18–35 year olds in 14 countries across North and South America, East and West Europe, Asia and Australia to investigate consumer perceptions of the Internet and other media. Consumers' perceptions of the Internet, when asked to explain how they felt about the Internet in relation to different animals, were as follows:

> *The dominant sense here was of something exciting, but also inherently malevolent, dangerous and frightening in the Internet.*

The positive aspect was expressed mainly through images of a bird but also a cheetah or dolphin. These captured the spirit of freedom, opening horizons, versatility, agility, effortlessness and efficiency.

In comparison with other media, the Internet was described as follows:

The Internet seemed less like a medium of communication than the others, and more like a reservoir of information.

This distinction was based on differences in the mode of operating: other media communicated to you whereas with the Internet the user had to actively seek and extract information for themselves. In this sense, the Internet is a recessive medium that sits waiting to be interrogated, whereas other media are actively trying to target their communications to the consumer.

Table 8.2 and Figure 8.6 present the final evaluation of the Internet against other media.

Table 8.2 Comparison of the properties of different media

	TV	**Outdoor**	**Print**	**Internet**
Intrusiveness	High	High	Low	Low
Control/ selectivity	Passive	Passive	Active, selective	Active, selective of consumption
Episode attention	Long	Short	Long	Restless, fragmented span
Active processing	Low	Low	High	High
Mood	Relaxed, seeking exceptional gratification	Bored, under-stimulated	Relaxed, seeking interest, stimulation	Goal-orientated, needs-related
Modality	Audio/visual	Visual	Visual	Visual (auditory increasing)
Processing	Episodic, superficial	Episodic/ semantic	Semantic, deep	Semantic, deep
Context	As individual in interpersonal setting	Solitary (in public space)	Individual, personal	Alone, private

Source: Branthwaite *et al.* (2000)

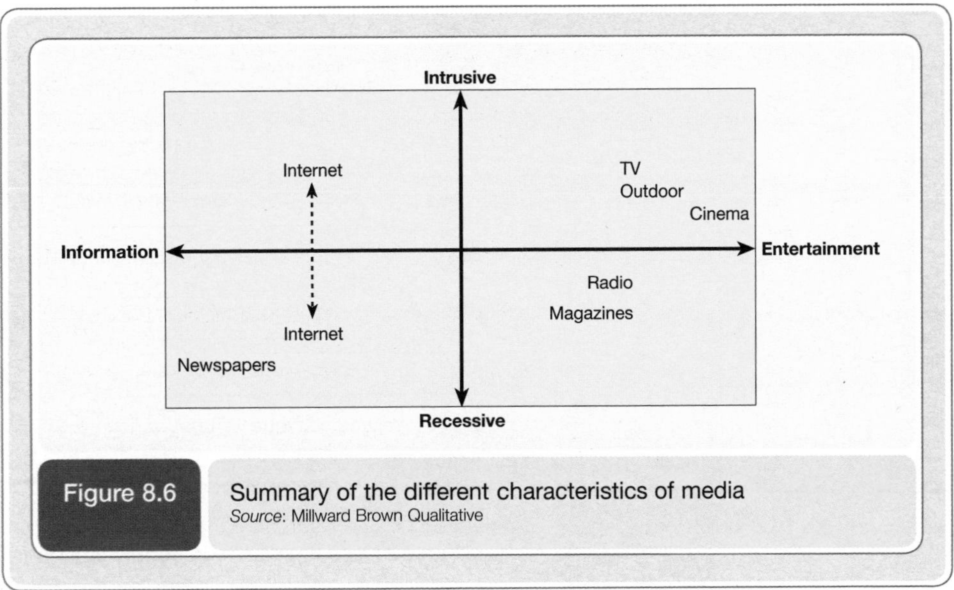

Figure 8.6 Summary of the different characteristics of media
Source: Millward Brown Qualitative

Step 1. Goal setting and tracking for interactive marketing communications

Digital marketers develop communications objectives for different timescales:

- *Annual marketing communications objectives.* For example, achieving new site visitors or gaining qualified leads could be measured across an entire year since this will be a continuous activity based on visitor building through search engines and other campaigns. Annual budgets are set to help achieve these objectives.
- *Campaign-specific communications objectives.* Internet marketing campaigns such as to support a product launch through online advertising and viral marketing. Specific objectives can be stated for each in terms of gaining new visitors, converting visitors to customers and encouraging repeat purchases. Campaign objectives should build on traditional marketing objectives, have a specific target audience and have measurable outcomes which can be attributed to the specific campaign.

The measures we cover in this section can be applied to both short and long-term. More depth on tracking through analytics and the specific measures used for measuring social media ROI is available in in Chapter 10.

Terminology for measuring digital campaigns

There are a bewildering series of terms used to set goals and track the effectiveness of digital campaigns, so we start this section by explaining the main measures you will encounter in models for campaign planning and reports from online campaigns. Figure 8.7 shows different measures from least sophisticated to more sophisticated as shown under the following headings. Basic tracking systems will only measure volumes of interaction, but more capable systems will cover volume, quality and value of interactions.

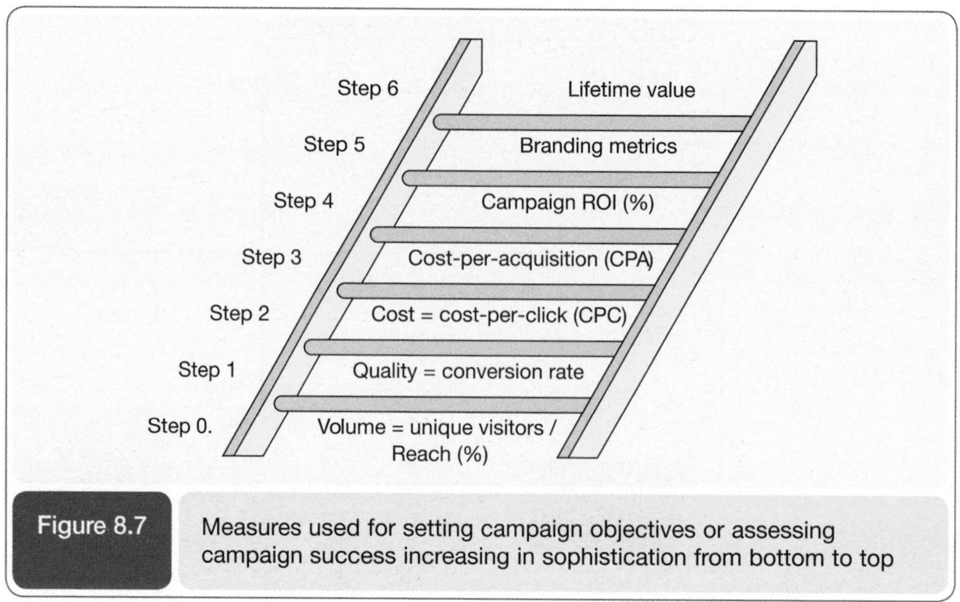

Figure 8.7 Measures used for setting campaign objectives or assessing campaign success increasing in sophistication from bottom to top

Visitor session (visit)
A series of one or more page impressions, served to one user, which ends when there is a gap of 30 minutes or more between successive page impressions for that user.

Unique visitor
Individual visitor to a site measured through cookies or the IP address on an individual computer.

0 Volume measures including clicks, visitor session and unique visitors

Traffic volume is usually measured as the number of click-throughs or visits to a site (**visitor sessions**) to a site or alternatively **unique visitors**. If possible, unique visitors is preferable to using page views or hits as a measure of effectiveness, since it represents opportunities to communicate with individuals but, as we will explain in Chapter 10, it may be technically difficult to calculate 'uniques' accurately as measurement is based on cookies. A more sophisticated measure is reach (%) or online audience share. This is only possible using panel data/audience data tools such as **www.netratings.com**, **www.comscore.com** or **www.hitwise.com**. *Example*: An online bank has one million unique visitors per month.

1 Quality measures including conversion rates to action and bounce rate

Traffic volume measures give no indication of whether the audience referred to the site engages with it, so we need quality measures to show us this. Conversion rate is the best known quality measure which shows what proportion of visitors from different sources within a defined time period convert to specific marketing outcomes on the web, such as lead, sale or subscription.

> *Example*: 10 per cent of visitors convert to an outcome such as logging in to their account, or asking for a quote for a product.

Visit or session conversion rate
An indication of the capability of a site in converting visitors to defined outcomes such as registration. Calculated by dividing the number of conversion events by the number of visitor sessions within a time period.

Visitor conversion rate
An indication of the capability of a site in converting visitors to defined outcomes such as registration. Calculated by dividing the number of conversion events by the number of unique visitors within a defined time period.

Conversion rates can be expressed in two different ways – at the visit level (**visit or session conversion rate**) or the unique visitor level (**visitor conversion rate**).

Eric Petersen (2004) explains it this way:

> the denominator you use [to calculate conversion rate] will depend on whether you're trying to understand how people behave during visits or the people themselves. If you're interested in people [and the overall buying process] use unique visitors, if you're interested in behaviour [on a single visit] use visits.

Examples:

$$\text{Visit conversion rate} = \frac{\text{10 conversion events}}{\text{1000 visits}} = 1\%$$

For an e-retailer this is the order conversion rate:

$$\text{Order conversion rate} = \frac{\text{10 sales}}{\text{1000 visits}} = 1\%$$

$$\text{Visitor conversion rate} = \frac{\text{10 conversion events}}{\text{800 visits}} = 1.25\%$$

For an e-retailer, this can be called the buyer conversion rate, also known as the browse-to-buy ratio or for a travel company 'look to book':

$$\text{buyer conversion rate} = \frac{\text{10 sales}}{\text{800 unique visitors}} = 1.25\%$$

Bounce rate
Proportion of visitors to a page or site who exit after visiting a single page only, usually expressed as a percentage.

A related measure that is useful to monitor during campaigns is the **bounce rate** which indicates the proportion of referred visitors to a page or site who exit after visiting a single page only, usually expressed as a percentage (i.e. that arrive at the site and bounce off it since they don't discover relevance!)

Reviewing bounce or engagement rates can improve the effectiveness of landing pages and the quality of referrers to a page. The benefit of using bounce rates rather than conversion rates is that there is a much wider variation in bounce rates for a page (i.e. typically 20% to 80%, compared to sub-10%), which enables problems with individual referrers, keywords or landing page conversions to be more readily identified. Bounce rates are calculated as follows:

$$\text{Bounce rate \%} = \frac{100 \times \text{single page visits to a page (or site)}}{\text{all visits starting on page (or site)}}$$

$$\text{Engagement rate \%} = (100 - \text{bounce rate \%})$$

2 Media cost measures including cost-per-click and cost-per-thousand

Cost-per-click (CPC)
The cost of each click from a referring site to a destination site, typically from a search engine in pay-per-click search marketing.

Cost-per-thousand (CPM)
The cost of placing an ad viewed by 1000 people.

The cost of visitor acquisition is usually measured as the **cost-per-click (CPC)** specific to a particular digital media channel, such as pay-per-click search engine marketing, since it is difficult to estimate for an entire site with many visitors referred from offline advertising.

Example: £2 CPC (500 clicks delivered from Google Adwords costing £1000).

Cost-per-thousand (CPM) (M = *mille*) is usually used as the currency when buying display ad space, for example, £10 CPM will mean that the ad will be served to 1000 visitors (technically visitor sessions). An effective CPM can also be calculated for other media channels, such as pay-per-click advertising, for comparison.

3 Acquisition cost measures including cost-per-action or acquisition

Cost-per-acquisition (CPA)
The cost of acquiring a new customer or achieving a sale. Typically limited to the communications cost and refers to cost per sale for new customers. May also refer to other outcomes such as cost per quote or enquiry.

A digital campaign will not be successful if it meets its objectives of acquiring site visitors and customers but the cost of achieving this is too high. So it is essential to have specific objectives and measures for the cost of using different digital media channels to drive visitors to the site and convert to transaction. This is stated as the **cost-per-acquisition (CPA)** (sometimes cost-per-action). Depending on context and market, CPA may refer to different outcomes. Typical cost targets include:

- cost-per-acquisition – of a visitor
- cost-per-acquisition – of a lead
- cost-per-acquisition – of a sale (most typical form of CPA, also known as CPS).

Allowable cost-per-acquisition
A target maximum cost for generating leads or new customer's profitably.

To control costs, it is important for managers to define a target **allowable cost-per-acquisition** such as £30 for generating a business lead or £50 for achieving sign-up to a credit card. When the cost of visitor acquisition is combined with conversion to outcomes this is the cost of (customer) acquisition.

Example: £20 CPA (for £2 CPC, 10% conversion with one-in-ten visits resulting in sale).

4 Return on investment (ROI) *or value* measures

Return on investment is used to assess the profitability of any marketing activity, or indeed any investment. You will also know that there are different forms of ROI, depending on how profitability is calculated. Here we will assume it is just based on sales value or profitability based on the cost per click and conversion rate.

$$\text{ROI} = \frac{\text{profit generated from referrer}}{\text{amount spent on advertising with referrer}}$$

A related measure, which does not take profitability into account is return on advertising spend (ROAS) which is calculated as follows:

$$\text{ROAS} = \frac{\text{total revenue generated from referrer}}{\text{amount spent of advertising with referrer}}$$

5 Branding measures

These tend to be most relevant to interactive advertising or sponsorship. They are the equivalent of offline advertising metrics, i.e. brand awareness (aided and unaided), ad recall, brand favourability and purchase intent.

6 Lifetime value-based ROI measures

Here the value of gaining the customer is not just based on the initial purchase, but the lifetime value (and costs) associated with the customer. This requires more sophisticated models which can be most readily developed for online retailers and online financial services providers. The technique for the calculation of LTV was outlined in Chapter 6.

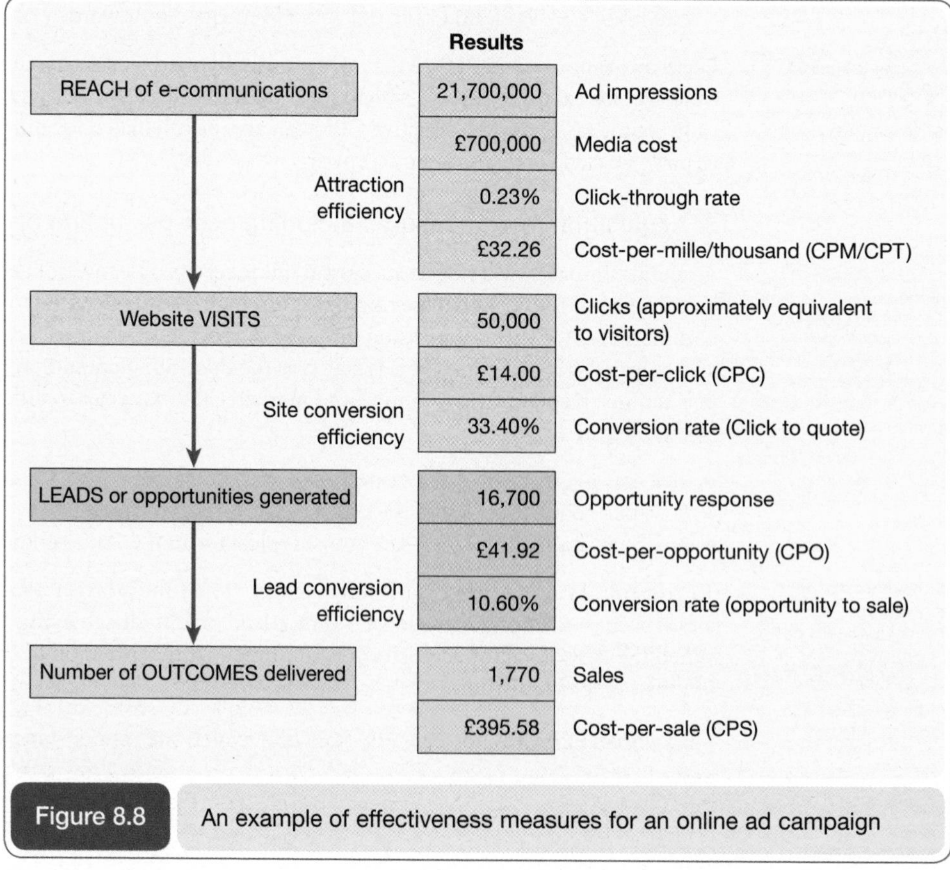

Figure 8.8 An example of effectiveness measures for an online ad campaign

Example: A bank uses a net present value model for insurance products which looks at the value over ten years but whose main focus is on a five-year result and takes into account:

- acquisition cost
- retention rates
- claims
- expenses.

This is valuable since it helps give them a realistic 'allowable cost per sale' which is needed to get return over five years. They track this in great detail – for example, they will know the ROI of different Google Adwords keywords and will then select keyphrase and bid strategies accordingly.

Figure 8.8 shows an example of an online ad campaign for an insurance product placing many of the core volume, quality and cost measures covered in this section in context. Here an opportunity or lead is when a quote is requested. Note that the cost of acquisition is high, but this does not take into account the synergies of online advertising with offline campaigns, i.e. those who are influenced by the ad, but do not click through immediately.

Examples of digital campaign measures

An interactive marketing communications plan should have five main types of goals included.

Online site promotion
Internet-based technique used to generate website traffic.

Offline site promotion
Traditional techniques such as print and TV advertising used to generate website traffic.

SMART
Specific, Measurable, Actionable, Relevant and Time-related.

Traffic building
Using online and offline site promotion techniques to generate visitors to a site.

1 *Traffic building goals.* These define targets for using **online site promotion** and **offline site promotion** to drive quality visitors or traffic to a website or other social presence which convert to the outcomes required (sales, lead, newsletter sign-up, social interaction) at an acceptable cost.

   Examples of **SMART traffic building** objectives which can be expressed as visitors, visits or sales:

   - Achieve 100,000 unique visitors or 200,000 visitor sessions within one year.
   - Deliver 20,000 online sales at an average order value of £50 and a cost-per-acquisition of £10.
   - Convert 30 per cent of existing customer base to active use (at least once every 90 days) of online service.
   - Achieve 10 per cent 'share of searches' within a market.

2 *Conversion or interaction goals.* Use onsite communications to deliver an effective message to the visitor which helps influence perceptions or achieves a required marketing outcome. The message delivered on-site will be based on traditional marketing communications objectives for a company's products or services. For example:

   - encourage trial (for example, achieve 4 per cent conversion of new unique visitors to registration or downloads of a music service such as iTunes or Napster)
   - build in-house permission-based list (grow e-mail database by 10,000 during year through data capture activities)
   - encourage engagement with content (conversion of 20 per cent of new unique visitors to product information area)
   - persuade customer to purchase (conversion of 5 per cent of unique new visitors)
   - encourage further purchases (conversion of 30 per cent of first-time buyers to repeat purchasers within a 6-month period).

To estimate a realistic number of conversions, we recommend creating conversion-based models like that shown in Figure 8.9. Take, for example, the objectives of a campaign for a B2B services company such as a consultancy company, where the ultimate objective is to achieve 1000 new clients using the website in combination with traditional media to convert leads to action. To achieve this level of new business, the marketer will need to make assumptions about the level of conversion that is needed at each stage of converting prospects to customers. This gives a core objective of 1000 new clients and different critical success factors based on the different conversion rates.

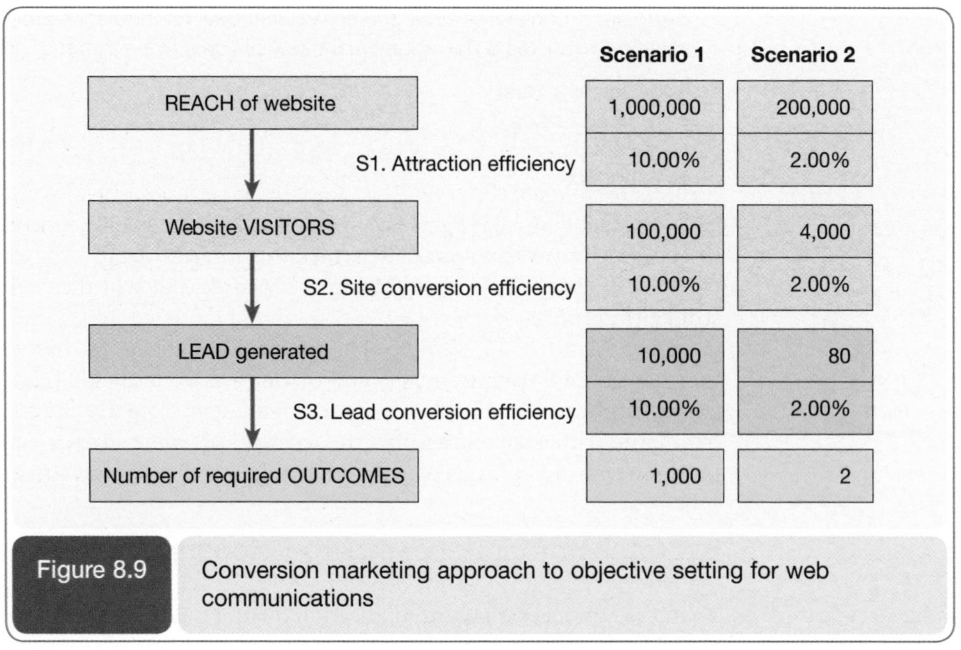

Figure 8.9 Conversion marketing approach to objective setting for web communications

Value event scoring
Value events are outcomes that occur on the site as indicated by visits to different page or content types which suggest that marketing communications are effective. Examples include leads, sales, newsletter registrations and product page views. They can be tagged and scored using many web analytics systems, for example Google refers to them as conversion goals.

If there are no products available for sale online, such as a luxury car manufacturer or a high-value B2B service offering white paper downloads, then it is less clear how to calculate ROI.

To get the most from campaigns which don't result in sale online and optimise their effectiveness, it is useful to put a value or points score on different outcomes, for example in the case of the car manufacturer, values could be assigned to brochure requests (5 points or £20), demonstration drive requests (20 points or £100) or simply visits to the site involving reviewing product features information (1 point or £1). This approach is known as **value event scoring**.

Through knowing the average percentage of online brochure requests or demo drive requests that convert to sales, and the average order value for customers referred from the website, then the value of these on-site outcomes can be estimated. This is only an estimate, but it can help inform campaign optimisation, by showing which referring sites, creative or PPC keywords and pages visited on the site which are most likely to generate desirable outcomes. Mini Case Study 8.2 gives an example of different types of events for a photo sharing site.

Mini Case Study 8.2 Spanish photo sharing website measures value events

Fotonatura (**www.fotonatura.org**), a Spanish photo sharing website, uses these micro-conversion goals in Google Analytics which give an overall conversion rate of 1.72%:

- Goal 1 – Registration (503 conversions)
- Goal 2 – Photo publication (3788 conversions)
- Goal 3 – Premium service registration (9 conversions)
- Goal 4 – Camera sales page (1049 conversions)

Source: Kaushik (2008)

3 *Third-party site reach and branding goals.* Reach, influence and engage with prospects customers on third-party sites such as online news and magazines sites, portals and social networks.

- Reach a targeted audience of 500,000 during the campaign.
- Create awareness of a product or favourability towards a brand (measured through brand research of brand awareness, brand favourability or purchase intent through using an online brand-tracking service such as Dynamic Logic, **www.dynamiclogic.com**).

Mixed-mode buying
The customer's purchase decision is influenced by a range of media such as print, TV and Internet.

4 *Multichannel marketing goals.* Integrate all communications methods to help achieve marketing objectives by supporting mixed-mode buying.
Examples of **mixed-mode buying** objectives:

- Achieve 20 per cent of sales achieved in the call centre as a result of website visits.
- Achieve 20 per cent of online sales in response to offline adverts.
- Increase average amount spent in store for every active site visitor from £3 to £4.
- Reduce contact-centre phone enquiries by 15 per cent by providing online customer services.

5 *Longer-term brand engagement goals.* One of the biggest challenges of online marketing, indeed marketing through any channel is to sustain long term interactions leading to additional sales. These are measured through lifetime value, loyalty and customer interactions.
A good example of developing SMART campaign objectives is provided in Chapter 9 in Mini Case Study 9.2 'Beep-beep-beep-beep, that'll be the bank then' (see page 534). In this campaign to promote a new interactive banking service the campaign objectives and results were to:

- capture 5000 mobile phone numbers from customers (200% of plan)
- acquire 3000 e-mail addresses (176% of plan)
- raise awareness about the new service (31,000 customers view demonstration)
- create 1000 new registrations (576% of plan).

This example shows the importance of capturing and maintaining up-to-date customer details such as e-mail addresses and mobile phone numbers.

Campaign response mechanisms

Digital media have increased the choice of response mechanisms. Reviewing response mechanisms is important since too narrow may limit response, but too broad and unfocused may not give the right types of response – marketers need to emphasise the response types or customer journeys most favourable to the overall success of the campaign in their creative and messaging. Policies for response mechanism across campaigns should be specified by managers to ensure the right approach is used across all campaigns.

Response mechanism will naturally vary depending on type of product. So, brands such as fast-moving consumer goods brands do not have to drive visitors to their own site; through advertising and creating interactive microsites on third-party sites, they can potentially be more effective in reaching their audience who are more likely to spend their time on online media sites than on destination brand sites.

Online response mechanism

The required response mechanisms should be specified in the digital campaign plan and the number of responses from each modeled. Figure 8.10 suggests the typical options of outcomes to online campaign media. From the creative displayed using media such as a display ad, pay-per-click ad or rented e-mail newsletter, there are five main options.

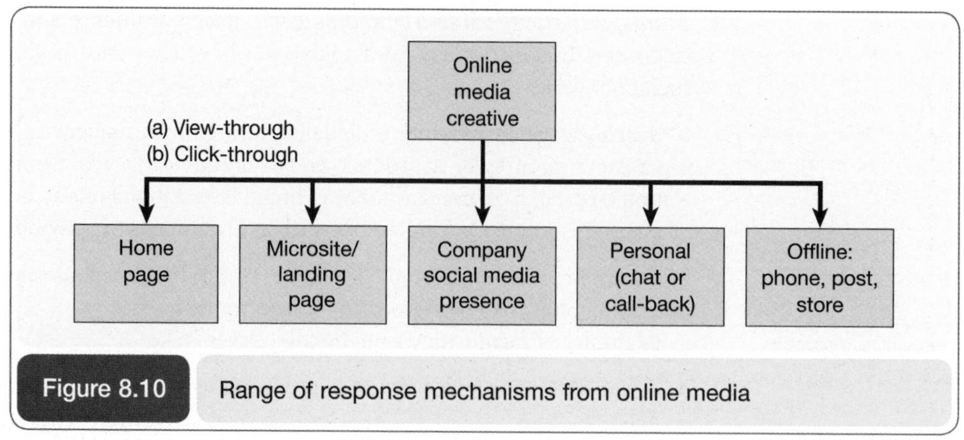

Figure 8.10 Range of response mechanisms from online media

1 Home page

Media site
Typical location where paid-for ads are placed.

Destination website
Site typically owned by a retailer or manufacturer brand which users are encouraged to click through to.

In the majority of cases, investment in online media will be wasted if visitors are driven from the **media site** to the home page of the **destination website.** Typically it is appealing to many audiences and offering too much choice – it won't effectively reinforce the message of the online creative or convert to further action.

2 Microsite/landing page

Landing page
A destination page when a user clicks on an ad or other form of link from a referring site. It can be a home page but more typically and desirably, it is a page with the messaging focused on the offer in the ad. This will maximise conversion rates and brand favourability.

URL strategy
A defined approach to how content is labelled through placing it in different directories or folders with distinct web addresses.

A focused **landing page** or specially created microsite can more effectively convert visitors to the action to help gain a return on the online campaign investment. Figure 8.11 shows an example of a landing page giving a range of response mechanisms, although offline is omitted. A **URL strategy** is used to make the page easy to label in offline creative. This specifies how different types of content on a site will be placed in different folders or directories of a website (this can also help with search engine optimisation). For example, if you visit the BBC site (**www.bbc.co.uk**) look at how the web address details vary as you move from one section to another such as News or Sport. An individual destination page on a website may be labelled, for example, www.company.com/ products/insurance/car-insurance. A further example is where site owners have to make a decision how to refer to content in different countries, either in the form:

http://<country-name>.<company-name>.com

or the more common

http://www.<companyname.com>.com/<country-name>

Campaign URL or CURL
A web address specific to a particular campaign.

Campaign URLs or CURLs are commonly used today, the idea being that they will be more memorable than the standard company address and blend in with the campaign concept. For example, an insurer used the CURL **www.quotemehappy.com**, a mortgage provider **www.hateyourmortgage.com** and a phone company **www.sleeptomorrow.com**, which are memorable elements of the campaign.

3 Personal (chat or call-back)

Call-back service
A facility available on the website for a company to contact a customer at a later time as specified by the customer.

In this case the creative or the landing page encourages campaign respondents to 'talk' directly with a human operator. It is usually referred to as a **call-back service** and integrates web and phone. Buttons or hyperlinks encourage a call-back from a telephone operator or an online chat. The advantage of this approach is that it engages the customer more and will typically lead to a higher conversion-to-sale rate since the customer's questions and objections are more likely to be answered and the personal engagement is more likely to encourage a favourable impression.

Figure 8.11 Alternative response mechanisms for a business-to-business landing page example

4 Offline: phone, post or store

Because part of a campaign is run online does not mean that offline responses should be excluded. Offline response mechanisms should not be discarded unless the cost of managing them cannot be justified, which is rarely the case.

Offline response goals for multichannel integration

Web response model
The website is used as a response mechanism for offline campaign elements such as direct mail or advertising.

We also need to include the right response mechanism for the offline media element of the campaigns such as TV ads, print ads or direct-mail pieces. The permission-based **web response model** is one that is frequently used today in direct marketing (Chapter 6). For example, this process could start with a direct mail drop or offline advert. The website is used as the direct response mechanism, hence 'web response'. Ideally, this approach will use targeting of different segments. For example, a Netherlands bank devised a campaign targeting six different segments based on age and income. The initial letter was delivered by post and contained a PIN (personal identification number) which had to be typed in when the customer visited the site. The PIN had the dual benefit that it could be used to track responses to the campaign, while at the same time personalising the message to the consumer. When the PIN was typed in, a 'personal page' was delivered for the customer with an offer that was appropriate to their particular circumstances.

Step 2. Campaign insight

Research into the marketplace context of a campaign is core to a planned approach. When a company is working with an agency, the marketer at the client company will incorporate initial campaign insight into a brief. This will give agency staff valuable information about the audience and marketplace for a proposition. The agency may then access more detailed insight during the campaign.

Fill (2007) describes this stage of communications planning as context analysis. He identifies these aspects of context which should be researched:

- *Customer context* including dimensions of segment characteristics; levels of awareness, perception and attitudes towards the brand or organisation; level of involvement; types of perceived risk and influence of different members of the decision-making unit.
- *Business context* including corporate and marketing strategy and plans; brand/organisation analysis and competitor analysis.
- *Internal context* including financial constraints; organisation identity; culture, value and beliefs; marketing expertise; agency availability and suitability.
- *External context* including key stakeholders; communications and needs; social, political, economic, legal and technological restraints and opportunities.

So, the context analysis references all existing plans such as business and marketing plans, internal and external information sources. Information from these will be collated and put into a campaign brief.

More detailed campaign insight will be accessed and analysed once the agency or internal team are working on the campaign. Large agencies use 'data planners' or 'customer communications planners' to review all available external data sources such as market, audience and internal data on customer profiles, past campaign results on the most effective channels in generating product sales to assist clients in strategic development and execution of campaigns. This data is then used to inform campaign targeting and media selection.

For example, a brief might specify that an FMCG client wants to run an online promotional campaign, with the goal of stimulating trial of products and adding to a prospect database through encouraging online registration. The campaign strategy or offer is based around offering daily prizes. The data planner involved uses all transactional data collected from previous similar campaigns campaign to be linked to socio-demographic data which is coupled with transactional information.

Customer insight for digital marketing campaigns

There is a wealth of customer insight information available for digital marketing campaigns, but it varies by sector. So it is important during the briefing or pre-planning stage to list all the possible information sources and then evaluate which are worthwhile, since some are free and some are paid syndicated research. We have introduced some of the techniques in Chapter 2, such as persona and customer scenario analysis, and also some of the information sources (see Table 2.2, Research tools for assessing digital markets, page 62).

Examples of the types of customer insight related to online competitor and audience behaviour that might be accessed at this stage in the campaign from third-party syndicated research sources include:

- *Site audience reach and composition.* What is the breakdown of audiences by age, gender or socio-economic group on different sites? This data is available from online audience panel providers such as Nielsen Netrating, Comscore and Hitwise.
- *Online buying behaviour and preferences.* For example, from the Forrester Internet User Monitor or the BMRB Internet Monitor or TGI.net. In the UK, TGI.net gives information on typical product preferences for a particular site – for example, the percentage of the audience whose last holiday was a city break. Additional surveys can be conducted via publisher sites.
- *Customer media consumption.* The usage of different offline and online media for different target demographics can be accessed from sources such as Hitwise.
- *Customer search behaviour.* The proportion of different phrases and their importance can be used to inform messaging.
- *Competitor campaign activity.* The activity of current advertising campaigns and previous seasonal campaigns. For example, in the UK, this is available from Thomson Intermedia.

- *Competitor performance.* This will give information on the audience size (reach) and composition of competitor sites and services like Hitwise can show which marketing techniques such as search engine marketing or affiliate marketing are successful in driving visitors to a competitor since referring sites and search terms can be accessed.

Wertime and Fenwick (2008) suggest a similar technique to persona development for campaigns which they describe as a 'participant print'. The main elements of the participant print are:

- *General profile.* This is basic demographic and psychographic information about customers. It may also include insight from previous online campaigns and activities such as search keywords and propensity to respond for different demographic groups (response rates).
- *Digital profile.*
  - *Digital usage habits.* The authors say this includes the usage of different digital media channels, types of sites used and digital platforms they use.
  - *Content consumption preferences.* This includes favoured sources of information related to the product category from portals specific to the product, comparison sites and specialist blogs.
  - *Content creation profile.* This reviews the propensity of the group to participate online. For example, in contests where they upload photos or ringtones, blogs or forums they comment on including neutral sites and competitor sites.
- *Individual profiles.* This is information about existing prospects and customers including profile information from customer databases, content preferences from web analytics and qualitative research with customers about their needs, wants and how they prefer to use digital channels.

An example of the type of indepth research available is the IPA Touchpoints survey which covers both surveyed usage of websites and other media, and opinions including why they use particular media. Hussein (2006) describes the purpose of this – he says the aim is to enable campaign planners to identify relevant target markets (demographic groups, attitudinal groups, activity groups, and so on) and fully understand them in terms of:

- how they spend their day (shopping, work, travelling)
- who they spend it with (friends, family, work colleagues)
- what they believe in (views and opinions on life, brands, media, advertising)
- what is important to them (time spent on activities, family values)
- how, when, where and why they consume particular media.

Further information on marketplace analysis, including links to the main data sources for digital campaign insights, are provided in Table 2.3.

Step 3. Segmentation and targeting

Campaign targeting strategy defines the target audience or type of people which you need to reach with your campaign communications. It's about defining, selecting and reaching specific audiences online. Targeting methods vary according to the market, campaign and e-communications tools involved. The key targeting issues to define for the online elements of a campaign are:

- quality of insight about customer or prospect available to assist with targeting
- range of variables or parameters used to target – e.g. audience characteristics, value, needs and behaviours
- identifying the targeting attributes or variables which will influence response
- specific targeting approaches available for the key e-communications tools – e.g. online advertising, search engine marketing and e-mail marketing.

Table 8.3 A range of targeting and segmentation approaches for a digital campaign

Targeting variable	Examples of online targeting attributes
1 Relationship with company	New contacts (prospects), existing customers, lapsed customers
2 Demographic segmentation	B2C: Age, gender, social group, geographic location B2B: Company size, industry served, individual members of decision-making unit
3 Psychographic or attitudinal segmentation	Attitudes to risk and value when buying, e.g. early adopter, brand loyal or price conscious
4 Value	Assessment of current or historical value and future value
5 Lifecycle stage	Position in lifecycle, related to value and behaviour, i.e. time since initial registration, number of products purchased, categories purchased in
6 Behaviour	Search term entered into search engine Responsiveness to different types of offers (promotion or product type) Responsiveness to campaigns in different channels (channel preference) Purchase history in product categories including recency, frequency and monetary value (Chapter 6)

The targeting approaches used for acquisition and retention campaigns will naturally depend on established segmentations and knowledge about customers. We have also discussed targeting approaches from a strategic basis in Chapters 4 and 6. From a campaign point of view, Table 8.3 shows some of the main targeting variables which can be reviewed in digital campaign planning.

Let's look at each targeting variable in a little more depth.

1 *Relationship with company.* Campaigns will often be intended to target new contacts *or* existing contacts. But remember, some communications – such as e-newsletters and e-mail campaigns – will reach both. Marketers have to consider whether it will be cost-effective to have separate communications for new, existing and lapsed contacts – or to target each of these groups in the same communications but using different content aimed at each.

   When visitors click through to your website from online and offline campaigns, copy should be presented that recognises the relationship or, again, provide a range of content to recognise each different relationship. Visit Microstrategy (**www.microstrategy.com**) to see how its registration page establishes the relationship.

2 *Demographic segmentation.* This is typically based on age, gender or social group. Online demographics are often used as the basis for which sites to purchase display advertising or for renting e-mail lists. Demographics can also be used to limit or focus who pay-per-click search ads are displayed to.

3 *Psychographic or attitudinal segmentation.* This includes attitudes to risk and value when buying, e.g. early adopter, brand loyal or price conscious. It is less straightforward to target on these attributes of a consumer since it is easier to buy media based on demographic breakdown. However, certain sites may be more suitable for reaching a particular psycho-

graphic audience. The psychographic characteristics of the audience are still an important part of the brief, to help develop particular messages. It is possible to collect attitudinal information on a site and add it to the customer profile. For example, Wells Fargo asks investors to select:

- the type of investment preferred (individual stocks or mutual funds); and
- what type of investor best describes you? (aggressive growth to more cautious).

4 *Value.* The higher value customers (indicated by higher average order value and higher modelled customer lifetime values) will often warrant separate communications with different offers. Sometimes digital channels are not the best approach for these customers – relationship managers will want direct contact with their most valuable customers; while digital channels are used to communicate more cost-effectively with lower value customers. It is also worth considering reducing the frequency of e-mails to this audience.

5 *Lifecycle stage.* This is very useful where customers follow a particular sequence in buying or using a service, such as online grocery shopping or online banking. As explained in Chapter 6, automated, event-triggered e-mail marketing can be developed for this audience. For example, bank First Direct uses a six-month welcome strategy based on e-mail and direct mail communications. For other campaigns, the status of a customer can be used for targeting – for example not-purchased or used service, purchased once, purchased more than five times and active, purchased more than five times and inactive, etc.

6 *Behavioural.* Behavourial targeting is one of the big opportunities provided by digital marketing. It involves assessing customers' past actions in following links, reading content, using online services or buying products, and then follows up on these with a more relevant message based on the propensity to act based on the previous action.

Online options for behavioural targeting can be illustrated by a travel company such as lastminute.com:

- *Pay-per-click search engine marketing* makes targeting possible according to the type of keyphrase typed when a potential customer searches for information. A relevant ad specific to a holiday destination the prospect is looking for 'e.g. Hotel New York' can then be shown.
- *Display advertising* makes behavioural targeting possible since cookies can be used to track visitors across a site or between sites and display relevant ads. If a site user visits the travel section of a newspaper site, then the ad about 'lastminute' can be served as they visit other content on this site, or potentially on other sites.
- *E-mail marketing* can be targeted based on customer preferences indicated by links they have clicked on. For example, if a user has clicked a link on a holiday in North America, then a targeted e-mail can be delivered relevant to this product or promotion. More sophisticated analysis based on RFM analysis (Chapter 6) can also be used.

When reviewing the options for which variables to use to target, the campaign planner must keep in mind that those selected for targeting should be those which are most likely to influence the level of response for the campaign. It is possible to target on may variables, but the incremental benefit of targeting on additional variables may not be worth the cost and effort. Figure 6.9 (page 334) indicates the general improvement in campaign response dependent on the type of targeting variables used. This approach is used by travel company Travelocity in their e-mail marketing. Speaking at the 2006 Internet Retailing Forum they described how they concentrate their efforts on behaviour suggesting purchase intent, i.e. when a visitor to their site clicks on a particular type of holiday, e-mails sent to the customer should be updated to reflect that.

Step 4. Offer, message development and creative

Many digital campaigns have direct response as the primary objective. Defining the right offer is vital to achieving these response objectives. But there are also likely to be brand objectives, to communicate the 'big idea' or concept behind the campaign or to position the brand.

In an online environment, there is very little time for the message to be delivered. Eyetracking studies suggest average gaze or dwell times for a whole page may be around ten seconds as suggested by Table 8.4, but individual fixation times on page elements such as page headlines or ads are much lower, so it is important the message is succinct and powerful.

Table 8.4 Variation in fixation time for different websites

Web page name	Visual complexity level	Average gaze time (seconds)	First fixation	Longest fixation	Scanpath shape
BBC UK	Complex	10.3	Upcoming show picture	Upcoming show picture	U, Z
Computer Science Manchester	Complex	10.1	Wide graphic/ picture	Wide graphic/ picture	Z
Gene Ontology	Complex	12.5	Title	Title C, I	
IMG Group	Complex	11.4	Horizontal menu	Right menu	Z, U
Vodafone UK	Complex	11.3	Flashing image	Flashing image	*
Google Results	Simple	9.3	Results	Logo, search keyword	Z, U
John Rylands Library Catalogue	Simple	6.0	Horizontal menu	Search source	Z
MINT Group	Simple	9.1	Logo	Logo	U
Peve Group	Simple	8.9	Centre graphic	Centre graphic	Z, I

Source: Harper (2006)

So given the limit page dwell times and fixations, a clear primary message is needed in the different forms of digital media where it is delivered:

- *Paid search* – within the headline of the ad.
- *Natural search* – within the <title> tag and meta description tag (see Chapter 9).
- *E-mail marketing* – within the subject line and the headline or title of the e-mail supported by images.
- *Display ads* – within the opening frame and possibly repeated in all frames.

The primary message should deliver relevance according to the context, so within paid search the primary message should be consistent with the search term entered by the user and should highlight the value proposition clearly. To successfully communicate our offer and message, we also need to ensure that the creative and copy helps achieve the five stages of information processing shown in Table 7.3 i.e. Exposure, Attention, Comprehension and Perception, Yielding and Acceptance, and Retention (page 407). Similarly, we also need to deliver a response as shown by well-known AIDA mnemonic which stands for:

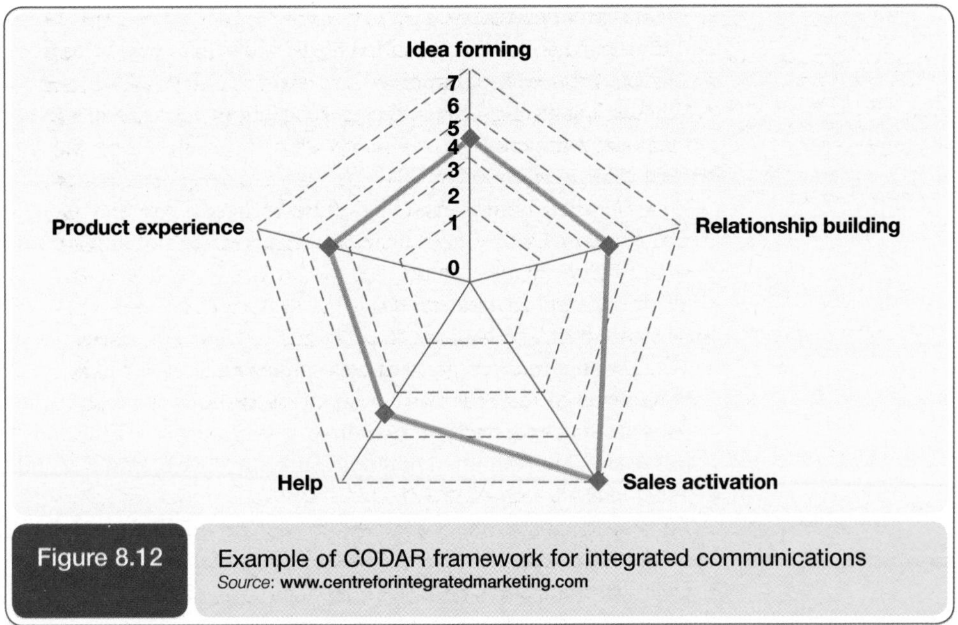

Figure 8.12 Example of CODAR framework for integrated communications
Source: **www.centreforintegratedmarketing.com**

- **A** wareness / **Attention**
- **I** nterest
- **D** esire
- **A** ction.

Having captured attention and developed interest with a primary offer and message, the creative needs to stimulate desire and action with the secondary offer and message, which:

- reassures prospects by giving a little more evidence of the offer or product benefits
- convinces the sceptic and encourages them to click
- can appeal to different types of person to the primary offer
- again, should have a clear call-to-action.

Jenkinson (2003) proposes that every marketing communication should contain a blend of five elements related to customer experience, with the significance or intensity of each element varying. He believes that this is useful for briefing the communication requirements from different communications media. The elements of this 'CODAR' framework are illustrated by the example in Figure 8.12.

- *Idea forming.* Generating ideas in the consumer's or client's mind, such as the brand promise, a value proposition or brand values.
- *Relationship building.* Building a relationship including affinity, emotional bonding, brand know-how or expertise, and database and/or personal knowledge about the customer.
- *Sales activation.* Stimulating the customer towards further investigation, trial or purchase.
- *Help.* Providing service and assistance to the customer relevant to their needs and wants – from informing the customer about availability of new technology/product to consultancy in the purchase process, in use status reporting, or resolution of a post purchase problem.
- *Product experience.* Using and interacting with the brand's deliverables, including store and website design, product availability, information such as a bank statement, value or pleasure in use.

Many lessons from direct marketing can be applied to digital communications. In his book, *Commonsense Direct Marketing*, Drayton Bird (2000) identified 'twenty-five pointers before you write a word or sketch a layout'. Here are the most relevant ones to be considered when developing online creative work:

- *What is the objective?*
  Gather names? Produce qualified leads? Make firm sales? Get free trials?
- *Are you clear on the positioning?*
  What will your message tell the prospect about your product or service? Does it fit in with the positioning?
- *Who are you selling to?*
  What are their hopes, fears, likes, dislikes, needs? Are they male or female? Young or old, rich or poor? Until you know these facts, you will not know what tone to adopt, let alone what to say.
- *What is it? And what does it do?*
  Obvious, but...
- *What need in your prospect does your product or service fulfil?*
  How many of the nine basic human motivations are relevant to potential customers of your product or service: make money, save money, save time and effort, help their families, feel secure, impress others, gain pleasure, improve themselves and belong to a group?
- *What makes it so special?*
  Interrogate your product or service. How does it differ from the alternatives? These are its features.
- *What benefits are you offering?*
  What it does rather than what it is.
- *What do you consider the most important benefit to be?*
  Ideally a unique benefit, but certainly the most appealing combination of benefits.

Perceptual mapping is a useful tool to review positioning and differentiation within the marketplace. It summarises how customers see a company's brand in relation to others in the marketplace. In perceptual mapping, two axes define fundamental characteristics of how people see products, services or brands. A classic method is to include a more rational dimension like price against a more emotional dimension such as making you feel safe.

Step 5. Budgeting and selecting the digital media mix

Traditional approaches such as those suggested by Kotler *et al.* (2001) can be used to set overall communications budgets. For example:

- *Affordable method* – the communications budget is set after subtracting fixed and variable costs from anticipated revenues.
- *Percentage-of-sales methods* – the communications budget is set as a percentage of forecast sales revenues.
- *Competitive parity methods* – expenditure is based on estimates of competitor expenditure. For example, e-marketing spend is typically 10–15 per cent of the marketing budget.
- *Objective and task method* – this is a logical approach where budget is built up from all the tasks required to achieve the objectives in the communications plan. This is a bottom-up approach that is often based on a model of the effectiveness of different digital media channels based on the measures of campaign effectiveness described in the objective setting section at the start of this chapter. Complete Activity 8.1 below to understand how these models are created.

Digital marketing campaign plans require three important decisions to be made about investment for the online promotion or the online communications mix. These are:

1. Level of investment in digital media as opposed to traditional media.
2. Mix of investment in digital media channels or e-communications tools.
3. Level of investment in digital assets.

1 Level of investment in digital media techniques in comparison to offline promotion

A balance must be struck between online and offline communications techniques based on the strengths and weaknesses of the different media options. A useful framework for considering the media characteristics which influence decisions on which to invest in has been developed by Coulter and Starkis (2005). Offline media are often superior in generating attention, stimulating attention and gaining credibility. Online media tend to be better at engagement due to personalisation, interaction and support of word-of-mouth. The offer can also often be fulfilled online for products that can be bought online. However, there are limits to the number of people that can be reached through online media (a limit to number searching on particular terms) and the cost is not necessarily always lower in competitive markets as shown in Mini Case Study 8.3.

Activity 8.1 A framework for selecting media

Coulter and Starkis (2005) identify these factors for media selection. We have added comments.

Quality

1 *Attention-getting capability (Attention)* – ability of an ad placed in this specific media to 'grab the customer's attention' due to the nature of that media.
2 *Stimulating emotions (Stimulation)* – ability of an ad placed in this specific media to convey emotional content and/or elicit emotional responses.
3 *Information content and detail (Content)* – ability of an ad placed in this specific media to convey a large amount of information and/or product description.
4 *Credibility/prestige/image (Credibility)* – ability of a specific media to lend prestige to a product through association (i.e. because that product is advertised within the media).
5 *Clutter* – degree to which it is difficult for a product advertised within a specific media to 'stand out' due to the large number of competitive offerings/messages.

[*Comment*: We would stress the capability of the media to generate a response, which is dependent on the combination of factors mentioned here that relate to brand awareness and influence. For online media, certain media such as pay-per-click search marketing tends to be more responsive than media buys of ads on portals since there is less clutter and the relevance is higher since the web user is searching.]

Time

1 *Short lead time* – degree to which an ad can be created and/or placed within a specific media in a relatively short period of time.
2 *Long exposure time* – degree to which the communication recipient is able to examine the advertising message within a specific media for an extended period of time.

[*Comment*: The ability to dynamically alter an ad during a campaign to select the best performing creative for each placement is particularly important online – for example optimising different creative executions of a display ad or a Google AdWords ad.]

Flexibility

1 *Appeal to multiple senses (Appeal)* – degree to which an ad placed within this specific media can communicate via sight, sound, taste, touch, and/or smell concurrently.
2 *Personalisation* – degree to which an advertising message placed within this specific media can be customised in order to target a specific individual or group of individuals.

3 *Interactivity* – degree to which the customer can respond to information conveyed in an advertisement placed within this specific media.

Coverage

1 *Selectivity* – degree to which an ad placed within this specific media is able to target a specific group of people.
2 *Pass-along audience (Pass-along)* – degree to which an ad placed within this specific media is seen by those other than the original message recipient.

[*Comment*: This is the viral marketing effect.]

3 *Frequency/repeat exposure (Frequency)* – degree to which any single ad placed within this specific media may be seen by any one particular individual on more than one occasion.

[*Comment*: Online this capability is available through behavioural targeting of display ads where cookies can be used to serve ads to the same person and develop the message with each new exposure if appropriate.]

4 *Average media reach (Reach)* – degree to which an ad placed within this specific media reaches a relatively wide audience.

Cost

1 *Development/production cost (Development cost)* – relative cost of developing or producing an ad for this specific media.
2 *Average media delivery cost (Delivery cost)* – average cost-per-thousand associated with this specific media.

[*Comment*: We should also add cost-per-response which is dependent on the click-through rate for each media and placement.]

The relative importance of these characteristics and the investment in different digital media will be dependent on the product and the type of campaign – whether it is direct-response-oriented or brand-oriented – and the scale of budget.

Figure 8.13 outlines typical options that companies have during a campaign, quarterly or annually. Which do you think would be the best option for an established company as compared to a dot-com 'pureplay' company? It seems that in both cases, offline promotion investment often exceeds that for online promotion investment. However, some pureplays do invest the majority of their budget in paid search and affiliate marketing, although they are likely to

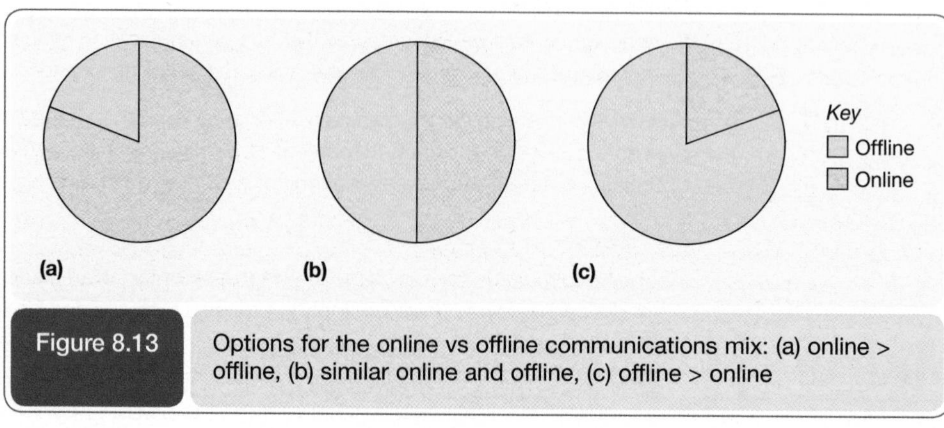

Figure 8.13 Options for the online vs offline communications mix: (a) online > offline, (b) similar online and offline, (c) offline > online

find there are limits to growth that this will impose. There are also increases to buying digital media suggested by Mini Case Study 8.3 which need to be considered. For existing companies, traditional media such as print are used to advertise the sites, while print and TV will also be widely used by dot-com companies to drive traffic to their sites.

Econometric modelling
A quantitative technique to evaluate the past influence or predict the future influence on a dependent variable (typically sales in a marketing context) of independent variables which may include product price, promotions and the level and mix of media investments.

Econometric modelling

Econometrics or **econometric modelling** is an established approach to understanding the contribution of different media in influencing consumers and ultimately generating sales and profit. It can also be used in a predictive way to plan for future campaigns. It is increasingly used in integrated campaigns to assess the appropriate media mix (see Cook (2004) for further explanation).

One of its main benefits is its ability to separate the effects of a range of influences such as offline or online media usage or other variables such as price, promotions used and to quantify these individual effects. A simple example might be for the sales of a drinks brand:

Mini Case Study 8.3 E-retailers cut-back on their digital communications spend.

Technology e-retailer dabs.com has traditionally used the following as their main communications tools:

- search engine marketing (the main investment)
- referrals from affiliates (this has been reduced)
- online display advertising on third party sites (limited)
- PR.

Jonathan Wall, Dabs marketing director, explains how dabs.com reappraised their use of e-communications tools. He said:

> *We stopped all our affiliate and price-comparison marketing in February because we wanted to see what effect it had on our business and if we were getting value for money. It was proving a very expensive channel for us and we've found [stopping] it has had virtually no effect, because we're seeing that people will still go to Kelkoo to check prices and then come to our site anyway. It's like they're having a look around first and then coming to a brand they know they can trust. We're continuing with paid-for search on Google, but that's all we're doing with online marketing at the moment.*

NMA (2005) also reported that Empire Direct had adopted a similar approach to its communication mix reporting that its co-founder and sales and marketing director Manohar Showan had revealed that the company has significantly moved from online to offline advertising. He said:

> *We've moved a lot more into national papers and specialist magazines – two years ago, if you'd asked me where we marketed and advertised ourselves, I would have said the majority was online. But now it's turned right round and online's the minority.*

NMA (2005) believes that the reason for this is not a mistrust of the very medium it's using to take sales but, instead, the result of a growing realisation that its acquisition costs were swelling online. Showan says:

> *We were very keen advocates of affiliate marketing and pay-per-click search. The trouble was we had to pay for every click and we were finding that the cost of acquiring each new customer was getting more and more. One big issue was that we were finding people would come to us through affiliates just to check information on a product they'd already bought, so we were basically paying for customers to find out how to hook up their new VCR. We still have affiliates – our main one is Kelkoo – and we still bid for clicks on Google, but not as much as we used to. One of the things we were finding with the search engines is that, with our own search optimisation and because so many people were coming to our site, we were normally very high up the list just through normal searching. In our experience, particularly with Google, if people can see what they want in the main list, they don't look to the right-hand side of the page.*

Sales = 100 +
+ 2.5 × own TVRs (television ratings)
– 1.4 × own price
+ 1.6 × competitor price
+ 1.0 × distribution
– 0.8 × temperature
– 1.2 × competitor TVRs

These relationships are typically identified using multiple linear regression models where a single dependent variable (typically sales) is a function of one or more explanatory or independent variables such as price, temperature, level of promotion.

Econometric models are developed from historic time-series data which record fluctuations dependent on different variables including seasonal variables, but most importantly, variations in media spend levels and the mix of media. In econometrics, sales fluctuations are expressed in terms of the factors causing them.

Digital marketing insight 8.2 Econometrics applications according to the Institute of Practitioners in Advertising

1 *Overall communication effectiveness (payback)*. This is the aggregate response of consumers to an advertising campaign over the entire period of its influence. Effects can often be reported by individual media. Sometimes it is also possible to quantify secondary effects where advertising increases (say) distribution, that in turn generates additional sales.
2 *Comparative campaign effects*. Econometric modelling can help to determine which campaign is the most potent influence on sales or other key measures.
3 *Efficiency*. Efficiency covers a diversity of issues:

- How big a budget is needed to:
  - reach sales targets
  - maintain adstock levels.
- How advertising should be flighted:
  - press vs television vs other media
  - burst vs drip
  - by time of year (media cost and relative effectiveness may be issues)
  - relative to previous activity (recency).
- What are the most effective coverage or frequency levels?
- Are particular weights of advertising more effective per unit of advertising – i.e. at what point does diminishing returns set in? The issue of diminishing marginal returns to scale with respect to advertising weight is one of the aspects of efficiency most often raised. It can imply ratings becoming less effective per additional rating point. It could refer to costs or responses that differ by region or time of year. All imply a resource allocation issue where econometrics can be helpful.

4 *Cross-brand effects: portfolio, umbrella and halo*. In some markets operators have a portfolio of products that may even be direct competitors – for example brewing or financial products. Advertising one of these could positively or adversely affect others. Thorough evaluation of advertising should investigate both the effects on the advertised brand and its stablemates.

5 *Competitive effects*. Competitive effects can be measured:

- on your own brand;
- on the competitor by modelling their sales (also showing your brand's effects on them).

Once the relative effects of own and competitive media activity are understood it becomes possible to calculate the budget levels required to offset competitive actions.

Source: Summarised from IPA (2004) *Econometrics Explained* by Louise Cook and Mike Holmes, edited by Les Binet

2 Selecting the right mix of digital media communications tools

When selecting the mix of digital media for a campaign or longer-term investments, marketers will determine the most appropriate mix based on their knowledge built up through experience of previous campaigns and taking input from their advisers such as experienced colleagues or agency partners.

Varianini and Vaturi (2000) have suggested that many online marketing failures have resulted from poor control of media spending. The communications mix should be optimised to minimise the cost of acquisition. If an online intermediary has a cost acquisition of £100 per customer while it is gaining an average commission on each sale of £5 then, clearly, the company will not be profitable unless it can achieve a large number of repeat orders from the customer.

Agrawal *et al.* (2001) suggest that e-commerce sites should focus on narrow segments that have demonstrated their attraction to a business model. They believe that promotion techniques such as affiliate deals with narrowly targeted sites and e-mail campaigns targeted at segments grouped by purchase histories and demographic traits are 10 to 15 times more likely than banner ads on generic portals to attract prospects who click through to purchase. Alternatively, pay-per-click ads on Google may have a higher success rate.

When this experience isn't there, which is often the case with new digital media opportunities, it is important to do a more structured evaluation including factors such as the ability of each medium to influence perceptions, drive a response, the cost of response and the quality of response – are respondents more likely to convert to the ultimate action such as sale? What is their likely lifetime value? For example some digital media channels such as affiliates are more likely to attract customers with a lower lifetime value who are more likely to switch suppliers.

Media planning and buying agency Zed Media have produced a useful summary of how a media mix might typically vary according to budget (see Figure 8.14).

The figure shows that for a direct response campaign with limited budget, investment in controllable, targeted media which typically have a lower cost-per-acquisition such as affiliates and paid search should be the main focus. If more budget is available, it may not be possible to buy further keywords or there may be benefits from generating awareness of the offering through more display advertising.

With a brand campaign where the focus is on generating awareness, the recommendations of Zed Media are reversed where they recommend that, even at lower budgets, more investment should be made in display advertising.

Deciding on the optimal expenditure on different communication techniques will be an iterative approach since past results should be analysed and adjusted accordingly. Marketers can analyse the proportion of the promotional budget that is spent on different channels and then compare this with the contribution from purchasing customers who originated using the original channel. This type of analysis, reported by Hoffman and Novak (2000) and shown in Table 8.5, requires two different types of marketing research. First, **tagging** of customers can be used. Here, we monitor, using specifically coded URLs or cookies, the numbers of customers who are referred to a website through different online techniques such as search engines, affiliate or banner ads, and then track the money they spend on purchases.

Tagging
Tracking of origin of customers and their spending patterns.

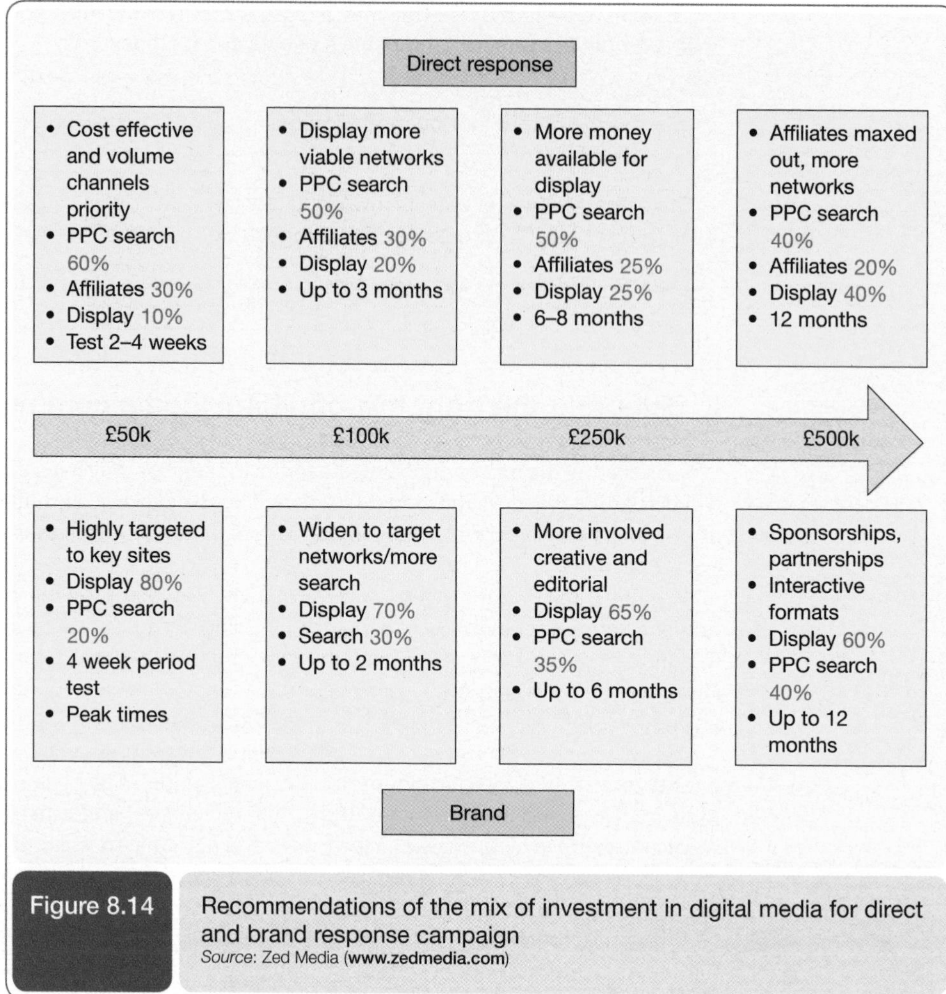

Figure 8.14 Recommendations of the mix of investment in digital media for direct and brand response campaign
Source: Zed Media (**www.zedmedia.com**)

Table 8.5 Relative effectiveness of different forms of marketing communications for a B2C company

Medium	Budget %	Contribution %	Effectiveness
Print (off)	20%	10%	0.5
TV (off)	25%	10%	0.25
Radio (off)	10%	5%	0.5
PR (off)	5%	15%	3
Word of mouth (off)	0%	25%	Infinite
Banners (on)	20%	20%	1
Affiliate (on)	20%	10%	0.5
Links (on)	0%	3%	Infinite
Search engine registration (on)	0%	2%	Infinite

Here are two examples of tracking tags placed on the referring hyperlink within the HTML code (e.g. <a href= 'tracking tag URLshown below'>Text or image prompting the user to link</a>). Such a tracking tag can be placed within a pay-per-click ad campaign, or a banner on an affiliate or display ad site:

1 http://www.ingdirect.co.uk/xos/aboutoursavingsaccount.asp?ct=1&siteid=339931;&placementid=11847966;&creativeid=0&adid=20323252
2 http://www.firstdirect.com/saveinvest/esavings.shtml?fd_msc=CC085

You can see that both examples point to a particular savings landing page. The 'query string' after the question mark is used to specify information about the referrer. In item 1, this is explicit with the site, placement (position on site), creative treatment and ad number all apparent. In item 2, a marketing source code is used for which there will be a separate reference or lookup table which contains information on the referring ad.

Attributing influence on sales to digital media channel

Last-click method of digital media channel attribution
The site which referred a visitor immediately before purchase is credited with the sale. Previous referrals influenced by other customer touch points on other sites are ignored.

Digital media de-duplication
A single referrer of a visit leading to sale is credited with the sale based on the last-click method of digital media channel attribution.

Digital media 'assist'
A referrer of a visit to a site before the ultimate sale is credited with the sale, often through a weighting system.

It is seldom the case that a customer will go straight to a site and purchase, or that they will perform a single search and then purchase. Instead, they will commonly perform multiple searches and will be referred to the ultimate purchase site by different types of site. This consumer behaviour is indicated by Figure 8.15. This shows that someone looking to purchase a car may be referred to a site several times via different digital communications channels.

A common approach to attributing the influence of different online media a customer consumes before purchase has been the **Last-click method of digital media channel attribution** introduced well by Lee (2010). He explains that this can give a misleading picture of which marketing channels are effective. In an analysis of visitors to an airline site (Figure 8.16) he shows that although the overall patterns of referrers to the site at first appear similar, there are some major differences. If you refer to Figure 8.16 you can see that, e-mail marketing, SEO for non-brand terms and PPC for brand terms are more significant when looking at the contribution of all sources.

Referring to Figure 8.15, you can see this has the benefit that we don't credit multiple affiliates with sale for affiliate marketing – only Affiliate 2 is credited with the sale, a process known as **Digital media de-duplication**. But it has the disadvantage that it simplifies the reality of previous influence or **digital media 'assists'** and previous referrals influenced by other customer touch points on other sites are ignored, such as the natural search or display ad in Figure 8.15.

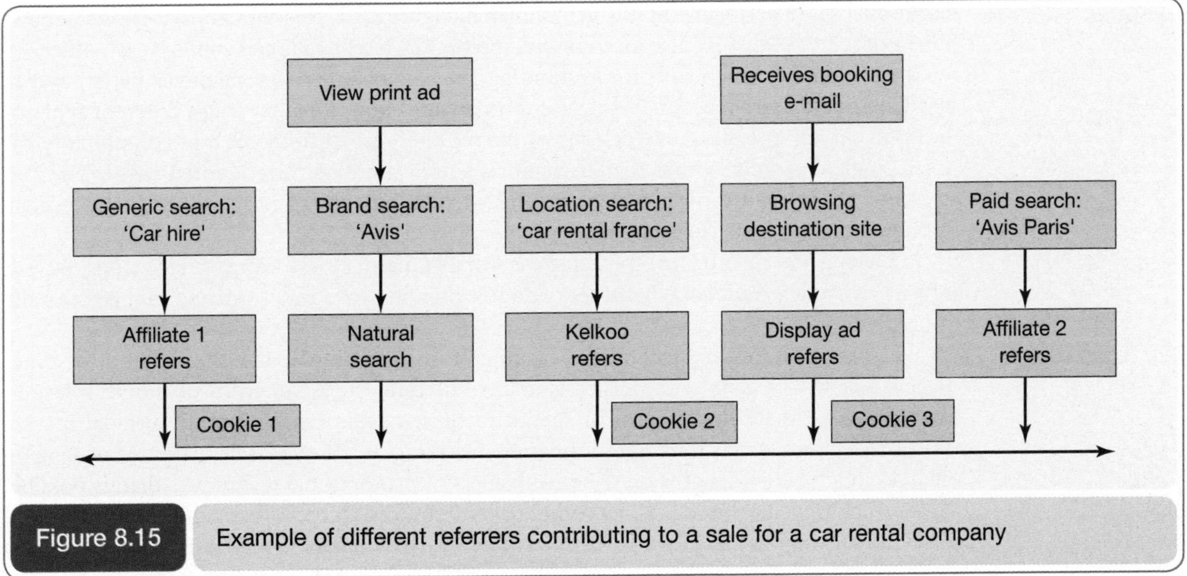

Figure 8.15 Example of different referrers contributing to a sale for a car rental company

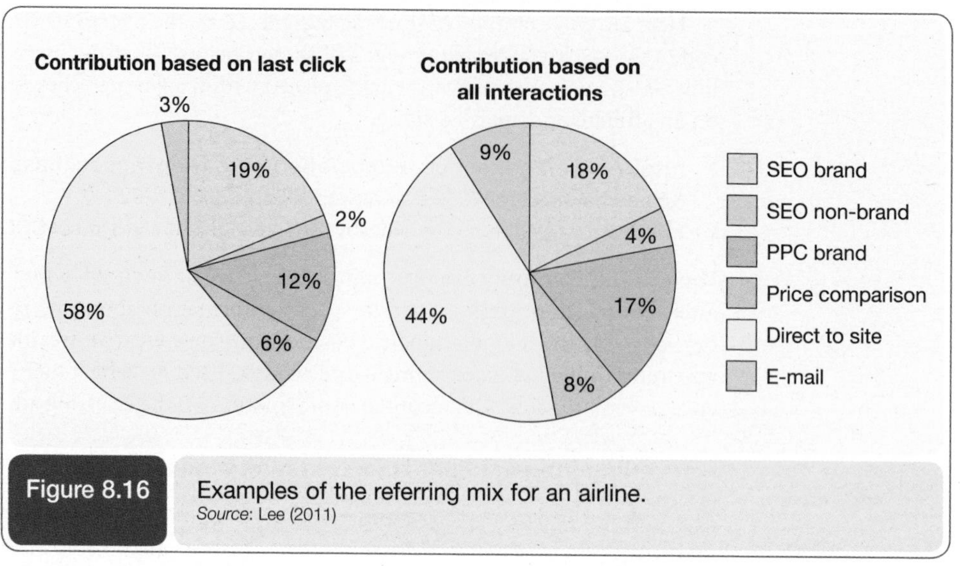

Figure 8.16 Examples of the referring mix for an airline.
Source: Lee (2011)

So, for the most accurate interpretation of the contribution of different media, the online marketer needs to use tagging and analysis tools to try to build the best picture of which channels are influencing sales and then weight the media accordingly. For example, a more sophisticated approach is to weight the responsibility for sale across several different referrers according to a model – so just considering the affiliates, Affiliate 1 might be credited with 30 per cent of the sales value and Affiliate 2 with 70 per cent for example. This approach is useful since it indicates the value of display advertising – a common phenomenon is the halo effect where display ads indirectly influence sales by creating awareness and stimulating sale at a later point in time. These are sometimes known as 'viewthrough' or post impression effects.

These allocation approaches won't be possible if agencies are using different tracking tools and reporting separately on different media channels – for example, the ad agency reports on display advertising, the search agency on pay-per-click, the affiliate manager on affiliate sales. Instead it is important to use a unified tracking system which typically uses common tags across all media channels. Common unified tracking solutions that consider all media are available from the likes of Atlas, Doubleclick Dart and some of the larger media agencies.

Further sophistication of tracking will be worthwhile for companies investing millions in digital media in order to understand the customer journey and the contribution of media. A useful analysis to perform is in the form shown in Figure 8.17. This anonymised example shows the importance of display ads, for example, and how different channels support each other.

It can then be worthwhile understanding the role of individual channels better, and in particular paid search. Marketers need to understand how consumers use different types of terms as shown in Table 8.6 which shows the repeated use of different types of search terms for a single customer (other digital channels such as affiliates are ignored here). The two columns on the right show how it is unrealistic to attribute the sale to the last search since the influence of the assists isn't shown.

Achieving and measuring repeat visits is worthwhile since according to Flores and Eltvedt (2005) on average, purchase intent sees a double digit increase after someone has been to a site more than once.

For some promotional techniques, tagging of links on third-party sites will not be practical. These will be grouped together as unattributed referrers. For word-of-mouth referrals, we have to estimate the amount of spend for these customers through traditional market research techniques such as questionnaires or asking at point of sale. The use of tagging enables much better insights on the effectiveness of promotional techniques than is possible in traditional media, but due to its complexity it requires a large investment in staff time and tracking software to achieve it. It is also very dependent on cookie deletion rates.

Channels	Sequence	% Conversions	Channel allocation
2	DS SD XS SX DX XD	34.01% 20.98% 8.35% 7.33% 2.24% 1.83%	74.75%
3	DDS SDS SXS DXD DXS XSX SDX	7.74% 5.30% 3.05% 1.02% 0.81% 0.41% 0.20%	18.53%
4	SDSD DSDS DXDX DSDX DSXD DXDS DXSD SDSX	1.63% 1.43% 0.41% 0.20% 0.20% 0.20% 0.20% 0.20%	4.48%
5	DSDSD SDSDS	1.02% 0.41%	1.43%
6	DSDSDS SDSDSD SDSDXS	0.20% 0.20% 0.20%	0.61%
7	DSDSDSD	0.20%	0.20%

Figure 8.17 Example of the sequence of visits to a site in generating conversions where two or more digital media channels were involved (Codes for channels: D = Display, S = Search, X = Aggregator)

Table 8.6 Example of weighted allocation of different searches

User id	Search query	Sale?	Value attributed: last click method	Value attributed: weighted method
123	Mobile phone (generic search)	No	£0	£40
123	Best camera phone (category generic search)	No	£0	£40
123	Nokia phone (product search)	No	£0	£40
123	Nokia N91 Orange (product + supplier search)	No	£0	£40
123	E-retailer brand name (branded search)	Yes	£200	£40

To see how a budget can be created for a digital campaign, complete Activity 8.2.

Activity 8.2 Creating a digital campaign budget

Purpose

To illustrate the type of budget created internally or by digital marketing agencies. Figure 8.18 shows an extract.

Activity

Download the spreadsheet from **www.smartinsights.com/conversion-model-spreadsheet** to understand how the different calculations relate to each other. Try changing the cost of media (blue cells) and different click-through rates (blue cells) for which typical values are shown for a competitive retail product. View the formulas to see how the calculations are made.

How would you make this model more accurate (i.e. how would you break down each digital media channel further?)

Input parameter table

Overall budget	£10,000
Average order value	£50
Gross profit margin	30.0%

Blue cells = input variables – vary these for 'what-if' analysis

Orange cells = output variables (calculated – do not overtype)

		Advertising		Search		Partners	
		Ad buys (CPM)	Ad network (CPM)	Paid search (CPC)	Natural search	Affiliates (CPA)	Aggregators
Media cost	Setup / creative / Mgt costs	£0	£0	£0	£0	£0	£0
	CPM	£10.0	£10.0	£4.0	£0.4	£10.0	£20.0
	CPC	£5.0	£5.0	£0.20	£0.20	£5.0	£10.0
	Media costs	£10,000	£10,000	£30,000	£10,000	£10,000	£10,000
	Total cost setup and media	£10,000	£10,000	£30,000	£10,000	£10,000	£10,000
	Budget %	10%	10%	30%	10%	10%	10%
Media impressions and response	Impressions or names	1,000,000	1,000,000	7,500,000	25,000,000	1,000,000	500,000
	CTR	0.2%	0.2%	2.0%	0.2%	0.2%	0.2%
	Clicks or site visits	2,000	2,000	150,000	50,000	2,000	1,000
Conversion to opportunity (lead)	Conversion rate to opportunity	100.0%	100.0%	100.0%	100.0%	100.0%	100.0%
	Number of opportunities	2,000	2,000	150,000	50,000	2,000	1,000
	Cost per opportunity	£5.0	£5.0	£0.2	£0.2	£5.0	£10.0
Conversion to sales	Conversion rate to sale	100.0%	100.0%	100.0%	100.0%	50.0%	100.0%
	Number of sales	2,000	2,000	150,000	50,000	1,000	1,000
	% of sales	1.0%	1.0%	72.7%	24.2%	0.5%	0.5%
	Cost per sale (CPA)	£5.0	£5.0	£0.2	£0.2	£10.0	£10.0
Revenue	Total revenue	£100,000	£100,000	£7,500,000	£2,500,000	£50,000	£50,000
Costs	Cost of goods sold	£70,000	£70,000	£5,250,000	£1,750,000	£35,000	£35,000
	Media costs	£10,000	£10,000	£30,000	£10,000	£10,000	£10,000
	Total costs (inc media)	£80,000	£80,000	£5,280,000	£1,760,000	£45,000	£45,000
Profitability	Profit	£20,000	£20,000	£2,220,000	£740,000	£5,000	£5,000
	Return on investment	25.0%	25.0%	42.0%	42.0%	11.1%	11.1%

Figure 8.18 Spreadsheet template for digital campaign budgeting
Source: **www.smartinsights.com/conversion-model-spreadsheet**

3 Level of investment in digital assets

Digital asset
The graphical and interactive material that supports a campaign displayed on third-party sites and on microsites. Includes display ads, e-mail templates, video, audio and other interactive media such as Flash animations.

The **digital assets** are the creative that support a campaign such as that shown in Mini Case Study 8.4, they include:

- display ad or affiliate marketing creative such as banners and skyscrapers
- microsites
- e-mail templates
- video, audio and other interactive media such as Flash animations, games or screensavers which form a microsite.

Mini Case Study 8.4 Lynx uses microsite to promote its 'Get More' campaign

In 2004 a new deodorant brand, Lynx Pulse, used online games, screensavers, viral e-mails, video clips and soundtracks, to extend the brand experience – from applying deodorant to interacting with the brand – for 1.4 million unique users.

A similar approach was repeated in 2008 using a similar range of digital assets in the 'Get In There' campaign which was part of a long-term 'Lynx Effect' brand concept supported at a campaign specific URL (**www.lynxeffect.com**, Figure 8.19). Rather than a short-term campaign, to maximise the impact the brief was to 'create a consistent long-term presence for the Lynx-Axe brand online'. Another difference from previous campaigns was the greater use of video and user generated content.

The reason for the campaign was highlighted by Karen Hamilton, regional VP of marketing, Lynx-Axe Europe explained the thinking behind the campaign to NMA (2008) when she said:

Figure 8.19 Lynx Effect campaign microsite (**www.lynxeffect.com**)

> *With our new campaign we feel we now have a digital presence that not only continues to give young guys the edge in the mating game but also provides us with an ongoing platform to deliver cutting-edge digital creativity. With Get In There, BBH came to us with a big idea that's rooted in the heart of our brand and understands the role of digital in our target audience's life. We have specifically created a large amount of exciting, diverse and tailored content that works across many different platforms.*

For the agency Jonathan Bottomley, planning director, BBH said:

> *Get In There is a rallying cry from the brand to get guys away from their computers, out of the chat rooms and to start meeting real girls rather than virtual girls.*
>
> *The idea had to break into the heart of guys' digital lives, so we created an extended network of linked content to sit on partner sites that guys visit all the time: YouTube, FHM, Flickr, Bebo. At the heart of the network is lynxeffect.com, which provides guys with tips, tools and widgets that they can use to approach girls. The idea is to give them an 'in', something to break the ice so that the fear of wondering what to say is reduced.*
>
> *There are killer weapons, such as the Lynx FX soundboard, which you can download to your mobile phone to turn it into a pulling machine. There are downloadable business cards, magic tricks and e-mail tools, all of which are refreshed regularly. For guys in need of inspiration, hidden camera footage showcases the exploits of the Lynx Guys, characters who are getting in there with the ladies, trying to show how its done.*

As with traditional media, there is a tension between spend on the advertising creative and the media space purchased to run the executions. There is a danger that if spend on media is too high, then the quality of the execution and the volume of digital assets produced will be too low.

Step 6. Integration into overall media schedule or plan

Integrated marketing communications
The coodination of communications channels to deliver a clear, consistent message to achieve marketing goals.

In common with other communications media, digital media are most effective when they are deployed as part of an **integrated marketing communications** approach. Kotler *et al.* (2001) describe integrated marketing communications as:

> the concept under which a company carefully integrates and coordinates its many communications channels to deliver a clear, consistent message about the organisation and its products.

The characteristics of integrated marketing communications have been summarised by Pickton and Broderick (2001) as the 4 Cs of:

- *Coherence* – different communications are logically connected.
- *Consistency* – multiple messages support and reinforce, and are not contradictory.
- *Continuity* – communications are connected and consistent through time.
- *Complementary* – synergistic, or the sum of the parts is greater than the whole!

The 4 Cs also act as guidelines for how communications should be integrated.

Further guidelines on integrated marketing communications from Pickton and Broderick (2001) that can be usefully applied to digital marketing are the following.

- Integrated communications planning is based on *clearly identified marketing communications objectives* (see later section).
- Digital marketing should involve *management of all forms of contact*, which includes management of both outbound communications, such as banner advertising or direct e-mail, and inbound communications such as e-mail enquiries.
- Internet marketing should utilise a *range of promotional tools*. These are the digital media channels illustrated in Figure 1.9 (page 28).

- *A range of media* should be used to communicate consistent messages about opportunities for customers to interact with a brand online. Marketing managers need to consider the most effective mix of online and offline media channels shown in Figure 1.9 to encourage interactions and drive traffic to their online presence.
- The communications plan should involve careful selection of the *most effective promotional and media mix*. This is discussed at the end of the chapter.

Additionally, we can say that integrated marketing communications should be used to support customers through the entire buying process, across different media.

Planning integrated marketing communications

The Account Planning Group (**www.apg.org.uk**), in its definition of media planning, highlights the importance of the role of media planning when they say that the planner:

> Needs to understand the customer and the brand to unearth a key **insight** for the communication/solution [Relevance].
>
> As media channels have mushroomed and communication channels have multiplied, it has become increasingly important for communication to cut through the cynicism and **connect** with its audience [Distinctiveness].
>
> ...the planner can provide the edge needed to ensure the solution reaches out through the clutter to its **intended audience** [Targeted reach].
>
> ...needs to **demonstrate** how and why the communication has performed [Effectiveness].

Media-neutral planning (MNP)

Media-neutral planning
An approach to planning ad campaigns to maximise response across different media according to consumer usage of these media.

The concept of **media-neutral planning (MNP)** has been used to describe an approach to planning integrated marketing campaigns including online elements. To read a review of the different interpretations see Tapp (2005) who notes that there are three different aspects of planning often encompassed with media-neutral planning:

- *Channel planning*, i.e. which route to market shall we take: retail, direct, sales partners etc. (we would say this emphasis is rare).
- *Communications-mix planning*, i.e. how do we split our budget between advertising, direct marketing, sales promotions and PR.
- *Media planning*, i.e. spending money on TV, press, direct mail and so on.

In our view, MNP is most usually applied to the second and third elements and the approach is based on reaching consumers across a range of media to maximise response. For example, Crawshaw (2004) says:

> The simple reason we would want media-neutral communications is so that we can connect the right message with our target audience, at the right time and place to persuade them to do what we want. This will lead to powerful, effective, value for money communications that solve clients' business challenges.

A customer-centric media-planning approach is key to this process. Anthony Clifton, Planning Director at WWAV Rapp Collins Media Group, is quoted by the Account Planning Group as saying (quoted in Crawshaw, 2004):

> Real consumer insight has to be positioned at the core of the integrated planning process and the planner must glean a complete understanding of the client's stakeholders, who they are, their mindset, media consumption patterns and relationship with the business – are they 'life-time' consumers or have they purchased once, are they high value or low value customers etc. This requires lifting the bonnet of the database, segmentation and market evaluation.

Digital marketing insight 8.3 Different forms of campaign integration

IPA (2011) report showed the popularity of alternative options for campaign inte-gration. The analysis of over 250 IPA Effectiveness Awards case studies, entered over a seven-year period (2004–2010) including examples from Hovis, O2, Virgin Atlantic, HSBC, E4 Skins, Johnnie Walker and more.

The report defines four options for integration:

1. *No integration* – single channel or campaigns using a number of channels but not integrating consistently across them. Analysis suggests that campaigns with no obvious integration or who use only one channel are good at reducing price sensitivity but have little impact on market share.
2. *Advertising-led integration* – channels unified around a common creative idea/ 'matching luggage' approach. Traditionally integrated advertising-led campaigns were reported to be more effective at share gain and customer acquisition.
3. *Brand idea-led 'orchestration'* – unified around a shared brand concept or need-state platform, often built around core brand values of the organisation. Analysis of campaigns suggests that brand idea-led campaigns are highly effective in retention, share defence and profit gain.
4. *Participation led 'orchestration'* – goal is to create a common dialogue or conversation, has emerged in latter years, partly driven by digital media. The analysis in the report suggests that participation-led campaigns underperform on hard sales measures but excel in rewarding existing users and on brand fame. Since they are relatively new, they are a small proportion of the total.

The research also found that multichannel campaigns are better at driving effectiveness than single channel activity: 78 per cent of cases with three channels demonstrate hard business effects versus 67 per cent of those with only one channel; there is however a point of diminishing returns beyond three channels. It's surprising this difference isn't larger, but multiple channels fare well when considering other measures.

Key activities in media selection and planning

The starting point for media planning, selection and implementation is to have clearly defined campaign objectives:

- For direct response campaigns, the most important are response volume, quality and cost.
- For campaigns where awareness and branding are the main outcomes, branding metrics become important.

Pickton and Broderick (2001) identify six activities in media implementation: target audience selection, media objectives, media selection, media scheduling, media buying and media evaluation.

A particularly important aspect for online media is that this evaluation and adjustment can – and should – occur during the campaign, in order to identify the best placements and creatives and to refine the ongoing media plan.

Learning from cross-media optimisation studies

Cross-media optimisation studies (XMOS)
Studies to determine the optimum spend across different media to produce the best results.

Many **cross-media optimisation studies (XMOS)** have shown that the optimal online spend for low-involvement products is surprisingly high at 10–15 per cent of total spend. Although this is not a large amount, it compares to previous spend levels below 1 per cent for many organisations.

Table 8.7 Optimum media mix suggested by XMOS studies

Brand	TV	Magazine	Online
Colgate	75%	14%	11%
Kleenex	70%	20%	10%
Dove	72%	13%	15%
McDonald's	71%	16% (radio)	13%

Source: Interactive Advertising Bureau (**www.iab.net/xmos**)

XMOS research is designed to help marketers and their agencies answer the (rather involved) question 'What is the optimal mix of advertising vehicles across different media, in terms of frequency, reach and budget allocation, for a given campaign to achieve its marketing goals?'

The mix between online and offline spend is varied to maximise campaign metrics such as reach, brand awareness and purchase intent. Table 8.7 summarises the optimal mix identified for four famous brands. For example, Dove (IAB, 2004) found that increasing the level of interactive advertising to 15 per cent would have resulted in an increase in overall branding metrics of 8 per cent. The proportion of online is small, but remember that many companies are spending less than 1 per cent of their ad budgets online, meaning that offline frequency is too high and they may not be reaching many consumers.

The reasons for using and increasing the significance of online in the media mix are similar to those for using any media mix as described by Sissors and Baron (2002):

- *Extend reach* – adding prospects not exposed by a single medium/other media.
- *Flatten frequency distribution* – if audiences viewing TV ads are exposed too many times, there is a law of diminishing returns and it might prove better to reallocate that budget to online media.
- *Reach different kinds of audiences.*
- *Provide unique advantages in stressing different benefits* – based on the different characteristics of each medium.
- *Allow different creative executions to be implemented.*
- *Add gross impressions if the other media is cost efficient.*
- *Reinforce messages by using different creative stimuli.*

Briggs *et al.* (2005) give the example of the launch of a new model of car. Their XMOS study provides these insights:

- Advertising works, but the price of some media has been bid up to make it inefficient compared to alternatives.
- TV generates the greatest level of absolute reach and produces high levels of purchase-consideration impact, but is less cost effective compared to magazine and online.
- Magazines and online category-related sites are similar in their impact, being very selective and efficiently delivering 'in-market' prospects.
- Electronic roadblocks are the most cost-efficient, and can produce significant daily reach (40 per cent or more); however, they are not as scalable as TV.
- While roadblocks delivered 40 per cent reach in a day, TV can deliver nearly twice the level in a single day.
- Due to changing media habits of consumers, Ford's campaign could be fine tuned to increase sales by 5 per cent without spending a dollar more.

For integrated communications to be successful, the different techniques should be successfully integrated through time as part of a campaign or campaigns.

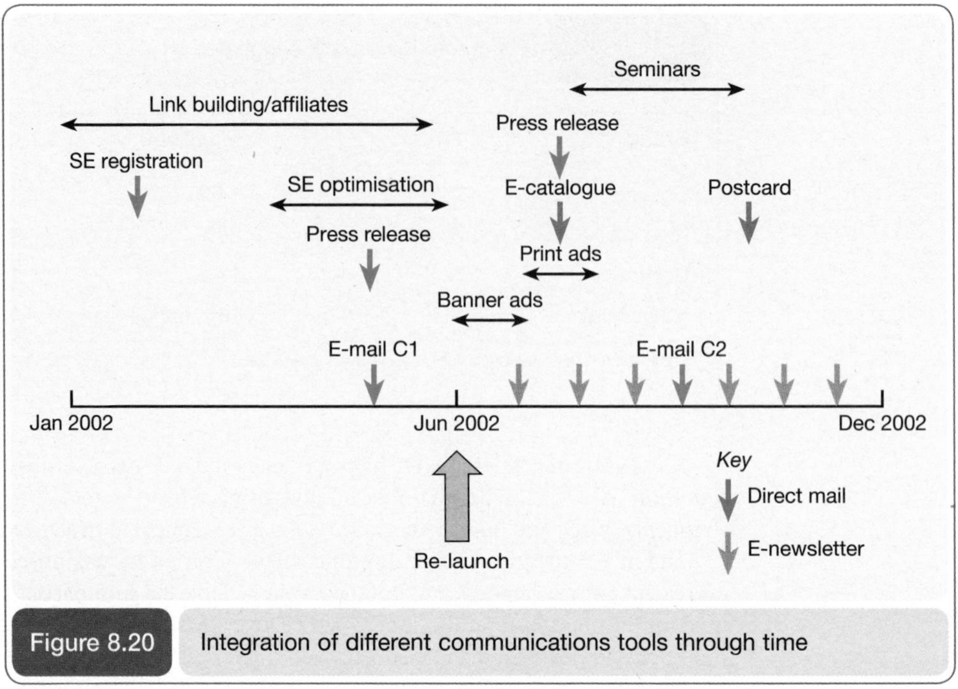

Figure 8.20 Integration of different communications tools through time

Figure 8.20 shows how communications can be planned around a particular event. (SE denotes 'search engine'; C1 and C2 are campaigns 1 and 2.) Here we have chosen the launch of a new version of a website, but other alternatives include a new product launch or a key seminar. This planning will help provide a continuous message to customers. It also ensures a maximum number of customers are reached using different media over the period.

In keeping with planning for other media, Pincott (2000) suggests there are two key strategies in planning integrated Internet marketing communications. First, there should be a media strategy which will mainly be determined by how to reach the target audience. This will define the online promotion techniques described in this chapter and where to advertise online. Second, there is the creative strategy. Pincott says that 'the dominant online marketing paradigm is one of direct response'. However, he goes on to suggest that all site promotion will also influence perceptions of the brand.

Finally, here are five questions about integration you must ask when creating a campaign:

1 *Consistent branding and messaging.* Is the branding and messaging sufficiently similar (coherent) throughout the campaign?
2 *Varying the offer, messaging and creative through the campaign.* Is offer and messaging varied sufficiently through the campaign? With each different medium and wave of the campaign, it can improve results to subtly vary the offer, message and creative. This might appear to conflict with the first guideline, but the two can be compatible, since:
   - different treatments and offers will appeal to different people and achieve different results
   - if each communication in a campaign is identical, then future campaign waves will be ignored
   - escalating or improving offers during a campaign can achieve better response.
3 *Frequency (number) and interval of communications.* Are you exposing the audience sufficiently or too much to your messages? This is a difficult balance to strike. In our view, some marketers often undercommunicate for fear of overcommunicating!

With online media buys, it's also important to think about frequency as well as reach. Increases in frequency will usually increase awareness as for any medium – though direct response will usually peak quite quickly before ebbing away.

If you have defined touch strategies that mandate a minimum or maximum number of communications within a period – and the interval between them – you should check that your plans fit in with these or that they do not constrain your campaign.

4 Sequencing of communications. You have the option to:

- launch your campaigns online first
- launch your campaigns offline first
- launch your campaigns simultaneously online and offline.

Here are some examples where your online and offline activities might not launch simultaneously:

- a campaign for an event promotion starts with a direct mail or an e-mail
- e-communications are reserved as contingency – in case offline response volumes are not high enough
- a promotion is launched online first (notified by e-mail) to appeal to loyal customers
- an unusual ad execution is launched online first to create a buzz
- a press release is announced first online so that it can be transmitted by particular advocates
- a timed or limited offer is launched online, because timing of receipt can be more accurately assured.

5 *Optimising timing.* Do communications get delivered and received at the optimal time? For online display advertising, PPC and e-mail marketing there are specific times of the day, days of the week or times of the month that your message will work best.

As a final example for this chapter, Mini Case Study 8.5 features many of the aspects of a great online campaign which take advantage of the online media. This campaign is:

- *Immersive* – uses rich media video clips and interactive maps to engage visitors.
- *Sustained* – runs over a period of two weeks to build campaign inertia and encourage ongoing engagement.
- *Participative* – visitors can feedback comments through the blog.
- *Integrated* – initial interest generated through print campaign and mailings to customer data.

Mini Case Study 8.5 The Tourism Ireland Taxi Challenge campaign

The Tourism Ireland Taxi Challenge is a great example of how an online campaign can involve people over a period of a few weeks to get people revisiting a site and interacting with a brand. Includes integration of a video microsite (Figure 8.21) combined with a forum. I would also like to see e-mail reminders pushed to people to get them to revisit and offer other promotions.

This campaign used the power and growth in popularity of broadband to create an experiential marketing campaign that showcased Ireland and allowed consumers to interact directly with the brand. It was based on a ten-day road trip around Ireland organised by the Irish Tourist board for the competition winners.

It is a great example of how an online campaign can involve people over a period of time. It includes user-generated content with a simple blog and a new video everyday. Daily content updates gave people a reason for revisiting the site. Users can view footage of the day's activities, leave comments, browse tourist information and download the trip itinerary.

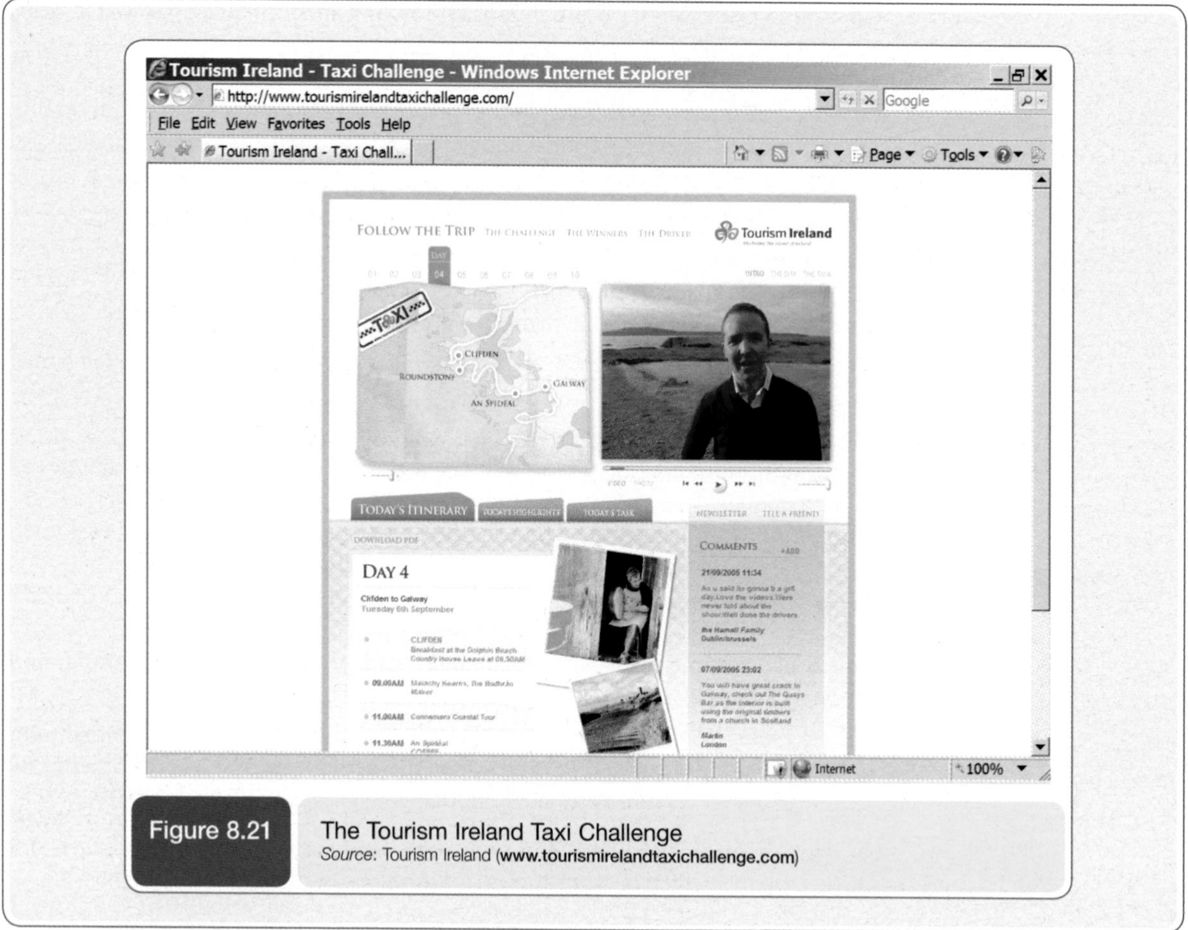

Figure 8.21 The Tourism Ireland Taxi Challenge
Source: Tourism Ireland (**www.tourismirelandtaxichallenge.com**)

Case Study 8 A short history of Facebook

Context

This case is about the social network FaceBook. According to its owners:

> *Facebook is a social utility that helps people communicate more efficiently with their friends, family and co-workers. The company develops technologies that facilitate the sharing of information through the social graph, the digital mapping of people's real-world social connections. Anyone can sign up for Facebook and interact with the people they know in a trusted environment.*

The case illustrates some of the challenges for an owner of a social network managing growth and seeking to avoid a decline in usage. It also highlights the challenges for partners and advertisers using a social network to reach and influence their audience.

The case is presented as key events during the development of Facebook which show the marketing communications challenges faced by Facebook and other social network owners. Facebook has a regularly updated statistics page at **http://www.facebook.com/press/info.php?statistics** which should be referenced to find the current usage levels of the network. In September 2011 the key figures are:

- *Size*: 750 million active users
- *Activity*: 50 per cent of users log on daily
- *Mobile platforms*: 250 millions active users access Facebook through their mobile devices. These users are twice as active as non-mobile users
- *Integration with other sites*: more than 2.5 million sites integrate with Facebook via social plugins (Figure 8.22)
- *70 localised (translated) versions* are available with 70 per cent of Facebook users outside the US.

Facebook launched and extended – 4 February 2004

Facebook was founded while Mark Zuckerberg was a student at Harvard University, as described in 2010 in the film *The Social Network*. Initially membership was limited to Harvard students. The initial viral effect of the software was indicated by the fact that more than half of the undergraduate population at Harvard registered on the service within the first month!

Zuckerberg used open source software PHP and the MySQL database to create the original 'TheFacebook.com' site and these technologies are still in use today. When Facebook first launched in February 2004, there were just three things that users could do on the site, although they are still core to the functionality of the site. Users could create a profile with their picture and information, view other people's profiles, and add people as friends.

Since 2004, Facebook has introduced other functionality to create the Facebook experience. Some of the most significant of these include:

- a wall for posting messages
- news feeds
- messages
- posting of multiple photos and videos
- groups
- applications
- social widgets or plug-ins enabling Facebook messages to be embedded on other sites
- facebook or social ads.

Intellectual property dispute – September 2004 and ongoing

There has been an ongoing dispute on ownership of Facebook since another Harvard-originated social networking site – 'HarvardConnection', which later changed its name to ConnectU – alleged in September 2004 that Zuckerberg had used source code to develop Facebook when they originally contracted him to help in building their site.

It is also alleged that another system predated Facebook. Aaron J. Greenspan, a Harvard student in 2003, created a simple web service that he called house SYSTEM. It was used by several thousand Harvard students for a variety of online college-related tasks – six months before Facebook started and eight months before ConnectU went online. Mark Zuckerberg was briefly an early participant. No suit has been filed by Greenspan, instead he has published a book about his experience.

Brand identity established – 23 August 2005

In August, Facebook bought the domain name facebook.com from the Aboutface Corporation for $200,000 and dropped 'the' from its name.

International expansion – 11 December 2005

Throughout 2005, Facebook extended its reach into different types of colleges and by the end of 2005 included most small universities and junior colleges in the United States, Canada and Mexico. It was also made available in many universities in the UK and Ireland, and by December Australia and New Zealand were added to the Facebook network, bringing its size to more than 2000 colleges and over 25,000 high schools. Eventually Facebook expanded to be available to anyone aged 13 and over.

Initial concerns about privacy of member data – 14 December 2005

Two MIT students downloaded over 70,000 Facebook profiles from four schools (MIT, NYU, the University of Oklahoma and Harvard) using an automated script, as part of a research project on Facebook privacy.

Facebook receives $25 million in funding – April 2006 and Microsoft invests – October 2007

In May 2005 Facebook received a $13 million cash infusion from venture firm Accel Partners, followed in April 2006 by a further $25 million from a range of partners including Greylock Partners, Meritech Capital Partners and investor Peter Thiel, the co-founder of PayPal. Facebook spokesman Chris R. Hughes explained the rationale for the investment when he said:

> *This investment supports our goal to build an industry-leading company that will continue to grow and evolve with our users. We're committed to building the best utility to enable people to share information with each other in a secure and trusted environment.*

Paul S. Madera, Meritech's managing director, said his firm was impressed by Facebook's rapid growth and its potential for further expansion in the coveted college-age market. 'They've been designated by their community as the chosen community portal,' Madera said. 'This is a company that the entire venture community would love to be a part of.'

In October 2007 Microsoft took a $240 million equity stake in Facebook. This stake was based on a $15 billion valuation of Facebook. Under the terms of this strategic alliance, Microsoft became the exclusive third-party advertising platform partner for Facebook, and began to sell advertising for Facebook internationally as well as in the United States.

New feed functionality launched – September 2006

New information feeds were launched in mid-2006 and these show the challenges of balancing the benefit of new functionality against disrupting existing user habits. ➔

Writing in the Facebook blog in September 2006 Mark Zuckerberg said:

> *We've been getting a lot of feedback about Mini-Feed and News Feed. We think they are great products, but we know that many of you are not immediate fans and have found them overwhelming and cluttered.*
>
> *Other people are concerned that non-friends can see too much about them. We are listening to all your suggestions about how to improve the product; it's brand new and still evolving.*

Later, in an open letter on the blog dated 8 September 2006, Zuckerberg said:

> *We really messed this one up. When we launched News Feed and Mini-Feed we were trying to provide you with a stream of information about your social world. Instead, we did a bad job of explaining what the new features were and an even worse job of giving you control of them. I'd like to try to correct those errors now.*

Categorising friends into different types (Friends Lists – December 2007) is one approach that has helped to manage this.

Facebook Platform for applications launched – 24 May 2007

The Facebook Platform provides an API (application programming interface) which enables software developers to create applications that interact with core Facebook features. The Facebook developer's resource (**http://developers.facebook.com**) explains there are three main components used to build FB apps:

1. *Interface (API)*. The Facebook API uses a REST-based interface. This means that our Facebook method calls are made over the Internet by sending HTTP GET or POST requests to our REST server. With the API, you can add social context to your application by utilising profile, friend, photo and event data.
2. *Query (FQL)*. Facebook Query Language, or FQL, allows you to use an SQL-style interface to more easily query the same data that you can access through other Facebook API methods.
3. *Facebook Markup (FBML)*. FBML Enables you to build full Facebook Platform applications that deeply integrate into a user's Facebook experience. You can hook into several Facebook integration points, including the Profile, Profile Actions, Canvas, News Feed and Mini-Feed. Note: In 2011 Facebook made the decision to deprecate 2011 (developer jargon to discontinue with sufficient time to enable migration to a new method). Instead Facebook now offers developers the possibility to create experiences within pages using standard HTML and Javascript as they would for building a normal site. These apps in the tabs of a company's page are hosted on the company's own server so can be created and tracked more readily.

By January 2008, over 18,000 applications had been built on Facebook Platform with 140 new applications added per day. More than 95% of Facebook members have used at least one application built on Facebook Platform.

According to the Facebook Applications Directory (**http://www.facebook.com/apps/**) listing in February 2008, the most popular FB applications were:

1. *FunWall*. Videos, Photos, Graffiti, Greeting Cards, Flash Embeds and more! 2,254,075 daily active users
2. *Who's in your Top Friends?* Add your Best Friends to your profile! 1,956,803 daily active users
3. *Super Wall*. Share videos, pictures, graffiti and more with your friends! 915,832 daily active users
4. *Bumper Sticker*. Stick your friends with funny stickers! 891,230 daily active users.
5. *Friends for Sale!* Buy and sell your friends as pets! 585,153 daily active users.
6. *Scrabulous*. Play Scrabulous (Scrabble) within Facebook – 632,372 daily active users.
7. *Texas HoldEm Poker*. Play Texas HoldEm with your FB friends – 557,671 daily active users.
8. *Movies*. Compare your taste in movies with friends – 528,996 daily active users.
9. *Compare People*. Find out who stands where in various categories: cutest, sexiest, smartest and many more. 428,432 daily active users.
10. *Are YOU Interested?* FUN application to see who is interested in YOU! 486,459 daily active users.

Some applications have been accused of FB application spam, i.e. 'spamming' users to request that the application be installed.

Facebook Platform for mobile applications was launched in October 2007. Although many Facebook users already interacted with their friends through mobile phones.

Facebook passes 30 million active users – July 2007

Facebook active users passed 30 million according to the Facebook blog in July 2007. Mashable (**http://mashable.com/2007/07/10/facebook-users-2**) reported that this represented a doubling in the first part of 2007.

Data produced by querying the Facebook ad targeting tool (**www.facebook.com/ads**), completed in November 2007 by blogger PK Francis, suggests that the majority of Facebook users in many countries are female: **http://midnightexcess.wordpress.com/2007/11/23/facebook-member-stats-an-update**.

Figure 8.22 Facebook social plug-ins (**http:developers.facebook.com/docs/plugins**)

In terms of user engagement metrics, Facebook (**http://www.facebook.com/press/info.php?statistics**) shows:

- some 68 million active users
- an average of 250,000 new registrations per day since January 2007
- it is the sixth-most trafficked site in the United States (comScore)
- more than 65 billion page views per month
- more than half of active users return daily
- people spend an average of 20 minutes on the site daily (comScore).

Advertisers assess reputational damage – Summer 2007

In August 2007, the BBC announced that six major mainly financial services firms (First Direct, Vodafone, Virgin Media, the AA, Halifax and the Prudential) had withdrawn advertisements from the networking website Facebook after they appeared on a British National Party page.

At a similar time, bank HSBC was forced to respond to groups set up on Facebook criticising them for their introduction of new student banking charges (although not until the case had been featured in the national media).

Facebook Ads and company Facebook pages launched – 7 November 2007

Some of the features of Facebook Ads (**www.facebook.com/ads**) include:

- Targeting by age, gender, location, interests and more.
- Alternative payment models – cost-per-click (CPC) or impression based (CPM).
- 'Sponsored Stories' or 'Social Ads' – ads can also be shown to users whose friends have recently engaged with a company Facebook page or engaged with the company website through Facebook Beacon.

At the time of the launch the Facebook blog made these comments, which indicate the delicate balance in getting

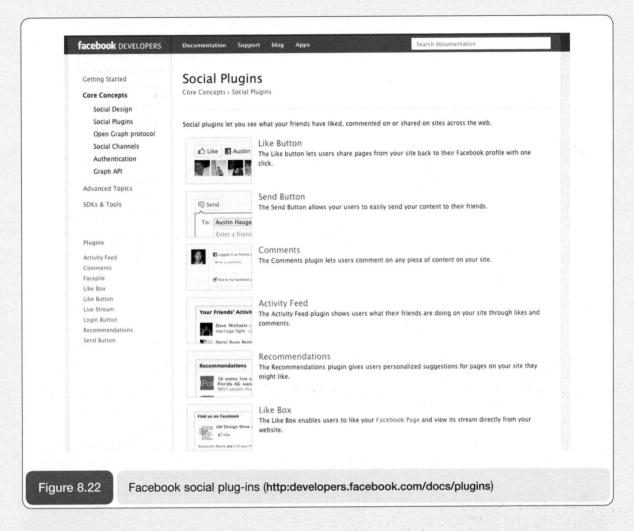

the balance right between advertising revenue and user experience. They said, first of all, what's not changing:

- *Facebook will always stay clutter-free and clean.*
- *Facebook will never sell any of your information.*
- *You will always have control over your information and your Facebook experience.*
- *You will not see any more ads than you did before this.*

Then, what is changing:

- *You now have a way to connect with products, businesses, bands, celebrities and more on Facebook.*
- *Ads should be getting more relevant and more meaningful to you.*
- *You now have the option to share actions you take on other sites with your friends on Facebook.*

These were originally implemented as 'social ads' and were based on a piece of technology known as 'Beacon' that tracks purchases or reviews made by Facebook users on outside sites, then reports these purchases to those users' friends.

For further information on Facebook advertising see **http://www.facebook.com/advertising** and **http://www.facebook.com/business** (contains in-depth guides to Facebook advertising).

Privacy concerns sparked by 'Beacon technology' – November 2007

Facebook received a lot of negative publicity on its new advertising format related to the 'Beacon' tracking system which Mark Zuckerberg was forced to respond to on the Facebook blog (5 December 2007). He said:

> *About a month ago, we released a new feature called Beacon to try to help people share information with their friends about things they do on the web. We've made a lot of mistakes building this feature, but we've made even more with how we've handled them. We simply did a bad job with this release, and I apologise for it. While I am disappointed with our mistakes, we appreciate all the feedback we have received from our users. I'd like to discuss what we have learned and how we have improved Beacon.*
>
> *When we first thought of Beacon, our goal was to build a simple product to let people share information across sites with their friends. It had to be lightweight so it wouldn't get in people's way as they browsed the web, but also clear enough so people would be able to easily control what they shared. We were excited about Beacon because we believe a lot of information people want to share isn't on Facebook, and if we found the right balance Beacon would give people an easy and controlled way to share more of that information with their friends.*
>
> *But we missed the right balance. At first we tried to make it very lightweight so people wouldn't have to touch it for it to work. The problem with our initial approach of making it an opt-out system instead of opt-in was that if someone forgot to decline to share something, Beacon still went ahead and shared it with their friends. It took us too long after people started contacting us to change the product so that users had to explicitly approve what they wanted to share. Instead of acting quickly, we took too long to decide on the right solution. I'm not proud of the way we've handled this situation and I know we can do better.*

New friends list functionality launched – December 2007

A criticism levelled at Facebook has been the difficulty in separating out personal friends and business acquaintances.

In December 2007, Facebook launched a significant new functionality called Friend Lists to enhance the user experience. Friend Lists enables users to create named groups of friends in particular categories, e.g. business or personal, and these private lists can be used to message people, send group or event invitations, and to filter updates from certain groups of friends.

December 2007/January 2008 – First drop in numbers using Facebook and new data centres to manage growth in users

Application spam has been considered one of the possible causes for the drop in visitors to Facebook starting from the beginning of 2008, when the website's growth fell from December 2007 to January 2008, its first drop since the website first launched.

To put this in context, the Facebook blog reported at the end of 2007 that nearly two million new users from around the world sign up for Facebook each week. This creates technical challenges – the blog reported that at end of 2007 full capacity was reached in their California datacentres. They explained that in the past they had handled this problem by purchasing a few dozen servers, but this time they had run out of physical space in the datacentres for new machines. But now Facebook assigns a user logging on to a relevant data centre – users in Europe and the eastern half of the US are connected direct to a new Virginia data centre whenever they're browsing the site and not making any changes, otherwise users are connected to California.

Facebook expands internationally – February 2008

Despite the hype generated among English speakers, Facebook only announced the launch of a Spanish site in February 2008 with local language versions planned for Germany and France. It seems that Facebook will inevitably follow the path taken by other social networks such as MySpace in launching many local language versions.

Facebook Messages and Places services introduced – November 2010

Although messaging between friends within Facebook has reduced the need for email communications, Facebook introduced its Messages services to reduce the need for users to use a rival search such as Gmail or Hotmail. Clearly intended to increase engagement on the site, e-mails sent from Facebook with the <username>@facebook.com address do not yet rival the volume of the other webmail providers.

Another major introduction in 2010 was Facebook Places which was seen as a rival to 'check-in' services such as Foursquare and Gowalla. However, this was integrated more closely into everyday Facebook status updates in 2011 with the less prominent 'Share where you are' feature.

June 2011 Google+ launched

After previous failed attempts to create social networking features that rivalled Facebook (Orkut, Google Wave), Google launched a series of new features united through a browser toolbar. The Circles feature readily enables you to readily group contacts – a big limitation of Facebook. The Sparks feature gives you a summary feed of the latest developments influenced by your friends' interests. Hangouts is group video chat offering a similar service to Skype and the Huddle feature is group chat. Instant upload enables upload of video and images from your mobile to a shared space. At the time of writing Google hasn't monetised these features through contextual ads such as featured in Gmail, but this should be expected in the future.

Facebook counters Google+ with new features – July 2011

In July 2011, Facebook introduced a series of features which seemed to directly target Google+ functionality. For example, Facebook made it easier to group friends in a similar ways to the Google Circles. Through an agreement with Skype Video calling is now also available within Facebook.

Sources: Facebook Statistics page (**http://www.facebook.com/press/info.php?statistics**); Facebook press room (**http://www.facebook.com/press.php**); Facebook blog (**http://blog.facebook.com**); Wikipedia (2008), Wikipedia Pages for Facebook (**http://en.wikipedia.org/wiki/Facebook**); for future updates relevant to this case study see: **http:/www.smartinsights.com/social-media-marketing/facebook-marketing.**

Questions

1 As an investor in a social network such as Facebook, which financial and customer-related metrics would you use to assess and benchmark the current business success and future growth potential of the company?

2 Complete a situation analysis for Facebook focusing on an assessment of the the main business risks which could damage the future growth potential of the social network.

3 For the main business risks to Facebook identified in your answer to Question 2, suggest approaches the company could use to minimise these risks

Summary

1 Key characteristics of interactive communications are the combination of push and pull media, user-submitted content, personalisation, flexibility and, of course, interactivity to create a dialogue with consumers.

2 We reviewed these elements of a digital marketing communications plan:

- *Step 1. Goal setting and tracking.* These can include goals for campaign volume (unique visitors and visits), quality (conversion to value events), cost (including cost-per-acquisition) and profitability.
- *Step 2. Campaign insight.* Information to feed into the campaign plan includes potential site audience reach and compositions, online buying behaviour and preferences, customer search behaviour and competitor campaign activity.

- *Step 3. Segmentation and targeting.* Key segmentation approaches are relationship with company, demographic segmentation, psychographic or attitudinal segmentation, value, lifecycle stage and behaviour.
- *Step 4. Offer and message development.* Includes identification of primary and secondary offers.
- *Step 5. Budgeting and selecting the digital media mix.* Should be based on conversion models reviewing all the digital media channels.
- *Step 6. Integration into overall media schedule or plan.* The principles of integration include coherence, consistency, continuity and complementarities.

Exercises

Self-assessment exercises

1. Review the reasons why continuous marketing activity involving certain digital media channels is preferable to more traditional burst or campaign-based activity.
2. Describe the unique characteristics of digital media in contrast to traditional media.
3. Give example goals for an online acquisition campaign in terms of response rates or engagement with creative, cost and overall campaign effectiveness.
4. Review the options for targeting particular audience groups online with different digital media.
5. How should a company decide on the relative investment between digital media and traditional media in a marketing campaign?
6. What are the options for integrating different types of digital media channels with traditional media?
7. How can different forms of customer insight be used to inform campaign execution?
8. What are the issues that a marketer should consider when defining their offer and message for an online campaign?

Essay and discussion questions

1. Discuss the analogy of Berthon *et al.* (1998) that effective Internet promotion is similar to a company exhibiting at an industry trade show attracting visitors to its stand.
2. Select a company of your choice and assess the effectiveness of the integration between their traditional communications, digital media channels and their website.
3. Select a recent campaign from a charity and with reference to their website campaign pages, identify how they should set campaign goals and review effectiveness.
4. How should companies decide on the granularity of targeting in digital media campaigns? Select two digital media channels to illustrate your examples.

Examination questions

1. Outline the range of goals that should be used to define success criteria for an online marketing campaign.
2. Using an example from a business-to-business company, describe the options available for targeting an audience through an e-mail newsletter.
3. Explain why integration between online and traditional media will make a campaign more effective overall.
4. Describe different options for testing the effectiveness of competing offers online.
5. Which do you think are the three most important changes in campaign communications introduced by the emergence of digital media channels?
6. Which considerations would determine the suitability of incorporating a mobile 'text-to-win' promotion into an offline campaign?
7. In which ways is the long tail concept relevant to campaign planning?
8. How should a confectionary brand assess the success of a campaign microsite in uplift of branding metrics?

References

Agrawal, V., Arjona, V. and Lemmens, R. (2001) E-performance: the path to rational exuberance, *McKinsey Quarterly*, No. 1, 31–43.

Berthon, P., Lane, N., Pitt, L. and Watson, R. (1998) The World Wide Web as an industrial marketing communications tool: models for the identification and assessment of opportunities, *Journal of Marketing Management*, 14, 691–704.

Berthon, P., Pitt, L. and Watson, R. (1996) Resurfing W^3: research perspectives on marketing communication and buyer behaviour on the World Wide Web, *International Journal of Advertising*, 15, 287–301.

Bird, D. (2000) *Commonsense Direct Marketing*, 4th edn, Kogan Page, London, UK.

Branthwaite, A., Wood, K. and Schilling, M. (2000) The medium is part of the message – the role of media for shaping the image of a brand, *ARF/ESOMAR Conference*, Rio de Janeiro, Brazil, 12–14 November.

Briggs, R., Krishnan, R. and Borin, N. (2005) Integrated multichannel communication strategies: evaluating the return on marketing objectives – the case of the 2004 Ford F-150 launch, *Journal of Interactive Marketing Communications*, 19(3), Summer.

Chaffey, D. and Smith, P.R. (2008) *E-marketing Excellence: Planning and Optimising Your Digital Marketing*, 3rd, Butterworth–Heinemann, Oxford.

Cook, L. (2004) Econometrics and integrated campaigns, *AdMap*, June, 37–40.

Coulter, K. and Starkis, J. (2005) Development of a media selection model using the analytic network process, *International Journal of Advertising*, 24(2), 193–215.

Crawshaw, P. (2004) Media neutral planning – what is it? Online article, Account Planning Group (**www.apg.org.uk**). No date given.

Deighton, J. (1996) The future of interactive marketing, *Harvard Business Review*, November–December, 151–62.

Fill, C. (2007) *Marketing Communications: Engagement, Strategies and Practice*, Financial Times Prentice Hall, Harlow, UK.

Flores, L and Eltvedt H. (2005) Beyond advertising – lesson about the power of brand new websites to build and expand brands ESOMAR, Montreal. ESOMAR, Online Conference, Montreal, June 2005.

Godin, S. (1999) *Permission Marketing*, Simon and Schuster, New York.

Harper, S. (2006) Pilot Eye Tracking Study, University of Manchester, School of Computer Science web research summary, available at: **http://hcw.cs.manchester.ac.uk/research/vicram/studies/eyetracking.php**.

Hoffman, D.L. and Novak, T.P. (1996) Marketing in hypermedia computer-mediated environments: conceptual foundations, *Journal of Marketing*, 60 (July), 50–68.

Hoffman, D.L. and Novak, T.P. (1997) A new marketing paradigm for electronic commerce, *The Information Society*, Special issue on electronic commerce, 13 (Jan–Mar), 43–54.

Hoffman, D.L. and Novak, T.P. (2000) How to acquire customers on the web, *Harvard Business Review*, May–June, 179–88, available online at: **http://ecommerce.vanderbilt.edu/papers.html**.

Hussein, I. (2006) IPA TouchPoints, *AdMap*, July–August, 46–48.

IAB (2004) XMOS Research Case Studies. Published at: **http://www.iab.net/insights_research/1672/1678/1690**.

IPA (2004) Econometrics Explained, by Louise Cook and Mike Holmes, Edited by Les Binet, a whitepaper published by the Institute of Practitioners in Advertising at: **www.ipa.co.uk**.

IPA (2011) *Integration: how to get it right and deliver results*, summary of a Institute of Practioners in Advertising members report, published 21 June 2011.

Jenkinson, A. (2003) Seeboard. A case study from the Centre for Integrated Marketing, **www.centreforintegratedmarketing.com**.

Kaushik (2008) Excellent Analytics Tip #13: Measure Macro AND Micro Conversions. Blog post, 26 March 2008 by Avinash Kaushik: http://www.kaushik.net/avinash/.

Kotler, P., Armstrong, G., Saunders, J. and Wong, V. (2001) *Principles of Marketing*, 3rd European edn. Financial Times/Prentice Hall, Harlow.

Lee, G. (2010) Death of 'last click wins': media attribution and the expanding use of media data, Garry Lee, *Journal of Direct, Data and Digital Marketing Practice*, 12(1), 16–26.

NMA (2005) Perfect Match, by Greg Brooks, *New Media Age*, 29 September: www.nma.co.uk.

NMA (2006) Banking on Search, *New Media Age*, 16 March 2006.

NMA (2008) Ad Watch – Lynx makes successful pass at digital with Get In There, *New Media Age*, 14–15, 7 February.

Novak, T. and Hoffman, D. (1997) New metrics for new media: towards the development of web measurement standards, *World Wide Web Journal*, 2(1), 213–46.

Peters, L. (1998) The new interactive media: one-to-one but to whom? *Marketing Intelligence and Planning*, 16(1), 22–30.

Petersen, E. (2004) *Web Measurement Hacks. Tips and Tools to Help Optimize your Online Business*, O'Reilly, Sebastapol, CA. www.oreilly.com/catalog/webmeasurehks/chapter/index.html.

Pickton, A. and Broderick, D. (2001) *Integrated Marketing Communications*, Financial Times/Prentice Hall, Harlow.

Pincott, G. (2000) Website promotion strategy, white paper from Millward Brown Intelliquest, available online at: www.intelliquest.com.

Schramm, W. (1955) How communication works, in *The Process and Effects of Mass Communications*, W. Schramm (ed.), 3–26. University of Illinois Press, Urbana, IL.

Shah, D. and Halligan, B. (2009) *Inbound Marketing: Get Found Using Google, Social Media and Blogs*, John Wiley & Sons, Inc, Hoboken, New Jersey.

Sissors, J. and Baron, R. (2002) *Advertising Media Planning*, 6th edn. McGraw-Hill, Chicago.

Tapp, A. (2005) Clearing up media neutral planning, *Interactive Marketing*, 6(3), 216–21.

van Doren, D., Flechner, D. and Green-Adelsberger, K. (2000) Promotional strategies on the World Wide Web, *Journal of Marketing Communications*, 6, 21–35.

Varianini, V. and Vaturi, D. (2000) Marketing lessons from e-failures, *McKinsey Quarterly*, No. 4, 86–97.

Walmsley, A. (2007) New media; the age of the trialogue, *The Marketer*, September, 12.

Wertime, K. and Fenwick, I. (2008) *DigiMarketing – The Essential Guide to New Media and Digital Marketing*, John Wiley and Sons, Singapore.

Further reading

Fill, C. (2005) *Marketing Communications – Contexts, Contents and Strategies*, 4th edn. Financial Times/Prentice Hall, Harlow. The entire book is recommended for its integration of theory, concepts and practice.

Novak, T. and Hoffman, D. (1997) New metrics for new media: towards the development of web measurement standards, *World Wide Web Journal*, 2(1), 213–46. This paper gives detailed, clear definitions of terms associated with measuring advertising effectiveness.

Wertime, K. and Fenwick, I. (2008) *DigiMarketing – The Essential Guide to New Media and Digital Marketing*, John Wiley and Sons, Singapore.

Zeff, R. and Aronson, B. (2001) *Advertising on the Internet*, 3rd edn. Wiley, New York. A comprehensive coverage of online banner advertising and measurement techniques and a more limited coverage of other techniques such as e-mail-based advertising.

Weblinks

Links on specific digital media channels such as e-mail marketing and search engine marketing are at the end of Chapter 9.

Sites focusing on approaches to running interactive marketing campaigns

- **ClickZ** (www.clickz.com/experts/). Has columns on different aspects of interactive communications including media planning.
- **iMediaConnection** (www.imediaconnection.com). Media site reporting on best practice in online advertising.
- **US Internet Advertising Bureau** (www.iab.net). The widest range of studies about Internet advertising effectiveness. In UK: www.iabuk.net.
- **Journal of Computer Mediated Communications** (http://www.blackwell-synergy.com/loi/jcmc). A free online peer-reviewed journal describing developments in interactive communications.
- **Media Buyer Planner** (www.buyerplanner.com). Developments in media planning with strong focus on online media.
- **Marketing Sherpa** (www.marketingsherpa.com). Articles and links on Internet marketing communications including e-mail and online advertising.
- **SmartInsights.com** (www.smartinsights.com). Advice on creating effective marketing campaigns include customer insight and attribution modelling.
- **World Advertising Research Centre** (www.warc.com). Covers offline and online media. Mainly subscription service, but with some free resources.

Chapter 9
Marketing communications using digital media channels

Chapter at a glance

Main topics

Case studies

Learning objectives

After reading this chapter, the reader should be able to:

- Distinguish between the different types of digital media channels
- Evaluate the advantages and disadvantages of each digital media channel for marketing communications
- Assess the suitability of different types of digital media for different purposes

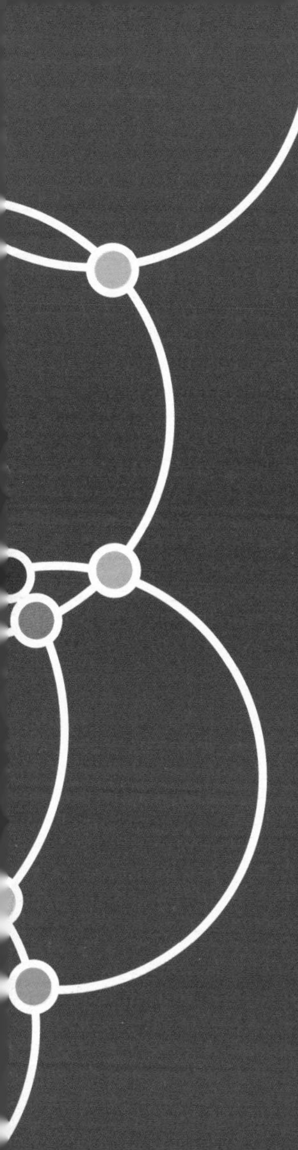

Questions for marketers

Key questions for marketing managers related to this chapter are:

- Which digital communications media should we select for different types of market?
- What are the success factors for using digital media that will make our campaigns more effective?

Scan code to find the latest updates for topics in this chapter

Links to other chapters

Related chapters are:

- Chapter 1 introduces the main options for communications with digital media.
- Chapter 8 reviews how to plan campaigns which use digital media channels. The section towards the end of the chapter on 'Selecting the right mix of digital media communications tools' in 'Step 5. Budgeting and selecting the digital media mix', is particularly relevant.
- Chapter 10 also considers the measurement of communications effectiveness.

Introduction

Digital media channel
Online communications technique such as search engine marketing, affiliate marketing and display advertising used to engage web users on third-party sites; encourage them to visit an organisation's site or purchase through traditional channels such as by phone or instore.

Digital marketing managers use many different **digital media channels**, such as affiliate, e-mail, social and search engine marketing, to attract visitors to their website. They also have options such as display advertising and widget marketing for communicating brand values to visitors of third-party websites. Traditional communications disciplines such as advertising, direct mail and PR remain important in generating awareness and favourability about brands and in encouraging visits to a companies online presence.

Choosing the most effective digital communications techniques and refining them to attract visitors and new customers at an efficient cost is now a major marketing activity, both for online business and multichannel businesses. In this chapter, we explain the differences between the different digital media options and review the strengths, weaknesses and success factors for using the communications techniques.

How is this chapter structured?

This chapter is structured around the six main digital media channels we have identified in Table 9.1 (Figure 1.9 on page 28 portrays a graphical summary). To enable easy comparison of the different techniques and to assist with assignments and revision, we have structured each section the same way:

- *What is it?* A description of the digital media channel.
- *Advantages and disadvantages?* A structured review of the benefits and drawbacks of each channel.
- *Best practice in planning and management.* A summary of the issues such as targeting, measurement and creative which need to be considered when running a campaign using each digital channel. This expands on the coverage given in the previous chapter on these issues.

As you read each section, you should compare the relative strengths and weaknesses of the different techniques and how consumers perceive different options in terms of trust (Activity 9.1). In the final section, we summarise their strengths and weaknesses for different applications.

Table 9.1 Summary of different digital media channels

Digital media channel	Description	Different communications techniques
Search engine marketing (SEM)	Gaining listings in the search engine results pages of the major search engines, Google, Bing, YouTube and popular country-specific engines. Also includes advertising on third-party publisher sites which are part of the search display networks	• Search Engine Optimisation (SEO) listing in the natural listing which does not attract a fee per click. Based on on-page optimisation and link-building • Pay-per-click (advertising) sponsored listings using Google AdWords for example
Online public relations (E-PR)	Maximising favourable mentions of your company, brands, products or websites on third-party sites such as social networks or blogs that are likely to be visited by your target audience. Also includes monitoring and, where necessary, responding to negative mentions and conducting public relations via a site through a press centre or blog, for example	• Syndicating content (e.g. press releases), gaining positive mentions, managing reputation on third-party sites, particularly forums and social networks • Use of owned media – own company feeds, blogs and feeds • Blogger and influencer outreach for earned media

Table 9.1 Continued

Online partnerships including affiliate marketing	Creating and managing long-term arrangements to promote your online services on third-party websites or through e-mail communications. Different forms of partnership include link building, affiliate marketing, aggregators such as price comparison sites, online sponsorship and co-branding	• Commission-based affiliate marketing • Creating long-term partnership relationships such as sponsorship, link-building or editorial
Interactive display advertising	Use of online display ads such as banners and rich media ads to achieve brand awareness and encourage click-through to a target site	• Site-specific media buys • Use of ad networks • Behavioural targeting
Opt-in e-mail marketing	Using legal, permission-based e-mailing to prospects or customers who have agreed to receive e-mails from an organisation. E-mails to communicate with prospects can be rented from a publisher or other list owner or companies can build up their own 'house list' containing customer or prospect details	• Acquisition e-mail activity including list rental, co-branded campaigns, advertising on e-newsletters • Retention and growth activity, e.g. house list for e-newsletters and customer e-mail campaigns • Automatic or event-triggered e-mail campaign activity
Social media marketing including viral and electronic word-of-mouth marketing	Social media marketing and viral marketing is effectively online word of mouth – compelling brand-related content is shared, forwarded or discussed electronically or discussed offline to help achieve awareness and, in some cases, drive response. Strong link with online PR activity	• Branded presence or advertising within social network • Creating 'viral agents' or compelling interactive content • Encouraging amplification of viral messages • Using customer advocacy effect • Widget marketing

The importance of each of these digital media channels in driving visitors will vary from company to company, but to give you an indication of how important they are on average see Digital marketing insight 9.1. You can see why search engine marketing is an important channel and this is why we start our coverage in this chapter with this. You can also see that direct traffic is high reflecting the importance of visits driven by traditional channels or visits from e-mail or social networks that are not being tracked separately. You can also see that links from other sites are also quite significant.

Digital marketing insight 9.1 How balanced is your referrer mix?

One approach to determining the most appropriate mix of digital media channels is this compilation across all sites that use the web analytics tool Google Analytics to measure site effectiveness (See Chapter 10 for a description of how these tools work). Figure 9.1 shows the average mix of referrers across sites tracked by Google Analytics.

This is a summary of the different terms in the pie chart:

- *Search engine* – this groups both natural and paid search (AdWords).
- *Referral* – this is traffic from other sites which have direct links to a site.

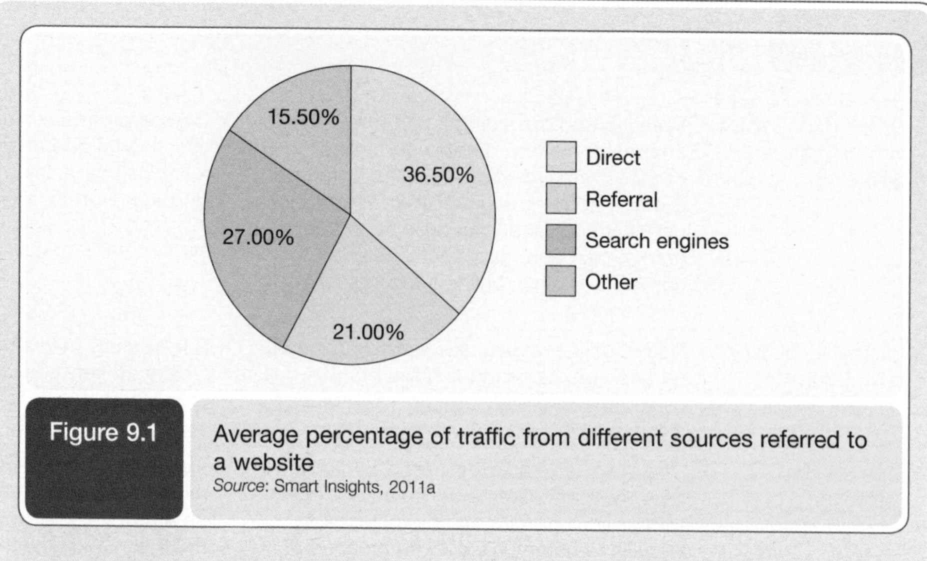

Figure 9.1 Average percentage of traffic from different sources referred to a website
Source: Smart Insights, 2011a

- *Direct* – direct traffic results from URL type ins, bookmarks or when e-mail marketing isn't tracked by marketers adding specific link tracking to their e-mail so that they show up in analytics. These days direct traffic will also include non-browser traffic from visitors clicking on apps for reading social messages like Hootsuite or Tweet-deck or other mobile apps linking to a site.
- *Other* – campaigns include AdWords when linked to the Google Account and any other campaigns like affiliates, display ads and e-mail campaigns when these have had marketing campaign tags attached. In this compilation AdWords is included under search engines.

Digital marketing in practice: The Smart Insights Interview

Kate Webb, online marketing manager at Vision Express, explains how the multichannel retailer prioritises its use of social media to meet business goals.

The Interview

Q. How big an impact has the increase in popularity of social media with consumers had on Vision Express?

Kate Webb: It's had quite an impact in terms of time and resource, especially in the early days. As a company we're relatively new to social media; we've only been active for just over a year. We spent a lot of time during the first three to six months listening, watching and learning what consumers were saying about our brand/looking for from our brand, in order to decide on how we should communicate, and where – which platforms.

During this time we have seen both our follower/fan numbers grow, but more importantly the engagement with our customers is increasing and we feel that our customers are really starting to converse with us as a brand.

Since being involved in social media we have seen an increase in the number of customers who mention us directly, or seek us out, rather than simply mentioning our brand name in passing conversation. To us this is an important development in building our customer relationship.

At Vision Express our social media activities are based on engaging with our existing customer base; we want to improve on relationships, or continue offline relationships, with our customers, online. In the optical industry we have a long purchase cycle, on average our customers come back to us every two years, so it is a long period during which to maintain our social media relationships.

We have found that for probably about one to two per cent, of our customer base, social media is their main point of contact with us. The type of communication varies between the different social media platforms, for example we find that Twitter is more of a customer service tool, whilst Facebook is a fun and engaging platform, suitable for promotional outreach.

There is still progress to be made, especially as social media grows and platforms are developed/changed, but we're confident we're on the right track to providing the same high level of service, that our customers get in our stores, online.

Q. What do you see as the key parts of a social media strategy that require management?

Kate Webb: I find that too often businesses think that social media is just about posting messages about the company on Twitter or Facebook, or getting an agency in to handle everything for them. But the key to making social media work, for me, is to have a strong strategy behind it, and to manage that strategy.

For me the key areas of focus in this strategy should be:

- *Brand/business persona*: I feel it's key to define a persona or personality for your business and to identify how you want to position your brand on social media, is the brand/business fun/funky, calm/serious, sensitive/nurturing or brash/loud? You need flexibility to evolve this over time as your relationship with customers grows.
- *Which platforms*: There are hundreds of social media platforms that we could all be involved in, so it's key to identify which platforms support your business objectives, and which ones you are going to get involved with. Otherwise resources and communication will simply be spread too thinly.
- *Goals/objectives*: It is important to ensure that your social media objectives or goals are aligned with that of your organisation. What is it that you want to achieve via social media. For Vision Express, our three critical goals are to:
  - Add value and service to our online customers, via informative dialogue, responsive customer service and feedback. This also works as a 2-way path, in that we then pass onto our store network all/any feedback we have received from our online customers.
  - Engage with our online customers, and build relationships with them. In order to do this effectively, we are working towards a one customer view database, which will enable us to match social media activity to in-store activity by our customers, thus enabling us to provide a tailored approach in our conversations.
  - Build brand awareness and consumer knowledge about our service offering. We want our customers to understand our company, and to recognise our values, ethics and personality, online & offline.
- *Analytics/results*: Be this sentiment or engagement levels, reporting on results/analytics needs to be regular, managed and analysed in order to adapt future strategy.
- *Technology advancements*: Social media platforms are changing all the time. Because of this it is imperative that we understand and gain knowledge of how these advancements/changes will affect our business's social media presence going forward. For example the development of Facebook's iframes in March this year, opened up a great opportunity for us to integrate our websites core offers into our Facebook page.

Q. How should a company assess the relevance of different social media opportunities to prioritise their focus?

Kate Webb: Having clear objectives and a clear strategy will help. Enabling you, on a case by case basis, to identify what social media opportunities work for which promotion/aspect of the business.

It's important for any business/brand not to spread their actions/activities too thinly, identify where the majority of your customers are and focus on engaging well with your customers on a few platforms.

As well as identifying which platforms to be active on, it's important to also understand to what extent you work with these platforms, does your business need/require interactive apps or games? Or is simple communication the key to your social media engagement.

I feel it is also important to identify where social media fits in with your overall online and offline presence, and ensure that it complements your other activities. Recently I have seen an increase in brands advertising both online and on TV their Facebook and Twitter presences, but not their website? To me, a brands website should take precedence, and social media presences should complement the website messaging and be aimed at engaging customers with the website.

If through doing these engagement activities we acquire customers, then great, but this isn't our primary focus.

Q. What advice would you give to a company starting a social media listening/ reputation management initiative?

Kate Webb: Listen, listen and listen some more. Social media isn't about who shouts the loudest, it's about engaging in conversation with your customers/prospective customers and about keeping them informed.

There are some free tools which you can use at the very beginning, such as Tweetdeck or Hootsuite, but bear in mind these are often limited to either one platform, or to scheduling outreach messages only.

If you are really serious about social media, and I think companies need to be these days, you need to enlist a social media monitoring platform, which will enable you to listen to what consumers are saying about your brand across micromedia (Twitter/ Facebook), blogs and forums.

You won't be able to respond to all consumer mentions, due to forum rules, but you can at least listen and feed this back into the business, so you can modify activities, or continue doing popular ones! Start small, don't overstretch your resources, and be realistic about the amount of time/resource and money social media can take up.

A few key things to remember are once you start talking, you need to continue the commitment to maintain the conversations, and ensure you gain inter-company awareness, there is nothing worse than talking to a customer via Twitter, and then having them go into store to be presented with 'We're on Twitter? I didn't know that'.

You will also need to get to know your customers, the ideal solution here is to integrate social media activities into your core customer database, so you have one customer view, but this can take time, money and resource. In the interim, the better social media monitoring tools these days are offering engagement platforms, which allow you to add notes and assign tasks, so you can build up a reasonable knowledge of your social media customers.

Q. Where do you think the responsibilities for managing social media marketing in a company should lie? How is it managed at Vision Express?

Kate Webb: By spending our first three to six months listening to what our customers were saying about our brand and what they were looking for from our brand, we managed to identify that our social media activities needed to be part of the whole business, not just an 'add-on' to our marketing activities.

It is important that social media activities have management 'buy-in' in any business. It needs to be integrated into core business activities if it is going to work properly. To integrate these activities into different departments correctly requires management support, the management structure need to understand why/how/who social media impacts on and affects both internally and within our customer base.

As a result, so far, we've integrated social media into a couple of key departments within the business, with the online marketing team as social media 'owners', in that we will identify the next strategic steps, bring in agency support, provide understanding of new developments and report on analytics and progress.

We have involvement from our customer care team, who respond on a day-to-day basis to customer enquiries/queries and feedback. We integrate social media into our marketing planning activities from the out-set, identifying whether a promotion is suitable for social media and if so, which platform it suits best, and we have our product department involved to provide a great level of product information and advice

To have social media as purely a marketing tool/activity will restrict a business in providing the right level of customer care, and will lead to sporadic/untimely and unfocused outreach.

Activity 9.1 How do consumers rate communications

Figure 9.2 shows consumer ratings of different forms of advertising. Review the alternatives and then discuss the implications for a marketer using these communications channels.

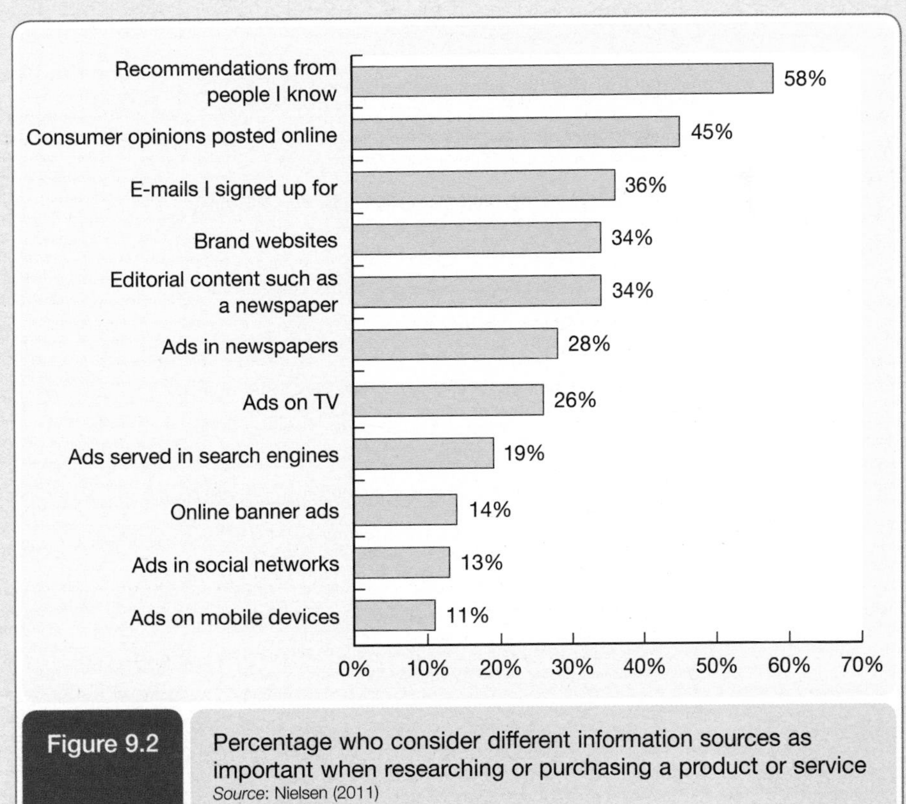

Figure 9.2 Percentage who consider different information sources as important when researching or purchasing a product or service
Source: Nielsen (2011)

Search engine marketing

Search engine marketing (SEM)
Promoting an organisation through search engines to meet its objectives by delivering relevant content in the search listings for searchers and encouraging them to click through to a destination site. The two key techniques of SEM are *search engine optimisation (SEO)* to improve results from the natural listings, and *paid-search marketing* to deliver results from the sponsored listings within the search engines.

Search engine marketing (SEM) is vital for generating quality visitors to a website as suggested by Figure 9.1. We all now naturally turn to a search engine when we are seeking a new product, service or entertainment. The main options include Google, Bing, the Google-owned YouTube, which is the second largest search engine by volumes of searches in many countries or other regional search engine. We also turn to search when we are familiar with a brand, shortcutting site navigation by searching for a brand, appending a brand name to a product or typing a URL into Google, which is surprisingly common, accounting for over 50 per cent of paid search expenditure according to Atlas (2007). This is known as **navigational (or brand) search**. Given the obvious importance of reaching an audience during their consideration process for a product or when they are locating a brand, search engine marketing (SEM) has become a fiercely competitively area of digital marketing.

There are two main types of SEM that are quite distinct in the marketing activities needed to manage them, so we will study them separately, although in practice they should be integrated:

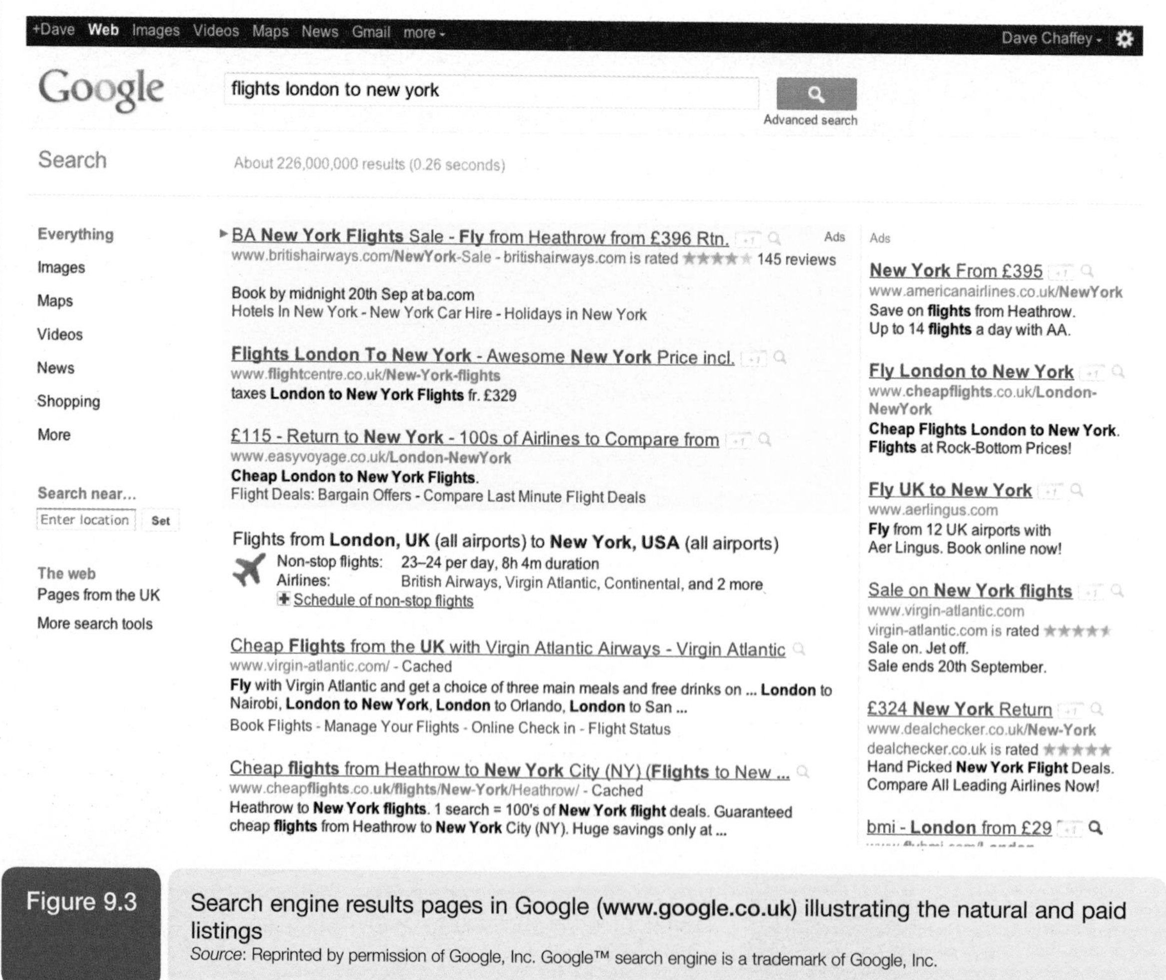

Figure 9.3 Search engine results pages in Google (www.google.co.uk) illustrating the natural and paid listings
Source: Reprinted by permission of Google, Inc. Google™ search engine is a trademark of Google, Inc.

Navigational (or brand) search
Searchers use a search engine such as Google to find information deeper within a company site by appending a qualifier such as a product name to the brand or site name. Organisations need to check that relevant pages are available in the search results pages for these situations.

Search engine optimisation (SEO)
A structured approach used to increase the position of a company or its products in search engine natural or organic results listings for selected keywords or phrases.

Natural or organic listings
The pages listing results from a search engine query which are displayed in a sequence according to relevance of match between the keyword phrase typed into a search engine and a web page according to a ranking algorithm used by the search engine.

Search engine results pages (SERPS)
The page(s) containing the results after a user types a keyphrase into a search engine. SERPS contain both natural or organic listings and paid or sponsored listings.

Universal search
The natural listings incorporate other relevant results from vertical searches related to a query, such as video, books, news, real-time social media recommendations, site links and images.

Paid search marketing (pay-per-click) marketing (PPC)
A relevant text ad with a link to a company page is displayed on the SERPs when the user of a search engine types in a specific phrase. A fee is charged for every click of each link, with the amount bid for the click mainly determining its position. Additionally, PPC may involve advertising through a displaynetwork of third-party sites (which may be on a CPC, CPM or CPA basis).

1 **Search engine optimisation (SEO)** involves achieving the highest position or ranking practical in the **natural or organic listings** shown in Figure 9.3 as the main body of the **search engine results pages (SERPS)** across a range of specific combination of keywords (or keyphrases) entered by search engine users.

As well as listing pages which the search engine determines as relevant for the search performed based on the text it contains and other factors, such as links to the page, the SERPs also contain other tools which searchers may find useful. Google terms these tools part of a strategy known as **universal search** for blended search. For example, Figure 9.3 shows a link to a price comparison service.

2 **Paid search (pay-per-click) marketing (PPC)** is similar to conventional advertising; here a relevant text ad with a link to a company page is displayed when the user of a search engine types in a specific phrase. A series of text ads usually labelled as 'sponsored links' are displayed above, or to the right of, the natural listings as in Figure 9.3. Although many searchers prefer to click on the natural listings, a sufficient number do click on the paid listings (typically around a quarter or a third of all clicks) such that they are highly profitable for companies such as Google and a well-designed paid search campaign can drive a significant amount of business for companies. There are also opportunities to create awareness and response from pay-per click ads displayed on third-party sites as we will see in the section on paid search marketing.

The importance of effective search engine marketing is suggested by Figure 9.4 which shows that generating the highest rankings for a company in the search engine results pages (SERPs) can generate many more visits because of a higher clickthrough rate. Note that click-through rate according to position will vary dramatically by type of keyword such as brand or generic keyword, but this research is based on 10,000 keywords across 250 B2C and B2B companies. To use search marketing effectively it's important to understand common customer behaviours, read Digital marketing insights 9.2.

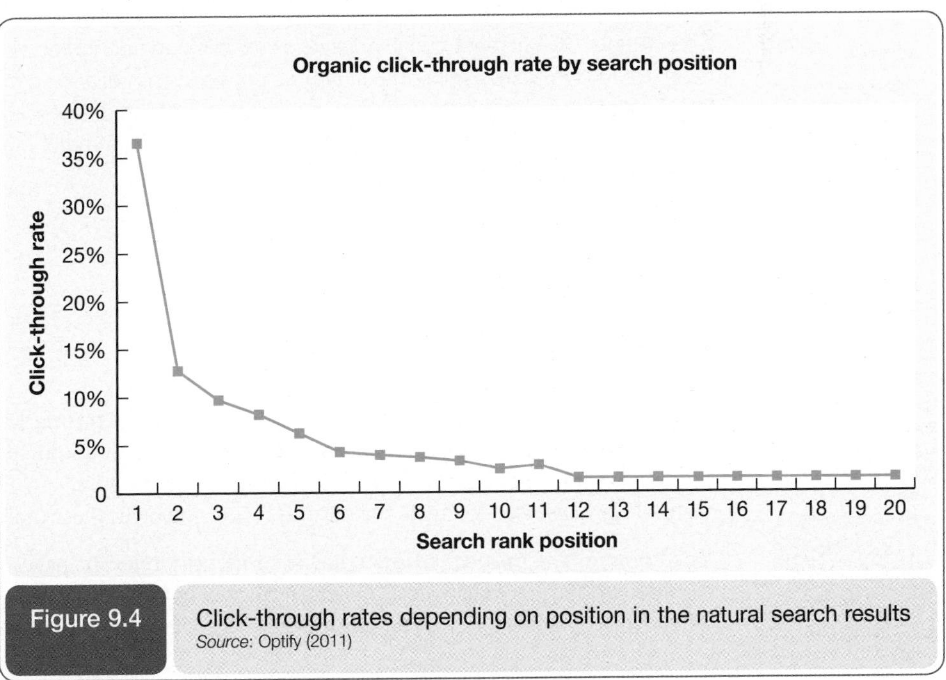

Figure 9.4 Click-through rates depending on position in the natural search results
Source: Optify (2011)

Digital marketing insight 9.2 Understanding consumer search engine behaviour

Search marketing firm Performics (2010) researched search preferences for a panel of 5000 users. The type of information they use search engines to find is shown in Figure 9.5. You can see this includes both information for online and offline purchase.

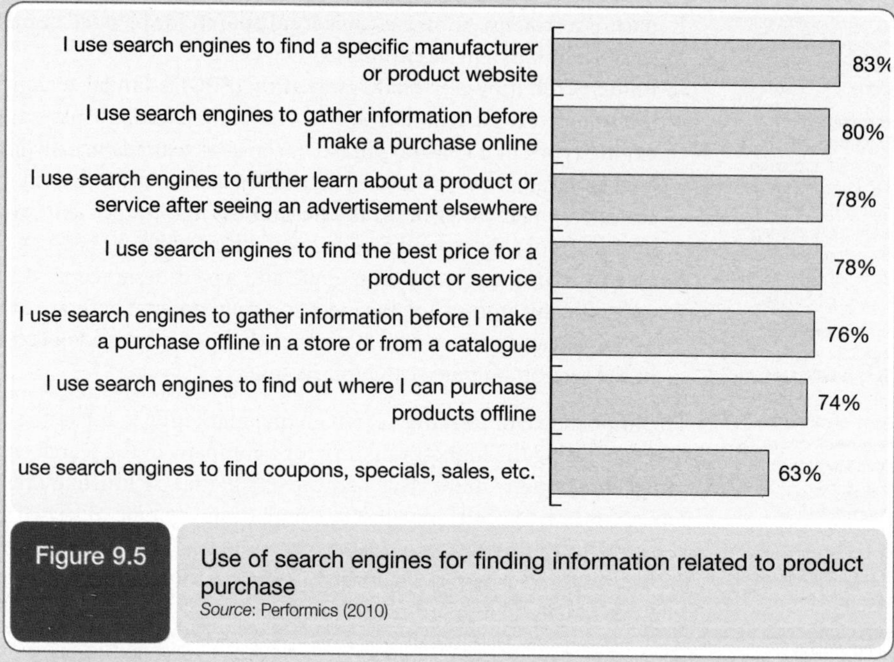
I use search engines to find a specific manufacturer or product website
83%
I use search engines to gather information before I make a purchase online
80%
I use search engines to further learn about a product or service after seeing an advertisement elsewhere
78%
I use search engines to find the best price for a product or service
78%
I use search engines to gather information before I make a purchase offline in a store or from a catalogue
76%
I use search engines to find out where I can purchase products offline
74%
use search engines to find coupons, specials, sales, etc.
63%

Figure 9.5 Use of search engines for finding information related to product purchase
Source: Performics (2010)

- More than three-quarters of respondents search to learn more about a product or service after seeing an ad elsewhere.
- Searchers are tenacious – if at first they don't succeed, they will modify their search and try again (89 per cent), try a different search engine (89 per cent), and go through multiple search results pages if necessary (79 per cent).
- 43 per cent at least occasionally view or click on sponsored video ads.
- Nearly two-thirds know the difference between natural and sponsored search results, with those age 18–29 most likely to be aware of the difference.
- 92 per cent click on the sponsored results, although many don't acknowledge this when asked.

Source: Performics (2010)

What is SEO?

Robots or spiders
Spiders are software processes, technically known as robots, employed by search engines to index web pages of registered sites on a regular basis. They follow or crawl links between pages and record the reference URL of a page for future analysis.

Improving positions in the natural listings is dependent on marketers understanding the process whereby search engines compile an index by sending out spiders or robots to crawl around sites that are registered with that search engine (Figure 9.6). The figure shows that the technology harnessed to create the natural listings involves these main processes:

1 *Crawling*. The purpose of the crawl is to identify relevant pages for indexing and assess whether they have changed. Crawling is performed by **robots** (bots) that are also known as **spiders**. These access web pages and retrieve a reference URL of the page for later analysis and indexing.

Although the terms 'bot' and 'spider' give the impression of something physical visiting a site, the bots are simply software processes running on a search engine's server which request pages, follow the links contained on that page and so create a series of page references with associated URLs. This is a recursive process, so each link followed will find additional links which then need to be crawled.

2 *Indexing.* An index is created to enable the search engine to rapidly find the most relevant pages containing the query typed by the searcher. Rather than searching each page for a query phrase, a search engine 'inverts' the index to produce a lookup table of documents containing particular words.

The index information consists of phases stored within a document and also other information characterising a page such as the document's title, meta description, PageRank, trust or authority, spam rating, etc. For the keywords in the document, additional attributes will be stored such as semantic markup (<h1>, <h2> headings denoted within HTML), occurrence in **link anchor text**, proximity, frequency or density and position in document, etc. The words contained in link anchor text 'pointing' to a page are particularly important in determining search rankings.

Link anchor text
The text used to form the blue underlined hyperlink viewed in a web browser defined in the HTML source. For example, a link: Visit Dave Chaffey's Digital Marketing site is created by the HTML code: <A href="http://www.smartinsights.com">Visit Dave Chaffey's Digital Marketing site</A>.

3 *Ranking or scoring.* The indexing process has produced a lookup of all the pages that contain particular words in a query, but they are not sorted in terms of relevance. Ranking of the document to assess the most relevant set of documents to return in the SERPs occurs in real time for the search query entered. First, relevant documents will be retrieved from a runtime version of the index at a particular data centre, then a rank in the SERPs for each document will be computed based on many ranking factors, of which we highlight the main ones in later sections.

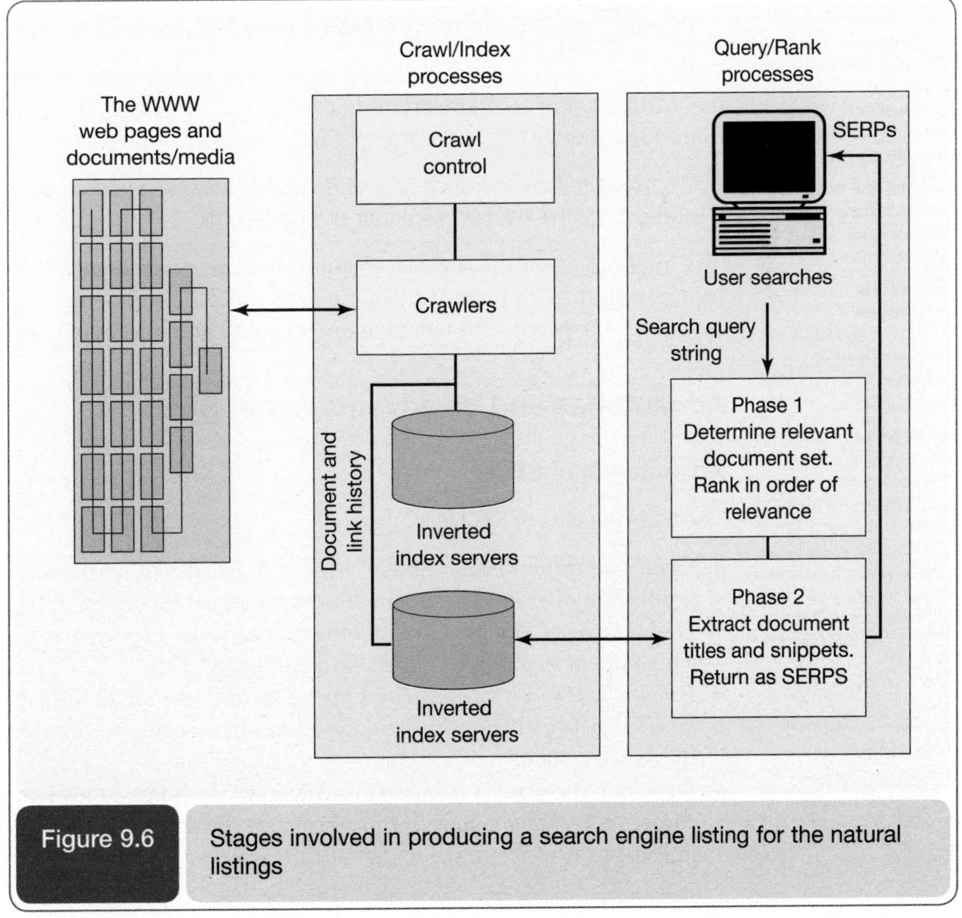

Figure 9.6 Stages involved in producing a search engine listing for the natural listings

4 *Query request and results serving.* The familiar search engine interface accepts the searcher's query. The user's location is assessed through their IP address and the query is then passed to a relevant data centre for processing. Ranking then occurs in real time for a particular query to return a sorted list of relevant documents and these are then displayed on the search results page.

Search engine ranking factors

Google has stated that it uses more than 200 factors or signals within its search ranking algorithms. These include positive ranking factors that help boost position and negative factors or filters which are used to remove search engine spam from the index where SEO companies have used unethical approaches such as automatically creating links to mislead the Google algorithms.

The two most important factors for good ranking positions in all the main search engines are:

- *Matching between web page copy and the key phrases searched.* The main factors to optimise on are keyword density, keyword formatting, keywords in anchor text and the document meta-data including page title tags. The SEO process to improve results in this area is known as **on-page optimisation**. We will cover some of details of best practice for this process in a topic later in this section.
- *Links into the page (inbound or* **backlinks**). Google counts each link to a page from another page or another site as a vote for this page. So pages and sites with more external links from other sites will be ranked more highly. The quality of the link is also important, so if links are from a site with a good reputation and relevant context for the keyphrase, then this is more valuable. Internal links are also assessed in a similar way. The processes to improve this aspect of SEO are **external link building** and **internal link architecture**.

On-page optimisation
Writing copy and applying markup such as the <title> tag and heading tag <h1> to highlight to search engine relevant keyphrases within a document.

Backlink
Hyperlink which links to a particular web page (or website). Also known as an inbound link. Google PageRank and Yahoo! WebRank are methods of enumerating this.

External link building
A proactive approach to gain quality links from third-party sites.

Internal link architecture
Structuring and labelling links within a site's navigation to improve the results of SEO.

Social graph
A term popularised by Facebook in 2007 when describing its Facebook platform. The social graph describes the relationship between individuals linked through social networks and other connections such as email or personal contact.

With the growing importance of sharing of links through social media the search engines now use the number of social mentions to a page and across a site to determine ranking positions (Smart Insights, 2010). For example, a representative of Bing said of assessment of Twitter:

> We take into consideration how often a link has been tweeted or retweeted, as well as the authority of the Twitter users that shared the link.

The implications of this are that if companies can get influencers with a larger influence to recommend their content or offers through social networks this can have the dual effect of reaching more people through their **social graph** and improving rankings.

Advantages and disadvantages of SEO

Advantages of SEO

The main benefits of SEO are:

- *Significant traffic driver.* Figure 9.1 showed that search marketing can attract a significant proportion of visitors to the site IF companies are successful in implementing it.
- *Highly targeted.* Visitors are searching for particular products or services so will often have a high intent to purchase – they are qualified visitors.
- *Potentially low-cost visitors.* There are no media costs for ad display or click-through. Costs arise solely from the optimisation process where agencies are paid to improve positions in the search results.
- *Dynamic.* The search engine robots will crawl the home page of popular sites daily, so new content is included relatively quickly for the most popular pages of a site (less so for deep links).

Disadvantages of SEO

Despite the targeted reach and low cost of SEO, it is not straightforward as these disadvantages indicate:

- *Lack of predictability.* Compared with other media SEO is very unreliable in terms of the return on investment – it is difficult to predict results for a given investment and is highly competitive.
- *Time for results to be implemented.* The results from SEO may take months to be achieved, especially for new sites.
- *Complexity and dynamic nature.* The search engines take hundreds of factors into account, yet the relative weightings are not published, so there is not a direct correlation between marketing action and results – 'it is more of an art than a science'. Furthermore the ranking factors change through time. See for example, SEOmoz (2011a) for the latest updates.
- *Ongoing investment.* Investment needed to continue to develop new content and generate new links.
- *Poor for developing awareness in comparison with other media channels.* Searchers already have to be familiar with a brand or service to find it. However, it offers the opportunity for less well-known brands to 'punch above their weight' and to develop awareness following click-through.

For these reasons, investment in paid search may also be worthwhile.

Best practice in planning and managing SEO

In this section we will review six of the main approaches used to improve the results from SEO. You will see that SEO is a technical discipline and that the techniques used change through time. For this reason SEO is often outsourced to a specialist SEO agency, although some companies believe they can gain an edge through having an internal specialist who understands the company's customers and markets well. You will see, though, that some of the on-page optimisation techniques recommended in this section are relatively straightforward and it is important to control brand and proposition messages. Content editors and reviewers within a company therefore need to be trained to understand these factors and incorporate them into their copywriting.

1 Search engine submission

While some unscrupulous search marketing companies offer to register you in the 'Top 1000 search engines', in reality registering in the top 5–10 search engines of each country an organisation operates in will probably account for more than 95 per cent of the potential visitors. Most existing companies will be automatically included in the search index since the search engine robots will follow links from other sites that link to them and do not require submission services.

Search engine submission
The process of informing search engines that a site should be indexed for listing in the search engine results pages.

For new companies, achieving **search engine submission** is now straightforward – for example, in Google there is an 'Add a URL' page (e.g. **www.google.com/addurl.html**), but it is more effective to get existing sites to link to a new site which the robots will follow. Unfortunately it can take time for a site to be ranked highly in search results even if it is the index: Google allegedly places new sites in a review status sometimes referred to as the *Google sandbox effect*. However, Google search engineers deny the existence of this and explain it is a natural artifact produced by new sites having limited links, history and so reputation. Either way, it is important to remember this constraint when creating startup companies or separate unlined microsites for a campaign since you may have to rely on paid search to gain SERPS visibility.

2 Index inclusion

Although a search engine robot may visit the home page of a site, it will not necessarily crawl all pages or assign them equal weight in terms of PageRank or relevance. So when auditing sites as part of an SEO initiative, SEO agencies will check how many pages are included within the search engine index for different search engines. This is known as **index inclusion.**

Index inclusion
Ensuring that as many of the relevant pages from your domain(s) are included within the search engine indexes you are targeting to be listed in.

Potential reasons for not gaining complete index inclusion include:

- Technical reasons why the search robots do not crawl all the pages, such as the use of SEO-unfriendly content management system with complex URLs.
- Pages identified as spam or of less importance or considered to be **duplicate content** which are then contained in what used to be known as the supplemental index in Google which don't rank so highly. In these cases it is sometimes best to use a specific 'canonical' meta tag which tells the search engine which the primary page is. If you are a multinational company with different content sites for different countries, then it is challenging to deliver the relevant content for local audiences with use of regional domains tending to work best.

Duplicate content
Different pages which are evaluated by the search engine to be similar and so don't rank highly, even though they may be for distinct products or services.

Companies can check the index inclusion through:

- Reviewing web analytics data which will show the frequency with which the main search robots crawl a site.
- Using web analytics referrer information to find out which search engines a site's visitors originate from, and the most popular pages.
- Checking the number of pages that have been successfully indexed on a site. For example, in Google the search '**inurl:www.smartinsights.com**' or '**site:www.smartinsights.com**' lists all the pages of Dave's site indexed by Google and gives the total number in the top-right of the SERPs.

3 Keyphrase analysis

Keyphrase (keyword phrase)
The combination of words users of search engines type into a search box which form a search query.

The key to successful search engine marketing is achieving **keyphrase** relevance since this is what the search engines strive for – to match the combination of keywords typed into the search box to the most relevant destination content page. Notice that we say 'keyphrase' (short for 'keyword phrase') rather than 'keyword' since search engines such as Google attribute more relevance when there is a phrase match between the keywords that the user types and a phrase on a page. Despite this, many search companies and commentators talk about optimising your 'keywords' and, in our opinion, pay insufficient attention to keyphrase analysis.

Key sources for identifying the keyphrases your customers are likely to type when searching for your products include your market knowledge, competitors' sites, keyphrases from visitors who arrive at your site (from web analytics), the internal site search tool and the keyphrase analysis tools such as the Google Keyword Tool listed at **www.smartinsights.com/search-engine-optimisation-seo.** When completing keyphrase analysis we need to understand different qualifiers that users type in. Here are examples of common types of qualifiers for 'car insurance':

- *comparison/quality* – compare car insurance
- *adjective* (price/product qualifiers) – cheap car insurance, woman car insurance
- *intended use* – high mileage car insurance
- *product type* – holiday car insurance
- *vendor* – churchill car insurance
- *location* – car insurance UK
- *action request* – buy car insurance.

According to the Google Keyword tool for a single month in 2011, for searches completed in the UK, the most popular exact phrases related to car insurance were:

- car insurance: 550,000
- cheap car insurance: 201,000

- car insurance quotes: 110,000
- compare car insurance: 49,500
- cheapest car insurance: 40,500
- car insurance comparison: 40,500
- temporary car insurance: 33,100
- car insurance groups: 27,100
- short-term car insurance: 27,000
- car insurance for young drivers: 22,200
- classic car insurance: 22,200

These data suggest the importance of ranking well for high-volume keyphrases such as 'cheap car insurance' and to consider products and services that target a need such as 'temporary' or 'short-term insurance'.

4 On-page optimisation

Although each search engine has its own algorithm with many weighting factors that change through time, fortunately there are common factors in the match between search terms entered and the occurrence of the words on the page that influence search engine rankings.

Occurrence of search term in body copy

The number of times the keyphrase is repeated in the text of the web page is a key factor in determining the position for a keyphrase. Copy can be written to increase the number of times a word or phrase is used (technically, keyphrase density) and ultimately boost position in the search engine. Note though that search engines carry out checks that a phrase is not repeated too many times such as 'cheap flights... cheap flights... cheap flights... cheap flights... cheap flights... cheap flights... cheap flights... cheap flights...' or the keyword is hidden using the same colour text and backgound and will not list the page if this keyphrase density is too high or it believes 'search engine spamming' has occurred. Today, other ranking factors like anchor text of backlinks pointing to the page from other sites are much more important.

In its guidance for Webmasters, Google states:

> Google goes far beyond the number of times a term appears on a page and examines all aspects of the page's content (and the content of the pages linking to it) to determine if it's a good match for your query.

These other factors include:

- frequency (which must be not too excessive, i.e. less than 2–4 per cent)
- occurrence in headings <h1>, <h2>
- occurrence in anchor text of hyperlinks
- markup such as bold
- density (the number of times)
- proximity of phrase to start of document and the gap between individual keywords
- alternative image text (explained below)
- document meta-data (explained below).

Alternative image text

Graphical images can have hidden text associated with them that is not seen by the user (unless graphical images are turned off or the mouse is rolled-over the image) but will be seen and indexed by the search engine and is a minor ranking factor, particularly in images linking to other pages. For example, text about a company name and products can be assigned to a company logo using the 'ALT' tag or attribute of the image tag as follows:

```
<img name="Logo" src="logo.gif" alt="Car insurance">
```

Document meta-data

'Meta' refers to information 'about' the page whichcharacterises it. The three most important types of meta-data are the document <title> tag, the document 'descriptions' meta tag and the document 'keywords' meta tag. These need to be unique for each page on a site(s) otherwise the search engine may assess the content as duplicate and some pages may be down-weighted in importance. Let's look at it in a little more detail:

1 *The document title.* The <title> tag is arguably the most important type of meta-data since each search engine places significant weighting on the keyphrases contained within it AND it is the call-to-action hyperlink on the search engine results page (Figure 9.3). If it contains powerful, relevant copy you will get more clicks and the search engine will assess relevance relative to other pages which are getting fewer clicks.

2 *The 'description' meta tag.* A meta tag is an attribute of the page within the HTML <head> section which can be set by the content owner. It doesn't directly affect ranking, but shows the information which will typically be displayed in the search engine results page. If it is absent or too short relevant 'snippets' will be used from within the body copy, but it is best to control messages and this can help identify the page as unique to prevent duplicate content problems. So, the page creator can modify this to make a stronger call-to-action in the search engine listings as in this case:

```
<meta name="description" content="Direct Line offers you great value car insurance
by cutting out the middleman and passing the savings directly on to you. To find out
if you could save, why not get a car insurance quote? Breakdown Cover Insurance
also available.">
```

To see how relevant and unique your <title> and meta descriptions are, use the Google 'site': syntax with a keyphrase – this will return all the pages on your site about a particular topic. For example:

```
<seo site:smartinsights.com>
```

To view meta tags for a site, select View, Source or Page Source in your browser.

3 *The 'keywords' meta-tag.* The meta keywords meta-tag is used to summarise the content of a document based on keywords. Some unscrupulous SEOs can still be heard to say to potential clients ('we will optimise your meta tags'). But this is not significant today since the keywords meta tag is relatively unimportant as a ranking factor (Google has never used them), although these keywords may be important to internal search engines. For example:

```
<meta name="keywords" content="Car insurance, Home insurance, Travel
insurance, Direct line, Breakdown cover, Mortgages personal loans, Pet insurance,
Annual holiday insurance, Car loans, uk mortgages, Life insurance, Critical illness
cover">
```

5 External linking

Boosting externals links is vital to SEO in competitive markets – on-page optimisation is insufficient, although it is less easy to control and often neglected. The founders of Google realised that the number of links into a page and their quality was a great way of determining the relevance of a page to searchers, especially when combined with the keyphrases on that page (Brin and Page, 1998). Although the Google algorithm has been upgraded and refined continuously since then, the number and quality of external links is still recognised as the most important ranking factor and this is similar for other search engines. As we mentioned above, links shared through social media are now also used as ranking factors.

PageRank
A scale between 0 to 10 used by Google named after Google founder Larry Page which is used to assess the importance of websites according to the number of inbound links or backlinks.

Generally, the more links a page has from good quality sites, the better its ranking will be. **PageRank** helps Google deliver relevant results since it counts each link from another site as a vote. However, not all votes are equal – Google gives greater weight to links from pages which themselves have a high PageRank and where the link anchor text or adjacent text contains text relevant to the keyphrase. It has been refined to identify sites that are 'authority sites' or hub sites for a particular type of search. For keyphrases where there is a lot of competition, such as 'car insurance', the quantity and quality of inbound links will be more important than keyphrase density in determining ranking.

While natural links will be generated if content is useful, a proactive approach to link-building is required in competitive markets. Chaffey and Smith (2008) recommend these steps to help boost your external links.

1 *Identify and create popular content and services.* By creating more valuable content and then showcasing them within your navigation, or grouping it within a few pages such as a 'Useful Resources' or a more extensive 'Resource Centre', you can encourage more people to link to your content naturally, or approach them and suggest they link or bookmark not only to the home page, but directly to the useful tools that have been created.
2 *Identify potential partner sites.* There are several options to find partner sites. It is helpful to try to identify the types of sites that you may be able to link with, for example:
   - directories of links (often less valuable)
   - traditional media sites
   - niche online-only media sites
   - trade associations
   - manufacturers, suppliers and other business partners
   - press release distribution sites
   - bloggers including customers and partners
   - social networks.

   Note: The section on online PR later in this chapter has more guidance on approaches for link-building.
3 *Contact partner sites.* A typical sequence is:
   - Step 1 – write e-mail encouraging link (or phone call to discuss from someone inside the company will often work best).
   - Step 2 – follow-up link.
   - Step 3 – setup links.

6 Internal link structures

Many of the principles of external link building can also be applied to links within sites. The most important principle is to include keyphrases used by searchers within the anchor text of a hyperlink to point to relevant content. It's also important to consider how to increase the number of internal links to pages which you want to rank well. A meshed structure with lots of interlinks can work better than a simple hierarchy.

PageRank varies for pages across a site. The home page is typically highest, with each page deeper within the site having a lower PageRank. There are several implications of this. First, it is helpful to include the most important keyphrases you want to target on the homepage or at the second level in the site hierarchy. Second pages that feature in the main or secondary navigation (text link menus referencing the keyphrase in the anchor text are best) are more likely to rank highly than pages deeper in the site that don't have many internal backlinks because they are not in the menu. Third, you need to review whether there are pages deeper within the site which feature products or services that are important, and which you need to rank for.

To summarise the complexities of SEO, see the compilation of the most important ranking factors based on a panel of experts defined by SEOMoz (2011b) Google Search Engine Ranking Factors.

Paid search marketing

Although SEO has proved a popular form of digital marketing, paid search marketing is still of great relevance since it gives much more control on the appearance in the listings subject to the amount bid and the relevance of the ad.

Each of the main search engines has its own paid advertising programme:

- Google Adwords (**http://adwords.google.com**)
- Microsoft Bing and Yahoo! adCenter (**http://adcenter.microsoft.com**)

What is paid search marketing?

We explained the principles of paid search marketing or sponsored links in the introduction to the section on search engine marketing . Although we said that the main model for paying for sponsored listings in the search engines is pay-per-click marketing, we have called this section paid search marketing since there are, increasingly, other options for payment on what is known as the content network.

Paid search content network

Display(or content) network
Sponsored links are displayed by the search engine on third-party sites such as online publishers, aggregators or social networks. Ads can be paid for on a CPC, CPM or a CPA basis. There are also options for graphical or video ads as well as text-based ads.

Contextual ad
Ad relevant to page content on third-party sites brokered by search ad networks.

Trusted feed
An automated method of putting content into a search engine index or an aggregator database.

Quality score
An assessment in paid search by Google AdWords (and now other search engines) of an individual ad triggered by a keyword which, in combination with the bid amount, determines the ranking of the ad relative to competitors. The primary factor is the click-through rate for each ad, but quality score also considers the match between the keyword and the occurrence of the keyword in the text, historical click-through rates, the engagement of the searcher when they click-through to the site and the speed at which the page loads.

Paid listings are also available through the **displaynetwork** of the search engines such as Google Adsense and Yahoo! Content Match. These **contextual ads** are automatically displayed according to the page content. They can be paid for on a CPC, CPM or CPA (pay-per-action) basis and include not only text ads but also options for graphical display ads or video ads. Google generates around a third of its revenue from the content network, so there is a significant amount of expenditure on the network.

Trusted feeds

Trusted feeds or paid for inclusion is no longer significant to search advertising for most organisations, so we will only cover them briefly. In trusted feeds used by Yahoo!, the ad or search listings content was automatically uploaded to a search engine from a catalogue or document database for inclusion in the search results. A similar approach is used by retailers to include their products in Google Product Search (see documentation for Google Merchant Blog for the latest techniques). Another related option is to advertise in RSS feeds.

What controls position in paid search?

In early pay-per-click programs, the relative ranking of sponsored listings was typically based on the highest bidded cost-per-click for each keyword phrase. So it was a pure auction arrangement with the cost-per-click dependent on the balance of the extent of competition in the marketplace against the revenue or profit that can be generated dependent on conversion rates to sale and retention. The variation in bid amounts for clients of one search bid management tool are shown in Table 9.2.

Contrary to what many web users may believe, today it is not necessarily the company which is prepared to pay the most per click who will get top spot. The search engines also take the relative click-through rates of the ads dependent on their position (lower positions naturally have lower click-through rates) into account when ranking the sponsored links, so ads which do not appear relevant, because fewer people are clicking on them, will drop down or may even disappear off the listing. The analysis of CTR to determine position is part of the **quality score**, a concept originally developed by Google but now integrated as part of the Microsoft Bing and Yahoo! search networks.

The quality score

Understanding the quality score is the key to successful paid search marketing. You should consider its implications when you structure the account and write copy. Google developed

Table 9.2 Variation in cost-per-click in different categories for US paid search campaigns

Category	CPC ($)
All finance	2.03
Travel	0.48
Automotive	0.53
Retail	0.43

Source: Efficient Frontier (2011)

the quality score because they understood that delivering *relevance* through the sponsored links was essential to their user's experience, and their profits. In their AdWords help system, they explain:

> The AdWords system works best for everybody; advertisers, users, publishers and Google too when the ads we display match our users' needs as closely as possible. We call this idea 'relevance'.
>
> We measure relevance in a simple way: Typically, the higher an ad's quality score, the more relevant it is for the keywords to which it is tied. When your ads are highly relevant, they tend to earn more clicks, move higher in Ad Rank and bring you the most success.

A summary formula for the Google quality score is:

> Quality score = (keyword's click-through rate, ad text relevance, keyword relevance, landing page relevance and other methods of assessing relevance)

So, higher click-through rates achieved through better targeted creative copy are rewarded as is relevance of the landing page (Google now sends out AdBots-Google to check them out). More relevant ads are also rewarded through ad text relevance, which is an assessment of the match of headline and description to the search term. Finally, the keyword relevance is the match of the triggering keyword to the search term entered.

If you have ever wondered why the number of paid ads above the natural listings varies from none to three, then it's down to the quality score – you can only get the coveted positions for keywords which have a sufficiently high quality score – you can't 'buy your way to the top' as many think.

Advantages and disadvantages of paid search marketing

Paid search listings, or sponsored links, are very important to achieve visibility in search engines when an organisation is in a competitive market given the competition to appear on the first page of the natural listing for target keyphrases.

As a result, many companies with an established paid search programme may generate more visits from paid search than SEO, although this wouldn't be true for companies that are class leaders in SEO.

Advantages of paid search marketing

The main benefit of paid search marketing are:

- *The advertiser is not paying for the ad to be displayed.* As we explained at the start of Chapter 8, wastage is much lower with paid search compared to traditional advertising. Cost is only incurred when an ad is clicked on and a visitor is directed to the advertiser's website. Hence it's a cost-per-click (CPC) model! However, there are increasingly options for paid search marketing using other techniques – Google also offers CPM (site targeting) and CPA (pay-per-action) options on its content network where contextual ads are displayed on third-party sites relevant to the content on a page.
- *PPC advertising is highly targeted.* The relevant ad with a link to a destination web page is only displayed when the user of a search engine types in a specific phrase (or the ad appears on the content network, triggered by relevant content on a publisher's page), so there is limited wastage compared to other media. YouTube users can also be targeted through Google's 'promoted video' PPC option. Users responding to a particular keyphrase or reading related content have high intent or interest and so tend to be good-quality leads.
- *Good accountability.* With the right tracking system, the ROI for individual keywords can be calculated.
- *Predictable.* Traffic, rankings and results are generally stable and predictable in comparison with SEO.
- *Technically simpler than SEO.* Position is based on combination of bid amount and quality score. Whereas SEO requires long-term, technically complex work on page optimisation, site re-stucturing and link building.
- *Remarketing.* Google offers retargeting through cookies placed on the searchers computer to display ads on the content network after someone has clicked on a paid search ad as a reminder to act. These can be effective in boosting the conversion rate to lead or sale.
- *Speed.* PPC listings get posted quickly, usually in a few days (following editor review). SEO results can take weeks or months to be achieved. Moreover, when a website is revised for SEO, rankings will initially drop while the site is re-indexed by the search engines.
- *Branding.* Tests have shown that there is a branding effect with PPC, even if users do not click on the ad. This can be useful for the launch of products or major campaigns.

Disadvantages of paid search marketing

However, there disadvantages to be managed:

- *Competitive and expensive.* Since pay-per-click has become popular, some companies may get involved in bidding wars that drive bids up to an unacceptable level. Some phrases such as 'life insurance' can exceed £10 per click.
- *Inappropriate.* For companies with a lower budget or a narrower range of products on which to generate lifetime value, it might not be cost effective to compete.
- *Requires specialist knowledge.* PPC requires a knowledge of configuration, bidding options and of the reporting facilities of different ad networks. Internal staff can be trained, but they will need to keep up-to-date with changes to the paid search services.
- *Time consuming.* To manage a PPC account can require daily or even hourly checks on the bidding in order to stay competitive. This can amount to a lot of time. The tools and best practice varies frequently, so keeping up-to-date is difficult.
- *Irrelevant.* Sponsored listings are only part of the search engine marketing mix. Many search users do not click on these because they don't trust advertisers, although these are mainly people involved in marketing!

Best practice in planning and managing paid search marketing

With PPC, as for any other media, media buyers carefully evaluate the advertising costs in relation to the initial purchase value or lifetime value they feel they will achieve from the average customer. As well as considering the cost-per-click (CPC), you need to think about the conversion rate when the visitor arrives at your site. Clearly, an ad could be effective in generating click-throughs or traffic, but not achieve the outcome required on the website such as generating a lead or online sale. This could be because there is a poor-incentive call-to-action or the profile of the visitors is simply wrong. One implication of this is that it will often be more cost effective if targeted microsites or landing pages are created specifically for certain keyphrases to convert users to making an enquiry or sale. These can be part of the site structure, so clicking on a 'car insurance' ad will take the visitor through to the car insurance page on a site rather than a home page.

Table 9.3 shows how cost-per-click can differ between different keywords that on generic (e.g. 'car insurance') and specific (e.g. 'women's car insurance'). It also shows the impact of different conversion rates on the overall CPA. The table also shows the cost of PPC search in competitive categories and why companies will strive to maximise their quality score to help reduce costs.

The cost per customer acquisition (CPA) can be calculated as follows:

$$\text{Cost per acquisition} = \frac{100}{\text{conversion rate \%}} \times \text{cost–per–click}$$

Given the range in costs, two types of strategy can be pursued in PPC search engine advertising. If budget permits, a premium strategy can be followed to compete with the major competitors who are bidding the highest amounts on popular keywords. Such a strategy is based on being able to achieve an acceptable conversion rate once the customers are driven through to the website. A lower-cost strategy involves bidding on lower-cost, less popular phrases. These will generate less traffic, so it will be necessary to devise a lot of these phrases to match the traffic from premium keywords.

Table 9.3 Examples of cost-per-click and CPA figures

Keywords	Clicks/day	Avg. CPC	Cost/day	CPA @ 25% conversion	CPA @ 10% conversion
'car insurance'	1323	€15.6	€20,640	€62	€156
'cheap car insurance'	199	€14.6	€2905	€58	€146
'woman car insurance'	4	€11.6	€46	€46	€116

Optimising pay-per-click

Each PPC keyphrase ideally needs to be managed individually in order to make sure that the bid (amount per click) remains competitive in order to show up in the top of the results. Experienced PPC marketers broaden the range of keyphrases to include lower-volume phrases. Since each advertiser will typically manage thousands of keywords to generate click-throughs, manual bidding soon becomes impractical.

Some search engines include their own bid management tools, but if an organisation is using different pay-per-click schemes, it makes sense to use a single tool to manage them all. It also makes comparison of performance easier too. Bid management software such as Acquisio (**www.acquisio.com**) and WordStream (**www.wordstream.com**) can be used across a range of PPC services to manage keyphrases across multiple PPC ad networks and optimise the costs of search engine advertising. The current CPC is regularly reviewed and your bid is reduced or increased to maintain the position you want according to different strategies and ROI limits, with amounts capped such that advertisers do not pay more than the maximum they have deposited.

As more marketers have become aware of the benefits of PPC, competition has increased and this has driven up the cost-per-click (CPC) and so reduced its profitability.

Although pay-per-click marketing does not initially appear as complex as search engine optimisation, in reality, there are many issues to consider. For example, the Econsultancy (2008b) guide to pay-per-click marketing identifies these paid search strategy issues which paid search marketers and their agencies must address.

1 **Targeting**
   - *Search ad network strategy.* Which of the search networks mentioned above do you use? Which are used in different countries?
   - *Content network strategy.* How do you treat the content network? Do you disable it? Create separate campaigns? Target specific sites using the Placement tool? Develop different creative? Use placement targeting in Google?
   - *Campaign structure strategy.* Campaign structure is important to ensure that searches using a specific search term trigger the relevant ad creative. Are AdGroups small enough to deliver a message relevant for the keyphrase entered?
   - *Keyword matching strategy.* How is creative targeted using the combination of broad match and negative match, phrase match and exact match?
   - *Search-term targeting strategy.* What are the strategies for targeting different types of keyphrases such as brand, generic, product-specific and different qualifiers (cheap, compare, etc.)?

2 **Budget and bid management**
   - *Budgeting strategy.* Is budget set as maximum cost-per-click (CPC) at the appropriate level to deliver satisfactory return on investment? Is daily budget sufficient that ads are served at full delivery (always present)?
   - *Listing position strategy.* Which positions are targeted for different keywords?
   - *Bidding strategies.* What is the appropriate maximum cost per click for different target keywords and campaigns to maximise effectiveness?
   - *Dayparting strategy.* Are ads delivered continuously through the day and week or are different certain days and times targeted (e.g. office hours, evening after ad breaks)?
   - *Bid management tool strategy.* Is a tool used to automate bidding? Which?

3 **Creative testing and campaign optimisation**
   - *Ad creative and copy strategy.* How are the 95 characters forming ad headlines, description and creative used to encourage click-through (and reduce click-through from unqualified visitors if necessary)? Is alternative copy tested? How are ads tested?
   - *Destination or landing page strategy.* How are landing pages improved?
   - *Campaign review and optimisation strategy.* What is the workflow for reviewing and improving success? Which reports are used? How often are they reviewed? By who? Which tests are used? What are the follow-ups?
   - *Specialist and innovative paid search techniques.* These include local, international, pay-per-call, mobile search.

4 **Communications integration.**

- *SEO integration strategy.* How is SEO integrated with paid search to maximise ROI?
- *Affiliate integration strategy.* How is affiliate marketing integrated with paid search to maximise ROI?
- *Marketing campaign integration strategy.* How is budget and creative changed during offline campaigns?

Beware of the fake clicks!

Whenever the principle of PPC marketing is described to marketers, very soon a light bulb switches on and they ask, 'So we can click on competitors and bankrupt them?' Well, actually, no. The PPC ad networks detect multiple clicks from the same computer (IP address) and say they filter them out. However, there are techniques to mimic multiple clicks from different locations, such as software tools and even services where you can pay a team of people across the world to click on these links. It is estimated that in competitive markets one in five of the clicks may be fake. While this can be factored into the conversion rates you will achieve, ultimately this could destroy PPC advertising so the search engines work hard to eliminate it.

Online public relations

What is online public relations (e-PR)?

Public relations (PR)
The management of the awareness, understanding and reputation of an organisation or brand, primarily achieved through influencing exposure in the media.

Digital media have become a very important element of **public relations (PR)**. Mike Grehan, a UK search engine marketing specialist, explains (Grehan, 2004):

> Both online and off, the process is much the same when using PR to increase awareness, differentiate yourself from the crowd and improve perception. Many offline PR companies now employ staff with specialist online skills. The web itself offers a plethora of news sites and services. And, of course, there are thousands and thousands of newsletters and zines covering just about every topic under the sun. Never before has there been a better opportunity to get your message to the broadest geographic and multi-demographic audience. But you need to understand the pitfalls on both sides to be able to avoid.

Online PR activity is closely associated with improving results from many of the other communications techniques described in this chapter, in particular SEO (link-building), partnership marketing and social media marketing. Furthermore, online PR has witnessed much innovation of Web 2.0-based approaches such as blogs, feeds, social networks and widgets which we will explore in this section.

But let's start with an understanding of traditional public relations – itself somewhat intangible. As you will know, 'PR' and 'public relations' are often used interchangeably. Unfortunately, PR is also an abbreviation for 'press release' or 'press relations'. Of course, the scope of PR is much wider than press releases. On its website, the UK Institute of PR defines PR as follows:

> Public relations is about reputation – the result of what you do, what you say and what others say about you. Public relations is the discipline which looks after reputation, with the aim of earning understanding and support and influencing opinion and behaviour. It is the planned and sustained effort to establish and maintain goodwill and mutual understanding between an organisation and its publics [its target audience including potential customers and stakeholders].

From a marketing communications and traffic building perspective, the main activities we are interested in are media relations which are used to influence potential customers. While websites are important tools for promoting investor relations and CSR (corporate social responsibility), this is not our main focus here.

Online public relations (e-PR)
Maximising favourable mentions of your company, brands, products or websites on third-party websites which are likely to be visited by your target audience. Online PR can extend reach and awareness of a brand within an audience and will also generate backlinks vital to SEO. It can also be used to support viral or word-of-mouth marketing activities in other media.

Online PR or e-PR leverages the network effect of the Internet. Remember that Internet is a contraction of 'interconnected networks'! Mentions of a brand or site on other sites are powerful in shaping opinions and driving visitors to your site. The main element of online PR is maximising favourable mentions of an organisation, its brands, products or websites on third-party websites which are likely to be visited by its target audience. Furthermore, as we noted in the section on search engine optimisation, the more links there are from other sites to your site, the higher your site will be ranked in the natural or organic listings of the search engines. **Online influencer outreach** is now an important activity to identify companies or individuals with a strong online following and then using these contact to influence their audience. Minimising unfavourable mentions, for example monitoring and influencing conversations in blogs and social networks through **online reputation management**, is also an aspect of online PR.

Mini Case Study 9.1 Renault use influencer outreach to support the growth

In 2010, Renault launched a new range of zero emission vehicles. Renault's objective was to get people talking about the range, and especially the star model, the TWIZY. Renault wanted to create links with opinion leaders sensitive to the automotive sector but also to ecology and new technologies.

To reach influencers and help spread the word about the new model, Agency BuzzParadise organised a special meeting at an international event, LeWeb. The idea was for Renault to use this platform to set up viral advertising aimed at a target sensitive to technological advances. Invitations were sent to 13 bloggers from France, Germany, Great Britain, Italy and Spain writing about High-Tech, Trends, Innovation and Scientific themes. These partners met for a conference session and to tests of vehicles in the ZE range.

As a result, 22 articles were created across the blogs and, through these, 900,000 exposures to the message were generated. This increased visibility for Renault and its TWIZY in the European blogosphere, social networks (Facebook, Twitter) and SEO (Google). The amplification effect of a relatively small number of bloggers is illustrated well by this reach figure. But it's worth remembering that visibility on blogs and social networks like this is usually ephemeral, meaning that the message is only visible for a short time within the blogosphere. So other techniques are also needed to give a more sustained delivery of messages and reminders to the audience. This is where traditional advertising and remarketing through displaying advertising to those who have already visited a company microsite play an important role.

Source: Buzz Paradise (2010), PR 2.0 for Renault, Case study: **http://www.buzzparadise.com/case-studies/pr-2-0-event-for-renault-le-web-2010/**

Differences between online PR and traditional PR

Online influencer outreach
Identifying online influencers such as bloggers, media owners or individuals with a large online following in the social networks and then approaching them to partner together to communicate with their audience.

Online reputation management
Controlling the reputation of an organisation through monitoring and controlling messages placed about the organisation.

Ranchhod *et al.* (2002) identify four key differences between online PR and traditional PR which are fundamentals of online PR that remain true today.

1 *The audience is connected to organisations.* Previously, there was detachment – PR people issued press releases which were distributed over the newswires, picked up by the media, and then published in their outlets. These authors say:

> The communication channel was uni-directional. The institutions communicated and the audiences consumed the information. Even when the communication was considered a two-way process, the institutions had the resources to send information to audiences through a very wide pipeline, while the audiences had only a minuscule pipeline for communicating back to the institutions.

2 *The members of the audience are connected to each other.* Through publishing their own blogs, social profiles or e-newsletters or contributing to reviews or discussions on others, information can be rapidly distributed from person to person and group to group.

Consumers will also have their own conversations about their needs and brands which will shape brand perception and purchase intent. The authors say:

> Today, a company's activity can be discussed and debated over the Internet, with or without the knowledge of that organisation. In the new environment everybody is a communicator, and the institution is just part of the network.

3 *The audience has access to other information.* Often in the past, the communicator was able to make a statement that it would be difficult for the average audience member to challenge – the Internet facilitates rapid comparison of statements. The authors say:

> It takes a matter of minutes to access multiple sources of information over the Internet. Any statement made can be dissected, analysed, discussed and challenged within hours by interested individuals. In the connected world, information does not exist in a vacuum.

4 *Audiences pull information.* Today this is often known as inbound marketing. Previously there were limited channels in terms of television and press. Today there are many sources and channels of information – this makes it more difficult for the message to be seen. The authors say:

> Until recently, television offered only a few channels. People communicated with one another by post and by phone. In these conditions, it was easy for a public relations practitioner to make a message stand out.

For the marketer or PR professional, managing PR, the main differences are:

- *Less easy to control.* There are many more places a brand can be discussed online, such as in blogs and forums, compared to traditional media where there are a smaller number of media outlets with news filtered through journalists and other editorial staff.
- *More options to create their own stories.* Since a company will have its own site, press centre, feeds and blogs, it is possible to bypass other media owners to some extent. Many companies have now created a 'social media newsroom'.
- *Need for faster response.* It is often said that 'bad news travels fast'. This has been facilitated online and a 'blogstorm' can soon arise where many bloggers are critical of a brand's action. Rapid response teams are needed. Some brands have created a social media command centre as part of a **social media governance** process based on **social media listening**. To see examples of social media governance policies in a range of sectors, see **www.socialmediagovernance.com**.
- *Easier to monitor.* Since Google and online reputation management tools index many pages, it is arguably easier to identify when a brand is discussed online.

Social media governance
A definition of how companies should respond to social mentions that may give rise to leads or reputational damage.

Social media listening
The process of using monitoring tools to review mentions of a brand and related keywords within social networks and other online sites.

Advantages and disadvantages of online public relations

Advantages of online public relations

The advantages of the proactive online public relations techniques which seek to build a buzz around a campaign or to gain favourable mentions and links on third-party sites are:

- *Reach.* E-PR can be a relatively low-cost method of directly reaching a niche audience or a mass audience if the brand is amenable to stories that are of interest to publishers. This is often the case for new online brands and startups such as Zopa (**www.zopa.com**). If buzz around an online campaign orchestrated through online PR is successful then additional reach and impact may also be generated by traditional media such as TV, print and radio.
- *Cost.* The costs for online PR are the agency or internal staff fees for developing the online PR plan, concepts and content. Since there are no media placement costs, this can be cost effective.

Mini Case Study 9.2 Dell and Gatorade launch social media command centres

In 2010/2011 Dell and Gatorade (Figure 9.7) independently launched 'social media command centres'. Watch the videos (available from the links for this chapter) to see how they planned to use them for reputation managing and reviewing the impact of social media.

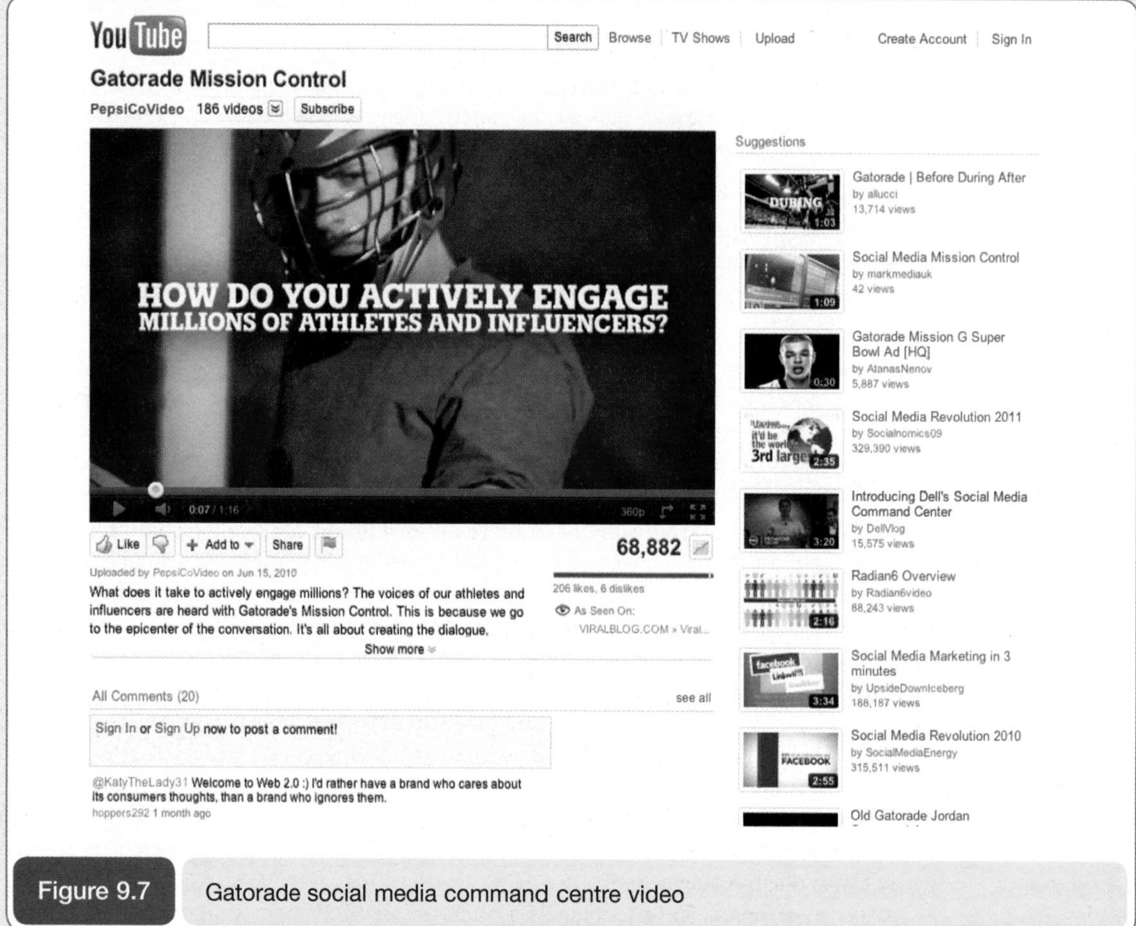

Figure 9.7 Gatorade social media command centre video

Clearly, these are big brands, what does this mean for smaller organisations? Some have even questioned their relevance for larger companies calling them white elephants. These are some implications of the need for social media listening highlighted by the approach of these big brands:

1. Put in place free or paid listening tools.
2. Use free tools initially to check the volume of conversation. If it's not significant, you probably don't need a 'mission control centre', but you should use a free tool to monitor your brand and respond appropriately – it's not just about monitoring the negatives as some seem to think, it's about reaching out to potential partners and collaborators too.
3. Set up social governance policies.
4. Find a method such that you can follow-up on potential partnership options – remember that Partnerships is the 8th P in the marketing mix.
5. Integrate your social media monitoring and reporting with other business and campaign reporting and web analytics systems.

Source: SmartInsights.com (2011b)

- *Credibility.* Independent comments that are made by a person independent from a company are considered more authentic and can so help raise trust about an online provider such as a retailer (see Figure 9.2). You can see that personal recommendations are particularly important and seem to be trusted more than content sites giving reviews and opinions (although these are still given credence by many web users).
- *Search engine optimisation.* E-PR can help generate backlinks to a site which are favourable for SEO, often from large sites such as online newspapers or magazines which have good link equity.
- *Brand-enhancement and protection.* Favourable stories can enhance the reputation of a brand among its target audience and amplification through influencers can help reach a new audience. But since unfavourable media mentions may damage a brand, so monitoring and response to these is a necessity for most brands.

Disadvantages of online public relations

The main disadvantage of e-PR is that it is not a controlled discipline like online advertising techniques such as pay-per-click marketing or display advertising where the returns generated will be known for a given expenditure. In other words, it could be considered a high-risk investment.

Many marketers are also wary of creating blogs or forums on their sites which may solicit negative comments. However, there are counter-arguments to this, namely that it is best to control and be involved with conversations about a brand on the site rather than when it is less controlled on third-party sites. For example, brands such as Dell (**www.ideastorm.com**) and Honda enable web users to make comments about their brands so this shows they are listening to customer comments and gain valuable sentiment that can feed into new product development ideas.

Best practice in planning and managing online public relations

In this section we will review the different types of online PR activities and techniques to improve results from these activities. The main activities that can be considered to be specifically involved with online PR include:

- communicating with media owners online (influencer outreach)
- link building
- web 2.0 content including blogs, podcasting, RSS feeds and widgets
- managing how your brand is presented on third-party sites
- creating a buzz – online viral marketing.

Communicating with online media owners (influencer outreach)

Forming relationships with publishers of media online gives a way to expand the reach of a brand. These influencers may include traditional journalists, but as we saw in Mini Case Study about Renault, bloggers or celebrities.

Journalists can be influenced online through a press-release area or social media newsroom on the website; creating e-mail alerts about news that journalists and other third parties can sign up to; news stories or releases submitted to online news feeds. Examples of feeds include PR Newswire: (**www.prnewswire.com**), Internetwire (**www.internetwire.com/iwire/home**), PressBox (**www.pressbox.co.uk**), PRWeb (**www.prweb.com**), Business Wire (**www.businesswire.com**). Press releases also can be written for search engine optimisation (SEO) since they will link back to the site.

An increasing number of journalists rely on blogs and feeds for finding sources for stories rather than traditional press releases, so engaging influencers through these is also important. Charles Arthur (**www.charlesarthur.com**), contributor to the *Guardian* in a posting 'Why I'm not reading PR e-mails to get news stories any more', says:

I'm not going to read things that are obviously press releases because the possibility of it just being annoying or irrelevant is too great; I'm going to go to my aggregator instead, because I've chosen every feed there for its potential interest. I pay more attention to my RSS feeds because they're sources I've chosen, rather than the e-mails I get from PR companies.

Link building

Link building
A structured activity to include good quality hyperlinks to your site from relevant sites with a good page rank.

Reciprocal link
Link agreed between yourself and another organisation.

Link building is a key activity for SEO. It can be considered to be an element of online PR since it is about getting your brand visible on third-party sites and creating backlinks related to your site.

Link building needs to be a structured effort to achieve as many quality links into a website as possible from referring websites (these commonly include **reciprocal links** which tend to be less valuable from an SEO perspective than one-way links). We have also seen that your position in the search engine results pages will be higher if you have quality links into relevant content on your site (not necessarily the home page).

McGaffin (2004) provides a great introduction to implementing a structured link building programme. The main principle of link building is as follows, McGaffin says: 'Create great content, link to great content and great content will link to you.' He describes how you should review existing links, link to competitors, set targets and then proactively enquire to suitable site owners for links.

Digital marketing insight 9.3 Reviewing the links into a site

You can use the syntax link:site in Google to see examples of links into a page on a site as judged by Google, e.g. **site:www.smartinsights.com**. But note that this also includes internal links and is not comprehensive. A better option to display links is the SEOmoz Site Open Site Explorer tool (**www.opensiteexplorer.com**). For alerts of new links or new mentions on other sites, Google's own alerts (**www.google.com/alerts**) are useful tools.

Web 2.0 atomised content

Web 2.0 concept
A collection of web services that facilitate interaction of web users with sites to create user-generated content and encouraging behaviours such as community or social network participation, mashups, content rating, use of widgets and tagging.

Blog
An online diary or news source prepared by an individual or a group of people. From 'Web log'. Business blogs are created by an organisation for communication to their audiences.

Many specialist online PR techniques such as blogs, podcasting and RSS feeds, are collectively referred to as **Web 2.0** which we introduced in the first chapter. Web 2.0 represents a revolution in web usage where previously passive consumers of content become active contributors. In Web 2.0 the web itself is merely a platform for interacting with content.

Blogs and blogging

Blogs give an easy method of regularly publishing web pages as online journals, diaries or news or events listings. Many blogs provide commentary or news on a particular subject; others function as more personal online diaries. A typical blog combines text, images and links to other blogs, web pages and other media related to its topic. The capability for readers to leave comments in an interactive format is an important part of many blogs. Feedback (trackback) comments from other sites are also sometimes incorporated. Frequency can be hourly, daily, weekly or less frequently, but several updates daily is typical.

There are many free services which enable anyone to blog (for example **www.wordpress.com** and **www.blogger.com**. The blogging format enables the content on a website to be delivered in different ways. For example, the SmartInsights blog has a lot of rich content related to Internet marketing which can be delivered in different ways:

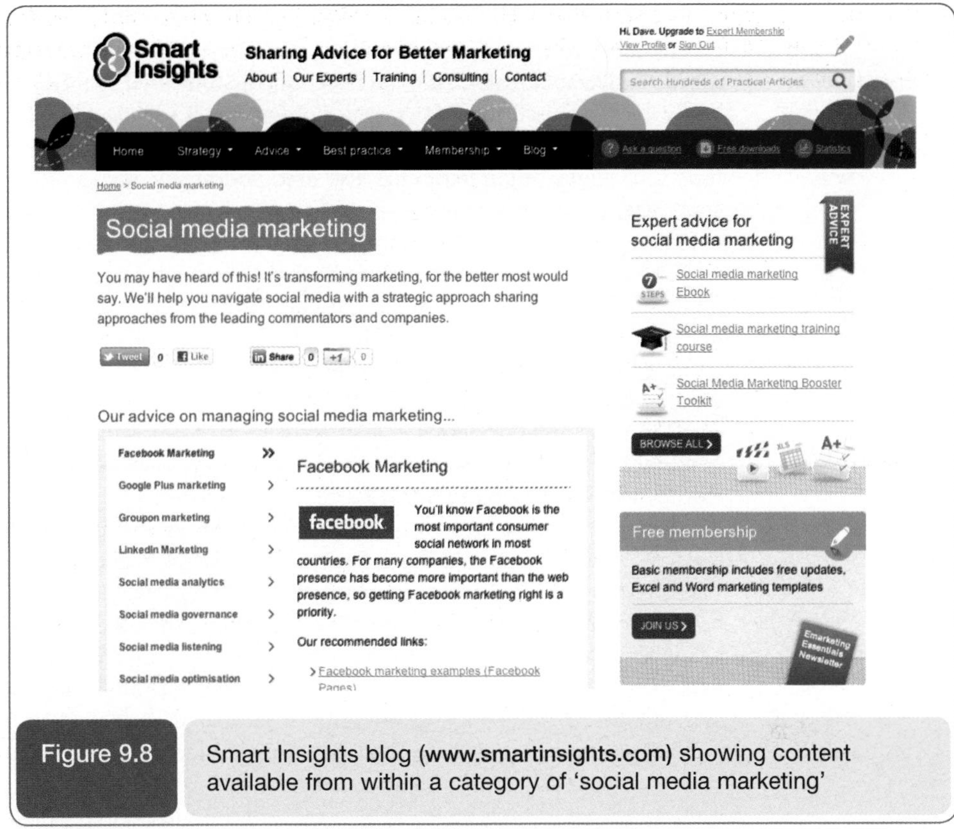

Figure 9.8 Smart Insights blog (**www.smartinsights.com**) showing content available from within a category of 'social media marketing'

- *By topic* (in categories or topics to browse) – example, social media marketing category (Figure 9.8).
- *By tag* (more detailed topics – each article will be tagged with several tags to help them appear in searches) – example, 'B2B' or 'case studies'.
- *By author* (features from different columnists who can be internal or external). Guest posting is an effective method for both guest author and blog to increase reach.
- *By time* (all posts broken down by the different methods above are in reverse date order).

Tagging and folksonomies

Tagging
Users or web page creators categorise content on a site through adding descriptive terms. A common approach in blog posts.

Folksonomy
A contraction of 'folk taxonomy', a method of classifying content based on tagging that has no hierarchy, i.e. without parent–child relationships.

A defining characteristic of Web 2.0 is **tagging** whereby users add their own metadata to content they produce, consume and share. On Flickr (**www.flickr.com**) and Del.icio.us (**del.icio.us**) for example, any user can attach tags to digital media items (files, bookmarks, images). The aggregation of tags creates an organic, free-form, 'bottom-up' taxonomy. The information architect Thomas van der Wal coined the term or 'folksonomy' derived from the idea of a 'folk-taxonomy' (Fitzgerald, 2006). **Folksonomies** are flat (that is, they have no hierarchy, and show no parent–child relationships) and, critically, are completely uncontrolled. A key implication of their lack of structure is that they do not support functions such as drill-down searching and cross-referencing.

Social bookmarking

Social bookmarking
Web users keep a shared version of favourite sites ('Favorites') online. This enables the most popular sites in a category to be identified.

Sites like Digg, Google, Reddit, StumbleUpon and Del.icio.us allow users to store, organise, search and manage favourite web pages on the Internet rather than on their PC. With such **social bookmarking** systems, users save links to web pages that they want to remember and/or share on bookmark hosting sites. These bookmarks are usually public but can be saved privately, shared only with specified people or groups, shared only inside certain networks, or some other combination of public and private domains.

Podcast
Individuals and organisations post online media (audio and video) which can be viewed in the appropriate players including the iPod which first sparked the growth in this technique.

Podcasts are related to blogs since they can potentially be generated by individuals or organisations to voice an opinion either as audio (typically MP3) or less commonly currently as video (video podcasts). They have been successfully used by media organisations such as the BBC which has used them for popular programmes such as film reviews or discussions and for live recordings such as the Beethoven symphonies that received over 600,000 downloads in June 2005 alone. Virgin Radio has also used podcasting, but cannot broadcast music (due to copyright restrictions), only the presenters! A big challenge for achieving visibility for podcasts is that content can only currently be recognised by tags and it is difficult to assess quality without listening to the start of a podcast. All the main search engines are working on techniques to make searching of voice and video content practical. In the meantime, some start-ups such as Odeo (**www.odeo.com**) and Blinkx (**www.blinkx.com**) are developing solutions.

In a business-to-business context, network provider Cisco (**www.cisco.com**) has used video podcasts for its Interaction network, which is used to sell the benefits of its services to small and medium businesses.

Photo, video and slide sharing sites

Photo sharing sites which are popular include Flickr (a Yahoo! service), Picasa (a Google service), Photobucket, Webshots Community, Kodak Gallery, ImageShack and SnapFish. These again rely on tagging to enable users to find related shots they are interested in and can be used to create mashups using widgets to embed the object into a blog or other site (see below for explanation of these terms). Some online campaigns for high-involvement products such as cars or holidays now invite customers to submit their own pictures via services such as Flickr to build ongoing interest in a campaign.

Video sharing sites include YouTube, Google Videos, Jumpcut, Grouper, Revver, Blip.TV, VideoEgg and Daily Motion. These sites have very similar features to photo sharing sites but some add more features in the form of subscriptions to channels and offer code to embed the players on social networks or blogs.

Another way of sharing content important in professional B2B markets is through slide sharing sites such as Scribd and SlideShare.net.

Really Simple Syndication feeds

Really Simple Syndication feed (RSS)
Blog, news or other content is published by an XML standard and syndicated for other sites or read by users in RSS reader software services. Now typically shortened to 'feed', e.g. news feed or sports feed.

Mashup
Websites, pages or widgets that combine the content or functionality of one website or data source with another to create something offering a different type of value to web users from the separate types of content or functionality.

Really Simple Syndication (RSS) is closely related to blogging where blog, news or any type of content such as a new podcast is received by subscribers using a feed reader. It offers a method of receiving news in a feed that uses a different broadcast method from e-mail, so is not subject to the same conflicts with spam or spam filters. Many journalists now subscribe to RSS feeds from sources such as the BBC (**http://news.bbc.co.uk/2/hi/help/3223484.stm**) which publishes RSS feed for different types of content on its site.

RSS is now being used to syndicate not just notices of new blog entries, but also all kinds of data updates including stock quotes, weather data and photo availability. Today, RSS is arguably important for integration of content shared from a blog through to social networks like Google, Facebook and LinkedIn

Mashups

Mashups (a term originally referring to the pop music practice, notably hip-hop, of producing a new song by mixing two or more existing pieces) are sites or widgets that combine the content or functionality of one website with another to create something offering a different type of value to web users from the other types of content or functionality. In practice they provide a way of sharing content between sites and stitching together sites through exchanging data in common XML-based standards such as RSS.

Examples of mashups include:

- Chicagocrime.org took police data for crime incidents and plotted them on street maps from Google Maps so that visitors could check in advance whether it was the sort of place you might get mugged, and when.

- Housingmaps.com combines Google Maps with Craigslist apartment rental and home purchase data to create an interactive housing search tool.
- Personal content aggregators such as Netvibes (**www.netvibes.com**), iGoogle (**www.google.com/ig**) or Pageflakes (**www.pageflakes.com**) often incorporate news stories from feeds and other data such as the latest e-mails or social network alerts. These are effectively a personal mashup.

Social networks

Social network
A site that facilitates peer-to-peer communication within a group or between individuals through providing facilities to develop user-generated content (UGC) and to exchange messages and comments between different users.

Widget
A badge or button incorporated into a site or social network space by its owner, with content or services typically served from another site making a widget effectively a mini-software application or web service. Content can be updated in real time since the widget interacts with the server each time it loads.

We have described **social networks** in more depth in other chapters, including Chapters 1, 2 and 6. From an online PR perspective, social networking sites can be valuable in these ways:

- They can be used to assess the 'Zeitgeist', i.e. what current trends and opinions are being discussed which can then be built into PR campaigns.
- They can assist in recommendations about brands and products. For example, Hitwise research (Hitwise, 2007) suggests that a high proportion of visits to fashion retail stores such as Top Shop were preceded by usage of social networks, suggesting that some visits are prompted by discussions.
- They can be used to solicit feedback about product experiences and brand perception, either by explicit requests or observing what is discussed. *New Media Age* (2008) quotes Miles Sturt, head of customer experience satisfaction at Nokia, saying buzz research can have an impact on the next model the company makes, rather than the one after:

> It gives us feedback on new handsets within three or four weeks, instead of the four to six months it takes to sit people down for market research interviews. That's important because our product teams start working on a refresh of a model straight after launch, so they can apply feedback to the next version of a handset rather than wait a few months for conventional market research that may have to wait for the launch after that.

But, as we note in the section on managing reputation, it is important to monitor comments and respond as appropriate.

Widgets

Widgets are different forms of tools made available on a website or on a user's desktop. They are a relatively new concept associated with Web 2.0. They either provide some functionality, like a calculator, or they provide real-time information, for example on news or weather.

Site owners can encourage partners to place them on their sites and this will help educate people about your brand, possibly generating backlinks for SEO purposes and also engaging with a brand when they're not on the brand owner's site. Widgets offer partner sites the opportunity to add value to their visitors through the gadget functionality or content, or to add to their brand through association with you (co-branding).

Widgets are often placed in the left or right sidebar, or in the body of an article. They are relatively easy for site owners to implement, usually a couple of lines of Javascript, but this does depend on the content management system.

The main types of widgets are:

- *Web widgets.* Web widgets have been used for a long time as part of affiliate marketing, but they are getting more sophisticated by enabling searches on a site, real-time price updates or even streaming video.
- *Google gadgets.* Different content can be incorporated into a personalised Google 'iGoogle' homepage.
- *Desktop and operating system gadgets.* Microsoft Windows and Apple Operating systems provide dashboard gadgets which make it easier to subscribe to information updates.
- *Social sharing widgets.* These encourage site visitors to share content they like, effectively voting on it. Share buttons provided by the networks or aggregators like AddThis.com

or ShareThis.com are now an essential part of many sites to assist in 'viral amplification'. Figure 9.9 gives an example where you can see how the popularity of different sharing services varies in different countries.

- *Facebook applications.* Facebook have created an API known as the Facebook platform (application programming interface) to enable developers to create small interactive programs that site owners can add to their sites to personalise them. Charitable site Just Giving has a branded app with several hundred users.

Atomisation

Atomisation
Atomisation in a Web 2.0 context refers to a concept where the content on a site is broken down into smaller fundamental units which can then be distributed via the web through links to other sites. Examples of atomisation include the stories and pages in individual feeds being syndicated to third-party sites and widgets.

Atomisation is a way of summarising a significant trend in Web 2.0 which incorporates some of the marketing techniques we have reviewed here such as posts on social networks, feeds and widgets.

In a Web 2.0 context atomisation describes how the content on a website can be broken down into smaller 'content objects' which are then shareable and can potentially be aggregated together with other content to provide content and services valuable for other site owners and visitors.

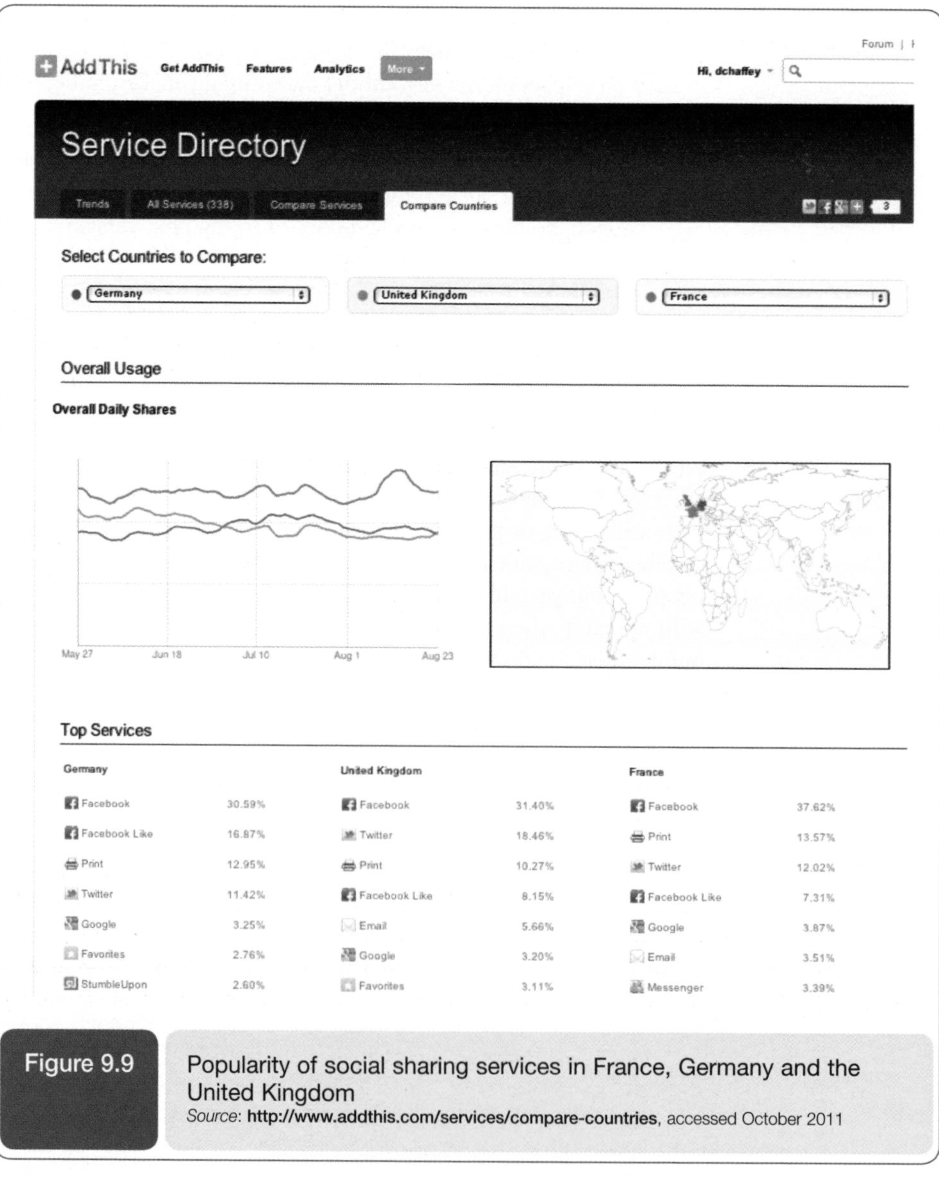

Figure 9.9 Popularity of social sharing services in France, Germany and the United Kingdom
Source: **http://www.addthis.com/services/compare-countries**, accessed October 2011

For site owners, options to consider for the application of atomisation include:

- Providing content RSS feeds in different categories through their content management system. For example, the BBC effectively provides tens of thousands of newsletters on their site at the level of detail or granularity to support the interest of their readers i.e. separate feeds at different levels of aggregation, e.g. sport, football, premier league football or a fan's individual team.
- Sharing social updates, images, videos or whitepapers. These can be embedded from specialist sites like Flickr, YouTube or Scribd using widgets made available by the site owner.
- Separating out content which should be provided as data feeds of new stories or statistics into widgets on other sites. For example, UK retail statistics widget dashboard for iGoogle created by Google.
- Development of web services which update widgets with data from their databases. A classic example is the Just Giving widget (**www.justgiving.com**) where money raised by a charity donor is regularly updated.
- Creating badges which can be incorporated within blogs or social networks by their fans or advocates. The membership body CIPD does this well through their 'link to us' programme (**www.cipd.co.uk/absite/bannerselect.htm**) which encourages partners to add banners or text links to their site to link with the CIPD site. Similiarly, Hitwise encourages retailers to link it through its Top 10 Award programme (an award for the Top 10 most popular websites across each of the 160+ Hitwise industries by market share of visits).

Online partnerships including affiliate marketing

We showed in Chapter 5 that partnerships are an important part of today's marketing mix. The same is true online. Resources must be devoted to managing your online partners. Many large organisations have specific staff to manage these relationships. In smaller organisations partnership management is often neglected, which is a missed opportunity. There are three key types of online partnerships which need to be managed: link building (covered in the previous section), affiliate marketing and online sponsorship. All should involve a structured approach to managing links through to a site. The main and most important form of partnership marketing for transactional e-commerce sites which we review in this section is affiliate marketing. We also review options for online sponsorship. Other forms of digital marketing communications reviewed in this chapter, which are often free in terms of the visitors generated, can also be considered as partner marketing, for example online PR, link-building and use of Web 2.0 syndication.

Affiliate marketing

Affiliate marketing
A commission-based arrangement where referring sites (publishers) receive a commission on sales or leads by merchants (retailers or other transactional sites). Commission is usually based on a percentage of product sale price or a fixed amount for each sale (CPA or cost per acquisition), but may also sometimes be based on a per-click basis, for example when an aggregator refers visits to merchants.

Affiliate marketing divides marketers and agencies as to its value. The discussion revolves around the value of affiliate marketing in generating incremental sales. There is no doubt that affiliates can generate more sales at a controlled cost, the question is whether these sales would have occurred anyway if a brand is well known. For example, Amazon has an affiliate programme but it could be argued that its brand is so well known and it has such a large customer base that it would receive most sales anyway. However, Amazon has run its programme for over ten years and although it has reduced commissions, it is still running and is used to promote new product offerings such as music downloads.

What is affiliate marketing?

Affiliate marketing is the ultimate form of marketing communications since it is what is known as a 'pay-per-performance marketing' method – it's a commission-based arrangement where the merchant only pays when they make the sale or get a lead. Compare this to the wastage with traditional advertising or direct mail! It can also drive a volume of business in a range of sectors – many banks, travel companies and online retailers get more than 10% of their sales from a well-run affiliate marketing programme. It's not so suitable though for business products or lower-priced consumer products since it will not be sufficiently profitable for the affiliates, and it may be difficult to recruit sufficient affiliates.

Figure 9.10 summarises the affiliate marketing process. You can see that when a visitor to an affiliate site (who may be an online publisher or aggregator) clicks through to a merchant site, this prospect will be tracked through a cookie placed on the visitor's PC. If the prospect later transacts within an agreed period, usually 1, 7, 30, 60 or 90 days, the affiliate will be credited with the sale through an agreed amount (percentage of sale or fixed amount).

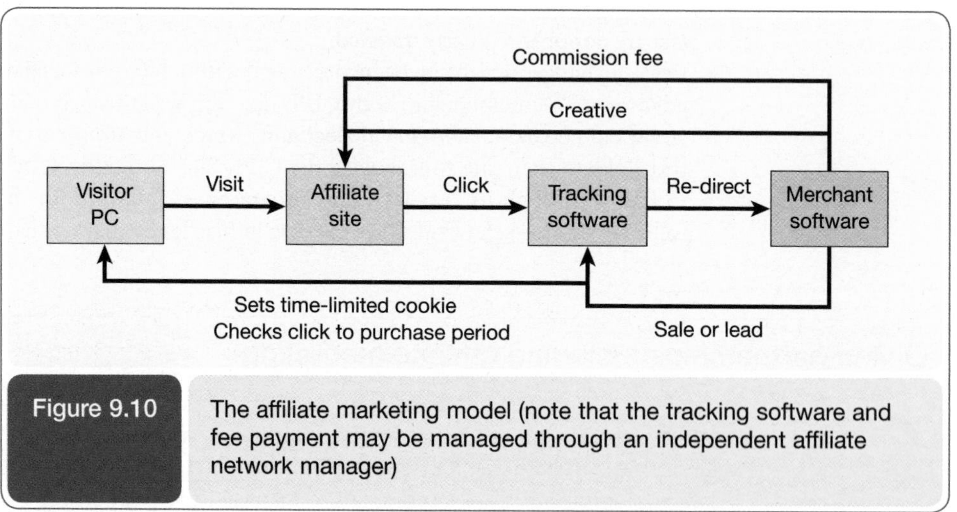

Figure 9.10 The affiliate marketing model (note that the tracking software and fee payment may be managed through an independent affiliate network manager)

Digital marketers need to be selective in choosing the right forms of affiliate marketing – not all may be desirable. These are the options of affiliate marketing models for you to consider.

- *Aggregators.* These are the major comparison sites like Kelkoo, USwitch and Moneysupermarket. These aren't strictly affiliates since some, such as Kelkoo and Shopzilla, charge on a cost-per-click, but USwitch and Moneysupermarket have a CPA model as well. Google Product Search (formerly Froogle) uses a similar model, but is a free option for retailers to submit a feed for which products may then be featured in the top of the Google SERPs.
- *Review sites.* For example CNet software or hardware reviews, or maybe startups like Reevoo or Review Centre. These all link to merchants based on cost-per-click or cost-per-acquisition deals.
- *Rewards sites.* These split the commission between the reward site and their visitors. Examples are GreasyPalm or QuidCo.
- *Voucher code sites.* MyVoucherCodes or Hot UK Deals are typical. If you have some great deals to entice first-time shoppers you should generate business, although many search by well-known brand.
- *Über-bloggers.* Martin Lewis's MoneySavingExpert.com is an incredibly popular site due to his PR efforts and great content. Although he has no ads, he is an affiliate for many sites he recommends.
- *Everyone else.* They don't tend to be high volume super-affiliates like all the above, but they're collectively important and you can work them via affiliate networks like Commission Junction or Tradedoubler. They often specialise in SEO or PPC.

Advantages and disadvantages of affiliate marketing

Advantages of affiliate marketing

Many of the benefits of affiliate marketing are closely related to search engine marketing since affiliates are often expert at deploying SEO or PPC to gain visibility in the search results pages. The main benefits of affiliate marketing are:

- *SERPS visibility.* Gain more visibility in the paid and natural listings of the SERPs (increase 'share of search' page).
- *Reach different audiences.* Can use different affiliates to target different audiences, product categories and related phrases.
- *Responsiveness to marketplace changes.* Affiliates may be more responsive than your in-house or agency teams in terms of algorithm changes for SEO or changes in bidding approaches for PPC. They are also great at identifying gaps in your search strategy. For example, they may be quicker at advertising on new products, or may use keyphrase variants that you haven't considered.
- *Target generic phrases in SERPs.* Enables you to reach customers through generic phrases (e.g. 'clothing') at a relatively low cost if the affiliates secure better positions in natural listings.
- *Increase reach in SERPs.* Increase the reach of your brand or campaign since affiliate ads and links featuring you will be displayed on third-party sites.
- *Generate awareness.* Can be used to generate awareness of brand or new products for which a company is not well known.
- *Diversity risk.* Use of affiliates reduces the risk caused by temporary or more fundamental problems with your SEM management or other digital marketing programmes.
- *Pay-per-performance.* The costs of acquisition can be controlled well.

Disadvantages of affiliate marketing

But there can be substantial drawbacks to an affiliate marketing programme which arise from the fact that your affiliates are mainly motivated by money. It follows that some of them may use unethical techniques to increase their revenue. Potential disadvantages are:

- *Incremental profit or sales may be limited.* You may be cannibalising business you would have achieved anyway.
- *Affiliates may exploit your brand name.* This is particularly the case where affiliates exploit brand names by bidding on variations of it (for example 'Dell', 'Dell Computers' or 'Dell laptop') or by gaining a presence in the natural listings. Here there is already awareness. It is important to prevent this and many affiliate programmes exclude brand bidding, although affiliates can have a role in displacing competitors from the listings for brand terms.
- *May damage brand reputation.* Your ads may be displayed on sites inconsistent with your brand image, such as gambling or pornography sites. Alternatively, creative may be out-of-date which could be illegal.
- *Programme management fees.* If using an affiliate network to manage your campaigns they may take up to 30% of each agreed affiliate commission as additional 'network override'.
- *Programme management time.* Affiliate marketing is founded on forming and maintaining good relationships. This cannot be done through the agency alone – marketers within a company need to speak to their top affiliates.

Best practice in planning and managing affiliate marketing

In this section we will review how affiliate networks can be used to improve the results from affiliate marketing and the main controls on affiliate marketing, i.e. commission, cookie periods and creative. It is important that these parameters are clearly defined in the affiliate agreement to reduce the likelihood of abuse.

Affiliate networks

Affiliate network
Third-party brokers also known as affiliate managers who manage recruitment of affiliates and infrastructure to manage a merchant's affiliate programme in the form of links, tracking and payment of a range of affiliates.

To manage the process of finding affiliates, updating product information, tracking clicks and making payments many companies use an **affiliate network** or affiliate manager such as the US/European networks Commission Junction (**www.cj.com**), Link Share (**www.linkshare.com**) or Trade Doubler (**www.tradedoubler.com**, mainly European). Since the affiliate network takes a cut on each sale, many merchants also try to setup separate relationships with preferred affiliates, often known as 'super affiliates'.

Since many of the important affiliates are members of more than one affiliate network programme, it is usually found that it is not worthwhile for a merchant to join more than two affiliate networks. They also need to be careful that several affiliates are not credited for multiple sales since this quickly becomes unprofitable for the merchant.

Affiliate marketing is often thought to apply solely to e-retailers where the affiliate is paid if there is a purchase on the merchant site. In fact, payment can occur for any action which is recorded on the destination site, for example through a 'thank you' post-transaction page after filling a form. This could be a quote for insurance, trial of a piece of software or registration for download of a paper. However, the majority of affiliate activity is within consumer sectors such as travel, finance and retail rather than business-to-business.

The value of affiliate networks in managing the relationships between merchants and publishers is such that it is rare for merchants to bypass them and so avoid the network override, although Amazon is one example of a merchant with their own programme.

Commission

In affiliate marketing, it is vital that commission is set at such a level that it incentivises affiliates to preferentially promote a merchants' products, while at the same time being profitable.

Earnings per click (EPC)
A relative measure of the effectiveness of a site or section of a site in generating revenue for the site owner through affiliate marketing for every 100 outbound clicks generated.

The affiliates or publishers are naturally obsessive about their **earnings per click (EPC)**. This is average earnings per click and is usually measured across 100 clicks.

EPC is a crucial measure in affiliate marketing since an affiliate will compare merchants on this basis and then usually decide to promote those with the highest EPC, which will be based on the commission levels and the conversion rates to sale for different merchants.

A merchant will set commission levels according to a product's awareness level within a merchant's portfolio of products or how much they feel they need to promote them. It will also be worth increasing commissions when there is a favourable promotion on a product since affiliates will then promote it, knowing that their EPC is more likely to increase. Less well-known products or newly launched products will often have more favourable commissions. For example at the time of writing, Tesco.com used affiliates for different products with different commission as follows:

- e-diets commission from £12 on 1–9 sales to £20 on 61+ sales
- wine at 2 per cent on lowest tier to 3 per cent on the Gold tier of sales of >£2500
- grocery and utilities – flat fee of £5 for first-time purchase only.

Cookie expiry period

Affiliates' EPC will also depend on the cookie expiry period agreed on the time between a visitor clicks the affiliate link and the sale is accredited to the affiliate. Common times are 7, 30 or 90 days. A longer cookie period will result in a higher EPC. Prussakov (2011a) recommends that 60 to 90 days is often best to incentivise affiliates in competitive markets with a longer decision-making period. Merchants don't typically want to pay multiple affiliates for a single sale. Instead, it is usually the last referring affiliate that is credited or a mix between the first and last. So a good tracking system is required to resolve this. Prussakov (2011b) uses the data presented in Figure 9.11 to argue that the majority purchase within a shorter-period, so a longer period gives a better incentive without adversely affecting profitability.

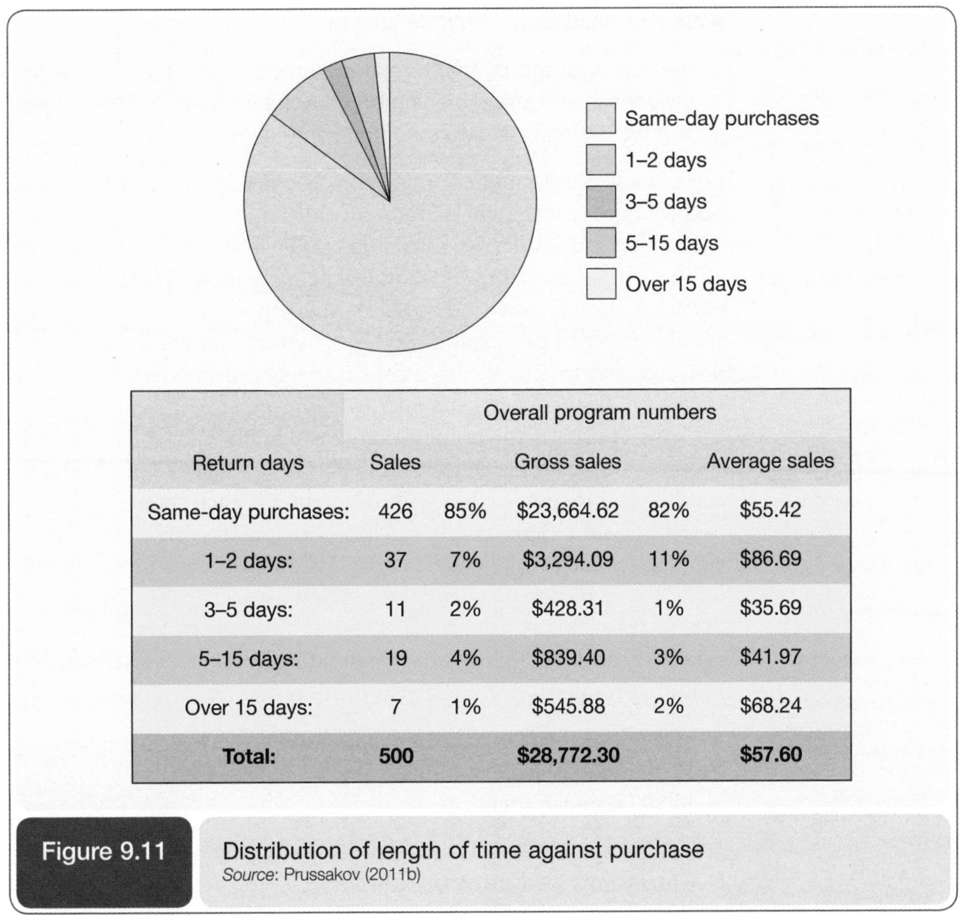

Overall program numbers					
Return days	Sales		Gross sales		Average sales
Same-day purchases:	426	85%	$23,664.62	82%	$55.42
1–2 days:	37	7%	$3,294.09	11%	$86.69
3–5 days:	11	2%	$428.31	1%	$35.69
5–15 days:	19	4%	$839.40	3%	$41.97
Over 15 days:	7	1%	$545.88	2%	$68.24
Total:	**500**		**$28,772.30**		**$57.60**

Figure 9.11 Distribution of length of time against purchase
Source: Prussakov (2011b)

Creative and links

Managing the creative which affiliates use to promote a merchant is a challenge since creative needs to be up-to-date in line with different promotions or it may be misleading, or even illegal. So this needs to be monitored by the affiliate manager. Many merchants now provide live product feeds to affiliate networks in order to keep their promotions and product pricing up-to-date.

There are risks of brand damage through affiliates displaying creative on content which a merchant might feel was not complementary to their brand (for example, a gambling site). This needs to be specified in the affiliate agreement – sites need to be reviewed carefully before affiliates are permitted to join a specific programme and additional sites used by each affiliate should be monitored.

Another form of brand or trademark abuse is when an affiliate bids on a merchant's brand name such that they may receive credit for a sale when a prospect was already aware of the merchant, as explained in Chapter 3 in the legal section. The limits of this should also be specified within the affiliate agreements and monitored carefully.

Online sponsorship

Online sponsorship is not straightforward. It's not just a case of mirroring existing 'real-world' sponsorship arrangements in the 'virtual world', although this is a valid option. There are many additional opportunities for sponsorship online which can be sought out, even if you don't have a big budget at your disposal.

Ryan and Whiteman (2000) define online sponsorship as:

> the linking of a brand with related content or context for the purpose of creating brand awareness and strengthening brand appeal in a form that is clearly distinguishable from a banner, button or other standardised ad unit.

For the advertiser, online sponsorship has the benefit that their name is associated with an online brand that the site visitor is already familiar with. So, for users of a publisher site, with whom they are familiar, sponsorship builds on this existing relationship and trust.

Paid-for sponsorship of another site, or part of it, especially a portal, for an extended period is another way to develop permanent links. Co-branding is a lower-cost method of sponsorship and can exploit synergies between different companies. Note that sponsorship does not have to directly drive visitors to a brand site – it may be more effective if interaction occurs on the media owner's microsite.

A great business-to-business example of online sponsorship is offered by WebTrends which sponsors the customer information channel on ClickZ.com (**www.clickz.com/experts**). They combined this sponsorship with different ads each month offering e-marketers the chance to learn about different topics such as search marketing, retention and conversion marketing through detailed white papers and a 'Take 10' online video presentation by industry experts which could be downloaded by registered users. The objective of these ads was to encourage prospects to subscribe to the WebTrendsWebResults e-newsletter and to assess purchase intent at sign-up enabling follow-up telemarketing by regional distributors. WebTrends reported the following results over a single year of sponsorship:

- list built to 100,000 WebResults total subscribers
- 18,000 Take 10 presentations
- 13,500 seminar attendees.

Co-branding
An arrangement between two or more companies who agree to jointly display content and perform joint promotion using brand logos, e-mail marketing or banner advertisements. The aim is that the brands are strengthened if they are seen as complementary. Co-branding is often a reciprocal arrangement which can occur without payment as part of a wider agreement between partners.

Contra-deals
A reciprocal agreement in the form of an exchange where payment doesn't take place. Instead services or ad space to promote another company as part of co-branding occurs.

Co-branding and contra-deals

Co-branding of sites or e-mails are closely related to online sponsorship. These **contra-deals**, as they are sometimes referred to, typically occur where there is an association between two brands and they are complementary but not competitive.

For example, one online publisher may offer subscribers the chance to sign-up with newsletters from a another company, a process known as 'co-registration'.

Co-branding can be a cost-effective form of online marketing, but specific resource such as 'online partnership manager' has to be put in place to set up and manage the relationships between partners. This will often be part of an affiliate manager's role.

Interactive display advertising

What is display advertising?

Display advertising
Display ads are paid ad placements using graphical or *rich media ad units* within a web page to achieve goals of delivering brand awareness, familiarity, favourability and purchase intent. Many ads encourage interaction through prompting the viewer to interact or rollover to play videos, complete an online form or to view more details by clicking through to a site.

Display advertising involves an advertiser paying for an advertising placement on third-party sites such as publishers or social networks. The process usually involves **ad serving** from a different server from that on which the page is hosted (ads can be served on destination sites in a similar way). Ad serving uses a specialist piece of software, possibly mounted on an independent server such as Doubleclick (now owned by Google). In 2008, Google launched its free ad manager service (**www.google.com/admanager**) to help site owners sell, schedule, optimise revenue, serve ads and measure directly-sold and network-based inventory.

Advertising is used on a range of sites in order to drive traffic to an organisation's **destination site**, or alternatively a **microsite** or nested ad-content on the media owner's site or on the destination site. The destination page from a banner ad will usually be designed as a specifically created direct-response page to encourage further action. For example, the nappy

Ad serving
The term for displaying an advertisement on a website. Often the advertisement will be served from a web server different from the site on which it is placed.

Destination site
The site reached on click-through.

Microsite
A small-scale destination site reached on click-through which is part of the media owner's site.

supplier Huggies placed an advertisement on a childcare site that led the parents clicking on this link to more detailed information on Huggies contained on the site and encouraging them to opt-in to a loyalty programme.

Display advertising is still colloquially known as banner advertising, but practitioners such as the trade body, the Internet Advertising Bureau (**www.iab.net** and **www.iabuk.net**), media owners such as publishers, advertisers and their agencies now commonly refer to 'display advertising'. This reflects the increasing range of ad formats we will discuss below.

Purchasing ad placements

When media is purchased, it is either purchased on a specific site such as *The Times* or *New York Times*, or it is purchased across several sites, which are known as an ad network.

Display advertising is purchased for a specific period. It may be purchased for the ad to be served on:

Run-of-site
Cost per 1000 ad impressions. CPM is usually higher for run-of-site advertisements where advertisements occur on all pages of the site.

- the **run-of-site** (the entire site)
- a section of site
- according to keywords entered on a search engine.

Traditionally, the most common payment is according to the number of customers who view the page as a cost-per-thousand (CPM) ad or page impressions. Typical CPM is in the range £10–£30. Other options that benefit the advertiser if they can be agreed are per click-through or per action such as a purchase on the destination site. Although initially media owners were able to control charging rates and largely used a per exposure model with the increase in unused ad inventory, there has been an increase in **results-based payment** methods particularly within ad networks.

Results-based payment
Advertisers pay according to the number of times the ad is clicked on.

Advantages and disadvantages of display advertising

Robinson *et al.* (2007) have noted that the two primary goals of online display advertising are first, using display adverts as a form of marketing communication used to raise brand awareness; and second, as a direct response medium focused on generating a response. Cartellieri *et al.* (1997) refer to a wider range of goals for online campaigns including:

- *Delivering content.* This is the typical case where a click-through on a banner advertisement leads through to a destination site giving more detailed information on an offer. This is where a direct response is sought. Today ads often embed videos or whitepapers to deliver content directly within the ad.
- *Enabling transaction.* If a click-through leads through to a merchant such as a travel site or an online bookstore this may lead directly to a sale. A direct response is also sought here.
- *Shaping attitudes.* An advertisement that is consistent with a company brand can help build brand awareness.
- *Soliciting response.* An advertisement may be intended to identify new leads or as a start for two-way communication. In these cases an interactive advertisement may encourage a user to type in an e-mail address or other information.
- *Encouraging retention.* The advertisement may be placed as a reminder about the company and its service and may link through to on-site sales promotions such as a prize draw.

These objectives are not mutually exclusive, and more than one can be achieved with a well-designed ad campaign.

Advantages of online advertising

- *Direct response.* Display advertising can generate an immediate direct response via click-through to a website enabling transaction for retail products for example.

- *Indirect response.* We will see in the section on the disadvantages of display advertising that click-throughs are so low that it suggests display advertising is not worthwhile. However, the indirect response should not be underestimated. This is where viewers of an ad later visit a website or search on the brand or category. Research by OPA Europe (2010) showed that for members sites, one third exposed to display advertising conducted searches for the advertised brands while 42 per cent visited advertised brand sites. Note that these results are for well-known brands and control figures were not presented to show the uplift compared to those non exposed.
- *Enhancing brand awareness and reach.* The visual imagery of a display ad can generate awareness about a brand, product or need. This is less practical in search engine marketing where searchers are already seeking a specific brand, product or need, although there are opportunities to make searchers aware of other, unknown suppliers. We also saw at the end of Chapter 8 that **XMOS (cross-media optimisation studies)** showed that online was useful for reaching audiences whose consumption of traditional media has decreased.

XMOS (cross-media optimisation studies)
Research designed to help marketers and their agencies answer the question 'What is the optimal mix of advertising vehicles across different media, in terms of frequency, reach and budget allocation, for a given campaign to achieve its marketing goals?' The mix between online and offline spend is varied to maximise campaign metrics such as reach, brand awareness and purchase intent.

Media multiplier or halo effect
The role of one media channel on influencing sale or uplift in brand metrics. Commonly applied to online display advertising, where exposure to display ads may increase click-through rates when the consumer is later exposed to a brand through other media, for example sponsored links or affiliate ads. It may also improve conversion rates on destination sites through higher confidence in the brand or familiarity with the offer.

- *Media-multiplier or halo effect.* Repeated exposure to ads online, particularly in association with other media, can increase brand awareness and ultimately purchase intent. Furthermore, practitioners report a **media multiplier or halo effect** of buying online ads which can help increase the response rates from other online media. For example, if a web user has been exposed to banner ads, this may increase their response to paid search ads and may also increase their likelihood of converting on a site since brand awareness and trust may be higher. Attribution modelling, which we introduced in Chapter 8, can help determine the contribution of display ads as shown in Digital marketing insights 9.2.

  This is suggested by research reported by MAD (2007) in the travel market which involved asking respondents what their response to an online ad that appealed to them would be. Surely it would be a click? In fact the results broke down as follows:

  - search for a general term relating to the advertisement (31 per cent)
  - go straight to advertisers site (29 per cent)
  - search for the advertiser's name (26 per cent)
  - click on banner to respond (26 per cent)
  - visit a retail store (4%).

  Of course, this methodology shows us reported behaviour rather than actual behaviour, but it is still significant that more than twice as many people are being driven to a search engine by banner advertising than by clicking directly on the banner! The research concludes that paid search marketing needs to be optimised to work with banner advertising, by anticipating searches that are likely to be prompted by the banner and ensure a higher rank for search results. For example, a brand featuring a Cyprus holiday offer will generate generic search terms like 'package holiday Cyprus' rather than brand searches.

  Abraham (2008) has also shown that online ads can stimulate offline sales. For one retailer with a turnover of $15 billion, research showed that over a three-month period, sales increased (compared to a control group) by 40 per cent online and by 50 per cent offline among people exposed to an online search – and display – ad campaign promoting the entire company. Because its baseline sales volumes are greater in physical stores than on the Internet, this retailer derived a great deal more revenue benefit offline than the percentages suggest.
- *Achieving brand interactions.* Many modern display ads comprise two-parts – an initial visual encouraging interaction through a rollover and then another visual or application encouraging interaction with a brand. This enables advertisers to calculate an interaction rate (IR) to assess the extent to which viewers interact with a brand ad.
- *Targeting.* Media buyers can select the right site or channel within a site to reach the audience (e.g. a specialist online car magazine or review site or the motoring channel within an online newspaper or TV channel site). Audiences can also be targeted via their profile through serving personalised ads, or ad in e-mail if visitors have registered on a site.

  Behavioural re-targeting options is used in an ad network to preferentially serve an ad to someone who seems to have an interest in a topic from the content they consume.

Effectively the ad follows the viewer around the site. For example, if someone visits the car section of a site, then the ad is served to them when they view other sections of the site. Re-targeting can work across an ad-network too and can even be sequential, where the messages are varied for an individual the more times they are exposed to the ad. Search re-targeting offers the option to display an ad after a visitor has searched on a particular term such as a car marque. Tracking of individuals is achieved through use of cookies.

- *Cost.* There are opportunities to buy online media at a cheaper rate compared to traditional media, although this is less true in focused, competitive markets such as financial services where there is limited premium inventory for media buyers to purchase.

  Ad networks from suppliers such as Blue Lithium or 24-7 Media give advertisers the options of advertising across a network of sites to reach a particular demographic, e.g. female 18–25, but at a lower cost than media buys on a specific site since the actual site used for the ad placement isn't known (hence these are sometimes known as '*blind network buys*'). Lower CPMs are achievable and in some cases CPC or CPA payment options are available. Site owners such as publishers use ad networks since it gives them a method of gaining fees from unused ad inventory which has not sold at premium rates.
- *Dynamic updates to ad campaigns.* In comparison with traditional media, where media placements have to be bought weeks or months in advance, online ads are more flexible since it is possible to place an advertisement more rapidly and make changes during the campaign. Experienced online advertisers build in flexibility to change targeting through time. Best practice is to start wide and then narrow to a focus – allow 20 per cent budget for high-performing ad placements (high CTR and conversion).

  A major change in the use of online advertising is through what are known as **Demand Side Platforms (DSPs)** that use an approach called **real-time bidding (RTB)**. The purpose of these is to exploit efficiencies through using technology to automatically bid on the most cost-effective ad inventory in an auction. Since individuals are tracked across different sites they can be targeted according to their interests shown by content view using a technique known as behavioural targeting. However, it is unclear whether privacy concerns such as those we covered in Chapter 3 will prevent this in future.

  Demand Side Platforms (DSPs)
  A service that enables ads to be managed across multiple ad networks and ad exchanges through a single interface designed for managing reporting and performance.

  Real-time bidding (RTB)
  Bids for buying ads against keywords can be managed in real-time in conjunction with a DSP.

  In an iMediaConnection (2003) interview with ING direct VP of marketing, Jurie Pieterse, the capability to revise creative is highlighted:

  > Another lesson we learned is the importance of creative. It's critical to invest in developing various creative executions to test them for best performance and constantly introduce new challengers to the top performers. We've also learned there's no single top creative unit – different creative executions and sizes perform differently from publisher to publisher.

- *Accountability.* As we will discuss later in the section, it is readily possible to measure reach, interaction and response to ads. However, it is more difficult to measure brand impact.

Disadvantages of online advertising

- *Relatively low click-through rates.* When discussing online ads, many web users will state they ignore ads and find them intrusive. Published click-through rates support this, with most compilations showing response rates of around 0.1 to 0.2 per cent, but with rich media formats such as video ads attracting higher click-through rates. This phenomenon is known among practitioners as banner blindness (see for example, Nielsen (2007)). The first 468 × 68 pixel banner ad was placed on Hotwired in 1995 and the call-to-action 'Click here!' generated a click-through of 25 per cent. Since then, the click-through rate (CTR) has fallen dramatically with many consumers suffering from 'banner blindness' – they ignore anything on a website that looks like an ad. Remember though, that for reasons such as awareness generation and the media multiplier effect, digital marketers should not dismiss online advertising as ineffectual based on click-through rates alone.

- *Relatively high costs or low efficiency.* When the low response rates are combined with relatively high costs of over £10 per thousand, this makes online ads an inefficient medium.
- *Brand reputation.* Brands can potentially be damaged in the consumers' mind if they are associated with some types of content such as gambling, pornography or racism. It is difficult to monitor precisely which content an ad is served next to when millions of impressions are bought across many sites, this is particularly the case when using ad networks.

Best practice in planning and managing display ad campaigns

Page and ad impressions
One page impression occurs when a member of the audience views a web page. One ad impression occurs when a person views an advertisement placed on the web page.

Reach
Reach defines the number of unique individuals who view an advertisement.

CPM
The cost of placing an ad viewed by 1000 people.

Interaction rate (IR)
The proportion of ad viewers who interact with an online ad through rolling over it. Some will be involuntary depending on where the ad is placed on screen, so it is highly dependent on placement.

Website auditors
Auditors accurately measure the usage of different sites in terms of the number of ad impressions and click-through rates.

Effective frequency
The number of exposures or ad impressions (frequency) required for an advertisement to become effective.

Clickthrough
A clickthrough (ad click) occurs each time a user clicks on a banner advertisement to direct them to a web page that contains further information. The click-through rate is expressed as a percentage of total ad impressions, and refers to the proportion of users viewing an advertisement who click on it. It is calculated as the number of click-throughs divided by the number of ad impressions.

View-through
Indicates when a user views an ad and subsequently visits a website.

In this section we will review how measurement, targeting and creative can be used to improve the results from display ad campaigns.

Measurement of display effectiveness

Different terms are used for measuring banner ad effectiveness. Each time an advertisement is viewed is referred to as an advertisement or **ad impression** – **page impressions** (page views) are other terms used. Since some people may view the advertisement more than one time, marketers are also interested in the **reach**, which is the number of unique individuals who view the advertisement. This will naturally be a smaller figure than that for ad impressions. Cost of ads is typically based on **CPM** or cost-per-thousand *(mille)* ad impressions as with other media. However, the popularity of CPC search advertising and CPA affiliate deals mean that these are options too.

As with other digital media, direct response to ads is measured through click-through rate. **Interaction rate (IR)** is a form of measurement that is unique to display ads. It refers to the many ads which encourage the site visitor to interact through a prompt to 'rollover' and another Flash creative will be loaded which may offer a clear brand message rendered in large font, a response form such as an insurance quote or a request to obtain a SIM or a game or poll. The engagement of the ad campaign for different placements can then be assessed through the interaction rate which will typically be ten times higher than the click-through rate if the targeting, offer and creative is right.

When payment is made according to the number of viewers of a site it is important that the number of viewers be measured accurately. To do this independent **website auditors** are required. The main auditing body in the UK is the Audit Bureau of Circulation Electronic, ABCelectronic (**www.abce.org.uk**).

There is much discussion about how many impressions of an advertisement an individual has to see for it to be effective. Novak and Hoffman (1997) note that for traditional media it is thought that fewer than three exposures will not give adequate recall. For new media, because of the greater intensity of viewing a computer screen, recall seems to be better with a smaller number of advertisements compared with old media. The technical term for adequate recall is **effective frequency.**

When a user clicks on the advertisement, he or she will normally be directed to further information, viewing of which will result in a marketing outcome. Usually the user will be directed through to part of the corporate website that will have been set up especially to deal with the response from the advertisement. When a user clicks on an advertisement immediately this is known as a **click-through**, but adserving systems (using cookies) also measure **view-through** which indicates when a user views an ad and subsequently visits a website within a defined period, such as 30 days. This increases overall response, but it should be borne in mind that users may have visited the site in response to other stimuli.

Interactive ad formats

As well as the classic 468 × 60 rotating GIF banner ad which is decreasing in popularity, media owners now provide a choice of larger, richer formats which web users are more likely to notice. Research has shown that message association and awareness building are much higher for flash-based ads, rich-media ads and larger-format rectangles (multipurpose units, MPUs)

Interstitial ads
Ads that appear between one page and the next.

Overlay
Typically an animated ad that moves around the page and is superimposed on the website content.

and skyscrapers. Other online ad terms you will hear include **interstitials** (intermediate adverts before another page appears) and the more common **overlays** (formerly more often known as *superstitials* or *overts*) that appear above content and, of course, *pop-up windows* that are now less widely used because of their intrusion. Online advertisers face a constant battle with users who deploy pop-up blockers or less commonly ad-blocking software, but they will persist in using rich-media formats where they generate the largest response.

Interactive ad targeting options

Online ads can be targeted through placing ads:

- *On a particular type of site (or part of site)* which has a specific visitor profile or type of content. So a car manufacturer can place ads on the home page of Handbag.com to appeal to a young female audience. A financial services provider can advertise in the money section of the site to target those interested in these products. To reach large mass-market audiences, advertisers can place an ad on a large portal home page such as MSN which has millions of visitors each day (sometimes known as a 'road-block' if they take all ad inventory).
- *To target a registered user's profile.* A business software provider could advertise on the FT to target registrants' profiles such as finance directors or IT managers.
- *At a particular time of day or week.*
- *To follow users' behaviour.* **Behavioural ad targeting** is all about relevance – dynamically serving relevant content, messaging or ad which matches the interests of a site visitor according to inferences about their characteristics. These inferences are made by anonymously tracking the different types of pages visited by a site user during a single visit to a site or across multiple sessions. Other aspects of the environment used by the visitor can also be determined, such as their location, browser and operating system. For example, FT.com using software from Revenue Science can identify users in eight segments: Business Education, Institutional Investor, Information Technology, Luxury and Consumer, Management, Personal Finance, Travel and Private Equity. The targeting process is shown in Figure 9.12. First the ad serving system detects whether the visitor is in the target audience (media optimisation), then creative optimisation occurs to serve the best ad for the viewer type.

Behavioural ad targeting
Enables an advertiser to target ads at a visitor as they move elsewhere on the site, visit other sites on an ad network return to the site, thus increasing the frequency or number of impressions served to an individual in the target market.

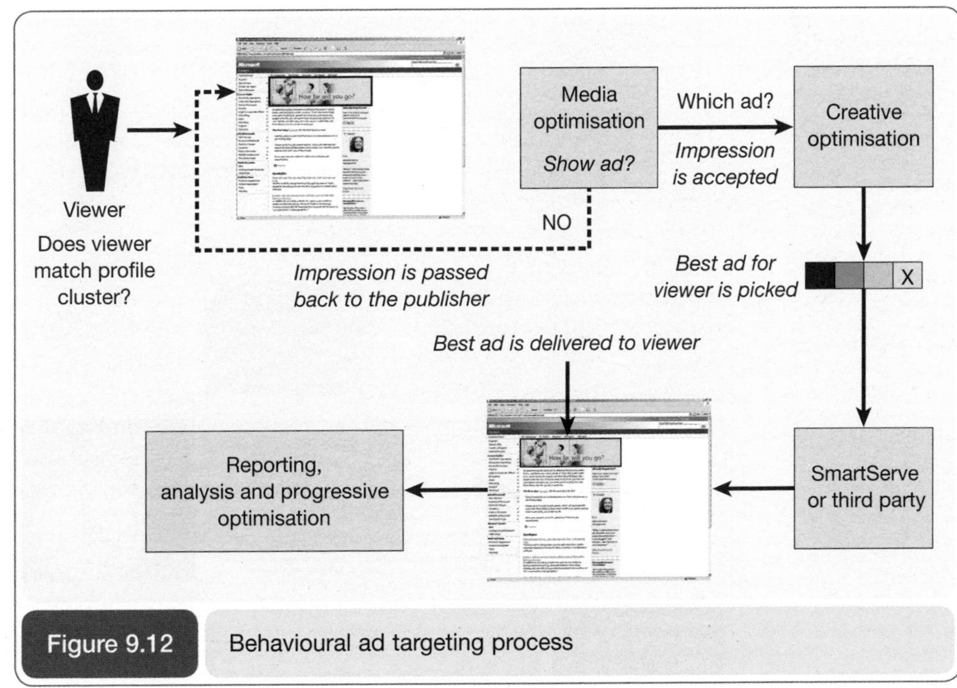

Figure 9.12 Behavioural ad targeting process

In 2010 behavioural targeting became available through Google's Adwords platform as Remarketing which made it available to many more advertisers.

Ad creative

As with any form of advertising, certain techniques will result in a more effective advertisement. Robinson *et al.* (2007) conducted research on the factors which increased click-through response to banner ads. The main variables they (and previous studies they reference include):

- banner size
- message length
- promotional incentive
- animation
- action phrase (commonly referred to as a call-to-action)
- company brand/logo.

Their research indicated that the design elements which made the most effective banner ads included a larger size, longer message, absence of promotional incentives and the presence of information about casino games. Surprisingly, the inclusion of brand name was not favourable in increasing click-through, although, as we noted, this may be because the ad generates a subsequent search on the brand. Please note that this study was restricted to online gambling ads.

Anecdotal discussions by the authors with marketers who have advertised online indicate the following are also important and worth considering:

- *Appropriate incentives are needed to achieve click-through.* Banner advertisements with offers such as prizes or reductions can achieve higher click-through rates by perhaps as much as 10 per cent.

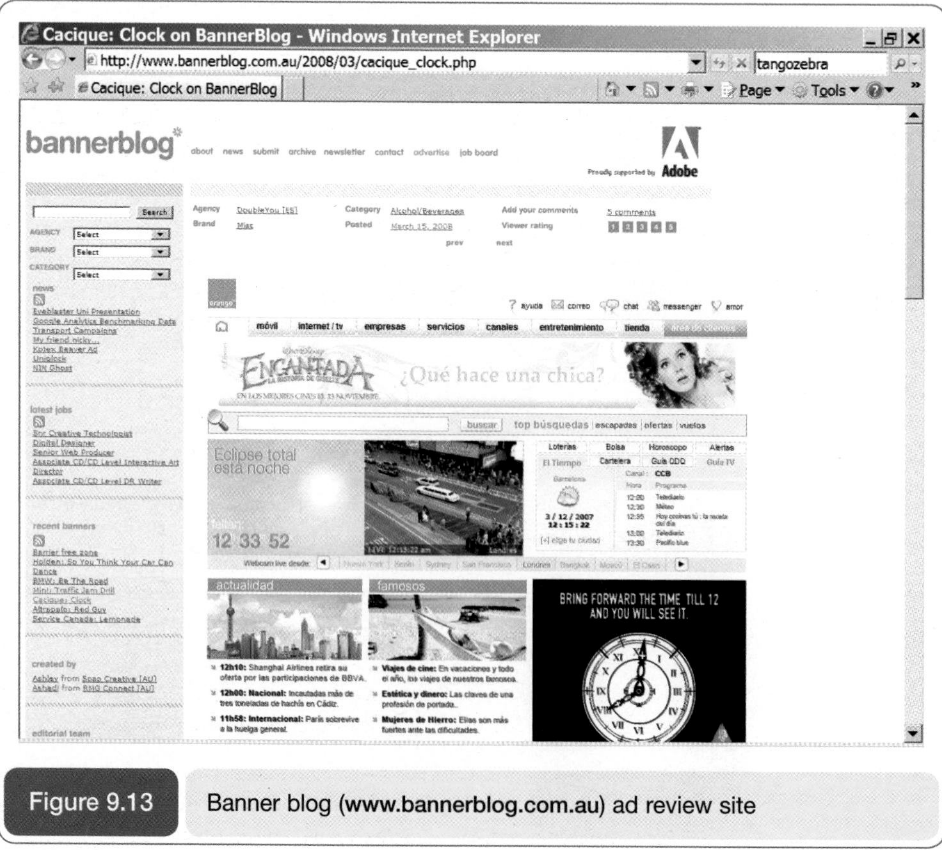

Figure 9.13 Banner blog (www.bannerblog.com.au) ad review site

- *Creative design needs to be tested extensively.* Alternative designs for the advertisement need to be tested on representatives of a target audience. Anecdotal evidence suggests that the click-through rate can vary greatly according to the design of the advertisement, in much the same way that recall of a television advertisement will vary in line with its concept and design. Different creative designs may be needed for different sites on which advertisements are placed. Zeff and Aronson (2001) note that simply the use of the words 'click here!' or 'click now' can dramatically increase click-through rates because new users do not know how banners work!
- *Placement of advertisement and timing need to be considered carefully.* The different types of placement options available have been discussed earlier in the chapter, but it should be remembered that audience volume and composition will vary through the day and the week.

Different styles of ad creative can be viewed by visiting the Ad Gallery of an ad serving company such as Tangozebra (**www.tangozebra.com**) or Eyeblaster (**www.eyeblaster.com**), or an ad review site such as Banner Blog (**www.bannerblog.com.au**, Figure 9.13) which features ads from many countries.

Opt-in e-mail marketing and mobile text messaging

We have grouped email marketing with text messaging since these are both 'push media' which share much in terms of their applications for prospect and customer communications. In this coverage we concentrate on e-mail marketing since mobile marketing was covered in Chapter 3.

What is e-mail marketing?

When devising plans for e-mail marketing communications, marketers need to plan for:

Outbound e-mail marketing
E-mails are sent to customers and prospects from an organisation.

Inbound e-mail marketing
Management of e-mails from customers by an organisation.

- **Outbound e-mail marketing**, where e-mail campaigns are used as a form of direct marketing to encourage trial and purchases and as part of a CRM dialogue.
- **Inbound e-mail marketing**, where e-mails from customers, such as service enquiries, are managed (this was discussed in Chapters 3 and 5 and isn't discussed further in this chapter).

The applications of outbound e-mail marketing communications broadly break down into customer acquisition and retention activities. e-mail activities within organisation tend to focus on customer acquisition as these ratings (on a 5-point scale) on the relative merits of different applications of e-mail by Chittenden and Rettie (2003) suggest:

- customer retention (4.5)
- sales promotion (4.4)
- gathering customer data (3.0)
- lead generation (3.0)
- brand awareness (2.7)
- customer acquisition (2.1).

Opt-in e-mail options for customer acquisition

For acquiring new visitors and customers to a site, there are three main options for e-mail marketing. From the point of view of the recipient, these are:

- *Cold e-mail campaign.* In this case, the recipient receives an opt-in e-mail from an organisation that has rented an e-mail list from a consumer e-mail list provider such as Experian (**www.experian.com**), Claritas (**www.claritas.com**) or IPT Limited (**www.myoffers.co.uk**)

or a business e-mail list provider such as Mardev (**www.mardev.com**), Corpdata (**www.corpdata.com**) or trade publishers and event providers such as VNU. Although they have agreed to receive offers by e-mail, the e-mail is effectively cold. For example, a credit card provider could send a cold e-mail to a list member who is not currently their member. It is important to use some form of 'statement of origination', otherwise the message may be considered spam. Cold e-mails tend to have higher CPAs than other forms of online marketing, but different lists should still be evaluated.

- *Co-branded e-mail.* Here, the recipient receives an e-mail with an offer from a company they have a reasonably strong affinity with. For example, the same credit card company could partner with a mobile service provider such as Vodafone and send out the offer to their customer (who has opted in to receive e-mails from third parties). Although this can be considered a form of cold e-mail, it is warmer since there is a stronger relationship with one of the brands and the subject line and creative will refer to both brands. Co-branded e-mails tend to be more responsive than cold e-mails to rented lists since the relationship exists and fewer offers tend to be given. The Digital marketing insight gives an example of where email marketing is used to increase awareness as part of an integrated campaign combined with display advertising.
- *Third-party e-newsletter.* In this visitor acquisition option, a company publicises itself in a third-party e-newsletter. This could be in the form of an ad, sponsorship or PR (editorial) which links through to a destination site. These placements may be set up as part of an interactive advertising ad buy since many e-newsletters also have permanent versions on the website. Since e-newsletter recipients tend to engage with them by scanning the headlines or reading them if they have time, e-newsletter placements can be relatively cost effective.Viral marketing, which is discussed in the next main section, also uses e-mail as the mechanism for transferring messages.

Digital marketing insight 9.4 SEAT combine e-mail with display advertising to increase awareness

This study analysed the advertising effectiveness of e-mail marketing and display advertising, looked at responses from over 1000 consumers to SEAT Ibiza ST campaigns. It used a classic 'hold out' approach where different respondents were reached through different combinations of media:

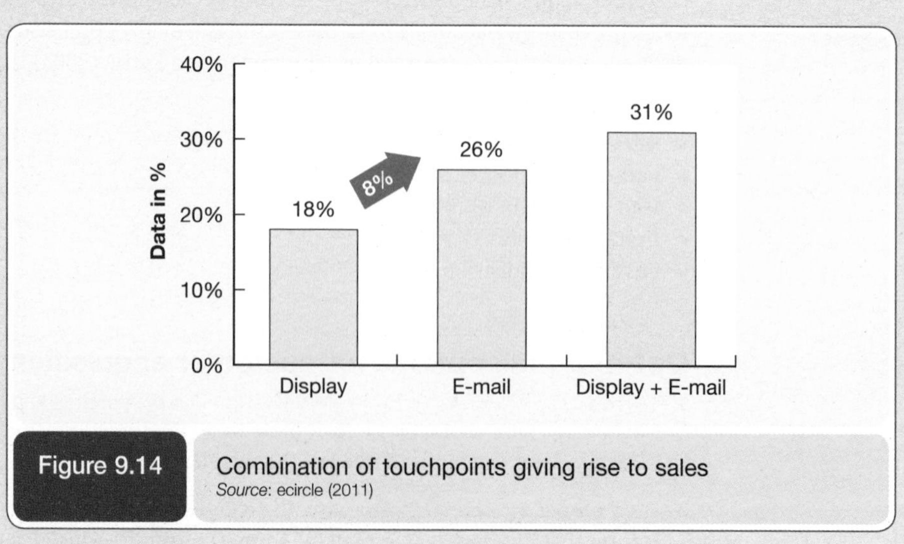

Figure 9.14 Combination of touchpoints giving rise to sales
Source: ecircle (2011)

- contact through an e-mail campaign
- contact with display advertising
- contact with both campaign channels.

The main results from the campaign which showed the integrated benefits of the campaign were:

1 The combination of display and e-mail advertising improves advertising recall by 13 per cent compared with just display advertising (Figure 9.14)
2 E-mail increases disposition to buy in 47 per cent of cases and is therefore ideal for increasing conversions
3 Spending power as a target group – by using e-mail you can precisely reach your target group
4 E-mail allowed the required reach of advertising to be reached three times more quickly than display advertising

Source: eCircle (2011)

Opt-in e-mail options for prospect conversion and customer retention (house list)

Opt-in
An individual agrees to receive e-mail communications.

House list
A list of prospect and customer names, e-mail addresses and profile information owned by an organisation.

E-mail is most widely used as a prospect conversion and customer retention tool using an **opt-in house list** of prospects and customers that have given permission to an organisation to contact them. For example, Lastminute.com has built a house list of over 10 million prospects and customers across Europe. Successful e-mail marketers adopt a strategic approach to e-mail and develop a contact or touch strategy which plans the frequency and content of e-mail communications as explained in Chapters 4 and 6. Some options for in-house e-mail marketing include:

- *Conversion e-mail.* Someone visits a website and expresses interest in a product or service by registering and providing their e-mail address, although they do not buy. Automated follow-up e-mails can be sent out to persuade the recipient to trial the service. For example, betting company William Hill found that automated follow-up e-mails converted twice as many registrants to place their first bet compared to registrants who did not receive an e-mail.
- *Regular e-newsletter type.* Options are reviewed for different frequencies such as weekly, monthly or quarterly with different content for different audiences and segments. These are commonly used to update consumers on the latest products or promotions or business customers on developments within a market
- *House-list campaign.* These are periodic e-mails to support different objectives such as encouraging trial of a service or newly launched product, repeat purchases or reactivation of customers who no longer use a service.
- *Event-triggered.* These tend to be less regular and are sent out perhaps every three or six months when there is news of a new product launch or an exceptional offer.
- *E-mail sequence.* Software can send out a series of e-mails with the interval betweene-mails determined by the marketer.

Advantages and disadvantages of e-mail marketing

Advantages of e-mail marketing

We saw in Chapter 6 that permission-based e-mail is an effective tool for building relationships with customers online. Despite the increase in spam, such that the vast majority of e-mails are spam or viruses (most estimates exceed 80 per cent), e-mail can still drive good response levels, particularly for house lists (retention e-mail marketing). Opt-in email communications provide a controlled push message which encourages response. An example of the continued power of e-mail marketing campaigns is shown in Figure 9.15. This shows research from GSI (2011) for the combination of touchpoints that can be attributed to sale from a single day, 29 November 2010, known in the US as 'CyberMonday' from 15GSI retail e-commerce sites. Since this is a known peak-day for sales, retailers are active in driving visitors to the site.

Owing to these advantages, in many countries such as the volume of e-mail marketing exceeds direct mail volumes. However, no one is suggesting direct mail will disappear immediately since it will typically have a higher impact than e-mail marketing and the two work best when integrated.

The main advantages of e-mail marketing are:

- *Relatively low cost of fulfilment.* The physical costs of e-mail are substantially less than direct mail.
- *Direct response medium encourages immediate action.* E-mail marketing encourages click-through to a website where the offer can be redeemed immediately – this increases the likelihood of an immediate, impulsive response. For this reason, it is one of the best methods of attracting existing customers to return to a site (it's a push media).
- *Faster campaign deployment.* Lead times for producing creative and the whole campaign lifecycle tends to be shorter than traditional media.
- *Ease of personalisation.* It is easier and cheaper to personalise e-mail than for physical media and also than for a website.

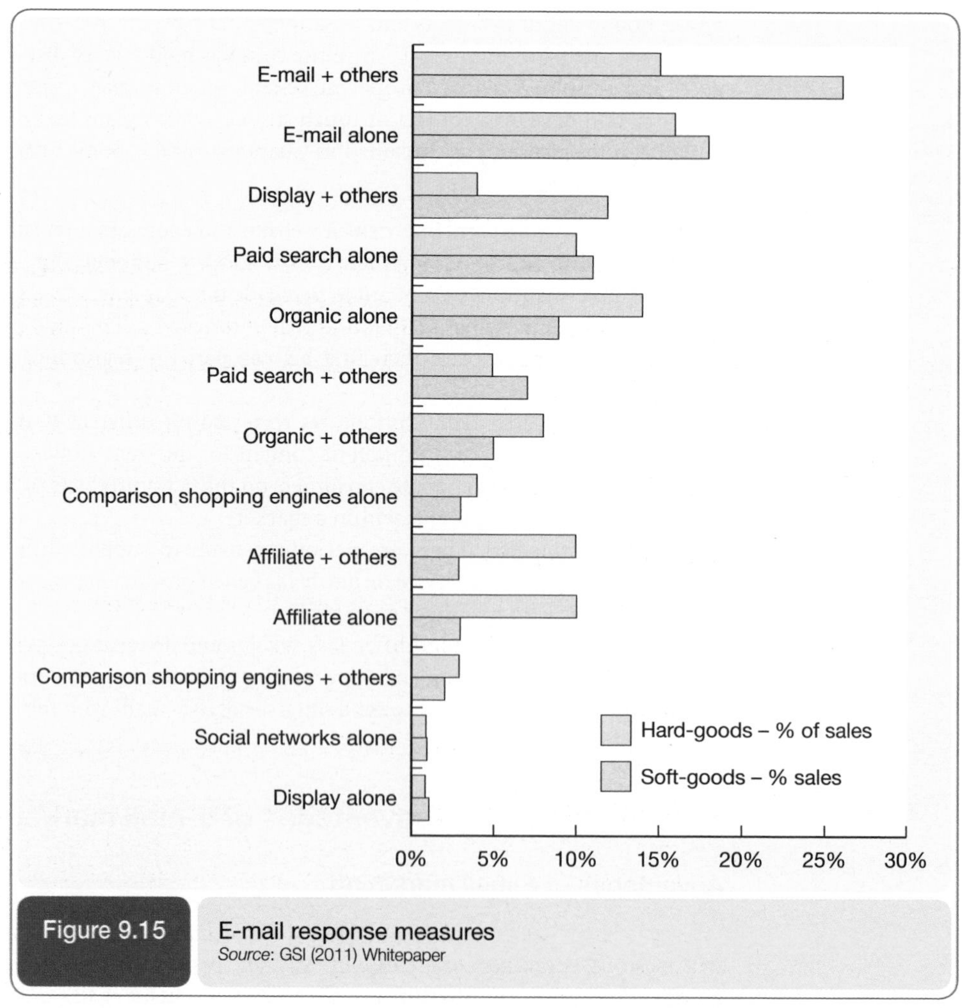

Figure 9.15 E-mail response measures
Source: GSI (2011) Whitepaper

- *Options for testing.* It is relatively easy and cost effective to test different e-mail creative and messaging.
- *Integration.* Through combining e-mail marketing with other direct media that can be personalised, such as direct mail, mobile messaging or web personalisation, campaign response can be increased as the message is reinforced by different media.

Disadvantages of e-mail marketing

Some of the disadvantages of e-mail marketing which marketers need to manage as they run their campaigns so that they are closely related to best practice are:

- *Deliverability.* Difficulty of getting messages delivered through different Internet service providers (ISPs), corporate firewalls and web mail systems.
- *Renderability.* Difficulty of displaying the creative as intended within the in-box of different e-mail reading systems.
- *E-mail response decay.* E-mail recipients are most responsive when they first subscribe to an e-mail. It is difficult to keep them engaged.
- *Communications preferences.* Recipients will have different preferences for e-mail offers, content and frequency which affect engagement and response. These have to be managed through communications preferences.
- *Resource intensive.* Although e-mail offers great opportunities for targeting, personalisation and more frequent communications, additional people and technology resources are required to deliver these.

Best practice in planning and managing e-mail marketing

In this section we will review how measurement, targeting and creative can be used to improve the results from e-mail marketing.

E-mail service providers

E-mail service providers (ESPs)
Provide a web-based service used by marketers to manage their e-mail activities including hosting e-mail subscription forms, broadcast and tracking.

E-mail service providers (ESPs) are a popular method companies use to manage their e-mail marketing. ESPs provides a web-based service used by marketers to manage their e-mail activities with less recourse to an agency. Rather than buying software that you host and manage on your server, the software is effectively used on a subscription basis, with a cost based on number of e-mails sent and runs on another company's server. The ESP manages four key capabilities including hosting of forms for managing e-mail subscriptions and landing pages, the broadcast tools for dispatching the e-mails and a database containing the prospect or customer profiles. They also provide tracking of effectiveness as shown by the example in Figure 9.16.

Measuring e-mail marketing

Figure 9.16 shows that the key measures for e-mail marketing are:

- *Delivery rate* (here indicated by 'non-bounce rate'). E-mails will bounce if the e-mail address is no longer valid or a spam filter blocks the e-mail.
- *Open rate.* This is measured for HTML messages through downloaded images. It is an indication of how many customers open an e-mail, but is not accurate since some users have preview panes in their e-mail readers which load the message even if is deleted without reading, and some e-mail readers such as Outlook Express now block images by default (this has resulted in a decline in open rates through time). Open rates for particular types of e-mail address, e.g. Hotmail.com, is also an indication of deliverability problems.
- *Click-through or click rate.* This is the number of people who click through on the e-mail of those delivered (strictly unique clicks rather than total clicks). You can see that response rates are quite high at around 10%.

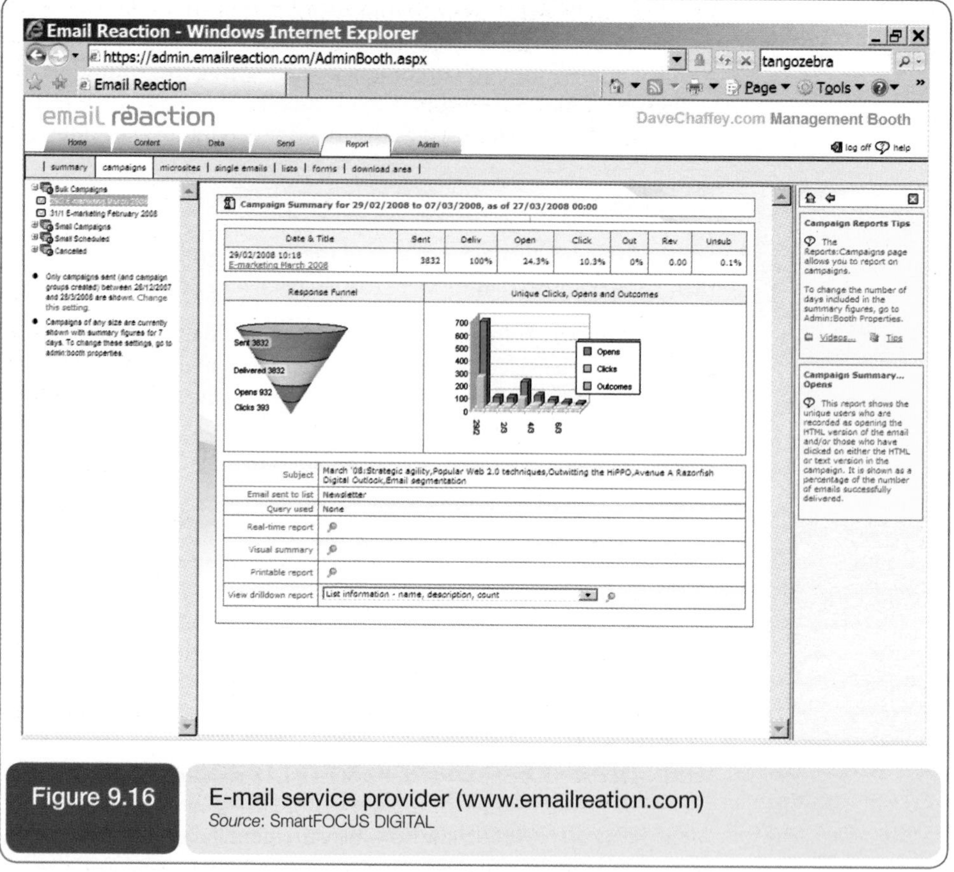

Figure 9.16 E-mail service provider (www.emailreation.com)
Source: SmartFOCUS DIGITAL

Additionally, and most important, are the marketing outcomes or value events (Chapter 8) such as sales and leads achieved when an e-mail recipient clicks through to the website. Retailers will also have additional methods of comparing e-mail campaigns such as revenue/profit per e-mail or thousand e-mails and average order value (AOV).

E-mail marketing success factors

Effective e-mail marketing shares much in common with effective direct e-mail copy. Chaffey (2006) uses the mnemonic CRITICAL for a checklist of questions that can be used to improve the response of e-mail campaigns. It stands for:

- *Creative.* This assesses the design of the e-mail including its layout, use of colour and image and the copy (see below).
- *Relevance.* Does the offer and creative of the e-mail meet the needs of the recipients? This is dependent on the list quality and targeting variables used.
- *Incentive (or offer).* The WIFM factor ('What's in it for me?') for the recipient. What benefit does the recipient gain from clicking on the hyperlink(s) in the e-mail? For example, a prize draw is a common offer for B2C brands.
- *Targeting and timing.* Targeting is related to the relevance. Is a single message sent to all prospects or customers on the list or are e-mails with tailored creative, incentive and copy sent to the different segments on the list? Timing refers to when the e-mail is received: the time of day, day of the week, point in the month and even the year; does it relate to any particular events? There is also the relative timing – when it is received compared to other marketing communications – this depends on the integration.

- *Integration.* Are the e-mail campaigns part of your integrated marketing communications? Questions to ask include: are the creative and copy consistent with my brand? Does the message reinforce other communications? Does the timing of the e-mail campaign fit with offline communications?
- *Copy.* This is part of the creative and refers to the structure, style and explanation of the offer together with the location of hyperlinks in the e-mail.
- *Attributes (of the e-mail).* Assess the message characteristics such as the subject line, from address, to address, date/time of receipt and format (HTML or text). Send out Multipart/MIME messages which can display HTML or text according to the capability of the e-mail reader. Offer choice of HTML or text to match users' preferences.
- *Landing page (or microsite)* – These are terms given to the page(s) reached after the recipient clicks on a link in the e-mail. Typically, on click-through the recipient will be presented with an online form to profile or learn more about them. Designing the page so the form is easy to complete can affect the overall success of the campaign.

A relevant incentive, such as free information or a discount, is offered in exchange for a prospect providing their e-mail address by filling in an online form. Careful management of e-mail lists is required since, as the list ages, the addresses of customers and their profiles will change, resulting in many bounced messages and lower response rates. Data protection law also requires the facility for customers to update their details.

Practical issues in managing e-mail marketing

Two of the main practical challenges for e-mail marketers or their agencies to manage are **deliverability** and **renderability.**

Deliverability
Refers to ensuring e-mail messages are delivered and aren't blocked by spam filters because the e-mail content or structure falsely identifies a permission-based e-mail as a spammer, or because the sender's IP address has a poor reputation for spam.

Renderability
The capability of an e-mail to display correctly formatted in different e-mail readers.

E-mail marketers have to ensure their e-mails are delivered given the increase in efforts by ISPs and web-e-mail companies to reduce spam into their end-users in-boxes due to the volume of spam. E-mail marketers do not want to be identified as a 'False positive' where permission-based e-mails may be bounced or placed into junk-mail boxes or simply deleted if the receiving system assesses that they are spam.

Web-based e-mail providers such as Hotmail and Yahoo! Mail have introduced standard authentication techniques known as Sender ID and Domain Keys which e-mail marketers should use to make sure the e-mail broadcaster is who they say they are and doesn't spoof their address as many spammers do. E-mail providers also assess the reputation of the e-mail broadcasters using services such as SenderScore (**www.senderscore.org**) based on the number of complaints and quality of e-mails sent.

It is also important that e-mail marketers do not use keywords in their e-mails which may identify them as spam. For example, e-mail filter such as Spam Assassin (**www.spamassassin.org**) have these types of rules which are used to assess spam:

• SUB_FREE_OFFER	• Subject starts with 'Free'
• SUBJECT_DRUG_GAP_VIA	• Subject contains a gappy version of 'viagra'
• TO_ADDRESS_EQ_REAL	• To: repeats address as real name
• HTML_IMAGE_RATIO_04	• BODY: HTML has a low ratio of text to image area
• HTML_FONT_BIG	• BODY: HTML tag for a big font size

Although the word 'free' in a subject line may cause a problem, this is only one part of the signature of a spam, so it may still be possible to use this word if the reputation of the sender is good.

Renderability refers to how the e-mail appears in different e-mail readers. Often images are blocked by readers in an effort to defeat spammers who use the fact that images are downloaded as the user views the e-mail to detect that the e-mail is a valid address. So e-mails that are only made up of images with no text are less likely to be effective than hybrid messages combining text and images. Formatting can also differ in different readers, so designers of e-mails have to test how e-mails render in common e-mail readers such as Hotmail and Yahoo! Mail.

A further challenge is trying to achieve ongoing engagement with list members. Some approaches that are commonly used include:

- Develop a welcome programme where over the first three to six months targeted automatically-triggered e-mails to educate subscribers about your brand, products and deliver targeted offers.
- Use offers to re-activate list-members as they become less responsive.
- Segment list members by activity (responsiveness) and age on list and treat differently, either by reducing frequency or using more offline media.
- Follow-up on bounces using other media to reduce problems of dropping deliverability.
- Best practice when renting lists is to request only e-mails where the opt-in is within the most recent six to nine months when subscribers are most active.

List management

E-mail marketers need to work hard to improve the quality of their list as explained in Chapter 6. DMA (2008) report that companies often fail to collect the most recent address with UK companies having e-mail addresses for only 50 per cent of their database. Respondents believed that the data and its selection accounted for over half of a campaign's success. The creative and offer are still considered significant while timing is viewed as having the least impact, accounting for just 10 per cent of the success of an e-mail campaign. The report noted that the majority of respondents gather new e-mail addresses through organic website traffic with offline (paper-based) activity accounting for 40 per cent and telemarketing for 31 per cent.

Mini Case Study 9.3 Beep-beep-beep-beep, that'll be the bank then – driving sales through mobile marketing

Say and Southwell (2006) creators of the text message banking system at First Direct (part of the HSBC Group, describe how if mobile marketing is carefully used with a trusted brand it can be effective. Their use of mobile marketing started in 2001 with product offer campaigns encouraging mobile users to log-on to the bank, call the contact centre or receive a direct mail pack for more information. Since there was a delay between requesting a direct mail pack and receiving one, a more responsive mechanism was for customers who replied to a text message with their e-mail address to immediately receive an e-mail with a link to a website featuring more information and an application form.

First Direct also use mobile short codes within their offline advertising encouraging those who read ads in newspapers about a product, for example, to follow-up on them immediately.

Short codes were also used for promotions. In one example, a 'text to win TXT2WIN' approach was used where customers were sent an e-mail or a direct mail pack with information about a new Internet Banking Plus account aggregation service plus details of a prize draw to win a holiday or ticket to a football match. To enter the competition, customers were asked to review an online demonstration, find an answer to a question, and text the answer to a shortcode number with their name, postcode and e-mail address.

The campaign objectives and results (in brackets) were to:

- capture 5000 mobile phone numbers from customers (200% of plan)
- acquire 3000 e-mail addresses (176% of plan)
- raise awareness about the new service (31,000 customers view demonstration)
- create 1000 new registrations (576% of plan).

This case shows the need for text message marketing to be carefully integrated with other direct channels such as web, e-mail and phone. It also shows the importance of capturing and maintaining up-to-date customer details such as e-mail addresses and mobile phone numbers.

Source: Say and Southwell (2006).

Mobile text messaging

We have concentrated our coverage on e-mail marketing in this section since the amount of marketing investment and levels of activity in e-mail marketing is much higher than mobile text messaging because it seems that receiving permission-based e-mails is more acceptable than receiving what may be perceived as an intrusive text message on a mobile device. Additionally, it enables more complex, visual messages to be delivered. However, Rettie *et al.* (2005) in an analysis of 26 text marketing campaigns (5401 respondents) demonstrated surprising levels of effectiveness. Her team found that overall acceptability of SMS advertising was 44 per cent, significantly higher than the acceptability of telemarketing and found relatively high response rates and brand recall compared to direct mail and e-mail marketing.

Social media and viral marketing

Social media marketing
Monitoring and facilitating customer-customer interaction and participation throughout the web to encourage positive engagement with a company and its brands. Interactions may occur on a company site, social networks and other third-party sites

Social media marketing is an important category of digital marketing which involves encouraging customer communications on a companies own site, or social presences such as Facebook or Twitter or in specialist publisher sites, blogs and forums. It can be applied as a traditional broadcast medium, for example companies can use Facebook or Twitter to send messages to customers or partners who have opted in. However to take advantage of the benefits of social media it is important to start and participate in customer conversations. These can be related to products, promotions or customer service and are aimed at learning more about customers and providing support so improving the way a company is perceived.

We've seen throughout this book that the opportunities of communicating with customers through social network sites, online communities and interactions on company sites are so great today that a social media strategy has become a core element of e-business strategy. Yet creating a social media or customer engagement strategy is challenging since it requires a change in mindset for the company since they may have to give up some control on their messaging to enable them to communicate with customers effectively. The change in approach required is clear from a movement that originated in the USA in 1999, known as the Cluetrain manifesto (**www.cluetrain.com**). The authors, Levine *et al.* (2000), say:

> Conversations among human beings sound human. They are conducted in a human voice. Most corporations, on the other hand, only know how to talk in the soothing, humorless monotone of the mission statement, marketing brochure, and your-call-is-important-to-us busy signal. Same old tone, same old lies. No wonder networked markets have no respect for companies unable or unwilling to speak as they do. Corporate firewalls have kept smart employees in and smart markets out. It's going to cause real pain to tear those walls down. But the result will be a new kind of conversation. And it will be the most exciting conversation business has ever engaged in.

Of course, more than a change in mindset is required – to achieve change on this scale requires senior management sponsorship, investment and changes to processes and tools as described in the next chapter on change management.

You can see that the Cluetrain manifesto is a call-to-action encouraging managers to change their culture and provide processes and tools to enable employees of an organisation to interact with and listen to customer needs in a responsible way.

Developing a social media communications strategy

When developing a social media strategy there seems to be a tendency for managers to turn straight to the tools they'll be using – should we start with Twitter or Facebook, or should we create a blog? This is the worst possible way to develop strategy, indeed it's not strategy, it's tactics! Strategy development for social media should be informed by demand analysis of customer channel adoption and the commercial potential of the approach.

Customer adoption of social media tools will vary according to customer segments and markets. So it's important to start by completing a marketplace analysis as described in Chapter 2 to see which social tools and engagement techniques are most effective for the target audience.

Next, the commercial benefits of social media need to be reviewed and goals defined. Some marketers will see social media primarily as a way of gaining new customers through the viral effect of social media as existing customers or contacts discuss or recommend your content or products. For others, the benefits may be centred more around how recommendations, reviews and ratings can increase conversion rate. Public relations specialists will want to listen to the conversations for positive and negative sentiment about brand and then seek to manage this by increasing the positives and managing the negatives. Finally, social media can be viewed as a customer engagement and retention tool. Here social media are used to deliver customer service or are used as alternative channel to email marketing to inform customers about new product launches or promotions.

POST is a useful framework for businesses to apply to help them develop a social media strategy summarised by Forrester (2007). POST is a simplified version of the SOSTAC framework introduced at the start of this chapter:

- *People.* Understanding the adoption of social media within an audience is an essential starting point. The Forrester social media profiling tool shows how usage varies for different demographic groups: **http://www.forrester.com/Groundswell/profile_tool.html.**
- *Objectives.* Set different goals for different options to engage customers across different aspects of the customer lifecycle from customer acquisition to conversion to retention. Josh Bernoff of Forrester recommends, 'Decide on your objective before you decide on a technology. Then figure out how you will measure it.'
- *Strategy.* How to achieve your goals. Bernoff suggests that because social media are a disruptive approach you should imagine how social media will support change. He says: 'Imagine you succeed. How will things be different afterwards? '*Imagine the endpoint and you'll know where to begin.*'
- *Technology.* Finally, decide on the best social media platforms and tools to achieve your goals; we reviewed the options for building communities and generating awareness through social networks at the end of Chapter 6.

Viral marketing

Viral marketing
Online viral marketing, or buzz marketing, is a form of electronic word-of-mouth marketing. Brands and promotions are discussed and awareness of them transmitted in two main forms, either as passalong e-mail or discussion in a social network.

Word-of-mouth (WOM) marketing
According to the Word-of-Mouth Marketing Association it is giving people a reason to talk about your products and services, and making it easier for that conversation to take place. It is the art and science of building active, mutually beneficial consumer-to-consumer and consumer-to-marketer communications.

Social media marketing can often be assisted through **viral marketing** that harnesses the network effect of the Internet and can be effective in reaching a large number of people rapidly as a marketing message is rapidly transmitted in the same way as a natural virus or a computer virus. It is effectively an online form of word-of-mouth communications which is sometimes also known as 'buzz marketing'. The two main forms of online viral marketing are through passalong-e-mails or discussions within social networks. When planning integrated campaigns, it is important to note that the online viral affect can be amplified through offline media mentions or advertising either on TV and radio or in print.

Word-of-mouth (WOM) marketing is an established concept closely related to viral marketing, but broader in context. The Word-of-Mouth Marketing Association (**www.womma.org/ wom101**) explain how WOM can be harnessed:

> Word-of-mouth can be encouraged and facilitated. Companies can work hard to make people happier, they can listen to consumers, they can make it easier for them to tell their friends, and they can make certain that influential individuals know about the good qualities of a product or service.

They go on to explain that all word-of-mouth marketing techniques are based on the concepts of customer satisfaction, two-way dialogue and transparent communications. The basic elements are:

- educating people about your products and services
- identifying people most likely to share their opinions
- providing tools that make it easier to share information
- studying how, where and when opinions are being shared
- listening and responding to supporters, detractors and neutrals.

WOMMA identify different approaches for facilitating WOM. The ones that are most relevant to online marketing are:

- *Buzz marketing.* Using high-profile entertainment or news to get people to talk about your brand.
- *Viral marketing.* Creating entertaining or informative messages that are designed to be passed along in an exponential fashion, often electronically or by e-mail.
- *Community marketing.* Forming or supporting niche communities that are likely to share interests about the brand (such as user groups, fan clubs and discussion forums); providing tools, content and information to support those communities.
- *Influencer marketing.* Identifying key communities and opinion leaders who are likely to talk about products and have the ability to influence the opinions of others.
- *Conversation creation.* Interesting or fun advertising, e-mails, catch phrases, entertainment or promotions designed to start word-of-mouth activity.
- *Brand blogging.* Creating blogs and participating in the blogosphere, in the spirit of open, transparent communications; sharing information of value that the blog community may talk about.
- *Referral programmes.* Creating tools that enable satisfied customers to refer their friends.

Positive WOM is believed to increase purchase intent. For example, Marsden *et al.* (2005) found that brands such as HSBC, Honda and O2 with a greater proportion of advocates measured through Net Promoter Score (NPS, Chapter 6) tended to be more successful. They recommend ten ways to encourage word-of-mouth, most of which can be facilitated online:

- *Implement and optimise referral programmes.* Reward customers for referring new customers, and reward the referee as well as the referrer.
- *Set up brand ambassador schemes.* Recruit brand fans as ambassadors who receive exclusive merchandise/offers to share with their contacts.
- *Use tryvertising.* A combination of 'try' or 'trial' and 'advertising', this is a twist on product sampling. The idea is that rather than provide free samples or trials to anyone in a target market, tryvertising involves sampling on a selective and exclusive basis to lead users – ideally with new products or services before they become widely available.
- *Use causal marketing.* Associate your brand with a good cause that builds on brand values (e.g. Nike anti-racism in sport).
- *Measure your Net Promoter Score (NPS).* Track your NPS (see page 338 for further details) at all brand touchpoints to find out what you are doing right, and what needs to be improved.
- *Start an influencer outreach programme.* Reach out to the 10% who tell the other 90% what to try and buy with special offers and programmes.
- *Harness the power of empowered involvement.* Create advocacy – let your lead clients, customers or consumers call the shots on your innovation and marketing with VIP votes and polls.
- *Focus innovation on doing something worth talking about.* Do something new that delivers an experience that exceeds expectations.

In an online context, word-of-mouth marketing is important since there is great potential for facilitating electronic word-of-mouth. It is very important for online marketers to understand how WOM can be generated and influenced since research, such as that conducted by Forrester (2007) quoted in the section on online public relations, shows that recommendations from friends, family or even other online consumers are trusted and are a major consideration in product and supplier selection.

E-mail forwarding or passalong viral marketing

Before the growth of social networking, e-mail forwarding was the main source of online viral activity. For example, research quoted by Dee *et al.* (2007) showed that for a US sample, around 60 per cent of web users frequently forwarded on by e-mail anything they think may be of interest to friends, family or colleagues. Today, social media are more important for the viral affect, but the methods to facilitate propagation of messages through email marketing should still be asssessed.

Chaffey and Smith (2008) distinguish between these types of viral e-mail mechanisms:

- *Passalong e-mail viral.* This is where e-mail or word-of-mouth alone is used to spread the message. This is classic viral marketing such as those showcased on the New Media Age Viral Chart (**http://www.nma.co.uk/resources/viral-brand-chart**) which involve an e-mail with a link to a site such as a video or an attachment. Towards the end of a commercial e-mail it does no harm to prompt the first recipient to forward the e-mail to interested friends or colleagues. The dramatic growth of Hotmail, reaching 10 million subscribers in just over a year, was effectively down to passalong as people received e-mails with a signature promoting the service. Word-of-mouth helped too. This mechanism is what most people consider to be viral, but there are the other mechanisms that follow too.
- *Web-facilitated viral (e-mail prompt).* Here, the e-mail contains a link/graphic to a web page with 'e-mail a friend' or 'e-mail a colleague'. A web form is used to collect the e-mail address to which the e-mail should be forwarded, sometimes with an optional message. The company then sends a separate message to the friend or colleague.
- *Web-facilitated viral (web prompt).* Here it is the web page such as a product catalogue or white paper which contains a link/graphic to 'e-mail a friend' or colleague. A web form is again used to collect data and an e-mail is subsequently sent.
- *Incentivised viral.* This is distinct from the types above since the e-mail address is not freely given. This is what we need to make viral really take off. By offering some reward for providing someone else's address we can dramatically increase referrals. A common offer is to gain an additional entry for a prize draw. Referring more friends gains more entries to the prize draw. With the right offer, this can more than double the response. The incentive is offered either by e-mail (the second option above) or on a web page (the third option). In this case, there is a risk of breaking privacy laws since the consent of the e-mail recipient may not be freely given. Usually only a single follow-up e-mail by the brand is permitted. So you should check with the lawyers if you are considering this.
- *Web-link viral.* But online viral isn't just limited to e-mail. Links in discussion group postings or blogs which are from an individual are also in this category. Either way, it's important when seeding the campaign to try to get as many targeted online and offline mentions of the viral agent as you can.

Social network-related viral marketing

Dee *et al.* (2007) also note the importance of social networks in influencing perceptions about brands, products and suppliers. Their research shows large differences in gender and age on the types of products discussed, but recommendations on restaurants, computers, movies and vehicles are popular in all categories.

Microsoft (2007), which part owns Facebook, has developed these approaches for taking advantage of social networking either through buying ad space, creating a brand space or brand channels that enable consumers to interact with or promote a brand:

- *Understand consumers' motivations for using social networks.* Ads will be most effective if they are consistent with the typical lifestage of networkers or the topics that are being discussed.
- *Express yourself as a brand.* Use the web to show the unique essence of your brand, but think about how to express a side of the brand that it is not normally seen.

- *Create and maintain good conversations.* Advertisers who engage in discussions are more likely to resonate with the audience, but once conversations are started they must be followed through.
- *Empower participants.* Social network users use their space and blogs to express themselves. Providing content or widgets to associate themselves with a brand may be appealing. For example, in the first six months of launching charity donation widgets, 20,000 have been used online and they became one of the biggest referrers to the JustGiving website and driving more people to fundraising pages to make donations (JustGiving, 2007).
- *Identify online brand advocates.* Use reputation management tools to identify influential social network members who are already brand advocates. Approach the most significant ones directly. Consider using contextual advertising such as Microsoft content ads or Google AdSense to display brand messages within their spaces when brands are discussed.
- *The Golden Rule: behave like a social networker.* Microsoft recommend this simple fundamental principle which will help the content created by advertisers to resonate with social networkers: behave like the best social networkers through:
  - being creative
  - being honest and courteous (ask permission)
  - being individual
  - being conscious of the audience
  - updating regularly.

Advantages and disadvantages of social media and viral marketing

The advantages and disadvantages of viral marketing are shared with those with online PR as covered earlier in the chapter. However, it can be argued that the risk in investment in viral marketing is higher since it is difficult to predict the success of a particular viral agent.

Advantages of social media and viral marketing

The main advantage of social media and viral marketing is that an effective viral agent can reach a large audience in a cost-effective way. We have also seen how consumers rate the opinions of their peers, friends and family highly, so they can be highly influential. Kumar *et al.* (2007) have discussed the potential value that can be generated through customer referrals in several case studies. Within social networks, major influencers can help spread the message more widely.

Disadvantages of social media and viral marketing

The main disadvantage of viral marketing is that this is a high-risk marketing communications technique, since it requires significant initial investment in the viral agent and seeding. However, there is no guarantee that the campaign will 'go viral', in which case the investment will be wasted.

With marketing within social networks it is challenging to engage audiences when they are socialising with their contacts and may not wish to interact with brands. It is also difficult to find the right types of content which will engage audiences and they will share with their contacts. Seeding to key influencers can help with distributing content, but seeding is a time-consuming specialist activity.

Of course, although positive viral marketing can spread rapidly, so can negative sentiments about a company, which we referred to in the section on online reputation management (see page 506).

Best practice in planning and managing viral marketing

Much discussion of practice in viral and word-of-mouth marketing centres around how and who to reach to achieve influence. Some, such as Malcom Gladwell and Seth Godin in their popular books *The Tipping Point and Unleashing the Idea virus* have suggested that influentials are important. Godin (2001) writes about the importance of what he terms 'the ideavirus' as a marketing tool. He describes it as 'digitally augmented word-of-mouth'. What differences does the ideavirus have from word-of-mouth? First, transmission is more rapid, second, transmission tends to reach a larger audience, and third, it can be persistent – reference to a product on a service. Godin emphasises the importance of starting small by seeding a niche audience he describes as a 'hive' and then using advocates in spreading the virus – he refers to them as 'sneezers'. Traditionally, marketers would refer to such a grouping as 'customer advocates' or 'brand loyalists'.

Others believe that the role of influencers in achieving word-of-mouth can be overstated. Balter and Butman, in their book, *Grapevine*, say:

> Everybody talks about products and services, and they talk about them all the time. Word-of-mouth is NOT about identifying a small subgroup of highly influential or well-connected people to talk up a product or service. It's not about mavens or bees or celebrities or people with specialist knowledge. It's about everybody.

While the influencers will have a greater impact, academics, Watts and Dodds (2007) concur, arguing that the 'influentials hypothesis' is based on untested assumptions and in most cases does not match how diffusion operates in the real world. They comment that 'most social change is driven not by influentials, but by easily influenced individuals influencing other easily influenced individuals'.

The role of social media in influencing consumers is discussed further in Chapter 2 in the section on consumer behaviour (see page 89).

To make a viral campaign effective, Justin Kirby of viral marketing specialists DMC (**www.dmc.co.uk**) suggested these three things are needed (Kirby, 2003):

- *Creative material – the 'viral agent'*. This includes the creative message or offer and how it is spread (text, image, video).
- *Seeding*. Identifying websites, blogs or people to send e-mail to start the virus spreading. Seeding can also be completed by e-mail to members of a house list or renting a list with the likely audience.
- *Tracking*. To monitor the effect, to assess the return from the cost of developing the viral agent and seeding.

Today, these factors are still relevant within online PR campaigns although we talk about 'shareable social objects' rather than 'viral agent' and 'influencer outreach' rather than 'seeding'.

Offline promotion techniques

The importance of offline communications in driving visitors to a website is well-known by site owners who find that greater levels of investment in offline advertising using TV, print or radio results in a greater numbers of direct visitors to websites (Figure 9.1). This can be tracked by web analytics which shows an increase in searches containing the brand or campaign name or the web address or direct visitors who enter the site URL into the address bar.

Research has identified that there is a clear correlation between investment in offline advertising and visits to a website. For example, Hitwise (2006) found in a study of brands including BSkyB, Orange and the AA that searches on brand terms and URLs increased-when offline media investment was combined with online. For example, when Sky's media campaign included both online and offline advertising (in September to November of 2005) the strongest result was achieved online with searches for the Sky brand increasing +20% and searches for the Sky URL more than doubling. When offline ran without the integration of online in March 2006, the same lift in searches was not evident. This research also shows the need for significant offline spend with Sky spending around 20 per cent online with print, TV and radio still remaining significant (see Figure 9.17).

The linkage between advertising and search has also been investigated by Graham and Havlena (2007) who additionally studied the role of advertising in generating word-of-mouth discussion online. They found 'strong evidence that advertising does stimulate increased visitation to the websites of advertised brands – an indicator of consumer interest and involvement with a brand'.

Online website promotion techniques such as search engine marketing and banner advertising often take prominence when discussing methods of traffic building. But we start with using offline communications to generate site visitors since it is one of the most effective techniques to generate site traffic and the characteristics of offline media are such (Figure 8.6, page 439) that they often have a higher impact and are more creative, which can help explain the online value proposition. **Offline promotion** refers to using communications tools such as advertising and PR delivered by traditional media such as TV, radio and print in order to direct visitors to an online presence.

Offline promotion
Using traditional media such as TV, radio and print to direct visitors to an online presence.

Despite the range of opportunities for using new online communications tools, traditional communications using offline media such as TV, print and direct mail and others shown in Figure 1.10 (page 30) remain the dominant form of investment in marketing communications for most. Even organisations which transact a large proportion of their business online continue to invest heavily in offline communications. EConsultancy (2008a) research into advanced adopters showed that even here the average expenditure on digital media channels as a proportion of communications budget was only 23 per cent. Consider the travel sector where both travel suppliers such as BA, Thomson and easyJet and intermediaries such as Expedia and Opodo transact an increasing proportion of their sales online, but are still reliant on offline communications to drive visitors to the web to transact.

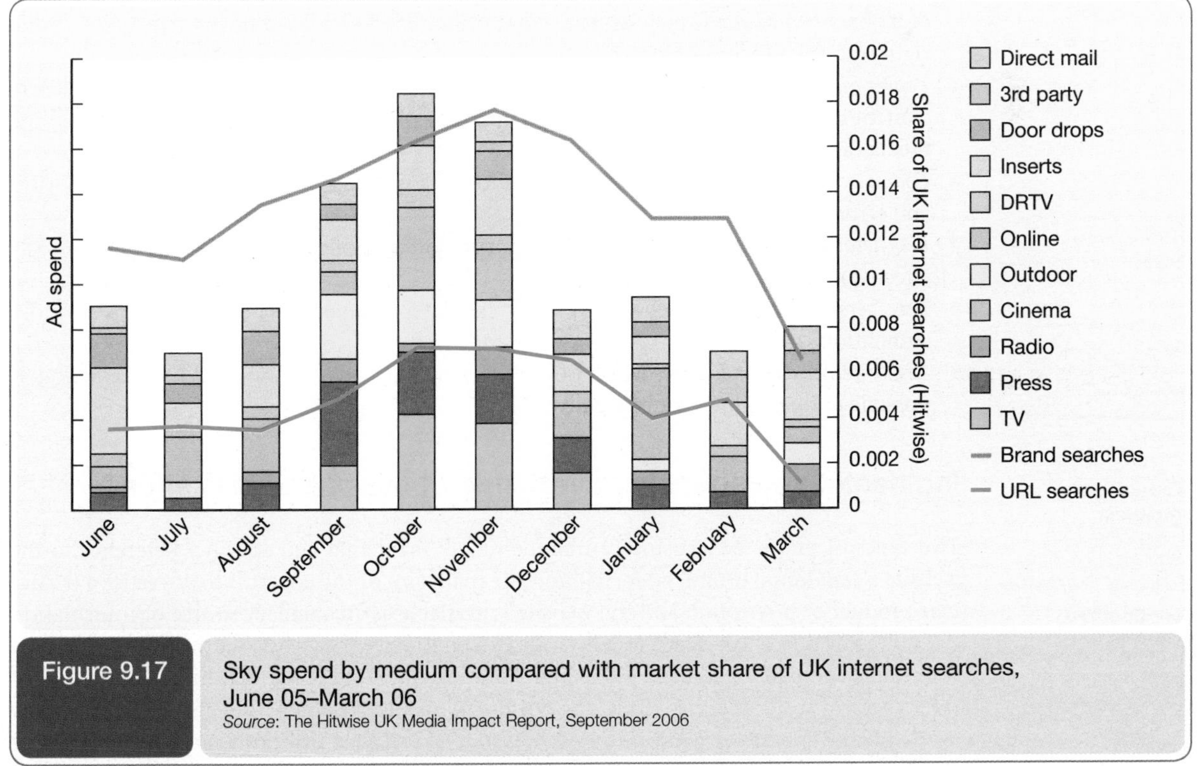

Figure 9.17 Sky spend by medium compared with market share of UK internet searches, June 05–March 06
Source: The Hitwise UK Media Impact Report, September 2006

When the web analytics data about referring visitors is assessed, for most companies who are not online-only businesses, we find that over half the visitors are typically marked as 'No referrer'. This means that they visited the site direct by typing in the web address into the address bar in response to awareness of the brand generated through real-world communications (others may have bookmarked the site or clicked through from a search engine).

So offline communications are effective at reaching an audience to encourage them to visit a site, but are also useful as a way of having an impact or explaining a complex proposition as, Mini Case Study 9.4 shows.

Advantages and disadvantages of using offline communications to support e-commerce

Offline communications work; they are effective in achieving four critical things:

- *Reach* – since newspaper, TV and postal communications are used by virtually all consumers.
- *Brand awareness* – through using high-impact visuals.
- *Emotional connection* – with brand again through visuals and sounds.
- *Explanation* – of the online value proposition for a brand.

A further benefit is that for any given objective, integrated marketing communications received through different media are more effective in achieving that objective. We mentioned this cumulative reinforcement effect of integrated marketing communications when referring to the 4 Cs of coherence, consistency, continuity and complementarities earlier in the chapter. Having said this, the disadvantages of using offline communications to encourage online channel usage compared to many online communications tools are obvious. In general the disadvantages of offline communications are:

- *Higher cost.* Return on investment tends to be higher for online communications such as search engine optimisation, pay-per-click marketing or affiliate marketing.
- *Higher wastage.* The well-known expression about 'half my advertising is wasted, but I don't know which half' may be true about offline marketing, but it isn't true online if the right tracking processes are in place.
- *Poorer targeting.* Targeting by behaviour, location, time, search keyword, site and site content is readily possible online. This tends to be more targeted compared to most offline media (apart from direct marketing).
- *Poorer accountability.* It is straightforward to track response online – offline it is expensive and error-prone.
- *Less detailed information.* The detailed information to support a decision can only be cost-effectively delivered online.
- *Less personalised.* Although direct mail can be personalised, personalisation is more straightforward online.
- *Less interactive experience.* Most offline communications are one-way – interaction is possible online with the right creative.

Incidental and specific advertising of the online presence

Incidental offline advertising
Driving traffic to the website is not a primary objective of the advert.

Specific offline advertising
Driving traffic to the website or explaining the online proposition is a primary objective of the advert.

Two types of offline advertising can be identified: incidental and specific. Reference to the website is **incidental offline advertising** if the main aim of the advert is to advertise a particular product or promotion and the website is available as an ancillary source of information if required by the viewer. Traditionally, much promotion of the website in the offline media by traditional companies has been incidental – simply consisting of highlighting the existence of the website by including the URL at the bottom of an advertisement. Reference to the website is **specific offline advertising** if it is an objective of the advert to explain the proposition of the website in order to drive traffic to the site to achieve direct response. Here the advert will highlight the offers or services available at the website, such as sales promotions or online customer service. Many state 'Visit our website!!', but clearly a more specific strapline can be developed which describes the overall proposition of the site ('detailed information and product guides to help you select the best product for you') or is specific to the campaign ('we will give you an instant quote online, showing how much you save with us').

Offline response mechanisms

The different response mechanics such as web response and URL strategy which we discussed in Chapter 8 in the section on campaign response mechanisms have to be used to maximise response since this helps to direct potential customers to the most appropriate content on the website. Different URLs are also useful for measuring the response of offline media campaigns since we can measure the number of visitors arriving directly at the URL by entering the domain name.

Public relations

Public relations can be an important tool for driving traffic to the website if changes to online services or online events are significant or if a viral campaign is discussed online. The days of the launch of a website being significant are now gone, but if a site is re-launched with significant changes to its services, this may still be worthy of mention. Many newspapers have regular features listing interesting entertainment or leisure sites or guides to specific topics such as online banking or grocery shopping. Trade magazines may also give information about relevant websites.

Jenkins (1995) argues that one key objective for public relations is its role in transforming a negative situation into a positive achievement. The public relations transfer process he suggests is as follows:

- from ignorance to knowledge
- from apathy to interest
- from prejudice to acceptance
- from hostility to sympathy.

These are, of course, goals of online PR which was discussed in more detail earlier inthis chapter.

Direct marketing

Direct marketing can be an effective method of driving traffic to the website. As mentioned earlier, a web response model can be used where the website is the means for fulfilling the response, but a direct mail campaign is used to drive the response. Many catalogue companies will continue to use traditional direct mail to mail-out a subset of their offering, with the recipient tempted to visit the site through the fuller offering and incentives such as competitions or web-specific offers.

Other physical reminders

Since we all spend more time in the real rather than the virtual world, physical reminders explaining why customers should visit websites are significant. What is in customers' hands and on their desk top will act as a prompt to visit a site and counter the weakness of the web as a pull medium. This is perhaps most important in the B2B context where a physical reminder in the office can be helpful. Examples, usually delivered through direct marketing, include brochures, catalogues, business cards, point-of-sale material, pens, postcards, inserts in magazines and password reminders for extranets.

Word-of-mouth marketing

It is worth remembering that, as we stated in the section on viral and word-of-mouth marketing, word-of-mouth plays an important role in promoting sites, particularly consumer sites where the Internet is currently a novelty. Opinion Research Corporation International, ORCI (1991), reported on a study among US consumers that showed that the typical Internet consumer tells 12 other people about his or her online shopping experience. This compares with the average US consumer, who tells 8.6 additional people about a favourite film and another 6.1 people about a favourite restaurant! It has been said that if the online experience is favourable then a customer will tell 12 people, but if it is bad they will tell twice as many, so word-of-mouth can be negative also. Parry (1998) reported that for European users, word-of-mouth through friends, relatives and colleagues was the most important method by which users found out about websites, being slightly more important than search engines and directories or links from other sites.

Activity 9.2 Selecting the best digital media channel mix techniques

Suggest the best mix of online (and offline) promotion techniques to build traffic for the following situations:

1 Well-established B2C brand with high brand awareness.
2 Dot-com start-up.
3 Small business aiming to export.
4 Common B2C product, e.g. household insurance.
5 Specialist B2B product.

Case Study 9 Innovation at Google

In addition to being the largest search engine on Earth, mediating tens of billions of searches daily, Google is an innovator. All online marketers should follow Google to see the latest approaches it is trialling.

Google's mission

Google's mission is encapsulated in the statement 'to organise the world's information ... and make it universally accessible and useful'. Google explains that it believes that the most effective, and ultimately the most profitable, way to accomplish its mission is to put the needs of its users first. Offering a high-quality user experience has led to strong word-of-mouth promotion and strong traffic growth.

Further details on the culture and ethics of Google is available at **http://www.google.com/intl/en/corporate/tenthings.html**. Notable tenets of the Google philosophy are:

1 Focus on the user and all else will follow.
2 It's best to do one thing really, really well.
3 You can make money without doing evil.

Putting users first is reflected in three key commitments in the Google SEC filing:

1 *We will do our best to provide the most relevant and useful search results possible, independent of financial incentives. Our search results will be objective and we will not accept payment for inclusion or ranking in them.*
2 *We will do our best to provide the most relevant and useful advertising. Advertisements should not be an annoying interruption. If any element on a search result page is influenced by payment to us, we will make it clear to our users.*
3 *We will never stop working to improve our user experience, our search technology and other important areas of information organisation.*

In the SEC filing, the company explains 'how we provide value to our users':

> *We serve our users by developing products that quickly and easily find, create, organise, and share information. We place a premium on products that matter to many people and have the potential to improve their lives.*

Some of the key benefits which are explained are: *Comprehensiveness and Relevance; Objectivity; Global Access; Ease of Use; Pertinent, Useful Commercial Information; Multiple Access Platforms and Improving the Web*.

The range of established Google services is well known and is listed at **http://www.google.com/options/**. Google's commitment to innovation is indicated by these more recent additions:

- Google+ announced 2011 – the social network to rival Facebook?
- Google TV (announced 2010) as part of a partnership agreement with Sony.
- Nexus One Phone using the Google Android mobile operating system launched in January 2010 (**www.google.com/phone**).
- Google Mobile advertising (although Google has offered text ads for some time, the 2009 acquisition of AdMob enables improvements in sophistication of this approach).
- Google Chrome OS (a lightweight operating system announced in 2009 and targeted initially at Netbooks).
- Google Chrome (a browser announced as a beta in 2008 and a full product for Windows in 2009).

For 2009, Google spent around 12 per cent of its revenue in research and development, an increase from less than 10 per cent in 2005, and a larger amount than Sales and Marketing (8.4 per cent).

Google revenue models

Google generated approximately 99 per cent of its revenues in 2007 and 97 per cent in 2008 and 2009 from its advertisers, with the remainder from its enterprise search products where companies can install search technology through products such as the Google Appliance and Google Mini.

Google AdWords, the auction-based advertising program, is the main source of revenue. Advertisers pay on a 'pay-per-click' cost basis within the search engines and someother services, but with cost-per-thousand payment options available on Google Networks members' web sites. Google has introduced classified style ad programmes for other media, including:

- Google Audio Ads (ads are placed in radio programmes)
- Google Print Ads
- Google TV Ads
- Google Promoted Video Ads within YouTube, user-initiated click-to-play video ads.

Google's revenues are critically dependent on how many searches it achieves in different countries and the proportion of searchers who interact with Google's ads. Research by ComScore (2008) suggests around 25 per cent of searches result in an ad click where sponsored search results are included (around 50 per cent of searches). Google is also looking to increase the number of advertisers and invests heavily in this through trade communications to marketers. Increased competition to advertise against a search term will result in increased bid amounts and so increased revenue.

International revenues accounted for approximately 53 per cent of total revenues in Q4 2009, and more than half of user traffic came from outside the US. In Q4 2009, 12 per cent of ad revenue was from the UK alone.

31 per cent of Google's revenue is from the Network of content partners who subscribe to the Google Adsenseprogramme.

Risk factors

Some of the main risk factors that Google declares include:

1. New technologies could block Google ads. Ad-blocking technology could, in the future, adversely affect Google's results, although there has not been widespread adoption of these approaches.
2. Litigation and confidence loss through click fraud. Click fraud can be a problem when competitors click on a link, but this is typically small-scale. A larger problem is structured click fraud where site owners on the Google content network seek to make additional advertising feeds.
3. Index spammers could harm the integrity of Google's web search results. This could damage Google's reputation and cause its users to be dissatisfied with products and services.

Google says:

> *There is an ongoing and increasing effort by 'index spammers' to develop ways to manipulate our web search results. For example, because our web search technology ranks a web page's relevance based in part on the importance of the web sites that link to it, people have attempted to link a group of web sites together to manipulate web search results.*

On 31 December 2009, Google had 19,835 employees. All of Google's employees are also equity holders, with significant collective employee ownership. As a result, many employees are highly motivated to make the company more successful. Google's engineers are encouraged to spend up to 10 per cent of their time identifying new approaches.

You can find updates on this case study by searching at **www.smartinsights.com** for 'Google Marketing updates'. For further reading, try Bala and Davenport (2008) – see Further Reading at the end of this chapter.

Question

Explain how Google generates revenue and exploits innovation in digital technology to identify future revenue growth. You should also consider the risk factors for future revenue generation.

Source: SEC, 2008

Summary

1 Online promotion techniques include:
   - *Search engine marketing* – search engine optimisation (SEO) improves position in the natural listings and pay-per-click marketing features a company in the sponsored listings of a search engine or on the display network
   - *Online PR* – including techniques such as influencer outreach, link building, blogging, and reputation management.
   - *Online partnerships* – including affiliate marketing (commission-based referral), co-branding and sponsorship.
   - *Online advertising* – using a range of formats including banners, skyscrapers and rich media such as overlays.
   - *E-mail marketing* – including rented lists, co-branded e-mails, event-triggered e-mails and ads in third-party e-newsletters for acquisition, and e-newsletters and campaign e-mails to house lists.
   - *Social media marketing* – engaging audiences on different social networks and on a company's own site through sharing content and developing great creative concepts which are transmitted by online word-of-mouth or viral marketing.

2 Offline promotion involves promoting the website address, highlighting the value proposition of the website and achieving web response through traditional media advertisements in print or on television.

3 Interactive marketing communications must be developed as part of integrated marketing communications for maximum cost effectiveness.

4 Key characteristics of interactive communications are the combination of push and pull media, user-submitted content, personalisation, flexibility and, of course, interactivity to create a dialogue with consumers.

5 Objectives for interactive communications include direct sales for transactional sites, but they also indirectly support brand awareness, favourability and purchase intent.

6 Important decisions in the communications mix introduced by digital media include:
   - the balance between spend on media and creative for digital assets and ad executions;
   - the balance between spend in traditional and offline communications;
   - the balance between investment in continuous and campaign-based digital activity;
   - the balance of investment in different interactive communications tools.

Table 9.4 provides a summary of the strengths and weaknesses of the tools discussed in this chapter.

Table 9.4 Summary of the strengths and weaknesses of different communications tools for promoting an online presence

Promotion technique	Main strengths	Main weaknesses
Search engine optimisation (SEO)	Highly targeted, relatively low cost of PPC. High traffic volumes if effective. Considered credible by searchers	Intense competition, may compromise look of site. Complexity of changes to ranking algorithm
Pay-per-click (PPC) marketing	Highly targeted with controlled cost of acquisition. Extend reach through content network	Relatively costly in competitive sectors and low volume compared with SEO
Trusted feed	Update readily to reflect changes in product lines and prices	Relatively costly, mainly relevant for e-retailers. No longer widely available.
Online PR	Relatively low cost and good targeting. Can assist with SEO through creation of backlinks	Identifying online influencers and setting up partnerships can be time-consuming. Need to monitor comments on third-party sites
Affiliate marketing	Payment is by results (e.g. 10% of sale or leads goes to referring site)	Costs of payments to affiliate networks for setup and management fees. Changes to ranking algorithm may affect volume from affiliates
Online sponsorship	Most effective if low-cost, long-term co-branding arrangement with synergistic site	May increase awareness, but does not necessarily lead directly to sales
Interactive advertising	Main intention to achieve visit, i.e. direct response model. But also role in branding through media multiplier effect	Response rates have declined historically because of banner blindness
E-mail marketing	Push medium – can't be ignored in user's inbox. Can be used for direct response link to website. Integrates as a response mechanism with direct mail	Requires opt-in for effectiveness. Better for customer retention than for acquisition? Inbox cut-through – message diluted among other e-mails. Limits on deliverability
Social media marketing, viral and word-of-mouth marketing	With effective viral agent, possible to reach a large number at relatively low cost. Influencers in social networks significant	Difficult to create powerful viral concepts and control targeting. Risks damaging brand since unsolicited messages may be received
Traditional offline advertising (TV, print, etc.)	Larger reach than most online techniques. Greater creativity possible, leading to greater impact	Targeting arguably less easy than online. Typical high cost of acquisition

Exercises

Self-assessment exercises

1. Briefly explain and give examples of online promotion and offline promotion techniques.
2. Explain the different types of payment model for banner advertising.
3. Which factors are important in governing a successful online banner advertising campaign?
4. How can a company promote itself through a search engine?
5. Explain the value of social media marketing.
6. How can online PR help to promote a new product?
7. How should websites be promoted offline?
8. What do you think the relative importance of these Internet-based advertising techniques would be for an international chemical manufacturer?
   (a) display advertising
   (b) paid search marketing
   (c) affiliate marketing.

Essay and discussion questions

1. How should companies evaluate the relevance and effectiveness of the digital media channels discussed in this chapter to their organisation?
2. Discuss the merits of the different models of paying for banner advertisements on the Internet for both media owners and companies placing advertisements.
3. Explain the factors that control the position of a company's products and services in the search engine results pages of a search engine such as Google.
4. Compare the effectiveness of different methods of online advertising including display advertisements, paid search marketing and affiliate marketing.

Examination questions

1. Give three examples of digital media channels and briefly explain their communications benefits.
2. Describe four different types of site on which online display advertising for a car manufacturer's site could be placed.
3. Click-through is one measure of the effectiveness of online advertising.
   (a) What is 'click-through'?
   (b) Which factors are important in determining the click-through rate of a banner advertisement?
   (c) Is click-through a good measure of the effectiveness of online advertising?
4. What is meant by co-branding? Explain the significance of co-branding.
5. What are 'meta tags'? How important are they in ensuring a website is listed in a search engine?
6. Name three alternative types of e-mail marketing that can be used for customer acquisition.
7. Briefly evaluate the strengths and weaknesses of affiliate marketing for a well-known retailer.
8. Which techniques can be used to promote a website in offline media?

References

Abraham, M. (2008) The off-line impact of online ads, *Harvard Business Review*, April, 86(4), 28.

Atlas (2007) Paying for navigation: the impact of navigational behavior on paid search, Research report by Nico Brooks, Director, Search Strategy, Published at: (**www.atlassolutions.com**).

Balter, D. and Butman, J. (2005) *Grapevine: The New Art of Word-of-Mouth Marketing*, Portfolio, New York.

Berthon, P., Lane, N., Pitt, L. and Watson, R. (1998) The World Wide Web as an industrial marketing communications tool: models for the identification and assessment of opportunities, *Journal of Marketing Management*, 14, 691–704.

Brin, S. and Page, L (1998) The anatomy of a large-scale hypertextual web search engine, *Computer Networks and ISDN Systems*, April, 30(1–7), 107–17, published at: **http://www-db.stanford.edu/~backrub/google.html**.

Cartellieri, C., Parsons, A., Rao, V. and Zeisser, M. (1997) The real impact of Internet advertising, *McKinsey Quarterly*, No. 3, 44–63.

Chaffey, D. (2006) *Total E-mail Marketing*, 2nd edn. Butterworth–Heinemann, Elsevier, Oxford.

Chaffey, D. and Smith, P.R. (2008) *E-marketing Excellence*, 3rd edn. Butterworth–Heinemann Elsevier, Oxford.

Chittenden, L. and Rettie, R. (2003) An evaluation of e-mail marketing and factors affecting response, *Journal of Targeting, Measurement and Analysis for Marketing*, March, 11(3), 203–17.

ComScore (2008) Why Google's surprising paid click data are less surprising, by Magid Abraham, 28 February, published at: **http:www.comscore.com/blog/2008/02/why_googles_surprising_paid_click_data_are_less_surprising.html**.

Dee, A., Bassett, B. and Hoskins, J. (2007) Word-of-mouth research: principles and applications, *Journal of Advertising Research*, December, 47(4), 387–97.

DMA (2008) UK National Client Benchmarking Report, published at: **www.dma.org.uk**.

Ecircle (2011) Display versus email. The SEAT Ibiza campaign illustrating how to effectively allocate your online advertising budgets. Research study published March.

EConsultancy (2008a) *Managing Digital Channels Research Report*, Dave Chaffey, available from: **www.e-consultancy.com**.

EConsultancy (2008b) *Paid Search Marketing, Best Practice Guide*, Dave Chaffey, available from: **www.e-consultancy.com**.

Efficient Frontier (2011) CPCs a strong month for finance, but weak for travel, 6 April, a blog post by Dr.Siddharth Shah: **http://blog.efrontier.com/insights/2011/04/march-2011-cps-a-strong-month-for-finance-but-weak-for-travel.html**

Fitzgerald, M. (2006) 'The Name Game: tagging tools let users describe the world in their own terms as taxonomies become folksonomies', *CIO Magazine*, 1 April.

Forrester (2007) Consumer Trends Survey North America – leveraging user-generated content, January, Brian Haven.

Gladwell, M. (2000) *The Tipping Point: How Little Things Can Make a Big Difference*, Little Brown.

Godin, S. (2001) *Unleashing the Ideavirus*, available online at: **www.ideavirus.com**.

Graham, J. and Havlena, W. (2007) Finding the 'missing link': advertising's impact on word of mouth, web searches, and site visits, *Journal of Advertising Research*, December, 47(4), 427–35.

Grehan, M. (2004) Increase your PR by increasing your PR. Article in *E-marketing News e-newsletter*, November. Source: **www.e-marketing-news.co.uk/november.html#pr**.

GSI (2011) The Purchase Path of Online Buyers. SucharitaMulpuru, March. Whitepaper published at http://www.gsicommerce.com/purchasepath/.

Hitwise (2006) UK media impact report, Analyst Heather Hopkins. Available online at: www.hitwise.com.

Hitwise (2007) Social networks can drive traffic – case study of ASOS and TopShop, blog posting by analyst Heather Hopkins, 1 March: http://weblogs.hitwise.com/heather-hopkins/2007/03/social_networks_can_drive_taf.html.

iMediaConnection (2003) Interview with ING Direct VP of Marketing, Jurie Pietersie: www.mediaconnection.com/content/1333.asp.

Jenkins, F. (1995) *Public Relations Techniques*, 2nd edn. Butterworth–Heinemann, Oxford.

JustGiving (2007) Justgiving Widget version 2.0, blog posting, 24 July: http://justgiving.typepad.com/charities/2007/07/justgiving-widg.html.

Kirby, J. (2003) Online viral marketing: next big thing or yesterday's fling? *New Media Knowledge*, published online at: www.newmediaknowledge.co.uk.

Kumar, V., Petersen, J. and Leone, R. (2007) How valuable is word of mouth? *Harvard Business Review*, October, 85(10), 139–46.

Levine, R., Locke, C., Searls, D. and Weinberger, D. (2000) *The Cluetrain Manifesto*, Perseus Books, Cambridge, MA.

MAD (2007) How online display advertising influences search volumes, published 4 June, MAD Network (*Marketing Week*), Centaur Communications: http://technology-weekly.mad.co.uk/Main/InDepth/SearchEngineMarketing/Articles/f66d813eeab74e93ad8f252ae9c7f02a/How-online-display-advertising-influences-search-volumes.html.

Marsden, P. Samson, A. and Upton, N. (2005) Advocacy drives growth, *Brand Strategy*, Dec 2005/Jan 2006, Issue 198.

McGaffin, K. (2004) Linking matters: how to create an effective linking strategy to promote your website, published at: www.linkingmatters.com.

Microsoft (2007) Word of the web guidelines for advertisers: understanding trends and monetising social networks. Research report available from: http://advertising.microsoft.com.

New Media Age (2008) Measuring Buzz. By Sean Hargrave, 17 January.

Nielsen, J. (2007) Banner blindness: old and new findings, Jakob Nielsen's Alertbox, published online, 20 August: http://www.usit.com/alertbox/ banner-blindness.html.

Nielsen (2011) State of the Media: Advertising Spend and Effectiveness. Q1 2011 summary published at: http://www.nielsen.com/us/en/insights/reports-downloads/2011/advertising-spend-effectiveness-q1-2011.html?status=success

Novak, T. and Hoffman, D. (1997) New metrics for new media: towards the development of web measurement standards, *World Wide Web Journal*, 2(1), 213–46.

OPA Europe (2010) The Silent Click. Building brands online in Europe: http://www.opa-europe.org/news/press-releases/265.

Optify (2011) The changing face of SERPS: organic clickthrough rate, whitepaper published Spring: http://www.optify.net/wp-content/uploads/2011/04/Changing-Face-of-SERPS-Organic-CTR.pdf.

ORCI (1991) Word-of-mouth drives e-commerce. Survey summary, May. Opinion Research Corporation International: www.opinionresearch.com.

Parry, K. (1998) *Europe gets wired. A survey of Internet use in Great Britain, France and Germany, Research Report 1998.* KPMG Management Consulting, London.

Performics (2010) Search engine usage study: 92% of searchers click on sponsored results, press release: http://www.performics.com/news-room/press-releases/Search-Engine-Usage- Study-92-Percent/1422.

PRCA (2005) Website definition of PR. The Public Relationships Consultants Association, www.prca.org.uk.

Prussakov, E. (2011a) *A Practical Guide to Affiliate Marketing. Quick Reference for Affiliate Managers and Merchants.* Self-published.

Prussakov (2011b) Back to Affiliate cookie duration return days question, blog post by Geno Prussakov, 12 September: http://www.amnavigator.com/blog/2011/09/12/back-to-affiliate-cookie-duration-return-days-question/.

Ranchhod, A., Gurau, C. and Lace, J. (2002) Online messages: developing an integrated communications model for biotechnology companies, *Qualitative Market Research: An International Journal*, 5(1), 6–18.

Rettie, R., Grandcolas, U. and Deakins, B. (2005) Text message advertising: response rates and branding effects, *Journal of Targeting, Measurement & Analysis for Marketing*, June, 13(4), 304–12.

Robinson, H., Wysocka, A. and Hand, C. (2007) Internet advertising effectiveness: the effect of design on click-through rates for banner ads, *International Journal of Advertising*, 26(4), 527–41.

Ryan, J. and Whiteman, N. (2000) Online advertising glossary: sponsorships. ClickZ Media Selling channel 15 May.

Say, P. and Southwell, J. (2006) Case study: Beep-beep-beep-beep, that'll be the bank then — Driving sales through mobile marketing, *Journal of Direct, Data and Digital Marketing Practice*, 7(3), 262–5.

SEC (2008) Annual report filing on form 10–K to US Securities and Exchange Commission (SEC) for Google Inc., 15 February.

SEOMoz (2011a) Google Algorithm Change History page: http://www.seomoz.org/google-algorithm-change.

SEOMoz (2011b) Google search engine ranking factors, published at: www.seomoz.org/article/search-ranking-factors.

Smart Insights (2010) 'Official': Facebook and Twitter DO influence natural search rankings. Author: Chris Soames, December 2010.

Smart Insights (2011a) Blog post: How balanced is your traffic mix? Author: Dave Chaffey. 4 July: http://www.smartinsights.com/digital-marketing-strategy/customer-acquisition-strategy/how-balanced-is-your-traffic-mix/.

Smart Insights (2011b), Social media command centres, blog post: 13 July. Author: Dave Chaffey. http://www.smartinsights.com/analytics-conversion-optimisation-alerts/social-media-command-centers/: http://www.smartinsights.com/search-engine-optimisation-seo/seo-strategy/customer-acquisition-strategy/facebook-twitter-influence-natural-search-rankings/.

Watts, D. and Dodds, S. (2007) Influentials, networks and public opinion formation, *Journal of Consumer Research* 34(4), 441–58.

Zeff, R. and Aronson, B. (2001) *Advertising on the Internet*, 3rd edn. Wiley, New York.

Further reading

Bala, I. and Davenport, T. (2008) Reverse engineering google's innovation machine, *Harvard Business Review*, April, 86(4), 58–68.

Fill, C. (2009) *Marketing Communications – Interactivity, Communitiesand Content*, 5th edn. Financial Times/Prentice Hall, Harlow. The entire book is recommended for its integration of theory, concepts and practice.

Novak, T. and Hoffman, D. (1997) New metrics for new media: towards the development of web measurement standards, *World Wide Web Journal*, 2(1), 213–46. This paper gives detailed, clear definitions of terms associated with measuring advertising effectiveness.

Weblinks

General digital media channel-related e-mail newsletters and portals

- **ClickZ Experts** (www.clickz.com/experts). Has columns on e-mail marketing, e-mail marketing optimisation and e-mail marketing case studies.
- **Econsultancy.com** (www.econsultancy.com). Best practice sections on different e-communications tools and newsletter features interviews with e-commerce practitioners.
- **Marketing Sherpa** (www.marketingsherpa.com). Articles and links on Internet marketing communications including e-mail and online advertising.
- **Smart Insights** (www.smartinsights.com) Advice on best practice and the latest updates on digital marketing edited by Dave Chaffey.

E-mail-related advice sites

- **Direct Marketing Association UK** (www.dma.org.uk). Best practice guidelines and benchmarks of response rates.
- **E-mail Experience Council** (www.emailexperience.org). A US organisation with compilations of practical tips on e-mail marketing.

Affiliates and aggregator advice sites

- **A4UForum** (www.a4uforum.co.uk). Used by affliates to discuss approaches and compare programmes.
- **Affiliate marketing blog** (http://blog.affiliatetip.com). Practical tips and the latest developments from affiliate Shawn Collins.
- **AM Navigator** (www.amnavigator.com/blog). Advice on managing affiliate programmes from Geno Prussakov).
- **Comparison Engines** (www.comparisonengines.com). A blog focusing on developments in shopping comparison intermediaries.

Internet advertising research sites

- **AtlasSolutionsInstitute** (http://www.atlassolutions.com). Microsoft owned ad-serving and tracking provider with research about consumer behaviour and optimising ad effectiveness.
- **Doubleclick** (http://www.doubleclick.com/insight/research). Google owned ad-serving and tracking provider with research about consumer behaviour and optimising ad effectiveness.
- **EyeBlaster** (www.eyeblaster.com) is one of the main providers of rich media ad-serving technologies. Its galleries have good examples.
- **iMediaConnection** (www.imediaconnection.com). Media site reporting on best practice in online advertising.
- **US Internet Advertising Bureau** (www.iab.net). The widest range of studies about Internet advertising effectiveness. In UK: www.iabuk.net.
- **Tangozebra** (www.tangozebra.co.uk) is a UK-based provider of ad-serving technology which showcases many of the most recent ad campaigns by industry category.
- **World Advertising Research Centre** (www.warch.com). Mainly subscription service, but some free resources.

Search-engine-related links

- **Google Webmaster tools** (www.google.com/webmasters). Provides a useful set of tools for sites verified by their owners including index inclusion, linking and ranking for different phrases in different locations.
- **Dave Chaffey's keyword suggestion tools** (www.davechaffey.com/seo-keyword-tools). The latest version of a range of free and paid tools for natural and paid search.
- **Reputation management** (www.davechaffey.com/online-reputation-management-tools).
- **Search Engine Watch** (www.searchenginewatch.com). A complete resource on SEO and PPC marketing. See Search Engine Land (www.searchengineland.com) for more commentary.
- **Webmasterworld** (www.webmasterworld.com). A forum, where search practitioners discuss best practice.

Viral marketing/Word-of-mouth research sites

- **Mashable** (www.mashable.com). Site focusing on developments and statistics related to social networks.
- **Viral and Buzz Marketing Network** (www.vbma.net). A European-oriented community of academics and professionals for discussion of the applications of connected marketing
- **Word-of-mouth marketing association** (www.womma.org). A US-oriented community of word-of-mouth marketing specialists.
- **O'Reilly Radar** (http://radar.oreilly.com). Commentary on the development of Web 2.0 approaches technologies from publishers O'Reilly, whose founder Tim O'Reilly coined the term Web 2.0.

Chapter 10

Evaluation and improvement of digital channel performance

Chapter at a glance

Main topics

Case studies

Learning objectives

After reading this chapter, the reader should be able to:

- Understand terms and tools used to measure and improve digital marketing effectiveness
- Develop an appropriate process to collect measures for digitalmarketing effectiveness
- Identify the activities necessary when managing an online presence

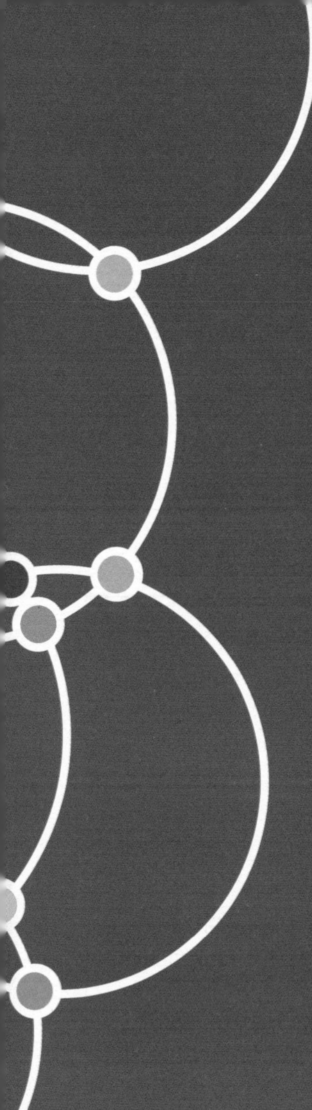

Questions for marketers

Key questions for marketing managers related to this chapter are:

- How do I measure and improve the effectiveness of digital marketing?
- How much resource do I need to put into managing and improving the site?

Scan code to find the latest updates for topics in this chapter

Links to other chapters

This chapter should be read in conjunction with these chapters:

- Chapter 4 describes the development of a digital marketing strategy. The aim of measurement is to quantify whether the objectives of this strategy have been achieved.
- Chapter 7 describes how to set up a website, and should be read before this chapter to introduce the reader to the concepts of website development.
- Chapter 8 describes methods of promoting a website. It should be read before this chapter since one aspect of measuring the effectiveness of Internet marketing is aimed at assessing the different promotional methods.

Introduction

Companies that have a successful approach to online marketing often seem to share a common characteristic. They attach great importance and devote resources to monitoring the success of their online marketing putting in place the processes to continuously improve the performance of their digital channels. This approach has been fundamental to the growth of Amazon as Case Study 10 in this chapter explains about their culture of metrics.

Alliance & Leicester, a traditional financial services provider who are now part of Santander, also have this approach. Stephen Leonard, their head of e-commerce, described their process as 'Test, Learn, Refine' (*Revolution*, 2004) while Graeme Findlay, senior manager, customer acquisition of e-commerce explained:

> Our online approach is integrated with our offline brand and creative strategy, with a focus on direct, straightforward presentation of strong value-led messages. Everything we do online, including creative, is driven by an extensive and dynamic testing process.

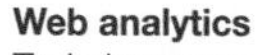

Web analytics
Techniques used to assess and improve the contribution of digital marketing to a business, including reviewing traffic volume, referrals, clickstreams, online reach data, customer satisfaction surveys, leads and sales.

The importance of defining an appropriate approach to measurement and improvement is such that the term **web analytics** has developed to describe this key digitalmarketing activity. A web analytics association (**www.webanalyticsassociation.org**) has been developed by vendors, consultants and researchers in this area to manage best practice. Their definition of web analytics is:

> Web analytics is the measurement, collection, analysis and reporting of Internet data for the purposes of understanding and optimising web usage.

You can see this is a 'catch-all' definition. How do you think it could be improved? We think it could reference the commercial aims of optimisation and the measurement of multichannel usage.

To succeed in a measured approach to improving results from Internet marketing we suggest that there are four main organisational prerequisites, which are broken down as shown in Figure 10.1 into the quality of the web analytics processes including defining the right improvement measures and purchasing the right tools and the management processes – such as putting in place a process where staff review results and then modify their marketing activities accordingly.

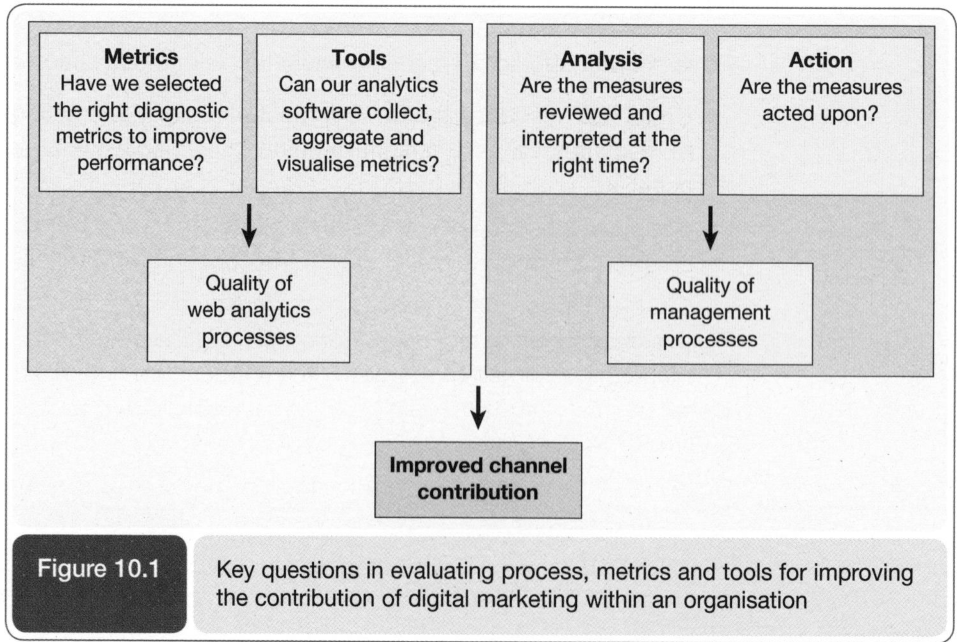
Metrics
Have we selected the right diagnostic metrics to improve performance?
Tools
Can our analytics software collect, aggregate and visualise metrics?
Analysis
Are the measures reviewed and interpreted at the right time?
Action
Are the measures acted upon?
Quality of web analytics processes
Quality of management processes
Improved channel contribution

Figure 10.1 Key questions in evaluating process, metrics and tools for improving the contribution of digital marketing within an organisation

This chapter is in two parts – the first part is about performance management, where we review the approach to improving performance through assessing appropriate measures, tools and the right process to apply them as suggested by Figure 10.1. In the second part, we review some of the issues involved with maintaining an online presence, looking at the tools and process for improving differentcompany web presences.

Digital marketing in practice — The Smart Insights interview

Avinash Kaushik, analytics evangelist at Google

Overview and main concepts covered

Avinash Kaushik is Google's analytics evangelist well-known for his books *Web Analytics An Hour a Day*, *Analytics 2.0* and his *Occam's Razor Blog*.

The Interview

Q. Some have criticised online customer engagement as being an abstract concept that can't be readily applied in the real world. Can you give some practical examples of how a site owner can apply the engagement concept to get better results?

Avinash Kaushik: Engagement is a nice goal to have. Create sites that customers will find engaging and they'll stick around or come back again or maybe do business with you.

But that term has been manipulated to a point where it means nothing any more (or everything to everyone) and is often used as an excuse to not do the hard work of figuring out what the real outcomes of the site are for the company and the website visitors.

My encouragement to website owners is to be initially sceptical when someone is trying to pawn off 'engagement' on them and ask the tough question: 'What do you really mean by engagement and how does it specifically apply to my business?'

Secondly, I encourage people to realise that on the most glorious spring day when the birds are chirping the right song, web analytics tools can measure the degree of engagement but they fall quite a bit short of measuring the kind of engagement. So they can report that visitors saw 19 pages on your site (degree) but they can't tell you if that was because the visitors were frustrated with your crappy navigation or thrilled with your content.

People use Google Analytics (or other tools) to measure easily various elements of the degree of engagement. Perhaps the simplest example is using the bounce rate for the core landing pages to identify pages that won't even entice visitors to make a one click! In two clicks you can also get loyalty (recency), frequency, length of visit and depth of visit to get a solid feel for if visitors are making repeat visits to the site of if they do it more frequently and marry that up with content consumption. Doing this by looking at trends over time is a fantastic way to understand if the site is delivering value for you customers.

For many 'social' websites, website owners also measure the number of people who sign up and then contribute by writing reviews or comments etc. These are all really good examples of 1) measuring the degree of engagement and 2) not confusing the real metric being measured by calling it engagement.

Q. Which are the best measures or reports you could point to which help marketers understand how well an e-commerce site is performing for retention?

Avinash Kaushik: I touched on some of the obvious ones above, the loyalty metrics (specifically recency and frequency). They immediately tell you if you are acquiring traffic that comes back again and again, and since GA will tell you recency by going as far back in history as you have data, that is a great way to know when customers come back (and perhaps also understand why). The other obvious thing to do for shorter time periods is to look at the trends for % of new visits, especially by the sources of your traffic.

Some retailers want to do retention analysis by looking at repeat purchases. For this, Google Analytics, like pretty much every tool out there, provides a very strong complement of ecommerce reports that allow you to segment the data by the types of purchasers (new or returning) which will help you understand their purchase behaviour and by applying filters to your data you can dig deeper into sources of traffics, trends in number of visits, content consumed etc.

This in conjunction with using even simple on-exit website surveys can give you a great picture of what is happening on your website and where you are missing the boat.

Q. Conversion optimisation. Today there is a lot more talk in large organisations about using techniques like AB or multivariate testing. How would you advise a small business owner to set out on this journey?

Avinash Kaushik: This might surprise you, but I am seeing a lot more traction in using optimisation techniques with smaller companies than with larger companies. There are a couple of interesting reasons:

1 A/B or MVT is now free with tools like Google Website Optimiser, so you can dispense with RFP's and all that 'stuff' and just go try the tool.
2 Smaller companies are much more willing to try new things and have less politics and entrenched opinions (and HiPPO's) that are hard to overcome. This is of course a tad bit sad because given the traffic and the sheer opportunities it really is a crime for larger companies to leave so much more revenue on the table, or the chance to optimise the customer experience which will improve loyalty and satisfaction.

My recommendations for any company are perhaps similar:

- Start with A/B testing. In my experience starting simple will ensure that you will get out of the gates fast and be able to start the critical process of cultural shift with easily understandable experiments. Then you can move to the 1.8 billion combination page test.
- For the highest impact try dramatic differences in your test versions. Trying shades of blue might sound interesting but the test might take a very very long time to provide you with statistically significant differences. But try a page with only text and one with text and images might get you on the path to understanding your customers faster.
- Run a report for your top 25 landing pages (entry pages) on your site, then look at the bounce rates for each of them. Pick three with the highest bounce rates, these are the pages letting you down the most. You'll win big by testing these first.
- Have an active 'customer listening channel'. Remote usability testing, market research, customer call centres or surveys (even a free excellent solution like 4Q, which I helped create with iPerceptions). The best focus points about what is not working on your site come from your customers (sadly not you) and likewise the greatest ideas on how to improve your site (and hence test) also come from your customers. Listen and you will prosper.

Q. What excites you most about potential developments in web analytics in the future?

Avinash Kaushik: The thing that excites me most is that no one has a clue where this is all headed. We have no idea what 'web analytics' will look like in five years. That is exciting because there is a ton of change and growth to come and being a part of helping play a small part in that change is simply fantastic.

There are new data collection methods to come, there are new ways of doing superior analysis of data, there is so much more we could do with Artificial Intelligence in optimising customer experiences, there are opportunities to bridge the various islands of data (on the web or outside) to create something amazing, there are ... it goes on and on.

They are going to get a lot better about what you should look at. Visualisation is great and tables are good but what is killing analysts right now is their ability to figure out, from megabytes and megabytes of data, what is actually worth looking at. Most tools still simply spew data out relying on the analyst (or the data consumer) to figure things out. That is a bad strategy, yet most tools follow it.

Visualisation has got a lot better – but I'm not seeing any form of intelligent recommendations. It's very tricky and the web analytics companies are too busy copying other functionality! It's good you mention that clickstracks features though. Using ClickTracks as an example, I demonstrated how to look at only the data that has shifted in importance by a statistically significant amount. Your top twenty of anything never changes, but using this type of report, What's Changed, you can look at just the data that really matters. Now it is easier to take action.

I expect all tools to get much much better at applying advanced mathematics and statistics to help their users identify where to focus their attention.

The other thing I would highlight as a evolution for web analytics tools is that they are going to do a lot more than page view reporting on your site. I don't mean doing clever things like event logging to measure Web 2.0 experiences, that is cool of course. I am referring to their ability to measure content no matter how it is distributed (widgets, rss, etc.) and where it is consumed (websites, feed readers, mobile phones, your home refrigerator or washing machine!).

Opportunity is, I suppose, what I find most exciting about the future of web analytics.

Performance management for digital channels

Performance management system
A process used to evaluate and improve the efficiency and effectiveness of an organisation and its processes.

Performance measurement system
The process by which metrics are defined, collected, disseminated and actioned.

Digital marketing metrics
Measures that indicate the effectiveness of digitalmarketing activities integrated across different channels and platforms in meeting customer, business and marketing objectives.

To improve results for any aspect of any business, performance management is vital. As Bob Napier, Chief Information Office, Hewlett-Packard was reported to have said back in the 1960s, 'You can't manage what you can't measure'. The processes and systems intended to monitor and improve the performance of an organisation, are known by business operations researchers as **performance management systems** and are based on the study of **performance measurement systems.**

Today, nearly all organisations have different forms of online presence, but the questions highlighted in Figure 10.1 aren't answered adequately. So, a good starting point is to understand the current improvement process and the organisational barriers which prevent a suitable improvement process.

In this section, we will review approaches to performance management by examining three key elements of an Internet marketing measurement system. These are, first, the *process* for improvement, and secondly, the measurement framework which specifies groups of relevant **digital marketing metrics** and, finally, an assessment of the suitability of tools and techniques for collecting, analysing, disseminating and actioning results. We will review three stages of creating and implementing a performance management system.

Stage 1: Creating a performance management system

The essence of *performance management* is suggested by the definition for performance *measurement* used by Andy Neely and co-workers of Cranfield School of Management's Centre for Business Performance. They defined performance measurement as (Neely *et al.*, 2002):

> the process of quantifying the efficiency and effectiveness of past actions through acquisition, collation, sorting, analysis, interpretation and dissemination of appropriate data.

Performance management extends this definition to the process of analysis and actioning change in order to drive business performance and returns. Online marketers can apply many of the approaches of business performance management to digital marketing. As you can see from the definition, performance is measured primarily through information on process **effectiveness** and **efficiency** as introduced in Chapter 4 in the section on objective setting, where we noted that it is important to include both effectiveness and efficiency measures.

Effectiveness
Meeting process objectives, delivering the required outputs and outcomes, 'doing the right thing'.

Efficiency
Minimising resources or time needed to complete a process 'doing the thing right'.

The need for a structured performance management process is clear if we examine the repercussions if an organisation does not have one. These include: poor linkage of measures with strategic objectives or even absence of objectives; key data not collected; data inaccuracies; data not disseminated or analysed; or no corrective action. Many of the barriers to improvement of measurement systems reported by respondents in Adams *et al.* (2000) also indicate the lack of an effective process. The barriers can be grouped as follows:

- *senior management myopia* – performance measurement not seen as a priority, not understood or targeted at the wrong targets – reducing costs rather than improving performance
- unclear responsibilities for delivering and improving the measurement system
- *resourcing issues* – lack of time (perhaps suggesting lack of staff motivation), the necessary technology and integrated systems
- *data problems* – data overload or of poor quality, limited data for benchmarking.

The Web Analytics Association (2011) Outlook survey of companies using web analytics gives insights on the specific challenges of performance management for digital marketing. The top 5 challenges for were:

- actionability of the data (36%)
- business decisions driven by analytics (35.3%)
- Social media (34.9%)
- executive management awareness and support for web analytics (34.9%)
- failure to take action on the data (31.0%)

In 2009, the largest hurdle organisations predicted was funding, but by 2011 this wasn't in the top 10, suggesting more buy-in to use of web analytics. The report also shows that the majority are happy with the capabilities of their web analytics tools. Instead, the top two issues reported suggest the problems of performance management, taking action based on the data.

To avoid these pitfalls, a co-ordinated, structured measurement process such as that shown in Figure 10.2 is required. Figure 10.2 indicates four key stages in a measurement process. These were defined as key aspects of annual marketing plan control by Kotler (1997). Stage 1 is a goal-setting stage where the aims of the measurement system are defined – this will usually take the strategic digital marketing objectives as an input to the measurement system. The aim of the measurement system will be to assess whether these goals are achieved and specify corrective marketing actions to reduce variance between target and actual key performance indicators. Stage 2, performance measurement, involves collecting data to determine the different metrics that are part of a measurement framework as discussed in the next section. Stage 3, performance diagnosis, is the analysis of results to understand the reasons for variance from objectives (the 'performance gap' of Friedman and Furey, 1999) and selection of

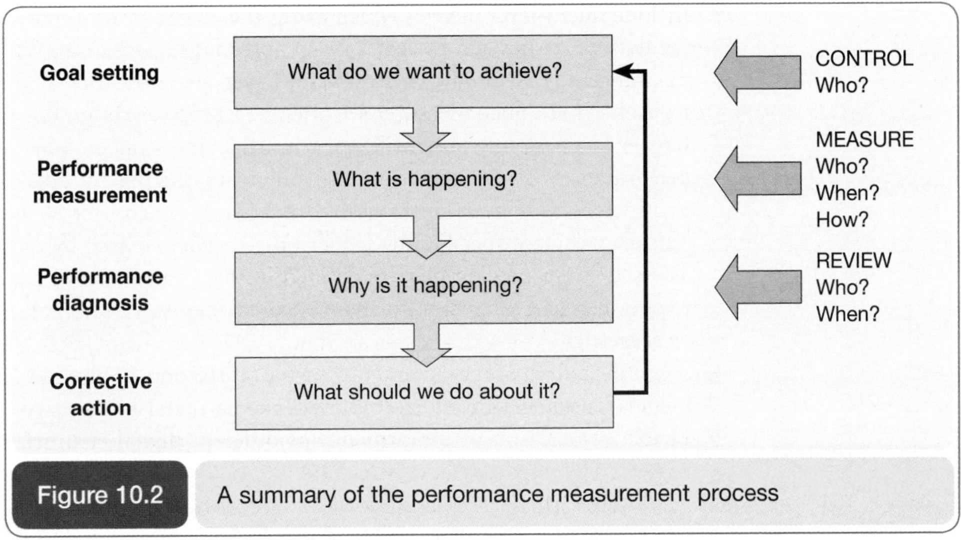

Figure 10.2 A summary of the performance measurement process

marketing solutions to reduce variance. The purpose of stage 4, corrective action, according to Wisner and Fawcett (1991), is:

> to identify competitive position, locate problem areas, assist the firm in updating strategic objectives and making tactical decisions to achieve these objectives and supply feedback after the decisions are implemented.

In a digital marketing context, corrective action is the implementation of these solutions as updates to content, design and associated marketing communications. At this stage the continuous cycle repeats, possibly with modified goals.

Stage 2: Defining the performance metrics framework

Measurement for assessing the effectiveness of digital marketing should assess the contribution of digital marketing at different levels:

1. Are corporate objectives defined in the digital marketing strategy being met?
2. Are marketing objectives plan achieved?
3. Are marketing communications objectives achieved?

These measures can also be related to the different levels of marketing control specified by Kotler (1997). These include strategic control (question 1), profitability control (question 1), annual-plan control (question 2) and efficiency control (question 3).

Efficiency measures are more concerned with minimising the costs of online marketing while maximising the returns for different areas of focus such as acquiring visitors to a website, converting visitors to outcome or achieving repeat business.

Chaffey (2000) suggested that organisations define a measurement framework or create a management dashboard which defines groupings of specific metrics used to assess digital marketing performance. He suggested that suitable measurement frameworks will fulfil these criteria:

- Include macro-level effectiveness metrics which assess whether strategic goals are achieved and indicate to what extent e-marketing contributes to the business (revenue contribution and return on investment). This criterion covers the different levels of marketing control specified by Kotler (1997), including strategic control, profitability control and annual-plan control.

- Include micro-level metrics which assess the efficiency of e-marketing tactics and implementation. Wisner and Fawcett (1991) note that organisations typically use a hierarchy of measures and they should check that the lower-level measures support the macro-level strategic objectives. Such measures are often referred to as *performance drivers*, since achieving targets for these measures will assist in achieving strategic objectives. Digital marketing performance drivers help optimise online marketing by attracting more site visitors and increasing conversion to desired marketing outcomes. These achieve the marketing efficiency control specified by Kotler (1997). The research by Agrawal *et al.* (2001), who assessed companies on metrics defined in three categories of attraction, conversion and retention as part of an e-performance scorecard, uses a combination of macro- and micro-level metrics.
- Assess the impact of the e-marketing on the satisfaction, loyalty and contribution of key stakeholders (customers, investors, employees and partners) as suggested by Adams *et al.* (2000).
- Enable comparison of performance of different digital channels with other channels as suggested by Friedman and Furey (1999).
- The framework can be used to assess e-marketing performance against competitors' or out-of-sector best practice.

When identifying metrics it is common practice to apply the widely used SMART mnemonic and it is also useful to consider three levels – business measures, marketing measures and specific digitalmarketing measures (see the objective setting section in Chapter 4).

Figure 10.3 shows a framework of measures, which can be applied to a range of different companies. The groupings of measures remain relevant, although they are centred on sites or online presence, measures for engagement with social media should also be considered. In Chapter 4, we also reviewed two alternative frameworks (see Tables 4.6 and 4.9) that can also be used for creating a performance dashboard.

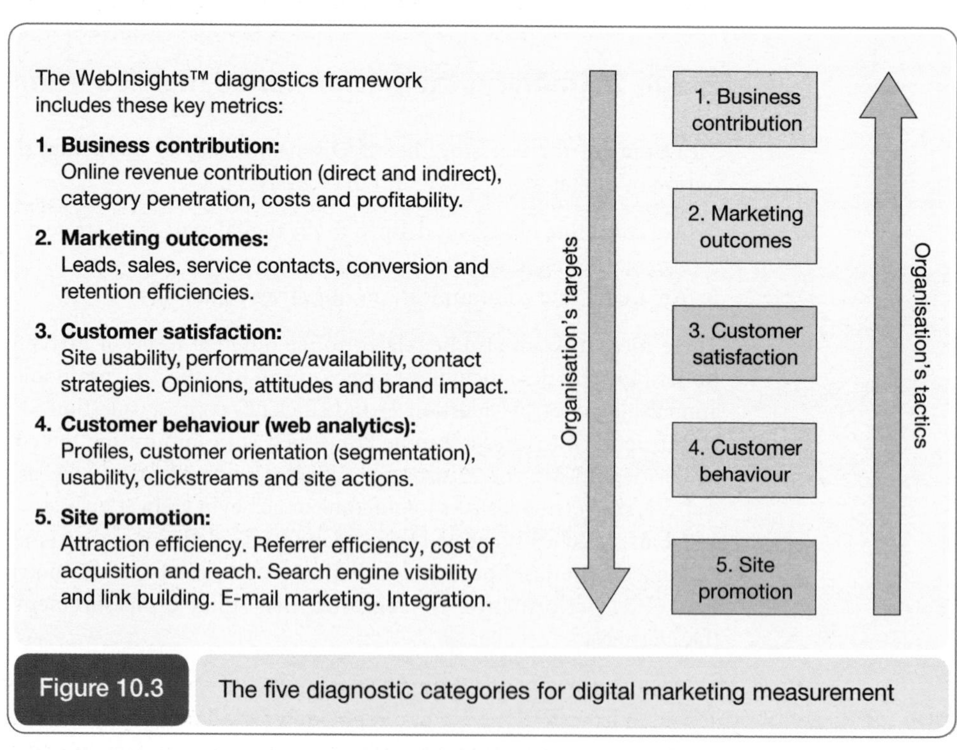

The WebInsights™ diagnostics framework includes these key metrics:
1. Business contribution:
Online revenue contribution (direct and indirect), category penetration, costs and profitability.
2. Marketing outcomes:
Leads, sales, service contacts, conversion and retention efficiencies.
3. Customer satisfaction:
Site usability, performance/availability, contact strategies. Opinions, attitudes and brand impact.
4. Customer behaviour (web analytics):
Profiles, customer orientation (segmentation), usability, clickstreams and site actions.
5. Site promotion:
Attraction efficiency. Referrer efficiency, cost of acquisition and reach. Search engine visibility and link building. E-mail marketing. Integration.
Organisation's targets
1. Business contribution
2. Marketing outcomes
3. Customer satisfaction
4. Customer behaviour
5. Site promotion
Organisation's tactics

Figure 10.3 The five diagnostic categories for digital marketing measurement

Channel promotion
Measures that assess why customers visit a site – which adverts they have seen, which sites have they been referred from.

Referrer
The site that a visitor previously visited before following a link.

Channel promotion

These measures evaluate the volume, quality and value of where the website, social presence or mobile site visitors originate – online or offline, and what are the sites or offline media that prompted their visit. Web analytics can be used to assess which intermediary sites customers are referred from (**the referrer**) and which keywords they typed into search engines when trying to locate product information. Similar information on referrer is not typically available for visits to social media sites. Promotion is successful if traffic meets objectives of volume and quality as explained in Chapter 8. Quality will be determined by whether visitors are in the target market and have a propensity for the service offered (through reviewing conversion, bounce rates and cost of acquisition for different referrers). In Chapter 8 we explored cost of acquisition and allocating sales to the appropriate digital referrer media (Step 5, see page 454).

Key measure

Referral mix. For each referral source such as paid search or display ads it should be possible to calculate:

- percentage of all referrals or sales (and influence in achieving sale last click or assist)
- cost-per-acquisition (CPA) or cost-per-sale (CPS)
- contribution to sales or other outcomes.

Channel buyer behaviour
Describes which content is visited and the time and duration.

Channel buyer behaviour

Once customers have been attracted to the site we can monitor content accessed, when they visit and how long they stay, and whether this interaction with content leads to satisfactory marketing outcomes such as new leads or sales. If visitors are incentivised to register on-site it is possible to build up profiles of behaviour for different segments. Segments can also be created according to visitor source and content accessed. It is also important to recognise return visitors for whom cookies or login are used. In Chapter 6 we saw how hurdle rates can be used to assess activity levels for return visits, e.g. 30 per cent of customers return to use the online service within 90 days.

Key ratios

Stickiness
An indication of how long a visitor stays on-site.

- Bounce rates for different pages, i.e. proportion of single page visits.
- Home page views/all page views e.g. 20% = (2000/10,000).
- **Stickiness**: page views/visitor sessions e.g. 2 = 10,000/5000.
- Repeats: visitor sessions/visitors e.g. 20% = 1000/5000

Channel satisfaction
Evaluation of the customer's opinion of the service quality on the site and supporting services such as e-mail.

Channel satisfaction

Customer satisfaction with the online experience is vital in achieving the desired channel outcomes. Online methods such as online questionnaires, focus groups and interviews can be used to assess customers' opinions of the website content and customer service and how it has affected overall perception of brand. Benchmarking services such as Foresee (**www.foreseeresults.com**) based on the American Customer Satisfaction Index methodology are published for some industries. These assess scores based on the gap between expectations and actual service.

Key measure

Customer satisfaction indices. These are discussed in Chapter 7 and include ease of use, site availability and performance, and e-mail response. To compare customer satisfaction with other sites, benchmarking services can be used.

Channel outcomes Record of customer actions taken as a consequence of a visit to a site.

Conversion rate Percentage of site visitors who perform a particular action such as making a purchase.

Channel outcomes

Traditional marketing objectives such as number of sales, number of leads, **conversion rates** and targets for customer acquisition and retention should be set and then compared to other channels. Dell Computer (**www.dell.com**) records on-site sales and also orders generated as a result of site visits, but placed by phone. This is achieved by monitoring calls to a specific phone number unique to the site.

Key marketing outcomes include:

- registration to site or subscriptions to an e-mail newsletter
- requests for further information such as a brochure or a request for a call-back from a customer service representative
- responding to a promotion such as an online competition
- an offline (phone or store) lead or sale influenced by a visit to the site
- a sale on-site.

Key measure

- Channel contribution (direct and indirect).

A widely used method of assessing channel outcomes is to review the conversion rate, which gives an indication of the percentage of site visitors who take a particular outcome. For example:

- Conversion rate, visitors to purchase = 2% (10,000 visitors, of which 200 make purchases).
- Conversion rate, visitors to registration = 5% (10,000 visitors, of which 500 register).

Attrition rate Percentage of site visitors lost at each stage in making a purchase.

A related concept is the **attrition rate** which describes how many visitors are lost at each step of a conversion funnel from landing page to checkout. Figure 10.4 shows that for a set time period, only a proportion of site visitors will make their way to product information, a small proportion will add an item to a basket and a smaller proportion still will actually make the purchase. A key feature of e-commerce sites is that there is a high attrition rate between a customer adding an item to a basket and subsequently making a purchase. It is surmised that this is due to fears about credit card security, and that customers are merely experimenting.

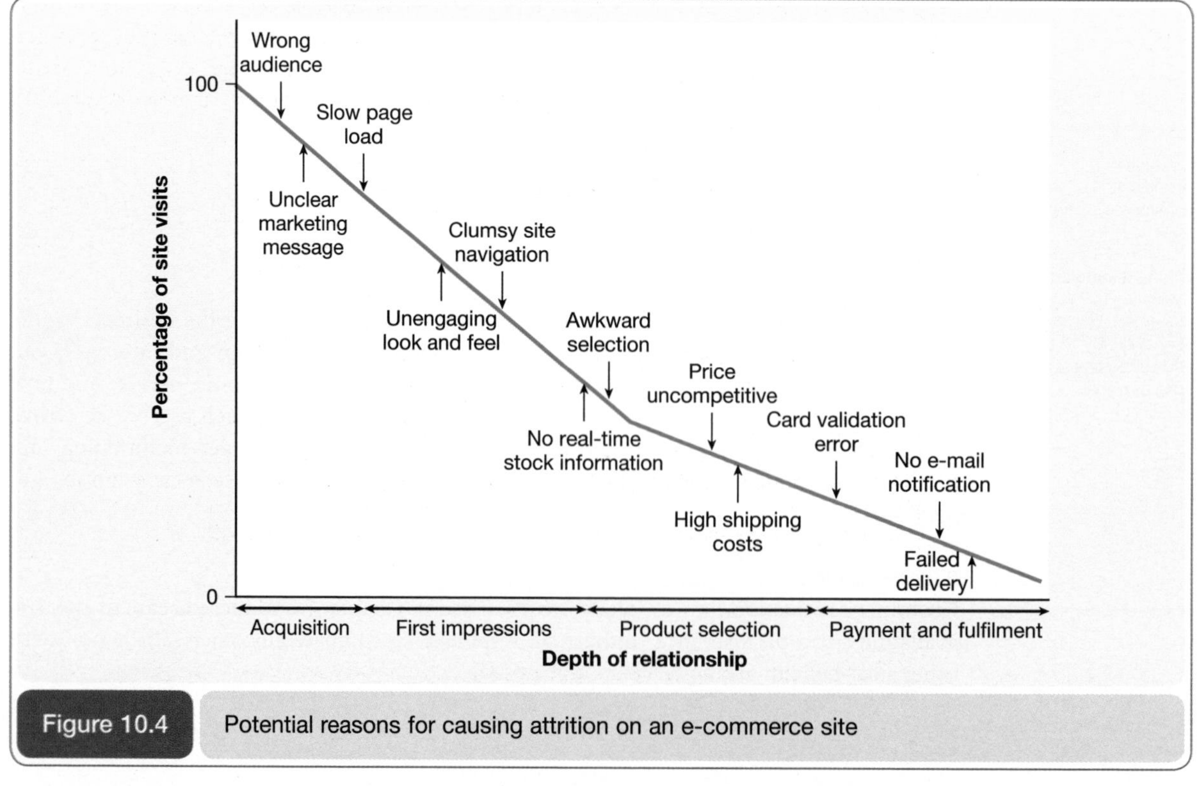

Figure 10.4 Potential reasons for causing attrition on an e-commerce site

Channel profitability The profitability of the website, taking into account revenue and cost and discounted cash flow.

Channel profitability

A contribution to business profitability is always the ultimate aim of e-commerce. To assess this, leading companies set an Internet contribution target of achieving a certain proportion of sales via the channel. Assessing contribution is more difficult for a company that cannot sell products online, but the role of the Internet in influencing leads and purchase should be assessed. Discounted cash flow techniques are used to assess the rate of return over time.

Multichannel evaluation

The frameworks we have presented in this chapter are explained in the context of an individual channel, but with the contribution of the channel highlighted as percentage sales or profitability. But as Wilson (2008) has pointed out, there is a need to evaluate how different channels support each other. Wilson says:

> Traditional metrics have been aligned to channels, measuring resource input or leads in at one end and the value of sales generated by the channel at the other end. For companies that have been operating in a single channel environment, this might have been relatively efficient – but it no longer works when the organisation diversifies to a multichannel approach.

He suggests the most important aspect of multichannel measurement is to measure 'channel cross-over effects'. This involves asking, for example: 'How can the impact of a paid search campaign be measured if it is as likely to generate traffic to a store, salesforce or call centre as to a website?' and 'How can the impact of a direct mail campaign be tracked if it generates website traffic as well as direct responses?'

An example of a balanced scorecard style dashboard developed to assess and compare channel performance for a retailer is presented in Figure 10.5.

Stage 3: Tools and techniques for collecting metrics and summarising results

Organisations need to select the most appropriate tools for collecting and reporting metrics which meet requirements such as reporting of marketing performance, accuracy, analysis and visualisation tools, integration with other marketing information systems (import, export and integration using XML standards), ease of use, configuration (e.g. creation of custom dashboards and e-mail alerts), support quality, cost of purchase, configuration and ongoing support.

Results (6) • Revenue • Multichannel contribution • Degree multichannel sells up • Costs per channel • Degree of sweating assets • Multichannel infrastructure costs	**Customers & stakeholders (5)** • Overall customer satisfaction • Customer propensity to defect • Customer propensity to purchase • Customer percepton of added value • Integration of customer experience
Core processes (3) • Productive multichannel usage • Price (relative to competitors/other channels) • Quality of integrated customer view	**People and knowledge (4)** • Staff satisfaction • Appropriate behaviours 'Living the brand' • Willingness to diversify/extend the brand • Knowledge of target customer

Figure 10.5 Multichannel performance scorecard example for a retailer
Source: Wilson (2008)

Techniques to collect metrics include the collection of site-visitor activity data such as that stored in web analytics systems and in site log files; the collection of metrics about outcomes such as online sales or e-mail enquiries and traditional marketing research techniques such as questionnaires and focus groups which collect information on the customer's experience on the website. We start by describing methods for collecting site-visitor activity data and then review more traditional techniques of market research .

Collecting site-visitor activity data

Site-visitor activity data
Information on content and services accessed by e-commerce site visitors.

Hit
Recorded for each graphic or text file requested from a web server. It is not a reliable measure for the number of people viewing a page.

Log file analyser
A separate program such as WebTrends that is used to summarise the information on customer activity in a log file.

Page impression
A more reliable measure than a hit, denoting one person viewing one page. Also known as page view.

Unique visitors
Individual visitors to a site measured through cookies or IP addresses on an individual computer.

Site-visitor activity data captured in web analytics systems records the number of visitors on the site and the paths or clickstreams they take through the site as they visit different content.

In the early days of Internet marketing, in the mid-1990s, this information was typically collected using log files. The server-based log file is added to every time a user downloads a piece of information (a **hit**) and is analysed using a **log file analyser** as illustrated by Figure 3.8. Examples of transactions within a log file are:

www.davechaffey.com – [05/Oct/2006:00:00:49 -000] 'GET /index.html HTTP/1.0' 200 33362

www.davechaffey.com – [05/Oct/2006:00:00:49 -000] 'GET /logo.gif HTTP/1.0' 200 54342

Despite their wide use in the media, hits are not a useful measure of website effectiveness since if a page consists of 10 graphics, plus text, this is recorded as 11 hits. **Page impressions or page views** and **unique visitors** are better measures of site activity. Auditing companies such as ABC electronic (**www.abce.org.uk**), which audit sites for the purpose of proving the number of visitors to a site to advertisers, use unique visitors and page impression as the main measures.

An example of visitor volume to a website using different measures based on real, representative data for one month is presented in Figure 10.6. You can see how hits are much higher than page views and unique visitors and are quite misleading in terms of the 'opportunities to see' a message. We can also learn from the ratio between some of these measures – the figure indicates:

- *Pages per visit (PPV)* – the average number of pages viewed per visitor to a site (this is indicative of engagement with a site since the longer a visitor stays on a 'sticky site', the higher this value will be). PPV is a more accurate indication of stickiness than duration on a site in minutes since this figure is skewed upwards by visitors who arrive on a site and are inactive before their session times out at 30 minutes.
- *Visits per (unique) visitor (VPV)* – this suggests the frequency of site visits. Readers will realise that this value is dependent on the period that data are collected over. These data are reported for a month during which time one would not expect many returning visitors. So it is often more relevant to present these data across a quarter or a year.

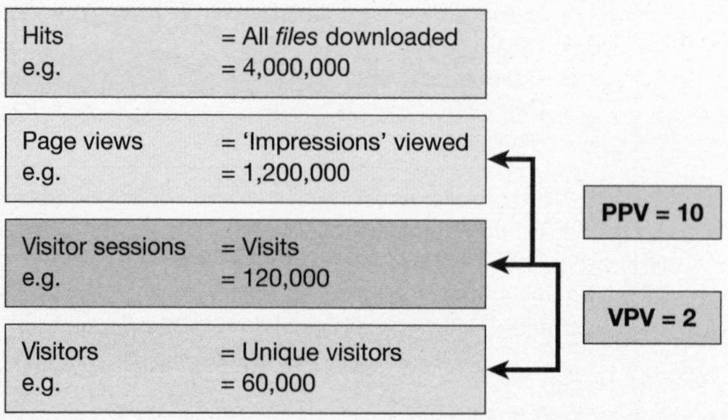

Figure 10.6 Examples of different measures of visitor volume to a website

Other information giving detailed knowledge of customer behaviour that can be reported by any web analytics package include:

- top pages
- entry and exit pages
- path or clickstream analysis showing the sequence of pages viewed
- country of visitor origin (actually dependent on the location of their ISP)
- browser and operating system used
- referring URL and domain (where the visitor came from).

Design for analysis

Measurement is often highlighted as an issue once the first version of a site has been 'up and running' for a few months, and employees start to ask questions such as 'How many customers are visiting our site, how many sales are we achieving as a result of our site and how can we improve the site to achieve a return on investment?' The consequence of this is that performance measurement is something that is often built into an online presence retrospectively. Preferable is if a technique known as **design for analysis (DFA)** is designed into the site so companies can better understand the types of audience and their decision points. For example, for Dell (**www.dell.com**), the primary navigation on the home page is by customer type. This is a simple example of DFA since it enables Dell to estimate the proportion of different audiences to their site and, at the same time, connect them with relevant content.

Design for analysis (DFA)
The required measures from a site are considered during design to better understand the audience of a site and their decision points.

Other examples of DFA include:

- Breaking up a long page or form into different parts, so you can see which parts people are interested in.
- A URL policy (see Chapter 8) used to recommend entry pages for printed material.
- Group content by audience type or buying decision and setting up content groups of related content within web analytics systems.
- Measure attrition at different points in a customer journey, e.g. exit points on a five-page buying cycle.
- A single exit page to linked sites.

Digital marketing insight 10.1 Focus on measuring social media marketing

Social media marketing has its own range of specialist measures, that can appear confusing, but are best understood in the context of a combination of website and PR measures.These show the volume, quality, sentiment and value of interactions. Analyst Altimeter (2011) has created a useful framework which is shown in Figure 10.7 that helps map out different social media measures in the context of level of business management

You can see that there are three levels of KPIs:

- *Business-level KPIs to measure contribution from social media*. These KPIs include contribution to revenue through direct sales attributed to social media. Softer measures include reputation and customer satisfaction (CSAT).
- *Reach and influence KPIs to review reach, share-of-voice and sentiment*. These show the relative comparison of a brand's reach.
- *Engagement KPIs to manage social media*. These are the easiest measures to collect, but the least valuable since they don't directly show contribution to business value. Although easy to collect, data is on interaction with social sites is often supplied separately by the owners of the different social presence and tools for managing social interaction. A new class of social analytics tools have been created to bring this data together. Figure 10.8 shows an example from the social media management tool Hootsuite where sharing of shortened URLs linking to different social media sites have driven traffic back to a main website. Direct traffic is where visitors click direct through from a social media messaging application like Hootsuite or Tweetdeck to the site.

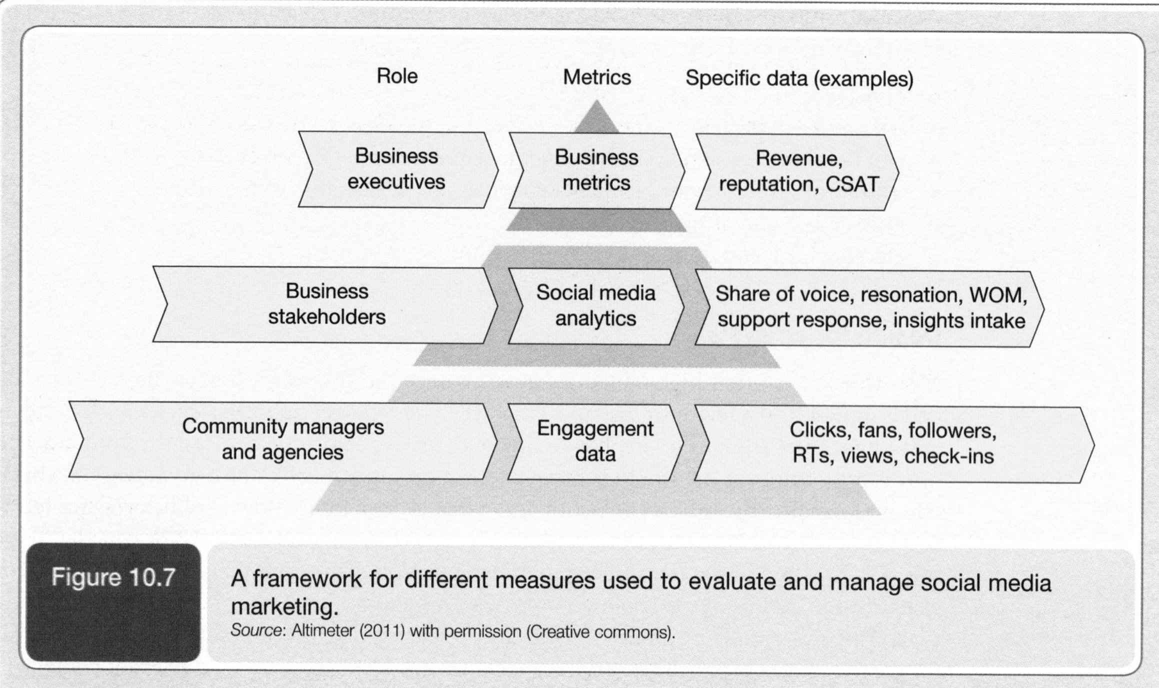

Figure 10.7 A framework for different measures used to evaluate and manage social media marketing.
Source: Altimeter (2011) with permission (Creative commons).

A common question within social media is how to assess the value of a consumer connecting with a brand, by liking on Facebook, following on Twitter or placing in a brand in a circle on Google+. Since the tracking of social media can't show what an individual does on the network, specific value is difficult to establish. Instead what we can assess is the relative purchase rates of visitors from social media sites to websites compared to other channels using measures like conversion rate and revenue per visitor.

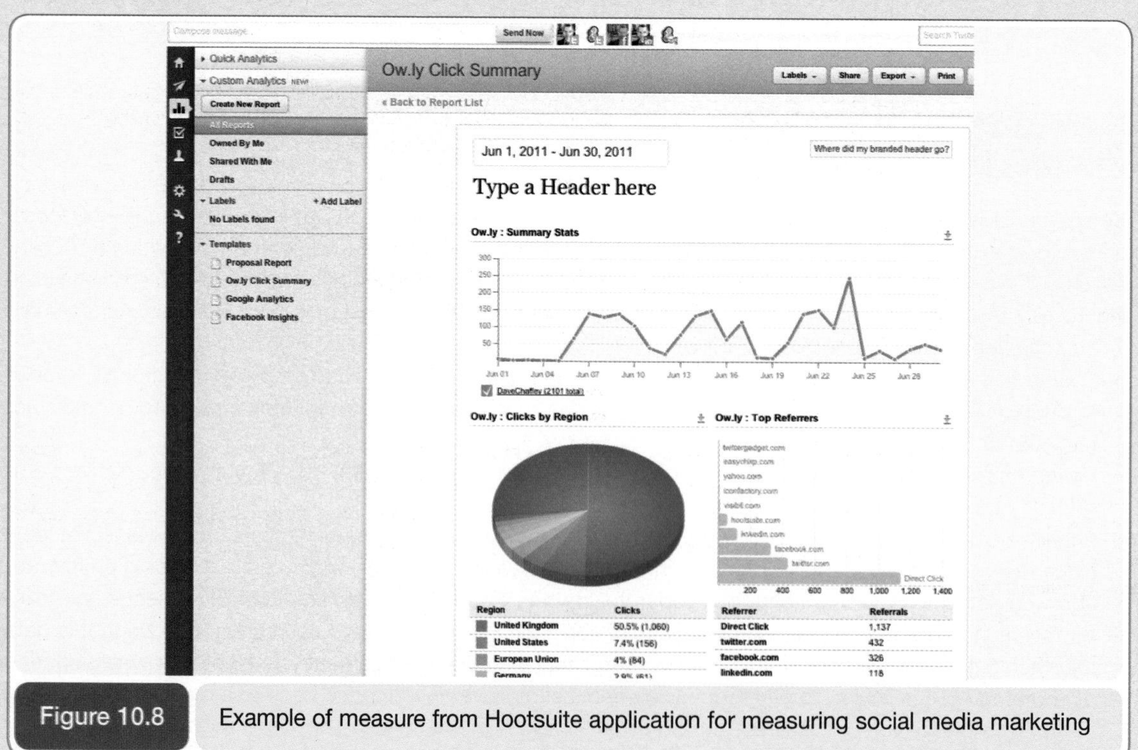

Figure 10.8 Example of measure from Hootsuite application for measuring social media marketing

AB and multivariate testing

AB testing
A/B or AB testing refers to testing two different versions of a page or a page element such as a heading, image or button for effectiveness. The alternatives are served alternately with the visitors to the page randomly split between the two pages. Changes in visitor behaviour can then be compared using different metrics such as click-through rate on page elements like buttons or images, or macro-conversion rates, such as conversion to sale or sign-up.

Often site owners and marketers reviewing the effectiveness of a site will disagree and the only method to be certain of the best-performing design or creative alternatives is through designing and running experiments to evaluate the best to use. Matt Round, then director of personalisation at Amazon, speaking at the e-metrics summit in 2004, said the Amazon philosophy, described further in Case study 10 is

> Data trumps intuition.

AB testing and multivariate testing are two measurement techniques that can be used to review design effectiveness to improve results.

AB testing

In its simplest form, A/B or **AB testing** refers to testing two different versions of a page or a page element such as a heading, image or button. Some members of the site are served alternately, with the visitors to the page randomly split between the two pages. Hence it is sometimes called 'live split testing'. The goal is to increase page or site effectiveness against key performance indicators including click-through rate, conversion rates and revenue per visit.

Table 10.1 Terminology for key website volume measures

Measure	Measure	Definition
1 How many? 'audience reach'	Unique users	A unique and valid identifier [for a site visitor]. Sites may use (i) IP + User – Agent, (ii) cookie and/or (iii) registration ID
2 How often? 'frequency metric'	Visit	A series of one or more page impressions, served to one user, which ends when there is a gap of 30 minutes or more between successive page impressions for that user
3 How busy? 'volume metric'	Page impression	A file, or combination of files, sent to a valid user as a result of that user's request being received by the server
4 What see?	Ad impressions	A file or a combination of files sent to a valid user as an individual advertisement as a result of that user's request being received by the server
5 What do?	Ad clicks	An ad impression clicked on by a valid user

Source: ABCe (**www.abce.org.uk**)

Control page
The page against which subsequent optimisation will be assessed. Typically a current landing page. When a new page performs better than the existing control page, it becomes the control page in subsequent testing. Also known as 'champion-challenger'

When completing AB testing it is important to identify a realistic baseline or **control page** (or audience sample) to compare against. This will typically be an existing landing page. Two new alternatives can be compared to previous control which is known as an ABC test. Different variables are then applied as in Table 10.2.

Table 10.2 AB test example

Test	A (Control)	B (Test page)
Test 1	Original page	New headline, existing button, existing body copy
Test 2	Original page	Existing headline, new button, existing body copy
Test 3	Original page	Existing headline, existing button, new body copy

An example of the power of AB testing is an experiment Skype performed on their main topbar navigation, where they found that changing the main menu options 'Call Phones' to 'Skype Credit' and 'Shop' to 'Accessories' gave an increase of 18.75 per cent revenue per visit (Skype were speaking at the 2007 e-metrics summit). That's significant when you have hundreds of millions of visitors! It also shows the importance of being direct with navigation and simply describing the offer available rather than the activity.

Multivariate testing

Multivariate testing is a more sophisticated form of AB testing which enables simultaneous testing of pages for different combinations of page elements that are being tested. This enables selection of the most effective combination of design elements to achieve the desired goal.

An example of a multivariate test is shown in Mini Case Study 10.1.

Mini Case Study 10.1 Multivariate testing at National Express Group increases conversion rates

The National Express Group is the leading provider of travel solutions in the UK. Around one billion journeys a year are made worldwide on National Express Group's bus, train, light rail and express coach and airport operations. A significant proportion of ticket bookings are made online through the company's website at **www.nationalexpress.com.**

The company uses multivariate testing provider Maxymiser to run an experiment to improve conversion rate of a fare-selection page which was the penultimate step in booking (Figure 10.9). The analysis team identified a number of subtle alterations to content (labelled A to E) and calls to action on the page with the aim of stimulating visitor engagement and driving a higher percentage of visitors through to successful conversion without changing the structure of the page or National Express brand identity. In order to aid more effective up-sell to insurance add-ons, changes to this call to action were also proposed.

It was decided that a multivariate test would be the most effective approach to determine the best performing combination of content. The variants jointly developed by Maxymiser and the client were tested with all live site visitors and the conversion rate of each combination monitored. 3500 possible page combinations were tried and during the live test the underperforming combinations were taken out to maximise conversion rates at every stage.

At the end of the testing period, after reaching statistical validity, results gave the best combination of elements showing a 14.11 per cent increase in conversion rates for the page, i.e. 14.11 per cent more visitors were sent through to the fourth and final step in the registration process, immediately hitting bottom line revenue for National Express (Figure 10.10).

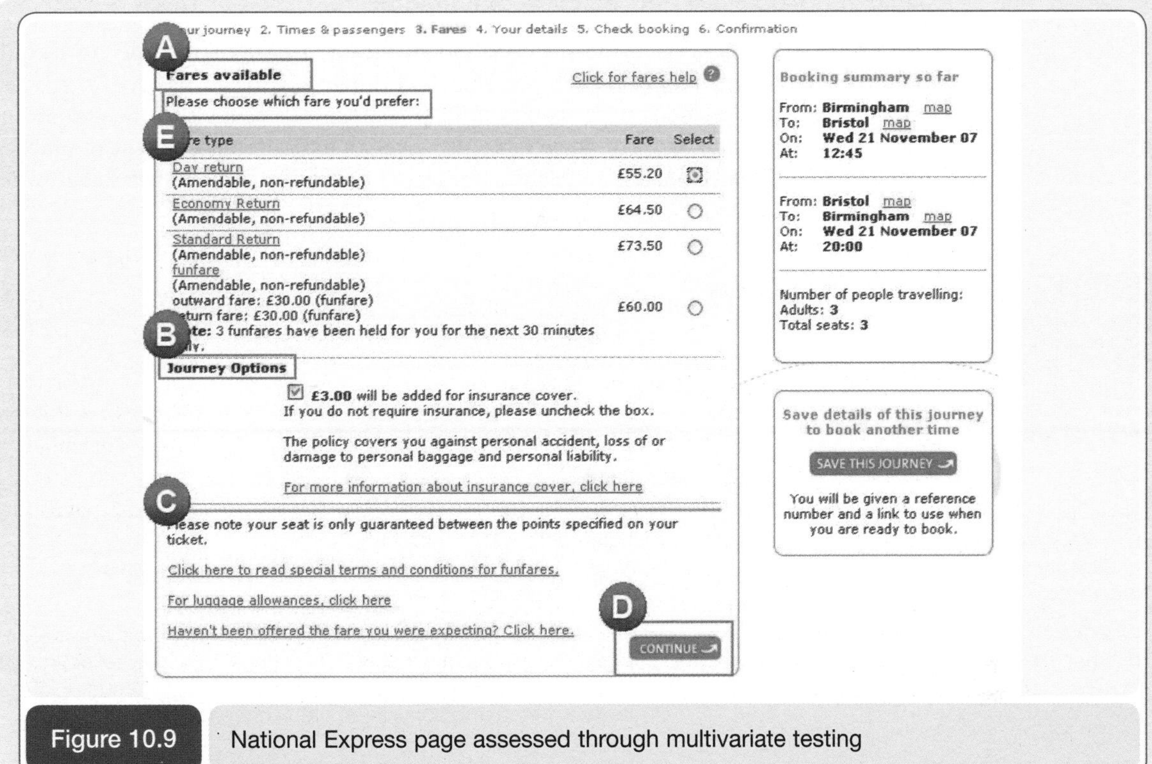

Figure 10.9 National Express page assessed through multivariate testing

Content combination	Maxybox A	Maxybox B	Maxybox C	Maxybox D	Maxybox E	Lift on control
1	Variant 3	Variant 2	Variant 4	Variant 3	Variant 1	14.11%
2	Variant 3	Variant 3	Variant 4	Default	Default	14.09%
3	Variant 6	Variant 3	Variant 4	Default	Default	11.15%
4	Variant 3	Variant 3	Variant 2	Default	Variant 3	10.57%
Default content	Variant 3	Variant 2	Default	Default	Default	0.00%

Conversion rate uplift by page combination:

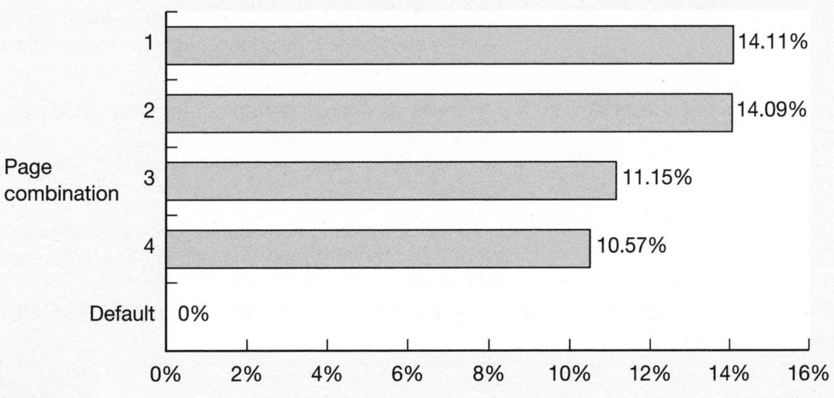

Figure 10.10 Results of multivariate testing for National Express

Clickstream analysis and visitor segmentation

Clickstream analysis refers to detailed analysis of visitor behaviour in order to identify improvements to the site. Each web analytics tool differs slightly in its reports and terminology, but all provide similar reports to help companies assess visitor behaviour and diagnose problems and opportunities. Table 10.3 gives an indication of the type of practical questions asked by web analyst and consultant Dave Chaffey (**www.davechaffey.com**) when reviewing clients' sites.

Table 10.3 A summary of how an analyst will interpret web analytics data. GA is terminology for Google Analytics (**www.google.com/analytics**), one of the most widely used tools

Analyst question	Typical web analytics report terminology	Diagnosis analyst used to improve performance
How successful is the site at achieving engagement and outcomes?	Conversion goals (GA) Bounce rates (GA) Pages/visit (GA)	• Is engagement and conversion consistent with other sites in sector? • What are maximum engagement and conversion rates from different referrers?
Where are visitors entering the site?	Top entry pages Top landing pages (GA)	• How important is home page compared to other page categories and landing pages? Does page popularity reflect product popularity? • Review messaging/conversion paths are effective on these pages • Assess source of traffic, in particular keywords from search engines and apply elsewhere
What are the sources of visitors (referrers)?	Referrers Traffic sources Filters set up to segment visitors	• Are the full range of digital media channels relevant for a company represented? • Is the level of search engine traffic consistent with the brand reputation? • What are the main link partners driving free traffic (potential for more?)
What is the most popular content?	Top content (GA)	• Is page popularity as expected? Are there problems with findability caused by navigation labelling? • Which content is most likely to influence visitors to outcome? • Which content is most popular with returning visitors segment?
Which are the most popular findability methods?	Site search (GA)	• How popular are different forms of navigation, e.g. top menu, sidebar menus, etc? • What are the most popular searches? Where do searches tend to start? Are they successfully finding content or converting to sale?
Where do visitors leave the site?	Top exit pages (GA)	• Are these as expected (home page, About Us page, transaction completion)? • Are there error pages (e.g. 404 not found) which cause visitors to leave?
Which clickstreams are taken?	Path analysis Top paths (GA)	• How can attrition in conversion funnels be improved? • What does forward path analysis show are the most effective calls-to-action? • What does reverse path analysis indicate about the pages which influence sales?

Path analysis

Aggregate clickstreams are usually known within web analytics software as forward or reverse paths. This is a fairly advanced form of analysis, but the principle is straightforward – you seek to learn from the most popular paths.

Viewed at an aggregate level across the site through 'top paths' type reports, this form of clickstream analysis often doesn't appear that useful. It highlights typically paths which are expected and can't really be influenced. The top paths are often:

- Home page : Exit
- Home page : Contact Us : Exit
- News page : Exit

Clickstream analysis becomes more actionable when the analyst reviews clickstreams in the context of a single page – this is **forward path analysis** or **reverse path analysis**.

Forward path analysis
Reviews the combinations of clicks that occur from a page. This form of analysis is most beneficial from important pages such as the home page, product and directory pages. Use this technique to identify: messaging/navigation combinations which work best to yield the most clicks from a page. These approaches can then be deployed elsewhere on the site or page. Work poorly and yield a relatively small percentage of clicks from a page.

Reverse path analysis
Reverse path analysis indicates the most popular combination of pages and/or calls-to-action which lead to a page. This is particularly useful for transactional pages such as the first checkout page on a consumer site; a lead generation or contact us page on a business-to-business site; an e-mail subscription page or a call-me back option.

On-site search effectiveness

On-site search is another crucial part of clickstream analysis on many sites since it is a key way of finding content, so a detailed search analysis will pay dividends. Key search metrics to consider are:

- number of searches
- average number of searches per visitor or searcher
- % of searches returning zero results
- % of site exits from search results
- % of returned searches clicked
- % of returned searches resulting in conversion to sale or other outcome
- most popular search terms – individual keyword and keyphrases.

Visitor segmentation

Segmentation is a fundamental marketing approach, but is often difficult within web analytics to relate customer segments to web behaviour because the web analytics data isn't integrated with customer or purchase data.

However, all analytics systems have a capability for a different, but valuable form of segmentation where it is possible to create specific filters or profiles to help understand one type of site visitor behaviour. Examples of segments include:

- First time visitors or returning visitors.
- Visitors from different referrer types including:
  - Google natural
  - Google paid
  - Strategic search keyphrases, brand keyphrases, etc.
  - Display advertising.
- Converters against non-converters.
- Geographic segmentation by country or region (based on IP addresses).
- Type of content accessed, e.g. are some segments more likely to convert? For example, speaking at Ad Tech London '06, MyTravel reported that they segment visitors into:
  - site flirt (two pages or fewer)
  - site browse (two pages or more)
  - saw search results
  - saw quote
  - saw payment details
  - saw booking confirmation details.

Selecting a web analytics tool

There has been consolidation of web analytics tools, such that there is now a basic choice of a free service such as Google Analytics or Yahoo! Analytics or a paid service from the main providers such as Omniture (owned by Adobe Systems), Coremetrics (owned by IBM) and WebTrends which may cost hundreds of thousands of dollars a year for a popular site. All will report similar measures for digital marketing activity to those explored earlier in the chapter, so often the selection of the best system will depend on factors such as:

- *Integration with other data sources* (for example, social media marketing, customer data and financial reporting). Figure 10.11 gives an indication of the types of data that need to be integrated; these include operational data, tactical and strategic data.
- *Accuracy*. Potential sources of inaccuracy are reviewed in Table 10.4 comparing traditional *log file analysis* to the more common *browser-based* or *tag-based* measurement system that records access to web pages every time a page is loaded into a user's web browser through running a short script, program or tag inserted into the web page. The key benefit of the browser-based approach is that it is potentially more accurate than server-based approaches. Figure 10.12 indicates how the browser-based approach works. The free version of Google Analytics uses sampling on large sites which can decrease accuracy.
- *Media attribution*. We saw in Chapter 8 that the 'last-click wins' model of attributing a referral source to sale is inaccurate and weighted models based on the whole customer journey are more accurate. The capability of analytics system to display this is important for companies investing a lot in online media.
- *Visualisation*. How data are displayed through reports and alerts. Vendors continually introduce new features in this area.
- *Customisation facilities*. For creating and distributing new reports and alerts
- Support services. For configuration of data feeds and reports and consulting to assist in auctioning the results. In 2011 the free service Google Analytics introduced a premium version for large corporate customers which included account management.
- *Privacy considerations*. Web analytics systems store personal data. As we saw in Chapter 4, it is important that data collection and disclosure about the method of collection by the system follow the latest laws about use of cookies.

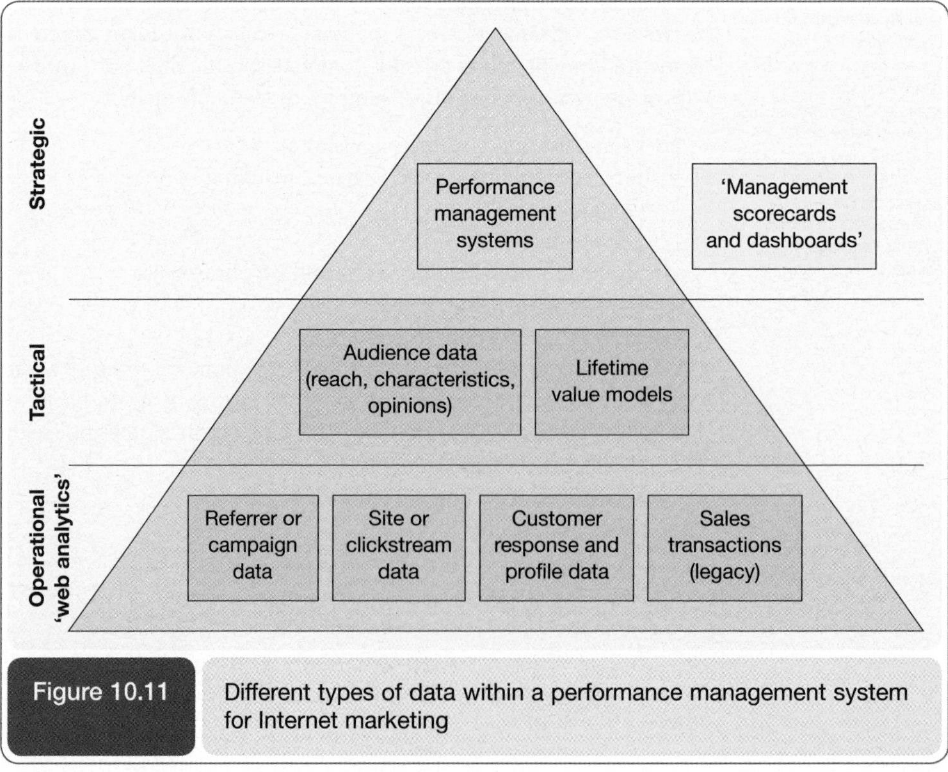

Figure 10.11 Different types of data within a performance management system for Internet marketing

Table 10.4 Inaccuracies caused by server-based log file analysis

Sources of undercounting	Sources of overcounting
Caching in user's web browsers (when a user accesses a previously accessed file, it is loaded from the user's cache on their PC)	Frames (a user viewing a framed page with three frames will be recorded as three page impressions on a server-based system)
Caching on proxy servers (proxy servers are used within organisations or ISPs to reduce Internet traffic by storing copies of frequently used pages)	Spiders and robots (traversing of a site by spiders from different search engines is recorded as page impressions. These spiders can be excluded, but this is time-consuming)
Firewalls (these do not usually exclude page impressions, but they do assign a single IP address for the user of the page, rather than referring to an individual's PC)	Executable files (these can also be recorded as hits or page impressions unless excluded)
Dynamically generated pages, generated 'on the fly', are difficult to assess with server-based log files	

Strategic data

Performance management systems for senior managers will give the big picture presented as scorecards or dashboards showing trends in contribution of digital channels to the organisation in terms of sales, revenue and profitability for different products.

An example of the output reporting from a web analytics service is shown in Figure 10.11.

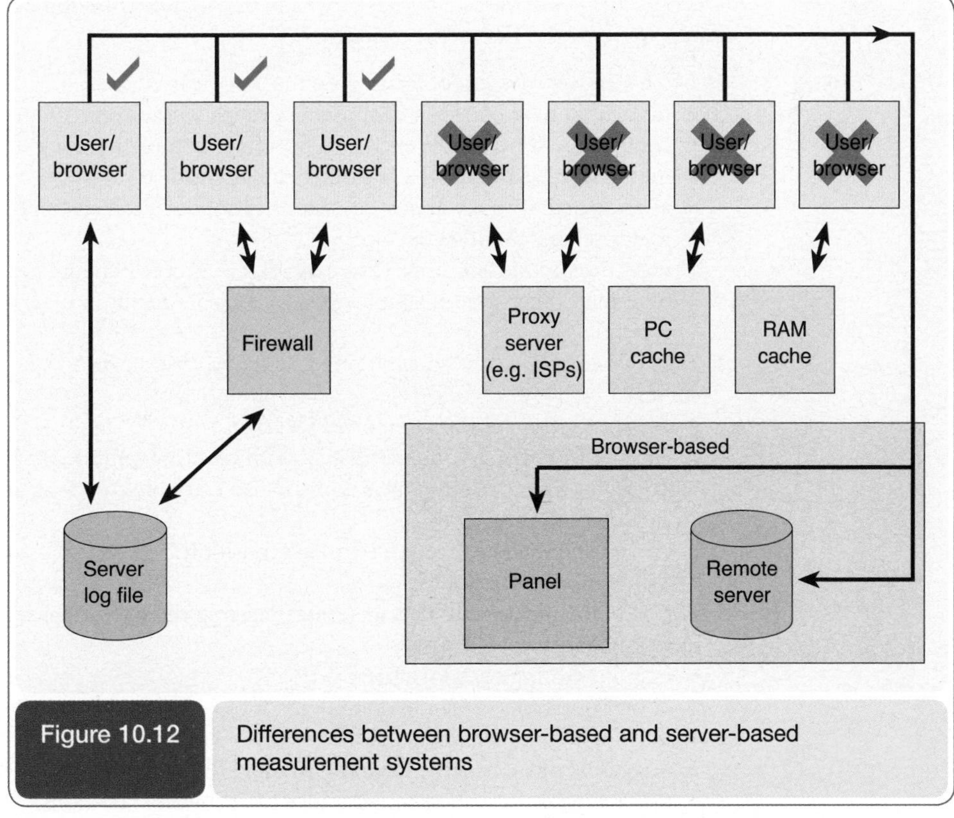

Figure 10.12 Differences between browser-based and server-based measurement systems

Marketing research using the Internet

Internet-based market research
The use of online questionnaires and focus groups to assess customer perceptions of a website or broader marketing issues.

Internet-based marketing research can help determine the influence of a website and related communications on customer perception of the company and its products and services. But it also has wider applications of gaining feedback from customers about a brand and how it could develop in future. SmartInsights (2010) identifies these five different classes of online feedback tools:

1 *Website feedback tools.* Provide a permanent facility for customers to feedback by prompts on every page. They are run continuously to enable continuous feedback including ratings on page content, and also products and services.
2 *Site user intent-satisfaction surveys.* These tools measure the gap between what the user had hoped to do on the site and what they actually achieved. We gave the example of 4Q in Chapter 7 that covers four questions to assess site effectiveness.
3 *Crowdsourcing product opinion software.* These are broader than web feedback enabling customers to comment about potential new services. This is the approach used by Dell in the IdeaStorm (**www.ideastorm.com**).
4 *Simple page or concept feedback tools.* Again a form of crowdsourcing, these tools give feedback from an online panel about page layout, messaging or services.
5 *General Online Survey Tools.* Tools like Zoomerang (**www.zoomerang.com**) and SurveyMonkey (**www.surveymonkey.com**) enable companies to survey their audience at a low cost.

The full options for conducting survey research include interviews, questionnaires and focus groups are summarised in Table 10.5. Each of these techniques can be conducted offline or online.

We will now briefly review the strengths and weaknesses of the different research techniques and some approaches to best practice.

Questionnaires

Malhotra (1999) suggested that Internet surveys using questionnaires will increase in popularity since the cost is generally lower, they can be less intrusive and they have the ability to target specific populations. This has proved to be the case. Questionnaires often take the form of pop-up surveys. The key issues are:

A *Encouraging participation.* Techniques that can be used are:
- interruption on entry – a common approach where every 100th customer is prompted
- continuous, for example click on a button to complete survey
- on registration on-site the customer can be profiled
- after an activity such as sale or customer support, the customer can be prompted for their opinion about the service
- incentives and promotions (this can also be executed on independent sites)
- by e-mail (an e-mail prompt to visit a website to fill in a survey or a simple e-mail survey).

B *Stages in execution.* It is suggested that there are five stages to a successful questionnaire survey:
1 attract (button, pop-up, e-mail as above)
2 incentivise (prize or offer consistent with required sample and audience)
3 reassure (why the company is doing it – to learn, not too long and that confidentiality is protected)
4 design and execute (brevity, relevance, position)
5 follow-up (feedback).

C *Design.* Grossnickle and Raskin (2001) suggest the following approach to structuring questionnaires:
- easy, interesting questions first
- cluster questions on same topic
- flow topic from general to specific
- flow topic from easier behavioural to more difficult attitudinal questions
- easy questions last, e.g. demographics or offputting questions.

Table 10.5 A comparison of different online metrics collection and research methods

Technique	Strengths	Weaknesses
Server-based log file analysis of site activity	• Directly records customer behaviour on site plus where they were referred from • Low cost	• Not based around marketing outcomes such as leads or sales • Size – even summaries may be over 50 pages long • Does not directly record channel satisfaction • Undercounting/overcounting • Misleading unless interpreted carefully
Browser-based site activity data	• Greater accuracy than server-based analysis • Counts all users, cf. panel approach	• Relatively expensive method • Similar weaknesses to server-based technique apart from accuracy • Limited demographic information
AB and multivariate testing	• Structured experiments to review influence of on page variables (e.g. messaging and buttons) to improve conversion from a website	• Often requires cost of a separate tool or module from standard web analytics package • Content management systems or page templates may not support AB/multivariate testing
Panel activity and demographic data	• Provides competitor comparisons • Gives demographic profiling representative • Avoids undercounting and overcounting	• Depends on extrapolation from data-limited sample that may not be representative
Outcome data, e.g. enquiries, customer e-mails	• Records marketing outcomes	• Difficulty of integrating data with other methods of data collection when service collected manually or in other information systems
Online questionnaires Customers are prompted randomly – every nth customer or after customer activity or by e-mail	• Can record customer satisfaction and profiles • Relatively cheap to create and analyse	• Difficulty of recruiting respondents who complete accurately • Sample bias – tend to be advocates or disgruntled customers who complete
Online focus groups Synchronous recording	• Relatively cheap to create	• Difficult to moderate and co-ordinate • No visual cues, as from offline focus groups
Mystery shoppers Example is customers are recruited to evaluate the site, e.g. **www.emysteryshopper.com**	• Structured tests give detailed feedback • Also tests integration with other channels such as e-mail and phone	• Relatively expensive • Sample must be representative

Typical questions that can be asked for determining the effectiveness of Internet marketing are:

- *Who is visiting the site?* For example, role in buying decision? Online experience? Access location and speed? Demographics segment?
- *Why are they visiting?* How often do they visit? Which information or service? Did they find it? Actions taken? (Can be determined through web analytics.)
- *What do they think?* Overall opinion? Key areas of satisfaction? Specific likes or dislikes? What was missing that was expected?

Focus groups

Malhotra (1999) noted that the advantage of online focus groups is that they can be used to reach segments that are difficult to access, such as doctors, lawyers and professional people. This author also suggests that costs are lower, they can be arranged more rapidly and can bridge the distance gap when recruiting respondents. Traditional focus groups can be conducted, where customers are brought together in a room and assess a website; this will typically occur pre-launch as part of the prototyping activity. Testing can take the form of random use of the site or, more usefully, the users will be given different scenarios to follow. Focus groups tend to be relatively expensive and time consuming, since rather than simply viewing an advertisement, the customers need to actually interact with the website. Conducting real-world focus groups has the benefit that the reactions of site users can be monitored; the scratch or slap of the head cannot be monitored in the virtual world!

Mystery shoppers

Real-world measurement is also important since the Internet channel does not exist in isolation. It must work in unison with real-world customer service and fulfilment. Chris Russell of eDigitalResearch (**www.edigitalresearch.com**), a company that has completed online customer service surveys for major UK retailers and travel companies, says 'we also needed to make sure that the bricks-and-mortar customer service support was actually supporting what the clicks-and-mortar side was promising. There is no doubt that an e-commerce site has to be a complete customer service fulfilment picture, it can't just be one bit working online that is not supported offline'. An eMysteryShopper survey involves shoppers not only commenting on site usability, but also on the service quality of e-mail and phone responses together with product fulfilment. Mystery shoppers test these areas:

- site usability
- e-commerce fulfilment
- e-mail and phone response (time, accuracy)
- impact on brand.

Site management process

As part of the process of continuous improvement in online marketing, it is important to have a clearly defined process for making changes to the online presence of a company. If pages remain static, as is the case with some brochureware sites we still see, then the opportunity to engage customers and prospects with a brand is missed. With search engines and social media sites featuring realtime data posted in blogs, companies who have a static site are also missing an opportunity to get better visibility. A static site also has a missed opportunity to make the site more effective at generating value for a business by increasing conversion rates using the AB and multivariate testing approaches we talked about in the last section.

The key to keeping a website dynamic is to have a clear content and e-communications strategy based on a content or social hub as we have seen in previous chapters. The site and content update process should be understood by all staff contributing content to the site, with their responsibilities clearly identified in their job descriptions. To understand the process, consider the main stages involved in publishing a page. A simple model of the work involved in maintenance is shown in Figure 10.13. It is assumed that the needs of the users and design features of the site have already been defined when the site was originally created, as described in Chapter 7. The model only applies to minor updates to copy, or perhaps updating product or company information. The different tasks involved in the maintenance process are as follows:

1. *Write.* This stage involves writing the marketing copy and, if necessary, designing the layout of copy and associated images.
2. *Review.* An independent review of the copy is necessary to check for errors before a document is published. Depending on the size of organisation, review may be necessary by one

person or several people covering different aspects of content quality such as corporate image, copy-editing text to identify grammatical errors, marketing copy, branding and legality.

3 *Correct.* This stage is straightforward and involves updates necessary as a result of stage 2.
4 *Publish (to test environment).* The publication stage involves putting the corrected copy on a web page that can be checked further. This will be in a test environment that can only be viewed from inside a company.
5 *Test.* Before the completed web page is made available over the World Wide Web a final test will be required for technical issues such as whether the page loads successfully on different browsers.
6 *Publish (to live environment).* Once the material has been reviewed and tested and is signed off as satisfactory, it will be published to the main website and will be accessible by customers.

How often should content be updated?

Website content needs to be up-to-date, in line with customer expectations. The web is perceived as a dynamic medium and customers are likely to expect new information to be posted to a site straightaway. If material is inaccurate or 'stale' then the customer may not return to the site.

After a time, the information on a web page naturally becomes outdated and will need to be updated or replaced. It is important to have both a content calendar for publishing future content and a mechanism defining what triggers this update process and leads to the cycle of Figure 10.13. The need for material to be updated has several facets. Trigger procedures should be developed such that when price changes or product specifications are updated in promotional leaflets or catalogues, these changes are also reflected on the website. Without procedures of this type, it is easy for there to be errors on the website. This may sound obvious, but the reality is that the people contributing the updates to the site will have many other tasks to complete, and the website can still be a low priority.

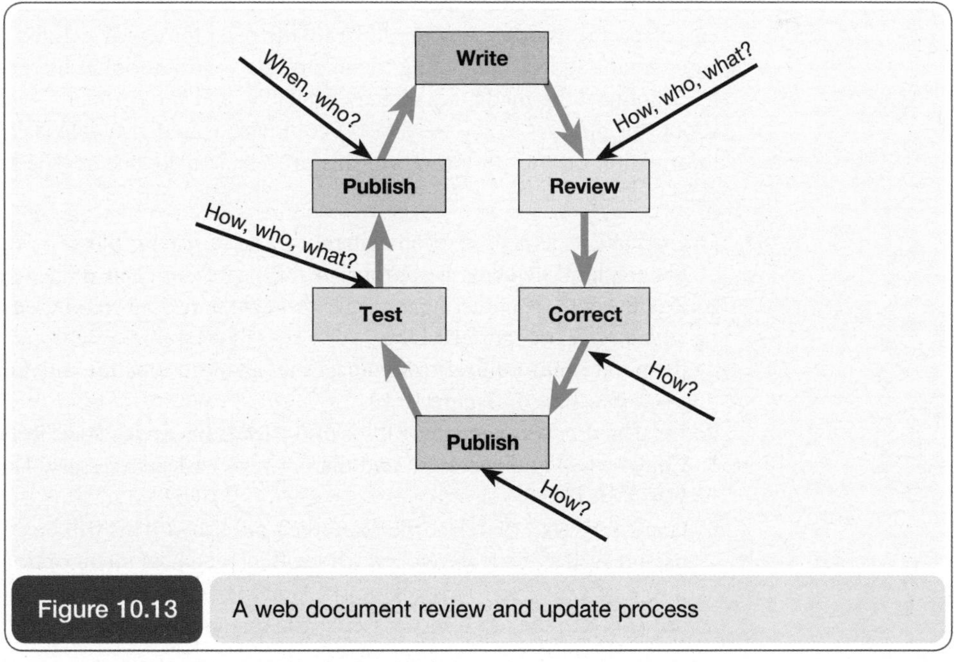

Figure 10.13 A web document review and update process

Responsibilities for site management

Maintenance is easy in a small company with a single person updating the website. Although they may be working on many tasks, one person is able to ensure that the style of the whole site remains consistent. For a large organisation with many different departments and offices in different countries, site maintenance becomes very difficult, and production of a quality site is only possible when there is strong control to establish a team who all follow the same standards. Sterne (2001) suggests that the essence of successful maintenance is to have clearly identified responsibilities for different aspects of updating the website. The questions to ask are:

- Who owns the process?
- Who owns the content?
- Who owns the format?
- Who owns the technology?

We will now consider these in more detail, reviewing the standards required to produce a good-quality website and the different types of responsibilities involved. Review of new site functionality is a strategic issue and was covered in Chapter 4.

Who owns the process?

One of the first areas to be defined should be the overall process for agreeing new site content and updating the site. But who agrees this process? For the large company it will be necessary to bring together all the interested parties, such as those within the marketing department and the site developers – who may be an external agency or the IT department. Within these groupings there may be many people with an interest such as the marketing manager, the person with responsibility for Internet or new-media marketing, a communications manager who places above-the-line advertising, and product managers who manage the promotion of individual products and services. All of these people should have an input in deciding on the process for updating the website. What, then, is this process? The process will specify responsibilities for different aspects of site management and detail the sequence in which tasks occur for updating the site. A typical update process is outlined in Figure 10.13. If we take a specific example we can illustrate the need for a well-defined process. Imagine that a large organisation is launching a new product – promotional literature is to be distributed to customers, the media are already available, and the company wants to add information about this product to the website. A recently recruited graduate is charged with putting the information on the site. How will this process actually occur? The following process stages need to occur:

1. Graduate reviews promotional literature and rewrites copy on a word processor and modifies graphical elements as appropriate for the website. This is the *write* stage in Figure 10.13.
2. Product and/or marketing manager reviews the revised web-based copy. This is part of the *review* stage in Figure 10.13.
3. Corporate communications manager reviews the copy for suitability. This is also part of the *review* stage in Figure 10.13.
4. Legal adviser reviews copy. This is also part of the *review* stage in Figure 10.13.
5. Copy revised and corrected and then re-reviewed as necessary. This is the *correct* stage in Figure 10.13.
6. Copy converted to web format and then published. This will be performed by a technical person such as a site developer, who will insert a new menu option to help users navigate to the new product. This person will add the HTML formatting and then upload the file using FTP to the test website. This is the first *publish* stage in Figure 10.13.

7 The new copy on the site will be reviewed by the graduate for accuracy, and needs to be tested on different web browsers and screen resolutions if it uses a graphical design different from the standard site template. This type of technical testing will need to be carried out by the webmaster. The new version could also be reviewed on the site by the communications manager or legal adviser at this point. This is part of the *test* stage in Figure 10.13.
8 Once all interested parties agree the new copy is suitable, the pages on the test website can be transferred to the live website and are then available for customers to view. This is the second *publish* stage in Figure 10.13.

Note that in this scenario review of the copy at stages 2 to 4 happens before the copy is actually put onto the test site at stage 6. This is efficient in that it saves the technical person or webmaster having to update the page until the copy is agreed. An alternative would be for the graduate to write the copy at stage 1 and then the webmaster publishes the material before it is reviewed by the various parties. Each approach is equally valid.

Content management systems with workflow capabilities are now commonly used to help achieve review of page updates. Revised copy for a page can be automatically e-mailed to all reviewers and then the comments received by e-mail can be collated.

To conclude this section, refer to Activity 10.1 which shows a typical website update process and considers possible improvements.

Activity 10.1 Optimising a content review process

Purpose

To assess how quality control and efficiency can be balanced for revisions to web content.

Activity

The extract below and Figure 10.14 illustrate a problem of updating encountered by this company. How can they solve this problem?

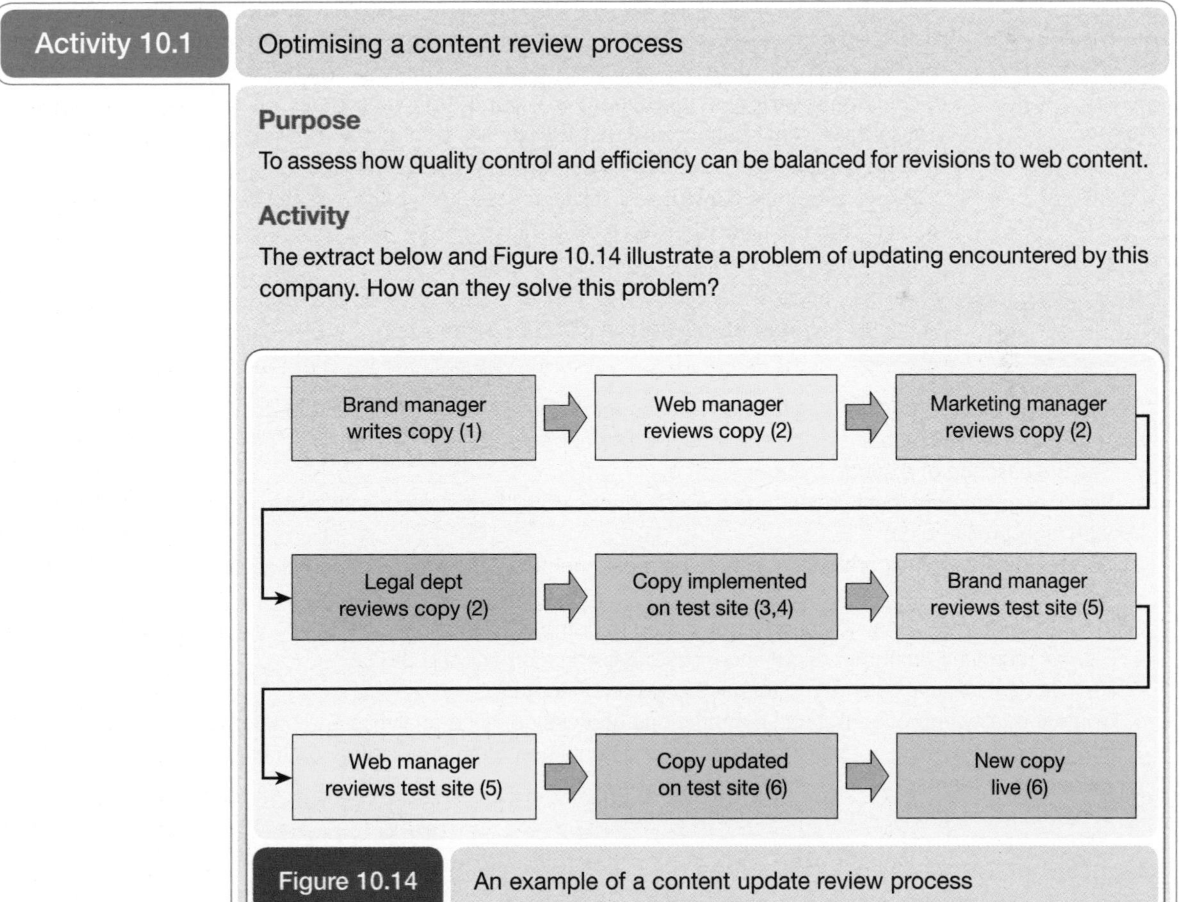

Figure 10.14 An example of a content update review process

Problem description

From the moment the brand manager identifies a need to update copy for their product, the update might happen as follows: brand manager writes the copy (half a day); one day later the web manager reviews the copy. Three days later the marketing manager checks the copy, seven days later the legal department checks the copy, two days later the revised copy is implemented on the test site and two days later the brand manager reviews the test site. The next day the web manager reviews the website, followed by updating and final review, before the copy is added to the live site two days later and over a fortnight from when a relatively minor change to the site was identified!

Who owns the content?

For a medium-to-large site where the content is updated regularly, as it should be, it will soon become impossible for one person to update all the content. It is logical and practical to distribute the responsibility for owning and developing different sections of the site to the people in an organisation who have the best skills and knowledge to develop that content. For example, in a large financial services company, the part of the business responsible for a certain product area should update the copy referring to their products. One person will update the copy for each of savings accounts, mortgages, travel insurance, health insurance and investments. For a PC supplier, different **content developers** will be required for the product information, financing, delivery information and customer service facilities. Once the ownership of content is distributed throughout an organisation, it becomes crucial to develop guidelines and standards that help ensure that the site has a coherent 'feel' and appearance. The nature of these guidelines is described in the sections that follow.

Content developer
A person responsible for updating web pages within part of an organisation

As realisation of content as a strategic asset grows, more senior roles are being created to manage content quality as shown by Mini Case Study 10.2.

Mini Case Study 10.2 Logitech appoint a content strategist

Computer peripheral provider Logitech advertised for a content strategist. This job description for a content strategist in a large company helps show us the key aspects of content strategy. These requirements summarise the essence of a sound content strategy:

1 Senior management must understand the importance of content strategy to invest in good quality resources with high-profile roles.
2 Content must be of exceptional quality to be most effective – the job descriptions says: '*useful*, *compelling* and *meaningful*'.
3 Involves a strategy for syndication – not limited to companies own site.
4 Blends improving customer experience, customer engagement and SEO.
5 Requires an editorial calendar to manage creation of content.
6 Content quality improved through a continuous process applying analytics and customer satisfaction.
7 Integrates copywriting, web platform design and implementation, marketing communications, PR and SEO resources or teams.
8 Supports goals and essence of company brand.

Content strategist responsibilities

- Drive the development and organisation of content that is useful, compelling and meaningful – directly on logitech.com and indirectly through distributed content.
- Create user flows, information hierarchies, wireframes and content strategy for Logitech.com in support of campaigns, product launches and ongoing improvement.

- Determine content requirements for logitech.com, inventory existing content, identify gaps, evaluate possible sources for additional material, and manage the process of getting that content into production.
- Creatively look for opportunities to improve content, consumer experience and SEO performance.
- Manage the Logitech.com editorial calendar to proactively keep content useful and up to date.
- Use analytics, consumer and usability testing and business requirements to help improve the experience and the content of Logitech.com in the long and short term.
- Work with the web, writing, PR and marcomm teams to determine the most effective ways to support campaigns and product launches on the web.
- Lead projects that make our web and component communication more intuitive and useful to consumers and internal partners.
- Work with brand architecture and terminology to guide the effective organisation of products and activities on Logitech.com.
- Drive the architecture of and improvements to the internal product content management system (worldwide product database to fit the needs of the organisation).
- Occasionally write or edit content – particularly meta-data, titles, alt text, and edit general content to optimise for natural search.

Content strategist requirements

- Four-year college degree in a relevant field required, Masters degree preferred.
- Five to seven years of experience in an information architecture role, with two to three years working on complex websites.
- Two to three years of experience being directly responsible for content strategy on a dynamic, complex or ever-evolving website.
- Experience with web content management systems, component content management systems DITA or otherwise and authoring systems XML or other.
- Strong strategic, analytical skills with a solid ability to articulate information requirements clearly.
- A creative and collaborative approach that elevates the creative and communication opportunities – rather than straight analysis.
- Expertise in content strategy – including strong experience in SEO and keyword analysis as well as planning flexible approaches to keep content accurate and fresh.
- Accomplishments in the effective use of syndication (in and out) and user generated content as well as working collaboratively with writers and designers.
- The ability to be measured by hard metrics – views, time on site, consumer feedback – as well as soft metrics – support of the brand vision and architecture, consumer perception.
- Demonstrated ability to visualise and communicate complex information using Microsoft Visio or similar software.
- Deep experience with all levels of UX strategy and testing – but the ability to act quickly on consumer insights and best practices.
- Solid work ethic, ability to perform under pressure, meet deadlines, prioritise and deliver multiple tasks on time.
- Willing to learn and contribute to a strong team environment.
- Enthusiastic about the products and the possibilities of Logitech.

Other Information

Logitech knows the value of strategic communication and content and now we're expanding our team to make the most of it. The global marketing team needs an expert who is ready to add his or her brain, talent and creativity to the cause of making our content work smarter, harder and around the globe. This is an opportunity for an IA/content strategy professional to put both strategy and executional excellence into practice every day and make an immediate and visible impact on the efficacy of a global organisation.

This role reports directly into the Global Director of Writing and Brand Architecture, with a direct and ongoing relationship with the Director of Global Web Marketing.

Sources: Job description: Information Architect/Content Strategist for Logitech, posted 29 September 2010, **http://jobs.mashable.com/a/jbb/job-details/379895**

Who owns the format?

Site design template
A standard page layout format which is applied to each page of a website.

The format refers to different aspects of the design and layout of the site, commonly referred to as its 'look and feel'. The key aim is consistency of format across the whole website. For a large corporate site, with different staff working on different parts of the site, there is a risk that the different areas of the site will not be consistent. Defining a clear format or **site design template** for the site means that the quality of the site and customer experience will be better since:

- *The site will be easier to use* – a customer who has become familiar with using one area of the site will be able to confidently use another part of the site.
- *The design elements of the site will be similar* – a user will feel more at home with the site if different parts look similar.
- The corporate image and branding will be consistent with real-world branding (if this is an objective) and similar across the entire site.

Site design templates were reviewed from a site design perspective in Chapter 7.

To achieve a site of this quality it is necessary for written standards to be developed. These may include different standards such as those shown in Table 10.6. The standards adopted will vary according to the size of the website and company. Typically, larger sites, with more individual content developers, will require more detailed standards.

Table 10.6 Website standards

Standard	Details	Applies to
Site structure	Will specify the main areas of the site, for example products, customer service, press releases, how to place content and who is responsible for each area	Content developers
Navigation	May specify, for instance, that the main Website designer/ menu must always be on the left of the screen webmaster usually achieves with nested (sub-) menus at the foot of the these through site templates screen. The home button should be accessible from every screen at the top left corner of the screen. See Lynch and Horton (1999) for guidelines on navigation and site design	Website designer/ webmaster usually achieves these through site templates
Copy style and page structure	General guidelines, for example reminding those writing copy that web copy needs to be briefer than its paper equivalent and ranking factors for SEO (Chapter 9). Where detail is required, perhaps with product specifications, it should be broken up into chunks that are digestible on-screen. Copy and page structure should also be written for search engine optimisation to keyphrases (Chapter 8)	Individual content developers
Testing standards	Check site functions for: • different browser types and versions • plug-ins • invalid links • speed of download of graphics • spellcheck each page	Website designer/ webmaster
Corporate branding	Specifies the appearance of company logos Website designer/ and the colours and typefaces used to convey webmaster and graphic the brand message design	Website designer/ webmaster and graphic design
Process	Web page or updating an existing page. Who is responsible for reviewing and updating?	All
Performance	Availability and download speed figures	Staff managing the server

Who owns the technology?

The technology used to publish a website is important if a company is to utilise fully the power of the Internet. Many standards, such as those in Table 10.6, need to be managed in addition to the technology.

As well as issues of integrating systems, there are detailed technical issues for which the technical staff in the company need to be made responsible. These include:

- availability and performance of the website server
- checking HTML for validity and correcting broken links
- managing different versions of web pages in the test and live environments and content management.

Content management systems

Content management Software tools for managing additions and amendments to website content.

Content management systems refers to when software tools (usually browser-based software running on a server) permit business users to contribute web content, while an administrator keeps control of the format and style of the website and the approval process. These tools are used to organise, manage, retrieve and archive information content throughout the life of the site.

Content management systems (CMS) provide these facilities:

- *Structure authoring* – the design and maintenance of content structure (sub-components, templates, etc.), web page structure and website structure.
- *Link management* – the maintenance of internal and external links through content change and the elimination of dead links.
- *Search engine visibility* – the content within the search engine must be stored and linked such that it can be indexed by search engine robots to add it to their index. This was not possible with some first-generation content management systems, but is typical of more recent content management systems.
- *Input and syndication* – the loading (spidering) of externally originating content and the aggregation and dissemination of content from a variety of sources.
- *Versioning* – the crucial task of controlling which edition of a page, page element or the whole site is published. Typically this will be the most recent, but previous editions should be archived and it should be possible to roll back to a previous version at the page, page element or site level.
- *Security and access control* – different permissions can be assigned to different roles of users and some content may only be available through log-in details. In these cases, the CMS maintains a list of users. This facility is useful when a company needs to use the same CMS for an intranet, extranet or public Internet site which may have different levels of permission.
- *Publication workflow* – content destined for a website needs to pass through a publication process to move it from the management environment to the live delivery environment. The process may involve tasks such as format conversion (e.g. to PDF or to WAP), rendering to HTML, editorial authorisation and the construction of composite documents in real time (personalisation and selective dissemination).
- *Tracking and monitoring* – providing logs and statistical analysis of use to provide performance measures, tune the content according to demand and protect against misuse.
- *Navigation and visualisation* – providing an intuitive, clear and attractive representation of the nature and location of content using colour, texture, 3D rendering or even virtual reality.

From this list of features you can see that modern CMSs are complex and many CMSs are expensive investments. Some open-source CMSs are available, without the need to purchase a licence fee, which have many of the features explained in this section. One example is Plone (**www.plone.org**) which is used by large organisations' websites such as NASA. Dave Chaffey uses Plone to manage the contents for updates to this book which readers can find on his website (**www.davechaffey.com**).

Initiatives to keep content fresh

It is often said that up-to-date content is crucial to site 'stickiness', but fresh content will not happen by accident, so companies have to consider approaches that can be used to control the quality of information. Generic approaches that we have seen which can work well are:

- Assign responsibility for particular content types of site sections.
- Make the quality of web content produced part of employees' performance appraisal.
- Produce a target schedule for publication of content.
- Identify events which trigger the publication of new content, e.g. a new product launch, price change or a press release.
- Identify stages and responsibilities in updating – who specifies, who creates, who reviews, who checks, who publishes.
- Measure the usage of content through web analytics or get feedback from site users.
- Audit and publish content to show which is up-to-date.

Case Study 10 Learning from Amazon's culture of metrics

Context

Why a case study on Amazon? Surely everyone knows who Amazon are and what they do? Yes, well, that's maybe true, but this case goes under the surface to review some of the 'insider secrets' of Amazon's success.

Like eBay, Amazon.com was born in 1995. The name reflected the vision of Jeff Bezos, to produce a large-scale phenomenon like the Amazon river. This ambition has proved justified since just eight years later, Amazon passed the $5 billion sales mark – it took WalMart 20 years to achieve this.

Amazon is now a global brand with over 76 million active customers accounts and order fulfilment to more than 200 countries. Despite this volume of sales, at 31 December 2007, Amazon employed approximately 17,000 full-time and part-time employees.

In September 2007, it launched Amazon MP3, à la carte DRM-free MP3 music downloads, which now includes over 3.1 million songs from more than 270,000 artists.

Vision and strategy

In their 2008 SEC filing, Amazon describe the vision of their business as to:

> *Relentlessly focus on customer experience by offering a wide selection of merchandise, low prices and convenience.*

This focus on the customer has been there from the start, the 1997 SEC filing said Amazon would 'obsess over the customer'. Success here is shown by consistently high ratings at the American Customer Satisfaction Index (**www.acsi.org**).

According to founder and CEO, Jeff Bezos, technology is very important to supporting this focus on the customer. Their 2010 Annual Report (Amazon, 2011) starts:

> *To our shareholders: Random forests, naïve Bayesian estimators, RESTful services, gossip protocols, eventual consistency, data sharding, anti-entropy, Byzantine quorum, erasure coding, vector clocks ... walk into certain Amazon meetings, and you may momentarily think you've stumbled into a computer science lecture. Look inside a current textbook on software architecture, and you'll find few patterns that we don't apply at Amazon. We use high-performance transactions systems, complex rendering and object caching, workflow and queuing systems, business intelligence and data analytics, machine learning and pattern recognition, neural networks and probabilistic decision making, and a wide variety of other techniques. And while many of our systems are based on the latest in computer science research, this often hasn't been sufficient: our architects and engineers have had to advance research in directions that no academic had yet taken. Many of the problems we face have no textbook solutions, and so we – happily – invent new approaches ... All the effort we put into technology might not matter that much if we kept technology off to the side in some sort of R&D department, but we don't take that approach. Technology infuses all of our teams, all of our processes, our decision-making, and our approach to innovation in each of our businesses. It is deeply integrated into everything we do.*

The quote shows how applying new technologies is used to give Amazon a competitive edge. A good recent example of this is providing the infrastructure to deliver the Kindle 'Whispersync' update to ebook readers. Amazon reported in 2011 that Amazon.com is now selling more Kindle books than paperback books.

For every 100 paperback books Amazon has sold, the Company sold 115 Kindle books. Kindle apps are now available on Apple iOS, Android devices and on PCs as part of a '*Buy Once, Read Anywhere*' proposition which Amazon has developed.

The analytics systems to review changes to the customer experience and their impact on profitability are also important to satisfaction. Round (2004) notes that Amazon focuses on customer satisfaction metrics. Each site is closely monitored with standard service avail-ability monitoring (for example, using Keynote or Mercury Interactive) site availability and download speed. Interestingly it also monitors per-minute site revenue upper/lower bounds – Round describes an alarm system rather like a power plant where if revenue on a site falls below $10,000 per minute, alarms go off! There are also internal performance service-level agreements for web services where t% of the time, different pages must return in x seconds.

From 1995 Amazon's consistent vision was to offer Earth's biggest selection and to be Earth's most customer-centric company. Consider how these core marketing messages summarising the Amazon online value proposition are communicated both on-site and through offline communications. Amazon.com adopts what it calls 'An Everyday Low Pricing' strategy, where its objective is 'not to discount a small number of products for a limited period of time, but to offer low prices everyday and apply them broadly across our entire product range'.

Of course, achieving customer loyalty and repeat purchases has been key to Amazon's success. Many dot-coms failed because they succeeded in achieving awareness, but not loyalty. Amazon achieved both. In their SEC filing they stress how they seek to achieve this. They say:

> *We work to earn repeat purchases by providing easy-to-use functionality, fast and reliable fulfilment, timely customer service, feature-rich content, and a trusted transaction environment. Key features of our websites include editorial and customer reviews; manufacturer product information; web pages tailored to individual preferences, such as recommendations and notifications; 1-Click® technology; secure payment systems; image uploads; searching on our websites as well as the Internet; browsing; and the ability to view selected interior pages and citations, and search the entire contents of many of the books we offer with our 'Look Inside the Book' and 'Search Inside the Book' features. Our community of online customers also creates feature-rich content, including product reviews, online recommendation lists, wish lists, buying guides, and wedding and baby registries.*

In practice, as is the practice for many online retailers, the lowest prices are for the most popular products, with less popular products commanding higher prices and a greater margin for Amazon. Free shipping offers are used to encourage increase in basket size since customers have to spend over a certain amount to receive free shipping. The level at which free shipping is set is critical to profitability and Amazon has changed it as competition has changed and for promotional reasons.

Amazon communicate the fulfilment promise in several ways including presentation of latest inventory availability information, delivery date estimates, and options for expedited delivery, as well as delivery shipment notifications and update facilities.

Customers

Amazon defines what it refers to as three consumer sets: customers, seller customers and developer customers. There are over 76 million customer accounts, but just 1.3 million active seller customers in its marketplaces and Amazon is seeking to increase this. Amazon is unusual for a retailer in that it identifies 'developer customers' who use its Amazon Web Services, which provide access to technology infrastructure such as hosting that developers can use to develop their own web services.

Members are also encouraged to join a loyalty programme, Amazon Prime – a fee-based membership programme in which members receive free or discounted express shipping in the United States, the United Kingdom, Germany and Japan.

Competition

In its SEC (2008) filing Amazon describes the environment for its products and services as 'intensely competitive'. It views its main current and potential competitors as: (1) physical-world retailers, catalogue retailers, publishers, vendors, distributors and manufacturers of its products, many of which possess significant brand awareness, sales volume and customer bases, and some of which currently sell, or may sell, products or services through the Internet, mail order or direct marketing; (2) other online e-commerce sites; (3) a number of indirect competitors, including media companies, web portals, comparison shopping websites and web search engines, either directly or in collaboration with other retailers; and (4) companies that provide e-commerce services, including website development, third-party fulfilment and customer service.

Amazon believes the main competitive factors in its market segments include 'selection, price, availability, convenience, information, discovery, brand recognition, personalised services, accessibility, customer service, reliability, speed of fulfilment, ease of use, and ability to adapt to changing conditions, as well as our customers' overall experience and trust in transactions with us and facilitated by us on behalf of third-party sellers'.

For services offered to business and individual sellers, additional competitive factors include the quality of their services and tools, their ability to generate sales for third parties they serve and the speed of performance for their services.

From auctions to marketplaces

Amazon auctions (known as 'zShops') were launched in March 1999, in large part as a response to the success of eBay. They were promoted heavily from the home page, category pages and individual product pages.

Today, competitive prices of products are available through third-party sellers in the 'Amazon Marketplace' which are integrated within the standard product listings. The strategy to offer such an auction facility was initially driven by the need to compete with eBay, but now the strategy has been adjusted such that Amazon describe it as part of the approach of low pricing. Amazon stocks around 26 per cent of its units through sellers, so enabling it to extend its range.

Although it might be thought that Amazon would lose out on enabling its merchants to sell products at lower prices, in fact Amazon makes greater margin on these sales since merchants are charged a commission on each sale and it is the merchant who bears the cost of storing inventory and fulfilling the product to customers. As with eBay, Amazon is just facilitating the exchange of bits and bytes between buyers and sellers without the need to distribute physical products.

Media sales

You may have noticed that unlike some retailers, Amazon displays relevant Google text ads and banner ads from brands. This seems in conflict with the strategy of focus on experience since it leads to a more cluttered store. However the Amazon (2011) report revealed that worldwide, media sales accounted for approximately 44 per cent of revenue ($14.88 billion of $34.204 billion). This suggests that marketplace revenues are included within media sales.

Marketing

Amazon does not reveal much about its marketing approach in its annual reports, but there seems to be a focus on online marketing channels. Amazon (2011) states 'we direct customers to our websites primarily through a number of targeted online marketing channels, such as our Associates program, sponsored search, portal advertising, email marketing campaigns, and other initiatives'. These other initiatives may include outdoor and TV advertising, but they are not mentioned specifically. In this statement they also highlight the importance of customer loyalty tools. They say: 'while costs associated with free shipping are not included in marketing expense, we view free shipping offers and Amazon Prime as effective worldwide marketing tools, and intend to continue offering them indefinitely'.

How 'the culture of metrics' started

A common theme in Amazon's development is the drive to use a measured approach to all aspects of the business, beyond the finance. Marcus (2004) describes an occasion at a corporate 'boot-camp' in January 1997 when Amazon CEO Jeff Bezos 'saw the light'. 'At Amazon, we will have a Culture of Metrics', he said while addressing his senior staff. He went on to explain how web-based business gave Amazon an 'amazing window into human behaviour'. Marcus says:

> *Gone were the fuzzy approximations of focus groups, the anecdotal fudging and smoke blowing from the marketing department. A company like Amazon could (and did) record every move a visitor made, every last click and twitch of the mouse. As the data piled up into virtual heaps, hummocks and mountain ranges, you could draw all sorts of conclusions about their chimerical nature, the consumer. In this sense, Amazon was not merely a store, but an immense repository of facts. All we needed were the right equations to plug into them.*

Marcus then goes on to give a fascinating insight into a breakout group discussion of how Amazon could better use measures to improve its performance. Marcus was in the Bezos group, brainstorming customer-centric metrics. Marcus (2004) summarises the dialogue, led by Bezos:

> *'First, we figure out which things we'd like to measure on the site', he said. 'For example, let's say we want a metric for customer enjoyment. How could we calculate that?'*
>
> *There was silence. Then somebody ventured: 'How much time each customer spends on the site?'*
>
> *'Not specific enough', Jeff said.*
>
> *'How about the average number of minutes each customer spends on the site per session', someone else suggested. 'If that goes up, they're having a blast.'*
>
> *'But how do we factor in purchase?' I [Marcus] said feeling proud of myself. 'Is that a measure of enjoyment?'*
>
> *'I think we need to consider frequency of visits, too', said a dark-haired woman I didn't recognise. 'Lot of folks are still accessing the web with those creepy-crawly modems. Four short visits from them might be just as good as one visit from a guy with a T-1. Maybe better.'*

'Good point', Jeff said. 'And anyway, enjoyment is just the start. In the end, we should be measuring customer ecstasy.'

It is interesting that Amazon was having this debate about the elements of RFM analysis (described in Chapter 6) in 1997, after already having achieved $16 million of revenue in the previous year. Of course, this is a minuscule amount compared with today's billions of dollars turnover. The important point was that this was the start of a focus on metrics, which can be seen through the description of Matt Round's work later in this case study.

From human to software-based recommendations

Amazon has developed internal tools to support this 'Culture of Metrics'. Marcus (2004) describes how the 'Creator Metrics' tool shows content creators how well their product listings and product copy are working. For each content editor, such as Marcus, it retrieves all recently posted documents including articles, interviews, booklists and features. For each one it then gives a conversion rate to sale plus the number of page views, adds (added to basket) and repels (content requested, but the back button then used). In time, the work of editorial reviewers, such as Marcus, was marginalised since Amazon found that the majority of visitors used the search tools rather than read editorial and they responded to the personalised recommendations as the matching technology improved (Marcus likens early recommendations techniques to 'going shopping with the village idiot').

Experimentation and testing at Amazon

The 'Culture of Metrics' also led to a test-driven approach to improving results at Amazon. Matt Round, speaking at E-metrics 2004 when he was director of personalisation at Amazon, describes the philosophy as 'data trumps intuitions'. He explained how Amazon used to have a lot of arguments about which content and promotion should go on the all-important home page or category pages. He described how every category VP wanted top-centre and how the Friday meetings about placements for next week were getting 'too long, too loud and lacked performance data'.

But today 'automation replaces intuitions' and real-time experimentation tests are always run to answer these questions since actual consumer behaviour is the best way to decide upon tactics.

Marcus (2004) also notes that Amazon has a culture of experiments of which A/B tests are key components. Examples where A/B tests are used include new home page design, moving features around the page, different algorithms for recommendations, changing search relevance rankings. These involve testing a new treatment against a previous control for a limited time of a few days or a week. The system will randomly show one or more treatments to visitors and measure a range of parameters such as units sold and revenue by category (and total), session time and session length. The new features will usually be launched if the desired metrics are statistically significantly better. Statistical tests are a challenge though as distributions are not normal (they have a large mass at zero, for example, of no purchase). There are other challenges since multiple A/B tests are running every day and A/B tests may overlap and so conflict. There are also longer-term effects where some features are 'cool' for the first two weeks and the opposite effect where changing navigation may degrade performance temporarily. Amazon also finds that as its users evolve in their online experience, the way they act online has changed. This means that Amazon has to constantly test and evolve its features.

Technology

It follows that the Amazon technology infrastructure must readily support this culture of experimentation and this can be difficult to achieve with standardised content management. Amazon has achieved its competitive advantage through developing its technology internally and with a significant investment in this which may not be available to other organisations without the right focus on the online channels.

As Amazon explains in SEC (2005):

> *using primarily our own proprietary technologies, as well as technology licensed from third parties, we have implemented numerous features and functionality that simplify and improve the customer shopping experience, enable third parties to sell on our platform, and facilitate our fulfilment and customer service operations. Our current strategy is to focus our development efforts on continuous innovation by creating and enhancing the specialised, proprietary software that is unique to our business, and to license or acquire commercially-developed technology for other applications where available and appropriate. We continually invest in several areas of technology, including our seller platform; A9.com, our wholly-owned subsidiary focused on search technology on www.A9.com and other Amazon sites; web services; and digital initiatives.*

Round (2004) describes the technology approach as 'distributed development and deployment'. Pages such as the home page have a number of content 'pods' or 'slots' which call web services for features. This makes it relatively easy to change the content in these pods and even change the location of the pods on-screen. Amazon uses a flowable or fluid page design, unlike many sites, which enables it to make the most of real-estate on-screen.

Technology also supports more standard e-retail facilities. SEC (2005) states:

> *We use a set of applications for accepting and validating customer orders, placing and tracking orders with suppliers, managing and assigning inventory to customer orders, and ensuring proper shipment of products to customers. Our transaction-processing systems handle millions of items, a number of different status inquiries, multiple shipping addresses, gift wrapping requests and multiple shipment methods. These systems allow the customer to choose whether to receive single or several shipments based on availability and to track the progress of each order. These applications also manage the process of accepting, authorising and charging customer credit cards.*

Data-driven automation

Round (2004) said that 'Data is king at Amazon'. He gave many examples of data-driven automation including customer channel preferences, managing the way content is displayed to different user types, such as new releases and top-sellers, merchandising and recommendation (showing related products and promotions) and also advertising through paid search (automatic ad generation and bidding).

The automated search advertising and bidding system for paid search has had a big impact at Amazon. Sponsored links were initially done by humans, but this was unsustainable due to the range of products at Amazon. The automated program generates keywords, writes ad creative, determines best landing page, manages bids, measures conversion rates, profit per converted visitor and updates bids. Again the problem of volume is there: Matt Round described how the book *How to Make Love like a Porn Star* by Jenna Jameson received tens of thousands of clicks from pornography-related searches, but few actually purchased the book. So the update cycle must be quick to avoid large losses.

There is also an automated e-mail measurement and optimisation system. The campaign calendar used to be manually managed with relatively weak measurement and it was costly to schedule and use. A new system:

- automatically optimises content to improve customer experience
- avoids sending an e-mail campaign that has low click-through or a high unsubscribe rate
- includes inbox management (avoid sending multiple e-mails/week)
- has a growing library of automated e-mail programs covering new releases and recommendations.

But there are challenges if promotions are too successful if inventory isn't available.

Your recommendations

'Customers Who Bought X ... also bought Y' is Amazon's signature feature. Round (2004) describes how Amazon relies on acquiring and then crunching a massive amount of data. Every purchase, every page viewed and every search is recorded. So there are now two new versions: 'Customers who shopped for X also shopped for ...', and 'Customers who searched for X also bought ...'. They also have a system codenamed 'Goldbox' which is a cross-sell and awareness raising tool. Items are discounted to encourage purchases in new categories!

He also describes the challenge of techniques for sifting patterns from noise (sensitivity filtering), and clothing and toy catalogues change frequently so recommendations become out-of-date. The main challenges though are the massive data size arising from millions of customers, millions of items and recommendations made in real time.

Partnership strategy

As Amazon grew, its share price growth enabled partnership or acquisition with a range of companies in different sectors. Marcus (2004) describes how Amazon partnered with Drugstore.com (pharmacy), Living.com (furniture), Pets.com (pet supplies), Wineshopper.com (wines), HomeGrocer.com (groceries), Sothebys.com (auctions) and Kozmo.com (urban home delivery). In most cases, Amazon purchased an equity stake in these partners, so that it would share in their prosperity. It also charged them fees for placements on the Amazon site to promote and drive traffic to their sites. Similarly, Amazon charged publishers for prime position to promote books on its site which caused an initial hue-and-cry, but this abated when it was realised that paying for prominent placements was widespread in traditional booksellers and supermarkets. Many of these new online companies failed in 1999 and 2000, but Amazon had covered the potential for growth and was not pulled down by these partners, even though for some, such as Pets.com, it had an investment of 50 per cent.

Analysts sometimes refer to 'Amazoning a sector', meaning that one company becomes so dominant in an online sector such as book retail such that it becomes very difficult for others to achieve market share. In addition to developing, communicating and delivering a very strong proposition, Amazon has been able to consolidate its strength in different sectors through its partnership arrangements and through using technology to facilitate product promotion and distribution via these partnerships. The Amazon retail platform enables other retailers to sell products online using the Amazon user interface and infrastructure through their 'Syndicated Stores' programme. For example, in the UK, Waterstones (**www.waterstones.co.uk**) is one of the largest traditional bookstores. It found competition with online so expensive and challenging, that eventually it entered a partnership arrangement where Amazon markets and distributes its books online in return for a commission online. Similarly, in the US the large book retailer Borders uses the Amazon merchant platform for distributing its products. Toy retailer Toys'R'Us have a similar arrangement. Such partnerships help Amazon extend its reach into the customer-base of other suppliers, and of course, customers who buy in one category such as books can be encouraged to purchase into other areas such as clothing or electronics.

Another form of partnership referred to above is the Amazon Marketplace which enables Amazon customers and other retailers to sell their new and used books and other goods alongside the regular retail listings. A similar partnership approach is the Amazon 'Merchants@' programme which enables third-party merchants (typically larger than those who sell via the Amazon Marketplace) to sell their products via Amazon. Amazon earns money either through fixed fees or sales commissions per unit. This arrangement can help customers who get a wider choice of products from a range of suppliers with the convenience of purchasing them through a single checkout process.

Finally, Amazon has also facilitated formation of partnerships with smaller companies through its affiliates programme. Internet legend records that Jeff Bezos, the creator of Amazon, was chatting to someone at a cocktail party who wanted to sell books about divorce via her website. Subsequently, Amazon.com launched its Associates Program in July 1996 and it is still going strong. Googling **www.google.com/search?q=www.amazon.com+-site%3 Awww.amazon.com** for sites that link to the US site, shows over four million pages, many of which will be affiliates. Amazon does not use an affiliate network which would take commissions from sale, but thanks to the strength of its brand has developed its own affiliate programme. Amazon has created tiered performance-based incentives to encourage affiliates to sell more Amazon products.

Marketing communications

In their SEC filings Amazon states that the aims of their communications strategy are (unsurprisingly) to:

- Increase customer traffic to our websites.
- Create awareness of our products and services.
- Promote repeat purchases.
- Develop incremental product and service revenue opportunities.
- Strengthen and broaden the Amazon.com brand name.

Amazon also believe that their most effective marketing communications are a consequence of their focus on continuously improving the customer experience. This then creates word-of-mouth promotion which is effective in acquiring new customers and may also encourage repeat customer visits.

As well as this, Marcus (2004) describes how Amazon used the personalisation enabled through technology to reach out to a difficult-to-reach market which Bezos originally called 'the hard middle'. Bezos's view was that it was easy to reach ten people (you called them on the phone) or the ten million people who bought the most popular products (you placed a superbowl ad), but more difficult to reach those in between. The search facilities in the search engine and on the Amazon site, together with its product recommendation features meant that Amazon could connect its products with the interests of these people.

Online advertising techniques include paid search marketing, interactive ads on portals, e-mail campaigns and search engine optimisation. These are automated as far as possible, as described earlier in the case study. As previously mentioned, the affiliate programme is also important in driving visitors to Amazon, and Amazon offers a wide range of methods of linking to its site to help improve conversion. For example, affiliates can use straight text links leading direct to a product page and they also offer a range of dynamic banners which feature different content such as books about Internet marketing or a search box.

Amazon also use co-operative advertising arrangements, better known as 'contra-deals', with some vendors and other third parties. For example, a print advertisement in 2005 for a particular product such as a wireless router with a free wireless laptop card promotion was to feature a specific Amazon URL in the ad. In product fulfilment packs, Amazon may include a leaflet for a non-competing online company such as Figleaves.com (lingerie) or Expedia (travel). In return, Amazon leaflets may be included in customer communications from the partner brands.

➜

Table 10.7 Financial results summary for Amazon for year ended 31 December 2007

	(All figures in millions)		
	2007	**2006**	**2005**
Net sales	$14 835	$10 711	$8 490
Cost of sales	11 482	8 255	6 451
Gross profit	3 353	2 456	2 039
Operating expenses (1):			
Fulfilment	1 292	937	745
Marketing	344	263	198
Technology and content	818	662	451
General and administrative	235	195	166
Other operating expense, net	9	10	47
Total operating expenses	2 698	2 067	1 607
Income from operations	655	389	432
Interest income	90	59	44
Interest expense	(77)	(78)	(92)
Other income (expense), net	(1)	(4)	2
Remeasurements and other	(7)	11	42
Total non-operating income (expense)	5	(12)	(4)
Income before income taxes	660	377	428
Provision for income taxes	184	187	95
Income before cumulative effect of change in accounting principle	476	190	333
Cumulative effect of change in accounting principle	–	–	26
Net income	$476	$190	$359

Sources: Internet Retailer (2003), Marcus (2004), Round (2004), SEC (2005), SEC (2008)

The associates programme directs customers to Amazon websites by enabling independent websites to make millions of products available to their audiences with fulfilment performed by Amazon or third parties. Amazon pays commissions to hundreds of thousands of participants in the associates programme when their customer referrals result in product sales. In addition, they offer everyday free shipping options worldwide and recently announced Amazon.com Prime in the US, their first membership programme in which members receive free two-day shipping and discounted overnight shipping. Although marketing expenses do not include the costs of free shipping or promotional offers, Amazon views such offers as effective marketing tools.

Questions

1 By referring to the case study, Amazon's website for your country and your experience of Amazon offline communications evaluate how well Amazon communicates their core proposition and promotional offers.
2 Using the case study, characterise Amazon's approach to marketing communications.
3 Explain what distinguishes Amazon in its uses of technology for competitive advantage.
4 How does the Amazon 'culture of metrics' differ from that in other organisations from your experience.

Summary

1 A structured measurement and improvement programme is necessary to collect measures to assess a website's effectiveness. Action can then be taken to adjust the website strategy or promotional efforts. A measurement programme involves:
- Stage 1: Defining a measurement process.
- Stage 2: Defining a metrics framework.
- Stage 3: Selecting of tools for data collection, reporting, optimisation and analysis.

2 Measures of Internet marketing effectiveness can be categorised as assessing:
- *Level 1: Business effectiveness* – these measure the impact of the website on the whole business, and look at financial measures such as revenue and profit and promotion of corporate awareness.
- *Level 2: Marketing effectiveness* – these measure the number of leads and sales achieved via the Internet and effect of the Internet on retention rates and other aspects of the marketing mix such as branding.
- *Level 3: Internet marketing effectiveness* – these measures assess how well the site is being promoted, and do so by reviewing the popularity of the site and how good it is at delivering customer needs.

3 The measures of effectiveness referred to above are collected in two main ways – online and offline – or in combination.

4 Online measures are obtained from a web-server log file or using browser-based techniques. They indicate the number of visitors to a site, which pages they visit and where they originated from. These also provide a breakdown of visitors through time or by country.

5 Offline measures are marketing outcomes such as enquiries or sales that are directly attributable to the website. Other measures of the effectiveness are available through surveying customers using questionnaires, interviews and focus groups.

6 Managing a website requires clear responsibilities to be identified for different roles. These include the roles of content owners and site developers, and those ensuring that the content conforms with company and legal requirements.

7 To produce a good-quality website, standards are required to enforce uniformity in terms of:
- site look and feel
- corporate branding
- quality of content.

Exercises

Self-assessment exercises

1 Why are standards necessary for controlling website management? What aspects of the site do standards seek to control?

2 Explain the difference between hits and page impressions. How are these measured?

3 How should social media marketing effectiveness be assessed?

4 Why should content development be distributed through a large organisation?

5 Describe the different types of measures that should be used to review and improve digital marketing.

6 How can focus groups and interviews be used to assess website effectiveness?

7 Explain how a web log file analyser works. What are its limitations?

8 Why is it useful to integrate the collection of online and offline metrics?

Essay and discussion questions

1 'Corporate standards for a website's format and update process are likely to stifle the creative development of a site and reduce its value to customers.' Discuss.

2 'Most companies collect data about digital marketing activities, but few derive much value from it'. Discuss possible reasons for this assertion.

3 You have been appointed manager of a website for a car manufacturer and have been asked to refine the existing online measurement and improvement programme. Explain, in detail, the steps you would take to develop this programme.

4 The first version of a website for a financial services company has been live for a year. Originally it was developed by a team of two people, and was effectively 'brochure-ware'. The second version of the site is intended to contain more detailed information, and will involve contributions from 10 different product areas. You have been asked to define a procedure for controlling updates to the site. Write a document detailing the update procedure, which also explains the reasons for each control.

Examination questions

1 Why are standards necessary to control the process of updating a website? Give three examples of different aspects of a website that need to be controlled.

2 Explain the following terms concerning measurement of website effectiveness:
   (a) hits
   (b) page impressions
   (c) referring pages.

3 Measurement of websites concerns the recording of key events involving customers using a website. Briefly explain five different types of event.

4 Describe and briefly explain the purpose of the different stages involved in updating an existing document on a commercial website.

5 Outline different types of measures for reviewing the effectiveness of social media marketing.

6 Give three reasons explaining why a website may have to integrate with existing marketing information systems and databases within a company.

7 You have been appointed manager of a website and have been asked to develop a metrics programme. Briefly explain the steps you would take to develop this programme.

8 If a customer can be persuaded to register his or her name and e-mail address with a website, how can this information be used for site measurement purposes?

References

Adams, C., Kapashi, N., Neely, A. and Marr, B. (2000) Managing with measures: measuring e-business performance, *Accenture white paper*. Survey conducted in conjunction with Cranfield School of Management.

Altimeter (2011) Framework: the social media ROI pyramid, 13 December 2010, by Jeremiah Owyang; **http://www.web-strategist.com/blog/2010/12/13/framework-the-social-media-roi-pyramid.**

Amazon (2011) Amazon 2010 full year report/SEC filing, available from: Amazon Investor relations site, published 27 January.

Chaffey, D. (2000) Achieving Internet marketing success, *The Marketing Review*, 1(1), 35–60.

Friedman, L. and Furey, T. (1999) *The Channel Advantage*, Butterworth-Heinemann, Oxford.

Grossnickle, J. and Raskin, O. (2001) *The Handbook of Online Marketing Research: Knowing your Customer Using the Net*, McGraw-Hill, New York.

Kotler, P. (1997) *Marketing Management – Analysis, Planning, Implementation and Control*, Prentice-Hall, Englewood Cliffs, NJ.

Lynch, P. and Horton, S. (1999) *Web Style Guide: Basic Design Principles for Creating Websites*, Yale University Press, New Haven, CT.

Malhotra, N. (1999) *Marketing Research: An Applied Orientation*, Prentice-Hall, Upper Saddle River, NJ.

Marcus, J. (2004) *Amazonia. Five Years at the Epicentre of the Dot-com Juggernaut*, The New Press, New York.

Neely, A., Adams, C. and Kennerley, M. (2002) *The Performance Prism: The Scorecard for Measuring and Managing Business Success*, Financial Times/Prentice Hall, Harlow.

Revolution (2004) Alliance & Leicester banks on e-commerce, by Philip Buxtone, *Revolution*: **www.revolutionmagazine.com**.

Round, M. (2004) Presentation to E-metrics, London, May 2005: **www.emetrics.org**.

SEC (2005) United States Securities and Exchange Commission Submission Form 10-K from Amazon. For the fiscal year ended 31 December 2004.

SEC (2008) United States Securities and Exchange Commission Submission Form 10-K from Amazon. For the fiscal year ended 31 December 2007.

SmartInsights (2010) Website Feedback Tools Review. Author: Dave Chaffey. Available at: **http://bit.ly/smartfeedback**.

Sterne, J. (2001) *World Wide Web Marketing*, 3rd edn. Wiley, New York.

Web Analytics Association (2011) Web Analytics Association Outlook: 2011 Survey report, February. Published at: **http://www.webanalyticsassociation.org**.

Wilson, H. (2008) *The Multichannel Challenge*, Butterworth-Heinemann, Oxford, UK. Copyright Elsevier.

Wisner, J. and Fawcett, S. (1991) Link firm strategy to operating decisions through performance measurement, *Production and Inventory Management Journal*, Third Quarter, 5–11.

Further reading

Berthon, P., Pitt, L. and Watson, R. (1998) The World Wide Web as an industrial marketing communication tool: models for the identification and assessment of opportunities, *Journal of Marketing Management*, 14, 691–704. This is a key paper assessing how to measure how the Internet supports purchasers through the different stages of the buying decision.

Friedman, L. and Furey, T. (1999) *The Channel Advantage*, Butterworth–Heinemann, Oxford. Chapter 12 is on managing channel performance.

Sterne, J. (2001) *World Wide Web Marketing*, 3rd edn. Wiley, New York. Chapter 11 is entitled 'Measuring your success'. It mainly reviews the strengths and weaknesses of online methods.

Weblinks

Web analytics resources

- **ABCe** (www.abce.org.uk). Audited Bureau of Circulation is standard for magazines in the UK. This is the electronic auditing part. Useful for definitions and examples of traffic for UK organisations.
- **E-metrics** (www.emetrics.org). Jim Sterne's site has many resources for online marketing metrics.
- **Marketing Experiments** (www.marketingexperiments.com). Summarises approaches to testing to improve website marketing effectiveness.
- **Smart Insights Web Analytics Strategy** (www.smartinsights.com/managing-digital-marketing/web-analytics-strategy). This Quick Guide from Dave Chaffey's site has all the main resources for students.
- **Web Analytics Association** (www.webanalyticsassociation.org). The site of the trade association for web analytics has useful definitions, articles and forums on this topic.
- **Web Analytics Demystified** (www.webanalyticsdemystified.com). A site to support Eric Petersen's books with a range of content.

Web analytics expertise

- **Avinash Kaushik's Occam's Razor blog** (www.kaushik.net). Avinash is an expert in web analytics and his popular blog shows how web analytics should be used to control and improve return on e-marketing investments.
- **EpikOne** (www.epikone.com/resources). A specialist web analytics blog and e-book by Justin Cutroni giving guidance on how to tailor Google Analytics.
- **Jim Sterne of Target Marketing** (www.targeting.com). Leading commentator on the topic.

Social media marketing analytics

These are the blogs of three of the leading commentators on social media marketing who discuss how to measure return from social media marketing.

- **Jay Baer** (www.convinceandconvert.com)
- **Brian Solis** (www.briansolis.com)
- **Jeremiah Owyang** (www.web-strategist.com)

Online marketing research resources

1. Digests of published market research data:
    - ClickZ Internet research (www.clickz.com/stats)
    - Market Research.com (www.marketresearch.com)
    - MR Web (www.mrweb.co.uk)
2. Directories of MR companies:
    - British Market Research Association (www.bmra.org.uk)
    - Market Research Society (www.mrs.org.uk)
    - International MR agencies (www.greenbook.org)
3. Traditional market research agencies
    - MORI (www.mori.com/emori)
    - NOP (www.nopworld.com)
    - Nielsen (www.nielsen.com)
4. Government sources:
    - European government (http://europa.eu.int/comm/eurostat)
    - OECD (www.oecd.org)

- UK government (**www.open.gov.uk, www.ons.gov.uk**)
- US government (**www.stat-usa.gov**)

5 Online audience data:
- Comscore (**www.comscore.com**)
- Hitwise (**www.hitwise.com**)
- Mori (**www.mori.com/emori**)
- Netratings (**www.netratings.com**)
- NOP World (**www.nopworld.com**)

Chapter 11

Business-to-consumer digital marketing practice

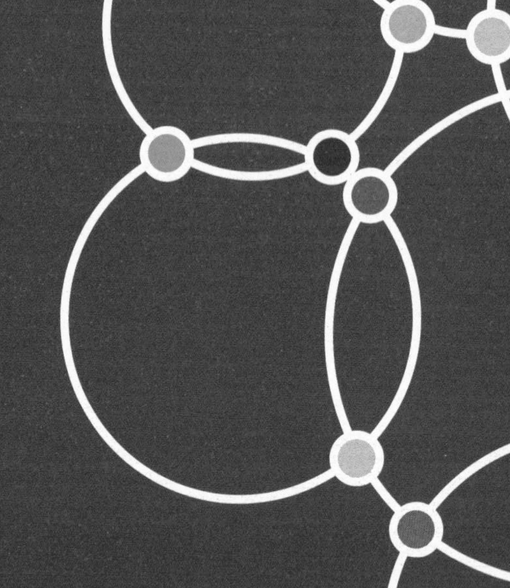

Chapter at a glance

Main topics

Case studies

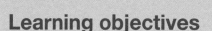

Learning objectives

After reading this chapter, the reader should be able to:

- understand online consumer behaviour, and more specifically how consumer profiles and online experiences shape and influence the extent to which individuals are likely to engage with the online trading environment
- explain the development of e-retailing and describe various types of online retailing activities and strategies
- begin to develop an understanding from a retailer's perspective of the strategic implications of trading online in consumer markets

Questions for marketers

Key questions for marketing managers related to this chapter are:

- What are the key decisions that a consumer-facing organisation should consider when developing an e-retail strategy?
- What are customer expectations of web-based services?
- How can we maximise commercial results for our site?
- How can we integrate social commerce and social media

Scan code to find the latest updates for topics in this chapter

Links to other chapters

This chapter builds on concepts and frameworks introduced earlier in the book. The main related chapters are as follows:

- Chapter 2, which provides an introduction to the characteristics of Internet consumer behaviour
- Chapter 4, which introduces strategic approaches to exploiting the Internet
- Chapter 6, which examines customer relationship management issues
- Chapter 7, covering issues relating to successful site development and operations

Introduction

Business-to-consumer (B2C) markets have made a significant contribution to the commercial development of the Internet encouraging wide-scale use of transactional e-commerce sites by a diverse and increasingly global range of consumers.

This chapter explores some of the key issues which have an impact on the growth and development of online B2C markets focusing on the retail sector. It begins by focusing on first the consumers (who they are, their expectations, how online experiences affect the motivation to shop online) and then retailers (the meaning and scope of the term *e-retailing* and the different ways in which digital and Internet technologies are used to create a virtual *retail channel*). The chapter concludes with a discussion of the factors affecting the development of successful e-retail strategies.

We start with a review summary of key digital marketing practice questions which applies to companies discussed in both chapters 11 and 12. These are key management questions marketers have to review to develop a digital marketing plan (see Digital marketing insight 11.1).

Digital marketing insight 11.1 — The Smart Insights planning template for digital strategy development

As an alternative perspective on strategy from that covered in Chapters 4 and 5, the PRACE framework we introduced in Chapter 1 gives a structure to review the opportunities and challenges for managing digital marketing in the different types of organisations covered in Chapters 11 and 12. These are some of the key strategic questions that need to be addressed by managers and can be viewed as a summary of actions to be taken.

Planning questions

These overview questions review strategies to maximise efficiency and effectiveness of the channel. Key questions to consider are:

Q1. Do we have a clear strategy to support growth of our online channels?
Q2. How do we align our online marketing activities to support our business goals?
Q3. Which audiences are we targeting and how do we attract them to do business with us online?
Q4. Which insights do we have about our customer characteristics (profiles), needs from online services (requirements and intent) and perceptions of our service (quality gap)?
Q5. Have we analysed our marketplace to understand the types of online sites and influencers that affect sales?
Q6. How is our value proposition and brand offer supported by online channels?
Q7. How do we integrate channels to support customer journeys?
Q8. How do we achieve sales growth through customer lifecycle strategies, i.e. reach strategy, interaction and conversion strategy and ongoing engagement strategy

Reach strategy questions

These questions should be asked to determine approaches to reach prospects, existing customers and raising awareness on a website or other online presences to encourage visits and interaction. Key questions here are:

Q1. Do we have visibility of actual and target performance for volume, quality and value for our online visitors?

Q2. What is the right channel media mix of paid, owned and earned media (inbound/content marketing) to meet our goals?
Q3. Have we maximised the efficiency of each channel? Which are the priorities?
Q4. Which audiences are we targeting not targeting through online media?
Q5. What are our core messages and offers to encourage use of online channels?
Q6. Are we putting sufficient time into managing relationships with partners and influencers?
Q7. How do we route traffic and manage customer journeys to maximise effectiveness?
Q8. How do we best integrate ALL channels?
Q9. How do we leverage the viral/word-of-mouth effect from viral channels?
Q10. Are our social presences effective and are we measuring reputation?

Act and conversion strategy questions

Act and conversion refers to achieving interaction and participation to deliver sales leads. For a retail site, this is initial engagement with a site to browse products and then add them to product categories. In financial services this is encouraging a quote or application while in travel this is encouraging interest in destinations. Conversion may happen online or offline, so steps are taken to facilitate these customer journeys. Key questions are:

Q1. How do we appeal to different audiences, needs, behaviour, referrers?
Q2. What are our key value messages?
Q3. How do we improve the customer experience to improve conversion and satisfaction across different hardware and software platforms such as desktop and mobile access?
Q4. How do we reduce friction to make more efficient customer journeys through the right call-to-action?
Q5. Is our content effective in supporting conversion?
Q6. Are social media and user-generated content ineffective in supporting conversion?
Q7. Are we maximising the value generated per visit?
Q8. Are we following up on leads effectively?
Q9. Are we using web analytics effectively to improve results through combining the right metrics, process, people and tools?

Engage and retention strategy questions

The final set of questions refer to approaches to build long-term relationships with customers through online media:

Q1. How well do we know the needs, wants, characteristics and value of existing customers?
Q2. How do we increase customer lifetime value?
Q3. What is the gap between customer satisfaction needs and delivery and do we improve satisfaction?
Q4. What content, offers, experiences will engage different audiences?
Q5. How should we manage customer communities to grow our brand?
Q6. How do we create an integrated lifecycle email + social media customer communications programme?
Q7. How can we use customer advocacy to improve results?

Key themes and concepts

This chapter considers online B2C markets from two distinct perspectives:

- *The consumer perspective* – the first part of the chapter focuses on the online consumer, namely his/her profile, which has been found to strongly influence the extent to which particular consumers shop online and also online shopping experiences, which are likely to shape online shopping intentions.
- *The company perspective* – the second part of the chapter examines the development of e-retailing, types of online strategies, factors likely to affect how retailers develop e-retailing activities, managerial and strategic challenges.

This chapter provides illustrative case studies, examples of consumer and retailer behaviour and graphics as supporting material. Academic articles are used to support underlying theoretical issues and concepts.

The consumer perspective: online consumer behaviour

Levels of consumer demand for online shopping and services ultimately determine the size of e-retail markets and when or if a market saturation point will be reached for online purchasing. Various influences, such as whether the consumer has access to the Internet, levels of competency in use of the technology and the perceived benefits of Internet shopping for different forms of products, have been identified as key factors likely to impact on whether an individual shops online.

Online retailing, or e-retailing as it will be referred to for the rest of this chapter, offers the consumer an experience very different from shopping in the high street: web-based stores can be open continuously around the clock; interactive promotions, which can be highly customised and permission-based; dynamic pricing enables real-time prices, which reflect current market demand e.g., eBay auctions; comparison shopping and recommendations shared by other site users. Indeed, many consumers, even if they do not intend to buy online, turn to the Internet to find information about a product in the early part of the buying decision-making process. An example of an online brand, which facilitates comparison of products and prices, is Kelkoo.com. The origins of the name from the French phrase '*Quel coût?*' can be interpreted as 'At what price?' or even 'What a bargain'.

As a result of the innovative characteristics of the online shopping environment, the online consumer experience can become an elective and very goal-orientated activity whereby consumers go to the Internet to seek the particular products and services they wish to buy. Perea *et al.* (2004) highlighted that while consumers are increasingly shopping online, it is not clear what drives them to shop in this way. They suggest there are various factors, including ease of use, enjoyment and consumer traits, which will determine whether an individual will become an avid Internet shopper. So who are the customers who shop online?

Who are the online customers?

Many researchers have written about online consumer behaviour and a very wide array of factors and variables have been cited as influencing the extent to which individuals are likely to shop online. Hoffman *et al.* (2004), focused on the impact of demographics, and highlighted inequities of Internet access based on race and gender that still occur. Source *et al.* (2005) looked at age and found that 'while older shoppers search for significantly fewer products than their younger counterparts they actually purchase as much as the younger consumer'. Doherty and Ellis-Chadwick (2006) suggest the large body of literature looking at online consumer behaviour variables can be grouped into two broad categories: studies of *consumer profiles* and studies of *consumer experiences.*

The consumer profile

A consumer's profile can strongly influence where, when and how an individual shops online and also have important marketing implications. We can break the consumer profile down into two distinct sub-categories: classification variables and character variables.

Classification variables are those personal attributes that tend to remain static throughout an individual's lifetime or evolve slowly over time. These variables are particularly useful for marketers as they can help to *identify* particular consumers and target groups. Moreover, according to Jobber (2007), profile segmentation variables can be used to group consumers together in a meaningful way so they can be reached by suitable media communications. See Table 11.1 for a list of classification variables and possible implications for online target marketing. Remember that while many consumers have desktop access to the Internet, there will be larger differences in access to smartphone and tablet devices, particularly between different countries and this will constrain the experiences these enable the merchant to offer.

Table 11.1 Consumer profile: classification variables

Profile variable	Online marketing impact
Age	Age can affect levels of access to technology, computer literacy and, eventually, the extent to which individuals use the Internet as part of their shopping routines.
Education	At the higher end of the educational spectrum (university and college graduates) the Internet is considered as essential if not indispensible.
Employment status	Employment places time constraints on online shopping behaviour, i.e. when and where individuals can access online shopping channels.
Gender	Male consumers still tend to make more purchases and buy higher ticket items online than females although the gap is narrowing significantly. In the UK, 71 per cent of males compared with 62 per cent of females accessed the Internet during 2007.
Geography	Location is an important consideration: where people live can affect the potential size of the online market; Asia now has the largest number of Internet users, followed by the European Union (EU). Interestingly the USA no longer has the highest number of Internet users.
Household size	Household size has the potential to affect the number of people involved in purchasing decisions and the direction of influence. For example, research has shown that in Europe children and teenagers can have a strong influence on purchasing based on their levels of computing competency.
Household type	Household type has the potential to affect product and service requirements; major shifts towards single person households has led to a shift in purchasing patterns and times of purchasing. Online, such households can create logistical difficulties when delivering bulky and perishable goods. Interestingly over three-quarters of all households with children have access to the Internet as opposed to just over half of households without children.
Income	Income affects purchasing power and also influences whether individuals have access to the Internet. In the UK, AB, C1, C2 social-economic groups are significantly more likely to have access to the Internet and to subsequently shop online than groupings D, E. Income is positively related to a tendency to shop online.
Mobility	Mobility affects channel access; less mobile targets may be encouraged to shop online. This also applies to macro-populations, which are poorly served by public and private transport.
Race and ethnicity	Race and ethnicity affects access to technology and economic circumstances. In the US, the number of African–Americans with Internet access is increasing to over 50 per cent but this sector of the population lags behind the Caucasians and Hispanics.

Character variables are less straightforward to understand and identify as they comprise any attributes of a consumer's perceptions, beliefs and attitudes, which might influence online behaviour and also shape an individual's intentions to shop online – e.g. innovativeness, enjoyment, skills and experience and emotions. It is important to recognise that character variables are more likely to develop, change and be significantly modified over time by online shopping experiences than classification variables. For example, if a consumer has negative beliefs about, say, privacy and security of online transactions, which are due to *lack of computer skills* these *beliefs* are likely to shape negative *attitudes* towards the Internet and reduce the *intention* to shop online. Conversely, if a consumer *believes* the Internet is, say, *easy to use*, they are more likely to have a positive *attitude* towards the idea of online shopping and ultimately have an increased *intention* to shop online. Each stance may be continually reinforced by positive or negative feedback from online shopping experiences. See Figure 11.1 for a model of how character variables interact.

Consumers' beliefs about a range of variables might ultimately shape their attitudes towards the Internet and their purchasing intentions. Examples include:

- *Security and privacy of information* – customers have an expectation that if they are prepared to provide detailed personal and financial information it will be stored securely. If this is not the case, personal belief, attitudes and intentions to shop online are likely to be negatively affected when a case of fraudulent credit card use or stolen identity occurs.
- *Risk* – online consumers are buying into a trading situation laden with uncertainty and a lack of cues to reinforce trading relationships and risk. Bauer (1960) identified six key types of risk likely to affect consumers: financial, product performance, social, psychological, physical and time/convenience loss. Online sales effectiveness can be increased significantly if the perception of risk is reduced. Willingness to purchase is considered to be inversely affected by perceived risk. Stone and Gronhaug (1993) state that 'risk is the subjective expectation of a loss'.
- *Trust* – is a potential outcome of risk reduction. Trust needs to be increased and perceived risk decreased for consumers to develop positive beliefs in the organisation's online reputation. Dimensions of trust include service provider expertise, product performance, firm reputations, satisfaction (with past interactions) and similarity. It should be noted that

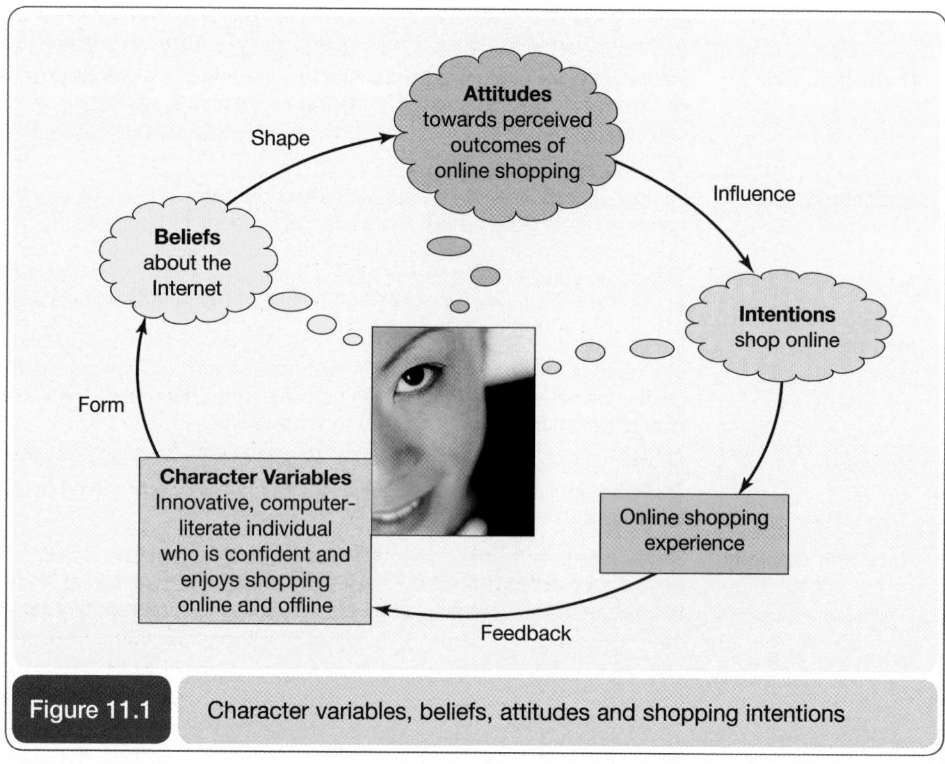

Figure 11.1 Character variables, beliefs, attitudes and shopping intentions

some researchers have suggested that not all online customers respond in the same manner. Newholm *et al.* (2004) conclude that e-retailers should adopt a differential approach to building trust and raise the point that types of customers and products can significantly affect how retailers should develop approaches for handling risk and trust. Indeed 'bargain hunters' are inherently risk takers and in this case it becomes the propensity to engage in risk taking, rather than being risk averse.

- *Perceived usefulness* – is positively associated with the intention to purchase and is defined as the extent to which an individual perceives that a new technology will enhance or improve his/her performance. Applied to online shopping, usefulness relates to the amount of time and effort required to learn how to shop online measured against the levels of service excellence provided by the retailer (Perea *et al.*, 2004).
- *Ease of use* – is an individual's perception that using a new technology will be free of effort and has been found to have particular influence in the early stages of a user's experience with a new technology (Davis, 1993).

In summary, *classification* and *character* variables have both been found to play an important role in predicting how consumers might behave over time, but it should be acknowledged that only character variables will be significantly affected by online shopping experiences (Doherty and Ellis-Chadwick, 2006). For example, gender may influence the extent to which an individual might shop online but gender will not be changed by online shopping experiences.

The consumers' online shopping experiences

Different aspects of the experience of online shopping have been found to have an effect on consumers' overall assessment of the online shopping process (Doherty and Ellis-Chadwick, 2006). Positive experiences in terms of convenience, service delivery, website security have all been found to increase customer satisfaction (Szymanski and Hise, 2000). Unsurprisingly, website design, ease of navigation, good levels of service and good value products have been found to increase consumer loyalty and also found to enhance the customer experience (Wolfinbarger and Gilly, 2003). E-retailers should aim to understand how customer expectations have been raised. Some of the key areas where customers have high expectations are:

- *Delivery* – the critical link between an online order and the delivery of the product is often referred to as the final or last mile. The last mile, including product transportation, is frequently considered the most important element of the order fulfilment process, i.e. 89 per cent of online shoppers rate on-time delivery high in importance and 85 per cent of buyers who receive their order on time would shop at the Internet merchant again. Thus, delivery-related issues have been shown to have a high level of importance to online shoppers (Esper *et al.*, 2003).
- *Timeliness* – the speed of digital communications has raised customer expectations in terms of response times and they expect a speedy shopping experience. It is no longer acceptable to take three or four days to respond to an online customer enquiry; an online customer expects that the response will be instantaneous or at least within a couple of hours. Additionally, they expect to be able to order goods and services at any time.
- *Availability* – the Internet creates a sales environment, which is not restricted by space constraints, therefore there is an increased expectation that not only will there be a wider range of goods for sale online but also the goods will be readily available for immediate delivery.
- *Convenience* – it should be easier and quicker to compare prices online; there should be easy access to a wide range of retailers without the inconvenience of having to travel to a number of different locations.
- *Customer service* – customer value is the foremost driver of competitive advantage in the Internet shopping environment and customer service can be measured by the consumer in terms of price savings, service excellence, time savings and experiential values such as entertainment, visual stimulation/reward, levels of interaction. At the start of Chapter 6 we read about the various dimensions of customer loyalty and how they can be translated into website features in Table 11.4. See Mini case study 11.1 for an example of online retail service delivery.

Mini Case Study 11.1 Best Buy offers, listens and responds in multiple channels

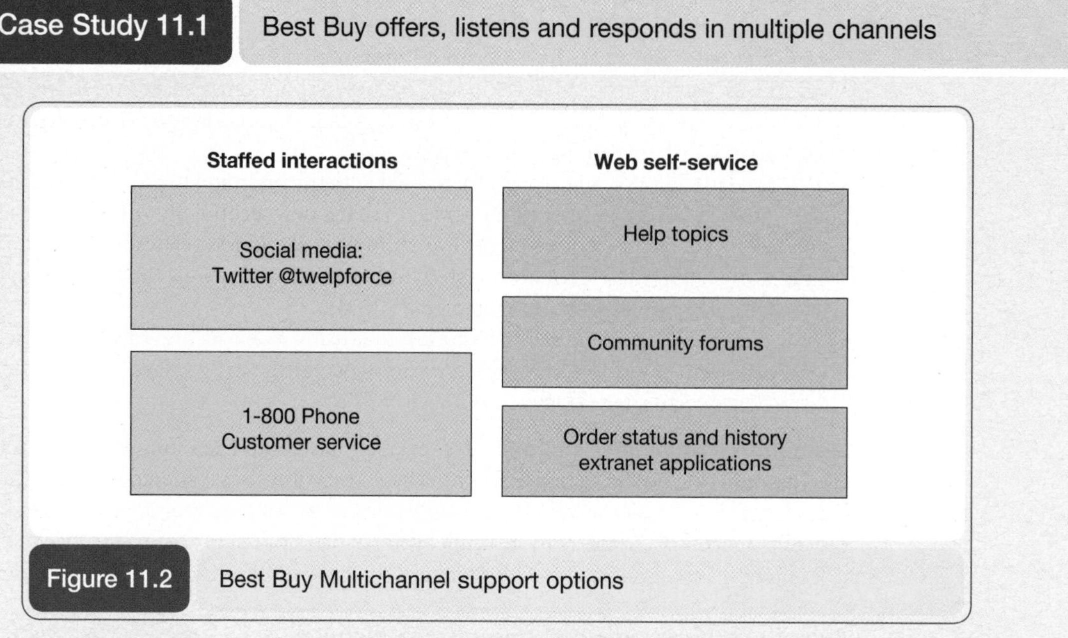

Figure 11.2 Best Buy Multichannel support options

Best Buy is a multinational retailer of technology and entertainment products operating in the United States, Canada, Europe, China and Mexico. The Best Buy family of brands and partnerships collectively generates more than $45 billion in annual revenue and includes brands such as Best Buy; Audiovisions; The Carphone Warehouse; Future Shop; Geek Squad, Jiangsu Five Star; Magnolia Audio Video; Napster; Pacific Sales; The Phone House; and Speakeasy. Providing quality customer service is a large part of the customer experience. Best Buy explains:

> *Approximately 155,000 employees apply their talents to help bring the benefits of these brands to life for customers through retail locations, multiple call centres and websites, in-home solutions, product delivery and activities in our communities.*

See a video explanation at: **http://www.bestbuy.com/about/**.

Figure 11.2 shows the customer support page for the Bestbuy.com. You can see that there are a wide range of choices of customer service including:

- The Twelpforce (**http://twitter.com/twelpforce**): immediate Twitter response followed by around 30,000 customers.
- Geek Squad online support: 'A live agent can fix your PC now! Prices starting at $49.99'.
- Discussion in communities.
- Standard e-mail and 'click to call' options: **http://www.bestbuy.com/about/**.

It is important to understand that the increase in customer expectations can have quite wide-reaching organisational implications. The gap between customer expectations of the online offer and the actual performance can have a significant impact on online performance. Now read Digital marketing insight 11.2 which explores the relationship between experiences and online success. Note that the similar E-SERVQUAL and WEBQUAL frameworks are described towards the end of Chapter 7.

Digital marketing insight 11.2 eTailQ

There has been a great deal of academic research looking at the relationship between quality and online success in consumer markets. Wolfinbarger and Gilly (2003) used the idea that quality is related to customer satisfaction and retention and ultimately customer loyalty. The study identified four dimensions of e-tailing and in doing so enabled the development of a reliable scale for the measurement of online retail quality called eTailQ. The four key dimensions identified by the study can help managers to understand customer judgements of a company website and how customers shape their attitudes based on their experiences of visiting say a retailer's website. The four dimensions in rank order of importance are:

1 **Website design:**
- easy navigation
- appropriate levels of information
- effective information search facility
- straightforward ordering
- appropriate personalisation
- appropriate product selection

2 **Fulfilment/reliability:**
- accurate display aimed at ensuring alignment between customer expectations and realisation
- delivery of the right product within promised time frame

3 **Customer service:**
- responsiveness to enquiries
- helpful
- willing service
- immediacy of response

4 **Privacy/security:**
- secure payment facilities
- secure and private personal information.

Customer judgement of the quality of the website visit is an important part of the customer's online experience and the outcome of the evaluation process could determine whether the customer (a) is sufficiently *satisfied* to return and make another purchase, (b) develops *loyalty* intentions and subsequently recommends a site to friends and family, (c) develops a positive relationship with the brand.

You can see that customer concerns from 2003 are similar in many ways to today. Consider which are different. We think that the most significant omissions in this framework are the integration between online and offline presences (click to reserve); integration with social commerce facilities (reviews and ratings) and social networks although the notion of 'community' is considered.

In summary, consumer demand for online shopping continues to grow at a rapid rate. As the Internet infrastructure expands and develops, more parts of the world are able to have access to the technology, which enables them to shop online. Political and economic development is also playing a part in enabling certain parts of the world to take part in the e-commence revolution.

Table 11.2 Loyalty variables

Loyalty variable	Website feature
Customisation	Personally, tailored product ranges, for example lists of regular grocery purchases, favourite products, brands, etc.
Contact interactivity	Two-way communications that demonstrate the dynamic nature of the online buyer/supplier customer relationship.
Cultivation	E-mail offers relating to past purchases, informing customers when there is a discount sale on items similar to their previous purchases.
Care	Real-time stock-out information/order tracking. Shoppers are looking for evidence that the retailer has paid attention to detail throughout the purchasing process.
Community	Product reviews from satisfied customers. Include a facility allowing and encouraging exchange of opinions among shoppers.
Choice	Online shoppers expect greater choice online. Therefore, the retailer needs to offer either wide or deep (or both) product and/or service choice.
Convenience	Easy access to required information and a simple transaction interface. Over-designed and cognitively complex sites tend to lose visitors before they make a purchase.
Character	Symbols, graphics, style, colours, themes can be used to reinforce brand image and convey brand personality.

Source: Based on Srinivasan *et al*., 2002

At an individual level more is now known about online consumer behaviour and for retail managers and marketers the key to online success is developing better understanding of the *consumer's profile* and the *consumer's behaviour when online shopping*. The web analytics tools we described in Chapter 10 are powerful in reviewing consumer behaviour. Online shoppers tend to have different profiles and characteristics to offline shoppers, which shape their shopping intentions. Online shoppers still tend to be younger, wealthier, better educated, have higher 'computer literacy' and more disposable income than the offline shopper. It is also important when planning e-retail strategies to consider that as the Internet becomes a more mainstream shopping channel there are likely to be a greater range of cultural differences as wider sectors of the global populations have greater access to online shopping channels. The next part of the chapter explores B2C markets from the retailer's perspective and looks at how organisations are developing the online shopping provision.

The retail perspective: e-retailing

This section explores online shopping from the retailer's perspective. More specifically, it considers the development of the online trading environment and e-retailing activities, trading formats and strategies and the strategic implications of trading online in consumer markets.

Development of e-retailing

In the early 1990s, when the development of the Internet as a trading environment began with the first exchanges of commercial e-mail, traditional retailers had little interest in trading online. However, for many retailers it was considered as a remote 'geekish' environment used solely by computer experts and scientists. It was not until the mid-1990s that larger retail companies began to consider how the Internet might impact on trade in the future and the challenges they might face.

In 1995, few retailers considered the Internet to be important as a channel to market but given the potential of Internet technologies to radically reconfigure the underlying processes of retailing, and because of the highly dynamic and innovative nature of the electronic marketplace, some companies began to test out online trading. Tesco began selling chocolates and flowers, and soon afterwards Sainsbury's and Dixons launched websites. Retailers in well-developed nations, particularly in the US and northern Europe, have spent recent years working out how to best use this new digital phenomenon to support and develop retail trading.

By 2008 most retailers considered it essential to have a website and the majority also offer their customers the option to shop online and where relevant, reserve and collect in-store. Online retailing has become increasingly popular and important to retailers and consumers around the world. In the UK, during the last ten years, the online shopping spend has increased to around 20 per cent of total annual retail sales.

E-retail formats and operational strategies

The introduction of online shopping has made classifying retailers by operational formats an increasingly complex task. Traditionally, retailers are classified by: types of retail organisation, e.g., multiples, independent, co-operative; format, e.g., store-based, home-based and each of these features of the operation can also be modified by the breadth and depth of product range offered, target markets served and number of outlets operated. Arguably, online shopping formats have evolved as part of the *natural* progression of the retail life cycle. Davidson *et al.*, (1976) introduced the idea of the retail lifecycle to explain the evolution of forms of retailing over time. Based on the premise that styles of retail operation have a lifecycle in much the same way products do and will start from an *introductory* phase where the operational style is innovative, and then move through into a *growth* stage as the business expands, into a *maturity* stage where the company begins to see greater profitability and then finally into *decline* stage, where the business is overtaken by more innovative competitors offering different retail styles and operational formats.

Operational categories

To begin to understand the operational styles and strategies of online retailers it is important to consider three main operational categories:

- *Bricks-and-clicks retailers* are generally long-established retailers operating from bricks-and-mortar stores in, say, the high street and then the Internet is integrated into their businesses either strategically or tactically as a marketing tool or a sales channel. According to Dennis *et al.* (2004) online shoppers prefer shopping at websites operated by established high-street retailers as they understand what a brand means in terms of value and the physical part of the operation gives an increased sense of security.
- *Clicks-and-mortar retailers* tend to be virtual merchants and design their operating format to accommodate consumer demands by trading online supported by a physical distribution infrastructure. Virtual channels have distinct advantages over traditional marketing channels in that they potentially reduce barriers to entry. The location issue, considered to be the key determinant of retail patronage (Finn and Louviere, 1990), is in the physical sense reduced, along with the need for sizeable capital investment in stores. The best-known virtual merchant using this format is Amazon.com, the world's largest online bookstore.
- *Pureplay retailers* – 'clicks-only' or virtual retailers operate entirely online. In reality it is almost impossible for a business to operate online without a point of access to the Internet. Therefore, generally speaking, the term 'pureplay' refers to retailers who do not have fixed-location stores and or own physical operational support systems, e.g. distribution warehouses. While this category has produced some very innovative retailers, in reality

few retailers actually outsource all warehousing, picking, packing, shipping, returns and replenishment requirement. Perhaps the key difference between these two com-panies is that one sells products and the other services. In the case of services, the customer takes themselves to the point of consumption rather than having goods delivered to their door. Other companies which fit this category are those which sell products in digitised form (Dennis *et al.*, 2004). The example of digitised products and the services industry is discussed in more detail in Chapter 12.

In addition to these three operational categories, there are new types of business that are targeting consumer markets. The growth in importance of *intermediaries* has led to the use of the term 'reintermediation' (see Chapter 1). In this case companies, not traditionally service shoppers, use the Internet and the web to connect buyers and sellers through the web and by e-mail. Shopping comparison and review sites such as Kelkoo (**www.kelkoo.com**) and Revoo (**www.revoo.com**) are in this category.

For many smaller retailers, making products available through marketplaces on other larger retail platforms can be significant. For example, 3M has a small retail operation at **www.3mselect.co.uk**, but is able to reach more shoppers through Amazon and eBay where awareness is achieved through it's products appearing in search results on these platforms. **Facebook commerce** (F-commerce) is another retail format possibility that became possible in 2011.

Facebook commerce (F-commerce)
Retailers create an online store within Facebook, often with a limited range of stock.

Manufacturers of consumer goods have also seen the opportunities offered by using the Internet as a sales channel to regain some of their power lost to the retailers in the past by the shortening of distribution channels. The process of disintermediation works by the manufac-turer excluding the retailer altogether and marketing directly to the customer, thus shortening the value chain and/or the supply chain by trading electronically and shifting the balance of power closer to the end-consumer. Early examples of disintermediation originated within the banking industry, when it was noticed that information technology and industry regulation had reduced the need for retail banks as intermediaries.

E-retailing operational strategies

The Internet trading environment is largely still in its introduction phase and as a result e-retailing is still evolving. Retail growth figures suggest that virtual merchants (brick-and-clicks, pureplays, intermediaries) are proving to be highly successful, while established retailers operating from fixed-location stores could find themselves increasingly being replaced by Internet-based retail formats. The implications are considerable, as the provision of online shopping is beginning to fundamentally alter the way that consumers shop, and in doing so revolutionise the retail environment.

Let's now look at models of how online retail presences can develop as company experience with the channel evolves. Dutch researchers Weltevreden and Boschma (2008) have devel-oped a capability typology which categorises potential operational strategies that retailers and other consumer formats might adopt and develop into information-based and sales-based (Table 11.3).

Information only strategies (adapted from Weltevreden et al., 2005)

- *Billboards strategy*: retailers use this type of website to provide information primarily to make customers aware of the company's existence. The site will not provide specific product information and only gives limited details about services offered.
- *Brochure strategy*: this type of website acts as a showcase providing information with a little more detail of specific products, say, new product lines.
- *Catalogue strategy*: this type of website provides detailed product information but offers little in terms of additional services.
- *Service strategy*: this type of website provides customers with access to a range of support services which can help build and develop customer relationships, e.g. searchable database of customer support information.

Table 11.3 Internet operational strategies

Strategy	Product information	Synergies/ additional services	Online sales physical channel(s)	Physical outlets	Website resembles	Physical outlets have limited functions
Billboard	None	None/limited	No	Yes	–	No
Brochure	Limited	None/limited	No	Yes	–	No
Catalogue	Extensive	None/limited	No	Yes	–	No
Service	Limited/extensive	Extensive	No	Yes	–	No
Export	Extensive	None/limited	Yes	Yes	No similarity	No
Mirror	Extensive	None/limited	Yes	Yes	Strong similarity	No
Synergy	Extensive	Extensive	Yes	Yes	Similarity	No
Anti-mirror	Extensive	None/limited	Yes	Yes	Similarity	Yes
Virtual	Extensive	Limited/ extensive	Yes	No	–	–

Source: Adapted from Weltevreden *et al.* (2005)

Online sales strategies

- *Export strategy*: in this case retailers sell online but the operation has no linkages to the physical retail presence the retailer may have in the high street. This strategy is sometimes adopted when entering a new market and can limit risk for a well-established brand.
- *Mirror strategy*: in this case a website has the look and feel of a retailer's offline operation but there are no linkages between the online and offline channel. The website is almost like an additional store.
- *Synergy strategy*: in this case there are strong links between the online and offline operations, e.g. cross-promotions, returns of goods ordered online can be taken back into the physical store.
- *Anti-mirror strategy*: here the website has become the dominant sales channel and physical stores are used to support the web operation rather than the other way around.
- *Virtual strategy*: the retailer either gives up the physical presence or does not develop one. It should be noted that in this case the distinction between category and strategy becomes blurred.

Perhaps the key question is how do retailers select the right strategy to adopt? There is a pattern of retail adoption, whereby retailers move from information-based strategies to online sales strategies. Traditional retailers are likely to begin by having an information-based website and then develop services before offering online sales. Typically, a newly established retail website aims to cover a range of business objectives but is likely to show limited evidence of targeting of content towards specific online consumers. However, as the web usage develops, the focus and strategic contribution of the online channels change. Figure 11.3 suggests how the strategic focus might change over time.

Retail channel
Retailers' use of the Internet as both a communication and a transactional channel concurrently in business-to-consumer markets.

As retailers develop their usage of the Internet for providing information, customer services and online sales it becomes a **retail channel**. This term was introduced by Doherty *et al.* (1999) to describe companies' multi-purpose adoption of the Internet, using it as both a communication and transactional channel concurrently in business-to-consumer markets. Traditionally the term *channel* describes the flow of a product from source to end-user. This definition implies a passive unidirectional system whereby the manufacturer or producer

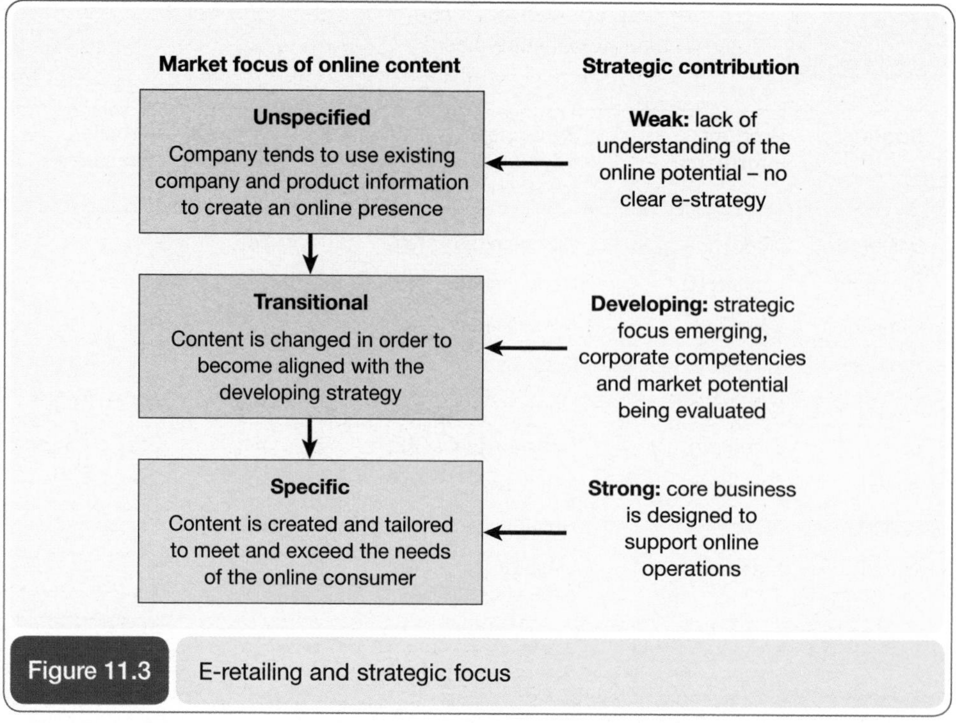

Figure 11.3 E-retailing and strategic focus

markets through a wholesaler or retailer to the consumer. This move may also suggest a shift towards a bidirectional retailer–consumer relationship, in which more power accrues to the customer (Hagel and Armstrong, 1997). As a result of the technological capacity e-retailers are becoming increasingly creative with how they are using the Internet and associated digital technologies to serve the needs of their customers. A high proportion of customers are multichannel customers who combine research based on use of a website with physical stores when making a purchase.

Implications for e-retail marketing strategy

For the retailer, the impact of an increasing number of consumers and businesses accepting the Internet and other forms of digital media as a stable channel to market is an increase in customer expectations, which creates competitive pressures and challenges. In part, this has been caused by new market entrants that have established their market position by, say, offering very wide and deep product choice, dynamic demand-driven pricing or instantaneous real-time purchase and delivery. The result is retailers are required to adopt a more dynamic and flexible approach to dealing with these raised expectations. Allegra Strategies (2005) identified a number of performance gaps and Table 11.4 presents some of the most significant gaps and the managerial implications.

For the e-retailers it is important to identify any performance gaps and develop strategies which help to close them. For example, in the case of logistics, research has found that utilising carriers (road haulage, air freight) that have higher levels of positive consumer awareness with appropriate online strategies (i.e. offering a choice of carriers) can contribute to the consumer's willingness to buy and overall satisfaction with the online buying experience. Therefore, development of strong awareness and brand image among consumers can prove to be a beneficial strategy for both the e-retailer and the carrier, since consumers have traditionally carried out the home delivery function themselves (i.e. shopping in 'brick-and-mortar' retail stores). Of course, this in itself raises the expectations of the care taken by the delivery agent, which has the implication of having to introduce better handling of goods as well as the speed with which the goods need to be delivered (Esper *et al.*, 2003). A further consideration is that the retailer and the chosen carrier need to be able jointly to satisfy the consumer so that they may benefit from co-branding.

Table 11.4 Performance gaps and managerial implications

Performance gap	Commentary	Managerial implications
The disparity between brand strength and website offer	• The gap between Internet use and the lack of website development means there is still the potential to capture browse and buy behaviour	• Companies need to develop websites to meet consumer expectations capture this behaviour • A failure to do so will result in lost sales as consumers browse and/ or buy elsewhere, i.e. the effect is both 'on' and 'off' line
The disparity between brand strength offline and online	• Retailer brand strength is frequently not reflected online. This may dilute current brand perception and leaves an opening for competitors to establish a stronger online brand presence even if they are weaker 'offline'	• The first 'dot-com' wave was concerned with establishing first mover advantage. This second wave is concerned with 'bricks-and-mortar' retailers establishing their brand strengths online, i.e. a 'brand' wave • Any lack of investment will deliver mind share advantages to competitors even if they have a lesser brand. In this second wave it will be difficult to recover a competitive position once any brand advantage has been lost
A lack of alignment between the nature of the online competitive environment and the maturity of consumer demand	• The most advanced entrants are from overseas or national catalogue companies, the larger retailers (to a variable extent) and specialist niche companies	• The market is still at an early stage in many retail categories. There remains a potential competitive advantage for a 'bricks-and-mortar' retailer to 'grab this window of opportunity'
Inertia in decision making	• There is a 'battle for budgets' within retailers, i.e. retrench and invest in core business at the expense of new channels • Some retail cultures run counter to non-traditional means of 'doing business'	• Barriers to customer contact need to be removed. Budgetary constraints are misaligned where the cost of doing nothing means lost opportunity at best, and at worst lost competitive advantage • The maturing outsourcing market may unblock the cost–benefit perception

Source: Allegra Strategies (2005)

How the online consumer accesses retailers' goods has given rise to various operational formats (discussed earlier in the chapter) and distribution strategies but this only forms part of the retailers e-strategy. Nicholls and Watson (2005) discuss the importance of creating e-value in order to develop profitable and long-term strategies and agree that logistics and fulfilment is a core element of online value creation but at two other important platforms: firm structure, and marketing and sales.

Firm structure can be used strategically depending on organisational capabilities and technology infrastructure. Porter (2001) described the emergence of integration and the potential impact on e-value chains. Integration can ensure faster decision making, more flexibility and attract suitable e-management specialists and capital investment (Nicholls and Watson, 2005). In the case of the UK grocery sector, larger retailers have adopted different approaches towards structuring their online operations. See Case study 11 for a detailed discussion of how ASDA, Morrisons, Sainsbury, Tesco and Waitrose have each adopted different strategic pathways to the development of online activities.

Marketing and sales can be used in customer-centric value creation strategies in the form of interactive marketing communications strategies (see Chapter 9 for a detailed discussion) and revenue streams. Indeed according to Dennis *et al.* (2004) there are four revenue stream business models, which in turn are based on advertising, merchandising and sales, transaction fees and subscriptions.

Strategic implications for retailers wishing to be successful online are far reaching and require a retailer to develop a carefully informed strategy, which is guided by a business model that can satisfy corporate objectives through the deriving value from corporate capabilities while effectively meeting the expectations of the online consumer. The target market and the product category can have a significant influence on success.

In conclusion, it is now widely acknowledged that there is a need for a company to have a coherent e-retail strategy underpinned by a clear vision of how to create sustained competitive advantage if a business is to gain the maximum benefits from operating online. An online retailer's strategy is likely to be affected by the category and operational strategy it adopts, the type of products and services it sells and the market segments it chooses to serve. Traditional offline retailers will need to defend their existing market share as new entrants online are increasingly shaping the future of the Internet as a retail environment. Retailers need to ensure that the value created by e-retailing is additional rather than a redistribution of profitability. It has been suggested that by removing the physical aspects of the retail offer the Internet increases competition.

Case Study 11 ASOS reinvents fashion retail

In the past, it has been suggested that it is not possible to develop a successful online fashion business. However, ASOS has grown into the UK's largest online fashion retailer in just under a decade. Indeed the ASOS Annual Report for 2011 proclaimed that 'Asos was the third most visited fashion website on the planet'. It averages 13 million unique visitors a month with 5.3 million registered users and 3.2 million active customers (defined as having shopped in the last 12 months). The main site **www.asos.com** targets the original UK market, but it is now growing share in other markets including France (**www.asos.fr**), Germany (**www.asos.de**) and the USA (**www.us.asos.com**). It has increased its country delivery list to 196.

The company's competitive strategy aimed at developing a unique market position by selling a specialist range of products, which have 'the designer fashion look'. Nick Robertson, the company's founder, started selling branded clothing as seen in films and on television. Not only did this enable to company the opportunity to create a market but it also benefited from celebrity endorsements in PR and promotional campaigns. ASOS now sells over 50,000 branded and own label clothing products and offers a much wider product range than its high street competitors. ASOS operates as a fast fashion retailer which has meant overcoming many challenges to get goods to the customers on time and at the same time manage the high rate of returns. ASOS, has set up systems which enable product lines to be replaced quickly. Operating at this level creates many challenges for ASOS so in order to deliver their promise of fast designer look fashion, and to constantly update product ranges ASOS has established an 'in-house' design team in Europe, which create catwalk lookalike items that are produced close to the customers, which aids delivery, and helps the higher returns rate of operating online rather than in-store.

> *ASOS introduced an 'independent designer section', which we established to provide a shop window to new design talent, has been very successful, and we plan to add an additional 30 designers to the 16 designers with whom we currently work.*
>
> *The most significant development in 2008/9, however, will be the launch of our branded clearance section, ASOSRed. eBay has proved that the Internet can be a very efficient channel for clearing end-of-season and markdown stock. We also know from research that eBay and other sites where this type of stock is available are popular with our customers. We firmly believe that by applying the ASOS presentation techniques to this end of season stock we will be able to enhance the image of the brands and the product and provide an overall better customer experience.*
>
> *The offer will initially consist of approximately 20 brands, expanding to around 50 brands within six months.*

Online value proposition

Product choice is at the core of the ASOS proposition with tens of thousands of branded and own-label products available with hundreds introduced each week. On pricing, ASOS is price competitive with its Price Promise (a price match offer): if you see a branded (non-Asos) product cheaper on another website, they will match that price. Asos describes its website as 'evolving constantly as we find better ways of presenting our products'. The essence of the brand communicated in its annual report is 'restless innovation for our customers'. The main elements which ASOS aspires to are: 'Inspire and power your fashion discovery'.

Other elements of the 'brand wheel' (see Figure 11.4) are:

- *External*: The world's best fashion, the best fashion experience, the service I want, inspire and engage me.
- *Internal*: Passionate about people, continuous improvement, fashion with integrity.

In 2010 ASOS.com launched its marketplace platform, which enables boutiques, vintage collectors, individuals and designers – established or unknown – to trade from their own virtual market stalls to customers across the world. It differs from other online marketplaces like eBay and Amazon in that each vendor can customise their shop front and, for £50 each month, will have access to an account manager at ASOS and some premium promotional spots on Marketplace.

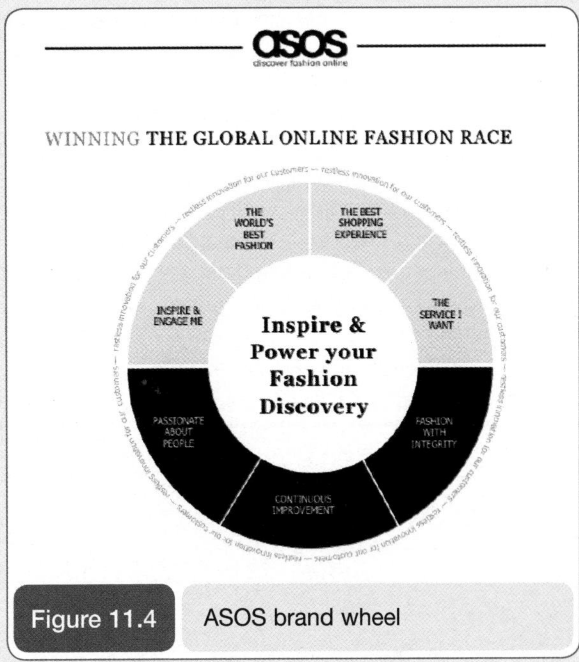

Figure 11.4 ASOS brand wheel

ASOS Service

Working with their logistics partner Unipart, Asos say they have been able to improve the speed and accuracy of deliveries to customers. Today, 95 per cent of all orders placed before 2.30 p.m. leave the warehouse the same day, even if the customer has not opted for next day delivery.

This has had the effect of moving the standard delivery terms from 3–4 days to 1–2 days. In October 2008 new delivery options were introduced including a named day service, including Saturday and both a.m. and p.m. delivery options. ASOS reported that they had invested in a customer contact management system which will enable us to respond to our customer care e-mails quicker and more efficiently. They also extended the customer care working hours to enable us to reduce the average response time from 60 minutes to 30 minutes.

Partnerships

Promotional tie-ups and associations are very important to ASOS. In June 2008 they launched a limited 100 design collaboration with the London College of Fashion. A capsule collection of 100 one-off pieces each sold on the ASOS website. The promotion received media coverage including two full page features in the national press. The collection sold out in minutes.

Marketing communications

In 2011 the ASOS magazine had a circulation of nearly 500,000. ASOS don't publish details of their online marketing, although they do invest in Google AdWords.

They are now less reliant on affiliate marketing which at one point contributed 30 per cent of revenue. There is much discussion about the value of this. Nick Robertson of ASOS said at the time of stopping the programme (in an incident known in affiliate marketing circles as 'Grubbygate') 'I'm not saying we couldn't do more in the online marketing space. Next year we'll reintroduce affiliate marketing, but as it should be. No silly commissions being paid to grubby little people in grubby studios growing income at our expense, getting in the way of genuine sales.'

Jess Luthi who previously worked on the programme justified investment as follows:

> *Affiliate refers a new visitor (average order basket at the beginning £35.00) affiliates gets £3.50 + network @ £1.05 = total commission payable £4.55. So its cost ASOS £4.55 for acquiring a new customer? Nope not quite, let's say a customer comes back and orders a further (I will be very generous here) say three times within the cookie of (I cant remember if it was 90 or 120, lets say 120 days) lets keep the basket at £35.00. This new customer has just cost ASOS £18.20 in total, after the cookie expires ASOS own the customer. If we take into account for overheads, let's say the customer cost ASOS, £20.20 (I have added £2.00 for odds and ends). But the customer has bought goods x 4 (goods have mark ups, they are not selling at cost) ASOS could not as long as I was there tell me what the life time value of a customer was, thing is they didn't know then.*

Search marketing

The range of terms ASOS target for search are evident from the <title> and description tags on their home page which are also used to communicate key brand messages:

> <title>ASOS | Shop women's fashion & men's clothing | Free Delivery & Returns</title>
>
> <meta name="Description" content="Discover the latest in women's fashion and men's clothing online. Shop from over 40,000 styles, including dresses, jeans, shoes and accessories from ASOS and over 800 brands. ASOS brings you the best fashion clothes online." />

Social media marketing

The company has made a significant commitment to community on its own site through the ASOS blogs at **http://community.asos.com/** and the social network sites where it has over 1.3 million Likes on Facebook. It runs regular events promoted integrated across the social networks and e-mail such as #ASOSSavvySunday:

> Look out for our weekly half-price timed sales, starting with the Big Dress Drop this Sunday at 6pm (London time). Naturally, our Facebook fans get exclusive early access to the sale at 5 p.m. BST.
>
> Not only that, but you get to choose – pick your favourite dresses and we'll add the five most popular into the sale at 50% off!
>
> What are you waiting for? Register here >> **http://asos.to/SavvySunday1**'

How ASOS target customers through e-mail marketing

According to the 2008 annual report, e-mail marketing accounted for 9 per cent of sales. Hash Ladha, the ASOS marketing and operations director, told *The Marketer* magazine in April 2009 that 'with 20,000 products live on the site at any time and 800 new product lines being added every week, that it's crucial that a customer's marketing message is personalised to include the kind of items they are most likely to buy'.

They have used the SmartFocus CRM system to define eight different customer types based on purchasing habits including frequent shoppers and those who bought specific brands. There are five female and three male customer profiles that identify a customer's propensity to spend (a value-based segmentation), their trigger points and whether they tend to shop at the weekend or during the week.

ASOS also ensures that its communications only include items in the appropriate spending bracket since there is a spectrum of goods on sale from bracelets for £5 to £1000 designer handbags. Through data mining, ASOS can even consider the customer's favourite colour.

The communications strategy integrates both online and offline media through:

- a print magazine sent to 500,000 active customers to encourage loyalty with some content repurposed as a 24-page supplement in magazines such as *Glamour* and *Cosmopolitan*.
- twice-weekly newsletters sent to the site's two million registered users

Both of these activities are a significant investment, with a team of ten dedicated to the two weekly e-newsletters.

The approach to re-activating lapsed customers through e-mail marketing is described by Ladha: 'We have three attempts over several weeks to try to reactivate them. If this fails, we might try a discount to entice them back. After that, they would become a non-target unless we ran a separate reactivation programme'.

Basket analysis

Basket analysis approaches were described in an interview with marketing and operations director Hash Ladha: 'One of the most interesting things we found was that men tend to buy for their partners as well as themselves. We previously thought this might work the other way around.'

Using this data, e-mail content was generated by the company's in-house editorial team. Generic content included a round-up of current fashion trends and 'best buy' recommendations. The personalised content took into account favourite brands and budget, recommending items below a certain price limit. E-mails were sent twice a week. Other strategies, such as encouraging customers to refer a friend to the company, and sending viral campaigns, were also used at this time. 'Our best customers visit the site every day. Shopping habits do vary, but most customers like to browse the site between spending,' says Ladha. He adds: 'A twice weekly e-mail gives them a direct link straight to the site and keeps it fresh in customers' minds.'

ASOS also wanted to lure lapsed customers back to its website. It targeted these individuals with tailored content that aimed to remind them why they had previously shopped online for designer and high-street clothing.

Source: ASOS (2011) Annual Report, 12 months to 31 March 2011. **http://www.asosplc.com/investors/financials/annual-interim-results**

Questions

1 Describe how ASOS applies the marketing mix online?
2 Summarise the integrated communications strategy used by ASOS?
3 What risks do you think managing as ASOS expands overseas?

Summary

1 This chapter has focused on e-tailing from two perspectives: the consumer and the retailer. In doing so the chapter has raised questions about the different types of customer that shop online and the various types of retail strategies used to create an online presence.
2 Online consumer behaviour is influenced by a number of factors, which shape and influence an individual's intention to shop online and have important managerial implications for retailers when developing target marketing strategies and looking for market development opportunities.
3 The online customer profile is made up of two distinct sub-categories: classification variables, and character variables, which are ultimately used to interpret the meaning of any online shopping experiences.
4 Online consumer behaviour is made up of a set of beliefs about the Internet, that are shaped from attitudes which influence an individual's intention to shop online. Over time an individual's behaviour can be modified by positive and negative online shopping experiences.
5 Websites that do not deliver a good online experience are unlikely to succeed. E-retailers need to develop a sound understanding of who their customers are and how best to deliver satisfaction via the Internet. In the future, more retailers may begin to develop more strategically focused websites, integrated into support systems.
6 Trading via the Internet challenges e-retailers to pay close attention to the online markets they want to serve and to understand that there are differences between the on- and offline customer expectations.
7 Website quality is important as it is a key determinant of customer satisfaction and eventually customer loyalty.
8 Given current levels of growth in adoption from both consumers and retailers, the Internet is developing into a well-established retail channel that provides an innovative and interactive medium for communications and transactions between e-retail businesses and online consumers.
9 The Internet and web present opportunities for companies to adopt different online retail formats to satisfy their customer needs, which may include a mix of Internet and physical-world offerings, e.g. bricks-and-mortar and pureplay retailers.

10 Retailers have developed a range of different strategies for using the web to interact with consumers from electronic billboards providing information to highly integrated online shopping and communication channels.

11 The virtual environment created by the Internet and associated technologies is a growing trading platform for retailing. This arena is increasing both in terms of the number of retail businesses that are online and the extent to which the Internet is being integrated into almost every aspect of a retailer's operations. As a result retailers must choose how they can best employ the Internet in order to serve their customers, rather than whether to adopt the Internet at all.

12 There are strategic advantages to be gained from deploying Internet technologies efficiently and effectively. Leading grocery retailers in the UK have demonstrated some of the opportunities for creating a sustained competitive advantage online based on various applications of IT resources and associated company capabilities.

Exercises

Going shopping online (based on consumer decision behaviour presented by Jobber (2007))

Select a product or service of your choice that you are about to, or would like to be able to, purchase. Visit as many websites as required until you find a product or service that could meet your needs if you were to make a purchase. Make sure you take note of all the sites you visit, the amount of time spent on each site and the type of information you might need to help you make your product/service choice.

Now try to analyse your online shopping experience by answering the following questions:

Questions	Possible solutions
1 What was the problem you were seeking to solve?	(a) If you were looking for a new pair of stylish sports shoes your problem could be defined as an image problem (b) If you were looking for a train ticket to get to work when your car is being serviced your problem could be defined as a lack of transport problem
2 What was the extent of your information searching?	How many websites did you visit? Did you think about consulting other sources of information? During this phase of the buying process we tend to build up an awareness set of possible brands which might solve our purchasing problem
3 What were the choice criteria which informed your decision making?	The next step is to reduce the possible options into a set of product choices you might actually consider purchasing. Then we screen our reduced choices using choice criteria to identify the final choice. You might have used, price or reliability to do this evaluation – alternatively you might have considered time (for example, where looking for a train ticket to get to work when your car is being serviced your problem could be defined as a 'lack of transport' problem)
4 What was your purchase solution (your preferred product or service)?	This is the site you would be most likely to purchase from.
5 Evaluate the websites you have visited in terms of how easy it was to find the information you needed to make your purchasing decision	Define the criteria which you used to select your answer in 4. You may want to refer back to the WEBQUAL criteria in Chapter 7.

Self-assessment exercises

1. Make a list of classification variables, which a retailer might use when trying to identify an online target market for (a) high-tech training shoes, (b) organic beauty products.
2. Explain the difference between 'classification' and 'character' variables.
3. Describe three different strategies an e-retailer might develop when creating an online presence.
4. Describe the different types of formats an online retailer might follow.
5. From a resource-based view, explain the difference between 'resources' and 'capabilities'.

Essay and discussion questions

1. Discuss whether you consider that all products on sale in the high street can be sold as easily via the Internet.
2. Select three websites that demonstrate the different ways in which a retailer might use the Internet to interact with its customers. Compare the contents of the websites and explain what the potential benefits are for the customers of each of the sites.

Examination questions

1. It was once predicted that the Internet would replace high street stores and that within ten years the majority of retail purchases would be made online. However, while online shopping is continuing to grow year-on-year it still represents a small part of the total retail spend. Explain why the early predictions have not been met from either the perspective of the consumer or the retailer.
2. Tesco.com has established a position of being the world's leading online grocer with an estimated sales turnover of £401 million and profits up 37 per cent to £21 million (as at 21 September 2005). However, Iceland was the first UK retailer to offer nationwide delivery of a range of groceries ordered via the web yet they have ceased to offer this service. Discuss why Tesco.com has been able to establish such a dominant market position.

References

Allegra (2005) Allegra Strategies Limited, London WC2N 5BW.

Bauer, R. (1960) Consumer behaviour as risk taking, *Proceedings of the American Marketing Association*, December, 389–98.

Davidson, W., Bates, A. and Bass, S. (1976) The Retail Life Cycle, *Harvard Business Review*, 54(6), 89–96.

Davis, F.D. (1993) User acceptance of information technology: system characteristics and behavioural aspects, *International Journal of Man–Machine Studies*, 38(3), 475–87.

Dennis, C., Fenech, T. and Merrilees, B. (2004) *E-retailing*, Routledge, Taylor and Francis Group, London.

Doherty, N.F. and Ellis-Chadwick, F.E. (2006) New perspective in Internet retailing: a review and strategic critique of the field, *International Journal of Retail and Distribution Management*, 24(4/5), 389–411.

Doherty, N.F., Ellis-Chadwick, F.E. and Hart, C.A. (1999) Cyber retailing in the UK: the potential of the Internet as a retail channel, *International Journal of Retail and Distribution Management*, 27(1), 22–36.

Esper, T., Jensen, T., Turnipseed, F. and Burton, S. (2003) The last mile: an examination of effects of online retail delivery strategies on consumers, *Journal of Business Logistics*, 24(2), 177.

Finn, A. and Louviere, J. (1990) Shopping centre patronage models; fashioning a consideration set segmentation solution, *Journal of Business Research*, 21, 277–88.

Hagel, J. III and Armstrong, A.G. (1997) *Net Gain – Expanding Markets through Virtual Communities*, Harvard Business School Press, Boston.

Hoffman, D., Novak, T. and Venkatesh, A. (2004) Has the Internet become indispensable? *Communications of the ACM*, July, 47(7), 37–42.

Jobber, D. (2007) *Principles and Practice of Marketing*, McGraw-Hill Companies, London.

Newholm, T., McGoldrick, P., Keeling, K., Macaulay, L. and Doherty, J. (2004) Multi-story trust and online retailer strategies, *The International Review of Retail, Distribution and Consumer Research*, October, 14(4), 437–56.

Nicholls, A. and Watson, A. (2005), *Implementing e-value strategies in UK retailing, International Journal of Retail and Distribution Management*, 33(6) 426–43.

Perea, T., Dellaret, B. and Ruyter, K. (2004) What drives consumers to shop online? A literature review, *International Journal of Service and Industry Management*, 15(1), 102–21.

Porter, M. (2001) Strategy and the Internet, *Harvard Business Review*, March, 62–78.

Rigby, E. (2005) Tesco to open online grocery warehouse, *Financial Times*, No. 27 October, 22.

Source, P., Perotti, V. and Widrick, S. (2005) Attitude and age differences in online buying, *International Journal of Retail and Distribution Management*, 33(2), 122–32.

Srinivasan, S., Anderson, R. and Ponnavolu, K. (2002) Customer loyalty in e-commerce: an exploration of its antecedents and consequences, *Journal of Retailing*, 78, 41–50.

Stone, R. and Gronhaug, K. (1993) Perceived risk: further considerations for the marketing discipline, *European Journal of Marketing*, 27(3), 39–50.

Szymanski, D. and Hise, R. (2000) E-satisfaction: an initial examination, *Journal Retailing*, 76(3), 309–322.

Weltevreden, J.W.J., Atzema, O.A.L.C and Boschma, R.A. (2005) The adoption of the Internet by retailers: a new typology of strategies, *Journal of Urban Technology* 12(3), 59–87.

Weltevreden, J. and Boschma, R. (2008) Internet strategies and performance of Dutch retailers *Journal of Retailing and Consumer Services*, 15(3), 63–178.

Wolfinbarger, M. and Gilly, M. (2003) eTailQ: dimensionalising, measuring and predicting eTail quality, *Journal of Retailing*, 79, 183–98.

Further reading

Dennis, C., Fenech, T. and Merrilees, B. (2004) *E-retailing*. Routledge, Taylor and Francis Group, London.

Mohammed, R., Fisher, R., Jaworski, B. and Addison, G. (2004) *Internet Marketing 2 edn with E-commerce*. McGrawHill, Maidenhead.

Chapter 12

Business-to-business digital marketing practice

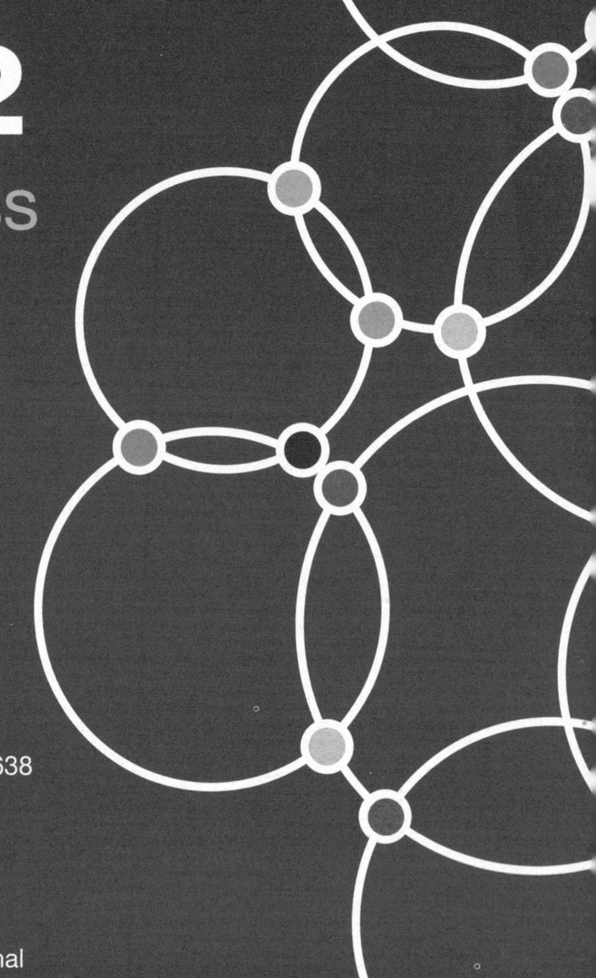

Chapter at a glance

Main topics

Case studies

Learning objectives

After reading this chapter, the reader should be able to:

- Explain the differences between online trading between business-to-business and business-to-consumer organisations
- Understand strategic options for organisations seeking to improve online efficiently and effectively identify the factors which are likely to influence whether an organisation operating in B2B markets is trading online

Questions for marketers

Key questions for marketing managers related to this chapter are:

- What are your organisation's sources of competitive advantage and are they applicable in online markets?
- How can your organisation benefit from creating online efficiency and online effectiveness?
- What is the strategic focus of your organisation's digital marketing strategy?

Scan code to find the latest updates for topics in this chapter

Links to other chapters

This chapter should be read in conjunction with these chapters:

- Chapter 2 describes the Internet micro-environment
- Chapter 3 looks at the Internet macro-environment
- Chapter 4 explores digital marketing strategy
- Chapter 5 describes the Internet and the marketing mix
- Chapter 11 examines business-to-consumer digital marketing

Introduction

Although we naturally tend to think of consumer examples when considering the potential for digital marketing, there are many ways digital marketing can support business-to-business organisations. If we return to the typology of website capabilities from Chapter 1, we can see how all of these can be relevant components for a B2B site:

- transactional e-commerce site
- services-oriented relationship-building website
- brand-building site
- portal or media site
- social network or community site

To understand how digital marketing can be best applied for B2B companies, we need to consider how the buying process operates in different B2B organisations. According to Jobber (2009), in organisational markets there are typically fewer customers who are likely to buy goods in bulk quantities and the buyer organisations tend to be larger and subsequently of great value to the supplier. What are the implications of this? Firstly, with fewer buyers the existence of suppliers and customers tends to be well known and it can be a very straightforward process to change over to web-based communications and trading. Choice criteria vary: impulse purchases, and those based on emotional motives are rare in organisational buying situations as buyers tend to be professionals who use technical and economic choice criteria to inform their decision making. This means that efforts to promote brands are different to those used for consumer brands and price setting tends to involve more negotiation between the seller and the buyer. Try Activity 12.1 to help understand the differences between B2B and B2C market characterisitics.

Activity 12.1 Which market characteristics distinguish B2B from B2C?

Purpose

To introduce the differences between B2B and B2C e-commerce that must be taken into consideration when devising strategy and tactics.

Activity

Consider how you think the characteristics summarised in the first column of Table 12.1 differ for B2C and B2B. Refer to Figure 12.1 when completing your answer.

Table 12.1 Differences in characteristics between B2B and B2C e-commerce

Characteristic	B2C	B2B
Proportion of adopters with access		
Complexity of buying decisions		
Channel		
Purchasing characteristics		
Product characteristic		
Use of content to support customers		
Use of community to support customers		

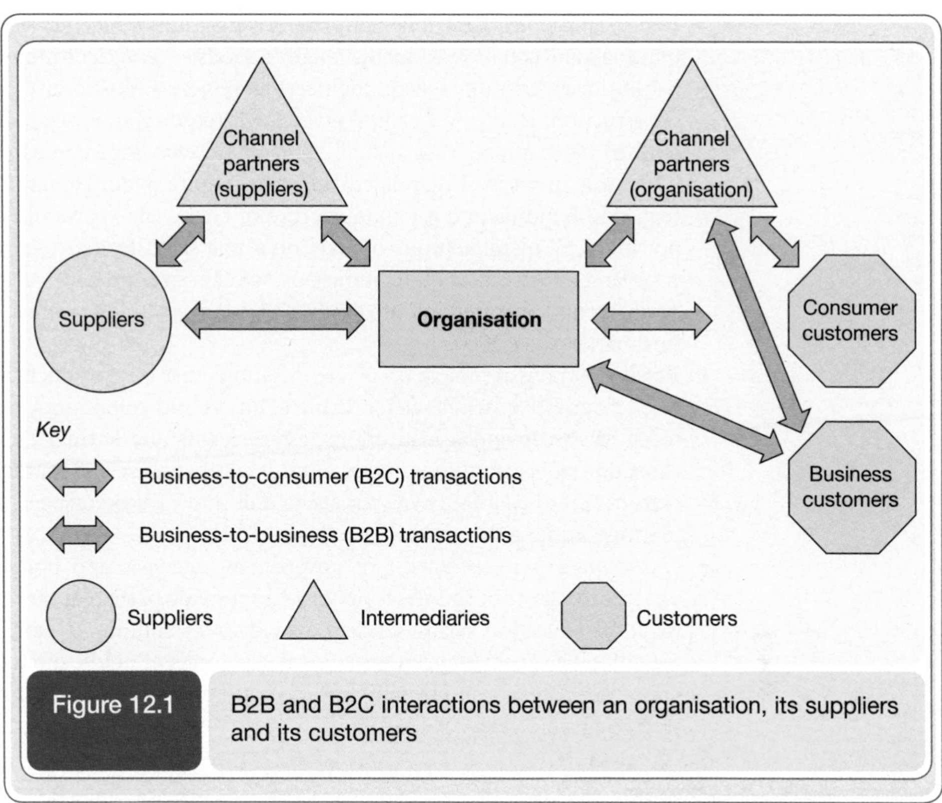

Figure 12.1 B2B and B2C interactions between an organisation, its suppliers and its customers

Kalaignanam *et al.* (2008) highlight that 'a business can leverage the potential of the Internet to enhance the *effectiveness* of its competitive strategy as well as the *efficiency* of its operations' and it is therefore important for marketing managers to be fully aware of where sources of competitive advantage can be found.

Key themes and concepts

This chapter explores business-to business (B2B) use of the Internet by focusing on:

- alternative types of B2B organisational marketing
- using digital marketing to support customer acquisition
- using digital marketing to support customer retention
- e-procurement
- electronic marketplaces
- factors that influence B2B adoption of the Internet
- the development of business strategies.

Types of B2B organisational marketing and trading environments

Traditionally, there are three main types of organisational markets in which businesses primarily trade with businesses: industrial, reseller and government. These markets cover hundreds of specialist markets which can be reviewed using Standard Industry Codes (SIC). Analysis of the main organisational markets reveals variations in company size, trading requirements, investments and trading potential. The three main types are:

- *Industrial markets* generally comprise organisations which are heavily dependent on raw materials and actually producing tangible goods – e.g. agriculture and hunting and forestry, fishing, heavy manufacturing, engineering, vehicles industry, electricity and gas supply and construction. Due to the capital investment required in many industrial sectors, markets tend to be dominated by a small number of very large companies. This is particularly noticeable in areas of manufacturing that require major capital funding and investment (e.g. ship building and the manufacture of chemicals). It should be noted that this does not mean all manufacturers operate on a vast scale. In the case of specialist engineering companies, they can be quite numerous, small in size and widely dispersed. Covisint (**www.covisint.com**), featured in Case Study 12.1, is an example of a business that has operated in this market since 2000.
- *Reseller markets* are made up of organisations that buy products and services in order to resell them – e.g. wholesalers, retailers, hotels and restaurants, transport, storage, communications, financial institutions, estate agents and letting. This covers a very diverse collection of organisations and as a result company size and market sector structures vary considerably. Euroffice (**www.euroffice.co.uk** and **www.euroffice.it**)is an example of a pureplay operating in this market (see Figure 12.2).
- *Government markets* consist of government agencies and bodies that buy goods and services to carry out specific functions and provide particular services – e.g. public administration, education, health services, armed forces, community, social and personal services activities. Government agencies control vast funds of public money generated from direct and indirect taxation. In many instances, purchasing requirements exceed those of large private commercial organisations.

Mini Case Study 12.1 Pureplay Euroffice prospers in the office supplies market

The SME office supplies market is estimated to be more than £1 billion in the UK. Euroffice was created in 1999 by founders George and Anthony Karibian and Christian Nellemann in 1999 when the online market was much smaller than today.The company now employs 49 people in both London and Milan. The majority of its suppliers are fulfilled by just three suppliers: Spicers, XMA and Kingfield Heath.

Figure 12.2 Euroffice (**www.euroffice.co.uk**)

Euroffice uses an internet-only business model. Its website offers over 27,000 products and services including office supplies, ink and toner cartridges, business machines, computer supplies, furniture and cleaning and maintenance. The core elements of its proposition evident from the site are:

- lowest price guarantee
- free next-day delivery
- free returns
- 30 day free credit accounts

The company uses state-of-the-art technologies to deliver a high level of service. It has achieved double-digit sales and triple-digit EBITDA growth, even during difficult economic downturns. Euroffice has received many industry awards and has been ranked on *The Sunday Times* Fast Track 100 on three occasions: 2004, 2005 and 2007. By 2010, Euroffice had sold to 250,000 SMEs with 80 per cent of its £30 million revenue from existing customers.

In 2009, Euroffice launched its Italian business in Milan. The following year, Darwin Private Equity acquired a majority stake in the company by backing a management buy-out (MBO) led by CEO Simon Drakeford.

Google is important to new customer acquisition with over 300,000 keywords targeted through Adwords and natural search. Euroffice has created its own bidding models and links to Google through APIs to support this. CRM is the main retention channel using email marketing and personalised web containers to target over 600 customer segments. Euroffice also has a loyalty points systems to encourage repeat customer systems and this accounts for around 10 per cent of business.

Sources: Econsultancy (2010) and company Wikipedia page

Using digital marketing to support customer acquisition in B2B marketing

The range of communications tools we introduced in Chapter 1 and detailed in Chapter 9 can also be effective in customer acquisition for B2B markets. Some of the key differences in applying these tools for B2B marketing are:

1 *Search engine marketing.* Within some specialist markets, search volumes can be much lower meaning that search marketing will deliver few leads although they can potentially be high value. Using the Google Keyword Tool (see Chapter 2) can reveal the scale of market demand. This can lead to intense competition, for example within professional services such as solicitors and lawyers leading to high cost per click in Google AdWords. In commodity B2B markets like office supplies (Mini Case Study 12.1) search volumes can be much higher and can be effective in customer acquisition.

2 *Online PR.* Given limited demand through search, online PR can be effective in generating awareness and demand for services. Content marketing based on whitepapers and videos which inform and educate are key communications tools, particularly in professional services markets (Smart Insights, 2011). According to Rene Power, five options for video marketing in B2B services include corporate videos, staff interviews or guidance, customer testimonials, video blogging and hosting conferences and presentations. Marketing Automation company Eloqua give a good example of how content marketing can be used to develop awareness through thought leadership (Figure 12.3). They have a separate resources section with a blog 'All About Revenue' acting as a content hub for different objects shared through social networks.

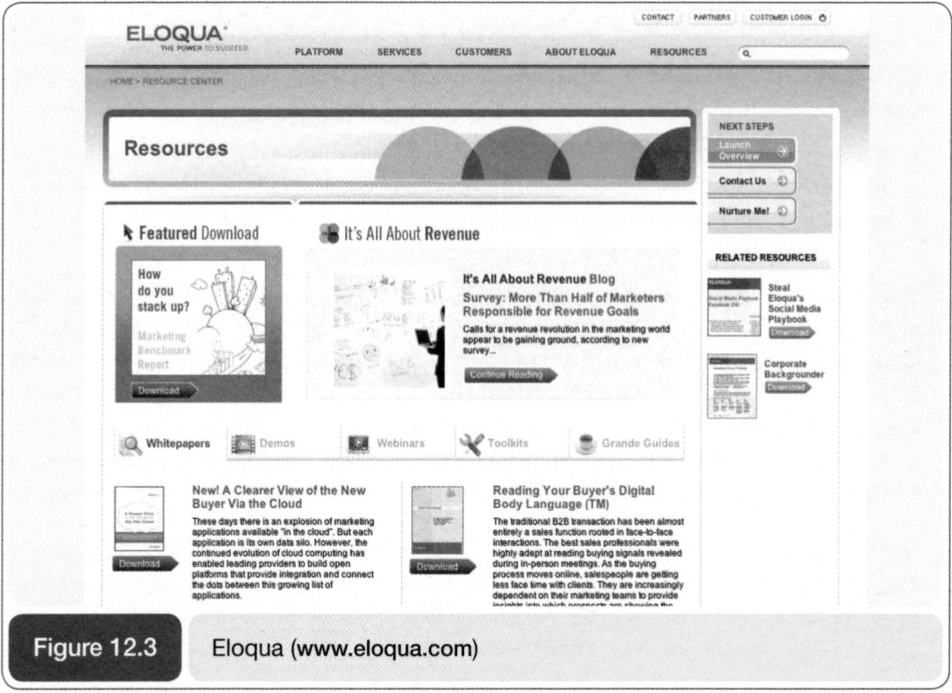

Figure 12.3 Eloqua (www.eloqua.com)

3 *Online partnerships.* Affiliate marketing tends to be less relevant for B2B marketing since the volumes available for consumer marketing aren't available to appeal to affiliates and often sites aren't e-commerce enabled. There may also be a different purchaser to specifier meaning that the affiliate can't be credited for the original lead. However, for retail B2B sites like Euroffice (Mini Case Study 12.2) affiliate marketing is still relevant. Other forms of partnership, particularly with influencers can be fruitful. For example, Eloqua has an ambassador programme with marketing commentators.

4 *Display advertising.* The use of online ads such as banners and rich media ads to achieve brand awareness and encourage click-through is equally relevant for demand generation in B2B marketers. Well known B2B brands like IBM are active in using this approach on technology trade marketing sites for instance.

5 *Opt-in e-mail marketing.* While using email to build relationships is prevalent within B2B marketing, there are options for using email for acquisition. Renting permission-based e-mail lists or placing ads in third-party e-newsletters can be effective.

6 *Social media marketing.* Specialist communities can be developed within B2B markets. For example, Eloqua have developed an independent 'TopLiners' community and they are also active within the main social networks including LinkedIn, the leading B2B social network.

Lead-generation and conversion optimisation for B2B marketing

Many business-to-business websites do not involve ecommerce transactions unlike the Euroffice example in Figure 12.2. Instead the model used is permission-based and within B2B marketing is often known as an inbound marketing or content marketing approach (explained in Chapters 1 and Chapter 6). The marketing model used to acquire customers is:

- *Stage 1.* Inbound marketing focusing on search, online PR and display advertising used to attract website visits.
- *Stage 2.* Engagement devices such as video, whitepapers or other forms of market education material is used to encourage the visitor to interact with site and share information via social media.

- *Stage 3.* Offering access to permission-based content valuable to the visitor is used to generate leads via encouraging the visitor to register on the site, supplying an e-mail address and profile information or sharing the content via social networks.
- *Stage 4.* Leads are followed-up through personalised email sequences or where appropriate outbound phone calls where leads are qualified as valuable.

Cisco is an example of an organisation deploying many of these content marketing approaches across the different social networks and blogs as shown in Figure 12.4.

Mini Case Study 12.2 How does Cisco communicate and execute its Human Network vision in social media?

Cisco started using social media as we know it today back in 2005 when they created the blog. Today they use a range of tools which support the development of the current brand message 'together, we are the human network'. Writing on this blog, John Earnhardt, director of corporate communications says:

> *We've learned that we can have richer and more engaging conversations through social media. We are a customer-centric company that doesn't fall in love with any specific technology. We ask customers and deliver what they want. Social media helps us listen and respond.*

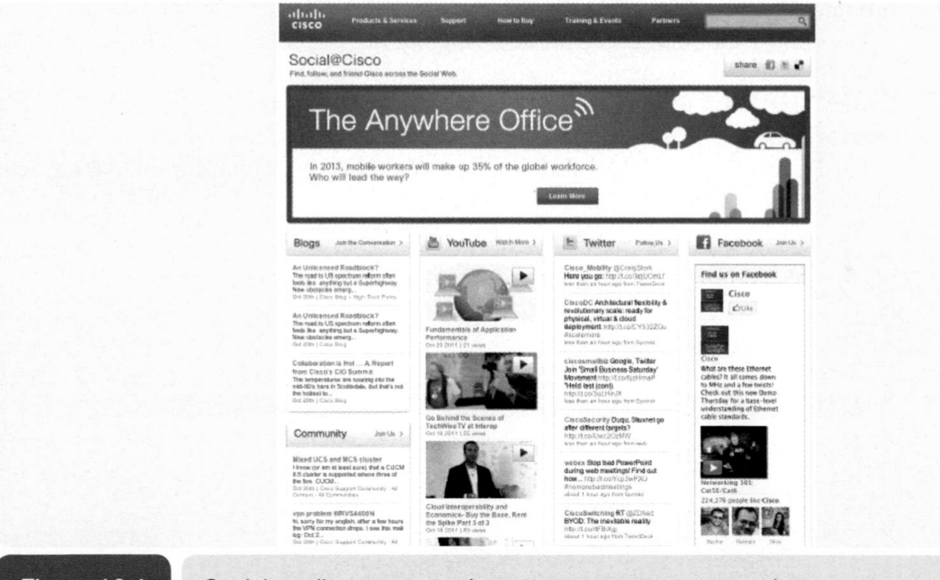

Figure 12.4 Social media aggregator (**http://socialmedia.cisco.com/**).

In 2007, Cisco started using video for press releases which are distributed on the Cisco YouTube channel: **http://www.youtube.com/CSCOPR** and **http://www.youtube.com/cisco**. One of the most popular videos was used for a campaign about 'the world's most interesting intern'. In 2008, the company's Twitter channel **http://twitter.com/#!/ciscosystems/** was started. This is mainly used for announcements previously distributed by press releases. It has nearly 100,000 followers. This was followed by the official Cisco Facebook fan page.

Today, visitors to the Cisco site can visit the social media aggregator (Figure 12.4). This gives access to all of these features:

1. *Corporate blog*. The corporate newsroom is a blog focusing on the company's latest news. It integrates the other blogs to give users easy access into the company.
2. *Twitter*. The @ciscosystems Twitter feed tweets news and information about the company, the Cisco team, and a link to Cisco's support page.

3 *Facebook*. The Cisco Facebook page appears to be more about interaction and entertainment, and ties together video and photographic media. It doesn't just provide information and news. The company also posts contests such as the current 'Super Fan' contest.
4 *YouTube*. The CISCOPR YouTube channel appears to get significant investment with well over 800 videos. There's everything from leadership and learning through to a fun series by the 'World's Most Interesting Intern'.
5 *Flickr*. Cisco's Flickr photostream has more than 50 pages of images and photos related to company events.

In addition to follow-up at Stage 4 where a user completes a form it is also possible to find some information from the IP address of some business users (technically this is known as a reverse domain lookup). Figure 12.5 shows how combining this information with analytics data about the source of the visit and type and amount of content viewed can be used for follow-up.

Customer retention in B2B marketing

Once relationships are formed, e-mail marketing is again important in maintaining a dialogue. Of course, phone and face-to-face interactions are important too. So many companies will use e-mail marketing for lower value customers and traditional channels for higher value customers.

We showed how Euroffice uses segmentation to vary offers through e-mail marketing (Chapter 4) and using the RFM analysis techniques (Chapter 6). They also use their 'Office Chatter' blog which is syndicated to Twitter to interact with their customers. This contains a blend of content such as 'deal of the day', polls and new product developments in office supplies.

Kalaignanam *et al.* (2008) also suggest three areas of relationship marketing activities where significant efficiency gains can be made:

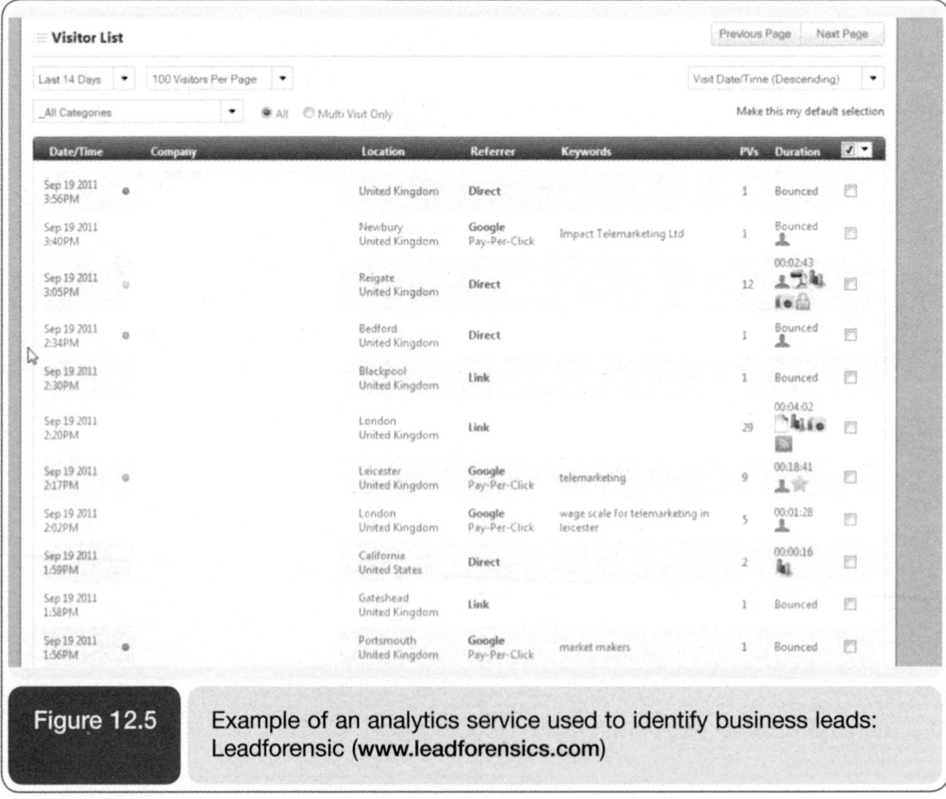

Figure 12.5 Example of an analytics service used to identify business leads: Leadforensic (www.leadforensics.com)

1 Post-sales customer relationship management

- *Buyer–seller relationships.* Relationships deepen as more and more companies become comfortable with trading in the online environment, and there is more standardisation of communication platforms through the use of Internet technologies. Buyers and sellers develop closer relationships and often work together in a very co-operative manner to achieve benefits for both parities using the Internet. Email and social media marketing can help facilitate these relationships.
- *Electronic billing* – some industries (e.g. telephone, utilities banking) serve very large customer bases (B2B and B2C) and many of the transactions are typically repeated, for instance quarterly gas bills. For such companies invoicing cost and the production of printed bills is expensive and therefore there is great potential for cost reduction through the application of electronic billing and automated payments. Euroffice featured at the start of this chapter provides tools to make placement of repeat orders more rapid.
- *Self-service technologies* – the airline industry is making significant changes to its cost base and in doing so improving levels of customer service by introducing self-service bag drops, the online check-in and getting flyers to print their own boarding cards. When linked to customer retention strategies (e.g. frequent flyer programmes) the capital cost for the installations of self-service technologies can quickly be redeemed. We self-service is commonly used by business-to-business technology companies, in particular software companies.
- *Online product registrations* – warranties are an important cue for buyers of the value of products and services; moreover, extended warranty schemes can aid customer retention rates and are responsible for a significant percentage of profits in certain industries – but operating such schemes can be very costly. Processing claims against warranties is labour-intensive and time consuming. Organisations can make significant cost savings through online product registration and warranty claim processing.
- *Online technical support* – in B2B markets customer relationship management is critically important. In high-tech industries much time can be spent dealing with teething problems resulting from the installation of a new software package. If the supplier can set up a system that can diagnose problems electronically then operating cost can be significantly reduced. Hewlett Packard and Dell are examples of companies where significant cost savings have been made as a result of using the website to distribute technical manuals and provide customer support.

2 Market research

- *Online surveys* – the cost of process is also reduced as the need for data input personnel is eliminated, and there is, potentially, improved quality due to reduction of data input errors.
- *Online focus groups* – by conducting electronic focus groups involving geographically dispersed participants, businesses can reduce information processing costs and factor costs but there are potential issues of generalisability and potential bias.

3 Knowledge sharing

- *New product development* (NPD) *knowledge sharing.* Product development cycles are generally becoming shorter and time to market much faster. The knowledge required for successfully implementing NPD projects often resides in different parts of the business, e.g. accounting, R&D, marketing or production. Consequently, an opportunity exists to leverage the Internet to facilitate sharing of intra-organisational knowledge. The Internet can be integrated into different stages of NPD for information gathering and transfer, both within and outside the organisation – e.g. customers, competitors and channel members.
- *Online advertising knowledge sharing.* The ability to digitise advertising content (e.g. artwork, audio and video files) and share it through online databases among departments

within the organisation and with advertising agencies enables streamlining of brand management and considerable savings. In the case of Coca-Cola huge efficiency gains were made by making available via the Internet over 100 years worth of corporate marketing and advertising icons. This provided easy access for anyone developing new marketing communication projects. Further benefits and efficiencies were gained by centralised storing and updating, and managing and disseminating best advertising practices. The system comprises downloadable video, photographs and marketing and advertising icons. A key benefit of the online knowledge system is that it enhances productivity gains by reusing existing brand knowledge.

- *Online sales knowledge.* Sharing information about sales leads has in the past been an inefficient, inaccurate and time-consuming activity and can result in duplication of effort. However, prospecting and qualifying sales leads and cross-referencing customers through an Internet-based contact management system can help eliminate redundancy and waste and significantly streamline the sales function. An example of other efficiencies related to the sales function occurs at trade shows. The promotional expenditure is the second largest area of spend in a business marketing communications budget and can account for as much as a quarter of the total show budget. Cost efficiencies can be made by using the Internet for pre-announcement of the show promotions, cross-promoting with other advertising and communication campaigns, using e-mail customer invitations.
- *Online service knowledge.* The Internet can be used to act as a platform to enhance the efficiency of intra-organisational learning through establishing problem–solution exchanges, e.g. online customer conflict-resolution centres.
- *Addressability.* The Internet can be used to find users and update customer databases, which can result in great efficiencies in targeting and the profitability of direct mail campaigns. Online communications offer an opportunity to create highly tailored, fast communications that can deliver high information content at comparatively low cost (Gattiker *et al.*, 2000).

Options for online inter-organisational trading

E-commerce trading between organisations usually occurs as part of the procurement process, which is part of the broader business activities of supply chain management. 'Procurement' refers to all activities involved with obtaining items from a supplier; this includes purchasing, but also inbound logistics such as transportation, goods-in and warehousing before the item is used. The key procurement activities and associated information flows within an organisation are shown in Figure 12.6. Online, this process is known as **e-procurement**.

Electronic procurement (e-procurement)
The electronic integration and management of all procurement activities including purchase request, authorization, ordering, delivery and payment between a purchaser and a supplier.

Knudsen (2003) and Smart (2010) have reviewed a simple classification of different types or applications of e-procurement. These are the main types:

1. *E-sourcing.* Finding potential new suppliers using the Internet during the information gathering step of the procurement process.
2. *E-tendering.* The process of screening suppliers and sending suppliers requests for information (RFI) or requests for price (RFP).
3. *E-informing.* Qualification of suppliers for suitability. It doesn't involve transactions but instead handles information about the supplier's quality, financial status or delivery capabilities.
4. *E-reverse auctions.* Enable the purchasing company to buy goods and services that have the lowest price or combination of lowest price and other conditions via Internet technology.
5. *E-MRO and web-based ERP.* These involve the purchase and supply of products which are the core of most e-procurement applications. The software used manages the process of creating and approving purchasing requisitions, placing orders and receiving the goods or service ordered.

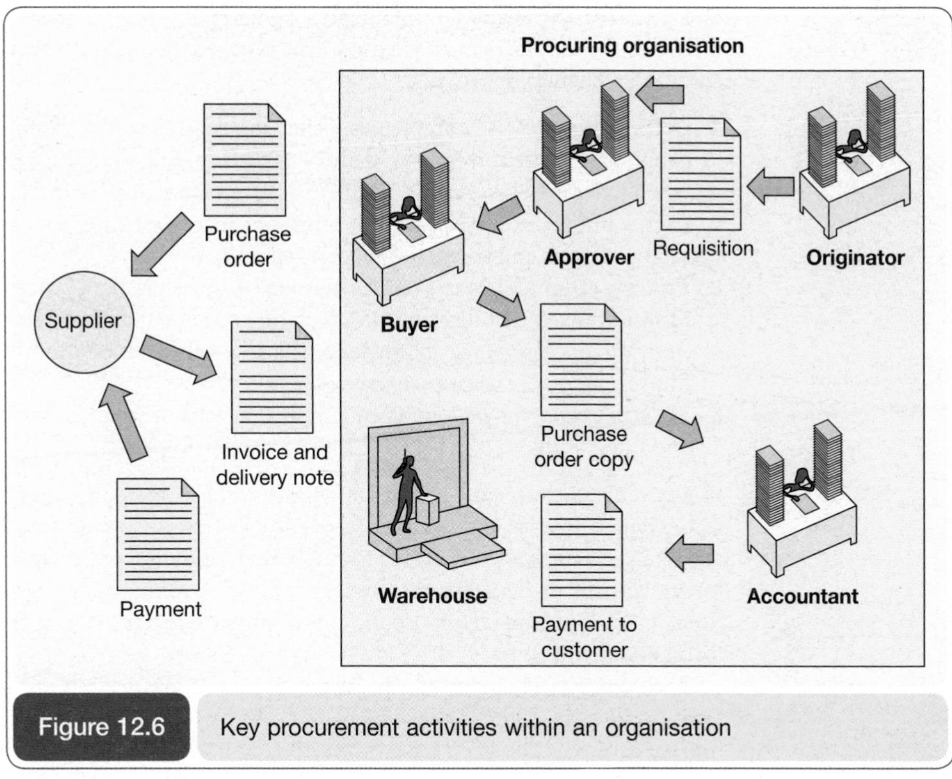

Figure 12.6 Key procurement activities within an organisation

Digital marketing insight 12.1 shows one example of a company offering an e-procurement solution.

Digital marketing insight 12.1 Perfect Commerce

In B2B markets many industrial sectors are made up of businesses which need procurement solutions. Perfect Commerce say they are able to turn purchasing into a strategic business function and this is a significant change that has come about as a result of successful application of Internet technologies. Indeed, Perfect Commerce's mission is 'power your profits' by providing bespoke procurement solutions for getting spending under control. Purchasing has become a business driver, due to the growing emphasis on efficient and effective spending. Indeed, according to Fernie *et al*. (2010) the restructuring of supply chains has been aided by the adoption of quick response systems and the rationalisation of primary distribution in conjunction with the steady growth in demand for online purchasing by shoppers. The outcome has been that Internet adoption has spread throughout the supply chain. Retailers are now using logistic solutions – like those offered by Perfect Commerce – to manage purchasing, such solutions are enabling the use of automated warehouses and inventory control (right down to the store level), which greatly reduces costs and stock holding. Internet technologies have facilitated the development of strategic sourcing tool and purchasing process that deliver significant benefits, e.g. controlling spend, increasing compliance, giving preferred suppliers greater visibility. The advantages for a retailer, for example, are that they can have a fully automated exchange system, which completely revolutionises purchasing, shipping, documentation across the supply chain. A system like the OSN can handle thousands of suppliers, millions of stock keeping units (products) and billions of pounds worth of transactions.

Source: Fernie *et al*. (2010)

Smart (2010) also reviewed the business benefits of e-procurement through case studies of three companies. He identifies five key drivers or supplier selection criteria for e-procurement adoption related to improving:

1 *Control* – improving compliance, achieving centralisation, raising standards, optimising sourcing strategy and improved auditing of data. Enhanced budgetary control is achieved through rules to limit spending and improved reporting facilities.
2 *Cost* – improved buying leverage through increased supplier competition, monitoring savings targets and transactional cost reduction.
3 *Process* – rationalising and standardisation of e-procurement processes giving reduced cycle time, improved visibility of processes for management and efficient invoice settlement.
4 *Individual performance* – knowledge sharing, value-added productivity and productivity improvements.
5 *Supplier management* – reduced supplier numbers, supplier management and selection and integration.

Process efficiencies result in less staff time spent in searching and ordering products and reconciling deliveries with invoices so potentially leading to reduced costs if employees can be reassigned. Savings also occur due to automated validation of pre-approved spending budgets for individuals or departments, leading to fewer people processing each order, and in less time. It is also possible to reduce the cost of physical materials such as specially printed order forms and invoices.

These potential benefits of e-procurement led to massive interest in the potential of electronic marketplaces to deliver these benefits. In the next section, we will review the evolution of these services.

B2B e-marketplaces

Electronic marketspace
A virtual marketplace such as the Internet in which no direct contact occurs between buyers and sellers.

Rayport and Sviokla (1995) introduced the term **electronic marketspace** and suggested the Internet created a new environment which had significant implications for the way in which businesses trade. The speed of development of computer, network and Internet technologies played a key role in the rapid expansion of the marketspace and subsequently the commercial practice of electronic trading. It should be remembered, however, that electronic trading *per se* is not a new phenomenon; commercial exchanges have taken place using electronic data interchange (EDI) and dedicated data links between organisations for several decades. Nevertheless, what is new is Internet technologies. Communication standards and protocols create a virtual trading environment where any organisation with a computer and access to the Internet has the potential to trade in global markets.

Many innovative marketplace models have developed, although the usage of marketplaces has not been as widespread as was predicted when the idea came to prominence in the late 1990s. For example, in the industrial market *e-auctions* are used by General Electric (GE) to trade with both established and non-established suppliers. The model is a web-based electronic bidding mechanism that operates in a similar way to those held in traditional auction rooms and tendering processes. In the GE case the aim is to drive costs down via a competitive, open-bidding process. The downward movement of prices is sometimes referred to as a 'reverse auction' as opposed to a bidding situation where prices are driven upwards. GE purchasing managers do not always select the lowest bid as they will assess the potential risks associated with the supplier: say, the ability to fulfil the order, quality and requirements for after-sales service issues, rejection rates and quality of goods. An emergent benefit of this model is that e-auctions allow companies to monitor competitive pricing, which helps the organisation reduce total costs.

While e-auctions focus on the sales side of purchasing, e-fulfilment focuses on the delivery of goods in a timely and appropriate fashion and is central to the re-engineering of the supply chain. According to a survey, 'fulfilment' will be an area of significant growth for businesses operating online. However, over 80 per cent of organisations cannot fulfil international orders of tangible goods because of the complexities of shipping, although there are some geographical locations (e.g. parts of Europe and Asia) that are better served by local warehouse support networks than others. Time will inevitably establish the validity of the proposition that online purchasing practices are sustainable business models.

Many different types of e-marketplaces emerged as a result of being based on different business models. Perhaps the most straightforward way to classify e-marketplaces is by type of user for example:

- *B2B independent e-marketplace* – an online platform operated by a third party which is open to buyers or sellers in a particular industry. By registering on an independent e-marketplace, members can access classified advertisements and requests for quotations or bids in a particular industrial sector. In Chapter 2 we looked at how Alibaba.com, one of the biggest online marketplaces, had developed. Members will typically be expected to pay a fee or make some form of payment.
- *Buyer-oriented e-marketplace* – an example of a portal which is normally run by a consortium of buyers in order to establish an efficient purchasing environment. Joining as a buyer, this type of marketplace can help lower, say, administrative costs or improve bargaining power with suppliers. As a supplier, an organisation can use a buyer-oriented e-marketplace to advertise and this can prove to be highly effective as the buyers will tend to be from a particular target segment.
- *Supplier-oriented e-marketplace* – sometimes known as a supplier directory, this is established and operated by a group of suppliers who are seeking to establish an efficient sales channel via the Internet to a large number of buyers. They are usually searchable by the product or service being offered. Supplier directories benefit buyers by providing information about suppliers for markets and regions they may not be familiar with. Sellers can use these types of marketplace to be found and to get leads.

Vertical and horizontal e-marketplaces provide online access to businesses vertically up and down every segment of a particular industry sector such as automotive, chemical, construction or textiles. Buying or selling using a vertical e-marketplace can increase operating efficiency and help to decrease supply chain costs, inventories and cycle time. A horizontal e-marketplace connects buyers and sellers across different industries or regions. You can use a horizontal e-marketplace to purchase indirect products such as office equipment or stationery.

In addition to e-marketplaces there are *online exchanges* or *trading hubs*, which are websites where buyers and sellers trade goods and services online and vary according to the size and number of companies using them and the type of commodity traded. There are already successful exchanges in markets as diverse as energy, textiles and logistics. Like online auctions, online exchanges allow trading between B2B organisations. Key growth factors for this type of trading environment are that large companies can use the exchanges to reduce stock holdings while small companies can bid collectively to earn volume discounts or to jointly deliver a large contract. The operational procedures can vary – for example, in some online exchanges suppliers are invited to provide a quote whereas in others buyers are invited to bid for specific products and services. In addition, there are commodity exchanges, where the price of a standardised commodity such as energy or telecoms bandwidth continuously changes as a result of changes in supply and demand. There are some important considerations for managers thinking about entering into online exchanges:

- Are all the required major suppliers already signed up to the exchange?
- Does the exchange operate a comprehensive list of products and services to facilitate price comparison?
- Could belonging to an exchange destabilise existing customer/supplier relationships?
- Does our organisation have adequate systems in place to support order fulfilment?
- What will be the effect of making information about prices and stock levels available to competitors, as well as potential customers?
- What are the cost comparisons between operating through an online exchange and existing sales and procurement systems?

An example of a trading hub is World Retail Exchange which is part of Global Sources (**www.globalsources.com**). Global Sources is an e-business solution and service within the global retail industry helping facilitate transactions with Asian suppliers through a range of tools varying from identifying and qualifying potential suppliers, to achieving agreement on product specifications, pricing and terms for purchase. This special programme provides an advantage to WWRE members in their Asian sourcing business processes.

Reasons for limited adoption of e-marketplaces

Johnson (2009) has investigated the reasons for limited adoption of online marketplaces. Based on interviews with purchasing managers in a range of sectors, he believes the most significant are potentially misguided perceptions of the benefits, risks and trust in partners. He gives one example of a marketplace servicing the aerospace and defence industry where it couldn't recruit sufficient small suppliers because the e-market charged the same fee to all suppliers regardless of their size. The e-market charged suppliers $4,000 per year to use its catalogue software tool to create their own electronic catalogues, and a yearly subscription fee of $390. Although most small suppliers could afford the subscription, many could not afford to pay $4,000 per year in order to create electronic catalogues on the e-market.

Case Study 12.1 shows the history of the automotive marketplace Covisint. This pattern of a transition from a marketplace portal to a hosted e-procurement service has been followed by other B2B marketplaces which were prominent around 2000 including CommerceOne and Ariba.

Case Study 12.1 Covisint – a typical history of a B2B marketplace?

This case studies a successful marketplace to prompt learning about what makes such a marketplace effective. It also illustrates the importance of online bidding in some industries.

The Covisint marketplace was originally created by Ford, GM and DaimlerChrysler (**www.covisint.com**). Today, Covisint is not a marketplace, but is described by its owners Compuware as a 'connectivity solution' with the strapline of 'enabling information ecosystems'. Its service is still used by motor manufacturers although they now don't use a single marketplace, rather each manufacturer uses technology to access its suppliers direct. This case study charts the evolution of the service.

2002: Covisint used extensively for bidding

Covisint (2002) described a high-level of activity on the exchange. Taking the example of DaimlerChrysler AG, 512 online bidding events processed through Covisint over a twelve-month period from 2001 to 2002. In total, this amounted to 10 billion. In May 2001, DaimlerChrysler staged the largest online bidding event ever, with an order volume of 3.5 billion in just four days. In total, 43 per cent of the total value of the parts for a future Chrysler model series was negotiated online with over 50 online bidding events in the third quarter of 2001 alone. As well as savings in material purchasing prices, DaimlerChrysler succeeded in reducing throughput times in purchasing by approximately 80 per cent, thus saving on process costs. According to Dr Rüdiger Grube, deputy member of the board of management responsible for corporate development:

> *The economic effects achieved with e-procurement in the first year of implementation have already covered the costs of previous investment in e-business and hold great potential for the future, too. Therefore, we will continue to pursue our e-business activities to the fullest extent in 2002 as well.*

With the online catalogue system 'eShop' which was part of the Covisint service at that time, DaimlerChrysler would be able to reduce process costs by 50 per cent after the completion of the blanket rollout, which would give approximately 15,000 users the possibility of ordering several millions of articles. By the end of 2002 about 1500 business partners would be connected to the electronic document exchange system 'eDocs', which would enable them to process approximately 500,000 document transmissions per year. Initial results using the 'FastCar' program for networking change management in automotive development at Chrysler show cuts in communication processes by 60–90 per cent. In 2001, over 600 managers connected to the system developed over 300 product improvement suggestions online with the 'New Product Change Management' used in the development department of Mercedes-Benz.

'e-Business activities are already closely intertwined from development through procurement, logistics, sales and marketing. To a great extent, they are already a part of everyday business', says Olaf Koch, vice president of corporate e-business. Dr Grube adds: 'We're a good deal closer to our goal of making DaimlerChrysler the first automotive company to be networked throughout the entire value chain.'

2004: Covisint purchased by Compuware

Line56 (2004) summarised the acquisition of Covisint by B2B software company Compuware. The article quotes Compuware CEO Pete Karmanos as predicting that the messaging and portal part of Covisint will contribute $20 million in 2005, and will eventually become a $100 million-plus business in the automotive industry alone. The primary e-procurement offering of Covisint is as a method of managing purchasing across the many different electronic business document formats including traditional EDI formats like ANSI X12 and EDIFACT along with XML purchasing formats such as OAGIS, STAR, RosettaNet and others. Different suppliers tend to have adopted different exchange formats, so a solution that integrates them is helpful. Covisint continues to offer a portal solution both for manufacturers and their suppliers, who in turn have tier 2 or 3 suppliers. A study for Covisint by AMR Research suggested that the Covisint Communicate service was found to help a company reduce the cost of developing and deploying a portal by up to 80 per cent and reduce the annual cost of maintenance by 50 per cent. You can see the portal solutions at: **https://portal.covisint.com/wps/public/tradingPartners/_l/en/**, one example being the Ford Supplier portal.

2008: Covisint used by more than 45,000 organisations in 96 countries

Today, Covisint describes itself as 'the leading provider of services that enable the integration of vital business information and processes between partners, customers and suppliers'. Many of its customers are still in the automotive industry, but now also in diverse industries including manufacturing, healthcare, aerospace, public-sector and financial services. The scale of operations is evident from these figures:

- translation and secure transportation over 40 million messages annually
- hosted infrastructure boasts 99.997 per cent uptime
- provides critical portal, messaging and/or security services for users at over 45,000 organisations worldwide.

For each industry it has developed specific services particular to data exchange within these industries. Covisint Connect offers EDI and web EDI facilities fore-procurement. Covisint Communicate has over 300 applications available, some typical modules of which are used by DaimlerChrysler AG including:

- *Accounts payable* – enables suppliers to research past and future payment/information, resolve issues prior to payment due dates and download document information to the desktop for further analysis.
- *Cooperative raw material acquisition* – provides suppliers with access to a cooperative raw material supply programme to leverage customers' purchasing power and maximise operational savings.
- *Product catalogue compilation tool* – collects and distributes information required to produce and update the company's catalogue of products.
- *Request for quote application* – enables customers to issue an online request for quotation process.
- *Supplier profile* – enables customers to maintain an accurate profile consisting of key information about the supplier.

Sources: Covisint web site (**www.covisint.com**); Covisint (2002) and Line56 (2004)

Question

By reviewing the case study and examples of the different supplier portals available on Covisint (www.covisint.com) explain why Covisint has prospered as a supplier of e-procurement portals and business document data exchange rather than as a neutral marketplace.

How digital technologies can support B2B marketing

For many years, it has been recognised that the Internet's power, scope and interactivity provide businesses with a unique opportunity to transform their businesses. The Internet has:

- become an important channel for promoting relationships with customers and other partners (Ansari and Mela, 2003)
- affected all of the elements of the marketing mix – promotion becomes highly interactive, pricing flexible and dynamic, products digital, and place virtual communication strategies of firms (Zettelmeyer, 2000)
- influenced the structure of the competitive market and increased trading opportunities with new partners (Varadarajan and Yadav, 2002)
- increased the capacity to deliver tangible gains through economic efficiencies (Vijayasarathy and Tyler, 1997).

How organisations make efficiency gains

Kalaignanam *et al.* (2008) have suggested there are three distinct areas where efficiency gains in marketing operations:

- *Decision information costs* – efficiencies can result from using information to facilitate decision making and reduce information processing costs.
- *Quality costs* are incurred to ensure that the products or operations conform to specifications. Internet technology can be used to significantly reduce these through gains in efficiency, – e.g. if a product does not conform to standards, the customer is likely to return the goods, which has implications for staffing, quality control and can even lead to a breakdown in customer relations.
- *Factor costs* increase in proportion to the level of activity. Traditionally, they are used in the context of production activities encompassing material and labour costs. Factor costs in marketing operations comprise labour costs, material costs and miscellaneous costs (e.g. travel and rentals).

Organisations can use the interactivity of Internet technologies to improve the efficiency of their marketing by focusing on these three types of costs.

The next section considers the factors which determine an organisation's levels of adoption of Internet technologies, which will also tend to determine its capacity to operate efficiently and effectively online.

Analysing the factors which influence the degree of adoption of Internet technologies

Some organisations have wholeheartedly embraced the use of Internet technologies whereas others 'have been far more timid either developing small scale, experimental applications or completely ignoring the Internet's potential altogether' (Ellis-Chadwick *et al.*, 2002). Table 12.2 summarises the key factors cited as affecting levels of business adoption of the Internet. It is possible to identify four key dimensions within these factors, which are likely to significantly affect online marketing planning and ultimately the effectiveness and efficiency of an organisations Internet operations. The dimensions (based on Ellis-Chadwick, 2008) are:

- *Financial dimension.* Businesses are beginning to consider carefully the Internet's potential to deliver economic gains. Ashworth *et al.* (2005) have stressed the importance of financial factors and how the extent to which business can benefit from economics of scale is likely to influence rates of Internet adoption. Businesses are also likely to evaluate the cost of operations, the availability of operational and development funding and the time line of online profitability. The outcome of analysis of financial variables is likely to critically affect the extent to which a business trades online, offers interactive services or invests in using the Internet to support its operations.
- *Operational dimension.* Grewal *et al.* (2004) highlighted the importance of the suitability of product range and the impact of logistical complexities of getting goods to buyers at acceptable costs and within an appropriate time frame as key determinants of whether businesses offer the Internet as a channel choice. For successful development of the online channel, businesses also need to have in place a suitable technological infrastructure, and a supportive and technologically integrated supply chain. A business's assessment of operational variables is likely to impact not only on the extent of development of online retail provision but also on the level of the online service provision. Other factors, which can be considered under the operational dimension, are company size and maturity and the choice of online format. Analysis of the operational factors is likely to influence the extent to which a business integrates online and offline channels.
- *Market dimension.* A business's perceptions and understanding of online market potential are cited as important indicators of the level and range of development of online market provision. Businesses tend to develop understanding of the market potential by assessing the suitability of the customer base (Grewal *et al.*, 2004). However, researchers suggest it is also important to understand the customer experience in a multichannel trading environment if the online channel is to be seriously developed. From this viewpoint, businesses should assess customers' perceived ease of use, convenience and levels of security in order to develop a realistic assessment of the market potential. Perceptions of online market potential, knowledge of markets served and market opportunities are likely to influence the extent to which businesses see the Internet as a new virtual world of trading opportunities.
- *Strategic dimension.* According to Doherty *et al.* (2003), strategic vision and leadership are critical to the development of a businesses use of Internet and web technologies. However, a clear vision needs to be supported by appropriate competencies and capabilities (Lee and Kim, 2007), say, suitable technological and Internet marketing expertise (Lee and Brandyberry, 2003), appropriate technological, financial and operational resources for a business to use the Internet effectively and efficiently to support its trading activities, develop a competitive positioning and capitalise on the opportunities created by trading in the new virtual world.

The implications are that for organisations wishing to engage successfully in developing transactional operations online there is a need to have certain factors in place. Perhaps most importantly well-resourced strategic leadership that can navigate a course, which not only creates a clear online positioning but also a sustainable competitive advantage, that is leveraged by maximising operational efficiencies and strategic effectiveness. But in addition, there should be evidence of a rich and fertile target market consisting of buyers who are motivated to buy online.

Table 12.2 Summary of the factors affecting adoption of the Internet

Factors influencing adoption	O'Keefe *et al.* (1998)	Doherty *et al.* (2003)	Grewal *et al.* (2004)	Lunce *et al.* (2006)	Ashworth *et al.* (2005)	Verdict (2007)	Lee and Kim (2007)
Capabilities and resources	✓	✓			✓		✓
Channel – relative advantage		✓					✓
Choice of online format			✓				
Company size	✓			✓			
Cost of operating sustainable online retail operations – economies of scale	✓	✓	✓		✓		
Ease of access, use and convenience			✓	✓		✓	
Economies of scale innovativeness					✓		✓
Internal expertise	✓	✓	✓		✓		✓
Level and type of information provision			✓				
Levels of customer service	✓		✓			✓	✓
Logistical infrastructure complexities		✓	✓		✓		✓
Maturity of online market positioning				✓			
Perceived and actual levels of security		✓	✓				✓
Product category and range	✓		✓	✓		✓	
Size and maturity of target market	✓	✓		✓	✓		
Strategic vision and commitment	✓	✓			✓	✓	✓
Sufficient financial capital				✓	✓		
Suitability of customer base	✓	✓	✓				✓
Suitable technological infrastructure		✓					✓
Supply chain management issues					✓	✓	

Source: Gunawan *et al.* 2008

Digital marketing strategies

The final part of the chapter considers B2B digital marketing strategies. It should be noted that it is not the aim of this section to revisit the process of planning online marketing strategies (which is discussed in Chapter 4), but to consider how digital marketing strategies might be used and integrated into organisational planning activities.

According to Nicholls and Watson (2005), many organisations are developing a better understanding of the importance of strategic thinking and how it can lead to development of successful online trading. In the past, companies have been accused of a lack of strategic planning, which was ultimately said to be the cause of their online failures (Porter, 2001). During the dot-com boom many companies were accused of a lack of strategic planning, which was ultimately said to be the cause of their business failures. E-strategy has been discussed at various levels from business re-engineering, new approaches to marketing planning to analysing and measuring specifics of web-based activities.

From a strategic planning perspective, Teo and Pian (2003) found that the level of Internet adoption has a significant positive relationship with an organisation's capacity to develop competitive advantage. This is in line with the earlier discussions of the factors, which affect levels of adoption. The implications are that organisations should seriously consider how to develop maximum capacity to benefit from the online trading environment. Organisations that hesitate are likely to be superseded by existing or new competitors. While in the current climate this sounds rather obvious, the business potential that can be derived from adopting Internet technologies is not always immediately clear. This situation helps to reinforce the importance of digital marketing planning as it can help to ensure that organisations reduce the risk of losing their competitive edge by missing out on the benefits of new technology. On the plus side, there are increasing opportunities to benefit from innovation, growth, cost reduction, alliance and differentiation advantages through planned adoption and development of Internet and digital technologies as more trading partners become part of the digital marketspace.

According to Nicholls and Watson (2005), in order to develop an online strategy it is critically important to use Internet technologies effectively and it is also vital to analyse the operational situation. Furthermore, it is important to assess the degree to which the offline and online management infrastructure, marketing and logistics functions are integrated. Figure 12.7 shows a model of e-value creation with key areas, which affect strategy development: the organisation's core strategic objectives, its business characteristics, internal resources and competencies. Different objectives need to be supported by different organisational structures and marketing strategies – e.g. greater cost reduction is likely to be achieved if technologies are integrated throughout the organisation. The characteristics of the organisation are likely to have a significant impact on Internet strategies – e.g. small companies will

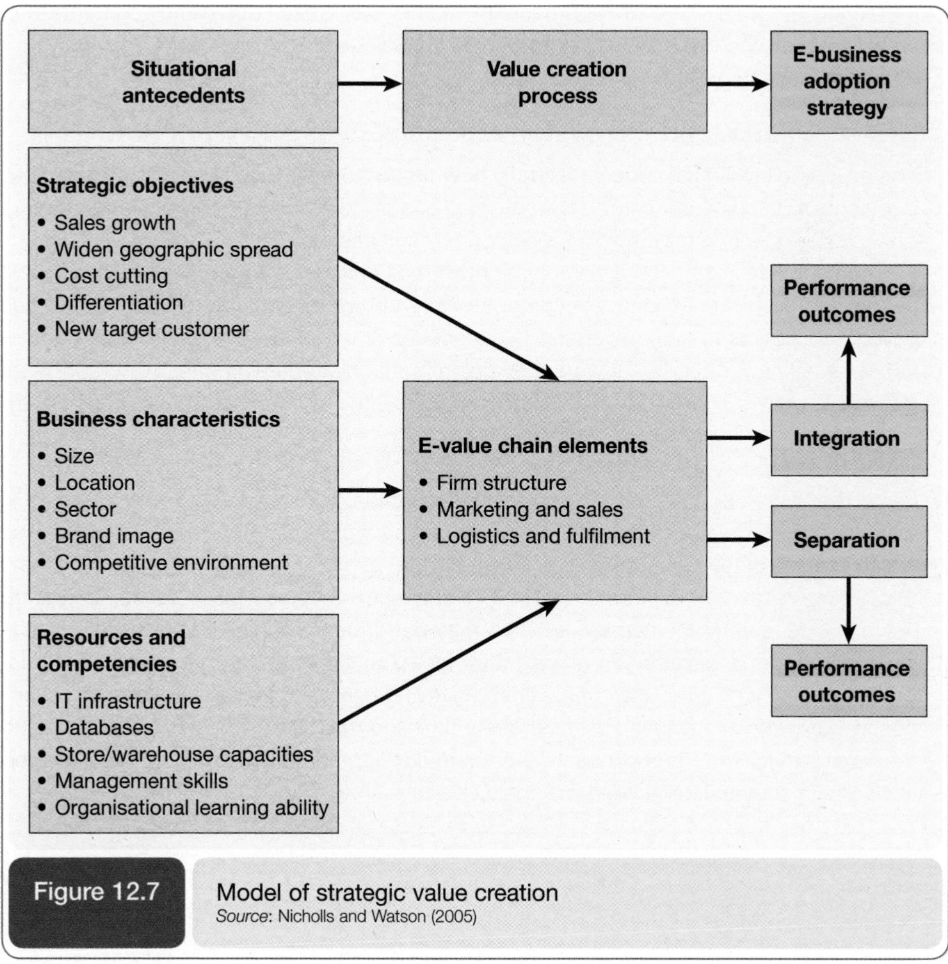

Figure 12.7 Model of strategic value creation
Source: Nicholls and Watson (2005)

have to consider carefully how to resource a fully transactional website and handle the logistics. Currently, a good deal of emphasis is placed on the supply-side of e-commerce strategies. Streamlining of procurement systems through the use of Internet technologies can make significant cost reductions, which can produce cost saving, managerial efficiencies in the purchasing function and financial benefits.

Mini Case Study 12.3 gives an example of a B2B services company that has taken a strategic approach to customer-centric strategy.

Mini Case Study 12.3 Customer-centric strategy at Thomson Financial

The Thomson Corporation is a global provider of integrated information-based solutions to business and professional customers. Thomson serve professionals in the fields of law, tax, accounting, financial services, scientific research and healthcare. Thomson Financial (**www.thomson.com/solutions/financial/**) provides information and software tools that help its customers make better decisions, faster.

Harrington and Tjan (2008) identified these steps in developing an online customer strategy for Thomson Financial.

Step 1: Map out your real market

Initially, in 2001, Thomson were using third-party reports to estimate market size. The approximately $15 billion financial-information market was divided into three categories: firms on the buy side, firms on the sell side, and corporate clients.

Using a more sophisticated approach the market was broken down into segments of users. Eight segments were identified and then, using a range of data including competitor reports, interviewing customers, Thomson Financial mapped out their share for each.

Step 2: Understand the customers' objectives and work flow

The next step involved finding out exactly how products were being used by different personas. For example, gathering information not only on the activities of a bank's head of research, who bought the product, but also on the behaviour of analysts doing research for their clients.

Thomson Financial used a combination of traditional survey methods and less traditional methods such as 'day in the life' observations of customers to chart users' activities. Key to this research was an approach called 'three minutes.' What were end users of a product or service doing three minutes before they used it and three minutes after? What were they doing for the next three minutes? Thomson kept asking that until we got a view of the full day. The aim was to make Thomson products part of as much of that day as practical.

Step 3: Develop products that provide what users value most

Once Thomson had a picture of users' needs, candidates for new features that would address unmet needs were identified. Candidate features and information were based on the biggest pain points for end users – which aspects of their jobs were so problematic that customers would pay to make them better? To determine this, Thomson surveyed more than 1200 investment managers, for instance, to find out the features those users valued most in the aggregate. Then they performed a conjoint analysis in which investment managers were asked to make trade-offs among attributes that might enhance the product. This gave a truer picture of their preferences. They saw that within the investment manager group there were three distinct clusters of needs: basic users, advanced users and real-time-focused users. The three clusters valued some but not all of the same things. They then concentrated future development efforts on creating three versions of our solution, each aimed at meeting the needs of one cluster.

Step 4: Keep the focus on users

Thomson highlight the importance of ongoing research and introduction of new functionality when they say:

> *We are continually evaluating and refining our customer strategy. Implementing it requires a flexible go-to-market plan, which we enable by including sales and product development people right up front in the research; by employing effective customer feedback loops that are built into a periodic review process; and by gradually scaling up the strategy across segments and businesses.*

In summary, it is perhaps reasonable to suggest that organisations are beginning to consider use of the Internet from a much more strategic perspective. Organisations operating in B2B sectors are generally well-placed to implement online strategies due to having well-established long-standing trading relationships with customers and members of the supply chain.

Source: Reprinted by permission of *Harvard Business Review*. Excerpt from Transforming Strategy One Customer at a Time, by R. Harrington and A. Tjan, March 2008.

Case Study 12.2 B2B adoption of the Internet: Inspirational Cosmetics

Internet adoption by organisations is, according to research, a process which involves different stages and each of the stages is affected by a number of variables. The stages summarised by Aguila-Obra and Padilla-Meléndez (2006) and the variables are shown in Tables 12.3 and 12.4.

Businesses at the initiation stage are likely to have a very basic level of Internet use but will move towards developing a very basic website and e-mail. By the time the adoption stage is achieved businesses are likely to have their own server in place. Changes to operations and managerial structure will have begun to take place by the time the routinisation stage is reached. Finally, when the infusion stage is reached many changes will have occurred including the development of different organisational units for managing the technology.

In addition to the impact of organisational, external and technology factors, firm size has an impact on the stage and speed of development. In other words the bigger the firm the more likely it is to have its own website and supporting technology infrastructure. Moreover, the larger the firm the greater the level and intensity of the business activity and the greater the number of employees involved.

Inspirational Cosmetics (IC) is a recently developed subsidiary of the giant pharmaceutical corporation Multichemical. IC is based in Stockholm and produces a range of high-quality cosmetic products and surgical applications. The company specialises in developing products for the 'anti-ageing' market. IC was established when the parent company, Multichemical, acquired a small Swedish company called Abbalaars, which produced highly effective anti-ageing creams from organically grown plants. The organisational structure of IC has been developed using a combination of local and international expertise. Local producers continue to supply high-quality organic materials for the production of facial creams. These producers are located all around Sweden and vary in size, in terms of number of employees from 5 to 500. The 'think global, act local' approach to the company development has also been applied to the development of the technology infrastructure. Multichemical provides an Internet infrastructure, which is capable of supporting a highly sophisticated range of Internet strategies. However, Abbalaars made limited use of the Internet internally: the company had a computer network linking all parts of the business but externally the website was a static site giving contact details and a short company history. IC has recently appointed an e-commerce director, Henrik Bjornesson, whose responsibility it is to develop online sales revenues and improve communications within the supply chain.

Table 12.3 Factors and variables affecting Internet adoption

Factors affecting adoption	Variables
External factors	• Organisational environment • Industry competition • External support • Internet user expectations • Global electronic markets
Technology factors	• Benefits of technology adoption • Barrier to technology adoption • Comparative advantage • Cost • Technology infrastructure
Organisational factors	• Perceived costs • Internal resources • Skills and expertise • Levels of investment • Business objectives • Organisational structure
Firm size	• Small • Medium • Large

Source: Based on Aguila-Obra and Padilla-Meléndez (2006)

Table 12.4 Stages of internet adoption and influencing factors

Stage	Influencing factors
Initiation	Firms tend to have limited access to technology resources and are unlikely to have internal computer network but firms at this stage are looking at opportunities created by the web. Investment and financial cost are key at this stage
Adoption/ adaptation	Firms will already have made an investment in technology but still need external support as they are beginning to use the web. Managerial expertise and external networks are key here
Acceptance/ routinisation	Firms are likely to have a fairly well-established technology infrastructure and are likely to be using the Internet and the web extensively for internal and external communications
Infusion	By this stage the firms have largely become self-sufficient in terms of operating and developing Internet and web technologies. Managerial skill will also be very well developed

Source: Based on Aguila-Obra and Padilla-Meléndez (2006)

Questions

1 Assess the stage of the Internet adoption for:
- multichemical
- inspirational Cosmetics
- the organic growers (suppliers).

2 Explain which factor and variables Henrik Bjornesson is most likely to consider when deciding how to achieve the business goals set by Rosemary Dulwich, the CEO of Inspirational Cosmetics.

3 Consider the likely stage of adoption of the suppliers of organic produce. Suggest ways in which Inspirational Cosmetics might develop its use of the Internet with these suppliers.

Summary

1. This chapter has examined B2B use of Internet technologies and in doing so it has considered the e-markets, the importance of efficiency and effectiveness to organisations operating online, the factors which affect adoption and has briefly looked at online marketing strategies.
2. We saw how companies can use e-procurement for efficiency.
3. Social media marketing can be applied to B2B markets for lead generation though content and inbound marketing techniques as we saw through the Cisco and Eloqua case studies. The chapter also examined B2B e-markets and considered the importance of e-markets in terms of growth and dispersion of use of Internet technologies across different industrial sectors.
4. We explored different types of e-market places and provided case examples of different types of e-market portals.
5. We summarised the factors that affect Internet adoption and suggested ways in which these factors cluster together into separate dimensions of influencing factors: financial, market, operational and strategic.
6. Digital marketing strategies are not always integrated into a business's wider planning activities. However, this is becoming more important as organisations increasingly integrate Internet technologies into the buying and selling activities.

Exercises

Self-assessment exercises

1. Evaluate and compare the factors likely to affect (a) a construction company, (b) an insurance brokerage contemplating setting up a transactional website aiming to develop online market share.
2. Explain the difference between online market efficiency and online market effectiveness.

Essay and discussion questions

1. Discuss why a business operating in an industrial market might be cautious about putting new product specifications on the company website.
2. Discuss the relevance of social media marketing to B2B organisations.
3. Explain how Internet technologies can contribute to the development of online business strategies.

Examination question

1. Discuss the extent to which B2B e-marketplaces are fundamentally different to traditional offline markets.
2. Explain the options for applying social media marketing to B2B marketing campaigns.

References

Aguila-Obra, A.R.D. and Padilla-Meléndez, A. (2006) Organisational factors affecting Internet technology adoption, *Internet Research*, 16(1) 91–110.

Ansari, A. and Mela, C.F. (2003) E-customisation, *J Mark Res*, May, 40, 131–45.

Ashworth, C. Schmidt, R., Pioche, E. and Hallsworth, A. (2005) An approach to sustainable 'fashion' e-retail: a five stage evolutionary strategy for clicks-and-mortar and pureplay enterprises, *Journal of Retailing and Consumer Service*, 13(4), 289–99.

Covisint (2002) Press release, 4 February. Covisint.com.

Doherty, N.F. and Ellis-Chadwick, F.E. (2003) The relationship between retailers' targeting and e-commerce strategies: an empirical analysis, *Internet Research*, 13(3), 170–82.

Econsultancy (2010) Q&A: Euroffice CEO Simon Drakeford on customer retention, blog post, 10 November, (http://econsultancy.com/uk/blog/6833-q-a-euroffice-ceo-simon-drakeford).

Ellis-Chadwick, F.E. (2008) Online retailing: open all hours? *International Journal of Business Environments*, 2(2).

Ellis-Chadwick, F.E., McHardy, P. and Wiesehofer, H. (2002) Online customer relationships in the European financial services sector: a cross-country investigation, *International Journal of Financial Services Marketing*, 6(4).

Fernie, J, Sparks, L. and McKinnon, A. (2010) Retail logistics in the UK: past present and future, *International Journal of retail Distribution Management*, 38(11/12), 894–914.

Gattiker, U.E., Perlusz, S. and Bohmann, K. (2000) Using the Internet for B2B activities: a review and further direction for research, *Internet Research Electronic Networking Application and Policy*, 10(2), 126–40.

Grewal, Iyer G. and Levy, M. (2004) Internet retailing: enablers, limiters and market consequences, *Journal of Business Research*, 57(7), 703–13.

Gunawan, G., Ellis-Chadwick, F. and King, M. (2008) An empirical study of the uptake of performance measurement by internet retailers, *Internet Research*, 18(4), 361–81.

Harrington, R. and Tjan, A. (2008) Transforming strategy one customer at a time, *Harvard Business Review*, March, 86(3), 62–72.

Jobber, D. (2009) *Principles and Practice of Marketing*, 6th edn. McGraw-Hill.

Johnson, M. (2009) Barriers to innovation adoption: a study of e-markets, *Industrial Management & DataSystems*, 110(2), 2010, 157–74

Kalaignanam, K., Kushwaha, T. and Varadarajan, P. (2008) Marketing operations efficiency and the Internet: an organizating framework, *Journal of Business Research*, 61(4), 300–08.

Knudsen, D. (2003) Aligning corporate strategy, procurement strategy and e-procurement tools, *International Journal of Physical Distribution & Logistics Management*, 33(8), pp. 720–34

Lee and Brandyberry, A. (2003) The e-tailer's dilemma, *ACM SIGMIS Database*, 34(2).

Lee, S. and Kim, K-J. (2007) Factors affecting the implementation success of Internet-based information systems, *Computers in Human Behaviour*, July, 23(4), 1853–80.

Line56 (2004) Compuware buys last of Covisint, Article by Jim Ericson, *Line56* (www.line56.com), 6 February.

Nicholls, A. and Watson, A. (2005) Implementing e-value strategies in UK retailing, *International Journal of Retail and Distribution Management*, 33(6), 426–43.

O'Keefe, R.M., O'Connor, G. and Kung, H.J. (1998) Early adopters of the web as a retail medium: small company winners and losers, *European Journal of Marketing*, 32(7/8), 629–43.

Porter, M. (2001) Strategy and the Internet, *Harvard Business Review*, March, 62–78.

Rayport, J. and Sviokla, J. (1995) Exploiting the virtual value chain, *Harvard Business Review*, November–December, 75–87.

Smart, A. (2010) Exploring the business case for e-procurement, *International Journal of Physical, Distribution & Logistics Management*, 40(3), 181–201.

Smart Insights (2011) Five ways to integrate compelling video into your B2B marketing, blog post by Rene Power, 25 August.

Teo, T. and Pian, Y. (2003) A contingency perspective on Internet adoption and competitive advantage, *European Journal of Information Systems*, 12(2), 78–92.

Varadarajan, R.P. and Yadav, M.S. (2002) Marketing strategy and the Internet: an organising framework, *J Acad Mark Sci*, Fall, 30, 296–313.

Verdict Research (2007) *UK e-retail 2007*, Verdict Research limited, Charles House, 108–110 Finchley Road, London, NW3 5JJ.

Vijayasarathy, L. and Tyler, M. (1997) Adoption factors and electronic data interchange use: a survey of retail companies, *International Journal of Retail Distribution and Management*, 25(9), 286–92.

Zettelmeyer, F. (2000) Expanding the internet: pricing and communications strategies when firms compete on multiple channels, *J Mark Res*, August, 37, 292–308.

Further reading

Benyon Davies (2004) *E-business*, Palgrave Macmillan.

Chaffey (2009) *E-business and E-commerce Management*, 4th edn, Pearson Education.

Harris, L. and Dennis, C. (2008) *Marketing the E-business*, 2nd edn, Routledge.

Laundon and Traver (2007) *E-commerce: Business, Technology, Society*, 4th edn, Prentice Hall.

Glossary

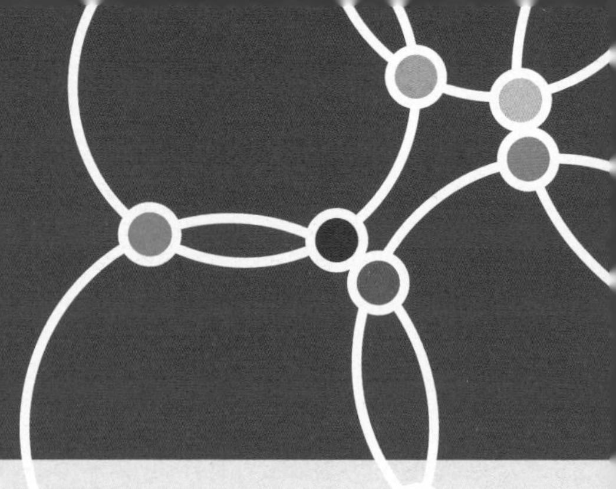

3G Third generation of mobile phone technology.

4G Fourth-generation wireless, expected to deliver wireless broadband at 20–40 Mbps (about 10–20 times the current rates of ADSL broadband service).

A

A/B testing A/B or AB testing refers to testing two different versions of a page or a page element such as a heading, image or button. The alternatives are served alternately with the visitors to the page randomly split between the two pages. Hence, it is sometimes called 'live split testing'. Changes in visitor behaviour can then be compared using different metrics such as click-through rate on page elements like buttons or images, or macro-conversion rates, such as conversion to sale or sign-up. AB testing is aimed at increasing page or site effectiveness against key performance indicators including click-through rate, conversion rates and revenue per visit. Since it does not consider combinations of variables tested, for best uplift multivariate testing is increasingly used.

Above the fold A term, derived from printed media, which is used to indicate whether a banner advertisement or other content is displayed on a web page without the need to scroll. This is likely to give higher click-through, but note that the location of the 'fold' within the web browser is dependent on the screen resolution of a user's personal computer.

Access platform A method for customers to access digital media.

Access provider A company providing services to enable a company or individual to access the Internet. Access providers are divided into Internet service providers (ISPs) and online service providers (OSPs).

Accessibility An approach to site design intended to accommodate site usage using different browsers and settings particularly required by the visually impaired and visitors with other disabilities including motor control, learning difficulties and deafness. Users whose first language is not English can also be assisted.

Accessibility legislation Legislation intended to assist users of websites with disabilities including visual disability.

Acquisition *See* **Customer acquisition.**

Active Server Page (ASP) A type of HTML page (denoted by an .asp file name) that includes scripts (small programs) that are processed on a web server before the web page is served to the user's web browser. ASP is a Microsoft technology that usually runs on a Microsoft Internet Information Server (usually on Windows NT). The main use of such programs is to process information supplied by the user in an online form. A query may then be run to provide specific information to the customer such as delivery status on an order, or a personalised web page.

ActiveX A programming language standard developed by Microsoft that permits complex and graphical customer applications to be written and then accessed from a web browser. ActiveX components are standard controls that can be incorporated into websites and are then automatically downloaded for users. Examples are graphics and animation or a calculator form for calculating interest on a loan or a control for graphing stock prices. A competitor to Java.

Ad creative The design and content of an ad.

Ad impression Similar in concept to a page impression; describes one viewing of an advertisement by a single member of its audience. The same as ad view, a term that is less commonly used.

Ad inventory The total number of ad impressions that a website can sell over time (usually specified per month).

Ad network Ad networks from suppliers such as Blue Lithium or 24-7 Media give advertisers the options of advertising across a network of sites to reach a particular demographic, e.g. female 18–25, but at a lower cost than targeting a single site since the actual site used for the ad placement isn't known (hence these are sometimes known as 'blind network buys').

Ad rotation When advertisements are changed on a website for different user sessions. This may be in response to ad targeting or simply displaying different advertisements from those on a list.

Ad serving The term for displaying an advertisement on a website. Often the advertisement will be served from a web server different from the site on which it is placed. For example, the server URL for displaying the advertisement is http://ad.doubleclick.net.

Ad space The area of a web page that is set aside for banner advertising.

Ad view Similar in concept to a page impression; describes one viewing of an advertisement by a single member of its audience. The same as ad impression, the term that is more commonly used.

Adaptive web design Also known as progressive enhancement, this design technique delivers different layouts and features according to what is supported by browser and screen resolution of the device.

Advertisement Advertisements on websites are usually banner advertisements positioned as a masthead on the page.

Advertising broker *See* **Media broker**.

Advertising networks A collection of independent websites of different companies and media networks, each of which has an arrangement with a single advertising broker (*See* **Media broker**) to place banner advertisements.

Affiliate A company promoting a merchant typically through a commission-based arrangement either direct or through an affiliate network.

Affiliate marketing A commission-based arrangement where referring sites (publishers) receive a commission on sales or leads by merchants (retailers). Commission is usually based on a percentage of product sale price or a fixed amount for each sale (CPA or cost-per-acquisition), but may also sometimes be based on a per-click basis, for example when an aggregator refers visits to merchants.

Affiliate networks Third-party brokers also known as affiliate managers who manage recruitment of affiliates and infrastructure to manage a merchant's affiliate programme in the form of links, tracking and payment of a range of affiliates.

Agents Software programs that can assist people to perform tasks such as finding particular information such as the best price for a product.

Aggregated buying A form of customer union where buyers collectively purchase a number of items at the same price and receive a volume discount.

Aggregators An alternative term to *price comparison sites*. Aggregators include product, price and service information comparing competitors within a sector such as financial services, retail or travel. Their revenue models commonly include affiliate revenues (CPA), pay-per-click advertising (CPC) and display advertising (CPM).

Agile software development An iterative approach to developing software and website functionality with the emphasis on face-to-face communications to elicit, define and test requirements. Each iteration or scrum is effectively a mini-software project including stages of planning, requirements analysis, design, coding, testing and documentation.

Allowable cost-per-acquisition A target maximum cost for generating leads or new customers profitably.

Alt tags Alt tags appear after an image tag and contain a phrase associated with that image. For example: <img src="logo.gif" alt="Company name, company products"/>.

Analysis phase The identification of the requirements of a website. Techniques to achieve this may include focus groups, questionnaires sent to existing customers or interviews with key accounts.

Anchor text (also known as link text) The (usually) clickable text element representing a hyperlink. Or more prosaically, the body copy that is hyperlinked.

Animated banner advertisements (animated GIFs) Early banner advertisements featured only a single advertisement, but today they will typically involve several different images, which are displayed in sequence to help to attract attention to the banner and build up a theme, often ending with a call to action and the injunction to click on the banner. These advertisements are achieved through supplying the ad creative as an animated GIF file with different layers or frames, usually a rectangle of 468 × 60 pixels. Animated banner advertisements are an example of rich-media advertisements.

Announcements *See* **Site announcements**.

Application Programming Interfaces Method of exchanging data between systems such as website services.

Archie A database containing information on what documents and programs are located on FTP servers. It would not be used in a marketing context unless one were looking for a specific piece of software or document name.

Asymmetric encryption Both parties use a related but different key to encode and decode messages.

Atomisation Atomisation in a Web 2.0 context refers to a concept where the content on a site is broken down into smaller fundamental units which can then be distributed via the web through links to other sites. Examples of atomisation include the stories and pages in individual feeds being syndicated to third-party sites and widgets.

Attrition rate Percentage of site visitors who are lost at each stage in making a purchase.

Audit (external) Consideration of the business and economic environment in which the company operates. This includes the economic, political, fiscal, legal, social, cultural and technological factors (usually referred to by the acronym STEP or SLEPT).

Audit (internal) A review of website effectiveness.

Auditors *See* **Site auditors**.

Authentication *See* **Security methods**.

Autoresponders Software tools or agents running on web servers that automatically send a standard reply to the sender of an e-mail message. This may provide information for a standard request sent to, say, price_list@company_name.com, or it could simply state that the message or order has been forwarded to the relevant person and will be answered within two days. (Also known as mailbots.)

Availability *See* **Security methods; Site availability**.

Avatar A term used in computer-mediated environments to mean a 'virtual person'. Derived from the word's original meaning: 'n. the descendant of a Hindu deity in a visible form; incarnation; supreme glorification of any principle'.

Average order value (AOV) The average amount spent for a single checkout purchase on a retail site for a particular customer group, e.g. first time purchasers.

B

Backbones High-speed communications links used to enable Internet communications across a country and internationally.

Backlinks Hyperlinks which link to a particular web page (or website). Also known as inbound links. Google PageRank and Yahoo! WebRank are methods of enumerating this.

Balanced scorecard A framework for setting and monitoring business performance. Metrics are structured according to customer issues, internal efficiency measures, financial measures and innovation.

Bandwidth Indicates the speed at which data are transferred using a particular network medium. It is measured in bits per second (bps).

- kbps (one kilobit per second or 1000 bps; a modem operates at up to 56.6 kbps).
- Mbps (one megabit per second or 1,000,000 bps; company networks operate at 10 or more Mbps).
- Gbps (one gigabit per second or 1,000,000,000 bps; fibre-optic or satellite links operate at Gbps).

Banner advertisement A typically rectangular graphic displayed on a web page for purposes of brand building or driving traffic to a site. It is normally possible to perform a click-through to access further information from another website. Banners may be static or animated (see **Animated banner advertisements**).

Behavioural ad targeting Enables an advertiser to target ads at a visitor as they move elsewhere on the site or return to the site, thus increasing the frequency or number of impressions served to an individual in the target market.

Behavioural loyalty Loyalty to a brand is demonstrated by repeat sales and response to marketing campaigns.

Behavioural traits of web users Web users can be broadly divided into directed and undirected information seekers.

Bid A commitment by a trader to purchase under certain conditions.

Blog Personal online diary, journal or news source compiled by one person, an internal team or external guest authors. Postings are usually in different categories. Typically comments can be added to each blog posting to help create interactivity and feedback.

Bluecasting Bluecasting involves messages being automatically pushed to a consumer's bluetooth-enabled phone or they can pull or request audio, video or text content to be downloaded from a live advert. In the future ads will be able to respond to those who view them.

Bluejacking Sending a message from a mobile phone or transmitter to another mobile phone which is in close range via Bluetooth technology.

Blueprints Show the relationships between pages and other content components; can be used to portray organisation, navigation and labelling systems.

Bluetooth A standard for wireless transmission of data between devices over short ranges (less than 10m), e.g. a mobile phone or a PDA.

Botnet Independent computers, connected to the Internet, are used together, typically for malicious purposes through controlling software. For example, they may be used to send out spam or for a denial of service attack where they repeatedly access a server to degrade its software. Computers are often initially infected through a virus when effective anti-virus measures are not in place.

Bounce rate Proportion of visitors to a page or site that exit after visiting a single page only, usually expressed as a percentage.

Brand The sum of the characteristics of a product or service perceived by a user.

Brand advocate A customer who has favourable perceptions of a brand who will talk favourably about a brand to their acquaintances to help generate awareness of the brand or influence purchase intent.

Brand equity The brand assets (or liabilities) linked to a brand's name and symbol that add to (or subtract from) a service.

Brand experience The frequency and depth of interactions with a brand can be enhanced through the Internet.

Brand identity The totality of brand associations including name and symbols that must be communicated.

Branding The process of creating and evolving successful brands.

Bricks-and-mortar A traditional organisation with limited online presence.

Broad and shallow navigation More choices, fewer clicks to reach required content.

Broadband technology A term referring to methods of delivering information across the Internet at a higher rate by increasing bandwidth.

Brochureware A website in which a company has simply transferred ('migrated') its existing paper-based promotional literature onto the Internet without recognising the differences required by this medium.

Broker *See* **Media broker**.

Browser *See* **Web browser**.

Bundling Offering complementary services.

Business model A summary of how a company will generate revenue, identifying its product offering, value-added services, revenue sources and target customers.

Business-to-business (B2B) Commercial transactions between an organisation and other organisations (inter-organisational marketing).

Business-to-business exchanges or marketplaces Virtual intermediaries with facilities to enable trading between buyers and sellers.

Business-to-consumer (B2C) Commercial transactions between an organisation and consumers.

Buy-side e-commerce E-commerce transactions between a purchasing organisation and its suppliers.

C

Call centre A location for inbound and outbound telemarketing.

Call-back service A direct response facility available on a website to enable a company to contact a customer by phone at a later time as specified by the customer.

Campaign-based e-communications E-marketing communications that are executed to support a specific marketing campaign such as a product launch, price promotion or a website launch.

Campaign URL (CURL) A web address specific to a particular campaign.

Capabilities Capabilities are intangible and are developed from the combined and coordinated behaviour and activities of an organisation's employees, and it is therefore 'embedded in the organisation and processes' (Makadok, 2001 – see Chapter 11). The definition of a capability is an organisation's ability to 'perform a set of co-ordinated tasks, utilising organisational resources, for the purposes of achieving a particular end result'

Card sorting The process of setting up a way of organising objects on the website in a consistent manner.

Cascading style sheets A simple mechanism for adding style (e.g. fonts, colours, spacing) to web documents. CSS enables different style elements to be controlled across an entire site or section of site. Style elements that are commonly controlled include typography, background colour and images, and borders and margins.

Catalogue Catalogues provide a structured listing of registered websites in different categories. They are similar to an electronic version of *Yellow Pages*. Yahoo! and Excite are the best known examples of catalogues. (Also known as directories.) The distinction between search engines and catalogues has become blurred since many sites now include both facilities as part of a portal service.

Certificate A valid copy of a public key of an individual or organisation together with identification information. It is issued by a trusted third party (TTP) or certification authority (CA).

Certification authority (CA) An organisation issuing and managing certificates or public keys and private keys to individuals or organisations together with identification information.

Change management Controls to minimise the risks of project-based and organisational change.

Channel buyer behaviour Describes which content is visited and the time and duration.

Channel conflicts A significant threat arising from the introduction of an Internet channel is that while disintermediation gives the opportunity for a company to sell direct and increase the profitability of products it can also threaten existing distribution arrangements with existing partners.

Channel marketing strategy Defines how a company should set specific objectives for a channel such as the Internet and vary its proposition and communications for this channel.

Channel outcomes Record customer actions taken as a consequence of a visit to a site.

Channel profitability The profitability of a website, taking into account revenue and cost and discounted cash flow.

Channel promotion Measures that assess why customers visit a site – which adverts they have seen, which sites they have been referred from.

Channel satisfaction Evaluation of the customer's opinion of the service quality on the site and supporting services such as e-mail.

Channel structure The configuration of partners in a distribution channel.

Clicks-and-mortar A business combining online and offline presence.

Clicks-only or Internet pureplay An organisation with principally an online presence.

Clickstream A record of the path a user takes through a website. Clickstreams enable website designers to assess how their site is being used.

Clickstream analysis Reviewing the online behaviour of site visitors based on the sequence of pages that they visit, the navigation and promotion they respond to, the ultimate outcomes and where they leave the site.

Click-through A click-through (ad click) occurs each time a user clicks on a banner advertisement to direct them to a web page that contains further information.

Click-through rate Expressed as a percentage of total ad impressions, and refers to the proportion of users viewing an advertisement who click on it. It is calculated as the number of click-throughs divided by the number of ad impressions.

Click-tracking Java technology can be used to track movements of individual users to a website.

Click ecosystem Describes the customer behaviour or flow of online visitors between search engines, media sites, other intermediaries to an organisation and its competitors.

Client–server The client–server architecture consists of client computers such as PCs sharing resources such as a database stored on a more powerful server computer.

Co-branding An arrangement between two or more companies where they agree to jointly display content and perform joint promotion using brand logos, e-mail marketing or banner advertisements. The aim is that the brands are strengthened if they are seen as complementary. Co-branding is often a reciprocal arrangement which can occur without payment as part of a wider agreement between partners.

Cold list Data about individuals that are rented or sold by a third party.

Collaborative filtering Profiling of customer interest coupled with delivery of specific information and offers, often based on the interests of similar customers.

Commoditisation The process whereby product selection becomes more dependent on price than on differentiating features, benefits and value-added services.

Common Gateway Interface (CGI) A method of processing information on a web server in response to a customer's request. Typically a user will fill in a web-based form and the results will be processed by a CGI script (application). Active Server Pages (ASPs) are an alternative to a CGI script.

Competitive intelligence (CI) A process that transforms disaggregated information into relevant, accurate and usable strategic knowledge about competitors, position, performance, capabilities and intentions.

Competitor analysis Review of Internet marketing services offered by existing and new competitors and adoption by their customers.

Competitor benchmarking A structured analysis of the online services, capabilities and performance of an organisation within the areas of customer acquisition, conversion, retention and growth.

Computer telephony integration The integration of telephony and computing to provide a platform for applications that streamline or enhance business processes.

Confidentiality *See* **Security methods**.

Consumer-to-business (C2B) Consumers approach the business with an offer.

Consumer-to-consumer (C2C) Informational or financial transactions between consumers, but usually mediated through a business site.

Consumer behaviour Research into the motivations, media consumption preferences and selection processes used by consumers as they use digital channels together with traditional channels to purchase online products and use other online services.

Consumer behaviour analysis In digital markets, this type of analysis involves research into the motivations, media consumption preferences and selection processes used by consumers as they use digital channels together with traditional channels to purchase online products and use other online services.

Contact or touch strategy Definition of the sequence and type of outbound communications required at different points in the customer lifecycle.

Content Content is the design, text and graphical information that forms a web page. Good content is the key to attracting customers to a website and retaining their interest or achieving repeat visits.

Content developer A person responsible for updating web pages within part of an organisation.

Content distribution (or delivery) networks (CDNs) A systems of servers distributed globally with copies of data stored locally to enable more rapid download of content. Their use has increased with increased use of streaming video and more complex web applications.

Content management Software tools for managing additions and amendments to website content.

Content management system (CMS) A software tool for creating, editing and updating documents accessed by intranet, extranet or Internet.

Content marketing The management of text, rich media, audio and video content aimed at engaging customers and prospects to meet business goals published through print and digital media including web and mobile platforms which is repurposed and syndicated to different forms of web presence such as publisher sites, blogs, social media and comparison sites.

Content network Sponsored links are displayed by the search engine on third-party sites such as online publishers, aggregators or social networks. Ads can be paid for on a CPC, CPM or a CPA basis. There are also options for graphical or video ads in addition to text-based ads.

Content strategy The management of text, rich media, audio and video content aimed at engaging customers and prospects to meet business goals published through print and digital media including web and mobile platforms which is repurposed and syndicated to different forms of web presence such as publisher sites, blogs, social media and comparison sites.

Contextual ads Ads relevant to page content on third-party sites brokered by search ad networks.

Continuous e-communications activities Long-term use of e-marketing communications intended to generate site visitors for customer acquisition (such as search engine, and affiliate marketing and online sponsorship) and retention (for example, e-newsletter marketing).

Contra-deals A reciprocal agreement in the form of an exchange where payment doesn't take place. Instead services or ad space to promote another company as part of co-branding occurs.

Control page The page against which subsequent optimisation will be assessed. Typically a current landing page. When a new page performs better than the existing control page, it becomes the control page in subsequent testing. Also known as 'champion-challenger'.

Convergence A trend in which different hardware devices such as televisions, computers and telephones merge and have similar functions.

Conversion marketing Using marketing communications to maximise conversion of potential customers to actual customers.

Conversion rate Proportion of visitors to a site, or viewers of an advert, who take an action such as registration or checkout. *See* **Visit conversion rate** and **Visitor conversion rate.**

Cookies Cookies are small text files stored on an end-user's computer to enable websites to identify the user. They enable a company to identify a previous visitor to a site, and build up a profile of that visitor's behaviour. *See* **Persistent cookies**, **Session cookies**, **First-party cookies**, **Third-party cookies.**

Core product The fundamental features of the product that meet the user's needs.

Core tenants A shopping centre or mall is usually a centrally owned managed facility. In the physical world, the management will aim to include in the mall stores that sell a different but complementary range of merchandise and include a variety of smaller and larger stores. The core tenants or 'anchor stores' as they are often called are the dominant large-scale store operators that are expected to draw customers to the centre.

Cost models for Internet advertising These include per-exposure, per-response and per-action costs.

Cost-per-acquisition (CPA) The cost of acquiring a new customer. Typically limited to the communications cost and refers to cost per sale for new customers. May also refer to other outcomes such as cost-per-quote or enquiry.

Cost-per-click (CPC) The cost of each click from a referring site to a destination site, typically from a search engine in pay-per-click search marketing.

Cost-per-targeted mille (CPTM) Cost per targeted thousand for an advertisement. (See Targeting.)

Cost per thousand (CPM) Cost per 1000 ad impressions.

Countermediation Creation of a new intermediary by an established company.

Cracker A malicious meddler who tries to discover sensitive information by poking around computer networks.

Cross-media optimisation studies (XMOS) Studies to determine the optimum spend across different media to produce the best results.

Cross-selling Persuading existing customers to purchase products from other categories than their typical purchases.

Customer acquisition Strategies and techniques used to gain new customers.

Customer-centric marketing An approach to marketing based on detailed knowledge of customer behaviour within the target audience which seeks to fulfil the individual needs and wants of customers.

Customer communications channels The range of media used to communicate directly with a customer.

Customer engagement Repeated interactions that strengthen the emotional, psychological or physical investment a customer has in a brand.

Customer engagement strategy A strategy to encourage interaction and participation of consumers with a brand through developing content and experiences with the aim of meeting commercial objectives. It is closely related to the development of content marketing and social media strategy.

Customer experience *See* **Online customer experience**.

Customer extension Techniques to encourage customers to increase their involvement with an organisation.

Customer insight Knowledge about customers' needs, characteristics, preferences and behaviours based on analysis of qualitative and quantitative data. Specific insights can be used to inform marketing tactics directed at groups of customers with shared characteristics.

Customer journey A description of modern multichannel buyer behaviour as consumers use different media to select suppliers, make purchases and gain customer support.

Customer lifecycle The stages each customer will pass through in a long-term relationship through acquisition, retention and extension.

Customer loyalty The desire on the part of the customer to continue to do business with a given supplier over time. *See* **Behavioural loyalty** and **Emotional loyalty**.

Customer orientation Providing content and services on a website consistent with the different characteristics of the audience of the site.

Customer profiling Using the website to find out customers' specific interests and characteristics.

Customer relationship management (CRM) A marketing-led approach to building and sustaining long-term business with customers.

Customer retention Techniques to maintain relationships with existing customers.

Customer satisfaction The extent to which a customer's expectations of product quality, service quality and price are met.

Customer scenarios (user journeys) Alternative tasks or outcomes required by a visitor to a website. Typically accomplished in a series of stages of different tasks involving different information needs or experiences.

Customer segments Groups of customers sharing similar characteristics, preferences and behaviours who are targeted with different propositions as part of *target marketing strategy*.

Customer selection Identifying key customer segments and targeting them for relationship building.

Customer touch-points Communications channels with which companies interact directly with prospects and customers. Traditional touch-points include face-to-face (in-store or with sales representatives), phone and mail. Digital touch-points include web services, e-mail and, potentially, mobile phone.

Cybermediaries Intermediaries who bring together buyers and sellers or those with particular information or service needs.

Cyberspace and cybermarketing These terms were preferred by science-fiction writers and tabloid writers to indicate the futuristic nature of using the Internet, the prefix 'cyber' indicating a blurring between humans, machines and communications. The terms are not frequently used today since the terms Internet, intranet and World Wide Web are more specific and widely used.

D

Data controller Each company must have a defined person responsible for data protection.

Data fusion The combining of data from different complementary sources (usually geodemographic and lifestyle or market research and lifestyle) to 'build a picture of someone's life' (M. Evans (1998) From 1086 to 1984: direct marketing into the millennium, *Marketing Intelligence and Planning*, 16(1), 56–67).

Data subject The legal term to refer to the individual whose data are held.

Data warehousing and data mining Extracting data from legacy systems and other resources; cleaning, scrubbing and preparing data for decision support; maintaining data in appropriate data stores; accessing and analysing data using a variety of end-user tools; and mining data for significant relationships. The primary purpose of these efforts is to provide easy access to specially prepared data that can be used with decision support applications such as management reports, queries, decision support systems, executive information systems and data mining.

Database marketing The process of systematically collecting, in electronic or optical form, data about past, current and/or potential customers, maintaining the integrity of the data by continually monitoring customer purchases, by enquiring about changing status, and by using the data to formulate marketing strategy and foster personalised relationships with customers.

Decryption The process of decoding (unscrambling) a message that has been encrypted using defined mathematical rules.

Deep linking Jakob Nielsen's term for a user arriving at a site deep within its structure or where search engines index a mirrored copy of content normally inaccessible by search engine spiders.

Deliverability Deliverability refers to ensuring e-mail messages are delivered and aren't blocked by spam filters because the e-mail content or structure falsely identifies a permission-based e-mail as a spammer, or because the sender's IP address has a poor reputation for spam.

Demand analysis Quantitative determination of the potential usage and business value achieved from online customers of an organisation. Qualitative analysis of perceptions of online channels is also assessed.

Demand analysis for e-commerce Assessment of the demand for e-commerce services among existing and potential customer segments using the ratio Access : Choose : Buy online.

Demand Side Platforms (DSPs) A service that enables ads to be managed across multiple ad networks and ad exchanges through a single interface designed for managing reporting and performance.

Demographic characteristics Variations in attributes of the population such as age, sex and social class.

Denial of service attack Also known as a distributed denial of service (DDOS) attack, this involves a hacker group taking control of many 'zombie' computers attached to the Internet whose security has been compromised. This 'botnet' is then used to make many requests to a target server, so overloading it and preventing access to other visitors.

Design for analysis (DFA) The required measures from a site are considered during design to better understand the audience of a site and their decision points.

Design phase (of site construction) The design phase defines how the site will work in the key areas of website structure, navigation and security.

Destination site Frequently used to refer to the site that is visited following a click-through on a banner advertisement. Could also apply to any site visited following a click on a hyperlink.

Destination store A retail store in which the merchandise, selection, presentation, pricing or other unique features act as a magnet for the customer.

Development phase (of site construction) 'Development' is the term used to describe the creation of a website by programmers. It involves writing the HTML content, creating graphics, and writing any necessary software code such as JavaScript or ActiveX (programming).

Differential advantage A desirable attribute of a product that is not currently matched by competitor offerings.

Differential pricing Identical products are priced differently for different types of customers, markets or buying situations.

Digital assets The graphical and interactive material that support a campaign displayed on third-party sites and on microsites, they include display ads, e-mail templates, video, audio and other interactive media such as Flash animations.

Digital audio broadcasting (DAB) radio Digital radio with clear sound quality with the facility to transmit text, images and video.

Digital brand A digital brand is a brand identity used for a product or company online that differs from the traditional brand. (Also known as an online brand.)

Digital cash An electronic version of cash in which the buyer of an item is typically anonymous to the seller. (Also referred to as virtual or electronic cash or e-cash.)

Digital certificates (keys) A method of ensuring privacy on the Internet. Certificates consist of keys made up of large numbers that are used to uniquely identify individuals. *See* **Public key**.

Digital marketing This has a similar meaning to 'electronic marketing' – both describe the management and execution of marketing using electronic media such as the web, e-mail, interactive TV, IPTV and wireless media in conjunction with digital data about customers' characteristics and behaviour.

Digital marketing metrics Measures that indicate the effectiveness of digitalmarketing activities integrated across different channels and platforms in meeting customer, business and marketing objectives.

Digital marketing strategy Definition of the approach by which applying digital technology platforms will support marketing and business objectives.

Digital media Communications are facilitated through content and interactive services delivered by different digital technology platforms including the Internet, web, mobile phone, interactive TV, IPTV and digital signage. *See* **Digital media channels**.

Digital media 'assists' A referrer of a visit to a site before the ultimate sale is credited with the sale, often through a weighting system.

Digital media channels Online communications techniques such as search engine marketing, affiliate marketing and display advertising used to engage web users on third-party sites; encouraging them to visit an organisation's site or purchase through traditional channels such as by phone or in-store.

Digital media de-duplication A single referrer of a visit leading to sale is credited with the sale based on the last-click method of digital media channel attribution.

Digital radio All types of radio broadcast as a digital signal.

Digital rights management (DRM) The use of different technologies to protect the distribution of digital services or content such as software, music, movies or other digital data.

Digital signage The use of interactive digital technologies within billboard and point of sale ads. For example, videos and bluetooth interaction.

Digital signatures The electronic equivalent of written signatures which are used as an online method of identifying individuals or companies using public-key encryption.

Digital television Information is received and displayed on a digital television using binary information (0s and 1s), giving options for better picture and sound quality and providing additional information services based on interactivity. *See* **Interactive digital TV**.

Direct marketimg Marketing to customers using one or more advertising media aimed at achieving measurable response and/or transaction.

Direct response Usually achieved in an Internet marketing context by call-back services.

Directed information seeker Someone who knows what information he or she is looking for.

Directories Directory websites provide a structured listing of registered websites in different categories. They are similar to an electronic version of *Yellow Pages*. Yahoo! and Excite are the best known examples of directories. (Also known as catalogues.)

Disintermediation The removal of intermediaries such as distributors or brokers that formerly linked a company to its customers.

Display advertising Paid ad placements using graphical or *rich media ad units* within a web page to achieve goals of delivering brand awareness, familiarity, favourability and purchase intent. Many ads encourage interaction through prompting the viewer to interact or *rollover* to play videos, complete an online form or to view more details by clicking through to a site.

Disruptive technologies New technologies that prompt businesses to reappraise their strategic approaches.

Distribution channels The mechanism by which products are directed to customers either through intermediaries or directly.

Domain name The web address that identifies a web server. *See* **Domain name system**.

Domain name registration The process of reserving a unique web address that can be used to refer to the company website.

Domain name system The domain name system (DNS) provides a method of representing Internet Protocol (IP) addresses as text-based names. These are used as web addresses. For example, www.microsoft.com is the representation of site 207.68.156.58. Domain names are divided into the following categories:

- Top-level domain name such as *.com* or *.co.uk*. (Also known as Global (or generic) top-level domain names (gLTD).)
- Second-level domain name. This refers to the company name and is sometimes referred to as the 'enterprise name', e.g. *novell.com*.
- Third-level or sub-enterprise domain name. This may be used to refer to an individual server within an organisation, such as *support.novell.com*.

Doorway pages Specially constructed pages which feature keywords for particular product searches. These often redirect visitors to a home page.

Download The process of retrieving electronic information such as a web page or e-mail from another remote location such as a web server.

Drip irrigation Collecting information about customer needs through their lifetime.

Duplicate content Different pages which are evaluated by the search engine to be similar and so don't rank highly, even though they may be for distinct products or services.

Dynamic pricing Prices can be updated in real time according to the type of customer or current market conditions.

Dynamic web page A page that is created in real time, often with reference to a database query, in response to a user request.

E

Early adopters Companies or departments that invest in new marketing techniques and technologies when they first become available in an attempt to gain a competitive advantage despite the higher risk entailed than that involved in a more cautious approach.

Early (first) mover advantage An early entrant into the marketplace.

Earned media The audience is reached through editorial, comments and sharing online.

Earnings-per-click (EPC) A relative measure of the effectiveness of a site or section of a site in generating revenue for the site owner through affiliate marketing for every 100 outbound clicks generated.

E-business *See* **Electronic business**.

E-cash *See* **Digital cash**.

E-commerce *See* **Electronic commerce**.

Econometric modelling A quantitative technique to evaluate the past influence or predict the future influence on a dependent variable (typically sales in a marketing context) of independent variables which may include product price, promotions and the level and mix of media investments.

Effective cost-per-thousand (eCPM) A measure of the total revenue a site owner can achieve through advertising or other revenue options. eCPM is calculated as advertising revenue achieved for every 1000 pages that are served for the whole site or a section. *See* EPC.

Effective frequency The number of exposures or ad impressions (frequency) required for an advertisement to become effective.

Effectiveness Meeting process objectives, delivering the required outputs and outcomes. 'Doing the right thing.'

Efficiency Minimising resources or time needed to complete a process. 'Doing the thing right.'

E-government The use of Internet technologies to provide government services to citizens.

Electronic business (e-business) All electronically mediated information exchanges, both within an organisation and with external stakeholders, supporting the range of business processes.

Electronic cash *See* **Digital cash**.

Electronic commerce (e-commerce) All financial and informational electronically mediated exchanges between an organisation and its external stakeholders. (*See* **Buy-side e-commerce** and **Sell-side e-commerce**.)

Electronic commerce transactions Transactions in the trading of goods and services conducted using the Internet and other digital media.

Electronic customer relationship management Using digital communications technologies to maximise sales to existing customers and encourage continued usage of online services.

Electronic data interchange (EDI) The exchange, using digital media, of standardised business documents such as purchase orders and invoices between buyers and sellers.

Electronic mail (e-mail) Sending messages or documents, such as news about a new product or sales promotion between individuals. A primitive form of push channel. E-mail may be inbound or outbound.

Electronic mail advertising Advertisements contained within e-mail such as newsletters.

Electronic mall *See* **Virtual mall**.

Electronic marketing Achieving marketing objectives through use of electronic communications technology.

Electronic marketspace A virtual marketplace such as the Internet in which no direct contact occurs between buyers and sellers.

Electronic procurement (e-procurement) The electronic integration and management of all procurement activities including purchase request, authorization, ordering, delivery and payment between a purchaser and a supplier.

Electronic shopping or ES test This test was developed by de Kare-Silver to assess the extent to which consumers are likely to purchase a particular retail product using the Internet.

Electronic tokens Units of digital currency that are in a standard electronic format.

E-mail marketing Typically applied to outbound communications from a company to prospects or customers to encourage purchase or branding goals. E-mail marketing is most commonly used for mailing to existing customers on a house-list, but can also be used for mailing prospects on a rented or co-branded list. E-mails may be sent as part of a one-off campaign or can be automated event-based triggered e-mails such as a Welcome strategy which can be broadcast based on rules about intervals and customer characteristics. *See* **Inbound e-mail** and **Outbound e-mail**.

E-mail service providers (ESPs) Provide a web-based service used by marketers to manage their e-mail activities including hosting e-mail subscription forms, broadcast and tracking.

E-marketing *See* **Electronic marketing**.

Emergent strategy Strategic analysis, strategic development and strategy implementation are interrelated and are developed together.

Emotional loyalty Loyalty to a brand is demonstrated by favourable perceptions, opinions and recommendations.

Encryption The scrambling of information into a form that cannot be interpreted. Decryption is used to make the information readable.

Enterprise application integration The middleware technology that is used to connect together different software applications and their underlying databases is now known as 'enterprise application integration (EAI)'.

Entry page The page at which a visitor enters a website. It is identified by a log file analyser. *See* **Exit page** and **Referring site**.

Environmental scanning and analysis The process of continuously monitoring the environment and events and responding accordingly.

E-retail According to Dennis *et al*. (2004), see Chapter 11, the business of e-retailing is defined as the sale of goods and services via the Internet or other electronic channels for individual consumers. This definition includes all e-commerce and related activities that ultimately result in transactions.

Ethical standards Practices or behaviours which are morally acceptable to society.

Evaluating a website *See* **Website measurement**.

Exchange *See* **Business-to-business exchanges or marketplaces**.

Exit page The page from which a visitor exits a website. It is identified by web analytics services.

Expert reviews An analysis of an existing site or prototype, by an experienced usability expert who will identify deficiencies and improvements to a site based on their knowledge of web design principles and best practice.

Exposure-based payment Advertisers pay according to the number of times the ad is viewed.

Extended product Additional features and benefits beyond the core product.

Extension *See* **Customer extension**.

External link building A proactive approach to gain quality links from third-party sites.

Extranet Formed by extending an intranet beyond a company to customers, suppliers, collaborators or even competitors. This is password-protected to prevent access by general Internet users.

F

Facebook commerce (F-commerce) Retailers create an online store within Facebook, often with a limited range of stock.

Faceted navigation Used to enable users to rapidly filter results from a product search based on different ways of classifying the product by their attributes or features. For example by brand, by sub-product category, by price bands.

Feed or RSS feed Blog, news or other content is published by an XML standard and syndicated for other sites or read by users in RSS reader services such as Google Reader, personalised home pages or e-mail systems. RSS stands for *really simple syndication*.

File Transfer Protocol (FTP) A standard method for moving files across the Internet. FTP is available as a feature of web browsers that is sometimes used for marketing applications such as downloading files like product price lists or specifications. Standalone FTP packages such as WSFTP are commonly used to update HTML files on web servers when uploading revisions to the web server.

Findability An assessment of how easy it is for a web user to locate a single content object or to use browse navigation and search system to find content. Like usability it is assessed through efficiency – how long it takes to find the content – and effectiveness – how satisfied the user is with the experience and relevance of the content they find.

Firewall A specialised software application mounted on a server at the point where a company is connected to the Internet. Its purpose is to prevent unauthorised access into the company by outsiders. Firewalls are essential for all companies hosting their own web server.

First-party cookies Served by the site currently in use – typical for e-commerce sites.

Flow Describes a state in which users have a positive experience from readily controlling their navigation and interaction on a website.

Focus groups Online focus groups have been conducted by w3focus.com. These follow a bulletin board or discussion group form where different members of the focus group respond to prompts from the focus group leaders.

Folksonomy A contraction of 'folk taxonomy', a method of classifying content based on tagging that has no hierarchy (i.e. without parent–child relationships).

Form A method on a web page of entering information such as order details.

Forward auctions Item purchased by highest bid made in bidding period.

Forward path analysis Forward path analysis reviews the combinations of clicks that occur from a page. This form of analysis is most beneficial when it is forward from important pages such as the home page, product and directory pages. This technique is used to identify messaging/navigation combinations which work best to yield the most clicks from a page. Similar, effective messaging approaches can then be deployed elsewhere on the site.

Frame A technique used to divide a web page into different parts such as a menu and separate content.

G

Gamification The process of applying game thinking and mechanics to engage an audience by rewarding them for achievements and sharing.

Global (or generic) top-level domain names (gLTD) The part of the domain name that refers to the category of site. The gLTD is usually the rightmost part of the domain name such as .co.uk or .com.

Globalisation The increase of international trading and shared social and cultural values.

Gopher Gopher is a directory-based structure containing information in certain categories.

GPRS This is approximately five times faster than GSM and is an 'always-on' service which is charged according to usage. Display is still largely text-based and based on the WAP protocol.

Graphic design All factors that govern the physical appearance of a web page.

Graphics Interchange Format (GIF) A graphics format used to display images within web pages. An interlaced GIF is displayed gradually on the screen, building up an image in several passes.

GSM The digital transmission technique standard used widely for mobile voice data.

H

Hacker Someone who enjoys exploring the details of programmable systems and how to stretch their capabilities.

Halo effect The role of one media channel on influencing sale or uplift in brand metrics. Commonly applied to online display advertising, where exposure to display ads may increase clickthrough rates when the consumer is later exposed to a brand through other media, for example sponsored links or affiliate ads. It may also improve conversion rates on destination sites through higher confidence in the brand or familiarity with the offer.

Hard launch A site is launched once fully complete with full promotional effort.

Hit A hit is recorded for each graphic or page of text requested from a web server. It is not a reliable measure for the number of people viewing a page. A page impression is a more reliable measure denoting one person viewing one page.

Home page The index page of a website with menu options or links to other resources on the site. Usually denoted by <web address>/index.html.

House list A list of prospect and customer names, e-mail addresses and profile information owned by an organisation.

HTML (Hypertext Markup Language) A standard format used to define the text and layout of web pages. HTML files usually have the extension .HTML or .HTM.

HTTP (Hypertext Transfer Protocol) A standard that defines the way information is transmitted across the Internet.

Hurdle rate The proportion of customers that fall within a particular level of activity. For example, the percentage of members of an e-mail list that click on the e-mail within a 90-day period, or the number of customers that have made a second purchase.

Hype cycle A graphic representation of the maturity, adoption and business application of specific technologies.

Hyperlink A method of moving between one website page and another, indicated to the user by text highlighted by underlining and/or a different colour. Hyperlinks can also be achieved by clicking on a graphic image such as a banner advertisement that is linked to another website.

I

Identity theft The misappropriation of the identity of another person, without their knowledge or consent.

I-Mode A mobile access platform that enables display of colour graphics and content subscription services.

Inbound customer contact strategies Approaches to managing the cost and quality of service related to management of customer enquiries.

Inbound e-mail E-mail arriving at a company.

Inbound e-mail marketing Management of e-mails from customers by an organisation.

Inbound Internet-based communications Customers enquire through web-based form and e-mail (*See* **Web self-service**).

Inbound link *See* **backlink**.

Inbound marketing The consumer is proactive in actively seeking out information for their needs and interactions with brands are attracted through content, search and social media marketing.

Incidental offline advertising Driving traffic to the website is not a primary objective of the advert.

Index inclusion Ensuring that as many of the relevant pages from your domain(s) are included within the search engine indexes you are targeting to be listed in.

Infomediary An intermediary business whose main source of revenue derives from capturing consumer information and developing detailed profiles of individual customers for use by third parties.

Information architecture The combination of organisation, labelling and navigation schemes constituting an information system.

Information organisation schemes The structure chosen to group and categorise information.

Initiation of the website project This phase of the project should involve a structured review of the costs and benefits of developing a website (or making a major revision to an existing website). A successful outcome to initiation will be a decision to proceed with the site development phase, with an agreed budget and target completion date.

Insertion order A printed order to run an advertisement campaign. It defines the campaign name, the website receiving the order and the planner or buyer giving the order, the individual advertisements to be run (or who will provide them), the sizes of the advertisements, the campaign start and end dates, the CPM, the total cost, discounts to be applied, and reporting requirements and possible penalties or stipulations relative to the failure to deliver the impressions.

Integrated marketing communications The co-ordination of communications channels to deliver a clear, consistent message.

Integrity *See* **Security methods**.

Intellectual property rights (IPRs) Protect the intangible property created by corporations or individuals that is protected under copyright, trade secret and patent laws.

Interactive banner advertisement A banner advertisement that enables the user to enter information.

Interactive digital TV (iDTV) Television displayed using a digital signal delivered by a range of media – cable, satellite, terrestrial (aerial). Interactions can be provided through phone line or cable service.

Interactivity The medium enables a dialogue between company and customer.

Interaction rate (IR) The proportion of ad viewers who interact with an online ad through rolling over it. Some will be involuntary depending on where the ad is placed on screen, so it is highly dependent on placement.

Internal link architecture Structuring and labelling links within a site's navigation to improve the results of SEO.

Intermediaries Online sites that help bring together different parties such as buyers and sellers.

Internet The physical network that links computers across the globe. It consists of the infrastructure of network servers and communication links between them that are used to hold and transport the vast amount of information on the Internet.

Internet-based market research The use of online questionnaires and focus groups to assess customer perceptions of a website or broader marketing issues.

Internet contribution An assessment of the extent to which the Internet contributes to sales is a key measure of the importance of the Internet to a company.

Internet EDI Use of electronic data interchange standards delivered across non-proprietary Internet protocol networks.

Internet governance Control of the operation and use of the Internet.

Internet marketing The application of the Internet and related digital technologies in conjunction with traditional communications to achieve marketing objectives.

Internet marketing metrics *See* **Metrics for Internet marketing**.

Internet marketing strategy Definition of the approach by which Internet marketing will support marketing and business objectives.

Internet Protocol Television (IPTV) Digital television service delivered using Internet protocol, typically by a broadband connection. IPTV can be streamed for real-time viewing or downloaded before playback.

Internet pureplay An organisation with the majority of its customer-facing operations online, e.g. Egg.

Internet Relay Chat (IRC) A communications tool that allows a text-based 'chat' between different users who are logged on at the same time. Of limited use for marketing purposes except for special-interest or youth products.

Internet service provider (ISP) Company that provides home or business users with a connection to access the

Internet. It can also host websites or provide a link from web servers to allow other companies and consumers access to a corporate website.

Interruption marketing Marketing communications that disrupt customers' activities.

Interstitial ads Ads that appear between one page and the next.

Intranet A network within a single company that enables access to company information using the familiar tools of the Internet such as web browsers and e-mail. Only staff within a company can access the intranet, which will be password-protected.

J

Java A programming language standard supported by Sun Microsystems, which permits complex and graphical customer applications to be written and then accessed from a web browser. An example might be a form for calculating interest on a loan. A competitor to ActiveX.

Joint Photographics Experts Group (JPEG) A compressed graphics standard specified by the JPEG. Used for graphic images typically requiring use of many colours, such as product photographs where some loss of quality is acceptable. The format allows for some degradation in image quality to enable more rapid download.

K

Key online influencers Individuals or publishers who an online target audience listens to and interacts with. Online influencer outreach or 'blogger outreach' can help companies reach and engage a wider audience.

Key performance indicators (KPIs) Metrics used to assess the performance of a process and/or whether goals set are achieved.

Keyphrase (keyword phrase) The combination of words users of search engines type into a search box which form a search query.

L

Lagging performance indicator A metric which indicates past performance. Corrective action can then be applied to improve performance.

Landing page A destination page when a user clicks on an ad or other form of link from a *referring site*. It can be a home page, but more typically and desirably a landing page is a page with the messaging focused on the offer in the ad. This will maximise conversion rates and brand favourability.

Last-click method of digital media channel attribution The site which referred a visitor immediately before purchase is credited with the sale. Previous referrals influenced by other customer touch-points on other sites are ignored.

Latency The average length of time that different customer types takes between different activities, e.g. log-ins, paying bills, first and second purchase.

Lead Details about a potential customer (prospect). (*See* **Qualified lead**.)

Leading performance indicator A measure which is suggestive of future performance and so can be used to take proactive action to shape future performance.

Lead generation offers Offered in return for customers providing their contact details and characteristics. Commonly used in B2B marketing where free information such as a report or a seminar will be offered.

Lifetime value (LTV) The total net benefit that a customer or group of customers will provide a company over their total relationship with a company.

Link anchor text The text used to form the blue, underlined hyperlink viewed in a web browser defined in the HTML source. For example: Visit Dave Chaffey's web log is created by the HTML code: <A HREF="http:// www.davechaffey.com">Visit Dave Chaffey's web log</A>.

Link building A proactive approach to gain quality links from third-party sites.

List broker Will source the appropriate e-mail list(s) from the list owner.

List owner Has collected e-mail addresses which are offered for sale.

Live website Current site accessible to customers, as distinct from test website.

Localisation Designing the content of the website in such a way that it is appropriate to different audiences in different countries.

Location-based marketing Location or proximity-based marketing is mobile marketing based on the GPS built into phones or based on interaction with other local digital devices.

Log file A file stored on a web server that records every item downloaded by users.

Log file analysers Web analytics tools that are used to build a picture of the amount of usage of different parts of a website based on the information contained in the log file.

Long tail concept A frequency distribution suggesting the relative variation in popularity of items selected by consumers.

Loyalty techniques Customers sign up to an incentive scheme where they receive points for repeat purchases, which can be converted into offers such as discounts, free products or cash. (Also known as online incentive schemes.)

M

Macro-environment Broader forces affecting all organisations in the marketplace including social, technological, economic, political and legal aspects.

Mailbots *See* **Autoresponders**.

Maintenance process The work involved in running a live website such as updating pages and checking the performance of the site.

Malware Malicious software or toolbars, typically downloaded via the Internet, which act as a 'trojan horse' by executing other unwanted activites such as keylogging of user passwords or viruses which may collect e-mail addresses.

Marketing-led site design Site design elements are developed to achieve customer acquisition, retention and communication of marketing messages.

Marketing intermediaries Firms that can help a company to promote, sell and distribute its products or services.

Marketing mix The series of seven key variables – Product, Price, Place, Promotion, People, Process and Physical evidence – that are varied by marketers as part of the customer offering.

Marketing planning A logical sequence and a series of activities leading to the setting of marketing objectives and the formulation of plans for achieving them.

Marketplace *See* **Business-to-business exchanges or marketplaces**.

Marketsite eXchange, eHub, metamediaries are terms used to refer to complex websites that facilitate trading exchanges between companies around the globe.

MarketSite™ is a trade mark of commerceOne and considered as the leading e-marketplace operating environment.

Marketspace A virtual marketplace such as the Internet in which no direct contact occurs between buyers and sellers. (Also known as electronic marketspace.)

Markup language *See* **HTML, XML**.

Mashup Websites, pages or widgets that combine the content or functionality of one website or data source with another to create something offering a different type of value to web users from the separate types of content or functionality.

Mass customisation The ability to create tailored marketing messages or products for individual customers or a group of similar customers (a bespoke service), yet retain the economies of scale and the capacity of mass marketing or production.

Mass marketing One-to-many communication between a company and potential customers, with limited tailoring of the message.

Measurement *See* **Website measurement**.

Media broker A company that places advertisements for companies wishing to advertise by contacting the media owners.

Media buyer The person within a company wishing to advertise who places the advertisement, usually via a media broker.

Media buying The process of purchasing media to meet the media plan requirements at the lowest costs.

Media fragmentation Describes a trend to increasing choice and consumption of a range of media in terms of different channels such as web and mobile and also within channels, for example more TV channels, radio stations, magazines, more websites. Media fragmentation implies increased difficulty in reaching target audiences.

Media multiplier or halo effect The role of one media channel on influencing sale or uplift in brand metrics. Commonly applied to online display advertising, where exposure to display ads may increase click-through rates when the consumer is later exposed to a brand through other media, for example sponsored links or affiliate ads. It may also improve conversion rates on destination sites through higher confidence in the brand or familiarity with the offer.

Media-neutral planning (MNP) An approach to planning ad campaigns to maximise response across different media according to consumer usage of these media.

Media owners The owners of websites (or other media such as newspapers) that accept advertisements.

Media planning The process of selecting the best combination of media to achieve marketing campaign objectives. Answers questions such as 'How many of the audience can I reach through different media?', 'On which media (and ad vehicles) should I place ads?', 'Which frequency should I select?', 'How much money should be spent in each medium?'

Media site Typical location where paid-for ads are placed.

Merchandising *See* **Web merchandising**.

Meta-data Literally, data about data – a format describing the structure and content of data.

Meta search engines Meta search engines submit keywords typed by users to a range of search engines in order to increase the number of relevant pages since different search engines may have indexed different sites. An example is the meta-crawler search engine or www.mamma.com.

Meta-tags Text within an HTML file summarising the content of the site (content meta-tag) and relevant keywords (keyword meta-tag), which are matched against the keywords typed into search engines.

Metrics for Internet marketing Measures that indicate the effectiveness of Internet marketing activities in meeting customer, business and marketing objectives.

Micro-environment Specific forces on an organisation generated by its stakeholders.

Micropayments (microtransactions) Digital cash systems that allow very small sums of money (fractions of 1p) to be transferred, but with lower security. Such small sums do not warrant a credit card payment, because processing is too costly.

Microsite Specialised content that is part of a website that is not necessarily owned by the organisation. If owned by the company it may be as part of an extranet. (*See* **Nested ad content**.)

Microsoft Internet Information Server (IIS) Microsoft IIS is a web server developed by Microsoft that runs on Windows NT.

Mixed-mode buying The process by which a customer changes between online and offline channels during the buying process.

Mobile-based apps A software application that is designed for use on a mobile phone, typically downloaded from an app store. iPhone apps are best known, but all smartphones support the use of apps which can provide users with information, entertainment or location-based services such as mapping.

Mobile commerce The use of wireless devices such as mobile phones for informational or monetary transactions.

Mobile marketing Marketing to encourage consumer engagement when using mobile phones (particularly smartphones) or tablet devices.

Multichannel marketing Customer communications and product distribution are supported by a combination of digital and traditional channels at different points in the buying cycle.

Multichannel marketing strategy Defines how different marketing channels should integrate and support each other in terms of their proposition development and communications based on their relative merits for the customer and the company.

Multichannel prioritisation Assesses the strategic significance of the Internet relative to other communications channels and then deploys resources to integrate with marketing channels.

N

Narrow and deep navigation Fewer choices and more clicks to reach required content.

Natural or organic listings The pages listing results from a search engine query which are displayed in a sequence according to relevance of match between the keyword phrase typed into a search engine and a web page according to a ranking algorithm used by the search engine.

Navigation The method of finding and moving between different information and pages on a website. It is governed by menu arrangements, site structure and the layout of individual pages.

Navigational search Searchers use a search engine such as Google to find information deeper within a company site by appending a qualifier such as a product name to the brand or site name. Organisations need to check that relevant pages are available in the search results pages for these situations.

Near Field Communications (NFC) Enables data exchange through wireless connections between two devices in close proximity to each other. Use of NFC enabled smartphones can facilitate contactless payments.

Nested ad content This refers to the situation when the person undertaking the click-through is not redirected to a corporate or brand site, but is instead taken to a related page on the same site as that on which the advertisement is placed. (Sometimes referred to as microsite.)

Net Promoter Score A measure of the number of advocates a company (or website) has who would recommend it compared to the number of detractors.

Non-repudiability *See* **Security methods**.

Notification The process whereby companies register with the data protection register to inform about their data holdings.

O

Offer An incentive in direct marketing or a product offering.

Offline site promotion Traditional techniques such as print and TV advertising used to generate website traffic.

Offline web metric Offline measures are those that are collated by marketing staff recording particular marketing outcomes such as an enquiry or a sale. They are usually collated manually, but could be collated automatically.

On-page optimisation Writing copy and applying markup such as the <title> tag and heading tags <h1> to highlight to search engines relevant keyphrases within a document.

One-to-one marketing A unique dialogue that occurs directly between a company and individual customers (or less strictly with groups of customers with similar needs). The dialogue involves a company in listening to customer needs and responding with services to meet these needs.

Online brand *See* **Digital brand**.

Online branding How online channels are used to support brands that, in essence, are the sum of the characteristics of a product or service as perceived by a user.

Online business model A summary of how a company will generate a profit identifying its core product or service value proposition, target customers in different markets, position in the competitive online marketplace or value chain and its projections for revenue and costs.

Online company presence Different forms of online media controlled by a company including their website, blogs, e-mail list and social media presences. Also known as 'owned media'.

Online customer experience The combination of rational and emotional factors in using a company's online services that influences customers' perceptions of a brand online.

Online incentive schemes *See* **Loyalty techniques**.

Online influencer outreach Identifying online influencers such as bloggers, media owners or individuals with a large online following in the social networks and then approaching them to partner together to communicate with their audience.

Online intermediary sites Websites that facilitate exchanges between consumer and business suppliers.

Online market ecosystem Interactions between different online systems related to a specific hardware or software technology which may be independent or developed by a particular brand.

Online promotion contribution An assessment of the proportion of customers (new or retained) who are reached by online communications and are influenced as a result.

Online PR (e-PR) Maximising favourable mentions of your company, brands, products or websites on third-party websites which are likely to be visited by your target audience. Online PR can extend reach and awareness of a brand within an audience and will also generate backlinks vital to SEO. It can also be used to support viral or word-of-mouth marketing activities in other media.

Online reputation management Controlling the reputation of an organisation through monitoring and controlling messages placed about the organisation.

Online revenue contribution An assessment of the direct contribution of the Internet or other digital media to sales, usually expressed as a percentage of overall sales revenue.

Online service providers (OSPs) An OSP is sometimes used to distinguish large Internet service providers (ISPs) from other access providers. In the UK, AOL, Freeserve, VirginNet and LineOne can be considered OSPs since they have a large amount of specially developed content available to their subscribers. Note that this term is not used as frequently as ISP, and the distinction between ISPs and OSPs is a blurred one since all OSPs are also ISPs and the distinction only occurs according to the amount of premium content (only available to customers) offered as part of the service.

Online service-quality gap The mismatch between what is expected and delivered by an online presence.

Online site promotion Internet-based techniques used to generate website traffic.

Online social network A service facilitating the connection, collaboration and exchange of information between individuals.

online tactical marketing segmentation Please supply

Online value proposition (OVP) A statement of the benefits of online services that reinforce the core proposition and differentiate from an organisation's offline offering and that of competitors.

Online web metrics Online measures are those that are collected automatically on the web server, often in a server log file.

Operational effectiveness Performing similar activities better than rivals. This includes efficiency of processes.

Opt-in A customer proactively agrees to receive further information.

Opt-in e-mail The customer is only contacted when he or she has explicitly asked for information to be sent (usually when filling in an on-screen form).

Opt-out A customer declines the offer to receive further information.

Opt-out e-mail The customer is not contacted subsequently if he or she has explicitly stated that he or she does not want to be contacted in future. Opt-out or unsubscribe options are usually available within the e-mail itself.

Outbound e-mail E-mail sent from a company.

Outbound e-mail marketing E-mails are sent to customers and prospects from an organisation.

Outbound Internet-based communications The website and e-mail marketing are used to send personalised communications to customers.

Outsourcing Contracting an outside company to undertake part of the Internet marketing activities.

Overlay Typically an animated ad that moves around the page and is superimposed on the website content.

Overt Typically an animated ad that moves around the page and is superimposed on the website content.

Owned media Different forms of online media controlled by a company including their website, blogs, e-mail list and social media presence.

P

Page impression One page impression occurs when a member of the audience views a web page. (*See* **Ad impression** and **Reach**.)

PageRank A scale between 0 to 10 used by Google to assess the importance of websites according to the number of inbound links or backlinks.

Page request The process of a user selecting a hyperlink or typing in a uniform resource locator (URL) to retrieve information on a specific web page. Equivalent to page impression.

Page view *See* **Page impression**.

Paid media Also known as bought media, a direct payment occurs to a site owner or an ad network when they serve an ad, a sponsorship or pay for a click, lead or sale generated.

Paid search marketing (pay-per-click PPC) A relevant text ad with a link to a company page is displayed on the SERPs when the user of a search engine types in a specific phrase. A fee is charged for every click of each link, with the amount bid for the click mainly determining its position. Additionally, PPC may involve advertising through a content network of third-party sites (which may be on a CPC, CPM or CPA basis).

Pay-for-performance communications The wastage from traditional media buys can be reduced online through advertising models where the advertisers only pay for a response (cost-per-click) as in pay-per-click search marketing or for a lead or sale as in affiliate marketing.

Pay-per-click PPC refers to when a company pays for text ads to be displayed on the search engine results pages as a sponsored link (typically above, to the right of or below the natural listings) when a specific keyphrase is entered by the search users. It is so called because the marketer pays each time the hypertext link in the ad is clicked on. If a link is clicked repeatedly, then this will be detected by the search engine as click fraud and the marketer will not be charged.

Payment systems Methods of transferring funds from a customer to a merchant.

People variable The element of the marketing mix that involves the delivery of service to customers during interactions with those customers.

Performance drivers Critical success factors that determine whether business and marketing objectives are achieved.

Performance management system A process used to evaluate and improve the efficiency and effectiveness of an organisation and its processes.

Performance measurement system The process by which metrics are defined, collected, disseminated and actioned.

Performance metrics Measures that are used to evaluate and improve the efficiency and effectiveness of business processes.

Performance of website Performance or quality of service is dependent on its availability and speed of access.

Permission marketing Customers agree (opt in) to be involved in an organisation's marketing activities, usually as a result of an incentive.

Persistent cookies Cookies that remain on a computer after a visitor session has ended. Used to recognise returning visitors.

Personal data Any information about an individual stored by companies concerning their customers or employees.

Personalisation Web-based personalisation involves delivering customised content for the individual through web pages, e-mail or push technology.

Personas A thumbnail summary of the characteristics, needs, motivations and environment of typical website users.

Persuasion marketing Using design elements such as layout, copy and typography together with promotional messages to encourage site users to follow particular paths and specific actions rather than giving them complete choice in their navigation.

Phishing Obtaining personal details online through sites and e-mails masquerading as legitimate businesses.

Phone-me A call-back facility available on the website for a company to contact a customer by phone at a later time, as specified by the customer.

Physical evidence variable The element of the marketing mix that involves the tangible expression of a product and how it is purchased and used.

Pixel The small dots on a computer screen that are used to represent images and text. Short for 'picture element'. Used to indicate the size of banner advertisements.

Place variable The element of the marketing mix that involves distributing products to customers in line with demand and minimising cost of inventory, transport and storage.

Plug-in A program that must be downloaded to view particular content such as an animation.

Podcasts Individuals and organisations post online media (audio and video) which can be viewed in the appropriate players (including the iPod which first sparked the growth in this technique). The latest podcast updates can be automatically delivered by *Really Simple Syndication*.

Portal A website that acts as a gateway to information and services available on the Internet by providing search engines, directories and other services such as personalised news or free e-mail.

Portfolio analysis Evaluation of value of current e-commerce services or applications.

Positioning Customers' perception of the product and brand offering relative to those of competitors.

Prescriptive strategy The three core areas of strategic analysis, strategic development and strategy implementation are linked together sequentially.

Price comparison sites *See* **Aggregators**.

Price dispersion The distribution or range of prices charged for an item across different retailers.

Price elasticity of demand Measure of consumer behaviour that indicates the change in demand for a product or service in response to changes in price.

Price transparency Customer knowledge about pricing increases due to increased availability of pricing information.

Price variable The element of the marketing mix that involves defining product prices and pricing models.

Pricing level The price set for a specific product or range of products.

Pricing model Describes the form of payment such as outright purchase, auction, rental, volume purchases and credit terms.

Primary persona A representation of the typical site user.

Privacy A moral right of individuals to avoid intrusion into their personal affairs. (*See* **Security methods**.)

Privacy and Electronic Communications Regulations Act A law intended to control the distribution of e-mail and other online communications including cookies.

Privacy statement Information on a website explaining how and why individuals' data are collected, processed and stored.

Process variable The element of the marketing mix that involves the methods and procedures companies use to achieve all marketing functions.

Product variable The element of the marketing mix that involves researching customers' needs and developing appropriate products. (*See* **Core product** and **Extended product**.)

Profiling *See* **Customer profiling**.

Promotion (online and offline) Online promotion uses communication via the Internet itself to raise awareness about a site and drive traffic to it. This promotion may take the form of links from other sites, banner advertisements or targeted e-mail messages. Offline promotion uses traditional media such as television or newspaper advertising and word-of-mouth to promote a company's website.

Promotion variable The element of the marketing mix that involves communication with customers and other stakeholders to inform them about the product and the organisation.

Propensity modelling A name given to the approach of evaluating customer characteristics and behaviour and then making recommendations for future products.

Prosumer 'Producer + consumer'. The customer is closely involved in specifying their requirements in a product.

Prototypes and prototyping A prototype is a preliminary version of part (or a framework of all) of a website that can be reviewed by its target audience, or the marketing team. Prototyping is an iterative process where website users suggest modifications before further prototypes are made and the final version of the site is developed.

Proximity marketing Marketing messages are delivered in real time according to customers' presence based on the technology they are carrying, wearing or have embedded. Bluecasting is the best-known example.

Psychographic segmentation A breakdown of customers according to different characteristics.

Public key A unique identifier of a buyer or a seller that is available to other parties to enable secure e-commerce using encryption based on digital certificates.

Public-key encryption An asymmetric form of encryption in which the keys or digital certificates used by the sender and receiver of information are different. The two keys are related, so only the pair of keys can be used together to encrypt and decrypt information.

Public-key infrastructure (PKI) The organisations responsible for issuing and maintaining certificates for public-key security together form the PKI.

Public relations The management of the awareness, understanding and reputation of an organisation or brand, primarily achieved through influencing exposure in the media.

Pull media The consumer is proactive in selection of the message through actively seeking out a website.

Push media Communications are broadcast from an advertiser to consumers of the message, who are passive recipients.

Push technology The delivery of web-based content to the user's desktop without the need for the user to visit a site to download information. E-mail can also be considered to be a push technology. A particular type of information is a push channel.

Q

Qualified lead Contact and profile information for a customer with an indication of the level of their interest in product categories.

Quality score An assessment in paid search by Google AdWords (and now other search engines) of an individual ad triggered by a keyword which, in combination with the bid amount, determines the ranking of the ad relative to competitors. The primary factor is the click-through rate for each ad, but quality score also considers the match between the keyword and the occurrence of the keyword in the text, historical click-through rates, the engagement of the searcher when they click-through to the site and the speed at which the page loads.

Quick Response (QR) code A QR code is a two-dimensional matrix bar code. QR codes were invented in Japan where they are a popular type of two-dimensional code used for direct response.

R

Reach The number of unique individuals who view an advertisement.

Real-time bidding (RTB) Bids for buying ads against keywords can be managed in real-time in conjunction with a DSP.

Really Simple Syndication (RSS) Blog, news or other content is published by an XML standard and syndicated for other sites or read by users in RSS reader software services.

RealNames A service for matching company names and brands with web addresses.

Reciprocal links Links which are agreed between yourself and another organisation.

Referrer The site that a visitor previously visited before following a link.

Referring sites A log file may indicate which site a user visited immediately before visiting the current site. (*See* **Click-through, Destination site** and **Exit page**.)

Referrer or referring site The source of a visitor to site delivered via a digital media channel. Typically a specific site, e.g. Google AdWords or a media site or an individual ad placement on the site.

Registration (individuals) The process whereby an individual subscribes to a site or requests further information by filling in contact details and his or her needs using an electronic form.

Registration (of domain name) The process of reserving a unique web address that can be used to refer to the company website.

Reintermediation The creation of new intermediaries between customers and suppliers providing services such as supplier search and product evaluation.

Relationship marketing Consistent application of up-to-date knowledge of individual customers to product and service design, which is communicated interactively in order to develop a continuous, mutually beneficial and long-term relationship.

Renderability The capability of an e-mail to display correctly formatted in different e-mail readers.

Repeat visits If an organisation can encourage customers to return to the website then the relationship can be maintained online.

Representation The locations on the Internet where an organisation is located for promoting or selling its services.

Repurposing Developing for a new access platform, such as the web, content which was previously used for a different platform.

Resource analysis Review of the technological, financial and human resources of an organisation and how they are utilised in business processes.

Resources Resources are defined as physical assets over which an organisation has control. This narrow definition of resources allows them to be clearly distinguished from capabilities (Beard and Sumner, 2004 – see Chapter 11).

Results-based payment Advertisers pay according to the number of times the ad is clicked on.

Retail channel Retailers' use of the Internet as both a communication and a transactional channel concurrently in business-to-consumer markets.

Retail format This is the general nature of the retail mix in terms of range of products and services, pricing policy, promotional programmes, operating style or store design and visual merchandising; examples include mail-order retailers (non-store-based) and department-store retailers.

Retention *See* **Customer retention**.

Return on advertising spend (ROAS) This indicates amount of revenue generated from each referrer. ROAS = Total revenue generated from referrer/Amount spent on advertising with referrer.

Return on investment (ROI) This indicates the profitability of any investment, or in an advertising context for each referring site.

ROI = Profit generated from investment/Cost of investment.

ROI = Profit generated from referrers/Amount spent on advertising with referrer.

Return path An interaction where the customer sends information to the iDTV provider using a phone line or cable.

Revenue models Describe methods of generating income for an organisation.

Reverse auctions Item purchased from lowest-bidding supplier in bidding period.

Reverse path analysis indicates the most popular combination of pages and/or calls-to-action which lead to a page. This is particularly useful for transactional pages such as the first checkout page on a consumer site; a lead generation or contact-us page on a business-to-business site; an e-mail subscription page; a call-me back option.

Rich media Advertisements that are not static, but provide animation, audio, sound or interactivity as a game or form to be completed. An example of this would be a banner display advertisement for a loan in which a customer can type in the amount of loan required, and the cost of the loan is calculated immediately.

Rich Internet Applications (RIA) Interactive applications which provide options such as product selectors or games. They may incorporate video or sound also. Typically built using technologies such as Adobe Flash, Ajax, Flex, Java or Silverlight.

Robot A tool, also known as a spider, that is employed by search engines to index web pages of registered sites on a regular basis. *See* **Spider**.

Run-of-site A situation where a company pays for banner advertisements to promote its services across a website.

S

Sales generation offers Offers that encourage product trial. A coupon redeemed against a purchase is a classic example.

Sales promotions The Internet offers tremendous potential for sales promotions of different types since it is more immediate than any other medium – it is always available for communication, and tactical variations in the details of the promotion can be made at short notice.

Satisficing behaviour Consumers do not behave entirely rationally in product or supplier selection. They will compare alternatives, but then may make their choice given imperfect information.

Saturation of the Internet Access to the Internet will reach saturation as home PC ownership reaches a limit, unless other access devices become popular.

Scenario-based analysis Models of the future environment are developed from different starting points.

Scenario of use A particular path or flow of events or activities performed by a visitor to a website.

Scripts Scripts can run either on the user's browser (client-side scripts) (*See* **Web browser**) or on the web server (server-side scripts).

Scrum A methodology that supports agile software development based on 15–30 day sprints to implement features from a product backlog. 'Scrum' refers to a daily project status meeting during the sprint.

Search engine Specialised website that uses automatic tools known as spiders or robots to index web pages of registered sites. Users can search the index by typing in keywords to specify their interest. Pages containing these keywords will be listed, and by clicking on a hyperlink the user will be taken to the site.

Search engine listing The list of sites and descriptions returned by a search engine after a user types in keywords.

Search engine marketing (SEM) Promoting an organisation through search engines to meet its objectives by delivering relevant content in the search listings for searchers and encouraging them to click-through to a destination site. The two key techniques of SEM are *search engine optimisation (SEO)* to improve results from the natural listings and paid-search marketing to deliver results from the sponsored listings within the search engines through pay-per-click (PPC) paid-search engine marketing and through content-network paid-search marketing (which may be on a PPC basis or on a CPM basis). SEM is about connecting the searchers with information which will help them find what they are looking for and will help site owners generate revenue or disseminate information.

Search engine optimisation (SEO) A structured approach used to increase the position of a company or its products in search engine natural or organic results listings (the main body of the search results page) for selected keywords or phrases.

Search engine ranking The position of a site on a particular search engine.

Search engine results pages (SERPs) The page(s) containing the results after a user types in a keyphrase into a search engine. SERPs contain both natural or organic listings and paid or sponsored listings.

Search engine submission The process of informing search engines that a site should be indexed for listing in the search engine results pages.

Secure Electronic Transaction (SET) A standard for public-key encryption intended to enable secure e-commerce transactions, lead-developed by Mastercard and Visa.

Secure HTTP Encrypted HTTP.

Secure Sockets Layer (SSL) A commonly used encryption technique for scrambling data such as credit card numbers as they are passed across the Internet from a web browser to a web server.

Security methods When systems for electronic commerce are devised, or when existing solutions are selected, the following attributes must be present:

- *Authentication* – are parties to the transaction who they claim to be? This is achieved through the use of digital certificates.
- *Privacy and confidentiality* – are transaction data protected? The consumer may want to make an anonymous purchase. Are all non-essential traces of a transaction removed from the public network and all intermediary records eliminated?
- *Integrity* – checks that the message sent is complete, i.e. that it is not corrupted.
- *Non-repudiability* – ensures sender cannot deny sending message.
- *Availability* – how can threats to the continuity and performance of the system be eliminated?

Seeding The viral campaign is started by sending an e-mail to a targeted group that are likely to propagate the virus.

Segmentation Identification of different groups within a target market in order to develop different offerings for each group.

Sell-side e-commerce E-commerce transactions between a supplier organisation and its customers.

Sense and respond communications Delivering timely, relevant communications to customers as part of a contact strategy based on assessment of their position in the customer lifecycle and monitoring specific interactions with a company's website, e-mails and staff.

Server log file *See* **Online web metrics**.

Service quality The level of service received on a website. Dependent on reliability, responsiveness and availability of staff and the website service.

Serving Used to describe the process of displaying an advertisement on a website (ad serving) or delivering a web page to a user's web browser. (*See* **Web server**.)

Session *See* **Visitor session**.

Session cookie A cookie used to manage a single visitor session.

Share of search The audience share of Internet searchers achieved by a particular audience in a particular market.

Share of voice The relative advertising spend of the different competitive brands within the product category. Share of voice (SOV) is calculated by dividing a particular brand's advertising spend by the total category spend.

Short code Five-digit numbers combined with text that can be used by advertisers or broadcasters to encourage consumers to register their interest. They are typically followed-up by an automated text message from the advertiser with the option to opt in to further information by e-mail or to link through to a WAP site.

Short Message Service (SMS) The formal name for text messaging.

Single customer view Customer profile information is kept consistent across systems to maintain customer data quality.

Site *See* **Website**.

Site announcements Usually used to describe the dissemination of information about a new or revised website.

Site auditors Auditors accurately measure the usage for different sites as the number of ad impressions and click-through rates. Auditors include ABC (Audit Bureau of Circulation) and BPA (Business Publication Auditor) International.

Site availability An indication of how easy it is to connect to a website as a user. In theory this figure should be 100 per cent, but for technical reasons such as failures in the server hardware or upgrades to software, sometimes users cannot access the site and the figure falls below 90 per cent.

Site design page template A standard page layout format which is applied to each page of a website. Typically defined for different page categories (e.g. category page, product page, search page).

Site map A graphical or text depiction of the relationship between different groups of content on a website.

Site measurement *See* **Website measurement**.

Site navigation scheme Tools provided to the user to move between different information on a website.

Site re-launch Where a website is replaced with a new version with a new 'look and feel'.

Site statistics Collected by log file analysers, these are used to monitor the effectiveness of a website.

Site 'stickiness' An indication of how long a visitor stays on a site. Log file analysers can be used to assess average visit times.

Site visit One site visit records one customer visiting the site. Not equivalent to User session.

Site-visitor activity data Information on content and services accessed by e-commerce site visitors.

Sitemapping tools These tools diagram the layout of the website, which is useful for site management and can be used to assist users.

Situation analysis Collection and review of information about an organisation's external environment and internal processes and resources in order to inform its strategies.

SMART metrics SMART metrics must be:

- Specific
- Measurable
- Actionable
- Relevant
- Timely.

Smartcards Physical cards containing a memory chip that can be inserted into a smartcard reader before items can be purchased.

Social commerce Social commerce is a subset of e-commerce which encourages participation and interaction of customers in rating, selecting and buying products through group-buying. This participation can occur on an e-commerce site or on third-party sites.

Social CRM The process of managing customer-to-customer conversations to engage existing customers, prospects and other stakeholders with a brand and so enhance customer-relationship management.

Social exclusion Part of society is excluded from the facilities available to the remainder.

Social bookmarking Web users keep a shared version of favourite sites ('Favorites') online. This enables the most popular sites in a category to be identified.

Social graph A term popularised by Facebook in 2007 when describing its Facebook platform. The social graph describes the relationship between individuals linked through social networks and other connections such as email or personal contact.

Social location-based marketing Where social media tools give users the option of sharing their location, and hence give businesses the opportunity to use proximity or location-based marketing to deliver targeted offers and messages to consumers and collect data about their preferences and behaviour. Businesses can offer consumers benefits to check-in, for example, to gain points, be the most regular visitor to that location, to gain rewards and prizes from advertisers, to share their location with friends, and, in the case of events, to meet like-minded people. Of course the privacy implications of this relatively new technology must be carefully reviewed.

Social media governance A definition of how companies should respond to social mentions that may give rise to leads or reputational damage.

Social media listening The process of using monitoring tools to review mentions of a brand and related keywords within social networks and other online sites.

Social media marketing Monitoring and facilitating customer-customer interaction and participation throughout the web to encourage positive engagement with a company and its brands. Interactions may occur on a company site, social networks and other third-party sites.

Social media strategy A definition of the marketing communications used to achieve interaction with social network users to meet business goals. The scope of social media optimisation also includes incorporation of social features such as status updates and sharing widgets into company websites.

Social network A site that facilitates peer-to-peer communications within a group or between individuals through providing facilities to develop user-generated content (UGC) and to exchange messages and comments between different users.

Social sign-on A user logs-in to a site using a social network service user name and password. This can enable connection between social memberships and company profile information.

Soft launch A trial version of a site launched with limited publicity.

Soft lock-in Electronic linkages between supplier and customer increase switching costs.

Software agents *See* **Agents**.

Spam Unsolicited e-mail (usually bulk mailed and untargeted).

Spamming Bulk e-mailing of unsolicited mail.

Specific offline advertising Driving traffic to the website or explaining the online proposition is a primary objective of the advert.

Spider Spiders are software processes, technically known as robots, employed by search engines to index web pages of registered sites on a regular basis. They follow links between pages and record the reference URL of a page for future analysis.

Splash page A preliminary page that precedes the normal home page of a website. Site users can either wait to be redirected to the home page or can follow a link to do this. Splash pages are not now commonly used since they slow down the process of customers finding the information they need.

Sponsorship Sponsorship involves a company paying money to advertise on a website. The arrangement may involve more than advertising. Sponsorship is a similar arrangement to co-branding.

Stage models Models for the development of different levels of Internet marketing services.

Stages in website development The standard stages of creation of a website are initiation, feasibility, analysis, design, development (content creation), testing and maintenance.

Static (fixed) web page A page on the web server that is invariant.

STEP A framework for assessing the macroenvironment, standing for Social, Technological, Economic and Political (including legal).

Storyboarding Using static drawings or screenshots of the different parts of a website to review the design concept with customers or clients.

Strategic agility The capability to innovate and so gain competitive advantage within a marketplace by monitoring changes within an organisation's marketplace and then to efficiently evaluate alternative strategies and then select, review and implement appropriate candidate strategies.

Strategic analysis Collection and review of information about an organisation's internal processes and resources and external marketplace factors in order to inform strategy definition.

Strategic market segmentation Selection of key audiences to target with value propositions developed for these audiences

Strategic positioning Performing different activities from rivals or performing similar activities in different ways.

Strategic windows Opportunities arising through a significant change in environment.

Strategy formulation Generation, review and selection of strategies to achieve strategic objectives.

Strategy process model A framework for approaching strategy development.

Streaming media Sound and video that can be experienced within a web browser before the whole clip is downloaded.

Streaming media server A specialist server used to broadcast audio (e.g. podcasts) or video (e.g. IPTV or webcast presentations). Served streams can be unicast (a separate copy of stream is served for each recipient), multicast (recipients share streams) or peer-to-peer where the media is shared between different recipient's computers using a Bitorrent or Kontiki approach.

Style guide A definition of site structure, page design, typography and copy defined within a company. (*See* **Graphic design**.)

Subject access request A request by a data subject to view personal data from an organisation.

Superstitials Pop-up adverts that require interaction to remove them.

Surfer An undirected information seeker who is often looking for an experience rather than information.

Symmetric encryption Both parties to a transaction use the same key to encode and decode messages.

Syndication Content or product information is distributed to third parties. Online this is commonly achieved through standard XML formats such as RSS.

T

Tagging Tracking of the origin or referring site or of visitors to a site and their spending patterns. Also tagging refers to where users or web page creators categorise content on a site through adding descriptive terms. A common approach in blog posts.

Target marketing strategy Evaluation and selection of appropriate segments and the development of appropriate offers.

Targeting (through banner advertisers) Advertising networks such as DoubleClick offer advertisers the ability to target advertisements dynamically on the World Wide Web through their 'DART' targeting technology. This gives advertisers a means of reaching specific audiences.

Technology convergence A trend in which different hardware devices such as TVs, computers and phone merge and have similar functions.

Telemarketing using the Internet Mainly used for inbound telemarketing, including sales lines, carelines for goods and services and response handling for direct response campaigns.

Telnet A program that allows remote access to data and text-based programs on other computer systems at different locations. For example, a retailer could check to see whether an item was in stock in a warehouse using a telnet application.

Template *See* **Site design page template**.

Test website A parallel version of the site to use before the site is made available to customers as a live website.

Testing content Testing should be conducted for plug-ins; for interactive facilities and integration with company databases; for spelling and grammar; for adherence to corporate image standards; for implementation of HTML in different web browsers; and to ensure that links to external sites are valid.

Testing phase Testing involves different aspects of the content such as spelling, validity of links, formatting on different web browsers and dynamic features such as form filling or database queries.

Third-party cookies Served by another site to the one being viewed – typical for portals where an ad network will track remotely or where the web analytics software places a cookie.

Tipping point Using the science of social epidemics explains principles that underpin the rapid spread of ideas, products and behaviours through a population.

Trademark A trademark is a unique word or phrase that distinguishes your company. The mark can be registered as plain or designed text, artwork or a combination. In theory, colours, smells and sounds can also be trademarks.

Traffic-building campaign The use of online and offline promotion techniques such as banner advertising, search engine promotion and reciprocal linking to increase the audience of a site (both new and existing customers).

Transactional sites Sites that support online sales.

Transaction log file A web server file that records all page requests.

Transfer Control Protocol/Internet Protocol (TCP/IP) The passing of data packets around the Internet occurs via TCP/IP. For a PC to be able to receive web pages or for a server to host web pages it must be configured to support this protocol.

Trialogue The interaction between company, customer and other customers facilitated through online community, social networks, reviews and comments.

Trusted feed A trusted feed is an automated method of putting content into a search engine index or an aggregator database.

Trusted third parties (TTPs) Companies with which an agreement has been reached to share information.

U

Undirected information seeker A person who does not know what information they are looking for – a surfer.

Uniform (universal) resource locator (URL) Text that indicates the web address of a site. A specific domain name is typed into a web browser window and the browser will then locate and load the website. It is in the form of: http://www.domain-name.extension/filename.html.

Unique visitors Individual visitors to a site measured through cookies or IP addresses on an individual computer.

Universal search The *natural listings* incorporate other relevant results from vertical searches related to a query, such as video, books, scholar, news, sitelinks and images.

Unsubscribe An option to opt out from an e-mail newsletter or discussion group.

Upload The transfer of files from a local computer to a server. Usually achieved using FTP. E-mail or website pages can be uploaded to update a remote server.

Up-selling Persuading existing customers to purchase more expensive products (typically related to existing purchase categories).

URL strategy A defined approach to how content is labelled through placing it in different directories or folders with distinct web addresses.

Usability An approach to website design intended to enable the completion of user tasks.

Usability/user testing Representative users are observed performing representative tasks using a system.

Usenet newsgroup An electronic bulletin board used to discuss a particular topic such as a sport, hobby or business area. Traditionally accessed by special newsreader software, these can now be accessed via a web browser from www.deja.com.

User-centred design Design based on optimising the user experience according to all factors, including the user interface, which affect this.

User journey *See* **Customer scenarios**.

User session Used to specify the frequency of visits to a site. Not equivalent to site visit.

V

Validation Validation services test for errors in HTML code which may cause a web page to be displayed incorrectly or for links to other pages that do not work.

Value chain A model that considers how supply chain activities can add value to products and services delivered to the customer.

Value event scoring Value events are outcomes that occur on the site as indicated by visits to different page or content types which suggest marketing communications are effective. Examples include, leads, sales, newsletter registrations and product page views. They can be tagged and scored using many web analytics systems, for example Google refers to them as conversion goals.

Value network The links between an organisation and its strategic and non-strategic partners that form its external value chain.

Value proposition of site The benefits or value of a website that are evident to its users.

Vertical portals These are generally business-to-business sites that will host content to help participants in an industry to get their work done by providing industry news, details of business techniques, and product and service reviews.

Video marketing The use of video to gain visibility in search marketing, video hosting sites and to engage site visitors.

View *See* **Page impression**.

View-through A view-through indicates when a user views an ad and subsequently visits a website.

Viral marketing A marketing message is communicated from one person to another, facilitated by different media, such as word of mouth, e-mail or websites. Implies rapid transmission of messages is intended.

Viral referral An 'e-mail a friend or colleague' component to an e-mail campaign or part of website design.

Virtual cash *See* **Digital cash**.

Virtual community An Internet-based forum for special-interest groups to communicate using a bulletin board to post messages.

Virtual mall A website that brings together different electronic retailers at a single virtual (online) location. This contrasts with a fixed-location infrastructure – the traditional arrangement where retail organisations operate from retail stores situated in fixed locations such as real-world shopping malls. (Also known as electronic mall.)

Virtual merchants Retailers such as Amazon that only operate online – they have no fixed-location infrastructure.

Virtual organisation An organisation that uses information and communications technology to allow it to operate without clearly defined physical boundaries between different functions. It provides customised services by outsourcing production and other functions to third parties.

Virtual private network Private network created using the public network infrastructure of the Internet.

Virtualisation The process whereby a company develops more of the characteristics of a virtual organisation.

Visit conversion rate An indication of the capability of a site in converting visitors to defined outcomes such as registration. Calculated by dividing the number of conversion events by the number of visitor sessions within a time period.

Visitor conversion rate An indication of the capability of a site in converting visitors to defined outcomes such as registration. Calculated by dividing the number of conversion events by the number of unique visitors within a defined time period.

Visitor session (visit) A series of one or more page impressions, served to one user, which ends when there is a gap of 30 minutes or more between successive page impressions for that user.

W

Walled garden A limited range of e-commerce services on iDTV (compared to the Internet).

WAP WAP is a technical standard for transferring information to wireless devices, such as mobile phones.

Web 2.0 concept A collection of web services that facilitate interaction of web users with a site to create user-generated content and encouraging certain behaviours online such as community or social network participation and user-generated content, mashups, content rating, use of widgets and tagging.

Web 3.0 concept Next-generation web incorporating high-speed connectivity, complex cross-community interactions and an intelligent or semantic web where automated applications can access data from different online services to assist searchers perform complex tasks of supplier selection.

Web accessibility Designing websites so that they can be used by people with visual impairment whatever browser/access platform they use.

Web addresses Web addresses refer to particular pages on a web server, which is hosted by a company or organisation. The technical name for web addresses is uniform or universal resource locators (URLs).

Web analytics Techniques used to assess and improve the contribution of e-marketing to a business, including reviewing traffic volume, referrals, clickstreams, online reach data, customer satisfaction surveys, leads and sales.

Web application frameworks A standard programming framework based on reusable library functions for creating dynamic websites through a programming language.

Web Application Protocol (WAP) A standard that enables mobile phones to access text from websites.

Web application server Software processes which is accessed by a standard programming interface (API) of a web application framework to serve dynamic website functionality in response to requests received from browsers.

Web browsers Browsers such as Mozilla Firefox and Microsoft Internet Explorer provide an easy method of accessing and viewing information stored as HTML web documents on different web servers.

Webmaster A webmaster is responsible for ensuring the quality of a website. This means achieving suitable availability, speed, working links between pages and connections to company databases. In small companies the webmaster may be responsible for graphic design and content development.

Web merchandising The aims of web merchandising are to maximise sales potential of an online store for each visitor. This means connecting the right products, with the right offer to the right visitor, and remembering that the online store is part of a broader experience including online and offline advertising, in-store visits, customer service and delivery.

Web radio Internet radio is when existing broadcasts are streamed via the Internet and listened to using plug-ins such as Real Media or Windows Media Player.

Web response model The website is used as a response mechanism for offline campaign elements such as direct mail or advertising.

Web self-service Content and services provided by an organisation to replace or complement in-store or phone customer enquiries in order to reduce costs and increase customer convenience.

Web servers Web servers are used to store the web pages accessed by web browsers. They may also contain databases of customer or product information, which can be queried and retrieved using a browser.

Website auditors Auditors accurately measure the usage of different sites in terms of the number of ad impressions and click-through rates.

Website content Accessible on the World Wide Web that is created by a particular organisation or individual. The location and identity of a website is indicated by its web address (URL) or domain name. It may be stored on a single server in a single location, or a cluster of servers.

Website measurement The process whereby metrics such as page impressions are collected and evaluated to assess the effectiveness of Internet marketing activities in meeting customers, business and marketing objectives.

Wide Area Information Service (WAIS) An Internet service that has been superseded by the World Wide Web.

Widget A badge or button incorporated into a site or social network space by its owner, with content or services typically served from another site making widgets effectively a mini-software application or web service. Content can be updated in real time since the widget interacts with the server each time it loads.

Wi-Fi ('wireless fidelity') A high-speed wireless local-area network enabling wireless access to the Internet for mobile, office and home users.

Wireframe Also known as 'schematics', a way of illustrating the layout of an individual web page.

Wireless Markup Language (WML) Standard for displaying mobile pages such as transferred by WAP.

Word-of-mouth marketing According to the Word-of-Mouth Marketing Association it is giving people a reason to talk about your products and services, and making it easier for that conversation to take place. It is the art and science of building active, mutually beneficial consumer-to-consumer and consumer-to-marketer communications.

World Wide Web A medium for publishing information on the Internet. It is accessed through web browsers, which display web pages and can now be used to run business applications. Company information is stored on web servers, which are usually referred to as websites.

X

XML An advanced markup language giving better control than HTML over format for structured information on web pages.

XMOS (cross-media optimisation studies) XMOS research is designed to help marketers and their agencies answer the question 'What is the optimal mix of advertising vehicles across different media, in terms of frequency, reach and budget allocation, for a given campaign to achieve its marketing goals?' The mix between online and offline spend is varied to maximise campaign metrics such as reach, brand awareness and purchase intent.

Index

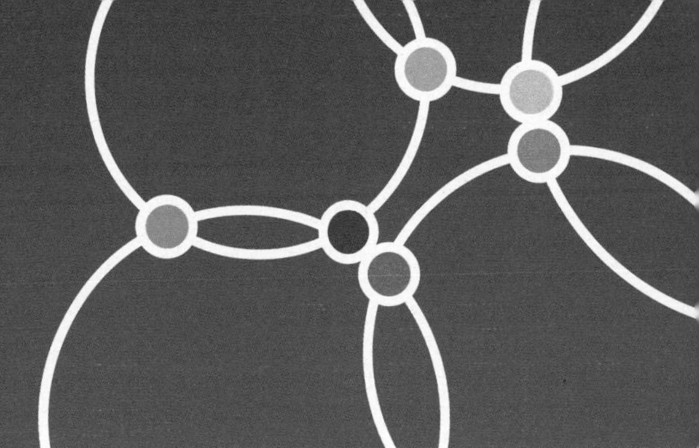